Ethical Challenges for Intervening in Drug Use: Policy, Research and Treatment Issues

Edited by

John Kleinig
John Jay College of Criminal Justice
Centre for Applied Philosophy and Public Ethics

and

Stanley Einstein
The Middle Eastern Summer Institute on Drug Use

The Uncertainty Series

Volume 1	**Organized Crime: Uncertainties and Dilemmas (1999)** S. Einstein & M. Amir (eds.)
Volume 2.1	**Policing, Security and Democracy: Theory and Practice (2001)** M. Amir & S. Einstein (eds.)
Volume 2.2	**Policing, Security and Democracy: Special Aspects of 'Democratic Policing' (2001)** S. Einstein & M. Amir (eds.)
Volume 3	**Drug Courts: Current Issues & Future Perspectives (2002)** L. Harrison, F. Scarpitti, M. Amir, and S. Einstein (eds.)
Volume 4.1	**Police Corruption: Paradigms, Models and Concepts — Challenges for Developing Countries (2003)** S. Einstein & M. Amir (eds.)
Volume 4.2	**Police Corruption: Challenges for Developed Countries — Comparative Issues and Commissions of Inquiry (2004)** M. Amir & S. Einstein (eds.)
Volume 5	**Ethical Challenges for Intervening in Drug Use: Policy, Research and Treatment Issues (2006)** J. Kleinig & S. Einstein (eds.)

Sam Houston State University, Criminal Justice Center
Box 1819, Huntsville, TX 77342-1819, USA
Telephone: (936) 294-3173 — Fax: (936) 294-4053
e-mail: books@oicj.org — www.oicj.org

ISBN: 0-942511-65-4 Paperbound
ISBN 13: 978-0-942511-65-9 Paperbound
ISBN: 0-942511-67-0 Hardcover
ISBN 13: 0-942511-67-3 Hardcover

Library of Congress Control Number: 2006935475

Cover designed by Ronit Berson

Contents

A Prologue to the Series

UNCERTAINTY is an international, interdisciplinary series of topic-focused books publishing invited state-of-the-art analyses one or more times a year. Each volume will contain a minimum of 10-15 review articles. They will focus on an issue, problem or process which remains unresolved. The topics will be ones which significantly affect the quality of life of the individual and the nature and effective functioning of our institutions, communities, and of society-at-large. Authors will help you, the reader, to move from concepts, definitions, theories, paradigms and their 'demands' to the implications of current generalizable empirical data, to the future of the issue's topic, noting remaining unresolved issues, the barriers to their understanding, planning and implementation and suggesting future research.

Each issue will include:

- *ABSTRACTS*
- *REFERENCES*
- *GLOSSARY*
- *RESOURCES*: Lists of selected printed, auditory, and visual materials from governmental and private organizations which the interested reader can write to for further information.
- *GRAPHICS:* Graphic materials, designed to help you, the reader, 'see' the issues, their parameters, 'demands' and (inter) relationships.

UNCERTAINTY, the series, is designed as a forum for minimizing individual and systemic uncertainties, to promote exploration of selected vital human concerns and to maximize the needed openness for preventing premature closure as we examine, think about, and create new paradigms of change. In our increasingly complex world in which solutions all too often raise, or themselves become problems, the paradox of the lawfulness of unpredictability is our reality; notions of *control, predictability* and '*cause and effect*' are mythical messages. In our complex world, the concept of predictability changes. The answer to the question 'Tell me what will happen?' *always* has some degree of uncertainty. 'Tell me what to anticipate or is plausible or likely?' is reasonable. The answers could be the same, scientifically speaking, but the meanings will be different. In our complex world, the dynamics of reality do not play dice, even though to all appearances, and to 'common sense,' life and reality is experienced as a dice game.

UNCERTAINTY is and can be a stimulus and tool for you.
Both the authors in each volume and the editors welcome queries and feedback.

The Editors

Dedication

To Bat El ("daughter of God")/ Natalie, born in 1986, removed from her home into a journey of survival in institutional life at age 13, and who removed herself from our world and her pain, at age 20, leaving behind a system of agencies that did the best that institutionalized systems can do,

and

To the many agency staff whose hearts and souls were moved and challenged by Natalie's honesty, passion and vulnerability and who now mourn her.

May we learn through Natalie's death what we could not learn while she lived.

Acknowledgments

Many people have made it possible for this volume to move from an idea through many necessary discussions to inviting contributors and finally to its actual publication. The willingness of professionals, friends, colleagues, and strangers to take the necessary time from their busy personal and professional responsibilities for this project was the critical ingredient.

Many people have helped in addition to the chapter contributors. These include: Abstract translators – Prof. Hua Ling Fu, Hong Kong (Chinese), Valery Gafurov, Ekaterinburg, Russia (Russian), Dr. Paolo de Mesquita Neto, Brazil (Portuguese), Dr. Allaman Allamani, Italy (Italian), Robert and Isabelle MacMath, Claire Courtial, and Alain Miget, Australia, Manuella Adrian, USA (French), Jonathan Lewy, Israel, and Dr. Eugene Kelly, USA, (German), Dr. Richard Hogan, USA (Spanish), Shmulik Szeintuch, Israel (Hebrew), Ayad Mohammed, Israel (Arabic) and Ms. Shirly Levy-Aldema, Israel graphic artist. The creativity of the graphic designer of this volume and of The Uncertainty Series, Ronit Berson, Israel, was and remains beyond what the editors expected. Dr. Stephen Coleman provided valuable editorial advice. We are most grateful to each of them.

Our families, friends, and colleagues continue to be most patient and understanding of us as we attempted to meet the demands of this volume which grew in scope and depth over time. Their support made it possible for us to continue. We, the editors, have learned a great deal while "sculpting" the volumes and have made new friends and have met new colleagues.

This volume, and The Uncertainty Series, continues because Dick Ward continues to believe in its importance. Many thanks!

We want to thank the publishers of *Substance Use and Misuse*, Taylor and Francis, for permitting the republication of the 5 articles in the Special Issue: *Ethical Issues of Substance Use Intervention*, Volume 39:3, 2004 which inspired the creation of the present two volumes.

List of Tables

List of Figures

List of Contributors

Manuella Adrian, M.Sc.Hyg., <madrian@the-beach.net>

Kendall Alexander, M.S.W., Island Grove Regional Treatment Center, 1140 M Street, Greeley, CO 80631, <KAlexander@islandgrovecenter.org>

A. Aukahi Austin, Ph.D., Department of Psychology, University of Hawai'i Mānoa, Mānoa , Hawai'i, USA

Allaman Allamani, M.D., Centro Alcologico Integrato, Villa Basilewsky, Via Lorenzo il Magnifico 104, 50129 Firenze, Italy "allaman allamani" <allamana@tin.it>

Linda A. Bennett, Ph.D., Department of Anthropology, College of Arts and Sciences, The University of Memphis, Memphis TN USA

Ellen Benoit, Ph.D., Assistant Project Director, National Development and Research Institutes, 71 West 23rd Street, 8th floor, New York, NY 10010 USA <Benoit@ndri.org>

Steve Clarke, Ph.D., LPO Box A260, ANU, Canberra ACT 2601, Australia <Stephen.Clarke@anu.edu.au>

Dean Cocking, Ph.D., Centre for Applied Philosophy and Public Ethics, Faculty of Arts, Building 22, Haydon-Allen Building, The Australian National University ACT 0200 Australia <dean.cocking@anu.edu.au>

Elliot Cohen, Ph.D., Dept of Humanities, Indian River Community College, 3209 Virginia Ave. Ft Pierce, FL 34981-5599 USA <ecohen@ircc.edu>

Stephen Coleman, Ph.D., Lecturer in Ethics in the School of Humanities and Social Sciences, University of NSW (@ADFA) and Senior Research Fellow, Centre for Applied Philosophy and Public Ethics <s.coleman@adfa.edu.au>

Ruth Edwards, Ph.D., Tri-Ethnic Center for Prevention Research, Colorado State University, Sage Hall, Ft. Collins, CO 80523, <redwards@lamar.colostate.edu>

Stanley Einstein, Ph.D., MEMSIDU, 113/41 Oleh HaGardom, East Talpiot, Jerusalem Israel <einstein@netvision.net.il>

Theodore Godlaski, M. Div., University of Kentucky College of Social Work 1 Quality St. , Suite 700, Lexington, KY 40507 USA <tmgodl1@uky.edu>

Dennis Gorman, Ph.D., Department of Epidemiology & Biostatistics School of Rural Public Health, 3000 Briarcrest Drive, Suite 310 Bryan, Texas 77802 USA <gorman@srph.tamhsc.edu>

William Gottdiener, Ph.D., Department of Psychology, John Jay College of Criminal Justice, City University of New York, 445 West 59th St. New York, NY 10019 USA <wgottdiener@jjay.cuny.edu>

Mane Hajdin, J.D., Ph.D., Dominican University of California, 50 Acacia Avenue, San Rafael, CA 94901 USA <mhajdin@dominican.edu>

Rodney Haring, LMSW, School of Social Work, University at Buffalo, State University of New York, 685 Baldy Hall, Buffalo, NY 14260 USA <rcharing@hotmail.com>

Douglas Husak, J.D., Ph.D., Department of Philosophy, Rutgers University, New Brunswick, New Jersey USA <husak@rci.rutgers.edu>

Jeannette L. Johnson, Ph.D., Friends Social Research, Inc., Social Research Center, 1040 Park Ave. Suite 103, Baltimore, MD 21210 USA <jjohnson@frisrc.org>

Tziporah Kasachkoff, Ph.D., Professor Emeritus of Philosophy, Graduate Center, CUNY; and Professor of Philosophy, Ben Gurion University, Beer Sheva, Israel <tkasachkoff@yahoo.com>

Jeanette Kennett, Ph.D., Principal Research Fellow, Centre for Applied Philosophy and Public Ethics, LPO Box 8260, The Australian National University Canberra ACT 2601 Australia. Visiting Principal Research Fellow, University of Melbourne. <Jeanette.Kennett@anu.edu.au>

John Kleinig, Ph.D., John Jay College of Criminal Justice, City University of New York, 899 Tenth Avenue, New York, NY 10019 USA <jkleinig@jjay.cuny.edu>

Neil Levy, Ph.D., Centre for Applied Philosophy and Public Ethics, University of Melbourne, Victoria 3010, Australia. <nllevy@unimelb.edu.au>

Tony Lynch, Ph.D., Philosophy, School of Social Science, University of New England, Armidale, NSW Australia <alynch@une.edu.au>

Stephen Magura, Ph.D., Director of Science and Research, National Development and Research Institutes, 71 West 23rd Street, 8th floor, New York, NY 10010 USA <steve.magura@ndri.org>

Steve Matthews, Ph.D., Senior Lecturer in Philosophy, School of Humanities and Social Sciences, Charles Sturt University, Wagga Wagga, NSW and Senior Research Fellow, Centre for Applied Philosophy and Public Ethics (an ARC funded Special Research Centre), Charles Sturt University, Canberra, and Visiting Senior Research Fellow University of Melbourne and the Australian National University <Stephen.Matthews@anu.edu.au>

Seumas Miller, Ph.D., Professor of Philosophy, Charles Sturt University and the Australian National University (joint position), Director of the Centre for Applied Philosophy and Public Ethics (an Australian Research Council funded Special Research Centre).

Michael Montagne, Ph.D., Professor of Social Pharmacy and Associate Dean of Graduate Studies, Department of Pharmaceutical Sciences, School of Pharmacy - Boston, Massachusetts College of Pharmacy & Health Sciences,179 Longwood Ave Boston MA 02115 USA <michael.montagne@bos.mcphs.edu>

Stephen J. Morse, J.D., Ph.D., Ferdinand Wakeman Hubbell Professor of Law and Professor of Psychology and Law in Psychiatry at the University of Pennsylvania, 3400 Chestnut Street, Philadelphia, PA 19104-6204 USA <smorse@law.upenn.edu>

Kenneth D. Pimple, Ph.D., Poynter Center for the Study of Ethics and American Institutions, Indiana University-Bloomington Indiana, USA <Pimple@indiana.edu>

Maurice Rickard, Ph.D., Research Fellow, Centre for Applied Philosophy and Public Ethics, Charles Sturt University, ANU Canberra ACT 2601, Australia <maurice.rickard@anu.edu.au>

Nancy R. VanDeMark, Ph.D., Arapahoe House, 3530 West Lehigh St., Denver, CO 80236 USA <nancy@ahinc.org>

Barbara C. Wallace, Ph.D., Department of Health and Behavior Studies, Teachers College, Columbia University, Box 114, 525 West 120th Street, New York, NY 10027, USA <BCW3@Columbia.edu>

Adrian Walsh, Ph.D., Philosophy, School of Social Science, University of New England, Armidale, NSW Australia <awalsh@metz.une.edu.au>

David Wasserman, Ph.D., Institute for Philosophy and Public Policy, University of Maryland, College Park, MD USA <dwasserm@umd.edu>

Shelly A. Wiechelt, Ph.D., University of Maryland, Baltimore County, School of Social Work, 1000 Hilltop Circle, AC-IV (B), Room 322, Baltimore, MD 21250 <wiechelt@umbc.edu>

Kylie Williams, M.A., Research Fellow, Centre for Applied Philosophy and Public Ethics, LPO Box 8260, The Australian National University, ACT 0200 Australia <Kylie.Williams@anu.edu.au>

Daniel Yalisove, Ph.D., John Jay College of Criminal Justice, City University of New York, 445 West 59th St. New York, NY 10019 USA <dyalisov@jjay.cuny.edu>.

Introduction

Anyway, no drug, not even alcohol, causes the fundamental ills of society. If we're looking for the source of our troubles, we shouldn't test people for drugs, we should test them for stupidity, ignorance, greed and love of power.

— P.J. O'Rourke

Interest in the "manufacture" and ingestion of psychoactive substances is as ancient as our historical records. Even in our earliest recorded history this interest was diverse. It has religious, celebratory, and therapeutic dimensions. Even then, though, the use of such substances was seen as potentially troublesome. The ancient story of Noah reports the untoward effects of alcoholic over-consumption (Gen. 9:20), a refrain that occurs time and again (Gen. 19: 32-38; Prov. 23: 29-35) in a tradition that also celebrates the wine that makes glad the heart of man (Ps. 104:15; cf. Eccles. 9:7), and includes the later Pauline injunction to take a little wine for the stomach (I Tim. 5:23). Other traditions reflect a similar diversity of response. To take just one example, in *The Laws*, Plato extols the "gift from Dionysus" but recommends that its consumption be tailored to different age groups: "Shall we begin by enacting that boys shall not taste wine at all until they are eighteen years of age; we will tell them that fire must not be poured upon fire, whether in the body or in the soul, until they begin to go to work – this is a precaution which has to be taken against the excitableness of youth; – afterwards they may taste wine in moderation up to the age of thirty, but while a man is young he should abstain altogether from intoxication and from excess of wine; when, at length, he has reached forty years, after dinner at a public mess, he may invite not only the other Gods, but Dionysus above all, to the mystery and festivity of the elder men, making use of the wine which he has given men to lighten the sourness of old age; that in age we may renew our youth, and forget our sorrows; and also in order that the nature of the soul, like iron melted in the fire, may become softer and so more impressible" (Plato, bk.II, 666).

Although many of the ancients focus on the products of fermentation, other substances were also known and ingested. Within the broadly Mediterranean area, the opium poppy is frequently referred to for its analgesic and sedative effects. Hemp has a long history in East Asia. Tobacco was chewed throughout the Americas, hallucinogenic mushrooms have a long social and religious history in Central America, and coca was used in South America long before it was exploited by the conquistadores.

For those of us who straddle the twentieth and twenty-first centuries, the situation remains a complex and confused one. Religious traditions both use and revile the use of mood-altering substances; our politico-legal system is "schizophrenic," sanctioning and even profiting from the manufacture and sale of alcohol and tobacco, while at the same time sometimes visiting almost unimaginably severe penalties on those caught with cannabis. The British (and later French) Opium Wars in China (1839–42 and 1856–60), and the use of coca after the Spanish conquest of South America, were cynical exploitations of drugs for profit by cultures formally dedicated to higher values. Irrationality is woven deeply into our socio-political order (Kahneman et al., 1982).

Figure I.1: Britain forces China to take Opium

Nor is the socio-political arena an appropriate domain for understanding the substances themselves. Much more is it a site of political power and dominance, as individuals and stakeholder groups vie to enshrine their more or less restrictive ideologies in legal format. For reasons that are often obliquely connected to the substances themselves, some are selectively "mystified" and "empowered" and fear of those who use them leads to their disempowering, marginalization, and stereotyping. Admonitions to "say no to drugs" or to join the "war against drugs" point to this fearsome power supposedly wielded by and threatened by these (or at least some of these) substances and their users.

This is deeply unfortunate. Psychoactive substances – drugs, if you will – are enormously diverse, and so are their effects, not only individually, but across their range. They deserve sensitivity in our understanding and response to them, not the inconsistent, heavy-handed (and curiously tunnel-visioned) reactions that are familiar to us. On the one hand, most drugs – even, and we might say especially, those that are most shrilly denounced – have valuable uses in the universe of human therapeutic responses. On the other hand, most drugs – including some of those that are not denounced but help to sustain the work of government through employment, taxation, etc. – are, if not used appropriately or with care, seriously disabling. They can be disabling not only to the users themselves but also to the networks they inhabit (and within which they act and interact) and the physical and social environment that we all share. Tobacco crops cause long-lasting depletion of potash, calcium, and nitrogen in the soil, and new species of shade-free coffee beans – café caturra – make much use of pesticides and herbicides. The cultivation of "illicit" drugs – especially in a world of black-markets – can be no less harmful to their social and physical environments. In some countries, the cultivation of drug crops has supplanted food production and promoted "slash and burn" practices (Courtright, 2001). This takes place against a background of global inequities in which well-off countries strong-arm those that are poorly off, offering alternatives that do little to alleviate their situation, make them competitive, or respect their local cultures and traditions.

Although contributors to the present volume are unlikely to be sympathetic to the status quo – a feat that almost defies comprehension – neither are they unmindful of the problematic character that most psychoactive substances may have. Whether it resides in the chemical properties of the substances in question or the individual or social environments in which they are used, or, more likely, in some combination of these, they are aware that the diversity of human interests in them and responses to them call for a nuanced and careful appraisal of the ways in which we respond and craft our social judgments.

What is particularly troubling is the way in which our social judgments concerning drug users have been hardened into a division US and THEM. We have privileged our judgments concerning the use of these substances, seeing those who use them as morally or pathologically impaired. No doubt their use or misuse may cause problems – as indeed may other forms of overindulgence – but we easily tend to express a special kind of opprobrium toward those who use drugs. Why so? And what reason do we have to be so sure of our judgments that we are justified in taking the condescending and repressive measures we do?

Broadly speaking – and this is very broadly speaking – we can track responses to drugs along two axes, medical and moral. The medical approach has room toward one end of its spectrum for a recreational and therapeutic understanding of drug use and, toward the other end, for drug use as a kind of disease or pathology requiring healing. Not every drug has a place along the spectrum and not every drug has usefulness for every user. What uses might be made and which users may be benefited, and how, are not likely to be determinable once and for all. Culture, time, and place remain constant factors in "medical" judgments.

The moral approach has room toward one end of its spectrum for a sacramental and labor-enhancing understanding of drug use and at the other end for its use as being criminal and self-destructive. Sometimes these spectra cross, as when the use of a previously illicit drug is permitted for medicinal purposes or when a visible, "tagged" drug user charged with drug-related crime is diverted to a treatment program.

There are, in fact, other axes. The two traditional responses suggest that drug use must be responded to rather than left to itself. And that is particularly so in cases in which its effects appear to be deleterious. And yet there is impressive evidence for thinking that in many cases, including those in which "intervention" of some kind is usually thought to be appropriate, what is sometimes referred to as "natural recovery" has outcomes that are not too different from those of "other-planned" interventions (Alcohol and Drug Abuse Institute, 2003; Shorkey et al., 2004; Klingemann, et al. 2001). In such cases, drug users, who in any case constitute a diverse group of people in both use and motivation (including those who are – somewhat tendentiously – said to be addicted) stop their use without the help from "professional" counselors or treatment providers of various kinds, whether tradition-based efforts or mutual aid programs such as Alcoholics Anonymous (AA) and Narcotics Anonymous (NA). This is important to remember in an area in which our interventions so often seem to be of limited value – and even exacerbating. Our rationalization that failure is "their" fault does not secure those efforts against searching scrutiny.

Yet in this volume we have chosen to focus on ethical issues raised by interventions into drug use. The significance of this focus calls for explanation and requires some explication. Human interactions can be assessed and appraised in a variety of ways – we can look at their political, economic, legal, religious, and cultural dimensions. Each has its appropriate place. But more fundamental than each of these is their moral appraisal, that is, their appraisal in terms of the basic currency of human intercourse: what we are in our relations to each other, individually, collectively, and institutionally. Without denying their internal logic or integrity, we nevertheless judge our political, economic, legal, religious, and cultural understanding and traditions in terms of their moral acceptability. We do not reverse the order. Morality constitutes the fundamental framework for our assessment of human conduct insofar as it affects the interests of others. We do not here draw a strong distinction between moral and ethical appraisals. Morality is general; ethics is role-related. Ethics as we understand it here is constituted by the requirements of morality as they are refracted through social roles – be they the roles of legislator, policy maker, or counselor.

Ultimately, such assessments will have at their base some conception of human flourishing or well-being that is expected and aspired to and which is affected (harmed or jeopardized) by some forms of drug use. What that conception is remains contested, and while that remains so our social responses will be sites of contestation.

Although several of the essays in this volume focus more particularly on some of the ethico-moral problems encountered by juridico-moral interventions – problems relating to criminalization, decriminalization, legalization, and interdiction – our main focus has been on broadly medical or therapeutic responses to drug use, and in particular problems encountered within the domain of drug user counseling. This has been a conscious decision. There is now a significant literature that deals with drug legislation – with legislation that bears on the cultivation, manufacture, distribution, and sale of certain drugs and with legal responses to those who use them – and a growing literature to suggest that such interventions are much less successful than their proponents would want them to be. Increasingly there is political room for viewing drug use as something warranting a broadly medicalized response, whether constructed on a "harm-reduction" model or, more socially, as a requiring the interventions of counseling or mutual-help, group therapy-support systems. Yet even those responses, desirable as they often appear to be, are in danger of co-optation to social processes and ends that perpetuate marginalization and discrimination.

This volume was initiated to meet the challenges of the increasing contemporary trend to "treat" substance users in the broadest sense of this concept, whether in institutional settings, ambulatory programs or even controlled environments such as prisons. We noticed – in the United States, at least, where drugs have for long been a social and political preoccupation – that, although there are many (often similar) professional codes of ethics for those who administer treatment and even some "bills of rights" for those who participate in treatment programs, there is a relatively sparse literature underpinning and even interrogating them. Counseling literature focuses heavily on questions of efficacy, and the ethical dimensions of treatment provision and therapeutic options are often left implicit. Such codes as there are tend to function in something of a scholarly vacuum. Counselors – often recovering addicts/users – are left to work out for themselves the underlying ethical resources and rationales that inform the codes to which they are asked to conform.

This may not be the same in every country. Interestingly, codes of ethics directed specifically to drug user counselors seem to be almost exclusively confined to the United States. Examples of these codes are reprinted in an Appendix to this volume, and a number of the authors have adverted to or discussed their provisions. In most other countries, however, drug user counseling is accommodated to general counseling codes, and in some of those cases there is a fairly well-developed literature for counseling in general. Is drug user counseling different from other kinds? Quite possibly not, though the fact that many of those who provide such counseling are themselves "recovering addicts" and the separate sites of drug user counseling from counseling of other kinds may lead to a detrimental isolation from their ethical roots and perspectives. In the present volume we have not sought to emphasize the differences, though we have attempted to focus more specifically on the ethical issues as they manifest themselves in the sphere of drug use.

A brief note on terminology. In the United States it is common to speak of "drug abuse." Although some of the authors in this volume remain comfortable using that terminology, the editors have some preference for the language of "misuse." Any substance, whether food or drugs, may be used or misused; abuse refers primarily to mistreatment of another, as in domestic or child abuse. Moreover, the increasing medicalization of drug use and our growing concern about over-moralization makes the language of misuse less tendentious than that of abuse.

Several of these essays began their life in a Special Issue (Kleinig, 2004) of *Substance Use and Misuse*, founded and edited by Stan Einstein. With some changes, those essays have been reprinted here, and we are grateful for the permission of Taylor & Francis and their five authors to do so.

No doubt we have not addressed every important issue relating to drug-user intervention. To have done so would have required a much longer volume, even an encyclopedia. Nor does this volume pretend to accommodate or respond to the myriad cultural traditions concerning drug use and interventions in the activities of those who use them. That may be thought a significant failure in an increasingly global world. But in the absence of a substantial literature that focuses explicitly on the moral and ethical dimensions of such, we believe that it is "better to light one candle than to curse the darkness." It is our hope that this volume will stimulate others to investigate, document, and publish that which we need to know in order to create and advance human well-being and beneficence in a highly politicized area associated with great confusion, pain, suffering, harm, built-in failures, malfeasance, and many ongoing dilemmas confronted by individuals, families, social networks, and communities, along with other formal-informal, institutional and non-institutional systems.

John Kleinig and Stanley Einstein
The Editors

References

Alcohol and Drug Abuse Institute (ADAI). (2003). Recovery from addiction without treatment (ADAI Bibliography #TX 265). University of Washington <http://depts.washington.edu/adai/lib/bibs/tx_265.htm>.

Becker, G.S. & Murphy, K. (1988). A theory of rational addiction. *Journal of Political Economy, 96*, 675-700.

Benzon, W.L. & Hays, D.G. (1990). The evolution of cognition. *Journal of Social and Biological Structures, 13*(4), 297-320.

Courtright, D.T. (2001). *Forces of habit.* Cambridge, MA: Harvard University Press.

Kahneman D., Slovic, P. & Tversky, A. (1982). *Judgment under uncertainty: Heuristics and biases.* Cambridge University Press.

Kleinig, J. (Ed.). (2004). Ethical issues of substance use intervention. *Substance Use and Misuse, 40*, 3.

Klingemann, H.K. & Sobell, L.C. (Eds.). (2001). Natural recovery research across substance use. *Substance Use and Misuse, 36,* 11.

Plato. (1871). *The Laws.* (trans. Benjamin Jowett) <http://classics.mit.edu/Plato/laws.html>.

Shorkey, C.T. (2004). Spontaneous recovery and chemical dependence: Indexed bibliography of articles published in professional chemical dependency journals. University of Texas at Austin <http://128.83.80.200/tattc/spontaneousrecovery.html>.

Part 1

Policy and Research Issues

1-1 Ethical Issues in Substance Use Intervention

John Kleinig, Ph.D.

Abstract

This chapter offers an overview of some of the ethical questions raised by governmental and medical interventions into drug use. With respect to the former, it begins with the liberal assumption that constraints on free action are to be justified by reference to its deleterious impact on others, but then qualifies that assumption by noting the social requisites of free action. With respect to medical interventions, it focuses on the codes that have been developed for treatment providers and their clients, and explores the ethical underpinnings of several of their central provisions—informed consent, privacy, confidentiality, non-discrimination, professionalism, and accountability.

Key Words: accountability, civil commitment, common good, communitarian, confidentiality, consent, control, discrimination, freedom, governmental intervention, harm, medical intervention, natural law, privacy, professionalism.

Introduction

For the purposes of this essay, the chemical substances I consider are those usually referred to as drugs. That already casts the net extremely broadly. Drugs are generally distinguished as non-food substances that alter an organism's structure or function, a characterization which, though broad enough to capture almost any substance that could be referred to as a drug, is probably too broad to generate any distinctive ethical questions. Even when we descend from the abstract heights of offering a comprehensive account to those substances more mundanely referred to as drugs, we are still confronted with an enormous array of substances, one that remains too large to generate any interesting general ethical questions. Witness to this broad array are the diverse social responses we find—allowing of course that these responses may in some cases be quite controversial and in need of review. Some drug-containing substances are available without restriction and if not used as food then often used with it—tea, coffee, and soft drinks containing caffeine, for example. Another cluster—including tobacco and alcoholic beverages—is publicly available though heavily taxed and formally restricted to adults. A more restricted group includes therapeutic agents available only on prescription (say, OxyContin), though some therapeutic drugs are available virtually without restriction—aspirin, for example. An interestingly problematic group—including certain glues and aerosols—comprises psychoactive substances that are generally available though not intended for ingestion. And finally there are psychoactive substances that are generally outlawed (though forms of some are available on a very restricted basis for therapeutic or palliative purposes)—marijuana, cocaine, heroin, LSD, and so on. The categorization is not comprehensive, but it indicates the diversity of substances that qualify as or contain drugs.

Although any ethical discussion of drug use intervention must restrict itself to or differentiate between this or that drug or group of drugs, it is important to keep in mind the wide range of substances that can be so characterized. In the passion of public debate, it is easy to forget that we are not talking about a simple natural classification, but one that is socially determined, albeit sometimes and to some degree by reference to the properties of substances and the effects they may have under certain conditions. But given the diversity of overlapping properties and the variety of circumstances, the lines we draw will always have a certain controversiality if not arbitrariness about them.

At one level, talk about "social determination" is innocuous: language/conceptualization is a human activity, and even if we sometimes aspire to a somewhat "photographic" scientific representation of the world, we ought not to forget the importance of a camera angle to the representation. In the case of the substances we refer to as drugs, however, we are dealing additionally with representations that are highly politicized, in which different social groups vie for "ownership" of the conditions of a substance's use. Debates over the legitimately sacramental use of peyote or the therapeutic use of marijuana highlight these struggles for ownership. The same goes for attempted divisions of drugs into "hard" and "soft": however much we attempt to provide a "scientific" justification for such classifications, they also reflect a contest for moral and/or political control.

Governmental intervention

If we begin the ethical discussion of substance use intervention with certain liberal assumptions, then the ethical onus of justification will be on those who wish to intervene. Let me expand. It is a fairly basic presupposition of morality that we are to conceive of human beings as possessing the (rational) capacities of perception, judgment, decision, and incremental learning. It is by virtue of these that individual humans should be permitted to go about their lives as they themselves determine. This does not mean that how they judge and decide is or should not be of concern to others, but it suggests that insofar as it does concern others, any engagement between or among them should initially be that of rational interlocutors. Those others may "intervene," but their intervention should take the form of presenting the object of intervention with reasons and arguments that that object can take into account in judging and deciding. The object-of-intervention's judgment and decision making should not be interfered with coercively but addressed rationally. Passion may not be inappropriate, but it is the passion that naturally accompanies certain kinds of rational considerations. Stronger—coercive—forms of intervention are generally appropriate only when a person's decisions are such as to prevent others from acting on their own reasons. Insofar as the interferer has failed to respect the rational standing of others, he or she might reasonably be restrained, or, at least in the event of some completed interference, be penalized or otherwise be made subject to their determinations.

As stated, these liberal assumptions are likely to garner fairly broad support. They are, however, not universally shared and in a larger discussion would need to be defended against some alternative accounts. There are, for example, certain natural law traditions that posit a human telos which, though rationally inscribed, is characterized by the realization of specifiable substantive goods. Such views are likely to allow for greater intervention than the liberal one I outlined. In addition, though, even these liberal assumptions are sometimes supplemented by additional considerations that bear on the degree of permissible social intervention. It is one such supplementation that I now wish to make.

This supplementary consideration reminds us that liberalism is itself a range of positions, some of which are in tension with others. The particular version of liberalism that underpins this essay does not conceive of individuals as effective sources of reasons independent of some sustaining social milieu in which they have been nurtured and within which their decision making takes place. The free and equal beings of ethical liberalism are not atomistic individuals tracing their paths in social space, but participants in and dependent on particular social milieux. The practical and conceptual wherewithal for many kinds of judgment and decision making come through the socially coordinated efforts of many, and so, although there may be some constraints on what others may do to one, there may also be some reasonable expectations on the part of others that one will contribute to and help sustain the social conditions of one's rational freedom. What is more, such activity, expressed through governmental agencies, may subsidize (through taxation) various undertakings that enable people to pursue their interests as "progressive beings." It was for this reason that when John Stuart Mill enunciated his "one very simple principle, as entitled to govern absolutely the dealings of society with the individual in the way of compulsion or control, whether the means used be physical force in the form of legal penalties, or the moral coercion of public opinion," he was also quick to qualify it. His basic principle—which, it turns out, was not so singular or simple —was that "the sole end for which mankind are warranted, individually or collectively, in interfering with the liberty of action of any of their number, is self-protection. . . . [T]he only purpose for which power can be rightfully exercised over any member of a civilized community, against his will, is to prevent harm to others." The qualification he added was that "there are also many positive acts for the benefit of others, which he may rightfully be compelled to perform; such as to give evidence in a court of justice; to bear his fair share in the common defence, or in any other joint work necessary to the interest of the society of which he enjoys the protection."

This qualification assumes some importance in the debate concerning drug use because, although liberals like Mill are adamant that paternalistic interferences cannot be justified, some socially sustaining interferences may be. Mill is clear that interference with an individual for "his own good, either physical or moral, is not a sufficient warrant. He cannot rightfully be compelled to do or forbear because it will be better for him to do so, because it will make him happier, because, in the opinions of others, to do so would be wise, or even right." Nevertheless, because an individual is both a "progressive" being and a "member of a civilized community" there are certain social obligations that he can be required to fulfil.

When it comes to drug use, then, we must look at particular drugs and see the ways in which they impact not only on the individual but, if more widely available, on the broader social milieu. That is, we must consider whether there would be social repercussions to drug availability that ought to mandate some constraints on their access. Mill believed that by and large there were not. One of Mill's later contemporaries, however, the Oxford philosopher T.H. Green (1836-82), confronted the issue at length and came to very different practical conclusions. Green was disturbed at the way in which liquor shops had sprouted up in British working class neighborhoods, depressing them and sapping their residents of the wherewithal for improving themselves and their condition. Although I am generally sympathetic to Mill, there is something in Green's more communitarian version of liberalism that deserves greater recognition.

Green's liberalism is more communitarian than Mill's because it focuses not primarily on the freedom of the individual but on a free society, and it does so by advocating an idea of the common good that functions as a constraint on what is socially allowable. Even so, Green's notion of the common good, though more idealist or perfectionist than anything in Mill, belongs to the same broad liberal tradition because it aims at the flourishing of individuals as free beings. Whereas Mill is bothered by the ways in which "society" may cripple the development of individuality (the "tyranny of the majority"), Green focuses on the importance of a relatively and broadly benign social environment to the enablement of individual flourishing (sustaining the "power on the part of the citizens as a body to make the most and best of themselves").

Green's views on the availability of alcohol are found in a variety of writings, though they are developed at greatest length in his 1880 lecture, "Liberal Legislation and Freedom of Contract," in which he argues for both land reform and constraints on the liquor trade. What he says needs to be read in the light of prevailing social conditions, at least so far as they existed in the poorer urban communities of England.

Although Green starts with the socially qualified assumption that people should be free to make their own choices in life, he explicitly rejects the libertarian conclusion that whatever people agree to in their dealings with others ought therefore to be permitted. He notes with approval recent labor legislation that constrained the contractual arrangements into which people might enter—legislation that limited the number of hours that children, young persons, and women could work in factories, and various other measures that affected workplace and residential safety and health for everyone. Although these constituted constraints on freedom of contract, Green argues that freedom, rightly understood, demands more than lack of constraint. The human freedom we prize is not "a freedom that can be enjoyed by one man or one set of men at the cost of a loss of freedom to others" but rather "a positive power or capacity of doing or enjoying something worth doing, and that, too, something that we do or enjoy in common with others. We mean by it the power which each man exercises through the help or security given him by his fellow-men, and which he in turn helps to secure for them." Freedom is not mere license but a valued and valuable capacity for self-improvement.

As already noted, whereas Mill's fundamental focus is on the free individual and his/her social requisites, Green's focus is on the free society, and the individual prerequisites for that. "When we measure the progress of a society by its growth in freedom, we measure it by the increasing development and exercise on the whole of those powers of contributing to social good with which we believe the members of society to be endowed; in short, by the greater power on the part of the citizens as a body to make the most and best of themselves." For Green, the freedom of the "wandering savage" is not to be compared to the freedom of "the humblest citizen of a law-abiding state." Society is the crucible of a freedom worth having, and freedom of contract "is valuable only as a means to an end," the end being "positive" freedom: "every one has an interest in securing to every one else the free use and enjoyment and disposal of his possessions, so long as that freedom on the part of one does not interfere with a like freedom on the part of others, because such freedom contributes to the equal development of the faculties of all which is the highest good for all." The state may have a role in ensuring this, Green believes, though it does not necessarily do so, and it does not necessarily do so by centralized means. It would be good were we to achieve the goal of freedom for the self-development of all through the "spontaneous action of individuals," but "we must take men as we find them," and "until such a condition of society is reached, it is the business of the state" to take steps to ensure that this interest of all is secured. "Left to itself, or to the operation of casual benevolence, a degraded population perpetuates and increases itself."

This is not a strong perfectionist goal: "it is the business of the state not indeed directly to promote moral goodness, for that, from the very nature of moral goodness, it cannot do, but to maintain the conditions without which the free exercise of the human faculties is impossible." And in his *Prolegomena to Ethics* he wrote that "no one can convey a good character to another. Everyone must make his own character for himself. All that one man can do to make another better is to remove obstacles, and supply conditions favourable to the formation of a good character." Thus, although Green did not accept the arguments of those who saw the presence of temptation as character building, he was also critical of "paternal government" that did "its best to make [morality] impossible by narrowing the room for the self-imposition of duties and for the play of disinterested motives."

Against such a background Green reviews existing liquor licensing laws, laws which, he says, prevent "the drink shops from coming unpleasantly near the houses of well-to-do people, and…crowd them upon the quarters occupied by the poorer classes, who have practically no power of keeping the nuisance from them." Although he thinks that something ought to be done to curb them, Green draws back from suggesting a particular solution—more stringent licensing rules versus the relocation of such shops, for example. The issue, he thinks, is one of creating social conditions that enable people to make the best of themselves, and this is not necessarily a matter of banning the sale of alcohol altogether (even though Green became a prohibitionist), but of diminishing the convenience of purchasing alcohol in neighborhoods that have been ravaged by it. Green is careful to indicate that the precise measures to be taken need to have regard to what people will tolerate: "to attempt a restraining law in advance of the social sentiment necessary to give real effect to it, is always a mistake."

Although one might—as many attempt to do—drive a broad wedge between Mill and Green, I suspect that they are closer in liberal spirit and social concern than is often acknowledged. To some extent their arguments differ because they are responding to different social dangers. For Mill it is the tyranny of the majority and authoritarian government; for Green it is the exploitative potential of inegalitarian capitalism, the need to "hinder hindrances" to self-development. Neither Mill nor Green advocate complete freedom of contract: both are opposed to a freedom that would allow people to sell themselves into slavery—though Mill's gnomic remarks on the subject leave it unclear as to whether he and Green share similar grounds for their opposition. And both recognize that what might seem to be or might begin as self-regarding behavior—alcohol consumption—may deleteriously affect others, and thus at some point justify governmental interference. Mill's focus, interestingly, is probably more individually intrusive than Green's. For whereas Green is (initially) concerned to regulate the number of liquor shops in working-class areas, Mill is willing to countenance direct interference with the individual whose drinking deprives his family of the support that they have a right to expect of him. Though certainly not coincident, the two positions are not completely exclusive. In the long run, a modified Greenian rather than Millian position has often prevailed with respect to alcohol: not prohibition, as Green ultimately favored, but significantly more stringent legal provisions relating to the sale and consumption of alcohol than those for other beverages.

Although Green and Mill cannot be completely reconciled, they seem to be most at odds over empirical considerations—whether the proliferation of drink shops is as individually and socially destructive as Green takes it to be. Whereas Green views the ready availability and aggressive retailing of alcohol in certain areas as having serious social consequences, Mill believes the effects of alcohol to be (for the most part) privately contained. As Green puts it (though without naming names): "It used to be the fashion to look on drunkenness as a vice which was the concern only of the person who fell into it, so long as it did not lead him to commit an assault on his neighbors. No thoughtful man any longer looks on it in this way." And whereas Mill did not focus on the possibly addictive and voluntariness-diminishing effects of alcohol, many of those in the Greenian camp did. In the debates over legislation, Mill and Green thus found themselves on opposing sides.

The point here is not to conflate Green and Mill—as I said, they cannot be completely reconciled—or even to argue for one against the other. My point is rather to suggest that there are subtleties to such debates that are not easily resolved by simple appeals to either Mill or Green. As with the tension between individual and community, of which this is yet another permutation, one wants to say not either/or but both/and.

Obviously the foregoing has broader implications for drug use intervention. First, in cases in which the use of a drug begins to have a significant impact on social life, there may be some reason for constraining its use. Green's concern is not with the use of state power to interfere with the choices of individuals per se, but with the use of state power to intervene in cases in which a cumulatively detrimental social effect has been brought about as a result of easy access to a substance to which a certain class of persons will be especially vulnerable. It is not drunkenness per se that Green targets but the ready availability of alcohol that results in drunkenness as a social problem. The same might be said of other drugs—not that people should be prevented from taking them, but that their availability should—so far as possible—not be such that their cumulative effect is socially detrimental.

There is, however, a further extension of Green's argument that might seem more troubling. It arises from what might be seen as the cumulative social effect of a variety of acts. Suppose that the existing social costs of alcohol are significant but not capable of being diminished without considerable social opposition. Suppose further that there is some other psychoactive substance to which a portion of the population wants access but which, like alcohol, would tend to be used excessively and detrimentally. Even if the second substance is not as socially disruptive as alcohol, prudent social policy might lead us to be more restrictive of its use than of the use of alcohol. It is not enough to compare it in the abstract with alcohol; what must also be assessed is the cumulative effect of their joint availability, given that the use of alcohol is already socially entrenched. That may involve consideration not only of the total social impact of the availability of two problematic substances, but also any added effects of their joint ingestion. Social policy decisions do not operate in a vacuum or with a blank slate but need to take socio-historical factors into account. One effect of that may be restrictive decisions that, taken alone, would have been invidious.

I do not put this forward as an argument for the social status quo on drug use—for example the acceptance of alcohol and tobacco and exclusion of marijuana and heroin—but simply as a general argument for seeing drugs (and other social practices that, if unconstrained, might be sufficiently deleterious socially to warrant intervention) historically and cumulatively and not simply discretely and comparatively. If, as a result, social policy favors invidious responses (say, by more severely restricting the use of a substance that is less harmful than one that is in entrenched common use), there is also reason for an incremental corrective social policy that will diminish the seeming hypocrisy of regulation.

A second inference to be drawn is that intervention need not take the form of direct or punitive prohibition, but may consist only in the imposition of certain costs that are likely to affect its use. There are many ways of affecting the consumption of substances that have socially deleterious effects. Criminalization is a particularly radical form of social intervention, since it not only attaches costs but also penalties to that which is prohibited and stigmatizes the offender. A great deal of the current debate focuses on criminalizing interventions into drug use (along with its possession and trafficking). But alternative forms of regulation may often—perhaps usually—be preferable. Substances may be taxed or made available only on prescription or limited to certain venues. Moreover, although the state, as the primary social repository of coercive power, may be ultimately responsible for the regulations we have, it also has the power to delegate that responsibility to others.

For the remainder of this essay, however, I wish to review some ethical issues prompted by a different form of drug use intervention—various treatment regimes designed to wean people from certain forms of drug dependence. First, however, it might be helpful to connect this discussion with the earlier one.

There is sometimes a very close relationship between governmental and medical intervention. More than one such relationship can be found. Sometimes it is between criminalization and treatment. Those who have violated criminal prohibitions against drug use may be offered treatment programs as an alternative to imprisonment. One might wonder why. If drug use is deserving of punishment, why should entering a treatment program be seen as an appropriate alternative? If treatment for drug use is seen as an appropriate response, why should its use be thought deserving of punishment? A partial explanation is probably that compelled and closely supervised treatment no less than imprisonment is seen as a penalty, though one that is appropriate only to those who see their "criminal dependence" as something to be dealt with. The background assumption is that even if a person is addicted to some prohibited drug—and thus has a compromised capacity to stop using it—he or she nevertheless retains the power to seek treatment for the addiction. The failure to do so is seen as deserving of penalty. Whether this is a correct account of addiction is not something I address here.

But the increasing use being made of drug (treatment) courts also gestures at a recognition that drug use—and dependence—is not to be construed on the model of other illegalities: it is in some sense a political gesture to those who have considered that drug use ought not to be penalized in the same way as other social offenses even if—under certain circumstances—some kind of response is called for.

Nor shall I address a further ethical issue, that which concerns the eligibility for treatment by those who have acquired and/or manifest some form of drug dependence. It is sometimes argued that those for whom drugs have become a problem have, in the words of the Victorian maxim, "made their own beds and must now lie in them." I shall assume that this issue has been resolved to the extent that those in question have access to some appropriate form of treatment, and that what are now to be considered are the ethical questions raised by various treatment regimes. This is not to say that the design and operation of socially accepted facilities for the treatment of people drug problems have always paid much attention to what is ethically acceptable. Given the proliferation of alternative programs and their high failure rates, there is some reason to believe that many such programs have not been either well-conceived or well-run.

A second type of relationship between governmental and medical intervention occurs when people are civilly committed to some treatment regime by virtue of their dependence. In civil commitment, those whose capacities are deemed to be so compromised that they constitute a danger to themselves and/or others are preventively detained, usually with a view to their treatment. There are several ethical issues here to which I will simply allude without further discussion. First of all, it cannot be presumed that because a person constitutes a danger to himself or others he is unable to take responsibility for the choices he makes. The capacity to take responsibility for one's choices needs to be independently established. Even though it may seem odd that a person would willingly choose a course likely to be detrimental to himself, we should not see such irrational choice as inherently responsibility-defeating. After all, those who engage in extreme sports—though foolish at one level—do so as the result of a formally respectable cost-benefit analysis. The excitement they get from exposing themselves to extreme danger may not be for everyone, but we have no reason to use its oddity to presume incapacity. It may well be that one of the reasons why drug user treatment programs are not more effective than they are is that they fail to establish a preferable alternative for users. Second, the judgment that a person constitutes a sufficiently significant danger to himself or others such that some intervention is justified is often highly speculative. We are not good predictors of dangerousness, and at least with respect to dangerousness to self, should be very reluctant to intervene. Even with respect to dangerousness to others, we need to have some confidence that we are frequently enough on target in our predictions to provide ethical cover for cases in which those who pose no danger to others are improperly detained. Rationality may be our distinctive capacity, but, as Kahneman and Tversky have shown, it is not one in which we excel.

Third, even if it is clear that a person is incapable of avoiding behavior that is dangerous to his well-being, we should not presume that he would choose to avoid such behavior if he could. The person may wish to continue in a state of dependence because, even with its dangers, it does not leave him worse off than he would be were he not dependent. Those who are dependent on certain drugs may not be capable of overcoming that dependence without assistance, but they are not thereby lacking the ability to judge whether their lives would be better were they no longer drug dependent and it may be that the issues that originally contributed to their dependence would remain as intractable as they were before.

Medical intervention

Treatment for substance mis/use remains a highly problematic and controversial issue. This is partly for reasons already touched upon—judgments about substance misuse are deeply intersected by various contentious moral, social, and political judgments. How we legitimately respond to drug use and even drug dependence will depend in some measure on the particular moral and social judgments we make and the political climate in which we must make them. But it is also connected with two other factors of importance. One, a factual issue, concerns the effectiveness of various treatments for drug users (or at least misusers). And the other concerns their costs, not merely monetary of course, but for those concerned and the society that must in some sense support such programs. Those costs will also need to be assessed against the significant possibility that those who begin to use drugs will eventually stop using them as part of some process of "natural recovery." For a good number of those who are treated, drug use might be seen as a "phase," albeit one that could have significant costs for the person and others while that person is going through it. Drug misuse might also be seen as a problem whose control or treatment is as effectively dealt with via informal strategies as by those of a more "medicalized" kind.

Were relatively simple, effective, and individualized treatments for substance misuse available, as there are, say, for broken limbs, that would certainly simplify matters. But drug use and dependence is not amenable to simple solutions. In part that is because it is in itself a complex matter, a function—in many cases at least, not only of chemical factors, and factors relating to individual conditions, but also complex social ones. Those social factors may encompass not only economics and class but also age, religion, ethnicity, and more individualized factors such as friendships, familial relations, employment circumstances, and so on. Much will depend on the dispositions of the candidate for treatment and the social conditions that will obtain subsequent to treatment.

And second, because drug user treatments have been only modestly successful, efforts to improve their efficacy have often been problematic. They have sometimes—either in themselves or through the ways in which they have been administered—had disproportionate costs for their clientele.

Some ethical questions concerning treatment, then, will be the same as those that must be faced by medical researchers who wish to introduce or at least experiment with novel therapies. There will need to be a review process that considers risks, benefits, and alternatives, one that ensures that those treated are appropriately informed concerning the course of treatment; care will need to be observed lest unfairly discriminatory practices are initiated; untoward eventualities will need to be accommodated; and so on. Other questions will be similar to those that need to be addressed with other treatment regimes, such as securing informed consent and assuring confidentiality. In addition, there will need to be some discussion and determination of how to handle those who fail to conform to the treatment regime (by testing, for example, with dirty urine). Are they to be excluded from further treatment in favor of others (assuming that such treatment programs constitute a scarce resource), or is the problem of dependence such that a certain level of deviance should be anticipated and accommodated?

Codes

Nowadays, much therapeutic intervention for substance misuse is addressed by professional codes of ethics or patients' bills of rights. Many who treat those with problems related to substance use belong to professional organizations that expect their members to observe certain ethical standards, primarily in relation to their clients and those close to them, but also with respect to fellow professionals, the law, third party payers, and sundry others. Representative of such documents are the Ethical Standards of the National Association of Alcoholism and Drug Abuse Counselors, the American Counseling Association's Principles for the Provision of Mental Health and Substance Abuse Treatment Services: A Bill of Rights, and the American Psychological Association's Mental Health Patient's Bill of Rights. However, they constitute only a small proportion of such statements as state and local agencies come to their own terms with the ethical challenges that confront them. Even if those who treat do not belong to formal associations, there is an increasing willingness on the part of courts to hold them to standards that are embedded in such associational documents.

For the most part, associational codes are worthy front-end statements. They specify conduct and expectations appropriate to the various parties involved in the therapeutic relationship—clients, professionals, third party payers, and so forth. Collectively, such documents attempt to cover the whole spectrum of contacts, from outreach to initial interview through the treatment regime to post-treatment associations. At each juncture of the "treatment" process, ethical questions arise and need to be confronted by the parties involved.

Like all such documents, however, they run the risks of ossification, legalism, heteronomy, and minimalism. Briefly, *ossification* involves a hardening of ethical judgment. Even if we believe that there is a right and wrong thing to do (as we may believe there to be a scientific fact of the matter), we need to beware of the temptation of thinking that our present formulation of that judgment is "final." Ethical judgment is a dynamic, ongoing activity, and one of the dangers inherent in codes is loss of a sense of that dynamism. *Legalism* occurs when a code of conduct is treated as though it were a set of quasi-legal rules, in which the emphasis comes to be on the "letter" to the neglect of their "spirit," and in which, connectedly, the focus comes to be on behavior to the neglect of attitude, on conformity to the neglect of disposition. *Heteronomy* results when people allow a code to substitute for their own reflective judgment on the issues at stake. It may be right to do what the code requires, but it is not right to do it just because the code requires it. What is done ought to be done for the reasons that make it appropriate to codify it, not because it is codified. And *minimalism* occurs when people treat the code of ethics as exhaustive of their ethical obligations to others. Codes generally specify minimum requirements, and not all or the whole extent of the ethical obligations that hold between the various relevant parties in treatments for substance use. Indeed, to the extent that codes are rule-driven rather than value-driven, they tend to concentrate on behaviors that have proven particularly problematic.

One of the reasons for the susceptibility of codes to the dangers I have noted is that, despite occasional hints in preambles, they have been severed from their ethical roots. They focus on ethical outcomes and forms (not meanings) rather than ethical values and their underpinnings. They speak of the need for informed consent, confidentiality, and so on, without indicating or articulating the deeper sources of such expectations in notions of human dignity, respect, justice, and so on. And so I offer here some of that articulation for the various responsibilities and rights that are enunciated.

Informed consent

Focusing first on the patient, client, or individual on whose behalf intervention occurs, the most fundamental requirement for intervention is informed consent. It was not always considered so. In a past era of therapeutic interventions, it was felt that health care professionals knew best and were justified in intervening paternalistically. Indeed, it was thought that the patient owed deference. Perhaps there was a modicum of truth in the underlying presumption. At least in an earlier era such professionals generally had training and knowledge with respect to the specific presenting symptoms that was far in excess of the training and knowledge of their patients.

But even then and increasingly obviously, this was and is only part of the story. Individual physicians often do not know as much as they claim, and it is better that the choice of treatment is not left exclusively in their hands (at least not without a second or third opinion). There is art as well as science in much medical judgment. Another consideration is the fact that health care professionals often have research as well as treatment agendas, and there have been (as there were in the Tuskagee experiments) major failures by such professionals to give priority to the health needs of their patients. Patients have been used. A third is the recognition that health care professionals sometimes have the rather limited agenda of addressing physical symptoms or illnesses rather than patients presenting with particular symptoms or illnesses. As a consequence, various issues likely to be of importance to patients' therapeutic decisions—such as their religious beliefs, family and economic situation—have been left out of account or given a weighting that failed to accord with the patients' own priorities. A fourth is the growing recognition that as the objects of therapeutic intervention, patients have a basic right to the final say with respect to their treatment, even if in a physician's judgment their decision is not the best one. There is now an additional factor: with the dispersal of up-to-date research information on the Internet, many patients are as well informed as their health care professionals, at least with respect to the kinds of treatment best suited to the specificities of their cases. So, for example, even if a physician is familiar with the literature on chemotherapy for breast cancer treatment, his patient may have a better idea of how that chemotherapy research bears on the situation of a post-menopausal woman with a 1.5 cm tumor, DCIS, and no nodal involvement. Understandably, physicians need to keep abreast of a wide-ranging literature that encompasses a diversity of patients and treatments. The patient, on the other hand, will be concerned with the way in which that literature bears on the specificities of her particular case.

Most fundamentally, the requirement of informed consent acknowledges that individuals in need of treatment are more than dysfunctional organisms. They are agents and not mere patients, decision makers who, by virtue of their standing as rational beings, have significant claim to be the final arbiters of what is done to them. They are sources of reasons of their own, not merely repositories for the reasons of others. They possess, as it is sometimes said, a certain dignity by virtue of their human standing and capacities, and it is by virtue of this dignity that they deserve respect and possess rights with respect to how others may treat them. Their consent acknowledges the fact that decisions about the treatment they undergo are ultimately theirs. Whatever the deficits of substance users, they are fundamentally persons who are able to take stock of their situation and make judgments about what is being proposed to them. This is not to deny that they may be impaired in certain ways; but though such impairments may require special consideration, they do not generally undermine the respect that is their due.

When people consent to treatment, they alter the normative relations in which others stand with respect to what they may do to them. They exercise a normative resource they possess so as to provide others with an otherwise unavailable normative resource. In consenting to treatment, people waive their claim not to suffer the interventions of others. For such consent to be valid, however, various conditions need to be satisfied.

The requirement that consent be informed is an intensifying or explicative requirement, because the genuineness of consent—what transforms mere assent into consent—is compromised if information that ought to have been made available to a deciding individual is withheld. In a therapeutic context, informed consent has come to require the fulfilment of at least the following conditions: that individuals be told about their prognosis, the therapeutic benefits and risks of the treatment, be informed of alternative treatments, have this information conveyed in language that is understandable, be given time to reflect on the information given, be encouraged to ask questions and have them answered by competent personnel, understand the financial implications of treatment including any constraints or requirements that are imposed by any third party payer, be informed about how any personal information will be used, be assured of a right to withdraw without penalty from treatment, and, if desired, be told how any complaints are to be made. Usually there is also a requirement that the information and consent be in writing.

It might also be appropriate for the person to inquire as to the performance of the treatment provider—whether the statistical prognosis has been replicated in the provider's own practice. To what extent should it be the responsibility of the person to be treated to ask appropriate questions and seek appropriate information and to what extent should it be the responsibility of the treater to make known information that may have a bearing on the decision? This is a difficult ethical question. *Caveat emptor* is too strong a requirement. Yet, despite the vulnerability of the patient, it may be inappropriate that all the burden be placed on the therapist. It may be too much to expect the therapist to volunteer that he is relatively inexperienced (after all, inexperience will at some point be the situation of every health provider, competent or incompetent). That is not to say that it would be inappropriate for the patient to raise the question, especially if he or she has doubts about what is being proposed.

What is true of therapeutic interventions generally holds also for substance user interventions. Those with problems of drug dependence ought—unless it can be established otherwise—to be presumed capable of understanding and consenting to treatment regimes. It is therefore incumbent on those who wish to intervene therapeutically to provide sufficient relevant information (of both a general and specific kind) in a manner that enables the individual in question to make a choice for him- or herself.

No doubt there are consequentialist benefits to such a requirement. A willing, cooperative patient is much more likely to benefit from the intervention, especially in drug cases in which social factors are likely to play a significant part in recovery. Nevertheless, it is the deontological recognition of an individual's entitlement to respect from others that provides the central rationale for the consent requirement.

In addition to informed consent's knowledge requirement, there are other, interlocking, requirements. First, there is a competence requirement. The person must not suffer from certain kinds of mental impairments—impairments that effectively undermine the person's capacity for making an autonomous decision. And second, there must be an absence of coercion. Signifying consent as a result of coercion is no consent at all.

Non-coerced consent may not be enough. A person may be competent enough to make a decision about the course of therapy, but be susceptible to unfair (rather than coercive) exploitation of vulnerabilities. A number of codes explicitly exclude sexual contact between therapist and client. This might at first seem a puzzling restriction on free relationships between adults who, in the way that adults do, could sometimes be expected to develop mutual attraction. But such exclusions, even if problematically absolute, recognize the vulnerability that underlies the therapeutic relationship, and thus the potential for exploitation of a human dynamic that even in other contexts is easily corrupted. For policy reasons, it is almost certainly better that intimate relationships be firmly excluded than that they be exposed to exploitable discretionary judgments. In some codes that do not absolutely rule out intimate relationships (say, after the therapeutic relationship has formally ceased) a burden is still placed on the therapist to ensure that no exploitation will occur.

Are there situations in which consent need not be sought? The sorts of cases that most readily come to mind are those in which, if the person is not treated, harm will be done to others. In the case of drug user treatment, this circumstance has most often been canvassed in the case of pregnant drug users. If it can be argued—as it often is—that certain forms of long-term harm are likely to be done in cases involving drug use, then it might be argued—on liberal grounds—that intervention for the sake of the fetus/child is justified. In the United States this issue has been obfuscated by efforts to criminalize pregnant drug users, a strategy that is not usually well-suited to the situations of either mother or child, but also tends to work discriminatorily to affect mostly those without the resources to handle their problem privately—that is, those who are poor, uneducated, and members of minority communities (conditions that often go together).

Privacy and Confidentiality

The same general ethical considerations that require informed consent on the part of those treated for drug mis/use also inform the recognition of privacy and need for confidentiality. Privacy is best thought of as a claim to control certain kinds of personal information. Its roots lie in the liberal conception of a human being as the possessor of certain capacities for thinking and feeling, and for progressive flourishing through the exercise of such capacities—what Mill spoke of as the capacity for individuality. The development and expression of individuality can be hampered in a number of ways. We generally think of a coercive invasion by others as the paradigmatic constraint. But we are not simply bodies in space vulnerable to physical interventions. Our status as persons signals a mode of being that can be interfered with just as dramatically—and perhaps even more insidiously—by invasions of privacy as by any crudely physical intervention. Important to our sense of self is the capacity to define the terms of our relations with others. In informational matters concerning our lives—particularly matters that are important to us—our moral autonomy is jeopardized if we do not have significant control over the terms under which that information is revealed to others. The way in which we relate to others comes to be determined by them rather than by us. It is not so much a matter of certain personal information being used against us—though that may be an additional consideration—as of our capacity to control our own behavior and the quality of our relationships with others. The mere voyeur may constitute no social threat; he impinges, rather, on our ability to be ourselves.

In certain circumstances, of course, the claim to control personal information is qualified by the effect that it may have on the legitimate claims or needs of others. Even though they derive from values of central significance, privacy and confidentiality are not absolutes. Where their observance places others at risk, a balancing process must be initiated. Thus, if an embittered drug user who has contracted AIDS through needle sharing threatens to infect others, it might be wondered whether professional confidentialities should be observed.

For various other social purposes there may also be legitimate disclosure requirements. In these cases, however, disclosure will be limited by those social purposes, and any wider dissemination of information will constitute a breach. In circumstances in which we may legitimately be expected or required to reveal personal information about ourselves to others or in which we choose to make certain information selectively available, those others will have certain obligations of confidentiality with respect to us—unless of course we waive that right and consent to their making such information more widely available. In furtherance of confidentiality, therapeutic codes of ethics often place limits on the disclosure—or risk of disclosure—of personal information gained during the therapeutic process. Thus there may be constraints on leaving phone messages, sending emails, or storing information on non-secured computers.

The problems that a person has with drug use are, to a significant extent, matters of private concern, and so those who provide treatment are not at liberty to make that information available to others—at least not in a way that is attributable. This applies not merely to gossip, which may be ethically problematic for other reasons, but also in teaching and research contexts. The advancement of knowledge through teaching and research does not generally require attributable information, and even though such advancement is socially valuable, it does not normally take precedence over the claims of privacy. A person who comes to a physician or therapist does not thereby consent to having his or her particularized information being made available to others. This is a common problem in teaching hospitals, where "trainees" often accompany physicians on their rounds. It is one thing for the patient's data to be included in some general compendium of treatment data; it is quite another for others to be present when a physician examines a particular patient.

Non-discrimination

In a society that formally frowns on certain kinds of drug mis/use, there is an ever-present likelihood that treatment services will be distributed in ways that reflect social judgments. Where the group of people visibly in need of such treatment is also distinguished on economic and/or racial grounds, there is an even greater likelihood that discrimination will occur. It will occur initially in the general allocation of resources to drug user treatment programs and additionally in decisions about who will be eligible for treatment. One of the sad ironies of many programs is that they make no provision for pregnant women or single mothers with problems related to drug use, even though this failure is likely to perpetuate problems onto to the next generation.

Such discrimination cannot normally be justified. The principle of respect for persons is also a principle of equal respect. Although certain public social resources may be distributed on grounds of achievement, effort, or some other legitimate consideration, what are seen as basic needs ought not to be differentially distributed except on grounds of differential need. To some extent, albeit still inadequately, this has been acknowledged if not fully recognized in cases in which straightforward physical needs are at stake. But in the case of drug use there is often an implicit judgment that those who need treatment must take responsibility for their own plight and are to be considered undeserving of social resources. What tends to be forgotten is not only that many physical ailments are the product of bad or careless choices but that many psycho-social ailments have their roots in factors over which people have had relatively little control. Even if they have had control, there may be strong reasons for giving them access to public therapeutic resources.

Economic and racial discrimination constitute only two of the many forms of illegitimate discrimination that might occur, and so, to varying degrees, different codes indicate that other forms—based, say, on religion, gender, marital status, sexual orientation, national origin, or mental and physical handicaps—are equally to be eschewed. The point is not to disallow any differentiations but to exclude those forms of discrimination that are irrelevant to the therapeutic task.

Professionalism

The trust placed in counselors and therapists makes it appropriate that counselors be committed to professionalism. By professionalism I understand a dedication by such people to providing therapeutic services to the best of their ability along with a further commitment to self-improvement. Competence is not simply a technical expectation but a moral demand. It includes technical skill of course, along with the kind of cultural competence that enables a therapist or counselor to empathize with the social and cultural background of the client. It also includes a constant upgrading of understanding, an appreciation that therapeutic understanding evolves and that what was adequate when credentials were obtained may no longer be so. At bottom, ensuring that one's skills and understanding are regularly updated is an expression of the respect that one has for patients.

Another aspect of the same expectation is that therapists not exceed the bounds of their competence. Being as competent as one can be includes a recognition of the bounds of one's competence, whether the limits be limits of what can be professionally achieved or have been created by some contingency in the therapist that impairs his or her performance. It involves, in addition, a recognition that if one is not able to secure a benefit for the patient, the therapist ought not to persist.

Accountability

Those who deliver treatment resources for drug use, whether as part of some publicly funded program or even, to some degree, as part of a private program, need to be held accountable for their actions. Those vested with the authority to distribute social resources are ultimately accountable to the larger society that secures those resources or from which they have been taken, and so there must be ways in which members of that larger social group can be assured that what they ensure is properly used. Even though the level of public accountability will be lower in the case of private agencies, it does not vanish altogether. Such resources are not gained or kept in a vacuum but by virtue of there being stable pre-existing social structures that set people on their way and secure them in their activity.

At its heart, accountability should be a personal concomitant of therapeutic professionalism. Ideally, treatment providers will, out of a commitment to the internal expectations of the therapeutic role, hold themselves to account for the quality of the service provided. It is because such internal constraints do not always function effectively that various external mechanisms, such as record-keeping, are needed and may be mandated via a code of ethics.

One's accountability extends beyond one's own conduct to responsibility for the "profession"—the mentoring of those in training and concern for the professional conduct of peers. Where a therapist becomes aware that a fellow professional is performing in a sub-par manner, there is some responsibility to try to remedy the situation—initially no doubt in a direct manner, but in certain serious or chronic cases through the offices of a professional association or even enforcement authorities.

Concluding Remarks

In this discussion of medical intervention, I have focused primarily on relations between treatment providers and the clients/patients. But these of course do not exhaust the ethically salient relationships in substance use intervention. There are relationships among the providers themselves, between third party payers and patients and third party payers and providers. Sexual harassment policies may be relevant to relations between providers, along with policies relating to dual treatment, respect for colleagues, and appropriate scholarly conduct in the case of published research materials. In relations between third party payers and patients, there may be individual and policy determinations of considerable ethical significance. What a third party payer will or will not compensate for (and to what extent), both as a matter of individual judgment as well as policy, is not just a matter of economics but also of fairness. Such "bottom line" considerations might also intrude to distort or interfere with treatment decisions. There are, in addition, many other relationships that may bear on whether and how treatment is conducted: between research institutes that need to test new therapies, suppliers of services to treatment institutions, legislators who regulate the provision of care and monitoring, and so on. Wherever relationships exist that impact on the interests of those involved in intervention, either as providers of treatment or as its potential beneficiaries, ethical issues will be involved.

John Kleinig, Ph.D, is Director of the Institute for Criminal Justice Ethics and Professor of Philosophy in the Department of Law & Police Science, John Jay College of Criminal Justice and in the PhD Programs in Philosophy and Criminal Justice, Graduate School and University Center, City University of New York. He also holds the Charles Sturt University Chair

of Policing Ethics in the Centre for Applied Philosophy and Public Ethics (Canberra, Australia). Educated in Australia, he taught philosophy at Macquarie University (Sydney) before coming to John Jay College in 1986. His philosophical interests are in the areas of ethics and social philosophy, with a focus on professional and practical ethics, particularly in the fields of education, bioethics, law, and criminal justice. He is the author of Punishment and Desert *(Martinus Nijhoff, 1973),* Philosophical Issues in Education *(Croom Helm/ St Martin's Press, 1972),* Paternalism *(Rowman & Allanheld/Manchester University Press, 1984),* Ethical Issues in Psychosurgery *(Allen & Unwin, 1985),* Valuing Life *(Princeton University Press, 1992), and* The Ethics of Policing *(Cambridge University Press, 1996). He is a member of the Editorial Board of* Substance Use and Misuse.

Acknowledgment

I am appreciative of the many suggestions received from Stanley Einstein—more than I have been able to accommodate on this occasion.

References

Adrian, M. (Ed.). (2001). Special issue: Do treatments and other interventions work? *Substance Use & Misuse, 36*(13), 1759-2023.

American Counseling Association. Principles for the provision of mental health and substance abuse treatment services: A bill of rights. <http://www.counseling.org/site /PageServer?pagename=resources_¬billrights> (8/3/03)

American Psychological Association. Code of Ethics, 1992 version, http:// www. apa.org/ethics/codeI992.html; 2002 version, <http://www. apa.org/ethics/code2002. html> (5/20/03).

American Psychological Association. Mental health patient's bill of rights. <http:// www.apa.org/pubinfo/rights/rights.html> (3/20/02).

Buscema, M., (Ed.). (1998). Artificial neural networks and complex social systems. *Substance Use & Misuse, 33*(1-3).

Connecticut, Certification Board, Inc. Alcoholism and substance abuse counselors' code of ethics. <http:www.ccb-inc.org/ethics.htm> (1/16/03).

Department of Health, Education and Welfare. (1973). *Final report of the Tuskegee Syphilis Study Ad Hoc Advisory Panel*, April 28, 1973, Washington, D.C.: US Government Printing Office, #747-022/5334.

Dombrowski, D.A. (1997). *Babies and beasts: The argument from marginal cases*. Urbana: University of Illinois Press.

Feinberg, J. (1984). *Harm to others*. NY: Oxford University Press.

Feinberg, J. (1986). *Harm to self.* New York: Oxford University Press, 291-300.

Green, T.H. (1883). In Bradley, A. C. (Ed.), *Prolegomena to ethics* (5th ed., 1907), Sect. 332. Clarendon: Oxford, 401.

Green, T.H. (1886). *Works*. Vol. II, (c) Sects. 17 & 18.

Green, T. H. (1888). Liberal legislation and freedom of contract (1881). In Nettleship, R. L. (Ed.), *Works*. Vol III. Longmans: London, 265-286.

Green, T.H. (1874). Speech at a meeting in Oxford on the Intoxicating Liquors Bill. *Oxford Chronicle*.

Harrison, L.D., and Scarpitti, F.R. (Eds.). (2002). Special issue on drug user treatment courts. *Substance Use & Misuse, 37*(12 & 13), 1441-1832.

Husak, D. (1992). *Drugs and rights*. Cambridge: Cambridge University Press.

Husak, D. The moral relevance of addiction. In this volume. Previously published in (2004) *Substance Use & Misuse, 39*(3), 399-436.

Iowa Board of Substance Abuse Certification, Code of Ethics for Alcohol and Drug Abuse Counselors. <http://www.ibsac.org/counsethics.pdf> (8/3/03).

Kahneman, D., Slovic, P., Tversky, A., (Eds.). (1982). *Judgment under uncertainty: Heuristics and biases*. Cambridge, UK: Cambridge University Press.

Kahneman, D. (1994). New challenges to the rationality assumption. *Journal of Institutional and Theoretical Economics, 150*(1), 18-36.

Kasachkoff, T. Drug addiction and responsibility for the health care of drug addicts. In this volume. Previously published in (2004) *Substance Use & Misuse, 39*(3), 489-509.

Kleinig, J. (1984). *Paternalism*. Totowa, NJ: Rowman & Allanheld, Ch. 7.

Kleinig, J. (1996). Ethics and codes of ethics. *The ethics of policing*. Cambridge, UK: Cambridge University Press, Ch.12.

Kleinig, J. (November, 1983). John Stuart Mill and voluntary slave contracts. *Politics, 18*(2), 76-83.

Kleinig, J, Lindner, C. (March, 1989). AIDS on parole: Dilemmas in decision-making. *Criminal Justice Policy Review, 3*(1), 1-27.

Lacoursiere, R.B. (2001). Burnout and substance user treatment: The phenomenon and the administrator-clinician's experience. *Substance Use & Misuse, 36*(13), 1839-1874.

Livingston County Council. Alcohol & substance abuse counselors' code of ethics. (Google Cache: <http://www.geocities.com/fmdesign 2002/ethics.html> (1/16/03).

Louisiana State Board of Certification for Board Certified Substance Abuse Counselors' Code of Ethics. <http://www.lsbcsac.org/bcsac¬ app_code.pdf> (5/12/03).

Maryland Substance Abuse and Mental Health Services. Consumer bill of rights and responsibilities. <http://www.samhsa.gov/mc/content/ cbr/index.htm> (1/16/03).

Mill, J.S. (1977). On liberty. In Robson, J. M. (Ed.), *Collected works of John Stuart Mill: Essays on politics and society*. Vol. XVIII. Ch. 1. Toronto: University of Toronto Press.

Mill, J.S. (1965). Principles of political economy [1848]. In John Robson, M., Bladen, V.W., (Eds.), *Collected works of John Stuart Mill*. Vols. II & III. Toronto: University of Toronto Press, 947-948.

Mill, J.S. (1972). Letter to Dawson Burns. *The Times*. 1868; November 7, reprinted in *The later letters of John Stuart Mill* 1849-1873 Mineka, F. E., Lindley, D. N., Toronto & London: University of Toronto Press & Routledge & Kegan Paul, 1480.

Missouri Substance Abuse Counselors' Certification Board, Inc., Code of Ethics. <http://www.dmh.missouru.gov/msaccb/ethics.htm> (8/3/03).

Morse, S. Medicine and morals, craving and compulsion. In this volume. Previously published in (2004) *Substance Use & Misuse, 39*(3), 437-60.

National Association of Alcoholism and Drug Abuse Counselors. Ethical standards. <http://naadac.org/documents/ display.php?DocumentID=ll> (8/3/03).

New Mexico Abuse Counselors. Code of ethics. <http://www.nmcpr.state.nm.us/nmac/parts/title 16/16.027.0018.htm> (5/19/03).

Nicholson, P. (1986). T. H. Green and state action: Liquor legislation. In Andrew, Vincent (Ed.), *The philosophy of T. H. Green*. Aldershot: Gower, 76-103.

Nolan, J.I., (Ed.). (2002). *Drug courts in theory and practice*. Hawthorne, NY: Aldine de Gruyter.

North Carolina Substance Abuse Professional Certification Board, Inc. Ethical principles of conduct. <http://www.ncsapcb.org/sacode-98.html> (1/16/03).

Ritchie, D.G. (1894). *Natural rights*. London: Allen & Unwin, 139.

Samuels, R., Stich, S., Faucher, L. (In press). Reason and rationality. In Niiniluoto, I., Sintonen, M., & Wolenski, J. (Eds.), *Handbook of epistemology*. Dordrecht: Kluwer. <http://ruccs.rutgers. edu/ArchiveFolder/Research%20Group/Publications/Reason/ReasonRationality.htm> (4/10/2003).

Sher, G. (2003, Winter/Spring). On the decriminalization of drugs. *Criminal Justice Ethics, 22*, 30-33.

Stich, S.P. (1985). Could man be an irrational animal? *Synthese, 64*, 115-135.

Sutherland, S. (1994). *Irrationality: Why we don't think straight?* New Brunswick, NJ: Rutgers University Press.

Tarasoff v. Regents of the University of California. (1974). 118 Cal.Rptr 129, 529 P. 2d 553.

Wasserman, D. Addiction and disability: Moral and policy issues. In this volume. Previously published in (2004) *Substance Use & Misuse, 39*(3), 461-88.

Glossary

communitarian: someone who holds the view that human flourishing requires "immersion" in a human community.

libertarian: someone who limits the role of the state to protection against "force, fraud, and theft."

other-regarding: affecting the interests of others.

perfectionism: as a political theory, the view that the state is justified in taking steps to ensure that certain individual excellences are secured.

self-regarding: affecting the interests only of the individual.

Telos: purpose, end.

Notes

1. For the purposes of the argument I confine myself to human beings who possess the capacities we typically associate with mature members of the species. What are sometimes referred to as marginal cases raise additional considerations. See, for example, Daniel A. Dombrowski, *Babies and Beasts: The Argument from Marginal Cases*, Urbana: University of Illinois Press, 1997.
2. J.S. Mill, *On Liberty*, Ch. 1, in *Collected Works*, Vol. XVIII: *Essays on Politics and Society*, ed. J.M. Robson, Toronto: University of Toronto Press, 1977. It was such a consideration that lay behind Mill's support for the subsidization of the arts. See J.S. Mill, *Principles of Political Economy* [1848], in John M. Robson & V.W.

Bladen (ed.), *Collected Works of John Stuart Mill*, Toronto: University of Toronto Press, 1965, Vols. II & III, pp. 947-48.

3. J.S. Mill, *On Liberty*, Ch. 1.
4. See especially, Joel Feinberg, *Harm to Others*, NY: Oxford University Press, 1984.
5. T.H. Green, "Liberal Legislation and Freedom of Contract" [1881], published in *Works*, ed. R.L. Nettleship, London: Longmans, 1888, Vol III, pp. 265-86. In this essay, Green also discussed existing land law.
6. Is a free society constituted simply by a collection of free individuals, or does a free society have conditions that affect what it is to be a free individual? Mill is closer to the first view and Green to the second.
7. For a good review, see Peter Nicholson, "T.H. Green and State Action: Liquor Legislation," in Andrew Vincent (ed.), *The Philosophy of T.H. Green*, Aldershot: Gower, 1986, pp. 76-103.
8. He is equally supportive of legislation that makes it compulsory for parents to send their children to school.
9. Cf. D.G. Ritchie's trenchant criticism of Herbert Spencer's Social Darwinism: *"In this country, no one is hindered by law from reading all the works of Mr. Herbert Spencer. This is negative liberty. But if a man cannot read at all, or if he can read but has not any money to spare for the purpose of buying so many volumes, or if he has no access to any public library, or if the managers of any library to which he has access refuse to permit such works on their shelves, or, if having access to them, he has no leisure in which to read them, or if he has not had such an education as enables him to understand what he reads, he cannot be said to get much good out of the fact that the law of the land does not prohibit him from reading Mr. Spencer's works," Natural Rights*, London: Allen & Unwin, 1894, p. 139.
10. Green's argument is very similar to those sometimes used in defense of affirmative action and compulsory education. To better the situations of those with a history of social oppression, it is not enough to remove formal constraints on them. Something positive must be done to improve their chances of making something of themselves.
11. *Prolegomena to Ethics*, ed. A.C. Bradley, Oxford: Clarendon, 1883, fifth ed. 1907, sect. 332, p. 401. That said, it needs to be acknowledged that Green believed that the full realization of human capabilities would have a moral cast to it. Thus he writes that *"the only good that is really common to all who may pursue it, is that which consists in the universal will to be good – in the settled disposition on each man's part to make the most and best of humanity in his own person and in the persons of others."* (sect. 244, p. 288). This is closely connected to his idealism, the view that the self-realization of one is possible only if the self-realization of all is attained (sect. 370, pp. 456-57); in other words, self-interest and the interests of others are intertwined.
12. Nicholson, "T.H. Green and State Action: Liquor Legislation," p. 90.
13. *Works*, Vol II, 1886 (c) sects. 17 & 18.
14. There is little doubt that Green saw the issue as one of class. He strongly identified with working-class progress, and saw both the proliferation of drink shops in

working-class areas and the lack of interest by conservatives in doing anything about it as a reflection of upper-class hegemony.

15. See John Kleinig, "John Stuart Mill and Voluntary Slave Contracts," *Politics*, 18, 2 (November, 1983), pp. 76-83.
16. Mill, however, makes it clear that, when what has the initial character of self-regarding conduct becomes other-regarding, interference with it is justifiable only insofar as it is other-regarding.
17. Although Green became a total abstainer and his sympathies were eventually with prohibition, he always kept an eye on what was politically—democratically—feasible. His older brother's life was destroyed by alcoholism, and this affected him emotionally; nevertheless, his focus is always on the cumulative social effect of drunkenness. The self- and other-regarding distinction is firmer for Mill than it is for Green.
18. T.H. Green, "Liberal Legislation and Freedom of Contract," p. 383.
19. See Mill's letter to Dawson Burns, published in *The Times*, November 7, 1868; reprinted in F.E. Mineka & D.N. Lindley, *The Later Letters of John Stuart Mill 1849-1873*, Toronto & London: University of Toronto Press & Routledge & Kegan Paul, 1972, p. 1480. See also Green's speech at a meeting in Oxford on the "Intoxicating Liquors Bill," *Oxford Chronicle*, May 16, 1874, p. 7. For further discussion on Mill and Green, see Nicholson, "T.H. Green and State Action: Liquor Legislation," pp. 87-91.
20. George Sher has recently put forward a similar argument in "On the Decriminalization of Drugs," *Criminal Justice Ethics*, Vol. 22, 1 (Winter/Spring, 2003), pp. 30-33. Important to making such an argument will be securing of a threshold of liberty so that the cumulative effect of constraint does not become oppressive.
21. The criminalization of drug use is discussed at length elsewhere, and I do not propose to consider it further here. Of particular significance is Douglas Husak's *Drugs and Rights*, Cambridge: Cambridge University Press, 1992. For a discussion that reflects his position, see his essay, "The Moral Relevance of Addiction," in this volume.
22. We might note the increasing use made of "drug (treatment) courts," along with the problems of equitable access and waiver of rights that they raise. See Lana D. Harrison and Frank R. Scarpitti (eds.), "Special Issue on Drug User Treatment Courts," *Substance Use & Misuse*, 37, 12 & 13, (2002), pp. 1441-1832; also James I. Nolan (ed.), *Drug Courts in Theory and Practice*, Hawthorne, NY: Aldine de Gruyter, 2002.
23. See Stephen Morse's essay, "Medicine and Morals, Craving and Compulsion," in this volume, which questions the deresponsibilitization of addiction.
24. However, for further discussion, see the essays in this volume by David Wasserman and Tziporah Kasachkoff, respectively "Addiction and Disability: Moral and Policy Issues" and "Drug Addiction and Responsibility for the Health Care of Drug Addicts."
25. Though civil commitment need not be and often is not initiated by governmental agents.
26. This may contribute to the "burnout" among treatment staff that some have identified. See R.B. Lacoursiere, "'Burnout' and Substance User Treatment: The

Phenomenon and the Administrator-Clinician's Experience," *Substance Use & Misuse*, 36, 13 (2001), pp. 1839-74.

27. See, in particular, D. Kahneman, P. Slovic, & A. Tversky (eds.), *Judgment under Uncertainty: Heuristics and Biases*, Cambridge, UK: Cambridge University Press, 1982; also S. Sutherland, *Irrationality: Why We Don't Think Straight?* New Brunswick, NJ: Rutgers University Press, 1994; S.P. Stich, "Could Man be an Irrational Animal?" *Synthese*, Vol. 64 (1985), pp. 115-35; D. Kahneman, "New Challenges to the Rationality Assumption," *Journal of Institutional and Theoretical Economics*, Vol. 150, 1 (1994), pp. 18-36; and R. Samuels, S. Stich, & L. Faucher, "Reason and Rationality," in *Handbook of Epistemology*, ed. Ilkka Niiniluoto, Matti Sintonen, & Jan Wolenski, Dordrecht: Kluwer, in press <http://ruccs.rutgers.edu/ArchiveFolder/Research%20Group/Publications/Reason/ReasonRationality.htm> (4/10/2003).
28. Groups such as Narcotics Anonymous and Alcoholics Anonymous.
29. See further, M. Buscema (ed.), "Artificial Neural Networks and Complex Social Systems," *Substance Use & Misuse*, Vol. 33, 1-3 (1998).
30. For a discussion of their effectiveness, see Manuella Adrian (ed.), "Special Issue: Do Treatments and Other Interventions Work?" *Substance Use & Misuse*, Vol. 36, 13 (2001), pp. 1759-2023.
31. The ethical obligations do not just go one way. Clients have obligations to treatment professionals, third party payers have obligations to clients, and so on. I shall deliberately speak interchangeably of "clients" and "patients." Each indicates something of importance: the former reminds us of the dignity and need to recognize full participation of those who are treated; the latter reminds us of their vulnerability and the exploitable inequalities that are usually present in the relationship.
32. <http://naadac.org/documents/display.php?DocumentID=11> (8/3/03)
33. <http://www.counseling.org/site/PageServer?pagename=resources_billrights> (8/3/03)
34. <http://www.apa.org/pubinfo/rights/rights.html> (3/20/02)
35. Consider, for example, the following:

    Alcoholism and Substance Abuse Counselors' Code of Ethics, Connecticut, Certification Board, Inc. <http:www.ccb-inc.org/ethics.htm> (1/16/03); Code of Ethics for Alcohol and Drug Abuse Counselors, Iowa Board of Substance Abuse Certification <http://www.ibsac.org/counsethics.pdf> (8/3/03); Code of Ethics, Louisiana State Board of Certification for Board Certified Substance Abuse Counselors <http://www.lsbcsac.org/bcsac_app_code.pdf> (5/12/03); Consumer Bill of Rights and Responsibilities, Substance Abuse and Mental Health Services, Maryland <http://www.samhsa.gov/mc/content/cbr/index.htm> (1/16/03); Code of Ethics, New Mexico Abuse Counselors <http://www.nmcpr.state.nm.us/nmac/parts/title16/16.027.0018.htm> (5/19/03); Ethical Principles of Conduct, The North Carolina Substance Abuse Professional Certification Board, Inc. <http://www.ncsapcb.org/sacode-98.html> (1/16/03); Code of Ethics, Missouri Substance Abuse Counselors' Certification Board, Inc., http://www.dmh.missouri.gov/msaccb/ethics.htm (8/3/03); Code of Ethics, Livingston County Council, Alcohol & Substance Abuse Counselors (Google Cache: <http://www.geocities.com/fmdesign2002/ethics.html> (1/16/03).

36. For a more extensive discussion, see John Kleinig, *The Ethics of Policing*, Cambridge, UK: Cambridge University Press, 1996, Ch.12: "Ethics and Codes of Ethics."
37. This study, which continued from 1932 to 1970, and was carried out under the auspices of the U.S. Department of Public Health, tracked the effects of syphilis on a large group of black males who believed that they were receiving treatment for their condition. Their consent to the risks associated with their involvement was never obtained, and at least forty of them died, most probably from lack of treatment that they could otherwise have obtained. For a fuller account and critique, see Department of Health, Education and Welfare, *Final Report of the Tuskegee Syphilis Study Ad Hoc Advisory Panel*, April 28, 1973, Washington, D.C.: U.S. Government Printing Office, 1973, #747-022/5334.
38. Some informational failures go to the substance of what is assented to and undermine consent altogether; other failures attach to collateral aspects of what is assented to so that even though the consent may have been fraudulently obtained we still allow that genuine consent was given. For a discussion of the complexities of this distinction, see Joel Feinberg, *Harm to Self*, New York: Oxford University Press, 1986, pp. 291-300.
39. Related to this will be the requirement—reflected in a number of ethical codes—that therapists or counselors not misrepresent their credentials, giving patients the impression that they are more qualified than they are.
40. I have discussed the balance between caveat emptor and the duty to disclose in John Kleinig, *Paternalism*, Totowa, NJ: Rowman & Allanheld, 1984, Ch. 7.
41. There are, however, problematic cases:
    (i) coercive offers, in which a benefit is offered under terms that a person has reason to expect on less costly terms than he is asked to consent to;
    (ii) exploitative offers, in which some vulnerability is used as a basis for extracting an agreement that the person would otherwise not be willing to give;
    (iii) unequal bargaining power, in which a person has little choice but to accept the terms that are offered; and
    (iv) extortion in which a threat is used to exact assent.
42. See, for example, Code of Ethics for Alcohol and Drug Abuse Counselors, Iowa Board of Substance Abuse Certification, Principle II <http://www.ibsac.org/counsethics.pdf> (8/3/03); Code of Ethics, New Mexico Abuse Counselors <http://www.nmcpr.state.nm.us/nmac/parts/title16/16.027.0018.htm> (5/19/03); Ethical Principles of Conduct, The North Carolina Substance Abuse Professional Certification Board, Inc., Sect. .0509 (4) <http://www.ncsapcb.org/sacode-98.html> (1/16/03); Code of Ethics, Louisiana State Board of Certification for Board Certified Substance Abuse Counselors, §1503 K <http://www.lsbcsac.org/bcsac_app_code.pdf> (5/12/03); Code of Ethics, Livingston County Council, Alcohol & Substance Abuse Counselors (Google Archive, 1/16/03).
43. See, for example, the American Psychological Association's Code of Ethics, §4.07 http://www.apa.org/ethics/code1992.html. A new code went into effect 6/1/03 (see §10.08): http://www.apa.org/ethics/code2002.html (5/20/03).
44. This is an important "if." Although there are cases in which long-term damage has been caused, and other cases in which some temporary deficit has been involved, there is little doubt that the magnitude and irreversibility of the problems have been

exaggerated by those with particular political agendas. In addition, of course, there is a question of the fetus's status. Here, however, we are not talking about abortion but about the bearing and subsequent life of a child who might be impaired.

45. I cannot argue, for example, that it is no business of others to know that I am carrying a dangerous and infectious disease, at least if its transmission can be effected by means of casual contact. Thus the Iowa Board's Code of Ethics (III.D) states: "Alcohol and Drug counselors reveal information received in confidence only when there is a clear and imminent danger to the client or other persons, and then only to appropriate workers, public authorities and threatened parties." The situation becomes more complicated in cases in which transmission will occur under more narrowly specified circumstances. See John Kleinig and Charles Lindner, "AIDS on Parole: Dilemmas in Decision-Making," *Criminal Justice Policy Review*, 3 (1) (March, 1989), pp. 1-27. Consider also Tarasoff v. Regents of the University of California, 118 Cal. Rptr 129, 529 P. 2d 553 (1974).
46. See Tziporah Kasachkoff, "Drug Addiction and Responsibility for the Health Care of Drug Addicts" in this volume.

1-2 The Moral Relevance of Addiction

*Douglas N. Husak, J.D., Ph.D.**

Abstract

I attempt to understand and assess the widespread belief that addiction is relevant to morality. I examine several accounts of how addiction might be significant from a moral point of view. Although I briefly discuss theories of virtue, I focus on three possible ways addiction might be relevant to moral blame. First, blame might be imposed for the act of using addictive drugs. Second, blame might be imposed for the condition of being addicted. Third, blame might be imposed for further risks persons are likely to undertake once they have become addicts. I conclude that each of these accounts has some plausibility, but none is entirely unproblematic. Addiction probably is relevant to morality, although its degree of importance is not as great as some commentators appear to believe. The moral relevance of addiction does not appear to rise to whatever level would justify a punitive response to addictive drug users.

Key Words: addiction, blame, compulsion, craving, virtue, voluntariness

Introduction

Many of us share a vague conviction that addiction is relevant to morality. But how? More precisely, to what is addiction morally relevant? This is the main issue I propose to address here. Part II will examine this question directly by distinguishing and evaluating three possible answers. Part I will begin by making a number of preliminary observations about morality and the nature of addiction. Although I am primarily interested in the moral relevance of addiction, I will comment on its legal importance as well—especially to criminal liability.[1] I have two reasons for straying from morality into law. First, I hope that a few clues about the moral significance of addiction can be gleaned by examining its relevance to the criminal law. Second, I suspect that an inquiry into the moral dimension of addiction is unlikely to be undertaken solely for its intrinsic interest. The judgment that addiction is morally important will probably be used in attempts to defend given responses to addicts. In particular, this judgment is almost certain to be invoked to support punitive action. We have less need to establish that addiction is morally significant if we propose to treat addicts for a supposed disease. But judgments about morality are central to the case for punishment. I will conclude that addiction is relevant from a moral point of view, but that the extent of its significance is likely to be exaggerated. Addiction appears to lack the degree of moral relevance that is needed to justify a punitive response either to drug addicts themselves, or to non-addicted users of addictive drugs who are at risk of becoming addicts.[2]

I.

The moral significance of addiction depends on two issues: first and most obviously, on the nature of addiction itself. Perhaps the standard way to proceed is to defend a particular conception of addiction, and then to examine its supposed moral implications. Clearly, this strategy is viable only if one begins with the correct account.[3] If one starts by presupposing either of two extreme views of addiction—each of which is almost certainly untenable—its moral significance would differ dramatically. A libertarian like Thomas Szasz, for example, can write a whole book about drugs without even including an entry on addiction in his index.[4] Apparently, the choices of addicts are just as free and voluntary as those of any other person.[5] Drug use may become a habit, but, like any other habit, the user can choose to stop simply by wanting to quit more than by wanting to persist.[6] At the opposite end of the spectrum, some theorists who endorse the disease model believe that addictive behavior is totally unfree and involuntary.[7] The drug use of persons who suffer from an addiction is analogous to a symptom of a disease—like fever from flu.[8] According to these diametrically opposed positions, addiction either has no affect on freedom or obliterates it altogether. Since freedom and voluntary choice are clearly relevant to morality, it is no surprise that theorists in these extreme camps derive radically distinct moral (as well as legal) implications from their respective conceptions of addiction.

In this paper, I will not pursue what I called the standard procedure. I will not defend or presuppose a particular conception of addiction in any detail. I will make only a minimal assumption about the nature of addiction.[9] I hope that this assumption is acceptable even to those whose views about addiction differ markedly. My central assumption is that the truth about addiction lies somewhere between the two extremes I just mentioned. Addiction undermines but does not preclude the freedom of the addict to engage in the behavior to which he is addicted. That is, addictive behavior is not a paradigm of free choice. Nor, however, is such behavior a paradigm of involuntariness. Addicts can and often do resist persisting in their addictive behavior;[10] many and perhaps most eventually quit altogether.[11] Those who succeed in changing their addictive behavior typically do so without undergoing treatment.[12] But they tend to experience considerably greater difficulty than if they had not been addicted.

My assumption focuses on what is typically described as the compulsion or craving component of addiction—feelings that are strong and powerful, but not literally irresistible.[13] I do not claim that compulsion or craving exhausts an adequate conception of addiction.[14] In all probability, a comprehensive account of addiction would supplement this component with others.[15] Researchers have advanced competing theories of the causes of the craving of addicts, but I hope to avoid commitment on this difficult issue as well. My only claim is that no adequate conception of addiction can exclude this component.[16] Unless someone craves or feels compelled to do something, we would not be warranted in saying that he is addicted to it.[17]

For the most part, I am content simply to assume that addiction includes a compulsion or craving that is difficult but not literally impossible to resist. Yet I believe this assumption is firmly supported by empirical evidence. If this assumption were correct, one would anticipate that the price elasticity of addictive substances to addicts would lie somewhere between that of luxuries like yachts and necessities like water. Nicotine, consumed almost exclusively by addicts, appears to exhibit the degree of price elasticity this assumption would predict.[18] Unlike behavior that is wholly involuntary, patterns of drug consumption among addicts are significantly influenced by their consequences. Rewards, punishments, feelings of guilt and shame, new information, and other forms of persuasion affect levels of drug use among addicts.[19]

If we focus solely on this component of addiction, it would seem to follow that persons can be addicted to all sorts of things. Craving or compulsion may take any object whatever, but is frequently exhibited with respect to foods like chocolate and emotional states like love.[20] It also might characterize behaviors like gambling[21] or watching television.[22] Our (so-called) intuitions or pre-theoretical judgments about the moral relevance of addiction are likely to differ depending on the object of the craving or compulsion. An athlete said to be addicted to exercise, for example, conjures up very different images than a parent said to be addicted to gambling. In what follows, however, I will discuss only one possible object of addiction as I have characterized it thus far. I will restrict most of my remarks to persons who crave or are compelled to use drugs.[23] I take no position on whether there is something special or distinctive about drug addiction as opposed to addictions to other objects.

My assumption about the nature of addiction has implications for the nature of freedom of choice. Sometimes (especially for legal purposes) we pretend that each action is free or unfree, voluntary or involuntary. We admit that a few stubborn borderline cases exist, but each such case must ultimately be sorted on one side of the line or the other. Behavior that is responsive to compulsion or craving lies somewhere at the borderline between free and unfree choice. Ultimately, however, it must be placed on one side of the line or the other. I reject this pretense. Freedom of choice comes in degrees. We can describe a model of perfectly free choice as well as a model of conduct that exhibits no degree of freedom whatever, but virtually all behavior in the real world lies on a continuum between these two extremes.[24] The distinction between the voluntary and the involuntary is one of degree—regardless of whether we focus on behavior or on the underlying neurobiology.[25] Instead of trying to decide whether given decisions are free or unfree, we should inquire (inter alia) to what extent they are voluntary or involuntary.

Again, I am mostly content to assume this view about the nature of freedom of choice. I will mention only one consideration that counts strongly in its favor. Consider the development of persons through infancy, childhood, adolescence and adulthood. No one can believe that there is a precise moment at which the behavior of given persons completes the transition from nonvoluntariness to voluntariness; presumably their conduct manifests more and more freedom as they mature. Rules and policies that identify a threshhold at which this transition is achieved—those that allow adolescents to make legally enforceable contracts at a given age, for example—are only crude attempts to approximate the point at which most persons can be presumed to be capable of a sufficient degree of free choice.

Some philosophers have thought it necessary to distinguish different senses of voluntariness. Michael Zimmerman, for example, contrasts two kinds of freedom: strict and broad.[26] Compulsion, as is paradigmatically exemplified in cases of duress, is compatible with strict freedom, but not with broad freedom. The bank teller who gives money to the robber at gunpoint is strictly free but broadly unfree. The teller's lament that he "had no choice" but to acquiesce in the gunman's threat refers to broad freedom; strictly, however, he had a choice. Zimmerman's distinction is helpful, but

I will not adopt it here. For present purposes, I believe that the distinction he draws between two kinds of voluntariness can be represented as a single continuum with no sharp boundaries on either side.[27]

I began by claiming that the moral significance of addiction depends on two issues, but I have not yet mentioned the second of these. Nothing has or lacks moral significance simpliciter; significance, moral or otherwise, is always relative to something. Addiction might be relevant to morality in either of two ways. First, addiction may be relevant to judgments about moral blame. According to this alternative, addiction affects whether or to what extent persons deserve or merit blame. The process of imposing blame involves two steps. First, the person to be blamed must have done something wrongful; no one can merit blame for conduct that is permissible.[28] But whether and to what extent someone should be blamed is not simply a function of the wrongfulness of his conduct. We must also decide whether the wrongful act is fairly attributed to him, that is, whether he is responsible for it. No one could ever escape blame by being excused for a wrongful act if persons were always responsible for the acts they perform.

But the moral significance of addiction need not consist in its relationship to blame. According to a second alternative, addiction may be relevant to judgments about virtue. Controversies about virtue, like those about blame, include two stages. First, one must defend a conception of human excellence or perfection. Next, he must show that addiction is incompatible with this conception, and thus qualifies as a vice.[29] In the present context, the details of the latter inquiry are especially important. It is tempting to suppose that the ideal human specimen has no addictions. The difficult problem is to identify the degree to which addiction undermines perfection. If addiction is only a minor and relatively unimportant vice, we have far less reason to be concerned about it.

We confront this same difficulty if we embrace the first alternative, and decide that addiction is relevant to judgments about blame. Wrongfulness and blame come in degrees. Ceteris paribus, the greater the wrongfulness, the more blame the wrongdoer merits. Unfortunately, we lack a precise measure, or even an adequate vocabulary, to quantify amounts of blame or vice. Yet judgments about degrees of blame or imperfection will prove absolutely crucial to any use to which we may want to put our conclusion that addiction is morally relevant. If addiction contributes to blame or vice to only a small degree, morality gives us far less reason to be worried about it than if its contribution turns out to be more substantial. We would not resort to costly and inefficient measures (such as those available to our system of criminal justice) to respond to acts that are only slightly wrongful or manifest only trivial vices.[30] Therefore, a thorough investigation of this topic must address not only whether, but also to what extent addiction is relevant to blame or virtue.

The second of the two accounts which I have mentioned—that locates the significance of addiction in its effect on virtue—encounters a problem with no analogue in alternatives that relate addiction to blame. A determination that addiction is a vice is less likely to be helpful in justifying given responses to addicts. In particular, we should be unwilling to invoke the criminal law to punish persons who lack virtue or excellence.[31] Many theorists have argued that criminal liability and punishment should be reserved solely for blameworthy conduct.[32] Thus I will have relatively little to say about virtue, and will focus primarily on those attempts to show that addiction affects whether and to what extent persons merit blame.

II.

Is addiction relevant to blame? Persons are never blameworthy simplicier; they are always to blame for something. Blame necessarily takes an object. We cannot begin to decide whether or to what extent addiction is relevant to moral blame without identifying what this object might be. Thus we need to specify for what we should blame the addict. At least three answers to this question are possible. First, blame might be imposed for the act of using the drug to which the person is addicted. Second, blame might be imposed for the condition of being addicted. Third, blame might be imposed for further risks persons are likely to undertake once they have become addicts. In this Part, I will comment on each of these three possible answers. In particular, I will discuss how given positions on some of these alternatives constrain what can be said about others. I will conclude that none of these three answers clearly establishes that addiction is very important from a moral point of view. But my discussions are cursory and inconclusive. At a minimum, I hope to provide an incentive for those commentators who hold contrary opinions to support their claims with greater care and detail.

A.

According to the first of these three possible answers, addiction is morally relevant to drug use itself. In other words, blame is imposed for the act of using the drug to which the addict is addicted. In what follows, I will offer several critical comments about this possible answer. I will conclude that this first answer has some plausibility, but should only be endorsed if two of its central assumptions can be defended: first, that the act of using the drug to which the person is addicted is wrongful; second, that the blame a person deserves for engaging in this wrongful act is affected by whether or not he is addicted.

Any critical discussion of this first answer must begin by examining the first of these two assumptions. Is drug use morally wrongful? Virtually no one really believes that persons are never permitted to use a drug; moral reactions depend on the reason for which the drug is taken. The moral permissibility of using drugs for medical purposes is rarely questioned[33]—although doubts could certainly be raised.[34] Moral condemnation is generally reserved for what I call recreational use—roughly, the consumption of a drug to produce pleasure or euphoria.[35] Unfortunately, however, the line between medical and recreational reasons for taking drugs has become increasingly blurred.[36] To the extent that the distinction between recreational and medical purposes has eroded, our moral judgments about drug use, which depend upon our ability to draw it, become more tenuous and difficult to defend.

At one time we had greater confidence in our ability to distinguish recreational from medical drug use. The latter, unlike the former, was designed to treat a disease or illness. But even this basis for distinguishing recreational from medical use is not as straightforward as it may seem. We need a theory of disease and illness in order to categorize a given act of drug use as medical, and no theory has proved unproblematic. In any event, the difficulties are even more formidable. Today, drugs are routinely used to treat syndromes and disorders that may be far less severe than full-fledged diseases or illnesses.[37] What exactly is a syndrome or disorder? The impoverished adolescent who takes cocaine to alleviate his boredom is not so easily distinguished from the middle-class housewife who uses Prozac to combat her depression. The worker who consumes caffeine in the morning to keep him alert is not so different from the executive who ingests valium in the evening to help him sleep. The husband who takes Viagra to increase his sexual potency is not so unlike the adolescent who smokes marijuana to enhance her passion. The foregoing examples are not unusual borderline cases that plague any effort to draw a precise contrast between two phenomena. They point out that we are hard-pressed to identify the reasons for taking drugs that should be condemned or condoned.[38]

Many commentators seem undisturbed by these difficulties; they insist in no uncertain terms that drug use is morally wrongful. William Bennett writes: "The simple fact is that drug use is wrong. And the moral argument, in the end, is the most compelling argument."[39] Barry Mcaffrey, the subsequent drug czar, concurs. President Bush cautions against any change in policy that would "undermine the message that drug use is wrong."[40] James Q. Wilson expresses this view eloquently. He writes:

> *"Even now, when the dangers of drug use are well-understood, many educated people still discuss the drug problem in almost every way except the right way. They talk about the "costs" of drug use and the "socioeconomic factors" that shape that use. They rarely speak plainly—drug use is wrong because it is immoral and it is immoral because it enslaves the mind and destroys the soul."*[41]

Despite these powerful allegations, some of us are less confident about the judgments they express. When moral intuitions conflict, we have no alternative but to identify and evaluate the reasons that lead many thoughtful people to conclude that recreational drug use is immoral.

What are these reasons? How can the mere act of taking a substance be wrongful? These questions give rise to perhaps the most basic and divisive issue in contemporary drug policy. Unfortunately, those who are convinced that the recreational use of drugs is wrongful almost never try to provide a detailed answer. That is, they rarely offer more than a cursory defense of their vehement moral condemnation of drug use.[42] Many commentators apparently regard this belief as self-evident. Clearly, this sort of response---or lack of response—is unhelpful. As long as beliefs about the wrongfulness of drug use are not supported, we have no basis to reply to those who disagree or are undecided, and do not regard these beliefs as obvious.

Sometimes, commentators appeal to public opinion polls to try to support their convictions about the immorality of drug use. They point to surveys that indicate that roughly two-thirds of Americans agree that illicit drug use is morally wrong. Sixty-four percent say that marijuana use is morally wrong. Seventy-six percent report they would continue to oppose the legalization of cocaine and heroin, even if they could be guaranteed that it would lead to less crime.[43] In fact, however, these polls reveal no consensus, but indicate the tremendous ambivalence that respondents feel about the morality of drug use. A sizeable percentage of the population is not prepared to condemn drug use. More importantly, moral controversies are simply not resolved by surveys of this kind. Consider, for example, vegetarians who insist that eating animals is wrongful. Perhaps these vegetarians have good reasons in favor of their beliefs, or perhaps they do not. But we do not prove them to be mistaken by reminding them that a majority of the public disagrees with their position. Unquestionably, vegetarians know that the majority rejects their beliefs; they are prepared to argue that most people are mistaken about the permissibility of eating meat. We could make no sense of the claim that the majority might be mistaken about morality if disputes of this kind could be resolved by a poll.

How might a moral case against drug use be constructed? Someone could believe that drug use is wrongful for either of two kinds of reasons.[44] First, the supposed immorality of drug use might consist in predictions about how such use is likely to affect subsequent behavior. Specifically, drugs might increase the probability that users will harm themselves or others. I will address this first possibility in Section C below. This account does not allege that drug use is wrongful per se; its supposed wrongfulness derives from further risks it is said to cause users to undertake.

A second possibility is that drug use might be immoral because of the psychological states it produces. In other words, the "high" of drugs might be wrongful to experience.[45] This alternative, however, seems implausible. In the first place, it is not altogether clear how or why a psychological state could be wrongful to experience. Moreover, the euphoria produced by licit drugs or prescription medications is almost never condemned as wrongful. Finally, psychological states that may be phenomenally indistinguishable from those caused by drugs—a "runner's high," for example—are more frequently approved than denounced. Therefore, the moral case against drugs is unlikely to be based on the nature of the experiences they cause.

Many of these same considerations count against supposing that recreational drug use is a vice. Most conceptions of human perfection are silent about whether or to what extent virtuous individuals engage in activities solely for recreational purposes. It is hard to see why persons who strive for excellence would never allow themselves to experience euphoria. An unwillingness to sample the pleasures of life might well qualify as pathological. Of course, some Christian conceptions of virtue are exceptions to this generalization. They recommend ascetic lifestyles, and caution against worldly enjoyment. Needless to say, such conceptions of virtue have not persuaded many contemporary moral philosophers.

It is crucial to notice that so-called intuitions about the alleged wrongfulness of drug use tend to be extraordinarily selective. Those drugs that are thought to be immoral coincide exactly with those drugs that happen to be illicit in the United States at the beginning of the 21st century. Still, the contrast between drugs that are addictive or non-addictive does not map closely onto the contrast between drugs said to be wrongful rather than permissible. Presumably, the use of some addictive drugs raises no plausible moral reservations whatever. Caffeine, for example, is almost certainly addictive; patterns of use are often compulsive.[46] LSD, on the other hand, is almost certainly non-addictive; even frequent users do not experience a craving. Some commentators who have addressed this problem have produced extraordinary defenses of the selectivity of their moral judgments. Consider, for example, the efforts of James Q. Wilson to justify the different approaches our criminal justice system adopts toward tobacco and cocaine. Both kinds of drugs, he admits, are harmful and addictive. But he claims that the criminal law should differentiate between them because cocaine, unlike tobacco, destroys the soul.[47] Of course, this allegation resists empirical confirmation, and is unlikely to persuade anyone who does not share the initial judgment that Wilson is trying to defend.[48]

Wilson's reference to the soul supports a conjecture that religion plays an important but widely neglected role in explaining why many commentators in the United States are prepared to denounce illicit drug use as morally wrongful. Although I cannot prove this suspicion, three distinct kinds of evidence help to support it. First, the paucity of respectable secular arguments against the morality of illicit drug use suggests that other kinds of considerations are at work. Second, the relative lack of moral fervor about drug use in much of Europe is most easily explained by the fact that religious faith tends to be less pervasive and politically influential than in most of the United States. Third and most importantly, no demographic variable—age, race, geographical location, income, political affiliation, or gender—correlates nearly as strongly with attitudes about illicit drugs as religion. Lifetime abstainers frequently credit religion for helping them to resist the lure of illicit drugs. Polls indicate that a majority of respondents who identify themselves as having "no religion" believe that marijuana should be "made legal." Protestants, by contrast, oppose legalization by a 69%-26% margin.[49] We should not underestimate the significance of religion if we hope to understand public attitudes about the morality of drug use.

To this point, my critical discussion of this first possible answer—according to which blame is imposed for the act of taking the drug to which the person is addicted—has simply challenged the central assumption that drug use itself is morally wrongful. But further difficulties emerge even if we concede this controversial claim and proceed to the second assumption. How does the supposed wrongfulness of drug use reveal the moral relevance of addiction? Is there good reason to draw a moral distinction between the wrongful drug use of addicts and that of non-addicts? I have supposed that addicts crave and use drugs compulsively. How and why should this difference between addicts and non-addicts affect the blame they merit for their wrongful acts? The most plausible answer to this question—an answer I will revisit in Section B—may not be congenial to those who insist that addiction is relevant to morality. Presumably, addiction could only reduce, not increase the blame a person merits for a given act of drug use. In other words, the blame an addict merits for his wrongful act of using drugs could only be less than, not greater than the blame merited by a non-addict who commits the same wrongful act.[50] In general, it is plausible to think that persons are less responsible for their wrongful acts—that is, their conduct is more difficult to attribute to them—as their behavior becomes less free and voluntary. Immoral acts that are easy to avoid are perhaps more blameworthy than equally immoral acts that are hard to avoid.[51] When addiction is implicated in a wrongful act, it is tempting to attribute blame to the addiction, rather than to the free and voluntary choice of the agent.

Does addiction really reduce the blameworthiness of a wrongful act of drug use? To answer this question, we might seek guidance from the criminal law. Anglo-American criminal law does not recognize a general defense for drug offenses when the defendant is addicted.[52] Nor do sentencing guidelines reduce the severity of punishment for the drug offenses perpetrated by addicts. Legal commentators do not tend to reserve judgment about blame until they learn whether a given act of drug use was committed by an addict or a non-addict. These facts provide some reason to doubt that addiction is morally relevant to the blame imposed for the act of using drugs.

Alternatively, we might try to answer this question by examining attitudes about the moral relevance of addiction when persons perform wrongful acts that do not involve drugs. Consider two individuals who perform the same wrongful act, such as gambling away the life savings of their families, under (otherwise) identical circumstances.

The first wrongdoer acts compulsively; his life exhibits patterns of gambling that are analogous to patterns of drug use among addicts. The second wrongdoer is non-compulsive; he gambles for the first and only time. Do we tend to differentiate between the blameworthiness of these two agents? Perhaps, or perhaps not. In either event, any distinction we might draw between them would probably be small.

Thus far, I have found no good reason to think that addiction is morally relevant to the blame merited for the act of using drugs. Drug use may not be wrongful at all, and addiction can only subtract from the blame of the user. But one rejoinder is available. Suppose that drug use is wrongful, and that addiction reduces the blame that persons merit for given wrongful acts of addictive drug use. Still, addicts could be more blameworthy than non-addicts for taking addictive drugs for the simple reason that they generally consume greater quantities than non-addicts.[53] If so, addiction might be relevant to the totality of acts of drug use performed by addicts, but not to given acts evaluated separately. We might illustrate this possibility by pretending that degrees of wrongfulness can be quantified precisely. Suppose that each act of drug use is somewhat wrongful, and that a non-addict merits blame for each such act to degree b. Addiction, let us further suppose, reduces the degree of blame by d, so that addicts merit $(b - d)$ for the same wrongful act. Still, addicts engage in more wrongful acts than non-addicts; they consume greater quantities of drugs. Suppose that non-addicts commit n wrongful acts; addicts commit mn. If $(b - d) \times (mn) > (bn)$, addicts would merit more blame overall than non-addicts for the sum total of their wrongful acts of drug use. I have no idea whether $(b - d) \times (mn)$ is really greater than (bn); nor do I have any helpful suggestions about how we might try to find out. But I can think of no other reason to conclude that addicts are more blameworthy than non-addicts for (what I have conceded to be) their wrongful act of using addictive drugs.

This first answer, then, depends on at least two assumptions that are as yet unsupported. If we hope to show that addiction is morally relevant because the act of using drugs is blameworthy, we must begin by providing some reason to think that drug use is wrongful. In addition, we must clarify why addiction should increase rather than decrease the quantum of blame that addicts merit. Perhaps these assumptions can be defended, but the task is formidable.

B.

According to the second possible answer I will examine, addiction is morally relevant because the status or condition of being an addict is itself blameworthy—or contrary to virtue.

As before, this second answer is sensible only if the status or condition of being an addict is morally wrongful (or a vice). I struggled to understand why acts of drug use might be thought to be wrongful; it may be somewhat easier to understand why it is wrongful to be an addict. The value of freedom and the capacity for voluntary choice are beyond controversy. Therefore, anything that destroys freedom must be very bad indeed. Of course, addiction obliterates the capacity for voluntary choice only according to one of the extreme views I mentioned in my initial remarks. As I have suggested, however, the real impact of addiction on freedom and voluntariness is less drastic.[54] According to the assumption with which I began, addiction merely undermines the degree to which the choice to use drugs is free and voluntary. Therefore, a critical discussion of this second possible answer must examine whether anything that limits or restricts (but does not destroy) freedom of choice is bad.

This proposition, I concede, is probably true. Anything that undermines freedom and our capacity for voluntary choice is likely to be bad. Virtue theory provides the more congenial framework for understanding this moral complaint about addiction. Arguably, the truly excellent being has no addictions; his choices are never compulsive, but are always completely free and voluntary.[55] The status or condition of being an addict is plausibly regarded as a vice.[56] But this concession does not end our inquiry. The deeper issue is not whether, but to what extent addiction is morally relevant. If addiction is not especially significant, we should not be too concerned about it from a moral point of view. But the contrary supposition—that addiction is of great moral relevance—has some surprising implications I will explore later in this Section. First, however, I will make a few general observations about the attempt to locate the moral significance of addiction in the status or condition of being an addict.

To begin, notice that the claim that addiction is relevant for either of the first two reasons—for using drugs, or for becoming addicted—provides a paternalistic rationale for blame (or the lack of virtue). In other words, the addict is blamed for what he does to himself. On this view, our judgments and responses are roughly comparable to those we exhibit toward persons who fail to develop their talents, eat too much, or fail to study. These failures are more likely to be construed as prudential than as moral. If someone balks at blaming persons for what they do to themselves, they should be reluctant to think that persons are to blame simply for using addictive drugs or for becoming addicted. In addition, even if paternalistic reasons do support moral blame, they provide a less plausible rationale for imposing criminal liability.[57] Although we might blame persons for failing to do what is good for them, we should be reluctant to go so far as punish them for their shortcomings. The harm of punishment is almost certainly greater than the harm person's cause to themselves by engaging in the conduct for which they are punished.

Moreover, I have previously suggested that persons who merit blame must have done something that is wrongful. This suggestion would indicate that blame can be imposed only for conduct.[58] This second possible explanation of the moral relevance of addiction, however, rejects or qualifies this suggestion; it imposes blame not for an action, but for a status or condition. Perhaps the status or condition in question can be reduced to one or more acts, so that blame for the status is reducible to blame for the acts that comprise the status. Since someone becomes a rapist, for example, by performing one or more acts of rape, there is nothing conceptually odd about blaming someone for being a rapist. But the status or condition of being an addict is not analogous; no one becomes an addict simply by performing one or more acts of drug use. Drug addiction requires a compulsion; it is not definable in terms of levels of use. Therefore, my earlier supposition must be rejected if we hope to make sense of the present possibility; the objects of blame must be taken to include not only conduct, but also statuses or conditions that cannot be reduced to acts. I doubt that this implication gives rise to a genuine problem. It is worth noting, however, that criminal law in the United States is typically said to reject status criminality; the Cruel and Unusual Punishment Clause of the Eighth Amendment is generally construed to preclude punishing persons for what they are, rather than for what they do (or fail to do).[59] Many commentators agree with the Supreme Court that a status or condition should not be an object of criminal liability.[60]

Is the status or condition of addiction an appropriate object of moral blame? Are all addictions blameworthy, or only some? Once again, judgments and attitudes about the moral plight of the addict turn out to be extraordinarily selective. Gary Watson invites us to imagine a person addicted to substance S who leads a healthy and productive life. Suppose further that

> *in a certain culture, otherwise similar to ours, the use of S is not only tolerated but respected as highly spiritually beneficial. The culture regards the dependency on this substance, which is to say, the vulnerability to various kinds of diminished self-control, as a small price to pay for the enrichment of human life provided by S. Fortunately, S is easily obtainable, perhaps even subsidized by the state for religious reasons.... In our imagined society, both the use of and dependence on S are regarded as entirely fitting and normal, on a par with the appetites for food and drink. The unfortunate minority who cannot tolerate S are thought to be missing something.*[61]

This example is designed to illustrate how the moral significance of an addiction depends not only on judgments about the value of human capacities but also on cultural views about the desirability of certain kinds of activities.

Even in our society, addictions to licit drugs are not always regarded as a vice. Whatever may be the case with alcohol and tobacco, there is no obvious reason why someone who uses caffeine compulsively must be said to fall short of human excellence. If I am correct, addiction per se may not be the heart of the moral problem after all. Instead, the object of blame might be the affects of the particular drug to which the person is addicted. Caffeine, after all, is relatively harmless to oneself or others, even when consumed compulsively. Many other addictive drugs are not so benign. I postpone the discussion of this possibility until Section C below.

We might examine other limitations on freedom and voluntariness to try to decide whether the status of addiction is blameworthy. Notice that no one lodges a moral protest against any number of conditions that undermine our freedom of choice but do not involve drugs. Are humans imperfect because we must eat, defecate, and cannot breath underwater? Perhaps. Of course, these limitations are natural and universal.[62] Still, any number of acquired conditions undermine freedom and voluntariness, but somehow manage to escape serious moral condemnation. Habits may provide the best examples. Like addictions, habits give rise to compulsive behavior and are notoriously difficult to break. Much of human behavior is routine and habitual. No one seems to think that the ideal human specimen lacks habits or routines. An analogy between addictions and habits raises the intriguing possibility that the condition of being an addict might actually be a virtue. "Good habits," unlike "good addictions," is a familiar locution. Why should the possibility of a good addiction be ruled out? A compulsion to do good deeds might well qualify as a virtue according to some accounts.[63] Definitions of addiction (or dependence) often stipulate that addictive behavior necessarily persists despite adverse consequences.[64] But we admire persons whose habitual commitment to the good is so strong that they persist in the face of enormous hardship. Again, moral judgments about addiction seem tenuous without further information about the affects of the particular addiction on oneself or others.

Someone who defends this second possible view about the moral significance of addiction might concede that my analogy is apt, as both habits and addictions undermine free choice to some extent. The morally relevant difference, he may insist, is one of degree; the impact on voluntariness is far more severe in the case of addictions. Habits inhibit freedom only slightly, whereas addictions all but devastate our capacity for voluntary action. This objection merits a response. The issue it raises is largely empirical; we need to determine whether habits are more or less changeable than addictions in response to rewards, punishments, feelings of guilt and shame, new information, and other forms of persuasion.[65] I will not try to settle that issue here. But the general point I have made above emerges once again. In order to assess the moral relevance of addiction, we must decide not only that compulsions undermine freedom, but also to what extent they do so. Otherwise, the moral relevance of addictions might be comparable to that of habits—which few philosophers have deemed to be especially relevant from the moral point of view.

What contribution can a philosopher make to this complex issue, without straying too far into unfamiliar empirical terrain? I propose to raise what I will call the problem of consistency. Clearly, coercive laws that have imprisoned hundreds of thousands of Americans require a justification. What is their rationale?[66] Commentators who have tried to defend the justifiability of laws proscribing illicit drug use frequently argue that addiction has a substantial impact on freedom or voluntariness. According to a popular train of thought, punitive laws are justified because they are designed to protect something of enormous value—our capacity for voluntary action. On this rationale, drug use is unlike other activities that pose risks to oneself. Most dangerous and unhealthy behaviors are not eligible for criminalization, since people participate in them freely. Even when individuals become obese by overeating compulsively and habitually, we would not dream of putting them behind bars.[67] But the drug use of addicts is alleged to be different in that it is less voluntary. To protect people from harming their precious capacity for free choice, the state is justified in prohibiting the use of addictive drugs.[68] Of course, punishments cannot really be very helpful to persons who are already addicted, if addiction really devastates the capacity for free choice. The claim that addicts are powerless to stop using drugs suggests that threats of punishment will do little to discourage them from persisting.[69] The rationale for criminalization, then, must be general deterrence—punishment can still be effective in dissuading potential addicts, whose capacity for voluntariness remains intact, from starting to use addictive drugs and becoming addicts.

Many responses can be made to this train of thought.[70] I will focus on the following problem. If the state cites its interest in protecting the capacity for free choice to try to justify its decision to criminalize addictive drug use, must it also reduce the blame imposed for acts of drug use among addicts on the grounds I sketched in Section A? Conversely, if the state reduces the blame of addicts for acts of drug use, does it also have a good reason to proscribe drug use? The line of reasoning in favor of an affirmative answer to these questions is as follows: Either (a) addiction does not have a major impact on freedom, or (b) addiction does undermine freedom to a significant degree. If (a) is true, and the freedom of addicts is mostly intact, the state interest in protecting freedom can hardly justify the enactment of drug proscriptions. We would not punish people to protect them from succumbing to a condition that is not especially severe, so some other rationale for drug proscriptions will have to be found. But if (b) is true, and addiction seriously undermines freedom, then the state interest in protecting our capacity for voluntary choice may provide a good reason to proscribe drug use. If addiction seriously undermines freedom, however, addicts should almost certainly be less blameworthy, and perhaps should be excused altogether, for their offenses of using drugs. Recall that the blame an addict merits for his wrongful act of using drugs can only be less than that of a non-addict for the same wrongful act.[71] The less free we suppose addictive behavior to be, the weaker our justification for punishment becomes. We might penalize people for behaviors we know to be somewhat involuntary, but we would not think of punishing them when their conduct is substantially unfree.

The problem of consistency I have described can be summarized quite simply: If it is justifiable to blame and punish addicts for using drugs, then their acts must be relatively free. But if drug use among addicts is relatively free, the criminalization of drug use cannot be justified by the need to protect voluntariness. Is this problem real? I think so. We should be skeptical when the state adopts incompatible positions about the impact of addiction on freedom and thus to the blame inherent in criminal liability. A legislator cannot emphasize the grave threat which addiction poses to freedom when called upon to justify the enactment of offenses of drug use, and yet downplay the impact of addiction on freedom when called upon to justify the punishment of addicts who commit the very offenses he has enacted.[72] Attempts to respond to the foregoing line of reasoning are among the most difficult and interesting projects in efforts to identify the moral relevance of addiction. In what follows, I will describe three possible replies to the problem of consistency. None of these replies, however, is entirely persuasive.

The first reply begins by returning to my initial assumption that freedom and voluntariness admit of degrees. Assume, for purposes of illustration, that the extent to which freedom is exemplified in a particular act can be quantified with precision. Let us represent fully voluntary conduct as "A", and wholly involuntary conduct as "Z". Suppose that the amount of freedom exemplified by the drug use of a typical addict is located along this spectrum at "T". Two distinct questions now arise in assessing the moral relevance of addiction. First, how little freedom must a wrongful choice exemplify before a person should be excused for making it? Second, how much freedom must a wrongful choice lack before the state has a good reason to enact criminal laws to prevent persons from making it? The answers to these two questions may well be different. The amount of freedom that must be lacking in order to excuse an act may not be identical to the degree of freedom that must be absent in order to justify proscribing it. Perhaps a choice must lack freedom to degree "P" before the state has a good reason to enact criminal laws to prevent persons from making it, although a choice must lack freedom to degree "V" before a before a person should be excused for it. The drug use of addicts may lack enough freedom ("T") to justify criminalization ("P"), but possess enough freedom to merit blame and defeat the claim for an excuse ("V"). If so, the problem of consistency is solved; the state can appeal to its interest in protecting freedom to support its decision to criminalize drug use while simultaneously withholding a defense from liability for the drug use of addicts.

I am unaware of anyone who has endorsed this reply to the problem of consistency. The myth of precision aside, I take this reply seriously, and do not pretend to have a persuasive response to it. Certainly, it would be a convenient simplifying hypothesis if the amount of voluntariness that must be lost by addictive drug use to justify the enactment of criminal legislation were the same amount that would require the recognition of an excuse for addicts. I see no good reason to believe that the former is less than the latter. Since imprisonment is such a terrible hardship to impose on persons, the diminution of freedom that is needed to justify criminalization may well be greater than the amount that would support granting an excuse of addiction. But I can think of little more to say against this first reply.

The second of my three replies to the problem of consistency invokes what might be called culpability-in-causing considerations.[73] These considerations endeavor to withhold an excuse from addicts for their drug use, despite conceding that addictive drug use may lack voluntariness altogether. How can we possibly justify blaming people for their involuntary acts? According to this reply, even a wholly involuntary act is ineligible for an excuse if the agent is somehow blameworthy for causing his own loss of freedom. Such is typically the case (or so the argument continues) with the drug use of addicts.

Culpability-in-causing considerations are not ad hoc, but govern the application of many excuses from blame and criminal liability, such as that of duress. This excuse is withheld when the defendant "recklessly placed himself in a situation in which it was probable that he would be subjected to duress."[74] Defendants who have recklessly placed themselves in various predicaments should have foreseen that they were likely to be subjected to threats that persons of reasonable firmness would be unable to resist. By parity of reasoning, the argument continues, the proposed defense should be unavailable to drug addicts. Although their freedom has been seriously compromised, they are justifiably blamed and punished for using drugs because they have freely performed a prior culpable act (viz., their use of addictive drugs prior to the time they became addicted) that they should have would subsequently result in addiction and deprive them of substantial amounts of voluntariness.

This second reply is plausible, and merits careful scrutiny. Let me hazard several possible rejoinders. First, consider a number of hard questions that might fuel suspicion about culpability-in-causing considerations generally. Exactly why is the defendant denied an excuse from blame when he culpably caused himself to be in a predicament in which an excuse is needed? Does the rationale involve estoppel-a rule of evidence whereby a person is barred from denying the truth of a fact that has already been settled? Can the blame of the prior voluntary act somehow transfer to the subsequent involuntary act? Are we simply acknowledging the epistemological difficulties of distinguishing those who pretend their voluntariness has been seriously undermined from those whose freedom is largely intact? In the absence of a more detailed account of culpability-in-causing rationales, a rejoinder is difficult to fashion. Moreover, is it really true that users should foresee that addiction and involuntariness are the likely results of their experimentation with drugs?[75] Perhaps not.[76] In addition, the severity of punishment that can result from denying the excuse seems grossly disproportionate to the gravity of the wrongful act the defendant has committed. Suppose a person freely places himself in the company of thugs. The wrongfulness of this act seems relatively minor. Suppose further that the thugs force him to assist in robbing a bank, and his excuse for this serious crime is denied altogether. Surely his blame as an accomplice to bank robbery should not be equated with that of the garden-variety bank robber who was not subjected to duress at all. Although the defendant who placed himself in the company of thugs might have foreseen his need to make some difficult choices, he may not have foreseen that anything as serious as bank robbery was likely to be among them.

A third and final reply to the foregoing problem of consistency is similar to the second, in that it purports to justify withholding an excuse from addicts who use drugs, even while conceding that their use is substantially involuntary. This reply does not blame the addict for his drug use, or for his previous free choice that caused him to become addicted, but rather for an altogether different free choice—his decision to forego various options that would allow him to discontinue his use of addictive drugs. All such options might be called treatments.[77] According to this reply, the addict becomes eligible for blame and punishment because of his free decision to forego whatever treatment would allow him to stop using drugs.

The most obvious rejoinder to this third reply is that treatment is often unavailable, and, when available, is not especially effective.[78] This reply is not definitive, however, because more promising treatments may be on the horizon.[79] A less obvious rejoinder involves what might be called "truth in blame" (or "truth in liability"). If addicts are "really" blamed and punished for some act other than their drug use, then addicts who use drugs should not be charged with violations of laws proscribing drug use, but rather with a new offense that proscribes their failure to seek treatment.[80] Implementing this proposal would raise enormous practical problems. What modes of treatment would suffice to preclude liability? How recently must treatment have been sought? How sincere and conscientious must the addict have been in his attempt to quit?

These questions would have to be answered. An addict who had sought treatment, or for whom treatment was unavailable, would not be liable for this new offense. Since the conduct of such persons would not satisfy the material elements of this new offense, the state would be required to bear the burden of proving that given defendants had not sought treatment before liability could be imposed.[81] Obviously, existing law imposes no such requirement; addicts who use drugs are blamed and punished, notwithstanding the fact that they had sought treatment, or that treatment was not available.

I am not wholly convinced by any of these three replies to the problem of consistency. Either the state should reduce the blame and punishment that addicts merit for using drugs, or it has less reason to criminalize addictive drug use. I suspect that the latter is true, and the state interest in protecting our capacity for voluntary choice does not justify drug prohibitions because the impact of addiction on freedom is not nearly as severe as popular opinion would seem to indicate.[82] Perhaps I am mistaken, however, and the state can consistently criminalize drug use to protect freedom while simultaneously denying a complete or partial excuse from blame for addicts. In any event, I hope to have cast doubt on the supposition that the criminal law can be selective with respect to the relevance of addiction to voluntariness and thus to the blame that underlies criminal liability. A state that endeavors to justify its decision to criminalize drug use by appealing to its interest in protecting the freedom of addicts is hard-pressed to deny the excuse of addiction I have sketched in Section A. At this point, however, I propose to place questions of consistency to one side in order to discuss the third and final basis for thinking that addiction might be relevant to morality.

C.

Perhaps blame has the third and final object I mentioned above—it is imposed for what addiction is more likely to lead the addict to do (or not to do). In other words, blame is imposed not for using drugs, or for becoming addicted, but rather because addiction increases the probability that addicts will commit other, subsequent wrongful acts. For simplicity, I will say that this third possibility imposes blame for various kinds of risks or risky behaviors that are increased when persons cross the line from casual use to addiction.

This alternative is just as plausible, and perhaps more so, than either of the two possibilities I discussed above. Neither drug use nor addiction appear to be especially relevant from a moral point of view, apart from further affects addiction is likely to have. A thought experiment to test this hypothesis asks us to imagine that we can know for certain that a given addiction will not cause the person to misbehave in any way. Would we still believe that his addiction is morally relevant? At the very least, its moral significance would wane dramatically. Compulsive drinkers of caffeine are not more likely to harm themselves or others than abstainers, so caffeine addiction is not regarded as morally relevant to any appreciable degree. But addictions to other substances may be different; they might increase the probability of a wide variety of risky behaviors—and therefore become a legitimate object of moral concern.

Blame for risks is widespread in both morality and law. Virtually all traffic offenses are designed to prevent persons from engaging in risky behaviors on the highways. For example, drivers are blamed and punished when they are drunk. Clearly, this behavior is condemnable because intoxication causes an impairment that increases the probability that the driver will be involved in a crash. Countless additional examples of blame and punishment for risky behaviors could be provided.[83]

Despite its plausibility, it is hard to assess this rationale for blame without a more specific description of the risky behaviors to which addiction is said to contribute. Usually the allegation is deliberately vague; addicts have been said to create risks of every imaginable kind of antisocial conduct.[84] Occasionally, however, a somewhat more concrete description is offered. According to James Q. Wilson, drug users "are not likely to be healthy people, productive workers, good parents, reliable neighbors, attentive students, or safe drivers."[85] Daniel Lungren, former Attorney General of California, argues against "legalizing drugs" by predicting "I don't think that you can argue against the fact that the costs in homelessness, unemployment, welfare, lost productivity, disability payments, school dropouts, lawsuits, medical care costs, chronic mental illness, accidents, crime, child abuse, and child neglect would all increase."[86]

Three obvious points must be made about such allegations. First, they must be supported by empirical evidence. I am aware of no data, for example, that show that (ceteris paribus) drug users (addicted or otherwise) are less reliable neighbors than abstainers. I am dubious that tests of such claims have ever been conducted. In the absence of empirical support, these accusations probably betray a simple prejudice against persons addicted to given kinds of drugs. Moreover, several of these allegations cannot begin to justify a punitive response to drug users. Even if we blame unreliable neighbors to a substantial degree, we certainly would not dream of punishing them. Other accusations, however, are clearly supported by epidemiological data and must be taken seriously.[87] Finally, this allegation must be assessed drug-by-drug. Cocaine addicts might engage in a host of risky behaviors, while heroin addicts may not create substantial risks of any significant harm. The degree of risk is not due to addiction per se, but is a function (inter alia) of the particular substance to which the person is addicted.

Beyond these three obvious points, matters become less clear. Several hard issues need to be addressed before we concede that this final alternative accurately captures the moral relevance of addiction. First, notice that most of the foregoing allegations do not really purport to blame the addict for other wrongful acts that he is more likely to commit. The bulk of these risks would not materialize but for the negative responses other persons take toward the addict. If drug addicts are more likely to lose their jobs than non-addicts, for example, it is probably because they are more likely to be discharged by their employers than to quit of their own volition. No one knows how many of these employees are fired simply for failing drug tests that are implemented by the vast majority of Fortune-500 companies today—and not because their drug use renders them incompetent in their job performance.

Many of these negative responses are pursued through our criminal justice system. In particular, users of illicit drugs obviously take enormous risks of arrest, prosecution, and punishment. Presumably, these risks are higher for addicts than for non-addicts, due to the greater quantities of drugs they tend to consume. But these risks are not direct consequences of addiction. Punishment is imposed by others; it is not something criminals inflict on themselves.[88] Blame becomes more difficult to justify when it is not applied for wrongful acts committed by the agent, but for consequences that follow from how others behave toward him.[89] To the extent that we believe addiction substantially undermines freedom, many of these responses become harder to defend. We do not blame the sick for their disease. The negative responses others adopt toward addicts are defensible only if we believe that addictive behaviors are largely the exercise of voluntary choice.

The greatest problem with this third and final alternative is that many and perhaps most of the risks commonly associated with addiction are due to or at least exacerbated by the fact that illicit drug use has been criminalized. Perhaps the most fundamental point of contention among drug policy experts is whether drug use or drug prohibitions produce greater hardships for society generally and for addicts in particular.[90] The addict, of course, is the person most likely to suffer if these harms materialize. No one should blame addicts for risky behaviors that are not caused by addiction itself, but by (frequently misguided) laws and policies implemented by others. I will mention just two of countless possible examples of this phenomenon. First, many of the health problems associated with addiction are compounded by the impurities in street drugs and the fact that addicts are reluctant to seek medical care because of their anxieties about arrest and prosecution.[91] Second, much of the poverty and squalor correlated with addiction is due to the high price of illicit drugs—a price that reflects the "crime tariff."[92]

Although most of the harms of addiction befall the addict himself, society suffers as well. But many of these harmful consequences could be ameliorated by relatively inexpensive social policies. Researchers have consistently found that needle exchange programs reduce HIV transmission among those who inject drugs, as well as among their sexual partners and children.[93] Despite their popularity throughout much of Europe, however, politicians in the United State still resist "harm-reduction" approaches to addiction.[94] "Zero tolerance" policies unashamedly aim to make the predicament of the addict as dreadful as possible in order to discourage others from engaging in drug experimentation. Social initiatives designed to minimize the harmful consequences of addiction inevitably conflict with those designed to reduce the prevalence of drug use.[95]

The claim that addiction increases the risk of crime is probably the most serious allegation among Lungren's litany of evils. Statistics from the Arrestee Drug Abuse Monitoring System (ADAM) indicate that a remarkable percentage of offenders in cities throughout the United States test positive for illicit drugs.[96] If addiction increases the risk of serious crime, we have ample reason to blame addicts, and even to punish them. But does addiction cause crime? Criminologists divide on this issue.[97] I will hazard a few observations, although I cannot begin to assess the empirical controversy here.[98] Longitudinal studies indicate that when both criminal conduct and delinquency are present, the onset of delinquency is more likely to precede than to follow the initiation of drug use.[99] Moreover, while delinquency typically ends in adulthood, addiction often persists.[100] These findings create difficulties for those who are convinced that drug use generally (and addiction in particular) cause crime. Despite insisting that addicts should be blamed and punished, Wilson's survey of the evidence leads him to conclude: "It is not clear that enforcing the laws against drug use would reduce crime. On the contrary, crime may be caused by such enforcement."[101]

Again, we should not be selective if we hold that the moral relevance of addiction consists in its causal connection to risky behavior. Alcohol is the drug most likely to lead to psychopharmacological crime. If we purport to blame addicts for the risks of violence and aggression, alcoholics would be the sensible place to begin.[102] More generally, if we propose to punish addicts for using drugs that are implicated in criminal behavior, no drug would be a better candidate for criminalization than alcohol. In 1998, the National Center on Addiction and Substance Abuse reported that 21% of persons in state jails or prisons for violent crime were under the influence of alcohol and no other drug at the time they committed their crime. Only 3% were under the influence of cocaine or crack alone, and 1% were under the influence of heroin alone.[103]

Moreover, if the moral relevance of addiction consists in its causal connection to risky behavior, we must also take account of its contribution to good behaviors. The earlier example from Watson shows that we cannot dismiss a priori the possibility that compulsive drug use could be beneficial.[104] More specifically, some drug use might actually reduce the risks of criminal behavior. For example, evidence suggests (if we are careful to control for other variables such as age) that smokers of marijuana, compulsive or not, might actually be less prone to aggression than abstainers; they are probably under-represented in the population of violent criminals.[105] The same may be true of persons addicted to other substances that sedate or operate as anti-depressants rather than stimulate.

Yet another important normative difficulty with blaming addicts for the risks associated with addiction—criminal or otherwise—is that these risks are distributed very unevenly throughout the population of addicts. The class of addicts turns out to be considerably broader than the class of persons who engage in risky behavior. The correlation between addiction and antisocial conduct is much closer among persons suffering from socioeconomic disadvantage.[106] What accounts for this fact? Drug addiction can lead to criminality and antisocial behavior in people who have the kinds of problems associated with poverty. Drug use—like other consensual crimes such as gambling and prostitution—can push people over a cliff. Whether an activity will push someone over a cliff depends on how close he was to the edge. Those with greater financial and social resources have a wider safety net, but disaster is only a short distance away for individuals who live at the social and economic margins of society. These people are more likely to take risks to solve whatever problems precede or are exacerbated by their drug use. We should be reluctant to blame people for an activity that leads them to fall off a cliff when the main problem is their proximity to the edge. The long-term solution is to move farther from the cliff.[107]

Finally, variables under the voluntary control of addicts affect the probability that their addiction will produce anti-social consequences. Among these variables are several precommitment strategies. The most well-known such strategies make it more difficult, costly, or even impossible to consume the addictive substance itself.[108] But these strategies can also help addicts to reduce the probability that they will engage in risky behaviors—even while they continue to use addictive drugs. I do not pretend to summarize the efficacy of these various strategies.[109] My point is that the probability of various antisocial acts is hardly a simple function of addiction. These risks are not invariant among all classes of addicts, but are affected by socioeconomic factors as well as by devices addicts can and do employ to minimize them—even while they persist in using drugs. To blame all addicts for increasing these risks without attending to the individual differences among addicts is too simplistic.

III. Conclusion

After making a number of preliminary observations about addiction and the nature of morality, I described two ways to understand the possible moral relevance of addiction. Addiction might be a vice, or, more importantly for purposes of justifying a punitive response, a basis for imposing blame. In either case, we need to decide for what we might blame the addict, or why we might suppose him to lack virtue. I have examined three possible answers to this question.

- First, blame might be imposed for the act of using the drug to which the addict is addicted.
- Second, blame might be imposed for the status or condition of being addicted.
- Third, blame might be imposed for subsequent risks or risky behaviors the addict is likely to undertake.

Each of these three answers provides a plausible (although hardly a compelling) reason to believe that addiction is morally relevant. But no answer provides a clear basis for concluding that addiction is especially relevant from a moral point of view. Addiction, if morally important at all, is probably not as significant as some commentators appear to think, and does not appear to rise to whatever level would justify a punitive response to addictive drug use.

Still, our intuitions that addiction is highly relevant to morality are not likely to be put to rest so easily. Perhaps a stronger case for the moral significance of addiction can be defended. At the very least, I hope that the preceding reflections will provide an incentive for persons who are persuaded of the moral relevance of addiction to support their position with greater care and detail.

Douglas Husak, J.D., Ph.D., is Professor of Philosophy and Law, Rutgers University. He specializes in the intersection of moral philosophy and criminal law. His books include Philosophy of Criminal Law (Rowman & Littlefield, 1987); Drugs and Rights (Cambridge University Press, 1992); and Legalize This! The Case for Decriminalizing Drugs (Verso, 2002).

Notes

* I would like to thank John Kleinig and Stanley Einstein for raising more difficulties with my argument than I could ever hope to address. I would also like to thank the students in Professor Jeffrey Fagan's seminar on Drugs, Law and Social Policy at the Columbia University School of Law for helpful suggestions on earlier drafts.

1. I discuss these matters in more detail in Douglas Husak, Addiction and criminal liability, *Law and Philosophy* 18 (1999), 655.
2. Impositions of criminal liability must satisfy a demanding standard of justification. See Douglas Husak, Limitations on criminalization and the general part of criminal law, in *Criminal Law Theory: Doctrines of the General Part*, ed. Stephen Shute and A.P. Simester (Oxford: Oxford University Press, 2002), 13.
3. Enormous controversy surrounds the nature of addiction. *"No consensual definition of the essence of addiction exists and any definition of addiction seems to generate as much controversy as illumination."* Stephen Morse, Hooked on hype, *Law and Philosophy* 19 (2000), 3, 11-12.
4. See Thomas Szasz, *Our Right to Drugs* (New York: Praeger, 1992).
5. Throughout this paper, I equate free and voluntary conduct.
6. Szasz, *Our Right to Drugs*, 162.
7. *"Addiction is the result of a series of small choices that provide large immediate benefits but much larger and unwanted long-term costs; by the time the costs are fully understood, the user lacks the ability to forgo the drug the next time it becomes available."* James Q. Wilson, *The Moral Sense* (New York: The Free Press, 1993), 94.
8. See, for example, A.I. Leshner, Addiction is a brain disease, and it matters, *Science* 278 (1997), 45.
9. Clearly, the viability of a theory of addiction depends on the phenomena it is designed to explain. See, for example, Terry E. Robinson and Kent C. Berridge, The neural basis of drug craving: an incentive-sensitization theory of addiction, *Brain Research Reviews* 18 (1993), 247.
10. Effective devices to resist engaging in addictive behavior include private rules, as described by George Ainslie, *Picoeconomics* (Cambridge, UK: Cambridge University Press, 1992), and *precommitment strategies*, as recounted by John Elster, *Ulysses and the Sirens* (Cambridge, UK: Cambridge University Press, 1984).
11. See Gene Heyman, Is addiction a chronic, relapsing disease? in *Drug Addiction and Drug Policy: The Struggle to Control Dependence*, ed. Philip B. Heyman and William N. Brownsberger (Cambridge: Harvard University Press, 2001), 81, 86.

12. See, for example, Dan Waldorf, Natural recovery from opiate addiction: some social psychological processes of untreated recovery, *Journal of Drug Issues* 13 (1983), 237. Harald Klingemann and Linda Sobell, Natural recovery research across substance use, *Substance Use and Misuse, 36*(11) (2001).
13. Many philosophers have questioned whether an internal compulsion can be literally irresistible and totally involuntary. See the discussion (and negative conclusion) in Gary Watson, Excusing addiction, *Law and Philosophy* 18 (1999), 589.
14. Nor is the phenomenon of craving especially helpful in explaining patterns of consumption among addicts. See Stephen Tiffany and Brian Carter, Is craving the source of compulsive drug use? *Journal of Psychopharmacology* 12 (1998), 23.
15. The most well-known diagnostic manual characterizes addiction (or "substance dependence") as a *"cluster of cognitive, behavioral, and physiological symptoms indicating that the individual continues use of the substance despite significant substance-related problems."* These symptoms frequently (but not always) include tolerance and withdrawal. American Psychiatric Association, *Diagnostic and Statistical Manual IV*, 175.
16. Conceptions of addiction did not always award a central place to compulsion, but have evolved over time to reflect social and political attitudes toward new drugs of abuse—especially cocaine—in the United States and Europe. See Ronald Akers, Addiction: the troublesome concept, *Journal of Drug Issues* 21 (1991), 777.
17. Craving is singled out as the common property of addictions in John Elster, *Strong Feelings* (Cambridge, MA: MIT Press, 1999), 62.
18. Theorists disagree about the price elasticity of nicotine and other drugs. See, for example, K.J. Meier and M.J. Licari, The effect of cigarette taxes on cigarette consumption, 1955 through 1994, *American Journal of Public Health* 87 (1997), 1126. For data that indicate a relatively high price elasticity for illicit drugs, see Jonathan Caulkins and Peter Reuter, What price data tell us about drug markets, *Journal of Drug Issues* 28 (1998), 593.
19. See Heyman, Is addiction a chronic, relapsing disease?
20. See Stanton Peele and Archy Brodsky, *Love and Addiction* (New York: Taplinger Pub. Co., 1975).
21. See Constance Holden: "Behavioral" addictions: do they exist? *Science* 294 (2001), 980.
22. See Robert Kubey and Mihaly Csikszentmihalyi, Television addiction is no mere metaphor, *Scientific American* 286 (February, 2002), 74.
23. This restriction is meaningful only if we have a reasonably good conception of what makes a given substance a drug. Although I am skeptical that an adequate account can be given, I will not press that point here. I will assume, however, that substances can be drugs even though they are licit; the status of a substance as a drug should not depend on whether or to what extent the law regulates its distribution or consumption.
24. See Joel Feinberg's valuable suggestions about voluntariness in his *Harm to Self* (New York: Oxford University Press, 1986), 113-117.
25. See P.S. Churchland, Feeling reasons, in *Neurobiology of Decision-Making*, ed. A.R. Damasio et.al., (Berlin: Springer-Verlag, 1996).

26. Michael J. Zimmerman, *An Essay on Moral Responsibility* (Totowa, N.J.: Rowman & Littlefield, 1988), 24ff.
27. Zimmerman admits to uncertainty (id., 25) about whether given conditions such as neuroses or obsessions deprive persons of strict or broad freedom. I believe this uncertainty indicates that the contrast between the two alleged types is likely to be a matter of degree rather than of kind.
28. This claim may require qualification. Suppose a person believes his act is wrongful, but he is mistaken, and his act is permissible. Is he nonetheless blameworthy? I put aside such complications as irrelevant to my inquiry.
29. Arguments that drug use constitutes a vice are critically discussed by David Richards, *Sex, Drugs, Death, and the Law* (Totowa, N.J.: Rowman & Littlefield, 1982).
30. For further thoughts, see Douglas Husak, Desert, proportionality, and the seriousness of drug offences, in *Fundamentals of Sentencing Theory*, ed. Andrew Ashworth and Martin Wasik (Oxford: Clarendon Press, 1998), 187.
31. See R.A. Duff, Virtue, vice and criminal liability—or do we want an Aristotelian criminal law?" *Buffalo Criminal Law Review* 6 (2002), 147. For a dissenting view, see Kyron Huigens, Virtue and inculpation, *Harvard Law Review* 108 (1995), 1423.
32. See, for example, Michael Moore, *Act and Crime* (Oxford: Clarendon Press, 1993).
33. Unless that drug is marijuana. Even in this case, resistance to the medical use of marijuana is likely to be either non-moral, challenging whether marijuana has a medical use, or instrumental, contending that the medical use of marijuana is bound to lead to wider, non-medical use. Generally, see George Annas, Reefer Madness—the federal response to California's marijuana law, *New England Journal of Medicine* 337 (1997), p.434.
34. For a discussion of the hazards of prescription drugs, see Jason Latrou, et.al., Incidence of adverse drug reactions in hospitalized patients, *Journal of the American Medical Association* 279 (1998), 1200. More recently, see Jay S. Cohen, *Overdose: The Case Against the Drug Companies* (New York: Jeremy P. Tarcher / Putnam, 2001).
35. Moral reservations are also expressed about a few other reasons for taking drugs. The use of drugs to enhance physical performance—such as anabolic steroids—often generates outrage. See John O'Leary, ed., *Drugs and Doping in Sport* (London: Cavendish Pub. Co., 2001). It will be fascinating to monitor attitudes about the use of drugs to enhance mental performance—when such drugs are perfected and become more widely available.
36. See Douglas Husak, *Legalize This! The Case for Decriminalizing Drugs* (London: Verso, 2002).
37. See Stanton Peele, *The Diseasing of America* (New York: Lexington Books, 1995).
38. If moral objections to drug use depend on the reason for which drugs are taken, we need to better understand what these reasons might be. For an interesting analysis, see Howard Parker, Judith Aldridge, and Fiona Measham, *Illegal Leisure* (London: Routledge, 1998).

39. William Bennett, Should drugs be legalized?" in *Drugs: Should We Legalize, Decriminalize or Deregulate?* ed. Jeffrey Schaler (Amherst, N.Y: Prometheus Books, 1998), 63, 67.
40. Remarks by President Bush in announcing the new head of the Office of the National Drug Control Policy (May 10, 2001).
41. James Q. Wilson, Against the legalization of drugs, *Commentary* 89 (1990), 21, 28.
42. Some moral philosophers assert that the use of given drugs will bring about a preponderance of disutility in the long run, but fail to explain why they are so confident in their calculations. See Rem Edwards, Why we should not use some drugs for pleasure, in *Drugs, Morality, and the Law* ed. Steven Luper-Foy and Curtis Brown (New York: Garland Pub. Co., 1994), 183.
43. See the 47 surveys described in Robert J. Blendon and John T. Young, The public and the war on illicit drugs, *Journal of the American Medical Association* 279 (1998), 827.
44. Of course, no one argument may establish the wrongfulness of each act of illicit drug use. We cannot conclude that all such acts are permissible from the fact that every single reason is inadequate. My modest point is that those who believe illicit drug use is wrongful must justify their position in more detail.
45. Statutes governing inhalants are explicit that mental states are the prohibited object of the offense. In California, for example, a criminal statute provides that *"any person who possesses nitrous oxide...with the intent to breathe, inhale, or ingest for purposes of causing a condition of intoxication, elation, euphoria, dizziness, stupefaction, or dulling of the senses...is guilty of a misdemeanor."* California Penal Code, §381(b) (2001).
46. Despite my confidence in this claim, the authors of DSM-IV assert that *"a diagnosis of Substance Dependence can be applied to every class of substances except caffeine." Diagnostic and Statistical Manual IV*, 175. The rationale for this exclusion is puzzling. Is it impossible to be dependent on a substance unless one risks or causes adverse consequences for oneself or others?
47. Wilson, Against the legalization of drugs.
48. A better reason to privilege licit drugs like tobacco and alcohol is their fiscal significance to western nations that dominate the world's economic and diplomatic affairs. See David T. Courtwright: *Forces of Habit: Drugs and the Making of the Modern World* (Cambridge, MA: Harvard University Press, 2001), 190.
49. Bureau of Justice Statistics, *Sourcebook of Criminal Justice Statistics* (2000), Table 2.83.
50. One commentator apparently regards this claim as a datum that any adequate theory of addiction should explain. He begins his paper by claiming: *"We tend to sympathize with addicts who behave illegally or immorally in service of their addictive cravings more readily than we do with those who act in exactly the same ways but who are not addicted. The addict who kills for money to buy crack seems less a moral monster than the unaddicted person who coldly plots the same murder for the same purpose."* Gideon Yaffe, Recent work on addiction and responsible agency," *Philosophy & Public Affairs* 30 (2001), p. 178.

51. Arguably, this general relationship between the degree of blame and the extent of avoidability underlies the exculpatory force of some criminal law defenses—most notably, duress. See Douglas Husak, *Drugs and Rights* (Cambridge, UK: Cambridge University Press, 1992), 109-117.
52. The leading case is *U.S. v. Moore*, 486 F.2d 1139 (1973).
53. Sometimes use is increased because persons cite their addictions to rationalize their behavior. The belief that addicts are powerless to curb their consumption becomes self-fulfilling. See Richard Eiser, Stephen Sutton, and Mallory Weber, "Consonant" and "dissonant" smokers and the self-attribution of addiction, *Addictive Behaviors* 3 (1978), 99.
54. See above, Part I.
55. Paradoxically, the capacity for complete freedom and voluntariness has not always been regarded as a property of a perfect god. See the discussion in *The Power of God* ed. Linwood Urban and Douglas N. Walton (New York: Oxford University Press, 1978), 54-58.
56. This view can be found in Wilson. He writes: *"A recovering alcoholic or drug abuser who relapses into his addiction becomes less than human."* I (charitably) construe him to mean that such a person becomes less excellent as a human. See *The Moral Sense*, 97.
57. See Douglas Husak, Legal paternalism, in *Handbook of Practical Ethics* ed. Hugh Lafollette (New York: Oxford University Press, 2002), 653.
58. I make no effort to define conduct, except to say that it includes actions as well as omissions or failures to act. See, for example, American Law Institute, *Model Penal Code*, §1.13(5).
59. *Robinson v. California*, 370 U.S. 660 (1962), is the most widely-cited case against the constitutionality of status criminality. But criticism of this interpretation has been voluminous; the constitutionality of punishment for a status is not as clear as Robinson may appear to indicate. See Douglas Husak, *Philosophy of Criminal Law* (Totowa, N.J.: Rowman & Allanheld, 1987), 100-102.
60. See Moore, *Act and Crime*, 19-20.
61. Gary Watson, Disordered appetites, in *Addiction: Entries and Exits* ed. John Elster (New York: Russell Sage Foundation, 1999), 3, 18.
62. Suppose that some but not all human beings were able to breathe underwater. It seems hard to believe that the rest of humanity would become guilty of a moral shortcoming.
63. Aristotelian virtue consists in a harmony between reason and passion. See *Nicomachean Ethics* VI.12, 1144a29-31.
64. See *Diagnostic and Statistical Manual IV*.
65. See Heyman, Is addiction a chronic, relapsing disease?
66. I explore this question in Husak, *Legalize This! The Case for Decriminalizing Drugs*.
67. We would not dream of punishing obesity, even though it may kill 300,000 Americans each year—a toll that may soon overtake tobacco as the leading cause of preventable deaths. See, U.S. warning of death toll from obesity, *New York Times* (December 14, 2001), A26, col.1.

68. Some commentators have endorsed this argument in the case of tobacco products. See Robert E. Goodin, *No Smoking* (Chicago: University of Chicago Press, 1989), 7.
69. But see George E. Vaillant, If addiction is involuntary, how can punishment help? in *Drug Addiction and Drug Policy: The Struggle to Control Dependence*, 144.
70. Most obviously, we can challenge the general deterrent effect of drug prohibitions. See, for example, Jeffrey Fagan, Do criminal sanctions deter drug offenders? in *Drugs and Crime: Evaluating Public Policy Initiatives*, ed. Doris MacKenzie and Craig Uchida (Thousand Oaks: Sage Publications, 1994). More recently, see Robert MacCoun and Peter Reuter, *Drug War Heresies: Learning from Other Vices, Times, & Places* (Cambridge, UK: Cambridge University Press, 2001), 72-100.
71. See above Part II (A).
72. When I say that a legislator cannot make such judgments, I do not mean to suggest that courts would find legislatures to lack the constitutional authority to make them. Under current law, state legislatures appear to have almost unlimited authority to create criminal offenses. See Louis Bilionis, Process, the Constitution, and substantive criminal law, *Michigan Law Review* 96 (1998), 1269.
73. I borrow this term from Paul Robinson, Causing the conditions of one's own defense: a study in the limits of criminal law doctrine, *Virginia Law Review* 71 (1985), 1.
74. See *Model Penal Code*, §2.09(2).
75. If the basis for denying a defense to the drug addict is his culpability in causing his own addiction, the excuse should remain available to those persons who lack such prior culpability. Some persons may not be especially culpable for becoming addicts. For example, people can become addicted to prescription medications they are initially permitted to take. Culpability-in-causing considerations provide no basis for denying these persons the excuse from blame or liability I have described.
76. For many years, a majority of students have reported that they do not believe much of what they are taught in their drug education programs in schools. Responsibility for this state of affairs is complex. See J.H. Brown, et.al., Students and substances: social power in drug education, *Educational Evaluation and Policy Analysis* 19 (1977), 65.
77. This conception may or may not recognize as treatment the substitution of one addictive drug (e.g., methadone) for another (e.g., heroin).
78. After leaving treatment programs, most patients resume drug use. See, for example, D.L. Thombs, *Introduction to Addictive Behaviors* (New York: Guilford Pub. Co., 1994). Ironically, recovery rates seem better among addicts who do not undergo treatment. See Heyman, Is addiction a chronic, relapsing disease?
79. See, for example, the Symposium on New Approaches in the Treatment of Substance Abuse, *Journal of Drug Issues* 27 (1997), 195-444.
80. Drug courts, which make punishment contingent on a failure to comply with a treatment regime, accomplish this result de facto. See James L. Nolan, Jr., *Reinventing Justice: The American Drug Court Movement* (Princeton: Princeton University Press, 2001).
81. *In re Winship*, 397 U.S. 358 (1970), requires the state to bear the burden of proof with respect to all material elements of a criminal offense.

82. See the discussion of the severity of withdrawal symptoms from opiate addiction in John Kaplan, *The Hardest Drug: Heroin and Public Policy* (Chicago: University of Chicago Press, 1983), 35.
83. The most serious criminal offense in most jurisdictions is reckless endangerment. See *Model Penal Code*, §211.2.
84. Some commentators purport to identify *"over fifty distinct classes of harms associated with drugs, most primarily borne by nonusers."* See MacCoun and Reuter, *Drug War Heresies: Learning from Other Vices, Times, & Places*, 60.
85. James Q. Wilson, Drugs and crime, in *Drugs and Crime*, ed. Michael Tonry and James Q. Wilson (Chicago: University of Chicago Press, 1990), 521, 524.
86. Daniel Lungren, Legalization would be a mistake, in *After Prohibition*, ed. Timothy Lynch (Washington: Cato Institute, 2000), 179, 180-181.
87. For example, addiction is known to increase the risks of homelessness. See Christopher Jencks, *The Homeless* (Cambridge: Harvard University Press, 1994). Moreover, addiction is a risk factor in child abuse. See Mark Chaffin, et.al., Onset of physical abuse and neglect: psychiatric, substance abuse, and social risk factors from prospective community data, *Child Abuse and Neglect* 20 (1996), 191.
88. Remarkably, some legal philosophers have contested this claim, contending that punishment is something offenders bring on themselves. See Herbert Morris, Persons and punishment, *Monist* 52 (1968), 475.
89. See Andrew von Hirsch, Extending the harm principle: "remote" harms and fair imputation, in *Harm and Culpability*, ed. A.P. Simester and A.T.H. Smith (Oxford: Clarendon Press, 1996), 259.
90. See, for example, Ethan Nadelmann, Drug prohibition in the United States: costs, consequences, and alternatives, *Science* 245 (1989), 939.
91. For example, pregnant women tend to avoid prenatal care, believing their babies will be taken away from them. These fears are not always irrational. See Dorothy Roberts, Representing race: unshackling black motherhood, *Michigan Law Review* 95 (1997), 938.
92. The phrase is found in Herbert Packer, *The Limits of the Criminal Sanction* (Stanford: Stanford University Press, 1968).
93. See Ricky Bluthenthal, et.al., Drug paraphernalia laws and injection-related infectious disease risk among drug injectors, *Journal of Drug Issues* 29 (1999), 1.
94. See Nick Heather, Alex Wodak, Ethan Nadelmann, and Pat O'Hare, eds., *Psychoactive Drugs and Harm Reduction: From Faith to Science* (London: Whurr Publishers, 1993).
95. See Mark Kleiman, *Against Excess: Drug Policy for Results* (New York: Basic Books, 1992).
96. See Office of Justice Programs, *Drug Use Forecasting Annual Report on Adult and Juvenile Arrestees* (Washington: U.S. Department of Justice, 2000).
97. For a recent survey, see Robert MacCoun and Peter Reuter, Drug control, in *The Handbook of Crime and Punishment* ed. Michael Tonry (Oxford: Oxford University Press, 1998), 207.
98. The best conceptual framework for understanding the drugs-crime connection is developed in Paul Goldstein, The drugs/violence nexus: a tripartite connection, *Journal of Drug Issues* 15 (1985), 493.

99. See Jonathan Shedler and Jack Block, Adolescent drug use and psychological health: a longitudinal study," *American Psychologist* 45 (1990), 612.
100. See J. Chaiken and M. Chaiken, Drugs and predatory crime, in Tonry and Wilson, *Drugs and Crime*, 203.
101. James Q. Wilson, Drugs and crime, in *Drugs and Crime*, 521.
102. See Jeff Fagan, Intoxication and aggression, in *Drugs and Crime*, 241.
103. National Center on Addiction and Substance Abuse, *Behind Bars: Substance Abuse and America's Prison Population* (1997), 33-34.
104. See Watson, Disordered appetites.
105. See Lynn Zimmer and John Morgan, *Marijuana Myths, Marijuana Facts* (New York: Lindesmith Center, 1997), 90.
106. See David Boyum and Peter Reuter, Reflections on drug policy and social policy, in Heyman and Brownsberger, *Drug Addiction and Drug Policy: The Struggle to Control Dependence*, 239, 244.
107. See William Stuntz, Race, class, and drugs, *Columbia Law Review* 98 (1998), 1795.
108. John Elster, *Strong Feelings* (Cambridge, MA: MIT Press, 1999), 186-187.
109. See Dan Waldorf, *Cocaine Changes: The Experience of Using and Quitting* (Philadelphia: Temple University Press, 1991).

1-3 Substance Misuse Treatment: Evidence-Based Policy or Fair Policy?

Maurice Rickard, Ph.D.

Abstract

There is a case to be made that decisions about what types of substance misuse treatment ought to be practiced are matters of public policy and social choice. It makes sense to want the policy process to make available the therapeutically (and ethically) evidence-based interventions. It also seems reasonable to expect that the policy and social choice processes about treatment practices be fair and just. That the decisions be properly authorized, in other words. One way to respect both of these plausible expectations is to conceptualize fairness in decision making about drug misuse treatment policy in such a way that it is conceptually conditional on the decisions delivered being the therapeutically right ones. The problem with this is that what is therapeutically correct or effective depends on one's view about what the purpose of drug misuse treatment is. The danger is to end up with a controversial conception of fair processes, rather than one that is maximally acceptable to all. This chapter explores some of the philosophical issues concerning fair treatment policy and evidence-based treatment policy, with particular respect to the question of the role of "stakeholders' in policy decision making.

Key Words: policy decision making, drug policy, fairness, evidence-basis, stakeholders, social cost

Introduction

According to the World Health Organization, psycho-active substance misuse (alcohol, tobacco, and illicit drugs) accounted for an estimated 12.4% of all deaths worldwide in the year 2000, and was the second highest set of health risk factors for mortality in developed nations. It also accounted for nearly 9% of the total years of life lost worldwide through illness (WHO 2002). The economic costs of substance misuse are substantial also. In 1995, the estimated social cost of substance misuse in the United States was $276 billion.[1] (SAMHSA, 1997). In Australia, the estimated cost was $34.4 billion in 1998-99 (Collins and Lapsley, 2002).[2] This is about twice what the Australian government spent on hospital care and medicine in 2003-04. The annual cost of illicit substance misuse in the United Kingdom is estimated to be between 2.9 billion and 5.3 billion pounds. (Godfrey et. al., 2002). Unlike many other social costs and consequences, those associated with substance misuse do not generally have comparable social benefits, so they constitute a substantial net social loss. Given this, it makes sense for society to take whatever measures are appropriate to stem the loss. In doing this, the state and its instrumentalities have a primary role. They are certainly primary in their centrality, social reach, and coordinative capacity—all of which contribute to effective social outcomes if practiced properly. But they are also primary in a normative sense, in terms of their authority—not the mere claim to authority the state often makes, nor the effects which that claim might have in getting things done, but the moral authority the actions of the state have when they are justifiable according to fair and just policy decision procedures. In other words, when they are authorized in the most philosophically defensible way.

It is crucial that public policy measures to address substance misuse be fairly and properly authorized. No doubt, the effectiveness of a measure is very important. But that importance tends to diminish if the measure or intervention is not ethically sound for one reason or another. Among the considerations relevant to ethical soundness, questions of the fairness or propriety of the decision to pursue a measure have a special place. Many of the chapters in this volume explore ethical issues in substance misuse treatment such as consent, privacy, confidentiality, non-discrimination, and so on, presumably with a view to clarifying what characteristics a treatment needs in order to be ethically sound in practice. Yet even if a treatment were ethically impeccable in these other respects if it were to be practiced, that might have less weight than it otherwise would, if the actual decision to practice the treatment was not an authorized one. That is, if it is simply not the sort of decision that the decider in question had the legitimate power or discretion to make, or if it is, the decision made does not conform to philosophical criteria for fair and just decision making in such matters, whatever one might take these to be.[3] Ethically sound and effective as an intervention might be, if it is not properly authorized in the circumstances, it ought not to be pursued. In this sense, whether a policy intervention is authorized is normatively prior in importance to whether it is effective or would be otherwise ethically sound in its practice.

This normative distinction between an intervention being authorized and it being effective (and ethical in its practice), signals a potential problem in the context of public policy. Is it conceptually the case that state authorized interventions should only be those that are most effective at addressing substance misuse (according to the available evidence)? Any claim to that effect would need to be established by argument, since it presupposes a particular philosophical view about what fair and authorized policy decision making consists in. There are competing philosophical accounts of that, against which the presupposed view would need to be defended. Few would dispute that it is worth every effort to try to fairly arrive at the best drug policy decisions, ones that conform to the available evidence concerning effectiveness and ethical propriety. The massive consequences of substance misuse speak in favor of that. But this is different from holding that drug policy decisions can be counted as fair or authorized only if they are the best policy decisions, or even good ones. This makes all the difference to the sorts of criticism that can be justifiably laid against those states and jurisdictions that do not always support drug policies that are consonant with the available evidence. There is no shortage of such states, even among the modern and enlightened ones. But governments are required to do only what is fair, and how we construe the relationship between fair policy and evidence-based policy will determine whether those states should be condemned for doing something impermissible or merely chastised for not doing their best.

From the point of view of stemming the misuse problem, it would indeed be ideal if the defining conditions for authorized policy making had built into them some sort of conceptual requirement that only good policies can count, or a promise at least, that it will be the good policies that are chosen. Building-in these in a well-justified way is no easy matter. This chapter maps out some of the broad philosophical complexities involved in trying to do that. The focus will be on policy relating to the clinical treatment of substance misuse, though the same set of complexities arise just as naturally with prevention, supply reduction, and law enforcement policy. The discussion will begin by briefly delineating the respects in which substance misuse treatment is legitimately the subject matter of public policy, rather than, say, mere individual or private discretion. It then turns to the question of evidence-based treatment policy, noting some of the major practical and normative impediments to its consistent pursuit. Finally, the discussion sketches out the major types of competing philosophical views about what makes a policy decision fair and justly authorized, and some of the problems they variously confront regarding evidence-based policy, and the issue of deciding whose interests and perspectives matter most.

Substance misuse treatment—why a matter of policy?

The question of which treatments should be available to which problematic drug users has been a particularly controversial one in the political and public arenas of the European Union, Australia, and North America over the last few decades. Issues such as methadone maintenance, heroin prescription, safe injecting facilities, treatments for prisoners, court-mandated treatments, to name the major ones, have variously been the subjects of considerable public controversy. What has significantly sustained the controversy in these cases, is the existence among citizens of differing conceptions of what the fundamental purposes of substance misuse treatment (and indeed, drug policy in general) are. This fact, in itself, proves to be one of the more persistent complexities in clarifying fairness in treatment policy making, particularly whose interests should be considered primary in those decisions (i.e., who the key stakeholders are). This complexity will be taken up later.

Before going into anything else, some preliminary reasons need to be given as to why substance misuse treatment ought to fall within the compass of public policy and social choice in the first place, and in what respects. Why should we consider it within the legitimate discretion of the state (ie., its authority) to make policy decisions about substance misuse treatment, and why isn't this simply a matter of the professional discretion of health care practitioners? In defense of the latter, one of the things to have solidly emerged in substance misuse treatment practice over the years is the fact that different patients have different histories, different pathologies and patterns of use, all of which suggest that no one treatment regime will suit all. Surely, it would be argued, doctors know best what treatments their individual patients will benefit from, certainly more than the state and its agencies, which may never come into contact with users who need treatment at all. It could also be argued, on a more normative plane, that the state has no business intervening in the privileged relationship between physician and patient, especially where the need for treatment is due to a patient's illegal activities.

These views arguably have limited force in weakening the potential role of public policy and social choice in relation to substance misuse treatment. There would certainly be no argument that health care practitioners who know their patients and their craft and have at their disposal a repertoire of tested and potentially effective interventions, are in the best position to decide the individual treatments to give their individual clients. Similarly, privacy and confidentiality between physician and patient ought to be respected. But these two dimensions of treatment provision do not exhaust all that is relevant to deciding about substance misuse treatment. First, it is worth making the general observation that people have a strong interest in knowing that the clinical treatments on offer (for whatever condition) are safe, and that the practitioners providing them are competent to do so. People who are not themselves physicians would not typically have the complex information necessary to judge these things. This information problem provides legitimate ground for the state to intervene and regulate for safety, qualifications, and effectiveness, where possible. So, even if the practitioner is in the best position to decide what treatments are suited to individual cases, the state has a legitimate claim to regulate what treatments will be legally available, who can legally provide them, and under what general conditions—all in the interests of public safety and the viability of the "market" in clinical services.[4]

There is also another set of respects in which substance misuse treatment should not be considered solely a private and individual matter. Healthcare practitioners, quite justifiably give overriding priority to the clinical needs of their individual patients. But drug misuse is not just a problem for individual drug misusers. In both consequences and, to an extent, causes, it is a collective and socially-shared problem. As indicated at the start, the costs of substance misuse are not only substantial, they are socially dispersed. Where, for example, HIV and HCV become more prevalent among substance users, the risks and costs are increased for the rest of society. Most non-drug users are at some risk of drug-related crime also. And apart from these direct risks, the economic costs of treatment, lost productivity, accidents, and so on, are often collectively shared in society, either by way of taxation or opportunity costs. To the extent that these risks and costs are shared by all or most members of society, those members can be argued to have a legitimate interest—via the agency of the state and its policies—in deciding how substance misuse is addressed, including in terms of treatment and rehabilitation. In this sense, members of society collectively can be argued to have a right or legitimate claim to decide about substance misuse treatment (via state-enacted policy).

But not only might this be grounded in rights, it might also be argued for on grounds of a responsibility that members of society have to collectively take part in addressing this problem. Although there is still a lot to be learnt about the psycho-social causes of individuals' problematic substance use, knowledge is gradually developing about some of the major factors that put people at risk, as well as protect them against developing problematic substance use. Although the exact relationship is complex, many of the risk and protective determinants of problematic substance use among youth appear to be social structural ones (Galea et al., 2004; Spooner et al., 2001). The predictive risk factors that have been posited include the likes of high levels of neighborhood disintegration, economic deprivation, and existing unaddressed substance misuse among family members. The posited protective factors include the likes of good family management practices, good integration into school settings, and strong integrated neighborhood communities (Toumbourou, 2002; Kilpatrick, et al., 2000; Loxley, et al., 2005). The prevalence of these risk factors and the absence of protective ones are unlikely to be due solely to broad societal forces, but it is still likely that they make a significant contribution. Given this, to whatever extent society is (causally) responsible for the contributing conditions of substance misuse, society can be argued to be (morally) responsible for addressing that misuse. And the most enduring way of doing that is through targeted policy interventions.[5]

Both these collective right and collective responsibility arguments, together, provide reason to think that the state is not only permitted to decide treatment issues through policy processes; they *have* to be so decided. If those arguments have force, the "what, who and how much" of substance misuse treatment practice is first and foremost a social policy matter. Just what types of treatment can be provided, who can be provided them and by whom, under what conditions (mandated through drug courts, community orders, etc.), and who should pay for them,[6] are all within the legitimate domain (i.e., authority) of social choice.[7] This conclusion, however, still leaves unresolved important issues about how to characterize fair policy decisions and outcomes, including the question of whose interests and perspectives should have greater or lesser weight in framing substance misuse treatment policy. These will be taken up shortly, with particular attention to evidence-based drug policy. As suggested, there are conceptual complexities involved in seeking to fairly secure such evidence-based outcomes. Some of these relate to certain of the empirical and normative characteristics of evidence-based drug policy, and these are noted in the next section.

Evidence-based substance misuse treatment policy—one thing or many?

The notion of evidence-based policy in substance misuse treatment is problematic from both empirical and normative points of view. Empirically, there is question as to what evidence is available to show which treatment interventions work, which do not, by how much, and whether indeed anything works at all. A key normative issue is what sort of evidence is even relevant to these questions, an issue generated by the existence of widely held differences in view about what the proper purposes of substance misuse treatment ought to be. Both of these have arguably interacted over time, contributing to treatment policy (and drug policy generally) becoming a "moralized" issue in the party politics of many modern western states.

Although an ever increasing amount of evidence is now being systematically collected about substance misuse treatment outcomes, the overall availability of rigorous data and evidence has for some time been quite low, especially data of the sort that could be usefully translated into clinical practice. The reasons for this are many. Substance misuse was not, until recently, seen by many as a health-related problem. In the case of illicit drug use, this has been exacerbated by the prevailing prohibitionist approach that casts substance misuse as a law and order matter, to be dealt with punitively rather than clinically (UN 2003). There is obviously less chance of useful long-term outcome data if there has been little systematic provision of treatment. This absence is particularly acute in the case of those in the criminal justice system with drug problems (Kothari et al., 2002). Even while the health and public health perspective on substance misuse is becoming more accepted in public policy, the prevailing prohibitionist policy culture still causes the goals of enforcement to dominate in state spending and popular attitudes. According to one estimate, between 1981 and 1998, US Federal budget expenditures on drug law enforcement increased over tenfold, while expenditures on substance misuse treatment, prevention and research were increased at only half that rate.[8] (Drucker, 1999). A national survey indicated that Australians consistently ranked treatment as a much lower budget priority than drug law enforcement in the case of illicit drugs (AIHW, 2005).

Even when prohibitionism has not dominated the health perspective, and particular substance misuse treatments have been provided for a long time, a culture of systematic evaluation has not always similarly been in place. A striking example of this is the legal prescription of heroin as a treatment for opiate dependence in the United Kingdom. Despite this treatment having been provided in that country since the 1920s (albeit on a small scale), there has been a dearth of evaluation and evidence on its effectiveness in that country (Stimson and Metrebian, 2003).

Notwithstanding these gaps in evidence, there is a rapidly accumulating body of research and investigation into the outcomes of different treatments for drug dependence, from pharmacological interventions to psychosocial ones. There is also increasing awareness of the impacts that differences among treatment clients and their possible co-morbidities can have on treatment outcomes.[9] All of this evidence is geared to throwing light on which type of intervention is more likely to produce positive treatment outcomes for which clients in what circumstances. But as well as this comparative data, evidence is sometimes presented to show simply that treatment "works"—that it does achieve what it seeks. More and more studies and evaluations are appearing that show, for example, that treatment in therapeutic communities can reduce subsequent drug use (e.g., Hubbard, et. al. 1997) and reduce arrest rates for ex-detainees (Inciardi, 2002); programs tailored to adolescent substance misusers can reduce criminal involvement and improve school performance (Hser et al., 2001); methadone maintenance treatment is effective in reducing the use of illicit drugs, in positive vocational and employment outcomes, in reducing criminal activity and imprisonment, in reducing injecting behavior and risk of HIV/HCV, and in reducing mortality (Hunt, 2003); heroin prescription can reduce criminal involvement, disease risks, and improve social functioning (van den Brink et al., 2002). There are also other studies indicating that, from an economic point of view, substance misuse treatment is very cost effective compared to the social consequences of non-treatment.[10]

However, alongside this body of evidence for treatment effectiveness, there is a parallel body that directly questions the success of existing substance misuse treatments. One recent review of treatment success observed that "despite its humanitarian intent and high-tech allure, treatment may not yield the positive results one would wish or which have been projected onto it" (Adrian, 2001, p. 1764). The review observes, for example, that in Canada almost 50% of all cases treated for alcohol dependence and psychosis in psychiatric hospitals are readmissions. The large scale US National Treatment Improvement Evaluation Study similarly concluded that half of the patients of a comprehensive range of treatment types for illicit substance misuse still used drugs one year after treatment. (Anon, 1996). How can this negative data be reconciled with the more positive evidence noted just above? How can policy be evidence-based, if the evidence is not consistent?

There is certainly nothing new about the existence of inconsistent data and evidence, especially in an area as complex and uncharted as health outcomes. Developing evidence-based policy in the context of inconsistent data is usually a matter of weighing and balancing it to determine what position if any seems most defensible. But in the case of evidence for substance misuse treatment effectiveness, the inconsistencies will often be of a less straightforward nature. Differences in evidence for substance misuse treatments often reflect differences in view about what effectiveness consists in. The negative data just cited tends to measure treatment success in terms of relapse rates and continued drug use, whereas the more favorable evidence takes into account a greater range of measures, such as social functioning, employment stability, criminal involvement, route of drug administration, infectious disease rates, as well as rates of use. As well as outcomes for individual users, these broader measures of treatment success encompass public health and population-based outcomes such as HIV/HCV prevalence and costs, crime and law enforcement-related losses, and so on. Importantly, these differences in data and evidence about treatment do not just reflect different measures; they reflect distinct conceptions of the goals and purposes of drug treatment. One takes the reduction or cessation of substance use to be the goal of treatment, while the other takes the reduction of drug-related harm to be the primary goal.

These two conceptions are not only different, they are also conflicting in many respects. The interventions that a *use reduction* goal might require can interfere with or be in tension with what a goal of *harm reduction* might recommend. For example, a use reduction goal will not condone needle exchange programs, a harm reduction measure that operates on the very assumption that people will continue to use injectable drugs.[11] Similarly, harm reduction goals will not easily countenance law enforcement measures, for example, that are geared to deterring use, but act also to deter problematic users from presenting at service providers to seek help for themselves or their families. So, these two goals can make very different and incompatible recommendations about treatment interventions. Moreover, the recommendations in each case can claim to be evidence-based.

Certainly it could readily, and possibly quite successfully, be argued that one goal is conceptually more fundamental than the other, and for that reason ought to be seen as the real primary goal.[12] However, this will not, of itself, change the fact that these two competing views are deeply entrenched in different people's attitudes to and understanding of drug policy. Historically, the goal of use reduction has pervaded policy thinking and has arguably acted to sustain the deterrence-oriented prohibitionist culture in general drug policy. To the extent that prohibitionism still dominates the drug policy landscape, the goal of use reduction still has a sound purchase in policy, as well as among those portions of the general population that support prohibitionism. Harm reduction is also rapidly gaining ground in policy and population attitudes. Perhaps the most important thing to observe about this entrenched difference of view about the goals of drug policy, is that it is not a merely "technical" factual difference. It is a difference of values. The competing views are views about the outcomes that substance misuse treatments and drug policies ought to seek. They are differences in conceptions of what it is good to bring about in society via policy.

Not only are these conceptions' values based simply in being conceptions of social ends, they also often carry with them moral symbolic associations about the character and deservingness of substance misusers. Aligned with the use reduction perspective there is sometimes a view that drug "addiction" is a moral failure, a lapse in character or even a perverse indulgence for which users should be punished or reformed, rather than something that is not fully within their control, and for which they need treatment assistance. Even where addiction and treatment is not the issue, but where liberalizing availability is, moral symbolic associations come into play, often reinforced by the media. One major US newspaper, for example, commenting on the recent US Supreme Court decision enabling the US federal government to override state laws allowing the medical use of cannabis, said *"Marijuana is banned because it is a mind-altering drug that people take for fun. The problem is not mainly that it is medically dangerous....It is that it is morally dangerous, that for too many people it is a ticket to idleness and irresponsibility."*[13] These various symbolic associations have led to drug policy becoming a "moralized" issue in the party politics of many modern democracies, along with issues such as gambling, prostitution, abortion, and the like (Mooney, 2001). Drug use (particularly illicit drug use) is often invoked by political parties for electoral purposes—usually under the promise of increased "law and order"—to mobilize certain values and constituencies and to signal party ideology. For example, in response to the (Democrat) Clinton administration's moves to increase the availability of methadone treatment in 1998, the (Republican) Mayor of New York City Rudolph Giuliani undertook to close down the methadone programmes run by his city, and was reported as calling Clinton's proposal a "terrible, terrible perversion of drug treatment," which "merely substitutes one addiction for another" (McCarthy, 1998, p. 1206).[14] Both media portrayal and political manipulation serve to reinforce the moral symbols associated with substance misuse, and further entrench in society the different conceptions of drug policy goals those symbols comport with.

The existence of these two socially entrenched, widely held, and ostensibly incompatible conceptions of the proper purposes of substance misuse treatment has important implications for how readily and strongly a requirement or expectation of evidence-based policy can be built into the philosophical conditions of fair and authorized treatment policy. Those philosophical conditions will need somehow to accommodate or deal with the following two problems.

- First, the very notion of evidence-based policy is normatively controversial given the possibility of differing conceptions of treatment effectiveness and success. This means that an account of fair and authorized policy decision making that somehow builds in an expectation of evidence-based policy outcomes is at risk of being biased and failing to be an impartial account of fairness.
- Second, the normative controversy about goals complicates pinning down the relevant "stakeholders" in defining the philosophical conditions for fair and authorized treatment policy decisions. Just whose interests are most or least at stake in the outcomes of treatment policy will depend on exactly what outcomes are sought, and this in turn will depend on the conception of treatment goals that one favors. The next section expands on these complexities.

Fair Policy—Who decides and what decisions?

It was argued earlier that questions about what treatment types should be available to what types of client and under what costs and conditions, should be considered policy matters, to be decided collectively through processes of social choice. Those decisions will only be acceptable ones, however, if they are fair. But there are differing accounts of what fair policy decisions involve. Policy decisions are products of public institutions, at least in justly constituted democracies. Those institutions range from parliamentary legislative and regulatory processes, to public committees and inquiries, to government departmental and quasi-departmental decisions. So, directly or indirectly, substance misuse treatment policy is linked to the political process. This observation can easily lead to the view that if the political process and the regulations and delegated authorities born of it are fair and democratic, any policy decisions made in accordance with those regulations and authorities will themselves be fair, whether the decision is to close down methadone programmes or to support the controlled prescription of heroin. Often, newly elected governments claim a "mandate" for their policies on that very basis. Even when the policies in question are not favored by the majority of the population or by those with the greatest expertise in the area, fair election to office, it is sometimes argued, carries with it the right to decide. Policies formed in a fair political context and as the result of fair decision processes are themselves fair in virtue of that, it could be argued, even if they might not be the best, or the most informed, or the most popular policies.

In reply to this, some see it as the role of a just government to bring about the best outcomes for the nation (whatever they might be), regardless of whether those outcomes accord with the views the majority happens to have, or the predilections and ideological preferences of the parties holding office. In line with this, it would be argued that it is not within the rightful discretion of governments or their agencies to act outside the genuine interests of the nation, and no such action is ever a fair or just one to perform. So, even if there were, say, little public sympathy toward the decriminalization of cannabis use, this may well be the best policy to pursue in the interests of the general population, or at least the interests of the key stakeholders. Public policy-making bodies should be constituted and regulated so that they make the right policy choices.

Running in parallel with these two scenarios are two different philosophical interpretations of fairness or justness. According to the first, purely procedural interpretation, whether a decision is fair or not depends solely on the process by which it came to be made. If the process or decision-procedure is fair, then the outcome that is decided is fair, whatever it turns out to be. It does not matter what the content of the actual decision is or what its consequences or impacts are, or how well it fits in with other states of affairs. There will be different views on what conditions need to be placed on the construction and conduct of a decision-process for it to count as a fair process. Typically the conditions specify what capacities, expertise, and relative powers the participants in the process should have, the information and interests they are allowed to consider and in what weight, how much each participant's own view contributes to the final decision made, how those views are aggregated, and so on. Different versions of procedural fairness will fill out the detail of these constraints and conditions differently. But the underlying premise is that if the right procedural conditions are put in place, then the outcomes, whatever they are, will be fair in virtue of them.[15]

The "pureness" of the pure procedural account pertains to the fact that none of the conditions of the process are defined or selected on the basis of a preconceived view or preference about what the outcome of the process should be like. Within the range of possibilities determined by its intended subject matter, the procedure remains silent about the outcomes it could produce. This is what adherents of pure procedural fairness usually take its fairness to consist in—the fact that its defining conditions do not, either conceptually or contingently, bias the process to any predetermined outcome or type of outcome.[16] If procedural conditions and constraints are selected or defined so as to increase the likelihood of certain decision outcomes over others, the procedure is no longer pure. Pure procedural accounts rely very heavily on specifications about the rights, interests, powers, capacities, and other relevant characteristics of the agents or participants in the decision process. To that extent, in answering the question of *how* fair decisions should be made, they also provide an answer as to *who* should decide them.

The second philosophical account of fairness is non-procedural and outcome-based. On this interpretation, the fairness of a decision is not defined in terms of the process by which it came to be made. What matters solely are the properties of the outcome. Different versions of outcome-based fairness take different properties to be relevant, for example, whether the choice promotes utility, or respects certain moral constraints, or serves people's interests equally or reflects a favored distributive pattern, and so on. If the state of affairs a decision seeks to implement does not reflect that favored property—if it does not for instance serve everyone's interests equally—then in virtue of that, it is simply not a fair decision. This will be so, on this account, even if the process by which the decision was made was very inclusive and even-handed and properly informed, or was otherwise fair looking. With this said, even though the nature of the process is not relevant to the *definition* of fair decisions or outcomes, the nature of the process is certainly relevant to whether a fair outcome is likely to be delivered or not. Adherents of outcome-based accounts will therefore seek to ensure that real life decision-processes are designed so as to guarantee or maximize the making of the right decisions, including who should play a role in the decision. For outcome accounts, the question of who decides—who is authorized—is simply answered as whoever is best placed to choose the right outcome, independently defined.

No argument will be made here to the effect that one or the other of these accounts of fairness, or any other account combining them, is the most plausible rendition of fairness overall. It seems very likely that the context and the subject matter for decision makes a difference. For example, in decision contexts where people have competing preferences about outcomes, a procedural approach, where there is no predetermined outcome and all can express their interests and determine a decision, seems to reflect fairness well. Similarly, in circumstances of conflict it seems fair (and pragmatic) to opt for a procedure of bargaining to achieve some workable "consensus" on how to move forward. On the other hand, where fundamental values are in question, like people's rights or potential harms, it would seem more just to opt for an outcome approach which ensures that the decision respects these values.

In the democratic political and policy context, perhaps the most plausible account of fairness consists in some combination of procedural and outcome-based criteria. One reason for thinking this is that modern parliamentary politics and policy making are competitive and are often about negotiating diverse preferences about wide ranging social outcomes, many of which potentially impact on fundamental interests, especially in the domains of health care and law enforcement (both relating to drug policy). Fairness in these diverse circumstances is not likely to be straightforward. Even so, it will still be the two accounts of fairness sketched above that are at work, albeit in combination. This means, however, that if there are problems with each account, there are likely to be problems with both when mixed together. And as it turns out, problems arise on each account of fairness when it comes to substance misuse treatment policy.

Stakeholders and impartiality—some problems

Each of the accounts sketched above purports to give a plausible theoretical picture of what fairness in decision making consists in. But in terms of what is one account supposed to be more plausible than the other? What are the properties of fairness that each seeks to capture better than the other, and in terms of which their relative success in doing so might be judged? Fairness is one of those notions that is hard to further analyze into more basic properties without lapsing into giving another (contestable) theoretical account of it. But with this said, there is one notion that fairness does seem intimately tied up with—*impartiality*. Fair decisions are fair in virtue of their being impartial between people's competing interests. This does not mean that impartiality requires everyone to end up exactly equal or to have exactly the same role or power in decision making. Impartiality more plausibly means respecting people's interests in proportion to their importance, urgency, or moral weight, and this will inevitably differ between people. The weight of people's interests will also differ when measured along different moral dimensions, including dimensions such as the consequences of a decision for them, how much more or less they have compared to others, what pre-existing rights and privileges they have, how deserving they are, what their level of knowledge or expertise is, what degree of legitimate authority they have, even maybe how lucky they are. Just which of these dimensions is most central to weighting the importance or urgency of different people's interests is itself subject to philosophical debate. But the point remains that impartiality is consistent with different roles or different outcomes for different people or groups of people, depending on the nature of their interests.

Procedural accounts take impartiality to be appropriately exemplified only when those with a legitimate interest in the possible decision outcomes have their interest represented in the decision-process in proportion to its proper weight and importance. That representation might be by way of the individuals themselves or their representatives participating in the process, with a "voice" in the final decision commensurate with the weight of their interest. Or, if the nature of the interest is sufficiently known, it can be represented through being factored into the information inputs to the process. Outcome accounts see impartiality as appropriately achieved if decision outcomes impact on or reflect the relevant parties' interests in proportion to their proper weight and importance. The decision processes suited to such outcomes will need to accurately factor in information about the relative weight of relevant interests. But this factoring in need not be by way of those interests being personally represented in the process.[17]

There will, of course, be a lot more to the two theoretical accounts of fairness than that. But whatever else is involved, to even begin to discharge their mission, both of them and any amalgamation of them will need to be able to identify who it is (either individuals or groups) who have interests that are relevant to the decision, and also their comparative weight. In other words, who the stakeholders are and who, or which interests, among them are more or less important.

This stakeholder terminology is very familiar in the context of drug policy. Among those who are often cited as stakeholders in drug policy decisions are users themselves, their families, neighborhoods and local communities, victims of drug-related crime, health professionals, and law enforcement agencies. Typically these groups are seen as stakeholders because they are impacted on, one way or another, by substance misuse or the various actions taken to address it. Drug policy formation in enlightened parts of the world is also increasingly taking stakeholder perspectives as important. However, problems arise when it comes to precisely delimiting the set of relevant stakeholders that is necessary for impartial policy decisions. These problems are connected with the existence of different and competing conceptions of the basic purposes of substance misuse treatment policy.

Consider pure procedural accounts of policy decision making. The stakeholders here will be the groups who are likely to be advantaged or disadvantaged by the possible outcomes of the policy decision process. In other words, those who have something at stake in the potential outcomes. The range of potential outcomes is clearly a function of the options and alternatives that are put on the table in the first place. There always has to be a relatively determinate idea of which options are to be included for choice and which not. But, importantly, this will significantly depend on what one takes to be the fundamental purposes of drug (treatment) policy. Policy alternatives that just do not fit in with how one conceives those purposes will either be excluded by default as viable options, or be given a very low priority for serious consideration. A different conception may well give those same options a higher priority and, with it, a higher likelihood of being the outcomes decided. For example, a "rave safe" initiative,[18] where facilities are provided for rave party-goers to test the safety and purity of the ecstasy they intend to consume, will be considered a no-priority or low priority option for a decision framed in terms of a use-reduction conception of drug policy. But that same initiative will be a high priority from a harm-reduction perspective. If stakeholders, and the relative importances among them, are identified in terms of the impacts of the decisions likely to be made, different conceptions of policy goals would appear to define different stakeholder sets. The problem here for procedural accounts is that impartiality, when it is defined in terms of stakeholder interests, seems to end up tied to particular conceptions of drug policy goals. And this fails to reflect the sort of impartiality that would be desired for fair policy decisions.

What has gone amiss here? There are two possibilities. Either it is mistaken to define impartiality in terms of stakeholder interests, or else it is mistaken to allow stakeholders and the relative importance of their interests to be delimited in terms of policy purposes. It is hard to shake the feeling that impartiality has to be defined in terms of people's interests, at least in some formal sense. Maybe the problem is how those interests are characterized. It was said just before that people's interests can be understood in different ways depending on the philosophical aims and arguments at hand. Maybe a purpose-neutral conception of people's interests would solve the problem. People's interests could perhaps be defined and compared in terms of their welfare or well-being, or some other purpose-neutral index. But it is not clear how this would contribute to a sounder way of distinguishing stakeholders from non-stakeholders in the possible outcomes of the decision process. It still remains the case that exactly who it is whose interests are more likely than not to be impacted on by the potential outcomes of a decision process, will depend on what the options are that are on the table for choice in the first place, and what the sense is of their relative priority. This is the case regardless of how people's interests are characterized. Moreover, even if the scope and nature of the policy options to be decided on are not defined or "closed" in terms of some conception of policy purposes, they will still be defined in some substantive, non-neutral way.

It would seem that the only way to avoid this would be to simply allow anything into the process as a possible option for responding to substance misuse, however unlikely and irrelevant it might seem from the point of view of serving any sensible goal, and then just allowing anyone to count as a stakeholder who could be affected by any of those possibilities if they happen to be chosen or not. Certainly, fully open decision procedures like this have their conceptual place (even if difficult in practice). But who counts as a stakeholder becomes so fluid and open that the notion of "stakeholder" no longer plays the robust role it was intended to have in defining policy decisions as procedurally fair or not. The conclusion this all seems to press for is that, even if a procedural approach to policy making can be impartial between stakeholders interests, it will not be impartial between ways of delimiting who is a stakeholder and among them whose interests are more or less important, unless the process is allowed to be so open and non-discriminating that the notion of "stakeholder" no longer marks a significant normative difference.

Does an outcome-based account of fair decision making avoid these problems? It was said earlier that impartiality on an outcome-based account is also defined in terms of stakeholder interests. But with this type of account, stakeholders and their interests are not identified *ex post* in a way that depends on the options that are up for consideration. Outcome-based fairness relies on an antecedent conception of which interests of which groups in what weight are relevant, and whatever policy option(s) impact on, or satisfy, or otherwise reflect those interests impartially, are the option(s) that the outcome account recommends as fair. But the same questions arise here as before. Where does this antecedent conception come from? Is it fairly and impartially chosen itself, or will it simply act to favor certain drug policy goals and purposes over others, by default? It would seem that both theoretical accounts of fairness in policy making are at risk of the same fundamental problem: even if a policy decision is fair in respecting people's relevant interests impartially, that decision will presuppose a particular view (among a possible many) of what interests are relevant. There will be questions as to whether that supposition has been fairly or impartially made. And that question is crucial. If the decision to treat certain interests as fundamental in the drug policy process has not been fairly made, then that may well undermine the fairness of the whole process, even when those interests are respected impartially. It has taken quite some time, for instance, for the perspectives and self-defined interests of substance users themselves to begin to be taken seriously in treatment policy, and drug policy in general. There may be a number of causes of this—including perhaps the influence of paternalistic attitudes to problematic users, or a default discounting of the perspectives of those involved in "illegal" activities.

Comprehensively fair policy—linking fairness and evidence

The last few observations suggest that to be fair at all, the drug policy-making process has to be fair comprehensively, with respect to two key concerns—what the relevant interests are, as well as how they are to be respected. Arguably to give a specification of the interests that drug treatment policy should fundamentally serve or respect is tantamount to giving (at least part of) a specification of the fundamental goals or purposes of substance misuse treatment policy. This suggests that comprehensively fair policy making needs to be conducted over two stages, the first being devoted to deciding what the basic purposes of treatment policy should be taken to be. But how is something like this to be decided fairly or impartially? Certainly, if the arguments above are anything to go on, this cannot coherently be decided in terms of criteria appealing to stakeholders or interests or such like. This would seem to straight away knock out of court outcome-based fairness accounts, since these intrinsically rely on antecedent accounts of interests, in terms of which fair outcomes are defined or identified. This suggests that the more appropriate decision criteria would be procedural ones, but, of course, ones that are sufficiently "open" in the interests that can be represented in the decision process. Clearly, a full defense of the procedures for fair social choices about the fundamental purposes of drug policy greatly exceeds the scope of this chapter. Something in the way of an inclusive deliberative social process where all can take part with equal voice, tends to suggest itself. Whatever that account turns out to be in detail, its fairly made decisions about the goals, purposes and interests to be served in drug policy will be fit to inform the second stage of fair policy making.

According to this thumbnail sketch, second stage decisions about which treatment policies to pursue in which circumstances will all be goal-directed, the goal being set by the "purpose" related decisions in the first stage (subject to whatever side-constraints might apply). If the first stage has been run properly, the goals will have been fairly chosen. With this said, though, there is no guarantee that these fairly chosen and "authorized" goals will be anywhere near the best goals for substance misuse treatment policy. Where does this leave the relationship between fair policy and evidence-based policy, the question that motivated this chapter in the first place? It appears, at first glance, that if there are no guarantees of the best goals being chosen, the two will be even further apart than ever. The relationship, however, is quite to the contrary. They could not be closer. One of the earlier sections of this chapter made the observation that what counts as (positive and negative) policy evidence is relative to policy goals. Evidence for a policy or intervention working, or against it working, is evidence about how well it achieves its assumed goals. This was noted in the context of ostensibly conflicting evidence for the success of drug treatments. The different bodies of evidence reflected different conceptions of the proper goals of substance misuse treatment—use-reduction vs. harm-reduction, and there may well be other goals. In policy terms, what counts as favorable or disfavorable evidence, is ineluctably goal dependent. This has implications for the sorts of policy interventions that (goal-directed) fairness will require in second stage decision making. It will require the choice of only those interventions that the evidence shows serve or otherwise reflects the fair purposes of substance misuse treatment policy. In the account that has been sketched here, fair policies will always (and necessarily) be evidence-based ones, keeping in mind that the notion of evidence in policy matters is a very dependent one.

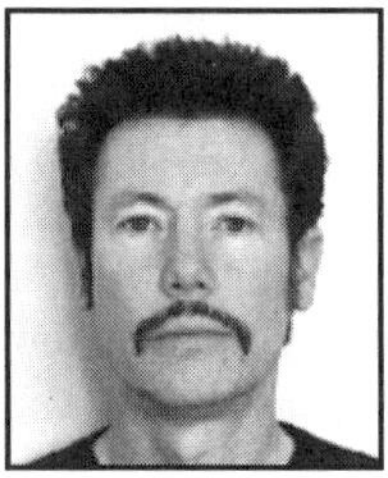

Maurice Rickard has a Ph.D. in political philosophy from La Trobe University and has taught and researched philosophy, bioethics, and ethics and public policy at a number of Australian universities. He also has a professional background in policy and legislative analysis and development in parliamentary and political environments, especially in health and drug policy. Maurice was the 2002 Australian Parliamentary Fellow, and a Senior Research Analyst

working at the Australian Parliament. Regrettably, in 2004-05 he made the mistake of wasting a year of his life at the Centre for Applied Philosophy and Public Ethics in Canberra, Australia. He is now a Ministerial Advisor in the Australian state of Victoria.

References

Adrian, M. (2001). Do treatments and other interventions work? Some critical issues. *Substance Use and Misuse, 36*(13), 1759-80.

Anon. (1996). Effectiveness of treatment proven in NTIES study. *Substance abuse report, 27*(19), 1-3

Australian Institute of Health and Welfare (AIHW). (2005). *National drug strategy survey 2004 results*, AIHW, Canberra.

Collins, D. J. & Lapsley, H. M. (2002). *Counting the cost: Estimates of the social costs of drug abuse in Australia in 1998/9.* Monograph Series no. 49. Commonwealth Department of Health and Ageing, Canberra.

Drucker, E. (1999). Drug prohibition and public health. *Public health reports, 114,* No 1, 14-29.

European Monitoring Centre for Drugs and Drug Addiction, (EMCDDA). (2004). *The state of the drugs problem in the European Union and Norway EMCDDA 2004 annual report.*

Galea S., Nandi A. and Vlahov D. (2004). The social epidemiology of substance use. *Epidemiologic Reviews, 26*(1), 36-52.

Godfrey, C., Eaton G., McDougall C., and Culyer A. (2002). *The economic and social costs of Class A drug use in England and Wales, 2000*, Home Office Research, Development and Statistics Directorate, July 2002.

Gowing L., Proudfoot H., Henry-Edwards, S., and Teeson, M. (2001). *Evidence supporting treatment: The effectiveness of interventions for illicit drug use.* Australian National Council on Drugs Research Paper No. 3, ANCD, Canberra.

Hser Y.I., Grella C.E., Hubbard R.L., Hsieh S.C., Fletcher B.W., Brown B.S., and Anglin M.D. (2001). An evaluation of drug treatments for adolescents in 4 US cities. *Archives of General Psychiatry, 58*(7), 689-95.

Hubbard R.L., Craddock S.G., Flynn P.M., Anderson J., and Etheridge R.M. (1997). Overview of 1 year follow-up outcomes in the Drug Abuse Treatment Outcome Study (DATOS). *Psychology of Addictive Behaviours, 11*(4), 261-278.

Hunt, N. (2003). *A review of the evidence base for harm-reduction approaches to drug use.* Available at <http://www.forward-thinking-on-drugs.org/review2-print.html>

Inciardi, J.A., Surratt H.L., Martin S.S., and Hooper R.M. (2002). The importance of aftercare in a corrections-based treatment continuum. In C.G. Leukefeld, F. Tims, D. Farabee (Eds.), *Treatment of drug offenders: Policies and issues.* New York: Springer Publishing Co., pp. 204-216.

Kilpatrick, D.G., Acierno, R. & Saunders, B. (2000). Risk factors for adolescent substance abuse and dependence: Data from a national sample. *Journal of Consulting and Clinical Psychology, 68.*

Kothari, G., Marsden, J. and Strang, J. (2002). Opportunities and obstacles for effective treatment of drug misusers in the criminal justice system in England and Wales. *British Journal of Criminology, 42*(2), 412-432.

Loxley, W., Toumbouroo, J., and Stockwell, T. (2005). A new integrated vision of how to prevent harmful drug use. *Medical Journal of Australia, 182*(2).

McCarthy, M. (October 10, 1998). Clinton administration plans to expand access to methadone. *The Lancet, 352,* p. 1206.

Mooney, C.Z. (ed.) (2001). *The public clash of private values. The politics of morality policy.* Seven Bridges Press: New York.

NHS Centre for Reviews and Dissemination. (2000). *Evidence from systematic reviews of research relevant to implementing the "wider public health" agenda.* Available at <www.york.ac.uk/inst/crd/wph.htm>

Parliament of Victoria. (1999). *Harm minimisation: Principles and policy frameworks.* Occasional paper No. 1, Drugs and Crime Prevention Committee. Available at <http://www.parliament.vic.gov.au/dcpc/Reports%20in%20pdf/Harm%20Minimisation.pdf>

SAMHSA (Substance Abuse and Mental Health Services Administration). (1997). *National estimates of expenditures for substance abuse treatment, 1997.* Rockville, MD.

Scanlon, A. (2002). State spending on substance abuse treatment. Policy Matters Issues Brief, National Conference of State Legislatures. Available at <http://www.ncsl.org/programs/health/forum/pmsas.htm>

Spooner, C., Hall, W. & Lynskey, M. (2001). *Structural determinants of youth drug use*, ANCD Research Paper 2. Australian National Council on Drugs, Canberra.

Stimson, G. and Metrebian, N. (2003, September). *Prescribing heroin: What is the evidence?* Joseph Rowntree Foundation.

Toumbourou, J.W. (2002). Drug prevention strategies: A developmental settings approach. DRUG INFO Clearinghouse, <http://druginfo.adf.org.au/article.asp?id=3343>.

UNDCP (United Nations Drug Control Program). (1996). *Economic and social consequences of drug abuse and illicit trafficking*, Technical Report No. 1996.

UN Office on Drugs and Crime. (2003). *Investing in drug abuse treatment.* United Nations, New York.

Van den Brink, W., Hendriks, V., Blanken, P., and Huijsman, I. (2002). Medical co-prescription of heroin. Two randomised controlled trials. Utrecht: Central Committee on the Treatment of heroin Addicts. Available at <www.ccbh.nl>

World Health Organisation. (2002). *World health report 2002.*

Notes

1. Social costs include the costs (quantified in $) to individuals, the community, and the state of health expenditures and losses, crime-related expenditures and losses, losses of productivity, and intangible losses caused by death and suffering.
2. Similar level, but less recent, cost estimates apply to the European Union. See UNDCP 1996 for estimates relating to illicit substance misuse.
3. Depending on what one takes these criteria to be, the decision might fail to conform in virtue of its substantive content, or in terms of the process by which the decision came about, or both.
4. If these information asymmetries are not addressed, there is a significant chance that the market in clinical service provision would completely fail, and this would be a massive social disaster.

5. Another, weaker, social responsibility argument might also be put forward based on the capacity of the state to intervene with strong or significant effects.
6. Demographic information suggests that treatment clients, for illicit substance misuse at least, are disproportionately likely to be socially and economically disadvantaged. For European data see Chapter 7 of EMCDDA, 2004. This will not necessarily be the same in the case of non-illicit substance use.
7. Much of the public policy focus, as with other social concerns, will be on resourcing. So, added to the list in the text will be questions about how much drug-related public intervention funding should go to treatment as opposed to law enforcement or justice administration or prevention, and also how much funding should go to drug use-related problems compared to other social priorities.
8. In 1981 the expenditures in those two areas were equal, and by 1998 the expenditure on enforcement was 66.3% of the total federal drug budget, and 33.7% for treatment, prevention, and research.
9. For a recent review of the existing evidence on treatment effectiveness for illicit drug misuse, see Gowing et. al., 2001, or UN Office on Drugs and Crime, 2003. For a more detailed review of existing evaluations of different substance misuse treatment interventions, see NHS Centre for Reviews and Dissemination, 2000.
10. For example, according to the California Drug and Alcohol Treatment Assessment, every $1 invested in treatment has a return of around $7 in savings from reduced incarceration, health costs, crime, and lost productivity (Scanlon, 2002).
11. This assumption is compatible with the role that needle-exchange programs often provide a point of access for users into further healthcare and treatment options, which may lead to them reducing their use. That role, however is not the primary purpose of such programs, which is to ensure that when users inject, they have access to appropriate injecting equipment.
12. It is argued in Parliament of Victoria 1999, for instance, that harm-reduction is conceptually the more fundamental policy goal.
13. *The Seattle Times*, June 9, 2005.
14. That the manipulation of drug policy symbols is often mere politics and rhetoric, and does not necessarily reflect real policy commitments, witness the approach of the current Australian federal government which, at the campaign and media level talks of its "Tough on Drugs" zero-tolerance of illicit drug use, but at the programme level maintains one of the most thoroughgoing harm-minimization policy strategies in the world.
15. It is worth noting also that on procedural accounts of fairness (pure or otherwise), a decision can be justified as fair in virtue of it being the actual outcome of a real decision-process that is fair, or in virtue of the fact it would be the outcome of a fair decision-process if such a process were conducted.
16. Or if they do, only in a very "thin" way.
17. In fact, if these representatives "voted" in a partialist way in the process (i.e., in line with their own interests), there would be little expectation of a decision outcome that reflected an impartial balancing of those interests.
18. Such as the drug information and monitoring service (DIMS) in the Netherlands.

1-4 Is Harm Reduction Psychotherapy Ethical?

William H. Gottdiener, Ph.D.

Abstract

Harm Reduction Psychotherapy (HRP) is a form of outpatient psychotherapy for individuals who are diagnosed with a substance use disorder (SUD) and who continue to use psychoactive substances. The treatment goal of HRP is to reduce the potential harm that might accompany psychoactive substance use. Sobriety is but one way to reduce harm, compared with traditional SUD treatments in which sobriety is the only acceptable goal. HRP is used because sobriety is not achievable and/or maintainable in all individuals who manifest an SUD or for every phase in a person's treatment. The chapter discusses whether or not HRP is an ethical treatment to provide individuals who are diagnosed with an SUD. Taking a Foucaldian perspective that personal liberty is essential to SUD treatment, and a psychoanalytic perspective that sobriety can be achieved only by a client who is ready to aim for that goal and has whatever is necessary – endogenously and exogenously – to initiate and maintain such a lifestyle adaptation, the author argues that HRP is the only ethical form of outpatient psychotherapy to provide individuals with an SUD.

Key Words: ethical treatment, Harm Reduction Psychotherapy (HRP), psychoactive substances, sobriety, substance use disorder (SUD), psychodynamic, self-medication

Introduction

What distinguishes harm reduction psychotherapy (HRP) is that its treatment goals include the reduction of any harms that might be associated with the use of psychoactive substances (Tatarsky, 2002). The significant consequence of HRP is that concrete treatment goals can vary widely along a continuum from controlled use of a substance to abstinence. HRP differs from traditional psychotherapeutic and psychosocial approaches to the treatment of substance use disorders (SUD) because the traditional approach employs an abstinence-only (AO) model of treatment, in which abstinence is the only acceptable treatment outcome. Clinicians who practice HRP employ it because they have observed via clinical experience that abstinence is not a realistic treatment goal for many individuals (Denning, 2000; Tatarsky, 2002; see also Rotgers, 2004).

Clinicians who practice traditional psychotherapies for individuals who are diagnosed with an SUD will engage in treatment only under specific conditions (see Kaufman, 1994 for a thorough example): (1) The client must commit to a goal of abstinence from all psychoactive substances, with the exception of nicotine and caffeine. (2) Clients must have graduated from either an inpatient or outpatient SUD detoxification program before entering psychotherapy. (3) Sobriety is maintained with concomitant use of self-help groups and/or structured outpatient treatment programs. (4) Psychotherapy sessions will not be held for an individual who is intoxicated. To do otherwise,would be tacitly to condone psychoactive substance use.

In contrast to the traditional psychotherapeutic approach to the treatment of SUDs, clinicians who practice HRP will engage in treatment under a wide variety of conditions (see Denning, 2000, and Tatarsky, 2002 for thorough examples): (1) The client can commit to abstinence, but such a goal will be determined by the needs of the individual clinical situation, and is not an *a priori* demand made by the therapist. (2) Clients do not have to enter or even graduate from a detoxification program before starting therapy, but they can if they want to do so. (3) Self-help groups and outpatient-treatment programs might be recommended in order to help the client develop self-care skills that will facilitate the client's ability to reduce the potential harm caused by psychoactive substance use, but such treatments are not required. (4) Psychotherapy sessions are likely to be held with a client who is intoxicated. When I treat a patient who comes to a session while intoxicated I find that it gives us a rare opportunity to examine the motivations and consequences of psychoactive substance use, in vivo, rather than as a tacit condoning of my client's psychoactive substance use. (5) Finally, clinicians who practice HRP often believe that they are conducting treatments that have realistic goals and therefore that they are giving their clients a better chance to remain in treatment, improve the overall quality of their lives, and increase the likelihood of achieving abstinence for those for whom that goal would be best (Denning, 2000; Tatarsky, 2002).

Although the clinical decision to pursue HRP or AO treatment seems to be couched within the context of what are practical and realistic treatment goals for clients to achieve, whether or not a clinician decides to employ HRP or AO is actually fraught with ethical issues that to my knowledge have not been clearly considered in the HRP literature. Therefore, the purpose of this chapter will be to start a dialogue on whether or not HRP is ethical to do.

Ethics of Harm Reduction

Public Health and Harm Reduction

The Harm Reduction (HR) movement is a public health movement and a political movement (Hathaway, 2001, 2002; Keane, 2003; Miller, 2001). As a public health movement, the HR philosophy consists of several components. First, there is acceptance that psychoactive substances will always be used by individuals no matter how intense the efforts at prohibition by any one community or government. Second, given that individuals will use psychoactive substances, the greatest good to the public health and to that of the individual user will be to facilitate the safety of that use (e.g., needle exchange programs to reduce the spread of blood-borne communicable diseases; legalization and regulation of psychoactive substances much the same way that alcohol production and distribution is legalized and its quality is monitored). Third, efforts at prevention of psychoactive substance use and efforts to treat users, including goals of prohibition and abstinence, are compatible with the goal of reduced harm.

Politics and Harm Reduction

Hathaway (2002, 2001) argues that proponents of HR have staked out an ethically and politically neutral argument to support HR efforts. The basic premise of the neutral position is that HR strategies are essential to reduce costs to the individual user and to society as a whole. Implicit in the neutral position is the notion that psychoactive substance use is inherently problematic and dangerous, and that people should avoid using psychoactive substances if at all possible. That many individuals indulge in psychoactive substance use and that a proportion of users become substance abusers or become substance dependent necessitates the need for HR interventions.

According to Hathaway, the ethically neutral and political position staked out by supporters of HR is problematic in several ways. First, it ignores the benefits of psychoactive substance use. Second, it ignores the fact that there is little danger (e.g., no direct health problems) for most users of psychoactive substances and that most users pose little danger (e.g., physical or psychological harm) to others. Third, and most importantly, it ignores the issue of whether or not people have the autonomy to choose how they want to live their lives.

Theoretical Rationale for the Practice of HRP

Although there are different political or ethical reasons why a therapist might practice HRP, there are also psychological theories of SUDs that support its use (Khantzian, 1985; Liese & Najavits, 1997). Psychoanalytical and cognitive-behavioral theories of SUDs posit that SUDs develop from early traumatic experiences. Trauma disrupts self-regulatory capacity. Psychoactive drugs are serendipitously discovered to provide temporary correction of self-regulatory problems. Because the underlying self-regulatory problems are not permanently fixed, the need to resume psychoactive substance use persists. If an individual becomes dependent on a psychoactive substance, then the condition might be chronic with periodic relapses expectable (McLellan, 2003).

Another way to understand the place of HRP in the therapeutic stratagem comes from psychoanalytic theory. According to Eissler (1953), the modal psychoanalytic therapeutic technique is interpretation of the patient's unconscious conflicts. Bringing those conflicts into conscious awareness is believed to reduce psychopathology. However, Eissler noted that many patients, for one reason or another, are incapable of considering the therapist's interpretations. As a result, the interpretation has no benefit for the patient, and, at worst, can exacerbate the patient's problems. Eissler suggested that the patient's ego is not yet receptive to the therapist's interpretation of unconscious conflict, and, therefore, the therapist must use alternative techniques to help make therapeutic gains, and with those gains, the patient might eventually be able to utilize the therapist's interpretations. (This discussion does not address the issue of the timing of interpretations, and the effect that proper timing has on treatment outcome. Such a discussion would consist of a complex and broad diversion from the topic at hand. The interested reader can find numerous discussions on the timing of interpretations. See Brenner, 1994 for an example).

An analogous situation can be postulated for many individuals who are diagnosed with an SUD. If abstinence is considered the model SUD treatment goal, it will work for those individuals whose egos are receptive to such a goal. For those individuals whose egos are not receptive to the goal of abstinence, however, HRP can be considered an alteration in technique to help the patient out. For some patients, such an approach might help their egos to get to a state in which they are receptive to the goal of abstinence.

Ethics of Harm Reduction Psychotherapy

As previously stated, the overall goal of HRP is to help a client reduce the harm that might accompany psychoactive substance use. However, within that goal is an ethical dilemma: by advocating harm reduction, the HRP therapist is not necessarily trying to stop his or her client from using psychoactive substances, which might not only be lethal to the client, but also lethal to others if the client behaves dangerously either to obtain the substances or while intoxicated. How, therefore, can an HRP therapist in good conscience ply his or her trade?

The HRP therapist can ply his or her trade by taking neither a neutral position nor by taking a liberal position to HR. It is possible that a particular therapist might view abstinence or prohibition as the best possible state of affairs for the individual client or even society, but realize that neither abstinence nor prohibition is likely to occur, and therefore that the best possible alternative would be to help reduce harm. Such a view would be realistic.

Another HRP therapist might take the politically liberal Foucauldian view that Hathaway (2001, 2002) advocates and assert that people have the right to use psychoactive substances and that they have the right to receive the treatment that they deem is in their best interest, which might or might not include the goal of abstinence. In addition, therapists have the right to practice HRP or not. Finally, the liberal Foucauldian position also suggests that there is no one path appropriate to the use of psychoactive substances and their treatment that can be universally applied so that everyone—clients and therapists alike—will be satisfied.

Diagnostic Considerations

The Diagnostic and Statistical Manual of Mental Disorders, fourth edition (DSM-IV, APA, 1994) distinguishes between substance dependence and substance abuse. These differences in diagnosis are important for the reader to be aware of because they have distinct implications for the ethics of HRP.

Substance dependence is defined as follows:

A maladaptive pattern of substance use, leading to clinically relevant significant impairment or distress, as manifested by three (or more) of the following, occurring at any time in the same 12-month period.

(1) tolerance, as defined by either of the following:
   (a) a need for markedly increased amounts of the substance to achieve intoxication or desired effect
   (b) markedly diminished effect with the continued use of the same amount of the substance
(2) withdrawal, as manifested by either of the following:

   (a) the characteristic withdrawal syndrome for the substance (refer to the Criteria A and B of the criteria sets for the Withdrawal from the specific substances)
   (b) the same (or a closely related) substance is taken to relieve or avoid withdrawal symptoms

(3) the substance is often taken in larger amounts or over a longer period than was intended

(4) there is a persistent desire or unsuccessful efforts to cut down or control substance use

(5) a great deal of time is spent in activities necessary to obtain the substance (e.g., visiting multiple doctors or driving long distances), use the substance (e.g., chain smoking) or recover from its effects

(6) important social, occupational, or recreational activities are given up or reduced because of substance use

(7) the substance use is continued despite knowledge of having a persistent or recurrent physical or psychological problem that is likely to have been caused or exacerbated by the substance (e.g., current cocaine use despite recognition of cocaine-induced depression, or continued drinking despite recognition that an ulcer was made worse by alcohol consumption)

Specify if:

With Physiological Dependence: evidence of tolerance or withdrawal (i.e., either Item 1 or 2 is present)

Without Physiological Dependence: no evidence of tolerance or withdrawal (i.e., neither Item 1 or 2 is present) (APA, 1994, p. 181).

Individuals who are diagnosed with substance dependence spend considerable time and effort obtaining and using psychoactive substances. Although for many individuals substance dependence involves physiological and psychological dependence, the diagnosis of substance dependence can be made solely in the context of psychological dependence.

Substance abuse is defined as follows:

A. A maladaptive pattern of substance use, leading to clinically significant impairment or distress, as manifested by one (or more) of the following, occurring within a 12-month period.

   (1) recurrent substance use resulting in a failure to fulfill major role obligations at work, school, or home (e.g., repeated absences or poor work performance related to substance use; substance-related absences, suspensions, or expulsions from school; neglect of children or household
   (2) recurrent substance use in situations in which it is physically hazardous (e.g., driving an automobile or operating a machine when impaired by substance use)
   (3) recurrent substance-related legal problems (e.g., arrests for substance-related disorderly conduct)

(4) continued substance use despite having persistent or recurrent social or interpersonal problems caused or exacerbated by the efforts of the substance (e.g., arguments with spouse about consequences of intoxication, physical fights)

B. The symptoms have never met the criteria for substance dependence for this class of Substance (APA, 1994, pp. 182-183)

Individuals who are diagnosed with substance abuse are not what most people would call hardcore drug addicts. Rather, they are individuals who, when they become intoxicated, fail to fulfill their obligations and put themselves and others at risk of danger. Such is the case of the individual who gets drunk only weekly, but always drives home from the bar while intoxicated. Unlike their substance dependent counterparts, individuals who are diagnosed with substance abuse generally show no signs of psychological or physiological dependence, and they do not experience withdrawal symptoms.

Ethical-Clinical Implications of Harm Reduction Psychotherapy for Substance Dependent versus Substance Abuse Diagnoses

It is possible to argue that it would be unethical to treat individuals who are diagnosed with either substance dependence or substance abuse in outpatient HRP, because the very nature of either disorder would prevent them from becoming adequately involved in their psychotherapeutic treatment. Proffering HRP to a substance dependent or abusing individual might be seen as leading that individual to think that benefits could accrue from treatment despite considerable use or abuse of psychoactive substances. Proffering HRP could also be seen as not taking seriously the dangers of SUDs.

If the HRP therapist holds that some individuals' egos cannot utilize the goal of abstinence—a theoretical point that is supported by McLellan's (2003) view that SUDs can be classified as chronic-relapsing conditions, then HRP is the only ethical treatment to offer individuals who cannot become abstinent. The clinical goals of the HRP therapist are to offer help to the patient to become able to lead a safer, more healthful life. Treating an individual who has a substance use disorder who continues to over-indulge in psychoactive substances is a way of trying to help that individual lead a safer life in spite of continued dangerous behavior. It is unclear to me how helping an individual to create a safer life would be unethical.

As stated previously, therapists who practice from an HRP perspective often treat clients who are intoxicated, which is rarely done by those who practice from an AO perspective because it is viewed as condoning the substance use. However, it is important to realize that treating someone who is intoxicated can be seen as similar to treating someone who is undergoing a bout of depression or anxiety while attending the psychotherapy session. In those cases the therapist does not tell the client to return once the depression has ended. That would be considered unethical. Then it seems that it is also unethical to send someone away who is diagnosed with an SUD and who is intoxicated during a session.

The Ethic of Harm Reduction Therapy is the Same as the Ethic of Abstinence-Only Treatment.

A Foucauldian argument of Harm Reduction asserts that individuals have the freedom to choose to direct their own lives, which also means that others have that same freedom (Sybylla, 2001). In the context of HRP, this would mean that if therapists have the freedom to direct their own lives, then so do individuals who choose to use psychoactive substances. That would also mean that psychotherapists are not free to interfere with another's freedom to use psychoactive substances, despite the harms that the substances might cause. Cast in this light, an ethical SUD treatment is one in which both therapist and client explicitly or implicitly agree on a way of exerting their individual freedoms. In actuality, both forms of treatment use the same ethical foundation. In both treatments the therapist and client agree that the therapist will not interfere with the client's psychoactive substance use except to the extent that the client will allow. Both forms of treatment belong on a continuum of how much the client is willing to limit his or her freedom to choose to use psychoactive substances. The therapist is employed by the client as an instrument to regulate the amount and quality of the client's freedom to use psychoactive substances: nothing more, and nothing less. Hence, the answer to the question posed in the title of this chapter is, "yes."

William H. Gottdiener, Ph.D. clinical psychologist, BA, Hunter College City University of New York (CUNY), Ph.D. The New School University in New York City, is assistant professor of psychology at John Jay College of Criminal Justice—CUNY where he primarily conducts research on the treatment of comorbid substance-use disorders (SUD) and posttraumatic stress disorder, self-regulation in individuals with SUDs, and psychosis and SUDs. Dr. Gottdiener has published his research in peer-reviewed scientific journals and invited book chapters and he is the recipient of several awards and grants from the National Institute on Drug Abuse (NIDA). He is also a supervising psychologist at St. Luke's-Roosevelt Hospital in New York City where he conducts his clinical research and a member of the hospital's faculty practice. The focus of Dr. Gottdiener's psychotherapy practice is the treatment of SUDs using Harm Reduction Psycho-therapy. His research and clinical work are largely informed by a psychodynamic theoretical perspective.

References

American Psychiatric Association. (1994). *Diagnostic and statistical manual of mental disorders (DSM-III-R)* (4th ed. revised). Washington, DC: American Psychiatric Association.

Brenner, C. (1994). *Psychoanalytic technique and psychic conflict.* Guilford, CT: International Universities Press.

Denning, P. (2000). *Practicing harm reduction psychotherapy: An alternative approach to addictions.* New York: Guilford.

Eissler, K. (1953). The effects of the structure of the ego on psychoanalytic technique. *Journal of the American Psychoanalytic Association, 1*, 104-143.

Hathaway, A. D. (2001). Shortcomings of harm reduction: Toward a morally invested drug reform strategy. *The International Journal of Drug Policy, 12*, 125-137.

Hathaway, A. D. (2002). From harm reduction to human rights: Bringing liberalism back into drug reform. *Drug and Alcohol Review, 21*, 397-404.

Khantzian, E.J. (1985). The self-medication hypothesis of addictive disorders. *American Journal of Psychiatry, 142*, 1259-1264.

Khantzian, E.J. (1999a). The self-medication hypothesis of substance use disorders: An update. In E. J. Khantzian (Ed.), *Treating addiction as a human process* (pp. 245-276). Northvale, NJ: Jason Aronson.

Kaufman, E. (1994). *Psychotherapy of addicted persons*. New York: Guilford.

Keane, H. (2003). Critiques of harm reduction, morality and the promise of human rights. *International Journal of Drug Policy, 14*, 227-232.

Liese, B. S., & Najavits, L. M. (1997). Cognitive and behavioral therapies. In J. H. Lowinson, P. Ruiz, R. B. Millman, & J. G. Langrod (Eds.), *Substance abuse: A comprehensive textbook-third edition* (pp. 467-478). Baltimore: Williams & Wilkens.

McLellan, A. T. (2003). The outcomes movement in addiction treatment: Comments and cautions. In J. L. Sorensen, Rawson, Richard A., Guydish, Joseph, Zweben, Joan E. (Eds.), *Drug abuse treatment through collaboration: Practice and research partnerships that work*. Washington, DC: American Psychological Association.

Miller, P. G. (2001). A critical review of the harm minimization ideology in Australia. *Critical Public Health, 11*(2), 167-178.

Rotgers, F. (2004). Introduction to the special issue: Innovations in clinical harm reduction. *Addiction Research and Theory, 12*(4), 301-303.

Sybylla, R. (2001). Hearing whose voice? The ethics of care and the practices of liberty: A critique. *Economy and Society, 30*(1), 66-84.

Tatarsky, A. (2002). Introduction: Harm reduction. In A. Tatarsky (Ed.), *Harm reduction psychotherapy: A new treatment for drug and alcohol problems* (pp. 1-15). Northvale, NJ: Jason Aronson.

1-5 Ethical Issues Raised by Non-Punitive Drug User Policies

Stephen Coleman, Ph.D.

Abstract

Over the last few decades there has been a strong push in many countries for the implementation of programs and policies that take a non-punitive attitude to the use and misuse of drugs, generally with the aim of minimizing the harm caused to the substance users. The aim of this chapter is to point out and discuss the particular ethical issues that some of these non-punitive drug policies raise. Particular policies examined include methadone maintenance treatment, needle exchange programs, provision of safe injecting facilities, prescription of heroin, and decriminalization of cannabis.

Key Words: medical model, moral model, methadone maintenance treatment (MMT), needle exchange programs (NEPs), secondary needle exchange programs, (SNEPs), safe injecting facilities, prescription, heroin, decriminalization, cannabis, chasing the dragon

Introduction

Many drugs, such as heroin and other opiates, cocaine, amphetamines, and psychotropic substances, are controlled, throughout the world, by laws that govern their supply, possession, and use. International treaties, such as the United Nations 1961 Convention on Narcotic Drugs and the United Nations 1988 Convention Against Illegal Traffic in Narcotic Drugs and Psychotropic Substances, commit signatory nations to treat the possession, use, and supply of such drugs and substances as punishable offenses. Thus those who use or misuse such substances outside the constraints of the law are generally subject to stiff penalties should their activities come to the attention of the relevant authorities.

Over the last few decades, however, there has been a strong push, particularly in the industrialized countries of Europe, in Australia, Canada, and, to a lesser extent, the United States, for the implementation of programs and policies that take a non-punitive (or at least a less punitive) attitude to the use and misuse of these controlled substances, generally with the aim of minimizing the harm caused to the substance users. The aim of this chapter is to point out and discuss the particular ethical issues that such non-punitive drug policies raise.

In his chapter in this volume, John Kleinig (2006) notes that the term "drug" can be applied to a great many different substances: publicly available and unrestricted foods (such as those containing caffeine), publicly available but restricted substances (such as tobacco and alcohol), therapeutic agents marketed as medicines (some of which are available only through prescription), psychoactive substances, some of which are generally available but are not intended for ingestion (such as glues and aerosols), and others that are generally outlawed (such as marijuana, cocaine, LSD, and so on). Since the topic of this chapter is drug user policy, when I use the term "drug" within this chapter it can be taken to be referring primarily (though not necessarily exclusively) to those substances deemed illegal by the law in the particular jurisdiction under discussion at the time.[1]

The Intellectual Basis of Drug Use Policies

It is important to recognize, at the outset, that the ethical issues raised by any particular drug use policy depend almost entirely on the view one takes of the use of drugs and of the behaviors exhibited by those who are addicted to drugs. Different approaches to the issue of the use and misuse of drugs are based on different models of drug dependence, and each of these models will suggest different techniques for correcting the problems caused by the use and misuse of drugs (Pendergast & Podus, 2000, p. 1646). Although several models have been proposed, for the purposes of this discussion I wish to consider only two—the medical model and the moral model—since these two models neatly sum up the two main approaches to formulating drug policy. Obviously there are variants of these two models, but in order to keep the discussion to a reasonable length, I will be forced to generalize, by referring only to the main features of these models.

The medical model, also known as the disease model, sees drug dependence as a disease and thus afflicted individuals as patients requiring medical attention. The moral model, on the other hand, sees drug taking as "a moral failing resulting from a lack of self-restraint on the part of affected individuals" (Pendergast & Podus, 2000, p. 1648) and thus sees those who misuse drugs (or who use drugs outside the restraints of law and social convention) as guilty of wrongdoing.[2] As can easily be seen from the laws regulating the use and possession of drugs, it is the moral model that has historically driven both social attitudes to the use of drugs and drug-user policy. Non-punitive drug-user policies subscribe to the medical model, or some variant of this model, and thus tend to fly in the face of existing laws, social attitudes, and established policy.

Under the medical model of drug use, ethical issues tend to arise only under certain specific circumstances—when, for example, a patient is not being given what is considered to be the best available treatment, or if the treatment proceeds without the informed consent of the patient, or the course of treatment is thought to be experimental and unlikely to benefit that particular patient directly. Thus, if a particular treatment is considered to be the best available treatment for the patient's condition, is known to benefit that patient directly, and if the patient has given informed consent to that course of treatment, then there are generally no ethical issues that need to be considered. However, were this same course of treatment to be considered under the moral model, the situation would be quite different. Under the moral model, no course of treatment for drug use or drug addiction can be seen to be adequate unless it deals, at least in some way, with the wrongdoing that is perceived to underlie the drug-using behavior.

Not all drug policies aim at the treatment of particular drug users. It is inevitable that some drug users within society will engage in potentially harmful behaviors related to their drug use, and thus some drug-use policies aim at reducing the amount of harm that such behaviors will cause. Such harm reduction policies will usually be perfectly acceptable within the medical model (which will generally view such harm reduction as a legitimate response to a public health issue), but will generally be unacceptable under the moral model, since these policies do not attempt to modify the actual source of wrongdoing—the drug-taking behavior of the user.

Sometimes when attempts are being made to decide between policies on a particular issue, the debate centers on evidence: the goal is clear, but there are real questions about which policy will best achieve that goal. That is not the case with drug policy. Although questions certainly remain about whether particular non-punitive policies, such as the prescription of heroin as a treatment for addiction to opiates, will be effective in dealing with the problems caused by drug addiction, other non-punitive policies, such as needle exchange programs, have clear scientific backing. Yet such policies are still seen as controversial. The reason for this controversy is that the debate about drug policy is not primarily about evidence, but about values (Buchanan, Shaw, Ford & Singer, 2003). Proponents of the medical model of drug dependence generally view the problems caused by the use of drugs little differently from the problems caused by a new strain of influenza virus: in both cases a proposed policy will, in their eyes, stand or fall on its scientific merits. Proponents of the moral model of drug dependence, on the other hand, will assess a proposed drug policy quite differently from a policy that has been proposed to deal with a new strain of influenza, since the moral model views drug policy as fundamentally an ethical issue rather than a scientific one. Thus presentation of purely scientific evidence about the impact of a particular drug policy is highly unlikely to convince a proponent of the moral model that the particular policy ought to be adopted.

In the following discussion, I will attempt to remain neutral as to which of these two models, medical or moral, is the most appropriate to adopt when assessing drug policy. In fact it may well be the case, as is argued by Stephen Morse (2006), that both have a role to play. Thus, rather than asserting that particular policies ought to be adopted, I will explain the goals of each of the major non-punitive policies and detail the scientific issues and evidence that might be accepted as sufficient reason to adopt the policy. I will then discuss any ethical issues that might arise under the medical model and explain why the moral model might find that particular policy inadequate or problematic.

Types of Non-Punitive Policies and Programs

Several different types of non-punitive policies and programs have been implemented in different countries. Most of these non-punitive policies focus on issues raised by the use of heroin. This is probably because heroin's addictive qualities, high risk of overdose, and risky usual method of administration (i.e., by injection), combine to make this drug, in the eyes of politicians and the public, the "worst" drug on the street market.[3] In any case, it appears that most long-term "problem" drug addicts come to be addicted to heroin (though many also use other drugs), so these non-punitive strategies tend to focus on the most serious problems of drug addiction. Thus most of the non-punitive policies that I wish to discuss in this chapter relate primarily to heroin use: methadone maintenance treatment, needle exchange programs, provision of safe injecting facilities, and the supply of heroin by prescription. The only non-heroin-related policy that I will examine is the decriminalization of cannabis.

Heroin-Related Policies

Methadone Maintenance Treatment (MMT) aims to provide individuals, generally those with a long established history of opiate dependence, a legally prescribed opiate (methadone) as a replacement for opiates (usually heroin) of dubious quality that have been illegally obtained. The original conception of MMT was that the supply of methadone would be necessary only while the patient was stabilized onto a regular dosage of opioids and that the dosage would then be gradually reduced until the patient was finally drug free. However, it has since been discovered that even stable MMT patients have a high rate of relapse into illegal opiate use once methadone has been withdrawn (Magura, 2001). Given that the long-term use of methadone is relatively safe for the patient, MMT is now regarded as being potentially, though rarely, a life-long treatment. Though methadone is available in a form suitable for intravenous use, it is usually prescribed in oral form.

The main benefit of MMT can be found in its minimization of the harms of street use of opioids, particularly the harms of intravenous use. When an addict stabilizes on oral methadone through MMT (assuming they are taking no illegal intravenous drugs), they are no longer subject to the risks of infections spread by transfer of blood, such as HIV and hepatitis B and C, they are no longer subject to the risks of poor IV technique, of health problems caused by the injection of impurities contained within the street purchased opioids, or to the risk of death or mental injury caused by opioid overdose (Townshend, Sellman & Coverdale, 2001). Other benefits for the MMT patient (again assuming that they are using no other illegal substances) include freedom from the need to locate and purchase illegal drugs on a regular basis and the need to find the money (often from criminal and/or other risky activities) to fund these purchases. However, MMT is often seen as controversial or problematic by proponents of the moral model since it does not attempt to end the user's reliance on opioids. An additional question that has been raised about MMT, as with all heroin-related non-punitive policies, is whether such programs ought to be publicly funded.

Needle exchange programs (NEPs),[4] unlike MMT, do not aim at ending the addict's reliance on street drugs, but rather attempt to reduce the risks of transmission of blood borne viruses such as HIV and hepatitis. Users of the needle exchange bring in used injection equipment and are provided with sterile replacement equipment, usually along with information about ways of minimizing the risks of contracting the aforementioned blood borne viruses and about safer injecting techniques. The goal of NEPs is to make sterile equipment and information about some of the risks of injecting drug use available to injecting drug users, and thus to encourage them to utilize clean equipment for injection and to practice better injection techniques and disease control, and thus reduce the likelihood of their contracting those diseases to which their lifestyle makes them prone (Delgado, 2004). NEPs may also provide other services such as temporary shelter, meals, opportunities for medical examinations, and referrals to a range of other services. NEPS are often criticized by proponents of the moral model for sending the wrong message about drug use to people in society (particularly young people in society), and for aiding and abetting the illegal drug trade by enabling people to use illegal drugs more safely (Bush, 2000).

All the criticisms that are applied to NEPS are often seen to carry even more weight against safe injecting facilities. Such facilities provide, in addition to sterile injecting equipment, a controlled location for injecting (or otherwise ingesting) drugs obtained elsewhere, with medical staff who are able to assist drug users in cases of emergency, such as when overdoses occur. These facilities aim to reduce the risks of illegal drug use even further than NEPs, by attempting to offset the problems of uncertain drug quality by ensuring that those users who inject within the confines of such centers will always be within close reach of medical assistance, should such assistance be required (Drug and Crime Prevention Committee, 1996). These facilities also provide social benefits, since members of the public are less likely to encounter addicts using drugs on the street, and they are also less likely to stumble across used injection equipment (such as syringes and needles) that forms a public health risk. However, they have been criticized for the possibility that they may send to society the message that injecting drugs is acceptable, and for the possibility that the existence of safe injecting facilities might draw drug users to frequent a particular area (i.e., the location of the safe injecting facilities) in greater numbers, thus devaluing property, increasing crime, and causing undue disturbance to businesses and members of the public in the local area (Drug and Crime Prevention Committee, 1996).

One of the most controversial proposals in the area of non-punitive policies is the suggestion that heroin ought to be provided as a prescription medicine for the treatment of opioid addiction. The benefits of such a proposal are similar to those of MMT, freeing drug users to pursue most (if not all) the activities of everyday life knowing that the drug to which they were addicted is always available. As well as normalizing the life of the addict, such a proposal has benefits for the rest of society (in the same way as MMT) in that drug addicts will not be required to pay extortionate street prices for the drugs that they require, and thus will not find it necessary to engage in high risk behaviors such as prostitution or criminal activity in order to acquire the money with which to purchase drugs.

Although the supply of heroin by prescription would generally enable the drug addict to continue to administer drugs intravenously, and thus still be at risk of acquiring HIV or hepatitis, such risks could be offset by the use of safe injecting facilities, or by the supply of sterilized injection materials along with the prescription drugs. One benefit of prescribing heroin over MMT is that such a program is likely to be more attractive to drug users, since it does not require them to change either their drug of choice (MMT requires the drug user to change from heroin to methadone) or their preferred method of ingestion (MMT will usually be provided as an oral dose, whereas prescription heroin could be supplied in a form suitable for injection or for "smoking," whichever was preferred by the drug user). Were prescription heroin to attract more drug users into treatment than other alternative treatments (such as MMT) then this would mean that there would be more heroin addicts in treatment, and fewer untreated heroin users in the community and—to the benefit of all—allow better control of the medical problems of this segment of society (Stimson & Metrebian, 2003).

The supply of heroin by prescription of course faces the same criticisms from proponents of the moral model as NEPs and the provision of safe injecting facilities, but to an even greater degree. It has been argued that since the government is providing heroin to drug users (in the form of prescription medicine) this sends a clear message that drug use is acceptable within the community (Short, Hawes & Kerin, 1997). It has also been suggested that providing heroin to addicts gives them no incentive to cease intravenous drug use, that the extra expense of providing pharmaceutical heroin over methadone cannot be justified, and that there is a risk that prescription heroin might be diverted onto the illegal market, thus creating more heroin addicts who would require treatment (Stimson & Metrebian, 2003).

Cannabis Policies

Policies that decriminalize (in one way or another) the use or possession of cannabis aim to maintain the legal prohibition on cannabis while at the same time reducing both the short- and long-term harmful effects of such a policy on those involved in only minor cannabis offenses. There is no universal agreement on what decriminalization means, and so, in jurisdictions where cannabis use has been "decriminalized," policies have varied widely. These policies include: reducing the severity of punishment for minor cannabis offenses; downgrading the severity of minor cannabis offenses to make them equivalent to motor vehicle traffic offenses, rather than criminal offenses; not prosecuting for possession of small amounts of cannabis; charging only as a last resort in cases of illegal drug use; introducing monetary penalties for minor cannabis offenses, payment of which will expiate the crime; and instigation of formal cautions for minor cannabis offenses, sometimes linked to mandatory drug education (Health Canada, 2003).

Despite the different approaches that have been taken to decriminalizing minor cannabis offenses, all these policies share some similarities. It has long been recognized that people with a criminal record face considerable difficulties within society, that criminal prosecution and conviction brings with it a stigma that may have long-term consequences for one's future education, job choices, and life prospects. Policies that decriminalize minor cannabis offenses all aim, in their various ways, at ensuring that such offenses do not carry the stigma of a criminal conviction and the consequences that such a conviction will bring.

Policies of decriminalization have been criticized for encouraging the use of cannabis, and for sending a message to society that the use of cannabis is considered to be acceptable.

The Ethics of Non-Punitive Drug Policies

Having briefly discussed the aims of some important non-punitive drug policies, and having also mentioned some of the criticisms that have been leveled at them, I now wish to examine in more detail the ethical issues raised by these policies. An essential part of the discussion of these ethical issues will be to examine why these policies might be seen as inadequate or problematic by proponents of the moral model of drug dependence.

I begin my discussion by examining those programs that focus on the problems associated with heroin addiction, addressing the programs in turn from the least controversial through to the most controversial. Only after dealing with all of these programs will I turn my attention to the issues raised by policies that decriminalize the use of cannabis.

Heroin-Related Policies—Methadone Maintenance

The first non-punitive drug program that I wish to discuss in detail is methadone maintenance. One of the main issues of MMT, when examined from the perspective of the medical model, is the fact that the aims of such a program tend to create a conflict for the providers of the treatment—a conflict between what is in the best interests of the patient and what is in the best interests of society. Although the normal medical situation is that the doctor treats the patient with sole concern for what is in the patient's best interests, in MMT the doctor may well be expected to put the interests of society ahead of the interests of the patient.

Consider the restrictions that normally apply to a patient who is being prescribed methadone as part of a methadone maintenance program. In the early stages of treatment, the patient is usually stabilized on a regular dose of methadone which must be taken "on site," which in most cases will mean that the methadone must be used by the patient either at the clinic providing the MMT, or at the local pharmacy where the methadone is being dispensed. Obviously the requirement of daily attendance at either a clinic or a pharmacy will be both quite onerous and disruptive of any attempts to get the patient to adopt a more normal life and daily routine, and so, after the patient has stabilized on a regular methadone dose, it is common to introduce "take-away" doses, which will be supplied to the patient for use on subsequent days. Such patients will no longer be required to attend the clinic or pharmacy every day, and will therefore enjoy more freedom in their life which may, for example, allow them to secure longer hours of employment. However, if it is found that MMT patients are "diverting" their takeaway dose (i.e., selling the methadone on the street or to other drug users), then penalties will usually be applied; either discontinuation of the takeaway regime, or, in more serious cases, exclusion from the MMT program.[5]

Here is where the ethical conflict lies for the providers of the program. If the aim of MMT is simply to treat the patients within the program, then it is clear that treatment ought to continue even in cases in which the patient is involved in diverting methadone doses, for the patient's health will certainly be best served by remaining within the program. Studies suggest that those who leave methadone programs before concluding treatment (or who are excluded from the program for disciplinary reasons) have a high rate of return to illegal drug use and a much higher fatality rate than those within MMT programs, and thus are at a much greater risk of harm than those who remain within MMT (Magura, 2001). But the diversion of methadone doses is also a serious problem, if not necessarily for the MMT patient involved in the diversion, then certainly for those in society as a whole, since the diverted dose may well result in harm or even death for its purchaser, especially if that individual is somewhat drug naïve. Penalties like exclusion from the MMT program for discipline breaches such as diversion of doses are intended to protect society from harm, but they do so at clear cost to the MMT patient. How ought a doctor involved in such a program to act, when the guidelines of the program are in clear conflict with the best interests of the individual patient?[6]

Similarly, the limits that are placed on MMT programs by external forces (usually by governments) also create a conflict for treatment providers. Many MMT programs are limited in various ways—through the number of patients that they may treat, through upper limits on the amount of methadone they may provide to each patient, or in the amount of time that a patient may be included in the program. These external limits may be imposed as a means of enforcing societal values (i.e., the moral model) and thus emphasize the view that the use of drugs is wrong, that drug users and drug addicts are to blame for their problems, and thus that there are certain limits on the aid that society is willing to provide these people. A good example of this trend was New York City Mayor Rudolph Giuliani's July 1998 announcement that he planned to "phase out and do away with methadone maintenance programs in the City of New York" over the next 2-4 years, and that all city controlled methadone clinics would henceforth adopt abstinence as the main goal of treatment (Mayor's Crusade, 1998). His basis for such an announcement was apparently the belief that MMT simply substitutes one drug of addiction for another, and thus that abstinence was a more moral goal of drug user treatment than long-term MMT.

Such external limits placed on MMT programs often conflict with the best interests of the patient, especially if the limits impinge upon recognized best medical practice. Patients in MMT programs have a much lower risk of contracting HIV and hepatitis than intravenous drug users not involved in such programs, and they also have a much lower rate of involvement in criminal offenses than untreated drug addicts (National Consensus, 1998). Thus it can be argued that the best interests of the drug user are served by providing easy access to MMT if the user seeks out such services, though this is at odds with limits being placed upon enrolments into such programs. It is also recognized that MMT will be ineffective if the prescribed dose of methadone is inadequate, as the patient is highly likely to continue to use heroin and/or other illegal drugs in such circumstances. Yet limits on the maximum dose of methadone that may be prescribed may mean that the required therapeutic dose cannot be prescribed. Limits on the length of time that patients may be included in an MMT program may also run counter to the best medical evidence. Research on mandatory short-term methadone-to-abstinence programs, the model proposed by Mayor Giuliani, suggests that such a policy is actually "roughest on the patients for whom methadone did the most good" (Winick, 2001, p. 42). Thus imposition of any of these external limits may create significant ethical dilemmas for medical staff involved in such a regulated MMT program.

Of course it may be the case that external limits are placed upon a program not because of a perceived need to enforce the moral model, but simply because of limited resources. Although such a situation may still give rise to ethical problems for those involved in administering such a program, these problems are hardly unique to drug-user treatment, for most (if not all) medical programs labor within the constraints of limited resources. However, the ethical dilemmas created by external limits are liable to be felt more keenly by those involved in drug-user counseling if it is perceived that these limits are being applied to enforce the values of the moral model, especially if the staff within the program are more inclined to follow the medical model, and thus must work within a program limited by external values with which they do not agree.

Interestingly, the discussion following Mayor Giuliani's much publicized announcement, and later back-down (Swarns, 1999), has left MMT as being a much more acceptable policy to proponents of the moral model. This is probably due in large part to the fact that the publicity given to the issue meant that experts in the field of drug use treatment were given sufficient media time to enable them to correct some misconceptions about addiction and about MMT. For example, if it is thought that addiction is actually a brain disease (Leshner, 1998), rather than merely a weakness of the will, then moral sanctions against addicts become much harder to justify (though such sanctions against those who are not yet addicts would fall into a different category). Similarly, greater understanding of the different ways in which heroin and methadone interact with the neural pathways of the brain has led to MMT being perceived less as a case of substituting one drug of addiction for another and more as long term pharmacological therapy, a category into which insulin therapy for diabetics and steroid therapy for rheumatoid arthritis could also be seen to fit. Again, moral sanctions against those involved in such therapy seems inappropriate.

Perhaps the main reason why MMT has come to be seen as at least somewhat acceptable within the moral model is that it does aim to deal with the cause of the problem, the patient's actual behaviour, in its attempt to interfere with the patient's cycle of drug misuse. However, policies that do not treat the cause but instead deal only with the symptoms, through harm reduction, are seen as far less acceptable under this model.

Heroin-Related Policies—Needle Exchange

The goal of NEPs is to enable injecting drug users to reduce the risks to which their lifestyle makes them prone (Delgado, 2004), with a particular emphasis on reducing the rate of spread of blood-borne viruses such as hepatitis and HIV, which generally run rampant through the injecting drug community. NEPs can realistically make little difference to some of the risks to which injecting drug users are exposed, such as health problems caused by impurities contained within street purchased drugs or the possibilities of drug overdose, and NEPs generally make few overt attempts to get drug users into treatment programs such as MMT.

The main ethical issue for the medical model is whether such programs are actually effective means of dealing with the public health problem of hepatitis and HIV, easily spread through the exchange of blood through the sharing of needles for drug injection. If NEPs are a cost efficient method for disrupting this viral transmission pathway, then this should be seen as a prima facie reason for their acceptance. The other main ethical issues raised by NEPs, under the medical model, revolve around the legal issues that might arise in relation to such programs.

For proponents of the moral model, issues such as the effectiveness of NEPs and legal complications that might arise in relation to such programs are only the start of the story. The biggest concerns for proponents of this model are the fact that NEPs do not attempt to change the immoral behavior of the drug user, and the concern that establishing such programs might be seen to condone drug use and even encourage some people, particularly impressionable young people, to experiment with drugs. Concerns such as these were clearly articulated by George W. Bush (2000) during his initial presidential campaign:

> *I do not favor needle exchange programs and other so-called "harm reduction" strategies to combat drug use. I support a comprehensive mix of prevention, education, treatment, law enforcement, and supply interdiction to curb drug use and promote a healthy, drug-free America, not misguided efforts to weaken drug laws. Drug use in America, especially among children, has increased dramatically under the Clinton-Gore Administration, and needle exchange programs signal nothing but abdication, that these dangers are here to*

stay. Children deserve a clear, unmixed message that there are right choices in life and wrong choices in life, that we are all responsible for our actions, and that using drugs will destroy your life. America needs a President who will aim not just for risk reduction, but for risk elimination that offers people hope and recovery, not a dead-end approach that offers despair and addiction.

The issue of whether NEPs are actually an effective means of slowing the spread of hepatitis and HIV is fairly straightforward. Although statements made by various United States Senators and Representatives have suggested that NEPs actually increase the rate of HIV transmission,[7] a large number of studies have shown that NEPs are effective in reducing the transmission of blood borne diseases such a hepatitis and HIV (Hurley, Jolley & Caldor, 1997; National Institutes of Health, 1997; Stimson, 1995).[8] Thus proponents of the medical model would see this as an effective answer to a public health issue, and would advocate the introduction of NEPs.

As I previously mentioned, the other main ethical problems for those enamored of the medical model relate to legal issues. In many jurisdictions, it is not only an offense to use or possess illegal drugs, but it is also an offense to possess drug paraphernalia, into which category all the equipment supplied by an NEP will fall. In cases in which the NEP has been formally established through either direct government intervention or the initiative of a local public health agency, such issues are unlikely to arise, since the drug laws with regard to the possession and distribution of drug paraphernalia may be amended in recognition of the existence of the NEP or subject to favorable local judicial interpretation. However, NEPs that have been established through other, less legally-recognized means may be forced to rely on the tolerance and discretionary powers of local law enforcement agencies in order to continue operating. Such a situation raises ethical issues for the local police as well as for the operators of the NEP.

The quote from George W. Bush highlights the main ethical issues of NEPs for those who favor the moral model; namely, that all strategies that aim at harm reduction rather than harm elimination (i.e., ending the use of drugs) are inappropriate, in that they do not take seriously society's perceived duty to fight the use of drugs and may in fact encourage the use of drugs among young people. In fact, although the position is rarely articulated, it is not inconsistent for a proponent of the moral model to think that drug users actually deserve to contract hepatitis or HIV as punishment for their immoral actions.[9] Those who hold such a view would of course be opposed to any harm reduction policy, such as the establishment of NEPs, that might allow such immoral actions to avoid punishment. One problem with holding such a view is that it is internally inconsistent. NEPs have been established to deal with a public health issue, the spread of hepatitis and HIV, rather than to enable drug users to "escape God's punishment" for their actions. The reason that the spread of these diseases is a public health issue is because it affects the whole community rather than simply IV drug users. If IV drug users contract HIV, they may spread it to other people through various means, not simply through the sharing of needles. A person who supports the view that IV drug users deserve to contract HIV ought nevertheless to support measures that attempt to prevent the spread of the disease to other innocent parties, such as sexual partners of the drug user, or the drug user's unborn children.

The issue of whether NEPs encourage drug use is one that proponents of the medical model are also concerned with, for even if NEPs are effective in reducing the spread of blood-borne viruses, it would certainly count against them if they actually encouraged drug use in the community. However, empirical studies of the effectiveness of NEPs in terms of their influence on the transmission rate of blood borne viruses, often also consider whether the existence of NEPs encourages illegal drug use. These studies have found no statistically significant increase in the use of such drugs subsequent to the establishment of a local NEP. This was acknowledged by then-Surgeon General David Satcher (2000):

> *After reviewing all of the research to date, the senior scientists of the Department and I have unanimously agreed that there is conclusive scientific evidence that syringe exchange programs, as part of a comprehensive HIV prevention strategy, are an effective public health intervention that reduces the transmission of HIV and does not encourage the use of illegal drugs.*

Of course, whether NEPs encourage the use of illegal drugs is an empirical question, and proponents of the moral model may be more interested in the symbolism of rejecting harm reduction in IV drug use than in empirical evidence. After all, in the aforementioned quote, George W. Bush (2000) states that "children deserve a clear, unmixed message that there are right choices in life and wrong choices in life, that we are all responsible for our actions, and that using drugs will destroy your life." This quote makes it clear that rejection of harm reduction strategies is more about delivering a clear symbolic message than about empirical facts.

The question that must be asked however, is to what extent, if at all, does support for harm reduction policies such as NEPs send out a message that drug use is acceptable? Harm reduction strategies in areas of life other than drug policy are not commonly thought to send such a mixed message. The use of seatbelts and airbags makes speeding safer, yet advocates of seat belts and airbags in automobiles are not thought to send a message that speeding is acceptable. The owner of a bar who rearranges the furniture and increases padding in an attempt to minimize the harm caused to patrons during fights would not be thought to send a message that fighting in the bar is acceptable. Banning gambling on credit is an attempt to reduce the harm of gambling, but this is not thought to send a message that excessive gambling is acceptable. If the drugs used by clients of the NEP remain illegal, then it is hard to see why the existence of NEPs might be thought to send such a message.

There is another reason to think that proponents of the moral model ought to support rather than oppose programs like needle exchange. Buchanan et al. (2003, p. 430) note that the argument in favor of NEPs is usually phrased in empirical, scientific terms, while the argument against NEPs is usually phrased in moral terms. They suggest that the main argument in favor of harm reduction policies in general, and NEPs in particular, is actually also a moral argument, albeit one that is rarely articulated. The cost of addiction and "substance abuse"[10] is overwhelmingly borne by the poorest sections of society, and harm reduction policies seek to reduce the burdens on those who can least afford to bear them. In the words of Buchanan et al. (2003, p. 438), "The staggering inequities of the intertwined epidemics of AIDS and substance abuse borne by poor people and people of color are the moral wrongs that we seek to redress." This is a moral argument, not a scientific one.

Heroin-related policies—Safe Injection Facilities

It is a relatively small step from a policy of needle exchange to a policy of providing safe injecting facilities for IV drug users. A policy of needle exchange attempts to reduce the harms caused to drug users by the use of shared or non-sterile needles. A policy of providing safe injection facilities does that as well, but attempts to reduce harm further by helping drug users to utilize safer IV techniques, and by ensuring that medical help will be available in the event it is required.

There are few ethical issues raised by the provision of safe injecting facilities that are not also raised by NEPs. The legal issues surrounding safe injection facilities are more complex, and thus provide more ethical issues for police, and concerns may be raised about the possibility of a "honey pot" effect; namely, that the presence of a safe injection facility may draw more drug users into an area. One other issue may arise if the safe injection facility provides drug users with only one means of ingesting drugs, as this situation may actually induce drug users into more risky methods of drug use. For proponents of the moral model, the main issue in providing safe injection facilities is again the perception that this sends the message that illegal drug use is acceptable.

Possibly the most difficult ethical issue regarding the provision of safe injection facilities is faced by the local law enforcement agencies. Drug users who wish to make use of the safe injection facilities will need to purchase their drugs elsewhere and then bring them to the safe injection facility. This means, of course, that all drug users who enter the facility will be in possession of illegal drugs and will thus be committing an offense. Drug users who make use of an NEP may be in possession of drug paraphernalia,[11] but even in jurisdictions in which this is an offense, it is generally a minor one compared to possession of an illegal substance.

Safe injecting facilities provide various social benefits—members of the public are less likely to encounter addicts using drugs on the street; they are less likely to stumble across used injection equipment that forms a public health risk; drug users are less likely to become victims of crime while under the influence of drugs—and thus police officers will benefit from drug users being able to use such facilities. It could even be argued that police have a duty to assist drug users in accessing such services. Yet, police still have a duty to uphold the law and thus the ethical issue arises for police in balancing these competing duties.

The possibility that the existence of safe injecting facilities might cause drug users to congregate in a particular area may be a valid concern but is one that can be addressed by simply establishing such a facility in an area in which public injecting is already a problem. A large part of this concern about the provision of safe injecting facilities comes down to the "not in my backyard" response, but the problem is not as easily resolved as it might be in some other cases. If a new prison is to be built, and no one wishes for it to be built in their local area, then it may be possible to build the prison in an isolated location, but such a solution does not work for the location of a safe injection facility. If such a facility is to be worthwhile, it needs to be accessible to as many potential users as possible. Because so many of the potential users of a safe injecting facility are extremely poor, often partly as a result of their illegal drug use, many will have no money to use public transport to reach a safe injection facility. Ideally, such a facility will need to be centrally located, in an area already frequented by illegal drug users, and be easily accessible by public transport, requirements that an isolated area will simply not satisfy.

One ethical issue that arises in the case of a safe injection facility but that does not arise in the case of an NEP is the possibility that it might encourage illegal drug users to adopt more risky drug use behaviors. Consider the administration of heroin. In most parts of the world, the preferred method of administration of heroin is by injection; thus the call for safe injection facilities. But this is not the only method by which heroin may be ingested. One other relatively common method is to "smoke" heroin. This method, which is more accurately termed inhalation, involves vaporizing the heroin without burning it, and then inhaling the resulting fumes (Stimson & Metrebian, 2003, p. 10). One form of this method—"chasing the dragon"—that originated in Hong Kong and spread to Europe via South East Asia, is the predominant method of heroin ingestion in the Netherlands. Many of the harms involved with heroin are related to the problems of intravenous use, and thus "chasing the dragon" is actually a preferable method of heroin ingestion since those who ingest it this way are not at risk of contracting hepatitis or HIV through shared needles, nor are they subject to injuries caused by poor IV technique, such as abscesses and infections, vein damage or collapse, deep vein thrombosis, or pulmonary embolism. Heroin overdose deaths are also more likely to occur among those who inject than among those who "chase the dragon" (Stimson & Metrebian, 2003, p. 13).

Clearly, in cases in which heroin users are accustomed to administering their drugs by methods other than injection, this ought to be encouraged. But if safe injection facilities provide facilities only for injection, then drug users who wish to make use of those facilities (perhaps because they wish to ensure their safety while under the influence of the drug) may be forced to inject. However, providing facilities for users to ingest by other means comes with its own problems. "Chasing the dragon" is a technique that requires some skill; poor technique can leave large amounts of vaporized heroin in the air, allowing it to be inhaled by injection facility staff. Even those skilled in the technique are unable to inhale all the vaporized heroin, and thus this method, while less risky for the drug user, may pose greater risks for those who work within the safe injection facility.

For proponents of the moral model, the most important issue that confronts the provision of safe injecting facilities is the same as that which confronts NEPs, namely, the perception that provision of such services sends a message to the community that the use of illegal drugs is acceptable. However, if the provision of NEPs does not send such a message, then it is hard to see how the provision of safe injecting facilities could do so. In fact it has been suggested that the provision of safe injecting facilities, rather than sending a message that illegal drug use is acceptable, might actually have the opposite effect. If the image of safe injecting facilities is well managed, a constructive message could be produced to the effect that such facilities are necessary precisely because the use of these illegal drugs is potentially so harmful (Drug and Crime Prevention Committee, 1996, p. 9).

In fact, there is a reason for thinking that safe injection facilities ought to be more acceptable to proponents of the moral model than NEPs are. One of the possible roles of safe injection facilities is to provide drug users with access to information about drug use treatment and to refer users to relevant treatment programs should those users so desire. Thus, the safe injection facilities serve as a means of facilitating contact with drug users, allowing those users to gain effective access to treatment that deals with the cause of their problems—the drug taking behavior—rather than merely reducing the likely harms of that behavior. Such a role would seem to be compatible with the moral model.

Heroin-related policies—Heroin Prescription

If safe injection facilities are only a short step away from NEPs under the medical model, then prescribing heroin is only a short step away from MMT. Both programs attempt to "normalize" the life of the drug user to the greatest extent possible, to allow drug users to distance themselves from the illegal drug market, and to not need to spend large amounts of their time securing a supply of the drug to which they are addicted, and the money with which to pay for it. Although methadone may be a medically preferred option, in that it acts in a much more lasting manner and tends to stabilize the endorphin responses due to its different interaction with the endorphin receptors, there may be benefits to providing those addicted to heroin with their drug of addiction on prescription. The main ethical issues for proponents of the medical model are whether such a policy would actually assist drug users, and whether such a program would be, were it to be found effective, cost efficient. For proponents of the moral model, the main ethical issue once again concerns the message that prescribing heroin would send to society about the acceptability of drug use. Other concerns under the moral model include questions about whether prescribing heroin to drug users would remove any incentive to end drug use, and whether these prescription drugs might be diverted onto the drug market, with its consequent dangers for other members of society.

Although there have been fewer studies of heroin prescription programs than for any of the other non-punitive policies that I have discussed in this chapter, the studies that have been undertaken suggest that there is a place for heroin prescription as a treatment protocol under the medical model. The largest trial of heroin prescription, undertaken in Switzerland, showed quite impressive outcomes in terms of prevention of heroin overdose deaths, reduced rates of new blood borne infections, reduction in involvement in crime of the participants of the trial, and increase in paid employment by trial participants (Uchtenhagen, Gutzwiller & Dobler-Mikola, 1997). The researchers involved in the trial also felt that the program was very cost efficient. If such results were able to be obtained in other heroin prescription programs, then all of the main questions asked under the medical model would certainly be answered.

Proponents of the moral model would be likely to be concerned about the fact that such a program does not seek to address the drug taking behavior of the participants, and thus fails to deal with the underlying moral problem. They may be somewhat reassured to hear that one of the findings of the Swiss heroin trial was that the longer patients were involved in the trial, the less likely they were to drop out of the program (which included also other treatment protocols such as MMT), and the more likely they were to transfer into the other treatment protocols within the program, with a significant percentage of the participants working toward abstinence from drug use (Uchtenhagen et al., 1997, p. 8). Of course, this still does not address the main question for proponents of the moral model, which is the message that prescription of heroin might send to society about the acceptability of drug use.

As I have noted before, it is difficult to see how a program such as this can realistically be seen to send a mixed message about the acceptability of drug use within society, especially since the drug that would be prescribed in these cases—pure pharmaceutical heroin, also known as diamorphine—is already prescribed for medical purposes. If prescribing the drug in other cases, such as for pain relief, does not send a mixed message about its acceptability within society, then it is difficult to see why prescribing the drug as a medical treatment for opiate addiction should be thought to do so. In this context it is worth remembering that a program of heroin prescription is not intended to be the only drug user treatment program available, but rather one of a number of possible treatments, to be offered alongside existing programs such as MMT. It is also the case that a heroin prescription program is generally envisaged only in cases in which the use of the prescribed drug can be supervised, as in a safe injection facility.[12] Finally, it is important to note that heroin prescription would be contemplated only in cases in which the drug user was actually already addicted to opiates, not in cases in which the drug user simply wanted to experiment with a different drug.

Cannabis policies

The last group of non-punitive policies that I wish to examine in this chapter are those regarding the use and possession of small amounts of cannabis. I have left such policies until last since they are, in an important respect, different from all the other non-punitive policies that I have discussed. The other policies I have discussed—MMT, NEPs, safe injecting facilities and the prescription of heroin—are all advocated by proponents of the medical model as a response to particular individual or public health problems caused by drug misuse and addiction, and are all opposed by advocates of the moral model. Policies that decriminalize the use and possession of small amounts of cannabis in one way or other are not proposed by advocates of the medical model in response to any health problem. These policies are proposed as a response to a social problem—the widespread use of cannabis in its various forms and the harms caused to individuals as a result of a criminal conviction and the subsequent possession of a criminal record.

Cannabis is almost certainly the most commonly used illicit drug in the western world, with studies suggesting that it has been tried by a third of adults in the USA (National Institute on Drug Abuse, 1992), and a similar percentage of adults in other English speaking countries such as Australia (Australian Institute of Health and Welfare, 2001). Studies suggest that the health risks of cannabis use are similar to the risks of use of legal drugs such as tobacco and alcohol (Hall, Solowij & Lemon, 1994), and most users of cannabis could be described as casual or social users of the drug.[13] For a casual user of cannabis, the health risks are minimal and thus the greatest harm likely for such a user will be caused by the criminal justice system itself, since the harms caused by conviction for the possession or use of cannabis, including the subsequent possession of a criminal record, greatly outweigh the likely harms caused by casual use of the drug. Given the widespread use of cannabis, punitive policies for possession and use of small quantities of the drug thus have the potential to harm a great number of people. This is why it is argued that the possession and use of small amounts of cannabis ought to be decriminalized.

Although the medical model does not apply to policies of decriminalization of cannabis, the moral model certainly does, for the use of cannabis, like the use of other illicit drugs, is seen as a moral failing. For proponents of the moral model, the main concerns about decriminalizing the possession and use of small amounts of cannabis are that such policies might encourage the use of this drug or that these policies might send a message to society that the use of the drug is acceptable, that the implementation of such policies does nothing to address the moral failing of the drug user, and the possible "gateway" effect of cannabis—allowing people to use cannabis might lead them to the use of other, harder, drugs.

Although answers to such concerns depend to some extent on the actual decriminalization policies proposed, it is possible to provide a partial answer to these concerns. With regard to the concern that decriminalization of cannabis might increase the use of the drug, it is possible to examine jurisdictions in which cannabis has been decriminalized to see whether this has in fact resulted in an increase in cannabis use. Although the evidence on this count is not conclusive, it appears that if the decriminalization of cannabis has any effect on levels of its use, then this effect is both slight and temporary (Single, 1989; Thies & Register, 1993; Single, Christie & Ali, 2000). Concerns about the possible message that might be sent through the implementation of such policies have been dealt with in earlier sections of this chapter. Suffice it to say here that any policy that decriminalizes the possession and use of small amounts of cannabis while simultaneously imposing stiff penalties on the possession or trafficking of larger amounts of the drug does not seem to be sending a message of acceptability about the drug.[14]

Answering the question whether decriminalization policies do anything to address the moral failing of the drug user is rather more difficult, and depends upon the form that decriminalization actually takes. Such a claim may have some weight against decriminalization policies that take no action at all against those found in possession of small amounts of cannabis, but it carries far less weight in cases in which decriminalization policies involve monetary fines for cannabis possession. The existence of a fine means that drug users are still being punished for their transgressions in much the same way that fines given to speeding motorists punish them for their moral failing in not complying with the speed limit. It is difficult to see why offenses involving drugs should be punished more harshly than other offenses, or why what is deemed a punishment in other cases would not be deemed a punishment in drug cases.

The final claim, that cannabis may serve as a "gateway" to the use of other drugs, is difficult to substantiate. Although it is true that most users of drugs such as heroin and cocaine began their illicit drug use with cannabis, it is also true that most users of cannabis do not progress to the use of "harder drugs".[15] What is clear however, is that virtually all users of illicit drugs began drug use through the legal drugs of alcohol and tobacco, and that there is much more evidence to support the view that these legal drugs are a gateway to illicit drug use than there is to suggest that the use of cannabis is a significant step toward the use of "harder drugs" (Single et al., 2000, p. 161).

Conclusions

The main non-punitive drug policies that have been suggested and implemented all raise ethical issues that need to be addressed. Many of these issues depend on the theory of drug use and dependence that one accepts—the medical model or the moral model. All of the non-punitive policies raise more issues for proponents of the moral model, and it is these issues that generally tend to frame the debate regarding the implementation of non-punitive policies. However, the issues raised by such policies for proponents of the medical model should also not be ignored.

Stephen Coleman, Ph.D., is Lecturer in Ethics in the School of Humanities and Social Sciences at the University of NSW (@ ADFA) and a Senior Research Fellow at the Centre for Applied Philosophy and Public Ethics. His philosophical interests focus on issues in police ethics, medical ethics, and the interaction between law and human rights. He is the author of The Ethics of Artificial Uteruses (Ashgate, 2004), numerous articles in peer-reviewed journals such as Philosophical Studies, Criminal Justice Ethics, Australian Journal of Professional and Applied Ethics, Journal of Professional Ethics, has contributed chapters to a number of edited collections, and is an Associate Editor of Criminal Justice Ethics.

References

Adlaf, E.M., Begin, P., & Sawka, E. (Eds.). (2005). Canadian Addiction Survey (CAS): A national survey of Canadians' use of alcohol and other drugs: Prevalence of use and related harms: Detailed report. Ottawa: Canadian Centre on Substance Abuse.

AIDS is the wrath of God. (2003, August 12). News24.com, Retrieved March 24, 2005, from http://www.news24.com/News24/World/News/0,6119,2-10-1462_1456423,00.html.

Australian Institute of Health and Welfare. (2001). 2001 National drug strategy household survey, First results. Canberra: AIHW.

Buchanan, D., Shaw, S., Ford, A. & Singer, M. (2003). Empirical science meets moral panic: An analysis of the politics of needle exchange. *Journal of Public Health Policy, 24*, 427-444.

Bush, G.W. (2000). Response of Governor George W. Bush to the AIDS Foundation of Chicago. Retrieved March 24, 2005, from http://www.aidschicago.org/pdf/GWB_response.pdf.

Delgado, C. (2002). Evaluation of needle exchange programs. *Public Health Nursing, 21*, 171-178.

Drug and Crime Prevention Committee, Parliament of Victoria. (1996). Occasional paper No. 2: Safe injecting facilities, Their justification and viability in the Victorian setting. Melbourne: Parliament of Victoria.

Hall, W., Solowij, N. & Lemon, J. (1994). *The health and psychological consequences of cannabis use*, National Drug Strategy Monograph Series No. 25. Canberra: Australian Government Publication Service.

Health Canada. (2003). Information: Cannabis reform bill. Retrieved February 2, 2005 from www.hc-sc.gc.ca/english/media/releases/2003/2003_34bk2.htm.

Hurley, S.F., Jolley, D.J. & Kaldor, J.M. (1997). Effectiveness of needle-exchange programmes for prevention of HIV infection. *The Lancet, 349*, 1797-1800.

Kleinig, J. (2005). Ethical issues in substance use intervention. In this volume. Previously published in (2004) *Substance Use & Misuse, 39*(30), 369-398.

Leshner, A. I. (1998). Addiction is a brain disease – and it matters. *National Institute of Justice Journal, 237*, 2-6.

Magura, S. (2001). Leaving methadone treatment: Lessons learned, lessons forgotten, lessons ignored. *Mount Sinai Journal of Medicine, 68*, 62-74.

The mayor's crusade against methadone. (1998, August 18). *New York Times*, p. A18.

Morse, S. J. (2005). Medicine and morals, craving and compulsion. In this volume. Previously published in (2004) *Substance Use & Misuse, 39*(30), 437-460.

National Consensus Development Panel on Effective Medical Treatment of Opiate Addiction. (1998). Effective medical treatment of opiate addiction. *Journal of the American Medical Association, 280*, 1936-1943.

National Institute on Drug Abuse, USA (1992). National household survey on drug abuse: Population estimates 1991; Revised, 20 November 1992. Rockville MA: National Institute on Drug Abuse.

National Institutes of Health. (1997, February 11-13). Interventions to prevent HIV risk behaviors. NIH Consensus Statement, 15, 1-41.

Pendergast, M.L. & Podus, D. (2000). Drug treatment effectiveness: An examination of conceptual and policy issues. *Substance Use and Misuse, 35*, 1629-1657.

Satcher, D. (2000, March 17). *Evidence-based findings on the efficacy of syringe exchange programs: An analysis of the scientific research completed since April 1998*. Washington DC: Department of Health and Human Services (Press Release).

Schechter, M. T. (2002). Science, ideology and needle exchange programs. *Annals of the American Academy of Political and Social Science, 582*, 94-101.

Short, J., Hawes, R. & Kerin, J. (1997, August 20). Heroin trials not on says Howard. *The Australian*, p. 1.

Single, E. (1989). The impact of marijuana decriminalization: An update. *Journal of Public Health Policy, 10*, 456-466.

Single, E., Christie, P. & Ali, R. (2000). The impact of cannabis decriminalization in Australia and the United States. *Journal of Public Health Policy, 21*, 157-186.

Stimson, G. V. (1995). AIDS and injecting drug use in the United Kingdom 1987-1993: The policy response and the prevention of the epidemic. *Social Science and Medicine, 41*, 699-716.

Stimson, G.V. & Metrebian, N. (2003). *Prescribing heroin: What is the evidence?* London: Joseph Rowntree Foundation.

Swarns, R. L. (1999, January 16). Mayor relents on plan to end methadone use. *New York Times*, p. A1.

Thies, C. & Register, C. (1993) . Decriminalization of marijuana and the demand for alcohol, marijuana, and cocaine. *Social Science Journal, 30*, 385-399.

Townshend, P. L., Sellman, J. D. & Coverdale, J. H. (2001). A preventive ethics approach to methadone maintenance programmes. *New Zealand Bioethics Journal, 2*, 7-13.

Uchtenhagen, A., Gutzwiller, F. & Dobler-Mikola, A. (Eds.). (1997). Programme for a medical prescription of narcotics. Summary of the Synthesis Report. Berne: Swiss Federal Office of Public Health.

Winick, C. (2001). A mandatory short-term methadone-to-abstinence program in New York City. *The Mount Sinai Journal of Medicine, 68*, 41-45.

Zinberg, N. E. (1984). *Drug, set, and setting: The basis for controlled intoxicant use*. New Haven: Yale University Press.

Glossary

cannabis: a term used to denote the various psychoactive preparations of the plant *Cannabis sativa*. Includes marijuana (from the leaf of the plant), hashish (from the resin of the flowering heads), and hashish oil.

decriminalization: the repeal of laws or regulations that define a behaviour, product, or condition as criminal, usually while still considering that behaviour, product or condition an infraction of the law (possibly punishable by a fine). Decriminalization is often distinguished from legalization, in which the behaviour, product or condition is no longer subject to any penalty of law.

heroin: a semisynthetic drug, derived from morphine, originally obtained from the opium poppy. In its various forms it can be injected, 'smoked', or snorted. It produces a 'high' and sedation when ingested; has a relatively short effect on the user.

medical model: the model of drug user treatment that sees drug dependence as a disease and thus afflicted individuals as patients requiring medical attention.

methadone: a synthetically produced, long-lasting opiate, available in both oral and injectable forms. When ingested it produces much less of a 'high' than heroin, less sedation, and has a much longer effect on the user.

methadone maintenance treatment (MMT): a treatment for opiate addiction that provides methadone as a substitute for other opiates (usually heroin) as a means of stabilizing the patient's endorphin response (disrupted by regular ingestion of 'high' inducing opiates) and meeting the physical need for opioids of the addicted patient. Intake of methadone is usually long-term; it may be reduced over time if abstinence is the ultimate goal of treatment.

moral model: the model of drug user treatment that sees drug dependence as a moral failing resulting from a lack of self-restraint, and thus afflicted individuals as persons guilty of moral wrongdoing.

needle exchange programs (NEPs): a harm reduction program in which intravenous drug users bring in used injection equipment and are provided with sterile replacement equipment. The aim of NEPs is to reduce the likelihood of transmission of blood borne viruses such as hepatitis and HIV, which are commonly spread through sharing of injection equipment.

safe injecting facilities: a harm reduction program which provides, in addition to sterile injecting equipment, a controlled location for injecting (or otherwise ingesting) drugs obtained elsewhere, with medical staff who are able to assist drug users in cases of emergency, such as when overdoses occur. The primary aim is to reduce the risks of injury or death caused by drug overdose.

Notes

* I would like to thank John Kleinig, Stanley Einstein and Nikki Coleman for their helpful comments on earlier versions of this chapter.

1. It should be noted that the list of substances denoted as illegal drugs, and thus prohibited by law, will vary wildly from country to country, and even within the

same country over a period of time. In most cases the list of banned substances will have more to do with public perception and politics than with the potential harms of the use of these substances.

2. I should make it clear at this point that being "guilty of wrongdoing" does not necessarily mean that one has broken the law. It is a moral, rather than a legal, conception of guilt that is in effect here, and while moral rules and laws often coincide, this is not always the case.
3. Of course, if the "worst" drugs are defined in terms of the absolute number of harms, injuries or deaths which they cause through their pharmacological actions, then nicotine and alcohol are easily at the top of the list.
4. In my discussion I do not distinguish between NEPs and the more recent secondary needle exchange programs (SNEPs), which provide needles and other equipment that they know will be used by people other than the actual exchanger.
5. Patients in an MMT program are usually stabilized on a very specific dose of methadone, intended to be the absolute minimum dose required in order to meet that patient's opiate needs. It may seem strange, therefore, to think of an MMT patient diverting a dose of the drug to which they are addicted, yet there are reasons why patients do become involved in dose diversion. If they cannot afford the costs of the MMT program, they may need to sell some of their methadone in order to ensure a continued, albeit somewhat inadequate, supply. Methadone also interacts differently with the body's endorphin receptors from drugs such as heroin, and thus does not induce the same "high," and so the MMT patient may divert methadone doses in order to purchase other drugs (such as amphetamines or cocaine) that do induce a "high."
6. It is illuminating to compare the situation faced by non-compliant patients within an MMT program with the situation of non-compliant patients being treated for chronic diseases such as diabetes or high blood pressure. Do diabetics, for example, face the possibility of exclusion from treatment or other sanctions if they fail to comply with treatment protocols?
7. Statements by various Representatives and Senators are quoted in Schechter (2002, p. 97). The study erroneously or inaccurately quoted by these people noted that HIV rates were higher among users of the NEP in Vancouver than among the general IV drug-using population of the city. Although a causal explanation for this fact was favored by those quoting the study – to support the view that NEPs cause higher rates of HIV transmission – the higher rates of HIV infection of the users of the Vancouver NEP could be better explained by the fact that users of the NEP were generally engaged in many more high risk behaviors (such as injecting in shooting galleries, involvement in prostitution, daily injection of drugs, etc.) than drug users in Vancouver who did not use the NEP.
8. A number of additional studies are cited in Buchanan et al. (2003).
9. Such a view is in line with the suggestion that AIDS is God's for punishment for homosexuality, a position commonly voiced in some circles. For a recent example, see "AIDS is the Wrath of God" (2003), discussing a speech by the Taiwanese Vice-President Annette Lu.

10. This volume's style utilizes the category *substance abuse* as a diagnostic category. Substances are used or misused; living organisms are and can be *abused*. Editors' note.
11. In some jurisdictions it is not an offense to be in possession of drug paraphernalia (sometimes known as "equipment for the administration of prohibited drugs"), in others possession of a hypodermic syringe or hypodermic needle is specifically excluded from the definition of drug paraphernalia. See for example the NSW Drug Misuse and Trafficking Act 1985 No 226, Section 11.1A.
12. This was the case in the Swiss heroin prescription trial.
13. For example, only 18.1% of Canadian cannabis users were found to be daily users of the drug (Adlaf, Begin & Sawka, 2005).
14. The proposed reforms to Canadian law regarding possession and use of small amount of cannabis are probably a good example here (Health Canada, 2003).
15. The reader is reminded that "gateway drugs", "soft drugs" and "hard drugs" are non-scientific stereotypes of selected illegal psychoactive "drugs" which empower and mystify "the drug" without in any way noting their pharmacological actions or the dimensions of the "drug experience" which is a function of the interaction between the substance, the user and the site of use. (Zinberg, 1984). Editors' note.

1-6 Thinking Ethically About Needle and Syringe Programs[1]

John Kleinig, Ph.D.

Abstract

Accepting—for the sake of argument—our current legal policies concerning heroin use and its users, what ethical questions are raised for needle and syringe supply or exchange programs? Do they weaken drug control laws, send the wrong message or obscure the right message, do little to eliminate the harm of drugs, detract from alternatives, and/or constitute a counsel of despair? I suggest that in the absence of established better alternatives, needle and syringe programs (NSPs) constitute a morally acceptable and in some cases even desirable option despite the continued criminalization of injection drug use. Yet they must be conceived and administered in ways that do not reinforce prevailing social prejudices.

Key Words: aggregative v. distributive; half-way house; counseling; criminalization; ethics; harm reduction; HIV/HCV transmission; moral message; needle and syringe programs; needle exchange programs; zero-tolerance

For reasons best known to itself, our society has chosen to criminalize the use of certain psychoactive drugs and, in addition, to stereotype and marginalize their users. That it should wish to control or discourage the use of such drugs is not, perhaps, surprising, given the multiple impacts of their unregulated use. That our policies of legislative response have sometimes taken the form of a stigmatized criminalization rather than of restricted access, prescription, taxation, and various other options—along with education and treatment—is to a considerable extent lost in the vagaries of our political history. But it is that to which we are currently heirs, and though those policies may seem—and I am sure are—frequently arbitrary and misguided, we are still left with the need to respond to the personal and social effects of drug use. Some of those effects will be intrinsic to the drugs themselves; others will relate more distinctively to drug-using practices.

Harm-reduction policies *appear* to offer a humane response, albeit primarily to drug-using practices. Rather than saying, in Victorian fashion, "You've made your bed, now you must lie in it,"[2] such policies seek to reduce some of the deleterious effects that are associated with a particular form of drug administration. These effects on both the users themselves and others who may be affected or infected by them—via transmissible viruses such as HIV and HCV[3]—are, I think most of us would accept, grossly disproportionate to whatever may be the inappropriateness of the drug use that transmitted them.[4]

I have been asked if I would comment on some of the *ethical* issues surrounding the use of what in Australia are known as NSPs (needle and syringe programs). Elsewhere, or, partly because of the ways in which they operate, they are known as NEPs (needle exchange programs), SEPs (syringe exchange programs), SNEPs (syringe and needle exchange programs),[5] and sometimes there are also references to SND (satellite needle distribution) or SNE (secondary needle exchange) programs and practices.[6]

Why should we look at the ethical dimensions of this issue, rather than, simply, at their *practicalities*—with which, I imagine, many of you are involved? At one level the answer is quite simple. Ethical concerns are basic to human interaction. They are the *fundamental currency* of interpersonal conduct. It is, most probably, an ethical concern—whether of compassion, beneficence, or justice—that prompts us to commit ourselves to social welfare or harm-reduction, a sense that we cannot simply stand on the sidelines as people risk catastrophic harm to themselves and to individual and collective others. We do not wait for bad consequences to occur in other spheres—we have safety standards and seatbelt regulations, for example—and there is no adequate reason for making an exception here.

But ethical concerns are fundamental in another and deeper sense. It is via ethical judgments that we assess and evaluate other norms of human interaction, whether they are political, economic, legal, or customary. We do not judge ethical standards by reference to these other ways of structuring and judging our behavior, but we appeal to ethical considerations in evaluating those others. If laws and governmental policies don't conform to ethical requirements, we have a strong reason for seeking to change them; if economic policies fall short of what we think is ethically acceptable, we have a strong reason to seek their restructuring; if political decisions are ethically suspect we have a powerful reason for protesting them. Being sensitive to the *ethical* issues surrounding NSPs is therefore of fundamental significance, even more fundamental than—though of course not independent of—whether they work. Not everything that might work is ethically required or even permissible, as we are reminded by current controversies about the use of harsh, even torturous, interrogation tactics,[7] and probably should be reminded by the tendentious language of the "war on drugs."

Not only are ethical issues fundamental, they are also *pervasive*; they arise at every point of our interactions. They are not restricted to special occasions. Even the simplest transaction—such as the purchase of a newspaper—is invested with ethical significance: whether I act politely and with respect toward the seller of the newspaper or with surliness and condescension. The same might be said about the delivery of drug paraphernalia: is distribution mechanical or is there recognition that the recipients are our fellows, albeit deeply affected by drugs? There are in addition even larger ethical questions lurking behind such transactions—in the first example, about whether a particular newspaper ought to be published and whether that vendor should stock it, and in the case of NSPs whether they ought to exist and, if so, who should operate them. We should remember, however, that these latter questions are distinct from, even though they may be related to, questions about whether the judgments we make ought to be enforced or otherwise officially sanctioned.[8] Ethical judgment is complex and nuanced.

Because of the way in which our society has chosen to respond to certain drugs and their users, some of these general questions tend to arise more visibly. Because we have chosen to criminalize the use of heroin and cocaine, ethical questions about the status of NSPs will tend to be more pressing than would be the case were those drugs' use not criminalized.

This is not the occasion to address some of these more fundamental issues, though they certainly need to be addressed. What I want to do here is review and offer an assessment of the kinds of ethical questions that are posed for NSPs within the existing Anglo-American sociopolitical system.

Accepting the sociopolitical status quo, the most fundamental question will be whether NSPs ought to exist. In the Australian context, fortunately, one is not forced to do too much work on this question, though I will later argue that there remain significant ethical issues concerning the ways in which such programs are implemented.

NSPs originated in Australia in the 1980s, and governmental support for harm reduction and, in particular, needle programs, has been significant, even if not always wholehearted.[9] However, were I giving this talk in the United States, where I normally reside, I would have a much tougher job, for the zero tolerance policies that often prevail frequently express themselves resolutely against NSPs.

In his 2000 presidential campaign, (then) Governor George W. Bush stated:

> *I do not favor needle exchange programs and other so-called "harm reduction" strategies to combat drug use. I support a comprehensive mix of prevention, education, treatment, law enforcement, and supply interdiction to curb drug use and promote a healthy, drug-free America, not misguided efforts to weaken drug laws. Drug use in America, especially among children, has increased dramatically under the Clinton-Gore Administration, and needle exchange programs signal nothing but abdication, that these dangers are here to stay. Children deserve a clear, unmixed message that there are right choices in life and wrong choices in life, that we are all responsible for our actions, and that using drugs will destroy your life. America needs a President who will aim not just for risk reduction, but for risk elimination that offers people hope and recovery, not a dead-end approach that offers despair and addiction.*[10]

There are several claims embedded in this campaign statement, and they constitute a useful peg on which to hang my discussion.

(A) There is the assertion that NSPs (or NEPs) are "misguided efforts to weaken drug laws." It is, of course, a claim we might wish to challenge. Maybe these are laws that we *should* seek to weaken—not necessarily, of course, because we are opposed to drug laws but because we think that the kinds of laws we have are inappropriate to the problem to which they are addressed. But, as I mentioned, I am here prescinding from that inquiry.

Taking it at its face value, how is this weakening intended (as suggested) or, if not intended, then consequent upon NSPs? Three possibilities are hinted at. One is that NSPs convey the message that drug use is not as seriously wrong as it really is: if you provide means whereby people can continue to do what the law forbids, then you weaken its condemnatory force. A second is that access to such means actually increases the amount of illicit behavior. And the third is that harm reduction is not enough; we should be aiming for harm-minimization or harm-elimination, and NSPs impede the latters' achievement.

(1) Take first the most intractable claim, namely, that *NSPs put a question mark against the law's condemnation of drug use*. There are really two issues embedded in this. One concerns *symbolism*, the other is about *ends*.

Let us concede that *some* means of delivering sterile equipment—say, vending machines—by being relatively neutral with respect to prevailing social judgments concerning drug use, *could* lead one to think that the only social judgment relevant to drug use concerns the transmission of disease.[11] For the moralistic opponent of drug use, that inference will be drawn, rendering both the symbolism and the ends of vending machine dispensation unacceptable.[12] Of course, whether that would be a legitimate reading of their availability is another matter. But it is not clearly excluded.

In the case of staffed NSPs, however, the situation is more complex. Consider first the issue of *ends*. It is at least arguable—and later on I will argue it—that an *optimal* program should embed needle distribution within a framework of services that seeks to overcome drug dependence.[13] Needle programs might reasonably be construed as *half-way houses* to keep users (as well as others) relatively safe until such users are ready to address their dependence constructively. If we add to this evidence that counseling, treatment, HIV and HCV prevention messages and testing, abscess wound care, and other clinical services (such as vaccination) are more likely to be sought and provided *in* the context of such programs than *outside* them,[14] then NSPs might be seen as important elements of social and public health policies designed to achieve ends that are not *too* different from those of existing drug laws.[15]

And the *symbolism* of NSPs, even if not moralistic, need not be unacceptable. True, the message will not be one of *moral* condemnation, but that does not prevent them from conveying the view that drug dependence is a bad thing: bad for those who are dependent and bad also for others. I take it from the fact that many program workers were once substance users that the message is ultimately about overcoming a condition—about "recovery," albeit in the context of safety. I concede that this may be thought insufficient by those who wish to convey an unnuanced message of moral condemnation.[16] But it is not a message of normative neutrality or of condonation. Other things being equal, being drug dependent is not a good thing to be.[17]

As with many morally fraught issues, it may not be possible to reconcile certain practices with certain symbolisms. The battle has to be fought at the level of basic ideology.[18] Nevertheless, at the level of social policy some rapprochement may be possible. If the overall social effect that is sought is the same *and* is achieved more effectively as well as with less harm, that is not a bad compromise. What is more, the existence of an NSP conveys no positive regard for the activities of non-dependant drug dealers. Both sides might reasonably view them as self-interestedly exploitative.

We might put the point even more strongly by saying that even if we should not only do what we can to reduce drug dependence but also believe that drug use is inappropriate, we will be morally better off not to adopt social policies that contribute nothing to its reduction and that will probably exacerbate the harms already caused by it. Opponents falsely believe that if NSPs are not available drug use will be diminished. That represents a serious misunderstanding of the dynamics of drug use as well as the drug-injecting population.[19]

NSPs, then, may constitute one vehicle for dealing with drug dependence, rather than an endorsement of it. Even if the moralistic message is not reinforced, neither is it explicitly opposed, and one purpose of that message—the discouragement of drug use—will be furthered by NSPs that *inter alia* are set up to offer access to treatment along with a variety of other services that assist not only users but those with whom they come into contact.

(2) I will return to the argument I have advanced, but before I do, let me comment on the second and third possible interpretations of the claim that NSPs weaken drug laws. The second possibility, that the presence of NSPs actually increases the use of drugs, even by those who already use them, does not seem to be borne out by the evidence that we have.[20] Bush's highly politicized claim—that drug use, especially among children, increased under the Clinton-Gore Administration—even if true, need not have had and almost certainly did not have any connection with the existence of NSPs. NSPs are not a form of advertising, the purpose of which is to initiate or increase drug consumption, even though one might want to argue that they seek to induce those who already inject certain drugs (IDUs) to do so in a way that is safer for themselves and others. If there is any message here, it is that until individual drug users are ready to come to terms with their drug use and the lifestyle that has come to be associated with it, they ought to take steps to minimize the likelihood of their or others suffering the worst side effects of that use.[21]

Suppose, though, that we had incontrovertible evidence that NSPs increased the number of drug users. Would that be a reason to oppose such programs? It would be a reason, but how strong a reason would surely depend on a calculus of consequences. We would need to weigh the costs of the increase against the costs of drug users not having access to clean drug using equipment. In particular we would need to weigh the costs of increased drug use against the diminution in HIV and HCV transmission. These latter costs are not merely the costs to a community in treatment and resources by those who contract them but also the disproportionate costs of those diseases to the individuals who contract them (whether users or others to whom they might have been transmitted). Even a minimally humane society does not leave by the roadside those whose reckless driving has resulted in an accident, and we cannot ignore the medical conditions of those whose drug use has resulted in their contraction of serious disease. Almost every study strongly argues that the social cost of NSPs is worthwhile.[22]

(3) The third possibility is that though NSPs *reduce*, they do not *minimize* or *eliminate*, harm and that we should focus on the latter. Now there may be an argument that other kinds of social strategies, because they are directly focused on overcoming drug dependence, will do more to minimize and ultimately eliminate harm. Such is the claim of some who support faith-based programs, in which the transformative power of a message is considered more important than (and is taken to be exclusive of) the employment of harm reduction strategies. But NSPs and harm minimization are not necessarily incompatible: it is ultimately an empirical claim whether NSPs or some other strategy or some combination of strategies will contribute most to the minimization of harm. It is all very well for those who support, say, faith-based alternatives to offer them as an additional strategy in dealing with drugs. But until there is adequate evidence that they do better, overall, in diminishing the harms of drug use, there is reason to support NSPs, particularly as we have ample evidence that NSPs are effective in reducing the primary and secondary harms caused by drug use. And even if faith-based or other programs do well, we would want to be sure that they are effective in reaching

a significantly similar clientele before arguing that NSPs should be abandoned.[23] Why should one size fit all?

(B) Connected to this is a further argument implicit in Bush's speech, namely, that there is some *incompatibility between NSPs and the menu of other options he prefers*—"a comprehensive mix of prevention, education, treatment, law enforcement, and supply interdiction." But there is no deep incompatibility here. True, to the extent that one has an NSP, there will need to be selective law enforcement—you won't station drug police at NSP premises, but—as existing Australian practice indicates—law enforcement is not thereby abandoned.[24] And, given that staffed NSPs do not increase drug use and also provide increased opportunity for and likelihood of needed and accepted treatment, they simply add to the menu of options available for diminishing dependence on drugs.

(C) Yet another implicit claim is that *NSPs wrongly signal that drug use is here to stay*. They are, Bush suggests, concessions to a false reality. But the false reality—at least as we are able to perceive it at present—is that drug use can be eliminated or is more likely to be eliminated in the absence of NSPs. Offering "hope" is inappropriate and irresponsible if it is not a *realistic* hope.[25] As the United States has discovered, the ability to control access to drugs is much more difficult than even hard-line interdiction promises, and the social costs of efforts to eliminate such access—whether to police and other enforcement personnel, to the criminal justice system, to the public through the crime costs of driving drug use underground, and to the health care system (to mention just some of them)—are massive. Indeed, one might well argue that our current policies have contributed more to the actual intractability of the "drug problem" than NSPs are likely to symbolize. But if, as mentioned earlier, there is no reason to think that NSPs increase drug use and in addition offer a modestly effective gateway to treatment, then they offer a much more realistic understanding of a social phenomenon than the one that in 2000 underpinned his own.

(D) Do NSPs *obscure the message* "that there are right choices in life and wrong choices in life, that we are all responsible for our actions, and that using drugs will destroy your life"? No more, I guess, than seatbelts and airbags and other harm-minimization strategies obscure the message that reckless driving is wrong and will endanger you. Moreover, what we mean by "right" and "wrong" here is left unclear: do we mean that, because of what drugs may do to you, drug taking is seriously *immoral, to the extent of being criminalizable*—or *unwise* and *imprudent*, like smoking and overeating and a sedentary existence? What is conveniently obscured by the Bush argument but which is much more readily acknowledged in the case of seatbelts and so forth is that many of those harmed by drug use are what, for the sake of argument, we might refer to as "innocents"—people who do not do drugs themselves but who have relations with drug users that *inter alia* risk the transmission of HIV/AIDS and other diseases. NSPs may not operate *moralistically*, but they do not obscure the message that some choices in life are bad. Indeed, insofar as they acknowledge and respond to the risk of harm they carry a clear message, and, if they also constitute a safe bridge or offer a gateway to treatment they reinforce that point. Access to treatment and other public health services, insofar as they are available via an NSP, also acknowledges responsibility for actions insofar as they provide realistic social choices. The only thing that is missing (though not explicitly rejected) is the censorious claim that the injection drug user is morally condemnable. The odds are that those who have reached the stage of injection drug use are not in a strong position to control their use and, moreover, that effective treatment will depend on their own cooperation. There are obviously some large questions here, but they are much more complex than the simplistic formula to which Bush appeals.

Bush's final remark, that NSPs constitute "a dead-end approach that offers despair and addiction," is of course a cheap parting shot.

- Why "dead-end," particularly if they offer a safe bridge or gateway to treatment; why dead end, if they diminish the amount of harm caused by a social problem?
- Why "despair" when they provide an opportunity for and even access to treatment to those who would otherwise, given our current social policies and provisions, not have realistic access; why despair, when they reduce the spread of harm to others?
- Why "addiction," when they do not increase drug use, and offer an alternative to it when users are ready to avail themselves of it and will be more likely to benefit from it in both the short and long term?

Before I conclude, however, I want to register a cautionary note about NSPs. As I understand it, most of the budget for needle programs in Australia goes to the provision of paraphernalia and not to staff and counseling support. Maybe that is as it should be, given the clientele.[26] Nevertheless, my reading of some of the support for this form of distribution, in particular a 2002 Report titled *Return on Investment in Needle & Syringe Programs in Australia* produced for the Commonwealth Department of Health and Ageing, gives me some pause.[27] The basic thrust of the Report, as I understand it, is one of minimizing social cost, where this is construed as a balancing of the economic costs of needle distribution against the economic costs of caring for those who contract AIDS or hepatitis C. The balance, the report argues, strongly favors the cost-effectiveness of NSPs.

I realize that this offers a powerful *political* argument for NSPs—one designed to "win over" those who might otherwise be persuaded by moralistic considerations into opposing them. And it is an argument that those who administer NSPs might well accept as a way of securing resources from an otherwise grudging provider. Nevertheless, I find something deeply troubling—ethically—in its symbolism no less deeply troubling than the moralistic opponents of NSPs find in their supposed symbolism. What is troubling is the seemingly cynical economic rationalism that legitimates public policy by reference to a particular "bottom line"—in this case taxpayers dollars, without real regard for the plight of those who are dependent on drugs. Of course, it does have some sort of regard for those who are drug dependent and in danger of contracting AIDS or hepatitis C. But the concern is with the cost of their care for the community, not with the deeper issue of their human situation and what might be done to enable its recovery. *If* we think that there is something humanly diminishing about drug dependence, then responsive programs—even harm reduction programs—ought to be funded and administered in ways that enable and encourage them to address the underlying issues and problems of dependence and not simply transmissible harms. This might not be an issue were we lacking evidence that needle programs offer a more effective and safer bridge to treatment than would be available in their absence. But that evidence exists, and though I would not argue that needle programs lack moral justification absent their responsiveness to the deeper problems of those who need their services, I think *that* justification is much less compelling than it might be.

Let me put the argument even more strongly. What I think drives the argument of the Report is the unstated belief that the spending of middle class tax dollars needs to be optimized and that it is optimized if we distribute syringes. Those dollars are not as efficiently spent if they are embedded in larger programs designed to assist those who are drug dependent to work toward a situation in which they can regain control over their circumstances and realize their human potentials. What that conveys is a social policy that is aggregative but not distributive. If you consider the social demographics of drug dependence and needle distribution, then you see that a program that focuses exclusively on dispensation without regard to the larger issue of drug dependence reinforces the deep racial, social, and class divisions in our communities. The symbolism, alas, is clear: we don't care too much about what happens to you as long as you don't cost us too much.

If NSPs are being funded only to the extent that taxpayer dollars are being spent most efficiently, then we need to expose their deeper implications and argue for something better. As was argued against slavery—that the *distribution* of social burdens was no less important than the *aggregation* of social benefit—so too we may argue in the case of social responses to drug dependence: social concern ought to be directed toward the most vulnerable and needy and not only to its most efficient exemplification.

In conclusion, I should note that these rather broad brushstroke ethical reflections do not exhaust those relevant to NSPs. As I mentioned at the beginning, every interpersonal transaction has an ethical dimension, and those engaged in the day-to-day operation of NSPs will constantly have to make ethically charged and often ethically difficult discretionary decisions, including

- the kinds of treatment programs that literature is provided for,
- the deployment and distribution of personnel and other limited resources,
- whether to supply paraphernalia to those suspected of selling what they receive to others,
- whether to charge for paraphernalia,
- whether premises should be used as a place for safer injection, or a refuge and source of community and other social services,

and so on and so forth. Discretion may be used well or badly, and though it will often be limited by broader social constraints (laws, rules, funding, and so forth), such discretion as is available may be exercised in ways that promote well-being, self-esteem, and autonomy or that reinforce the marginalization, dehumanization, stereotyping, and inequities that are visited upon the disempowered in our communities.[28]

John Kleinig, Ph.D. (ANU) is Director of the Institute for Criminal Justice Ethics and Professor of Philosophy in the Department of Law & Police Science, John Jay College of Criminal Justice and in the PhD Programs in Philosophy and Criminal Justice, Graduate School and University Center, City University of New York. He also holds the Charles Sturt University Chair of Policing Ethics in the Centre for Applied

Philosophy and Public Ethics (Canberra, Australia). Educated in Australia, he taught philosophy at Macquarie University (Sydney) before coming to John Jay College in 1986. His philosophical interests are in the areas of ethics and social philosophy, with a focus on professional and practical ethics, particularly in the fields of education, bioethics, law, and criminal justice. He is the author of Punishment and Desert (Martinus Nijhoff, 1973), Philosophical Issues in Education (Croom Helm/ St Martin's Press, 1972), Paternalism (Rowman & Allanheld/Manchester University Press, 1984), Ethical Issues in Psychosurgery (Allen & Unwin, 1985), Valuing Life (Princeton University Press, 1992), and The Ethics of Policing (Cambridge University Press, 1996). He is editor of the journal, Criminal Justice Ethics and a member of the Editorial Board of Substance Use and Misuse.

Glossary

aggregative social policies: directed to maximizing social benefits, construed in various ways (for example costs in taxpayer dollars, demand on social welfare resources, etc.)

distributive social policies: concerned with how social burdens are shared, whether equitably or inequitably, or whether inequitable social distributions are made moreso.

faith-based programs: those administered by groups who consider that social welfare (and well-being) should have an irreducibly religious or perhaps spiritual dimension.

recovery: usually considered to be a process whereby those who have been drug dependent regain an acceptable level of physical, psychological, and social well-being.

shooting galleries: locations that offer relatively safe and often supervised facilities for drug injection.

zero-tolerance policies: those that allow for or encourage little no discretion in the enforcement of laws, particularly those relating to vice or petty offenses.

Notes

1. This paper was originally delivered as a keynote address at the Anex Harm Reduction Conference, Melbourne, Australia, June 7, 2005. I wish to acknowledge the assistance of Ricky Bluthenthal, Stephen Coleman, Stan Einstein, Alex Kral, John Ryan, Mukta Sharma, and Tom Stopka.
2. This hard saying also makes tendentious suggestions about responsibility for drug dependence. For discussion, see Tziporah Kasachkoff, "Drug Addiction and Responsibility for the Health Care of Drug Addicts," *Substance Use & Misuse*, 39 (3) (2004): 489-509, reprinted in this volume.
3. NSPs may also reduce HBV and bacterial infections.
4. There are, unfortunately, those who see it either as God's punishment on certain kinds of behavior or, less personally, as some form of natural sanction (cosmic justice).
5. In some jurisdictions injecting equipment is provided only on a one-to-one exchange basis; sometimes that is simply an aspiration; sometimes there is no exchange requirement or even expectation. The name used need not be tightly correlated with practice. In decisions about how a program is to be administered, trade-offs will be

involved. A strict *exchange* program may minimize the number of abandoned – and infected or otherwise dangerous – needles; on the other hand, a strictly administered exchange program may, for various reasons, increase the likelihood of using infected paraphernalia. In general, the less tolerant a jurisdiction, the more likely it is that exchange will be "expected." It is not unreasonable to think that a program that dispenses according to need (rather than some form of exchange) will diminish the likelihood of reuse/sharing and thus of riskier behavior. Generally, programs – and communities – that distribute according to need will also provide facilities (often also in public restrooms) for needle disposal. Strict one-for-one exchanges sometimes encourage needle reuse because IDUs who carry paraphernalia all the time face an increased likelihood of apprehension by police. For some comparative discussion, see Alex H. Kral, Rachel Anderson, Neil M. Flynn, & Ricky N. Bluthenthal, "Injection Risk Behaviors Among Clients of Syringe Exchange Programs With Different Syringe Dispensation Policies," *Journal of Acquired Immune Deficiency Syndromes, 37*, no. 2 (October 1, 2004): 1307-12. On syringe disposal under different regimes, see Jennifer Lorvick, Ricky N. Bluthenthal, Lauren Gee, Rachel Anderson, Neil M. Flynn, Andrea Scott, Mary-Lou Gilbert, Alexis Martinez, "Disposal of Used Syringes by Clients of Syringe Exchange programs, California, 2003," presentation at the National Harm Reduction Conference, New Orleans, November, 2004, which suggested that although unsafe disposal practices may increase somewhat with need-based programs, the differences are not significant. At the same time, 1-1 exchange programs were associated with a greater level of needle sharing.

6. The acronyms can be confusing, since "S" may dummy for "syringe," "satellite," or "secondary." SND is defined as: *"receiving a new syringe from another individual through trading, purchasing, borrowing, or being given the syringe outright, or supplying a syringe to another individual through trading, selling, lending, or giving a syringe outright."* SNE occurs when programs allow users to exchange needles not only for themselves but also for others. See Mark W. Tyndall, J. Bruneau, S. Brogley, P. Spittal, M.V. O'Shaughnessy, M.T. Schechter, "Satellite Needle Distribution Among Injection Drug Users: Policy and Practice in Two Canadian Cities," *Journal of Acquired Immune Deficiency Syndromes 31*(1) (Sept 1 2002):98-105; Mark W. Tyndall, J. Bruneau, S. Brogley, P. Spittal, M.V. O'Shaughnessy, M.T. Schechter, "The Role Of Secondary Needle Exchange: Policy And Practice In Two Canadian Cities," <http://www.pulsus.com/cahr2002/abs/abs325.htm>.
7. See, for example, Mark Danner, *Torture and Truth: America, Abu Ghraib, and the War on Terror* (New York: New York Review of Books, 2004).
8. One might, for example, question the appropriateness of permitting owners of private "shooting galleries" to operate such programs, given what we know of their history and the difficulties of ensuring that sterile needles are exchanged.
9. Alex Wodak, "Needle Exchange and Bleach Distribution Programmes: The Australian Experience," *International Journal of Drug Policy 6*, no. 1 (1995): 46-56; N. Crofts, C.K. Aitken, & M.J. Kaldor, "The Force of Numbers: Why Hepatitis C is Spreading Among Australian Injecting Drug Users while HIV is Not," *Medical Journal of Australia* 170 (1999): 220-221.

10. George W. Bush, *Response of Governor George W. Bush to the AIDS Foundation of Chicago* (2000): http://www.aidschicago.org/pdf/GWB_response.pdf.
11. Needle vending machines – unlike condom dispensers – may have other problems associated with them, given that needles are inherently dangerous. Nevertheless, if, as may be the case, the clientele of vending machines differs significantly from that of staffed NSPs, that may be a reason for having both. See Alex Wodak & Annie Cooney, *Effectiveness of Sterile Needle and Syringe Programming in Reducing HIV/AIDS Among Injecting Drug Users* (Geneva: World Health Organization, 2004), 21.
12. This is not to reject them – only to say that they probably cannot be reconciled to the outlook of those who take this position. It might be open to their defenders to argue that whatever the merits of that outlook, it ought not to be translated into social policy. However, those who take such a position often hold in addition that their views ought to be legislatively enforced.
13. Here I follow the World Health Organization in using the term "drug dependence" to cover what it previously distinguished as "addiction," "habituation," and "drug dependence." The virtue of the old distinction was that it recognized a range of drug-related "dependencies," with varying implications for ethically appropriate responses. The problem with the old categorization was the artificial way in which it divided up drug users: dependent users will display varying degrees of control (or lack thereof) with respect to their condition, and ethical social responses will need to have regard to this.
14. R. Heimer, "Can Syringe Exchange Serve as a Conduit to Substance Abuse Treatment?" *Journal of Substance Abuse Treatment 15*, no.3 (1998): 183-91; H. Hagan, J.P. McGough, H. Thiede, S. Hopkins, J. Duchin, & E.R. Alexander, "Reduced Injection Frequency and Increased Entry and Retention in Drug Treatment Associated with Needle-Exchange Participation in Seattle Drug Injectors," *Journal of Substance Abuse Treatment 19,* no. 3 (2000): 247-52; R.N. Bluthenthal, A. Gogineni, D. Longshore, & M. Stein, "Factors Associated with Readiness to Change Drug Use Among Needle-Exchange Users," *Drug & Alcohol Dependence 62* (2001): 225-30. Merely entering a program of course is no guarantee of its success – a "therapeutic engagement" or "alliance" is often critical. There is evidence, however, that retention is also improved for those who enroll through NSPs.
15. Though it must be remembered that existing drug laws are directed against users and not simply those who are drug dependent.
16. In their case the only response is to require that they defend what they assert.
17 This is not, of course, to deny that there may be other dependencies – some of which are socially promoted – that are not good to have. Consistency in social policy is not one of our strong points.
18 Obviously this will not accommodate the views of those who think drug users ought to contract AIDS and die. My purpose here is to try to be responsive to positions about which reasonable people might disagree, not to satisfy every position, no matter how extreme. See the discussion in D. Buchanan, S. Shaw, A. Ford, & M. Singer, "Empirical Science Meets Moral Panic: An Analysis of the Politics of Needle Exchange," *Journal of Public Health Policy 24*, nos. 3-4 (2003): 427-44.
19. This also goes for the issue of establishing NSPs in prisons.

20. The very few studies that suggest – or are exploited to suggest – otherwise can be accounted for in other ways. See for example the discussion of increased HIV/AIDS in Vancouver in M. Schechter, S. Strathdee, P.G.A. Cornelisse, *et al.*, "Do Needle Exchange Programs Increase the Spread of HIV Among Injection Drug Users?: An Investigation of the Vancouver Outbreak," *AIDS, 13* (6) (1999): pp. F45-51.
21. Such programs often distribute literature, provide referrals and other materials and advice that will assist in diminishing the harms of drug use: safer injection practices, overdose prevention (naloxone), condom use, HIV and HCV counseling and testing, hepatitis A and B vaccination, and STD testing and treatment. They may also provide additional services: meals, showers, shelter, primary medical care (including abscess wound care), bleach, social welfare, and housing assistance.
22. Health Outcomes International Pty Ltd, in Association with The National Centre for HIV Epidemiology and Clinical Research and Professor Michael Drummond, Centre of Health Economics, York University, *Return on Investment in Needle & Syringe Programs in Australia* (Canberra, ACT: Commonwealth Department of Health and Ageing, 2002); Alex Wodak & Annie Cooney, *Effectiveness of Sterile Needle and Syringe Programming in Reducing HIV/AIDS Among Injecting Drug Users* (Geneva: World Health Organization, 2004).
23. In a world of limited resources, there is always a danger that ideology will blindly trump effectiveness in decision making.
24. We should not see such discretionary enforcement judgments as peculiar to drug use. Police constantly make judgments about which laws to enforce, and when and how to enforce them. Full enforcement is a formalistic myth. A registration card can function to distinguish persons with drug paraphernalia but choose to "shoot up clean" from those who do not.
25. No society has been "drug free" any more than it has been "crime free." There is a basic fallacy involved in responding to both in an increasingly Draconian fashion. For some history see, D. T. Courtright, *Forces of Habit* (Cambridge, MA: Harvard University Press, 2001); R.J. MacCoun & P. Reuter, *Drug War Heresies: Learning from Other Vices, Times and Places* (Cambridge, UK: Cambridge University Press, 2001; R. Porter & M. Teich (eds.), *Drugs and Narcotics in History* (Cambridge, UK: Cambridge University Press, 1995).
26. I am, however, a bit skeptical, given other studies that suggest the value of NSPs as gateways.
27. Health Outcomes International Pty Ltd, in Association with The National Centre for HIV Epidemiology and Clinical Research and Professor Michael Drummond, Centre of Health Economics, York University, *Return on Investment in Needle & Syringe Programs in Australia* (Canberra, ACT: Commonwealth Department of Health and Ageing, 2002).
28. See Erving Goffman, "On Cooling the Mark Out: Some Aspects of Adaptation to Failure," *Psychiatry, 15* (1952): 451-63, on ways in which agents of social change can be co-opted into becoming agents of social control.

1-7 Addiction and Disability: Moral and Policy Issues

David Wasserman, J.D.

Abstract

This chapter discusses the conceptual, ethical, and policy issues raised by the legal classification of drug addiction as an impairment, and of some non-using drug addicts as people with disabilities. It focuses on the questions of (1) what moral judgments, if any, underlie the classification of addiction as an impairment; (2) whether it makes sense to apportion the burdens of drug addiction between chemical, biological, social, political, and other causes; (3) how considerations of distributive justice may compel or constrain measures to ease the burdens of drug addiction; and (4) whether it is justifiable to deny the current users of illegal substances legal protections available to the current users of legal substances.

Key Words: addiction, disability, distributive justice, impairment, discrimination

Introduction

Most ethical discussion of drug policy in the past 30 years has focused on the justification for imposing criminal sanctions on drug use and sale, and on the extent to which the criminalized behaviors, from the initial use of drugs thought to be addictive to the commission of crimes to support addiction, can be regarded as voluntary or rational (Corrado, 2001; Yaffe, 2002). These two issues are related but distinct: some opponents of criminalization invoke a right to certain kinds of self-regarding behavior; others claim that some of that behavior should be regarded as involuntary, and thus exempt from criminal sanction, without being a matter of right. Proponents of criminalization, on the other hand, deny both a right to engage in drug use or sale, and the involuntariness of such behavior. In this chapter, I will try to sidestep this debate without ignoring it, in addressing a different set of ethical issues: those raised by the classification of drug and alcohol addiction as impairments, and of individuals addicted to drugs as disabled, protected against discrimination on that basis.

The anti-discrimination laws of the United States and other western countries classify addiction as an impairment, and treat some or most addicts as people with disabilities (Bickenbach, 2000). These legislative classifications reflect two important but potentially conflicting developments: first, addiction is increasingly regarded as a disease or disorder of the brain, with a biological and genetic basis, rather than a moral failing or mere bad habit; second, addiction is increasingly recognized as a stigmatized condition, subject to discriminatory attitudes and practices that may impose burdens on the addict greater than its adverse biological effects. Although both these developments support greater leniency in the criminal law, they pull in opposite directions elsewhere. The first development involves the relatively recent "medicalization" and "pathologizing" of a condition—drug dependency or addiction—previously viewed as a vice or a moral weakness; indeed, substance addiction has become the paradigm for a much wider class of "conditions" which are categorized as pathological and which range from an excessive fondness for junk food to an excessive attachment to abusive partners. If the problem is classified as medical, the appropriate response appears to be clinical: behavior modification, psychotherapy, or supposedly more benign substitute substances or activities. The second development resists the medicalization of addiction, attributing many or most of its burdens to social attitudes and practices. If hostile, discriminatory attitudes and practices are to blame for the addict's unhappy lot, or for the addiction itself, then the appropriate response appears to be social: to reform those attitudes and practices. These developments are not necessarily conflicting, but they suggest or emphasize different causes and responses.

Both developments rest to some extent on empirical claims: the former, on the claims that addiction has a biological and genetic explanation, and that addicts differ on average from non-addicts in their genetic constitution and their neurobiology; the latter, on the claim that the addiction itself, and/or many or most of the burdens attributed to the addiction or the addictive substance, are in fact promoted or exacerbated by the social and legal environment. Again, both claims could be true: those who become addicted might be biologically or genetically predisposed to a condition made even more probable, and more harmful, by the social environment. But both developments also rest to some extent on moral convictions: in the case of the former, on the conviction that certain types of dependency are unworthy or degrading; in the case of the latter, on the conviction that many hostile attitudes and practices towards addiction and addicts display contempt, prejudice, or an overly narrow conception of well-being.

In this chapter, I will argue that analyzing addiction in terms of disability provides us with a useful way of understanding what is burdensome about being addicted, how biological and social factors interact making it burdensome, and whether we should favor some kinds of intervention over others in mitigating or eliminating its burdens.

Drug Addiction and Drug Addicts under the Americans with Disabilities Act and the Interactive Model of Disability

Under current disability law in the United States, notably the 1973 Rehabilitation Act and the 1990 Americans with Disabilities Act (ADA), drug addiction is classified as an impairment, and many or most drug addicts qualify as disabled (Rehabilitation Act of 1973, Americans with Disabilities Act of 1990). The partial list of physical and mental impairments in the regulations accompanying the ADA includes "drug addiction" (29 C.F.R. sec. 1630 (2)). A current, former, or suspected addict is classified as an "individual with a disability" if her addiction "substantially limits one or more major life activities"; if she has a record of (past) addiction that substantially limits her, or if she is substantially limited because she is "regarded as having" an addiction (ADA, sec. 3 (2)). (Neither the law nor the accompanying regulations define "substantially limited" or specify who must "regard" the individual as addicted, but the determination of actual addiction is typically made by health professionals, while the perception of addiction is typically in the eyes of prospective employers, administrators, or insurers.) The self-inflicted character of some addictions is no bar to their inclusion under the ADA. There is no exception for impairments acquired through voluntary conduct—the person who becomes addicted because of reckless abuse is as eligible for the protections of the ADA as the person who becomes paraplegic because of reckless driving. But a drug addict enjoys the protection of the ADA only if she has stopped using the drug: the law specifically disqualifies those currently engaged in "illegal use of drugs" as individuals with disabilities (ADA, sec. 510). There is no exclusion for those currently engaged in the legal use of alcohol.

Under the ADA, like the disability discrimination laws of most English-speaking and European countries, the classification of a condition as a disability has three essential elements:

- First, the condition, in this case drug addiction, is a physical or mental disorder or dysfunction;
- Second, the condition (or a history of the condition, or the belief that a person has the condition) substantially limits major life activities, which include self-care, the routine "activities of daily living," and working to the exercise of the senses.
- Third, the condition is stigmatized—as is the user, the use, and the substance used (Bickenbach, 2000; Wasserman, 2000).

The first two features are explicit elements of most of contemporary legal schemes; the third provides a rationale for the protection against discrimination afforded by those schemes. The third feature is implicitly treated as a major cause of the second: impairments are seen as disabling, substantially limiting major life activities, in large part because of the "myths, fears and stereotypes" they evoke—attitudes that are embodied in discriminatory, but often invisible, physical arrangements and social practices.

In requiring physical and mental impairment (or a record or perception of such impairment) as an eligibility condition, while treating the eligible individuals as a group subject to discrimination, the ADA is informed by the prevailing model of disability as an interaction among biological, social, political, and other environmental factors. This model highlights the critical role of social practices in creating disability, and of changes in those practices in alleviating disability. It reflects a broad consensus among disability scholars and policy makers that the disadvantages associated with most impairments are a product of biological features, environmental factors, and personal goals. As Ron Amundson explains in a representative passage:

> *A person with a disability [impairment] is handicapped only with respect to a particular environment and a particular goal. This is because the structure of the environment determines which goals are accessible to people with certain disabilities. Blind people are handicapped with respect to access to information because so much information in the present social environment is stored only in visually accessible form. Wheelchair users are handicapped with respect to travel because so little public transportation is accessible to wheelchairs (Amundson, 1992, p. 110).*

Under the ADA, an impairment does not become a disability unless it "substantially limits one or more major life activities," which will often depend on the physical and social environment of the person with the impairment (ADA, sec. 3 (2)).

This interactive model is double-edged in its application to drug addiction: it provides a basis for claiming that many of its disadvantages result from mutable social and legal arrangements, and for requiring a modification of those arrangements to better accommodate addicts. But it also provides a basis for resisting, as unduly burdensome, wholesale changes in the social and legal practices that make life harder for drug and alcohol addicts.

The interactive model also suggests a different contrast from those central to the decriminalization debate: not between punishing and treating drug addicts, nor between drug use as voluntary or involuntary behavior, but between responding to drug addiction with therapeutic and corrective measures and responding with accommodation and social reform; between modifying the individual, whether by threats or therapy, and modifying her environment, whether by changes in the legal regime that makes drug use and sale criminal, or by changes in the social practices that help to stigmatize addicts—treating them not as diverse individuals but as a homogenous group that is depraved, idle, or dangerous.

In the rest of this chapter, I will examine three issues raised by the application of disability law, and the interactive model of disability, to drug addiction and drug addicts.

- First, I will consider the interplay of science and values in the classification of certain forms of dependency as addictions, and thus, as physical or mental impairments.
- Second, I will look at the issues of distributive justice suggested by the ADA's demand for the "reasonable accommodation" of drug and alcohol addicts, and more broadly, by the attribution of many or most of the disadvantages of addiction to social and legal practices.
- Finally, I will examine the "current use" exclusion for illegal drugs in light of the analysis in the previous two sections, arguing that the exclusion may be partially justified in terms of the moral judgments underlying the impairment classification and the different burdens of reasonable accommodation posed by drug and alcohol use in modern societies.

Drug Addiction as an Impairment

There is a lively philosophical debate over the "value-neutrality" of the disease classification; about whether it is part of the meaning of "disease" and "impairment" that the condition in question is undesirable or disadvantageous (Wachbroit, 1998). Most writers on the subject embrace "normativist" accounts that regard those classifications as value-laden, so that it is part of the meaning of "disease" and "impairment" that they are undesirable conditions (Engelhardt, 1986; Amundson, 2000). But there are several vigorously-defended non-normative accounts (Boorse, 1975; 1977; Wachbroit, 1992), according to which those classifications are based on biological or bio-statistical judgments of species-typical functioning, which entail nothing about the desirability of such functioning. Proponents of non-normativist accounts recognize, of course, that it is usually advantageous to function at or above a species-typical level, but they note that there are circumstances in which it may not be, adducing such familiar examples as flat feet on a potential draftee. They argue that the criteria by which functions are, or should be, deemed normal or species-typical are either statistical or scientific—based on the best available biological theory—not prudential, aesthetic, or moral.

Even non-normativists recognize, however, that actual disease classifications are not strictly descriptive; that they are influenced by cultural and moral judgments, and bounded by time and place. Homosexuality ceased to be classified as a psychiatric disorder, for example, at a time when public, or at least professional, attitudes towards same-sex relationships were becoming more benign and tolerant. More recently and more relevantly, nicotine was officially recognized as addictive by the medical establishment in the United States only after a generation of research established beyond any reasonable doubt that the tobacco containing it was highly toxic in almost any form in which it was consumed.

The examples of homosexuality and nicotine suggest that however value-neutral the impairment classification may be in theory, the classification of a habit, dependency, or craving as addictive appears to be particularly susceptible in practice to a host of normative considerations. Although certain objective criteria are often said to characterize addiction, such as tolerance and withdrawal (in the idiom of decision theory, diminishing marginal utility and increasing total utility) (Bickenbach, 2000; Elster and Skog, 1999), it is doubtful that these criteria have been consistently applied in classifying substances and activities as addictive. Some dependencies lacking these features are commonly regarded as addictions, and some dependencies having these features are not. For example, the habitual use of some drugs may be labeled as addictive even if users experience increasing marginal utility, or "reverse tolerance;" whereas an increasingly discriminating passion for classical music might yield both diminishing marginal utility and increasing total utility without being labeled as addictive.

In the past decade, there has been some movement towards a more objective basis for classification. Several neurological mechanisms associated with addiction have been identified, and a mutation has recently been found that protects against some addictions. Researchers hold out the prospect of more biologically precise definitions of addiction that will leave less room for moral evaluation and social prejudice (Gardner, 1999; Leschner, 1996). There will doubtless be other findings in the near future that will allow a more precise biological characterization of addiction. But most substances now classified as addictive received that classification well before there was a clear scientific basis for doing so. It has yet to be shown that all or most dependencies classified as addictions have the same neurological basis, that all or most dependencies not so classified lack it, or that there are genetic predispositions to all or most addictions.

Clearly, the classification of drug and alcohol addiction as impairments has been influenced not only by the scientific evidence, which has been spotty and weak for most of the history of that classification, but by the prevailing conviction that their objects are unworthy of the dependency and attachment which they induce, unlike, say, the dependency on, or attachment to, a child, a lover, or an artistic project. What Gary Watson says about excusing addiction may apply as well to classifying addiction as an impairment: it "turns as much on our sense of choiceworthy forms of human life as on questions of individual responsibility…" (Watson, 2001, p. 118).

The questions of the scientific basis, or the value-neutrality, of the addiction classification is complicated by the fact that several distinct impairments of functioning may be associated with dependency upon a given substance or activity.

- First, there are the defining features of the dependency itself—tolerance and withdrawal. Obviously, these will differ in magnitude, in neurobiological mechanism, and in other respects across substances, activities, and individuals.[1] There is a need for some kind of threshold to separate mere familiarity from tolerance, and mere longing from withdrawal.
- Second, there is the tendency to acquire the kind of dependence that qualifies as addiction. Such tendencies may be genetic or acquired, they may vary more or less continuously among individuals, or within the same individual as a function of a range of factors. They may be more or less general across substances and activities.
- Third, there are the effects of the substance or activity, apart from those effects that help establish whether the substance is addictive. Some effects may appear benign, like heightened concentration or equanimity; others innocuous or ambivalent, like a euphoric glow unresponsive to immediate circumstances; still others malign, such as uncontrollable anger or bleeding. These varying effects may or may not be associated empirically with the addictive or non-addictive properties of the substance or activity, but they are separable conceptually—what is neurobiologically a highly addictive substance could have very benign effects as long as it was used.

One could have competing normative and non-normative accounts of impairment at any of these three levels—the actual addiction, the predisposition to addiction, and the psychological and social effects of the substance. For example, one might look for the underlying impairment not in the addiction itself, but in a predisposition to become addicted, or the lack of a predisposition against addiction—a predisposition that could well have a genetic basis. The addiction itself would be seen as somewhat analogous to a type of injury suffered disproportionately by those with a constitutional defect, like a weak immune system or brittle bones.[2]

The discovery of different genetic or neurobiological predispositions to specific addictions would raise the question of why a predisposition to drug or alcohol dependency should be regarded as an impairment, if predispositions to more favored forms of dependency, e.g., to people or to causes, were not. A non-normativist might well argue that the latter should be regarded as impairments if they involved similar departures from species-typical function, while a normativist would argue that we should only classify the latter as impairments if we saw such predispositions as undesirable or disadvantageous. If a more general predisposition to addiction were discovered, it would probably be regarded as an impairment by normativists as well, unless they regarded it as desirable or advantageous to have a broad propensity for becoming dependent on a wide variety of substances and activities to which the individual might be fortuitously exposed.

The robust role of moral judgment in the classifications of certain habits and dependencies as addictive is suggested not only by the obvious role of such judgments historically, but in the role that they currently play in the continuing expansion of the addiction category. We may recognize that many past judgments which informed the addiction classification were informed by a variety of prejudices and misconceptions—from the racist image of the insidiously seductive Chinese opium den to the somewhat more innocent exaggeration of the intensity of the "cravings" and withdrawal symptoms associated with various narcotics. But we should not be so ready to distance ourselves from all the moral judgments that informed earlier campaigns against drug addiction. For example, to the extent that the pleasures yielded diminish an addict's interest in her family or culture, or appear to anesthetize her against the pervasive poverty and social injustice which she faces, we would also be inclined to condemn the addiction, if not the addict herself. In famously condemning religion as the opiate of oppressed people, for example, Marx was condemning not only religion but opiates, treating both as sources of false or blunted consciousness about oppression and exploitation.

The pervasive impact of moral attitudes in the social understanding of addiction is further reflected in the current expansion of the addiction category. At the same time that some reformers are assailing the moral judgments underlying current drug policy, other reformers are busily augmenting the list of addictions, guided by strong moral judgments about the undesirability of various types of non-chemical dependency.

These movements have broadened the category of "addiction" to cover many activities and substances not previously regarded as disorders, but rather as vices or weaknesses. To risk sounding like Ian Hacking (Hacking, 2001), some people have always gambled too much, eaten too much, and loved unwisely, but it is only in the past few decades that we have seen the appearance of drug addicts, food addicts, and women-who-love-men-who-hate-women: the concept, category, and label are of far more recent vintage than the behaviors grouped under it. The moral judgments lying behind the emergence of these new addictions are more complex than simple condemnation: gambling and gluttony have long been condemned as vices, but they are now seen as highly destructive appetites, disapproved because of the actual and imagined, direct and indirect, harms which they cause the individual and his family rather than for any intrinsic evil. In the case of women who love unwisely, the moral change has come more in the evaluation of the men whom they love and the relationships which they enter—those men and those relationships are now judged abusive, and the predilection to enter into them seen as self-destructive. The shift in judgment cannot be attributed to scientific discovery: while there is some evidence of a biological basis for "overeating," there is less for gambling, and none, so far as I know, for loving abusive men.

Not surprisingly, the treatment of some of these "cravings" and predilections as "pathological" is fiercely contested, generally on moral, not scientific grounds. One writer reacted to the isolation of an injectable, appetite-suppressing hormone by asking, "Since when is appetite a pathology that needs to be medicated away?" (Amey, 2002). But this protest sounds like a rearguard action: the disapproval of certain foods, certain relationships, or a high level of "consumption" of either, is likely to lead to the social classification of habitual consumption as addictive, with or without the benefit of neurological or genetic evidence that would set it apart from the indulgence of more acceptable appetites.

We get an even sharper sense of the importance of moral judgment and social attitudes in the classification of "cravings" as pathological (if not always addictive) by considering a hypothetical case, where desires now thought acceptable come to incur widespread disapproval. Most people in the U.S. currently approve, and are willing to subsidize through private and public health insurance, expensive attempts of infertile couples to achieve pregnancy though an array of techniques, notably in-vitro fertilization. But what if we came to accept the views now held by some proponents of adoption and population control, that having children with a biological or genetic link is a luxury, and an increasingly costly one, in a heavily overpopulated world with hundreds of millions of abandoned and neglected children? We might possibly come to think of the desire for a biological connection as suspect, even if many of us shared it, and think of people who went to extravagant lengths to satisfy it as suffering from a pathological compulsion, a "biophilia" [to give a different meaning to E.O. Wilson's term (Wilson, 1984)] that led them to disregard personal and social costs and other commitments in their pursuit of a genetic link to the children they raised. Although this prospect is fanciful, it reminds us that we should be aware of the moral attitudes that prompt us to regard certain cravings as acceptable and reasonable, and others as unreasonable and debased.

In the case of moral judgments about illegal drugs, we have much to learn from the debates over antidepressants, although these drugs are legal and not (in most senses and most cases) addictive. Opposition to the wide prescription and heavy use of those drugs is not based solely, or primarily, on adverse effects—unlike the past generation of tricyclics, the current generation of selective serotonin reuptake inhibitors (SSRIs) does not flatten affect like a bulldozer—but on the sense, articulated by Peter Kramer in *Listening to Prozac* (Kramer, 1993), that they threaten to alter, if improve, central or defining features of our personality, character, and affect, and that they make our emotional lives too easy and euphoric. These concerns, when expressed in stronger terms, are sometimes dismissed as "pharmacological Calvinism" (Mills, 2002). I do not wish to take sides in this debate, merely to point out that its intensity suggests that it is ethical more than empirical; that issues about the appropriateness of chemical interventions are not resolved merely by monitoring their effects with a variety of scientific methodologies.

Drug Addicts as Disabled

I noted earlier that there are two elements of disability in contemporary law besides an actual or perceived impairment: substantial limitations associated with the impairment, and the stigmatization of the impairment or those bearing it. A body of research supports the common-sense impression that these latter two conditions are partially independent; that the pain, reduced longevity, or dysfunction associated with an impairment is only loosely correlated with its degree of stigmatization (Albrecht et al., 1982). There is little doubt that drug addicts are stigmatized, and that their stigmatization substantially limits their major life activities. If there was ever a group facing the "myths, fears, and stereotypes" that United States disability law is intended to protect against, it is drug addicts. By the late 1980s or earlier 1990s, the dominant popular and media stereotype of the black ghetto in the United States had shifted from the "Welfare Queen" to the "Crack Addict." In many ways, the new stereotype was far more invidious than the old. The Welfare Queen was, at least, resourceful and enterprising, and there was lots of room in her plushly-upholstered Cadillac for her children and consorts. The Crack Addict was, in contrast, listless, sallow, and emaciated, and her hollow-socketed eyes looked out for only one thing—the rock. She would readily trade her body and even her children for a pipeful of crack. The Crack Addict had no inner, and dwindling outer, resources; unlike the Opium Addict, in his ornate and aromatic den, she lived in a fetid shell of an apartment; unlike the Heroin and Cocaine Addicts, who might have great, if dissipated, musical or artistic talent, she had nothing to offer, or lose. And while the Welfare Queen became the icon for reduced financial support and increased bureaucratic oversight, the Crack Addict became the icon for an even more disturbing trend: a dramatic increase in prison terms for crack cocaine, contributing to unprecedented rates of incarceration for young African-Americans. These stereotypes are pervasive and deeply entrenched; they clearly contribute to limiting the opportunities for employment, community involvement, and other social participation available to people who are, have been, or are perceived to be, addicted to illegal drugs.

Apportioning the Burden of Addiction to Medical and Social Causes: A Red Herring

For purposes of classifying an impaired individual as a person with a disability, it does not matter how much the substantial limitations associated with the impairment are caused or mediated by the drug or the addiction itself, or by cultural, economic, and legal factors: all that is required is a biomedical impairment, a substantial activity limitation, and some causal nexus between the two. But it may appear to matter a great deal in deciding how to respond to disability. In the case of addiction, there is a protracted debate among researchers and policy analysts about the extent to which the burdens and limitations associated with addiction to various drugs are attributable to the "direct" pharmacological effects (I put "direct" in quotes because even those effects may be mediated by social and cultural context) of the drug or the addiction, to the pre-existing social and economic conditions of the users or addicts, to the illegality of the drugs and the social and economic effects of prohibition, or to the stigmatization of users and addicts (Vassel, 1994).

Like most questions in social science, this one is not likely to get a definitive answer. Its investigation is complicated by the fact that mediating factors such as pre-existing poverty and unemployment, illegality, and stigma are so closely associated with each other. Natural "experiments" partially disassociating these factors, like differences in the legal regimes of neighboring countries, have limited generalizability, and they are subject to varying interpretation (Vassel, 1994). But we can venture one broad generalization: addiction to some illegal drugs, though perhaps not very many, would be physically or psychologically harmful to almost all users in almost any conceivable social and legal setting, while the adverse impact of addiction to many or most other illegal drugs varies enormously with social context.

The search for a more precise answer to the question of how much of the burden of addiction is attributable to medical or social causes may be misguided and distracting.

1. The question may be misguided because it is not susceptible to a meaningful answer—even drug policy experiments far more varied and controlled than those that have been, or ethically could be, undertaken could never yield a quantitative answer, because we lack any metric for differences in social and legal context, let alone the common metric for biological, pharmacological, social, and legal factors that we would need to meaningfully apportion influence among those factors.

2. The question is distracting because the apportionment of causal influence does not have clear implications for the appropriateness of different interventions. Even if we believed that the direct effects of the drug, or the neurochemical imbalances of the addict, were the main cause of the drug's adverse impact, we might find that various social interventions, from finding the addict a job to returning custody of her children, were more effective at mitigating its adverse

impact than a pharmacological response. Or, more controversially, we might conclude that even if the adverse impact of the drug and the addiction were mainly due to social and economic circumstances, it was less expensive and disruptive to change those circumstances than to mitigate the effects of the drug and the addiction pharmacologically.

Our view of the proper social and legal response to addiction depends on how we assess the costs of addiction and the costs changing social and legal practices to make addiction less burdensome. Assessing these costs requires scientific input, of course, but the assessment is ultimately not a scientific one. It depends on the (dis)value we place on various forms of dependency, and on the (dis)value we place on the effects of proposed changes in legal and social practice. Those valuations, in turn, reflect our conceptions of well-being and distributive justice. In the U.S., disability law leaves room for such broad assessments in requiring social and environmental accommodations to impairments, but only if they are "reasonable," and do not impose "undue hardship." Legal commentators often complain about the vagueness and elasticity of those terms (MacCoun, 2001), but they could hardly be more precise and still capture the values that are relevant to assessing interventions.

The Role of Moral Judgments about Addiction in Assessing Competing Interventions

It is in assessing alternative interventions that the debate about the "normativity" or "value-neutrality" of the impairment classification becomes relevant. While that debate is in one respect quite academic, concerning the proper understanding of health and disease, as strictly biological concepts or as hybrid biological, social, and moral concepts, it may also have significant practical implications. Although non-normativists are often accused of conferring scientific legitimacy on judgments that are really based on cultural values or prejudices (Amundson, 2000), they take no position on the desirability of conditions classified as disease or impairments, insisting that what is abnormal biologically may be desirable or valuable socially, prudentially, or morally. Christopher Boorse, for example, a leading non-normativist, asserts that:

> *At least in some circumstances, a disease state may be preferable to normality; it is advantageous to have cowpox in a smallpox epidemic, rubella prior to pregnancy, myopia or flat feet during a military draft, or oviduct blockage if one wishes no more children.... (Boorse, 1995, p. 369)*

In the debate over alternative interventions, they can be seen as occupying a middle ground between opposing groups of normativists: between those who see impairments as inherently undesirable, and as such, as appropriate targets for correction; and those who see impairments as stigmatized variations, reflecting cultural bias against the abnormal and unconventional (Altman, 2001; Williams, 2001). While on the latter view, such variations should not be exempt from modification, since there may be practical reasons for modifying them, the principal aim of social policy should be to eliminate or reduce the biases informing their classification and burdening those with conditions so classified.

The alignment of views on appropriate interventions is actually more complex than this, since few who regard impairments as inherently undesirable would deny that the impairment classification was heavily influenced, at least at the margins, by cultural bias, while few who assign such bias the dominant role in the impairment classification would deny that many impairments are inherently undesirable, albeit to a much lesser extent than generally believed.

These differences in emphasis can be illustrated by the conflicting approaches to drug addiction. Virtually no one, except a few romantic poets and radical psychiatrists, regards drug addiction, or the propensity to drug addiction, as inherently valuable; as a "positive good." A range of people, however, from welfare economists to civil-rights activists, view addiction as a rational, reasonable, or at least understandable response to oppressive social conditions; as blunting the desire to achieve goals already foreclosed by poverty or race. While most of those who take this view would see the eventual reduction or elimination of addiction as desirable, many would advise against too much emphasis on treating addiction itself, rather than its underlying social and economic causes. Others, with broadly similar professional orientation and ideology, see addiction as demeaning and self-destructive, even, or particularly, in the social and economic settings where it is most prevalent. They would regard measures to fight addiction and drug use as an integral part of any adequate program of social reform. While these positions may not be formally inconsistent, they often lead to conflicting priorities.

These competing views on addiction policy roughly correspond to competing views on general disability policy. The correspondence is rough because some disability scholars and activists regard some impairments as inherently neutral, or even desirable.[3] Most disability scholars and activists, though, would likely agree that most impairments are at least marginally disadvantageous in most environments. But they would also insist that any policy that treats them exclusively as medical problems, ignoring their physical and social environments, is inadequate and even oppressive (Bickenbach, 1993). Beyond this, however, moderates and radicals diverge.

On the moderate view, treating impairments as a medical problem is not mistaken but overly narrow. Many conditions classified as impairments warrant medical or other clinical intervention, but they are also markers for discrimination. They are not only a source of legitimate medical claims, but a trigger for hostile social responses. As such, they should be the target of social interventions to reduce stigma and discrimination.

On the radical view, the medical model is mistaken or highly suspect, largely an expression of moral condemnation or aesthetic aversion in a spuriously scientific idiom. Disability policy should focus entirely on removing the stigma and discrimination which they evoke. Even if conditions such as blindness, paraplegia, or addiction can reasonably be seen as disadvantageous by individuals who have them, their decision to seek medical or clinical intervention should be regarded as a personal one. The impairment classification has little or no policy relevance. Radicals and moderates agree that medical judgments and therapeutic interventions should not play the dominant role in disability policy that they traditionally have.

We could draw a rough parallel between the radical and moderate views and the two major approaches to drug policy reform: full legalization—of possession and even sale—which would treat addiction to those drugs no differently from dependency on many now-legal substances and activities, and harm reduction, which sees addiction as a genuine impairment but also sees the burden of addiction as due in significant part to oppressive laws, policies, and public attitudes (MacCoun, 2001). Neither approach is committed to seeing addiction as desirable, or even neutral, merely as no worse inherently or instrumentally than many dependencies induced by legal substances or activities. Both take the view that social policy should be directed towards constructing a more accommodating social environment for addicts, in addition to, if not instead of, attempting to eliminate or reduce addiction.

The Constraints of Distributive Justice in Assessing Competing Interventions

We cannot decide on an appropriate policy towards disability in general, or addiction in particular, merely by rejecting an exclusive focus on clinical intervention, and recognizing the importance of social reform. As I suggested earlier, creating a more accommodating environment may have significant costs, and involve tradeoffs with other values and other vulnerable groups.

A "fantasy" presented by Gary Watson for a different purpose suggests the extent to which cultural, social, and legal factors affect the burden of addiction, but also that the assessment of measures to reduce that burden may be morally complex:

> *[W]hether and how often the addict's special vulnerability is indeed realized depends to a large extent on social norms and her economic circumstances. I'm told that it's possible for a well-supplied and well-regulated heroin addict to live an otherwise healthy and productive life. (Cocaine and amphetamines are another matter.)*
>
> *In any case, imagine that this is so for a certain severely addictive substance, S, and that in a certain culture, otherwise similar to ours, the use of S is not only tolerated but respected as highly spiritually beneficial. This culture regards the dependency on this substance, which again entails a vulnerability to various kinds of diminished self-control in circumstances of deprivation, as a small price to pay for the enrichment of human life provided by S. Fortunately, S is readily obtainable, perhaps even socially subsidized by the society for religious reasons....*
>
> *In our imagined society, both the use of and dependence on S are regarded as entirely fitting and normal, on a par with the appetites for food and drink. Someone who acquires the addiction to S has not thereby run afoul of any social or legal obligation to maintain self-control. The threat of being deprived of one's S is here on a par with the coercive predicament created by the prospect of imminent starvation. (Watson, 2001, p. 616)*

It is unclear, and may not be necessary to decide, whether we would regard such "sacred addiction" in this imaginary society as an impairment, even if S had such effects as a temporary loss of self-control, orientation, or consciousness. We might, adopting a value-neutral conception, classify it as an impairment, but deny that it was a disability, since, in the society Watson describes, such addiction would enhance rather than limit major life activities despite, or perhaps because of, its temporary effects. But this hardly answers the question of whether we would be willing to accept the vast cultural and social changes needed to prevent such a strong addiction from becoming a disability. The answer is almost surely no. We quite reasonably find limited value in the heightened impulsivity and diminished consciousness that S induces, and while we might and should be willing to make greater allowance for such states than we do, we would not and should not support the radical transformation of our society that would be necessary to sanctify or sacralize them.

What is important about Watson's fantasy for our purposes is that it suggests that the full accommodation of drug addicts may require far more than small changes in the physical and social environment. This general point has been recognized with respect to the accommodation of other impairments. Dan Wikler (Wikler, 1979), Alan Buchanan (Buchanan, 1996), and others, have argued that changes in our entire "scheme of social cooperation"—the formal and informal rules that govern our interactions and allocate their tangible and intangible benefits—would be necessary to more fully integrate people with mild or moderate cognitive impairments. Although their claims about the burdens of accommodation may be overstated, they highlight not only the critical role that social practices play in substantially limiting major life activities, but the substantial, if often intangible, burdens of changing those practices. Watson's fantasy suggests how much our society might have to change for the addiction to certain drugs to enhance rather than limit the opportunities and prospects of those addicted to them.

Such vast changes would impose significant burdens on non-addicts. It might be that societies which sacralize drug use among some parts of the population have sustained themselves by enslaving or otherwise ruthlessly exploiting other segments of the population. Even if we shared the enthusiasm for S found in Watson's imaginary society, we might regard the kind of society in which it could be sacralized as oppressive and grossly inegalitarian, with a small priestly class supported by the ceaseless toil of a drug-free peasantry.

We can get a more realistic picture of the costs of more modest accommodations by looking at societies that have decriminalized the possession or sale of certain drugs. Extrapolating from recent experiments in the decriminalization and limited legalization of marijuana and other drugs [reviewed in (MacCoun, 2001)], MacCoun and Reuter conclude that:

> *[L]egalization of cocaine, marijuana, and heroin would lead to large reductions in drug-related crime and mortality, but also to large increases in drug use and addiction. Poor urban minority communities, which have been devastated by drug violence and drug incarcerations, might benefit substantially, but the larger body of middle-class Americans would likely be worse off. (MacCoun and Reuter, 2002)*

Our society may be unwilling to make the tradeoffs described by MacCoun and Reuter, but we need to recognize that there is nothing "natural" about much of the burden of drug addiction in our society; that, if their conclusions are correct, we have chosen to impose heavy burdens on poor addicts to limit the addiction of middle-class youth. A recognition that we have made such distributional choices should take some of the sanctimony out of our opposition to drug abuse and incline us to adopt drug policies as benign as possible, consistent with preventing the proliferation of drug use and addiction. Those policies, which would generally fall under the rubric of "harm reduction," might well reduce the proportion of drug addicts who qualified as disabled, and reduce the burden on those who still did.

Accommodation may also impose a significant cost in reduced productivity. To the extent that drug use is limited to an unemployed or underemployed underclass (that may be encouraged by the lack of adequate legal employment), it will have little impact on productivity, except for the diversion of law enforcement resources for interdiction, arrests, prosecutions, etc. The widespread use of many drugs to the middle and upper classes might have a far more adverse effect on productivity, the myth of the cocaine-snorting bond trader to the contrary. These are broad social costs, not the economic burdens on specific employers and facilities on which ADA litigation typically focuses, but they are important to consider in assessing the difficulty of making drug use less disabling by a change in legal regime. A consideration of such costs makes it clear that the fact that disabilities are, in an important sense, socially constructed, does not mean that social reconstruction is easy or cheap. Alleviating the burdens of drug addiction may be far more costly, albeit in less tangible ways, than alleviating the burdens of blindness or paraplegia. It may, for example, be far less expensive and disruptive to provide braille literature and signage than to change work schedules, divisions of labor, and social expectations to accommodate the likely effects of legalizing certain drugs.

Similar issues of morality and justice are raised by changes in the legal regime governing alcohol consumption and gambling. A generation of scholars pointed out the adverse effects of prohibition in making alcohol expensive and unsafe, in corrupting law enforcement, and in promoting organized crime (Kobler, 1973). More recently, revisionist scholars have pointed out the damaging effects of repeal, such as an upsurge in liver disease and other drinking-related medical conditions (Edwards et al., 1994). It is likely that the burdens of repeal, even more than the burdens of prohibition, were borne disproportionately by the poor.[4]

In considering the tradeoffs involved in accommodating addictions, the U.S. experience with alcohol since prohibition is especially sobering. Alcohol possession, use, and sale by adults have been legal for almost seventy years, although heavily encumbered by regulation and taxes. Despite the legality, and widespread use and general acceptance of alcoholic beverages, addiction to alcohol continues to place substantial limits on the major life activities of many alcoholics. There are many other forms of accommodation besides the removal of criminal prohibitions and sanctions that might reduce those limits, but some are financially prohibitive and some are morally unacceptable. We could, for example, require employers to tolerate indefinite absences, negligent performance, and sexual harassment by alcoholic employees, which would make it much easier for some alcoholics to hold and maintain jobs, but we would quite reasonably regard such tolerance as financially ruinous and morally repugnant.[5]

The "Current Use" Exclusion

Many of the accommodations available to alcoholics, limited as they are, are not available to current drug users. This has struck commentators (Hennen, 1997; Vanko, 1996) as unprincipled or moralistic. Most of the commentary on the ADA and drug addiction has challenged the availability of the "current use" exclusion to drug but not alcohol addicts. This exclusion is alleged to be a transparent political compromise, or to reflect the ambivalent view of drug addiction under the ADA and in public opinion, as a moral failing and as a disease. Although I will not defend the "current use" exclusion, I will argue that it is less anomalous or unprincipled than it is often claimed to be; that it is broadly consistent with the moral judgments underlying the classification of drug addiction as an impairment, and with the eligibility of non-substance using addicts for the protection of the ADA. The kind of appetites acquired by the drug addict are seen as debased and destructive; and the illegality of those drugs, while obviously not reducing the strength of the addiction to them, is regarded as reducing the excuse or justification for acting on the addiction. The fact that current alcohol users are not similarly excluded may reflect a mistaken judgment about the adverse impact of alcoholism, but it may also reflect a more defensible deference to the authority of the law, or a more realistic view of the social resources for accommodating alcohol addiction.

There are at least two rationales for this exception that do not involve the demands of congressional politics or the pious condemnation of illegal drug use. The first concerns the comparative difficulty of accommodating current alcohol and drug users. Over long years of experience with alcoholism, we have developed a set of social practices, such as designated drivers and familiar hangover remedies, for mitigating the harmful effects of alcohol abuse, and much experience in employing them. While some of these practices, like designated drivers, could be readily adapted to current drug use, others might be harder to employ. But this is a difference in degree, not kind. It would explain why the accommodations needed by the current users of illegal drugs would more often be held to be unreasonable, or unduly burdensome, but not why such accommodation is categorically refused them. Moreover, given the widespread uncertainty about the adverse effects of various mitigating measures and practices, it would be hard to claim significant harm reduction from measures that were not readily adaptable to drug misuse and addiction (as, say, the practice of designating driving would be).

It is thus hard to deny that there is a moral judgment informing the current use exception for illegal drugs. It need not, however, be a judgment based on the mistaken view that illegal drugs or their abuse is intrinsically worse than alcohol or its abuse. It may reflect a reasonable concern about the cumulative impact of additional addictions on a society already burdened with one it cannot shed. While our society could reduce that cumulative impact somewhat by imposing further restrictions, and taxes, on alcohol consumption, those measures might also have adverse effects, e.g., a resurgence of bootlegging, or might have only a negligible impact on addiction. The denial of the ADA's protections and accommodations to current users of illegal drugs may also reflect a demand for greater self-restraint in avoiding activities that our society has made illegal than in avoiding activities it has not. Because current drug use involves a breach of legal and civic duty while current alcohol use does not, we might reasonably treat the former as more blameworthy than the latter, even if the addictions driving them are of equal strength.

Watson makes this general point in an analogy from addiction to duress (Watson, 2001). He argues that the availability of a duress defense is not based entirely on the magnitude of the threatened consequences or the choice-impairing impact of the threat, but also on the judgments that it is more acceptable to do certain things under a given level of threat or pressure than others. Many states deny a duress defense for murder, for example, even though the threat or pressure to commit murder may certainly be as great as the threat or pressure to commit any lesser offense; the denial is based on the view it is an especially great wrong to kill another person, however severe the threat or pressure. Watson himself contrasts the hunger for food and for drugs: the law might excuse theft in response to the "internal duress" of food hunger, or at least hunger tied to nutritional needs, when it wouldn't excuse theft in response to the internal duress of drug addiction, even if the cravings, and the immediate consequences of their frustration, were as severe. Stealing to feed oneself is considered more acceptable than stealing to feed one's drug habit, because the desire for food is regarded as worthier than the desire for drugs, whatever the strength of those desires.[6] (Here, however, alcohol addiction would be treated no differently from drug addiction, since a craving for alcohol is also considered far less morally compelling than a craving for food. Indeed, in the criminal law, alcohol addiction generally provides no more of an excuse for prohibited conduct than does drug addiction, whether such conduct is in the direct or indirect service of the addiction, or merely encouraged by it.)

We know that addicts can often devise and implement "Odyssean" strategies in moments of lesser temptation, to prevent themselves from succumbing in moments of greater temptation. They can try to avoid contact with the people with whom they have "done drugs" or the places where they have done them, and they can preemptively raise the sanctions for relapse by various forms of self-blackmail. These are undoubtedly difficult steps, but they do not require the addict to resist the full force of his compulsion. Alcoholics do not have to take similar steps to be eligible for the protection of the ADA (though that protection is limited—their failure to take such steps might well render them unqualified for their jobs or unfit for public facilities and accommodations). But it does not seem clearly unreasonable to require more effort of those whose relapse would violate the legal prohibitions enacted by a liberal-democratic regime, even if the distinctions between what was and was not prohibited might, from a detached, ahistorical perspective, appear somewhat arbitrary.

The "current use" exclusion does, however, put further pressure on the acceptance of drug addiction as voluntarily-acquired impairment. Unlike the person who loses leg function in a skiing accident, or who becomes addicted to alcohol from heavy drinking after a messy divorce, the person addicted to heroin, cocaine, or amphetamines is almost certain to have acquired his impairment through repeated felonies—the repeated possession of illegal substances. Although these felonies involve no direct harm to other people, they do involve a violation of laws that procedurally if not substantively, have some moral authority for anyone who accepts the legitimacy of a liberal-democratic state. The past may only be prologue to his current status as an earnestly recovering addict, but there does seem to be a continuing tension in the criminalization of the acts that led to his addiction, on the one hand, and the legal treatment of his addiction as establishing his membership in a protected minority group.

Concluding Thoughts

Public attitudes towards impairments and the people who bear them, are marked by profound ambivalence, vacillating between pity and admiration, between the impulse to treat and correct and the impulse to accept and accommodate, and between optimism about the prospects for reforming addicts or their social environments and pessimism about the likelihood of lasting personal or social reform. Public attitudes towards addiction and use are even more sharply ambivalent, ranging from fear and loathing, pity and condescension, to indignation at the social conditions that foster and burden addiction. The legal treatment of addiction as an impairment reflects, and evokes, both sorts of ambivalence. The ADA embodies, without fully reconciling, these conflicting attitudes. For this reason, as well as others I cannot address here, concerning the delicate political balances struck in its legislative drafting and passage, and the increasing conservatism of its judicial interpretation, it is unlikely to advance the civil rights of recovering drug addicts as significantly as it has the rights of other people with substantial impairments.

David Wasserman, B.A. (Philosophy), Yale University; M.A. (Psychology), University of North Carolina; J.D., University of Michigan, is a research scholar at the Institute for Philosophy and Public Policy in the University of Maryland's School of Public Affairs. He has written about the moral underpinnings of criminal law and legal practice, the concept of discrimination, and issues in procedural and distributive justice. His present research focuses on ethical and policy issues in disability, health care, reproduction, and genetic technology. In addition to numerous articles and book chapters, he has published A Sword For the Convicted: Representing Indigent Defendants on Appeal (Greenwood, 1990). He has co-authored Disability, Difference, Discrimination, with Anita Silvers and Mary Mahowald (Rowman and Littlefield, 1998), and co-edited Genetics and Criminal Behavior, with Robert Wachbroit (Cambridge, 2001).

References

29 C.F.R. sec. 1630 (2).

Americans with Disabilities Act of 1990 (ADA).

Albrecht, G., Walker, V., Levy, J. (1982). Social distance from the stigmatized: A test of two theories. *Social Science and Medicine, 16,* 1319, 1327.

Altman, B.R. (2001). Disability definitions, models, classification schemes, and applications. In Albrecht, G., Seelman, K., Bury, M. (Eds.), *Handbook of disability studies*. Thousand Oaks, CA: Sage Publications, 97-122.

Amey, R. Appetite suppressing hormone found. [Bioethics] Community email, 8/7/2002, http://www.egroups.com/community/Bioethics.

Amundson, R. (1992). Disability, handicap, and the environment. *Journal of Social Philosophy, 23*(1).

Amundson, R. (2000). Against normal functions. *Studies in the History and Philosophy of Biological and Biomedical Sciences, 31*(1).

Bickenbach, J. (1993). *Physical disability and social policy*. Toronto: University of Toronto Press.

Bickenbach, J. (2000). The ADA v. the Canadian Charter of Rights: Disability rights and the social model of disability. In Francis, L., Silvers, R. (Eds.), *Americans with disabilities: Exploring the implications of the law for individuals and institution.* New York: Routledge.

Boorse, C. (1975). On the distinction between disease and illness. *Philosophy and Public Affairs, 5,* 49-68.

Boorse, C. (1977). Health as a theoretical concept. *Philosophy of Science, 44*(4), 542-573.

Boorse, C. (1995). Concepts of health. In VanDeveer, D., Regan, T. (Eds.), *Health care ethics: An introduction*. Philadelphia: Temple University Press, 359-393.

Buchanan, A. (1996). Choosing who will be disabled: Genetic intervention and the morality of inclusion. *Social Philosophy and Policy, 13*(2).

Corrado, M. (2001). Addiction and responsibility. *Law and Philosophy* (special issues).

Dolnick, E. (1993). Deafness as culture. *Atlantic Monthly* September (37), 38.

Edwards, G., Anderson, P., Babor, T.F., Casswell, S., Ferrence, R., Giesbrecht, N., Godfrey, C., Holder, H.D., Lemmens, P., Makela, K., Midanik, L.T., Norstrom, T., Osterberg, E., Romeslj o, A., Room, R., Simpura, J., Skog, O. (1994). *Alcohol policy and the public good.* Oxford: Oxford University Press.

Elster, J., Skog, O. (1999). Introduction. In Elster, J., Skog, O. (Eds.), *Getting hooked: Rationality and addiction.* New York: Cambridge University Press.

Engelhardt, H.T. Jr. (1986). *The foundations of bioethics*. New York: Oxford University Press.

Galston, W., Wasserman, D. (1996, Spring). Gambling away our moral capital. *The Public Interest,* 58-71.

Gardner, E. (1999). The neurobiology and genetics of addiction: Implications of the "reward deficiency syndrome" for therapeutic strategies in chemical dependency. In Elster, D. (Ed.), *Addiction entries and exits*. New York: Russell Sage Foundation, 57-119.

Hacking, I. (2001). Degeneracy, criminal behavior, and looping. In Wasserman, D., Wachbroit, R. (Eds.), *Genetics and criminal behavior*. New York: Cambridge University Press.

Hennen, A. (1997). Protecting addicts in the employment arena: Charting a course towards tolerance. *Law and Inequality, 15*: 157.

Kobler, J. (1973). *Ardent spirits: The rise and fall of prohibition*. New York: Putnam.

Kramer, P. (1993). *Listening to Prozac*. New York: Viking Press.

Leshner, A. (1997). Addiction is a brain disease, and it matters. *Science, 278,* 45-47.

MacCoun, R. & Reuter, J. (2001). *Drug war heresies: Learning from other vices, times, and places*. New York: Cambridge University Press, 385-395.

MacCoun, R. & Reuter, P. (2002). Cocaine, marijuana, and heroin. *The American Prospect, 13*(10): 25-28.

Mills, C. (2002). In Gehring, V., Galston, W. (Eds.), *One pill makes you smarter: An ethical appraisal of the rise of Ritalin: Philosophical dimensions of public policy*. New Brunswick, NJ: Transaction Publishers, 257-263, 261.

Rehabilitation Act of 1973, Sec. 504.

Vanko, K. (1996). In search of common ground: Leveling the playing field for chemically dependant workers under the Americans With Disabilities Act of 1990. *University of Illinois Law Review*, 1257.

Vassel, R. (1994). The Americans With Disabilities Act: The cost, uncertainty, and inefficiency. *Journal of Law and Commerce, 13*: 397.

Wachbroit, R. (1998). Health and disease, Concepts of. *Encyclopedia of Applied Ethics, 2*: 533-538.

Wachbroit, R. (1992). Normality as a biological concept. *Philosophy of Science, 61,* 579-591.

Wasserman, D. (2000). Stigma without impairment: Demedicalizing disability discrimination. In Francis, L., Silvers, A. (Eds.), *Americans with disabilities*. New York: Routledge.

Watson, G. (2001). Excusing addiction. *Law and Philosophy*, 589-619.

Wikler, D. (1979). Paternalism and the mildly retarded. *Philosophy and Public Affairs, 8*(4), 63-87.

Williams, G. (2001). Theorizing disability. In Albrecht, G., Seelman, K., Bury, M. (Eds.), *Handbook of disability studies*. CA: Thousand Oaks, 123-144.

Wilson, E.O. (1984). *Biophilia*. Cambridge, MA: Harvard University Press

Yaffe, G. (2002). Recent work on addiction and responsible agency. *Philosophy & Public Affairs, 30*(2), 178-221.

Glossary

addiction: the habitual consumption of a substance or performance of an activity, caused or sustained by a psychological or neurobiological dependency, sometimes characterized as having two features: diminishing marginal utility and increasing total utility.

"Current Use" exclusion: the denial of the legal protections of the Americans with Disabilities Act (ADA) to those individuals currently using illegal substances.

disability: under the standard legal definition of the ADA, an individual with a disability is one with a physical or mental impairment that substantially limits her performance of one or more major life activities, such as walking, seeing, hearing, self-care, or working.

distributive justice: fairness in the distribution of resources, welfare, opportunities, or capabilities. Both the appropriate subject of the distribution—resources, welfare, etc.—and the criteria of fairness in its distribution, are matters of protracted debate among philosophers and political scientists.

impairment: a physical or mental abnormality or dysfunction, with the standard of normality or functionality determined biologically, statistically, by moral and prudential value, or by some combination of these.

normativists: philosophers of science who maintain that it is part of the meaning of "disease," "dysfunction," and "impairment" that conditions so classified are undesirable.

non-normativists: philosophers of science who deny that it is part of the meaning of "disease," dysfunction," and "impairment," that conditions so classified are undesirable, however likely it is that such conditions will be disadvantageous and burdensome.

Notes

1. For example, a chain-smoking Orthodox Jew, forbidden to smoke on the Sabbath, may be addicted, but he rarely manifests or complains of the "classical" withdrawal symptoms after a full day of religious-based withdrawal.
2. It is not clear that there would be any practical difference in treating a predisposition to addiction as an impairment. Because the addiction itself is treated as an impairment, a person who acquired it in the absence of such a predisposition would still be regarded as impaired, as there is no exception for "voluntary" impairments. And it is not clear that a predisposed individual would qualify as disabled in the absence

of addiction, unless his predisposition was known (e.g., by genetic testing), and was itself a source of substantial limits on life activities. Of course, there could be adverse consequences for the individual who was screened as "predisposed," such as the denial of employment or insurance.

3. This view has gained the strongest following among people who are deaf, bolstered by their acquisition of a distinctive language and culture. Many deaf people do not regard themselves as having an impairment or disability at all, and regard medical interventions like cochlear implants as a form of cultural imperialism They would treat deafness, like homosexuality, as a stigmatized variation, whose de-medicalization is a critical step towards equality.
4. Critics of state-sponsored or -authorized gambling have made similar claims. Although both state lotteries and legalized casinos are more often promoted as revenue-generating than addiction-accommodating, they also raise issues about fairness and well-being. Their critics have pointed out that the former are profoundly regressive, with the poor being induced to pay more than they can afford for services for which they should have as a matter of right, and for tax reductions from which they do not benefit. Critics point out the similarly regressive impact of casino-gambling, both in the disproportionate number of poor people who frequent casinos and in the disproportionate impact of their inevitable gambling losses on themselves and their families.
5. The ADA does require that employers provide "otherwise qualified" practicing alcoholics "reasonable accommodation," unless (a bit redundantly), such accommodation would pose an "undue hardship" on the employer. While I am not aware of any case law on the subject, I suspect that such accommodation would include not firing an alcoholic employee for tardiness due to occasional off-duty benders, and not sending him home just because he stank of gin. The ADA's exception for "direct threats" to safety sharply limits the accommodations that need to be made for any job posing safety risks, but in this post-industrial era, most jobs do not.
6. As we become more discriminating about the goodness of various kinds of food, we may become differentially tolerant of the hunger for them, and of illegal acts committed to satisfy that hunger. A "junk food addict" who steals a bag of Doritos may expect less sympathetic treatment than a "food addict" (a label we would hesitate to apply) who steals a loaf of (whole-grain) bread to satisfy a craving of equal intensity.

1-8 Disability and Substance User Treatment/Rehabilitation: Ethical Considerations

Ellen Benoit, Ph.D. and Stephen Magura, Ph.D., C.S.W.

Abstract

Before 1996, individuals in the United States who were chronically addicted to drugs or alcohol could receive certification as being disabled, entitling them to income support from the Social Security Administration (SSA), as long as they were participating in treatment. Legislation in March 1996 required the SSA to eliminate addiction from eligible disabilities and remove from its rolls everyone who had been receiving benefits as disabled substance users. This change raises significant ethical questions, which we address from the perspective of distributive justice, i.e., any system designed to allocate material and social goods to members of society based on specified principles. We examine the policy's distinction between "deserving" and "undeserving" persons in need and analyze how the medically ambiguous nature of "addiction" fosters competing "just desert" claims in the debate over eligibility. For example, does becoming disabled as a result of substance misuse constitute a form of voluntaristic behavior? Finally, we consider the consequences of the SSA reclassification for policy stakeholders, including beneficiaries, treatment providers, and the public.

Key Words: addiction; disability; policy analysis; substance dependency treatment; ethics; distributive justice; recovery; treatment compliance; need; reciprocity; volition; responsibility

Introduction

There are two relatively recent legislative changes concerning disability that affect substance users. The Americans with Disabilities Act (ADA) of 1990 makes it illegal for employers or potential employers to discriminate against drug users and alcoholics who are in recovery. The Contract with America Advancement Act of 1996 (hereinafter the 1996 Act) discontinued Social Security disability benefits for individuals whose disabilities are the result of drug or alcohol misuse. In this chapter we will focus on the changes in Social Security disability benefits, because the ADA is addressed elsewhere in this volume (see Wasserman). We will begin by describing both pieces of legislation, because together they constitute the bulk of policy measures addressing the needs of people disabled by substance misuse. (We are concerned only with disability that can be attributed to substance misuse. Many substance users are also disabled by other physical or mental ailments, but when we refer to "disabled substance users" we mean those disabled by drug addiction or alcoholism, whether the disability is caused by the pharmacology of substances or by the manner of their use and associated lifestyle.)

After explaining changes in regulations concerning disability and substance users, we will explore the ethical considerations inherent in the Social Security reforms, emphasizing issues of distributive justice. We will also identify the stakeholder groups in the affected system of intervention and the consequences faced by each group, with an eye toward understanding the broader implications of the change in disability policy. It is important to note that although we discuss policy judgments about who may be deserving or undeserving of aid, this is a critical essay in which we attempt to define issues and alternative viewpoints without advocating any specific position.

Legal changes regarding disability and addiction

Under the Americans with Disabilities Act, which was passed in 1990, it is illegal to discriminate against people addicted to drugs or alcohol who are in recovery. The ADA was passed after many years of organized lobbying by disabled individuals and their advocates; the rationale was to extend to disabled people the same civil rights that were granted to women and minorities in the 1960s (Baffuto and Boggs, 1990; Tomko, 2002). With respect to illegal drugs under the ADA, past misuse is considered a covered disability. Although the ADA does not use the term "recovery," it offers protection to a person who "has successfully completed a supervised drug rehabilitation program and is no longer engaging in the illegal use of drugs" or "is participating in a supervised rehabilitation program and is no longer engaging in such use" (ADA, 1990, Sec. 104 [b]). In addition to meeting these criteria, which describe what is commonly referred to as being in recovery, an individual must also be able to perform the essential functions of the job held or desired; under these circumstances employers must make "reasonable accommodations" to the person's needs (ADA, 1990; Colbridge, 2000). Such accommodations may include additional sick leave or vacation time to attend rehabilitation/treatment programs or a flexible work schedule (to fit methadone clinic hours, for example). Interestingly, the ADA distinguishes between the use of illegal drugs and the use of alcohol, which is legal. Active alcoholics are protected by the ADA, as are alcoholics in recovery, but current users of illegal drugs are not (ADA, 1990). The ADA is silent on the logic of this distinction, but Wasserman (2004: 481) suggests that what appears to be preferential treatment for alcoholics may instead reflect "deference to the authority of the law, or a more realistic view of the social resources for accommodating alcohol addiction."

To gain ADA protection, individuals must show that they are otherwise qualified for the position and that they can perform the essential functions of the job (with or without reasonable accommodation). They also must demonstrate that they are disabled as defined by the Act, which means that their impairment substantially limits one or more life activities, that they have a record of such impairment, and that they are regarded as having the impairment. The question of whether addiction is self-inflicted is not a factor (Colbridge, 2000; Wasserman, 2004).

Unlike the ADA, which explicitly includes addiction in its definition of disability, the 1996 revision to Social Security policy eliminated drug addiction and alcoholism from its list of disabilities rendering individuals eligible for benefits. Moreover, the legislation mandated that all individuals receiving Social Security benefits for substance-related disabilities be removed from the rolls as of January 1997 (H.R. 3136, P.L. 104-121). The programs affected by the legislation were Social Security Disability

Insurance (SSDI), which bases benefits on prior work experience, and Supplemental Security Income (SSI), which is based on financial need instead of work experience (U.S. Social Security Administration, 2005). When the legislation was passed in March of 1996, an estimated 209,000 individuals disabled by substance misuse were receiving SSI and SSDI benefits (Davies, Iams, and Rupp, 2000).

The change in Social Security disability policy posed significant challenges to both substance users and to the treatment community, if only because it eliminated a source of subsistence income for substance users and complicated the efforts of treatment professionals to help them. Many counselors took on the added responsibility of helping their clients re-qualify for benefits under another disability category; the lost income also provoked some clients to resume criminal activity (Benoit, Young, Magura, and Staines, 2004; Swartz, Martinovich, and Goldstein, 2003). These problems were exacerbated by the 1996 Act's passage just five months before the Personal Responsibility and Work Opportunity Reconciliation Act (PRWORA) terminated the hoary U.S. system of "welfare as we know it," i.e., Aid to Families with Dependent Children (AFDC), and replaced it with the much more restrictive Temporary Assistance to Needy Families (TANF). PRWORA placed special restrictions on welfare-eligible drug users and imposed work requirements and time limits on cash assistance for all recipients. Combined with the removal of SSI and SSDI as alternative sources of support, treatment counselors and their clients came under pressure to accelerate rehabilitation and prepare drug users to (re-) enter the work force (see Benoit, Young, Magura, and Staines, 2004).

Substance users had been eligible for Social Security disability benefits since SSI was established in 1972, under its "drug addicts and alcoholics" (DA&A) category; SSDI was added in 1974. SSI made benefits conditional upon participation in treatment programs and required that DA&A beneficiaries have "representative payees" to receive payments for them and manage their income. After completing a rehabilitation program, SSI recipients were required to undergo a continuing disability review (CDR) to determine whether they were still disabled and eligible for benefits. SSDI did not require beneficiaries to attend treatment, but it did assign representative payees for those recipients who were determined to be legally incompetent or unable to manage their benefits (GAO, 1994a). Note that the SSA directed all disabled beneficiaries to follow recommended treatments if that could restore the ability to work, although those who failed to comply did not jeopardize their benefits, as was the case with disabled substance users (Hunt and Baumohl, 2003).

From the start, however, there were problems with monitoring SSI treatment compliance and with interpreting the definition of disability to include substance misuse. As a result, a large number of lawsuits and attempts to adjust definitions gave SSI and SSDI a troubled history and helped make the programs politically unpopular. In 1994, the General Accounting Office (GAO) reported that only 20 percent of SSI's DA&A beneficiaries were participating in treatment programs, although virtually all DA&A recipients had representative payees (GAO, 1994a).

Problems were numerous. To begin with, public treatment capacity was inadequate in many parts of the country. In addition, the SSA was required by law to rely on Medicaid to cover treatment costs, but Medicaid coverage varied by state. Despite the fact that the SSA had developed a network of public and private referral and monitoring agencies (RMAs) to refer recipients to treatment and monitor their progress, the system was difficult to implement and was largely ineffective. One problem was the legislated reimbursement formula that did not pay providers until a client sustained nine continuous months of employment. But Congress also failed to allocate adequate funds to the SSA to pay the RMAs, with the result that in many states no agency was willing to provide the required services. In 1994 the SSA was mandated by Congress to expand RMA duties and establish contracts with them in all 50 states, but the agency did not manage to implement the reforms until after March of 1996, when Congress terminated the DA&A program (Hunt and Baumohl, 2003).

Although the list of impairments that qualify as disabilities has changed, the SSA has used the same core definition of disability for decades:

> *...the inability to engage in any substantial gainful activity (SGA) by reason of any medically determinable physical or mental impairment(s) which can be expected to result in death or which has lasted or can be expected to last for a continuous period of not less than 12 months. (Social Security Administration, 2005)*

Not surprisingly in the case of substance misuse, the requirement that disability be "medically determinable" has historically been a source of difficulty in evaluating applicants' eligibility for benefits. Before 1972, the SSA required evidence of irreversible organ damage in order to classify substance misuse as disabling, but this criterion proved impractical for substances other than alcohol. The fact that most symptoms of addiction are behavioral fed conflicting interpretations of disability criteria, prompting some of the litigation and redefinitions described above. In 1985 the SSA removed the requirement for organ damage and established Substance Addiction Disorders as a new disability listing under mental disorders (Hunt and Baumohl, 2003).

The decision to classify an individual as disabled is made by Disability Determination Services (DDS) offices in each state, where DDS workers review medical evidence solicited from health-care practitioners and institutions that have treated the individual. The key question is whether substance misuse is "material" to the applicant's condition—in other words, whether the applicant would remain disabled even if he or she stopped using drugs or alcohol. If the answer is no, then addiction is deemed to be material to the disability and benefits are not awarded. But before 1996, the same answer would have established addiction as a disability and entitled the applicant to benefits! In order to qualify for SSI or SSDI benefits now, applicants must demonstrate that they have a physical or mental disability other than alcohol or drug addiction, or which is not induced by continuous drug or alcohol use.

Note that the SSA definition of disability requires that applicants be unable to engage in "any substantial gainful activity," which is understood as the ability to exert significant mental or physical effort for remuneration or profit. Thus, benefits are available only to those who are unable to work, although the concept of "work" is problematic here. Drug addicts often work in the underground economy, say in drug sales or prostitution; but they may or may not be employed in the legal economy. To the SSA, this is gainful activity that proves an applicant is not disabled, as we explain below. In contrast, ADA protection is available only to those who can work for a legal employer – the disabling condition must inhibit other "major life activities." Consequently, it seems that U.S. disability policy toward substance misusers offers protection against actions intended to prevent them from working, but it explicitly denies them benefits if they cannot work. They are entitled to legal protection only if they can work and they attempt to do so.

Defining addiction as disabling—and as not disabling

Congress eliminated addiction as a disability in March 1996, after years of reports that SSI and SSDI beneficiaries were noncompliant with treatment requirements and that these programs essentially were doing little more than subsidizing substance misuse, despite numerous attempts to reform the system. There was also concern because the number of addicts receiving benefits had more than doubled—from fewer than 100,000 in 1989 to about 250,000 by the end of 1993—perhaps as a result of cutbacks in state general assistance programs, court decisions favoring applicants and outreach programs (GAO, 1994a,b; Hunt and Baumohl, 2003). The political climate in Washington was hostile toward public assistance of virtually any kind, perhaps most evident in the passage of PRWORA in August 1996. This was largely a legacy of political dominance by conservative Republicans, from the Reagan administration with its rhetoric against "welfare queens" in the 1980s through the 1994 elections when Republicans gained control of Congress. Moreover, the intensified criminalization of the "War on Drugs" since the 1980s had eroded public understanding of substance misuse and demonized substance users (Gordon, 1994; Reinarman and Levine, 1997). Politicians railed against the practice of paying disability benefits to people who "inflict it on themselves" (U.S. House, 1994). Mass media reports characterized the Social Security disability program as one in which "the first day of every month is like Christmas" for addicts who receive "easy money" from SSI and SSDI and then proceed to squander it on drugs or alcohol (Hunt and Baumohl, 2003:37; Irvine and Goulden, 1992; Ruddy, 1994; Satel, 1994:18). While some critics went on to offer constructive suggestions for reform (e.g., Satel, 1994), the debate was moralistic in tone and dominated by depictions of disabled substance users as irresponsible citizens who either refused to work or were incapacitated by a self-inflicted condition—in either case, undeserving of public aid.

The fact that federal policy has simultaneously classified addiction as disabling in the ADA (except for active users of illegal drugs or individuals using prescription drugs illegally) and as not disabling by the SSA reflects the subjective nature of policymaking, but it also illustrates the degree to which the concepts of addiction and disability are socially constructed. Like other social problems, including poverty, racism and crime, disability is subject to political interpretation. This means that policies regarding disability will be unstable, likely to change in concert with prevailing culturally-constructed definitions of addiction and disability. In the 1980s and 1990s, politicians found that they could win elections by tapping into public fear of crime and social disorder with rhetorical images of drug addicts as violent criminals or shiftless feeders at the public trough, or both. During the same period, the U.S. policy of criminalizing drug use created institutions with deep vested interests in mass incarceration and with the resources to exert pressure on policymakers to protect those interests. One can argue that the removal of addiction from the list of disabilities qualifying for SSI and SSDI reflects the demedicalization of substance misuse, a reversal of the dominant conception of addiction as a disease, which had prevailed even within the Social Security Administration. Before 1996, SSA criteria for disability benefits included the following language: "Substance addiction can be a disabling medically determinable impairment. No additional physical or medical impairment is required. Eligibility for disability benefits involving substance addiction is determined like any other medical disorder" (GAO, 1994a).

The assumptions behind defining addiction as a disability were consistent with those behind the sociological conceptualization of illness, or what Parsons (1951) called "the sick role"—the status is beyond the control of the afflicted individual and therefore the individual is excused from ordinary obligations (such as work) and entitled to social support. The pre-reform SSI regulations mandated that disabled substance users participate in treatment in order to receive benefits. This was of course essential for rehabilitation; the goal was for beneficiaries to become self-sufficient through sustained, legal employment. However, it can also be seen as "substantial gainful activity" in itself, a substitute for the (legal) "work" that disabled people cannot do. The policy ensured that disabled substance users were doing something useful to earn their support. This too follows the Parsonian model, requiring that sick individuals demonstrate a desire to recover by actively seeking treatment and following the course prescribed by medical professionals. This component of the model is intended to legitimate the genuinely sick by distinguishing them from malingerers, a function similar to that of the SSA's requirement that disability be "medically determinable."

Requiring beneficiaries to actively engage in rehabilitation in exchange for benefits raises questions of personal motivation. It also evokes the debate over the effectiveness and/or moral rightness of coerced treatment. There is no evidence that SSA considered whether DA&A recipients were "treatment ready;" it may have been considered by RMAs, but their incentives, weak as they were, favored pushing clients through treatment. Although some substance users find external pressure motivating, even subtle coercion can undermine the therapeutic effectiveness of an ostensibly voluntary treatment program (Magura, 2000). There is also no evidence that SSA recognized that treatment participation may actually include frequent relapses, given that its policy was to punish relapse by canceling benefits. On the other hand, there was apparently no limit to the length of time one could spend moving in and out of treatment, collecting benefits during periods of participation. Judging by SSI recipients' low rates of treatment participation, the SSI program would seem to have been an ineffective source of rehabilitation for most disabled substance users. But whether this reflects the flaws of coercive policy or simply poor agency management remains an open question.

The assumptions behind the SSA's 1996 redefinition of disability are quite different. The notion that addiction is not disabling presumes that one can work while addicted and that therefore income support is not needed. Obligations are not excused, and one is expected to actively seek and participate in a program of rehabilitation or treatment. The claim that disabled substance users have only themselves to blame for their condition suggests that assistance is undeserved. As Hunt and Baumohl (2003) point out, this view does not completely demedicalize addiction, because the expectation that substance users will seek treatment at least tacitly acknowledges some form or level of illness, although not rising to the level that merits public aid.

The Parsonian conceptualization of illness can be seen as a form of the biopsychosocial model that is widely accepted in the United States as a basis for understanding addiction. It combines elements of three models: biomedical, psychological, and social. Thus it recognizes the distinction between disease, understood as malfunctioning of biological or psychological processes, and illness, defined as the psychosocial experience and meaning of disease (Kleinman, 1980). With respect to chronic drug users, the biopsychosocial framework recognizes that addiction is not simply a biomedical condition and that it is not caused solely or perhaps even primarily by the pharmacology of a drug of choice. It allows the argument that chronic and compulsive consumption in the face of negative consequences is irrational behavior. This raises the question of how much agency is exercised by the user, which fosters varied socially constructed definitions of the disabling condition.

According to Kleinman (1980), the first clinical function of a health care system is to cast disease into a particular cultural form (illness); such definition is the first stage of healing. Within the system the definition of illness is influenced by external cultural, social, political, and economic factors. In the United States, this means that addiction can be defined simultaneously as illness and as bad behavior—i.e., as illness caused by bad behavior. Perhaps to a greater extent than with purely physiological ailments, treatment providers place the onus for recovery on the patient, who may also be identified as a lawbreaker when using illegal drugs.

The biopsychosocial model—and each of the perspectives it draws from—is but one possibility among many for understanding illness and/or disability (which is often defined as chronic illness). Other models are informed by a variety of knowledge bases and belief systems such as religious or spiritual beliefs or folk traditions, all of which highlight the importance of cultural dimensions. Each model has implications for treatment and they can coexist, so that spiritual healing may be sought from shamans even when Western medicine is also used. Disability is generally understood in Western cultures as a condition in which physical and/or psychological impairments prevent a person from performing normal roles or activities. In the United States, the salient activity is work (legitimate employment); certainly it is central to the Social Security Administration's disability policies. But in other cultures, where understandings of illness are rooted in spiritual rather than biomedical traditions, disability may have a different meaning, or a condition in a specific setting may not be defined as a disability at all. Epilepsy, for example, is considered a disabling brain disorder in the U.S., but to the Hmong people of Laos it manifests the loss of the soul, and in some other cultures it is seen as a divine enabling gift (Fadiman, 1998; Hershenson, 2000).

Income security and distributive justice

The determination to withhold or grant income security benefits implies considerations of distributive justice, i.e., any system designed to allocate material and social goods to members of society based on specified principles (Lamont, 2003). Basing that determination on whether an applicant can work and may be complicit in his or her own disability raises the question of "just deserts." The simplest way to express a desert claim is, "X deserves A in virtue of B" (Kleinig, 1971: 71). In the United States, social policies addressing income security are based on conservative principles, especially that of reciprocity. That is, although the state recognizes need, it limits assistance to citizens who contribute to society and behave responsibly (Anderson, 2004). This posture stands in contrast to liberal principles, in which need is a sufficient basis for support. Another way of explaining the conservative position is to say that individuals, even those in need, must do something or have something that makes them deserving of assistance from the state. In fact, the distinction between the "deserving" and "undeserving" poor has a long history in the United States. Those who are poor as a consequence of accident, disabling illness, or old age, for example, have been deemed to merit assistance. Poor people who cannot cite those causes have been vilified as lazy and/or immoral, even if they have been denied economic opportunity through no fault of their own but by, say, racial discrimination (Gordon, 1994; Katz, 1989; Patterson, 2000). The reclassification of disabled substance users from "deserving" to "undeserving" is simply one of its more recent manifestations.

Lamont (1994) identifies two distinct types of reasons for arguing that an individual does not deserve a certain benefit:

- one, that the person does not possess the quality forming the basis of desert; and
- two, that the quality possessed [is not a legitimate basis of desert]

Both of these reasons are relevant to the question of whether the disabled substance user should receive taxpayer-funded income support. However, it might be more accurate to restate the second reason by saying that the substance user possesses a quality that delegitimates his or her otherwise acceptable basis of desert.

The political reasons for denying disability status to "substance abusers" seem to belong in the first category. The quality that constitutes desert basis is clear from the Social Security Administration definition of disability as an impairment that prevents "substantial gainful activity" by an individual, that is, one must be unable to work. Denying this desert basis to drug addicts and alcoholics implies that they are able to work. In fact, this claim has been explicitly upheld in administrative law findings that drug dealing and prostitution require enough physical and mental effort to be considered "substantial gainful activity" and that if it could be "plausibly established" that an individual had earnings from such activity, he or she would be deemed ineligible for SSI or SSDI benefits (Hunt and Baumohl, 2003: 15).

There is some logic to this rationale. It is often argued that work in the illicit drug trade or prostitution requires business and interpersonal skills that are also valued in the legal economy (Bourgois, 1996; Dunlap and Johnson, 1994). Thus, it does not sound unreasonable to claim that an individual who can function gainfully in underground markets could do as well in legal employment and therefore is not disabled. One may counter that there are qualitative differences between the two economies, even if we assume that someone could actually make a living in illicit markets. Most work in the legal economy includes fixed and regular hours and requires conformity to conventional norms of behavior to an extent not found in illicit markets. It is possible, therefore, that an individual dependent on drugs or alcohol may be able to function at a level that is adequate for sporadic drug transactions and assorted "hustling," but which falls well short of what is necessary to sustain legal employment and true self-support.

It might be more plausible to argue that an addict who can function gainfully in the underground economy can also meet the requirements of treatment and rehabilitation. This argument would not necessarily conflict with a finding of disability, if participation in treatment were seen as requiring less effort than "substantial gainful activity."

On the foregoing view, if drug addicts and alcoholics do not possess the desert basis for benefits—disability—then that is enough to deny them aid. But does the second type of reason for denial also apply—do drug addicts and alcoholics possess a quality that delegitimates desert? This is a more complex issue than the first type of reasoning. It may be that drug users possess several qualities that could be considered undeserving, although some may be the same attributes that make legitimate employment impossible (as described above). The formal regulations concerning SSI and SSDI are silent on conditions that do not meet the criteria for disability, including one characteristic of substance users that was frequently invoked in the political rhetoric leading up to reform: that their condition is "self-inflicted." From this perspective, being unable to control one's drug or alcohol use is a moral weakness, a willful violation of the principal of reciprocity that underlies citizenship. To say that someone does not deserve to get something is different than saying that they deserve not to get it, although by offering this rationale for denying benefits to substance users, Congress seems to elide the distinction.

To say that a substance user—or anyone else—does not deserve a certain benefit is not equivalent to saying the person is not entitled to that good. The concept of desert is related to, but distinct from, the concept of entitlement. The problem of defining addiction as disability for Social Security purposes nicely illustrates this distinction. Before 1996, it was possible to argue that drug addicts and alcoholics were entitled to benefits because of the way the law was written, but they did not actually deserve those benefits. Indeed, this would seem to be exactly the argument that prevailed when the DA&A program was terminated by Congress. In the absence of that program, the converse argument might well be made today: that drug addicts and alcoholics deserve benefits even though they are not entitled to them under the law. This argument would most likely be made by addicted persons and their advocates. One may also argue that in an ideal world, everyone is entitled to whatever he or she deserves. And in ordinary conversation, "entitled" is often used interchangeably with "deserving." But in the real world entitlement is an institutional concept, less dependent on moral values than the concept of desert. The institution chooses a desert basis—in this case disability—but the resulting entitlement is a rule or regulation, not a moral value (Kleinig, 1971; Lamont, 1994).

The SSA's reclassification of addiction also highlights the distinction between desert and need. What do substance users need? If they are to engage in rehabilitation they need access to treatment, at a minimum, and of course this treatment should be evidence-based and adhere to standards of quality (Magura, 2000). There is an extensive scientific literature showing the effectiveness of treatment, but of course outcomes vary considerably for individuals, relapses after treatment unfortunately are common, and thus treatment often needs to be repeated periodically; fast and permanent "cures" are rare. On the other hand, natural recovery undoubtedly also occurs, perhaps more frequently than commonly thought (Klingemann and Sobell, 2001).

But whether or not they are in treatment, addicted people need a source of income or support, like everyone else, simply to live. Some substance users can work during rehabilitation, depending on the nature of their employment and of their treatment program. Others, unable to support themselves through employment, need assistance. According to Kleinig (1971), one may deserve a certain social benefit without needing it, or one may need it without deserving it. Under current regulations, the message is that substance users may very well need income support, but they do not deserve it, and thus they are deemed unentitled to it. Before 1996, however, Social Security disability policy kept desert and need in parallel. Substance users' need for income support was recognized simply by their inclusion in the category of disabled; but in order to be entitled, they also had to participate in treatment. Thus the institution (SSA) supplied a desert basis (participation in treatment) for the entitlement.

Distinguishing need from desert in the way that is done by Social Security disability policy raises questions of volition and responsibility (Cupit, 1996; Lamont, 1994). Individuals may be involuntarily disabled, which explains their need, but that does not guarantee assistance under principles of reciprocity, which require that one give something in return for aid. This is a conservative interpretation of distributive justice principles (Anderson, 2004). In theory even a conservative interpretation could suspend the requirement of reciprocity in cases where it is established that one has been injured through no fault of one's own and therefore deserves compensation. This exception would be clearest when one's injury or disability could be attributed to another's negligence or bad act, but that is not generally the finding with drug addicts and alcoholics. Proving one's inability to work and then participating in treatment and rehabilitation met the criterion of reciprocity for disabled substance users until 1996. It is sometimes argued that need cannot be considered a desert basis because need requires no action on the part of the beneficiary. In Kleinig's (1971) example, the child from a deprived background may need extraordinary encouragement from teachers but cannot be said to deserve it, because he/she has not given anything in exchange for it and the child is not responsible for his/her background. [Distributive justice, of course, may operate with need as well as desert—as noted on p. 159.]

Lamont (1994), arguing that desert claims involve external moral values, points out that theorists vary in the level of volition required for desert claims. (See also Kleinig, 2001.) At the low end of the spectrum, minimal levels of volition would seem to converge with need. After all, most SSI and SSDI recipients are involuntarily needy—and involuntarily disabled—although that is precisely the point of controversy in the case of substance users. SSA policy does not consider disabled substance users equal to the "deserving poor" because it does not accept the presumed cause of their need as legitimate. Nor does it recognize the distributive justice argument that such individuals may deserve compensation simply because they are not responsible for their plight.

Indeed, one can argue the alternative, that substance users have done something to establish the condition (disability) on whose basis they apply for aid. Such is the case in the political rhetoric that portrays disabled substance users as undeserving because their condition is self-inflicted. Contrary to the reciprocity argument that a deserving party must be responsible for the quality that entitles them to a benefit, this claim denies benefits because the applicant is deemed responsible for what would otherwise be the deserving attribute. It evokes the conceptualization of "voluntary victims" that Kasachkoff (2004) employs in considering the question of society's obligation to provide health care to addicted drug users. Voluntary victims are individuals who engage in risky behavior—for example, illicit drug use, unprotected sex, skydiving, and mountain climbing—with full knowledge of the possible consequences. When those individuals become ill or injured or otherwise need assistance as a result of the risky activity, one school of thought holds that society is not obligated to help them, because they have brought their afflictions on themselves. This principle has resulted in individuals in some localities being charged for the costs of their rescues when they get into trouble.

The principle is not applied consistently, however, even to substance use. One of the most glaring contradictions is the status of tobacco smoking. Although incontrovertibly causing lung cancer and contributing hugely to heart disease, among other ailments, smokers who become disabled due to their smoking are eligible for disability benefits. There would be a revolution if their benefits were denied, thus pragmatism easily trumps the principle of the "voluntary victim" in the case of tobacco. Society has chosen to define smokers as truly addicted, thus not in control of their behavior, at least setting a precedent that might once again be extended to other substances that science says also induce loss of control. Eating disorders resulting in obesity with its negative health consequences is a similar example.

Thus let us briefly consider, just how voluntary is drug/alcohol addiction? (Kasachkoff, 2004). The argument against regarding addiction as a disability clearly presumes volition, but the presumption may be rebuttable. Consider first the simple fact that most people who use drugs and alcohol do not become dependent on them. How do we explain the ones who do? Granted that the initial act of drinking, smoking, inhaling, injecting, or ingesting a drug by some other means is a voluntary one, regardless of any concomitant social pressures. For most people, subsequent drug or alcohol consumption remains voluntary—and controlled. The salient characteristic of what is termed "addiction" is that consumption has become involuntary in some sense; control has been lost; negative consequences, actual or anticipated, no longer stem the behavior. Although the causes of addiction are still not well understood—genetic predisposition, pharmacology, brain chemistry, environment, or any combination, are all candidates—the symptomatic loss of control is not generally disputed by treatment professionals. The potentially involuntary nature of drug/alcohol use for some people has been essential to understanding addiction as a medical condition, and one that may be disabling, since the 18th century (Conrad and Schneider, 1992). Indeed, in 1975 a federal circuit court ruled that the Social Security Administration must consider "loss of control" when evaluating the role of alcoholism in disability (Griffis v. Weinberger, 1975; Hunt and Baumohl, 2003). (The decision was later interpreted to include addiction to other drugs as well.)

Whether or not addicts are responsible for their condition does not directly answer the question of whether they are disabled. Some may meet the SSA's burden to prove that they cannot engage in "substantial gainful activity," while others may not. Substance addictions vary in type, intensity, and consequences for social and economic functioning. But considering responsibility introduces the possibility of problems with the Social Security Administration's determination of what conditions qualify as disabling. To create a blanket exclusion for addiction on the presumption that it is a self-inflicted condition is not only logically erroneous, but ethically inconsistent (if not actively discriminatory). The SSA includes volition in its desert basis only in the case of drug addicts and alcoholics. Other individuals who may be disabled by other voluntary activities—including reckless and sometimes illegal ones like riding a motorcycle without a helmet, or smoking—are not similarly judged. They are just as entitled to benefits as applicants who did not knowingly take chances with their health and can arguably be labeled "innocently" disabled (by accident or non-substance-use-related disease, for example).

Perhaps the deserving/undeserving split that Social Security makes is analogous to reward and punishment. As Cupit (1996) argues, reward and punishment are modes of response that presuppose the recipient's capability for responsible behavior. However, no one has advocated for actively punishing disabled substance users, unless the withholding of benefits can be seen as punitive. But that may be a difficult claim to make, because current SSA policy simply declares disabled substance users ineligible for benefits. It may be more persuasive to argue that previous (pre-1996) SSI/SSDI policy was punitive, because it sanctioned people who failed to comply with treatment requirements by terminating the benefits they had been receiving. While such a policy was intended to serve as an incentive, it also ignored the reality of the treatment experience, which commonly includes multiple relapses to substance use. Essentially, it can be viewed as punishing posited "vulnerable people" for failing to live up to unreasonable expectations about treatment as an infallible "cure."

Perhaps the 1996 change represents a shift toward libertarianism, if that is understood as being similar to conservatism in requiring individuals to make a productive contribution in order to justify receiving something of value (Anderson, 2004). The difference is that according to libertarian principles, it is the market, not the state, that determines the distribution of goods. In a world governed by libertarian principles the concept of assistance, in the sense of state aid to the needy, is virtually meaningless. And in such a world, SSI would in all likelihood not exist. (One could argue that perhaps SSDI would exist, because it is a benefit earned by employment.) Nevertheless, the revised policy seems to take a libertarian approach to substance misusers by moving them from the arena of the state to that of the market. Declaring that they are not disabled, can enroll in a short course of curative treatment if they so choose, and thus can support themselves through work, is to say that they can survive in the marketplace.

Consequences and implications

One argument for terminating benefits was the fact that the number of drug users receiving disability payments had soared, more than doubling between 1989 and 1994 (GAO, 1994b). At the time benefits were discontinued, the 209,000 targeted recipients constituted the largest number of drug users in the program's history, although they also represented only 2.6 percent of the total SSI/SSDI caseload (Davies et al., 2000). The General Accounting Office and the Congressional Budget Office estimated that most of the targeted recipients would be eligible for continued benefits because of other impairments, such as psychiatric and physical disabilities: more than half, according to the GAO, and 75 percent according to the CBO (GAO, 1994a; Hunt and Baumohl, 2003). Given this, and because the 1996 Act allowed drug users to reapply for eligibility under other impairments, it might be assumed that terminating benefits for addiction as a disability would have little overall impact. In fact, however, most targeted recipients did lose their benefits. By the end of 1997 only about 35 percent of former recipients had reapplied and retained benefits, and 28 percent had not even filed new applications (Hunt and Baumohl, 2003).

Chronically addicted individuals may not be disabled in the eyes of the SSA, but they may well be unemployable. Many lack job skills and/or work habits valued by the legal employment market, and many have extensive histories of criminal activity during periods of active substance use, making them undesirable to employers. Such individuals need income support to live without reverting to crime, even though they may not "deserve" such support under the reciprocity principle. Thus the implications of Social Security's change in disability criteria reach beyond individual substance users to a broader pool of stakeholders including drug dependency treatment providers, social service agencies, and the general public.

For the public, the consequences involve both safety and economics. Extensive research conducted over several decades has firmly established strong and varying links between drug use and crime. In the multi-city study of former SSI recipients, Swartz, Martinovich and Goldstein (2003) found that subjects who lost their DA&A benefits and were unable to requalify under another disability were one to two and a half times as likely to report committing drug or property-related crimes as were those who requalified for benefits. Most of the crimes were drug or property related, and the researchers found that criminal activity increased during the two years of the study. Subjects who reported using heroin or cocaine or both were more likely than nonusers to be involved in crimes. Although the authors do not report whether any of the crimes involved violence, the pattern of activity may fall under what Goldstein (1985) calls economic compulsive violence, in which drug users commit robbery or other income-producing crimes. This is particularly true with respect to those addicted to illicit drugs such as cocaine and heroin, by definition expensive and available only on the black market, which is regulated partly by violence. Because alcohol is legal, of course, it is less likely to foster economically inspired crime. However, alcohol is more closely linked to violent behavior than any other drug because of its psychopharmacological effects (Parker and Auerhahn, 1998).

For several decades U.S. taxpayers have funded policies that have emphasized incarcerating illicit drug users, an approach that is not cost-effective and perhaps socially self-defeating as well. A growing body of research indicates that imprisonment is more expensive than publicly funded treatment and income supports combined. The cost of treatment varies with modality and ranges from an annualized average of approximately $5,100 per client for a standard outpatient program to about $22,000 per client in a therapeutic community (Roebuck, French and McLellan, 2003). Given that SSI and SSDI paid disabled substance users an average of about $5,500 annually, the total cost to taxpayers of a program that paid income support and treatment could be estimated at between $10,000 and $28,000 (GAO, 1994b). In contrast, the average annual cost of incarceration is more than $22,000 per inmate in federal prison and $23,000 in state prison; in New York state it is about $36,000 (Bureau of Justice Statistics, 2004). These amounts do not include the cost of providing in-prison drug dependency treatment, which averages approximately $4,100 per prisoner annually (Roebuck et al., 2003). The cost-effectiveness of treatment is actually greater than these numbers indicate. Other research has shown that treatment substantially reduces societal costs such as crime, violence, and lost productivity, and that achieving the same benefits through additional domestic law enforcement would cost up to 15 times as much (Center for Substance Abuse and Treatment, 1997; Rydell and Everingham, 1994).

The loss of SSI and SSDI benefits would logically turn disabled substance users to other sources of income support, such as General Assistance, TANF and Food Stamps. Indeed, Congress anticipated that higher spending in those programs would partially offset the savings to be realized by removing drug users from the Social Security disability rolls. Some of those programs would face an influx of new applicants for services at a time when they were under pressure to reduce their own rolls. However, certain alternative forms of public income security became more difficult to secure after 1996, particularly for substance users. Under PRWORA, for example, individuals convicted of drug offenses became ineligible for public housing and were banned for life from TANF benefits and food stamps. PRWORA does allow states to opt out of the TANF ban, and so far eight states and the District of Columbia have done so. (The eight are: Connecticut, Michigan, New Hampshire, New York, Ohio, Oklahoma, Oregon, and Vermont.) An additional 20 states have modified the ban to deny benefits for only certain drug offenses or for a limited time period (Allard, 2002).

Welfare-eligible drug users may be required to enroll in treatment as a condition of receiving benefits, but time spent in treatment does not count toward satisfying the new work requirements that PRWORA also imposed (Benoit et al., 2004). Nevertheless, requirements such as these may also have a positive effect if they indeed motivate substance users to persevere in rehabilitation and if welfare and treatment agencies diligently monitor client progress.

Ellen Benoit, Ph.D., is a project director in the Institute for Special Populations Research at NDRI. Her research has focused on social policies related to public health and social control, particularly as they affect low-income substance users. She has published articles on poverty and the illegal drug trade, the impact of welfare reform on drug user treatment, and sociodemographic contexts of drug use and dependence.

Stephen Magura, Ph.D., C.S.W., is Director of Science and Research at NDRI and has been the Principal Investigator of many studies sponsored by the National Institute on Drug Abuse, the National Institute on Alcohol Abuse and Alcoholism, and the National Institute on Child Health and Development. These studies have included drug abuse clinical trials, treatment outcome evaluations, health services research, social epidemiology studies, HIV prevention research and policy analysis. Dr. Magura has authored or edited several books and special journal issues, including Outcome Measures for Child Welfare Services (1986), Experimental Therapeutics in Addiction Medicine (1994), a special issue of Health and Social Work on "Chemical Dependency" (1994), and special issues of Substance Use & Misuse on "Program Quality in Substance Dependency Treatment" (2000) and "Contemporary Vocational Rehabilitation for Substance Users" (2004). He serves on the Editorial Boards of five professional journals, is an elected member of the College on Problems of Drug Dependence (CPDD) and the Research Society on Alcoholism (RSA), serves on federal advisory committees and is a faculty member of the Middle Eastern-Mediterranean Summer Institute on Drug Use.

References

Allard, P. (2002). *Life sentences: Denying welfare benefits to women convicted of drug offenses*. Washington, D.C.: The Sentencing Project.

Anderson, E. (2004). Welfare, work requirements, and dependant-care. *Journal of Applied Philosophy 21*(3): 243-256.

Baffuto, T. and Boggs, E.M. (1990). What ADA has meant and what it can mean for people with mental retardation. *American Rehabilitation 16*(4): 10-14.

Benoit, E., Young, R., Magura, S. and Staines, G. (2004). The impact of welfare reform on methadone treatment: Policy lessons from service providers in New York City. *Substance Use and Misuse 39*(13&14): 2355-2390.

Bourgois, P. (1996). *In search of respect: selling crack in El Barrio*. Cambridge: Cambridge University Press.

Bureau of Justice Statistics. (2004). *State prison expenditures, 2001*. NCJ202949. Washington, DC: U.S. Department of Justice.

Center for Substance Abuse and Treatment. (1997). *National treatment improvement evaluation study, 1997 highlights*. Rockville, MD: Substance Abuse and Mental Health Services Administration.

Colbridge, T.D. (2000). Defining disability under the Americans with Disabilities Act. *FBI Law Enforcement Bulletin*, October 2000: 28-32.

Conrad, P. and Schneider, J.W. (1992). *Deviance and medicalization: From badness to sickness*. Philadelphia: Temple University Press.

Cupit, G. (1996). Desert and responsibility. *Canadian Journal of Philosophy 26*(1): 83-100.

Davies, P., Iams, H. and Rupp, K. (2000). The effect of welfare reform on SSA's disability programs: Design of policy evaluation and early evidence. *Social Security Bulletin 63*(1): 3-11.

Dunlap, E. and Johnson, B.D. (1994). Family and human resources in the development of a female crack-seller career: Case study of a hidden population. *Journal of Drug Issues 26*(1): 175-198.

Fadiman, A. (1998). *The spirit catches you and you fall down: A Hmong child, her American doctors, and the collision of two cultures*. New York: Farrar, Straus & Giroux.

General Accounting Office. (1994a). Social Security: Disability Benefits for Addicts and Alcoholics are Out of Control. GAO/T-HEHS-94-101.

General Accounting Office. (1994b). Social Security: Major Changes Needed for Disability Benefits for Addicts. GAO/HEHS-94-128.

Goldstein, P. (1985). The drugs-violence nexus: A tripartite conceptual framework. *Journal of Drug Issues 14*: 493-506.

Gordon, D.R. (1994). *The Return of the Dangerous Classes: Drug Prohibition and Policy Politics*. New York: W.W. Norton & Co.

Griffis v. Weinberger. (1975). 509 F.2d 837 (9th Cir. 1975)

Hershenson, D.B. (2000). Toward a cultural anthropology of disability and rehabilitation. *Rehabilitation Counseling Bulletin 43*(3): 150-157, 177.

Hunt, S.R. and Baumohl, J. (2003). Drink, drugs and disability: an introduction to the controversy. *Contemporary Drug Problems 30*: 9-76.

Irvine, R. and Goulden, J.C. (1992). Social Security subsidizes junkies. *The AIM Report XXI-8*: 1-2.

Kasachkoff, T. (2004). Drug addiction and responsibility for the health care of drug addicts. *Substance Use and Misuse 39*(3): 489-509.

Katz, M.B. (1989). *The undeserving poor: From the war on poverty to the war on welfare*. New York: Pantheon Books.

Kleinig, J. (1971). The concept of desert. *American Philosophical Quarterly 8*(1): 71-78.

Kleinig, J. (2001). Deserts, philosophical concept of. In Baltes, P.B. & Smelser, N.J. (eds.-in-chief), *International Encyclopedia of the Social and Behavioral Sciences*, Amsterdam: Elsevier, Vol. V, pp. 3529-35.

Kleinman, A. (1980). *Patients and healers in the context of culture: an exploration of the borderland between anthropology, medicine and psychiatry*. Berkeley: University of California Press.

Klingemann, H. and Sobell, L. (2001). Introduction: Natural recovery research across substance use. *Substance Use & Misuse 36*(11): 1409-1416.

Lamont, J. (2003). Distributive Justice. *The Stanford Encyclopedia of Philosophy* (Fall 2003 Edition), Zalta, E.N. (ed.), URL = <http://plato.stanford.edu/archives/fall2003/entries/justice-distributive/>.

Lamont, J. (1994). The concept of desert in distributive justice. *The Philosophical Quarterly 44*(174): 45-64.

Magura, S. (2000). Introduction: Program quality in substance dependency treatment. *Substance Use and Misuse 35*(12-14): 1617-1627.

Parker, R.N. and Auerhahn, K. (1998). Alcohol, drugs, and violence. *Annual Review of Sociology 24*: 291-307.

Parsons, T. (1951). *The social system*. New York: The Free Press.

Patterson, J.T. (2000). *America's struggle against poverty in the twentieth century*. Cambridge: Harvard University Press.

Reinarman, C. and Levine, H.G. eds. (1997). *Crack in America: Demon drugs and social justice*. Berkeley: University of California Press.

Roebuck, M.C., French, M.T. and McLellan, A.T. (2003). DATStats: results from 85 studies using the drug abuse treatment cost analysis program (DATCAP). *Journal of Substance Abuse Treatment 25*: 51-57.

Ruddy, C. (1994). Easy street. *Reader's Digest 144*(863): 102.

Rydell, C.P. and Everingham, S.S. (1994). *Controlling cocaine*. Prepared for the Office of National Drug Control Policy and the United States Army. Santa Monica, CA: Drug Policy Research Center, RAND Corporation.

Satel, S. (1994). Hooked. *The New Republic*, May 30: 18-19.

Social Security Administration. (2005). Disability evaluation under social security. Social Security Administration Office of Disability Programs. SSA Pub. No. 64-039.

Social Security Advisory Board. (2003). *The Social Security definition of disability*. Washington, D.C.: Social Security Advisory Board.

Swartz, J.A., Campbell, K., Baumohl, J. and Tonkin, P. (2003). Drug treatment participation and retention rates among former recipients of Supplemental Security Income for drug addiction and alcoholism. *Contemporary Drug Problems 30*: 335-364.

Swartz, J.A., Martinovich, Z. and Goldstein, P. (2003). An analysis of the criminogenic effects of terminating the Supplemental Security Income impairment category for drug addiction and alcoholism. *Contemporary Drug Problems 30*: 391-424.

Tomko, C.M. (2002). The economically disadvantaged and the ADA: Why economic need should factor into the mitigating measures disability analysis. *Case Western Reserve Law Review 52*: 1033-1065.

U.S. House of Representatives. Committee on Ways and Means. (1994). *Exploring means of achieving higher rates of treatment and rehabilitation among alcoholics and drug addicts receiving federal disability benefits*. February 10, 1994. Serial 103-75. Washington, DC: U.S. Government Printing Office.

Wasserman, D. (2004). Addiction and disability: moral and policy issues. *Substance Use and Misuse 39*(3): 461-488.

Glossary

ADA (Americans with Disabilities Act): Federal legislation enacted in 1996 to protect disabled individuals from discrimination in employment and in public places.

AFDC (Aid to Families with Dependent Children): Federal program of cash and noncash aid to poor families, until it was eliminated in 1996.

desert: A quality or attribute that merits reward or punishment.

disability: Chronic physical or mental impairment that prevents an individual from engaging in normal roles or activities.

distributive justice: a system designed to allocate material and social goods to members of society based on varying principles, such as need, equality, individual characteristics or market transactions

entitlement: A rule instituting a claim to benefits on the basis of some specified desert.

Food Stamps: Federal program enabling low-income individuals and families to buy eligible food in authorized stores with coupons and electronic benefits.

General Assistance: State-level programs of cash and noncash benefits for needy individuals ineligible for benefits from TANF or other family assistance programs.

pharmacology: the reactions and properties of drugs.

recovery: With respect to drug addiction, the process by which an individual discontinues drug use and participates in a supervised rehabilitation program.

representative payee: Person appointed by SSA to receive and manage funds for an SSI recipient who is determined to be unable to do so.

SSA (Social Security Administration): Federal agency that administers retirement, survivors and disability insurance programs and Supplemental Security Income for the blind, aged and disabled.

SSDI (Social Security Disability Insurance): Federal program of disability assistance in which benefits are based on prior work experience.

SSI (Supplemental Security Income): Federal program of disability assistance in which benefits are based on financial need regardless of work experience.

TANF (Temporary Assistance to Needy Families): Federal, time-limited program of cash and noncash aid to poor families. It replaced AFDC in 1996.

voluntary victims: Individuals harmed as a result of engaging in risky behavior with full knowledge of the possible consequences.

voluntaristic behavior: Willful conduct; behavior driven by volition rather than by coercion or forces beyond an individual's control.

1-9 Conflicts of Interest in the Evaluation and Dissemination of Drug Use Prevention Programs

Dennis M. Gorman, Ph.D.

"But the problem remains; the overadvocacy trap continues to sabotage program evaluation" (Campbell, 1988, page 299).

Abstract

This chapter examines the implications of recent developments in the evaluation and marketing of drug use prevention programs for research integrity, and specifically for the threats to this that arise from conflicts of interest. It begins with a description of what is meant by the term "conflict of interest" and a review of the main types of conflicts that have been discussed in the medical and public policy literatures in recent years. This is followed by a more detailed discussion of the individual and institutional conflicts of interest that exist in drug use prevention research.

Key Words: accountability; conflict of interest; drug use prevention; evaluation research; program dissemination; public policy; evidence-based policy and practice; expert committees

Introduction

Many of the ethical issues discussed in the chapters of this book pertaining to treatment also apply to the provision of prevention services. These include issues of informed consent, the place of morality in service provision, professional competence and conduct, and the range and possible latitude of service provision. It is beyond the scope of the current chapter to discuss all these issues. Rather the focus here is on one particular ethical issue that has become increasingly important in the field of drug use prevention in recent years, namely, conflict of interest.

The reason that conflict of interest has become an important issue in the area of drug use prevention relates to the way in which prevention programs are now evaluated and disseminated. Indeed, what is especially interesting about the area of drug use prevention in this regard is that over the past 15 years it has sought to become more scientific in the conduct of program evaluations while at the same time becoming more business-like in the way that it markets and disseminates these programs. The impetus for these changes came in large part from criticism directed at the efficacy of government-funded interventions of the mid-1980s, notably those of the Center for Substance Abuse Prevention (CSAP) and the US Department of Education's Safe and Drug-Free Schools and Communities Program (Gorman, 1997; 1998; US General Accounting Office, 1997). With the demand for more accountability and need to demonstrate the efficacy of publicly-funded programs, the terms "science-based," "research-based" and "evidence-based" have increasingly been used in the advocacy of primary prevention programs by researchers, program administrators, and the federal agencies that fund these interventions (e.g., Biglan & Taylor, 2000; Botvin, 2000; Schinke, Brounstein & Gardner, 2002; National Institute on Drug Abuse, 1997; 2003; US Department of Education Safe, Disciplined, and Drug-Free Schools Expert Panel, 2002). As with any product, consumer confidence is increased when an intervention is labeled "evidence-based" (especially by a seemingly independent party such as a government-sponsored "expert committee"), and thus to be "scientific" is to be marketable in the world of prevention practice.

In this chapter I will explore the implications of these trends in the evaluation and marketing of drug use prevention programs for the integrity of the research that is conducted, and specifically for the threats to research integrity that arise from conflicts of interest. I begin by describing what is meant by the term conflict of interest and reviewing the main types of conflicts that have been discussed in the medical and public policy literatures in recent years. This is be followed by a more detailed discussion of the importance of considering the role of conflict of interest in the conduct and dissemination of drug use prevention research.

The Nature and Types of Conflict of Interest

As Smith (1994) observes, suggesting that an agency or individual has a conflict of interest is far removed from being an accusation of outright bias, dishonesty or fraud. It simply means that there are two potentially competing interests simultaneously at play in the same situation. Along similar lines, Tobin notes that the term conflict of interest refers to "a set of conditions in which professional judgment concerning a primary interest, such as the validity of research, might be influenced by a secondary interest, such as financial gain" (Tobin, 2003, page 1161). He further draws an important distinction between the term "conflict of interest" and that of "bias." The former is a condition that is determined by circumstance, while the latter is a behavior determined by outcome. Thus, bias exists when the researcher's judgment concerning his/her primary interest (i.e., the production of objective knowledge) has been clearly influenced by some secondary and competing interest. In contrast, a conflict of interest exists irrespective of whether the researcher's judgment and behavior can be demonstrated to have been adversely influenced – that is, it exists simply as a condition of the researcher having two competing interests (DeAngelis, 2000; Tobin, 2003). Whether this potential for bias translates into actual bias is an empirical question. Further, Tobin (2003) argues, it is for the reader of a research report to decide whether this potential exists, rather than for the researcher to decide through refusal to report the existence of any such conflict of interest.

There are a number of secondary interests of a researcher that have the potential to influence his/her judgment concerning his/her research, and hence the validity of the results produced. Some of these are inherent in nearly all forms of research, for example the pressure for career advancement, and related demands to publish in peer-reviewed journals (Tobin, 2003). The secondary interest that has attracted most attention in the area of biomedical research, however, is that of financial conflict of interest. One reason for this, as Tobin (2003) observes, is that while non-financial conflicts such as pressure to get promoted are inherent in all research activities, financial conflicts are not.

They are often optional on the part of the researcher, and readers of a research report have little way of knowing whether they are present unless they are disclosed by the researcher. A second type of conflict of interest that has received attention in recent years, and that is especially relevant to the evaluation of intervention policies and programs intended to prevent undesirable behaviors such as drug use, is that which results from adherence to a specific set of attitudes, beliefs, values or theories that are not amenable to change or modification when faced with conflicting evidence (Bachrach & Newcomer, 2002; MacCoun, 2005). This we will call "ideological" conflict of interest. An obvious example of this in the area of substance misuse is the dismissal by adherents of the disease model of alcoholism of evidence that demonstrates a return to low risk drinking by individuals who formerly met diagnostic criteria for dependence and the related failure of the treatment industry to consider moderation services (Klingemann, 2001; Sobell & Sobell, 2005).

Financial Conflicts of Interest

Analysis of the effects of financial conflicts of interest on research integrity has occurred most frequently in the area of biomedical research, specifically the effects of pharmaceutical industry sponsorship of clinical trials of drug efficacy. Indeed, there exists a sufficiently large body of research in this area that a number of meta-analyses have recently appeared that summarize the literature pertaining to the scope of industry sponsorship and its relationship to study design and methods, outcomes reported, and limitations on investigator behavior such as restrictions on publication (Bekelman, Li, & Gross, 2003; Lexchin, Bero, Djulberg & Clark, 2003). These analyses show that financial relationships between the pharmaceutical industry and researchers are widespread (about 25% of researchers have industry affiliations) and that there exists a systematic bias in the reporting of study outcomes favoring the products of those companies sponsoring the research. The latter finding is consistent across a range of diseases, drugs and drug classes, and types of study design (Lexchin et al., 2003). In addition, industry sponsorship has been found to be associated with both publication delay and publication bias (i.e., publishing positive results more often than negative results).

In terms of study design and methods, industry-sponsored research tends to use inappropriate control conditions (e.g., inactive controls or low doses of comparison drugs), but in other respects appears to be of similar quality to research funded through other sources. However, the studies that have assessed quality have tended to focus on design issues such as the presence of randomization, and have paid less attention to issues related to data analysis and reporting. The few studies that have examined these aspects of industry-sponsored studies have found fundamental shortcomings such as selective reporting among numerous outcome variables, changes in measurement scales before analysis, multiple subgroup analysis, and selective use of alpha levels above 0.05 and one-tailed significance tests (Gotzsche, 1989; Bero & Rennie, 1996).

There is nothing unique to the pharmaceutical industry that would lead one to consider it the only industry that might have a vested interest in the outcome of the research that its sponsors into the effects of its products. As Tobin (2003) observes, the desire to deliver a sound return on an investment is fundamental to the business ethic. A curriculum publisher will go out of business if it consistently loses money just as a pharmaceutical company will if there is no demand for its products. Thus, the desire to create profit (or, at the very least, remain financially solvent) has the potential to conflict with that of the scientist's desire to create knowledge whenever the two come into contact, whatever the nature of the business. However, detailed analyses of this issue are rare outside of the studies of the research funded by the pharmaceutical industry (Stelfox et al., 1998), the tobacco industry (Bero, Galbraith & Rennie, 1994; Barnes & Bero, 1998) and the food industry (Levine et al., 2003). As I will discuss later, we tend to be naturally suspicious of these large scale industries in which profit motive clearly outweighs concerns about public health, but somewhat naïve when it comes to considering these issues when either a researcher or research sponsor is seen to be well-intentioned.

Ideological Conflicts of Interest

As noted above, the term "ideological conflict of interest" refers to conflicts that derive from the researcher's theoretical and conceptual belief systems, and this is especially important in areas of research that are value-laden or in which ideological divisions run deep (Bachrach & Newcomer, 2002; MacCoun, 2005). As MacCoun (2005) observes, while financial conflicts are likely to be more of a problem in areas such as medicine and engineering than in public policy, the reverse is true of ideological conflicts since policy goals often pertain to issues about which individuals hold very strong opinions. He cites a number of areas of policy analysis that are matters of perpetual dispute and in which many of the main protagonists hold very divergent and contradictory views. These areas include the death penalty, HIV/AIDS, drug prohibition, needle exchange, sex education and gun control. While there are times when such strongly held beliefs and passions appear to lead to outright scientific misconduct (Kennedy, 2003) or to overt political pressures (Kaiser, 2003), our concern here is with those instances when they exercise a more subtle threat to research integrity through either the researcher or the sponsor assuming an advocacy role that conflicts with the objectivity that is fundamental to the role of scientist. Such subtle influences may affect the very basic questions that the research addresses (e.g., not looking for iatrogenic effects of a program) as well as the use of specific data analysis and presentation practices (e.g., use of one-tail significance tests and post-hoc sample refinement). In short, they result not in fraud or outright deception, but in what Feinstein (1988) calls "distortions" and "delusions."

In those cases in which a researcher is committed to a particular outcome *a priori* because it fits his or her preconceived belief system, then advocacy is likely to displace the skepticism and critical rationalism that one generally associates with the scientific world view (Gorman, 2005a; MacCoun, 2005). Advocacy-oriented research typically involves the selective use and emphasis of evidence to promote a hypothesis (without outright fraud or concealment) rather than the critical testing of that hypothesis. And, as MacCoun (2005) notes, while there is nothing inherently wrong with taking such an advocacy role provided this is made explicit and occurs within an adversarial system of evaluating evidence (i.e., one that assumes that facts will be selectively presented in a manner that is most favorable to one's position), there is a problem when an assertion of values is presented as an assertion of facts. The public tends to think of the scientific role as inherently inquisitorial (not adversarial), and the scientist as objective and manifesting disinterest (not passionate and committed) (MacCoun, 2005; Merton, 1973; Institute of Medicine, 2002). Thus, if a researcher is committed to a particular worldview (e.g., abstinence from drug use, harm reduction) or to a particular preventive technology (e.g., social skills training, community mobilization) then this should be made clear so that the consumers of the information that he/she produces can take this into account.

Conflicts of Interest in Drug Use Prevention Research

There are a number of reasons why consumers of evaluation studies in the area of drug use prevention should attend to issues of conflict of interest. First, data analysis and presentation practices similar to those found in the evaluation of pharmaceutical products have been observed in studies that assess the methodological quality of research in the area of drug and alcohol use prevention. Second, the potential for financial conflicts clearly exists within the drug use prevention field as program developers frequently evaluate their own programs and the federal agencies that fund research are under pressure to produce programs that are effective in meeting the country's goals in the "War on Drugs". Third, and related to the latter issue, there is also a potential ideological conflict of interest since both program developers and program sponsors are often committed to a certain set of ideas and opinions about the nature of drug use (e.g., behavioral psychology, zero tolerance) that are embedded within the interventions that they promote.

Each of these issues will be discussed in turn, starting with the concerns about data analysis and presentation. This will be followed by a discussion of some of the specific issues regarding conflicts of interest in the evaluation and dissemination of drug use prevention programs. This discussion will separate out sources of individual conflicts of interest (which focus primarily on those that arise when program developers evaluate their own interventions) from those that arise from the institutional and political context of drug use prevention research. For although we tend to think of conflict of interest as primarily a property of individuals, there are important social and political sources of conflict, and most individual instances are best understood within a complex organizational system of inputs and outputs (Bachrach & Newcomer, 2002; Institute of Medicine, 2002). Such political and institutional conflicts are often difficult to identify and assess, but include pressures from funding agencies, the demands of organizations that produce and market commodities that result from academic research (e.g., pharmaceutical products or curricula), and pressures from third parties that have a vested interest (either philosophic or financial) in the outcome of the research. The chapter concludes with a brief examination of the process whereby "research-based" or "evidence-based" prevention programs have been selected by federal agencies in the United States, since this is where both individual and institutional conflicts most obviously come together.

Data Analysis and Presentation Practices

As noted above, following criticism of drug use prevention programs in the early 1990s (specifically, the absence of evidence demonstrating their effectiveness), federal agencies such as CSAP, the US Department of Education, the National Institute on Drug Abuse (NIDA), and the National Institute of Justice began to emphasize the importance of research in determining which interventions to fund. One manifestation of this was a series of publications describing those interventions that had apparently been demonstrated to be effective in rigorous experimental and quasi-experimental evaluations (e.g., Schinke et al., 2002; National Institute on Drug Abuse, 1997; 2003;

US Department of Education Safe, Disciplined, and Drug-Free Schools Expert Panel, 2002). A number of intervention programs, such as the Life Skills Training Program, Seattle Social Development Project, Midwestern Prevention Project, and Project ALERT received multiple endorsements across these publications (Gorman, 2005; Gandhi, Murphy-Graham, Petrosino, Remignanti & Weiss, in press). And, indeed, all of these programs have been tested in large-scale experimental or quasi-experimental evaluations (e.g., Botvin et al., 1995; Ellickson & Bell, 1990; Hawkins, Catalano, Kosterman, Abbott & Hill, 1999).

While advocates of these programs contend that these evaluations are methodologically sound (e.g., Botvin & Griffin, 2005; Hawkins & Catalano, 2005), others argue that many of the positive program effects reported in evaluation studies emerge through use of data analysis practices that are not consistent with rigorous hypothesis testing. These practices include multiple subgroup analysis (Gerstein & Green, 1991; Gorman, 1998; Gandhi et al., in press; Manski, Pepper & Petrie, 2001), post hoc sample refinement (Gorman, 2002; 2005a), use of one-tail significance tests with no prior indication of unidirectional results (Brown, 2001; Glantz & Mandel, 2005; Gorman, 2003), changing the way that outcome variables are constructed from study to study (Brown, 2001; Gorman, 2003; 2005b; Gandhi et al., in press), and calculation of attrition rates using measurement points other than the pretest as the denominator (Gorman, 2002; 2005a).

Critical assessment of the data analysis and presentation practices used in the evaluation of drug use prevention programs is a fairly new development in the field of drug studies, and it is not entirely clear what the underlying reason for the use of such practices might be. Are these researchers engaged in advocacy and hypothesis promotion, or are they simply trying to ensure that the programs are given a fair test under conditions of maximum program fidelity (MacCoun, 2005)? Elsewhere, I have argued that these data analysis and presentation practices emanate from an essentially inductive/confirmationist approach to knowledge generation, in which a theory about the potential broad reach of a program is constructed from selective empirical observations and then, in turn, the scattered positive effects that emerged from subsequent evaluations are marshaled in support of the theory and its program (Gorman, 1996; 2005c). This approach to knowledge generation is fundamentally at odds with the critical rationalist view that emphasizes deduction and falsification, and that is at the heart of the scientific approach to program evaluation (Campbell, 1988; Gorman, 2005a). Conflict of interest and bias does not play a role in this type of explanation since the data analysis and presentation practices simply emerge from a particular way of trying to understand the world, albeit a nonscientific (or pseudoscientific) way.

Others, however, have suggested that conflict of interest might help us understand the use of irregular data analysis and presentation practices in the fields of evaluation and primary prevention studies (Barach & Newcomer, 2002; MacCoun, 2005; Moskowitz, 1993). This is an area that warrants both more open discussion within the evaluation field and more empirical analysis along the lines of that conducted on evaluations of pharmaceutical products sponsored by drug companies (e.g., Bekelman et al., 2003; Lexchin et al., 2003). Evaluation research must recapture the idea that rigorous, open debate is the most fundamental feature of science, as well as being the most efficient way to assess the relative merits of competing hypotheses (Bachrach & Newcomer, 2002; Campbell, 1988; Gorman, 2005a).

Individual Sources of Conflicts of Interest

In the field of drug use prevention, it is the norm rather than the exception for program developers to evaluate their own programs. It is also not unheard of for program developers to have financial arrangements with the publishing companies and consulting firms that market and disseminate their programs (Bachrach & Newcomer, 2002; Littell, 2006; Moskowitz, 1993). In such circumstances, the role of program evaluator and that of program owner/marketer can quite reasonably be conceived as potentially conflicting primary and secondary interests. Quite simply, a string of negative results are unlikely to boost sales of the program. In addition, even when a program developer does not have a direct financial relationship with a publisher or distributor, he/she may still build an entire academic career around the evaluation of a "successful" intervention. This can lead to enhanced professional standing and prestige, which can indirectly lead to financial benefits such as promotion, job offers, new funding, and stipends for presentations and committee work (Bachrach & Newcomer, 2002).

It is worth noting in this respect that those few evaluations of school-based curricula that have been undertaken by independent research teams have shown that the social skills and competency approaches that dominate federal research-based lists are largely ineffective (D'Onofrio, Moskowitz & Braverman, 2002; Harrington, Giles, Hoyle, Feeney & Yungbluth, 2001; Peterson, Kealy, Mann, Marek & Sarason, 2000). This is in keeping with the findings from meta-analyses of educational and criminal justice interventions that show that independently conducted evaluations routinely produce lower effect sizes than evaluations conducted by program developers (Borman, Hewes, Overman & Brown, 2003; Lipsey, 1995; Petrosino & Soydan, 2005). Lipsey (1995) notes that there are two possible explanations of this finding – the cynical view that has the developer/evaluator engaged in hypothesis promotion, and the high fidelity view that has the developer/evaluator better able to implement the program as designed and intended. Which of these is at play in any particular body of research is obviously an empirical question. The fact that data analysis practices such as multiple subgroup analysis typically do not appear in independent evaluations of drug use prevention programs means that the use of different data analysis practices is at least worth considering as an explanation of the different results reported in independent and non-independent evaluations.

In light of these issues regarding program evaluators evaluating there own programs, caution should be excercised in interpreting the findings that result for any such evaluation. One should be especially cautious when the developer/evaluator has a conflict of interest. Most medical journals now require detailed disclosure of financial conflicts (e.g., Smith, 1994; Tobin, 2003). Unfortunately, many drug and alcohol journals, as well as evaluation and prevention journals, do not mandate any such detail disclosures. So, for example, while some of the papers describing evaluations of Life Skills Training program contain a statement acknowledging the program developer's publishing agreement with Princeton Health Press, Inc. (e.g., Botvin et al., 1995, page 1106; Griffin, Botvin & Nichols, 2004, page 207), others contain no such disclosure (e.g., Botvin, Griffin, Diaz & Ifill-Williams, 2001; Griffin, Botvin, Nichols & Doyle, 2003). Similar discrepancies exist with other well-known programs such as the Seattle Social Development Project and PATHS, with some publications stating financial conflicts of interest (e.g., Greenberg, 2004, page 5; Hawkins, Kosterman, Catalano, Hill

& Abbott, 2005, page 25) and others not (e.g., Catalano, Haggerty, Oesterle, Fleming & Hawkins, 2004; Kam, Greenberg & Kusche, 2004). It should be made clear that this problem does not reside with the program developers; when asked to disclose conflicts of interest they will obviously comply. Rather, it is a problem with the editorial policies of journals, and these should be rectified by introducing policies similar to those of the major medical journals.[1]

Institutional and Political Sources of Conflict of Interest

Beyond potential financial conflicts of interest, drug use prevention is an area of research in which individuals and agencies frequently adhere to strong theoretical and ideological beliefs. For example, a number of the federal agencies that fund evaluations in this area are not doing so simply to advance basic science but have as their primary concern the development of effective interventions that they can then disseminate as part of the broader set of drug control policies collectively termed the "War on Drugs" (Government Accounting Office, 2003; Petrosino, 2003). Thus, program evaluations take place within a complex political and cultural context in which the production of interventions that meet specific goals and objectives (e.g., reduced adolescent drug use), not just the generation of knowledge (e.g., does Program X reduce adolescent drug use?), is of pre-eminent importance. This is especially true as policy makers and practitioners are more and more held accountable for delivering effective interventions within the constraints of limited budgets (Petrosino, 2003). Here the potential conflict resides in the researcher's desire to produce "good news" about an intervention program, especially if he/she wishes to secure additional funding in the future.

The federal government spends close to $12 billion a year on illicit drug control, of which about $1.5 billion goes to prevention activities (Office of Natural Drug Control Policy, 2003). The Performance Measures of Effectiveness (PME) System developed by the Office of National Drug Control Policy (ONDCP) in the early 1990s sets specific goals in the areas of supply and demand reduction (Office of National Drug Control Policy, 1999). The first of these is to: "Educate and enable America's youth to reject illegal drugs as well as alcohol and tobacco" (Office of National Drug Control Policy, 1999, page 19). Each of the five ONDCP goals is broken down into a set of measurable objectives. Three of the nine objectives included under Goal 1 refer to the use of research and science to guide and inform prevention efforts (Objectives 4, 8 and 9; Office of National Drug Control Policy, 1999, pages 86, 95 and 97). For example, Goal 1, Objective 4 is to "Provide students in grades K-12 with alcohol, tobacco, and drug use prevention programs and policies that are research based" (Office of National Drug Control Policy, 1999, page 86). The Department of Education and Department of Health and Human Services are designated as the "reporting agencies" for these objectives, and therefore clearly have an interest both in the identification of evidence-based prevention programs and the widespread dissemination of these. It is unlikely that this fact is lost on prevention program developers and evaluators.

We have little trouble in recognizing that there might be potential conflicts of interest when the sponsor of a research project is an obvious "bad guy," or at least an organized entity that does not have the advancement of public health as its primary goal. As noted above, one of the best examples of this is the pharmaceutical industry whose profit motive is seen to outweigh its commitment to disease eradication and health promotion. Two other examples from within the field of drug studies are the tobacco industry (Barnes & Bero, 1998; Malone & Bero, 2003) and the alcohol industry (Babor, Edwards & Stockwell, 1996). Here, as with the pharmaceutical industry, we tend to be highly suspicious not only of the industry's motives due to its desire to turn a profit but also of the findings of any investigator that accepts its funding. Concern is not so much with blatant "sell out" on the part of the investigator, but with more subtle influences that might be at play. For example, a recent case study of the relationship between the tobacco industry and the eminent researcher Ernst L. Wynder concluded that his views concerning the evidence on the adverse effects of passive smoking were consistent with his own research findings and could not be shown to be directly linked to the industry funding that he received (Fields & Chapman, 2003). However, commenting on this paper, Malone and Bero (2003) argue that one cannot rule out the less obvious effects that this relationship may have had on Wynder's research such as which questions to ask, which designs to use, which analysis to conduct, and how to interpret findings. Along similar lines, the editor of Addiction went so far as to withdraw from publication a paper by Elleman-Jensen (1991) that the journal had published ten years earlier on the grounds that its author failed to disclose a "working relationship" with the tobacco company Phillip Morris (Edwards, 2001). This despite the fact that there was no criticism of the paper's scientific worth or evidence to suggest that the research leading to the paper was funded by tobacco interests. Rather, the decision to withdraw the paper was made "strictly on the conflict of interest question" (Edwards, 2002, page 757). Edwards concluded that had the conflict been declared at the time of submission, the paper would have been rejected.[2]

Given the obvious financial interests of entities such as the tobacco industry, and the potential conflict of these with the goals of public health, it is not difficult to persuade consumers of research to be skeptical of studies that receive funding through these sources. However, what happens when the research sponsor is well-intentioned and has as one of its primary goals the advancement of the nation's health? Does this entirely preclude the possibility of conflict of interest? What happens, for example, if the sponsor wants to eliminate illicit drug use through, amongst other means, zero-tolerance school-based education and has spent billions of dollars in pursuit of this goal over the past two decades? And since these are tax payer dollars the sponsor is under some pressure to produce results (US General Accounting Office, 1997). Should we therefore be suspicious of any researcher who has received funding from this sponsor or whose university-based research program is primarily funded by it? For does he or she not also know – like the recipient of tobacco industry dollars – what the research sponsor would like to hear in the way of good news? And does he or she not also know that being the bearer of bad news (in the form of a set of findings that fail to reject the null hypothesis that Program X does not prevent drug use) might also jeopardize any future funding?

Objectivity and Independence in the Selection of Evidence-based Interventions

As should be clear from the above discussion, the drug use prevention field has embraced the idea of producing evidenced-based lists of intervention programs through consensus committee with an enthusiasm that is perhaps unprecedented in the arena of public policy. There has, however, been very little discussion of the potential problems with this approach, especially for the conduct of rigorous scientific evaluations.

But, as Feinstein (1988) observed, while establishing consensus may be necessary to satisfy political incentives (such as meeting the goals and objectives set by ONDCP) it has little to do with the practice of science. Indeed, he adds that in the most extreme manifestations of these procedures, consensus gives rise to a dogma that demands conformity and seeks to silence the dissent and debate through which a scientific discipline develops and evolves. In line with this, MacCoun (2005) notes that while collective decision-making may be well-suited for reducing random error, it is less well-suited to dealing with correction of individual bias and may actually serve an amplifying rather than an attenuating function.

In addition to these general concerns about the functioning of expert committees, there are two specific issues pertaining to the committees that have been convened in the drug use prevention field that are pertinent to the present discussion of conflict of interest.[3] First, researchers are often members of the expert panels that are convened by federal agencies to select evidence-based programs, and their programs end up being included on the lists that are produced. For example, the 15-person panel that produced the Safe, Disciplined and Drug-free Schools list included a number of practitioners and evaluators whose programs the Panel designated as exemplary (Saunders, 2002; US Department of Education Safe, Disciplined, and Drug-Free Schools Expert Panel, 2002, page iii). As noted above, the potential for bias in evaluation research increases with the number of roles that a single individual assumes in addition to that of researcher (Bachrach & Newcomer, 2002). In cases where program developers sit on expert panels there are at least three potentially conflicting roles being assumed by each individual – program developer, program evaluator, and official expert. If the developer also has a financial stake in the program, then there exists a fourth potential conflict.

Second, the federal government is both the financial sponsor of many of the programs designated as evidence-based on these lists and the guardian of the processes through which such status is conferred. For example, at least seven of the nine programs that appeared on the list of exemplary programs of the US Department of Education Safe, Disciplined, and Drug-Free Schools Expert Panel (2002) received funding from federal government agencies such as the Centers for Disease Control, NIDA, and National Institute on Mental Health. The two NIDA lists that have been produced also contain numerous programs funded by the federal government, including many that have received financial support from NIDA itself (National Institute on Drug Abuse, 1997; 2003).

In other areas in which these types of inter-relationship between product sponsor, researcher and review body exists – notably, in recommendations concerning drug efficacy that come from consensus committees sponsored by the pharmaceutical industry – questions concerning conflict of interest are legitimately raised (Freemantle & Maynard, 1994; Sheldon & Davey Smith, 1993; Smith, 1994). It is assumed that because the industry spends vast sums of money on the development of the product, it has a vested interest in the product being perceived as effective. Therefore, industry claims concerning the efficacy of the product, as well as the claims of those that it directly funds, must be viewed with caution, at the very least.

The few empirical assessments of the use of expert committees in the area of drug use prevention certainly give cause for concern. In an examination of two evaluations of school-based programs that appeared on the US Department of Education's list of nine "exemplary" programs, it was found that the preponderance of evidence reported in these studies showed that they had little or no effect on behavioral outcomes (Gorman, 2002). Also, both evaluations were methodologically flawed, especially in regard to recruitment and retention of participants. These findings suggest that the criteria used to designate programs exemplary (e.g., effect on a behavioral outcome, rigorous study design) were either poorly defined or not operationalized and applied properly by the committee members in the process of program selection. Similar concerns were raised by Gruner and colleagues (in press) in their review of five programs that appear on a number of recent best practice lists such as those of NIDA, CSAP, and the US Department of Education.

Conclusions

The foregoing discussion suggests that we should attend more seriously to issues pertaining to conflict of interest in the arena of drug use prevention research than we currently do. Indeed, this should be a legitimate area of academic inquiry, just as it is in research pertaining to the pharmaceutical, tobacco, and alcohol industries. We have seen that both in the conduct of evaluation research and program dissemination there are sufficient potential individual and institutional conflicts that we should not only assess these but also put structures in place that protect the integrity of the research that is conducted. It does not make sense to abandon the healthy skepticism we exhibit in other areas in which inter-relationships exist between program sponsors, developers, marketers and evaluators simply because the sponsor is a governmental agency and not a private company, or because the commodity that is produced and marketed is designed to achieve a laudable goal such as the reduction of drug use. Such skepticism serves not only science, but also the public good by ensuring that the interventions that we label as "exemplary," "model," and "evidence-based" truly warrant such designations.

Dennis M. Gorman, Ph.D., is a Professor in the Department of Epidemiology & Biostatistics at the Texas A&M Health Science Center School of Rural Public Health. He is currently a member of the editorial board of Substance Use and Misuse. His research interests include ecological studies of the relationship between alcohol availability and violence, evaluation of public policies to reduce alcohol- and drug-related problems, and the use and misuse of science in the evaluation of primary prevention programs. He has published over 50 articles in these areas. He received his doctorate in Medical Sociology from the University of Essex in 1988.

Acknowledgement

This work was funded by a grant from the Smith Richardson Foundation, Inc. The opinions expressed are those of the author and do not necessarily reflect those of the Foundation.

References

Bachrach, C. & Newcomer, S.F. (2002). Addressing bias in intervention research: summary of a workshop. *Journal of Adolescent Health, 31*: 311-321.

Babor, T.F., Edwards, G. & Stockwell, T. (1996). Science and the drinks industry: cause for concern. (Editorial). *Addiction, 91*: 5-9.

Barnes, D.E. & Bero, L.A. (1998). Why review articles on the health effects of passive smoking reach different conclusions. *Journal of the American Medical Association, 279*: 1566-1570.

Bekelman, J.E., Li, Y. & Gross, C.P. (2003). Scope and impact of financial conflicts of interest in biomedical research. *Journal of the American Medical Association, 289*: 454-465.

Bero, L.A. & Rennie, D. (1996). Influences on the quality of published drug studies. *International Journal of Technology Assessment in Health Care, 12*: 209-237.

Bero, L.A., Galbraith, A. & Rennie, D. (1994). Sponsored symposia on environmental tobacco smoke. *Journal of the American Medical Association, 271*: 612-617.

Biglan, A. & Taylor, T.K. (2000). Increasing the use of science to improve child-rearing. *Journal of Primary Prevention, 21*: 207-226.

Borman, G.D., Hewes, G.M., Overman, L.T. & Brown, S. (2003). Comprehensive school reform: a meta-analysis. *Review of Educational Research, 73*: 125-230.

Botvin, G.J. (1986). Substance abuse prevention research: Recent developments and future directions. *Journal of School Health, 56*: 369-374.

Botvin, G.J. (2000). Preventing drug abuse in schools: social and competence enhancement approaches targeting individual-level etiologic factors. *Addictive Behaviors, 25*: 887-897

Botvin, G.J., & Griffin, K.W. (2005). Prevention science, drug abuse prevention, and Life Skills Training: Comments on the state of the science. *Journal of Experimental Criminology, 1*: 63- 78.

Botvin, G.J., Baker, E., Dusenbury, L., Botvin, E.M. & Diaz, T. (1995). Long-term follow-up of a randomized drug abuse prevention trial in a white middle-class population. *Journal of the American Medical Association, 273*: 1106-1112.

Botvin, G.J., Griffin, K.W., Diaz, T. & Ifill-Williams, M. (2001). Preventing binge drinking during early adolescence: one- and two-year follow-up of a school-based preventive intervention. *Psychology of Addictive Behaviors, 15*: 360-365.

Brown, J.H. (2001). Youth, drugs, and resilience education. *Journal of Drug Education, 31*: 83-122.

Campbell, D.T. (1988). The experimenting society. In E.S. Overman (Ed.) *Methodology and Epistemology for Social Science: Selected Papers—Donald T. Campbell* (pp. 290-314). Chicago: University of Chicago Press.

Catalano, R. F., Haggerty, K. P., Oesterle, S., Fleming, C. B., & Hawkins, J. D. (2004). The importance of bonding to school for healthy development: Findings from the Social Development Research Group. *Journal of School Health, 74*: 252-261.

DeAngelis, C.D. (2000). Conflict of interest and the public trust. *Journal of the American Medical Association, 284*: 2237-2238.

D'Onofrio, C.N., Moskowitz J.M. & Braverman, M.T. (2002). Curtailing tobacco use among youth: evaluation of Project 4-Health. *Health Education & Behavior, 29*: 656-682.

Edwards, G. (2001). A paper which must be withdrawn from publication. (Editorial note). *Addiction, 96*: 1099.

Edwards, G. (2002). Addiction's decision to withdraw a published paper from citation on the grounds of undisclosed conflict of interest. *Addiction, 96*: 1099.

Elleman-Jensen, P. (1991). The social costs of smoking revisited. *Addiction, 86*: 957-966.

Ellickson, P.L. & Bell, R.M. (1990). Drug prevention in junior high: a multi-site longitudinal test. *Science, 247*: 1299-1305.

Fields, N. & Chapman, S. (2003). Chasing Ernst L. Wynder: 40 years of Philip Morris' efforts to influence a leading scientist. *Journal of Epidemiology & Community Health, 57*: 571-578.

Feinstein, A.R. (1988). Fraud, distortion, delusion, and consensus: the problems of human nature and natural deception in epidemiological science. *American Journal of Medicine, 84*: 475-478.

Freemantle, N. & Maynard, Al. (1994). Something rotten in the state of clinical and economic evaluations? (Editorial). *Health Economics, 3*: 63-67.

Gandhi, A.G., Murphy-Graham, E., Petrosino, A., Remignanti, S. & Weiss, C.H. (in press). The devil is in the details: examining the evidence for "proven" school-based drug abuse prevention programs. *Evaluation Review*.

Gerstein, D.R. & Green, L.W. (1993). *Preventing drug abuse: What do we know?* Washington, DC: National Academy Press.

Glantz, S.A. & Mandel, L.L. (2005). Since school-based tobacco prevention programs do not work, what should we do? (Editorial). *Journal of Adolescent Health, 36*: 157-159.

Gorman, D.M. (1996). Etiological theories and the primary prevention of drug use. *Journal of Drug Issues, 26*: 505-518.

Gorman, D.M. (1997). The failure of drug education. *The Public Interest, 129*: 50-60.

Gorman, D.M. (1998). The irrelevance of evidence in the development of school-based drug prevention policy, 1986-1996. *Evaluation Review, 22*: 118-146.

Gorman, D.M. (2002). Defining and operationalizing "research-based" prevention: a critique (with case studies) of the US Department of Education's Safe, Disciplined and Drug-Free Schools Exemplary Programs. *Evaluation and Program Planning, 25*: 295-302.

Gorman, D.M. (2003). The best of practices, the worst of practices: the making of science-based primary prevention programs. *Psychiatric Services, 54*: 1087-1089.

Gorman, D.M. (2005a). Drug and violence prevention: Rediscovering the critical rational dimension of evaluation research. *Journal of Experimental Criminology, 1*: 1-23.

Gorman, D.M. (2005b). Does measurement dependence explain the effects of the Life Skills Training Program on smoking outcomes? *Preventive Medicine, 40*: 479-487.

Gorman, D.M. (2005c). The centrality of critical rational reasoning in science: a response and further comments on the Life Skills Training program, the Seattle Social Development Project, and prevention studies. J*ournal of Experimental Criminology, 1*: 263-275.

Gotzsche, P.C. (1989). Methodology and overt and hidden bias in reports of 196 double-blind trials of nonsteroidal anti-inflammatory drugs in rheumatoid arthritis. *Controlled Clinical Trials, 10*: 31-56.

Greenberg, M. T. (2004). Current and future challenges in school-based prevention: the researcher perspective. *Prevention Science, 5*: 5-13.

Griffith, K.W., Botvin, G.J., Nichols, T.R. & Doyle, M.M. (2003). Effectiveness of a universal drug abuse prevention approach for youth at high risk for substance use initiation. *Preventive Medicine, 36*: 1-7.

Griffin, K.W., Botvin, G.J. & Nichols, T.R. (2004). Long-term follow-up effects of a school-based drug abuse prevention program on adolescent risky driving. *Prevention Science, 5*: 207-212.

Harrington, N.G., Giles, S.M., Hoyle, R.H., Feeney, G.J. & Yungbluth, S.C. (2001). Evaluation of the All Stars Character Education and Problem Behavior Prevention Program: effects on mediator and outcome variables for middle school students. *Health Education & Behavior, 28*: 533-546.

Hawkins, J.D. & Catalano, R.F. (2005). Doing prevention science: A response to D.M. Gorman and a brief history of the quasi-experimental study nested with the Seattle Social Development Project. *Journal of Experimental Criminology, 1*: 79-86.

Hawkins, J.D., Catalano, R.F., Kosterman, R., Abbott, R. & Hill, K.G. (1999). Preventing adolescent health-risk behaviors by strengthening protection during childhood. *Archives of Pediatric & Adolescent Medicine, 153*: 226-234.

Hawkins, J.D., Kosterman, R., Catalano, R.F., Hill, K.G. & Abbott, R.D. (2005). Promoting positive adult functioning through social development intervention in childhood: long-term effects from the Seattle Social Development Project. *Archives of Pediatric & Adolescent Medicine, 159:* 25-31.

Institute of Medicine (2002). *Integrity in Scientific Research: Creating an Environment that Promotes Responsible Conduct.* Washington, DC: National Academies Press.

Kaiser, J. (2003). Studies of gay men, prostitutes come under scrutiny. *Science, 300*: 403.

Kam, C.-M., Greenberg, M.T. & Kusche, C.A. (2004). Sustained effects of the PATHS curriculum on the social and psychological adjustment of children in special education. *Journal of Emotional & Behavioral Disorders, 12*: 66-78.

Kennedy, D. (2003). Research fraud and public policy. *Science, 300*: 393.

Klingemann, H. K.-H. (2001). Natural recovery from alcohol problems. In: Heather, N., Peters, T.J. & Stockwell T. (eds.). *International Handbook of Alcohol Dependence and Problems* (pages 357-374). New York: Wiley.

Levine, J., Gussow, J.D., Hastings, D. & Eccher, A. (2003). Authors' financial relationships with the food and beverage industry and their published positions on the fat substitute olestra. *American Journal of Public Health, 93*: 664-669.

Lexchin, J., Bero, L.A., Djulbegovic, B. & Clark, O. (2003). Parmaceutical industry sponsorship and research outcome and quality: systematic review. *British Medical Journal, 326*:1167-1176.

Lipsey, Mark W. 1995. What do we learn from 400 research studies on the effectiveness of treatment with juvenile delinquents? In: McGuire, J. (ed.) *What works? Reducing reoffending*. New York: Wiley.

Littell, J.H. (2006). The case for multisystemic therapy: Evidence or orthodoxy? *Children and Youth Services Review, 28*: 458-472.

MacCoun, R. (2005). Conflicts of interest in public policy. In: Moore, D.A., Cain, D.M., Loewenstein, G. & Bazerman, M. (eds.). *Conflicts of Interest: Challenges and Solutions in Business, Law, Medicine, and Public Policy* (pages 233-262). London: Cambridge University Press.

Malone, R.E. & Bero, L.A. (2003). Chasing the dollar: why scientists should decline tobacco industry funding. *Journal of Epidemiology & Community Health, 57*: 546-548.

Manski, C.F., Pepper, J.V. & Petrie, C.V. (2001). *Informing America's Policy on Illegal Drugs: What we don't know keeps hurting us*. Washington, DC: National Academy Press.

Merton, R.K. (1973). *The sociology of science*. Chicago: University of Chicago Press.

Moskowitz, J.M. (1993).Why reports of outcome evaluations are often biased or uninterpretable: examples from evaluations of drug abuse prevention programs. *Evaluation and Program Planning, 16*: 1-9.

National Institute on Drug Abuse (1997). *Preventing drug use among children and Adolescents: A Research-Based Guide*. Bethesda, MD: US Department of Health and Human Services.

National Institute on Drug Abuse (2003). *Preventing drug use among children and adolescents: A research-based guide for parents, educators, and community leaders (Second Edition)*. Bethesda, MD: US Department of Health and Human Services, .

Office of National Drug Control Policy (1999). *National Drug Control Strategy—Performance Measures of Effectiveness: Implementation and Findings*. Washington, DC: Executive Office of the President.

Office of National Drug Control Policy (2003). *National Drug Control Strategy: FY 2004 Budget Summary*. Washington, DC: Executive Office of the President.

Pedersen, K.M. & Christiansen, T. (2002). A fair hearing or academic kangaroo court? *Addiction, 97*: 227-229.

Peterson, A.V., Kealy, K.A., Mann, S.L., Marek, P.M. & Sarason, I.G. (2000). Hutchinson Smoking Prevention Project: long-term randomized trial in school-based tobacco use prevention—results on smoking. *Journal of the National Cancer Institute, 92*: 1979-1991.

Petrosino, A. (2003). Standards for evidence and evidence for standards: the case of school-based drug prevention. *Annals of the American Academy of Political & Social Science, 587*, 180-207.

Petrosino, A. & Soydan, H. (2005). The impact of program developers as evaluators on criminal recidivism: results from offender treatment meta-analyses. *Journal of Experimental Criminology, 1*: 435-450.

Rothman, K.J. (1993). Conflict of interest: the new McCarthyism in science. *Journal of the American Medical Association, 269*: 2782-2784

Saunders, D.J. (2002). Your tax dollars on drugs. *San Francisco Chronicle*, August 22nd.

Schinke, S., Brounstein, P. & Gardner, S. (2002). *Science-Based Prevention Programs and Principles, 2002*. Rockville, MD: Center for Substance Abuse Prevention, Substance Abuse and Mental Health Services Administration.

Sheldon, T.A. & Davey Smith, G. (1993). Consensus conferences as drug promotion. *The Lancet, 341*: 100-102.

Smith, R. (1994). Conflict of interest and the BMJ. (Editorial). *British Medical Journal, 308*, 4-5.

Sobell, M.B. & Sobell, L.C. (2005). Time to tear down the wall: comment on Dawson et al. *Addiction, 100*: 294-295.

Stelfox, H.T., Chua, G., O'Rouke, K. & Detsky, A.S. (1998). Conflict of interest in the debate over calcium-channel antagonists. *New England Journal of Medicine, 338*: 101-106.

Tobin, M.J. (2003). Conflict of interest and AJRCCM: restating policy and a new form to upload. *American Journal of Respiratory and Critical Care Medicine, 167*: 1161-1164.

US Department of Education Safe, Disciplined, and Drug-Free Schools Expert Panel (2002). *Exemplary and Promising Safe, Disciplined, and Drug-Free Schools Programs 2001*. Jessup, MD: US Department of Education.

U.S. General Accounting Office (1997). *Safe and Drug-Free Schools: Balancing Accountability and Local Flexibility*. Washington, DC: US General Accounting Office.

Glossary

adversarial system of evaluation: a system of discourse that assumes that one can selectively present data in a manner that is most sympathetic to one's favored position.

advocacy-oriented research: Research that has as its primary goal the promotion of a specific position or idea.

bias: systematic and deliberate distortion of the truth.

conflict of interest: set of conditions in which professional judgment concerning a primary interest might be influenced by a secondary interest.

deductive/falsification approach: developing testable hypotheses from theories and then subjecting these hypotheses to rigorous tests capable of falsifying them

evidence-based: policy or program that is based on sound scientific evidence.

expert committee: group of individuals assumed to be authorities in particular area that is convened for the purpose of producing some pronouncement on the state of knowledge or practice in that area.

financial conflict of interest: conflict that derives from the researcher or research sponsor having a financial interest in the product that is being evaluated in the research that he/she is conducting or sponsoring.

ideological conflict of interest: conflict that derive from the researcher's theoretical and conceptual belief systems not being subject to change on the basis of empirical evidence.

inductive/confirmationist approach: Developing general statements (theories) from disparate observations, and then "confirming" these statements on the basis of subsequent disparate observations.

irregular data analysis and presentation practices: practices that diverge from those that are used by scientists in an effort to subject hypotheses to rigorous tests of falsification.

program integrity: delivering and implementing an intervention program in a manner consistent with the design of the program.

research integrity: conducting research according the standards of rigorous scientific practice.

Notes

1. For an opposing opinion concerning conflict of interest statements see Rothman (1993). It should also be noted that some journals (such as *Prevention Science*) do require such disclosures; other journals in the field should follow this lead.
2. Citation of this case should not be taken as an endorsement of the decision of the Addiction editor. Pedersen and Christiansen (2002) raise a number of issues pertaining to the veracity of the accounts upon which the decision was made and the nature and extent of Elleman-Jensen's relationship with Phillip Morris. Since Elleman-Jensen is deceased and cannot provide his side of the story, and since the editorial decision appears to have been made unilaterally, there is some legitimate cause for concern with the process by which such a serious action was taken.
3. For a discussion of the types of criteria and selection procedures used in some of the main expert committees that have been used to select model drug use prevention programs see Gorman (2002; 2005a), Gandhi et al. (in press) and Petrosino (2003).

1-10 Drug Addiction and Responsibility for the Health Care of Drug Addicts

Tziporah Kasachkoff, Ph.D.

Abstract

Taking care of those who are in need of health care is something that we, as a society, feel ourselves committed to insofar as public funds make that possible. Is this commitment in any way qualified by the fact that a person's medical maladies are the result of that person having voluntarily embarked on activities whose deleterious consequences for health were known and appreciated by that person beforehand? Specifically, is society's obligation to provide health-care services to those who have addicted themselves to illicit drugs attenuated by the fact of that addiction? Some argue that it is, whereas others consider this position morally untenable. This essay explores the question of who is right on this matter and why.

Key Words: choice, fairness, justice, innocent victim, responsibility, sympathy, voluntary assumption of risk, voluntary victim

Because of the strain that medical afflictions such as AIDS, smoking-induced emphysema, alcoholism, and drug addiction have come to place on our health-care resources, it has been argued (at least in the popular press) that we as a society need not fund the health-care attention sought by those whose illness, disease, or other medical affliction results from their own voluntarily engaged-in high-risk activity.

This view found expression in the "Letters" section of Newsweek, written by a reader in response to a story the magazine had run on the strain that the spread of AIDS had placed both on our health care resources and on the sufferers themselves. She asks:

> *why AIDS stricken children or adults infected through non sexual contacts get sympathy while infected homosexuals and drug users don't. Isn't it obvious? When people engage in high-risk behavior they have to accept the consequences. If I play hopscotch on the freeway and get hit by a car, should I expect sympathy?*[1]

Although the correspondent claims that the "consequences" of high risk activity must be borne by the risk takers—consequences, we might assume, that are medical and financial—she calls into question the legitimacy of high risk takers expecting even our sympathy should they, as a result of their high-risk behavior, find themselves in medical need. (Perhaps as well, there is the suggestion of a connection between a legitimate lack of sympathy with those who suffer from self-induced misfortunes and the justified refusal of aid to those who suffer those misfortunes.)

Many issues are raised by these suggestions: whether those who become ill as a result of voluntarily engaging in dangerous activity have a right to sympathy, solicitude, care, some sort of social benefits, or the use of medical resources that are both scarce and supported by taxpayers' dollars; whether, even if there is no moral right to sympathy or care or resources or benefits on the part of those whose health care needs are brought about by their own activity, we as a society should nonetheless provide these things (or some of these things) to meet the needs of the ill regardless of how the illness has been brought about.

In this essay I shall focus on the following two questions:

(1) Whether, generally speaking, drug abuse is rightly viewed as falling within the category of high-risk activity that is voluntarily engaged in, and the considerations that might incline us to answer this question in one way rather than another; or

(2) Whether, in deciding who should receive publicly funded medical resources, we should take into account whether a person's misfortune has come about as a result of her being a "voluntary victim."

The category I shall dub "voluntary victims of illness" is meant to derive its normative significance from its contrast with a category of persons sometimes referred to as "innocent victims" of misfortune. People who bring misfortune on themselves, it is argued, fall outside the range of our moral obligation to care for others—or, at the very least, our duty of benevolence is, with respect to them, attenuated. Unlike the "innocent," these sufferers have brought about their own suffering. Having knowingly engaged in high-risk behavior, they are rightly asked to shoulder responsibility for the afflictions consequential to their conduct, afflictions that would have been avoided had it not been for that conduct.

The argument I shall focus on in this paper is less severe than it might be. It does not argue that we are wrong to fund those who fall into the "voluntary victims" category but rather that it is not wrong not to fund or care for them. Although we may extend to "voluntary victims" exactly what we might extend to others, anything that we do extend is only supererogatory; it is not morally mandated or required. (Of course, there might be those—indeed there are those—whose judgment is less lenient, that judgment being that we not only have the right but also the duty not to put society's resources at the service of those who have "made themselves" ill. Such a strong position might make reference to what is unfair with respect to others—say, asking others to pay costs that they have not themselves incurred[2]—or it might make reference to the social disutility of others' paying—and perhaps resenting paying—costs which, had the victims of illness been forced to pay themselves, might have served to deter their health-risking behavior in the first place.) Clearly, holders of the strong position that it is positively wrong to aid the voluntarily ill will find the weak view that it is not obligatory to aid the voluntarily ill true, but misleading. For if the weak view is true, it leaves open the possibility—which the strong view rejects—that reasons of charity or supererogation may justify coming to the aid of those whose disabilities have been brought about by their own voluntary activities.

The first thing to note about the category "voluntary victim" is its vagueness and potential breadth: it might be applied to all of those who become ill or incapacitated as a result of voluntarily embarking on activities, projects, or lives, knowing the detrimental consequences, or risks of detrimental consequences, to their health. It thus covers or seems to cover those who suffer the ill effects of the voluntary use of illicit drugs, of smoking, of a diet rich in animal fats, of caffeine consumption, of what has come to be called "unprotected" sex, of mountain climbing and jaywalking and—now that we know there is a connection between stress and heart disease—of voluntarily working in stress-related occupations (such as the military or certain levels of business).

Of course, some of these high-risk activities court more serious injury than others, and some (such as jaywalking) may be easily foregone, while others (such as mountain climbing or skiing for the sports enthusiast) may be avoided only at the cost of severe negative repercussions on other valuable facets of that person's life. Still others (such as some nicotine, caffeine, or drug-related behavior) may be linked to physiology or psychology to such an extent that the characterization of the behavior as "voluntary" can be made only with qualification. It appears, then, that the category "voluntary victims" is a grab bag label applied not only to those whose behavior may unambivalently be viewed as voluntary but also to those whose behavior may be taken as voluntary in some ways but not in others, and, as well, to those whose behavior could not, without qualms, be called voluntary at all.

The extraordinary variety of actions and behaviors at which the voluntary victims argument has been targeted reflects one or more of a number of failures—the failure to distinguish between different degrees and even kinds of voluntariness; the failure to acknowledge that the voluntariness with which one does something has to do with one's knowledge and understanding of the facts and risks involved in what one does and the extent of one's knowledge and understanding of these things; the failure to recognize that voluntariness has to do with whether one appreciates the significance of the information concerning the facts and risks for one's own particular life and future—say, how the scientific or statistical evidence might translate into possibilities for one's own future—as well as the degree to which one appreciates the significance of this information; the failure to recognize that determinations of voluntariness must consider whether desisting from dangerous activity is difficult to achieve, as well the extent of the difficulty; and the failure to appreciate that voluntariness has to do with whether there is a cost to changing one's habits or preferences, as well as the amount of that cost.

In this essay I shall focus on the "voluntary victims" argument as it is sometimes applied to those who come to be in need of medical attention on account of their addiction to illicit drugs. According to the "voluntary victims" argument, the lot of drug abusers, sad as we might see it, assumes its tragic proportions precisely because it is, so the argument goes, "self inflicted." When we have to decide how to allocate our limited resources, certainly this feature—that of self infliction or of voluntary assumption of risk—is germane to deciding where our responsibilities lie.

It seems plausible enough to regard people who engage in behaviors in which they are not forced to engage and who engage in these behaviors while knowing the associated risks, as people who voluntarily assume the risks associated with that behavior. After all, we are not talking here of the forced injection of illicit drugs, nor of children, nor of people who have been denied or have been unable to gain information that was publicly available, nor of those whose mental abilities have precluded or prevent their understanding either the notion of risk in general or the specific risks associated with the behavior in question. Rather, we are talking about the behavior of adults who intravenously inject illicit drugs, knowing both the risk (and sometimes the certainty) of addiction to the drug they inject and the consequences of addiction to that drug.

Still, the question of voluntariness remains. The argument to be made for the non-voluntariness of intravenously administering drugs and so of incurring the risks associated with that activity is, at least for those already addicted, fairly standard: there is physical as well as psychological dependency; there is urgency; withdrawal is difficult and, depending on the extent of the addiction, often literally sickening and sometimes even lethal. As well, in many countries that have laws prohibiting the use of certain drugs, and in some states in the United States, it is illegal not merely to buy the prohibited drug but also to purchase the syringes with which to inject them, and so the black market, at black market prices, must provide both the drugs and the syringe with which to inject the drugs.[3] For this reason, not only are the drugs expensive and scarce, but the syringes as well. Clearly, in this situation there is, for the addict, pressure to reuse syringes, sometimes to borrow them, and sometimes to lend them. Because of this, given the urgency of the situation, risky behavior continues despite knowledge of modes of transmissions, despite the knowledge that AIDS and other transferable diseases are prevalent, and despite knowledge of the consequences of contracting these diseases. Those working in the public health sector know that programs of risk reduction must proceed on the premise that (consistent with what has been found from efforts to control the spread of various sexually transmitted diseases) dissemination of factual information is not enough to effect a change in behavior.[4] There must be means available for changing the behavior that one knows is risky, and the means must not come at too high a cost. For most drug addicts, this means, at the least, cheap and easy access either to sterilizing bleach or to new sterile needles; unfortunately, needle cleaning apparatus and supplies are unrealistic for many who inhabit the world of drug dependency.

In recognition of both the connection between needle sharing and transmission of the HIV virus and other diseases from addict to addict, and of the difficulty that most addicts are likely to encounter in obtaining cheap and easily available sterile needles, campaigns have been introduced in various cities in Europe and in the United States to distribute new needles free of charge to the addict population, or to exchange their used needles for free new ones.[5] (Some of these campaigns have been less successful than expected for a variety of reasons, some of them political.)[6] But of significance is the finding that needle distribution programs often have an "internal" reason for failure: the sharing of drug injection equipment among IV-drug users reflects not merely the (rectifiable) economic scarcity of the equipment but, as well, the way that positive social relationships among users find expression. For example, "washes"—the small amount of drug left in the syringe after injection—are often offered by one addict to others in need of a fix as a way of establishing or expressing friendship and loyalty in an environment that often constitutes the sole benign social world for the addict.[7] As one sociologist working in the field has written:

> *The running-partner [a shooting buddy with whom an IV-drug user typically shoots up and engages in other "bonding activities"] relationship is the strongest positive relationship within the IV drug use subculture.... It would be considered a major insult to refuse to use one's partner's works [drug injecting paraphernalia] if one did not have works of his or her own readily available. Refusal to share one's own works so that the partner remained in a state of withdrawal would place a severe strain on the relationship. It would undermine*

> *the teamwork and synchronicity of intense experience that are the bases of the running buddy relationship.*[8]

> *Refusing to share a needle with someone whom one wanted to maintain a close personal relationship with... [is] considered very difficult or impossible. Refusal to share implies that one believes that the other person has and/or can transmit AIDS. Such an implication would severely strain a personal relationship among IV drug users, just as it would among members of conventional society.*[9]

> *The sharing of works for injecting drugs is thoroughly integrated into the IV drug subculture. It starts with initiation into injecting, as an important practical and symbolic part of the running partner relationship, and becomes a business in the shooting galleries, in which sharing of works extends to persons who may not know each other. The sharing of works symbolizes a wide range of positive relationships among IV drug users, from the romantic initiation, to the social bonding of running buddies, to the practical mutual advantages for a user and a gallery owner. Significant reductions in the sharing of needles may thus require fundamental changes throughout the culture.*[10]

Perhaps the author of these remarks overstates (and maybe even over romanticizes) the case, especially in light of a study of needle-sharing practices in New York City, the city with the largest drug addict population, half of whom are believed to be HIV-positive. That study indicates that of the interviewed addict population, only one in three admitted to sharing needles (though another 25 percent admitted renting or buying used needles). Six months into a (three year) free-needle exchange program, the number of addicts who admitted sharing needles had dropped ten percent.[11] Still, it is hard to deny the significance of epidemiologists' recognition that "each epidemic represents a particular blend of ecological circumstances and social responses that develop within highly specific economic, political and social contexts,"[12] and for this reason the high-risk behavior of addicts, both generally, and in connection to AIDS and other diseases, is not to be seen, and not to be described, as a simple act which is autonomous in relation to the surrounding social and cultural environment of the actor. Rather it is embedded within a (sub)culture characterizable by certain values, social roles, and rules for the allocation of status and standing.[13] In short, the behavior at issue in IV-drug use cannot easily be changed without considerable disruption that is both social and emotional. This makes sense of the otherwise surprising results of some psycho social studies conducted in New York City at the height of the AIDS epidemic there. What was found was that for persons who were both addicted to drugs and in the habit of sharing needles, sharing information about AIDS—about the illness itself and about its mode of transmission—had no significant effect on risky behavior. Not only did knowledge of both the deleterious consequences and the high risk of such consequences not produce much deterrent effect, neither did the sort of "knowing" often thought very important to behavior modification—namely, the knowing that comes through emotional engagement with those who have already become victims of suffering as a result of their dangerous drug-related activities. Indeed, even the knowledge often thought most important to motivating behavior change—namely, understanding how the experiences of others might relate to one's own possibilities, produced no significant change in behavior. What researchers found was that over 90 percent of those who did not change their behavior believed that they would eventually become infected with AIDS if they continued to do as they were doing. Indeed, of all the predictors of risk reduction behaviors in New York City among needle-sharing addicts, the best was whether or not one's buddies were believed to be changing their own behavior in response to the threat of AIDS. One might surmise from this that the addict's response to risk takes into account the responses of others who share like lives and like risks, like status and like stigma. In this way the addict affirms his behavior and his behavioral changes within what counts, for him or her, as the socially relevant group. This confirms what we know—that much drug-addicted behavior is interpersonal in nature, and therefore modification of that behavior not only affects, but is affected by, the social conditions within which the behavior takes place and against which it must be understood.

I'm not suggesting here that all assumption of risk on the part of every or even most intravenous drug users is completely non-voluntary, and that we must adopt a hard determinist line that holds that to explain a piece of behavior by reference to physical or social or psychological antecedents or conditions is to show that there were no alternatives open to the agent. Nor would I suggest that because behavior may not, in a given instance, be fully voluntary, it may not be voluntary enough.[14] My point is only to stress that the voluntariness of risky behavior on the part of an IV-drug user depends not only on whether the behavior is perceived by the particular drug user to be dangerous, but whether, in addition, avoiding the danger is, from the standpoint of that user's other, perhaps quite reasonable values, so costly that her desisting is an unreasonable expectation. Drug users vary—in their perceptions, their knowledge, the amount of control they have over their environment, the resources they have available for change, the cost of making use of those resources, and their view of the alternatives open to them were they to make use of the resources for change. Because of this—because intravenous drug-users are not a homogeneous group—we should not be tempted to assume, as application of the "voluntary victims" argument to them does, that their behavior—insofar as it results in drug-related ailments and afflictions—is, without further qualification, always and fairly to be characterized as voluntary.

Clearly, in order to say with confidence that someone's behavior, even someone's rather dangerous behavior, was voluntary, we need to know many things about her. We need to know not merely that there was access to generally available information about the disease and its mode and rate of transmission, but also that the agent did not extrapolate wrongly from these data to her own case; that the evidence was presented in a way that gave a clear indication of the dangers involved; that the risks involved were not only heard, but understood; and that they were not only understood but seen to be surmountable, and surmountable at costs that were not felt by the agent to be prohibitive.

But suppose it is conceded that the "voluntary victims" argument is sometimes misdirected toward behavior that may not be genuinely voluntary or, better put, not sufficiently voluntary to rise above some threshold of voluntariness relevant to the ascription of responsibility. (For all I have argued up to this point is that the argument is not always applied in ways that are consistent with its own principles.) If the argument is restricted to individuals whose behavior we know to be voluntary (or voluntary enough), can the category "voluntary victims" be used as the basis for picking out those who should be excluded from health care resources that are secured at public expense?

According to the argument, our obligation to provide health care resources or services is at least reduced (if not entirely dissolved) if the illness or disease was a foreseen or likely outcome of voluntary conduct. So it is the combined presence of voluntariness on the one hand and high-risk behavior on the other that is presented as grounding a negative moral judgment concerning our obligations toward persons who engage in behavior characterized by these features.

The argument has as its defined target all who voluntarily engage in behavior that is known to be high risk: mountain climbers, some intravenous drug takers, some smokers, some who overindulge in drinking and eating or in drinking and eating certain things, some who engage in unprotected sex, skiers, some in high-stress careers, and some Evel Knievels, to mention only a few. Of course, most of the voluntary high-risk behavior noted here is engaged in for reasons of pleasure or profit. But voluntary high-risk activities may be undertaken for reasons of morality, or even sometimes of health itself. The priest who visits the infectious sick to console them and the physician who attends the infectious ill in an effort to heal them, will be no less "voluntary victims" as defined by the "voluntary victims" argument, should they contract disease through their knowing and uncoerced professional contact, than are the patients who contract their diseases through social or personal or sexual contact. There is nothing to distinguish these cases in terms of the only two factors announced by the argument as determinative: (1) the foreseen risks, and (2) the voluntary actions that courted those risks. The category "voluntary victims" is meant to capture a combination of considerations that are morally relevant to distinguishing between those to whom we ought to provide health care attention and those to whom we need not, but its net is cast so wide that it enmeshes those who, despite their deliberate and knowing involvement, even precisely because of their deliberate and knowing involvement—the Mother Teresas and the Albert Schweitzers of the world come to mind here—not only deserve our medical (and sympathetic) attention, but ought to be special targets of these attentions.

Of course, those who use the voluntary victims argument against those whose plight is self-induced do not mean it to be used against those who in the course of doing good bring misfortune upon themselves. Those who assume risks in the course of benevolent projects are meant to be excluded from the application of the argument, but consistent with the principles of the argument they should not be. The argument is meant to support the not uncommon view that we are not morally obligated to make good the loss incurred by individuals in the course of their voluntary but risky pursuit of their pleasures, but applied consistently, it justifies not coming to the aid of those who, with like knowledge and voluntariness, suffer losses as a result of risks they take in the course of noble, sometimes even self sacrificial, pursuits. Consistently applied, the "voluntary victims" argument will judge harshly any agent who suffers as a result not only of his misdeeds but even of his good deeds—so long as there is nothing to distinguish between the doings of these different kinds of deeds in terms either of their known risk or the voluntariness with which these risks have been assumed.

But notwithstanding this requirement of consistency, we will not find anyone appealing to the category "voluntary victim" in relation to a Mother Teresa who becomes ill as a result of ministering to the sick. And this suggests that the argument is actually working in reverse of its declared direction: rather than its using the voluntary assumption of risk as the ground for arriving at a moral judgment about specific behaviors (or about the agents of specific behaviors) and therefore about how we should respond to them, the argument uses a prior moral judgment about the agent and about the response to him or her that is morally appropriate, and this becomes the basis for the attribution of voluntariness. This explains the "voluntary victims" argument's selectivity—its targeting of those whose behavior is not merely risky but counter to socially sanctioned norms—IV-drug users, for example, who are often considered by conventional society as "objects of fear, mistrust, hostility, scorn, and to a limited extent, pity;"[15] homosexuals, who are not uncommonly objects of derision and fear, and who, among segments of conventional society are regarded, on account of their sexual activity, as sinners whose health-related sufferings are divine and merited punishment; over-indulgers in food and wine; and, of late, smokers.

The type of reasoning we find in the "voluntary victims" argument—that of attributing to an agent a particular intentional or volitional relation to the foreseen consequences of her act on the basis of a prior moral judgment concerning her responsibility for those consequences—is not exclusive to that argument.[16] But though this type of reasoning is neither original with nor unique to the "voluntary victims" argument, its use in the "voluntary victims" argument has often been offensive in a way that it isn't elsewhere (which is not to say that, as found in the law, it is not confusing or even wrongheaded).[17] The reason for its offensiveness in the voluntary victims argument is that, first, the moral judgments appealed to by the argument are smuggled into, rather than declared by, the argument. The argument does not, after all, announce its judgments or spell them out; we realize them only by seeing how the argument is applied, and by coming to appreciate the moral significance of the argument's selective application. Second, the judgments on which the argument relies are often those about which there is great contention. And, finally, the use to which the argument puts the judgments it makes is itself highly contentious.

But suppose we were to make explicit the moral judgments on the basis of which voluntary victims are identified, and suppose, too, that we restrict the argument's application to those "victims" about whom (or about whose activities) we can come to moral agreement. How, then, shall we assess the argument that we have no (or, at the most, reduced) obligation to provide—with publicly-funded but limited health care resources—for those whose suffering has come about as a result of their own voluntary doing when that doing is not merely harmful to the agent but subject to explicit and legitimate moral disapproval? Should our duties of care for sufferers be mediated by our assessment of the morality of the harmful act that has resulted in their misfortune?

The first thing to notice is that the question raised here presumes that, generally, we have some moral obligation to provide for those in need of medical help. Were we not to accept this, the "voluntary victims" argument for diminished responsibilities to those whose suffering results from voluntary but morally disapproved of behavior would be redundant. The question raised, then, is whether, within the context of a general moral obligation to provide health care resources to the needy, the fact that one's needs have been brought about by one's own voluntary and morally objectionable behavior, justifies withholding resources necessary to meet those needs.

Various arguments might be offered to support a positive answer to this question and so to an affirmation of the legitimacy of the "voluntary victims" argument. Let me suggest what these might be:

(1) Insofar as we are dealing with social or public policy, it is straightforwardly utilitarian justified not to extend medical resources to sufferers whose misfortune has been brought about by behavior that we as a society wish, and have good moral reason for wishing, to deter. While the specific behaviors that we are morally justified in discouraging are, of course, open for discussion—and no doubt will be the focus of contention—once we as a society have decided on those behaviors which are to be discouraged, social policies with respect to those behaviors—and with respect to those whose voluntary participation in those behaviors has resulted in the need for publicly-financed medical attention—ought to reflect that decision. Since negative societal attitudes, especially as expressed through social policies, operate as deterrents to behavior, insofar as society is justified in discouraging those behaviors, it is also justified in taking measures that are necessary to effect that end.[18] Our general moral obligation to provide assistance to the medically needy is thus overridden in those cases in which honoring that obligation would be counterproductive to the legitimate interest we have in discouraging the voluntary and immoral behavior that produced the need for medical assistance.

(2) Insofar as social concern gets expressed through publicly-funded care, society has the right to express its disapproval of moral wrongdoing by directing its resources elsewhere. The issue here is not deterrence (though a deterrent effect may well be produced along the way). Rather, the point is that recognizing a diminished duty of care toward those who injure themselves in the course of doing wrong may be justified by its expressive function: this is the way society's moral condemnation finds public articulation. On the other hand, caring for those who have injured themselves in the course of doing good symbolizes moral validation, and expresses solidarity with those pursuits and with those persons. This is why the "voluntary victims" argument has no application to the world's Mother Teresas and Albert Schweitzers. It has no application there because it has no point there.

(3) Our obligation to attend to the health-care needs of others must be sensitive to considerations of fairness in distributing the—necessarily limited— resources that we must draw on to attend to those needs. These considerations speak against our regarding those whose needs have been generated by immoral and high-risk behavior as having the same right as others to the resources that must be divided among them. Specifically, those who have voluntarily sacrificed their health in the interests of immoral pursuits have thereby surrendered their rights to draw on limited and publicly-funded resources that might instead be made available to others of like need but of different history. Fairness dictates that high-risk and seriously morally defective behavior counts decisively against the right to public and scarce resources (which still leaves open the possibility that despite the absence of a right on the part of the recipient—and so of an obligation on society's part with respect to her—society might nonetheless decide to provide, where it can, for everyone in need regardless of the history of those needs).

Let us examine each of these arguments:

(1) The first maintains that, when society has a morally justified interest in discouraging high-risk and immoral behavior, furtherance of that interest may override

our general obligation to aid the medically needy should that behavior generate health impairments that put the agent in medical need. When discouraging immoral and dangerous behavior is of greater value than meeting our general obligation of medical care, then we have support, in the form of utilitarian considerations, for the "voluntary victims" argument.

These utilitarian considerations do not, however, establish the legitimacy of the "voluntary victims" argument. For even were we to agree both that some behaviors are morally undesirable and that some behaviors are so undesirable that they should be deterred, the utilitarian argument as outlined begs the question at issue. It is one thing to say that social policies restricting health-care resources ought to be made an instrument of social deterrence when the value of that deterrence demands it; it is another thing to state the conditions under which the value of social deterrence does demand it and thus to specify under what conditions society is justified in withholding its medical resources for the purpose of achieving that deterrence. What we want is the second but what is offered is only the first, namely, the pleonasm that when deterrence morally outweighs the value of caring for those in medical need, our moral obligation to provide that care is overridden by that interest. But of course this claim does nothing to help us to discern the conditions under which society's legitimate interest in deterring seriously socially undesirable behaviors does outweigh its obligation to make available its health-care resources to those who are in medical need.

But there are further difficulties with the utilitarian support offered in defense of the "voluntary victims" argument. The claim that the importance of deterring certain immoral behaviors may outweigh our obligation to provide medical care for the agents of those behaviors comes perilously close to the claim that if society is justified in discouraging certain behaviors it is also justified in taking any measures that will effect that end. And this latter claim is surely false. Given the value we place on health and the value we place on those things the pursuit of which requires health, withholding medical resources as a means of social control—even over extremely offensive conduct and even over conduct that should be controlled—strikes us as especially heartless. Because of this, in order for considerations of deterrence to outweigh our obligation to the medically needy those considerations would have to assume an importance that we, as a liberal society, do not generally give it. Indeed, given the value we place on access to health care, the deterrence of socially undesirable behavior by means of measures that will inevitably (if not by design) negatively affect a person's medical welfare, can find sanction only if deterrence of undesirable behavior comes to be viewed as having paramount importance.

Furthermore, the claim that society's legitimate interest in deterring certain behaviors may justify withholding medical resources from those whose behavior has resulted in the need for those resources provides no rationale for limiting, in the interests of deterrence, the withholding of resources from those whose behavior has been both risky and morally objectionable. Behavior that is sufficiently socially objectionable to warrant deterrence is not limited to conduct that is morally objectionable. Nor is it limited to behavior that is objectionable on the ground that it recklessly courts a high risk of deleterious consequences. So our choosing to regard the withholding of health-care resources as a justifiable vehicle of social control opens the door for a far more extensive—and correspondingly less legitimate—political use of health care services than intended even by promoters of the "voluntary victims" argument. This is a danger that has to be taken into account by those who might wish to craft social policies of deterrence using access to medical resources as means.

(2) The suggestion that society has a right to express its disapproval of certain behaviors through, among other things, the social policies it institutes, is, I believe, well taken. But the question here, analogous to the question raised above, is whether social policies detrimental to another person's health may justifiably be used to give expression to social values even when the values themselves are not in dispute, and even when there is moral justification—perhaps even a moral mandate—for these values to find public expression. To claim that health care resources may justifiably be withheld only when doing so will convey a sufficiently important moral message concerning the behavior that has created the need for those resources leaves unanswered the question that this answer begs: when is the moral message of society so important that its expression through health care restrictions is morally permissible?

Moreover, we should realize that the values we intend to convey through the adoption of particular policies are not the sole values that will find public expression through those policies. Our choosing to express moral disapproval through the withdrawal of healthcare resources will carry its own moral message—not merely with regard to the disapproved of behavior but with regard to the character of a society that chooses to express its condemnation in this way. In liberal societies, use of health care categories and health care resources for the express purpose of delivering moral messages has never found justification: however morally important these messages may be and however important may be their public affirmation, access to necessary health care is too fundamental to the well-being and functioning of persons to assign it this political role.

(3) The third argument is primarily about fairness and desert. On this account, the "voluntary victims" argument attempts to make distribution of health-care resources more just rather than more efficient. Since our resources are limited, so must access be, and it is only fair to deny access to those who make themselves less deserving recipients. The "voluntary victims" argument provides a criterion for desert by taking into account the history of how the medically needy have come to be that way.

There is, I believe, something to be said for this last consideration. That a person did not have to be in the unfortunate state she finds herself in, that she knowingly and voluntarily took on certain risks she need not have, and took on those risks in the course of morally disapproved of pursuits, speaks against providing her with resources that otherwise could be placed in the service of those whose medical disabilities were not self-induced, could not have been avoided, and were incurred in the course of activities that did not impose on others. Although it may not be true—and perhaps even be callous—to say that the suffering of voluntary victims is a case of their "getting what they deserve," it may still be true that voluntary victims= entitlements to society's limited health-care resources are not to be derived solely from the fact of their medical needs.[19] For, one might argue, the history of one's medical misfortune determines what constitutes a fair, publicly funded, response.

Viewed in this way, the "voluntary victims" argument may seem a reasonable argument from fairness: in voluntarily engaging in high-risk activities, risks which cannot be justified by appeal to the moral worth of the activities themselves, those unfortunates who suffer as a result of risks they have taken cannot now make a claim upon the sacrifice of others in dealing with their misfortune. (Indeed, the argument may not only be fair enough, it may even be kind enough, for "voluntary victims'" lack of a rightful claim to limited medical resources means only that we have no strict obligation to provide for their needs. It does not mean that we should not out of kindness or decency provide, where we can, resources that cannot be claimed as a right.)

But the fairness argument may encounter the following objection: since we are all taxpayers and so all contributors to the public purse, and since in addition, none of us engages in behavior that is completely free of risk, we can all be presumed to tacitly accept that, collectively, we will bear the burden of the risks that others assume. While some may jeopardize their health by mountain climbing and skiing, others will assume less obvious but perhaps no-less-costly risks associated with the voluntary choice of a sedentary life. In the end, the contribution of each will be matched by the varying demands of each. It is unfair to single out some voluntary risk takers as entitled to health care and others as not.

This answer to the "voluntary victims" argument, though not sound, points to an important feature which the voluntary victims argument, construed as an argument from fairness, must address: the degree of risk that various activities have and therefore the varying reasonableness of their public subsidization. The claim that since all activities have some element of risk, it is unjust to target some but not others is unsound because it assumes that all behaviors court the same (or approximately the same) level of risk, a level which it is reasonable for us, as a society, to subsidize. But this is false. Although what constitutes reasonableness when it comes to risk is certainly culturally determined, it is still true that we do not all engage in activities which court the same level of risk, and society has the right to decide on a threshold level of risk beyond which it may decide that demands on the public purse are no longer reasonable demands.

But if the voluntary victims argument is a reasonable one, why does the Newsweek correspondent's remarks seem so mean-spirited, small, and perhaps even ruthless? I suggest that it is because, as stated by the correspondent (and as usually heard), the argument, construed as an argument from fairness, falls short of the mark not merely of generosity but of fairness itself. Although it takes into account one matter relevant to just treatment, namely, whether a person has (or has not) done something that may abrogate what might otherwise be her entitlements, it fails to be sensitive to other issues that must figure in the determination of a fair response.

First, it fails to consider the extent to which a person's suffering may be disproportionate to the significance of the act that brought it about. When the Newsweek correspondent asks "If I play hopscotch on the freeway and get hit by a car, should I expect sympathy?" she means to be giving a well directed instance of the "voluntary victims" argument. But given the terrible suffering in which such accidents generally issue, any suggestion that the heedless hopscotch sufferer should not receive the medical resources necessary to help her serves as a reductio ad absurdum. Although fairness may support diminished entitlements for those who have voluntarily assumed the risk of becoming victims and assumed that risk in the course of activities that do not morally redeem them, it also demands that we invoke some criterion of proportionality between the risks taken and the extent of the suffering that ensues. We may not balk at someone saying that Jones, who went out in the cold without a sweater, got what he deserved when he comes down with the sniffles, but if he ends up suffering from a life threatening case of pneumonia, his misfortune, relative to his carelessness, is sufficiently severe to render this judgment heartless.

Second, in its focus on three features of behavior as jointly sufficient for triggering a negative decision regarding the deployment of medical resources—voluntariness, dangerousness, and lack of worthwhile contribution—the "voluntary victims" argument offers a criterion for the distribution of health-care resources that appears to be independent of a presumption of scarcity. Without this presumption, application of the "voluntary victims" criterion may still be grounded in a principle of fairness, but the use of that principle will be quite different. In the case of scarcity, the principle is employed to restrict distribution of resources to some when those resources are necessary to improve the lot of those who—on this criterion—are more deserving. But in circumstances of unlimited resources or, more plausibly, in circumstances in which the costs of helping are sufficiently insignificant (say, in circumstances in which all that is needed is a dose of low cost penicillin) appeal to the "voluntary victims" argument as an appeal to a principle of fairness plays quite a different role. Here the argument is not that the resources made available to "voluntary victims" unfairly jeopardizes the stock of resources available to others who are more deserving. It is, rather, that, regardless of the bounty of our resources, it is unjust for us to be made to pay the bill for others' voluntary risk taking, especially when those risks have been assumed in the course of activities deemed morally repugnant or foolish. Simply put, it is unjust to sanction others taking what we regard as unacceptable risks at our expense. Here the appeal is to a principle of justice that figures in a larger, libertarian, account of the requirements of social justice and to that extent, it is an argument from justice that, relative to the "voluntary victims" argument more narrowly conceived, invites considerably more contention.

Let me conclude by noting a consideration, not touched upon above, that suggests that employment of the "voluntary victims" argument in the setting of health-care policy may be more problematic—both morally and politically—than might first appear. Given that the "voluntary victims" argument relies on a distinction between those who have behaved voluntarily and those who have not, health care policy that relies on this argument will necessarily saddle health-care officials with making judgments that are generally not possible and where possible, in many cases not desirable. Judicious assessments of voluntariness typically involve knowledge of the kinds of things that health care policy makers are in neither a position to know nor, in a free society, ought to be especially privy to. Voluntariness is not easy to discern in matters such as those we have been discussing and leaving that discernment to officials whose duty it is to implement health-care policies that will affect the welfare and well-being of those in need of healthcare services is a move in the wrong direction.

Tziporah Kasachkoff, Ph.D. (USA) is currently Professor of Philosophy at Ben Gurion University of the Negev in Be'er Sheva, Israel, where she teaches courses in theoretical and applied ethics, and political and social philosophy. She has been associated for more than 30 years with the City University of New York, where she has taught students at two ends of the educational spectrum: at the Borough of Manhattan Community College, where students begin their college career, and at the

Graduate Center, where students take courses for their Masters and Doctorate degrees in Philosophy. Professor Kasachkoff is editor of the American Philosophical Association's Newsletter on Teaching Philosophy, has edited a collection of essays on the teaching of philosophy entitled In the Socratic Tradition: Essays on Teaching Philosophy, Rowman & Littlefield, 1998, and is now completing a revised version of that collection which will be published under the title Teaching Philosophy: Theoretical Reflections & Practical Solutions (Rowman & Littlefield, 2004). She is also the editor with Steven Cahn of Morality and Public Policy (Prentice-Hall, 2002) and the author of numerous articles on ethics, social policy, and ethics issues in health care. One of Professor Kasachkoff's chief professional interests is in the teaching of philosophy and the teaching of the teaching of philosophy. In 2000, she was the recipient of the American Association of Philosophy Teachers Award of Merit for Outstanding Leadership and Achievements in the Teaching of Philosophy.

References

Agar, M. H.. *Ripping and Running: A Formal Ethnography of Urban Heroin Addicts*, New York: Seminar Press, 1973 and Coombs, R.H., L.J. Fry, and P.G. Lewis, (eds.) Socialization in Drug Abuse Cambridge, England: Schenkman, 1976

Baum, A., and Nisselof, S.E.A. "Psychological Research and the Prevention, Etiology, and Treatment of AIDS," *American Psychologist*, November, 1988, vol. 43: 900-906.

Brandt, Allan M., No Magic Bullet: A Social History of Venereal Disease in the United States Since 1880, (New York: Oxford University Press, 1987.

Breslow, L. *Review of the Public Health Services' Response to Smoking*, U.S. Congress Office of Technology Assessment, 1982, pp. 146 148.

Feinberg, Joel. *Harm to Self, The Moral Limits of the Criminal Law*, New York: Oxford University Press, 1986, Vol . III, chs. 20, 21, and 23.

Finnis, John. "Intention and Side Effects" in *Liability and Responsibility: Essays in Law and Morals*, eds., R.G. Frey and Christopher W. Morris, (New York: Cambridge University Press, 1991), pgs. 32 61.

Goodin, Robert. *No Smoking: The Ethical Issues* (Chicago, Ill: Chicago University Press, 1989), p. 28.

Jarlais, Don C., Friedman, Samuel R., and Strug, David. "AIDS and Needle Sharing within the IV Drug Use Subculture," *The Social Dimension of AIDS: Method and Theory,* eds., Douglas A. Feldman and Thomas M. Johnson, (New York, Westport, Conn., and London: Praeger Press, 1986), p. 116.

Letters to the Editor, *Newsweek*, November 18, 1991.

Mireya Navarro, Mireya . "New York Needle Exchanges Called Surprisingly Effective," *New York Times*, February 18, 1993, pp. A1, B4.

"Needle Nostrum?" *U.S. News & World Report 104*:14 June 20, 1988;

"Realism on AIDS," *The Nation, 246*:181, February 13, 1988.

Riese, Guenter B. See "Epidemics and History: Ecological Perspectives and Social Responses," *AIDS: The Burdens of History*, ed., Elizabeth Fee and Daniel M. Fox, (Berkeley: University of California Press: 1988), pp. 33-66.

Smith, A. D. "Britain Tries Needle Exchange," *World Press Review 35*:31 2 June, 1988; "Experiment Worth Trying," *Commonweal 115*:645, December 2, 1988

Williams, Glanville. *The Sanctity of Life and the Criminal Law*, London: Faber & Faber, 1958, p. 286.

Glossary

hard determinist (sometimes called "incompatibilist"): someone who holds the view that (1) freedom and determinism are incompatible (a causally determined event is one that cannot but have occurred), (2) every human event is determined by antecedent conditions, and, therefore, (3) no human action is free.

reductio ad absurdum: the refutation of a claim by showing that its acceptance leads to an absurdity.

utilitarian: someone who holds the ethical position that actions (policies, regulations, laws, etc.) are morally justified insofar as those actions (etc.) lead to a greater amount of happiness for a greater number of people than plausible alternatives.

Notes

1. Letters to the Editor, *Newsweek*, November 18, 1991.
2. In the United States, for example, 40% of the costs of treating smoking-induced illness are borne by the public. (L. Breslow, *Review of the Public Health Services' Response to Smoking*, U.S. Congress Office of Technology Assessment, 1982, pp. 146 148; Robert Goodin, *No Smoking: The Ethical Issues*, Chicago, Ill: Chicago University Press, 1989, p. 28.)
3. In the United States, most states do not criminalize the possession or use of syringe needles without a prescription. New York used to criminalize it, but no longer does. See Mireya Navarro, "New York Needle Exchanges Called Surprisingly Effective," *New York Times*, February 18, 1993, pp. A1, B4.
4. Historically, efforts to combat sexually transmitted diseases through apprising potential victims of the facts, risks, and prevalence of the disease have generally proven unsuccessful. See Allan M. Brandt, *No Magic Bullet: A Social History of Venereal Disease in the United States Since 1880*, New York: Oxford University Press, 1987.
5. A. D. Smith, "Britain tries needle exchange," *World Press Review 35*:31–2 (June, 1988); "Experiment Worth Trying," *Commonweal 115*:645 (December 2, 1988); "Needle Nostrum?" *U.S. News & World Report 104*:14 (June 20, 1988); "Realism on AIDS", *The Nation, 246*:181 (February 13, 1988). See also Mireya Navarro, "New York Needle Exchanges Called Surprisingly Effective."
6. Influential religious, political and ethnic leaders have often gone on record as opposing such programs for a variety of reasons, chief among them being their not wanting "to send the wrong message" to drug addicts. The argument is that distribution by a government agency of free sterile needles to be used for intravenous drug injection serves to undermine the law which makes the selling and buying of street drugs illegal. Others have objected that clean needle distribution programs "lead to the notion that we have a permanent disability of addiction that is intractable, and that is a shame" (Mitchell S. Rosenthal, president of Phoenix House, a drug rehabilitation center in New York City, as quoted in Mireya Navarro, "New York Needle Exchanges Called Surprisingly Effective."

7. See A. Baum and S.E.A. Nisselof, "Psychological Research and the Prevention, Etiology, and Treatment of AIDS," *American Psychologist*, November, 1988, vol. 43: 900-906.
8. Don C. Jarlais, Samuel R. Friedman, and David Strug, "AIDS and Needle Sharing within the IV Drug Use Subculture," *The Social Dimension of AIDS: Method and Theory*, ed. Douglas A. Feldman and Thomas M. Johnson, Westport, CT and London: Praeger Press, 1986, p. 116.
9. Don C. Jarlais, Samuel R. Friedman, and David Strug, "AIDS and Needle Sharing within the IV Drug Use Subculture," p. 121.
10. Don C. Jarlais, Samuel R. Friedman, and David Strug, "AIDS and Needle Sharing within the IV Drug Use Subculture," pp. 119-120.
11. See Mireya Navarro, "New York Needle Exchanges Called Surprisingly Effective."
12. See Guenter B. Riese, "Epidemics and History: Ecological Perspectives and Social Responses," *AIDS: The Burdens of History*, ed. Elizabeth Fee and Daniel M. Fox, Berkeley: University of California Press, 1988, pp. 33-66.
13. The term "subculture" is widely used within sociological writings on IV drug use to describe the social network found among IV drug users. See, for example, Don C. Jarlais, Samuel R. Friedman, and David Strug, "AIDS and Needle Sharing within the IV Drug Use Subculture;" also M.H. Agar, *Ripping and Running: A Formal Ethnography of Urban Heroin Addicts*, New York: Seminar Press, 1973 and R.H. Coombs, L.J. Fry, and P.G. Lewis, (ed.) *Socialization in Drug Abuse*, Cambridge, UK: Schenkman, 1976.
14. For useful discussion of the notion of the standards of voluntariness, see Joel Feinberg, *Harm to Self, The Moral Limits of the Criminal Law*, New York: Oxford University Press, 1986, Vol III, chs. 20, 21, and 23.
15. Don C. Jarlais, Samuel R. Friedman, and David Strug, "AIDS and Needle Sharing within the IV Drug Use Subculture," p. 113.
16. See, for example, Glanville Williams, *The Sanctity of Life and the Criminal Law*, London: Faber & Faber, 1958, p. 286.
17. For a good discussion of this issue, see John Finnis, "Intention and Side-Effects." in *Liability and Responsibility: Essays in Law and Morals*, eds. R.G. Frey and Christopher W. Morris, New York: Cambridge University Press, 1991, pp. 32-61.
18. I am grateful to Dahlia Dehri for this point, and as well for discussion of the paper generally.
19. I speak of "*entitlements*" here rather than "*desert*" because it is not clear that fairness in the distribution of health care resources is fundamentally a question of moral merit. As I see it, the question before us is whether it is fair to demand that society draw on the public purse to subsidize the unfortunate fallout from freely chosen and dangerous pursuits. One may answer this question of fairness without appealing to the notions of moral merit and desert.)

1-11 Ethical Issues in Drug User Treatment Research

Kenneth D. Pimple, Ph.D.[1]

Abstract

Drug user treatment research should be guided by (a) the basic ethical considerations that prevail in all forms of scientific research, including honesty and candor; assigning proper authorship credit; and refraining from intimate or harassing behavior toward research subjects; and (b) ethical principles specific to research using human subjects enumerated in the Belmont Report as respect for persons, beneficence (and non-maleficence), and justice. An additional principle not explicitly mentioned in the Belmont Report but gaining wide acceptance is inclusion, or access to treatments. Researchers are morally (and in some cases legally) bound to adhere to these principles, and the drug user treatment research community as a whole has an obligation to do its best to shape the research agenda and social policy according to these principles.

Key Words: research ethics, human subjects research, authorship, Belmont Report, respect for persons, informed consent, beneficence, non-maleficience, risk-benefit analysis, justice, well-being, inclusion

1. Introduction

In this paper I examine ethical issues in drug user treatment research primarily through the prism of the fundamental and broad ethical principles elucidated in the Belmont Report. These three principles—respect for persons, beneficence, and justice—have informed and shaped policies and regulations governing human subjects research in the United States since the 1980s, and I will refer to them as the Belmont principles.

I believe that the Belmont principles are well-conceived, nearly comprehensive, and probably valid in any cultural setting (note the descending degree of certainty).

1. It seems clear that anyone wanting to argue that the Belmont principles are ill-conceived would bear the burden of proof.
2. That the principles are nearly comprehensive can be defended with the observations that, as far as I am aware, only one or perhaps two other principles with broad application (non-maleficence and inclusion) have been adduced. I count these as "one or perhaps two" because it can be plausibly argued that non-maleficence is implied by beneficence (Section 3.3), particularly in the context in which beneficence is described in the Belmont Report; thus whether non-maleficence should be considered a separate principle is a matter of interpretation. Furthermore, it could be argued that justice (Section 3.4) implies the principle of inclusion (Section 3.5), though clearly this implication is weaker than the implication of non-maleficence.

3. The cross-cultural validity of the Belmont principles, which I endorse only tentatively, may be a weak point of my discussion in this paper because if there are countries in which one or more of the Belmont principles are not valid, this essay will have limited application in those places. Even so, it may be useful as a point of contrast, and should be informative.

My goals are dual: To introduce relevant basic tenets of research ethics and to apply them in a practical manner to the topic of drug user treatment research. Keeping my discussion practical will maximize its relevance to some researchers while limiting its relevance to others (the latter being, I should think, a smaller group). My knowledge of drug treatment research is very thin, and my understanding of the contexts in which such research takes place is no better than that of an educated and moderately well-informed American layman. In countries where the cultural, social, medical, political, and legal contexts differ from those of the United States, some of the points I raise will likely be irrelevant and others bewildering. Furthermore, there will no doubt be important issues for these other contexts upon which I will not touch. For these shortcomings I apologize, and offer as expiation only that they result not from chauvinism but from ignorance.

I begin by briefly discussing relevant aspects of research ethics that apply generally, not just to the subset of research that involves human subjects. Then I cover the Belmont principles and the above-mentioned refinements. I conclude with a few words about the responsibility of the community of drug user treatment researchers in creating and sustaining an ethically sound program of research. Throughout, I draw on relevant codes of conduct in drug user treatment and drug user treatment research.[2]

2. General research ethics

The most fundamental principle of research ethics is easily stated: Be honest and candid. Being honest means reporting your findings as accurately and clearly as you are able; it also means refraining from falsifying or fabricating data or reports. Being candid means going beyond merely telling the truth to telling as much of the truth as is relevant. This means reporting doubts, exceptions, blind alleys, negative results, and so forth, whenever doing so would generally be helpful and whenever failing to do so would be harmful.

This is easily stated but can be difficult to implement. Even researchers who intend to be honest might find themselves wondering exactly how much has to be reported and what can be left unsaid without also being dishonest. Limited journal space may make candor difficult. Nevertheless, without honesty, science is crippled, and every researcher should make every effort to overcome all obstacles to honesty and candor.

The various codes of ethics specifically covering drug user treatment research do not have much to say about the ethics of research, and do not mention the importance of honesty. This is not surprising; honesty is so important that it is typically taken for granted. The two principles that are outlined in the codes covered in this section are widely accepted across research disciplines. The other principles mentioned in the codes apply only to human subjects research and are covered elsewhere in this paper.

2.1 Assigning proper credit in authorship (NAADC Principle 6; Connecticut Certification Board, Inc., Principle 6; Iowa Board of Substance Abuse Certification, Principle VI; North Carolina 0506)

Authorship has been called "the coin of the realm" in research (Wilcox 1998), and this is not an over-statement of the importance of authorship credit. The number and quality of one's publications can make or break a promotion or a grant application. It is not surprising that some researchers are tempted to accept, demand, or steal authorship credit to which they are not entitled.

No exact criteria for conferring or claiming authorship have been universally accepted, but many journals now specify their own criteria. A few negative criteria, however, do seem to be universally condemned. Gift authorship, or honorary authorship, conferred on someone who did not work on the research project but only contributed indirectly—by providing lab space or funding, or by being the lab director or dissertation advisor—is not morally acceptable. Some degree of substantive contribution to the research being reported is always necessary for authorship.

In a similar vein, plagiarism—presenting another person's words or ideas as if they were your own—is universally condemned, and is a way of unjustly taking credit.

2.2 No harassment or sexual relations with subjects (Iowa Board of Substance Abuse Certification, Principle VI)

Relationships characterized by power differentials are prone to abuse by the more powerful party. It is widely accepted across professions that professionals—including researchers, physicians, professors, lawyers, and ministers—have an obligation to keep their relationships with their subjects (patients, students, clients, congregation members) on a professional footing, which excludes sexual intimacy between a professional and his or her client.

The role of human subject carries an innate dependency and vulnerability that must not be abused by a researcher. It seems likely, moreover, that many human subjects in drug treatment research are vulnerable for other reasons, including their dependence on drugs and other factors that often co-occur with drug dependency, such as poverty, a criminal history, lack of education, health problems, and membership in an underprivileged ethnic or racial minority. Insofar as these or other characteristics of a human subject make her or him more susceptible to coercion, whether overt or subtle, the researcher has an especially heavy moral obligation to refrain from exploiting the subject.

3. The Belmont Report

The Belmont Report is the foundational document in the United States on the ethics of research with human subjects. In the introduction it distinguishes between research and practice. Then it outlines three core ethical principles (hereafter referred to as Belmont principles), with three corresponding applications, that should guide all research with human subjects.

3.1 Research versus practice

A good deal of research undertaken in medical settings, including some drug treatment research, includes procedures and interventions identical to those undertaken in medical treatments. Furthermore, in some circumstances, health care providers are justified in employing unproven or novel treatments that may seem "experimental." When is a procedure research, and when is it practice?

The key feature of medical treatment is that it is intended to benefit the patient. The key feature of medical research, however, is that it is intended to benefit some future patient or population of patients. Medical research may, incidentally and happily, prove beneficial to the human subjects enrolled in it. Furthermore, benefit to subjects may be a secondary goal of medical research, but, in contrast to medical practice, it is not the primary goal.

The difference here may be simply stated: In medical practice, the physician does something for the patient. In medical research, the researcher does something to the subject. The patient's well-being is central; the subject's wellbeing is peripheral.

Since the *raison d'etre* of medical treatment is to benefit the patient, protections for the patient are intrinsic to medical treatment. But the same does not hold for medical research. When a patient becomes a subject, additional protections are necessary. As the Belmont Report puts it, "the general rule is that if there is *any element* of research in an activity, that activity should undergo review for the protection of human subjects" (emphasis added).

This distinction holds for seemingly minor or trivial aspects of an overall activity, such as the methods for recording data and the data collected. If you ask even one question of your subjects that you would not ask of your patients, the activity has an element of research and should be treated as research, because when you ask that extra question you cross the line from helping your patient to using him.

3.2 Respect for persons

The first principle of the ethical conduct of research with human subjects is respect for persons. There is no avoiding the fact that in research, human beings are used as a means to an end—the end being the development of generalizable knowledge. Treating people as a means to an end is always ethically problematic, and usually ethically unacceptable, because it reduces them to the level of a mere thing, an object, or a senseless tool.

Human beings are distinguished from most (possibly all) other animals by their capacity for autonomy, or self-determination. We can form our own goals and our own means to attain those goals. Interference with a person's autonomy is a serious moral breach because it is, in this sense, simultaneously an interference with her or his very humanity. Emmanuel Kant's Categorical Imperative abjures us never to treat a human being as a means only, but always also as an end.

In order to honor a research subject's autonomy, the researcher must be careful to ensure that the subject takes part in the research knowingly and willingly. If participation as a research subject reflects a person's autonomous decision, the principle of respect for persons is upheld. The usual application of the principle of respect for persons is informed consent.

Please note that the requirement of respect for persons applies even if the research poses no risk. It is generally easy to see that it is wrong to make people take risks as research subjects against their will, but it may be less obvious that making a person a research subject without consent even in a study with no other risk is also wrong. Perhaps the language of "respect for persons" can make this clearer: Tricking someone into taking part in research (by, for example, failing to tell her the true aim of the study, or collecting information from him under the guise of a routine medical history) is insulting—it is disrespectful.

3.2.1 Informed consent (NAADAC Principle 9a)[3]

The ultimate goal of all drug treatment research must be to provide a benefit to society in general (if only in the form of scientific knowledge), to future individuals who profit from improved treatments, to the particular subjects enrolled in a particular study, or some combination of the three. Research involving human subjects which does not have a reasonable expectation of achieving one or more of these three kinds of benefits is generally ethically unacceptable.

Even in the cases where a research project can reasonably be supposed to have a direct therapeutic benefit to the research subjects, they cannot morally be enrolled into the research unless (a) they are provided adequate information about the research, (b) they adequately understand this information and its potential benefits and harms, (c) they agree voluntarily (without duress, coercion, or undue influence) to take part in the research, and (d) they have adequate decision-making capacity to so agree.

A potential subject's ability to provide informed consent can be compromised in a variety of ways; here I will discuss impaired cognition, impaired judgment, coercive settings, dependent circumstances, and youth.

3.2.1.1 Impaired cognition (b) or impaired judgment (d)

A variety of circumstances or characteristics, such as lack of education, mental retardation, intoxication, brain damage, and the like, can render a person unable to understand the purpose of a study, the study's risks and benefits, and so on – in short, unable to understand what's going on. The same and other characteristics may hinder a person's ability to make sound judgments. A person with impaired understanding and judgment can be termed incompetent (to make her or his own decisions). Securing informed consent to participate in research from an incompetent person is problematic.

It is generally agreed that it is unacceptable to subject a person to risky research that does not confer a direct therapeutic benefit without that person's consent. A variation on any of these three qualifiers – risk, benefit (to the subject, not to society), and consent – can change the equation. For example, it may be acceptable for a guardian or legal representative to provide proxy consent to enroll her or his incompetent ward into a risky research project that does offer direct therapeutic benefit.

3.2.1.2 Coercive settings (prison, hospital) and circumstances (need for treatment) (c)

Even when a person's intrinsic cognitive functions and judgment are intact, other circumstances can cast doubt upon her or his ability to provide voluntary consent. For example, the extreme dependence of persons confined to a nursing home or hospital, the coercive pressure inherent in prisons and jails, and the vulnerability of the impoverished sick are all likely to render potential research subjects unusually easy to coerce. In general, people in these circumstances should not be the first choice to use as research subjects, and if they are used, it should only be in studies that have reasonable expectation of providing them a direct therapeutic benefit.

3.2.1.3 Research with minors (b, c, d)

Minors are typically regarded as being less capable than adults at understanding, making free decisions, and having sound judgment. For this reason, informed consent for taking part in research must be provided by one or both parents or guardians.

Typically minority status is defined by age, but the age of majority can vary depending on the area of law (16 to drive, 18 to vote, 21 to drink alcohol). An arbitrary age of majority for research purposes is desirable for logistical reasons, but problematic for ethical reasons. Researchers should strive to be sensitive to the actual capabilities of the young people they study and provide adequate protections.

3.2.2 Confidentiality must be maintained

It seems to be common to think of confidentiality in terms of risk – if confidentiality is breached, for example, a research subject's insurability might be compromised. This is true as far as it goes, but even when a breach of confidentiality poses no risk of harm to the subject, respect for persons demands that her or his privacy be zealously protected.

3.3 Beneficence

The second Belmont principle is beneficence, or doing good. According to this principle, research must be designed so as to maximize the potential good and minimize the potential harms resulting from the research. The minimization of harms can also be termed non-maleficence. Note that both benefits and harms can accrue to individual research subjects during the course of the research and to society as a whole during and (especially) after the research. This implies four values to optimize when designing research:

	Benefit	**Risk**
Subjects	Maximize	Minimize
Society	Maximize	Minimize

It is difficult, even in theory, to optimize more than one variable. If the mandate to maximize and minimize benefits and risks is taken at face value, one would conclude that minimizing risk to subjects, for example, would mean reducing the risk of research participation to zero. This is certainly possible, but only at the cost of eliminating many lines of research, and rendering impossible the prospect of simultaneously maximizing benefit to society.

It seems clear that the Belmont Report is not asking for the impossible, but only the exceedingly difficult. These values do not have to be absolutely optimized, but balanced against each other and optimized together. This will almost always mean that risks to subjects are not reduced to the absolute minimum, but only to the minimum possible in the light of the other values. Balancing these four values requires acute judgment and careful deliberation.

The usual application of the principle of beneficence is cost-benefit analysis, in which these four values are weighed against each other in the light of the probable outcomes – both short-term (to individual subjects) and long-term (to society) – of the proposed research. Overall, for a research project to be ethically acceptable, the probable benefits must outweigh the probable risks.

3.3.1 Confidentiality must be maintained (NAADAC Principle 8, New Mexico Regulation 16.27.18.17)

As mentioned above in the context of respect for persons (Section 3.2.2), confidentiality must be maintained. Maintaining confidentiality is a matter of non-maleficence because breaches of confidence can be harmful, especially in research on sensitive issues such as illegal behavior. A disclosure that a research subject regularly uses a controlled substance could lead to her or his imprisonment.

3.3.2 Interventional research should be beneficial and non-maleficent (NAADAC Principle 7)

Interventional research here is distinguished from observational research or research in which existing data, such as medical or criminal records, are examined.

In this context, interventional research can be described as research in which subjects are asked to take one or more drugs[4] according to a research protocol, or to refrain from taking drugs they are were taking before enrolling in the study, or to alter aspects of their daily life (for example, by taking counseling, or by taking part in a 12-step program, or by staying away from old friends who may be a bad influence). This is research that is both designed to make a change in the individual subject and to learn whether the prescribed change brings about one or more target changes – does attending AA meetings reduce the consumption of alcohol?

In this example, if the target change is realized the subject enjoys a direct benefit. But whether the target change is realized in the study population or not, society may benefit from the research; for example, if the study shows that only a small portion of subjects benefit from attending AA meetings, society can benefit from this knowledge by directing efforts to stem alcoholism accordingly.

For the most part, designing non-interventional research so as to avoid harms to subjects – for example, by diligently protecting confidentiality – is adequate, and no effort need be made to provide a benefit to subjects as long as some benefit is expected to accrue to society. However, interventional research should always be designed to ensure that there is reasonable expectation that individual subjects will enjoy benefits from participating in the research.

The best case is always that in which the individual subject enjoys some therapeutic benefit – that is, in which her or his drug dependence is decreased, or harmful side effects of drug dependence are reduced. When such direct benefits to subjects are not possible, careful consideration should be made to providing compensation (usually in the form of money) to balance the risks of taking part in the research.[5]

3.3.3 Research results should be applied

Drug treatment research that carries any degree of risk to human subjects can only be justified by reference to its potential benefit to the subjects and/or society (usually embodied in future drug users). Non-therapeutic research, by definition, cannot be beneficial to the subjects of the research, but in both therapeutic and non-therapeutic research other people (including, possibly, the subjects) might benefit from the research findings sometime in an unknown future. In both forms of research, but especially in non-therapeutic research, the probability that research results will be applied to the benefit of society should be part of the cost-benefit analysis.

It appears that the findings of drug treatment research are not applied to real-world problems as effectively as they should be. Jon Morgenstern cites two papers by Miller and colleagues (Miller et al. 1986, 1995), calling them "a comprehensive review of the outcome literature for alcoholism treatment" and noting that their findings demonstrated that "there is an almost inverse relationship between interventions with demonstrated efficacy and those used in the current alcoholism treatment system" (Morgenstern 2000:1660; see also p. 1670ff on effective models for technology transfer).

It would be admittedly hard on researchers to say that they should not pursue their line of study because policy makers will not make use of the findings. Policy development is not, after all, the direct responsibility of researchers. However, any researcher who justifies putting subjects at risk on the basis of a claim that the results will have future benefits has a moral responsibility to be reasonably accurate about the chances of those benefits actually being reaped. If nothing else, this suggests that the drug treatment research community should actively encourage the use of effective treatments and discourage the use of ineffective ones. The best methods for doing so are beyond the scope of this paper and the expertise of the author.

3.3.4 Longitudinal research

The most beneficial treatments for drug use would have a long-term effect. Short-term research that only shows, for example, that an intervention is effective for a few weeks is welcome, but inadequate. Longitudinal research should be pursued whenever possible.

3.4 Justice

The third Belmont principle is justice, narrowly construed: "Who ought to receive the benefits of research and bear its burdens?" According to this principle, the benefits and burdens of research should be distributed across society in accord with moral principles. The usual application of the principle of justice concerns the selection of subjects.

The importance of this principle is clear in the light of past abuses in which people to whom researchers had easy access, including institutionalized mentally retarded children, prisoners, and hospital patients,[6] were exploited as research subjects. The principle of justice demands that people should not be enrolled as subjects of research merely because they are easy targets – including people with drug dependency problems. This demand also echoes the principle of respect for persons and its injunction that people with diminished autonomy should be accorded additional protection.

But the principle of justice also demands that one segment of the population should not be asked to bear the risks associated with research when (a) that segment of the population is unlikely to reap the benefits of research or (b) the benefits of research will redound to a larger or different segment of the population. For example, research on treatments for drugs that are mostly used by the wealthy, or on treatments that will likely be available only to the wealthy, should not be done using only or mostly poor people as subjects.

3.5 Inclusion (post-Belmont)

The Belmont Report was written in response to abuses by researchers that put human subjects at risk without adequate (sometimes without any) justification, and often without informed consent or, sometimes, any consent. It was also an era when biomedical research with human subjects was, compared to today, more experimental –more uncertain, more risky, more speculative, and less likely to yield practical benefits. Thus the Belmont Report has a protective tone; its emphasis is, understandably, on the protection of subjects from the risks of research.

A number of technical and social factors have led to an emphasis on inclusion in research. Perhaps the prototype was activism by the AIDS community. When a diagnosis of AIDS was a death sentence and there was no treatment available outside of trials, the risk of taking part in research tended to be about the same as or less than the alternative. AIDS activism led to many changes in human subjects research, but for our purposes the most important was the impression it made on the research community and the wider society that, at least sometimes, being excluded from research can be more risky than being included.

The principle of inclusion applies to individuals, populations, and even diseases: Individual patients should be given access to experimental treatments; neglected populations (such as women and children) should be represented in research; and neglected diseases (such as breast cancer) should be studied. (Mastroianni and Kahn 2001)

Thus, insofar as (a) people in need of effective drug treatment can benefit from taking part in treatment trials; (b) drug users have been neglected as a population (whether considered as the population of drug users, poor people, criminals, prisoners, or racial or ethnic minorities); or (c) drug user treatment is under-studied compared to other diseases that exact a similar toll, a case can be made that the amount of drug user treatment research should be increased.

4. The research community

Individual researchers have an important role to play in living up to the ethical standards outlined in this paper. However, while each individual researcher has complete control over whether he or she gives credit where credit is due (Section 2.1) or refrains from harassing or research subjects (Section 2.2), individuals have limited control over whether the treatments they develop will be applied (Section 3.3.3) or whether the areas of drug treatment most in need of research will receive the attention they deserve (Section 3.5). Problems of the latter sort are social problems that can only be addressed by groups of people.

As a community, then, drug treatment researchers have a responsibility to do what they can to uphold the principles outlined in this paper. Through their work in professional societies, as reviewers of manuscripts and grant proposals, as advisors to research institutions and governmental agencies, and other channels, they should always bear in mind the big picture.

Funding agencies have enormous influence over the lines of research that are pursued; federal and state law makers have a good deal of say over which treatments will be applied. Insofar as researchers can influence these bodies and others that control the direction of research and the impact research has on society, they have an obligation to exert that influence to uphold the principles and standards of the field.

5. Conclusion

It has been noted that "different approaches to [drug user] treatment are based on different assumptions or models regarding the nature of [drug] dependence and the appropriate techniques for correcting the problem" (Prendergast and Podus 2000:1646). To mention only two models, the disease model "regards drug dependence as a progressive, often fatal disease, requiring pharmacological or other medical intervention for afflicted individuals" (1647), and the moral model "sees drug use as a moral failing resulting from a lack of self-restraint on the part of affected individuals" (1648).

According to the disease model, a treatment would be considered effective to the degree that dependence were decreased or eliminated ("cured") and secondary symptoms or conditions were diminished. But while some advocates of the moral model would applaud success along the lines of the disease model, others might argue that it does not go far enough: Insofar as drug dependence is a moral failing, it cannot be said to have been dealt with effectively without moral change. "In its extreme form, the moral model is associated with the belief that drug-dependent individuals do not deserve treatment, certainly not at public expense; instead, they deserve punishment" (Prendergast and Podus 2000:1648).

Since different models of the nature of drug dependence require different criteria for evaluating treatment success, models are of central importance to public policy. However, I would argue that these differences are not germane to the ethics of drug user treatment. According to the standards of research ethics, all human beings must be accorded equal respect, whether they are regarded as suffering from a disease or from a moral failing. This means that researchers must adhere to the principles of respect for persons, beneficence, justice, and inclusion, as well as the basic tenets of general research ethics, no matter which model of drug dependence guides their research.

Kenneth D. Pimple, Ph.D., is Director of Teaching Research Ethics Programs at the Poynter Center for the Study of Ethics and American Institutions, an endowed center at Indiana University-Bloomington. He is also an Affiliate Faculty at the Indiana University Center for Bioethics. He has nearly fifteen years of experience in organizing faculty workshops on ethics and research ethics.

Since 1993 he has directed the Teaching Research Ethics project (TRE), which offers an annual workshop for researchers from the sciences and other fields. In its eleven years, the workshop has attracted 428 participants from 40 states, the District of Columbia, and 9 foreign countries (29 participants total from Brazil, Canada, Denmark, Germany, Israel, Kuwait, Mexico, Norway, and the United Kingdom), representing 141 universities and other institutions.

Since 1999 he has directed Scientists and Subjects: An Online Seminar on the Ethics of Research with Human Subjects, an annual seminar funded by the National Institutes of Health.

In 2001 he was commissioned by the Institute of Medicine Committee on Assessing Integrity in Research Environments to write three background papers for its major publication, Integrity in Scientific Research: Creating an Environment that Promotes Responsible Conduct (Washington, D.C.: National Academies Press, 2002).

His publications in the field of research ethics include "General Issues in Teaching Research Ethics," in Research Ethics: Cases and Materials, ed. Robin Levin Penslar (Bloomington: Indiana University Press, 1995); "The Ethics of Human Cloning and the Fate of Science in a Democratic Society," Valpairaso University Law Review 32(2):727-737 (1998); and "Six Domains of Research Ethics: A Heuristic Framework for the Responsible Conduct of Research," Science and Engineering Ethics 8(2):191-205 (2002).

He has been invited to make presentations on the responsible conduct of research and on teaching research ethics in a wide variety of venues and served on advisory boards for the National Science Foundation, the National Institutes of Health, and other organizations.

References

Hornblum, A.M. (1998). *Acres of Skin: Human Experiments at Holmesburg Prison.* New York: Routledge.

Jonsen, A.R. (1998). *The Birth of Bioethics*. Oxford University Press.

Mastroianni, A., and Kahn, J. (2001). Swinging on the pendulum: Shifting views of justice in human subjects research. Hastings Center Report May-June:21-28.

Miller, W.R., and Hester, R.K. (1986). The effectiveness of alcoholism treatment methods: What research reveals. In Miller, W.R. and Heather, N. (Eds.), *Treating Addictive Behaviors: Process of Change* (pp 121-174). New York: Plenum Press.

Miller, W.R., Brown, J.M., Simpson, T.L., Hamdmaker, N.S., Bien, T.H., Luckie, L.F., Montgomery, H.A., Hester, R.K., and Tonigan, J.S. (1995). What works? A methodological analysis of the alcohol treatment outcome literature. In R. K. Hester and W. R. Miller (Eds.), *Handbook of Effective Alcoholism Treatment Approaches: Effective Alternatives*. Needham Heights, MA: Simon & Schuster.

Morgenstern, J. (2000). Effective technology transfer in alcoholism treatment. *Substance Use and Abuse 35*(12-14):1659-1678.

National Commission for the Protection of Human Subjects of Biomedical and Behavioral Research (1979). *The Belmont Report: Ethical Principles and Guidelines for the Protection of Human Subjects of Research*. Washington, D.C.: U.S. Government Publishing Office. http://www.hhs.gov/ohrp/humansubjects/guidance/belmont.htm

Pendergast, M.L., and Podus, D. (2000). Drug treatment effectiveness: An examination of conceptual and policy issues. *Substance Use and Abuse 35*(12-14):1629-1657.

Rothman, D.J. and Rothman, S.M. *The Willowbrook Wars*. New York: Harper and Row.

Wilcox, L. J. (1998). Authorship: The coin of the realm, the source of complaints. *Journal of the American Medical Association 280*:216-217.

Notes

1. I wish to thank the editors of this volume and Jennifer E. Livesay, Ph.D., for critical comments on earlier drafts of this paper.
2. A list of codes was provided by the co-editors, to whom I am grateful.
3. NAADAC Principle 9a does not mention research, but its insistence on informed consent in other settings makes it clear that informed consent in research is consis-

tent with the values espoused by NAADAC. Principle 9a reads: "The NAADAC member shall inform the client and obtain the client's agreement in areas likely to affect the client's participation including the recording of an interview, the use of interview material for training purposes, and/or observation of an interview by another person."

4. "Drugs" here includes medicines and alcohol.
5. NAADAC Principle 7d actually specifies that "The NAADAC member shall not use or encourage a client's participation in any demonstration, research or other non-treatment activities when such participation would have potential harmful consequences for the client or when the client is not fully informed." It is unclear whether research which includes a component of treatment (and therefore benefit) falls under this prohibition.
6. For information on the abuse of mentally retarded children at the Willowbrook State Mental Hospital see Rothman and Rothman 1984; on the abuse of prisoners at Holmesburg Prison, see Hornblum 1998; on the abuse of patients at the Jewish Chronic Disease Hospital (as well as other abuses), see Jonsen 1998.

1-12 Decisions Involving Research and Ethics: Misusing Drug Use(r) Statistics

Manuella Adrian, M. Sc.Hyg.

"Insincerity in the search after truth is one of the most degrading of sins."
— Francis Galton

Abstract

Scientific research has provided us with one of the most powerful means to improve the lot of humankind. However, its very power can be the source of a host of moral and ethical dilemmas for those who use it. Most attention into the ethics of research is currently directed toward human subject research and is oriented to reduce the likelihood of harm to participants, with reasonably well developed guidelines having emerged since the Nuremberg trials over the past half-century. Also recognized are the ethical dilemmas that stem from the goals of research particularly as regards militaristic research. Less well known are areas of ethical concern arising from the scientific method itself, from research methods and interpretations of data which are also described in this paper. We review some of the basic tenets of the scientific method used in conducting research investigations in the area of substance use and misuse starting with the basic principles enunciated by Isaac Newton to establish causality and exploring some of the newer conceptual frameworks used to determine points of intervention where we may act in order to obtain the results we want even when strict linear causality cannot be applied, using examples not only from the substance use area but also from a more general scientific framework when such illustrations may be useful. We will then consider the ethical and moral problems that may result from the nature of the subject matter being investigated, its organization and funding, as well as the use of inappropriate methods and techniques – including some of the issues that need to be considered with the use of human subjects – which may result in erroneous conclusions that may be harmful to patients, to scientists and to society as a whole.

Key Words: research ethics; conceptual framework; research methods; statistics and data; addiction

Introduction

Research is intended to provide us with information and knowledge that we did not have before. Scientific research uses a particular way of reasoning and examining facts through systematic observation and experimentation, so as to establish causation.

The explanatory power achieved as a result of identifying the causes of phenomena allows us to predict, and hence control, the results, or consequences, of certain actions, activities, or events. We can direct our efforts and undertake actions to achieve specific consequences; this allows us an instrumental means to achieve our goals. Because of the numerous successes of the scientific method in explaining what we observe in the world, and its ability to allow us to achieve instrumental control over the material world in which we live, it has become the predominant mode of perceiving and understanding our experiences. Whereas pure research is oriented wholly to identifying causes and consequences in an almost abstract way, applied research is oriented to identifying the practical means whereby we can achieve the goals of satisfactorily resolving certain situations that we consider to be problematic.

In this paper we will review some of the basic tenets of the scientific method used in conducting research investigations in the area of substance use and misuse starting with the basic principles enunciated by Isaac Newton to establish causality and exploring some of the newer conceptual frameworks used to determine critical points where we may intervene in order to obtain the results we want, even when strict linear causality cannot be applied. We will use examples not only from the substance use area but also from a more general scientific framework when such illustrations may be useful. We will then consider the ethical and moral problems that may result from the nature of the subject matter being investigated, its funding, as well as the use of inappropriate methods and techniques (including some of the issues that need to be considered with the use of human subjects), which may result in erroneous conclusions that may be harmful to patients, to scientists, and to society.

Goals of Scientific Research

Generally, the goals of practical applied research have an ameliorative aspect to them. In the most general way, we want to make things better. Whereas we may feel it is right to increase joy and decrease suffering, we may need to qualify this goal depending on what is meant by "joy" or "suffering" and, even more importantly, whose joy or suffering we are contemplating. Should research be directed at improving the lot of the many or the few or even a very selected few? Liberal egalitarian democracies would vote with improving the lot of the many through the undertaking of public works (e.g., dams, highways, public sewer systems) and the provision of public services (e.g., education, social welfare, health services). Less egalitarian societies, whether they be landed or moneyed aristocracies, oligarchies, or totalitarian regimes run by despots, where there are considerable power differentials between the social classes, may favor allocating resources to suit the needs, or caprices, of the powerful few regardless of the harm it may do to the many: hence, the financing of research into successfully cloning pets for the rich, rather than research into providing affordable quality education and basic health care services to all people. Although I obviously consider this to be a less than optimum allocation of resources, it is, nevertheless, a relatively benign peccadillo in comparison to directing research and development into transforming the pesticide Zyklon-B into the poison gas used in Nazi concentration camp extermination chambers during the Holocaust (Cornwell, 2004).

Ardent pacifists criticize all military research. Thus, American scientific research that led to the Atom Bomb has been criticized, especially in view of the massive number of horrific deaths resulting in Hiroshima and Nagasaki (where the bombs were dropped). In addition, arguments have been made by some, including historian Alperovitz (1996) and General MacArthur, supreme commander of Allied forces in the Pacific during World War II, that dropping the atom bombs was "completely unnecessary" (Tanaki, 1996:3) and had little impact on the outcome of World War II, as Japan was already near military collapse by then. Others have argued, however, that this amounts to arguing on the basis of 20/20 hindsight as the information was not available at the time and that, in any case, dropping the atomic bomb served to "avoid a bloody invasion, thereby saving both Japanese and American lives" (Lance Murrow, quoted in Tanaki, 1996: 4). Moreover, the number of lives saved as a result of medical research, along with diagnostic and therapeutic procedures involving nuclear products that benefit roughly 50,000 persons per day (Atomic Energy of Canada Limited [AECL], 2002-2005) have by now far surpassed the 280,000 lives lost when the Atom Bomb was first used (Otherground, LLC and World-War-2.info., 2003).

Institutional Goals And Individual Researchers' Ethics

Before we put aside the issue of the ethics of the goals to which research is directed, we must consider the dilemma of the scientist who is working, knowingly or not, on a project whose goals he would consider incompatible with his personal sense of morality. In the case of the Atom Bomb, the magnitude of the devastation that would ensue after a successful detonation in the field was unknowable before it occurred. Whereas some of the scientists who worked on the development of the atom bomb—including Leo Szilard (1898-1964 Current Era[1]), who first convinced Albert Einstein (1879-1955 CE) to write the letter to American President Roosevelt that led to the building of the Atom Bomb—became actively contrite over the deaths that had resulted from their efforts and became active in the "Ban the Bomb" post-war peace movement, others, such as Edward Teller (1908-2003 CE), gave more importance to the need to prevent future political and military domination by repressive totalitarian regimes and were instrumental in developing the yet more powerful, and more powerfully deterrent, H-bomb. Clearly, these are areas where it is not easy to know the right thing to do. The decision may be dependent on the particular circumstances of each situation where an individual scientist's sense of personal morality and professional ethics must come into play.

One difficulty, of course, is that one person's sense of morality may be another person's sense of careerism, expediency, or voluntary ignorance that would allow one to state, quite truthfully, that one was "only following orders." Whereas the post World War II Nuremberg court war crimes tribunal pretty much rejected the "following-orders" defense, it is not clear to what extent coercive, highly hierarchical organizations (including the military), or totalitarian regimes allow an individual the luxury of outright refusal without forcing that person to pay the ultimate price, resulting not only in their own death (occasionally after torture) but also that of their family and loved ones. Some German university scientists who appeared to embrace the notion of a Nazification of science "might have been under some pressure to conform" (Cornwell, 2004: 199). Indeed, according to the British mathematician G. H. Hardy "[a]nxiety for one's own position, dread of falling behind the rising torment of folly, determination at all costs not to be outdone, may be natural if not particularly heroic excuses" (Cornwell, 2004:199).

A passive-aggressive response may sometimes be more effective. Should one be outwardly and vocally opposed to a course of action or area of scientific research, one is likely to be removed and replaced by someone who is more compliant. By appearing to be outwardly acquiescent, one is likely to be kept on the job where a degree of inefficiency, ineptitude, and incompetence may be a more effective means of resistance, if not to say sabotage, in the long run. Some have claimed that this is what accounted for German physicist Heisenberg's (1901-1976 CE) ambiguous actions during World War II. Although a vocal supporter of the Nazi regime, this world renowned physicist—to whom we owe the idea of Heisenberg's Uncertainty Principle—proved himself amazingly inept at the practicalities of producing a German Atom Bomb (Cornwell, 2004). Historically, some peoples who, by dint of history and geography, have been conquered repeatedly over the centuries would almost seem to have adopted this strategy of passive-aggressive resistance as a survival strategy. How else to explain East Bloc Balkan countries where, under the sway of Moscow during the Cold War, the obligatory learning of the Russian language in school coincided with a sudden and amazing Russian linguistic incapacity among students, amazing in view of the usual multilingualism of educated persons in the Balkans (Anonymous, 1974).

It may be necessary to consider such subterfuges and compromises within the grey areas between black and white, where distinctions between right and wrong are not incontrovertible, and when a researcher's purely scientific activities put his or her life in danger. For example, because the American government was undertaking a "drug war" against the Medellin drug cartel, a Colombian scientist specializing in drug addiction who was attending a scientific conference in the 1980s funded by an American government grant and held in the U.S., became frightened for his life lest Colombian drug lords interpret attendance at the conference as inimical to the drug trade. Scientists at the conference agreed to change part of the official title of the scientific report emanating from the conference from "drug addiction" to "medical problems of toxico-dependence." This eliminated the potentially controversial term "drug" and emphasized the medical aspects, without in any way changing the actual topics or papers presented at the conference and published in the report. This represents a far lesser compromise than that of Galileo (1564-1642 CE) who, faced with the Inquisition, recanted his astronomical findings, which were scientifically valid, accurate, and true, even if they contradicted religious Catholic Church doctrine of the time.

Some research organizations, in order to attract qualified staff who may be morally opposed to certain areas of research (e.g., tobacco research), may recruit staff with the understanding that they will not be expected to work in these areas. Whereas a large research organization may be able to accommodate the personal preferences of its staff, this is not always the case, especially for smaller companies. The exigencies of the marketplace, whether driven by the interests of customers in for-profit organizations, or by the topics of interest or subject matter of grants and granting agencies in the not-for-profit or public sector, may determine the areas in which research efforts will be directed. If there is a sudden increase in the need for persons doing research in tobacco marketing or in military avionics, and a sudden drop in interest and funding for projects in other areas, it may not always be possible to assign personnel to the projects of their choice. Indeed there may be no other projects underway other than the ones that a researcher may find morally repugnant. In the realities of the work world the morally uncompromising scientist may have no other choice but to resign.

Alternatively, in the realities of the work world, the employer of a morally uncompromising scientist may have no other choice but to terminate his or her employment. No employer faced with what is essentially an insubordinate employee would have any difficulty in justifying termination even in the most pro-labor of labor-law jurisdictions. The massive industrial and other work world restructuring that started in the late 1980s was justified on the basis of maintaining or enhancing profitability and shareholder value. Clearly, scientist employees who were not doing productive work because they refused to work in certain areas of enquiry when no other areas of work were available could not be seen as enhancing profitability. Most employers in Canada, for instance, would terminate uncompromising scientist-employees as part of the re-structuring process without the issue of insubordination ever needing to arise. In the U.S., where most states operate in an employment-at-will labor law context, terminations can occur at any time without the employer having to present any cause. The scientists must then decide whether their personal or family financial security is worth compromising by refusing the assigned, but morally repugnant work, and at the same time determine whether they are prepared to compromise their personal or professional ethical standards. Consider the dilemma created when the marketing research firm that hired a newly minted PhD social scientist with a strict anti-tobacco ethic, with the understanding that the scientist will not do any tobacco research, suddenly obtains a large contract from a tobacco company requiring the specific skills of the social scientist. The ultimate parting of the ways is inevitable.

National Differences in Ethical Standards and their Effects on Orienting Selected Research Topics.

Despite international standards for human rights enshrined in the *Universal Declaration of Human Rights* adopted by the United Nations and its member countries in 1948, the ethical standards that guide individual scientists' moral behavior, especially as they may apply it in their professional scientific work in terms of the types of research they carry out or the types of interventions they may consider, may differ in different parts of the world. At an addiction conference in Canada several years ago, addiction researchers from Germanic countries presented abortion as an obvious and logical means of preventing the occurrence of fetal alcohol syndrome in children born to women who consumed alcohol during pregnancy. However, abortion, although legal, is still considered controversial in North America, and such an intervention undertaken for such a purpose, to the uncomprehending amazement of the Germanic researchers, elicited, literally, a very audible collective gasp of shock from the Canadian scientific audience in attendance.

This author had a somewhat similar reaction when a paper she presented on controlling the availability alcohol (Adrian, Ferguson, & Her, 1996) in order to reduce its deleterious effects was met with skepticism at a harm reduction conference held a decade ago in Italy, where the audience made up of addiction experts accepted the concept of drug-related harm but could not fully appreciate the harmful effects of alcohol. In retrospect, this is not surprising: Italy is a "wet" culture, in which alcohol is an integral part of everyday life for most people, being regularly consumed with meals in the form of wine or as aperitifs and *digestivi* throughout the day. This pattern of consumption generally results in silent problems such as liver cirrhoses rather than more obvious displays of public drunkenness or alcohol-associated violence. In addition, Italian social norms and mores strongly inhibit public displays of drunkenness, hence alcohol-related problems may become largely invisible even to a professional audience.

In contrast, at approximately the same time, an audience of addiction experts at a Canadian health conference was very suspicious of professional scientific presentations on the potentially beneficial health effects of alcohol, such as its possible role in reducing cardiovascular morbidity (see for example, Pinder & Sander, 2004; den Heijer et al., 2004; Niroomand et al., 2004; Renaud, 2004). The audience, used to a "safe" low level of drinking threshold of "2 drinks a day for men" and "one drink a day for women" in Canadian research, was stymied by the Italian cut-off for low drinking level of "5 drinks a day," and unable to appreciate fully the implications of the information that was presented. It is interesting to note that the "2 drinks a day" threshold was set because the original Canadian population survey (National Alcohol and Drugs Survey [NADS], 1989, conducted by Statistics Canada and Health and Welfare Canada) on which it was based used a sequence of questions and data categories that could accommodate only a small range of calculated drinking levels, with the "2 drinks a day or less" category being the only one available for the "low" category.

Similar events undoubtedly surround the current research-based public health message that the "only safe level of smoking" is "not to smoke," which permeates not only the social zeitgeist but also the unconscious and unexamined assumptions of addiction researchers who may have difficulty dealing with the idea that tobacco could have beneficial effects: for example, it reduces the tremors of Parkinson's disease (Alves, 2004; Hernan, 2001) and is an effective anorexiant. Even tobacco smoke,[2] which is the vehicle into the lungs for most of the carcinogenic elements in tobacco, can be used to chase off mosquitoes and other biting insects in the outdoors. Similar controversy and limitations may be attendant on the studies of the possible medical uses of marijuana in reducing the symptoms of Parkinson's (Venderova, 2004), the nausea associated with cancer therapy or AIDS-associated anorexia (Fride, 2005), or in improving mood in the depressed (Denson, 2005). The American government's refusal to countenance the use of medical marijuana (Hopkins, 2005) is likely to delay our progress in obtaining knowledge that could be useful and beneficial in this area.

Bogus Research Goals

Another emerging problem area is that of bogus research, when research methods, including surveys, are used not to obtain information to increase our knowledge of human behavior, but to persuade, to propagandize, to market, and to sell products or services to the unwary respondent. This author has been on the receiving end of so-called telephone interviews on "the importance of the arts in our city" which were actually part of the pre-set telephone solicitor's fund-raising spiel for an otherwise prestigious and respected local big-city opera company. The author has also received numerous mailed questionnaires over the years sponsored by one or another of the various official registered political parties or powerful national lobbying groups in both the U.S. and Canada, supposedly to identify community concerns over social issues, which were in reality a series of questions with an increasingly hysterical tone ("the scourge of drug addiction in our streets"), obviously intended to alarm the respondent until the only solution to the dire social conditions raised in the questionnaire was to donate generously in response to the final fund-raising pitch question. Although it may be tempting to fault researchers who thus pervert the principles of objectivity of scientific research, in actuality the basic methods of questionnaire design and survey sampling are widely taught in a variety of programs, including business and marketing, journalism, and public relations, as well as the social and health sciences, not to mention engineering, architecture, statistics, and mathematics programs throughout our colleges and universities. Indeed, a person may acquire elementary questionnaire-building skills almost by "osmosis" as a result of having been surveyed many times, starting in early school years. It is therefore not surprising that marketing in the guise of research can be easily undertaken by persons who have never been exposed to the principles and ethics of scientific research.

The Scientific Research Method

The scientific research method is used to examine and understand the world we live in. Its adherents use scientific reasoning and observation or experimentation using particular research designs appropriate to answering our questions about how the world works. The intent is to provide accurate and valid knowledge that may be applied to solve problems in the material world.

Scientific Reasoning and Research Design

Let us now consider the nature of the scientific method itself. Scientific reasoning and its ways of reasoning and establishing causality was codified by Isaac Newton (1646-1727 CE) in his *Principia* into four rules:

1. we are to admit no more causes of natural things such as are both true and sufficient to explain their appearances,
2. the same natural effects must be assigned to the same causes,
3. qualities of bodies are to be esteemed as universal, and
4. propositions deduced from observation of phenomena should be viewed as accurate until other phenomena contradict them (Weisstein, 2005).

In its most basic essence, the scientist attempts to explain the world (or portions of it) by observing phenomena, attempting to identify those that are linked to one another in recurring patterns. This is the first phase of *induction*, in which intuition and pattern recognition skills are paramount in helping to devise hypotheses (as yet unproven ideas) about how the world works. In the second phase of *deduction*, hypotheses are formulated precisely and stringently so as to be testable. Systematic observation and data collection are used to test whether hypotheses can be disproven by empirical or experimental data. This is derived from Newton's 4th rule of scientific reasoning (things are true until proven otherwise).

Many persons are under the impression that science proves things. In reality, this is not the case. In generating a testable hypothesis we logically postulate *a priori* (i.e., before the experiment is conducted or the data collected) what the expected results should be were our hypothesis to be correct. Empirical results are then examined using a variety of logical and statistical techniques to determine if they support the hypothesis. Should the results not support the hypothesis, this invalidates the hypothesis. The hypothesis is deemed to be not correct, necessitating the investigator to go back to the drawing board and attempt to find another explanation and offer another hypothesis to account for the observations. The new hypothesis must then itself be tested in new experiments and observations intended to find its flaws in order to disprove it. Although the logic and rigor of scientific reasoning was first established for physics, it has been amply demonstrated to be appropriate to other realms of investigation, such as medicine and the social sciences, including the field of addictions.

Should numerous and different experiments to test a hypothesis be undertaken over the years in many different locations and circumstances (this is derived from Newton's 3rd rule of universality) and no results be obtained that would contradict the hypothesis, it then becomes reasonably well established and, over the centuries, may become a scientific Law (for example, the Law of Gravity). In the field of addictions, the "law of alien poisons" holds that psychoactive substances which are new to a culture are seen as more problematic than those that are already well-known in a society: thus consumption of alcohol is traditional and normative in Italy, problematic in North America and illegal in India. In contrast, the use of cannabis-containing substances has been traditional for thousands of years in India, but is illegal in Europe and North America where it was introduced more recently. One wonders what beneficial effects would result from the recognition that other addiction-related phenomena are sufficiently well-established to be considered a "law," including the relapsing nature of addiction and addictive behaviors which needs to be taken into account when establishing program goals that are more likely to be helpful to persons with addiction-related problems.

In studies of addiction that attempt to explain why alcohol, tobacco, or drug addiction occurs—however these "loaded" and politicized terms, concepts and processes may be defined, and by whom—Newton's 1st rule would mean that the availability of alcohol, tobacco, or drugs is a necessary condition such that alcohol, tobacco, or drug addiction cannot occur without the presence of alcohol, tobacco, or drugs (or substances that the user believes to be alcohol, tobacco, or drugs), but that is not a sufficient cause since alcohol, tobacco, or drugs may be available at a party, for instance, without all persons present at that party necessarily using any of these substances or for users to become addicted. In addition, "availability" is not equivalent to "accessibility" and/or the "opportunity" to begin to use, continue to use, and/or to make changes in ones pattern and manner of use. These parameters are rarely, if ever, investigated. This may account for the failure of attempting to eradicate alcohol, tobacco, and drug addiction through Prohibition or other forms of institutionalized "drug control."

The sufficient cause for drug addiction is now thought to be a complex interaction of the drug's pharmaco-active characteristics and the individual's biological and psychological propensities, as well as aspects of his or her socio-cultural, political, and economic environment. This is the bio-psycho-social model that would probably meet Newtons's 1st rule of sufficient cause if we could specify its nature precisely enough as to render it testable. The lack of necessary specificity is demonstrated by the 52 theories posited to explain the etiology of drug use (Lettieri, et al, 1980).

Laboratory experimentation vs. observational studies

One difficulty with investigating human behavior is that, in the real world, human behavior does not occur within the strictures of the laboratory where we can eliminate or control, more or less, possible confounders. In the real world of everyday life it is difficult, if not impossible, to conduct true experiments. At best we can observe, carefully and systematically, what is happening in those real world circumstances when, where, and how the behavior of interest occurs. Such observational studies, called *natural experiments*, can yield interesting and useful information about why the behavior occurs. The careful design of prospective (or retrospective-prospective) studies, as is done in epidemiology or other population-based studies such as studies of criminality, political behavior, management and administrative practices, and the like, can serve the needs of public health, social justice, or administrative efficiency; but not all of the actual needs.

One difficulty with a natural experiment is that it is sometimes difficult to identify what is a crucial aspect of the situation and what is mere happenstance. In addition, the investigator has no control over the situation so as to be able to exclude the possibly extraneous. The result is that causality is difficult to establish outside the laboratory. The difference between a generalizable documented pharmacological action ("drug effect") and an experienced, reported "drug experience," within a controlled laboratory environment is yet another commonly known example of the complexity affecting the move from data to information to knowledge and perhaps even to wisdom, if and when substance use(r) intervention is evidence-based and not stake-holder driven or based upon principles of faith.[3]

In addition, rarely do authors note the necessary critical conditions for the concepts and processes that they posit to operate [begin, continue, change, stop or not begin at all] generally and, more specifically, the nexus between such conditions and the processes/concepts/dimensions. For example, we are now in the era of posited "risk factors" and "protective factors." What are they, empirically? What are their dimensions? And what are the necessary critical conditions for them to operate or not?

Confounders

Because of the complexities inherent in living and adaptive systems, research into systems of human behavior may be faced with confounding factors that complicate the "pure" cause-and-effect relationship.

Confounders, in a sense, correspond to the necessary cause of Newton's 1st rule of research. Nothing would happen without them, yet by themselves they are not enough to effectuate an observable effect. In a sense, their role is a bit like that of enzymes or catalysts in chemical reactions. The reaction would not occur, or not occur as readily or speedily, without the presence of the catalyst. The catalyst takes an active role in the actual chemical reaction, forming a temporary chemical bond to a substance in an intermediate phase of the reaction, before releasing its chemical bonds to the newly formed final chemical product of the reaction, so that the catalyst can return to its initial chemical state. The catalyst itself remains unchanged at the end of the chemical cycle it has facilitated, and, having returned to its original form, becomes available to start a new cycle of reactions. In social science research, these catalysts of human behavior are called mediators or moderators, depending on their role. Mediators enhance the effect of a causative agent whereas moderators dampen this effect.

A cause will have a larger effect or a bigger and more noticeable consequence in the presence of a mediator, and a smaller effect in the presence of a moderator. Confounders may be an order of magnitude greater than the cause-and-effect relationship they influence. Ambient economic conditions may affect the likelihood of a person's spending propensity, as consumer confidence tends to soar in economic boom times, and this may occur in addition to the effect of personal spending power (income) (see Figure 1 for a schema outlining this relationship).

Figure 1.12.1: Causation and confounders.

				Personal Spending Power
				↓
Economic Boom Times	→	Soaring Consumer Confidence	→	Greater Personal Spending

Note: The direction of the arrows indicates the direction of causality, from cause to consequence.

Although individual behavior at the micro-level may eventually affect confounders operating at the macro-level, the effect would scarcely be perceptible within the time frames used for most studies, and hence confounders would appear unchanged much like catalysts in a chemical reaction. However, confounders need not all be macro-level events. Personal spending propensity for alcohol (e.g., purchasing a larger quantity or choosing more expensive alcoholic beverages) may increase as personal income increases, but it may also be moderated by the need to save for a child's college education (which will diminish short-term spending), and mediated by a child's upcoming nuptials (which will further increase spending for items such as imported French champagne for the wedding).

Such complex relationships are difficult to model partly because of their inherent complexity, and partly because the mathematical techniques needed to do so are viewed as complex and may not have been covered in the usual course syllabi or textbooks of statistics used in graduate courses in many social sciences programs. As a result, some researchers may lack the technical skills needed to study certain phenomena. Thus even if these researchers can ask the right question, they may be unable to devise a method to formulate an answer.

One major difficulty that arises from this situation is that researchers may not even be aware that they have such gaps in their knowledge base, so that the possibility of filling the gap becomes remote. Indeed, not all researchers are as insightful as Nobel prize-winning physicist Richard Feynman (1918-1988 CE) who, during a sabbatical year devoted to doing work outside of his own specialty, discovered that he needed "a map of the cat," as he phrased it for lack of knowledge of the appropriate terminology. Fortunately he was sufficiently self assured and fearless (or maybe oblivious) about the potential for appearing foolish to ask a helpful librarian who interpreted his request and provided him an anatomical chart of the cat (Feynman, 1984). A similar relevant issue relates to the consequences of not categorizing problems (see below Categories of Problems).

Critical Control Points

The lack of an incontrovertible sufficient cause identified from among a multiplicity of possible causative factors is not necessarily a deterrent to making socially useful and effective interventions when multiple intervention approaches, often based on competing theoretical models, are in current use. However, there may be some anxiety about whether current intervention approaches are appropriate when a causative factor in a particular model that gains ascendancy is not demonstrated to be a sufficient cause. For example, early in the field of AIDS, the presence of HIV was considered to be the predominant cause of AIDS. One problem is that not all persons with HIV go on to develop AIDS (at least not within the time frame that the disease had been studied so far). Hence, with the data available and the disease model in use at that time, HIV could not have logically been the sufficient cause of AIDS (see Newton's 1st rule, above). Considerable controversy arose in the scientific literature about the emphasis on the role of HIV in the development of full blown AIDS.

While not necessarily identifying the sufficient cause, observational studies of natural experiments can pinpoint a nexus point where several potentially causative factors converge into critical control points. The idea of the critical control point is derived from Hazard Analysis Critical Control Point (HACCP) analysis, and corresponds to "a single measurable element that covers a multitude of potential sins" (Grandin & Johnson 2005:267). If the intent of applied research is to be ameliorative and instrumental, the identification of such critical control points may be sufficient to orient our instrumental interventions. If we use the perspective of Hazard Analysis Critical Control Point (HACCP) analysis, it may be that HIV is a marker representing the critical control point in AIDS, regardless of its exact role as a causative factor.

Complexity

The classical rules of scientific enquiry may also need to be re-examined to take into account recursive processes. In some cases, empirically established relationships are still *a-theoretical*, in the sense that they are not yet organized into a self-contained explanatory system that can account for all observations within a class of phenomena (as is the case, for example, with Newtonian physics), or that is close to accounting for many of the empirical observations obtained so far (as is the case with Einstein's theory of special relativity). Up to quite recently, substance use—of whatever variety, as well as abstinence—were, and for many continue to be, linear cause-and-effect phenomena which may be complicated. However, it is becoming increasingly clear that human behavior is complex, and models to account for it must include dynamic processes and other sophisticated analytic techniques (Ferguson & Lim, 1998; Buscema, 1998; Barabasi, 2003) that incorporate both personal individual factors (age, gender, ethnicity, psychological factors) as well as structural factors (social, economic, and cultural) (Alexander, et al, 1987; Adrian, 2003). Models derived from Artificial Neural Networks (ANN) theory (Buscema, 1998) may meet their predetermined parameters without necessarily corresponding to the Newtonian model of causality. This does not preclude them from permitting useful instrumental interventions.

Having noted this, one is challenged by the ongoing reality regarding a great deal of contemporary substance use intervention research. With the advent of artificial science and its theoretical underpinnings (chaos, complexity, uncertainty, and network theories), it is now posited that much of human behavior is complex, dynamic, multi-dimensional, level/phase structured, non-linear, law-driven and bounded by culture, time, place, age, gender, ethnicity, etc. This obviously includes substance use related behaviors. Two important issues derive from this:

1. Using linear models/tools to study non-linear processes/phenomena can and does result in misleading conclusions and can therefore also result in inappropriate intervention;
2. The concepts prediction and control have different meanings and dimensions from those they have in the more traditional linear cause-and-effect paradigms. (Buscema, 1998; Barabási, 2003).

Given that this information/knowledge has been available for a number of decades, one is challenged to understand why much of the research continues to use simplistic, linear, cause-and-effect research designs and data analysis. And given that actual as well as potential harm is a reality, this ongoing "tradition" can be considered at the very least to be a harbinger of ethical dilemmas. The equally traditional "cop out" of too early closure through using the code "transfer of technology" problems doesn't resolve this issue.

Misunderstanding of Scientific Results

Linear models are easier to understand and explain and tend to be taught first in undergraduate or graduate research courses. Because graduate students and aspiring researchers do not necessarily take more advanced research courses, they are rarely exposed to more sophisticated non-linear models. One would therefore expect that all researchers and consumers of research products (those who read the scientific literature without necessarily being researchers themselves) would therefore have a basic understanding of the linear cause-and-effect relationships reported in a scientific article. Based on this author's experience in communicating scientific information to the public, including policy makers and media, as well as consulting and teaching courses in research and evaluation, it is clear that there is no guarantee that this expectation will be met.

Media and science writers (who are often not trained in science, but in writing, and who have taken for credit courses such as "statistics without numbers") have expectations of a degree of omniscience and certainty found only in religious belief and not in science-based information; one relatively sophisticated ATOD [Alcohol, Tobacco and Other Drugs] science writer had difficulty accepting on an emotional level that our science-based knowledge is probabilistic in nature, and hence, approximate, imperfect, incomplete, and constantly subject to revision. Another television science reporter had no difficulty with the statistical approximation and regularly asked for the standard error of any survey-based alcohol and drug information, certain that the scientist would be tripped up and reveal that he was "lying with statistics" (viz. *How to Lie With Statistics* by Huff & Geiss, 1954; and the more sophisticated version by Holmes, 1990), little knowing what other numerous causes may account for the imprecision of our estimates.

Comments by a researcher suggesting possible areas where further research is needed by speculating on the possible social consequences of the physical findings in children born to women using cocaine and crack during gestation (e.g., weighing an average of half a pound below normal at birth and averaging about 5 IQ points less by age seven) was transformed by the popular press into the crack babies epidemic "which became an emblem of the havoc drugs wreak and a pretext for draconian drug laws. Hospitals began secretly testing pregnant women for cocaine, and jailing them or taking their children. Tens of thousands of kids were swept into foster care" (Blake, 2004), and many more labeled as "crack babies" have faced prejudice and discrimination during their school years and through their lives

The way that scientists think and communicate is hard to understand except in the broadest terms by those not trained in the scientific method. Concepts, hypotheses, methods, results, findings, and conclusions expressed with all due caution by researchers may be misunderstood in their subtleties by non-scientists, including media, policy makers and the interested lay public with the result that there is an inherent "vulnerability" of research as a model and ideology which can be, has been, and is misused—as a result of which it is a source of individual and systemic harm.

The Teaching of Research Methods

While one would hope that most scientists have a basic understanding of scientific thinking, this is not necessarily the case, and ethical problems associated with the logic of scientific reasoning are derived from a misunderstanding of basic scientific reasoning and the processes involved in conducting scientific research. In graduate research programs considerable time is spent on the particularities of data collection, such as the construction of questionnaires, including the sequence of questions in a questionnaire, the use of closed or open ended questions, Likert scales and the like, as well as the training of interviewers, developing methods of ensuring adherence to research protocols by research assistants, interviewers, field observers, and/or clinical research staff. However, far less attention is given to the logic of research design, that is to say the formulating of a research question (rather than a questionnaire) and determining what type of data (regardless of the means of collecting it) will best answer the question. One reason is that the minutiae of data collection, (formulate questions, send questionnaires to the printer, mail questionnaires, data entry of questionnaires) are closer to everyday activities and are thus far easier for most people to understand.

Categories of Problems

Horst Rittel (Rittel et al., 1989) has suggested that problems can and should be usefully categorized into two types: "tame problems" and "wicked problems." "Tame problems" are solved in the traditional known and tried "water fall paradigm"; gather data, analyze data, formulate solution, implement solution. "Wicked problems" can only be responded to individually, each time anew, with no ultimate, repeatable solution. This distinction, regarding a taxonomy of problems, has yet to be considered in terms of its utility, "demands," and implications for substance use prevention programs and processes and the research designed to study them.

Categories of Questions

The cyberneticist Heinz von Foerster (von Foerster et al., 1960) posited that there are two types of questions: "illegitimate questions" and "legitimate questions." The former, illegitimate questions, are those for which the answers are not known. A legitimate question is one for which the answer is known. Rarely is the question asked, with regard to an ever-growing list of posited critical parameters in the substance use field ("risk factors," "protective factors," "gateway drugs," "vulnerability," etc.): What are the critical endogenous and exogenous conditions which are needed for these posited processes to operate (to begin, to continue, to change, to cease), or not to begin at all? Is this a random event? Are there built-in ethical issues which merit raising?

The tradition of asking legitimate questions and not needed illegitimate ones is not only a barrier to achieving needed knowledge but can and does present ethical challenges by misusing limited human, fiscal, and other resources. For example, "drug user" treatment models continue to be categorized as:

1. long term residential,
2. short term in-patient,
3. out-patient drug free,
4. out-patient maintenance, and
5. detoxification

In reality these 5 non-models represent place, time, and techniques. And from a treatment reality perspective there are 4 treatment models:

1. tradition-based,
2. professional model-based,
3. mutual-help-based (AA, NA, GA, OA, etc.), and
4. self-help based treatment or change ("natural recovery").

The ongoing legitimate research question which is asked, in a variation of themes, is: Which of the five models is more effective?

The illegitimate question for which we badly need some generalizable answers is: What are the necessary critical conditions for one of the actual 4 treatment models, each with its range of traditions, policies, goals, staff, and techniques, etc. to engage a person in a planned change process and to achieve treatment goals which are viable, acceptable, etc. given the strengths and limitations of available, accessible endogenous and exogenous resources?

Paradoxical research topics in the field of addictions

The addiction field does not have a unique overarching theoretical framework to explain addiction and its problems. As a result there can be no unique overarching goal in treatment. Some specialists believe that only abstinence is an appropriate goal; others believe that controlled drinking (Sobell & Sobell, 1973, 1978), or a Lindesmith (1968) type intervention providing state regulated consumption of non-therapeutic narcotics (van den Brink et al., 2003), is the answer, whereas others dispute this vigorously (Pendery, Maltzman, & West, 1982). Nevertheless, programs may maintain a homogeneous treatment goal of abstinence for a heterogeneous population of drug users. Others may be funding a study of "evidence-based" treatment of substance users when treatment quality and appropriateness are absent.

Even if the goal of treatment is to promote abstinence, the reality is that addiction is a relapsing type disorder (e.g., "binge drinking") with longer or shorter intervals between binges. However, not all programs recognize these inherent contradictions and program evaluations rarely take them into account. When diagnosing "substance abusers" as manifesting a chronic relapsing disease, researchers would then study their abstinence rates post treatment. Even more paradoxically, the posited chronic drug user patients enrolled in a methadone maintenance treatment program may be expelled for "dirty urines" of non-narcotic drugs.

Some research projects appear to be enamored of the methodological technicalities of research without taking into account the realities of the sites where they are to be carried out. For example, researchers may be positing "treatment matching" in articles and at conferences as a preferred evidence-based treatment model in publicly funded programs whose budgets could not support such a plan and then not making provisions for supplying the funding to demonstrate this empirically. Others may be researching the effectiveness of harm reduction programs for reaching marginalized drug users who do not utilize public resources which more often than not have formal and informal policies which keep "them" at a distance, and then not studying the possibility that these programs may be co-opted into maintaining the marginalization.

Ethics Committees

The fact that an ethics committee or review board of an institution has given the "green light" for a study can give rise to a number of unresolved ethical issues.

- What are the implications of collecting data from individuals who then are not very likely to benefit directly from their participation; what's in it for THEM?
- What are the implications of an institution collecting data from substance users when its formal or informal policies are not to serve the substance user?

A cynical veteran of institutional ethics committees once noted that these committees' primary responsibility is not to prevent harm to the research subject but to prevent harm (in the form of lawsuits) to the institution.

Logic and Statistics

The rigorous logic of scientific thinking used in establishing causality may be far more intimidating, especially to persons with no prior training in logic, philosophy of science, or inadequate backgrounds in those most intimidating of subjects: mathematics (which generally provides the earliest introduction to logical reasoning) and statistics (which codifies probabilistic reasoning). Early math-phobia may be caused by having to learn basic mathematical reasoning from teachers who often don't understand it themselves and whose major qualifications for teaching mathematics is not a knowledge of mathematics but a knowledge of pedagogy and teaching techniques. In such circumstances, it is only the most gifted (such as Pascal [1623–1662 CE] , who, though as a young boy forbidden to learn mathematics, rediscovered the basic propositions of classical Pythagorean geometry by himself, before going on to found the field of probability and statistics) (Ball, 1908), or the most dogged and desperate, who will proceed to learn mathematics or statistics on their own. Many will continue to struggle with lifelong innumeracy and shaky foundations in logical thinking. The result is that ill-designed research projects will generate massive quantities of data from which it is sometimes difficult, or at any rate laborious and time intensive, to derive useful information to increase our fount of knowledge. Projects can include many hundreds of thousands of data points derived from medical records, school records, social assistance records, delinquency records, legal and criminal records, IQ and other test results, residence and driving information, etc., that extend over many years and many jurisdictions. Such massive quantities of data need to be organized into a coherent whole with the researcher essentially imposing a narrative or a background conceptual framework on the data in order to be able to organize it in such a way that the contrast between subgroups of a population can become apparent and used to answer research questions.

There are many ways of structuring data bases, and how they are structured determines to some extent the types of questions they can answer. An early iteration of a drug and alcohol data base was structured temporally in terms of political and geographic jurisdictions, e.g., provinces within a country by year (Popham, Schmidt et al., 1958). A cost-benefit framework (Adrian, 1980) was used to organize an expanded alcohol and drug statistics data bank (Adrian, 1979; 1980b, 1981, 1983, 1985a,b; Adrian, Jull, & Williams, 1989a,b; William, Chang & Truong 1992a,b). Yet another way of structuring a data base is in terms of geography where a distinction was made between urban, semi-urban and rural (Rose, 1998).

The data could then be used to quickly answer not only descriptive questions on how many consumed what substances and in what quantities or forms and in what jurisdiction, but also to answer questions regarding:

1. the economic benefits derived from the production, manufacture, trade, and taxation of substances (e.g., government revenue derived from the sale of tobacco and alcohol amounts to almost 2% and 4% respectively of all government revenue in Canada),
2. the numbers of workers in tobacco processing and manufacture and their salaries and wages,
3. the value of tobacco imports, or
4. the health consequences of use in terms of
    a. mortality from falling asleep while smoking in bed, or
    b. mortality from tobacco-related disorders such as chronic bronchitis, asthma, emphysema, and a proportionate share of deaths due to neoplasms, stroke, hypertension and heart disease (Adrian, Jull, & Williams, 1989b:451-454, 455, 456, 457, 460-462, and 463 respectively).

A socio-geographic framework can be expanded to answer questions regarding epidemiology of substance use in terms of risk exposure (Adrian & Jull, 1991; Adrian, Ferguson, & Her, 1996) and evaluation of prevention interventions (Adrian, Ferguson, & Her, 2001), or of alternative treatment modalities (Ogborne, Adrian et al., 1991; Smart et al., 1993; Adrian, Ogborne et al., 1994; Adrian, Ferguson et al., 1998). These issues could not have been investigated so readily and in as timely a manner (or indeed at all) had access to an organized data base not been available. Inefficiencies in data management resulting in slowness in obtaining accurate answers to issues that have a serious impact on people's lives have an ethical dimension when they prevent or delay a person from obtaining necessary evidence-based effective treatment.

The Problem of Numbers

A recurring problem in research projects is to have too large a number of explanatory variables relative to the sample size. Consider a study with a sample of about 1,500 observations, a perfectly respectable sample size and one that is not uncommon in most population-based survey research studies such as might be done by the Gallup poll. Now, consider that we have a behavior, such as drinking, that we think may be affected by the following seven demographic variables: Gender, Age, Race/ethnicity, Marital status, Education, Employment status, and Income level. Because of the number of categories in each variable (e.g., the variable "gender" has 2 categories "male" and "female," etc.), it is quickly possible to reach a total number of 37 (=2+7+4+5+7+5+7) separate categories (see table 1).

Table 1.12.1: Variables and their categories in a typical study

Variable	Categories	Number of categories
Gender	Male, Female,	2
Age	Under 15 years of age 15 to 17, 18 to 24, 25 to 34, 35 to 44, 45 to 64, 65 and over	7
Race/ethnicity	White Black or African-American Hispanic or Latino Other	4
Marital status	Never married Married Widowed Separated Divorced	5
Education	Less than ninth grade Ninth to twelfth grade (no diploma) High school graduate or GED, Some college, no degree Associate degree, Bachelor's degree, Advanced degree (graduate school, professional degree)	7

Variable (cont.)	Categories (cont.)	Number of categories (cont.)
Employment status	Employed full time, Employed part-time, Unemployed, Student, Retired	5
Income level	Less than $5,000 $5,000 to $14,999 $15,000 to 24,999 $25,000 to 34,999 $35, 000 to 49,999 $50,000 to 74,999 $75,000 and over	7
Total variables 7	Total categories 37	

These categories correspond to those used in the U.S. Census (U.S. Census Bureau, 2004)

Although the total number of variables (7) and categories (37) are clearly fewer than the total sample size of 1,500, a major problem arises if we wish to consider the effect of the categories of each variable upon each other using a factorial design to test for interaction effects (also known as "cross-tabulation"). Please note that according to some authors, "factorial designs are the only effective way to examine interaction effects" (Trochim, 2001:200). The total number of possible cross-tabulations of variables and their categories (called, respectively, "factors" and "levels" in factorial design) would produce 68,600 (=2x7x4x5x7x5x7) cells, a number which far exceeds the total number of observations (n=1,500) in the sample. The number of cells with no observations in them would be high. Analysis of these types of data using factorial design will pose not only statistical difficulties (for example, to use certain statistical tests there have to be some 30 observations in each cell), but cross-tabulation results will be difficult to interpret meaningfully. Once again, the reality that powerful techniques, such as ANN (Buscema, 1998), have been available for a number of decades and are appropriate for such data analysis research yet are not used is an example of data analysis ethical issues in the substance use(r) research field.

Another problem is to have a larger number of variables than of observations. This can arise when researchers use multiple pre-existing complex research instruments within a study in order to increase the reliability and validity of their research (as well as the likelihood of a positive review for funding purposes when the grant reviewer recognizes one of the already validated instruments in their field). One difficulty can arise when multiple and partly duplicative questionnaire instruments are used in a project; in order not to invalidate a previously validated instrument, one may be reluctant to eliminate duplicate questions even when these may be redundant within the context of the whole questionnaire. The not infrequent but rarely mentioned situation of the respondent giving different answers to the same duplicated question asked in multiple sections of a multi-part questionnaire raises even more questions about data validity and the quality of the results and conclusions drawn from them.

In this author's experience the situation of too many variables relative to the sample size can also arise when:

1. the minimum sample size for the study has been improperly specified,
2. there are problems of ascertainment or recruitment,
3. the researcher is dealing with a rare event,
4. the sample has been chosen from the wrong population, or
5. the wrong sampling framework has been used, etc.

The situation can also occur when a project involves multiple members, each of whom may contribute to a questionnaire, but some of whom may leave before data analysis has been fully specified or begun, while remaining team members have no interest or knowledge of that area. One very large data bank of medical procedures in Canada for years routinely, laboriously, and expensively coded whether procedures had been done on the right- or left-hand side of the body ("handedness"). The person who had set up the data collection protocol left shortly after the project was begun, and the handedness data, which went on to puzzle programmers and data analysts for years to come, was never analyzed.

A different set of issues arises from the use of the "omnibus" survey questionnaire. An omnibus survey incorporates a wide array of questions on a variety of unrelated topics. They are usually administered by commercial survey companies, such as the Gallup Poll, but also government statistical bureaus, such as Statistics Canada (the Canadian federal agency that according to *The Economist* has been the world's leader in statistical accuracy) that conduct periodic (often weekly) surveys of the population. Questions can address any topic including opinions and behaviors such as knowledge of marijuana legislation (Adrian, 1980c), as well as car purchasing intentions, toothpaste brand preference, etc. all in the same survey. Each set of questions is intended to be independent of any other. However, it is possible (and indeed highly likely) that the lingering memory of a preceding set of questions may color one's understanding (and responses) to subsequent questions. Since the sequence of questions may influence responses, a different sequence of the same set of questions may elicit different responses and the validity of responses, research results, conclusions, and policy recommendations may be questionable.

Since we use model building to generate testable hypotheses, it is incumbent upon the researcher to specify parsimoniously those variables expected to have a causative effect (independent variables) and those that are consequent (dependent variables). If we include a specific variable we should have a very good reason to do so and we should include it only if we intend to use it. To do otherwise is not only to embark on a "fishing expedition" but also to burden the respondents unduly by using up their time answering questions unlikely to ever be used.

Statistics and Research: Statistically Significant vs. Meaningful Results

Many researchers equate statistical significance with substantive significance, although this is incorrect. A large enough sample size will, however, achieve statistically significant findings even when these findings are not substantive (i.e., they are not meaningful in the real world). An early version of a Canadian alcohol and drug statistics compendium widely used in policy recommendations made much of the 0.1% increase in a particular indicator. However, most alcohol and drug related events are relatively rare at a population level. A public health specialist pointed out to the economist who had prepared the report that, for public health monitoring or planning purposes, an extra death from liver cirrhosis per year out of a total of over 2,000 such deaths was for all intents and purposes negligible.[4] Conversely, very small changes may not be statistically significant yet be enormously important in the real world. The current U.S. population is approximately 300 million, of whom about 2 million die yearly. Should the number of deaths increase by 1, this would not be statistically significant. Yet if the death was due to inhalation anthrax, smallpox, or pneumonic plague, all of which are enormously: infectious, have a high case fatality rate, and have applications in bio-terrorism, this would be enormously and substantively significant in the real world today.

One problem that arises from a too-small sample size is that it may be difficult to test hypotheses without accepting a low level of statistical significance. The significance of the size of an effect is linked to the number of observations, or sample size, on which it has been made. The sample size should be set according to the expected size of the effect and how much the researcher wants to be right—which is itself dependent on how unwilling the researcher is to be wrong. The researcher can be wrong by thinking there is an effect when there is none (Type I error, or alpha error), or thinking there is no effect when there is one (Type II error, or beta error). The alpha level corresponds to the *level of significance*.

The conventional set-point level of significance in research has been the 5% or 0.05 *probability level* (p). In other words, the results one has found may be due to chance alone 5 times out of 100 (or one out of 20 times). Lower probability levels are deemed preferable ($p \leq 0.01$ is better than $p \leq 0.05$), and higher levels are deemed worse. At $0.05 \leq p \leq 0.10$, the results are deemed "suggestive," a compromise due to the fact that in some fields large sample sizes are difficult to achieve (e.g., economists who use aggregate time series data are unlikely to find more than a few decades' worth of data).

According to Brian Ferguson (2005):

> *Suppose you start with the hypothesis that there is an effect from some hypothesized cause, but that it will be quantitatively small. Then, given the value of alpha that you want to work at—5% or 1% or whatever—you can calculate the minimum sample size necessary to detect that effect at the specified alpha level. Then you collect a sample of that size, and if you can't find it in a sample of that size, it probably isn't really there. It's different, of course, when you aren't sampling but have to use whatever data are available—then you might not have a large enough sample to estimate a small effect...That's different from hypothesizing an effect, finding it not to be significant, and saying that if we had a larger sample size it would be significant so we'll treat it as if it were significant.*

"The Truth but Not the Whole Truth": Less than Accurate Research Findings and the Problem of Outliers

Research findings do not always correspond to ideal patterns that perfectly correspond to what we hope to find. The data may contain "noise," random fluctuations that obscure the meaning (message) of our findings. Minuscule errors in observation can introduce random fluctuations in the data. Hence, we may find "outliers" that fall outside the scope or pattern of our findings. The astute researcher needs to put aside such noise and concentrate on the essence of the message. However, it is not always clear what is an outlier and what is the main finding. Sometimes in the early phase of development of a field, there is a tendency to concentrate on the main or most evident pattern in order to make the fundamental discoveries, and it is only as a field develops that the hidden meaning of outliers becomes evident. A recent review of Mendel's research notes indicate that, in his work with garden peas, he discarded the outliers in his data so as to establish the rules of dominant and recessive inheritance of genetic traits (Mendelian inheritance). However, outliers themselves may provide crucial evidence. It was fluctuations in the observed planetary orbit of Neptune relative to its calculated orbit that led to the discoveries of the planets Uranus and Pluto, and fluctuations in the luminosity of distant stars that is the current basis for discovering extra-solar planets. A published "anecdote" merits recounting from the drug user treatment field. During the 1950s, Riverside Hospital, built to treat tuberculosis and situated between the land of the Bronx and Rikers Island prison, treated civilly committed drug users from the age of 13 years and 1 day to 21 years minus 1 day. The legal papers were valid for three years. For years the literature referred to research implemented there which documented, empirically, that there were 7 times as many male drug users as female drug users and that only 2% of patients interviewed a year after treatment were abstinent, as reported in the Alksne Report (1959). The report did not note that there were 7 times as many beds for males, who were housed in the hospital building, as there were for females, who were housed in a separate building, or that the average time for once-a-week individual treatment was only two months (8-9 sessions at most) for the patients who had been interviewed in a follow-up a year after their treatment.

Policy research and evaluation

In some cases, evaluation research is undertaken to examine the effect of some existing organizational policy or program. Such research may have considerable impact on people's lives including that of the persons who have developed the policy or program, those who deliver and administer the program, and the persons to whom the policy or program is directed and who are the subjects of or participants in the program. Clearly the stakes are high. Often the data that are available were set up for administrative rather than research purposes. So while there may be considerable data available, they may not be the right data to answer a specific researcher's question. It is only relatively recently (in the last decade or two) that many grantors or other funders began to have a requirement to incorporate an evaluative component in service programs. Although evaluative data may be collected, the needs of evaluation over time may vary, and burning issues of today were never dreamt of when the programs (and their evaluation data components) were set up five or ten years earlier. Hence it may be necessary to use proxy data that provide more or less accurate approximate measures of the variables of concern. Results based on proxy measures may differ from those that would have been obtained with the actual data had they existed, and hence conclusions as to the effectiveness of a program may be unduly optimistic or pessimistic.

Because of the importance or divisiveness of the issues, outside researchers may be contracted to do the evaluation. They may be more, or less, familiar with the specific service delivery field, with the issues and administrative practices of the particular program, or with the data that is available. For example, recently a World Bank staff member was given the responsibility for setting up a "harm reduction" program for drug users in Bangladesh. This person's background in economics and/or systemic administration may be helpful in doing cost benefit analysis or helping to determine cost-efficient operational procedures, but a lack of knowledge of psychological and medical problems or health-related issues may hamper that person's ability to help in the planning, implementing, overseeing, and researching of what needs to be researched in a Third World country's introduction to harm reduction for Injection Drug Users (IDUs). Program staff may be more or less forthcoming. Data that are provided may be incomplete, and crucial elements may be unavailable, as when inexperienced junior trainees accidentally overwrite and obliterate several years of data. Again, results could be unduly optimistic or pessimistic. In addition, in some cases there may simply not be enough data to make a judgment. Governments or corporations, however, may have pressing issues that require rapid action to avert impending disasters and cannot wait the several years it may take to collect better data. Real world decision making must often take place under conditions of uncertainty, in which the best input of the researcher is to provide an approximate, probabilistic, and possibly "gut-level, best guess" answer. While far from an ideal answer and far from the ideal rigorous research model, in some cases seasoned researchers with a good sense of the issues and the data can indeed make reasonable, meaningful statements on an issue, so long as the issue is not an ideological one on which they have their own ideological stance.

More troubling is the situation in which an organization with a predetermined agenda sets up a "needs assessment" or other such study which is intended to bolster a particular position. The issue of "stake holders" (individuals as well as systems) and their influence remains under-developed in substance user research. Some have questioned whether, for example, NIDA's commitment for a number of years to study drug use as a "disease of the brain" was based upon empirically driven data, the director's agenda, or other considerations. Often, the researcher is put in the position of having to find the data to justify or "back up" a decision that has already been made. Contradictory findings must be ignored or discredited. And while it is fair play in the research game to attempt to find the flaws in a theory, hypothesis, experiment, or other study, as that is the way that one tests the validity of a hypothesis (by seeking to disprove it), such critical analysis is intended to be applied to all research findings, including those that support, as well as those that take an oppositional view to one's own opinion on an issue.

False results

A more egregious problem arises when the researcher, convinced that there is an effect (but that it is not apparent because of the sample size) and under time pressure to produce results, may help the situation along. At least this was the reason given by the Sloan-Kettering cancer researcher for painting the skin of the mice that he was using the color they would have been had his experiment worked. The rest of the scientific community called it scientific misconduct, or fraud. (A synopsis of the case can be found at http://www-personal.umich.edu/~bobden/scientific_misconduct.pdf).

Problems relating to the science of research

Because the point of research is to gain an accurate understanding of the world or those parts of it that we are researching, it is incumbent upon researchers to use their best skills to find the truth, notwithstanding that in our *de facto* reality there is no "truth." False results obviously cannot meet those requirements. Results pre-determined before the research is conducted may or may not correspond to the real world situation: we have no way of knowing since the research to test their validity has obviously not been done! Results based on a lack of the right question, or use of the wrong reasoning, the wrong research design or method or statistics or data, are unlikely to provide a valid understanding of the phenomena being investigated. If one of the fundamental tenets of conducting research is to get at the truth, then this cannot be achieved through this approach. To contend otherwise would be misleading.

The Funding of Research and Research Management

Grants-based funding

The emphasis on the minutiae of data gathering is evident in many grant proposals, where far less attention seems to be given to the asking of interesting questions, "illegitimate questions" or to consideration of how such questions could best be answered through research design and the formulation of testable hypotheses. Because much of the health or addiction research in the U.S. is grant driven and proposals are peer reviewed as well as institutionally reviewed by the grantee and the grantor, proposals must be based on concepts that are familiar to the reviewer. Hence, it is possible that "major breakthrough"-type research will likely not be favorably reviewed because it is viewed as being too new and untried. (*The Journal of Irreproducible Results* once ran a spoof article on how the granting agency reviewers had rejected as untried God's proposal to create the universe.)

Another difficulty is the fact that it takes a relatively long time for discoveries to be made. One needs to have a degree of basic and background knowledge, become interested in the right problem, ask the right question, and be insightful in interpreting results before an initial discovery can be made. From initial discovery to practical application a twenty-year time-span is not unusual. It took 40 years between Einstein's famous $e=mc^2$ equation in his 1905 paper (Gribbin & Gribbin, 2005) and the first atom bomb (1945), and even longer to the first atomic submarines and nuclear power generation reactors. It took several decades between synthesis of LSD and its use, first in the field of psychotherapy for which it showed promise initially, followed by its increasing use as an unregulated recreational drug before the health consequences became known. Yet, consider the ethical implications that in funded NIDA/NIAAA[5] research the usual time span for a grant is no more than three years, a period insufficient for studying complex, multi-dimensional concepts and processes in an era of "evidence-based" intervention.

Sometimes it seems that the research that is accepted is likely to increase our understanding of an issue only marginally. Progress is a matter of inches rather than the leaps and bounds that may be needed with certain critical issues. In the grants environment of funding, grant proposals are institutionally reviewed by the grantor. When a funding agency, such as NIDA, claims that it funds 85% of all research in a field, the requirements of a granting agency can determine the research agendas of a whole field. This presents an interesting paradox. In theory, researchers are expected to undertake research in order to fill gaps they discover in our understanding. In practice, areas of research are dictated by the policy interests of grantors (viz. "he who pays the piper calls the tune"). In some cases, agencies that are government grant funded but administratively independent of government, so called Non-Government Organizations (NGOs) or quasi-non-government organizations (QUANGOS), or other independent organizations, including "think-tanks" such as the Rand Corporation, Mathematica, The Research Triangle Institute, The Hudson or Cato Institutes in the U.S., and Informetrica, The Atlantic Institute for Market Studies or the Fraser Institute in Canada, or university professors and researchers, are selected to carry out research on topics that are of particular interest to government and which have policy implications so that their implementation results in policy change. Having policy research being conducted by NGOs, QUANGOs, think-tanks, university professors and other such, allows governments to conveniently distance themselves from any research results or conclusions that may be embarrassing or controversial. Such policy reports are then tabled (i.e., "presented" in parliamentary procedural terms), but the policies they advocate are not implemented. Proportionately, there are far more NGO or contract based research organizations in the U.S. than in Canada. The proportion of policy vs. "pure" research carried out by university based professors varies between countries, being for instance higher in Canada or the U.K. and lower in the U.S, whereas the reverse is true of NGO research. Many NGOs or contract research organizations have well-known political or ideological biases (e.g., the CATO and Fraser institutes are conservative, other NGOs are known to be liberal) and the selection of a particular NGO to carry out certain research almost guarantees a particular type of conclusion and policy advice on the issue. Historically, in Canada, a higher proportion of university-based policy research was likely to be implemented, whereas in the U.S. not only was there a lower proportion of policy research undertaken by academics, but such research also had a lower likelihood of being implemented. This has allowed professors in the U.S. to be much freer in their choice of research topics and conclusions, since they have a lesser need to be pragmatic and circumspect in their stated conclusions. In the U.S., public funds will most likely continue to support a broad range of substance use and misuse intervention processes, efforts, and concepts or ideologies. The "researcher" in the U.S., whatever his/her discipline, status, or number of years in this field, *knows* (or chooses not to know)—based upon endless evidence—that the likelihood that his/her documented generalizable findings will more than likely not be used for needed macro policy-making generally, nor, more specifically, for making viable micro changes with which to effect needed processes and outcomes.[6]

The difficulty is that researchers, understandably, want to use their research results to make policy recommendations which they believe to be optimal in terms of their effect on the individual. Policy makers, also understandably, want conclusions that are pragmatic in that they can be implemented to yield reasonably good results for most people, even when these are less than optimal for any particular individual. As the late Monique Begin, Minister of Health and Welfare Canada and member of the federal Cabinet under Prime Minister Pierre Trudeau, often repeated in public interviews "Politics is the art of the possible." Thus policies that are adopted often appear to be cobbled from less than optimal but highly feasible compromises. In mathematical terms, political compromise corresponds to the use of optimal control theory which "has as its objective the maximization of the return from, or the minimization of the cost of, the operation of physical, social, and economic processes" (Kirk, 1970). Researchers whose field is oriented toward individual processes (e.g., physicians, psychologists, social workers, and other clinicians), may be frustrated by what they consider to be a betrayal of their truths, whereas policy makers are frustrated by a lack of appreciation of what they consider to be their practical needs. Is it a funded researcher's and author's responsibility, at the very least, to remind the reader to consider "this" as an issue which may merit someone's interest and concern?

Government grants

When grantors are government agencies they may be limited in terms of what they can fund depending on the ideologies and belief systems of political leaders and governments in power, even when these beliefs systems are not supported by our current scientific knowledge. For example, Russian genetics was hampered for decades by the Lysenko (1898-1976 CE) (http://www.encyclopedia.com/searchpool.asp?target=@DOCTITLE%20Lysenko%20%20Trofim%20Denisovich) model based on Lamarck's (1744-1829 CE) (http://www.ucmp.berkeley.edu/history/lamarck.html) theory of inheritance of acquired characteristics. According to this model, if you cut off a rat's tail the next generation of rats would be born tailless, clearly something that does not happen in nature. Lysenko genetics corresponded to a rigid communist era political ideology that believed in the perfectibility of man, with the new man who would replace the degenerate scion of defunct western political regimes, the product of the new communist social system. It is beyond the scope of this paper to debate political ideology, especially of defunct political regimes, but clearly the results in terms of advancement of Soviet genetics and agricultural crop yields were less than spectacular. Similarly in the U.S., certain lines of research have been blocked for a number of years because of ideological and political opposition. For example, U.S. research using stem cells that may offer promise for persons suffering from neurological disorders, including those that may be related to substance use or misuse, is hampered by the conservative Moral Majority's opposition to abortion whence many stem cells originate. Similarly, U.S. research into the use of condoms to prevent the spread of AIDS is relatively limited in view of official positions on sexual morality by conservative groups. The application of evidence-based research findings to reduce AIDS due to injection drug use or sex may be even more limited due to ideological positions. Although condoms became available in federal prisons in Canada more than a decade ago, and condom distribution in European prisons is increasing (Schaller & Harding, 1995) they were only available in seven jails and prisons in the US (Anonymous, 2003), and completely unavailable in Ireland (Jurgens, 2002).

Non-government grants

The development of non-governmental granting agencies administered by persons with a special interest in specific diseases that they or their family members may have offers a more immediate impact on solving practical problems. These disease-specific agencies such as the *Christopher Reeve*[7] *Paralysis Foundation* described as "committed to funding research that develops treatments and cures for paralysis caused by spinal cord injury and other central nervous system disorders… [and] also vigorously work[ing] to improve the quality of life for people living with disabilities" (http://www.christopher-reeve.org/about/aboutmain.cfm), or the *Michael J. Fox*[8] *Foundation for Parkinson's Research* described as "dedicated to the aggressive pursuit of all ethical avenues of research promising improved therapies and ultimately a cure for people living with Parkinson's disease" (http://www.michaeljfox.org/), are less interested in fundamental or basic research and much more interested in practical results that are likely to offer a cure or hope of a cure in the near future. Similarly, the *Bill and Melinda Gates*[9] *Foundation*, described as "dedicated to closing the tremendous gaps in health… work[ing] to ensure that lifesaving advances in health are created and shared with those who need them most…[and] mak[ing] sure that there are systems in place to adopt and sustain [them]" (http://www.gatesfoundation.org/AboutUs/LetterfromBillMelindaFrenchGates/default.htm) is interested in making existing technologies and solutions available to deal with urgent health problems of the developing world. The addition of experienced and reputable researchers on their review committees is intended to prevent their funding of crackpot projects rather than ensuring continued scientific orthodoxy.

"Hard money," salaried research, and in-house research

In some cases, research is funded on a "hard monies" basis rather than being grant dependent. Permanent institutional staff are paid a salary that allows them to conduct research within the areas of interest or responsibility of their employer's mandate, but with a considerable amount of latitude as to the exact research questions or research methods used, so long as these are not too financially onerous relative to the size of the organization and usual standards of safety of human subjects is maintained (see below). Resident scientists, in addition to their pre-determined projects, carry out independent research. This in-house research model has been used by a number of governmental research organizations in Canada and the U.S. For instance, the staff of Statistics Canada and of Health and Welfare Canada, federal government departments, in conjunction with other researchers, have regularly conducted research in the alcohol (Riley [government author name underlined] & Adrian, 1993), drug (Adrian, Layne, & Williams, 1996) and tobacco areas (Adrian, Lundy, & Eliany, 1996) and in special populations (Eliany & Clarke, 1992) for many years, whereas part of the National Institute on Alcohol Abuse and Alcoholism not only supports but also "**conducts** [author's emphasis] biomedical and behavioral research" (http://www.niaaa.nih.gov/) (See Allen et al., 1993 for an example of a peer reviewed article based on such research conducted partly by funding agency staff.).

Several difficulties arise with the in-house model of research management. This research may encroach on the time that the staff person should be devoting to his or her job-specific tasks (and vice versa). The institutional researcher may be competing with grants-based researchers in terms of research topics to be undertaken. Grants-based researchers who depend on grants for their livelihood may not get any funding if they find that their idea has already been done by someone who did not have to compete through the onerous grants mechanism for funding. On the other hand, in-house research will have produced results far more quickly to the benefit of advancing knowledge in the field than if one had to send out a Request For Proposals (RFP) and wait for potentially interested researchers to discover the RFP, prepare a grants submission that must be peer reviewed, and possibly revised and resubmitted, before the project can be started. The turn around time can often take several years.

One difficulty is that, in some cases, in-house government research may be slow to be commercialized and reach the marketplace and the potential patients, clients, or customers (including government in its role as buyer) who may need these products and services. Certainly, this was one of the dilemmas underpinning government "make or buy" policies intended to ensure goods and services are available in a timely manner and on a least-cost basis, when large-scale government manufacturing is impractical or unlikely in a privatizing political and economic climate, as in the U.S., which is privatizing many of the functions previously undertaken by government, including not only public schools and prisons but also some of the ancillary military support functions which are now being carried out by private contractors. Although some would argue that private enterprise may be more innovative and efficient than the public sector, which often has an entrenched and immovable bureaucracy to contend with, others raise concerns that the private profit motive may be resulting in reduced benefits to the public good when the dedication and public spirit of conscientious career public servants is replaced with the "me-first" personal attitude and indifference to the good of the public of overworked and overstressed employees seeking to maximize their current income while keeping an eye out for their next job pending the next lay-off.

It is not always clear which is the better approach of research management to optimally improve our knowledge, serve the public good, and meet the financial daily living requirements of highly qualified staff. In Canada, a considerable amount of alcohol, tobacco, and drug treatment research is conducted by agencies that are based in or affiliated with hospitals which are funded by the provincial ministries of health. Provincial fiscal restraint measures were introduced in the 1990s and were expected to achieve a 30% reduction in expenditures by attrition of permanent salaried staff. More numerous, and more highly paid, administrative staff with experience in industrial restructuring were hired to conduct layoffs of nurses and researchers (including alcohol, tobacco, and other drug researchers), some of whom were rehired as non-permanent (and more highly paid) contract workers or consultants by the Ontario Health Ministry for example (since the duties of the laid-off staff still had to be carried out), while others left their profession or the province, seeking employment in other areas.

One of the consequences of the fall of communism is that many highly trained professional and scientific personnel in the former Soviet Bloc countries, who had been highly valued by the previous regime and received good salaries and numerous job perks (e.g., having country residences, being allowed to travel abroad), suddenly became unemployed or received salaries that were insufficient to meet their daily needs in the newly privatized economies. Deprived of their daily bread and of a social system that may have been inequitable and despotic but that they at least understood and through which they could negotiate their way, some remained in a state of shock waiting for the government to intervene and others emigrated or sold their services to whoever would employ them (the spectacle of the university professor waitressing because it paid better was not entirely uncommon). In some cases, certain scientific staff who had worked in the oil and gas industries became owners of industrial enterprises. One major concern identified in the western press was the extent to which those who had worked in the military, with armaments, or in the nuclear industry, would be tempted to sell to terrorist organizations their knowledge or the nuclear arsenal to which they had access. Soros' *Open Society Institute*, established to "help countries make the transition from communism (http://www.soros.org/about/overview), [and to] promot[e] the restructuring of transitional economies, focusing on building viable market economies and creating new jobs" (http://www.soros.org/initiatives) was one of the few that offered a stipend to former Soviet scientists to allow them to continue to conduct research, thus obviating the need to peddle their skills or specialized knowledge to less than benign potential employers. The *Lindesmith Center*, a leading drug policy institute with a keen interest in Eastern Europe, including the fostering of drug research, was created in 1994 under the direction of Ethan Nadelmann (2000) with the philanthropic support of George Soros.[10]

Research Methods Applied to Human Subjects Research

The issue of research ethics is taken most frequently to be synonymous with the area of human subjects research. Indeed, it is when we work with humans that the greatest harm can occur if strict ethical standards are not applied. One problem is that the ultimate recipient of treatment or other interventions is a human being, and there is no guarantee that the intervention will work or at least not make matters worse or prove fatal to the recipient. In order to protect the human, the tradition has been to try things out first on lesser beings. Thus, early scientific experiments on nerve conduction were carried out on frogs by Galvani (1737-1798 CE) and Volta (1745-1827 CE)—and repeated by generations of high school and college students since—and mice were used initially to study respiration by Lavoisier (1743-1794 CE). However, at some point there is a need to see if the same process will also work on humans. In the early days of medical science, gradations of more or less valuable human lives were used when first switching from animals to humans. The young, the old, the very sick, the terminally ill or about-to-die, the poor, prisoners, slaves, foreigners, the uninformed and the gullible, and racial and ethnic minorities were all at one time used as the first human subjects for untested or dangerous interventions.

The first blood transfusion was carried out between a sheep and a young peasant lad (the boy survived). The first vaccine—cowpox, somewhat protective against smallpox—was tested by Edward Jenner (1749-1823 CE) on the son of his gardener (Brown, 1996; Edward Jenner Institute for Vaccine Research, undated).

The march of the French Revolution and Napoleon's armies across Europe was accompanied by enormous advances in medicine and surgery as new techniques were tried on horribly wounded and moribund soldiers by young military surgeons (who were not linked to the conservative university medical schools). Similar advances were made in all modern wars: the American Civil War (McGiveney, undated) saw the introduction of the syringe (the necessary cause for injection drug use); modern plastic surgery was an offshoot of World War I (Penn Surgery, 2005); mobile blood transfusions were perfected by Canadian doctor Norman Bethune during the Spanish Civil War (CBC, 2005); effective sunscreen was first developed for American troops in the Viet Nam war. All of these advances were eventually made available to the civilian population, but not until they had been proven effective in large populations of soldiers. For example, the early successes with military surgical anesthesia eventually led to civilian anesthesia, including the use of anesthesia by the English Queen Victoria when she gave birth. U.S.

soldiers in the Pacific who were deployed to witness Atom Bomb testing on Pacific islands were unwitting, and probably unintended testees of the effects of radioactive dust from nuclear explosions (Asimov, 1979). The awful wounds of soldiers not only required but allowed for more creative medical solutions since it was also unheard of for soldiers to sue the military for any medical misadventure they may have experienced as a result of their military career. It is not until recently that veterans' groups have become involved in seeking compensation consequent to the effects they suffered as a result of the use of the defoliant Agent Orange in the Viet Nam War, or that of armor-piercing uranium bullets and nerve gas prophylaxis during the First Gulf War.

Hospital charity wards were routinely used by medical students to gain the skills they would need when they began to treat paying customers. Early vaccines were tested in prisoners (who may have hoped for reduced sentences if they participated), or on mentally retarded or other inmates of psychiatric institutions (who may not have understood what was being done to them), or on "foreigners." One of the first large-scale tests of Dr. Jonas Salk's killed polio vaccine was done in the 1950s in Montreal, Canada, where horrific polio epidemics had occurred in the Montreal region for several years prior, and parents were eager to allow anything that would offer some protection to their children. (This author well remembers having classmates in Montreal who had had polio with its consequent neuro-motor deficits.) Some early versions of what may become a vaccine for AIDS are currently being tested with greater or lesser success in prostitutes, injection drug users, and other at-risk populations in developing countries (Waldholz & King, 1999; CNN.com, 1999; Elias, 2003; Cromie, 2003). This has been criticized by some as yet another instance of the developing world exporting one of its risks which it is unwilling to bear to a place that has no power to protest, or to bear the financial burden of the full extent of the risks. Even the pro-business newspaper, *The Wall Street Journal* (2005), has noted that:

> *With more than 1 billion people, India provides a huge pool of potential trial subjects [for clinical trials], meaning tests could be organized quickly, and costs are lower than in the developed world, [but] some ethical questions have also risen, such as whether poor or sick Indians might be duped into taking drugs they don't understand, reducing them to Third World human guinea pigs.*

The ultimate test of the macho medical researcher was, and continues to be even today, a willingness to use himself as the first recipient of a new vaccine or treatment. The developer of Western Equine Encephalitis vaccine would always inform his students at the University of Pittsburgh that he was the first human recipient of the vaccine (Western Equine Encephalitis vaccine is used in horses and at the present time is not licensed for use in humans (http://www.cdc.gov/ncidod/dvbid/arbor/weefact.htm).) Australian physician Barry Marshall (one of the two discoverers) infected himself with *Helicobacter pylori* to prove that ulcers were an infectious disease that could be cured with antibiotics (AstraZeneca, 2004).

More relevant to the substance use and misuse field was the study done on himself by Dr. Albert Hofmann (1970, 1971), Director of Research, Department of Natural Products, Sandoz Ltd., Basel, Switzerland, to test the pharmaco-activity of a specimen of *Psilocybe mexicana Heim* that had been sent to his laboratory. Previous animal tests had been inconclusive, whereas "human beings provide a more sensitive index of substances with psychic effects than animals" (Hofmann, 1970). It was necessary to determine if there was in fact a pharmaco-active effect in the sample prior to undertaking chemical analysis to isolating the pharmaco-active ingredient. "With the aid of this reliable test in human beings, it was then possible to extract the active principles from the mushroom and to purify and crystallize them. The main active component was named psilocybin, and an accompanying alkaloid, usually present only in small amounts, named psilocin" (Hofmann, 1970).

Similarly, in 1955, the Canadian psychiatrist Osmond conducted a series of experiments on himself to test the effect of *Rivea corymbosa* seeds, called Ololiuqui by the Aztec and which has been used since pre-Hispanic times in religious ceremonies and magic medicinal practices. After taking 60 to 100 seeds, Dr. Osmond passed into a state of apathy and listlessness accompanied by increased visual sensitivity (Hofmann, 1970, 1971).

During World War II, Danish pharmacologists Erik Jacobsen (head of research) and Jens Held, working on developing medication to kill intestinal parasites based on Disulfiram, then an ointment used to treat the skin disease scabies, found that after exposure to Disulfiram during laboratory work, they developed nausea and other unpleasant symptoms during meals when they consumed alcohol (e.g., beer, aquavit). This accidental self-experimentation led to the use of Disulfiram (or Antabuse) in aversive alcohol therapy with chronic alcoholics (Gratzer, 2002).

Not all human experimentation has been benign. Experimentation on humans was first described two thousand years ago by Suetonius, the Roman historian who, in his *The Twelve Caesars*, described how the effect of poisons would be tested on slaves, or how one of the Roman emperors would ligature the penises of male slaves who had been made to drink wine to increase their propensity to urinate, to see how this would affect them (they died of uremic poisoning within a few days), as well as conducting vivisections on human slaves. The latter was considered particularly horrific, not because of the human suffering it caused, but because cutting open a human body, except in battle-related activities, was sacrilegious (Galen, the famous 2nd century Roman physician whose textbooks were widely used during the Middle Ages, pictures the human fetus growing inside its mother's forked double womb based on animal dissections).

In the 20th century, the Nazis carried out human experiments on Jewish, Gypsy, and other concentration camp prisoners who were infected with typhus, cholera, smallpox, diphtheria, malaria, and other infectious diseases to test vaccines or treatments (although the outcomes were usually fatal) or simply to follow the course of the disease to the point of death to provide information to help the German military (Cornwell, 2004). To see how long a person could survive in the cold, imprisoned Russian soldiers were forced to swim in freezing water until they died, some begging to be shot because of the pain (Shirer, 1960). As part of these series of experiments, and more relevant to the substance field, are the Nazi mescaline experiments to develop a "mind control" drug to use on unruly people. The experiments were run by Dr. Kurt Plotner on Jews, gypsies, and Russians at the Dachau concentration camp. The mescaline was administered covertly, and subjects experienced extreme disorientation, thinking they had gone raving mad since they had no idea this was being caused by an external agent. Some subjects became furious, others melancholy or gay as though drunk; "sentiments of hatred and revenge were exposed in every case" (Marks, 1979 p.5), and caused certain people to "reveal their most intimate secrets" (Marks, 1979 p.6).

There were also American studies carried out on human subjects without their knowledge or consent. Among the better known and (in)famous are the Tuskegee, Alabama (USA) syphilis studies on poor Black men initiated in 1932, ostensibly offering treatment for the disease, but in fact merely studying the life course of the disease. Despite the availability of effective penicillin treatment after World War II, the study was continued until the 1970s when newspaper stories broke (Babbie, 2004). Again more relevant to the substance use and misuse field are the attempts to develop a "truth" drug under the direction of Dr. Wilfred Overholser using mescaline, barbiturates, and, in 1943, *Cannabis indica* in St. Elizabeth's Hospital in Washington by the Office of Strategic Services, the US wartime intelligence agency (Marks, 1979 p.6).

Deceptive practices have been used in human behavior research to circumvent the possibility that participants' behavior may be influenced by trying to please the researchers should they know what the researchers were trying to prove. For example medical researchers use placebo control groups in case the effect is due to suggestion rather than to the new medication. In some behavior research, study participants may not be told the real reason for the research, or may be given incomplete information. For example, Milgram (1963, 1965) studied the extent to which people are willing to harm others when following orders by getting college students to supposedly administer electric shocks to others as part of a learning experiment. The deceptive practices of this study have been criticized as unethical since many students became deeply troubled as a result of thinking they had administered what they thought were near lethal shocks. More relevant to the substance use and misuse field are the covert studies of the effects of LSD. D-lysergic acid diethylamide, or LSD (known initially as LSD-25), was first developed in 1938 in the Sandoz pharmaceutical-chemical research laboratories in Basle, Switzerland, for its possible applications in obstetrics-gynecology (LSD is mildly uterotonic). Its pharmaco-active effects were discovered in 1943 by chemist Albert Hofmann (1970; Beresford, 1999), who had accidentally ingested a small amount. LSD was used initially in psychotherapeutic contexts, before its use eventually became popular in the drug subculture of the 1960s through the impetus of Dr. Timothy Leary, a Harvard professor who advocated psychedelic experiences. Military use of LSD was considered, according to Brigadier General J. H. Rothschild (1964), commanding general of the United States Army Chemical Corps Research and Development Command, since a "military commander under the effects of LSD-25 would lose his ability to make logical, rational decisions and issue coherent orders. Group cooperation would fall apart...." CIA experiments with LSD were conducted on many unwitting subjects, most often prisoners or patrons of brothels set up and run by the Agency, which had installed two-way mirrors in the establishments to allow for observation of the drug's effects (Andrews, 2001), sometimes with fatal results. On November 19, 1953, an Army scientist and germ warfare specialist named Frank Olson was slipped a solid dose of LSD in his drink. After spending eight days stumbling about in what many observers described as a paranoid, depressed state, Olson jumped through his hotel window in New York and fell ten stories to his death (Andrews, 2001; Hofmann, 1980).

Standards for Ethical Human Subjects Research.

A number of standards to ensure that the research is carried out according to the highest ethical standards have been instituted, following the Nuremberg war crimes tribunal. These standards are constantly being revised by national and international organizations. The U.S. government, through The National Cancer Institute of The National Institutes of Health, maintains a web site at: http://cme.cancer.gov/clinical-trials/learning/humanparticipant-protections.asp that provides training to persons who will be conducting government funded human subjects research.

In essence, the current standards require that research involving humans must ensure that "respect for persons, beneficence, and justice" is provided to participants (Belmont, 1979). Whatever is done to human participants must first do no harm and protect participants from harm by maximizing anticipated benefits and minimizing possible risks of harm. It must provide a benefit, "a valued or desired outcome enjoyed by the participant (therapeutic benefit), or accruing to a group under study, or to their family members, or to scientific knowledge (nontherapeutic benefit)." The distribution of burdens and benefits must be fair. Persons must give their *informed consent* before they can become voluntary participants in research without coercion, duress, or undue inducement. They must be able to freely withdraw from the study at any time. The information that they provide cannot be used against them and is expected to be kept *confidential* and not be divulged to unauthorized personnel including family, employers, insurance, police, and government.

However, difficulties persist in the interpretation and the implementation of these standards. For example, confidentiality can be maintained in certain studies involving persons engaged in certain illegal activities (e.g., illegal drug use which is regulated by Federal statute) if a certificate from the Federal government is issued to permit this. However, some illegal activities (such as child abuse, involving persons under the age of 18 years) are governed by State law and, currently in the state of Florida, any instance of child abuse, in particular child sexual abuse (which may or may not also involve the use of psycho-active substances), must be reported to the authorities. Hence, the contradiction between research confidentiality and legal reporting requirements.

Mechanisms to ensure that no harm is done are sometimes imperfectly put into effect. John Solomon (2005) of the Associated Press reports that American children in foster care, predominantly consisting of the poor and minorities, were used for 20 years as early recipients of experimental AIDS treatment. Despite the elaboration of a system of checks and controls to ensure oversight of compliance with voluntary participation and to ensure that potentially harmful incidents were monitored, a recent audit showed that these monitoring systems were rarely fully implemented, although arguably through their participation in this program these children had access to advanced and state-of-the-art therapies to which they would not otherwise have had access. Certainly this parallels the thinking of concerned parents who allowed the polio vaccine to be tested on their children in Canada (see above).

Some Concluding Remarks

The point of research, and especially applied research, is to gain an accurate understanding of the world in order to be able to improve the lot of humankind. It is incumbent upon researchers to use their best skills to find the truth so that our interventions can be both beneficial and successful. The choice of research goals, topics, questions, design, methods, staff, study subjects, funding (adequacy as well as stable, ongoing sources), necessary temporal ranges for the "demands" of what is being studied, and oversight mechanisms are all important, not only from an ethical viewpoint but for the most pragmatic of reasons: what is laboratory research today will form the world in which we, each one of us, will live tomorrow. Lest this seem too abstract and far-fetched a statement, this author well remembers the invention of "Light Amplification by Stimulated Emission of Radiation" which earned its co-discovers, Charles H. Townes (1915-) and Arthur L. Schawlow (1921–1999) (The Columbus Optical SETI Observatory, 2004), Nobel prizes in physics in 1964 and 1981, respectively (Lucent Technologies, 1998). The device was first touted in the press as a potential death ray for use in military applications, but is now a common device found in most offices and homes as a computer peripheral known as the Laser Printer.

People's lives are short and resources are limited. It is incumbent upon us as moral beings to make the best use of the latter to increase the well-being of the former. We must strive to make the best, most effective, and efficient use of what we have, including all persons' abilities, interests, energies, and life experiences, in an ethical context. We cannot afford, for instance, to waste and/or misuse *de facto* limited human and other types of resources by refusing to allow the contributions of specific people or groups of people such as minorities or women in those jurisdictions in which they are socially devalued and prevented from obtaining an education that can not only better their lives but also contribute to increasing the well-being of all.

Data and information must be treated with respect and parsimoniousness. It is unfair to drown respondents with an ever increasing burden of questions that will likely never be analyzed. Such data as are collected should be analyzed, using the most appropriate, available resources within the *de facto* realties as is being increasingly realized through the secondary analysis of data. The value of the contributions of respondents must be recognized and respected, especially when such contributions may have been made at considerable personal sacrifice, resulting from public or private tragedies. Barring stem cell research because stem cells come from fetal tissue would be logical only if fetal deaths occurred solely to provide stem cells. In a world in which miscarriages and abortions occur as a matter of course, it may be more respectful of the lives lost if some good were to come from them by increasing our medical knowledge so as to allow others to live, and to live better lives. It is not clear if the same argument could be made with regard to knowledge gained from past coerced human experimentation not currently used.

We must recognize that although ethical systems and written standards of ethical research may help us to formulate some choices, ultimately we are each unique, and each situation is unique and requires an appropriate and sometimes difficult choice of action. Because persons and situations are also in a constant process of change, choices may need to be modified and improved in response to newer circumstances and greater knowledge. In the ambiguities of changing circumstances there may be a need to reverse earlier choices and take a new approach that will, it is to be hoped, lead ultimately to better decisions.

Manuella Adrian, M. Sc. Hyg. (USA-Canada), *scientist, administrator, lecturer, public health researcher and educator. Early in her career she was a policy analyst with the Canadian Ministry of State for Science and Technology (MOSST) where she investigated different models of research organization used in a number of countries in North America and Western Europe. More recently, she has been director of research at the Kansas Health Institute, head of the statistical research program at the Addiction Research Foundation of the province of Ontario in Canada, research economist/sociologist with Health and Welfare Canada. Consultant to the World Health Organization, (WHO), the Pan American Health Organization (PAHO). Appointments with universities in Canada (Guelph, Toronto, Carleton) and the USA (Florida International, Nova SouthEastern, Kansas). Member of the editorial board of Substance Use and Misuse, and a faculty member of the Middle Eastern Summer Institute on Drug Use (MESIDU) in Israel and the Middle Eastern—Mediterranean Summer Institute on Drug Use (MEMSIDU) in Italy. Research interests include: addictions, psychoactive drugs, population health, health behaviors, epidemiology; special populations (women, youth, elderly, minorities), social costs, cost benefit/ cost effectiveness, measuring quality of life (QALYs/ DALYs), health care financing, health care management, needs-based planning, evaluation and outcome studies of health care and public health initiatives, estimates of market size and post-marketing surveillance of pharmaceuticals. Quantitative methods including research design, applied statistics, analyses of large data bases, ecological studies, multivariate techniques. Over 200 Professional Publications, including 26 books and monographs, 15 book chapters, 34 articles (Social Science and Medicine; Medical Care; J. Applied Economics; J. Public Health Policy; American J. Health Promotion; American J. Drugs & Alcohol; Canadian Medical Association J.; Canadian J. Public Health; British J. Addictions; J. Studies on Alcohol; Drug Use and Misuse; International J. Addictions; American Statistician), newspaper articles and videoscripts.*

References

Adrian, M. (Complier [Comp.]) (Comp.) (1979). *Statistical Supplement to the Annual Report of the Alcoholism and Drug Addiction Research Foundation of Ontario 1977-78*. Toronto: Alcoholism and Drug Addiction Research Foundation, 150pp.

Adrian, M. (1980a). The Whys and Wherefores of Information Systems: Nature and Magnitude of Alcohol Situation in Ontario. *Toxicomanies -revue internationale de recherche et information scientifique, 13*(3-4):189-201.

Adrian, M. (Comp.) (1980b). *Statistical Supplement to the Annual Report of the Alcoholism and Drug Addiction Research Foundation of Ontario 1978-79*. Toronto: Alcoholism and Drug Addiction Research Foundation, 212pp.

Adrian, M. (1980c). *Attitude Towards Marijuana Legislation: Report of a National Household Survey -1978*. Toronto: Addiction Research Foundation, Substudy No. 1112.

Adrian, M. (Comp.) (1981). *Statistical Supplement to the Annual Report of the Alcoholism and Drug Addiction Research Foundation of Ontario 1979-80*. Toronto: Alcoholism and Drug Addiction Research Foundation, 275pp.

Adrian, M. (Comp.) (1983). *Statistics on Alcohol and Drug Use in Canada and Other Countries, Data Available by August 1982*. Toronto: Alcoholism and Drug Addiction Research Foundation, 324pp

Adrian, M. (Comp.) (1985a). *Statistics on Alcohol and Drug Use in Canada and Other Countries -Volume I: Statistics on Alcohol Use, Data Available by September 1984*. Toronto: Alcoholism and Drug Addiction Research Foundation, xxii, 313pp.

Adrian, M. (Comp.) (1985b). Statistics on Alcohol and Drug Use in Canada and Other Countries -Volume II: Statistics on Drug Use, Data Available by September 1984. Alcoholism and Drug Addiction Research Foundation, Toronto, xxiv, 367pp.

Adrian, M. (2003). How can sociological theory help our understanding of addictions? *Substance Use Misuse 2003, 38*(10):1385-1423

Adrian, M., Ferguson, B.S., & Dinin, C. (1998). Is community-based treatment an add-on or a substitution for hospital treatment of alcoholism? Some evidence from Canada. *Medical Care. 36*(9):1419 29

Adrian, M., Ferguson, B.S., & Her, M. (1996). Does allowing the sale of Quebec wine in grocery stores increase consumption? *Journal of Studies on Alcohol*. 1996; 57(4):434-448.

Adrian, M., Ferguson, B.S., & Her, M. (2001). Can Alcohol Price Policies Be Used To Reduce Drunk Driving? *Substance Use Misuse. 36*(13):1923-1958

Adrian, M., & Jull, P. (1991). The effect of low alcohol beverages on alcoholism levels in Canada in 1986. In: Naranjo, C., & Sellers, E. (Eds.) *Novel Pharmacological Interventions for Alcoholism*. New York: Springer-Verlag, pp. 251-253.

Adrian, M., Jull, P., &Williams, R. (comp.) (1989a). *Statistics on Alcohol and Drug Use in Canada and Other Countries -Volume II: Statistics on Drug Use, Data Available by 1988*. Toronto: Alcoholism and Drug Addiction Research Foundation, xxx, 526pp., 172 tables, 37 illustrations, appendices, index

Adrian, M., Jull, P., &Williams, R. (comp.) (1989b). *Statistics on Alcohol and Drug Use in Canada and Other Countries -Volume I: Statistics on Alcohol Use, Data Available by 1988*. Toronto: Alcoholism and Drug Addiction Research Foundation, xxvi, 407pp., 132 tables, 22 illustrations, appendices, index.

Adrian, M., Layne, N., & Williams, B. [Introduction by Room R.] (1996). *Canadian Youth and Drugs: A Health Promotion and Social Marketing Resource Guide*. Health Canada and Addiction Research Foundation, 141pp.

Adrian, M., Lundy, C., & Eliany, M. (Eds.) (1996). *Women's Use of Tobacco, Alcohol and Other Drugs. / Les Canadiennes et l'usage d'alcool, de tabac et d'autres drogues*. Toronto: Addiction Research Foundation, xxxviii, 265pp.

Adrian, M., Ogborne, A.C., Rankin, J.G., Ferguson, B.S., & Jull, P. (1994). Community-based facilities may be replacing hospitals for the treatment of alcoholism: The evidence from Ontario. *American Journal of Drug and Alcohol Abuse. 20*(4):495-515

Alexander, J., Giesen, B., Munch, R., & Smelser, N. (1987). *The Micro-Macro Link*. University of California Press

Allen, J.P., Fertig, J.B., Towle, L.H., Bryant, K., Altshuler, V.B., Vrublevsky, A.G., & Valentik, Y.V. (1993). Structure and correlates of alcohol dependence in clinical samples in the United States and Russia. *Addiction, 88*(11):1535-1543.

Alperovitz, G. (1996). *The Decision To Use The Atomic Bomb*. U.K: Vintage

Alves, G., Kurz, M., Lie, S.A., & Larsen, J.P. (2004). Cigarette smoking in Parkinson's disease: influence on disease progression. *Movement Disorders*. 2004 Sep;19(9):1087-1092.

Andrews, G. (2001). *MKULTRA : The CIA's Top Secret Program in Human Experimentation and Behavior Modification*. Healthnet.

Anonymous (1974). Balkan engineer who could speak five languages (but not Russian) explaining that not speaking Russian, despite more than 10 years of obligatory study of the Russian language in the school system, was a means of unobtrusive political resistance in his country. Personal communication.

Anonymous (2002). US: condoms distributed to gay inmates in LA. *Canadian HIV AIDS Policy Law Review. 6*(3):18-9.

Anonymous (2005). Medical ethics: The testing of AIDS drugs. *Sun-Sentinel.Com.* Posted May 8, 2005, retrieved may 8, 2005, from http://www.sun-sentinel.com/news/opinion/editorial/sfl-2editshapemay08,0,7738271.story.

AstraZeneca (2004). *Helicobacter pylori: The key to a cure for peptic ulcer patients?* Retrieved May 4, 2005, from http://www.patienthealthinternational.com/features/2885.aspx.

Asimov, I. (1979). *In Memory Yet Green: The Autobiography of Isaac Asimov, 1920-1954*. New York: Doubleday.

Atomic Energy of Canada Limited (AECL) (2002-2005). *Medical Applications: Canadian History*. Retrieved June 3, 2005, from http://www.aecl.ca/index.asp?layid=3&csid=421&menuid=58.

Babbie, E. (2004). *The Practice Of Social Research. 10th Edition*. Belmont, California (USA): Wadsworth/ Thomson Learning.

Ball, W.W.R. (1908). *A Short Account of the History of Mathematics. 4th Edition.* Retrieved July 4, 2005, from http://www.maths.tcd.ie/pub/HistMath/People/Pascal/RouseBall/RB_Pascal.html.

Barabási, A.L., (2003). *Linked: How Everything Is Connceted to Everything Else and What It Means for Business, Science and Everyday Life*. New York: Plume-Penguin Books.

Belmont Report (1979). *Ethical Principles and Guidelines for the Protection of Human Participants of Research*. National Commission for the Protection of Human Subjects of Biomedical and Behavioral Research.

Beresford, J. (1999). *Discovery of LSD The Albert Hofmann Foundation-Lysergic Acid Diethylamide (LSD-25)*. Retrieved June 21, 2005, from http://www.hofmann.org/lsd/

Blake, M. (2004). The damage done: Crack babies talk. *Columbia Journalism Review*. Sep/Oct. Retrieved June 20, 2005, from www.cjr.org/issues/2004/5/voices-blake.asp.

Brown, K.S. (1996). DNA vaccines: A fluke emerges. *The Scientist 10*[7]:14, Apr. 01, Retrieved May 8, 2005, from http://www.geocities.com/issues_in_immunization/developments/dna_vaccines_jenner.htm

Buscema, M. (1998). Artificial Neural Networks, *Substance Use & Misuse, 33*(1-3)

Canadian Broadcasting Corporation [CBC] (2005). *Blood Transfusions in Spain*. Broadcast November 30, 1980. Retreived May 8, 2005, from http://archives.cbc.ca/IDC-1-74-1345-8062/people/bethune/clip3

Center for Disease Control [CDC] (2005). *Western Equine Encephalitis*. Fact Sheet. Retrieved May 4, 2005, from http://www.cdc.gov/ncidod/dvbid/arbor/weefact.htm

CNN.Com (1999). Massive trial of AIDS vaccine to begin in Thailand. *CNN Interactive*. Posted February 10, 1999, Retrieved May 8, 2005, from http://edition.cnn.com/HEALTH/9902/10/aids.vaccine.trial/

Cornwell, J. (2004). *Hitler's Scientists: Science, War, and the Devil's Pact*. New York: Penguin

Cromie, W. J. (2003). New AIDS vaccine tested in U.S., Africa: trials in Boston, St. Louis, Botswana. *Harvard University Gazette*. Posted May 29, 2003, Retrieved May 8, 2005, from http://www.news.harvard.edu/gazette/2003/05.29/01-aidsvax.html

den Heijer, T., Vermeer, S.E., van Dijk, E.J., Prins, N.D., Koudstaal, P.J., van Duijn, C.M., Hofman, A., & Breteler, M.M. (2004). Alcohol intake in relation to brain magnetic resonance imaging findings in older persons without dementia. *American Journal of Clinical Nutrition*, 2004 Oct; 80(4):992-7.

Denson, T.F., & Earleywine, M. (2005). Decreased depression in marijuana users. *Addictive Behaviors*. 2005 Jun 17; [Epub ahead of print]

Edward Jenner Institute for Vaccine Research. (undated) *Edward Jenner*. Retrieved May 8, 2005, from http://www.jenner.ac.uk/ns/jenner.htm

Eliany, M., & Clarke, J. (1992). *The Use Of Alcohol And Other Drugs By Older Canadians And Its Consequences*. Health and Welfare Canada. Minister of Supply and Services Canada, 1992 Cat. No. H39-259/1992E. Retrieved June 23, 2005, from http://www.hc-sc.gc.ca/hecs-sesc/cds/publications/alcohol_drugs/toc.htm

Elias, P. (Associated Press) (2003). Experimental AIDS vaccine fails major test in Thailand. *SunHerald.com*. South Mississippi's Home Page, Posted on Wed, Nov. 12, 2003, Retrieved May 8,2005, from http://www.sunherald.com/mld/sunherald/business/7244349.htm

Ferguson, B.S. (2005). *Statistics*. e-mail. 5/3/2005 9:39 PM

Ferguson, B.S., & Lim, G.C. (1998). *Introduction To Dynamic Economic Models*. Manchester University Press

Feynman, R.P., Leighton, R., & Hutchings, E. (ed.) (1984). *"Surely You're Joking, Mr. Feynman!": Adventures of a Curious Character*. New York: W. W. Norton & Co.

Fride, E., Bregman, T., & Kirkham, T.C. (2005). Endocannabinoids and food intake: newborn suckling and appetite regulation in adulthood. *Experimental Biology and Medicine* (Maywood, N.J.). 230(4):225-34

Fox, M.J. (2002). *Lucky Man*. New York: Hyperion.

Galton, F. Quoted In: Brookes, M. (2004). *Exreme Measures: The Dark Vision And Bright Ideas Of Francis Galton*. New York: Bloomsbury, p. 170.

Grandin, T. & Johnson, C. (2005). *Animals In Translation: Using The Mysteries Of Autism To Decode Animal Behavior*. New York: Scribner.

Gratzer, W. (2002). *Eurekas and Euphorias: The Oxford Book of Scientific Anecdotes*. Oxford (UK): Oxford University Press, pp. 135-130.

Gribbin, J. & Gribbin, M. (2005). *Annus Mirabilis : 1905, Albert Einstein, And The Theory Of Relativity*. New York : Chamberlain Bros.

Hernan, M.A., Zhang, S.M., Rueda-deCastro, A.M., Colditz, G.A., Speizer, F.E., & Ascherio, A. (2001). Cigarette smoking and the incidence of Parkinson's disease in two prospective studies. *Annals of Neurology*. 2001 Dec;50(6):780-6.

Hofmann, A. (1970). The discovery of LSD and subsequent investigations on naturally occurring Hallucinogens. In: Ayd, F.J., Jr. & Blackwell, B. (eds.) *Discoveries in Biological Psychiatry*. J.B. Lippincott, Retrieved May 2005, from http://www.psychedelic-library.org/hofmann.htm

Hofmann, A. (1971). Teonanaìcatl And Ololiuqui, Two Ancient Magic Drugs Of Mexico. *Bulletin of Narcotics*. 1:3-14.

Hofmann, A. (1980). *From Remedy to Inebriant. LSD- My Problem Child.* McGraw-Hill, Retrieved June 21, 2005, from http://nepenthes.lycaeum.org/Drugs/LSD/ProbChild/Preface.html

Holmes, C.B. (1990). *The Honest Truth About Lying With Statistics*. Charles C. Thomas.

Hopkins, T.J. (2005). US Supreme Court says no to medical marijuana. *British Medical Journal*. Jun 18;330(7505):1408.

Huff, D., & Geis, I. (1954) *How to Lie With Statistics*. WW Norton.

Jurgens, R. (2002). HIV/AIDS in prisons: recent developments. *Canadian HIV/AIDS Policy & Law Review.* 7(2-3):13-20.

Kirk, D. E. (1970). *Optimal Control Theory: An Introduction*, Prentice Hall

Lettieri, D.J., Sayers, M., & Pearson, H.W. (eds.) 1980, *Theories on Drug Abuse*. National Institute on DA Research Monograph No. 30, Rockville, MD. NIDA

Lindesmith, A.R.,(1968). *Addiction and Opiates*. Chicago, Aldine Pub. Co.

Lucent Technologies (1998). *The Invention Of The Laser At Bell Laboratories 1958-1998*. Retrieved May 9, 2005, from http://www.bell-labs.com/history/laser/invention/

Marks, J.D. (1979). *The Search for the Manchurian Candidate: The CIA and Mind Control*. W. W. Norton & Company.

McGiveney, J. (undated). *Drug Enforcement Administration Historical Interviews. James McGivency* [sic] Tape 162. James McGiveney Retired Chief DEA Public Affairs. Retrieved May 15, 2005, from http://www.usdoj.gov/dea/deamuseum/transcripts/james-mcgiveney_11042003.pdf

Milgram, S. (1963). Behavioral Study Of Obedience. *Journal of Abnormal Social Psychology. 67*:371-378. Cited In: Babbie, E. (2004). *The Practice of Social Research*. 10th Edition. Belmont, California (USA): Wadsworth/ Thomson Learning.

Milgram, S. (1965). Some conditions of obedience and disobedience. *Human Relations*. 18:57-76. Cited In: Babbie, E. (2004). *The Practice of Social Research. 10th Edition*. Belmont, California (USA): Wadsworth/ Thomson Learning.

National Institutes of Health [NIH] (undated) *Human Participants Protection Education for Research Teams*. Online Course, sponsored by The National Cancer Institute (NCI) Of The National Institutes Of Health. http://cme.cancer.gov/clinicaltrials/learning/humanparticipant-protections.asp

Nadelmann, E. (2000). *Drug Policy Reform: Principles, Perspectives, and Politics*. Lindesmith Center-Drug Policy Foundation. RAND Science and Drug Policy 2000 Speaker Series October 23, Retrieved May 15, 2005 from http://www.rand.org/multi/dprc/seminars/nadelmann.html

Newton, I. *The Principia: Mathematical Principles of Natural Philosophy*. Quoted in: Weisstein, E.W. (2005). *Eric Weisstein's World of Physics*. Retrieved April 30, 2005, from http://scienceworld.wolfram.com/physics/Torque.html

Niroomand, F., Hauer, O., Tiefenbacher, C.P., Katus, H.A., & Kuebler, W. (2004). Influence of alcohol consumption on restenosis rate after percutaneous transluminal coronary angioplasty and stent implantation. *Heart*. 2004 Oct;90(10):1189-93

Ogborne, A.C., Adrian, M., Newton-Taylor, B., & Williams, R. (1991). Long term trends in male drunkenness arrests in Metropolitan Toronto: Effects of social setting Detoxication Centres. *American Journal of Drug and Alcohol Abuse 17*(2):187-197.

Otherground, L.L.C. & World-War-2.info. (2003). *World War 2 Atomic Bomb* Retrieved April 30, 2005, from http://www.world-war-2.info/atomic-bomb/

Pendery, M.L., Maltzman, I.M., & West, L.J. (1982). Controlled drinking by alcoholics? New findings and a reevaluation of a major affirmative study. *Science*, 217, 169-175.

Penn Surgery (2005). *Plastic Surgery*. The University of Pennsylvania Health System. Retrieved April 30, 2005, from http://www.uphs.upenn.edu/surgery/clin/plastic.html

Pinder, R.M., & Sandler, M. (2004). Alcohol, wine and mental health: focus on dementia and stroke. *Journal of Psychopharmacology*, 2004 Dec;18(4):449-56.

Popham, R.E., & Schmidt, W., with the assistance of Williams, R.G., Bronetto, J., [and] Cooper, C.P. Foreword by Seeley JR. (1958). *Statistics of Alcohol Use and Alcoholism in Canada, 1871-1956; First Report*. Toronto: University of Toronto Press. xv, 155 p. (chiefly tables).

Renaud, S.C., Gueguen, R., Conard, P., Lanzmann-Petithory, D., Orgogozo, J.M., & Henry, O. (2004). Moderate wine drinkers have lower hypertension-related mortality: a prospective cohort study in French men. *American Journal of Clinical Nutrition*, 2004 Sep;80(3):621-5.

Riley, R., & Adrian, M. (1993). Proposal for a Composite Index of Alcohol Problems. *Health Reports*. (Statistics Canada, Catalogue No. 82-003); 5(4):383-398.

Rittel, H., & Noble, D. (1989). *Issue-Based Information Systems for Design*. Working Paper 492, The Institute of Urban and Regional Development, University of California, Berkeley, California, email: iurd@uclink.berkeley.edu.

Rose, T.P. (1998). Social And Childhood Indicators Of Childhood Wellbeing. In: Singh, G.K., Wilkinson, A.V., Song, F.F., Rose, T.P., Adrian, M., Fonner, E., & Tarlov, A.R. *Health and Social Factors in Kansas: A Data and Chartbook, 1997-98*. Topeka, KS: Kansas Health Institute, vi, 304 pp, tables, illustrations pp 47-57

Rose, T.P. & Song, F. (2000). Social and educational indicators of childhood wellbeing in Kansas. In:. Tarlov, A.R. & St. Peter, R.F. (Eds.) *The Society And Population Health Reader. Volume II: A State Perspective*. Health and Society Series. New York: The New Press. Pp. 97-103.

Rothschild, J. H. (1964). *Tomorrow's Weapons*. Cited in "LSD And Psychotherapy" In: Brecher, E.M. & Editors of Consumer Reports Magazine *Licit and Illicit Drugs* Retrieved April 30, 2005, from http://www.a1b2c3.com/drugs/lsd02.htm

Schaller, G., Harding, T.W. (1995). [AIDS prevention in European prisons] [in French] *Sozial-und Präventivmedizin 40*(5):298-301

Shirer, W.L. (1960). *Rise And Fall Of The Third Reich*, New York: Simon & Schuster

Smart, R.G., Mann, R.E., & Adrian, M. (1993). Health and productivity savings from increased alcoholism treatment in Ontario. *Canada Journal of Public Health 84*(1):62-63

Sobell, M.B., & Sobell, L.C. (1973). Alcoholics treated by individualized behavior therapy: One year treatment outcomes. *Behavior Research and Therapy*, 11, 599-618.

Sobell, M.B., & Sobell, L.C. (1978). *Behavioral Treatment of Alcohol Problems: Individualized Therapy and Controlled Drinking*. New York: Plenum Press.

Solomon, J. (2005). Aids drugs tested on foster children: Protection law skirted, review finds. *South Florida Sun-Sentinel*, May 5, 2005, p. 9A. retrieved Amy 8, 2005, from http://www.sun-sentinel.com/news/nationworld/sfl-aaids05may05,1,602743.story?ctrack=1&cset=true

Takaki, R. (1996). *Hirohisma: Why America Dropped The Atomic Bomb*. Back Bay Books

Tesoriero, H.W. (2005). Purdue Pharma, H.D. Smith plan test of electronic tracking of drugs. *The Wall Street Journal*. Tuesday, May 31, P. D7, Col. 1-2.

Texas Department of State Health Services (updated 01 March 2005). *Section 6.6. Determine CCPs Principle 2*. Retrieved May 15, 2005, from http://www.tdh.state.tx.us/bfds/foods/bvw/bvwmanual/pdf/Section%206-9.pdf

The Columbus Optical SETI Observatory (2004). *Arthur Schawlow, Nobel Laureate and Co-inventor of the Laser, Dies*. Retrieved May 9, 2005, from http://www.coseti.org/schaobit.htm

The Wall Street Journal Online (WJS.com) (2005). Drug Cos mull ethics of using India for clinical trials. *The Wall Street Journal* DOW JONES NEWSWIRES. May 2, 2005 11:23 p.m. Retrieved May 9, 2005.

Trochim, W.M.K (2001). *The Research Methods Knowledge Base, 2nd Edition*. Cincinnati, Ohio (USA): Atomic Dog Publishing.

United Nations (undated). *The Universal Declaration of Human Rights*. United Nations, Office of the High Commission, High Commissioner For Universal Rights (OHCHR) Retrieved June 23, 2005, from http://www.unhchr.ch/udhr/lang/eng.htm

U.S. Census Bureau (2004). *Statistical Abstract of the United States, 2004-2005. Section 1.Population*. Last Revised: Wednesday, 08-Dec-2004 16:52:23 EST. Retrieved May 8, 2005, from http://www.census.gov/prod/2004pubs/04statab/pop.pdf

von Foerster, H., Mora, P.M., & Amiot, L.W., (1960). Doomsday; Friday, 13 November, A.D, 2026. *Science*, 132, 1960. pp. 1291-1295.

van den Brink, W., Hendriks, V.M., Blanken, P., Koeter, M.W.J., van Zwieten, B.J., & van Ree, J.M. (2003). Medical prescription of heroin to treatment resistant heroin addicts: two randomised controlled trials. *British Medical Journal 327*:310 (9 August), doi:10.1136/bmj.327.7410.310 Retrieved July 4, 2005.

Venderova, K., Ruzicka, E., Vorisek, V., & Visnovsky, P. (2004). Survey on cannabis use in Parkinson's disease: subjective improvement of motor symptoms. *Movement Disorders*. 2004 Sep;19(9):1102-6.

Waldholz, M., & King, R.T. Jr. (Staff Reporters of The Wall Street Journal) (1999). Rhone-Poulenc Is Testing AIDS Vaccine In Africa; VaxGen Plans Trial in Thailand. *The*

Wall Street Journal, Posted Tuesday, February 9, 1999, Retrieved May 8, 2005, from http://www.aegis.com/news/wsj/1999/WJ990208.html

Weisstein, E.W. (2005). *Eric Weisstein's World of Physics*. Retrieved April 30, 2005, from http://scienceworld.wolfram.com/physics/Torque.html

William, B., Chang, K., & Throung, M.V. (Comp.) (1992a). *Canadian Profile: Alcohol, Tobacco and Other Drugs, 1992* Toronto: Alcoholism and Drug Addiction Research Foundation.

William, B., Chang, K., & Throung, M.V. (Comp.) (1992b). *Annual Sourcebook: Alcohol, Tobacco and Other Drugs, Ontario Profile, 1992* Toronto: Alcoholism and Drug Addiction Research Foundation.

Glossary

case fatality: Case fatality refers to the odds of dying of a disease. A high case fatality rate means the odds of dying of the disease are very high.

confounders: Co-occuring circumstances or events that make it seem as though there is a relationship between the "causal" event and the "consequence" when there is none, or that conversely makes it seem as though there is no relationship when in fact there is one. The presence of confounders can also make a relationship seem larger or smaller than it actually is. Careful research design may help to eliminate or reduce the effect of confounders.

critical control points: For every significant hazard identified in the hazard analysis, there must be a point, procedure, or operation at which control can be applied to prevent, eliminate or reduce the hazard to an acceptable level. These steps are Called Critical Control points or CCP (Texas Department of State Health Services (2005).

fishing expedition: This is a situation where we really have no idea what is, or might be, going on, but we hope that, someday, out of the morass of material we have accumulated, we may get lucky, and something will pop up so we can make some sense of it.

marker: A marker is an indirect measure—and often a very precise measurement—, when the actual measure or observation may be difficult to obtain. For example, a positive breathalyzer test would be a marker indicating that the person has consumed alcohol, even if the physical act of consumption of alcohol was not actually observed.

outliers: Statistical outliers are values which are far outside of the normal range of values for that particular sort of data. For example, a blood alcohol content (BAC) of 0.08 is the legal limit for intoxication in Canada, ranging from about 0.05 to 0.10 depending on the jurisdictions. However, emergency departments occasionally have intoxicated patients with BACs that are barely detectible on toxicology. Such low readings would be considered outliers.

prospective and retrospective: A prospective study is a study undertaken today and that will yield its results sometime in the future; it can be used to study such questions as "how many smokers today will develop cancer over the rest of their future life?" A retrospective study is one that uses current data to examine events of the past; it would be used to find out "How many persons with cancer today smoked in the past?" Finally a retrospective prospective study would look at "How many persons who were smokers 50 years ago went on to develop cancer up to today?"

recursive: Recursive processes have multiple iterations where the cause in one iteration becomes the consequence in the next iteration, and so on until certain pre-set parameters are met.

Notes

1. Dates of birth and death are given in Current Era (CE) years and are based on 'Weisstein, 2005', unless noted otherwise
2. Many older physicians trained in the first half of the 20th century started smoking as medical students when they used tobacco to mask the stench of partly dissected cadavers in human anatomy class.
3. The "Just say No" program etiologically was reported to have begun from a Judeo-Christian perspective with the giving of the 10 Commandments...and we know how effective that has been.
4. Depending on the phenomena, a 0.1% change may be very significant. Daily trades on the New York Stock Exchange average $50 billion, and a 0.1% change would correspond to $50 million a day, which would be most substantively significant for a brokerage house whose income depends on volume of trade.
5. National Institute on Drug Abuse (NIDA) and National Institute on Alcohol Abuse and Alcoholism (NIAAA).
6. "Transfer of Technology" is the politically correct shibboleth which covers this.
7. Now deceased, actor Christopher Reeves, star of the Superman movies, became paralyzed due to a spinal cord injury after a horse riding accident.
8. Actor Michael J. Fox (2002), star of the Back to the Future movies and of several long-running television series, developed Parkinson's Disease in his thirties.
9. Bill Gates, founder of Microsoft corporation and richest man in the world for more than a decade according to the business magazine Fortune, and his wife Melinda now run the largest private philanthropic foundation in the world.
10. American financier and philanthropist George Soros immigrated from a Communist East European country.

1-13 Ethics in Prevention Research with Children

Jeannette L. Johnson, Ph.D. and Nancy R. Vandermark, Ph.D.

Abstract

Understanding the ethical decisions involved in the research on the prevention of drug use can be both complicated and simple. Prevention research is complicated because it occurs with children, and the issues surrounding the protection of the child and its rights are vitally significant. With children, these rights must be attended to with clarity of purpose, respect, and tenderness. Ethics in prevention research is simple because the answer to understanding effective preventative interventions can only be found during childhood. There are no alternatives to understanding how to prevent disease, disorder, or dysfunction without first conducting research with children. It is the conjunction of both the complications and the simplicity that makes the ethical issues in prevention research thorny.

Key Words: ethics, prevention science, children, resilience, cultural difference

Introduction

Many challenges face us as researchers in the changing world of research ethics (Kirschner, 2003), and ethical guidelines constantly change with these evolutions. This chapter attempts to summarize current thought concerning the ethics involved in conducting research on drug use prevention with children. Many books, chapters, and peer reviewed articles have addressed research ethics with children (Drotar, 2000; Hoagwood, Jensen, and Fisher, 1997; Sieber, 1992). Hoagwood, Jensen, and Fisher (1997), for example, have devoted an entire volume to understanding the application of contemporary ethical thought on the scientific study of children and adolescents with mental disorders. In this book, they outline the legal, regulatory, and moral parameters guiding study with children and adolescents. Although the book addresses mental disorders in children specifically, the basic tenets of research ethics with children, no matter what the research, remain the same. A subsequent article by Fisher et al. (2002) produced guidelines for making ethical decisions in the conduct of mental health research with minority children and youths. In this chapter we will review these recommendations for their relevance to prevention research, after first considering current guidelines for conducting research with children.

Current Guidelines

In 1974, the National Research Act (National Research Act, 1974) mandated the establishment of Institutional Review Boards (IRBs) to protect individuals who participated in research at institutions receiving federal funding for biomedical or behavioral research. The National Research Act stated that the IRB must determine that all of the following requirements are satisfied in order to approve research:

(1) Risks to subjects are minimized: (i) by using procedures which are consistent with sound research design and which do not unnecessarily expose subjects to risk, and (ii) whenever appropriate, by using procedures already being performed on the subjects for diagnostic or treatment purposes.

(2) Risks to subjects are reasonable in relation to anticipated benefits, if any, to subjects, and the importance of the knowledge that may reasonably be expected to result. In evaluating risks and benefits, the IRB should consider only those risks and benefits that may result from the research (as distinguished from risks and benefits of therapies subjects would receive even if not participating in the research). The IRB should not consider possible long-range effects of applying knowledge gained in the research (for example, the possible effects of the research on public policy) as among those research risks that fall within the purview of its responsibility.

(3) Selection of subjects is equitable. In making this assessment the IRB should take into account the purposes of the research and the setting in which the research will be conducted and should be particularly cognizant of the special problems of research involving vulnerable populations, such as children, prisoners, pregnant women, mentally disabled persons, or economically or educationally disadvantaged persons.

(4) Informed consent will be sought from each prospective subject or the subject's legally authorized representative, in accordance with, and to the extent required by §46.116.

(5) Informed consent will be appropriately documented, in accordance with, and to the extent required by §46.117.

(6) When appropriate, the research plan makes adequate provision for monitoring the data collected to ensure the safety of subjects.

(7) When appropriate, there are adequate provisions to protect the privacy of subjects and to maintain the confidentiality of data.

   (b) When some or all of the subjects are likely to be vulnerable to coercion or undue influence, such as children, prisoners, pregnant women, mentally disabled persons, or economically or educationally disadvantaged persons, additional safeguards have been included in the study to protect the rights and welfare of these subjects.

Ethics committees are not standardized in their application of protections for children (Hall, 1991), and while most professional organizations have guidelines for conducting research, they are criticized for not coping satisfactorily with the ethical issues related to children (Sieber, 1994). For example, the Code of Ethics for the National Association of Social Workers (revised in 1999, http://www.nasw.org) makes no specific provisions for conducting research with children. Similarly, the most recent Code of Ethics developed by the American Psychological Association (APA, 2002), which became effective June 1, 2003, still does not have specific guidelines for conducting research with children. The research guidelines found under Code 8, Research and Ethics, are of special import to prevention research:

(8.02) Informed Consent to Research

(a) When obtaining informed consent as required in Standard 3.10, Informed Consent, psychologists inform participants about (1) the purpose of the research, expected duration, and procedures; (2) their right to decline to participate and to withdraw from the research once participation has begun; (3) the foreseeable consequences of declining or withdrawing; (4) reasonably foreseeable factors that may be expected to influence their willingness to participate such as potential risks, discomfort, or adverse effects; (5) any prospective research benefits; (6) limits of confidentiality; (7) incentives for participation; and (8) whom to contact for questions about the research and research participants' rights. They provide opportunity for the prospective participants to ask questions and receive answers. (See also Standards 8.03, Informed Consent for Recording Voices and Images in Research; 8.05, Dispensing With Informed Consent for Research; and 8.07, Deception in Research.)

(b) Psychologists conducting intervention research involving the use of experimental treatments clarify to participants at the outset of the research (1) the experimental nature of the treatment; (2) the services that will or will not be available to the control group(s) if appropriate; (3) the means by which assignment to treatment and control groups will be made; (4) available treatment alternatives if an individual does not wish to participate in the research or wishes to withdraw once a study has begun; and (5) compensation for or monetary costs of participating including, if appropriate, whether reimbursement from the participant or a third-party payor will be sought. (See also Standard 8.02a, Informed Consent to Research.)

Code 8, in its entirety, does not make mention of the special research issues involved in the case of children. The entire Code 8, Research and Ethics, of course, is pertinent to research with children; but it is written in such a language that it is left up to the reader how to apply the ethical guidelines to children. Surprisingly, the Society for Prevention Research, an international organization focused upon the advancement of science-based prevention programs and policies through empirical research and whose membership includes scientists, practitioners, advocates, administrators, and policymakers, does not address ethical guidelines for conducting research with children. The Society has issued an excellent document (Society for Prevention Research, Standards of Evidence, 2005) to determine the necessary criteria that must be met for preventive interventions to be judged efficacious or effective. To date, however, they have not issued ethical standards for conducting prevention-based research with children.

The United States Government has issued a set of policies for the protection of human subjects (United States Government Code of Federal Regulations, 2001) that applies, with few exceptions, to all research involving human subjects conducted, supported or otherwise subject to regulation by any Federal Department or Agency. There are additional protections for children involved as subjects in research (Subpart D). Table 1 reports the Office of Human Research Protection Code of Federal Regulations that specifically addresses the conduct of research with children.

Table 1.13.1: Office of Human Research Protection Code of Federal Regulations, Subpart D, Additional DHHS Protections for Children Involved as Subjects in Research.

46.401 To what do these regulations apply?

(a) This subpart applies to all research involving children as subjects, conducted or supported by the Department of Health and Human Services.

(1) This includes research conducted by Department employees, except that each head of an Operating Division of the Department may adopt such non-substantive, procedural modifications as may be appropriate from an administrative standpoint.

(2) It also includes research conducted or supported by the Department of Health and Human Services outside the United States, but in appropriate circumstances, the Secretary may, under paragraph (i) of §46.101 of Subpart A, waive the applicability of some or all of the requirements of these regulations for research of this type.

(b) Exemptions at §46.101(b) (1) and (b) (3) through (b) (6) are applicable to this subpart. The exemption at §46.101(b) (2) regarding educational tests is also applicable to this subpart. However, the exemption at §46.101(b)(2) for research involving survey or interview procedures or observations of public behavior does not apply to research covered by this subpart, except for research involving observation of public behavior when the investigator(s) do not participate in the activities being observed.

(c) The exceptions, additions, and provisions for waiver as they appear in paragraphs (c) through (i) of §46.101 of Subpart A are applicable to this subpart.

§46.402 Definitions.

The definitions in §46.102 of Subpart A shall be applicable to this subpart as well. In addition, as used in this subpart:

(a) "Children" are persons who have not attained the legal age for consent to treatments or procedures involved in the research, under the applicable law of the jurisdiction in which the research will be conducted.

(b) "Assent" means a child's affirmative agreement to participate in research. Mere failure to object should not, absent affirmative agreement, be construed as assent.

(c) "Permission" means the agreement of parent(s) or guardian to the participation of their child or ward in research.

(d) "Parent" means a child's biological or adoptive parent.

(e) "Guardian" means an individual who is authorized under applicable State or local law to consent on behalf of a child to general medical care.

§46.403 IRB duties.

In addition to other responsibilities assigned to IRBs under this part, each IRB shall review research covered by this subpart and approve only research which satisfies the conditions of all applicable sections of this subpart.

§46.404 Research not involving greater than minimal risk.

DHHS will conduct or fund research in which the IRB finds that no greater than minimal risk to children is presented, only if the IRB finds that adequate provisions are made for soliciting the assent of the children and the permission of their parents or guardians, as set forth in §46.408.

§46.405 Research involving greater than minimal risk but presenting the prospect of direct benefit to the individual subjects.

DHHS will conduct or fund research in which the IRB finds that more than minimal risk to children is presented by an intervention or procedure that holds out the prospect of direct benefit for the individual subject, or by a monitoring procedure that is likely to contribute to the subject's well-being, only if the IRB finds that:

(a) the risk is justified by the anticipated benefit to the subjects;

(b) the relation of the anticipated benefit to the risk is at least as favorable to the subjects as that presented by available alternative approaches; and

(c) adequate provisions are made for soliciting the assent of the children and permission of their parents or guardians, as set forth in §46.408.

§46.406 Research involving greater than minimal risk and no prospect of direct benefit to individual subjects, but likely to yield generalizable knowledge about the subject's disorder or condition.

DHHS will conduct or fund research in which the IRB finds that more than minimal risk to children is presented by an intervention or procedure that does not hold out the prospect of direct benefit for the individual subject, or by a monitoring procedure which is not likely to contribute to the well-being of the subject, only if the IRB finds that:

(a) the risk represents a minor increase over minimal risk;

(b) the intervention or procedure presents experiences to subjects that are reasonably commensurate with those inherent in their actual or expected medical, dental, psychological, social, or educational situations;

(c) the intervention or procedure is likely to yield generalizable knowledge about the subjects' disorder or condition which is of vital importance for the understanding or amelioration of the subjects' disorder or condition; and

(d) adequate provisions are made for soliciting assent of the children and permission of their parents or guardians, as set forth in §46.408.

§46.407 Research not otherwise approvable which presents an opportunity to understand, prevent, or alleviate a serious problem affecting the health or welfare of children.

DHHS will conduct or fund research that the IRB does not believe meets the requirements of §46.404, §46.405, or §46.406 only if:

(a) the IRB finds that the research presents a reasonable opportunity to further the understanding, prevention, or alleviation of a serious problem affecting the health or welfare of children; and

(b) the Secretary, after consultation with a panel of experts in pertinent disciplines (for example: science, medicine, education, ethics, law) and following opportunity for public review and comment, has determined either:

(1) that the research in fact satisfies the conditions of §46.404, §46.405, or §46.406, as applicable, or (2) the following:

(i) the research presents a reasonable opportunity to further the understanding, prevention, or alleviation of a serious problem affecting the health or welfare of children;

(ii) the research will be conducted in accordance with sound ethical principles;

(iii) adequate provisions are made for soliciting the assent of children and the permission of their parents or guardians, as set forth in §46.408.

§46.408 Requirements for permission by parents or guardians and for assent by children.

(a) In addition to the determinations required under other applicable sections of this subpart, the IRB shall determine that adequate provisions are made for soliciting the assent of the children, when in the judgment of the IRB the children are capable of providing assent. In determining whether children are capable of assenting, the IRB shall take into account the ages, maturity, and psychological state of the children involved. This judgment may be made for all children to be involved in research under a particular protocol, or for each child, as the IRB deems appropriate. If the IRB determines that the capability of some or all of the children is so limited that they cannot reasonably be consulted or that the intervention or procedure involved in the research holds out a prospect of direct benefit that is important to the health or well-being of the children and is available only in the context of the research, the assent of the children is not a necessary condition for proceeding with the research. Even where the IRB determines that the subjects are capable of assenting, the IRB may still waive the assent requirement under circumstances in which consent may be waived in accord with §46.116 of Subpart A.

(b) In addition to the determinations required under other applicable sections of this subpart, the IRB shall determine, in accordance with and to the extent that consent is required by §46.116 of Subpart A, that adequate provisions are made for soliciting the permission of each child's parents or guardian. Where parental permission is to be obtained, the IRB may find that the permission of one parent is sufficient for research to be conducted under §46.404 or §46.405. Where research is covered by §46.406 and §46.407 and permission is to be obtained from parents, both parents must give their permission unless one parent is deceased, unknown, incompetent, or not reasonably available, or when only one parent has legal responsibility for the care and custody of the child.

(c) In addition to the provisions for waiver contained in §46.116 of Subpart A, if the IRB determines that a research protocol is designed for conditions or for a subject population for which parental or guardian permission is not a reasonable requirement to protect the subjects (for example, neglected or abused children), it may waive the consent requirements in Subpart A of this part and paragraph (b) of this section, provided an appropriate mechanism for protecting the children who will participate as subjects in the research is substituted, and provided further that the waiver is not inconsistent with Federal, State, or local law. The choice of an appropriate mechanism would depend upon the nature and purpose of the activities described in the protocol, the risk and anticipated benefit to the research subjects, and their age, maturity, status, and condition.

(d) Permission by parents or guardians shall be documented in accordance with and to the extent required by §46.117 of Subpart A.

(e) When the IRB determines that assent is required, it shall also determine whether and how assent must be documented.

§46.409 Wards.

(a) Children who are wards of the State or any other agency, institution, or entity can be included in research approved under §46.406 or §46.407 only if such research is:

(1) related to their status as wards; or

(2) conducted in schools, camps, hospitals, institutions, or similar settings in which the majority of children involved as subjects are not wards.

(b) If the research is approved under paragraph (a) of this section, the IRB shall require appointment of an advocate for each child who is a ward, in addition to any other individual acting on behalf of the child as guardian or in loco parents. One individual may serve as advocate for more than one child. The advocate shall be an individual who has the background and experience to act in, and agrees to act in, the best interests of the child for the duration of the child's participation in the research and who is not associated in any way (except in the role as advocate or member of the IRB) with the research, the investigator(s), or the guardian organization.

The Ethics of Conducting Prevention Research

Several authors have suggested that it is important for researchers to consider the ethical issues that might arise when conducting research with ethnic minority populations (Alvidrez and Arean, 2002). This is especially significant for prevention researchers, as preventative intervention programs frequently target risk behaviors in diverse populations. Moreover, the rapidly changing demographics of the United States causes researchers to conduct research with populations that are different from those of even ten years ago. For example, in the year ending Sept. 30, 2002, almost 1.1 million immigrants were admitted to the United States. The three leading countries from which they came were Mexico (219,380), India (71,105) and China (61,282). The United States projects a dramatic increase in ethnic minorities for the next 50 years. Table 2, below, shows the United States Census predictions for projected population changes by race. From 2000 to 2050, the percentage increase for Asians, other races, and Hispanics is expected to be 213%, 217%, and 188%, respectively. Even from 2000 to 2010 (the upcoming five years), Asians, other races, and Hispanics are expected to increase their populations by 33%, 31%, and 34%, respectively.

Table 1.13.2: Projected Population Change in the United States, by Race and Hispanic Origin: 2000 to 2050
(In thousands except as indicated. As of July 1. Resident population.)

Numerical or percent change and race or Hispanic origin	**2000 - 2050**	**2000 - 2010**	**2010 - 2020**	**2020 - 2030**	**2030 - 2040**	**2040 - 2050**
Numerical Change						
Total	137,729	26,811	26,869	27,779	28,362	27,908

White alone	74,078	16,447	15,634	15,102	13,959	12,936
Black alone	25,543	4,636	4,911	5,077	5,434	5,485
Asian Alone	22,746	3,557	3,747	4,592	5,412	5,438
All other races 1/	15,362	2,171	2,576	3,009	3,557	4,049
Hispanic (of any race)	66,938	12,134	12,000	13,299	14,530	14,975
White alone, not Hispanic	14,554	5,383	4,824	3,240	1,155	-48
Percent Change						
Total	48.8	9.5	8.7	8.3	7.8	7.1
White alone	32.4	7.2	6.4	5.8	5.1	4.5
Black alone	71.3	12.9	12.1	11.2	10.8	9.8
Asian Alone	212.9	33.3	26.3	25.5	24.0	19.4
All other races 1/	217.1	30.7	27.9	25.5	24.0	22.0
Hispanic (of any race)	187.9	34.1	25.1	22.3	19.9	17.1
White alone, not Hispanic	7.4	2.8	2.4	1.6	0.6	0.0

Notes:

1/ Includes American Indian and Alaska Native alone, Native Hawaiian and Other Pacific Islander alone, and Two or More Races

Source: U.S. Census Bureau, 2004, "U.S. Interim Projections by Age, Sex, Race, and Hispanic Origin," <http://www.census.gov/ipc/www/usinterimproj/>

Internet Release Date: March 18, 2004

How will the changes in the United States population affect prevention science? It most likely means that we have to pay even more careful attention to cultural differences than ever before. For this reason, in 2001, a group of national leaders was convened to examine research ethics for mental health science involving ethnic minority children and youth (Fisher et al., 2002). Four categories of mental health research that facilitate ethical behavior were identified, and within each category, several recommendations were made. Category 1 includes recommendations for the application of cultural perspectives, category 2 includes recommendations for informed consent procedures, category 3 includes recommendations for confidentiality and disclosure procedure, and category 4 includes recommendations for including participant and community procedures. We believe these recommendations to be so important for the application to prevention research that we include them in their entirety below (Fisher et al., 2002, pages 4-19):

Category 1: Application of cultural perspectives to the evaluation of research risks and benefits.

Recommendation 1: Investigators need to carefully consider and explicitly describe the theoretical, empirical, and social frameworks driving the definitions of race, ethnicity, or culture that are used to select participant populations. This will ensure the scientific validity of the research question and will allow research findings to be evaluated within the context of continuously changing scientific and societal conceptions of these definitions.

Recommendation 2: In designing their research, investigators need to consider within-group variability and individual differences among ethnic groups that may influence children's mental health and responsiveness to treatment. Such factors include ethnic identification, acculturation, language, education, socioeconomic status, regional variation, and personal and familial immigration history. Although a single study may not examine all of these factors, the selection of variables and the discussion of findings should reflect an awareness of their possible influence on development and on the disorder or symptoms under investigation.

Recommendation 3: Whenever possible, investigators should select instruments that have been standardized on members of the research participants' racial or ethnic group. When culturally appropriate tests have not yet been developed or sufficiently evaluated, investigators should take steps to ensure that their instruments are assessing conceptually and operationally the mental health characteristics under study. One way to accomplish this is to examine the cultural, developmental, and item equivalence of instruments for each population studied. In the case of non-English-speaking or multilingual participants, investigators should use translated versions of standardized instruments that have been subjected to rigorous standards of measurement equivalence to ensure that the desired psychological constructs are properly measured.

Recommendation 4: Programmatic research is needed on questions that examine historical and contemporary forms of prejudice and discrimination as implicating factors in the development of well-being among ethnic minority children and adolescents. Racial and ethnic intolerance within peer groups, schools, employment settings, juvenile justice proceedings, and health care systems should be included in studies of person-context interactions contributing to positive and poor developmental outcomes if research is to fully inform mental health services for ethnic minority children and youths.

Recommendation 5: Mental health research should examine participant's developmental capacities for coping and resilience in addition to factors that may influence vulnerability to mental disorders. Researchers examining the roles of race, ethnicity, and culture on the development of children and youths should consider how minority status may add a layer of mental health vulnerability imposed by social and institutional prejudices rather than by ethnic group characteristics, values, and traditions.

Recommendation 6: Prior to testing an intervention developed for members of the majority culture or an ethnic minority population, researchers should have adequate theoretical, clinical, practical, or empirical bases for hypothesizing that it will be effective in the particular ethnic group recruited for the study. This includes knowledge of that group's cultural values, traditions, socioeconomic status, education, or other relevant variables that may facilitate or interfere with responsiveness or resistance to different treatment conditions under study.

Recommendation 7: Investigators testing a promising mental health treatment should consider ethnic disparities in access to quality mental health services when selecting as a control condition a treatment currently available to the community versus the best quality of treatment available nationwide.

Recommendation 8: Investigators must provide all members of the research team with training in the cultural competencies necessary to conduct research with the racial and ethnic populations involved in the study in order to ensure the highest quality of data collection. Principal investigators should also encourage staff to provide ongoing feedback about participants' responses to recruitment practices, experimental procedures, instruments, and all aspects of the research. This feedback will allow investigators to evaluate the effectiveness of the procedures and the need for culturally appropriate methodological adjustments.

Recommendation 9: Investigators and research team members from all ethnic backgrounds can benefit from examination of their own cultural biases. Through self-reflection and exchange of views, the research team can examine and address different cultural conceptions of the research, mental health goals, and scientific procedures aimed at understanding and promoting positive development of ethnic minority children and youths.

Category 2: Development and implementation of respectful informed consent procedures.

Recommendation 10: Investigators can enhance informed consent protections through individual and community awareness mechanisms aimed at educating prospective participants, their guardians, and their communities about the research process and participants' rights. Such mechanisms include the use of recruitment handbooks and the dissemination of information through community-based speakers, bureaus, mass media, parent-child associations, health care centers, and religious organizations. Informed decisions to participate are also facilitated by providing prospective participants and their guardians with time to consider the information and to discuss it with family members or community elders.

Recommendation 11: Informed consent procedures must be conducted in a language understood and preferred by prospective participants and their guardian or guardians; researchers should recognize that children and adolescents may have different language competencies and preferences than adult members of their families. Investigators should also ensure that consent forms translated from English or other languages are adequate. These forms should be translated using procedures that ensure equivalency.

Recommendation 12: When necessary, investigators must use the services of interpreters who have the language and knowledge competencies necessary to ensure that consent is informed, rational, and voluntary. Having children serve as interpreters to obtain parent permission is not permissible because it may result in misinformation or may undermine respectful parent-child relationships. In small and cohesive ethnic communities, individuals qualified to serve as interpreters may have other role relationships with prospective participants and their families. Through careful and respectful questioning, investigators must determine whether these multiple relationships could be exploitative or otherwise harmful to participants, must select alternative interpreters when feasible, and must take steps to ensure that consent is voluntary and that participant confidentiality is protected.

Recommendation 13: Informed consent procedures for research involving ethnic minority groups should reflect sensitivity to participants' concerns about signed forms. Investigators may seek a waiver for this requirement when appropriate, and, if granted, they should continue to provide prospective participants and their guardians with a detailed oral or written consent statement about the research and to document that oral consent has been obtained.

Recommendation 14: When designing informed consent protocols, investigators should make an effort to understand expectations about guardian permission and child assent that reflect cultural attitudes, values, and histories related to the roles of family members and community structures in decisions regarding the welfare of children and adolescents. Investigators should respect these relationships while fulfilling legal obligations and should recognize that their primary obligation is participant protection.

Recommendation 15: When deciding whether to request a waiver of guardian consent, investigators should consider the meaning and consequence of the waiver to parent-child relationships within the norms and behavior of the ethnic group from which participants are recruited. Investigators should be sensitive to potential institutional biases regarding parental competence that may influence waiver decisions. A guardian's reluctance to return consent forms is not a justification for waiving guardian permission.

Recommendation 16: Assent procedures for children need to be tailored to reflect the participants' developmental level, experience, and cultural expectations about adult authority. Assent procedures should provide sufficient opportunities for children or adolescents to express their wishes about agreement or refusal to participate in the research. When the requirement for guardian permission has been waived, investigators should identify participant advocates who have the language skills and cultural competencies necessary to protect the rights of the children or adolescents.

Recommendation 17: Selection of fair and noncoercive compensation for research participation needs to reflect consideration of cultural, economic, and developmental factors influencing the value and meaning of monetary payments or other compensation alternatives as legitimate recompense for the time and effort contributed to a research project. Consultation with prospective participants and community leaders can assist in determining compensation that is perceived as fair and noncoercive by members of the cultural group recruited for research participation.

Recommendation 18: Informed consent procedures conducted in service settings must clarify the differential roles of investigators and professional staff, the relationship and obligations of the investigator to the service agency and to the participant, and the extent to which participation in the research is distinguishable from receipt of services. Investigators must also provide prospective participants and their guardians with clear explanations of the purpose of assessments and interventions conducted to gain scientific knowledge, those conducted exclusively for receipt of treatments or services, and those used in legal investigations or child welfare evaluations.

Recommendation 19: Investigators should work with institutions to develop safeguards to ensure that prospective participants understand that research refusal or withdrawal does not result in termination of services or other negative consequences. Reconsent procedures at appropriate intervals for longitudinal studies should be implemented to ensure that participation remains voluntary.

Category 3: Developing and Implementing Culturally Sensitive Confidentiality and Disclosure Policies

Recommendation 20: When working with rural or small and unique ethnic populations, investigators need to be aware of the added difficulties of protecting the confidentiality of individuals and their communities. During the recruitment, implementation, and dissemination stages of research, investigators should take extra precautions to protect the privacy and identity of research participants, their families, and their communities.

Recommendation 21: When research involves multiple informants, investigators must take precautions not to reveal confidential information about the participants to the informants. When research is conducted in institutional settings, investigators must take steps to protect participant privacy and recognize that institutional staff may have different disclosure and reporting obligations or that they may use the knowledge in ways that participants and their guardians may find undesirable.

Recommendation 22: Criteria for disclosing information about an ethnic minority child's mental health status or risk behaviors need to include careful consideration of mandated reporting laws. Criteria should also be culturally valid and should include culturally appropriate means of assessing the following: (a) clinical levels of risk, (b) the truthfulness of reports, (c) whether a problem needs immediate attention, (d) whether a child or adolescent is already receiving services for the problem, and (e) sensitivity to the child or adolescent's expectations about the investigator's protective role.

Recommendation 23: Members of different ethnic groups may differ in their expectations for and valuing of confidentiality when it relates to information indicating that a child or an adolescent has a mental health problem or is engaged in high-risk or health-compromising behaviors. Confidentiality and disclosure policies should reflect consideration of and respect for these differences to the extent that is possible given that such policies may be determined by state, local, or federal law or by IRB standards for that community.

Recommendation 24: Once culturally valid criteria for disclosing confidential information have been established, investigators should, whenever possible, identify culturally appropriate persons and agencies that can best serve the interests of participants in need of referral or immediate intervention. Working with community members, schools, child welfare agencies, courts, law enforcement agencies, and mental health facilities, investigators can build culturally sensitive systems of protection that define when, how, and to whom a problem will be reported in a manner consistent with laws governing reporting.

Recommendation 25: The specific confidentiality and disclosure policies selected for a study must be explained to prospective participants and their guardians during informed consent procedures. Such information includes an explanation of reporting requirements, such as those related to mandated child abuse reporting or duty-to protect laws. When possible, participants and guardians should be allowed to choose among available disclosure and service referral procedures.

Category 4: Community and Participant Consultation: The Importance of Community and Participant Perspectives

Recommendation 26: Community and participant consultations involve an ongoing reciprocal and respectful dialogue among scientists, prospective participants, their families, and other community stakeholders. This dialogue is aimed at strengthening scientific merit and responsibility during research design, implementation, and dissemination. In some communities, this may require that researchers establish a relationship with the community long before the study is commenced. This relationship can inform the study's goals and aims and engage community members as true collaborators.

Recommendation 27: Consultation is not a means of obtaining blind acceptance of an already worked-out protocol. Respectful and successful community and participant consultation often depends on relationships of trust that are established early in the research design phase and are continued through the data interpretation, implementation, and dissemination phases. When a substantial number of participants and community representatives indicate concern about the balance of risks and benefits, recruitment or informed consent procedures, confidentiality policies, research compensation, or dissemination plans for a proposed project, investigators should work to modify these procedures to best meet the standards of scientific rigor and participant protection.

Recommendation 28: Multicultural research teams, especially those in which the ethnicity of frontline workers differs from that of the principal investigators, need to carefully consider the community outreach role of each team member to ensure that principal investigators maintain awareness of and are response to community and participant concerns.

Recommendation 29: When seeking community consultation and collaboration, investigators should draw on a definition of community that includes representatives who have a knowledge base about the cultural and mental health concerns of the individuals who will participate in the research. When the mental health problems of children and adolescents are the focus of investigation, this may require drawing community representatives from multiple ethnic groups.

Recommendation 30: When conflicts over ethical procedures emerge among prospective participants, their family members, and community stakeholders during the design phase of the research, investigators should strive to modify experimental procedures in a manner that continues to ensure scientific validity while adequately addressing the needs of all parties. Researchers should recognize that their primary responsibility is to ensure the protection of the rights and welfare of those who participate in the research.

Recommendation 31: Research proposals describing plans for community consultation should emphasize the strategies that will be used to identify and ensure sufficient community input and the role that community and participant consultation will play at different stages of the research.

Recommendation 32: A description of the ways in which the consultation process contributed to the evaluation and enhancement of ethical procedures should be included in research reports to contribute to the ethical development of the field of mental health science involving ethnic minority children and youths.

These recommendations offer significant guidance to prevention research with children in such areas as identification of developmentally appropriate measures, ensuring fully informed assent and consent, assessing parental competence and avoiding coercion. It would serve the prevention field to adopt the document. Additionally, the recommendations offer advice in less apparent areas such as strategies to build collaboration and trust, the role of the family and community in research, and weighing the benefits and costs of certain experimental procedures. These recommendations, if implemented in prevention research, could provide a sound base on which to build future research strategies. Expanding the intent of the recommendations, we offer some additional areas for consideration in advancing prevention research.

Beyond Current Ethical Standards

The social sciences have long been held captive by academic and research paradigms that utilize models of risk; hence, we have described people, families, cultures, and whole nations using a research language that emphasizes their risk status, rather than their strength. By applying this model, people and cultures are typically described by their disease rate, their lack of success, or by what they have not accomplished. Because of this, we have come to understand individuals, families, and cultures by what they are not, especially compared to the dominant culture.

In contrast to this model, Werner (1989a) introduced the concept of resilience through her longitudinal study of children born into poverty on the island of Kauai, Hawaii. These children were ethnically diverse; they were Japanese, Philippine, and part or full Hawaiians. When the children were born, Hawaii was not yet the 50th state of the United States, and the island of Kauai was not yet the tourist Mecca that we now know it to be. In 1955, Kauai was an island where running water and electricity were privileges that not all families enjoyed. By today's standards, the environment might be considered impoverished. She followed these individuals well into their forties and showed that even under the most adverse of conditions, individuals can mature into competent, caring adults. (Werner, 1989a; Werner, 1989b; Werner and Smith, 1992; Werner and Smith, 2001).

Werner and Smith (Werner, 1989a; Werner, 1989b; Werner and Smith, 1992; Werner and Smith, 2001) document the life course of these individuals with extensive multivariate, longitudinal data that includes biological and psychological assessments. Their evaluation of these children occurred at birth, infancy, early and middle childhood, late adolescence, and adulthood. Using a natural history method, the life trajectories of these individuals were documented allowing the assessment of the long-term consequences of perinatal and prenatal complications, rearing conditions, development, and long-term adaptation. Among many provocative findings, their study suggested that children who grow up in poverty are more likely to experience a wide variety of deleterious child health and developmental outcomes. Recent evidence bears this out as the research in child poverty has been linked to low-quality prenatal and medical care; low birth weight; delays in physical, cognitive, and social development; school dropout; teen pregnancy; and eventually unemployment (Corcoran, 1995; Duncan and Brooks-Gunn, 1997; Huston, Garcia Coll, & McLoyd, 1994; Masten, 1994; McLeod & Shanahan, 1993). In the Kauai study approximately two-thirds of the children growing up in poverty eventually developed serious problems as adults; however, the remaining third developed and matured into competent, caring adults. Even though most of the children grew up in similar environments, the strikingly different outcomes of those who grew up to become competent, caring adults begged the question: How come? Understanding resilience across individuals, cultures, and entire societies can help reshape a research model of loss and disease into one that values the strengths and vitality of the past, present, and future of the culture, and prevention research is in a unique position to do so. It would be a disservice not to.

Resilience, as a concept, has received much criticism over the last couple of decades, in part, because some researchers perceive resilience as a romanticized notion of careworn psychological theories, such as trait theory (Glantz & Johnson, 1999). Nevertheless, there is some general acceptance that the process of resilience is what helps people sustain lives of health and hope, despite adversity. Children demonstrate resilience when they draw on inner strengths, skills, and supports to keep adversity from derailing their lives. Resilience, to many researchers, refers to successful adaptation despite risk and adversity (Masten, 1994), or unexpected achievement in spite of stress (Bartelt, 1994). The newly founded field of positive psychology has established a new science of hope and optimism (Gillham, 2000) that prevention research could benefit from. To date, there has been little empirical collaboration between the two fields.

Resilience speaks to the very nature of contemporary experience. Very early on, America was viewed as a 'melting pot' that molded immigrants into an American amalgam. Through conformity and hard work we could all prosper as Americans. Cultural homogeneity, as opposed to cultural heterogeneity, was the goal. To be part of the non-dominant culture was to be inferior. Thus, all immigrants and Indigenous People were held to this model of conformity through a variety of societal and governmental actions. For example, Indigenous Peoples have undergone continuous challenges to their political, economic, social, and cultural well being (Waller, Okamato, Hankerson, 2002). As a result of invasion and colonization, Indigenous Peoples suffer uniquely. Deliberate attempts were made to destroy Native people and the impact of historical actions has left its mark on Native people today. For example, in 1971, 34,538 Native children were in Bureau of Indian Affairs (BIA) residential boarding schools (Hogan and Siu, 1988). Children were often sent to schools hundreds of miles away from home.

These children were taken from their families, destroying family bonds and cultural influences. The children were not allowed to practice their Native language, spiritual beliefs, or healing traditions. They were also taken from their homes and adopted out to substitute care (foster or adoptive homes) at a rate that is 20 times higher than that of White children (Johnson, 1981). For example, in the 1960s and 1970s, over 25% of all Native children were taken from their families and placed in foster care, adoptive homes, or institutions (Weaver & White, 1997) until 1978 with the passing of the Indian Child Welfare Act. Yet, today, they remain strong in spite of devastating adversity. The question again begs asking: Why?

Iris Heavyrunner and Joann Morris (2002) suggest that what is missing from the American amalgam is an understanding of that which makes our society stronger, instead of weaker—cultural resilience. This concept predates the discovery of Native People and demonstrates a traditional process in action. Understanding the different cultural contexts of resilience may help us to understand better the process of resilience. Furthermore, understanding that cultural heterogeneity is a strength, and not a weakness, could enhance our understanding that other cultures may carry with them lessons about resilience for the dominant culture.

Many agree that race and culture are important determinants of outcome, and some suggest that lives are constrained by the larger forces of racial and cultural contexts (Montgomery et al., 2000). Understanding multicultural issues becomes increasingly important as the percentage of ethnic minority students in schools continues to increase. Counselors, health practitioners, and teachers must broaden their cultural knowledge base and develop new strategies that are responsive to the unique experiences of young people; recognizing that these experiences offer both challenges and opportunities for the individual. Taylor (1994) underscores the importance of understanding the determinants of culture as a way to speak specifically to the strategies for building the resilience of individuals and families facing economic and social disadvantages.

For the prevention scientist, adoption of the resilience model helps us to tackle the complex and thorny issues present in conducting prevention research with children. First, we can begin to understand the holistic and complex interrelationships that allow children, families, and cultures to not only to survive, but also to grow strong. These are important prevention messages. For example, understanding the role of family values among Native American families may be a key to their resilience. Native Americans (as in many other cultures) value an extended family tribal structure that concerns the whole family's social and economic well-being. They think about the collective whole, rather than the self, in a 'we' rather than an 'I' mental framework. The value of the group and the strength of the family are potential processes that lead to healthy outcomes among Native Americans. For example, Native Americans often participate in community focused child care and value the elderly. Elders among Native Americans often garner respect, and their opinions are valued, rather than discarded. This is in direct contrast to an individualistic model, where success is often equated with independence, and not interdependence. Native American society is a good starting point, but similar observations have been made about immigrant and refugee families, as well as other non-Western cultures. Underscoring the nature of Native American thinking, as well as many other indigenous cultures, is the concept of 'relationship'—namely, of things that are related to each other. The emphasis of life is relational and therefore, non-linear. Studying this relational perspective has important implications for prevention science. How can we describe the importance of 'relationship' to individual and cultural strength? How can we measure it? What are the implications for dominant research paradigms? These may be the tasks for the next generation of prevention research.

Table 3 shows how the variety of prevention delivery formats can influence ethical considerations in prevention science. We have discussed only one area. Using this background as a framework, prevention research might need to adopt a set of ethics for its research paradigms that encompass the nuances of working with different children in different venues. The 32 recommendations presented by Fisher et al. (2002) would be an excellent starting point. By adopting these recommendations for ethics in conducting prevention research with children, we will be in a better position to design public policies and interventions that meet the needs of all of the children in the United States, and not just those of the dominant culture.

Table 1.13.3: Prevention Delivery Effects on Ethical Considerations

Type of Variation	Prevention Programs
Age	Target different ages of children thus making it difficult to have a standardized consent format that is appropriate for all ages.
Venue	Occur in numerous venues: churches, schools, after-school programs, and community centers. Each venue may have its own specific consent requirements.
Ethno-cultural Group	Target different ethno-cultural groups thus making it important to develop consent forms that are linguistically equivalent for each group.
Group Size	Have different requirements for the delivery of the program, thus making it difficult to develop a standardized set of confidentiality requirements because large group delivery programs may require different types of confidentiality agreements compared to small group delivery programs.
Gender	May be designed for males, for females, or for mixed-gender groups. Gender specific programs may influence decisions about consent form content.

Jeannette L. Johnson, Ph.D., is a cross-cultural psychologist who has extensive experience in community-based prevention research, with an emphasis on understanding the role of risk and protective factors in high-risk youth and examining models of vulnerability. She is currently a Senior Research Analyst at Friends Research Institute in Baltimore, MD. In the past she was a Distinguished Professor at SUNY-Buffalo and the Director of the Research Center on Children and Youth. Dr. Johnson is of Native American heritage (Huron) and has

extensive experience with Native American communities. She has conducted community-based substance use and HIV/AIDS prevention research as well as treatment research with chronic substance users. She is a contributing editor for several journals, including Substance Use and Misuse, the author and co-author of many professional publications, and a faculty member of the Middle Eastern Summer Institute on Drug Use (MESIDU) in Israel, Italy, and Spain.

Nancy R. Vandermark, Ph.D., is the Director of Colorado Social Research Associates, the Research and Program Evaluation division of Arapahoe House, Inc. She worked as a Chief Operating Officer and Program Manager with Arapahoe House, the largest substance use prevention and treatment provider in Colorado, for 12 years and the research and evaluation department for the past three years. Her work has included overseeing and evaluating detoxification and treatment programs for adults and adolescents, including specialized programs for individuals involved with the child welfare system, women, survivors of interpersonal violence, offenders, homeless persons, adolescents and individuals with serious and persistent mental illness. She has developed programs in a variety of settings including hospitals, schools, community treatment programs, jails, battered women's shelters and child welfare agencies. Dr. Vandermark has been the Project Director or Principal Investigator on six federally funded services research grants from the Substance Abuse and Mental Health Services Administration addressing parental substance use and misuse, integrated interventions for women with substance use-related problems, mental illness and trauma and services for children.

References

Alvidrez, J. & Arean, P.A. (2002). Psychosocial treatment research with ethnic minority populations: Ethical considerations in conducting clinical trials. *Ethics & Behavior, 12*(1), 103-116.

American Psychological Association. (2002). Ethical principles of psychologists and code of conduct. *American Psychologist, 57*, 1060-1073.

Bartelt, D. (1994). On resilience: Questions of validity. In M. C. Wang and E. W. Gordon, (Eds.), *Educational resilience in inner-city America: Challenges and prospects* (pp. 97-108). Hillsdale, NJ: Erlbaum.

Corcoran, M. (1995). Rags to rags: Poverty and mobility in the U.S. *Annual Review of Sociology, 21*, 237-267.

Duncan,G. J., & Brooks Gunn, J. (1997). Income effects across the life span: Integration and interpretation. In G. J. Duncan & J. Brooks Gunn (Eds.), *Consequences of growing up poor* (pp. 596-610). New York: Russell Sage Foundation.

Drotar, D. (2000). Handbook of research in pediatric and clinical psychology: Practical strategies and methods. *Issues in clinical child psychology.* Dordrect, Netherlands: Kluwer Academic Publishers, pp. 305-326.

Fisher, C.B., Hoagwood, K., Boyce, C., Duster, T., Frank, D.A. Grisso, T., Levine, R.J., Macklin, R., Spencer, M.B.B., Takanishi, R., Trimble, J.E., Zayas, L.H. (2002). Research ethics for mental health science involving ethnic minority children and youths. *American Psychologist, 57*(12), 1024-1040.

Gillham, J. E. (Ed.). (2000). *The science of optimism and hope: Research essays in honor of Martin E. P. Seligman.* Philadelphia, PA: Templeton Foundation Press.

Glantz, M. D., & Johnson, J. L. (Eds.). (1999). Resilience and development: Positive life adaptations. *Longitudinal research in the social and behavioral sciences.* New York, NY: Kluwer Academic/Plenum Publishers.

Hall, D. (1991). The research imperative and bureaucratic control: The case of clinical research. *Social Science and Medicine, 32*(3), 333-342.

Heavyrunner, I., & Morris, J. S. (2002). Traditional native culture and resilience. Retrieved October 2, 2002, from http://www.coled.umn.edu/CAREI/Reports/Rpractice/Spring97/traditional.htm.

Hoagwood, K., Jensen, P.S., Fisher, C.B. (Eds.). (1997). *Ethical issues in mental health research with children and adolescents*. Hillsdale, NJ: Lawrence Erlbaum Associates.

Hogan, P. T. & Siu, S. (1988). Minority children and the welfare system: An historical perspective. *Social Work*, November-December, 493-498.

Huston, A. C., Garcia Coll, C. T., & McLoyd, V. (Eds.). (1994). Special issue on child development and poverty. *Child Development, 65*(2), 275-715.

Johnson, B. B. (1981). The Indian child welfare act. *Child Welfare, 60*(7), 435-445.

Krischner, K.L. (2003). The challenge of human subject research in the new millennium. *Topics in Stroke Rehabilitation, 9*(4), 92-95.

Masten, A. S. (1994). Resilience in individual development. Successful adaptation despite risk and adversity. In M. C. Wang and E. W. Gordon, (Eds.), *Educational resilience in inner-city America: Challenges and prospects* (pp. 3-25). Hillsdale, NJ: Erlbaum.

McLeod, J. D., & Shanahan, M. J. (1993). Poverty, parenting, and children's mental health. *American Sociological Review, 58*(3), 351-366.

Montgomery, D., Miville, M. L., Winterowd, C., Jeffries, B., & Baysden, M. F. (2000). American Indian college students: An exploration into resiliency factors revealed through personal stories. *Cultural Diversity and Ethnic Minority Psychology, 6*(4), 387-396.

National Research Act. Pub. L. No 93-348, 88 Stat.342 (12 July 1974) (codified as amended in scattered sections of 42 U.S.C.).

Sieber, J.E. (1992). Planning ethically responsible research: A guide for students and internal review boards. *Applied social research methods series, Vol. 3*1. Thousand Oaks, CA: Sage Publications.

Sieber, J.E. (1994). Will the new code help researchers to be more ethical? *Professional Psychology: Research and Practice, 25*(4), 369-375.

Society for Prevention Research. (2005). Standards of evidence. Retrieved on June 3, 2004, from http://www.preventionresearch.org/StandardsofEvidencebook.pdf

Taylor, R. (1994). Risk and resilience: Contextual influence on the development of African-American adolescents. In M. C. Wang and E. W. Gordon, (Eds.), *Educational resilience in inner-city America: Challenges and prospects* (pp. 216-224). Hillsdale, NJ: Erlbaum.

United States Government Code of Federal Regulations, Title 45, Public Welfare, Department of Health and Human Services National Institutes of Health, Office for Protection from Research Risks, Part 46, Protection of Human Subjects, Effective Dec 13, 2001. (Retrieved on Dec 20, 2004 from http://www.hhs.gov/ohrp/)

Waller, M. A., Okamato, S. K., & Hankerson, A. A. (2002). The Hoop of learning: A holistic, multisystemic model for facilitating educational resilience among indigenous students. *Journal of Sociology and Social Welfare, 29*(1), pp. 97-116.

Weaver, H. N. & White, B. J. (1997). The Native American family circle: Roots of resiliency. In H. N. Weaver and B. J. White (Eds.), *Voices of first nation people.* New York, NY: Haworth Press, pg. 67-79.

Werner, E. E. (1989a). Children of the garden island. *Scientific American, 260*(4), 106-111.

Werner, E. E. (1989b). High-risk children in young adulthood. A longitudinal study from birth to 32 years. *American Journal of Orthopsychiatry, 59*, 72-81.

Werner, E. E. & Smith, R. S. A. (1992). *Overcoming the odds: High risk children from birth to adulthood.* Ithaca, NY: Cornell University Press.

Werner, E. E. & Smith, R. S. (2001). *Journeys from childhood to midlife: Risk, resilience, and recovery.* Ithaca, NY: Cornell University Press.

Glossary

culture: The thoughts, speech, action, attitudes, artifacts, norms, customary beliefs, social forms, and traits of a group.

resilience: The self-righting ability to recover from adversity.

Prevention Science: The theory, research, and practice of prevention.

indigenous: Originating in a particular region or environment.

1-14 Reflections on Ethical Issues in Research with Aboriginal Peoples

Theodore M. Godlaski, M. Div., Jeannette Johnson, Ph.D., and Rodney Haring

If the Great Spirit had desired me to be a white man he would have made me so in the first place. He put in your heart certain wishes and plans; in my heart he put other and different desires. Each man is good in the sight of the Great Spirit.It is not necessary, that eagles should be crows.

— Sitting Bull (Teton Sioux)

They told us that Indian ways were bad. They said we must get civilized. I remember that word, too. It means 'be like the white man.' I am willing to be like the white man, but I did not believe Indian ways were wrong. But they kept teaching us for seven years. And the books told how bad the Indians had been to the white men—burning their towns and killing their women and children. But I had seen white men do that to Indians. We all wore white man's clothes and ate white man's food and went to white man's churches and spoke white man's talk. And so after a while we also began to say Indians were bad. We laughed at our own people and their blankets and cooking pots and sacred societies and dances. I tried to learn the lessons—and after seven years I came home...

— Sun Elk, from Taos Pueblo, telling of his experiences at Carlisle Indian School in 1890 (Nabokov, 1991, p. 222).

Abstract

This article is a reflection on the salient ethical issues that arise in research work with aboriginal or native peoples. The primary source of ethical concern is the cultural appropriateness of the research purpose, design, methods, protocol, and publication/dissemination plan. Although cultural appropriateness is not a well-defined construct, the lack of concern for Native ways of thinking, social structure, communication, and worldview can be evident in harm done as a result of ill-conceived research endeavors. The authors draw on recent work in this area to provide guidelines for culturally sensitive research.

Key Words: aboriginal, culture, cultural appropriateness, cultural sensitivity, dominant culture, ethnic gloss, Four Directions, genocide, historical trauma, harmony, human subjects protection, indigenous people, Institutional Review Boards (IRBs), mainstream culture, native peoples, non-linear thinking, non-materialism, spirituality, American Indian, Native American

Introduction

The issue of overriding importance in research with aboriginal or native peoples is not really unique to these groups. Cultural appropriateness or cultural sensitivity is an ethical factor that underlies research and intervention with any group. However, aboriginal peoples may have structures of belief, customs, and historical experiences so different from those of researchers trained in mainstream institutions and universities that special care needs to be taken when these same researchers apply their methodologies to indigenous peoples.

Native populations suffer from critical health problems of all kinds, including those involving substance use. This is not a new phenomenon. What is most telling is that in the past three decades their health has not markedly improved, at least in the United States, relative to the non-native population. The U.S Commission on Civil Rights, an independent and bipartisan commission established by Congress in 1957, issued a report to the President and Congress of the United States in 2004 on the state of health care among Native Americans (U.S. Commission on Civil Rights, 2004). In the opening chapter to that report they state the following:

> *Today, Native Americans continue to experience significant rates of diabetes, mental health disorders, cardiovascular disease, pneumonia, influenza, and injuries. Specifically, Native Americans are 770 percent more likely to die of alcoholism, 650 percent more likely to die from tuberculosis, 420 percent more likely to die from diabetes, 280 percent more likely to die from accidents, and 52 percent more likely to die from pneumonia or influenza than the rest of the population of the United States, including whites and minorities. As a result of these increased mortality rates, the life expectancy for Native Americans is 71 years of age, nearly five years fewer than the rest of the U.S. population. A comparison of earlier life expectancy data illustrates one of the problems facing the IHS (Indian Health Service) in eliminating disparities. In 1976 the life expectancy for Native Americans was 65.1 years, compared with 70.8 years for other Americans. Although life expectancy for Native Americans has since then improved by six years, their life expectancy relative to other Americans has improved very little. (pp. 7-8)*

In relation to Native-American mental health problems, the report of the U.S. Commission on Civil rights states:

> *The most significant mental health concerns today are the high prevalence of substance abuse, depression, anxiety, violence, and suicide. Substance abuse, most notably alcoholism, has been the most visible health disorder crisis. Depression is also emerging as a dominant concern. These two illnesses are most commonly attributed to isolation on distant reservations, pervasive poverty, hopelessness, and intergenerational trauma, including the historic attempts by the federal government to forcibly assimilate tribes. (U.S. Commission on Civil Rights, 2004, p. 12)*

The American Academy of Pediatrics released information in 2002 indicating that Native American and Alaskan Native youth 14 to 24 years of age were twice as likely to die by suicide, and native children 5 to 10 years of age were three times more likely to die by suicide than comparably aged non-native children. The need for improved understanding of the factors contributing to this intolerable and shameful situation are clear, as are the need to develop and test appropriate interventions that are better able to assist native people in addressing these problems. All this implies the need to do research that will yield valid results and genuinely benefit native peoples.

From the onset, it is important to note that this chapter does not pretend to exhaustively discuss the ethical issues raised in work with indigenous peoples. It is meant more as a reflection on some of the most prominent concerns in this area. Further, there is no desire to homogenize indigenous, native, or aboriginal people. There are vast differences in cultural patterns and historical experiences among these groups. There is more variation among tribal groups than there are similarities. Tribes have different traditions, ceremonies, food, and manners of being—in short, different cultures. For example, among Native Americans, variation extends to geographic areas, which are, in effect, distinct cultural areas as well: the Arctic, Sub-Arctic, Northwest Coast, Plateau, Plains, East, California, Great Basin, and Southwest (Driver, 1969; Manson, Shore, Barron, Ackerson & Neligh, 1992). Another indication of this heterogeneity is the more than 200 spoken Indian languages (Fleming, 1992). Likewise, there are vast differences among native peoples concerning their degree of enculturation into the mainstream culture: ranging from those who are indistinguishable from the mainstream, to those who are multicultural and move easily between the native and mainstream cultures, to those for whom the mainstream culture is both alien and incomprehensible.

Finally, the intent here is not to homogenize researchers. Those for whom culture is a central preoccupation of their discipline, such as anthropologists, tend to think long and hard about the cultural implications and appropriateness of what they do. Those for whom culture is a distant and poorly understood notion, such as psychologists and physicians, tend not to think so long and hard, seeing things as mainly an individual affair. There is a range of those in between, such as sociologists and social workers, who may understand culture for what it is or who may see it as the outgrowth of social behavior.

As preface, let us posit a working definition of culture. Marsella (1985) defines culture as learned experience that is transmitted across generations that is externally represented in such forms as artifacts (e.g., clothing, foods, technologies), roles (e.g., parents, mother, father, occupations), and institutions (e.g., family, religious, educational, economic). Culture is also internally represented in such forms as worldviews, values, beliefs, attitudes, or cognitive styles. Moreover, he suggests that behavior cannot be separated from the cultural context in which it develops and is sustained, and that, moreover, culture influences all aspects of our lives.

Cultural Sensitivity

It is important to recognize that cultural sensitivity or appropriateness is a poorly defined notion, lacking clear construct indicators, a clear theoretical grounding, and is—at present—very difficult or even impossible to measure (Ridley et al., 1994). Some of the difficulty comes from a kind of reductionism that fails to recognize that one individual may participate in multiple cultures at any given point in his/her life. For example, one of the authors knows a Native American Medicine Man who is also a devout Presbyterian, a single father who attends Parents Without Partners, a recovering member of Alcoholics Anonymous, an elected public official, and chairperson of his local political party. Each of these roles takes place within a different culture with its own specific beliefs, customs, history, and language. To be sure, all overlap the others more or less, with some sharing a good deal in common (male member of a specific Native American group and Medicine Man) while others have very little that is in common (Chairperson of a local political party organization and member of Parents Without Partners). Despite the differences, the individual mentioned seems to have no difficulty at all moving gracefully from one role to another, and does not perceive any inherent contradictions among them. Just as with individuals, groups also may participate in multiple cultures. As a general rule, the more isolated and self-sufficient a group, the less it will have in common with the mainstream culture, and the greater the need for researchers to have a clear understanding and respect for cultural differences of all kinds.

Charles Ridley and colleagues (1994) propose that cultural sensitivity may have a good deal to do with the development of specific perceptual schemata: generalized and dynamic mental structures or formats that enable individuals to identify culturally relevant perceptions, organize this information in a meaningful way, interpret the meaning and significance of behaviors in the light of this organized data, and anticipate and project future behaviors. This schemata is elaborated through ideographic data gained from direct experience and can consist of spoken language, nonverbal behaviors, cognitions, emotions, physiologic responses, sensations, spirituality, and the vast number of interactions among these (Ridley et al., 1994). The first and essential step in developing such schemata is an awareness of one's own cultural baggage so that new information is not blocked, misinterpreted, distorted, or minimized.

For a researcher, or anyone else for that matter, to become aware of his/her own cultural schemata is no easy task. So pervasive and omnipresent are cultural realities that they are, almost by definition, accepted as necessary and true without question or examination. This is no less true for the dominant culture and the culture of academia than it is for any other culture. It brings to mind the Sufi story of the fish who hears of a marvelous substance which is the source and sustenance of all life called water, and goes in search of it.

Henderson and colleagues (1992) said that cultural sensitivity in research has something to do with a heightened awareness of the effects of culture on the individuals and phenomena being studied, the structure of the research endeavor itself, and—most importantly—the researchers. When working with indigenous peoples, researchers from the "dominant" culture may approach the process much like health care providers who travel from the developed world to the developing world, with a sense that they have something to contribute to native culture and want to do it in a "culturally sensitive" way (Parfitt, 1994). The problem, ethical and social, comes from a lack of awareness of the effect of the "dominant" culture whose assumptions of a better way blocks any openness about whether the native culture needs, wants, or is even interested in what the researchers want to provide. Consequently, it would seem best to involve indigenous people from the very beginning, as the research is being planned. Rogler (1989) recommends learning about and immersion in the culture of the population to be studied as a necessary part of the planning phase of the project. Understanding of the social and cultural structures allows development of appropriate sampling techniques, appropriately targeted interventions, and can direct the researcher to gain sanction from appropriate gatekeepers. Such involvement should include discussion about whether the indigenous group sees the research goal as important and whether the research plan and methods are acceptable. Perhaps most important, the indigenous group should be able to benefit clearly from the results of the research. This is a very serious point. Native groups have long had a healthy suspicion about what policy makers do with information about them. In this way they have been in the vanguard of those wise enough to understand that governments can and often do use information about a group to its disadvantage if there are groups with greater economic and political power who will benefit.

Research in the Indigenous Community

Kowalsky and colleagues (1996) make some instructive observations about gaining research access to native communities. They maintain that it is a staged process that researchers must respect. The stages are as follows:

1. Stopping: in this stage the researchers may be prevented by formal or informal means from accessing subjects until the community as a whole agrees that the research is appropriate and the researchers' intentions can be assessed.
2. Waiting: in this stage some limited or partial access may be granted so that the community can judge the trustworthiness of the researchers and whether the research is worth the time and energy of community members.
3. Entry: in this stage communication between the community and the researcher can begin because the community has judged the research valuable and the researcher worthy of trust.

It is striking how different this is from most behavioral research and how much it must run contrary to the cultural expectations of most researchers about their welcome into any environment. The ability to enter into this process would require that the researcher come to see his/her role as instrumental and secondary to the good of the community. Frankly, for many researchers, especially those from university settings, this would be a radical role reversal. Yet without the process of acceptance into an aboriginal community any research endeavor would at best, simply fail and, at worst, be doggedly pursued but produce invalid and misleading data. This second state would most likely produce harm to all involved.

Although it is dangerous to generalize, there are some common elements in the cultures of native peoples that can provide guidance to researchers in approaching work with aboriginal communities. Many Native communities are drawn together by core values such as an emphasis on spirituality, recognition of the sacredness of all living things, and respect for the land and the natural world in which they live. Native peoples may also have quite different ways of explaining and experiencing illness, especially emotional problems, than those of the mainstream culture. There is a large body of ethnographic data indicating that Native Americans and Alaskan Natives experience emotional distress that is not identified in the Diagnostic and Statistical Manual of the American Psychiatric Association (Grant & Brown, 2003). It is important that researchers have both understanding and familiarity with how distress is experienced differently in Native groups so that suffering is not minimized or ignored because it does not fit comfortably into conventional definitions.

The film industry's image of an American Indian living in a teepee and running around in a breech cloth is not the case today. Rather, life in American Indian communities is a mix of contemporary lifestyles and traditional roots. Although values and lifestyles differ from tribe to tribe, many American Indians live in modern-day homes and carry on daily routines much the same as non-Natives. However, one major difference is the inclusion of different traditional tribal values and customs. This may include such things as daily prayers of thanks to mother Earth and its belongings, utmost respect for family and community, a mix of spirituality, following values laid down by elders, and looking ahead for future American Indian generations. The values that are held sacred to most indigenous peoples place them in harmony with the spiritual, or unseen, world. These values have been carefully detailed by Don Coyhis (1999), and are briefly summarized here. His target audience is clinicians but his insights are equally valuable for researchers.

- Cooperation—In the non-native world, competition and independence are respected forms of behavior, but in the Native worldview, these values are not held in such high esteem. Instead, cooperation, which encourages a way of being, as opposed to competition that encourages a state of doing, is placed high as a value. Cooperation among families, tribes, and communities recognizes that it takes a combined effort to achieve a state of harmony in the physical world.
- Harmony with Nature—In the point of view of many aboriginal peoples, cooperation with nature is as important as cooperation with people. Natives show this by valuing animals, the earth, and understanding that everything is connected. This is a way of experiencing the world that grows out of animistic traditions, in which everything is imbued with spirit and worthy of gratitude and respect. It is also a way of experiencing the world in more or less direct opposition to the Judeo-Christian tradition of a world of objects created specifically to be subdued and exploited by and for humankind.
- Group Emphasis—One distinction related to a value system is the interdependence between individuals and the citizens of a community (Brieland, 1977). In the 16th century, values of this nature were found in American Indian cultures of the Northeast U.S. This was recognized by a narrative account written in an early European travelers journal, "the chiefs are generally the poorest among them, for instead of their receiving from the common peoples as among the Christians, they are obliged to give to the mob" (Megapolensis, cited in Van Meteran, 1535-1612). In this narrative, the value of sharing was exhibited when chiefs, shared and/or gave away personal items for the increased well-being of the tribal society. Traditionally, Indian people make their first decision based on what is good for the tribe, what is good for the clan or the family, and finally, what is in the best interest of the individual. The individual's benefit does not come first. Emphasizing the individual first could embarrass Native people. Further, many research instruments tend to have a "dominant" cultural emphasis on the individual's experience and needs as central. Such a frame of reference may be both confusing and distasteful to Native people.

- Religion—In the traditional Native worldview, religion, or spirituality, is a way of life, and it is not something that a person goes to or does on just one day of the week. Spirituality is expressed through prayer, ceremony, or "ways"—specific methods of ritual or appropriate action that suffuse daily life. American Indians range on various planes of spirituality and religion. However, spirituality is an important aspect to keep in mind when working with American Indian client groups. Spirituality not only represents a religious practice, it represents a way of life and a guide for daily routines. Much like the use of humor, conversation of spirituality should be included only after a trusting relationship has been built; even then counselors should await cues from the client to initiate discussion. Conversation of spirituality and religion should form from the client rather than be initiated and probed from the counselor. Spirituality and religion are often maintained as sacred and intellectual property of the individual and tribe and should be approached only when the client wishes to share.
- The Four Directions—Understanding the value of the "four directions" is instrumental in understanding Native thought, especially among Native Americans. The four directions are sometimes represented in the medicine wheel, which is a part of some, but not all, Native American tribes. The four quadrants of the medicine wheel represent life and are symbolized by the mental, spiritual, emotional, and physical parts of the individual. The four directions can also represent the four directions of the earth: east, west, south, and north. Among the Navajo, these four directions can also represent: 1) the East, representing the beginning of life and the process of thinking (Nitsahakees); 2) the West, representing life (Iina), the importance of relationships; 3) the South, representing the process of planning and the development of physical abilities and health; and 4) the North, representing hope.
- Non-materialism—Most Native peoples are raised in non-materialistic environments that emphasize that the best things in life are not things. Motivation to succeed is not to gain or buy things. Thus, when non-native workers work within the Native community (such as healthcare practitioners or educators) they may attempt to inspire using motivational purposes of success such as buying houses, or cars, or wealth in general. These purposes have little impact on Native peoples. Additionally, in some Native groups, wealth is determined by what one gives away rather than by what one possesses. In these groups the poorest individual is the one who hoards the most goods.
- Names—A person's name is very important in most aboriginal tribes. The linguistic name is a source of strength and identity. When the administrators at Carlisle (a boarding school for teaching Native children to be more "white") took the Indian children's names away, they knew what they were doing in the long, painstaking process of "killing the Indian." In taking away the linguistic Indian name—which had been a source of strength, cultural pride, and psychic identity—and making the "new" names very common, written everywhere, used again and again, they in effect erased all spiritual aspects of the children's identities. Traditionally, Indian children did not have their names spoken often. When someone was referred to, it was usually either by relationship or by a

nickname. But the children knew who they were: they belonged to the name, and the name belonged to them, and to no other. Naming and self-naming was a fluid, ongoing process that changed throughout a person's life according to circumstance, personal experience, loss, triumph, foolishness, or social commentary. So a person could have (at least) a birth name, a baby name, several nicknames, a child name, a "young adult" name, an adult name, and an elder name. In addition, there might be a "secret" or ceremonial name, known only by the individual and the holy person who gave that name. Most Native people will introduce themselves by first introducing the names of their family, as does Black Elk:

> *"I am a Lakota of the Ogalala band. My father's name was Black Elk, and his father before him bore the name, and the father of his father, so that I am the fourth to bear it. He was a medicine man and so were several of his brothers. Also, he and the great Crazy Horse's father were cousins, having the same grandfather. My mother's name was White Cow Sees; her father was called Refuse-to-Go, and her mother, Plenty Eagle Feathers. I can remember my mother's mother and her father. My father's father was killed by the Pawnees when I was too little to know, and his mother, Red Eagle Woman, died soon after." (Black Elk Speaks, as told through John G. Neihardt, 1932, p. 7)*

This also has the effect of placing the individual within the context of family, clan, and tribe. In the aboriginal world one gains identity from this network of relationships and not from individual accomplishments.

- The Circle—In his book "The American Indian Mind in a Linear World," Fixico (2003) discusses how aboriginal non-linear thinking uses circles and cycles to see, describe, and interpret the world and his or her experience. To think like a Native means that things, feelings, knowledge, and events are seen in the context of each other, and that this contextual relationship is cyclical. The circle of life includes everything seen and unseen, and these circles and cycles are evident in seasons, the elements, life, and death. Viewing life through a non-linear lens lets the person see his/her relationship to both past and future as a continuum that includes both ancestors and legacies. All things are related, and everything is involved. An approach to life that is circular will provide context and relationship. Groups become more important than individuals, and individuals are not left in isolation but related to all things around them. Thus, thinking is inclusive, and not exclusive.

Researchers in the Community

Researchers need to recognize that they are often viewed negatively in Native communities. Native people have often been exploited, not just by governments and corporations but also by researchers who have come in from the outside to study Native people and to gather data. Often, Native communities have not been informed of the study findings or experienced any benefits of the research. Fear of exploitation has led many Native people to avoid involvement in research projects altogether (Weaver, 1997). It is of no value to protest personal innocence in such matters. Researchers must recognize that there is such a thing as historical guilt by association. Just as in the area of human subjects protection or research integrity, there is a presumption of guilt until innocence can be proved. So too with many Native groups. Researchers must patiently demonstrate respect, integrity, and good faith until the jury comes back in to find them worthy of trust and cooperation.

The Native American Leadership Commission on Health and AIDS (Native American Leadership Commission on Health and AIDS, 1994) made the following recommendations for researchers to guide their work with aboriginal peoples in a culturally appropriate way:

- allow time to develop collaborative relationships with Native people prior to beginning the project;
- hire and include Native people in all phases of the research project;
- allow time to obtain a Tribal Council Resolution in support of the project (3-6 months);
- work with Native people to modify materials and procedures for cultural appropriateness;
- work with Native people to develop culturally appropriate procedures and protocols;
- share information from the project in publications and media that are used by Native community members;
- involve gatekeepers who have access to word-of-mouth communication;
- include members of the target community in developing plans about publication and information dissemination;
- allow time for members of the Native community to review project findings prior to publication to avoid misunderstanding;
- respect cultural norms such as modesty;
- provide a mechanism for empowerment and/or continuation of the project after funding ends;
- emphasize benefits for the family and tribe rather than the individual;
- involve elders in leadership roles;
- involve gatekeepers in the project to enhance credibility and ensure that messages get to the community;
- include community members as co-authors on publications;
- projects should always benefit the community rather than simply surveying the community to collect information.

A failure to understand traditional cultures can lead to problems not just for researchers but also for those whose job it is to safeguard subject safety: Institutional Review Boards (IRBs). Meadows and colleagues (2003) recount preparation for a qualitative study of health needs for middle-age women in a Canadian aboriginal group in Alberta. The researchers had to convince the IRB to allow significant modification in the informed consent process. First, they argued for the use of an oral rather than written informed consent. Many Native cultures are essentially oral cultures that place little value in, and may even be put off by, written forms. Given the history of many North American aboriginal tribes with written documents like treaties, it is small wonder that any written document would be viewed with suspicion and contempt. Second, they argued for a simplified informed consent that included the intent of the project, the amount of time and effort required for participation, and the expected benefit to the tribe. For readers who are unfamiliar with informed consent documents, most are at least three pages long and contain numerous sections explaining the qualifications and affiliation of researches, any potential individual risks and benefits involved, the presence or lack of compensation for participation, the consequences or lack of consequences in case of refusal to give consent, the availability or lack of availability of assistance in case of any problem, the methods for maintaining confidentiality in the storage and reporting of data, who may have access to data aside from the researchers, and several other sections that apply to vulnerable populations (pregnant women, children, those under court or criminal justice control). The researchers argued that inclusion of all the elements usually required would make the oral consent confusing, upsetting, and insulting to the participants. Fortunately, the IRB had considerable experience in research protocols involving aboriginal peoples and eventually agreed with the researchers that insisting on what was usually required would be inappropriate and potentially harmful in this case. The moral of the story is that what is meant to protect subjects in one culture may harm them in another. Additionally, it would probably be a good idea if Institutional Review Boards that seldom reviewed protocols involving aboriginal peoples deferred to Institutional Review Boards with extensive experience and expertise in this area.

Communication

It is important to note that communication style among Native peoples tends to be quite different from the communication style among non-native people. Of course, communication styles vary, but there are several common elements:

- Patience—Concepts of time appear to be different for aboriginal people, but this is only because the Native person takes more time to make decisions and consider possibilities and ways of being. Patience is a way of being, a way of seeing, a way of thinking, and a way of conducting oneself in the world. Silence is common among Native Americans, and is a manifestation of patience, which in turn is a respectful way of communicating. One form of communication that is often inherent in many American Indian cultures is the practice of silence. Silence is often mistaken for shyness. However, for American Indians it often represents a period of reading body language and non-verbal communications. It is also a time in which American Indian clients may evaluate and test the specialists attempting to assist them.
- Listening and observing—Most Native people may appear quiet and not as talkative as non-Natives, but this quietude is a skill that is taught, encouraged, and valued among most aboriginal people. Natives do a lot more listening than they do talking, and this behavior is seen as a sign of respect. Seeing, knowing, experiencing, and understanding involves listening intently and observing keenly the seen and unseen world, and understanding the relationship between these worlds. According to Fixico (2003), Native thinking not only involves listening for sounds, but hearing while understanding the unseen. For example, in Talking Circles and Healing Circles—typical formal methods for commu-

nication and problem solving used by many Native American groups—each person talks in turn while everyone else listens closely without interruption or probing. Each person addresses his/her own experience and may have reference to what another person in the circle has said but never asks for clarification or elaboration. The underlying belief is that it is the responsibility of the listener to understand and that the speaker has said all he/she thinks appropriate, asking for more is rude and presumptuous. Another type of communication to be aware of when working with American Indian clients may be defined as "turn-taking." This process is represented by allowing the client to talk at his/her own pace and respectfully waiting until the completion of the story. Often times, American Indian clients will elaborate concerns in a thoughtful and meaningful story. By allowing the client to complete his/her story without interrupting or probing for information too early, the client can bring forth the meaningful end of a particular incident, thought, or story conclusion. At the end of a given story, the "turn-taking" then transfers to the specialist or counselor. By taking turns talking, this process allows less "butting in" and produces a respectful manner of communication.

- Oral tradition—Story telling is the foundation of aboriginal oral tradition. Patience, listening, and observing are a part of the oral tradition of Native people and are essential skills for understanding the metaphors and relationships inherent in storytelling. Oral tradition typically passes stories down from generation to generation; these stories preserve the culture, transmit the history, tell personal biographies, entertain, educate, and inform. Stories serve different functions. For example: creation stories help explain the beginning of the physical and spiritual universe. Some stories are metaphors for explaining cultural values. American Indian culture is typically visual and oral, and stories are typically used as a means of conveying information or teaching morals and values. In some Native groups, like the Tlingit of Alaska's Southeast coast, oratory is a highly evolved art form. Individuals from this culture can speak eloquently and at length about any subject that concerns them, drawing from a wealth of tradition, history, and myth to illustrate meaning.
- Modesty value—In many Native cultures there are different behaviors around eye contact, and Coyhis (1999) estimates that close to half of the Native cultures do not maintain eye contact. To be modest is to be polite, respectful, and to honor the other person. Modesty is manifested by not staring into the eyes of the other, but looking away. Mainstream education often teaches health care specialists to maintain strong eye contact, stress leaning forward in your chair towards the client, and to some extent maintain strong eye contact. When working with American Indian clients, this practice may decrease the amount of comfort. Recommendations to positively increase the comfort zone may include sitting to the side of the client, maintaining some eye contact but not constantly staring, and to let the client initiate, engage, and control the eye contact process.
- Non-linear thinking—Indians are non-linear thinkers. To think like an Indian means that things, feelings, knowledge, and events are seen in their context to each other, and that this contextual relationship is cyclical. Viewing life

through a non-linear lens lets the person see their relationship to both their past and their future as a continuum that includes both ancestors and legacies. All things are related, and everything is involved. An approach to life that is circular provides context and relationship. Groups become more important than individuals, and individuals are not left in isolation but related to all things around them. Thus, thinking and communication becomes inclusive, and not exclusive. To the typical non-Native, the discourse of Native people may seem circumstantial and illogical. The non-Native is used to moving from supposed cause to perceived effect both in thought and speech, creating a chain of causal events that largely ignores anything that seems secondary. The Native will typically address all the factors—past and present, individual and common, material and immaterial, proximate and distant—that relate to a subject, and it is only after all have been addressed that it becomes apparent how they relate.

- Humor—Humor is often a part of many American Indian cultures. However, a comfortable rapport should be established before attempting to include this during the intervention. American Indian clients may use humor in many ways. It can be a way to increase comfort level with the specialist or counselor. Humor may also serve as part of the story-telling process. Finally, humor may serve as a defense mechanism against pain, trauma, distress, or an embarrassing situation.
- Indian Time—A common phrase used across Indian Country is "Indian Time." "Indian Time" is represented by coming to meeting a little later then expected. In the non-Indian world being a little late is often confused with not being prepared or not being able to budget time. From an American Indian perspective it is often a way of respecting, honoring, and communicating with those you meet along the way. As a specialist or counselor working with American Indian clients, it is important to take into consideration "Indian Time." To many American Indians, communicating with people along their travels is well-warranted, and being a little late is often commonplace.

Assessment

These differences in style of thinking and communication give rise to concerns regarding the use of conventional evaluation/assessment techniques with Native people. It is a serious ethical concern that research design and methods yield true and useful information about the population studied and do so without unnecessary discomfort. If the methods used are sufficiently culturally inappropriate that they give invalid information or are offensive in a way that prompts Native people to answer in such a way as to end the session as quickly as possible, harm has been done.

Exclusive reliance on quantitative techniques may be too reductionistic to adequately portray realities in a manner meaningful to Native people. That is, if the purpose of assessment is expected to be useful to Native people, the purpose must reflect the values, beliefs, and other epistemological assumptions of the Native community. The assessment process itself should respect the wide range of linguistic, tribal, and cultural differences. There is very little in the literature that addresses measurement with aboriginal peoples, and most assessment does not concern itself with the diversity of the population.

Very little assessment technology for Native people focuses on specific tribal groups but instead has a generic category called, for example, American Indian or Native American. Frequently, aboriginal people are treated as if they do not have distinct tribal identity. Trimble (1991) refers to this approach as an 'ethnic gloss' and argues that it fails to capture the significant differences that exist within most racial and ethnic groups. Using ethnic glosses with American Indians, or any other Native people, are especially problematic because of the extreme diversity of the population; nevertheless, ethnic gloss has been the predominant approach used in assessing American Indians. As a result, little refined work related to measurement is available for this population. Elaborating on the population descriptions or sample through administering detailed demographic or ethnic identification measures can minimize ethnic gloss. In addition, assessing aboriginal peoples requires moving beyond a framework that uses an individualistic approach to one that utilizes a sociocultural framework that will focus on the individual in context.

American Indians might be one racial or ethnic group in the mind of non-Native researchers, but culturally they are many. In the face of inadequate assessment, several steps can be taken to improve current instrumentation: 1) Improve existing standardized instruments to make them less culturally inappropriate than they are currently for all cultural groups in which they are used. Careful attention to the translation and back-translation process can be extremely important. 2) Draw upon qualitative/ethnographic research approaches in the development and administration of semi-structured assessment formats that permit flexibility in the way in which questions are framed and rephrased. 3) Serious attention needs to be given to the valid administration of assessments by professionals who are familiar with the culture and the language and who are skilled in conducting assessments.

Despite questions about the validity of existing tests for Native Americans, they endure a considerable amount of testing. But these standardized tests, often normed on the principles of Western culture, conflict with many aspects of Native American culture. For example:

- The content of standardized assessments measures experiences that may not be common to reservation Indians or other more isolated Native groups.
- Native peoples, who value patience in response, may be penalized by timed assessments merely because they are taught to take time when responding.
- Most Native peoples have visually oriented cultures, and tests relying only on written responses penalize them.
- Native peoples approach written tasks differently. Individuals who are accustomed to cooperating with each other and sharing information may not be able to proceed readily when faced with the solitary task of writing a response to a question.

A few studies have examined the use of standardized instruments with Native American youth and adults. McCullough, Walker, and Diessner (1985) used the Wechsler Scales of Intelligence with Native American youth in the Columbia River Basin and also reviewed the literature on intelligence testing with Native American youth. These studies found a large difference between verbal and performance scale tests, with performance scale scores being one to two standard deviations higher, calling into question the validity of the full scale IQ score. Self-report personality inventories, such as the California Psychological Inventory (CPI) or the MMPI, have been used extensively. For example, use of the CPI has been reported in a few studies (Davis, Hoffman, & Nelson, 1990) suggesting a lower profile for Native Americans but these differences have been attributed to acculturation and role expectations.

It can be reasonably argued that all assessment is essentially a culturally negotiated product and implies some degree of social compromise—at a practical level, these types of principles are articulated in the works of theorists like Guba and Lincoln (1989), and Patton (1990). Guba and Lincoln (1981, 1989) recommend using naturalistic inquiry methods in order to maintain the cultural integrity of the assessment process and to respect multiple perspectives. Naturalistic inquiry allows for and encourages all stake-holders in the enterprise to tell their story. They state that the standardized or survey interview does not take account multiple worldviews. Wolf and Tymitz (1977) suggest that naturalistic inquiry is aimed at understanding actualities, cultural realities, and perceptions that exist untainted by the obtrusiveness of formal measurement or preconceived questions. Naturalistic inquiry is a more valuable method for assessing Native peoples because it is geared to the uncovering of stories told by real people, about real events, in real and natural ways. Culturally responsive evaluation can employ semi-structured interviews that can be designed to allow respondents to "tell their own story," in their own words, minimizing the bias imposed by the method. This means that in the actual conduct of data collection respondents would not be discouraged from offering whatever they considered important. Using storytelling as a means of assessment serves the purpose of recognizing that each respondent is, in a very meaningful way, a stakeholder in the process. Storytelling, dialogue, and metaphoric expression enable us to decipher language. In listening to stories we acknowledge the complexities of language and culture. In her essay, The Moral Necessity of Metaphor, Ozick (1986, p.28) writes:

> *"Through metaphor, the past has the capacity to imagine us, and we it. Those who have no pain can imagine those who suffer. Illuminated lives can imagine the borders of stellar fire. We strangers can imagine the familiar hearts of strangers."*

A metaphor is a kind of story that calls us to consider a radically different way of knowing. In her book, The Sacred Hoop: Recovering the Feminine in American Indian Tradition, Paula Gunn Allen (1986, p. 42) contends that allowing people to "give voice" to their life journey, i.e., telling their story, allows a "holistic image to pervade and shape consciousness, thus providing a coherent and empowering matrix for action and relationship." Zemke (1990, p. 65) notes that stories can play a stabilizing role in our culture and believes that "without air our cells die, without a story our selves die." A story provides structure for our perceptions and assessments of reality. In many aboriginal tribal groups, a story is seen as having a life of its own. Such stories carry energy -- a truth, a lesson, an insight, an evaluative reflection -- that can enter our being and connect us to a powerful source of truth making and perceptual affirmation. Many Native healers have viewed English words as being "cages for ideas" (Chambers, 2005, p. 1) and become frustrated with their inability to express authentically the gestalt of their cultural reality and life experience when non-Native researchers probe for explanations that fit into a structuralist worldview.

Data Collection

In many Native societies, individuals play very distinct roles in relation to each other. There are some things that can be discussed only with specific individuals or in the context of specific rituals. There are things that many aboriginal women would not discuss with a man even of their own family and, conversely, things that no aboriginal man would discuss with any women even of his own family. This being the case, how likely would it be that an aboriginal woman would discuss such matters with a male stranger who might be Non-native or not of her tribe? And what emotional and social distress does asking about such matters cause to such a woman? These limits are things that any responsible researcher working with an aboriginal group must educate him/herself about, making appropriate provisions in the data collection protocol. This implies using appropriate Native individuals for data collection whenever possible. Doing so can raise other problems. Most Native peoples are not afflicted with the same Calvinist work ethic as many non-Native researchers. Coming from a gathering and hunting tradition, there may be times when other activities will take precedence over collecting data. Further, if the data collection methods are culturally inappropriate, Native data collectors may have difficulty sticking to a script that makes little sense to them and which they may find ignorant and even offensive.

There is great sensitivity to the data itself. The rights and welfare of human participants are protected in accordance with 45 CFR Part 46 (US Government, Code of Federal Regulations, http://www.hhs.gov/ohrp/) that applies, with few exceptions, to all research involving human subjects conducted, supported or otherwise subject to regulation by any Federal Department or Agency. IRB's must approve research procedures that protect the privacy and confidentiality of persons who participate in research, and typically this involves: (1) A unique ID number used instead of names, and names should not be written on answer forms; (2) Keys to ID numbers are kept separate from data in locked storage areas; (3) Only research staff administer the questionnaires so that an individual's answers cannot be seen by any other staff member or anyone else; (4) Data is typically stored without any personal identification, and should be securely kept in project research offices under the supervision of the principal investigator; (5) Only relevant trained project staff may examine or work with any data; and (6) Variable labels and reports should not use pejorative terms about sample characteristics and group differences. When American Indian tribal members are not principal investigators nor members of the research staff, these provisions for the data, accordingly, cannot be made available to the tribe. These policies conflict with the past experiences of many Native Americans as it is a reminder of past treatment: culture is taken away. The researcher who is in the community needs to be in constant partnership with the Native community to insure that the data that is collected, and necessarily protected, is also owned by the community so that the researcher does not continue the long history of taking away and not giving back. Giving back the data to the community does not necessarily mean handing over the raw data, which would be against research ethical policy, but giving back to the community could be something as simple as having regular meetings to show how data collection is proceeding and what is happening with the project, preparing reports that show what some of the findings are, making the data available to young Native investigators for use in their own graduate studies, or including indigenous staff on the research team. There are many ways that the policy is workable that does not offend the Native culture. A culturally responsive researcher would find these ways.

Historical Trauma

There is a final point to consider whose ethical implications are so large as to be daunting (for an extended and thoughtful treatment see Duran & Duran, 1995). Aboriginal peoples, worldwide, have been subject to prejudice, persecution, dislocation, and genocide. Few Native groups have escaped massive trauma both historically and presently. The example of Native Americans is both graphic and instructive.

From 1492 to approximately 1890, Native Americans endured a four hundred year military struggle that ended in Wounded Knee, South Dakota on December 29, 1890. This is considered as the last battle of the Indian Wars, and the Indians lost. When the Europeans first arrived in North America, there were many culturally, politically, and geographically dispersed groups of indigenous people, rather than just one. Estimates of the indigenous population at the beginning of the European invasion of North America vary between 7 and 18 million (Stiffarm, 1992). Thornton (1987) estimates that by 1800 only about 600,000 American Indians remained. By 1900, the U.S. Census counted only 237,196 American Indians (U.S. Bureau of the Census, 1937). During the nineteenth century, approximately two thirds of the Indian population died. The near extinction of North America's indigenous population is unparalleled; depending on the original population estimate used, during the first 400 years of European occupation, the American Indian population was reduced by between 96.6 percent and 98.7 percent. In 1890 the Federal government declared that the "Indian Wars" were officially over due to the reduction in the American Indian census (Stiffarm, 1992). This constitutes the largest genocide ever committed.

In the latter part of the 19th century, after most Indian people were forcibly removed from their traditional lands and placed on reservations, there were concentrated attempts to shift reservation land from communal or tribal ownership to individual ownership. These efforts culminated in the General Allotment Act of 1887 (Dawes Act). There are many accounts of the devastation caused by this law (Hirschfelder & Montano, 1993; Waddell and Watson, 1971) and by 1933 more than two thirds of the Indian land base had passed into non-Indian hands (Sorkin, 1978).

During the same time period as the enactment of the General Allotment Act, another initiative established off-reservation boarding schools. These schools operated from the late 1800s until the middle of the twentieth century with the explicit purpose of removing Indians from reservations and teaching them the skills needed to live among Whites (Meriam, 1977). Indian children were often forcibly removed from their families and placed in Bureau of Indian Affairs (BIA) boarding schools hundreds of miles from their home reservations. These children were forced to learn White ways through such means as cutting their hair short, wearing European style clothing, and being punished for speaking their tribal language.

Indian Reformers, predominantly Quakers and missionaries, began to explore ways to 'civilize' the Indians. Based on the notion that Indians should be assimilated into the White culture, the idea of Indian boarding schools was patterned after the Hampton school, a government boarding school for African-American children founded in 1868 by Samuel Chapman Armstrong. By mid 1879, the Secretary of the Interior and Secretary of the War Department granted permission to use a deserted military base, Carlisle Barracks in central Pennsylvania, as the site of the first Indian boarding school. The first students included 82 boys and girls from the Dakota Territory who traveled together by train, without parents, to Carlisle, PA to attend the Carlisle Industrial Indian School. Luther Standing Bear, one of the first students to travel to Carlisle, described the journey in his book, "My People, the Sioux" (Bear, 1928). He depicted his journey as traveling on a moving house; he described how the children stopped at various train stations and whole towns would come to stare at them. Apparently, the journey had been publicized in the newspapers. When they finally arrived at the school, the transformed military post, there was no food, no bedding, no clothing and they had to sleep on the floor. The Bureau of Indian Affairs was in charge and, despite marketing the journey, it fell short (Carlisle Industrial Indian School, 2005, http://home.epix.net/~landis/histry.html).

One of the first things that occurred to the children arriving at Carlisle was an official name change. Indian children were not allowed to keep their Indian names. Once the children's name had changed, school officials enforced it and they were not allowed to use their Indian names or risked punishment. As related by Ota K'te, Plenty Kill, who later became known as Luther Standing Bear:

> *"One day when we came to school there was a lot of writing on the blackboards. We did not know what it meant.... None of the names were read or explained to us, so of course we did not know the sound or meaning of any of them. The teacher had a long pointed stick in her hand, and the interpreter told the boy in the front seat to come up. The teacher handed the stick to him, and the interpreter told him to pick out any name he wanted.... When the long stick was handed to him, he turned to us as much to say, 'Shall I—or will you help me—to take one of these names?' He did not know what to do for a time.... Finally, he pointed out one of the names written on the blackboard. Then the teacher took a piece of white tape and wrote the name on it. Then she cut off a length of the tape and sewed it on the back of the boy's shirt. Then that name was erased from the board.... Soon we all had names of white men sewed on our backs." (Standing Bear, 1928, in Allen, 1994, pp. 116-117)*

Indian children were forbidden to speak their native language and perform any native rituals. They were Christianized and taught to ridicule and despise anything that had to do with Native ways or thought. In short, they were the subjects of a kind of cultural genocide by forcible re-education. Any infraction of any rule was met with severe corporal punishment. As has been later learned, sexual abuse of both boys and girls was a fairly common practice.

One result of this destruction of Indian cultural traditions was that many of these children ended up in urban areas rather than returning to their reservations. The effects of boarding schools are still with us and can be seen in contemporary American Indian society. For example, Walker (1981) found that about thirty percent of a sample of outpatients from the Seattle Indian Health Board Clinic had attended boarding schools and that this attendance was associated with alcohol problems. Maria Brave Heart Yellow Horse, a prominent American Indian researcher, argues that the effects of cultural trauma, such as depression and substance abuse, have been inherited by most American Indians today (Brave Heart, 2003). As the use of boarding schools dropped off in the middle of the twentieth century, the increased placement of Indian children in non-Indian foster and adoptive homes represented a less institutionalized version of accomplishing assimilation. For example, a 1969 survey conducted by the Association on Native American Affairs found that approximately 25-35 percent of all Indian children were separated from their families (Guerrero, 1979). During the 1960s and 1970s Minnesota Indian children were placed out of home at a per capita rate five times greater than non-Indian children; in Montana the ratio of Indian foster care placement was 13 times greater; in South Dakota 40 percent of all adoptions were of Indian children and the rate of foster care placement was 16 times greater than for non-Indian children (Byler, 1977). Reaction to the placement of Indian children in non-Indian homes culminated in the Federal Indian Child Welfare Act of 1978 (Wares et al., 1994) that mandated a priority order for placement of Indian children to be adopted first, by their family; secondly, by the tribe; third, by other Native Americans; and, finally non-Indians. Many urban Native Americans were separated from their tribes and families through adoption by non-Indian families (Spicer, 1995).

In 1900, only about 0.5 percent of all Indian people were urban. By 1940, the numbers were still fairly small, at approximately 7 percent. It was after World War II that a dramatic shift occurred. In the 1950s the Federal Government of the United States made its final efforts at dissolution of Native American culture. The government offered large inducements of housing, jobs, and other supports if Native Americans would move off reservations to large urban areas – predominantly San Francisco, Los Angeles, and New York. The reality of this relocation was that Native families were dumped in urban areas with no support and left to survive on their own as best they could. Many did not survive. Those who did survive display characteristics similar to forced refugees (Duran & Duran, 1995). In 1990, 56 percent of the American Indian population was living in urban communities (Davis, 1994; Hirschfelder & Montano, 1993; Snipp, 1996), and by 2000, over 60 percent lived in urban areas (Forquera, 2001). Table 4 shows this urban population growth across time.

Table 1.14.1: Growth in the Urban American Indian Population

Year	Percent Urban
1900	.5
1940	7.0
1950	13.4
1960	27.9
1970	44.5
1980	52.0
1990	56.0
2000	64.0

The effects of such long trauma are profound and may underlie many of the problems experienced in Native communities. It is like a kind of Post Traumatic Stress Disorder that affects both individuals and groups, arising out of a shared historical experience. Questions arise about whether a Native person could or would express his/her grief, sadness, and rage with anyone let alone a non-Native. Further, it implies that both non-Native and Native researches have some obligation to direct their efforts toward the fuller understanding and ultimate healing of so great a harm. Finally, it implies that the institutions responsible for so great a harm make active restitution in every way possible.

Summary

This chapter provides very general guidelines to some of the ethical issues involved with conducting research with indigenous communities. It is not intended to be comprehensive; indeed, this is not possible given the great diversity and multiculturalism embedded within indigenous cultures. Rather, we hope to increase sensitivity to the important role that cultural factors play in designing research, applying methodologies, and shaping the content of our own responses. The cultural nuances of communication are especially important in research, and by providing some description of these, perhaps the reader might be led to explore the topic further. For this we highly recommend the book by Jamake Highwater (2003) "The Primal Mind: Vision and Reality in Indian America). As he opens his book he states, "The greatest distance between people is not space but culture" (Highwater, 2003, p. 3). Designing our research to bridge this distance is our next ethical task.

Theodore M. Godlaski, M.Div.., (USA), is Assistant Clinical Professor of Psychiatry School of Medicine, former member of the staff of the Center on Drug and Alcohol Research at the University of Kentucky and currently a member of the faculty of the School of Social Work. Prior to coming to the University, he developed and directed treatment programs in both the public and private sector. He also consulted both nationally and internationally on program design and operation. He is

currently involved in three research projects. Two are directed toward examining the outcome of substance user treatment and one focuses on the affect, for Native Alaskans, of inclusion of traditional Tlingit healing practices in an inpatient treatment program. He is a current member and former Chairperson of the National Ethics Committee for NAADAC. He has a long standing interest in clinical research with rural populations and has been a MESIDU faculty member both in Israel, Italy and in Spain. He is a member of the Editorial Board of Substance Use and Misuse.

Jeannette L. Johnson, Ph.D., Dr. Johnson is a cross-cultural psychologist who has extensive experience in community-based prevention research, with an emphasis on understanding the role of risk and protective factors in high risk youth and examining models of vulnerability. She is currently a Senior Research Analyst at Friends Research Institute in Baltimore, MD. In the past she was a Distinguished Professor at SUNY-Buffalo and the Director of the Research Center on Children and Youth. Dr. Johnson is of Native American heritage (Huron) and has extensive experience with Native American communities. She has conducted community-based substance use and HIV/AIDS prevention research as well as treatment research with chronic substance users. She is a contributing editor for several journals - Substance Use and Misuse; the author and co-author of many professional publications. and a faculty member of the Middle Eastern Summer Institute on Drug Use (MESIDU) in Israel, Italy and Spain.

Rodney Haring, LMSW, Ph.D. Candidate, is an enrolled member of the Seneca Nation of Indians and resides on the Cattaraugus Reservation in New York State. He is a licensed master level social worker and a doctoral candidate at the State University of New York at Buffalo, School of Social Work. His dissertation work and interests revolve around recreational tobacco use, narrative therapy, online social work techniques, and research methods with Indigenous Peoples.

References

Allen, P. G. (1986). *The sacred hoop: Recovering the feminine in American Indian traditions* Boston: Beacon Press.

Allen, P. G. (1994). *Voice of the Turtle: American Indian Literature, 1900-1970.* New York: Ballantine Books.

American Academy of Pediatrics (2002). Significant health disparities threaten Native American children and youth. Retrieved on July 14, 2005, from http://www.aap.org/advocacy/washing/american_indian.htm.

Bear, Standing L. (1928). *My People, The Sioux.* (E.A. Brininstool, Ed.) Cambridge: The Riverside Press.

Brave Heart, M. Y. H. (2003). The Historical Trauma Response Among Natives and Its Relationship with Substance Abuse: A Lakota Illustration. *Journal of Psychoactive Drugs, 35*(1), 7-13.

Brieland, D. (1977). Historical overview and the working definition of social work practice. A reprint from 1958. *Social Work, 3*(2), 12-28.

Byler, W. (1977). The destruction of American Indian families. In Unger, S. (Ed.), *The Destruction of American Indian Families*, (pp. 1-11). New York, NY: Association on American Indian Affairs.

Chambers, W. (2005). Anti-pluralism and Sleeptalking: The dominant epistemology in practice Indigenous Perspectives 1: Knowledge. Retrieved from the Internet on July 13, 2005 from www.iaiancad.org/nep/course/indig1/knowledge/chapters/sleeptalking.htm

Coyhis, D. (1999). *Understanding Native American Culture*. Colorado Springs, CO: Coyhis Publishing.

Davis, M. B. (1994). *Native America in the Twentieth Century*. New York, NY: Garland Publishing, Inc.

Davis, G. L., Hoffman, R. G., & Nelson, K. S. (1990). Differences between Native Americans and Whites on the California Psychological Inventory. *Psychological Assessment: A Journal of Consulting and Clinical Psychology, 2*(3), 338-342.

Driver, H.E. (1969). *Indians of North America*. Chicago, IL: University of Chicago Press.

Duran E. & Duran B. (1995). *Native American postcolonial psychology*. Albany, NY: State University of New York.

Fleming, C.M. (1992). American Indians and Alaska Natives: Changing societies past and present. In M.A. Orlandi, R. Weston, & L.G. Epstein (Eds.), *Cultural Competence for Evaluators: A Guide for Alcohol and Other Drug Abuse Prevention Practitioners Working with Ethnic/Racial Communities* (pp. 147-171). Rockville, MD: Office for Substance Abuse Prevention.

Fixico, D. L. (2003). *The American Indian Mind in a Linear World: American Indian Studies & Traditional Knowledge*. New York, NY: Routledge.

Forquera, R. (2001). *Urban Indian Health*. Seattle, WA: Henry J. Kaiser Family Foundation.

Grant J, & Brown, T. (2003) American Indian and Alaskan Native Resource Manual, NAMI Retrieved on July 14, 2005 from, www.nami.org/Content/ContentGroups/Multicultural_Support1/CDResource

Guba, E. G., & Lincoln, Y. S. (1989). *Fourth generation evaluation*. Newbury Park, CA: Sage.

Guba, E. G., & Lincoln, Y. S. (1981). *Effective evaluation: Improving the usefulness of evaluation results through responsive and naturalistic approaches*. San Francisco: Jossey-Bass.

Guerrero, M. (1979). Indian Child Welfare Act of 1978: A response to the threat to Indian culture caused by foster and adoptive placements of Indian children. *American Indian Law Review, 7*, 51-77.

Henderson, D. J., Sampselle, C.M., Mayes, I., & Oakley, D. (1992). Toward culturally sensitive research in a multicultural society. *Health Care for Women International 13*(4), 339-350.

Highwater, J. (1981). *The Primal Mind: Vision and Reality in Indian America*. Bridgewater, NJ: Replica Books.

Hirschfelder, A. & Montano, M. (1993). *The Native American Almanac*. NJ: Prentice Hall.

Kowalsky, L.O.; Verhoef, M.J.; Thurston, W.E.; & Rutherford, G.E. (1996). Guidelines for entry into an aboriginal community. *The Canadian Journal of Native Studies, 16*(2), 267-282.

Manson, S.M., Shore, J., Barron, A., Ackerson, L., & Neligh, G. (1992). Alcohol abuse and dependence among American Indians. In Helzer, J. and Canino, G. (Eds.), *Alcoholism in North American, Europe, and Asia*. New York: Oxford University Press.

Marsella, A. (1985). Culture, self, and mental disorder. In Marsella, A., DeVos, G. & Hsu, F. (Eds.) *Culture and Self: Asian and American Perspectives*, (pp. 209-228). New York: Travistock Publications.

Meadows, L. M., Lagendyk, L. E., Thurston, W. E., & Eisener, A. C. (2003). Balancing culture, ethics and methods in qualitative health research with aboriginal peoples. *International Journal of Qualitative Methods, 2*(4). Article 1. Retrieved on July 11, 2005 from, http://www.ualberta.ca/~iiqm/backissues/2_4/pdf/meadows.pdf

McCullough, C.S., Walker, J.L., Diessner, R. (1985). The use of Wechsler Scales in the assessment of Native Americans of the Columbia River Basin. *Psychology in the Schools, 23*, 23-31.

Meriam, L. (1977). The effects of boarding schools on Indian family life. In Unger, S. (Ed.), *The Destruction of American Indian Families* (pp. 14-17). New York, NY: Association on American Indian Affairs.

Nabokov, P. (1991). *Native American Testimony: A Chronicle of Indian-White Relations from Prophecy to the Present, 1492-1992*. New York, NY: Viking.

Native American Leadership Commission on Health and AIDS. (1994). *A Native American leadership response to HIV and AIDS*. New York: American Indian Community House.

Neihardt, J. G. (1932). *Black Elk Speaks Being the Life Story of a Holy Man of the Ogalala Sioux*. Lincoln, NE: University of Nebraska Press.

Ozick, C. (May, 1986). The moral necessity of metaphor. *Harper's Magazine*, 64-65.

Parfait, B. (1994). Value orientations of expatriate nurses in the developing countries. *International Journal of Nursing Studies, 31*(3), 279-288.

Patton, M. (1990). *Qualitative evaluation and research methods: 2nd edition*. Newbury Park, CA: Sage.

Ridley, C.R., Mendoza, D.W., Kanitz, B.E., Angermeier, L., & Zenk, R. (1994). Cultural sensitivity in multicultural counseling: A perceptual schema model. *Journal of Counseling Psychology, 41*(2), 125-136.

Rogler, L.H. (1989). The meaning of culturally sensitive research in mental health. *American Journal of Psychiatry, 146*(3), 296-303.

Snipp, C.M. (1996). The size and distribution of the American Indian population: Fertility, mortality, migration, and residence. In Sandefur, G.D., Rindfuss, R.R & Cohen, B. (Eds.), *Changing Numbers, Changing Needs: American Indian Demography ad Public Health* (pp. 17-52). Washington, D.C.: National Academic Press.

Sorkin, A. (1978). *The Urban American Indian*. Lexington, Massachusetts: DC Health and Company.

Spicer, E.H. (Ed.). (1961). *Perspectives in American Indian Culture Change*. Chicago: University of Chicago Press.

Stiffarm, L. (1992). The demography of Native North American: A question of American Indian survival. In Jaimes, M.A. (Ed.), *The State of Native America: Genocide, Colonization, and Resistance* (pp. 23-54). Boston, MA: South End Press.

Thornton, R. (1987). *American Indian holocaust and survival: A population history since 1492*. Norman, OK: University of Oklahoma Press.

Trimble, J. E. (1991). Ethnic specification, validation prospects, and the future of drug use research. *The International Journal of the Addictions, 25*(2A), 149 170.

United States Bureau of the Census (1937). *Fifteenth Census of the United States 1930: The Indian Population of the United States and Alaska*. Washington, D.C.: U.S. Government Printing Office.

U.S. Civil Rights Commission (September, 2004). Broken promises: Evaluating the Native American health care system. Retrieved on July 14, 2005 from, http://www.usccr.gov/pubs/nahealth/nabroken.pdf.

Van Meteren, E. (1609). *Narratives of New Netherland 1609-1664*. (J.F. Jameson, Ed.). New York, NY: Charles Scribners Sons.

Waddell, J.O., & Watson, O.M. (1971). *The American Indian Urban Society*. Boston: Little, Brown and Company.

Walker, R.D. (1981). Treatment strategies in urban Indian alcoholism program. *Journal of Studies on Alcohol, Supplement 9*, 171-184.

Wares, D., Wedel, K., Rosenthal, J., & Dobrec, A. (1994). Indian child welfare: A multicultural challenge. *Journal of Multicultural Social Work, 3*(3), 1-15.

Weaver, H.N. (1997). The challenges of research in Native American communities: Incorporating principles of cultural competence. *Journal of Social Service Research, 23*(2), 1-15.

Wolf, R. & Tymitz, B. (1976-1977). Ethnography and reading: Matching inquiry mode to process. *Reading Research Quarterly, 12*, 5-11.

Zemke, R. (1990). Storytelling: Back to a basic. *Training, 27*(3), 44-48.

Glossary

Native American or **American Indian** and **Alaskan Native:** refer to people having origins in any of the original peoples of North and South America (including Central America), and who maintain tribal affiliation or community attachment. It includes people who indicated their race or races by marking this category or writing in their principal or enrolled tribe, such as Rosebud Sioux, Chippewa, or Navajo.

Indigenous: The word indigenous is derived from the latin word indigena, meaning nativ, indigenous, aboriginal, and has several, related meanings that generally refer to the native people of a place.

BIA: Congress established the Bureau of Indian Affairs (BIA) within the United States War Dept. in 1874 but later transferred BIA to the Dept. of the Interior due to dissatisfaction over Army administration of Native American affairs. The BIA had jurisdiction over trade with Native Americans, their removal to the West, their protection from exploitation, and their concentration on reservations. The Bureau of Indian Affairs evolved into a land-administering agency, a process speeded up by the Dawes Act of 1887, the Burke Act of 1906, and the Wheeler-Howard Act of 1934, now acting as trustee over Native American lands and funds. The bureau also promotes agricultural and economic development, provides a health program, social services, Native American schools, and reclamation projects for Alaska Natives and Native Americans in the United States.

Reservation: An Indian reservation is land reserved for a tribe because the tribe relinquished its other land areas to the U.S. through treaties. Reservations vary in size, ranging from a few acres for the smallest to the Navajo reservation, which spreads across three States and is about the same size as the State of West Virginia. The Navajo Reservation, at over 16 million acres, covers parts of Arizona, New Mexico, and Utah. Many of the smaller reservations are less than 1,000 acres with the smallest less than 100 acres. On each reservation, the local governing authority is the tribal government. Although only 36 percent of the Indian population in 2000 resided on reservations, for many Indians, including urban Indians, reservations represent the foundation of Indian identity and a symbol of what it means to be Indian. The 279 Federal and State reservations, located primarily in the western part of the continental United States, are the last remaining lands belonging to a group that once inhabited all of North America. Only 18 reservations had populations in excess of 5,000 in 2000. Most American Indians do not live on reservations or trust lands, but instead live in urban areas (http://factfinder.census.gov/home/aian/aianaff2000.html).

Tribal Affiliation: The term 'tribe' is commonly used to delineate distinct groups of aboriginal people who share social, cultural, and political ties. Among American Indians, the term tribe can be used interchangeably with confederacy, nation, band, community, village, and corporation. Although most Americans are familiar with a few tribal groups, like the Navajo, Sioux, or Lakota, Cherokee, Chippewa, Apache, and Hopi, few are aware of the many others. Tribal membership is determined by the enrollment criteria of the tribe from which Indian blood may be derived, and this varies with each tribe. Generally, if linkage to an identified tribal member is far removed, one would not qualify for membership. A person must belong to or be enrolled in a federally recognized tribe in order to be recognized as an Indian. Individuals enrolled in federally recognized tribes are issued a Certificate of Degree of Indian Blood (CDIB) from the Bureau of Indian Affairs. This is commonly referred to as blood quantum, and Indians with CDIB are sometimes referred to as card-carrying Indians. For the most part, tribal membership is limited to individuals who have at least one-fourth degree of Indian Blood, but there is some variation across tribes. For example, 21 tribes require at least one-half blood quantum, while some require only one-eighth, one-sixteenth, or one-thirty-second. It is not necessary to be of 100 percent American Indian racial heritage to be recognized as Indian by the Federal Government. In 1910 only 56.5 percent of American Indians were 'full bloods', and by 1930 the percentage had dropped to 46.3. This trend has continued for the past 70 years and is due in large part to high rates of marriage and childbearing between Indians and non-Indians. It has been projected that within the next century the proportion of the American Indian population with less than one-fourth blood quantum will increase to about 60 percent. American Indians, Alaska Natives, and Native Hawaiians are the only groups in the United States that are required to prove their degree of ancestry through documentation of blood quantum.

Indian Removal Act: Congress passes the Indian Removal Act in 1830, legalizing the removal of all Indians east of the Mississippi River to west of the Mississippi

River. Approximately 100,000 Indians are resettled in the area that is now Oklahoma. The process of removal is often brutal, with whole tribes being forced to walk several hundred miles. Walking along the trail until about 1839, more than 15,000 men, women and children die. The route they traversed and the journey itself became known as "The Trail of Tears" or, as a direct translation from Cherokee, "The Trail Where They Cried" ("Nunna daul Tsuny").

Little Big Horn: Between 1875 and 1886 in disputes over White settlement and gold mining on the Sioux reservation in the Black Hills of south Dakota, Colonel Custer is sent to apprehend the Sioux leader, Sitting Bull. In 1876, Custer and his troops are defeated in the Battle of Little Big Horn, in Montana. The army retaliates with great strength and, within one year, has forced most of the Indians onto reservations or into exile in Canada with Sitting Bull. Crazy Horse is killed in captivity, and Indian Police later kill Sitting Bull (in 1890) after he returns to the Standing Rock reservation. The graves of those killed in the battle are located around a granite monument marking the spot of Custer's "last stand."

Sitting Bull: (1831–1890) was a great Native American chief and the Sioux leader in the battle of the Little Bighorn. He rose to prominence in the Sioux warfare against the whites and the resistance of the Native Americans under his command to forced settlement on a reservation led to a punitive expedition. Sitting Bull and some of his followers escaped to Canada, but returned (1881) on a promise of a pardon and were settled on a reservation. In 1885 he appeared in Buffalo Bill's Wild West Show, but his championship of the Native American cause was not at an end. He was killed by Native American police on a charge of resisting arrest. He was buried in North Dakota, but in 1954 his remains were removed to South Dakota.

Wounded Knee: In 1890 nearly 300 Indians are massacred at Wounded Knee, a creek rising in SW South Dakota and flowing into the White River on the Pine Ridge reservation. This is the site of the last major battle of the Indian wars. After the death of Sitting Bull, a band of Sioux, led by Big Foot, fled into the badlands, where they were captured by the 7th Cavalry on Dec. 28, 1890, and brought to the creek. On Dec. 29, the Sioux were ordered disarmed; but when a medicine man threw dust into the air, a warrior pulled a gun and wounded an officer. The U.S. troops opened fire, and within minutes almost 200 men, women, and children were shot. After this point in time, essentially all Indians are placed on reservations or assimilated into the White world.

Part 2

Treatment Issues

2-1 On the Competence of Substance Users to Consent to Treatment Programs

*Steve Clarke, Ph.D. and Neil Levy, Ph.D.**

No man is good enough to govern another man without that other's consent.
— Abraham Lincoln, Speech, 1854

Abstract

Many thinkers hold that regular drug users are incompetent to consent to medical treatment. In this article, we set out minimum criteria for agents to count as competent to give informed consent, and argue that regular drug users—even those who are considered addicted to a drug—typically meet these conditions. Though addiction does impair autonomy, it does not impair it to a degree incompatible with the provision of informed consent. Studies of the behaviors of addicts show that they generally retain sufficient control over their behaviors and their decision making to qualify as competent to consent.

Key Words: autonomy, beneficence, consent, craving, dual processor, informed consent, paternalism, withdrawal

Consent

In this chapter we consider whether or not, and in what circumstances, substance users can be considered competent to consent to participate in substance user treatment programs. Let us begin by focussing on the nature of consent and asking ourselves what it is to provide consent. In asking ourselves what it is to provide consent we are reflecting on one of the most central organising concepts in contemporary Western liberal societies. In the words of one of the editors of this volume:

> *We would not be far wide of the mark if we suggested that the prevailing social ideology is structured round the presumption that interpersonal and political relationships ought to be, and for the most part are, based on the mutual consent of the parties involved. (Kleinig 1982, p. 91)*

It might be thought that consenting to x simply involves making it known, explicitly or implicitly, that you are willing to allow x to take place. If so then consent could be analysed using the tools of speech-act theory alone.[1] However, the utterance of the words "I consent" is not generally considered to be sufficient for the provision of genuine or "effective" consent. Consent is not usually considered to have been effectively provided unless additional conditions have been met. The most commonly mentioned additional condition for consent to be effectively provided, over and above the utterance or implication of the phrase "I consent," is the informedness condition. An attempt to provide consent will typically be judged to be ineffective unless it is grounded on a proper basis of relevant information; hence the phrase "informed consent," which is ubiquitous in contemporary medical ethics.[2]

The view that informedness is a necessary component of consent in medicine is a relatively recent development in the governance of relations between patients and medical professionals. Until the last quarter of the Twentieth Century, medicine was dominated by a culture of paternalism. Although patients were asked to provide consent to an operation or a course of medical treatment, they were typically expected to do so without the provision of what would now be considered highly relevant information. They were not expected to decide whether or not a suggested operation or course of medical treatment was the appropriate one to take, but simply expected to indicate that they were willing to let their fate be decided by a particular doctor who was a participant in a highly trusted profession.[3]

The hitherto dominant culture of medical paternalism was undermined by a series of scandals in medicine, including the collusion of German doctors in experiments that involved the use of non-consenting subjects in concentration camps in the Nazi era (Lifton, 2000) and the notorious Tuskegee experiments in Alabama, conducted between 1932 and 1970 (Department of Health, Education, and Welfare, 1973). It was further undermined by the rise to prominence of dissenters to paternalism within medicine, such as Jay Katz (1984). The dominant ideology of contemporary medicine is one that emphasizes the importance of the value of patient autonomy. Nowadays, it is expected that patients will be provided with sufficient relevant information to enable them to autonomously decide whether or not to undergo an operation, or undertake a course of medical treatment. It is also expected that they will be assisted in interpreting unfamiliar information and using it to make an enlightened decision regarding their medical care (Appelbaum et al., 1987, pp. 156-173). Mutatis mutandis for research subjects and medical experiments.

The importance of obtaining informed consent is enshrined in the codes of practice of most professional organizations in the field of medical treatment in America and other Western liberal democracies. This includes substance user counselors.[4] Counselors who are members of the American Counseling Association (ACA) are required to adhere to a code of ethics, which makes the following stipulations (A.3) regarding informed consent:

> *When counseling is initiated, and throughout the counseling process, as necessary, counselors inform clients of the purposes, goals, techniques, procedures, limitations, potential risks, and benefits of services to be performed, and other pertinent information. Counselors take steps to ensure that clients understand the implications of diagnosis, the intended use of tests and reports, fees, and billing arrangements. Clients have the right to expect confidentiality and to be provided with an explanation of its limitations, including supervision and/or treatment team professionals; to obtain clear information about their case records, to participate in the ongoing counseling plans; and to refuse any recommended services and be advised of the consequences of such refusal.*[5]

NAADAC, the American association for addiction professions, also has an ethics code that is binding on all counsellors who are certified by NAADAC. It includes the following stipulations:

> *7d: The NAADAC member shall not use or encourage a client's participation in any demonstration, research or non-treatment activities when such participation would have potential harmful consequences for the client or when the client is not fully informed.*
>
> *9: It is the responsibility of the NAADAC member to safeguard the integrity of the counseling relationship and to ensure that the client has reasonable access to effective treatment. The NAADAC member shall provide the client and/or guardian with accurate and complete information regarding the extent of the potential professional relationship.*[6]

Many courts have considered that effective informed consent is provided when there is an adequate disclosure of relevant information and when the consent obtained is based on this disclosure. However, philosophers and bio-ethicists have tended toward more comprehensive definitions. According to Beauchamp and Childress, informed consent can usefully be understood as comprising five "elements." These are: (1) competence, (2) disclosure, (3) understanding, (4) voluntariness, and (5) [bare] consent (2001, p. 79; also Faden and Beauchamp, 1986, pp. 274-275). So, informed consent to an operation or a course of medical treatment is not provided unless prospective patients are competent to provide consent, receive a thorough disclosure of relevant information, understand that disclosure sufficiently well, are able to voluntarily consent to that operation or course of medical treatment, and communicate that they do consent to it.

Much more could be said about any and all of these elements of informed consent. For example, there is a current debate about exactly what categories of information should be disclosed for the purposes of informed consent. On some views, only information about reasonably foreseeable risks and alternative forms of treatment need be disclosed (Schuck, 1994). Others require in addition a disclosure of the nature of the procedure, benefits of treatment, and a prognosis if treatment is declined (Appelbaum et al., 1987, pp. 49-57). And it has recently been argued that comparative information about available surgeons' performance ability should be disclosed to patients as part of the informed consent process (Clarke and Oakley, 2004). There are further questions that can be raised about what understanding amounts to and what constitutes voluntariness. It is not clear how comprehensive a grasp of relevant information is required for information to count as having been understood. And it is not clear what sorts of influences count as undermining of voluntariness.[7] Here we concentrate on the issue of competence to consent, which is particularly difficult to deal with in the context of substance user treatment. There are apparently plausible arguments to the conclusion that many substance users are not competent to consent to treatment programs. For example, Charland (2002) has recently argued that heroin addicts are not competent to consent to treatment. We argue that this conclusion is too bald. Before examining this argument, however, we attend to an analysis of the concept "competence."

Competence

Philosophical discussions of competence focus on two main issues, the nature of competence itself and standards or tests of competence. To be competent is to have the capacity or ability to perform a particular task to a certain degree of proficiency. The degree to which one must be proficient at performing a task, in order to be appropriately judged to be competent, is a degree that is relative to a particular task. I may be a competent tennis player and an incompetent golfer at the same time. Competence is a threshold concept. I am judged to be either competent or incompetent at performing a task according to whether or not my abilities at that task reach a particular level of proficiency. Nevertheless, it can be appropriate to speak of degrees of competence. I can be barely competent or highly competent, incompetent despite having some proficiency, or highly incompetent. Such comparative judgements are made relative to a threshold between competence and incompetence for a given task. Now the world does not divide neatly into classes of competent and incompetent performances of particular tasks. More typically, there is a continuum of qualities of performance to be discerned and the distinction that we draw when we divide this continuum into the classes "competent" and "incompetent" is in large part a value judgment. We might choose to set the threshold at a variety of different levels depending on the outcomes that we wish to promote.[8]

Levels of competence are not fixed, but can vary over the course of time and in light of the influence of a variety of factors. The authors of this paper were not competent to ride bicycles when they were two year olds, but they are now. However, they are still not competent to ride bicycles when they are drunk or severely sleep deprived. Competence to consent to medical treatment centrally involves having the ability to make decisions about one's health related interests. Again, this is not an ability with a level that is set in stone. Two-year-olds are not competent to consent to arthroscopic knee surgery, but most adults are. But adults are still not competent to provide consent to arthroscopic knee surgery when they are severely sleep deprived. The ability to make decisions is not one indivisible kind of activity. We may be competent to decide for whom to vote but not competent to decide to run for political office. Similarly, we may be competent to decide to consent to routine arthroscopic knee surgery but not competent to decide to consent to complicated brain surgery.

Having the ability to make a competent decision about one's own health care involves a number of different abilities. First, one must be capable of acquiring, comprehending and retaining information. Second, one must be capable of processing that information so as to formulate a decision. Third, one must be able to express such a decision. Fourth, one must be able to act autonomously.[9] Autonomy in the context of decision making refers to the ability to govern one's self, to direct the broad course of one's own future. It is sometimes confused with the ability to make decisions free from the influence of others. It is doubtful that any individual could have such an ability, but in any case this is not the sense of autonomy that is in play here. To claim that someone is capable of deciding autonomously is to claim that they are capable of accumulating and processing relevant information, including information gained from others and making a decision of their own on the basis of that information.

Having the ability to make a competent decision involves exercising all of the above capacities, so fair tests of competence will involve consideration of the ability of people to exercise all of these capacities. If someone cannot understand relevant information, or cannot make a decision on the basis of such information, or cannot express a decision or cannot act on the basis of their own volition, then that person cannot be competent to make significant decisions about health care, or about other important matters. Insisting that we detect evidence of all of the above capacities in people before we decide that they are competent to make decisions about their own health care can make it sound like we are setting the threshold of competence in patient decision making quite high. However, it is usual to insist that the threshold of competence in patient decision making be set low. It is often argued that there is an initial presumption of competence in medical decision making. The onus is upon those who doubt that someone is competent to make a decision regarding a particular medical procedure or course of treatment to demonstrate that that person is incompetent. In other words, we presume that people are competent to decide about their own health care unless it can be proven that they are incompetent to do so (Welie and Welie, 2001, p. 132).

Our initial presupposition of competence in patient decision making may seem somewhat mysterious. We do not presume that someone is competent to drive a car or conduct surgery until proven otherwise. In these cases we make an initial presupposition of incompetence, placing the onus upon prospective drivers or surgeons to prove that they meet the standards that we require to be licensed to drive, or licensed to perform surgery, before we allow them to drive or conduct surgery. The initial presupposition of competence in patient decision making is justified by our desire to respect peoples' autonomy.[10] We judge that it is better to allow many false positives—incompetent people deciding to undergo medical treatment wrongly judged to be making competent decisions—than to allow even a few false negatives—competent people being deprived of the opportunity to decide for themselves whether or not to undergo medical treatment—if we are to respect peoples' autonomy in patient decision making.

When making judgments that patients are incompetent to make decisions regarding their own health care, health care professionals are making judgments about their patients' decision-making abilities. However, medical training does not typically give one expertise in the intricacies of decision making.[11] In practice, medical professionals who are called upon to make a judgment of incompetence in patient decision making are able to draw upon a variety of socially agreed rules that guide such judgments. We typically judge people under a certain age to lack the competence to make important decisions about their own health care. And typically we do not expect people who are drunk or in a state of shock to be competent to make such decisions. We either wait until we judge that they are in a fit state to make such decisions, or if we are unable to wait, we ask their closest relatives or others who play significant roles in their lives to make such decisions on their behalf. In cases that do not fall clearly into these categories of exclusion we must see very clear evidence of decision-making failure before we decide that people are incompetent to decide about their own medical treatment.

It is commonly argued that the level of ability that we insist upon before deciding that someone is competent to make a particular decision should vary in line with the seriousness of the consequences of that decision (Grisso and Appelbaum, 1998). There is something intuitively right about this line of reasoning. When there is much at stake, as a consequence of allowing a decision to be made that could be made incompetently, it seems that we should be more willing to act so as to prevent those consequences from happening. Our respect for the autonomy of patients is a very important value in medical care, but it is not the only value to be concerned about. Medical ethicists talk about the value of beneficence—concern for the welfare of patients, and this must be balanced against the value of autonomy.[12] And the need to be concerned for the welfare of patients will be heightened in cases where there is much at stake as a consequence of a patient's decision to consent to an operation or course of medical treatment.

Some medical ethicists have argued for a variant of the above line of reasoning. Instead of arguing that it is appropriate to insist on a more stringent test of competence when the consequences of a decision to consent to a course of medical treatment are more serious than in other cases, Buchanan and Brock (1990) appear to argue that competence itself varies with the consequences of a decision. According to them, "the greater the risk relative to other alternatives…the greater the level of communication, understanding and reasoning skills required for competence to make that decision" (Buchanan and Brock, 1990, pp. 55).

Buchanan and Brock's (1990) line of reasoning is dubious at best. A certain level of competence is required to bet ten dollars on a horse to win a race at particular odds. But it does not seem plausible to think that if a gambler bets the same amount of money at twice the odds, or if she raises her bet to twenty dollars, she will require a higher level of competence to make her decision to bet. Rather, it seems plausible to think that once she is competent to bet on horses to win races she is similarly competent to do so across a wide range of variations of odds and stakes. Her decision-making procedure is exactly the same across a great range of variations of stakes and odds. Of course we will be more concerned about the outcome of her more reckless bets and so considerations of beneficence will prompt us to scrutinize these more closely. But this heightened concern of ours is best understood as driven by considerations of beneficence and not by consideration of alleged and unexplained variations in decision-making competence.[13]

Buchanan and Brock's (1990) line of reasoning faces another problem, which is that it seems difficult to reconcile with contemporary behavioural decision-making research. According to influential contemporary research in psychology the mind is best understood as a "dual processor" (Kahneman and Frederick, 2002). We use conscious deliberative logical reasoning in some instances and then effortlessly switch to non-conscious intuitive processing in other instances. If Neil needs to add 51 + 24 he does so in a deliberate systematic rule-driven way, applying the principle of addition. However, if he needs to decide whether a person likes him or is only pretending to like him, he does so using non-conscious processing. It might be thought that all decision making about risks involves conscious processing, but psychological research points to the opposite conclusion. Lay people, when asked to balance the expected benefits of a medical procedure against the risks typically involved, do so in an intuitive non-conscious way. For the many of us who are untrained in the intricacies of statistics, conscious processing is applied to only very simple mathematical calculations and intuitive processing is applied to the majority of calculations involving risks.[14]

Intuitive processing of risk information proceeds quite differently from conscious deliberative processing information. Rather than applying systematic rules, we utilize a number of simplifying heuristics to make the task of assessing risks tractable. Utilized in the wrong contexts these heuristics can lead to a variety of fallacious results, such as those made famous by Tversky and Kahneman (1974, 1983) in a series of much-discussed experiments. Tversky and Kahneman's results are sometimes taken to support the conclusion that people are generally incompetent to manipulate statistical information and that they require better statistical education. However, we would argue, along with Gigerenzer et al. (2002), that the use of such heuristics is quite appropriate in the vast majority of the circumstances in which we actually find ourselves, and that it is unrealistic to expect people to cease employing intuitive processing in the context of complex risk-assessment tasks.[15]

Given that we generally process risk information in an intuitive manner, and utilize simplifying heuristics when we do so, it seems that Brock and Buchanan (1990) are wrong to hold that there is a straightforward correlation to be found between degrees of risk and the level of reasoning skills involved in deciding how to deal with those risks. Some severe risks may be dealt with quite easily if there happen to be suitable heuristics available to assist us in processing the relevant risk information. Conversely, some quite mild risks may be difficult for people to respond to appropriately if there are not suitable heuristics available to help them process the relevant risk information.

Addiction and Consent

As we have seen, the general presumption of competence on behalf of adults to consent is defeated when we know that the person is in a state incompatible with such competence: drunk, in shock, sleep-deprived, suffering from certain kinds of mental illness, and so on. There is little doubt that the immediate effects of many drugs, legal and illegal, are also incompatible with competence to consent. Heroin, like many legal sedatives, causes drowsiness, LSD causes hallucinations as well as confusion, and cocaine may cause reckless behaviours. However, it is more controversial whether addiction to drugs, rather than their acute effects, is incompatible with competence to consent.

For the purposes of this article, we characterize addiction in terms of tolerance and dependence. A person exhibits tolerance to the effects of a drug if she needs progressively higher doses to achieve the same effects. A person is dependent upon a drug if she satisfies two or more of the following: she takes it regularly, experiences cravings for it or withdrawal symptoms if she abstains for longer than usual, she has made unsuccessful attempts to cut down her use of the drug, and the drug has significant adverse impacts upon the quality of her life.[16]

The definition offered above is deliberately neutral on the psychological effects of addiction. It is these further psychological effects that decide whether addiction is compatible with the capacity to give informed consent. Many thinkers argue that addiction is characterized by a loss of autonomy. Autonomy, as we have already seen, is the ability to govern oneself. According to these thinkers, addicts cannot govern themselves because they are governed by their drugs. Drug taking for addicts is posited to be compulsive by some theorists. It follows from this that addicts—notwithstanding their heterogeneous status and functioning—cannot choose to abstain from it. This view of addiction is widely held, by specialists and the general public alike. Louis Charland, for instance, argues that heroin addicts "suffer from a compulsive need to seek and use" their drug and as a result cannot abstain from it. Because their brain "has almost literally been hijacked by the drug" (Charland 2002, p. 37; p. 43), addicts do not act of their own volition when they buy and use drugs.

Law courts and law enforcement agencies typically reject the claim that addicts do not act of their own free will when they buy and use drugs. Many philosophers are equally sceptical of the claim. Although it is easy to see how one can be compelled to move by a physical force, it is much harder to see how a force acting on the mind can be compulsive (Feinberg, 1970). Some go as far as to claim that addiction has no negative impact upon autonomy at all (Foddy and Savalescu, 2006).

Evaluating this debate requires us to get clear on the nature of addiction. Despite the claims of thinkers like Charland, it is clear that addicts are not literally compelled to procure and use drugs. If they were, it would be very mysterious how addicts could ever give up their drugs. But give up they do, very often on their own as clearly documented in the "natural recovery" literature (Sobell et al., 2000; H.K.Klingemann and L.C. Sobell, 2001). The evidence, both from studies of individual addicts and from studies of population-wide drug-taking behaviors, converges on the conclusion that drug taking is, to some extent at least, under the control of those who engage in it.

Consumption of heroin and cocaine, including the consumption by those who are by any standards addicts, is price sensitive in a manner that would be surprising if addictive desires were compulsive (Elster, 1999; Neale, 2002). Price sensitivity is also a feature of alcoholism (Fingarette, 1988). Consumption is price sensitive both within and outside the laboratory; moreover, alcoholics are sensitive to cost even after consuming an initial priming drink. In experiments in which addicts were asked to perform a certain amount of work in order to receive their drug, they rebelled when they regarded the price as too high, even when their only alternative was abstention. Moreover, the features of addiction which are normally thought to cause compulsion—fear of withdrawal and cravings—have been shown to be far too weak to overwhelm the volitional resources of addicts. The typical addict goes through withdrawal several, perhaps many, times. Indeed, some deliberately abstain for prolonged periods in order to lower their tolerance for the drug, and thereby decrease the dose they will need to achieve the high they want (Ainslie, 2000). Addicts do indeed experience cravings—more intensely for some drugs than for others—and withdrawal is indeed an unpleasant experience (though once again the extent to which this is so varies from drug to drug; cocaine addiction seems to be almost entirely a matter of craving and not withdrawal). But the evidence reviewed above demonstrates that these forces, singly or combined, are not sufficient to move the addict against her will.[17]

It is clear, then, that positions like Charland's are wrong. Addiction is not characterized by compulsion. It does not follow, however, that addicts are competent to consent to participate in medical treatment and research. Autonomy can be impaired sufficiently to undermine competence to consent, without being destroyed entirely. The threshold for competence is set low, but not that low. Severely sleep-deprived individuals lack competence to consent, even though they exercise some significant degree of control over their actions. Perhaps, then, addiction is incompatible with competence to consent, despite the fact that it is rarely or never literally compulsive.

It is surely true that addiction has some negative impact upon autonomy. Those of us who have ever struggled with an addiction—whether to caffeine, tobacco, or to heroin—know that this is far too hasty. Addicts often say that they use their drug against their will, and there does seem to be some sense in which this is true. After all, not only is there the phenomenological evidence, to which many of us can attest, that breaking an addiction is difficult, but there is also the evidence that comes from the fact that addiction often results in severely adverse consequences for addicts and for those close to them. Addicts frequently engage in illegal, dangerous, or degrading activities in order to procure their drug, and as a result sometimes lose their paid employment. All too often, they end up in jail.[18] If drug use was purely a matter of autonomous choice, we should not expect their lives to spiral out of control so dramatically. The question, therefore, is not whether addiction impairs autonomy, but whether the impairment is significant enough to undermine competence to consent.

There may be no general answer to the question of whether addiction is consistent with competence to consent. Instead, the answer may vary depending upon the drug in question and how recently the addict consumed it (and perhaps according to the significance of the course of action to be consented to). Different drugs may impair autonomy to different degrees; caffeine addiction has quite different effects upon the agent's ability to comprehend information and make a decision than heroin addiction. Moreover, an addict currently experiencing cravings—intrusive, intense and persistent desires for a drug—or undergoing withdrawal seems to be less autonomous than one who has recently consumed the drug (once the initial effects of intoxication, if any, have passed).

Addiction can impair autonomy either by undermining the agent's ability to process relevant information or by undermining his or her ability to act on that information. The sedative effects of narcotics, for instance, have much the same negative impact upon the ability to make decisions as does sleep deprivation. It seems likely that in many cases drugs' effects upon the ability to process information are more important so far as autonomy is concerned. It is widely recognized that addictive cravings have the effect of "crowding out" other considerations (Elster, 1999). While in the grip of these cravings, addicts overestimate the pleasure that they will receive from drugs and underestimate the costs of continuing to consume them. They find it difficult to keep considerations that weigh against consumption in mind. For some addicts, and with regard to some drugs, cravings are very likely inconsistent with the ability to take in and process information sufficiently well to enable the provision of informed consent.

Fortunately, cravings tend not to persist for very long. There is good evidence that cravings are cue and belief dependent; addicts experience cravings most powerfully when they encounter cues associated with drug use or when they believe that their drug is imminently accessible (Loewenstein, 1999; Elster, 1999). With this information, it is possible for counsellors to take steps to ensure that clients are able to understand information imparted to them, and come to an autonomous decision on its basis. They should avoid situations likely to trigger cravings. This is not a simple linear process and it is useful to once again remember that there are associated critical conditions, which are necessary for cravings to occur or not to occur. In practice, this means, among various options, talking with addicts and substance users of various types in circumstances in which they have not previously taken drugs. This means that crucial discussions should not take place in the addict's home, but should take place in the offices of the counsellor or some neutral environment. The informed consent procedure should also not take place in the immediate aftermath of drug consumption, since many drugs cloud decision making for a shorter or longer period after consumption. It is useful to remember that medicinal "drugs" can and do facilitate decision making when anxiety, depression, and confusion are operating. Nor should these discussions occur while the addict is undergoing withdrawal. Fortunately, it is relatively easy to avoid the cues, which trigger cravings, and it is normally obvious whether the addict has recently consumed or is undergoing withdrawal. It is therefore not very difficult to ensure that addicts are as well placed as other people to appreciate the information imparted to them.

Very much the same kinds of circumstances that impair addicts' ability to appreciate information also undermine their ability to act autonomously. For addicts, as indeed, for all of us, continuously persisting desires are extremely difficult to resist; if desires persist long enough, they may be literally impossible to resist (Baumeister et al., 1998; Baumeister, 2002). It is therefore extremely likely that cravings help to explain the impairment in volition which is reported by, and observable in the behaviors of, addicts. Cravings are not all that difficult to resist in the short term, but the longer they persist, the harder continued resistance becomes (Levy, 2006). This hypothesis helps to explain the fact that addicts who are attempting to give up their drug typically have little difficulty in abstaining long enough to go through withdrawal, but are extremely likely to return to drug use weeks or even months later (Loewenstein, 2000; Ainslie, 2001). Since the cravings which undermine volitional resources are, among other considerations, cue- and belief-dependent, in the manner already outlined, the same steps which can be taken to avoid triggering cravings should also be effective in ensuring that addicts are able to exercise autonomous control over their actions.

So long as appropriate steps are taken—so long, that is, as counsellors ensure that the cues likely to trigger cravings are avoided, that clients are not experiencing withdrawal symptoms, or are under the pharmacological and/or "drug experience" influence of mind-distorting drugs—there is no general barrier to holding addicts competent to give informed consent. Meeting these conditions will usually not be very difficult. We therefore conclude that addiction is not an obstacle for drug users providing informed consent to participate in treatment programs.

Steve Clarke, Ph.D., is a senior research fellow at the Centre for Applied Philosophy and Public Ethics, Charles Sturt University as well as a research fellow in the Program on the Ethics of the New Biosciences in the James Martin 21st Century School at the University of Oxford. He is a broad-ranging philosopher who works mostly in philosophy of science and applied ethics. He has recent publications in such journals as Philosophy of the Social Sciences *and the* Journal of Medicine and Philosophy. *He was the joint winner (together with Justin Oakley) of the 2004 Eureka Prize for Research in Ethics. See: http://www.amonline.net.au/eureka/research_ethics/index.htm.*

Neil Levy, Ph.D., is a senior research fellow at the Centre for Applied Philosophy and Public Ethics, University of Melbourne as well as a research fellow in the Program on the Ethics of the New Biosciences in the James Martin 21st Century School at the University of Oxford. He is the author of four books and over fifty articles on all areas of philosophy and ethics.

References

Ainslie, G. (2000). A research-based theory of addictive motivation. *Law and Philosophy, 19* (1), pp. 77-115.

Ainslie, G. (2001). *Breakdown of will.* Cambridge: Cambridge University Press.

American Counseling Association, ACA code of ethics and standards of practice http://www.counseling.org/Content/NavigationMenu/RESOURCES/ETHICS/ACA_Code_of_Ethics.htm

American Counseling Association. (2005). Code of ethics draft. http://www.counseling.org/CF_content/index.htm

Appelbaum, P.S., Lidz, C.W. and Meisel, A. (1987). *Informed consent: legal theory and clinical practice.* New York: Oxford University Press.

Baumeister, R.F., Bratslavsky, E., Muraven, M. & Tice., D.M. (1998). Ego-depletion: Is the active self a limited resource? *Journal of Personality and Social Psychology 74*, pp. 1252-1265.

Baumeister, R.F. (2002). Ego depletion and self-control failure: an energy model of the self's executive function. *Self and Identity 1*: 129-136.

Beauchamp, T.L. and Childress, J.F. (2001). *Principles of biomedical ethics.* (Fifth Ed.) New York: Oxford University Press.

Buchanan, A. and Brock, D. (1990). *Deciding for others: The ethics of surrogate decision-making.* Cambridge: Cambridge University Press.

Charland, L.C. (2002). Cynthia's dilemma: consenting to heroin prescription. *American Journal of Bioethics, 2*, pp. 37-47.

Clarke, S. (2001). Informed consent in medicine in comparison with consent in other areas of human activity. *Southern Journal of Philosophy 39*, pp. 169-187.

Clarke, S., and Oakley, J. (2004). Informed consent and surgeons' performance. *Journal of Medicine and Philosophy 29*, pp. 11-35.

Cowart, M.R. (2004). Understanding acts of consent: using speech act theory to help resolve moral dilemmas and legal disputes. *Law and Philosophy, 23*, pp. 495-525.

Department of Health, Education and Welfare. (1973, April 27). Final report of the Tuskegee syphilis study ad hoc advisory panel. Washington DC: US Government Printing Office, #747-022/5334.

Elster, J. (1999). *Strong feelings: emotion, addiction and human behaviors.* Cambridge, MA: MIT Press.

Faden, R.R. and Beauchamp, T.L. (1986). *A history and theory of informed consent.* New York: Oxford University Press.

Feinberg, J. (1970). What is so special about mental illness? In *Doing and deserving.* Princeton: Princeton University Press, pp. 272-292.

Fingarette, H. (1988). *Heavy drinking: the myth of alcoholism as a disease.* Berkeley: University of California Press.

Foddy, B. and Savulescu, J. (2006). Addiction and autonomy: Can addicted people consent to the prescription of their drug addiction? *Bioethics, 20*, pp. 1-15

Gawande, A. (2002). *Complications: a surgeon's notes on an imperfect science.* Profile Books: London.

Gigerenzer, G. (2002). *Reckoning with risk.* London: The Penguin Press.

Gigerenzer, G., Czerlinski, J., and Martignon, L. (2002). How good are fast and frugal heuristics? In Gilovich, T., Griffin, D. and Kahneman, D. (Eds.), *Heuristics and biases: the psychology of intuitive judgement*. Cambridge: Cambridge University Press, pp. 559-581.

Grisso, T., and Appelbaum, P.S. (1998). *Assessing competence to consent to treatment: a guide for physicians and other heath professionals*. New York: Oxford University Press.

Kahneman, D. and Frederick, S. (2002). Representativeness revisited: attribute substitution in intuitive judgement. In Gilovich, T., Griffin, D. and Kahneman, D. (Eds.), *Heuristics and biases: the psychology of intuitive judgement*. Cambridge: Cambridge University Press, pp. 49-81.

Katz, J. (1984). *The silent world of doctor and patient*. New York: The Free Press.

Klein, G. (1998). *Sources of power: how people make decisions*. Cambridge MA: MIT Press.

Kleinig, J. (1982). The ethics of consent. In Nielsen, K. and Patten, S.C. (Eds.), *New Essays in Ethics and Public Policy*. Guelph, Ontario: Canadian Association for Publishing in Philosophy, pp. 91-118.

Kleinig, J. (2004). Ethical issues in substance use intervention. *Substance Use and Misuse 39*, pp. 369-398. Reprinted in this volume pp, xx –xx.

Kleinmuntz, B. (2000). Why we still use our heads instead of formulas: toward an integrative approach. In Connolly, T., Arkes, H.R. and Hammond, K.R. (Eds.), *Judgement and decision-making: an interdisciplinary reader (2nd Ed.)*. Cambridge: Cambridge University Press, pp. 681-712.

Klingemann, H.K. and Sobell, L.C. (2001). Natural recovery research across substance use. *Substance Use and Misuse 36* (11), pp. 1409-1416.

Levy, N. (2006) Addiction, autonomy and ego-depletion: A response to Bennett Foddy and Julian Savulescu, *Bioethics, 20*, pp. 16-20.

Lifton, R.J. (2000) *The Nazi doctors: killing and the psychology of genocide*. New York: Basic Books.

Loewenstein, G. (2000). Willpower: a decision theorist's perspective. *Law and Philosophy, 19,* pp. 51-76.

National Association for Alcohol and Drug Addiction Counselors (NAADAC). Ethical standards for counsellors. <http://naadac.org/documents/display.php?DocumentID=11>

Neale, J. (2002). *Drug users in society*. New York: Palgrave.

Schuck, P. H. (1994). Rethinking informed consent. *The Yale Law Journal, 103*, pp. 899-959.

Sobell, L.C., Ellingstad, T.P., & Sobell, M.B. (2000). Natural recovery from alcohol and drug problems: methodological review of the research with suggestions for future directions. *Addiction, 95*, pp. 749–764.

Tversky, A., and Kahneman, D. (1974). Judgement under uncertainty: heuristics and biases. *Science, 185*, pp. 1124-1131.

Tversky, A. and Kahneman, D. (1983). Extensional versus intuitive reasoning: the conjunction fallacy in probability judgement. *Psychological Review, 90*, pp. 293-315.

US Department of Justice, Drugs and Crime Facts, <http://www.ojp.usdoj.gov/bjs/pub/pdf/cfjs00.pdf>.

Welie, J.V.M., and Welie, S.P.K. (2001). Patient decision-making competence: outline of a conceptual analysis. *Medicine, Health Care and Philosophy, 4*, pp. 127-138.

Wicclair, M. (1991). Patient decision-making capacity and risk. *Bioethics, 5*, pp. 91-104.

Glossary

autonomy: the state of being self-governing. On minimal accounts of autonomy, self-governance amounts to freedom from external constraints. More elaborate accounts involve consideration of the internal states of autonomous agents.

beneficence: action done for the benefit of others. This includes acts of altruism, charity, kindness, and mercy.

consent: to give consent is to alter the normative relations of others to oneself by providing those others with an entitlement to perform an act or set of acts.

craving: an intense and intrusive desire to consume a drug or other substance. Cravings are produced by regular consumption of many, though by no means all, drugs of dependence.

dual processor: a system that integrates two distinct types of operations. The human mind is said to be a dual processor because it integrates rapid automatic intuitive processes with slower deliberative conscious calculations.

informed consent: consent that is grounded on a sufficient basis of relevant information. It is standard in contemporary medicine to require that the informed consent of a patient be obtained before an operation or course of treatment takes place.

paternalism: interference in the activities of others that is justified by appeal to the promotion of their welfare or the prevention of harms that may beset them.

withdrawal: regular consumption of many drugs produces neurochemical adaptation to their effects. After adaptation, abstention from drug use produces the symptoms of withdrawal, which are very unpleasant. Dependence upon different drugs produces different experiences of withdrawal. Anxiety, irritability, and sleeplessness, as well as physical symptoms such as muscle cramps and diarrhoea are characteristic of the more serious withdrawal symptoms. In the case of alcohol, withdrawal can be fatal.

Notes

* Requests for information should be addressed to: stephen.clarke@anu.edu.au

1. For a recent analysis of consent in terms of speech act theory, which acknowledges limitations to this approach, see Cowart (2004).
2. One of the authors of this paper argues that informedness is a necessary component of all consenting relationships, properly understood, whether these take place in medicine or in other spheres of human activity. See Clarke (2001).
3. Changes in the culture of medicine in the latter part of the twentieth century are vividly described by Gawande (2002, pp. 208-227).
4. For convenience we will employ the broad term "substance use counselors." However it should be noted that we do not mean to imply that all such counselors are cut from the same cloth, as it were. As one of the editors of this volume has pointed out to us, there are no unique models or techniques applicable to the treatment of all substance users.
5. The ACA is currently developing a draft code which makes the following explicit stipulations regarding informed consent:
   A.2a Informed Consent. Counselors offer clients the freedom to choose, whether to enter into or remain in a counseling relationship. For clients to make informed choices they need adequate information about the process and the counselor. Counselors have an obligation to review in writing and verbally with clients the rights

and responsibilities of both the counsellor and the client. Counselors recognize that informed consent is an ongoing part of the counselling process. Counselors appropriately document discussions of informed consent throughout the counselling relationship (ACA 2005).

6. Kleinig (2004, p. 384, footnote ai.) provides references to the ethics codes of a number of state and local level organisations for substance user counselors. Most of these codes include some sort of requirement for counsellors to obtain the informed consent of their clients.
7. For surveys of the many philosophical and legal issues that the doctrine of informed consent raises, including the issues of what understanding amounts to and what constitutes voluntariness, see Faden and Beauchamp (1986) and Appelbaum et al. (1987).
8. The issue of setting a threshold in the context of judgments of surgeons' performance ability is discussed in Clarke and Oakley (2004, pp. 20-21).
9. Similar analyses of competent decision-making are due to Beauchamp and Childress (2001, p. 73) and Welie and Welie (2001, p. 135).
10. Of course this presupposition would not have been considered justifiable in the older medical culture of paternalism. In the older paternalistic culture patients were presumed generally to lack the competence to make a sensible autonomous decision regarding their own medical treatment.
11. Our doubts about the ability of medical professionals to appreciate the intricacies of patients' decision-making abilities are fueled by evidence of the decision-making shortcomings of medical professionals, especially in relation to their ability to comprehend statistical information. See, for example Gigerenzer (2002, Chs. 5-7).
12. On the need to balance competing norms in medical ethics see Beauchamp and Childress (2001, pp. 18-23).
13. For further discussion of Buchanan and Brock's (1990) argument relating decision-making capacities to risk levels see Wicclair (1991).
14. For a comparison of intuitive and statistical techniques in risk assessment see Kleinmuntz (2000).
15. For an extended defence of the use of intuition in risk related decision-making see Klein (1998).
16. This definition combines features of the definition of addiction in the *Diagnostic and Statistical Manual* of the American Psychiatric Association (DSM-IV) and the *International Classification of Diseases* (ICD-10) published by the World Health Organization (WHO).
17. At least this seems true of between-episode behaviour. Within episodes, the behavior of those addicted to some drugs—most notably cocaine—seems sometimes to be genuinely compulsive. See Elster (1999 pp. 167-169, n. 8).
18. The US Department of Justice estimates that in 1997 19% of federal prisoners and 16% of state prisoners were serving sentences for crimes committed to raise money to buy drug. 25% of property offences were committed for the same purpose (US Department of Justice, Drugs and Crime Facts, <http://www.ojp.usdoj.gov/bjs/pub/pdf/cfjs00.pdf>).

2-2 Medicine and Morals, Craving and Compulsion

Stephen J. Morse, J.D., Ph.D.

Abstract

Thinking about addictions has been dominated by two models: the medical model, which treats addiction as a disease and related behaviors as signs and symptoms, and the moral model, which views addiction and related behaviors as indications of moral failure. This paper describes both models and their implications, with special emphasis on the moral model. The meaning of compulsion or coercion caused by internal psychological states, such as craving, is explored to determine if addicts may fairly be held morally and legally responsible for their behavior, such as seeking and using substances. It is argued that diminished rationality better explains than compulsion why addicts might be excused for their behavior, but it is concluded that most addicts can be held responsible for most addiction-related behavior. Nonetheless, both models have desirable characteristics, and sound public policy should not be based solely on either. The implications for criminal justice of employing both models to guide policy are explored.

Key Words: craving, duress, loss of control, compulsion, morals, non-responsible, voluntary

Introduction

Thinking about whether agents are responsible for becoming addicted and for conduct associated with their addictions has been hindered by inadequate understanding of how models of addiction relate to responsibility. Although no uncontroversial definition of addiction exists, and "addiction" and "addict" are not formal diagnostic terms, I shall use both for ease of exposition. I define addiction phenomenologically–as do many researchers–as persistently arising feelings of intense craving to consume substances and attempting to seek and use those substances. I treat addiction as an all or none category, but the criteria are continuum concepts, and there is no scientifically determined cutting point for deciding when a person "is addicted."

Even sophisticated people tend to think that if addiction is a disease, the addict is akin to an automaton, a puppet manipulated by the substance induced neurophysiological strings of a biological disorder. Consequently, they also think that the addict is not responsible for behaviors, such as seeking and using drugs, that are an integral feature of his addiction. Conversely, many people think that addiction is purely a result of moral weakness.

This essay suggests that medical and moral models of addiction both have attractive features and that sensible social policy need not succumb either to medical or to moral triumphalism. Other models are of course used, but medical and moral models dominate discussions of moral and legal responsibility. I begin with a "fable" from real life, the case of Mr. Leroy Powell, which concretely presents the clash between the alternative models of addiction. I then contrast the two models in some detail. I pay special attention to the moral model, because sophisticated versions of it are almost certainly less familiar to those in the therapeutic professions.

This article next turns to the central question of responsibility. I conclude that there is good reason to hold most addicts responsible for addiction-related behavior, such as seeking and using drugs, even if many might not be responsible for initially becoming addicted. I also claim that holding addicts responsible should not prevent social acceptance of either treatment-oriented responses that are consistent with the medical model or criminal law reforms that would diminish "the war on drugs" and its associated costs.

A Real Life "Fable": The Case of Leroy Powell

In December of 1966 in Austin, Texas, Mr. Leroy Powell was arrested, charged, and convicted of public intoxication. His defense counsel argued that because Mr. Powell was afflicted with "the disease of chronic alcoholism,...his appearance in public [while drunk] was not of his own volition," and thus to punish Mr. Powell for this symptomatic behavior would be a violation of the Eighth Amendment prohibition of cruel and unusual punishment (Powell v. Texas, 1968, p. 517). Mr. Powell's defense was supported by the testimony of an expert psychiatrist, one Dr. David Wade, who testified that a "chronic alcoholic" is an "involuntary drinker," who is "powerless not to drink," and who "loses his self control over his drinking." (p. 518)

Based on his examination of Mr. Powell, Dr. Wade concluded that Powell was, a "chronic alcoholic," who "by the time he has reached [the state of] intoxication...is not able to control his behavior, and...has reached this point because he has an uncontrollable compulsion to drink" (p. 518).

Dr. Wade also opined that Powell lacked "the willpower to resist the constant excessive consumption of alcohol." The good doctor admitted that Powell's first drink when he was sober was a "voluntary exercise of will" but qualified this answer by claiming that alcoholics have a compulsion that is a "very strong influence, an exceedingly strong influence," that clouds their judgment. Finally, Dr. Wade suggested that jailing Powell without treatment would fail to discourage Powell's consumption of alcohol and related problems. One could not find a more clear expression of the medicalized, disease concept of addiction to ethanol.

Powell himself testified about his alcoholism. Indeed, there was no dispute about whether he was a chronic alcoholic. He also testified that he couldn't stop drinking. Powell's cross examination concerning the events of the day of his trial is worth quoting in full.

> Q: You took that one [drink] at eight o'clock [a.m.] because you wanted to drink?
>
> A: Yes, sir.
>
> Q: And you knew that if you drank it, you could keep on drinking and get drunk?
>
> A: Well, I was supposed to be here on trial, and I didn't take but that one drink.

Q: You knew you had to be here this afternoon, but this morning you took one drink and then you knew that you couldn't afford to drink any more and come to court; is that right?

A: Yes, sir, that's right.

Q: Because you knew what you would do if you kept drinking, that you would finally pass out or be picked up?

A: Yes, sir.

Q: And you didn't want that to happen to you today?

A: No, sir.

Q: Not today?

A: No, sir.

Q: So you only had one drink today?

A: Yes, sir. (p. 519)

On redirect examination, Powell's attorney elicited further explanation.

Q: Leroy, isn't the real reason why you just had one drink today because you just had enough money to buy one drink?

A: Well, that was just give to me.

Q: In other words, you didn't have any money with which you could buy drinks yourself?

A: No, sir, that was give to me.

Q: And that's really what controlled the amount you drank this morning, isn't it?

A: Yes, sir.

Q: Leroy, when you start drinking, do you have any control over how many drinks you can take?

A: No, sir. (p. 520)

Powell wanted to drink and had that first drink, but despite that last answer, his compulsion did not cause him to engage in the myriad lawful and unlawful means he might easily have used to obtain more alcohol if his craving was desperately compulsive. And no one, I hope, wishes to suggest that poverty is a useful treatment for chronic alcoholism.

Addicts are not automatons. If they have good enough reason not to seek and use, in most cases they do not. The questions are whether those reasons are available to them when they seek and use drugs or whether they are compelled to seek and use, even if they recognize and endorse the reasons not to. The United States Supreme Court refused to "constitutionalize" a legal non-responsibility defense in Powell in 1968, but the question this paper addresses is whether people like Powell are morally responsible.

The Medical Model of Addiction

The medical model treats the insistent "craving" and the related seeking and using conduct of people with addictions to substances as signs and symptoms of an underlying disorder. Investigators have proposed biological, behavioral, psychodynamic, and other etiological explanations, and various hypotheses have received empirical support, but no causal model can claim uncontroversial validity. Nonetheless, all medical modelers agree that addicts are sick, and recent investigative methods and scientific understanding of the brain have fueled increasing emphasis on the "brain disease" view. The following quote from Alan Leshner (1997), is representative.

> *Dramatic advances over the past two decades in both the neurosciences and the behavioral sciences have revolutionized our understanding of drug abuse and addiction. Scientists have identified neural circuits that subsume the actions of every known drug of abuse, and they have specified common pathways that are affected by almost all such drugs. Researchers have also identified and cloned the major receptors for virtually every abusable drug, as well as the natural ligands for most of these receptors. In addition, they have elaborated many of the biochemical cascades within the cell that follow receptor activation by drugs. Research has also begun to reveal major differences between the brains of addicted and nonaddicted individuals and to indicate some common elements of addiction, regardless of the substance (p. 45).*

A medicalized view of drug addiction has important implications for understanding the addict's conduct. Most fundamentally, the medical model usually assumes that the person is not responsible for having the underlying disorder or for exhibiting the signs and symptoms. After all, with few exceptions, diseases are unwelcome states that people "contract." The signs and symptoms are not human action, but instead are simply mechanistic biophysical effects of the underlying pathology. It thus makes sense to say that most signs and symptoms are not intentional–they just happen to people and that the "sufferer" could not help but exhibit them. The model is mechanistic and it is easy to conclude that the diseased agent is not responsible for desiring consumption and for behavior related to satisfying that desire. The appropriate response, it seems, is non-judgmental and therapeutic, rather than evaluative and punitive.

Many people influenced by the medical model who study or work with drug addicts—and with others who manifest some impulse or desire disorders, such as pedophilia or "compulsive" gambling—recognize that addictions are unlike many other disorders in significant respects. As a result, the purely medical view may be difficult to maintain. Seeking and using behavior is distinguishable from most signs of disease because it is intentional action, rather than simply the state or movement of a body. It is plausible to assume that the addict might be able to exert some degree of intentional control over the aberrant behavior and that encouraging the agent to "take responsibility" for the conduct might be therapeutically efficacious. Consequently therapists might well insist that their addicted clients must take responsibility for their conduct as a precondition for genuine improvement. Therapists can treat acceptance of responsibility as simply instrumental, but some surely also believe that some degree of moral responsibility is warranted. Thus, the medical model of "disorders of desire" is not necessarily inconsistent with moral evaluation of at least the conduct that is a sign of the disorder. Nonetheless, the lure of mechanism powerfully impels medical modelers to conclude that addicts have little, if any, control over their desires and conduct and are not morally responsible for them. As a corollary, many believe that criminal blame and punishment are unjustified.

The foremost treatment implications of the medical model—which arose only recently as an alternative to the view that addiction was a sin and properly punishable—are that a therapeutic response is clinically and morally warranted. One interesting moral and legal question is whether treatment can be imposed on the addict without his consent and as a condition for the release of agents who are confined because they acted on their desires. Therapeutically beneficial treatment can be used parentalistically or as a mechanism of social control, both of which are fraught. This question is complex, and answering it goes beyond the scope of this article, but suffice it to say that most people who "suffer" from addictions are competent most of the time to make treatment decisions. If treatment is imposed on them, it must be justified by hard parentalism, by a pure police power rationale, or by both.

The Moral Model of Addiction

The moral model focuses precisely and centrally on the reality that seeking and using behavior is intentional action and not simply a state or movement of a sick agent's body. Any moral theory posits that intentional human action is an appropriate object of moral assessment. Therefore, drug-related conduct, like any other intentional behavior, may properly be morally evaluated. Some moral theories also claim that it is proper morally to evaluate the virtue of an agent's thoughts and desires, but others do not because thoughts and desires per se do not harm others or, more arguably, the agent. Moreover, the law's concern is conduct, not thoughts and desires, because only conduct violates or threatens the rights of others. Indeed, the United States Supreme Court has held that the Constitution forbids criminal blame and punishment of agents simply for being addicted (Robinson v. California, 1962). The question for morality and law, then, is whether an addict is morally responsible for the conduct motivated by the craving for the drug.

In our moral and legal system, responsibility is a necessary, crucial variable for making decisions concerning blame, liberty, and confinement. Judgments of moral and legal responsibility are only possible, however, according to some implicit or explicit theory of responsibility. Theories of responsibility are highly contested, differing substantially about the criteria for both responsibility and excuse (see Kutz, 2002). Nevertheless, it is clear that our moral and legal thought, at least implicitly—and sometimes explicitly—adopts a theory of responsibility that makes an agent's general capacity for rationality and the absence of unjustified compulsion or coercion the touchstones of responsibility. In turn, if the agent's general capacity for rationality was compromised or the agent acted under compulsion, excuse and non-responsibility may be warranted. Judges, lawyers, commentators, behavioral scientists, and others often discuss the general question of responsibility as if it were a question of free will or free choice, and on occasion they characterize the compulsion or coercion criterion for excuse as a "volitional" question. These are misleading characterizations, however, that do not and cannot explain the criteria for responsibility and excuse that both the law and ordinary morality adopt (See Morse, 1998 & 2002).

The identified criteria for responsibility—the general capacity for rationality and lack of unjustified compulsion—are normative and not self defining. Moral and legal practices must provide justifiable criteria that decision makers can fairly apply. We need not provide a specific definition. Whatever criteria for rationality and compulsion are adopted will be the criteria according to which the responsibility of addicts must be assessed. Differing definitions will produce different outcomes. Some may excuse many addicts and others may excuse few, but rationality and compulsion will provide the parameters of the decision.

As Herbert Fingarette and Ann Fingarette Hasse have persuasively shown, (1979) the presence of a disease per se does not answer the question of responsibility within a moral and legal model, even if the presence of the disease and its signs and symptoms are uncontroversial. Although human action may perhaps be properly considered the sign of an underlying disorder, it is nevertheless true that the effect of disease on responsibility must be cashed out in terms of rationality and compulsion. Having a disease is not an excuse per se when human action is at issue (Moore, 1985). As the next section discusses, from the perspective of the moral model, many and perhaps most addicts seem responsible for behavior, such as seeking and using, that is associated with and perhaps symptomatic of the addiction.

Responsibility for Addiction and Addiction-Related Conduct

First, it is helpful to distinguish responsibility for becoming an addict from responsibility for behavior associated with addiction. Many people might not be responsible for becoming addicted because it happened when they were teenagers or even earlier, stages of life when the person has not yet developed the full capacity for rationality. On the other hand, knowledge of the addictive potential of legal and illegal substances, such as ethanol, nicotine, caffeine, the opiates, cocaine, and others, is widespread in our culture. Indeed, few are unaware, at least as an intellectual matter, that the "slope" from recreational substance use to addicted craving may in some cases be slippery and steep. Consequently, when virtually all adults begin to use drugs voluntarily, they are aware or should be aware of the potential for addiction and may fairly be held responsible if they become addicted. Further, if agents are responsible for becoming addicts, then there is a plausible argument that they may also be fairly held responsible for completely foreseeable conduct that addiction routinely produces. This is not to suggest that they must be treated without compassion or that needed treatment should be withheld. It is simply to recognize, as we already do most clearly in the case of sexually transmitted diseases, the trivially true observation that on occasion people can be responsible for contracting a disease.

The more interesting moral and legal question is the addict's responsibility for behavior associated with addiction, even assuming that they are not responsible for becoming addicted. Holding someone responsible for behavior caused by a condition for which they are not responsible may seem inconsistent, but much of our behavior is caused by characteristics of the person, such as one's character, for which one is not fully responsible. Causation is not an excusing condition. All behavior is caused by something. If causation were an excuse, everyone or no one would be responsible for all behavior. The question, therefore, is always whether a genuine excusing condition obtains, and once again, a theory of irrationality or compulsion will be necessary to furnish an excuse.

The Compulsion Theory of Excuse for Addiction-Related Behavior

During periods of intense craving, the addict's essential claim is that his desires, his cravings, are so strong, so powerful, that he cannot control them, that he cannot help himself.[1] Again, however, even if the desires are the product of a disorder, that does not per se imply that the agent must be excused. Even if they are signs of disease, seeking and using are intentional human actions. The drug addict desires either to avoid the pain of withdrawal or to experience pleasure, or both. The addict believes (correctly) that consuming the substance will satisfy the desire. The addict therefore forms and acts on the intention to seek and use. The addict is not an automaton and addiction associated behavior is far more calculated than the tic-like conduct associated with disorders like Tourette's Syndrome.

The desire to take drugs, like all desires, might be produced by genetic predisposition, by socialization experiences, by particular situations, or by a host of other causes, but a desire is simply a desire, however it is produced. Desires and temptations, whether "normal" or "abnormal," may be strong or weak, persistent, or sudden and transient. It is of course easier in the colloquial sense to behave wisely, morally, and legally if an agent does not have strong desires to behave unwisely, immorally, or illegally. Moreover, failure to satisfy strong desires can cause very unpleasant feeling states, such as tension, anxiety, and frustration. When anyone is in the grip of a powerful, insistent desire of any type, it is frustrating and even painful not to satisfy it. Consider the experience of an addicted smoker for nicotine on a very long, smoke-free flight. Nonetheless, what does it mean to say that an agent "can't help it" when the agent yields to strong desires that will cause unpleasant feelings if they are not satisfied? Having a strong desire is not a genuinely excusing condition in general for engaging in wrongful or prohibited behavior, and the moral modeler asks why a strong desire for forbidden drugs in particular should furnish an excuse.

If an agent's body is literally forced to move, say, by operation of a genuine reflex, then the agent does not act at all because the concept of action in both morality and law requires intentional bodily movement. Conduct caused by strong desires, however, is surely human action and not a biophysical mechanism. Note, too, that the strength of the desire, and not its normality or abnormality, is what motivates the conclusion that perhaps the agent can not help himself. The alleged abnormality of a desire is not a proxy for its strength. After all, we would not conclude that an agent who yields to a weak desire can not help himself, even if the desire is abnormally caused or abnormal in itself. For example, assuming that we could measure accurately the strength of a pedophile's desire for sexual contact with children, we would not conclude that a pedophile with weak desires was unable to control himself in the presence of children.

Let us consider whether the legal meaning of "involuntariness," which seems to be synonymous with lack of capacity to control oneself, can help us understand what we generally mean conceptually by loss of control. Two doctrines in criminal law negate responsibility because the agent allegedly acted "involuntarily": the absence of an act and compulsion or duress. An agent is clearly not even *prima facie* responsible unless the agent's harmful bodily movements are intentional actions. Even if an agent acts intentionally, however, if the agent acts in response to compulsion or duress, he or she will be held non-responsible because the agent has been placed in a hard choice situation and we could not fairly hold the agent accountable for yielding to a sufficient threat.

In the case of no action, the bodily movement is literally involuntary, literally a mechanism, because it is caused by something other than the agent's intention. In the case of duress, involuntariness is both metaphorical and a legal label affixed to agents who are considered to be non-responsible. In either case, if the agent causes harm, we conclude that the agent could not help it and we hold him or her non-responsible. Again, in the case of no action, the agent literally could not have prevented the bodily movement from occurring. In the case of duress, one acts intentionally, but we can not fairly expect the agent to act differently. Consequently, we say metaphorically that addicts cannot help acting as they did and we ascribe non-responsibility. Can either theory explain loss of control as this standard is used when evaluating the responsibility of drug addicts?

I believe that the metaphor of "mechanism" is the most misleading source of the intuition that some people cannot control actions intended to satisfy some desires, especially if we believe that the desires are produced by neurochemical or other brain abnormalities. This mechanistic metaphor is powerful because mechanistic events are not proper objects of responsibility ascription. Thus, if yielding to a strong "abnormal" desire is "just like" a biophysically involuntary bodily movement, then yielding is apparently not a responsible action. This is simply an analogy, however, and it is flawed. Recall that a desire is simply a desire, whether it is caused by biological abnormalities or the alignment of the planets. There is no literal physical compulsion, as there is in cases of reflex, spasm, and the like. It is literally true that an agent can not help a reflexive bodily movement, but is it true that an agent cannot help acting to satisfy at least some strong desires in some situations?

To cash out the mechanistic metaphor, examples of the following kind are given (Morse, 2000). Assume that an agent needs to urinate, but is unable to find an appropriate place to do so. As time passes and the bladder continues to fill, the desire to urinate will become increasingly powerful and unpleasant. At some point, however, the person's bladder will empty because the pressure on the urethral (urinary) sphincter will mechanically force it to open; he or she will no longer be able to "hold it in," no matter what the cost might be for doing so. For example, suppose the agent is threatened with death for permitting his bladder to empty. The agent will surely exercise control for a very lengthy period, but all agents will finally empty their bladders because, ultimately, voiding will be a product of a literally uncontrollable mechanism. The sphincter "fails" because the physical pressure on it is too great.

Strong desires are allegedly analogous to the full bladder. Increasing desire is analogized to increasing pressure on the sphincter and we are supposed to conclude that people are no more responsible for yielding to some desires than they are for emptying their bladders. But desires aren't physical forces, actions aren't mechanisms, and people aren't sphincters. There are no "desire units" that will finally mechanistically force the "action switch" to flip if enough "desire units" are added. Assuming that an addict wants to live, if we threaten him with immediate death for seeking and using a substance, he will not seek and use. What reasons would have motivational salience in an individual case is of course an open question and individual agents will respond to different reasons. The point is simply that the actions of addicts are actions and not mechanisms and thus they are potentially reason responsive. The example might also suggest that if it takes a gun to one's head to motivate a person not to engage in certain actions, then it must be very hard not to perform those actions. Again, this is true in a colloquial sense best explained in terms of a rationality defect, as explained below, but it does not mean that there is anything wrong with the agent's will. The analogy to literal mechanism fails, but if the mechanistic picture is in one's head, it is easy to conclude that the addict can not control himself.

Now let us consider whether a compulsion or duress theory may explain the conclusion that some agents who suffer from intense and allegedly abnormal desires cannot control themselves. Assume that an agent is being threatened with a horrible death unless she kills a group of people. Duress is an excuse to crime only if an agent is threatened with death or grievous bodily harm, a person of reasonable firmness would yield in the situation, and the agent is not at fault for placing herself in the threatening situation (American Legal Institute, 1985). In the example, there is a powerful reason to ask the agent not to kill the group. The agent has no right to prefer her innocent one life to the equally innocent lives of many. Killing would of course be an action under the circumstances and the agent had no volitional or control problem. The agent's reasoning is intact and prefer her will, her volition operates effectively to terminate the threat and to save her own life (Moore, 1993). Nevertheless, the reason to excuse the agent would be that she faced a dreadfully hard choice and we could not fairly expect the agent not to yield when threatened with death. When threats become sufficient, most people, including those of impeccable virtue, might find it almost impossible not to yield, no matter what the cost might be for doing so.

The agent faced with the threat of frustration of strong internal desires is essentially claiming an "internal duress" excuse, a "non-culpable hard choice" generated by the craving. But is the frustration of desire the equivalent of the experience of death, grievous bodily harm, or agonizing pain? Unlike the literal involuntariness of mechanism, the metaphorical involuntariness of duress is a continuum concept. Frustration and related unpleasant feeling states may be psychologically painful, but even if the desire and its strength are not the agent's fault, think how much psychological pain must be threatened to consider an agent not responsible.

It seems unlikely that most rational agents threatened with dysphoria face a sufficiently hard choice to warrant non-responsibility. Dysphoria and fear of it are continuum concepts and difficult to measure, but let us suppose that we could evaluate such states reasonably accurately based on inferences from self report, behavioral manifestations, and the like. I suspect that the feared dysphoria of unconsummated cravings is not as severe as the fear of death or grievous bodily harm. If this is right, few sufferers from internal compulsion would succeed with a hard choice excuse, albeit we might feel sympathetic towards their plight. Note, further, that if the agent's primary reason for yielding is the positive pursuit of pleasure rather than the avoidance of threatened psychological pain, then there is no hard choice, and "internal duress" would not obtain.

In some cases, the threat of dysphoria might be great enough to excuse simple possession for personal use and use. Even then, however, these are considered serious wrongs and perhaps the threat of, say, experiencing withdrawal symptoms, would not be deemed sufficient. Moreover, such dysphoria would never justify other crimes, such as stealing to obtain money to buy drugs. And again, even if we did excuse for this reason in some cases, there is no control defect. The agent's will operates effectively indeed to end the psychological pain by satisfying the desire. The non-responsibility condition, if one obtains at all, would be a sufficiently hard choice that the agent faces through no fault of his or her own.

Loss of control as a non-responsibility condition is a colloquial concept that gains undeserved credibility when it is analogized to "involuntariness" caused by a genuine mechanism or most cases of duress. Nonetheless, is there a residual, commonsense meaning of loss of control that makes sense? Human beings can be subject to strong desires that leave them feeling subjectively unfree and that appear to have coercive motivational force. Indeed, in many cases these desires or urges may be experienced as "ego alien," as if they were being imposed on the agent rather than being part of the agent. It is surely harder to behave well when one has strong desires to do wrong because the prospect of satisfaction is so pleasant, the prospect of frustration is so painful, and the combination of these prospects tends to diminish our ability to be able to bring reason to bear about what we should do. But desires and fears of frustration and related feeling states are once again not physical forces that literally force one' s body to move if they reach sufficient intensity. They work through the agent's practical reason. Indeed, most self control mechanisms that we use to control the untoward effects of our desires are techniques that facilitate the use of reason, prevent us from acting when we act "unthinkingly," or prevent us from being in situations in which we recognize that we act "unthinkingly."

Loss of control as an independent state or condition that undermines responsibility does not gain much support from related scientific or clinical data. Loss of control is not a technical term, but empirical research concerning addictions, impulses, impulsivity, and disorders of impulse control is probably the most relevant to the legal meaning of loss of control. In basic and clinical science, however, there is no consensus about either the conceptual meaning, the definition, or the measurement of these terms (Parker & Bagby, 1997). Some definitions are simply question-begging about the agent's ability to control his or her conduct. For example, the American Psychiatric Association's (APA) diagnostic and statistical manual (DSM IV TR) defines the "essential feature" of an impulse control disorder as, "the failure to resist an impulse, drive or temptation to perform an act that is harmful to the person or to others" (APA, 2000, p. 663). But why does the person fail to resist, and is the reason one that suggests that the person is not responsible for the failure? The DSM IV TR explains further: "...the individual feels an increasing sense of tension or arousal before committing the act and then experiences pleasure, gratification, or relief at the time of committing the act. Following the act there may or may not be regret, self reproach, or guilt" (APA, 2000, p. 663). But does the presence of increasing tension or arousal mean that the agent cannot control himself, and can we validly measure such states and the supposed loss of control?

In this general area of research, good objective measures of the operative terms, such as tension and arousal, often do not exist and thus make valid empirical research impossible. Those measures with some apparent validity often do not correlate. In a crude, commonsense fashion, we can estimate the strength of a desire by observing how much the agent is willing to sacrifice to satisfy it, but this is a far cry from a repeatable, objective measure (Donovan, 1988). Even when the research is good, in the absence of a successful account of "uncontrollability," research cannot tell us whether failure to resist is "controllable" because the research concerns human action and not mechanisms. There have been attempts to measure loss of control directly, but these efforts have been question-begging failures because they circularly include loss of control as one of the criteria for the inability to control oneself (Morse, 2000). This research does not investigate how many "desire units" are necessary mechanically to flip the "action switch."

I am not making the unjustifiably skeptical claim that good research has taught us nothing in the domain of behavioral control. Indeed, we know a great deal about the variables that contribute to what Thomas Schelling memorably describes as the "intimate contest for self command" (Ainslie, 2001; Bandura, 1997; Rachlin, 2000; Schelling, 1984). For example, all things being equal, agents who discount time steeply by preferring immediate to long-term rewards, or who are reward insensitive are more likely to behave wrongly than agents who discount time shallowly or who are reward sensitive. Unfortunately, however, we have no scientific measure of whether, ultimately, an agent can control himself, and rational capacity defects are the variables that in most cases cause an agent to find it difficult to control himself (Hart, 1968). It was precisely for these types of reasons, for example, that during the ferment of insanity defense reform in the early 1980s, the American Psychiatric Association (1983) and the American Bar Association (1984) recommended abolition of the control or volitional prong of the insanity defense.

Quite simply put, we cannot distinguish between an irresistible desire and one simply not resisted. I fully believe addicts when they report that they subjectively feel that their desires are "uncontrollable." Moreover, experiencing some urges as ego alien may seem to increase those urges' coercive motivational salience. Nevertheless, despite the honesty of subjective reports of alleged uncontrollability, we do not know whether this is objectively the case. Such feelings, however honest they may be, cannot substitute for conceptual and empirical demonstration that people cannot control themselves.

The Irrationality Theory of Excuse for Addiction-Related Behavior

A perhaps more plausible basis for excusing the craving addict is a theory of irrationality. Some people with disorders of desire may have an irrationality claim because on occasion the desire becomes so insistent that it substantially compromises the agent's capacity for rational deliberation (Kennett, 2001). Those who work with addicts recognize that when the desire reaches its peak, addicts can often think of nothing else other than their craving, their desire to consume the substance at almost any cost. The strength and salience of the desire make it exceedingly difficult and perhaps impossible for the agent to use ordinary self management techniques, including distracting oneself and employing competing reasons, to avoid the undesirable conduct. Fundamental components of rationality—the capacities to think clearly and self consciously to evaluate one's conduct—are compromised. The agent may not recognize the various options at all or may not be able coherently to weigh and to assess those that are recognized. For moral and legal purposes, the precise mechanisms by which desires can compromise rationality are less important, however, than the clear evidence that they can.[2]

Another argument straightforwardly assimilates such cases to irrationality cases by claiming that some desires are themselves irrational and the agent who suffers from them is therefore irrational. From the radically subjective viewpoint of thinkers from Hume to modern rational choice, it is impossible to give an adequate account of the irrationality of desires. They are just brute "givens" that are not evaluable in terms of rationality. Nozick (1993), claims that we have no adequate theory of the substantive rationality of desires. Some philosophers disagree, but no satisfyingly adequate account has been provided. In any case, the desire to take drugs either to obtain pleasure or to avoid pain seems entirely rational.

Moreover, if the desire is weak, however abnormal it may be, it is difficult to imagine why a weak desire should excuse. In the face of weak desires, we can fairly expect agents to exercise self control if yielding to the desire will cause harm to others or to themselves. Strong desires can of course interfere with our ability to reason well, to bring good reason to bear, but then it is not the content of the desire, but the effect of the desire's strength on cognitive abilities that is doing the excusing work. And from this point of view, there is no reason to distinguish allegedly abnormal from normal desires. Wanting something too much can be an affliction and seem irrational, but once again, it will potentially furnish an excuse only because intense wanting may disable rational capacity.

Diachronous Responsibility

Although I think that the irrationality claim is persuasive in many cases and, alternatively, many are attracted to the internal duress account, neither potential excusing condition implies that addicts cannot be held responsible for addiction-related behavior. Agents can be responsible for placing themselves in a non-responsible state, a form of responsibility that we may term diachronous.[3]

In the quiescent state when the addict is not experiencing intense craving, neither theory of excuse obtains. In that state, compulsion can furnish no plausible ground for an excuse. Even if desires can be compelling, the craving is not motivating the addict at that time. Moreover, addicts in the quiescent state exhibit no defect of rationality. They understand what they are doing, their instrumental rationality is intact, and they understand the moral and legal rules governing conduct associated with addiction. Indeed, in some cases they may fully endorse those rules and addicts often are ambivalent about their habits or even despise themselves for yielding to their desires. Now, as a result of addiction and the addict's life style, some addicts may lead lives that have caused such mental, physical, social, and economic deterioration generally that the addict's general capacity for rationality is virtually always compromised. Such cases exist, but surely they are a minority.

The source of the hard choice or rational disability is typically a characteristic desire the agent experiences. Although the agent's conduct may seem excusable when the desire is intense and creates a threat of dysphoria or disables the agent's rationality, during those periods when the desire is more quiescent and the agent can think straight, the agent will almost always be aware that periods of non-responsibility will arise. Intense desires are seldom one off events that surprise the agent, and both such desires and consequent action can usually be avoided by preparation. If the agent fails to take such steps, then the agent can be held responsible for actions that are excusable at the moment that they occur. For example, an agent threatened with death or bodily harm unless the person commits a crime cannot claim a duress excuse if he or she culpably placed himself or herself in a situation in which the threat would be made (American Law Institute, 1985, Section 2.09). Thus, in most cases, the agent will be held responsible because he or she was capable of taking steps to prevent irrational states or internal compulsion from occurring.

During the quiescent stage, then, addicts have no excusing claim and know or should know that as the craving increases they will suffer from decreasing rationality, decreasing ability to access the reasons not to engage in addiction-associated behavior. Consequently, the moral modeler might fairly argue that the addict has a duty to take steps to bind himself to the mast when his desires are less insistent, especially if the addiction associated behavior is legally forbidden or if the costs are externalized because the behavior harms families, friends, and society more generally.

Implications of Holding Addicts Responsible

The implications for "treatment" of the moral model depend entirely on the context in which treatment will occur. Outside the legal system, this model suggests that blaming the addict, asking the addict to take moral responsibility for his or her behavior, is appropriate and not a case of entirely blaming the victim. Whether it is useful to blame the addict is an empirical question. One may not wish to do so because it may be considered counter therapeutic, slowing the recovery process. But if it were therapeutically indicated, the therapist would be morally justified in treating the addict as responsible.

In the criminal justice system, the moral model's appropriate response depends on the applicable theory of punishment for responsible agents. On a purely retributive theory, the appropriate "treatment" is proportionate blame and punishment. Even if an offender agreed voluntarily to undergo some type of biological or behavioral intervention that would reduce the probability of re-offending to zero, there would be no justification for reducing the offender's condign sentence. If, however, a mixed theory blending retributive and consequential concerns is regnant—as it is today in most American jurisdictions—then interventions that reduce the likelihood of recidivism should sensibly be offered and would reduce the offender's sentence to the lower end of a range that desert might set. Offering interventions under such conditions would probably not be considered coercive because it is an offer and not a threat (McKune v. Lile, 2002). The prisoner is not entitled to receive intervention. An interesting question is whether the state may impose treatment, especially invasive treatments, on non-consenting, competent prisoners. Such treatment might be justified by considerations of specific prevention, but almost certainly this rationale would yield to the prisoner's liberty right to be free of treatments that seek to change thoughts, feelings, and behavior.

Finally, the moral model has no necessary implications for the scope of criminalization of drug-related behavior. Simply because it may not be unfair to hold addicts responsible for such behavior, it does not follow that the State would be wise to prohibit such behavior and to blame and punish those who offend. Strong criticism of American criminal law's drug policies can be mounted on purely consequential grounds, such as the increase in related crime and corruption that necessarily accompanies criminalization, and there are powerful arguments generally for decriminalization (see, Husak,

2002 and MacCoun & Reuter, 2001). On the other hand, it seems clear that alternative responses other than criminal law cannot be fully justified by the objection that addicts are not responsible.

Mixing Medicine and Morals

Under the right conditions and when properly used, the medical and moral models both have attractive features and the potential for abuse. Treating people as sick rather than bad can tend to produce kinder, more understanding treatment. The medical model also is likely to spawn research that might identify the causes of undesirable behaviors and the types of *ex ante* and *ex post* interventions that may reduce the frequency of such behavior. On the other hand, applying the medical model to intentional behavior can lead to unwarranted demeaning of the dignity and personhood of human agents and unwanted parentalistic treatment. Unless carefully used, it may create injustice by treating responsible agents as not responsible. The moral model has the great virtue of treating people as subjects, as people, rather than as objects, and thus endowing them with dignity and respect. Also, if justice demands that people be held responsible, only a moral model can properly do this. On the other hand, moral models can become harshly moralistic or punitive because those who offend morality and the law can be demonized as sinful "others" who deserve whatever harsh treatment they receive. Moreover, their application can blind people to the virtues of more rehabilitative approaches to aberrant behavior.

The medical and moral models need not be inconsistent. Let us assume, quite reasonably, both that addicts, or anyway many of them, are properly characterized as suffering from a disease and that many such offenders are nonetheless morally responsible for their conduct according to some justifiable conception of responsibility. Blame, the expression of condemnation for violation of an expectation by a responsible agent, might be therapeutic even within a purely treatment context. Within the criminal justice system, responsible offenders might be fairly convicted and punished for drug-related offenses, but society might also encourage research and provide various treatment programs to potential offenders and those being punished for their offenses. As Justice Marshall recognized in his opinion in Powell v. Texas (1968), a criminal justice response may be useful in dealing with conduct a disease in part produces.

On the other hand, if addicts as a class are not responsible for their conduct, then blame and punishment would never be warranted, despite the substantial resentment that drug offenses engender. Or, if addiction-associated conduct is not deemed to be the sign of an underlying disorder and no excusing condition is otherwise found, it is possible that an entirely moral response might be appropriate. In that case, no civil commitment would ever be justified to prevent drug-related conduct. But even then, a non-medicalized program of research to identify the causes of and the measures to prevent drug-related conduct would be justifiable if such conduct imposes costs on society.

Conclusion: Powell Revisited

Leroy Powell was capable of not taking the first drink and of stopping drinking if he had sufficient reason to do so, such as going to court. It is undeniable, of course, that not drinking was very hard for Powell under virtually all conditions. But, assuming the wisdom of criminalizing public drunkenness, there seems little reason not to hold Leroy Powell criminally responsible for such behavior. As Powell himself conceded, he knew that once he started drinking there was a risk that he would behave unreasonably boisterously in public. It was his duty at that point to take whatever steps were necessary to prevent this from happening. This may seem to be an unreasonable demand. After all, the cost to him of prevention would be very high, and the cost to society of his public drunkenness is relatively trivial, but society can evidently neither justify nor excuse his public drunkenness. He must bear the cost if he wishes to avoid jail.

The observations concerning the balance of costs between Powell and society do suggest, however, that a purely criminal justice approach seems unwise. It would be far more sensible to provide Powell with decent treatment if that would lower the risk that he and society would have to bear the costs of law enforcement, prosecution, and punishment. Of course, such treatment will not be everywhere available on an equal basis. Let us assume, however, that if society were persuaded of the virtues of the treatment alternative in cases like Powell's, some attempt would be made to provide adequate resources to make this alternative realistic.

On the other hand, the coercive threat of criminal penalties can be a powerful motive for an addict to accept treatment that will lower the risk of recidivism (Satel, 2001). In the United States, for example, drug courts have been used to divert offenders to outpatient treatment rather than prison after they have pled guilty. The drug courts retain powerful leverage over the offender. Treatment retention is higher and recidivism is lower for those in these programs than control subjects. Although there is controversy about these programs, they do suggest the wisdom of retaining a criminal justice option (Harrison et al., 2002).

In short, neither a unitary medical nor moral model is likely to be the best response to the complicated personal and social issues that addiction-related behaviors present.

Stephen J. Morse, J.D., Ph.D., is Ferdinand Wakeman Hubbell Professor of Law and Professor of Psychology and Law in Psychiatry at the University of Pennsylvania. In addition to being a lawyer and psychologist, Morse is a board certified forensic psychologist and was awarded the Distinguished Contribution to Forensic Psychology Award from the American Academy of Forensic Psychology. He has written extensively in the areas of criminal law and mental health law, with particular emphasis on questions of responsibility and control.

References

Ainslie, G. (2001). *Breakdown of Will.* Cambridge, U.K.: Cambridge University Press.

American Bar Association. (1984). *ABA Criminal Justice Mental Health Standards.* Chicago: ABA.

American Law Institute. (1985). *Model Penal Code and Commentaries.* Philadelphia: ALL

American Psychiatric Association Insanity Defense Work Group. (1983). Statement on the insanity defense. *American Journal of Psychiatry 140*: 681-688.

American Psychiatric Association. (2000). *Diagnostic and Statistical Manual of Mental Disorders. 4th ed.* Text Revision; Washington: APA.

Bandura, A. (1997). *Self-Efficacy: The Exercise of Control*. New York: W.H. Freeman and Company.

Donovan, D.M. (1988). Assessment of addictive behaviors: implications of an emerging biopsychosocial model. In: Donovan, Dennis M., Marlatt, G. Alan, eds. *Assessment of Addictive Behaviors*. New York: The Guilford Press, 3-58.

Elster, J. (1999). *Strong Feelings: Emotion, Addiction, and Human Behavior*. Cambridge, MA: MIT Press, 169-179.

Fingarette, H., Hasse, A. (1979). *Mental Disabilities and Criminal Responsibility*. Berkeley, CA: University of California Press.

Harrison, L., Scarpitti, F., Amir, M., Einstein, S. eds. (2002). *Drug Courts: Current Issues and Future Perspectives*. Huntsville, TX: Office of International Criminal Justice.

Hart, H.L.A. (1968). *Punishment and Responsibility*. Oxford: Oxford University Press.

Husak, D. (2002). *Legalize This! The Case for Decriminalizing Drugs*. London: Verso.

Kennett, J. (2001). *Agency and Responsibility: A Common-Sense Moral Psychology*. Oxford: Oxford University Press.

Kutz, C. (2002). Responsibility. In: Coleman, J., and Shapiro, S., eds. *The Oxford Handbook of Jurisprudence & Philosophy of Law*. New York: Oxford University Press, 548-587.

Leshner, A.I. (1997). Addiction is a brain disease, and it matters. *Science 278* (45-47): 45.

MacCoun, R.J., Reuter, P. (2001). *Drug War Heresies: Learning from Other Vices, Times and Places*. Cambridge, UK: Cambridge University Press.

McKune v. Lile. (2002). 536 US. 24.

Moore, M.S. (1993). *Act and Crime: The Philosophy of Action and Its Implications for Criminal Law*. Oxford: Oxford University Press.

Moore, M.S. (1985). Causation and the excuses. *California Law Review 73*: 211-259.

Morse, S.J. (1998). Excusing and the new excuse defenses: a legal and conceptual review. In: Tonry, Michael, ed. *Crime and Justice: A Review of Research*. Vol. 23. Chicago: University of Chicago Press, 329-406.

Morse, S.J. (2000). Hooked on hype: addiction and responsibility. *Law and Philosophy 19*: 3-49.

Morse, S.J. (2002). Uncontrollable urges and irrational people. *Virginia Law Review 88*: 1025-1078.

Nozick, R. (1993). *The Nature of Rationality*. Princeton, NJ: Princeton University Press.

Parker, J.D.A., Bagby, R.M. (1997). Impulsivity in adults: a critical review of measurement approaches. In: Webster, C.D., Jackson, M.A., eds. *Impulsivity: Theory, Assessment, Measurement*. New York: The Guilford Press, 142-157.

Powell v. Texas. (1968).392 U.S. 514.

Rachlin, H. (2000). *The Science of Self-Control.* Cambridge, MA: Harvard University Press.

Robinson v. California. (1962). 370 U.S. 660.

Satel, S.L. (2001). Is drug addiction a brain disease? In: Heyman, Philip B., Brownsberger, William N., eds. *Drug Addiction and Drug Policy: The Struggle to Control Dependence.* Cambridge, MA: Harvard University Press, 118-143.

Schelling, T.C. (1984). *Choice and Consequence: Perspectives of an Errant Economist.* Cambridge, MA: Harvard University Press, 54.

Notes

1. Such episodes are of course not limited to the powerful desire for controlled substances. Consider, for example, the desire of an addicted smoker for nicotine on a long, smoke free flight. Note that questions of responsibility rarely arise in such instances. We take it for granted that the smoker can control his craving for nicotine. Such examples are useful for comparison, however, because there is little reason to believe that the craving for nicotine is always less intense than the craving for controlled substances.
2. For a description of the mechanisms, see Elster, Jon. (1999). *Strong Feelings: Emotion, Addiction, and Human Behavior.* Cambridge, MA: MIT Press, 169 179.
3. I borrow this term from Jeanette Kennett.

2-3 Counselor-Client Relationships and Professional Role Morality

Kylie Williams, M.A. and Dean Cocking, Ph.D.

Abstract

This chapter presents a pluralist conception of the role morality appropriate to professional counseling. The role obligations, sensitivities and territory of human problems relevant to counseling are especially broad in scope and fraught with potential conflicts. The nature and settings of involuntary drug user treatment programs presents special problems for counselor-client relationships. Indeed, for many writers, these problems fatally compromise the moral goods and guiding goals fundamental to counseling. We agree that some key values are often compromised in involuntary settings. We argue, however, that much of the role conflict here is best understood as accommodated within our pluralist conception, rather than reflecting a counseling practice altogether dissociated from its appropriate constitutive goals.

Key Words: counselor, substance misuse, disease model, involuntary treatment, coerced treatment, therapeutic alliance, coercion, involuntary context, ethics, plurality, professional role morality, social control, agency, professional roles, values, harm minimization, involuntary settings, substance user counsellors, diversionary programs, drug courts, needle exchange programs, therapeutic jurisprudence, paternalism, client autonomy, self-determination, confidentiality, discretion, client well-being, trust, confidence and disclosure, therapeutic competence, relapse, voluntary treatment

Introduction

The nature and circumstances of counselor[1]-client relationships present especially difficult challenges for the project of providing a clear, well-demarcated and unambiguous theoretical account of the proper responsibilities, concerns, and sensitivities of the professional counselor. One well-recognized set of reasons for this is provided by the role obligations, legal and otherwise, that counselor's have to their employer—typically, the state—and to the wider interests of others and society. As many writers have discussed (Lowenberg and Dolgoff, 1985; Millstein, 2000; Reamer, 1990; Robinson and Reeser, 2000; Tunney, 2002), these obligations often conflict and prove difficult to reconcile with obligations and concerns that counselors have with respect to their clients' needs and interests.

However, these latter obligations and concerns also present a source of reasons that fuel the difficulties regarding the proper role responsibilities and concerns of counselors, for the appropriate territory of the counselor's concern with respect to their client is often quite global. Unlike most professions, not only are counselors often involved in treating a diverse range of clients, a very broad range of a client's needs, interests, relationships and related histories is often relevant to the counseling context. In other professional-client relations, such as doctor-patient, pedagogical, or lawyer-client relations, the needs and interests of the client relevant to the relationship are typically quite narrow and circumscribed, i.e., (respectively) to the client's physical health or educational or legal interests. In the counseling case however, the counselor will often need to take a much broader account of the person's life. Thus, counselors often need to be concerned not only with a client's physical health, educational, or legal interests, but perhaps with all these as well as issues concerning their clients' familial relationships, personality, social environment, support, and so on.[2]

This broad scope of concerns, along with meeting the requirements from the state and the wider relevant interests of others and society, places counselors at the intersection of human nature and complex social, legal and economic circumstances. In so doing, the professional counseling role seems especially broad in scope and fraught with potential conflicts. Moreover, since simple or straightforward solutions are generally unavailable and problem solving typically involves significant time, negotiation and skill, it is frequently a requirement of this process that some significant rapport and trust develop between counselors and their clients. As a consequence (again, unlike many of their professional counterparts) it would often not be appropriate for counselors to detach or situate themselves at too great a distance from a broad range of significant aspects of their client's lives and circumstances.[3]

In this chapter, we focus on counselor-client relationships that address drug user problems, and in particular on the rise of involuntary drug user treatment contexts and the problems that such environments might be thought to pose for the prospects of successful counselor-client relationships. While we agree with various writers that involuntary settings present special and significant difficulties for such relationships, and we suggest some problems of our own in this regard, we nevertheless reject the view, common to discussions of the ethics of counselor-client relations, that the professional role morality appropriate to counseling is thereby fatally and necessarily compromised in such settings.

Our discussion will proceed as follows. First, since our discussion of counselor-client relationships is cast within the context of involuntary substance treatment programs (primarily court-mandated community and residential programs), we present a brief history of the rise of such programs. In our second and third sections we develop an account of the ethical implications of involuntary contexts, including voluntary treatment participation within closed institutions such as prisons,[4] for counseling-client relationships and for the role morality of professional counseling in general. Here, as mentioned, we agree that involuntary contexts present a range of serious problems for the development of successful therapeutic relationships. In the final section, however, we point also to the significant reasons that can support counselor involvement with clients in involuntary contexts, and we highlight the atypical scope of appropriate counselor concern for their client by reference to a general analysis and account of the role morality of professional-client relationships.

Here, while we agree that certain key values are often compromised in involuntary settings, we aim to show that the atypical sources of complexity and conflict that characterize counseling-client relations can best be accommodated within a pluralist conception of the professional role morality appropriate to counseling. On this pluralist conception, a broad and sometimes conflicting range of client problems, circumstances, and wider obligations are the appropriate territory of the profession.[5] We conclude that much of the conflict typical of counselor-client relationships—especially within involuntary settings—reflects these plural and sometimes conflicting aspects of the role, rather than a counseling practice altogether dissociated from its appropriate constitutive goals.

The rise of court-mandated treatment alternatives

A long-held view in the field of treatment for substance misuse has been that for treatment to be successful individuals must first acknowledge that they have a problem and, second, must want to do something about it, i.e., they must seek treatment voluntarily. The placement and involvement of counselors to deal specifically with clients who have been mandated by the courts to attend treatment programs will therefore immediately seem problematic to many in the field.

The relatively recent emergence of court ordered drug-user treatment programs over the last fifteen or so years has primarily come in response to the explosion in substance misuse, related crime, and recidivism. And given the magnitude of the situation that has emerged, the reluctance on the part of those with substance use problems to voluntarily address their problems has been one of the key rationales supporting mandated or coerced treatment.[6] Research into the area of mandated or coerced treatment supports this contention concerning the reluctance to seek voluntary treatment, with findings from various studies suggesting that less than ten percent of alcohol and other substance abusers enter treatment, and, once in treatment, dropout rates of 30–60 percent are typical (Fagan, 1999; Newcomb, 1992; Polcin and Weisner, 1999).[7]

Legal mandates supporting the involuntary treatment rationale—namely, that many individuals require external pressure to seek and remain in treatment—gain their moral warrant primarily from the doctrine *parens patriae*. On the doctrine of *parens patriae*, sovereign entities such as the state may act as the definitive guardian for the good of those whose interests, capacities, and safety are significantly compromised by mental illness, ill health, age, disability, or substance misuse. For these individuals, paternalistic legal pressure and sanction can provide both the initial force to start them on treatment (Fagan, 1999) and continuing force to maintain the opportunity to engage in therapeutic processes, where they might otherwise resist or rescind before the rehabilitative benefits are secured.

Various writers on the subject of substance misuse and addiction point to three perspectives—medical, legal, and moral—that have historically influenced policy and legal responses to substance misuse. As Fagan (1999) observes, the legal perspective starts with the basic assumption that people are inherently rational and responsible for their own behavior and that, by virtue of this, possess the capacity to exercise freedom of choice and the power to control their own actions. On this view, the legal model represents a moralized account of addiction in which dependencies are seen as the result of human weakness, immorality, and defects of character. In accord with this view, the legal model has exerted considerable influence in terms of state and legislative responses to criminal or anti-social behavior, where punishment, such as incarceration, is thought to presumptively deter and control behavior.

However, with the emergence of a therapeutic or medical approach to substance misuse in the 1960s, legal-moralized accounts of addiction began to give way to the influence of a disease model of addiction and dependency (Fagan, 1999). As a corollary to the influence of the medical model and its reformulation of the nature of addiction, intervention and treatment was premised on the notion of individuals as victims of an illness over which they had little or no control.

The contribution of the disease model, while still subject to debate and controversy, cannot be underestimated for its influence and pre-eminence in shifting the focus away from legalistic and moralized accounts of human deficiency and culpability to a focus on illness, rehabilitation, and public health. Yet despite the ascendancy of the medical model and its focus on etiology, the multivariate and complex causes of substance misuse and addiction have proven difficult to reconcile on a purely biological basis. As a result, concern with the basis of addiction began to shift to the treatment and management of symptoms (Fagan, 1999). In more recent times, the aims of treatment have become much broader than simply seeking a cure (Bloch and Singh, 1994), and a number of models have since emerged to explain addiction and inform treatment modalities. Holistic[8] approaches, for instance, incorporate key features of a range of models including, but not limited to, biological, social, and psychological factors that have been thought to contribute to and sustain substance dependency.

While drug user offenders and issues of drug criminality have traditionally been the domain of the legal system, a combination of factors, including social disadvantage, mental illness, recreational use, increased availability of both licit and illicit substances, and the emphasis on arrest and prosecution have exacted a considerable toll on the ability of the legal system to effectively address and cope with the influx of drug-related cases. Mumola (1999) writes that in the 1997 Survey of Inmates in State and Federal Correctional Facilities (U.S.), over 570,000 of the Nation's prisoners (51 percent) reported the use of alcohol or drugs while committing their offense. Although only a fifth of State prisoners were drug user offenders, 83 percent reported past drug use, and 57 percent were using drugs in the month before their offense, compared to 79 percent and 50 percent, respectively, in 1991. Also, 37 percent of state prisoners were drinking at the time of their offense, up from 32 percent in 1991. Figures among the Federal prisoner population show a sharp increase in reports of substance misuse. Although the proportion of federal prisoners held for drug-related offenses rose from 58 percent in 1991 to 63 percent in 1997, the percentage of all Federal inmates who reported using drugs in the month before the offense rose from 32 percent to 45 percent. A fifth of Federal prisoners reported drinking at the time of their offense in 1997, up from a tenth in 1991.

With courts and correctional facilities frequently encountering recidivist offenders and increased incarceration rates, strategies to reduce drug and alcohol misuse associated with criminal activity were introduced in a variety of guises ranging from diversionary programs through to corrections-based substance user treatment, community initiatives, and, more recently, the advent of drug courts as well as different types of needle exchange programs. The United States has been at the helm of such court-mandated initiatives, concerned to deal with the extensive social, legal, and economic devastation wrought by alcohol, prescription, and illicit substance misuse. In the United States alone, it has been estimated that the annual economic cost of substance misuse to the U.S. economy is over $414 billion. Alcohol and drug misuse are factors in the placement of more than 75 percent of children entering foster care, while at least half of adults arrested for major crimes—including homicide, theft, and assault—tested positive for drugs at the time of their arrest. Among those convicted of violent crimes, approximately half of state prisons inmates and 40 percent of federal prisoners had been drinking or taking drugs at the time of their offence (Substance Abuse, 2001).

In recognition of the strain placed on both the court and jail systems, the first drug court was launched in Florida in 1989.[9] Since then more than 600 drug courts have been established throughout the United States (Nolan, 2003). However, while the advent of drug courts bodes well for the future development and expansion of judicial rehabilitative initiatives, Belenko and Peugh (2005: 279) counsel that although there exist over 1,000 operational drug courts, they only serve approximately 5 percent of the potential offender population and tend to target non-violent offenders. In New York State, the recent enactment of changes to the so-called Rockefeller minimum sentencing laws—first enacted in the 1970s—could be interpreted as a cautious start by legislators to address the very real problem of soaring incarceration rates.[10] Yet with the most recent comprehensive survey finding 36 states had enacted some form of mandatory minimum sentencing for drug offences by 1996 (Bureau of Justice Assistance, 1998), the continued presence of minimum sentencing laws and the popularity of tough law and order campaigns will almost certainly contribute to rising incarceration rates among the drug-involved prison population (Belenko and Peugh, 2005).

While the economic cost of housing such a burgeoning state and federal prison population provides a powerful incentive for the development of new alternatives to incarceration, another influential factor has been the theoretical paradigm of therapeutic jurisprudence itself. As a comparatively new theory, therapeutic jurisprudence is founded on the notion that substantive rules, legal procedures, and the role of the judiciary can either assist or hinder the socio-psychological consequences for individuals involved with the legal system. Although this does not imply that therapeutic concerns assume greater importance than other causes or consequences,[11] it nevertheless highlights the role of the law as a potential therapeutic agent and so supports the idea that it be applied in a therapeutically constructive way. As Scott and Leip (2001) explain, although the theory was applied by legal and academic scholars and originally attached to mental health law, it was later adopted in response to issues of domestic violence, homelessness, and family law. The definition has now evolved into "the use of social science to study the extent to which a legal rule or practice promotes the psychological and physical well being of the people it affects" (Slobogin, 1995:193, cited in Scott and Leip, 2001).

While therapeutic jurisprudence grew out of mental health law, it also cut its teeth on civil commitment, the insanity defense, and incompetency to stand trial, by examining the way in which a system that is designed to help people recover or achieve mental health often backfires, causing results contrary to what is intended (Wexler, 2000). Having now expanded to encompass a range of legal concerns, therapeutic jurisprudence has played an influential role in the development of court-mandated rehabilitative alternatives to sentencing and a host of other initiatives aimed at maximizing the social and psychological well-being of individuals and communities grappling with substance misuse. For instance, offenders in some drug courts now participate in several legal and treatment processes that are collectively aimed at producing positive changes for the offender and hence society (Scott and Leip, 2001).

In Australia, the advent of a therapeutic jurisprudence framework to manage and assess the increasingly complex issues associated with substance misuse—in most cases non-violent heroin users—has gained discretionary and empirical support with some courts choosing to divert heroin users into rehabilitation programs rather than conviction and jail. However, prior to the inception of drug courts, Australia has, since 1985, advanced the principle of harm minimization as the basis of its National Drug Strategy. According to the Australian Institute of Health and Welfare (2003), harm minimization refers to policies and programs designed to reduce drug use-related harm and aims to improve health, social, and economic outcomes for both the community and the individual through a wide range of integrated approaches, including supply reduction, demand reduction, and harm reduction strategies. Some programs, like the C.R.E.D.I.T. (Court Referral Education, Drug Intervention, and Treatment) program in Victoria, offer treatment programs as part of bail conditions.[12] Such initiatives form part of a wider interventionist approach that is increasingly becoming the norm in criminal courts throughout Australia.

Not unlike the United States, the misuse of licit, illicit, and other substances in Australia also exacts a considerable economic and social toll. Collins and Lapsley (2002) in their seminal study of the economic and social cost of drug misuse in Australia have estimated the tangible social costs in the years 1998-1999 to be approximately 18.3 billion or approximately 5.5 percent of GDP. A comprehensive statistical analysis of drug use in Australia conducted by the Australian Institute of Health and Welfare (2003) found that in 2000-01, 83 percent of illicit drug arrests were related to drug consumption rather than provision or sale of drugs, while 10.2 percent or 1,852 of sentenced prisoners were imprisoned for drug-related offenses. Of these, 81 percent were imprisoned for dealing or trafficking drugs. In addition, results based on the 2001 Drug Use Careers of Offenders Survey show that 70 percent of sentenced male prisoners used an illicit drug in the six months prior to their arrest, while 20 percent were dependent on alcohol and 44 percent on an illicit drug (Australian Institute of Health and Welfare [AIHW], 2003). In recognition of the need for alternative judicial approaches to the encroaching "drug problem," Australia's first Drug Court began a three-year trial in NSW, operating out of Parramatta Court, in 1999. Other state jurisdictions such as Victoria, South Australia, Western Australia, Queensland, and the Northern Territory have followed with their own Drug Court trials currently underway.[13]

Counseling within Involuntary Settings—Ethical difficulties

Given the proliferation of judicial and social initiatives concerned with diversionary strategies and rehabilitative incentives, counselors are now frequently recruited to work with a range of involuntary clients who have been mandated or coerced into drug user treatment and rehabilitation programs. Situated in state and judicial services whose mandates are traditionally concerned with justice, the protection of society, and the regulation and monitoring of behavior, it is not uncommon to find counselors working with community-based or residential court-mandated clients, clients of statutory departments, and prisoners ordered to undergo drug user rehabilitation counseling within private and public correctional facilities. Counselors also inevitably work with clients who are coerced informally via ultimatums, pleadings and demands from family or other concerned parties.[14]

In dealing with mandated or involuntary clients, various theorists and practitioners in the field of professional counseling have raised ethical concerns and provided empirical evidence regarding the compromise of the trust and rapport thought essential to counselor/client relations when counselors adopt what may be loosely described as a conflicting or dual role in their work with involuntary clients (Lowenberg and Dolgoff, 1985; Millstein, 2000; Reamer, 1990; Robinson and Reeser, 2000; Tunney, 2002). For many theorists, the dual role represents an uneasy alliance, in which professional values concerned with client self-determination, empowerment, and well-being come into conflict with often rigid institutional and state mandates concerned with safety and justice. Ethical complications and difficulties are thought to arise, in part, from the very nature of the coercive inducements extended toward clients who would otherwise resist rehabilitative opportunities and from tension experienced by workers occupying the dual role of client advocate and state/organization employee.

The literature concerned to examine and analyze the ethical and practical dilemmas posed by the institutional setting is vast. In discussions of institutional treatment for people with substance dependence, much has been written about the disjuncture between the core values informing the helping professions, such as counselors and social workers, and the unease that workers feel as co-opted agents of the state by institutional settings and norms. Conversely, others point to the valuable and worthwhile goals aimed at by the institutional setting and how this, in turn, provides for the appropriate occupational presence of counselors—particularly where the ameliorative objectives are not just concerned with rehabilitation and a restoration of agency, but are also in keeping with broader social objectives concerned with justice, the law, and civic responsibility (Haynes, 1998; McLaughlin, 2002; Sachs & Newdom, 1999; Swenson, 1998; Wakefield, 1988, June & September).

The tension between professional values and institutional policies presents unique and distinctive challenges for the role of the professional counselor, raising a number of relevant normative questions concerned with the dual role of counselors in the involuntary context. For instance, how might a concern to develop and foster a mutual partnership in problem solving be compromised by the involuntary status of clients? How should the rationale for coercion be understood? As an adjunct to traditional criminal justice systems, how might the professional counselor in partnership with the criminal justice system appropriately balance their shared obligations and still uphold substantive professional values such as discretion, confidentiality, and self-determination? How ought the professional role of counselors—appropriately understood to encompass a broad range of interests, skills, expertise, and needs—be accommodated within the institutional setting?

In answering these and other ethical concerns, we turn now to an introduction of the sorts of ethical issues thought distinctive of involuntary settings and the dual role of counselors within such contexts. To do this, we focus upon three substantive professional counseling values—self-determination/autonomy, confidentiality, and discretion. In so doing, we draw out the conflicting and competing nature of the demands thought to compromise these values—and thereby the role of professional counselors—and we provide an overview of the specific sorts of objections leveled against the amalgamation of therapy with justice. In the final section of our discussion, we move toward some resolution of these concerns by showing how our pluralist account of the role morality appropriate to professional counseling can accommodate the central conflicts that drive many of these concerns. Some concerns, we also argue, can be rejected since they rest on misunderstandings, for instance, in regard to the sort of client autonomy that is typically at stake, or the failure to allow for justified forms of paternalism.

Court-mandated involuntary treatment contexts: ethical implications of the dual role

There is a plethora of values and principles to which professional counselors from a range of professional groups, such as social workers, psychologists, and the like, are typically committed. Although some basic differences exist in terms of emphasis and orientation, for the most part, the role of professional counseling is concerned to promote client autonomy by promoting the client's capacities (typically limited or damaged) for self-determination, client well-being, and successful therapeutic relationships or partnerships. For many theorists and practitioners, however, key features of these values can conflict with the goals of criminal justice, where the means of social control such as punishment, regulation of behavior, confinement, and client monitoring are commonplace. In particular, the retributive, paternalistic, and controlling aspects of such forms of treatment are thought especially at odds with the concern to promote the client's capacity for autonomy, and hence at odds with the counselor's fundamental professional responsibility in this regard.

Indeed, Honea-Boles and Griffin (2001) argue that court-mandated coercion of clients into therapy not only violates the fundamental concern of counselors with the client's right to self-determination, but in so doing also violates the codes of ethics of several prominent relevant professional organizations, such as The American Psychological Association, the National Association of Social Workers, and the American Counseling Association. Certainly clients entering treatment in order to avoid a custodial sentence, or to secure their parental rights, or to resist social or family ostracism, often do so at the cost of limiting certain personal freedoms and rights, such as their confidentiality and informed consent. Moreover, limited client autonomy has been shown to bring about a range of other unhelpful factors—such as client resentment, uncooperativeness, self-censure, etc.—that mitigate against an effective counselor-client relationship and thereby compromise the prospects of positive recuperative outcomes within involuntary contexts. More direct challenges to the counseling role presented by the involuntary setting—such as limited discretion and strict adherence to institutional rules—can also have negative implications for client-worker relations and recovery.

The concerns expressed by theorists opposed to the merger of therapeutic services with justice also point to how the involuntary context shifts power away from the client toward the professional as expert. The effects highlighted here are the further exclusion and erosion of client rights and autonomy. Practices such as client monitoring, supervision, infringement, and reporting are seen as inimical to values, such as confidential self-disclosure and respecting informed consent, thought central to the promotion of client autonomy. On this view, where the counselor is perceived as an agent of the state working for the state, as opposed to an agent of change working with clients, then suspicion, distrust, and mendacity can compromise the working relationship. Limitations upon client self-determination and autonomy are also thought exacerbated by the lack of access to alternative treatments and choices, including the choice of counselor, that typically feature in the involuntary setting (Brophy and McDermott, 2003: 87).

The lack of choice, particularly as it extends toward the selection of a counselor, is a significant problem supported by substantial empirical evidence concerning the various factors thought to distinguish a successful therapeutic collaboration. Of particular interest here are the many theorists and practitioners in the field of counseling who now champion the importance of relational approaches that involve reciprocity and a sense of undertaking a joint venture toward success. And this encompasses various therapeutic aims in a range of fields including, but not limited to mental health, drug and alcohol rehabilitation and aged care (Faver, 2004; Ganzer and Ornstein, 2002; Kiehn and Swales online; Sampson, 2003; Spira and Kenemore, 2002; Wellin and Jaffe, 2004). Such theorists contend that professional counselors are "central actors in shaping the character and humanity of care" (Wellin and Jaffe, 2004: 284) and emphasize the development of a therapeutic alliance between the counselor and client as crucial to the recovery or resolution of many psychological troubles.

In a meta-analysis of 24 studies, Horvath and Symonds (1991) found a significant association between the therapeutic alliance and positive outcomes. While in a controlled clinical trial that investigated the relationship between the therapeutic alliance and treatment outcomes for depressed outpatients across a range of psychotherapeutic modalities and clinically managed pharmacotherapy trials, Krupnick, Sotsky, Simmens, Moyer, et al. (1996) found the therapeutic alliance to have a significant effect on positive clinical outcomes for both psychotherapies and for active and placebo pharmacotherapy. Furthermore, an investigation by Horvath and Luborsky (1993: 562) into a range of studies concerned with Rogerian Therapist-Offered Conditions (TOC)—such as regard, empathy, unconditionality and congruence—showed that: "it is the client's perception of the therapist as an empathic individual, rather than actual therapist behavior that yielded the most robust correlation with outcome."

With the empirical evidence pointing toward a strong correlation between the therapeutic alliance and positive outcomes, limitations on the choice of counselor within the involuntary setting may well present a significant stumbling block to the procurement of positive therapeutic outcomes. Although one might *prima facie* think that an acceptable level of therapeutic competence would suffice to provide a professional service to clients, it turns out that such therapeutic competence may not be enough to enable the development of the sort of trust and rapport required to deliver positive therapeutic outcomes. Prochaska and DiClemente (1984) have articulated a basic process concerned with the stages of change typically involved in the therapeutic encounter. In short, while there are different ways to conceptualize progress toward recovery, commonly recognized stages of treatment include:

1. involving a person in a collaborative, trusting relationship (engagement);
2. helping the engaged individual to develop the motivation to become involved in recovery-oriented interventions (persuasion or motivation);
3. helping the motivated individual to acquire skills and supports for managing illness and pursuing goals (active treatment); and
4. helping the person who is in stable remission to develop and use strategies for preventing relapses (relapse prevention).

Such stages of change can be difficult to implement in involuntary settings, particularly those characterized by organizational cultures whose policies and programs significantly limit client autonomy, restrict the normal parameters of professional discretion, and elevate the core regulatory mandate of the institution above other guiding therapeutic values. The first stage of the treatment process—engagement—often involves time, significant negotiation, and reciprocal relations of trust and honesty between the client and worker. As mentioned, empirical data concerned with the evaluation or effectiveness of successful client outcomes strongly suggests that a professional relationship along the lines of a therapeutic alliance between the counselor and client may be pivotal to the procurement of positive therapeutic outcomes. If we take this to be, at the very least, testament to the importance of developing a mutually caring and trusting therapeutic relationship, then where the first stage of recovery is compromised by features of the involuntary context, the procurement of the further stages, which crucially rely on the establishment of a collaborative partnership, will similarly be compromised.

The ethical concerns raised by institutional restrictions upon counselors using discretion or keeping confidentiality[15] also assumes currency primarily because of the disvalue this extends to the development of the therapeutic relationship. Not only might clients self-censure potentially helpful or useful information, restrictions to confidentiality can ignore and exacerbate the nature of addiction where relapse, denial and psychological fragility are common. Many writers and experts on the subject of addiction view relapse as a composite and expected occurrence in the rehabilitative process (Anglin, Hser and Grella, 1997; Grella and Joshi, 1999; Hser, Grella, Chou and Anglin, 1998; MacMaster, 2004). However, strict institutional environments, governed by mandates concerned with legal compliance, client monitoring, and the provision of rehabilitative services, may not be well placed to accommodate flexible approaches to rehabilitation. Subsequently, the sanctions typically attached to relapse, such as custodial sentences, or the removal of one's children into state care, leave little room for failure or the application of professional discretion and may significantly disadvantage clients whose relapse, in other contexts, could well be interpreted as a natural progression toward recovery.

Strict institutional contexts therefore, may inadvertently alter the way client-worker relations are perceived and disrupt the development of trust, confidence, and disclosure. Where clients feel threatened by restrictions to confidentiality and powerless over the way in which their personal information is used, then even seemingly innocuous admissions such as recurring thoughts of drug use, or exasperation at the involuntary context might be minimized or censored by the client in order to avoid increased supervision, breaching on issues of non-compliance, augmentation of confinement, or being labeled as uncooperative.

In this context, restrictions on the proper use and application of professional discretion are perhaps of special significance. Discretion is widely recognized as a defining and crucial value inherent to most professional roles. Our police service for instance, administers and enforces laws, yet has scope for the use of discretion in situations in which laws do not clearly apply, do not apply at all, or, if applied, would cause much greater harm. In setting out some of the concerns brought about by the involuntary context, we provide the following case study as an illustration of how the use of professional discretion can conflict with a range of other interests, and of how all things considered, a too limited or controlled prohibition on its use, can stifle flexible, fluid approaches and damage the therapeutic process.[16]

A teenage student is referred to the school counselor by teachers concerned with the gradual negative change in the student's demeanor and behavior. Although the counselor and student develop a close rapport and the student is able to express a number of concerns and feelings, the student's mental and physical health continues to rapidly decline, and family and mental health experts quickly become involved in the care and support of the student. The normally placid, studious, and gentle demeanor of the student is soon replaced by confusion, disorientation, suicidal ideation, and physical aggression. It soon transpires, via telephone conversation with the student, the student's parents, and the school counselor, that the student has been misusing amphetamines, and using heroin and cannabis for approximately four months. The Adolescent and Child Psychiatrist is informed, and the student is diagnosed as suffering from drug-induced psychosis. While the student is kept home during the acute phase of the illness and initial withdrawal, teaching staff are informed of the student's fragile mental health and given strategies to assist the student upon return to school, i.e., lessened work load, need for quiet time, managing specific behaviors, etc. As the school has a strict and uncompromising drug policy, the student's parents ask the counselor to withhold any information concerning the student's drug taking as they fear, among other concerns, that the student's confidentiality, reputation, recovery and social supports within the school will be compromised if the student is expelled. As the student has not used drugs on school premises, the counselor agrees. Upon the student's return to school, the student appears to be progressing well, reports from teachers and family confirm that the student is making steady progress, and the student continues to visit the school counselor for additional support. The counselor, however, is soon alarmed when the student appears unannounced in the counselor's office and hands over a small quantity of white powder wrapped in foil. The student explains that former drug acquaintances had been waiting at the school gates for the student to arrive, where they offered the student "a freebie." Knowing there are no "freebies," the student feels intimidated and cornered and reluctantly accepts the foil. Feeling anxious and confused, the student carries the small quantity of drugs until early afternoon before deciding to consult the counselor and hand over the drugs.

Ordinarily, the responsibility of the counselor to act in accordance with school policy concerning the possession of drugs on school grounds is to first recognize the situation as a criminal matter. School policy and procedure dictate that the counselor must report the student to the School Principal, who in turn notifies the local police, child statutory authorities, and the student's family. However, this situation presents the counselor with a number of ethical concerns and competing interests. The school counselor knows that the school takes an uncompromising view of illicit substances on school grounds and that the student may well be expelled. Although the school has a policy of due process for students under threat of expulsion, any such hearing concerning the student's future at school will not safeguard the privacy of the student or the student's family. The counselor also recognizes the force of the student's trust and understands that the student has made significant progress toward recovery, and the conspicuous arrival of police along with the student's parents and the sudden absence of the student from class and school would inevitably arouse suspicion and compromise the student's confidentiality. The counselor also knows that the student's mental health and drug rehabilitation rely, in significant part, upon the stability of routine, anonymity of the specific problems, continuing education, and continued association with school friendship groups. Disclosure to the school would significantly compromise or disrupt the student's chance of continuing a stable path to recovery. The counselor also understands the legal obligation to report the drugs to the police and that failure to do so, or destruction of the drugs constitutes a criminal offense. The counselor is not only confronted with the prospect of significant legal sanction and the loss of employment with the school; the counselor also faces disqualification from the relevant regulative and professional body with whom he is registered. In weighing up the various considerations and obligations the counselor decides to put the interests and well-being of the student first. The counselor does not inform the school. Instead, in consultation with the student and the student's parents, the drugs are disposed of and the counselor convenes a meeting with the police and the School Principal to discuss concerns and form strategies to address student safety and drug dealing near the school and to develop specific drug education and awareness programs in accord with the school's health syllabus.

As such cases show, the appropriate use of professional discretion is sometimes what is called for in circumstances in which strict compliance with relevant institutional procedures and laws (both legal and organizational) would have resulted in far greater adverse consequences to the client, such as the student's expulsion from school, the discontinuance of support from the school counselor, social and family stigma, and the loss of significant school friends. In addition to making a judgment regarding the student's best interests from a large range of relevant concerns, the counselor was also attentive to the institutional and broader social concerns at which the regulations of the institution and the law were directed, such as, student safety and drug education. Thus, the case also highlights the breadth and complexity of the professional counseling role and the broad scope of concerns with which the counselor should be rightfully engaged.

In sum, the arguments leveled against involuntary settings are clearly quite compelling and highlight a number of ways in which the moral agency of clients and the development of the sort of trust and rapport essential to successful therapeutic alliances may be compromised. With the literature suggesting that key features of the counseling relationship play a significant role in determining successful rehabilitative outcomes—and in light of the empirical evidence that suggests the long-term success of involuntary treatment is, as yet, indeterminate (Dennis, Scott, Funk, Foss, 2005; Lang and Belenko, 2000; Leukefeld and Timms, 1993)—involuntary contexts clearly provide problematic terrain for the proper deployment of professional counseling practice. Indeed, Shearer claims (2003) that, with respect to court-ordered counseling, the role and practice of psychotherapists working with court-mandated clients is a form of "therapy as punishment." Coercion of clients into treatment, he argues, conflicts with informed consent and thereby fatally undermines treatments that must be made on the basis of informed choice (Herring, 2002 cited in Shearer, 2003, p.10). On this view, the "ethical minefield" (Shearer, 2003) thrown up by the involuntary context cannot be reconciled with the human rights and recuperative interests that are compromised when counselors work with coerced clients.[17]

However, both critics and supporters of the involuntary context can agree that the ethical issues raised by the convergence of a therapeutic framework with state/institutional objectives are complex and potentially inimical to the interests of clients and the professional role of counselors. Moreover, they should also agree on the importance of the focus on problems that call into question the nature and legitimacy of professional counseling within the involuntary context. Nevertheless, while objections leveled toward the merger of therapy with justice have helpfully drawn attention to the sorts of problems thought distinctive of involuntary settings and the dual role of counselors, we think that such objections do not provide a case for excluding professional counselors from the involuntary context altogether. As we go on to argue, we think a too exclusive focus on the objections proffered in regard to involuntary contexts tends to reflect a narrow, incomplete conception of the sorts of values that are at stake and of the nature and range of problems that counselors are rightfully thought to confront and manage.

However, before we go on to set out our pluralist approach to the role of the counselor, we ought to provide some account of concerns specific to prison-mandated treatment as this arena may quite rightly be thought to present distinctive and additionally problematic terrain for the proper deployment of professional counseling practice. Certainly correctional facilities represent a unique challenge to counselors who work with a range of clients in extremely concentrated, punitive and often violent environments. Not only does the correctional context pose a number of distinctive ethical challenges by way of its punitive nature, it can also magnify the range and extent of the sort of problems we have already outlined.

Pendergast et al. (2002: 10) for instance, argue that entering treatment in prison is psychologically and procedurally quite distinct from entering community-based involuntary treatment. They argue that within the prison environment, there is less concern with procedural justice, and prisoners are often ill-informed about the reasons for entering treatment or what the treatment may entail. There are few opportunities to choose other alternatives, and prisoners may lose privileges and preferred living conditions within the prison setting. Some researchers (Moos and Finney, 1995) also point to how the regimented and punitive nature of correctional facilities can inhibit flexible and personalized approaches to treatment.

To this end, Pendergast et al. (2002) claim that it is not clear that findings on coerced treatment within community-based or residential environments can be generalized to prison-based treatment programs. Another difficulty in assessing the specific sorts of problems we might expect from stricter involuntary settings is that although prisons have been concerned to provide treatment options, such options have been largely voluntary, and any assessment of the impact of forced treatment within the prison system has minimal empirical evidence from which we can yet draw conclusions (Prendergast, Farabee, Cartier, Henkin, 2002).

Other factors thought to complicate participation and positive outcome rates among correctional inmates are simply the overwhelming number of inmates with treatment needs. Lang and Belenko (2000: 145) argue that even though the availability of substance-user treatment within the correctional system has always been inadequate relative to need, and the number of inmates in treatment has actually fallen in recent years, a focus on enforcement and punishment has shifted policies away from rehabilitation, with the result that the number of inmates in need of such treatment has continued to climb. While it is difficult to pinpoint with any precision the sorts of problems unique to mandated treatment within correctional facilities,[18] what we can glean from the literature is that the problems for professional counselors appear institutionally systemic, rather than reflective of any incongruity regarding the role and place of counselors within the justice system. What this suggests is that most of the barriers to treatment are associated with scarce resources, law and order policies, burgeoning prison populations, timing of sentences, and pressure to homogenize treatment programs.

Moreover, while the literature on treatment outcomes is fraught with conflicting findings, some results do suggest that voluntary participation in treatment during incarceration may yield a reduction in recidivism, relapse, and criminal behavior—particularly where the therapeutic involvement is focused on continuing care and long-term recovery management (Dennis, Scott, Funk and Foss, 2005; Farabee, Prendergast and Anglin, 1998). In light of the possible benefits associated with treatment, and in light of the range of longitudinal studies that suggest voluntary treatment of substance abuse disorders (in the non-offending population) is associated with significant reductions in substance use, related problems, and costs to society (Dennis, Scott, Funk and Foss, 2005), we can, along with Siddall and Conway (1988) and Allison and Hubbard (1985), cautiously suggest that treatment programs and therapeutic relationships appear to support a range of positive outcomes. Based on these findings, we can extend this analysis further to hypothesize that mandated treatment within correctional institutions may well provide the catalyst for change for a number of treatment resistant individuals. A summary of findings by Farabee et al. (1998, cited in Prendergast et al. 2002: 7), from a range of studies published between 1976 and 1996, appears to support this hypothesis, with the overall evidence suggesting that coerced clients do at least as well as voluntary clients across a broad range of treatment programs.[19] While undoubtedly, many of the sorts of ethical and practical problems outlined earlier in the paper can be found within the correctional system, the evidence does not suggest that counselors working in such environments thereby compromise therapeutic outcomes or their professional integrity altogether. On the contrary, it would appear that despite the significant barriers to their practice, counselors do manage to effect positive change in the lives of many drug dependent inmates.

Let us now turn to some resolution of the sort of concerns we have canvassed by showing how our pluralist account of the role morality appropriate to professional counseling can accommodate the central conflicts that drive many of these concerns. As mentioned earlier, however, we will also argue that some of the concerns we have seen can be rejected.

Professional Roles and Counselor-Client Relationships: A Pluralist Account

It is generally accepted that certain professional roles, such as the role of doctor or lawyer, are largely defined by their constitutive goals and that those goals generate substantive rules governing conduct within the role. These conduct-governing rules have guiding regulative force because an agency governed in this way is thought to serve some important human or moral good embodied in the constitutive goals of the professional role. Thus, the key goods of human health and justice provide the primary constitutive goals for the medical and legal professions respectively and generate substantive conduct-governing rules, such as, in the case of lawyers, that one be a zealous advocate of one's client's legal interests, or, in the case of general practitioners, that one take special interest in the health of one's own patients.

It is also generally recognized that such substantive rules directing one toward preferential treatment of one's own clients or patients can bring one into conflict with other ordinarily accepted moral claims or the legitimate claims of others. Thus the lawyer's zealous advocacy of his client's interests may come at the expense of compassion for the victim of crime, and the doctor's keeping the confidentiality of her own patient may come at some risk to others. Argument over whether or not such preferential treatment of one's clients is justified will, ultimately, turn on whether it can plausibly be claimed to serve the relevant human or moral good in question and whether its service to this good is worth the cost. It is often argued, for instance, that patients need to be able to trust their doctors to act in their interests rather than in the conflicting interests of others, since if patients cannot do so, they will not seek help when they should, or they will not disclose information a doctor needs in order to make an accurate diagnosis and institute appropriate treatment. If such things are true, then they provide powerful reasons in favor of patient confidentiality to justify the costs of other conflicting claims. And as we have seen in the counseling case, the development of some significant forms of trust, including confidentiality-related forms of trust, is widely and rightly thought important to securing positive therapeutic outcomes.

It would not be peculiar to the professional role of counselors, therefore, that they might be properly directed to pay preferential treatment to the interests of their client and to sometimes do so at the expense of some conflicting legitimate claim or demand. One thing we have tried to show as peculiar, however, compared to other professional roles, such as that of the doctor or lawyer, is the breadth and depth of the counseling role, including occasions for preferential treatment of one's client's interests and the potential conflicts that might arise. For, unlike doctor's or lawyers, the prism provided by the constitutive goals of one's professional relations with one's client as their counselor is not limited by such relatively narrow concerns as physical health or legal justice. On the contrary, it is commonplace for the quite global interests of the client as a person to be the proper territory of the professional counselor's concern and interest. Thus, for instance, as we saw in the case of the school counselor and teenage client, the counselor's appropriate interest in the client encompassed an interwoven complex of psychological, educational, familial, social, legal, and drug use-related problems, and properly addressing this complex of concerns came at the expense of certain other obligations, such as strict institutional reporting practices.

Nevertheless, while we think the territory of appropriate concern for one's clients' interests may be atypically broad and deep, and that the fact of conflicts from within the substantive conduct-governing rules appropriate to the counseling role, especially in the involuntary context, is correspondingly atypically problematic, we do not think such conflicts indicate that the counseling role is fatally undermined by the involuntary context. Rather, as with the more traditional professional roles within the medical and legal professions,[20] many of the conflicts within the counseling profession are better understood to result from conflicts from within the substantive conduct-governing rules appropriate to the counseling role. And as such, the real concern, as with other professions, is how such conflicts might best be balanced and how the more extreme of such conflicts might best be avoided so as to not too greatly undermine the pursuit of positive therapeutic outcomes or risk some other high cost, such as significant harm to others.

So, for instance, a client-centered concern with confidentiality does not provide a singular focus for the medical practitioner or have any absolute status regarding how, all things considered, they should be guided. Rather, the value of confidentiality provides one substantive conduct-governing rule to be balanced within a plural and conflicting value system, including, for instance, harm to others. Accordingly, the concern to keep confidentiality might be trumped, say, by the risk to others of deadly infectious disease. Similarly, on this way of theorizing about the role morality appropriate to the professions, the counseling role can also be seen to be largely guided by plural substantive conduct-governing rules,[21] which, in various ways, may conflict.[22]

Indeed, in so far as the appropriate territory of the counselor's role is atypically broad in scope, a corresponding plurality of appropriate conduct-governing rules should be expected. Clearly, for instance, the procurement of positive therapeutic outcomes for one's client is a central guiding goal of counseling. However, especially in the context of clients who are drug offenders and under court-ordered involuntary treatment, the counselor is also rightly guided by concern for others or society more generally. Thus, the counselor will often rightly also be subject to the obligations imposed by, say, fairly strict monitoring and reporting practices.

Such concerns will, in certain cases and circumstances, conflict in various ways with some of those concerns we have already canvassed, such as, providing allowance for relapse, imposing too strict limits on professional discretion, and developing collaborative and trusting relationships. But on a pluralist conception, in which in addition to these concerns the counselor is also rightly concerned to constrain, say, the drug offender's freedoms in various ways (for the good of the client or others), such conflicts are the appropriate territory of the professional counselor's role, rather than evidence of the role as fatally undermined. The real issue is how these plural concerns may be balanced and some of the more damaging conflicts avoided. Thus, as we have mentioned, there is a developing recognition that therapeutic jurisprudence in the form of certain sorts of involuntary treatments will be hopelessly ineffective if it seeks only simple, say medical or punitive, cures. (Much less is this approach concerned only with safety and justice at the expense of the client's prospects for recovery or worthwhile counselor-client relations.) As we set out in section 1, a broader and more in-depth "holistic" approach is being undertaken to achieve more adequate understandings and therefore treatments, in order to promote more effective positive change for the offender-client, such positive changes including, greater participation of offender-clients in the legal and treatment processes and greater focus on psychological, social, and economic factors influencing the use and misuse of licit and illicit substances.

We saw earlier that inconsistencies in expressed professional values and goals have been presented by various writers and thought to result in a dichotomy within the professional counseling role along lines concerned, on the one hand, with the promotion of client autonomy, and, on the other hand, with the so-called social control function of counselors within the involuntary context. On our pluralist account however, while the territory of appropriate concern for one's client is distinctively broad in the counseling case, the dichotomy presented here should be regarded as a false one. Indeed, the key mistake of the alleged dichotomy is that it fails to recognize, much less capture and assimilate, the range of important considerations—again, especially regarding the context of involuntary status—that reflect the breadth of territory in human problems and the wider social interests facing the profession. Support for the involvement of counselors within the involuntary context need not be about social control in any pejorative sense, nor buttress any story of compromised autonomy. Rather, counselors are appropriately guided by related plural concerns with their client's interests and those of others, society, and the state and are especially well-placed to deal with the range of problems brought about by, for instance, impaired functioning and limited autonomy arising from severe and persistent substance use.[23]

As mentioned early in our discussion, one key justification for the involvement of counselors within the involuntary context is provided by the doctrine of *parens patriae*, in which external intervention and assistance by the state may be justified for those who represent a significant harm to themselves or others by virtue of their substance dependency and related failures of rationality or autonomy. Such interventions are, therefore, in many cases, better seen as efforts to rehabilitate and promote autonomy where it has been compromised by mental illness, injury, disease, and/or substance use. Those who argue that such approaches are ruled out by concerns attached to the involuntary context, such as with client autonomy and confidentiality (see, e.g., Shearer, 2003), seem to have too strong or idealized a notion of these values, applying them as inviolable in a given case or across the board to all clients.

In addition to the case from paternalism, a second justification for the therapeutic jurisprudence approach and the involvement of counselors in involuntary contexts is presented by the sheer magnitude of the social, psychological, and legal problems presented by criminal offenders. As set out in section 1, the social and legal costs are now staggering and so, appropriately, the state and legal system is gradually coming to terms with understanding and so better treating offenders suffering such problems. Against those who would exclude the involuntary context altogether from the appropriate domain of counseling, it is important to notice that the social work profession in particular has for some years advocated a unity of purpose to assist in the management of client needs, while attempting to address broader-based social concerns and policies. The basic foundations of generalist practice that utilize both micro and macro knowledge and skills not only allow for the justification of divergent roles and functions, but recognize that this divergence is frequently a necessity if client needs and broader social interests are to be reconciled (Burman, 2004).

One significant contribution from social work theory has been to draw attention to broad, structural features, to highlight how the counselor and client should not be regarded as separate from the socio-economic and political milieu. Rather, counselors and other allied professionals are seen to play a central and significant role in personal, social, and political spheres—including the merger of therapeutic services with justice. Such analyses link individual problems with structural socio-economic and political features, shifting the focus away from "moralized" accounts of individuals as the sole cause or locus of their problems and toward the ways in which social determinants such as class, age, gender, race, poverty, and so on, can contribute to personal problems and difficulties. Fook (1993:21), for instance, in her explication of radical casework provides a succinct analysis of the basic tenets undergirding a broadened, structural approach to counseling and writes:

> *One of the challenges for a radical approach to casework then is to carry the notion of social further than family or other people. A radical approach to casework should focus on socio-economic factors such as class and power interests and associated ideological beliefs in meeting the individual problem. This, of course, entails two chal-*

> *lenges: attaining a broadened focus, and attaining an ability to use this focus in casework practice.*[24]

In locating the role and purpose of professional counseling in such broader contexts, it is inevitable that counselors will begin to look beyond the individual to wider social spheres, not only to determine the nature of certain relationships, e.g., how poverty or disadvantage can contribute to increased risk of substance misuse, but also to determine how counselors can bring to light and challenge broader social concerns that foster personal problems. For instance, counselors frequently navigate and traverse the legal system in their dealings with individuals and groups. How the law impacts on individuals and how individuals can best realize their legal rights is, to a large extent, a necessary requirement for the proper performance of the professional counseling role. With input into the direction of law and social policy, the very nature of the professional role is such that it is situated in a socio-legal context. It would thus be a severely limited and detrimental conception of the counselor's guiding concerns and obligations to imagine, along with various writers, that the involuntary domain is necessarily inappropriate to the counseling role.

Conclusion

Although there are conflicting values or interests within the institutional setting, and many problems presented for proper counselor-client relations and client recovery, these problems should not be thought to dismiss the role of professional counselors within the institutional environment. On the contrary, the much-maligned nature of the institutional setting can provide a range of social goods and opportunities that are specifically in keeping with the aims of the counseling profession. Indeed, some of the core professional principles governing counseling practice can be accommodated within most institutional settings, even where such settings are punitive in orientation.

Thus, even in those institutions strictly concerned with incarceration and retribution, there may be scope for workers to adopt the role of client advocate or lobbyist to protect the restricted interests of clients and challenge institutional culture, without compromising core professional values. It is mistaken to think that the roles of the counselor as an agent of the state and as an agent of change for the client are mutually exclusive. Given the compromised autonomy of many clients due to drug use-related or psychological problems, social disadvantage, and the like, and the counseling roles undertaken to address what has become a social and legal problem of enormous proportions, it is crucial to see that these dual "hats" can and need to be worn together.

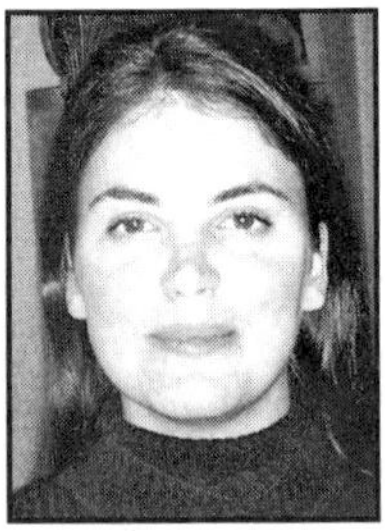

Kylie Williams, MA, is research fellow at the Centre for Applied Philosophy and Public Ethics, Australian National University, Canberra. Educated in Australia, Kylie has a degree in social welfare and has worked as a professional counselor dealing with child, adolescent, and family issues within a range of contexts including the institutional and community sectors. She received her Masters in Social Policy and Planning from Charles Sturt University in New South Wales, Australia, in 2002. Kylie has also taught a range of welfare and social policy subjects at Charles Sturt University, including community policing with the Police Field Education Unit. Over the last two years, she has worked

as a Research Assistant on two projects concerned with the impact of mental illness on identity and agency and is currently undertaking a Bachelor of Arts (honours) in Philosophy through Charles Sturt University. Her current research interests include: welfare and applied ethics and the implications of professional detachment on the therapeutic alliance; an examination of the normative claims attached to mental illness and its relation to identity; the ethics of prostitution and the wider sex industry; and a critical examination of the rise and implication of post-modernist thought within the fields of social work and welfare practice.

Dean Cocking, Ph.D., is senior research fellow at the Centre for Applied Philosophy and Public Ethics, Australian National University, Canberra. He received his Ph.D. from Latrobe University, Melbourne, Australia, in 1996. His current research interests include: the ethics of friendship; professional role morality; and normative understandings of the self.

References

Allison, M. and Hubbard, R.L. (1985). Drug abuse treatment process: A review of the literature. *International Journal of the Addictions, 20*, pp: 1321-1345.

Anglin, M.D., Hser, Y.I., Grella, C.E. (1997). Drug addiction and treatment careers among clients in the Drug Abuse Treatment Outcome Study (DATOS), *Psychology of Addictive Behaviors, 11*, pp: 308-323.

Australian Institute of Health and Welfare (AIHW) (2003). Statistics on drug use in Australia 2002. AIHW cat.no. PHE 43. Canberra: AIHW (Drug Statistics Series no.12).

Belenko, S. and Peugh, J. (2005). Estimating drug treatment needs among state prison inmates. *Drug and Alcohol Dependence, 77*, pp: 269-281.

Brophy, L. and McDermott, F. (2003). What's driving involuntary treatment in the community? The social, policy, legal and ethical context, *Australasian Psychiatry, 11*, Supplement, pp: 84-88.

Bureau of Justice Assistance, (1998). 1996 National Survey of State Sentencing Structures. September 1998. NCJ 169270. [online] http://www.drugstrategies.org/criticalchoices/CC_Ch06.html#_edn67

Collins, D. J. and Lapsley, H. M. (2002). Counting the cost: estimates of the social costs of drug abuse in Australia in 1998-99, National Drug Strategy Monograph Number 49, Canberra DoHA.

Dixon, N. (2001) RBR 3/01 Drug Courts. Research Brief. Publications and Resources, Queensland Parliamentary Library, Parliament House Queensland, pp: 1-23. [online] http://www.parliament.qld.gov.au/Parlib/Publications_pdfs/books/rbr0301nd.pdf

Fagan, R. (1999). The use of required treatment for substance abusers, *Substance Abuse. 20*(4), pp: 249-261.

Farabee, D., Prendergast, M., Anglin, M.D. (1998). The effectiveness of coerced treatment for drug-abusing offenders. *Federal Probation, 62*(1), pp: 3-10.

Faver, C. A. (2004). Relational spirituality and social caregiving. *Social Work, 49*, (2), pp: 241-250.

Fischer, J. (1978). *Effective casework practice*. McGraw-Hill: New York.

Fook, J. (1993). *Radical casework: A theory of practice*. Allen & Unwin: St Leonards.

Freeman, K. (2003). Evaluating Australia's First Drug Court: Research Challenges. Paper presented at the Evaluation in Crime and Justice. Trends and Methods Conference, convened by the Australian Institute of Crime in conjunction with the Australian Bureau of Statistics, Canberra, 24-25 March, 2003. http://www.aic.gov.au/conferences/evaluation/freeman.pdf

Ganzer, C. and Ornstein, E.D. (2002). A sea of trouble: A relational approach to the culturally sensitive treatment of a severely disturbed client. *Clinical Social Work Journal, 30*(2), pp: 127-144.

Goldstein, E.G. (1996). What is clinical social work? Looking back to look ahead. *Clinical Social Work Journal, 24*(1), pp: 89-104.

Grella, C.E. and Joshi, V. (1999). Gender differences in drug treatment careers among clients in the national drug abuse treatment outcome study. *American Journal of Drug and Alcohol Abuse, 25*, pp: 385-406.

Harrison, et al, (2002). *Drug Courts: Current Issues and Future Perspectives*. Office of International Criminal Justice (OICJ), Huntsville, TX.

Haynes, K. (1998). The one hundred year debate: Social reform versus individual treatment. *Social Work, 43*(6), pp: 501-512.

Herring, B. (2002). Ethical guidelines for addiction treatment professionals. *Counselor, 3*(2), pp: 14-19, cited in Robert A. Shearer (2003, p.10).

Hiersteiner, C. and Peterson, K. (1999). Crafting a useable past: The care centered practice narrative in social work, *Affila, 14*(2), pp: 144-161.

Honea-Boles, P. and Griffin, J.E. (2001). The court mandated client. Does limiting confidentiality preclude a therapeutic encounter? *TCA Journal, 29*(2), pp: 149-160.

Horvath, A.O. and Symonds, B.D. (1991). Relation between working alliance and outcome in psychotherapy: A meta-analysis. *Journal of Counseling Psychology, 38*, pp: 139-149.

Hser, Y.I., Grella, C.E., Chou, C.P., and Anglin, M.D. (1998). Relationships between drug treatment careers and outcomes: Findings from the National Drug Abuse Treatment Outcome Study, *Evaluation Review, 22*, pp: 496-519.

Krupnick, J.L., Sotsky, S.M., Simmens, S., Moyer, J., Watkins, J., Elkin, I., Pilkonis, P.A . (1996). The role of the Therapeutic Alliance in Psychotherapy and Pharmacotherapy Outcome: Findings in the National Institute of Mental Health Treatment of Depression Collaborative Research Program. *Journal of Counseling and Clinical Psychology, 64*, (3), pp: 532-539.

Leukefeld, C.G. and Tims, F.R. (1993). Drug abuse treatment in prisons and jails. *Journal of Substance Abuse Treatment, 10*, pp: 77-84.

Lowenberg, F.M. and Dolgoff, R. (1985). *Ethical Decision-making for social work practice (2nd edn.)*. Peacock: Itasca, Ill.

MacMaster, S.A. (2004). Harm reduction: A new perspective on substance abuse services, *Social Work, 49*(3), pp: 356 – 364.

Margolin, L. (1997). *Under the cover of kindness: The invention of social work*. University Press of Virginia: Charlottesville.

Matiation, S. and Jürgens, R. (1998). Legal Issues Relating to Aboriginal People & HIV/AIDS: Discrimination, Jurisdictional Divisions, Testing & Confidentiality (Abstract number 2931) Canadian HIV/AIDS Legal Network, Montréal, Québec, Canada. Poster presentation at the 12th World AIDS Conference, Geneva, 28 June - 3 July 1998.

McLaughlin, A. (2002). Social work's legacy: Irreconcilable differences, *Clinical Social Work Journal, 30*(2), pp: 187-198.

McSweeney, T., Turnbull, P.J. and Hough, M. (2002). Review of criminal justice interventions for drug users in other countries. A paper presented for the National Audit Office. Criminal Policy Research Unit, South Bank University, London. December, pp: 1-8. [online] http://www.nao.org.uk/publications/nao_reports/03-04/0304366_international.pdf

Millstein, K. (2000). Confidentiality in direct social-work practice: Inevitable challenges and ethical dilemmas. *Families in Society, 81*(3), pp: 270-283.

Moos, R.H. and Finney, J.W. (1995). Substance abuse treatment programs and processes: linkages to patient's needs and outcomes, *Journal of Substance Abuse, 7*, pp: 1-8.

Mullaley, B. (1998). *Structural social work: Ideology, theory and practice, (2nd edn.)*. Oxford University Press: Toronto.

Mumola, C.J (1999). Bureau of Justice Statistics Special Report. Substance Abuse and Treatment, State and Federal Prisoners, 1997 [online] http://www.ojp.usdoj.gov/bjs/pub/pdf/satsfp97.pdf

Newcomb, M. (1992). Substance abuse and control in the United States: Ethical and legal issues, *Soc. Sci. Med, 35*(4), pp: 471-479.

Nolan, J.L. Jr. (2003). Reinventing Justice: The American Drug Court Movement. Princeton University Press, Princeton.

Prendergast, M.L., Farabee, D., Cartier, J., Henkin, S. (2002). Involuntary treatment within a prison setting: Impact on psychosocial change during treatment. *Criminal Justice and Behavior, 29*(1), pp: 5-26.

Polcin, D.L. and Weisner, C. (1999). Factors associated with coercion in entering treatment for alcohol problems, *Drug and Alcohol Dependence, 54*, pp: 63 – 68.

Prochaska, J.O. and DiClemente, C.C. (1984). *The trans-theoretical approach: Crossing the traditional boundaries of therapy*. Homewood, IL: Dow-Jones/Irwin.

Reamer, F.G. (1990). *Ethical dilemmas in social service (2nd edn.)*. Colombia University Press: New York.

Robinson, W. and Reeser, L. (2000). *Ethical decision-making in social work*. Allyn and Bacon: Boston.

Sachs, J. and Newdom, F. (1999). *Clinical work and social action: An integrative approach*. Haworth Press: New York.

Sampson, E.E. (2003). Unconditional kindness to strangers: Human sociality and the foundation for an ethical psychology, *Theory and Psychology, 13*(2), pp: 147-175.

Scott, S. and Leip, L.A. (2001). Testing Therapeutic Jurisprudence Theory: An Empirical Assessment of the Drug Court Process, *Western Criminology Review 3*(1), [Online] http://wcr.sonoma.edu/v3n1/senjo.html.

Shearer, R.A. (2003). Court ordered counseling: An ethical minefield for psychotherapists. *Annals of the American Psychotherapy Association, 6*(3), pp: 8-11.

Siddall, J. W. and Conway, G. (1988). Interactional variables associated with retention and success in residential drug treatment. *International Journal of Addictions, 23*, pp: 1241-1254.

Specht, H. and Courtney, M. (1994). *Unfaithful angels: How social work has abandoned its mission*. The Free Press: New York.

Spence Coffey, D. (2003). Connection and autonomy in the case management relationship. *Psychiatric Rehabilitation Journal, 26*(4), pp: 404-412.

Spira, M. and Kenemore, E. (2002). Cancer as a life transition: A relational approach to cancer wellness in women. *Clinical Social Work, 30*(2), pp: 173-186.

Substance Abuse: The Nations Number One Health Problem, Feb. (2001). Prepared by Brandeis University's Schneider Institute for Health Policy, for The Robert Wood Johnson Foundation, Princeton, New Jersey.

Swenson, C. (1998). Clinical social work's contribution to a social justice perspective. *Social Work, 43*(6), pp: 527-537.

The American Probation and Parole Association (APPA) (1996). Substance abuse treatment. Position Statement [online] http://www.appa-net.org/about%20appa/substanc.htm

Tunney, K. J. (2002). Tangled Relationships: Managing Boundary Issues in the Human Services. *International Social Work, 45*(4), pp: 534 (2 pages).

Turnbull, P. J., McSweeney, T., Webster, R., Edmunds, M. and Hough, M. (2000). Drug treatment and testing orders: Final evaluation report, Home Office Research Study, No. 212, London Home Office.

Wakefield, J. C. (1988). Psychotherapy, distributive justice, and social work part 1: Distributive justice as a conceptual framework for social work, *Social Service Review, (June), 62*(2), pp: 187-211.

Wakefield, J.C. (1988). Psychotherapy, distributive justice, and social work part 2: Psychotherapy and the pursuit of justice, *Social Service Review, (September), 62*(3), pp: 353-382.

Wellin, C. and Jaffe, D. (2004). In search of "personal care:" Challenges to identity support in residential care of elders with cognitive illness. *Journal of Aging Studies, 18*, pp: 275-295.

Wexler, D. (2000). Therapeutic jurisprudence: an overview. *Thomas M. Cooley Law Review, 17*, pp: 125-139.

Notes

1. We use the term counselor broadly conceived, to capture the range of occupational interests concerned with therapeutic work with individuals and groups—such as social work, psychology, specialised substance user counselors, nurses, group workers, psychiatrists and other allied professional groups who engage in therapeutic practice.
2. Stan Einstein has suggested to us that this introduces a 'system network approach' where human behaviour is characterized in terms of dimensions that are, among other things, complex, dynamic, multi-dimensional and non-linear. See, e.g., Buscema, M. 'Artificial Neural Systems', *Substance Use and Misuse*, 33 (1-3), (1998). We thank Einstein for his suggestion and references here.
3. We focus directly on the issue of professional detachment and the forms of detachment appropriate (or otherwise) to counsellor-client relations in our 'Professional Detachment and the Therapeutic Alliance' (unpublished paper).

4. We thank John Kleinig for alerting us to the importance of the distinction between treatment within closed institutions, such as prisons, and the types of coercive treatment involved in court ordered attendance to therapeutic programs. Clearly the prison setting itself, along with related security requirements, present special problems, e.g., regarding privacy, access to a range of resources and treatment options, beyond, say, the monitoring and attendance requirements imposed by court ordered treatment programs. Also, 'significant others' such as family and friends may not be able to participate much in the process, even where such participation might be critical. We thank Stan Einstien for putting the latter point to us.
5. We think this quite generally true of the counselling profession since we think it generally true that an especially broad range of problems become implicated in counsellor-client relationships. This allows of course, that sometimes things are simpler and that sometimes things are also complicated by a broad range of problems in other professional relationships, such as the lawyer-client relationship. The case of drug-user counselling we think is clearly one where such complications are commonplace.
6. Of course, irrespective of whether or not the misuse of licit or illicit drugs has increased, "treatment" has primarily increased because we have "medicalized" types of drug users and use. Also, the 'natural recovery' literature has well documented that many drug users have stopped on their own accord without any formal treatment. See, e.g., H.K. Klingemann and L.C. Sobell (eds.) Natural Recovery Research Across Substance Use, *Substance Use and Misuse, 36*: 11, 2001. We thank Stan Einstein for putting both these points to us.
7. We do not mean to suggest here that this shows something deficient in the substance user, rather than, say, the counselor, the program or "significant others". Again, we thank Stan Einstein for suggesting this qualification.
8. The holism we primarily have in mind in this part of our discussion concerns how "drug problems" can be—indeed, typically are—, expressive of a wide set of client problems and issues, including, e.g., medical, psychological and economic problems. The breadth of problems here also raises the question of the drug counselor's expertise to handle such a range of problems. Indeed, often the drug counselor cannot handle such a breadth of issues alone, and so drug treatment is to some extent divided off from other treatments. Another sense of holism also pertinent to our discussion concerns how counseling practise is not just concerned with the individual client but often also with wider social, economic and political issues (especially regarding the counselor's obligations to society and the state and the relevance of broader, social, economic and political understandings to counselors' approaches to their clients and their delivery of appropriate services). We thank John Kleinig for bringing these distinctions to our attention.
9. See, Harrison, et al, *Drug Courts: Current Issues and Future Perspectives*, Office of International Criminal Justice (OICJ), Huntsville, TX, (2002). We thank Stan Einstein for this reference.
10. Belenko and Peugh (2005: 269) report that between 1980 and 2002, the total number of inmates in the United States quadrupled from 501,886 to 2,033,331, with the number of state inmates increasing by 309% to 1,209,640, while Federal prisoner numbers increased by 538% to 151,618 and local jail inmates increased

from 265% to 665,475. The alarming rise in incarceration rates has been attributed to drug related crime and high rates of substance use and dependence.

11. Therapeutic concerns, for instance, need not come at too great an expense of other legal values, such as justice and due process.
12. See, http://www.aic.gov.au/research/drugs/responses/drug_courts.html for an overview of drug court and drug policy initiatives across the various state jurisdictions in Australia.
13. For a comprehensive overview, evaluation and comparison of drug courts and other judicial initiatives in Australia, Great Britain and the United States, see Freeman (2003); McSweeney et al (2002); Turnbull et al (2000); Dixon (2001); Harrison et al (2002).
14. Acts of paternalism typically involve violating a moral principle, usually liberty. Whether one's liberty is justifiably violated or not, i.e., whether it really is in one's best interests that one's liberty is constrained—is an open question. We suggest later in the paper, that confusion resulting from a failure to distinguish between justified and unjustified forms of paternalism seems to have fuelled many of the reservations counsellors and writers have regarding therapeutic treatment in the involuntary setting.
15. These institutional restrictions come in addition to the normal constraints placed on confidentiality, such as where violating confidentiality may avoid significant harm to others or the client.
16. The above incident is based on an actual case. Specific details have been changed to protect the identities of those involved.
17. For a comprehensive account of the various objections regarding the dual focus in professional counseling practice, see, for example, Margolin (1997); Mullaly (1998) and Specht & Courtney (1995). The latter lament the growth of therapy, describing the role of clinical social workers as "secular priests in the church of individual repair" (p.28) and see a tendency in practitioners to foster self-indulgence and radical individualism in an age marked by "meaninglessness" (p.13). Mullaly (1998), on the other hand, sees the current nature of clinical practice as one of control and coercion informed and supported by neo-conservative ideology.
18. At the time of publication, Prendergast, Farabee, Cartier and Henkin (2002: 10) claim that prior to their paper, "Involuntary treatment within a prison setting", that all published studies of prison-based treatment were based on subjects who had volunteered for treatment.
19. Although, as Prendergast et al. (2002) counsel, such results should be interpreted cautiously given the variance in study design, the terminology used to characterise coerced treatment, the interaction of coercion (external pressure) and motivation (internal pressure) and the dearth of studies on coerced prison based treatment.
20. So, e.g., while the medical practitioner's constitutive goal to promote human health may license them a certain degree of partiality toward their own patients, such partiality may conflict with the significant health interests of others and these conflicting considerations would also fall under the ambit of concern provided by their constitutive goal of promoting human health.
21. As we mention earlier in regard to the need to allow for professional discretion, we do not imagine such rules to cover all circumstances. In most professions one will

face difficult circumstances not well accommodated or settled by one's guiding rules (much less by formal regulations governing one's conduct).

22. e leave open whether the plural values and conflicts of which we speak can be accommodated by the particular values of broad-based moral theories such as Kantianism or Consequentialism. For our purposes here, this question is beside the point. For even if they can, these plural values and conflicts remain. They will merely have been accommodated under principles concerned with one's categorical duties or the maximization of good consequences.
23. Again, as indicated by our case of the school counselor and teenage client, a complex of psychological, educational, family, legal, social and drug problems is the appropriate territory of the counselor's concern regarding his client since these may and often do together undermine the client's capacities for reasonable amounts of autonomy and prospects for pursuing a worthwhile life.
24. Fook (1993: 147) also argues that, *"maximising information to clients, and thereby maximising their choices within a restricted situation, can give clients some autonomy. Decreasing self-blame by alerting people to the political and social reasons for certain imposed limitations can also be potentially liberating."*

2-4 Conceptualizing the Professional Relationship in Drug User and Alcohol Misuser Counseling

Elliot D. Cohen, Ph.D.

Abstract

Codes of ethics, statutes, and case law yield basic ethical duties or requirements incumbent upon professionals who counsel drug users and alcohol misusers. However, if these therapists are to counsel effectively, then they must also incorporate more aspirational, person-centered criteria into their counseling practices. Starting with an analysis of the fundamental values that undergird effective therapy and integrating several professional models of relating in healthcare, this chapter builds a viable, eclectic model of the therapist-client relationship.

Key Words: fiduciary model, professional ethics, trust, autonomy, morality of duty, morality of aspiration, technical repair model, contractual model, partnership model, paternalistic model, special purpose friendship, non-consensual disclosure, respect, informed consent, self determinism

Introduction

This chapter develops the framework for an eclectic model of the therapist-client relationship in the context of drug user and alcohol misuser counseling. The emerging model recognizes two integrated levels of relating, first at the level of fulfilling institutional requirements or duties; second, at a more idealistic, aspirational level. The second level is constrained by the first level of institutional duties. Both levels derive from recognizing an intrinsic teleology to counseling practice and the values inherent in it. This internal set of purposive values also sets parameters within which paternalistic intervention can sometimes be justified.

In professional ethics, conceptual models of the professional-client relationship can have implications for practice and the ability of professionals to provide efficient services to their clients. These models help to guide practice by setting broad therapeutic values and goals. For example, helping professions such as law and health care (including both mental health and medicine) have sometimes been conceived according to a fiduciary model, which takes trust as a fundamental value guiding practice. According to this model, because professionals possess knowledge and skills that clients lack, clients must trust professionals to apply their expertise in a manner conducive to clients' interests. Accordingly, a fiduciary model stresses other values that are conducive to trust such as honesty, candor, loyalty, competence, and fairness.[1] As will become evident, the eclectic model developed here includes a fiduciary component.

Conceptual models of the professional-client relationship need to be distinguished from conceptual models that attempt to describe the status of clients themselves. For example, in recent years, drug addicts and alcoholics have been viewed according to a disease model.[2] One alternative model has conceived "heavy drinking" as a "central activity" rather than as a disease,[3] and, historically, prior constructs have viewed such activities as moral transgressions. These models can have profound implications for treatment. If people with drug and alcohol use habits are ill, they may be justly "medicated" or treated for an underlying "pathology." If instead they have devoted themselves to a destructive activity, then therapy can help them to embrace a more constructive central activity. On the other hand, if they are guilty of a moral transgression, then they may be justly punished rather than treated.

Treatment models must also be distinguished from models of the professional-client relationship. A prominent treatment model is that of Alcoholics Anonymous (AA) and Narcotics Anonymous (NA). AA and NA are based on mutual help: addicts help other addicts, though this does not involve a professional-client relationship.[4] On the other hand, though professional treatment models typically include AA or NA support groups within their therapeutic regime, they also utilize treatment modalities that are commonly used in other areas of counseling practice, such as cognitive-behavior therapy, learning theory, and aversive conditioning.[5]

Models of the professional-client relationship cut across various treatment modalities and are based on more general ethical concepts, in particular, alternative definitions of what it means to be moral. There are two such definitions that under gird alternative models of the professional-client relationship. A discussion of each follows.

The Moralities of Duty and Aspiration

The concept of being "moral" (or "ethical") is equivocal. On the one hand, it can signify acting dutifully, that is, doing what is required within a prevailing culture. This sense of acting morally has been called the morality of duty. On the other hand, it can signify going beyond what is merely required, seeking excellence in relating to others. This sense has been called the morality of aspiration.[6]

The morality of duty speaks in concrete, well definable terms; it is subject to legal enforcement, and it typically prescribes what not to do. For example, the duties not to steal, kill, or commit adultery fit this characterization.

In contrast, the morality of aspiration is more idealistic and abstract in character and speaks in affirmative terms about what one ought to do rather than about what one must not do. For example, it is desirable to be brave, temperate, honest, and friendly, but no one is fined or imprisoned just for failing to be any of these. While these "virtues" are not expected of a person as a matter of course, one may, indeed, be praised for attaining them.

The distinction between the morality of duty and that of aspiration also applies within professional cultures. For example, in the counseling profession, codes of ethics typically forbid a therapist from having sex with clients.[7] Therapists who violate this professional duty may not only incur sanctions such as having their licenses revoked, they may also be subject to fines or imprisonment;[8] but, of course, no one would praise counselors for abstaining from having sex with their clients.

Similarly, in the legal profession, a lawyer who coaches a client to commit perjury may be disbarred and is subject to criminal prosecution for subornation of justice. In contrast, in the prevailing culture, lawyers are encouraged to—they ought to—provide pro bono legal service to indigent clients and to donate time and professional expertise to charitable causes, but these are not generally regarded as duties, and they are not typically held in breach of professional duty for failure to do so.[9]

The relationship between professionals and their clients, and more specifically, between health care professionals (including drug use and alcohol misuse counselors) and their clients, can be alternatively conceptualized depending on whether the relationship is construed in terms of the morality of duty or the morality of aspiration. This distinction is itself imbedded in specific models of professional relating. What follows is a brief discussion of some relevant versions of such models in health care.

Models of Relating in Health Care

According to one duty-based model, the health care relationship can be narrowly construed in terms of qualified delivery of a technical service, much as a consumer with a leaky drain seeks out the technical assistance of a competent, licensed plumber.[10] While health care clearly does involve the application of technical expertise, a model purely in these terms unduly depersonalizes the relationship by relegating the person seeking health care to some inanimate property of the person (like a kitchen sink) in need of "repair."[11]

Another model conceives the relationship in terms of a contract between the seeker of health care and a health care provider. Such a model emphasizes the need for a contractual understanding in order to keep both parties "honest," since mutual trust outside of a legally enforceable contract is not a realistic possibility.[12] Each therefore has duties or obligations (binding professional and legal requirements) to the other arising out of this contract. For example, the health care provider has a duty to provide competent services for a fee, and the health care seeker must accept the fee as part of the contractual understanding. As such, this model conceives of health care relationships as falling primarily within the scope of a morality of duty.

Another model conceives the relationship in terms of a partnership. On this model the health care seeker works collaboratively with the health care provider in attaining a common goal of improved health. Although each is deemed to have distinctive competencies (the health care seeker is not presumed to have the medical knowledge held by the provider), the two partners are equal insofar as each must respect the autonomy and dignity of the other.[13]

In contrast to a contractual model, the partnership model emphasizes the cultivation of mutual trust and autonomy. On this model, the health care provider does not have a special knowledge of what is in the best interest of the health care seeker, who remains free to interpret the value dimensions (although not the technical aspects) of health care according to his particular values.

The partnership model of relating in health care fits the morality of aspiration. In contrast to the contractual model, which defines morality in terms of basic, enforceable requirements, the partnership model provides a model of excellence (of what we ought to strive for) in health care. For example, in the counseling relationship, a therapist who takes a paternalistic approach to treatment, who is generally closed to clients' collaborative efforts in setting counseling goals, and who does not value mutual trust, can be criticized for not performing as he should, and for being a poor therapist; but he would not typically be held for breach of duty or incur legal sanctions simply for such failings.

According to one further model, the professional relationship emerges as a kind of "special purpose friendship" according to which, as in a medical context, "the patient expresses trust and confidence in the physician while the doctor's friendship for the patient should consist above all in a desire to give effective technical help—benevolence conceived and realized in technical terms."[14] Although this model embodies moral aspirations of trust and confidence, it does so unilaterally, in contrast to a partnership, which stresses mutuality. Further, "special purpose" friendship models unilateral benevolence (in the form of provision of competent service) but does not embody the element of mutual respect for autonomy, that is an essential feature of a partnership and, indeed, of friendship in its ordinary sense. Further, a bond of friendship typically signifies a stronger psychological bond, a form of connectedness not signified by a partnership.

According to still another model, the health care seeker is conceived in terms of a child or at best an adolescent who must be "taken care of" by the health care provider who "knows best" what is good for the latter.[15] This paternalistic model has little room for respect for the autonomy of the health care seeker, and trust is unilateral. As in a "special purpose" friendship, the health care seeker must trust that the health care provider will use his technical expertise to do the right thing for the health care seeker.

In mental health, none of the above models are per se adequate, although each captures some essential aspect of the therapeutic relationship. The concept proposed in this chapter starts with the premise that mental health counseling, and in particular, addictions counseling, is an institutional practice with an "intrinsic teleology" that dictates the terms of this relationship. Thus, instead of applying a model from outside the practice, the goal is to construct an eclectic model that grows out of the very nature of therapy.[16]

The Inherent Values of Therapy

Clients enter therapy for a multitude of reasons, including alleviation of anxiety, depression, guilt, inability to cope, dysfunctional relationships, drug and alcohol addictions, and codependency. The central purpose of therapy is, in turn, to assist clients to relieve their psychological pain and suffering, and to attain greater and more permanent and meaningful modes of pleasure and adaptation to life situations. In broad utilitarian terms, it is to promote client welfare.

Insofar as clients live in the world, not apart from it, they also bear relations to others. These relationships include family, friends, and other third parties, and diverse social institutions including mental health agencies and insurance companies. The teleology of therapy therefore looms wider than treatment of the individual client. Indeed, as announced in Tarasoff, a therapist has a legal duty of due care extending not just to the client per se but also to third parties who might be endangered by the client's behavior.[17] Insofar as therapists collectively promote the welfare of clients and safeguard the welfare of others in the process, therapy has, within its purview, the broad utilitarian mission of promoting social welfare.[18]

It is in this social context that the ethical parameters of the therapist-client relationship must be considered. The case of counseling clients who have drug and alcohol addictions is no exception, and while there are idiosyncratic features of this client population and its counseling institutions and treatment approaches that need to be accommodated, there are also certain common treatment values arising out of the inherent utilitarian counseling mission that help to define the therapist-client relationship.

Two central values vital to this mission are cultivation of client trust and facilitation of client autonomy.[19] A client's reposing of trust in the therapist is vital to successful treatment because otherwise clients are not likely to make pertinent disclosures and to cooperate openly in the therapeutic process. Regardless of which therapeutic modality is employed (from cognitive behavioral to affective approaches), without this reposed trust, the probability of successful treatment is immensely diminished.[20]

Second, and related, clients who feel disempowered and non-autonomous are not likely to make constructive changes in their lives. Clients who have alcohol and drug addictions particularly confront such disempowerment insofar as they have "lost the power of choice in drink."[21] The subscription to a higher power in AA is itself a tool aimed at trying to regain such self-determination.

These two values of trust and autonomy are interfacing, and mutually supportive. The therapist who attains her client's trust creates an environment in which the client can feel safe enough to cooperate in therapy, make pertinent disclosures, and make behavioral changes. A therapist who treats clients with the respect and dignity of a self-determining agent, instead of creating dependencies and disempowering them, thereby creates a therapeutic climate under which clients are likely to repose greater trust, which, in turn, sets the stage for further constructive change.

Accordingly, the therapist-client relationship must, to be viable, embody those conditions that facilitate trust and client autonomy. Without such conditions, the relationship will be ill equipped to promote the central, utilitarian objective of the therapeutic mission.

Counseling Persons

The ethical tradition based on the theory of Immanuel Kant addresses fundamental issues of respect for client autonomy and trust in the form of the "categorical imperative" to treat persons as "ends in themselves" instead of as "mere means" and to make "universal law" of one's motives for action. According to this major ethical tradition, persons are rational, self-determining agents and must not be treated as mere objects. Whereas agents are centers of intrinsic worth and command unconditional respect, objects have only instrumental worth—value conditioned upon the particular uses others might have for them. And though a rational person could consistently will a universal law to discard a mere object, say, an old hat, after it is no longer useful, rational persons could not consistently will to treat persons like old hats, since they themselves would not will to be so treated.[22]

This Kantian respect for rational autonomy implies active participation of clients in the therapeutic process and to this extent embodies a partnership model. The counselee cannot be viewed as a mere consumer purchasing a product since therapy portends a joint venture between counselor and counselee. The latter, unlike mere product consumers, are themselves part of the process. Therapy, unlike the enlistment of a plumber to repair a leaky faucet, arises out of an interdependent, collaborative journey. Nor is this relationship best construed in terms of patient, which implies passivity. Counselees are not simply patients paternalistically maneuvered and treated by the therapist as though their participation could be detached from the process without dismantling it.

Counselees may well be construed as therapy partners insofar as this term assumes active agency rather than passivity or disengagement. The more ubiquitous general term client is also satisfactory since it does not exclude and in some contexts even requires active engagement. For example, in the lawyer-client relationship, clients are presumed to retain "the ultimate authority to determine the purposes to be served by legal representation, within the limits imposed by law and the lawyer's professional obligations."[23]

True, bio-genetic factors posited to lead to drug addiction raise questions about the acceptability of a model that emphasizes Kantian respect for rational autonomy. But even if it is assumed that drug addiction is a disease,[24] it still does not follow that the individual "suffering from" this disease is non-autonomous. Unless the addicted individual acknowledges the problem instead of denying it, and accordingly exercises the willpower and discrimination to make suitable behavioral, cognitive, and emotional changes, the prospect for recovering is dismal. To charge that such an individual has little or no autonomy in bringing about such life changes is self-defeating insofar as successful therapy assumes the individual's capacity for making such changes in the first place.[25] Insofar as a therapeutic approach empowers addicted individuals to make such changes, it portends viable therapy. Insofar as an approach recognizes and treats such individuals as therapy partners, as clients but not as passive recipients, it empowers them to make these changes.

Confidentiality and Informed Consent as Conditions of Ethical Therapy

Practices involving the deception of clients, even if done for therapeutic purposes, can violate the stated Kantian injunctions. One form of deception that clearly militates against promotion of therapist-client trust is nonconsensual disclosure of client information reposed in confidence. Clients who entrust their therapists with their deepest secrets only to have this trust betrayed are thereby treated as mere objects manipulated. Indeed, no rational agent would will such betrayal to be universal law, as no rational agent would want herself to be so treated. Respect for client confidentiality accordingly emerges as a necessary condition of ethical therapy.

The potential for violation of confidentiality is compounded when, as is often the case in drug user and alcohol misuser counseling, therapy occurs in a group setting. In such a case, the therapist has a compelling duty to make clear the importance of confidentiality among group members as well as between therapist and client. Without assurance of such a bond of confidentiality, it is doubtful that many clients would venture to make profoundly personal disclosures.

Kant speaks of a "community of ends" in which each of us is connected to others by virtue of our rational, autonomous nature.[26] The group setting can be empowering inasmuch as it provides the occasion for each member of the group to participate in a "community of ends" in which each group member is tied to the next by a bond of respect for their rational dignity, which includes respect for privacy. Indeed, even if just one group member could not be counted on to keep this trust, no group member could feel safe to disclose, and the potential for meaningful and successful therapy would thereby be jeopardized. With the substantial emphasis in drug and misuser counseling on support groups, and given the extreme loss of control stemming from drug or alcohol addiction, group counseling provides a useful means for clients to regain some of their rational autonomy as members of a therapeutic community of ends. Therapists who counsel in groups must therefore convey this rationale and importance of confidentiality as a group responsibility, and model a firm commitment to it.

Inasmuch as therapists' duty to protect extends to vulnerable third parties whose welfare may be endangered by clients' actions, therapists' duty of confidentiality may sometimes conflict with the duty toward such endangered individuals. One context in which such conflict may occur is that in which an HIV seropositive client is sexually active with an identifiable sex partner who is unaware of the client's HIV seropositivity.[27] Given the high rate of HIV in clients who are or have been intravenous drug users, this problem may be of special concern to counselors who work substantially with this client population.

The American Counseling Association has explicitly addressed this problem, and has provided the following permissive disclosure rule:

> *Contagious, Fatal Diseases. A counselor who receives information confirming that a client has a disease commonly known to be both communicable and fatal is justified in disclosing information to an identifiable third party, who by his or her relationship with the client is at a high risk of contracting the disease. Prior to making a disclosure the counselor should ascertain that the client has not already informed the third party about his or her disease and that the client is not intending to inform the third party in the immediate future. (See B.1.c and B.1.f)*[28]

Currently, addiction counseling codes of ethics provide no explicit guidance regarding the ethical disposition of contagious, fatal diseases. The above-cited ACA rule may therefore provide some constructive guidance in helping addictions counselors confront this moral quandary.[29]

Such an exception to confidentiality need not transgress Kantian respect. Confidentiality need not be "absolute" to respect clients as rational, self-determining agents—as "ends in themselves." As noted by other contributors to this volume, codes of counseling ethics generally provide for disclosure of confidential information to the extent necessary to prevent clear and imminent danger to the client or other.[30] But such disclosure need not violate respect for client self-determination if the client is adequately informed upon inception of therapy that this exception exists. It is the failure to adequately apprise clients of such exceptions to confidentiality on inception of therapy that treats clients as objects manipulated and is an ethical violation.

Especially in the case of drug user counseling, where there is increased risk of encountering sexually active, HIV seropositive clients, therapists may explicitly mention as a possible exception to confidentiality, the danger posed to the sex partners of such clients. Thereby, in the event that a therapist decides to disclose confidential information to the extent necessary to protect the endangered, identifiable sex partner, the client will have already been informed of the possible exception before confiding in the therapist. In this manner, the therapist will have respected the client's self-determination as much as reasonably possible in this difficult situation. Further, prior to disclosure, the therapist should apprise the client of the intent to disclose. In this way, the therapist will have given the client an opportunity to make the disclosure himself without usurping his autonomy. Indeed, respect for the dignity of the client as a rational, self-determining agent militates against the therapist's disclosure to the endangered third party without such prior notification.[31]

Involuntary Treatment of Incompetent Clients

Obtaining clients' informed consent to treatment respects their inherent dignity as rational, self-determining agents only if they have, in the first place, the capacity for rational judgment. If a client who poses imminent danger to self or others is involuntarily committed or detained, no ethical breach of this Kantian standard of respect need occur. For example, involuntary commitment of an intoxicated individual to "dry out" need not in itself constitute an ethical breach since the individual lacks the requisite cognitive capacity for informed consent.[32] Such a paternalistic measure can be justified in relation to the broad utilitarian mission of therapy (to safeguard client welfare) without Kantian transgression of respect for client autonomy—insofar as no such capacity exists to be transgressed.[33]

This is in contrast to involuntary, paternalistic measures that restrict the liberty of clients who do, in fact, possess the requisite rational capacity for consent. There is both legal and moral justification for permitting a competent client to engage in behavior that is contrary to the client's welfare. For example, courts have recognized the right of a competent, adult Jehovah's Witness to refuse a life-saving drug transfusion, while they have refused to recognize the authority of the adult Witness to decide against such life-saving measures for their minor (incompetent) children.[34]

While no hard and fast line can be drawn between judgment that is competent and that which is not, the case of an alcohol or drug impaired individual who lacks the ordinary capacity for self-protective judgment is not debatable. The cocaine addict who is suffering from paranoid ideation and the alcoholic who has delirium tremens or is publicly intoxicated on a busy city street is beyond the pale of respect for self-determination and can be paternalistically restricted without ethical breach of due Kantian respect, but only so long as this state of incompetence persists.

Such limiting cases to the standard of respect for self-determination should not be over-generalized and applied to treatment of alcoholics and drug-addicted clients simply because they are alcoholic or drug addicted. Within the said broad parameters of client welfare, treatment programs cannot transgress Kantian respect for informed consent without defeating their very mission of client welfare. In this sense, such respect must remain an inviolable aspect of the therapist-client relationship.

Unconditional Positive Regard, Congruence, and Empathetic Understanding as Further Conditions of Ethical Therapy

Treating clients with the dignity of "ends in themselves" requires what psychologist Carl Rogers called "unconditional positive regard," that is, an unconditional, warm, caring, nonjudgmental acceptance of the person of the client. This is not to be confused with avoidance of constructive criticism of clients' misdeeds, however. For example, the Alcoholics Anonymous (AA) twelve-step treatment program requires that clients honestly admit to themselves what they have done wrong, and attempt to rectify these wrongs in action.[36] Here, though, the emphasis is on making behavioral change, not on denigration of entire selves. Similarly, cognitive-behavioral treatment approaches to alcohol and drug addictions such as Rational-Emotive Behavior Therapy (REBT) prescribe as a rational standard, the avoidance of globally damning self-assessments, and target instead making lasting behavioral changes.[37] Insofar as totally worthless beings are incapable of taking such positive steps in the first place, imputations of total worthlessness (for example, "I am a rotten person") are self-defeating from the standpoint of therapy.

Regardless of the therapeutic modality employed, in respecting client dignity through unconditional positive regard, therapists foster a non-threatening, trustful environment in which clients can feel free to explore and work through their life issues. Given that therapy aims at increasing clients' control over their addictions and over their lives, to the extent that unconditional positive regard portends such a supportive environment, it also emerges as a vital condition of therapeutic progress.

Clients are not likely to trust their therapists if they are perceived as disingenuous, or "phony." On the contrary, the more congruent the therapist is, that is, the more genuine she is, putting on no professional or personal façade, the more likely it is that the client will, herself, become more open and candid.[38]

In drug user and misuser counseling, it is often the case that therapists are themselves recovering drug addicts or alcoholics. Unlike non-drug addicts and non- alcoholics, these therapists can relate to their clients through self-disclosure about common experiences directly related to their drug and alcohol use-related problems. This can enhance the perception of therapists' authenticity for this specific client population. Further, given this shared experiential base, therapists' capacity to empathize with clients' circumstances can be enhanced, further facilitating client trust and self-disclosure.[39]

On the other hand, given this intimacy between therapist and client, there is also increased risk that therapists in recovery will counter-transfer. Since such loss of professional objectivity and distance can have detrimental effects on client welfare, the recovering status of drug user and alcohol misuser counselors can also be a handicap if not cautiously approached.

The most straightforward manner to address this problem is for the therapist to refer the client to another therapist if she believes that loss of objectivity due to counter-transference threatens client welfare. Depending on the nature and extent of the counter-transference, another possibility is for the therapist to seek supervision from another therapist who is capable of maintaining professional distance. In this case, Kantian respect for client self-determination would require that the therapist inform the client of her intent to seek supervision due to counter-transference. The client is entitled to all information necessary to give informed consent to therapy, which includes such information having potential bearing on client welfare.[40] So informed, the client would be free to decide whether she wishes to continue in counseling with the therapist under supervision, or seek counseling from a different therapist.

Dual Role Relationships, Non-Maleficence, and Due Care

It is a standard of counseling practice that therapists "avoid dual role relationships with clients that could impair their professional judgment or increase the risk of harm to clients."[41] However, insofar as drug user and alcohol misuser therapists are "recovering," they may find themselves attending the same AA meetings as their clients, and this has potential to impair the objectivity of both client and therapist. Since the therapist is seen to be struggling with problems similar to those for which the client seeks therapy, the therapist may lose credibility as a competent service provider in the eyes of the client. Conversely, the therapist may find it difficult to separate his role as group member from his role as therapist.

In such cases, recovering therapists may attempt to avoid this problematic dual role relationship by attending groups comprising other therapists. However, this may similarly affect objectivity in relating to these colleagues—for example, in providing referrals, and in seeking consultation with them.

Another possibility is to discuss this problem with clients upon inception and to make therapy provisional on the avoidance of membership in the same AA support group. The therapist can inform the client of the problematic nature of such a dual role relationship thereby providing her with informed consent. As the problematic dual role relationship can arise non-electively, that is, as a result of the client's (not the therapist's) decision to enter the same group, this approach has the virtue of preempting in advance the uncomfortable situation of having to deal with the problem later.[42] The client is accordingly given adequate forewarning and can make an informed judgment about whether to accept these terms or to seek therapy with another therapist such as one who is not himself recovering. This treats the client as a rational, self-determining agent and is therefore in concert with the Kantian standard.[43]

Since this approach avoids potential for significant harm, it may arguably be taken as a standard of due care for drug user and alcohol misuser counselors who themselves attend group meetings as part of their own process of recovering. This approach satisfies the standard of practice forbidding a counselor from engaging in activities that "seek to meet the counselor's personal needs at the expense of a client."[44] At the same time, it satisfies the requirement that the client be informed of "limitations that may affect the relationship at or before the time that the counseling relationship is entered."[45]

Conceptualizing the Therapist-Client Relationship

The model of the therapist-client relationship in drug user and misuser counseling that emerges from the above considerations incorporates (nonexclusively) aspects of contractual, partnership, friendship, and paternalistic models of health care. Given the primacy of the therapeutic goal of promotion of client welfare (as qualified herein) and its connection to cultivating mutual trust and facilitation of client autonomy, the emergent eclectic model is defensible on the basis of an "intrinsic teleology" that dictates its key terms.

On this mixed approach, the therapist who agrees to treat a client incurs a duty of due care to the client, which includes providing competent therapy without compromising client welfare. Due care here includes therapists' avoidance of meeting personal needs through provision of therapy at the expense of clients' needs. An instance of the latter is the duty to avoid membership in the same support group as one's client. The therapist also incurs a duty to obtain informed consent from the client at the inception of treatment. This includes, among other things, apprising the client of the import and limits of confidentiality. In discharging this duty, the therapist should, for example, inform the client of the duty to disclose in cases of imminent harm to self or other, including, in some instances, harm arising from fatal, contagious diseases such as

AIDS. In group counseling, the therapist has a duty of due care to make sure that all participants in the group understand the significance of confidentiality as a condition of therapy and of the need to preserve it. To this extent, the relationship is contractual in character and belongs to the morality of duty: it can be described in the language of institutional duties or requirements, and is definable in terms that carry legal as well as ethical significance. A therapist who breaches the relationship at this level may be taken to account for malpractice.

However, insofar as therapists and clients have mutual responsibilities to treat each other as rational, self-determining persons, and to build their relationship on a firm foundation of mutual trust, they are therapy partners, each working collaboratively and respectfully in their respective roles toward client recovery. Here the relationship goes beyond the standard protocol of duties and speaks instead in the more abstract moral terms of personal aspiration—responsibility, freedom, personhood, and trust—rather than purely in terms of requirement.

Unconditional positive regard, empathy, and congruence solidify this bond between these two partners, and mutual experiences with drug or alcohol addiction and sharing in the same personal goal of recovering, create an even more intimate solidarity that sounds more like friendship. At this level, the discourse is in terms of personality attributes, attitudes, and virtues—genuineness, honesty, connectedness, care, and acceptance.

Still this friendship must fall short of personal involvement as therapists must work within an institutional, contractual framework constrained by duties such as avoiding dual role relationships that have the potential to destroy professional distance and objectivity—for instance, avoiding membership in the same support groups, and staying on guard against counter-transference, thus providing adequate referrals or seeking appropriate supervision in case therapists' ability to serve clients' welfare is impaired.

At the same time, therapists recognize that there are logical limits to the possibility of working collaboratively as partners and "special purpose" friends. A client who is intoxicated or otherwise not sufficiently rational to meet the terms of the therapeutic contract, or to repose the trust and mutual respect for autonomy embedded in the relationship, may thus be involuntarily treated, paternalistically, until such time as competent to partake in therapy.[46]

The Functionality of the Proposed Model

The contractual, partnership, and friendship dimensions of the therapist-client relationship derive from the intrinsic teleology of therapy as defined herein. The point has been to devise an ethical model that works in junction with a broad range of therapeutic interventions and treatment models to promote client welfare. Therapists respect their contractual duties in providing informed consent, keeping confidences, and avoiding conflicts of interest and problematic dual role relationships. While these duties are themselves limited by client welfare (as well as that of third parties), they provide a basic level of institutional safeguards that preserves the integrity and functionality of the therapeutic relationship.

But this basic level of practice codified in ethics rules and legal statutes does not touch the more abstract, aspirational dimensions of the relationship deriving from the intrinsic teleology of counseling. To wit, therapists are not likely to meet this mark unless they also function as partners and friends in the aforementioned ways.

These are not alternative, exclusive roles that take turns so that it is necessary to know when to turn one off and the other on, and conversely. Therapists who exemplify the aspirational dimensions of their relationship instead display unconditional positive regard, congruence, and empathy in the process of working collaboratively, freely, and respectfully as partners in a joint venture. The two roles are mutually supportive. The dimensions of trust and solidarity coalesce in a relationship founded on both. In this regard, the whole is greater than the sum of the parts so that talk of levels of interaction is only a useful way of analyzing the parts but not the whole.

The idea of mutual help imbedded in AA and NA programs works for similar reasons. So does a "higher power." These therapeutic tools provide a stable support in which to repose trust (or faith) in confronting the addiction that has subdued the mind, body, and spirit. The alcoholic who has looked for stability in a culture of drink, only to sink lower and lower into loneliness and despair, is now offered a viable support in the form of a constructive, collaborative, goal-driven, therapeutic friendship that respects and cultivates personal autonomy. Unlike a culture of drugs and alcohol, this is a culture of empowerment.

The eclectic, holistic model conceptualized is not one that can be emulated just by following the rules in a code of ethics or in a book of statutes. Such obedience, even if steadfast and well-intentioned, does not capture the aspirational dimensions of the relationship just described. To be sure, mere obedience to rules can satisfy what duty requires, but what duty requires is not enough to promote the ultimate mission of therapy. What is requisite here is better described in the language of virtues and character, not merely in terms of actions in conformity to rules.[47] The emotional and attitudinal dimensions of the relationship involve habits or dispositions that comprise a person's character. For this reason, the model developed here is quite selective. Those who lack these emotional and attitudinal qualifications (or at least the potential to develop them) need not apply. Those unable to empathize and care, and to relate authentically are not satisfactory candidates. Those who are phonies, even if good show persons, lack the acumen to meet the demands of this model. They may have talents suitable elsewhere in the health care delivery system (for example, as health care administrators), but they are not likely to serve well on the front lines of this collaborative, person-oriented, therapeutic process.

Elliot D. Cohen, Ph.D. is chair of the Department of Humanities and professor of philosophy at Indian River Community College in Fort Pierce, Florida. Cohen also serves as the editor of the International Journal of Applied Philosophy, is the applied ethics editor of FREE INQUIRY, the editor of International Journal of Philosophical Practice, and the director of the Institute of Critical Thinking. Cohen works as an ethics consultant for several health care facilities and, in addition to numerous published articles, is the author or editor of twelve books. His recent book, What Would Aristotle Do? Self-Control Through the Power of Reason, is focused on philosophical counseling. Cohen is a founder and executive director of the American Society for Philosophy, Counseling, and Psychotherapy. Cohen earned his doctoral degree from Brown University.

Notes

1. Michael Bayles, *Professional Ethics*, 2nd Ed. (Belmont, CA: Wadsworth, 1989).
2. There is in fact no single disease model, but several such models, each with its own features and criteria for success and failure.
3. See Herbert Fingarette, *Heavy Drinking: The Myth of Alcoholism as a Disease* (Berkeley & Los Angeles: University of California Press, 1989).
4. By "professional" in this context I am broadly referring to degreed practitioners with specialized, formal training such as licensed mental health counselors, licensed clinical social workers, licensed clinical psychologists, psychiatric nurses, and certified addictions professionals.
5. See, for example, Samuel T. Gladding, *Counseling: A Comprehensive Profession* (Upper Saddle River, NJ: Prentice-Hall, 2003); see also U.S. Department of Health and Human Services, "Brief Interventions and Brief Therapies for Substance Abuse," retrieved on June 16, 2005 from http://ncadi.samhsa.gov/govpubs/BKD341/34c.aspx.
6. See Lon L. Fuller, *The Morality of Law* (New Haven: Yale University Press, 1969).
7. For example, according to provision A.7.(a) of the American Counseling Association (ACA) *Code of Ethics* "Counselors do not have any type of sexual intimacies with clients and do not counsel persons with whom they have had a sexual relationship."
8. For example, see Florida Statute 491-0112
9. In fact, the American Bar Association's 1969 *Code of Professional Responsibility* explicitly divided its rules into Disciplinary Rules (DRs) and Ethical Considerations (ECs). The former were deemed duties or requirements backed by sanctions whereas the latter were deemed aspirations. See Preliminary Statement, American Bar Association, *Model Code of Professional Responsibility*, retrieved on June 15, 2005 from http://www.abanet.org/cpr/ethics/mcpr.pdf
10. James Childress & Mark Siegler, "Metaphors and Models of Doctor-Patient Relationships: Their Implications for Autonomy," in Thomas Mappes & David DeGrazia (eds.), 5th Edition, *Biomedical Ethics* (New York: McGraw Hill, 2004).
11. Robert M. Veatch, "Models for Ethical Medicine in a Revolutionary Age," *Hastings Center Report 2*(3) (1972), 5-7. Also available at http://falcon.tamucc.edu/~sencerz/Veatch_Models.htm
12. Childress & Siegler, "Metaphors and Models of Doctor-Patient Relationships"; Howard Brody, "The Physician-Patient Relation," in Robert M. Veatch (ed.), *Medical Ethics*, 2nd Edition (Boston: Jones & Bartlett Publishers, 1997), 75-101; Robert M. Veatch, "Models for Ethical Medicine."
13. Childress & Siegler, "Metaphors and Models of Doctor-Patient Relationships"
14. Childress & Siegler, "Metaphors and Models of Doctor-Patient Relationships," p. 74. Compare also the Charles Fried, "The Lawyer as Friend," in Elliot D. Cohen (ed.), *Philosophers at Work: Issues and Practice of Philosophy*, 2nd Edition (Fort Worth: Harcourt, 2000), 84-93.
15. Childress & Siegler, "Metaphors and Models of Doctor-Patient Relationships"; Ronald Munson, *Intervention and Reflection: Basic Issues in Medical Ethics*, 7th Edition (Belmont, CA: Wadsworth, 2004), pp. 108-109.

16. This eclectic approach is developed more fully in Elliot D. Cohen & Gale S. Cohen, *The Virtuous Therapist: Ethical Practice of Counseling and Psychotherapy* (Belmont, CA: Wadsworth, 1999).
17. *Tarasoff v Regents of University of California*, 551 P.2d 334 (Cal. 1976) In this important case, Prosenjit Poddar, a voluntary outpatient at a hospital attached to the University of California, killed Tatiana Tarasoff in October 1969, having told a psychologist two months earlier that he planned to do so. The psychologist informed the campus police. Poddar was briefly detained and then released. He appeared to be rational and he promised to stay away from the girl. Ms. Tarasoff, was neither informed about Podder's plans to kill her nor about his detention. In essence, Ms. Tarasoff's parents sued the University because there had not been a breach in client confidentiality. The judges' decision was that: "The protective privilege [of client confidentiality] ends where the public peril begins."
18. Cohen & Cohen, *The Virtuous Therapist.*
19. Cohen & Cohen, *The Virtuous Therapist.*
20. This also applies to therapies that employ aversive or pharmacological treatments. These therapies cannot simply be administered apart from a broader therapeutic environment. It is within this broader environment that cultivation of client trust is of paramount importance.
21. *Alcoholics Anonymous*, 4th Edition (New York: Alcoholics Anonymous World Services, Inc., 2001), p. 24.
22. Immanuel Kant, *Groundwork of the Metaphysics of Morals*, trans. H.J. Paton (New York: HarperCollins, 1964), sect. 2.
23. American Bar Association, *Model Rules of Professional Conduct*, Rule 6.2(C). Retrieved on June 15 from http://www.abanet.org/cpr/mrpc/mrpc_toc.html.
24. As mentioned previously, not all models accept this premise. See, for example, Fingarette, *Heavy Drinking*.
25. This assumption is typically made by treatment modalities that accept the disease model, including the popular Minnesota Model developed by the Hazeldon Foundation as well as the AA model. See Gary L. Fisher & Thomas C. Harrison, *Substance Abuse: Information for School Counselors, Social Workers, Therapists, and Counselors*, 3rd Edition (Boston: Allyn & Bacon, 2004), Ch. 7.
26. Kant, *Groundwork of the Metaphysics of Morals*, sect. 2.
27. Elliot D. Cohen, "Confidentiality, Counseling, and Clients Who Have AIDS: Foundations of a Model Rule," *Journal of Counseling and Development*, American Counseling Assoc., Jan./Feb. 1990.
28. ACA, *Code of Ethics*, B.1.d.
29. The ACA rule was adapted from my proposed model rule. See Elliot D. Cohen, "Lethal Sex: Conditions of Disclosure in Counseling Sexually Active Clients with HIV," *International Journal of Applied Philosophy 17*(2) (Spring 2004): 255-67.
30. See, for example, Seumas Miller, "Privacy, Confidentiality, and the Treatment of Drug Addicts," in this volume.
31. Elliot D. Cohen, "Confidentiality, HIV, and the ACA New Code of Ethics: The `Contagious, Fatal Diseases` Rule," *Journal of Mental Health Counseling 19* (1997): 349-63.

32. This does not mean that ethics transgressions cannot occur in the method of treatment involuntarily reposed. For example, subjecting the client to experimental treatments or ones with irreversible, harmful side effects would raise moral problems.
33. Elliot D. Cohen, "Paternalism that Does Not Restrict Individuality: Criteria and Applications," *Social Theory and Practice, 12*(3) (Fall 1986): 309-35.
34. *In re Clark*, 185 N.E.2d 128, 132 (Ohio, 1962)
35. Carl R. Rogers, *On Becoming a Person* (Boston: Houghton Mifflin, 1961).
36. Alcoholics Anonymous, p. 67.
37. Albert Ellis & Emmett Velten, *When AA Doesn't Work For You : Rational Steps to Quitting Alcohol* (New York: Barricade Books, 1992).
38. Rogers, *On Becoming a Person.*
39. Rogers, *On Becoming a Person*; Cohen & Cohen, *The Virtuous Therapist.*
40. Cohen & Cohen, *Virtuous Therapist*; See also *Canterbury v. Spence*, 464 F.2d 772 (DC Cir. 1972).
41. ACA, *Standards of Practice*, Standard 3; Iowa Board of Substance Abuse Certification, *Code of Ethics for Alcohol and Drug Counselors*, Principle 2.
42. For a discussion of "non-elective" dual role relationships, see Cohen & Cohen, *The Virtuous Therapist*, Chapter 6.
43. Nor should popular stereotypes about substance users as rigid and inflexible, short-circuit respect for them as self-determining. A central goal within the intrinsic teleology of therapy is the empowerment of already disempowered individuals. Clients are not empowered when they are treated as objects. The perception that their lives are outside their control is typically what brings these clients to therapy in the first place. In treating clients as rational, self-determining persons, therapists model respect and provide the opportunity for clients to exercise control over their lives.
44. Louisiana State Board of Certification for Board Certified Substance Abuse Counselors (LSBCSAC), *Rules*, Sec. 1503 B.
45. LSBCSAC, Sec. 1503 J.
46. Nor is such paternalism incompatible with friendship in the ordinary sense, since a friend would not typically permit his or her friend to remain in such a state of incompetence without trying to help the friend.
47. Cohen & Cohen, *The Virtuous Therapist.*

Figure 2.4.1: Levels of Therapist-Client Relating

Level 1 Morality of Duty

Contractual Relationship:

Therapist meets professional duties that promote client trust

- Therapist maintains client's confidentiality and requires the same among group members in group therapy
- At inception of therapy (and throughout as necessary), therapist attains client's fully informed consent to therapy, including apprising client of exceptions to confidentiality, as when client has a fatal, contagious disease (such as HIV) and is sexually active or sharing needles with a vulnerable third party.
- Therapist exercises due care in the provision of therapy including avoidance of compromising dual role relationships such as membership in the same support group as client.

Level 2 Morality of Aspiration

2a Partnership:

Therapist and client share in collaborative, joint venture based on mutual trust and respect for autonomy

- Client respects therapist's judgment in setting therapeutic conditions such as the therapeutic modality used (cognitive, behavioral, affective, psychopharmacological, etc.)
- Therapist is tolerant of client's personal values in setting goals, for example, not requiring that client accept therapist's own religious perspective such as the Christian deity as opposed to a "higher power" as the client conceives it.
- Therapist empowers client to exercise willpower and discrimination to make suitable behavioral, cognitive, and emotional changes in attaining therapeutic goals, and does not create client over-dependency by advising about personal matters.

2b Friendship:

Therapist forges deeper, interpersonal bond with client

- Therapist is congruent (genuine) in relating to client and does not hide behind a professional façade, modeling the same for client
- Therapist displays unconditional positive regard (intrinsic caring) for client as a person and exhibits respect for client as center of intrinsic value even when disagreeing with client's destructive behavior.
- Therapist uses personal experience as an addict to achieve empathetic understanding of client's subjective world but without counter-transference or loss of professional objectivity.

2-5 Ethical Issues Raised by Mutual-Help Approaches for Substance User Treatment: The Place of Twelve-Step Organizations

Allaman Allamani, M.D.

Abstract

The intrinsic differences between the ways in which mutual help groups and formal professional treatment agents and agencies relate to and work with misusers of alcoholic beverages and other drugs have ethical implications. More particularly, the ethic of Twelve-Step groups is universalistic, based as it is on spirituality, otherness, and solidarity. Even if their efficacy in producing abstinence can be scientifically studied, they are best described as "communities of healing"(Seppala, 2001). On the other hand, where professionals are involved in substance user treatment programs, the ethic appears to be utilitarian; it is oriented towards the interests of either the individual or the social group. Even if when interacting the two diverse perspectives may have produced tension or conflict, co-operation among mutual help fellowships and the health care system is presently diffused and world-wide.

Key Words: Alcoholics Anonymous, desperation, therapist-patient relationship, ethics, Higher Power, moral freedom, mutual help fellowships, otherness, relapse, responsibility, solidarity, spirituality, treatment, Twelve Steps, universalistic, utilitarian

1. Ethical issues

Ethical issues arise when we have a problematic choice between competing behaviors (Lavoie et al., 1994). Human behaviour is a context for seeking "the good" and avoiding evil; its categories are those of convenience, usefulness, and beauty as well as those of right and moral principles, and is underlain by the key concepts of freedom/autonomy, will, and responsibility.

In some instances it is clear how to resolve the competing choices, because beneficence or malfeasance is manifest, as is the case when a clinician betrays his patient's legitimate expectations by deceiving him about the effectiveness of a treatment that he is going to receive for his illness; or when the doctor's main motivation is self-promotion and financial gain. On other occasions, particularly when autonomy and control are at issue, the resolution is less clear-cut, as when a health professional transmits her client's data without the client's awareness to another health service for purposes of amelioration, or when she uses her authority to impose her view on her client over the mutual help group opinion, that is treated as ancillary to the professional perspective.

In addition, ethical questions are often raised in the treatment field about issues of "life and death" and the appropriate therapeutic interventions to pursue. The persons involved may have to struggle between two conscientious choices, each of which is morally correct within a particular system of values (Lavoie et al., 1994). In such cases, the final choice may be difficult, if not excruciating, for both parties: the patient must decide whether to undergo the only painful medical treatment for a severe illness or to withdraw from it; the clinician will have to decide whether to continue the administration of medicaments or to stop them in the case of a terminal condition.

Ethical conflicts can and do occur in relation to the choices that can be made regarding the treatment system to which to refer a client. These conflicts may be especially pressing for health and social-welfare professionals in the complex field of substance user treatment, as well as for the general public, when facing what often times seems to be an either/or choice—professional treatment models and institutions versus the option of mutual help groups, of which Alcoholics Anonymous is the prototype.

Moreover, the situation of the alcoholic or of the drug user is heavily freighted with a social moral stigma, the view that addiction is a "moral disease." The opinion of professionals and society-at-large swings between the prevalent idea that the addict's morally inadequate behavior is the cause of his/her consequent problems, for which he/she is responsible, and the less widespread idea that the addict's "disease"—a substance use disorder, for example—and its related ego weakness makes her or him nonresponsible for the consequent personal and social harm. These opinions continue to have consequences by excluding drug addicts from potentially life-saving practices such as costly medical treatment for Hepatitis C or—in the case of alcoholics—liver transplants (Rehm et al, 2003).

Alcoholics Anonymous and its parallel associations, such as Narcotics Anonymous and Overeaters Anonymous, are seen as so "peculiar" when compared with the world of traditional professional models of health care and its medical science-based principles, that they appear to be in collision with it. For such mutual-help-based models are:

- self-referring, that is they are self sufficient and anonymous;
- based on spiritual experiences; and
- based on the presence of a Higher Power.

The aim of this chapter is not to review the underpinnings of medicine. It is sufficient to be reminded that medicine is mainly based on objective biological theory, founded in the cause-effect principle. Its practice has a diagnostic side involving the domain of chemistry and physics, and a therapeutic side encompassing a set of evidence-based physical interventions, including surgical action and medicament administration. In addition, when psychology, which is mostly interested in humans as functioning and adapting persons—is concerned with treatment, it is focused on diagnosis, therapy, and on the evaluation of its clinical programs. That is, it is based on a scientific set of theories open to objective examination. Both medicine and psychology are therefore founded on rational theories and on practices that relate to those theories. This rationalist position is somehow shared by "complementary" or "alternative medicines" as recently practiced in the Western world, such as acupuncture, homeopathy, and osteopathy.

This chapter's focus, on the one hand, is to better understand the genesis and dimensional underpinnings of Alcoholics Anonymous—that is whether and how it clashes or co-operates with the teaching and administration of medicine and of health care; on the other hand, it is concerned with the ethical frameworks of A.A. and the health sector, and whether they are compatible.

In general, any new therapeutic approach to treating the human condition has an initial self-protecting phase as it attempts to demonstrate its effectiveness, and later as it seeks to establish both its visibility and autonomy. Conflicts with the medical system are particularly acute. In a second phase, such approaches will be integrated into the prevailing system where they may become part of a menu of compatible alternatives. This might have already occurred in the history of A.A., and it is especially true for some "alternative" medicines. For example, after some years of serving a few social elites in the western world, acupuncture treatment began to be studied in experimental contexts, and may now be integrated with other medical treatments in different programs—as a pain reliever in several conditions, affecting early hypertension, or as a detoxifying agent in addiction (WHO, 1991; Bullock, 1990). The usual pathway is that the new approach, which has lower scientific status in western thought, is brought within medical boundaries because of its practical therapeutic effects, that is, on the basis of a utilitarian ethic. This pathway is constituted according to the function that science has in contemporary western society, where it is generally trusted for its universal significance. However, the status inequality of alternative therapeutic approaches enables the contrasts and contradictions to survive for a long time.

When considering ethics in the West, it is reasonable to suggest that our keynote author would be Immanuel Kant, whose *Critique of Practical Reason* (2001) aimed at describing universal moral laws:

(a) act in such a way that your individual behavioral norm can also be construed as a universal behavioral law;

(b) act in such a way as to treat yourself as well as the other persons as an end and not only as a means.

In these laws, Kant stressed the relevance of the human universal, or collective, that stretches beyond the individual and encompasses the whole of humanity. These universal moral laws govern human behavior, requiring mutual respect, solidarity, and reciprocity.

Kant rejected merely utilitarian ethics, which—since the English philosophers of the 18th century—had focused on maximizing the needs of the individual or group good as the basic norm for human behavior. An example of utilitarian ethics is that of a person going to the doctor to relieve his or her symptoms and feel better, and a physician's responding to that need. Even the professional desire to include the patient's problem within the larger domain of medical knowledge in order to treat him or her, may be considered part of a group desire to extend medicine's area of competence. Indeed, all organizations, including health organizations, have an intrinsic tendency to support themselves, one corresponding to a utilitarian ethic of self-preservation (see Illich, 1976).

Because, in the following pages, we will attempt to support the view that Alcoholics Anonymous and the other 12-step groups essentially work according to universalistic principles, and not to utilitarian ones, its ethical divergence from the ethics of the health system make more problematic the co-operation between this fellowship and the health professions.

When he referred to the Jewish-Christian statement "Love God above everything and your neighbor as yourself," Kant called it the "law of all laws," leading one to appreciate the importance of Love, and of the Other, in the realm of the moral freedom

(Kant, 2001). In fact, God ("as we understood Him"), love, and the presence of the other, are fundamental in Alcoholics Anonymous, as we shall discuss later.

The universality of the "law of love" can be argued from a multi-cultural perspective. It has similar expressions in other religious cultures, for example, in the Buddhist concept of "compassion" toward any living being.

The issue of the objective reality of God has to do more with religion than with Kant's approach to morality, and has both a subjective and a psychological dimension. The psychiatrist Carl Gustav Jung, who paid much attention to these topics, explained the subjective principle of God by means of his distinction between ego and Self. Self, that is, the deeper level that an individual attains beyond the ego boudaries, is the deposit of images of the unconscious collective archetypes, i.e., of human collective values. In Jungian terms, both God and Spirit are archetypes of the Self, the former being a human experience potentially brought into awareness during the evolution of each individual (Jung, 1959). The American psychologist William James had a similar approach to religious phenomena, which he interpreted within a psychological framework (James, 1958). The relationship between the experience which an individual has of God and of the other, and the reality of God and of the other in the outer reality of the individual—in other words, the relationship between the experience of God/other and the existence of God/other—was at the heart of a controversy between Martin Buber and Jung (Buber, 1958).

Responsibility is a key-concept in ethics. From the perspective of the cofounder of A.A., Bill Wilson, "responsibility" is both an individual and a communal process encompassing the history of A.A. as a fellowship. It is a healing process that leads from immaturity to true maturity. To quote from the Declaration at the 30th Anniversary Convention of A.A. in Toronto in 1965, "I am responsible. When anyone, anywhere, reaches out for help, I want the hand of A.A. always to be there. And for that: I am responsible". In another context, Bill summarized it as follows: "The word 'responsibility' is the keynote of any democracy and of Alcoholics Anonymous also" (Wilson to Tiebout, 4 Nov. 1964, in Kurtz, 1991, p 141).

The above-mentioned ideas can help us better to focus on the ethical aspects of mutual help Twelve-Steps groups and their potential as well as on their interactions with the health professions and their models of care.

2. The Genesis of Alcoholics Anonymous

Alcoholics Anonymous (A.A.) was founded during the third decade of last century, in 1935, through the development of a specific philosophy whose dimensions and very essence differed from contemporary, western medically-based planned intervention, as the result of an experienced "solution"[1] that was not derived from medical clinics and hospitals.

Most of the words used to describe the foundation of A.A. are not medical: they are desperation, helplessness, agony, abyss, death, miracle, rightness, freedom, love, and God. In addition, the typical history of an A.A. member is to feel "close to death" and "hit the bottom" and, afterwards, to personally experience a resurrection. This self-witnessed process—which is more than just a personal report—sounds strange to medical practice, notwithstanding that medicine and other professional models of treatment are designed and mandated to cure and save from illness and death, to relieve from pain and from pathology, and to restore health and even autonomy.

We can recognize the typical words and ideas of A.A. in the history of Bill Wilson, an alcoholic, and the founder of A.A. The basic "experiences" of Alcoholics Anonymous occurred during December 1934. Bill, having once again become drunk, came yet again to Towns Hospital in Manhattan, New York, once more to be dried out by Dr. Silkworth. And Dr. Silkworth, even if unenthusiastic about Wilson's plans, gave him a bed again. This was the alcoholic "revolving door syndrome" well-known to professionals.[2] This was the last and most severe of Bill's innumerable relapses. It is written in *Pass It On* (Alcoholics Anonymous 1984):

> *Now, he [was] waiting for the end. "The terrifying darkness had become complete"—Bill said—"In the agony of spirit, I again thought of the cancer of alcoholism which had now consumed me in my mind, and spirit and soon the body." The abyss gaped before him. In his helplessness and desperation, Bill cried out, "I'll do anything, anything at all! If there be a God, let Him show Himself!"*

Bill possessed a sharp intelligence, had a great love of life, had a loving wife and was excellent in the stock exchange business in New York. He could have been a very happy and successful man. But this dramatic step was just the last one in a long series of relapses not only into drinking, but also into personal, family, and workplace disasters. He already had several experiences of hospitalization for alcoholism and had now reached the depths of his powerlessness. Such feelings were presumably more painful to him when he compared his own existence with that of someone who had been able to abstain. He had, in fact, been visited by an alcoholic friend, Ebby T., who had stopped drinking because he had "got religion." Ebby had a conversion experience with the Oxford Group, a nondenominational Christian evangelical movement (Kurtz, p. 24-25). This visit impressed Bill, and he started thinking again about his life options. His friend Ebby found a way out. But what about himself?

The following describes what happened to Bill after experiencing the "terrifying darkness":

> *What happened next was electric. Suddenly, my room blazed with an indescribably white light. I was seized with an ecstasy beyond description.... Then, seen in the mind's eye, there was a mountain. I stood upon its summit, where a great wind blew. A wind, not of air, but of spirit. In great, clean strength, it blew right through me. Then came the blazing thought: "You are a free man." ...finally the light and the ecstasy subsided.... I became acutely conscious of a Presence which seemed like a veritable sea of living spirit.... "This, I thought," must be the great reality. The God of the preachers".... I remained in this state for a long time. I seemed to be possessed by the absolute, and the curious conviction deepened that, no matter how badly things may go, there could be no question of the ultimate rightness of God's universe.... I knew that I was loved and that I could love in return (Alcoholics Anonymous, 1984).*

What is described here is a culminating experience that originated in experienced powerlessness, and from which sprang forth a request for help from a not attending Higher Being. Then the pneumatic breath of "spirit" shared the living spirit with the person—Bill—who was dead to it before, drawing him into a process of new individuality, through which an absolute reality of freedom, rightness, and love was experienced. A saving strength arose from the acceptance of weakness, that is, a deep religious insight (Kurtz, 1991, p. 150).

After that day Bill's life changed. But this was not enough. Something more had to happen. For five months he abstained while unsuccessfully trying to help other alcoholics to abstain. He also tried to return to work, but in the end his attempts to "win" in the Wall Street scene proved to be a failure. On a Saturday afternoon in May, he found himself alone in a hotel in Akron, Ohio, close to the hotel bar where some revellers were meeting. Bill started to panic because the lure of alcohol returned.

"God," he thought, "I am going to get drunk." One idea rose out of all his recent intensive experiences: "I need another alcoholic" (Kurtz, 1991, p. 27).

Bill turned to the hotel church directory and through a phone call to an Episcopalian minister listed there, he got a list of ten names from the local Oxford Group. He made nine calls, none of which was able to refer him to the kind of person he was looking for. But the last person on the list gave him the name of Henriette Sieberling, a distinguished lady in Akron, who was able to get him an appointment with Dr. Bob for the following afternoon:

> *Doctor Robert Holbrook Smith, a prominent Akron surgeon...had tried all the medical cures and the religious approaches yet somehow he could not stay sober.... He had extracted from his wife a promise that they would not stay longer than fifteen minutes .... But...Wilson began telling Smith the tale of his experiences with alcohol: the hopes, the promises, and the failures of both; the drinking camaraderie...his doctor's diagnosis.... Bob had occasionally nodded his head, muttering "Yes...that's just like me." Now...for the first time in his life, Dr. Bob Smith began to open his heart. (Kurtz, 1991 p.27-29)*

Bill was not preaching. Nor was he trying to make his interlocutor conform to his own ideas, as he had done in his last months. On the contrary, he was sharing his life. In turn, Bob understood that Bill Wilson was able to control his drinking problem through an approach that was not oriented to "get" but rather to "give." Dr. Smith had never before realized that now obvious fact.

By now it was nearing midnight. Bob invited Bill to return home with himself and his wife. Nearly one month later, on June 10, 1935, Dr. Bob had his last drink. Alcoholics Anonymous was founded (Kurtz, 1991, p.32-33).

The encounter of Bill and Bob more clearly showed that the spiritual pathway was not per se sufficient to save Bill from alcoholism, since he needed to acknowledge the importance of the other. The important "other" Bill had met at first was Ebby; later on it was Bob; Bill and Bob had discovered that, in order that one become, and remain, sober, the other one too had to be sober.

The two, along with other alcoholics who followed and have met in A.A., found an identity in shared weakness. Oneness came from the acceptance of limitations. Their individual differences in strength and weakness were acknowledged, as reflected in the diverse source that gave birth to Alcoholics Anonymous—the strange mix of Bill and Bob, two men so different in personality that in other circumstances they "would never have spent ten seconds together" (Kurtz, 1991, p 151).

3. The Principles of Alcoholics Anonymous

The founding events of Alcoholics Anonymous are the spiritual experience and the encounter with the other. To what kind of ethic can they be referred? And how commensurable are they with the standards, processes, and roles of medical and other treatment disciplines?

One cannot deny that part of the motivation that drove Bill in his last hospitalization was utilitarian. He was looking for personal relief from alcoholism through medicine and its hierarchical "doctor-patient" relationship. There was also a motivation for some sort of spiritual change, stimulated by the conversation with his visiting alcoholic friend Ebby. This appeared to be instrumental for his "readiness" to do something other than what he had already done to bring about a longed for improvement in his life. The domain of health in contemporary western society is anchored in and is sensitive to both a personal request from an identified "patient" to be "cured" of his/her pain or suffering, and a planned clinical intervention that is designed to treat the patient's problem, system, or condition. Mutuality is not part of this design.

However, the encounter Bill had with the "white light" transformed this utilitarian motivation into a spiritual experience of universal significance. This is clearly demonstrated from the words reported in the records of what happened: "rightness," "great reality," "universe," "absolute," "God." Such transformation is also shown by the missionary attitude and conviction that Bill manifested after that special moment and the effort he invested in a movement fashioned to reach every alcoholic in the world.

In a similar way the encounter that Bill had with Bob was born out of Bill's need not to fall down yet again into a drinking binge. He felt depressed from the failures experienced by both his work-role self and his efforts to "cure" alcoholics, and felt an urgency about, as well as the need to seek, his personal safety.

The encounter did not involve preaching but sharing by two different persons—the essence of mutual help. The encounter changed from an individual necessity into a collective experience in which the interaction moved from a well-known, bounded, complicated "I-you" approach into one of a complex "us."[3] The turning point of this change is encapsulated in Bob's head nodding and muttering, "Yes, that's just like me." Two "me's" or one "I-you" dyad have become a time-bound and task-driven "us," the unity of a shared weakness, reflected by an acceptance of their differences.

What made these changes—from personal interest to something of universal significance—possible?

Bill Wilson found it appropriate to call his peak experience a spiritual "conversion." He found this concept in the American psychologist William James's *The Varieties of Religious Experience* (James, 1958), a book that Ebby gave him to read when he was still a patient at the New York hospital. According to James, who first published his studies on the psychological implications of the religious and spiritual dimension in 1902, such an experienced conversion occurs when one "surrenders" after pain and suffering, from being in a hopeless and death-like condition. Then a new life can come about. Being "born again" or "reborn" are both secular-based and religiously-driven experiences that facilitate treatment and healing. James observed that this passive approach, which recalls the despair and abandonment leading to salvation, that Martin Luther preached at the time of the Reformation, was revived in the 19th century American "mind cure movement"—and became contemporary, thanks to the more recent psychotherapies of "letting go" (see Lowen, 1973; Grof, 1993). It involves an acknowledgment that our ego is small and that a "greater ego" is present (James, 1958). The hopelessness of the condition of the alcoholic and, as Bill put it later in his life, "deflation at depth," are the pathway to a spiritual experience. According to the first two Steps of the A.A. program, alcoholics have had to admit that they "were powerless over alcohol" and that their "lives had become unmanageable" so that they "came to believe that a Power greater than ourselves could restore" them "to sanity" (Alcoholics Anonymous, 1976). The process is made meaningful by the fact that such acknowledgment is not just to oneself but also to others during the meeting. The accepting and sharing context enables the participants to break through their painful feelings of shame—constantly present in their lives as a counterpart to their feelings of being judged by the public (Kurtz, 1982). By contrast, the context of confidentiality and protection that is specific to the professional relationship encourages the individual to retain his shameful view of himself and would be an unsurmountable obstacle to his facing and acknowledging his problem.

Alcoholics are supposed to "turn" their will and their life "over to the care" of a Higher Power or God, defined, according to the Third Step, "as we understood Him" (The Twelve Steps and Twelve Traditions, 1988). Bill and the founders of Alcoholics Anonymous attempted to attenuate the idea that belief in God is a prerequisite for attending A.A. meetings: A.A. is said to be a non-religious program, inclusive of all creeds, which atheists can also attend, being allowed to address the Higher Power as "the group," the "group conscience" or, as somebody humorously said, "his own hat."

There is another way of considering God. Contemporary man has incorporated Him into himself, when he challenges natural and social limits and interprets human evolution as unending progress. By contrast, A.A. stands as an offbeat trend to modernity. In the beautiful *Not God: a History of Alcoholics Anonymous*, Ernst Kurtz clarifies that:

> *Not-God means first "You are not God"…. This message of Alcoholics Anonymous to its members is that they are not infinite, not absolute, not God…. Also, because the alcoholic is not God, not absolute, not infinite, he or she is essentially limited. Yet from this very limitation—from the alcoholic's acceptance of personal limitation, arises the beginning of healing and wholeness. (Kurtz, 1991, p.3)*

From the outside, A.A.'s appeals to a Higher Power may be compared with the medical appreciation of placebo effects, by means of which even in traditional medicine the importance of beliefs about efficacy is recognized as a relevant component in the process of healing. Of course, from a psychological viewpoint, a belief system has more to say about the believer than about the objects of belief that figure centrally in religion. The argument between psychology and religion would probably be endless—whether the great strength of religious founders like Abraham and Mohammed to change their peoples' lives came from their subjective faith or rather from the object of their faith (God). Indeed, a psychological perspective on the patient/physician relationship would acknowledge the placebo effect involved in the patient's beliefs in the doctor or the pill or treatment prescribed by the doctor (Fish, 1973)—tendentiously ascribing omnipotence or a kind of deity to the individual physician or to the medical category, a process that we might consider a useful deception. The "powerful placebo" is there the main player. From within the Twelve-Step experience, however, the appeal to a Higher Power is hardly comparable to belief in the efficacy of a treatment because, paradoxically, it is at first generated by a profound feeling of non-power, non-God, and, from a condition of hopelessness.

Although it would be difficult to argue in a clinical context that a Higher Power had any impact on a disease, it would be acceptable to maintain that an encounter with the other, the second founding principle of A.A., is pertinent to the domain of medicine and treatment that adheres to traditional professional models. Indeed, ever since the birth of medicine, the relationship between patient and physician has been the basis of any clinical action. For the most part, the relationship has had the character of an "authority/dependence" interaction, in which the patient is the passive recipient of actions and the therapist has the active role of planning the therapeutic process. The accumulation of medical knowledge and machinery has magnified the difference between the two roles, to the point at which both legal concerns and the claims by patients to have an active partnership in the theraputic process have generated the practice of ethically-based informed consent of the client prior to any relevant medical action. However, informed consent seemed to become a legal stratagem for protecting the doctor or the health system in the event of untoward outcomes. Moreover, the authority/dependence relationship has persisted and appears to support a utilitarian ethic in which the patient's role usually confirms and reinforces the dominant position of medical hierarchy in controlling clients' symptoms and illness. This lack of a partnership dimension and of genuine patient/therapist communication creates ethical problems and may be at the root of many malpractice allegations.

In the twentieth century revolution against the medical understanding of the patient as a passive object, Freudian psychoanalysis gave special attention to the significance of "the other" in the patient/clinician interaction, and to the concepts of transference and counter-transference (Freud, 1977; Jung, 1954). However, even though Sigmund Freud and his followers opened up the vast realm of the human subject and of his unconscious in theoretical formulations, leading to a great interest in the patient and the patient's viewpoint in clinical practice, a professional asymmetry is still apparent in the psychotherapeutic setting and process.

By contrast, Bill and Bob's encounter had its critical moment when Bob reflected Bill's life in his own. This is what still happens today when a newcomer attends an A.A. meeting, or even when an A.A. fellow meets an alcoholic person in clinical facilities for the first time. Within a non-judgmental and accepting environment s/he perceives that "the other" alcoholic is him/her, and the personal need to be treated tends to become a free and collective sharing. What happens there is, according to Kurtz, "identifying, not comparing," differences among alcoholics being "valued as enriching" because "the sense of incompleteness shared leads to...acceptance that the partial completeness of others complements rather than destroys...one's own partiality" (Kurtz, 1991, 220-221).

Many, if not most, clinicians would be at the very least puzzled were they do compare the "diagnosed" and/or experienced "needs" within the rules of uni-directional confidentiality of their clients with what goes on in open or closed "here and now" multi-dimensional A.A. meeting interactions. In fact there seems to be a difference between the clinical world and the mutual help one in respect of both its lexicon and the interpretation of the reality experienced. The client may come, for example, to the doctor's office, clinic, or hospital out of desperation and hopelessness, in search of help; and the professional—of any discipline—perceives his helping role as making a diagnosis and taking responsibility for the dependent patient (who is expected to be "compliant"). Since the "alcoholic problem"[4] is basically dependence on a substance—to be chronically addicted—and inherently to reject dependence-promoting authorities, taking decisions for the "identified patient," that is, acting as an authority, is paradoxical. Moreover, the traditional professional role is often felt by the "patient" to be judgmental. All-too-often this feeling may elicit both emotions of guilt and shame in the "dependent client."

This puzzle was probably recognized by the main actors in the story that "pre-founded" A.A. They were Rowland H., an American alcoholic of financial means who had had numerous unsuccessful treatment attempts, and the famous Swiss psychiatrist Carl Gustav Jung, from whom Rowland sought psychotherapy in 1931. The treatment, which continued for one year, appeared to be successful. When Rowland returned after he had gone back to the US and relapsed, Jung refused to treat him any more, telling him that his condition was hopeless. Jung nevertheless indicated that there might be a hope, if Rowland could undergo an existential transformation. Rowland therefore sought out the Oxford group, which promoted a change in life by practicing spiritual principles, and was started a few decades earlier by an evangelical minister (Kurtz, 1991, pp 24-25). Rowland was abstinent while attending the Oxford group and passed the spiritual message on to his alcoholic friend Ebby T., who in turn became abstinent and subsequently met Bill W. In a sense, Alcoholics Anonymous was founded by a chain of "others." But from another perspective, both Jung's and Rowland's admission of the failure of traditional, professional-driven psychotherapy turned into the opportunity for a higher awareness. This "higher awareness" was the origin and the basis of Alcoholics Anonymous. According to Jung's comment many years later, as Bill quotes him:

> *the healing process could not be activated by further medical and psychiatric treatment, but there could be a hope, only on condition that the alcoholic could become the subject of a spiritual or religious experience—in short, a genuine conversion.* Jung added: *the only right and legitimate way to such an experience is that it happens to you in reality, and it can only happen to you when you walk on a path which leads you to higher understanding. You might be led to that goal by an act of grace or through a personal and honest contact with friends, or through a higher education of the mind beyond the confines of mere rationalism.* And again: *craving for alcohol was the equivalent on a lower level of the spiritual thirst of our being for wholeness, expressed in medieval language: the union with God. (Alcoholics Anonymous, 1984)*

One conclusion from this paragraph is to consider and acknowledge that different principles are appropriate to A.A. and the medical/clinical disciplines, at both ethical and practical levels. Whereas A.A. relates to the dimension of spirit and universality and aims at healing a person's whole life, clinical disciplines relate to the dimension of biology and psychology, and to the care of the individual's micro ↔ macro personal needs and status, in which "context" is, at best, background.

Such difference in the values given to persons generates problems of mutual understanding and of reciprocal conduct. Twelve-Step people may be considered too "rigid" or deluded by some clinicians, whereas the former could view the latter as taking a limited or theoretical approach and not really understanding alcoholics and their needs. Only a respectful reciprocal attitude will help here.

4. Alcoholics Anonymous—A Method

Alcoholics Anonymous ranks as the method most commonly used world-wide for the recovery of persons suffering from alcohol-use-related problems as well as "alcoholic-related" problems (Al-Anon and Al-Ateen) and has consolidated its efficacy over 70 years. No less than its principles, its "non-organizational" organization is "peculiar" since it:

- is based on personal anonymity,
- avoids outside economic contributions,
- has autonomy at the local group level, and
- facilitates nation-wide representativeness.

A.A. is an autonomous and self-supporting fellowship of women and men not allied with other political, labor union, health care, religious, or private organizations. It is known that the program is based on 12 Steps—the recovery program, 12 Traditions—guiding the decisions of the fellowship at large, and 12 Concepts—the principles of the service structure of A.A. (The Twelve Steps and Twelve Traditions, 1988; The A.A. Service Manual, 1991-2).

As to A.A. anonymity, Tradition Twelve says that "Anonymity is the spiritual foundation of all our Traditions, ever reminding us to place principles above personalities" (The Twelve Steps and Twelve Traditions, 1988). Anonymity means that the sharing union with others is rooted in acceptance of weakness and of limitation, that is, acceptance of "self and others as other-than-perfect" (Kurtz, 1991, p 197). Anonymity is a preventive precaution against relapses into "ego expansion"; it underlines the fact that the alcoholic attending a meeting is considered a real subject, irrespective of her/his family name and profession, and it implies freedom and openness in interactions with others, the fellowship's aim being alcoholic salvation. The text of the parallel association, Narcotics Anonymous, adds the further idea: "Throughout our Traditions we speak in terms of 'we' and 'our' rather than 'me' and 'mine'" (Narcotics Anonymous, 1988, p. 69).

As to the self-sufficiency of each group, Tradition Seven says that "Every A.A. group ought to be fully self-supporting, declining outside contributions" (The Twelve Steps and Twelve Traditions, 1988). A.A. requests no economic contribution of any kind whatsoever and depends solely on contributions by its members; in other words, its costs to the community are nil. Groups do not compromise their integrity by investing financially, nor do they open themselves up to any kind of outside contributors that may distract them from their unique purpose—personal recovery. This also implies that participation is available to anyone regardless of means, that it is up to the free decision of each group member to put money in the group basket during each meeting, and that expenses are kept to a minimum (Seppala, 1991, p.166-7).

A.A. has no official opinion about alcoholism. Even though it has greatly influenced the disease concept of alcoholism developed by Jellinek (1962), and may refer to the DSM American Psychiatric Association classification of disease (DSM-IV TR 2000), A.A. does not endorse any particular definition of alcoholism, leaving it to the appropriate disciplines. This attitude is represented in Tradition Ten: "Alcoholics Anonymous has no opinion on outside issues; hence the A.A. name ought never be drawn into public controversy" (The Twelve Steps and Twelve Traditions, 1988). Rather than disease, A.A. often uses the term "illness," which conveys the experience of suffering, hopelessness, and weakness and their recognition during group meetings. The group experience allows its members to believe that "alcoholism" is not just a biological, psychological, or social disease, but also a spiritual one. A.A. does not promote any religion, even if it supports an engagement in practices that may be religious, such as praying and meditating, making a moral inventory of oneself, admitting "our own wrongs" and "making direct amends of them" (Alcoholics Anonymous, 1976).

The basic unit of A.A. is the group meeting. As it is said in the second Tradition, in the group "there is but one ultimate authority—a loving God as He may express Himself in our group conscience." And "our leaders are but trusted servants; they do not govern." The only requirement for A.A. membership is "a desire to stop drinking." Tradition Nine adds that A.A. "ought never be organized," but that "service boards or committees" may be created "directly responsible to those they serve" (The Twelve Steps and Twelve Traditions, 1988).

The stories of Alcoholics Anonymous fellows invariably show a route that traverses from the dependence upon the substance to dependence upon "others" and God, or Spirit, and from a confusion between one's self and the outside world to the acceptance of one's limitations. By attending the group and by following the 12 step program, the individual conflict between dependence and control turns into the condition of being part of a whole, represented by the group. The end of this process, described by Damian McElrath as a spiritual Odyssey (McElrath, 1987), is to "walk" the Twelve Steps in order to attain the necessary, freeing, spiritual awakening, that is to acknowledge one's weakness and salvation through sharing experiences with "the other" alcoholic.

According to Tradition One, "Our common welfare should come first; personal recovery depends on A.A. unity" (The Twelve Steps and Twelve Traditions, 1988). Indeed, one "overarching theme" of the story of Alcoholics Anonymous has been how the fellowship has maintained its unity over the years in the face of ever increasing diversity. Ernst Kurtz argues that this is due to A.A. pluralism, which he characterized as joyous, established at Bill's first meeting with Bob, thanks to their converging diversities. Fellowship implies "finding strength in a oneness that derived from accepting weakness" and "the capacity to experience oneness in such a way that differences are perceived as enriching rather than threatening" (Kurtz 1991, 256).

The Fellowship's organizational features, particularly anonymity and any member's freedom to attend or not attend several weekly meetings, make the available information about group membership and attendance less than satisfying, considering the current statistical standards promoted by professional models of treatment that rely on clinical trials and on "evidence-based treatment." All A.A. data are collected on a voluntary basis. As a result, from a statistical viewpoint, Twelve-Step surveys that have been so far implemented within the fellowship in a few countries must be considered simple indicators of group activity (see, for example, Alcoholics Anonymous Membership Survey, 2001, for North America; Allamani, 2000, for Italy).

5. Universality and Versatility

The worldwide spread of A.A. demonstrates its universality. From its beginning, A.A. was intended to be as inclusive as possible in helping anyone with an alcohol problem and, over time, alcoholics and their family members. Even if A.A. principles were created in the 19th century, within a predominantly Christian, white, male, American culture, the "group conscience" nature of each A.A. meeting, as well as the A.A—concepts of giving "careful consideration to minority opinion" (concept 5) and of reaching all important decisions "whenever possible by substantial unanimity" (concept 12) (The A.A. Service Manual, 1991-2, p S108)—probably facilitated the groups' sensitivity to and awareness of having to adapt to different local needs. For example, in US groups, women's attendance grew to 35% in the 1990s and, among African Americans, A.A. is said to be more and more accepted and effective (Seppala, 1991, p. 177-8). In the mid-1950s, especially in South-East Asia, more and more of those chemically addicted and whose religious tradition was Buddhist undertook the program (Kurtz, 1991, p.226-7).

More generally, there has been a tremendous spread of A.A. throughout the world. It is currently to be found in 171 countries or territories on every continent. Its main Big Book has been translated into more than 30 languages, including, among others, Swahili, Arabic, Tagalog, and Korean. In fact, no planned effort has been made to export A.A. through political, commercial, national, or cultural interests or pathways. On the contrary, the diffusion of A.A. has evidently been based on the efforts of individuals who, having experienced this mutual-help program, have attracted other alcoholics while actively dealing with their own drinking problem. This process has taken a number of years at different "speeds," depending on the particular country. As Klaus Mäkela observes: "Until recently, A.A. has for the most part spread from drunkard to drunkard as an authentic grass-roots movement. This is in clear contrast to many other innovations bearing the imprint of American culture, such as the new religious movements of the last decades" (Mäkela et al., 1996, p.33).

The core of A.A. "is spiritual and relative. The truth of this is borne out by the variety of cultures, including those in Eastern Europe and Asia, embodying a wide variety of religious beliefs as well as degrees of atheism and agnosticism, where the Twelve-Step movement has taken root and begun to flourish" (Smith et al., 1994).

An overview of the ways in which A.A. works in different countries and its variability within countries shows that the fellowship operates differently in each context, showing a great cultural flexibility. In some countries, the relationship between A.A. and the professional treatment system developed with a sort of reciprocal distance. In other cases there has been accommodation and even convergence (Eisenbach-Stangl & Rosenqvist, 1998, p. 7-22; Mäkela et al., 1996, p. 185-189).

- Austria is a typical case of A.A. functioning in isolation, with little contact with the professional treatment system;

- in Finland, for a subpopulation of alcoholics, it developed as a respected alternative to professional treatment;
- in the United States and in Iceland, A.A. became an important component of the treatment system;
- in some European countries, such as Poland, A.A. has grown as a result of the development of public treatment programs for alcoholics—functioning as after-care and complementing state-funded programs;
- in Mexico, however, where A.A. rapidly increased while the welfare system was less developed, this has not been the case;
- in countries such as Italy, the development and functioning of A.A.—its availability and accessibility—may have given an essential stimulus to the public treatment system for alcoholics (Allamani & Petrikin, 1996).

On a whole, the picture is a diversified one, A.A. often growing up irrespective of the size of the treatment system (Mäkela et al., 1996, p. 187).

The versatility of the founding principles of A.A. is shown by the fact that Alcoholics Anonymous has been the basis for other 12-step associations and for many mutual-help groups all over the world. Such associations address a diversity of adaptational and life-style problems of dependence or compulsivity. The following are the most popular of such mutual-help programs:

- Al-Anon (Relatives and Friends of Alcoholics), and Al-Ateen (Adolescent Children of Alcoholics), addressing the needs of non-alcoholic members of a family in which there is an alcoholic person;
- Narcotics Anonymous (NA), which helps illicit drug addicts;
- Cocaine Anonymous, focusing on cocaine addicts;
- Overeaters Anonymous (OA), for persons affected by bulimia and other eating disorders;
- Nicotine Anonymous, for people who are dependent on tobacco smoking;
- Co-dependence Anonymous, for individuals pathologically dependent on their partners;
- Sex and Love Addicts (SLA), for persons compulsive on sex, and
- Gamblers Anonymous (GA), addressed to people dependent on gambling, as well as GamAnon, family members of gamblers.

According to recent estimates, the number of groups worldwide are (DiClemente, 2003):

– Alcoholics Anonymous	98,000
– Al-Anon	32,000
– Narcotics Anonymous	21,000
– Cocaine Anonymous	2,000
– Marijuana Anonymous	1,000

6. Co-operation between Professionals and Twelve-Step Fellowships

As noted above, there is a double reason to differentiate between the Twelve-Step movement and the medical and professional disciplines so that the former is not seen as or characterized as "treatment." In its beginning,

(a) A.A. sprang out of a treatment failure and

(b) was founded on a recognition of/belief in the importance of human spirituality.

Spirituality was the lever that overturned the commonplace view that alcoholics behave immorally and have no hope of a cure. Also, spirituality can be viewed in two ways from a clinical perspective. According to the first, it belongs to the domain of miracles that are beyond the rational reach of science and its practice and therefore cannot be explained by reference to biological or psychological theories. The absence of reasons to explain a healing constitute the negative indication of a miracle, often appealed to by the fellows of Alcoholics Anonymous when recalling the moments at which they changed from drunkenness to abstinence. The second way typically describes spirituality in medical terms as a neurosis with no place in medical and psychiatric treatment.

In both cases, the spiritual program is controversial from the perspective of the professional training of health professionals, most of whom are not educated in non-traditional approaches to disease. Even if both scientific and lay information is nowadays more and more diffused concerning "complemental" medicines or psychotherapies or treatments, such as psychosomatics, acupuncture, homeopathy, osteopathy (WHO, 1990), and also on body-mind working, and even on the spiritual experience of illness (Grof & Grof, 1989), only a few professionals are also trained in such approaches. Moreover, the spiritual emphasis of Twelve-Step programs may be not easily accepted even by clergy because of suspicions about their religious vagueness. To take an example, for many years Catholic parishes in Italy were reluctant to provide a room for A.A. meetings, a situation that changed only in 2000 when an official letter of appreciation was sent by Pope John Paul II to Italian A.A. General Services.

The success of A.A.'s mutual-help program when compared and contrasted with the failure of clinical treatments of alcoholism might have placed Alcoholics Anonymous and health professions on opposite sides. For example, A.A. members are not usually favorable toward the use of medicaments to prevent drinking, because they believe that the support from ever-present mutual-help groups is able to do that which needs to be done (Tonigan & Kelly, 2004). Nevertheless, Alcoholics Anonymous and professionals do collaborate. Members of the former would never have survived without the active help of nonalcoholic doctors and nurses, as well as members of other professions such as journalists and clergy. Some of them helped shape A.A. (Alcoholics Anonymous, 1957):

- Dr. William Silkworth, who took care of Bill W. during many of his stays at Towns Hospital in New York and who developed the concept of alcoholism as a "mind obsession" (Kurtz, 1991, pp 21-22);
- Sister Ignatia of the Sisters of Charity of St Augustine, supporting the hospitalization of alcoholics;
- the New York Oxford Group leader and Episcopal clergyman Samuel Shoemaker;

- the Saturday Evening Post writer Jack Alexander, whose 1941 article about A.A. sparked the surge of interest towards the association; and
- the businessman John D. Rockefeller, who introduced the principle of self-support and convinced the new association to avoid economic dependence on other organizations.

One example of co-operation between professionals and A.A. is the remarkable role that the former have had on the A.A. General Service Board of Trustees, which has the responsibility of the fellowship. In the beginning, the Board had four non-alcoholic and three alcoholic trustees. One underlying motive for this was, Bill Wilson said in 1947, "suppose all of us alcoholics should get drunk at once, who then would hang on to the money?" (Alcoholics Anonymous, 2000-01). Since then, the idea of "responsibility" developed slowly out of the "dependence" and "immaturity" that affects the history of recovering alcoholics. In the decade 1955-1966, a change occurred. A.A. alcoholic members realized that A.A. had come of age, and that they could now responsibly handle responsibility, so that the General Service Board of Trustees ratio was changed to 14 recovered alcoholics and 7 non-alcoholics. The former (who are supposed to leave the service in the case of relapse) are divided up into Regional Trustees and General Service Trustees, either elected or approved by the Conference of the Group Delegates; the latter are chosen by the General Service Board and approved by the Conference. The non-alcoholic Trustees, according to the bylaws, are professionals from different disciplines who "have not been afflicted by the disease of alcoholism and who express a profound faith in the recovery program upon which the fellowship of Alcoholics Anonymous is founded" (The A.A. Service Manual, 1991-92, S109); in other words, they are supposed to know the program well and to support both the fellowship at large and the Board of Trustees in particular. Bill Wilson wrote in November 1951 Grapevine: "because of their detached position they have often shown better judgment than we mercurial and prejudiced alcoholics [and] have…stabilized our Headquarters operation" (Alcoholics Anonymous, 2000-01).

Is the Twelve-Step program really a treatment program? On the one hand, "yes," because it is intended to arrest substance use and serve as a framework for extended recovery. On the other hand, there is a broad range of treatment technologies—medications and psychiatric care are just two of them—that have nothing to do with Twelve-Step principles (Magura, 2005). In any case, A.A. and the other Twelve-Step programs are not based on a medical model, since the posited "disease" of alcoholism is considered to be a spiritual disease; but for clinical purposes they are often understood as a general "mutual aid" approach.

It may be useful, at this point, to consider the definitions of "treatment," "disease," and "health" in terms of their dimensions in order to be better able to explore ethical issues and considerations. In perhaps over-simplistic terms, treatment is a planned, goal-driven change process which is tradition-bound, professional model bound, mutual aid bound, or self-treatment driven. The reader is referred to the "natural recovery" literature for the latter model (see Klingemann et al., 2001). Moreover, some authors claim that, at least in the field of alcohol misuser treatment, changes in alcohol consumption are brought about not by treatment interventions per se, but rather by the individual's choice to enter a treatment context (Bergmark & Oscarsson, 2005).

In reality, there are many models of illness (bio-chemical, actuarial, functional, experiential, social, political, religious, animistic, economic, and others) as well as of health, each with its own dimensions, concepts, processes, "demands," and, in terms of this chapter, ethical considerations.

In many countries, A.A. has been and continues to have a major influence in shaping the formal treatment for "addiction," "drug abuse," "drug use," and other coded terms and has been, so far, important for health professionals in the context of after-care treatment. At the end of the 1940s, a short term residential mixed program called the "Minnesota Model" was created that incorporated some of the Twelve Steps, offered A.A. groups during treatment, and encouraged long-term attendance at A.A. after discharge. Since the 1960s, the Minnesota program has become more medicalized and psychologized and has been especially successful in the USA, Iceland, and Sweden (Eisenbach-Stangl & Rosenqvist, 1998, p.10-11).

There are data that document the interchange between Twelve-Step and formal, professional-based treatment programs. In a number of US surveys, 52-66% of clients entering some form of treatment for drug use attended Twelve-Step meetings 1-3 months beforehand (Magura, 2007). In 2001, 34% of A.A. North Americans members were referred to A.A. by a treatment facility (other referrals being done by other A.A. members, by the member him/herself, or by the member's family [Alcoholics Anonymous, 2001]). Similarly, in Italy, the health system has been responsible for about 25% of those who come to A.A. meetings (Allamani, 2000).

In conclusion, the differences between the two worlds of the mutual-help driven A.A. and the clinical treatment sector has sometimes and in some places resulted in A.A. remaining aloof and distant from health care professionals, their institutions, and models. This limited interaction has, however, not prevented opportunities for co-operation between the two nor the pragmatic utilization of A.A. in clinical contexts. Actually, the two worlds are not opposed. Alcoholics Anonymous is said to add a spiritual dimension to the clinical approach without competing with it. In fact, Tradition Ten states that "Alcoholics Anonymous has no opinion on outside issues; hence the A.A. name ought never be drawn into public controversy" (The A.A. Service Manual, 1991-92, p S107). Thus the Fellowship in no way intends to interfere with the somatic or psychological skills of professionals, whether they be general practitioners, pharmacotherapists, psychologists, hospital-based, or belong to a broad range of university specialists.

7. Effectiveness

Within the A.A. fellowship, the effectiveness of the Twelve-Step program—as measured by abstinence from alcohol and a long-term life of sobriety if you regularly attend the group meetings—is said to be evidenced by the diffusion of the movement worldwide, and by the hundreds of thousands of people attending the meetings. It is also added that the programs "have stood the test of time." Even if there may be a few ethical reasons why A.A. ought to be interested in/committed to research—as ways of increasing its cooperation with traditional treatments—there is a concern in A.A. that the traditions of public anonymity and economic independence might be threatened by entering a standard study. This, together with the attitude that change is not necessary for A.A. (Seppala, 2001, p. 25), explains A.A.'s lack of interest in scientific research about itself.

Also, the current identification of Twelve-Step groups by health professionals as suitable after-treatment programs along with the relatively high percentage of referrals to Twelve-Step groups by treatment facilities (Magura, 2007), are also taken to be indicators of a broad consensus among professionals about the effectiveness of such groups.

But a caveat may be appropriate at this point. Since Kropotkin's intriguing volume (Kropotkin, 1921), much has been written and spoken about "mutual-help" as a concept, a process, an ideology, and as a model for change, but we can still not adequately generalize, empirically, about the critical conditions for effective "mutual-help" to commence, continue, and change when necessary, for particular people and in particular contexts.

If the Twelve-Step program is a spiritual one, how can its spiritual dimension be demonstrated to affect the disease condition? Nowadays the issue of how spirituality affects one's illness or disease does not pertain only to the Twelve Steps. There is an increasing body of research that studies the positive influence of spiritual and religious practices on both physical and mental health—e.g., blood pressure and the immune system (Seeman et al, 2003).

If a contemporary researcher is going to credit or discredit the "spirituality's" effect on the alcoholic's motivation to change by asserting the position that it is merely a subjective matter, s/he may suppose that spirituality is effective only for addicts who are believers and not for atheists and agnostics. However, the Twelve-Step program has been shown to be beneficial for both atheists and agnostics, even if to a different extent.

Recent American studies on the Alcoholics Anonymous program and spirituality seem to support the effectiveness of spirituality. Unfortunately they overlooked the distinction between God and Spirit, which is felt to be a substantial one for A.A. In a study from a small data sample (N=47) of two A.A. groups, longevity in A.A. predicted a preferred spiritual coping style (Horstmann & Tonigan, 2000). Another study, part of a larger one (project MATCH) examining 621 aftercare clients' and 415 outpatient clients' subjective impressions about A.A., documented that spiritual experience and God-consciousness were positively related with A.A. meeting attendance and practicing of prescribed A.A. behaviors (Tonigan et al., 2000). Although continuous measures of religiosity have not been shown to be predictive for A.A. attendance, the binary categorical values of Belief in God or not were able to indicate meaningful differences; in fact among the project MATCH 1,526 outpatient and after-care clients, 12-Step treatment was significantly less likely to "take" among those who identified themselves as atheist or agnostic. By contrast, when atheists or agnostics attended A.A., their abstinence increased in the same proportions as believers in God (Tonigan et al., 2002).

A researcher can also envisage Twelve-Step programs as a "black box" producing effects, and measure its success or failure in the same way as any other treatment program. Project MATCH was the most well-known US study, involving nine Centers with over 20 sites, 75 therapists, 952 outpatients and 774 after-care patients, testing three distinct alcohol user treatments:

- 12 sessions of Cognitive Behavioral Treatment,
- 12 sessions of Twelve-Step Facilitation, and
- 4 sessions of Motivational Enhancement Therapy.

The results of these three different treatment philosophies were approximately the same so far as helping patients to achieve significant changes in their drinking behaviors.

A Twelve-Step based therapy demonstrated, for the first time, equal and sometimes slightly better abstinence from drinking outcomes for many patients. After-care patients treated after some residential treatment had greater A.A. attendance as well as better abstinence from drinking outcomes. Patients who participated in mutual-help groups in the year after treatment maintained more abstinence, less substance use, less distress, fewer psychiatric problems, and more employment (Project MATCH, 1997).

8. Ethical controversies

Alcoholics Anonymous and other Twelve-Step Fellowships are the most prestigious, but they are not the only mutual help groups, most of which are non-spiritually oriented (Richardson & Goodman, 1983). Among those who also offer mutual help and care to alcoholics are: the French Vie Libre, the Swedish Links, the Polish A.A. Clubs, the Croatian and Italian Clubs for Treated Alcoholics, the American Rational Recovery System, and the Secular Organisation for Sobriety or SOS (Mäkela et al., 1996, p 207-211).

On the whole, mutual help groups manifest common features that distinguish them from the professional treatment model world. Included among these features are:

- participants in the mutual help groups share the same problem, whereas that is not the case with professional health workers;
- participants in mutual help groups all share their experience and have a symmetrical interaction among themselves, whereas the clinician and the client operate in the hierarchically-based asymmetrical fashion that is typical of the interactions between an authority and a dependent person;
- professionals are educated to be suspicious of passion, whereas passion is an important ingredient in mutual-help group activities; and
- in Twelve-Step meetings there is no leader and no suggestions are given beyond the sharing, whereas advice is mandatory in most clinical settings.

These differences remind us that Alcoholics Anonymous and the clinical treatment professions belong to different ethical categories: in brief, the former to a collective ethic, in which each participating person is represented as an end to the other; and the latter to an individualistic or group ethic, in which the actors behave instrumentally to relieve the patient's symptoms and increase the domain of health profession competence. The contemporary growth of professional interest in the effectiveness and dimensions of mutual help groups makes the ethical issues more evident. Ethical controversies and their resolutions have accompanied the history of all mutual help groups (Richardson & Goodman, 1983). A major problem is associated with "power." The social position of professionals, along with their networks and their "guilds," is able to provide them with the necessary power to influence the functioning of mutual help groups, generating an opposing reaction from them because their rights have been overlooked, though this is possibly hidden by virtue of the professionals' dominant position. To quote an example from Francine Lavoie, Andy Farquharson, and Mellen Kennedy (Lavoie et al., 1994), the professionals' dilemma can be to decide whether to facilitate mutual help meetings in a community, "so that a group finally gets started," or to wait until such a group "emerges under its own initiative"; in a parallel way the self-helpers' dilemma can be whether to rely on their own resources, or to use outside advice on organizational issues. In the case of the professionals, the question will concern the consequences of facilitating or not facilitating the group, though there are also additional questions to be raised about their motivations, whether they may be linked to personal professional agendas—e.g., organizational pressure to implement groups, or personal choice of more leisurely work schedule—or to broader values such as promoting better services to the community.

Many ethical questions concerning spirituality, religiosity, and powerlessness can also be raised with regard to Twelve-Step groups. Since it would be both space- and time-consuming to address all of them, only seven questions have been chosen as a representative "sample," each of which is provided with an answer that it is hoped will stimulate the reader to explore the issue in greater depth.

(a) Q: Why should a formal professionally-based treatment agent or agency refer a substance user, of whatever type, to a religious program like Twelve-Step?

A: Twelve-Step principles are based on a spiritual experience of addiction and healing, and can be understood only from such a perspective. However, they are not a religion and do not compete with any religion. Any participant has the opportunity to address his/her principle of existential meaning in his/her own way through the idea of the Higher Power. The positive attempt by professionals or lay people to understand the effectiveness of the meetings in social terms such as "solidarity" (I-you → "us") and "philanthropy" (available and accessible mutual help) are the views of outsiders that "remain at literal, concrete levels of analysis and fail to consider the nature of symbolic communication and the purposes it serves" (Seppala, 2001, p.175).

(b) Q: Being 'born" in a Christian cradle, is a Twelve-Step program inappropriate for different non-Christian cultures? Is it completely non-denominational—does spiritually-based mutual-help work as well for Muslims, Jews, and Buddhists?

A: A.A. has moved away from the ideologically Christian-religious oriented Oxford Group toward a transcultural perspective; moreover, it acknowledges the lay psychologist William James and psychiatrist Carl Gustav Jung among its main inspirations. On the whole, Twelve-Step groups look at and relate to addiction as a life-time process in which fellow human beings can inclusively receive as well as give, regardless of who has "the problem." Their anonymity and their focus on "principles, not personalities" may help to explain how they have diffused from the original white, American, Protestant, urban culture and environment into a global movement.

(c) Q: Is there a Twelve-Step mutual-help version that is suitable for atheists?

A: It is estimated that at least 5 percent of the United States population affirms atheism (Gallup & Lindsay, 1999), and that atheism and agnosticism may be even more diffused in other countries. The Big Book (Alcoholics Anonymous, 1976) faces this issue in chapter four "We agnostics" and Appendix II "Spiritual experience," in which just spirituality and the belief in a Higher Power, and not religion, are considered to be compatible with whoever is beginning to attend A.A. groups, and where we are reminded that most of the spiritual experiences in A.A. are what "the psychologist William James calls the 'educational variety'" since they generally "develop slowly over a period of time." Indeed it takes time for some A.A. fellows who attend the meetings to turn from a nonexistent or tepid spirituality to a definite form of spirituality, or even go back to the religion that they had abandoned years before.

(d) Q: Is the issue of "powerlessness" contradictory or even dangerous for a program considered to contribute to the "cure" of alcoholism and other addictions?

A: According to the Twelve-Step principles, dependence on alcohol and other psychoactive substances is a person's lifelong condition, and addiction is a disempowering situation deeply affecting her/his relationship with both the substance and others. The program's First Step is not to succumb, but to admit or to acknowledge that "we are powerless" and that "our life is unmanageable" (The Twelve Steps and Twelve Traditions 1988).

(e) Q: Could there be State support for a program that included the A.A. mutual-help Fellowship option?

A: As noted earlier, there are many examples of co-operation between A.A. (and other Twelve-Step fellowships) and health services. However, Tradition Seven states: "every A.A. group ought to be fully self-supporting, declining outside contribution," and fellows are strict about this issue. Any type of co-operation is not of a funded activity and A.A. does "it" for the need to implement the Twelfth-Step, "carry the message to alcoholics" (The Twelve Steps and Twelve Traditions, 1988).

(f) Q: How are we to understand those for whom A.A. "does not work"? Is it helpful, for example, to consider such a reality like a "medicine" that works for some but not for others?

A: The A.A. Twelve-Step program is not a medical treatment, with its specific indications and contraindications. Nevertheless its literature stresses that it is not for everybody, or for everybody at all phases and stages in their life, even if it is intended to help as many alcoholics as possible. However the professional who refers a client to Twelve-Step meetings should be ready to interpret a patient's criticism about the meetings as a possible denial of her or his alcoholic problem. In addition, the referring professional, as well as the alcoholic, need to be aware of and sensitive to a *de facto* reality: a group and a meeting is a complex network that may not be suitable for a specific person, or at that particular point in her or his life. Given the large numbers of Twelve-Step groups in many parts of the world and their general availability and accessibility, such a problem is likely to be resolvable.

(g) Q: How is it that some therapeutic communities applying Twelve-Step principles share underlying assumptions about rights, responsibilities, obligations, and techniques that can be viewed as institutionalizing the violation of the other as a basic necessity for achieving ultimate personal growth and freedom?

A: Coercion, with its all-too-often built in humiliation and violation of the other as a means to freedom or personal autonomy, is not a Twelve-Step approach. Such utilitarian ways of relating to "the other" is distant from A.A.'s and other fellowships' acceptance of spirituality and of sharing with and respecting others. Instead, the utilitarian approach—violation of the other and coercion—is specific to those health and/or court institutions, or to those therapeutic communities that may see A.A. or other fellowships as a means to attain the addict's good.

In conclusion, as far as a professional clinician is concerned, Twelve-Step programs should not be perceived as a formal treatment model, governed and changed by science-derived evidence, but rather as mutual help groups perceive themselves, as communities of healing (Seppala, 2001, p. 175). From this perspective, probably the best first step that professionals might take is to get sufficiently close in order to become aware of and to try to resolve the ethical issues raised by their interaction with mutual help approaches. One way to begin to do this is to recognize that "we" accept choices that are made not only on the basis of research results but also on the basis of beliefs and experiential know-how (Lavoie et al., 1994).

Allaman Allamani, MD (Italy) *Born in Albania in 1943, educated in Italy. Psychiatrist; Family Therapist, Researcher; since 1993 Coordinator of Centro Alcologico, Florence Health Agency. Author or co-author of 125 articles, editor or co-editor of 10 books. He is a member of the Editorial Board of Substance Use and Misuse and a faculty member of the Middle Eastern Summer Institute on Drug Use. From 1973 to 1993 he worked as a gastroenterologist clinician in the Gastroenterology Unit of Careggi Hospital in Florence. In the 1970s he co-founded the Tuscany section of the Italian Psychosomatic Society and the Centre of Interactional and Family Therapy in Prato, Italy; in the 1980s also co-founded the Tuscan section of the Italian Society of Alcohology. In the 1980s he contributed to the diffusion in Italy of the holistic ideas of Professor Jules Grossman from California, who through his workshops promoted a synthesis between the William Reich approach and a spiritual ad meditative perspective. In the same decade he contributed to a Regione Toscana project on Therapeutic Communication for helping professions together with Vera Maillart and others. Later on he started a comprehensive Alcohol Problem Treatment and Prevention program in Florence, also focused on eating problems, based on low access threshold, family and motivational approach, and co-operation with mutual-help groups. He developed the first community action alcohol projects in Italy in the Florence area. Well known to the Italian 12 step movements, he was the first non-alcoholic trustee of Italian Alcoholics Anonymous from 1997 to 2003. He is trustee of the Psychosomatics Training Institute, Florence, and member of the Kettil Bruun Society. He lives in Florence and has regular visits in California, where his adolescent son resides.*

Acknowledgement

Thanks to Shlomo Einstein, whose extremely rich comments and suggestions have been often incorporated in the text, giving it the best possible shape. Also I am grateful for the help he gave me in editing the text. I am grateful to John Kleinig whose positive criticisms helped me to reformulate my ideas even if not in agreement with his. Thanks to Theodore Godlaski for providing me some literature. And finally, thanks to Italian A.A. for the opportunity I have had to experience the world of A.A., especially during my service as non-alcoholic trustee at the Italian General Service Board during 1997-2003.

References

Alcoholics Anonymous. (1976). *Alcoholics Anonymous*. A.A. World Service Inc., New York.

Alcoholics Anonymous. (1957). *Alcoholics Anonymous Come of Age*. A.A. World Service Inc., New York.

Alcoholics Anonymous. (1965). Declaration at the 30th Anniversary Convention of A.A. in Toronto in 1965.

Alcoholics Anonymous. (Winter 2000-2001). *About A.A. A Newsletter for professionals*. A.A. World Service Inc., New York.

Alcoholics Anonymous. Membership Survey, 2001. A.A. World Service, New York, New York.

Alcoholics Anonymous. (1991-1992). *The A.A. Service Manual combined with Twelve Concepts for World Service*. 1991-1992 Edition. Alcoholics Anonymous World Services Inc., New York.

Alcoholics Anonymous. (1988). *The Twelve Steps and Twelve Traditions*. Alcoholics Anonymous World Services Inc., New York.

Allamani, A. & Petrikin, C. (1996). Alcoholics Anonymous and the Alcohol Treatment System in Italy. *Contemporary Drug Problems, 23*(1): 43-55.

Allamani, A., Cameron-Curry A., Zavan V., Cibin, M., Jean, G. (2000). Alcoholics Anonymous in Italy, An overview. *Alcologia, 12*(2): 61-66.

Allamani A. (2000). Alcolisti Anonimi: storia di un percorso italiano [Alcoholics Anonymous: history of an Italian pathway]. *Itaca, 4*, 10: 88-101.

American Psychiatric Association. (2000). *DSM-IV-Tr Diagnostic and Statistical Manual of Mental Disorders*. American Psychiatric Association.

Bergmark, A., Oscarsson, L. (2005). The concept of treatment for substance abuse—context, modality and choice. *Paper presented at the Annual Alcohol Epidemiology Symposium of the Kettil Bruun Society*, University of California, Riverside, May 30-June 3, 2005

Buber, Martin. (1953). *Gottesfinsternis* [God's eclipse]. Manesse Verlag Zurich.

Buscema, M. (1998). Artificial Neural Networks, *Substance Use & Misuse, 33*:1-3.

Bullock, M.L. (1990). Controlled trial of acupuncture for severe recidivist alcoholism. *Lancet, 335*: 20-21

Di Clemente, C. (2003). Auto mutuo aiuto, Spiritualità e Cambiamento. [Mutual self help, Spirituality and Change] *Paper presented at the second Italian conference on the co-operation between professionals and 12 step associations*. Piacenza, Italy, November 2003.

Eisenbach-Stangl, I., Rosenqvist P. (1998). *Diversity in Unity. Studies of Alcoholics Anonymous in eight societies*. NAD Publication n. 33, Helsinki

Gallup, G., Lindsay, D.M. (1999). *Surveying the religious landscape: trends in US beliefs*. Harrisburg, PA: Morehouse.

Fish, J.M. (1973). *Placebo Therapy*. Jossey-Bass, San Francisco

Freud, S. (1977). *Introductory Lectures on Psychoanalysis*. Engl Transl. Liveright Publisher Corp.

Grof, C. (1993). *The thirst for wholeness. Attachment, Addiction and the Spiritual Path*. HarperCollins, New York

Grof, S. & Grof, C. (1999). *Spiritual Emergency: When Personal Transformation Becomes a Crisis*. J.P. Tarcher, Los Angeles

Horstmann M.J., Tonigan, J.S. (2000). Faith development in Alcoholics Anonymous: a study of two A.A. groups. *Alcoholism Treatment Quarterly. 18*(4): 75-84

Illich, I. (1976). *Medical Nemesis: The Expropriation of Health*. Pantheon Books, New York.

James, W. (1958). *The Varieties of Religious Experience*. Mentor, New York.

Jean, G., Cibin, M., Pini, P., Aliotta, V., Bocchia, M., Allamani, A., Fanella, F., Fedi, R., Contreras, L., Perazza, D., Bocchia, M., Nuovo, M., Zavan, V. (2003). Interazione tra servizi alcologici e Alcolisti Anonimi [Interaction between alcohol treatment centers and Alcoholics Anonymous]. In: *Libro Italiano di Alcologia* [Italian Book of Alcohology] a cura di A. Allamani, D. Orlandini, G. Bardazzi, A. Quartini, A. Morettini, SEE Firenze.

Jellinek, E.M. (1962). *The Disease Concept of Alcoholism*. College and University Press, New Haven, CT.

Jung, C.G. (1954). *The practice of psychotherapy: essays on the psychology of the transference and other subjects*. Engl Transl. Pantheon Books, New York.

Jung, C.G. (1959). *Aion: researches into the phenomenology of the Self*. Engl Transl. Pantheon Books, New York.

Kant, I. (2001). *Critique of Practical Reason*. Engl transl. Cambridge University Press, West Nyack, New York, U.S.A.

Klingemann, H., Sobell, L.C., Barker, J., Blomqvist, J., Cloud, W., Elllinstad, T., et al. (2001). *Promoting self change from problem substance use. Practical implications for policy, prevention and treatment*. Kluwer Academic Publishers, Dordrecht.

Kropotkin, P. A. (1921). *Mutual Aid: A Factor of Evolution*. University Press New York

Kurtz, E. (1991). *Not-God. A History of Alcoholics Anonymous*. Hazelden

Kurtz, Ernst (1982). Why A.A. works. The intellectual significance of Alcoholics Anonymous. *Journal of Studies on Alcohol, 43*: 38-80.

Lavoie, F., Farquharson, A., Kennedy, M. (1994.) *Ethical issues in professional and mutual-help group collaboration: results of three workshops and proposal for further discussion*. Produced by mutual-help Canada.

Lowen, A. (1973). *Depression and the Body: The Biological Basis of Faith and Reality*. Penguin Books

Magura, S. (2007). The relationship between Addiction Treatment and 12-step Fellowships: current knowledge and research questions. *Substance Use and Misuse, forthcoming in Vol. 42*, 2007. This article is based on a paper presented at the 8th annual Middle Eastern Mediterranean Summer Institute on Drug Use, Rome-Florence, Italy, February 13-18, 2004 as part of planning for the For Whom is it Permitted, For Whom is it Forbidden Exhibit.

Mäkela, K., Arminen, I., Bloomfield, K., et al. (1996). *Alcoholics Anonymous as a mutual mutual-help movement. A study in eight societies*. The University of Wisconsin Press, Madison

McElrath, Damian. (1987). *A Spiritual Odyssey*. Hazelden Foundation, Hazelden.

Narcotics Anonymous. (1988). *Narcotics Anonymous*. Narcotics Anonymous World Services Inc, Van Nuys CA.

Project MATCH Research Group. (1997). Matching alcoholism treatments to client heterogeneity: Project MATCH post treatment drinking outcomes. *Journal of Studies on Alcohol, 58*: 7-29.

Rehm, J., Fisher, B., Hayden, E. (2003). Abstinence ideology and somatic treatment for addicts—ethical considerations. *Addiction Research and Theory 11*(5): 287-293.

Richardson, A., Goodman, M. (1983). *Self Help and Social Care: Mutual Aid Organisation in Practice*. Policy Studies Institute, London.

Rittel, H., Noble, D. (1989). Issue-Based Information Systems for Design. *Working Paper 492*, The Institute of Urban and Regional Development, University of California, Berkeley, California <iurd@uclink.berkeley.edu>.

Seeman, T.E., Dubin, L.F., & Seeman, M. (2003). Auto mutuo aiuto, Spiritualità e Cambiamento [Mutual self help, Spirituality and Change]. *Paper presented at the second Italian conference on the co-operation between professionals and 12 step associations*. Piacenza, Italy, November 2003.

Seppala, Marvin D. (2001). *The Twelve-Step Principles*. McGraw Hill, Hazelden.

Smith, D.E., Buxton, M.E., Bilal, R., Seymour, R.E. (1994). Cultural points of resistance to Twelve-Step program recovery. In: *Principles of Addiction Medicine*, C. Chase ed, Chapter 3

Tonigan, J.S., Miller, W.R., Connors, G.J. (2000). Project MATCH client impressions about Alcoholics Anonymous. *Alcoholism Treatment Quarterly. 18*(1): 25-41.

Tonigan, J.S., Miller, W.R., Schermer, C. (2002). Atheists, Agnostics and Alcoholics Anonymous. *Journal of Studies on Alcohol 63*(5): 534-541.

Tonigan, J.S., Kelly, J.F. (2004). Beliefs about A.A.A and the use of medications: a comparison of three groups of A.A. exposed alcohol dependent persons. *Alcoholism Treatment Quarterly 22*(2): 67-78

World Health Organisation. (1991). *Traditional medicine and modern health care. Progress report by the Director-General*. Geneva (unpublished document, A44/10).

Glossary

chronicity: quality of the diagnosis of a long-term disease promoting the creation of long term specialized treatment programs

conversion experience: a new perspective on life revealed when one "surrenders" after struggling against hopeless pain and suffering

encounter with the other: a sharing process between two different persons -the essence of mutual help.

ethics: attitude seeking "for the good" whose values draw upon the domain of right, freedom-autonomy , and responsibility.

higher Power: the spiritual dimension that is acknowledged to get help in the Twelve-Step program

mutual help fellowships: group of individuals who mutually help each other about a common problem

otherness: the acknowledgment of the shared differences of the other person in a group

powerlessness: inability to confront the illness and the world demands

recovery: according to the Twelve Steo program, both being abstinent and entering a process of personal maturity

relapse: go back to drink again and to be a passive object of fear

revolving door: the circular process of moving from abstinence to relapse, amd vice versa

solidarity: the sharing experience of similar problems among individuals

spirituality: a fourth human dimension beyond the fields of biology, psychology, sociology

universalistic: collective, attributable to each individual

universal right: one aspect of each human need for justice

utilitarian ethics: ethics giving value to the good of the individual or of the group

Notes

1. Horst Rittel has suggested that problems can and should be usefully categorized into two types: *"tame problems"* and *"wicked problems"* The former are solved in a traditional known and tried "water fall paradigm"; gather data, analyze data, formulate solution, implement solution. The latter "wicked problems" can only be responded to individually, each time anew, with no ultimate, repeatable solution. This distinction, regarding a taxonomy of problems, has yet to be considered in terms of its utility, "demands" and implications for substance use prevention programs and processes. Nor have ethical parameters associated with this thesis been considered (Rittel and Noble 1989).
2. *"Chronicity"*, as measured by 'lapse' and 'relapse' is a critical dimension in the relatively recent "medicalization" of a range of types of uses and users (DSM-IV TR) and can be considered as a factor for the creation of specialized treatment programs for "THEM," separate from the mainstream of medical care. "Chronicity" is a shared and sharing process which facilitates mutual help between strangers who have all "been there" before.
3. *'Complicated'* and *'complex'* are often confused and used interchangeably. They are quite different in their essence. A *complicated system* is a combination of many units, each maintaining its identity along the way and outside of the system. Consider a screw in a 747 Jumbo jet. If you modify the screw a little bit the system won't work; complications will occur. In a *complex system* each component changes, over time, losing its identity outside of the system: caterpillar ↔ cocoon ↔ butterfly ↔ egg ↔ .... Each process faces its own ethical challenges.
4. This shibboleth continues to "empower" and mystify alcohol, and/or other "drugs" and to "disempower"

2-6 The Moral Goal of Treatment in Cases of Dual Diagnosis

Jeannette Kennett, Ph.D. and Stephen Matthews, Ph.D.

Abstract

Substance use and misuse occurs at a very high rate among people with mental health problems, and the relationship between the two conditions is complex. In this chapter we argue that treatment of substance use in dual diagnosis clients must begin from an understanding of the losses suffered by those with mental illness. We outline the fundamental condition of effective agency, unified agency, which is disrupted in mental illness, and show how this is needed to secure access to central social and moral goods such as continuing employment and satisfying relationships. We argue that drug use will be disvaluable primarily in so far as it too prevents access to this set of agential goods and focuses the agent on synchronic well-being to the exclusion of diachronic well-being. The goals and methods of treatment for dual diagnosis patients should thus reflect the primary impairment to unified agency.

Key Words: agential goods, autonomy, diachronic well-being, dual diagnosis, effective agency, ground projects, moral disvalue, moral goods, restorative function, self-medication, synchronic well-being, unified agency

Introduction

Substance use and misuse occurs at a very high rate among people with mental disorders, and the relationship between the two conditions is complex.[1] Until fairly recently the special needs of this group went largely unacknowledged, and even now services are limited, fragmented, and many individuals are denied adequate treatment for their conditions. What are the moral issues for therapy raised or sharpened by examination of this most marginalised set of clients? In this paper we argue that treatment of substance use in dual diagnosis clients must begin from an understanding of the losses suffered by those with mental illness. We outline the fundamental condition of effective agency, unified agency, which is disrupted in mental illness, and show how this is needed to secure access to central social and moral goods. We claim that drug use is disvaluable primarily in so far as it too impairs access to this set of agential goods. The person with co-occurring mental illness and substance use problems is thus doubly disadvantaged.

Drug use by the mentally ill is often claimed to be an attempt by the ill person to self-medicate their psychiatric symptoms. We examine the self-medication hypothesis and through listening to the voices of affected individuals, argue that the evidence points more broadly to the use of drugs to alleviate or compensate for the disabled agency, distress, and exclusion from social goods suffered by those with mental illness. Drug use may thus in some circumstances have a restorative function for the individual concerned. We then consider what implications our account of the losses imposed by mental illness and of our understanding of the self-medication hypothesis have for the goals, methods, and background moral assumptions of drug treatment programs for dual diagnosis clients and of the attitudes and values that should inform such programs.

Unified Agency, Ground Projects, and Diachronic Welfare

It is a cliché to say it, but valuable lives are meaningful and fulfilling. What underpins these features is slightly less obvious. The value of a life might be registered merely in terms of the aggregation of the well-being a person experiences moment-by-moment through their life, but such an approach, though it might be adequate for (say) a cat or a parrot, would fail to properly account for those goods which we hold to be most central to a flourishing human life, and which are only available to us because we are temporally extended agents.[2] Compare a life composed of a series of short term, but on the whole pleasant, experiences and sensations, such as might arise from eating or bathing or being massaged or listening to nice music, with a life in which the person, say, developed enduring, happy relationships, was a hardworking and much appreciated committee member for the local hospital, wrote a well-received biography, and pursued a passion for growing orchids. Suppose this second life also contained significant early hardship and illness (to which the later charitable work was in part a response) such that it is clear that the aggregate of momentary well-being or synchronic well-being in the first life was greater than in the second life. Nevertheless the second person might look back on her life with greater satisfaction. It is plausible to suppose that hers is the more valuable life.[3]

Flourishing lives, it seems, are marked by such things as relationships which stand the test of time. They are marked by challenges and also by the rewards that accrue to a person who has stuck at a task and completed it despite perhaps many obstacles being placed in the way. Anyone who has successfully parented a child, or who has managed an organisation over an extended period, or who has completed a PhD, or undertaken elite sports, knows that their achievement unavoidably involved difficult, boring, and sometimes painful experiences. Nevertheless, as we often say "it was worth it". We should say then, that though good lives may come in many different forms they all have significant diachronic value.

Let's be a little more systematic in giving expression to the diachronic goods. What we are talking about is a range of moral and social goods that accrue to persons who successfully engage in projects and occupy certain roles. For us, these terms are used in a quasi-technical way. Our projects include, in a broad sense, any ongoing activities, large or small. Performing a short piece of music would constitute a project of the small variety, but it would be a project nonetheless because in describing it as a performance we need to invoke the performer's agency at each of its points. More important though, to our identity and diachronic well-being, are the success of what Bernard Williams has called 'ground projects'. According to Williams (1981, p.5), we each have "a set of desires, concerns or…projects…which help to constitute a character." A person's ground projects are the force "which propel…him into the future, and give…him a reason for living". While any desire, even the simple desire for a glass of water, propels us some way into the future, the cluster of projects and concerns which give our lives their particular shape and character are longer term. Through taking on these projects we provide ourselves with reasons that extend into the future and shape the actions and decisions we will take then. In adopting, pursuing, juggling, modifying, and completing our various projects we extend our agency across time and to a significant extent, become authors of our own unique life stories.[4]

Ground projects typically include such things as learning a skill, playing a sport, studying, pursuing a career, raising a family, maintaining a friendship, or working for a political or moral cause. The loss or failure of these projects (or most of them) would, suggests Williams, remove the meaning from the person's life. We can see why by focusing on our various roles. Seeing through our projects depends upon the capacity to occupy and sustain certain roles over extended periods of time. Roles, in this sense, are close cousins of projects. So, for example, it is in the role of parent that one takes on the project of raising children. It is in the role of fiction writer that one takes on the project of writing a novel; and so on. The roles we occupy are critical to our identity, to how we see ourselves and how we are seen. Writer's block is frightening, not just because it threatens the completion of the novel but because it threatens my conception of myself as a writer. The so-called 'empty nest syndrome' is not simply about a mother missing her children when they leave home. She mourns the loss of her role even while she acknowledges the success of her project.

The capacities required to sustain roles and see projects through are the very capacities that constitute us as effective agents. Christine Korsgaard (1989) argues that effective agency is unified agency. Effective agents must have the capacity to deliberate, choose, and act in accordance with their choices. In order to act successfully however, both at each particular time and over time, they must eliminate conflict among their disparate motives and adopt a unity of purpose. Because most of our worthwhile and significant relationships, projects, and roles are longitudinal, judgments about how we manage and balance the demands of each must be made with a temporally extended conception of our agency. Whenever we act for the sake of a project extending over time we unify ourselves.

The capacity for unified agency contains both forward-looking and backward-looking elements. Faced with choices now about what I will do tomorrow, next week, next year, or beyond, my decision commits me pragmatically (at least) to viewing myself tomorrow, next week, etc., as the very same agent as the choice-maker I am now. From a backward-looking perspective the actions I undertake now may only make sense when I consider them as part of plans made at some earlier time. For my behaviour now, understood as mere bodily movement, constitutes no action that can be ascribed to me in rational terms, unless it can be viewed as behaviour performed as the outcome of some deliberation which aims at fulfilling a certain end.

Successful agency thus presupposes a unity of self over time. This is a presupposition that is required by both the actor, and by those with whom he interacts. (Many of our projects are, after all, joint projects, or require the assistance of others for their success.) Unified agency is also critical to an understanding of autonomy. Autonomy is a self-governing capacity. To govern yourself successfully you need to be able to make sense of yourself at any particular time as implementing the projects, and occupying the roles, of the larger temporal unit to which you belong. It is in virtue of this capacity that individuals are able, as Korsgaard (1999) puts it, to constitute themselves into persons.[5] Critical to this analysis is that unified agency is not merely something a person happens to possess at particular times. It is something you possess only if you are disposed in a systematic way to exercise control over your affairs over continuous periods of time.

In order to appreciate more fully the significance of the unity of agency to the success of our roles and projects and so to our diachronic welfare we only need to consider cases in which it is absent. Suppose you were unable to complete tasks that were of importance to you. You might enroll in a course in which you were initially greatly interested; but after a while you would get distracted from your original purpose and you would lose the motivation to attend classes, write essays, and so on, and eventually drop out. Or you might find it impossible to maintain relationships. You might find yourself attracted to a person, and initially it would be fun. But inevitably an aspect of their personality would grate, and you would terminate the relationship and move on to the next. Suppose your problem here was quite general: you simply lacked the capacity to see through any project over an extended period. Consequently, you failed to complete courses that you had taken up with enthusiasm; you had no long-term friends; you continually lost or left the jobs you took; and so on. Such a picture is one of a life pitted with failures, one that lacks in a global sense the values that mark a meaningful human life.

Now to clarify we are not saying that unity of agency is guaranteed to deliver the diachronic goods we have been speaking of. Mere longevity of a career, relationship, or whatever is not of value. Clearly, for example, a relationship plagued by unmitigated boredom, dislike, or even violence, is a bad thing; if it cannot be repaired it is better terminated. In the film American Beauty (1999), the central character Lester Burnham has what might have seemed by one bland description the perfect suburban lifestyle: a long and stable family existence, steady job, beautiful wife and home. From the outside he seems to have a pretty good life partly because he has managed to obtain these diachronic goods. In the film narrative what might have seemed the perfect suburban existence is the source of Burnham's anger and bitterness. The capacity for unified agency, which Burnham presumably possessed, is never sufficient for attaining diachronic well-being. In addition to sustaining attention to certain projects and relationships within a life, they must go well: for example, careers must be fulfilling, and relationships must flourish; projects in general must be of some worth to the agent.[6] However, and importantly, the great goods that may attach to marriage, parenting, work, and so forth are conditional upon the capacity for unified agency. The inability to unify oneself thus blocks access to these goods.

Agency Failures and Diachronic Losses

The case above of someone who fails to complete their projects, or to fulfil valuable roles, was described in an abstract way. But of course there are concrete cases of this. Elsewhere (Kennett and Matthews, 2003; Kennett forthcoming) we have argued that what is centrally disvaluable about mental illness is the way it denies sufferers access to the diachronic goods—the goods that depend upon unified agency. Take again the example of a person studying for a degree. Unless that person is able to be governed over time by the set of reasons—to attend classes, to study, and so forth—generated by this project, the project will fail. A person whose mental condition impairs or interrupts their capacity to extend their agency over time is especially vulnerable to the failure of their ground projects. There are a variety of reasons why their agency may be ineffective. Some of these different reasons can be traced to features that are particular to the different disorders. So, for example, major depressive illness severely undermines motivation; dissociative conditions may induce amnesic gaps; disordered thought and speech, and hallucinatory episodes in schizophrenia may make it impossible to sustain attention to a project or to work co-operatively with others. In broad terms, recurrent or chronic mental illness often means that sufferers cannot rely on their future selves being appropriately affected by their present plans and decisions. Their projects are thus derailed or given up, and they lose the social roles that are so important to identity and self-esteem. Their losses are compounded by the reactions of those around them who shy away from socially odd behaviour, distress, anger, or unresponsiveness. The goods of close loving relationships may thus be lost or are unattainable.[7] The stigma of mental illness cements social rejection and exclusion. The evidence from Link (1982/1987) is that experiences of social rejection and stigma have a negative effect on employment prospects, quality of life, self-esteem, and social functioning on the mentally ill even after controlling for the severity of psychiatric conditions. Wright et al (2000: 80) found that:

> *Even for patients who have had extensive experience in the mental patient role, subsequent experiences of rejection increase and crystallize patients' self-deprecating feelings. The impact of these new experiences of rejection appears to persist over time and, indirectly, contribute to a decrease in some client's feelings of mastery and control a year later.*

Directly or indirectly then, the symptoms of mental illness affect sufferers' capacities to be effective agents, and this is something people without a mental illness take completely for granted.

Drug use too can lead to impairments of agency and diachronic losses. It seems obvious that cravings for particular drugs, or states of intoxication and withdrawal may interfere with the pursuit of more worthwhile activities and the discharge of the individual's responsibilities.[8] Khantzian (p3) suggests that drug dependence leads to 'disuse atrophy'. "Chronic drug use interferes with a person using and developing their psychological capacities (cognitive, perceptual, emotional) to deal with life challenges." The individual who devotes himself each day to obtaining his hit often cannot sustain appropriate attention to his work or family. He is dominated by short term concerns. While he may often enough prefer abstaining to using, for the very reasons that he would then be able to meet the demands and reap the benefits of studying, work, or caring for family, his preferences are vulnerable to reversal when the cravings hit.[9] Those who misuse drugs thus fail to unify themselves over time in the service of their ground projects, and their projects and the social roles associated with them are lost or endangered. Indeed, in cases where there are not these kinds of losses we do not think that drug use is particularly morally problematic.[10]

The moral dimension of the disvalue arising out of disunity is most clearly seen when we consider the negative effects on those others (e.g., children, friends, spouses, students) who depend on the agent fulfilling their social and moral roles and attending to their projects. When a person's agency is disrupted in the ways we've described, others too will be denied access to significant diachronic goods. The disvalue to both parties typically includes moral disvalue.[11] This is no more prominent than in cases where illness or substance misuse, or both, disrupt the relationship between parents and children. In this connection consider Lloyd Wells' description of his patient Mary, who has a serious dissociative disorder: "...She was taken aback by the speed with which her son had grown up, and her sense of discontinuity in his life. "I've been cheated," she said. "Almost eighteen years have gone by since my son was born, and I haven't even had the opportunity to live most of it..." (Wells, 2003: 301). Her son also suffered long term disadvantage from his mother's gross disunity. As we have argued elsewhere (Kennett and Matthews, 2003), in order for both Mary and her son to properly engage in the mother-son relationship, it is necessary to sustain attention to this ground project in a continuous way. Disunified agency is precisely the condition in which such sustained attention fails to take place. Wells reports (p.301) that, "the boy rather plaintively said on one occasion how hard it was to go to school never knowing who would be at home when he returned". In many of her altered states Mary lacked the capacity to engage in any rich interpersonal relations, let alone meet the demands of parenting. The resulting loss to her son was profound.

For those in the grip of a chronic mental illness, the losses to self become magnified through lost friendships—both existing ones, and those that might have been forged but for the social isolation that comes from conditions such as schizophrenia, and major depressive illness. These are moral losses given the weight of moral value we attach both to important social roles, such as parenting, and to close friendship. The losses arise from the negative effects of disruptions to agency on the web of social connections which give meaning and value to the lives of all involved. And as we will argue, the treatment of such pathologies of agency, reaching their nadir in dual diagnosis cases, is best recognised as a moral issue (and not just a medical issue). In advocating this, however, we distinguish our position from the stern moralism that, for example, characterises approaches to drug use in the so-called 'war on drugs' which is too often a 'war' on persons who are already marginalised and vulnerable. As Mary's case makes clear, the moral losses that make treatment and support of sufferers a moral enterprise do not necessarily imply any moral wrongdoing on the part of those whose agency is under threat.

When mental illness co-occurs with substance misuse the agential losses described above can be expected to multiply. Sufferers are increasingly marginalised. In addition to losses of jobs, relationships, and education, their basic subsistence needs, health needs, and even their liberty is threatened. The problem is especially pressing once we recognize the extraordinary rates of co-morbidity and its associated features of homelessness, imprisonment, and stigmatization of co-morbid individuals, both within services, and the general community. We now turn to these issues.

The Size of the Problem

Rates of co-morbidity

It's widely agreed that substance use and substance use disorders such as dependency and addiction occur at a very high rate among those with both serious and less serious mental disorders and vice versa. In the US the 1991 Epidemiologic Catchment Area (ECA) study found a lifetime prevalence rate of substance use disorders of 16.7%

in the general population, but this figure skyrocketed for those with mental disorders. Prevalence rates for schizophrenia sufferers provided in the study were 47%, for affective disorders 32%, and for anxiety disorders 23.7%. According to Todd et al (2004) UK studies have found 1 year prevalence rates of substance misuse problems among those with psychotic illness or first episode psychosis of 36.3% and 37%. In Australia the National Survey of Mental Health and Well Being (NSMHWB) conducted in 1997 also found high rates of co-morbidity and low rates of treatment seeking. Other recent Australian research (for example, Siegfried et al, 1999) has found prevalence rates of 59.8% for substance use among outpatients with schizophrenia. In their paper on meeting the treatment needs of multiply diagnosed consumers, Steele and Rechberger (2002) provide an overview of the staggering number of individuals in the United States, diagnosed with at least one co-occurring mental health disorder and substance abuse disorder. According to their figures obtained via the Substance Abuse & Mental Health Services Administration - National Advisory Council (SAMHSA NAC, 1997), in any given year, the number of co-morbid individuals approximates 10 million people. Of the 7.2 million adults (18-54) who have dual disorders and were living in identified households, the majority were found not to have received treatment at all—not even in the primary health care sector (SAMHSA NAC, 1997, cited in Steele and Rechberger, 2002).

Problems associated with co-morbidity

There is evidence from Lowe and Abou-Saleh (2004) that co-morbidity is associated with an increased risk of violence, suicide, and worse clinical and social outcomes. Alvidrez et al, (2004), and Kavanagh et al, (2000), cite a variety of studies which indicate that co-occurring substance misuse in those with a serious mental illness is associated with exacerbation of symptoms, decreased medication compliance, disrupted relationships and an increased risk of hospitalization, homelessness, incarceration, victimization and serious infections. This is confirmed by the over-representation of those with both mental illness and substance misuse in homeless and prison populations.

(i) Homelessness

According to the US group NAMI (formerly known as the National Alliance for the Mentally Ill) one in twenty persons with a severe mental illness is homeless (See Human Rights Watch Report, 2002). If we include people with no secure accommodation it is likely to be much higher. In a study by Catherine Robinson (2002) of mentally ill homeless people living in Sydney and Brisbane around 85% reported that they had been diagnosed with one or more mental disorders and interviewers' impressions were that around 70% had a high and regular drug or alcohol intake. They also reported high rates of imprisonment and illness, low rates of employment, and high levels of assault and other trauma.

(ii) Imprisonment

The US Human Rights Watch group estimates that one in six U.S. prisoners is mentally ill at any given time. The prevalence of mental illness in the prison population is three times higher than in the general population, and many of these have problems with substance misuse. The Mental Health Co-ordinating Council (NMHCC), a peak body for non-government organisations in New South Wales, reports that of people with a mental illness in NSW prisons 86% had a history of substance misuse, 76% had active substance misuse at arrest, and 66% of their crimes related to substance misuse, usually non-violent. They argue that a zero-tolerance approach to drug offences automatically brings people with dual diagnosis within the criminal justice system. The trauma of prison life may lead to a worsening of symptoms and makes treatment for both the mental illness and drug use problematic. The result is increased rates of suicide, self harm attempts, and inmates with mental illness becoming victims of violence (NMHCC fact sheet).

(iii) Stigmatization within services/exclusion from services

In a 1991 paper on mental patients with substance misuse problems Salloum and colleagues note that,

> *these patients have been invariably depicted as being difficult, manipulative, dangerous, noncompliant with, and abusive of medications. They have been described as displaying a pattern of "attention seeking and help rejecting" behaviour to service providers, and they are in a chronic state of "crisis."*[12]

Attitudes among mental health professionals may have changed somewhat with an increased focus on this patient group. A recent Australian survey found that the majority of mental health worker respondents were positive about treatment interventions and held non-discriminatory, non-moralistic attitudes towards users (See Pinikahana et al, (2002).

However another recent Australian survey found that 82% of mental health staff found dealing with dual diagnosis clients "moderately or very difficult", mainly due to lack of resources, training, and fragmentation of services (Kavanagh et al., 2000). And another study found that 60% of staff thought that management of this group was inadequate and 73% of them believed that this was mainly because this group was very difficult to treat. Only 20% nominated lack of services as the problem (Siegfried et al., 1999). A Victorian Government website acknowledges that it is common for practitioners to blame clients for being difficult and unresponsive to treatment rather than to question whether the treatment and support services offered are appropriate.[13] Punitive or detached responses to clients in inpatient settings aggravate their sense of alienation and lack of worth. As one of Robinson's (2003) respondents poignantly says:

> *I was in the mental health ward at the hospital the other day. You're enclosed in a room you can't get out of and there's a mattress on the floor... That's not going to make you get better, that's not going to help you. (p.29)*

Overwhelmingly, Robinson (2003) says, her respondents criticised the failure of mental health staff to spend time with their clients, to listen to them and to assist them to work through their problems through counselling and practical support. She argues that the stigma suffered by those with mental disorders is exacerbated for those with a dual diagnosis and that mental health and support and accommodation services are "sites of continued stigma and discrimination" (p.4). Stigmatising attitudes are clearly a barrier to effective treatment since the client is not treated as an equal partner in treatment. A trusting relationship seems essential for successful therapy, but treatment which is discriminatory, hostile, or moralistically toned engenders resentment and withdrawal on the part of the client. Worse yet, if a person with a dual diagnosis feels blamed for their condition, it is hard for them to resist the thought that to some extent, they deserve such blame. As we argue, this effect is precisely not what is required when they are attempting to re-connect with the social world.

The Self-Medication Hypothesis

Why, given the poorer outcomes and greater impairment reported for dual diagnosis patients, do people suffering mental illnesses use non-prescribed drugs at such a high rate? Three main hypotheses have been suggested (Harris, 2005; Hides, 2004; Goswami, 2004). First, the secondary mental illness model suggests that substance use may cause mental illness. Second, the shared vulnerability model suggests that the mental illness and the substance use may have a common cause. Third, the substance use may be secondary to the mental illness. Specifically, it may be an attempt to alleviate or self-medicate painful psychological states or other psychiatric symptoms.

Our main focus here will be on the self-medication hypothesis (SMH). Although heavy use of certain substances, for example, amphetamines and alcohol, may trigger psychosis or depression, the National Co-morbidity Survey carried out in the United States in the early 1990s found that for the great majority of individuals with co-occurring substance misuse and mental health disorders, the mental disorder developed first.[14] And though something like a common cause or vulnerability might underlie some cases of co-morbidity—for example Hides et al (2004) postulate that personality factors such as neuroticism or impulsivity could be critical—the causes of many mental illnesses are not well established. We do not think in any case that these other two hypotheses are incompatible with the SMH. Personality factors may influence the coping strategies chosen by the client one of which may be self-medication. Further it is relevant that the SMH originated in addiction literature where it is proposed that substance use is a response to severe distress caused by "'integration failure', i.e., failure to achieve the kind of social acceptance, competence, personal autonomy, or ability to experience negative emotions at the lowest level that can reasonably be expected..." (Gelkopf et al., 2002: 142). Mental illness can, we've argued, cause, as well as be partly constituted by, such "integration failures" or, in our terms, failures of unified agency. We do not claim then that the SMH provides a complete account of substance use and misuse in individuals with a co-occurring mental disorder since the interactions between the two are complex, but we do think that, properly interpreted, it is well supported and consistent with our account of the diachronic values which are at stake in these conditions. We claim that in a significant number of cases substance use is motivated at least in part by desires for social participation and acceptance or by the distress that comes from social exclusion. An understanding of how motives for substance use are connected with the values attached to agency and identity should lead to an ethical framework for treatment which eschews punitive and paternalistic approaches to the user and incorporates those values into all aspects of therapy.

Although the SMH is intuitively highly plausible, it has been challenged. As it was originally formulated (Goswami et al, 2004: 140) it proposes that the users' choice of drugs is not random but "is based on the specific pharmacological ability of the substance to improve specific symptoms or patterns of emotional distress." So formulated it seems to contain a success condition and has been interpreted in this way by a number of researchers in the mental health field (Goswami, 2004; Lammertink et al., 2001). If the SMH is true, they suggest, we should (a) expect mentally ill drug users to display less severe psychiatric symptoms than their non-drug using counterparts; (b) expect patterns of drug use to vary by type of disorder, and (c) expect that different reasons should also be given for the use of different substances and those reasons should not be "exclusively hedonistic…but should also be symptom oriented." (Goswami, 2004, p.141). We think that seeing substance use and misuse fundamentally as a response to the distress and disability of mental disorder does not commit us to hypothesis (a) and perhaps not to (b).

First and most obviously (a) appears to conflict with the evidence cited above of more severe symptoms and worse outcomes for the dually diagnosed mentally ill. If the SMH commits us to (a) then it looks false. But the SMH is not best read as predicting quite generally that users with mental illness will be better off than non-users with mental illness. The issue is more complex. For the SMH would also predict that those suffering more severe symptoms and distress will have stronger motivations for drug use, and this would constitute at least a partial explanation of the observed correlation between substance misuse and poorer outcomes for dual diagnosis patients. They were among the worst off to begin with. Goswami et al. (2004) argue that conducting studies of hospitalised patients with severe psychopathology in whom attempts at self-medication must already have failed, introduces a bias in testing this thesis. In their recent study they compared the severity of symptoms of matched groups of outpatients with schizophrenia and found that the dual diagnosis group was significantly less symptomatic than the schizophrenia only group. This raises the possibility that some individuals with less severe mental illness do manage their symptoms through self-medication. If they are reasonably successful they will not come to the attention of service providers and so evidence in favour of the hypothesis will be systematically excluded from assessments of it.

In assessing the SMH against the evidence of poorer outcomes in users we need also to distinguish between negative outcomes that can be traced directly to the substance use, i.e., to the psycho-pharmaceutical effects of the drugs used, and negative outcomes resulting from social and institutional policies toward users. Housing programs for the mentally ill often exclude substance users, so they end up homeless; homeless people fare worse in general health, in personal safety, and in their access to other benefits such as psychosocial rehabilitation services, training and employment (Alvidrez et al., 2004; Robinson, 2003). Where their substance use is criminalised they are also exposed to the ills of the criminal justice system and they suffer a double dose of social disapproval and exclusion. Small wonder if their mental health problems are exacerbated in such harsh circumstances.

Distinguishing between immediate and longer-term effects of substance use is also critical. Certain substances might ease psychiatric symptoms and distress in the short term and so account for their use in line with the SMH, yet exacerbate them or create other problems over the longer term, so accounting for the negative outcomes reported for dual diagnosis patients. For example alcohol use might provide temporary relief from anxiety or depression but is likely to worsen these conditions over time or with heavy use. In a recent study (Alvidrez et al., 2004, p. 351) respondents saw most drug use as providing only a temporary fix.

> *Just when somebody is depressed, usually they want to drink to forget about it, then it only makes it worse...*
>
> *It can only subdue it a bit but it won't completely help your bravery or your fairy tales to become better through drugs.*

We argue therefore that the SMH does not stand or fall on the success criterion, narrowly interpreted. We think it is rather a theory about the motivations and expectations of users. If I take glucosamine sulphate in the belief that it will reduce my arthritic symptoms and improve my life—instilled perhaps by talking to some friends—then I am surely self-medicating whether or not my symptoms improve and even if, objectively, they worsen. Of course we should be very interested in whether, when, and what self-medication works. To the extent that self-medication is successful this will have significant moral implications for treatment policy and broader social policy. Criminalising such use seems particularly unjust, as do threats to remove clients from treatment programs should they fail to abstain.

The evidence for prediction (b), that patterns of use will vary by disorder, is mixed and suggests that factors such as price, availability, social competence, and legal consequences also influence choice of drugs (Lammertink et al., 2001; Gandhi et al., 2003). The existence of other factors influencing choice doesn't of itself undermine the SMH but might make it difficult to substantiate by comparing group patterns of use. Nevertheless there is significant evidence that substances are chosen for specific therapeutic effects. For example there is clear evidence that alcohol is chosen to reduce anxiety across a range of disorders and some evidence that it does reduce anxiety.[15] A review article (Plume, 1995) examining the relationship between Attention Deficit Hyperactivity Disorder (ADHD) and self-medication with cocaine cites studies which found that 50% of inpatient cocaine abusers met the criteria for mood disorders and other studies showing a strong relationship between cocaine use and ADHD. Cocaine has similar properties to the medications used to treat ADHD and Plume cites a large number of studies to support her conclusion that users with ADHD "frequently report a paradoxically placid response to cocaine as well as temporary relief from hyperactive symptoms" (Plume, 1995, p.3). The author also cites several case studies where treatment with medication for ADHD led to relief both from ADHD symptoms and from the desire to use cocaine (Plume, 1995). In looking to see whether there is evidence to connect choice of drugs to particular disorders it is also important to keep in mind that drug users may have undiagnosed disorders.[16] A focus on psychiatric inpatient samples may once again have a distorting effect on the overall picture and lead to premature dismissal of (b) and rejection of the SMH.

The most plausible prediction from the SMH is (c) which focuses on the goals and expectations of the user. Spencer et al (2002) distinguish between self-medication models, social affiliation models, and motivational models of drug use. The motivational model, according to them, suggests that drug use is mediated by cognitive processes including "thoughts, memories, and perceptions that determine a person's expectations about the direct and indirect effects that [drugs] will have on the person's affect"

(Spencer, et al, 2002, p.234). They argue that this model is better placed to explain drug use. We think the self-medication model is best interpreted as a motivational model. It connects symptoms and effects of the disorder to the agent's motives for using drugs. As originally formulated it is primarily concerned with coping motives: in cases where there is co-occurring mental illness we see no reason why it could not include social motives, and enhancement of well-being motives, given the deleterious effects of mental illness on these aspects of life. We examine user's accounts of their motives to see if they are consistent with the hypothesis that their substance use is an attempt to self-medicate. We include here motives connected to alleviation of, or compensation for, the disabling effects of their mental illness on their social agency.

Many of the stated reasons for substance use do not differ significantly between those with and without a mental illness. Does this speak against the SMH in cases of dual diagnosis? We do not think so.

First, as we have already noted, it is likely that there are significant levels of undiagnosed mental illness and disorder amongst those who misuse drugs.

Second, common motives won't count against the hypothesis if the practice of self-medication is widespread among drug users. As we've noted, the SMH originated in the addiction literature. Common motives are thus just what we should expect.

Third, the implied suggestion that mentally ill drug users just want to get high (and the implied disapproval of such hedonistic motives) leaves us with no explanation as to why the mentally ill are so much more inclined to hedonism than the rest of us. On the face of it this seems unlikely. But higher rates of drug use among the mentally ill compared with the broader community would be predicted by the SMH since the increased distress, fragmentation, and social disability suffered by those with mental illness provide particularly powerful motives for use. In line with this suggestion a recent study of 18,849 respondents on past 30 day use of alcohol, marijuana, and other illicit drugs and past year unmet need for and use of mental health care, concluded that substance use "varies with past year unmet need for mental health care and mental health care use in ways consistent with the self-medication hypothesis." (Harris and Edlund, 2005, p.117). Another study found that posttraumatic stress disorder was a significant predictor of time to relapse for women after discharge from inpatient substance misuse treatment (Brown et al., 1999). Compared with non-PTSD patients they "relapsed faster, drank more on those days where they did drink, and had more heavy drinking days during the follow-up period." (p.115) Significantly they also reported higher levels of "psychiatric distress" and evidenced "a greater likelihood of meeting diagnostic criteria for current major depressive disorder, bipolar disorder, panic disorder, and a cluster B personality disorder." (p.120) Spencer et al (2002) also found that increases in symptoms in individuals with psychotic disorders predicted increased motives for use. They argue that "motives are the generative mechanism through which symptoms lead to dependence on alcohol and cannabis" (p.243).

Fourth, if dual diagnosis clients' reasons for drug taking reflected those of the general population as being fundamentally hedonistic, then their usage should not be sensitive to its effect on their symptoms. But there is some reason to think that it is sensitive in this way. A measure of this sensitivity, as we saw above under the evidence for (b), is that counterfactually, usage is responsive to the severity of symptoms. That is, other things being equal, someone self-medicating would be motivated to reduce their usage were their symptoms to diminish in severity. As mentioned, cocaine usage in individuals with ADHD is sensitive in just this respect. Such claims of a general counterfactual dependence between usage and symptom relief are very difficult to test because of the fact that most often drug usage involves (at least) two effects: the high, and the relief of symptoms. The ADHD case studies are special because these individuals did not experience the normal high response, but only the calming reaction. So, in a very real sense, these studies do test the counterfactual dependence claim by controlling for the hedonistic motives. So we think they importantly support both the prediction from (c), as well as further work into considering the reasons why people with a mental illness self-medicate.

Fifth, the attribution of hedonistic motives may in part be an artifact of study designs which ask respondents to provide simple yes or no answers to items on a list. This restricts the options and responses available, forcing on the respondent opinions or intentions, which he or she might otherwise not have thought of or expressed. It presents the user with possible motives for drug use that may be present to some degree and so are assented to, but that might not be very salient to their decision making or might simply be instrumental. Hedonistic motives such as 'to get high' or 'to feel good' which are common to drug users with and without mental illness are thought to be inconsistent with the SMH. But such effects might be sought primarily as the means by which other more important goals connected to effective agency and central social goods, such as to 'increase socialization', 'increase confidence,' or 'decrease anxiety', can be met. E. J. Khantzian, the 'father' of the self-medication hypothesis, describes the case of Bob an alcoholic who had 'always felt lonely and isolated as a child and recalled a "restriction, suppression, repression, oppression and depression"'. In recalling the effect of his first drink Bob said:

> *I began to feel free—free to feel. I felt happy, even giddy—unashamed, unpretentious and uninhibited. I felt that I finally was a member of the human race. 'One of the guys,' and equal to others'. (Khantzian n. d., p.2)*

People living with the stigma and disability of mental illness might be excused for seeking to feel like 'one of the guys and equal to others' through one of the very few means available to them.

A recent qualitative study of community-dwelling clients, which used open-ended questions to elicit reasons for drug use, supports the view that drug use is motivated by desires related to living a normal life. Alvidrez et al. (2004) found that "respondents generally described using drugs to remove negative feelings or to regain normal functioning rather than to 'feel good' or 'get high'". For example:

> *[You use drugs] in order to get a boost of energy, help you regain resources and get back in touch with things, which is my motivation, to get back up to a normal functioning level. (p.351)*

An early case study of the psychotropic effects of methadone and opiate drugs reports that none of the patients spoke of "using drugs in order to achieve a euphoric state. Their use of opiates was intended to help them lead quasi normal lives." (McKenna (1982: 6).) And in a personal account of the use of opiates and methadone maintenance to deal with bipolar disorder, one woman says:

> *So I was faced with a dilemma. These anti-depression drugs were awful. They were doing horrible things to me and they weren't even working effectively. When I took heroin though, I felt great...The depression cleared up. I used to go to my bedroom and shut myself away from everybody for most of the day, but now I was out playing with the kids, reading them stories, coping with their behaviour. I was coping with life for the first time in two years.*[17]

Alvidrez et al. (2004, p.348) report that a range of quantitative and qualitative studies on self-reported reasons for use have consistently shown that severely mentally ill patients report using drugs "to alleviate depression, anxiety, low self-esteem and boredom; to escape reality; and to be more socially engaged." Robinson (2003, p.33) argues that among participants in her study of homeless mentally ill people, drug and alcohol use, over-dosing and other harmful behaviours should be "understood as 'symptoms' of forms of social exclusion as well as of...trauma and mental disorder". The use of drugs as a coping or even survival mechanism was clearly evident.

Drugs and alcohol were used to medicate the extreme pain of traumatic events as well as to 'quieten' aspects of mental disorders such as hearing voices. Bill (57) commented that without drug and alcohol use, he would not have survived the terror of having to sleep rough and would have committed suicide. In Tara's case, despite having had a stroke and blood clot related to alcoholism, her abusive husband encouraged her addiction to...'benzos' (benzodiazepines) as a way to manage behaviours associated with obsessive compulsive disorder (Robinson, 2003, p.25).

While the use of drugs may be a strategic choice in dire circumstances it also reinforces those circumstances. In some cases the outcomes are tragic. Anne Deveson tells of the last time she saw her son Jonathan, a homeless schizophrenia sufferer.

> *He had a large bundle of white pills, wrapped in polythene, and he went to take two of them.*
>
> *'Please Jonathan' I begged, 'put them away.'*
>
> *'Listen,' he said, 'they gave my father morphine for the pain in his cancer, and it helped him, right, and no-one's going to tell me not to take stuff for my pain, right?'*
>
> *Later Deveson found him banging his head and crying:*
>
> *I took him to the couch and held him in my arms and stroked his head and kissed his head, and all the while his body was heaving with sobs, while he shuddered out disconnected statements like, 'I can't go on...the pain in my head...terrible, terrible...look at me...look at what I've fucking become...oh God! (Deveson 1998, p.255))*

Jonathan whose physical health was already precarious from living on the streets, died of an overdose a few days later, aged 24. But it would be a mistake to think that his primary problem was his drug use rather than the circumstances to which that use was a response. His story as recounted by Deveson reveals systematic institutional failure to provide appropriate care and support to him and his family. It is a case study in inadequate resources, fragmentation of services and barriers to services that result in exclusion of the most complex and needy cases.

Evaluative Goals and Frameworks for Therapy

The accounts given by dual diagnosis clients of their reasons for substance use and its effects are consistent with the fundamental tenets of the self-medication hypothesis and with our account of the disabling effects of mental illness on agency, and so on access to the central human goods that are conditional on effective agency. What are the moral implications of this reading of their substance use and misuse? First and foremost, moral condemnation seems utterly out of place. Their drug use no more indicates a bad character than does a resort to morphine to relieve the suffering of cancer. While we should not deny the obvious dangers and disadvantages of heavy or illicit drug use we should also acknowledge users' reasons of self-medication in order to gain insights into appropriate treatment approaches and institutional design. Thus we should acknowledge that drug use may aim to be, and sometimes succeeds in being functional for individuals in difficult circumstances. It may help them to manage their condition, to re-negotiate their social world, or simply provide a much needed escape from the trauma of their lives.

That clients with a dual diagnosis self-medicate is evidence of the effort they are making to help themselves to function socially and to manage their lives. It is evidence of an expression of their autonomous agency, and of their need and desire to access the primary social goods of projects, roles and relationships. Viewed this way, treatment programs that regard drug use either as just a medical problem, a disease to be managed and controlled—thus treating the patient as a medical object—or as something to be punished as foolish or immoral—thus treating the patient like a disobedient child—are subject to criticism because they inevitably leave out the person who is struggling to regain a meaningful life. Traditional hierarchical models of treatment, such as the medical model, build inequity into their structure and so undermine, rather than support autonomous agency.

An individual with a dual diagnosis is a person whose capacity for competent agency is threatened. Such competence is not something that may be switched on the way a light is switched on, because our capacity for agency comes in degrees. The process of restoring agency is thus likely to be gradual. It follows that treatment programs which do not take account of the difficulty of their client's lives and the fragility of their agency, which implicitly or explicitly view their drug use as morally wrong or as the involuntary expression of a disease, and so see abstinence as the fundamental goal of treatment, or which take a confrontational approach to drug use and see current use or relapse as a barrier to participation in treatment, are failing their clients in both the sympathy and the respect that is due to them.

In the remainder of this final section we review some specific treatment goals. Our thesis is that these goals are to be measured against the over-arching aim of clients to restore to themselves, and those they care about, the means to attain the primary social goods of successful ground projects and important social roles.[18]This requires that treating agencies see dysfunctional aspects as failures related to the whole person and their context, and address them with eyes for their inter-relations. Treatments that disaggregate the client into separate dysfunctional aspects are almost certainly doomed to fail. Thus treatments that see a patient as merely a presently-disabled object, abstracted from their history of trauma, abuse, and illness, and from a future with real social possibilities, won't see the need to restore to the patient strategies for a continuing or ongoing agential unity. This may seem to state the obvious, but some programs, to which we refer below, fail to invoke such understandings in their dealings with clients.

It is worth noting again in this context the constitutive connection between extended agency and ground projects: it is in taking on a project and being guided by the reasons arising from it that I extend my agency and thus unify myself. Thus it is no good for a treatment program to be nominally concerned about the restoration of a patient's agency or autonomy without at the same time recognising that the building of meaningful ongoing roles and projects is just what it is to restore that agency or that autonomy.

Specific Treatment Frameworks

(i) Tolerating relapse: abstinence versus harm minimisation

The fundamental moral goal of treatment is the restoration and support of well-functioning agency in part through the creation of pathways to social goods.[19] There may be a variety of steps to restoring agency but importantly they need to be decided upon by the client in partnership with the clinician or counsellor. Will an emphasis on abstinence secure the goals of treatment? In some circumstances abstinence might be a means to the end but it is a mistake to confuse it, as some programs do, with the end itself. We argue that confusing the client's fundamental interest in rebuilding their life and in regaining or developing the capacity to extend their agency, with a mere instrumental factor such as abstinence, will tend to prevent real progress and to obscure the central problems inherent in these cases.

Consider in this connection the example of a person on a methadone program. Notice first that in such a case there is no abstinence from the methadone itself. Yet those stabilized on such programs benefit from improved functioning and access to social goods such as employment and education that result from their release from the time-consuming, risky, and expensive activities of securing illegal drugs. But now consider the effects of imposing on a client in such a program the strict requirement of abstinence from all drugs apart the methadone. Take a client who attends a methadone clinic and is told their treatment will stop if they breach a rule to stay clean. Any amount of illicit drugs in their system will be regarded as a breach and result in termination of the program. Thus for the treating institution the goal here appears to be driven by a mistaken assessment of what is morally important. The goal is for the person to be drug free, because the moral menace just is the presence of illicit drugs in the person's system. This results in treatment that regards the client suspiciously as a potentially naughty child who must be monitored and told what to do. It presupposes a punitive, controlling attitude on the part of the treating agency, which is unilateral in its focus. Such an attitude is likely to be strongly resented by those clients who otherwise might have expected to be helped to live a normal or at least near-normal life. The client views his or her drug problem as preventing access to some central social goods, like maintaining close relationships and holding down a job. So there is a natural and appropriate expectation that the goal of treatment include a view of the patient within this social context. The client, therefore, might legitimately expect this fundamental goal of treatment s/he holds to be shared by the agency delivering the treatment.

The moral force of this expectation and the moral shortcomings of treatment programs which ignore it are beautifully illustrated by the following extended extract from a personal account of methadone treatment.

> *There are differing opinions on how to judge the 'success' of any treatment. For the 'drug-free-world' lobby, no treatment is successful unless the client becomes completely drug-free.*
>
> *This is too black and white...Not everyone can live up to these expectations, it is just setting people up to fail. By these criteria an anti-depressant treatment is not successful, no matter how happy or functional the patient is, until they stop taking anti-depressants; heart medication is not successful, no matter how many years it adds to a patient's life, until the patient is free of the medication. It isn't a requirement in other treatments, why should it be a requirement in methadone treatment?*
>
> *A more reasonable target is to see if the client's life improves: health, living conditions, social reintegration, employment, education, family relationships. I mean, who cares if the person is swallowing a small amount of liquid once a day, so long as he/she is healthier and happier than before. When the person is ready to become drug-free, then let it happen, but it is counter-productive to push and push until they are pushed over the edge.*
>
> *...Some clinics and doctors have draconian rules, in the client's best interests of course, but that doesn't stop us from feeling as if we are being treated like prisoners rather than ordinary human beings...Surely someone with drugs in their urine is more in need of treatment; whose interest is it in to discontinue their program? ...not the client or his/her family, they lose a stabilising influence in their lives; not society, one more person has a reason to steal and cheat...Just dispensing methadone is not enough, much better results come by working through the client's problems. Working through problems with clients, not telling them what's best for them and they'll do it whether they like it or not, is the way of the future. Taking each client as an individual, tailoring their treatment to best suit the client's needs.* ***As addicts begin to be regarded as humans with rights and feelings, so the treatments become humane and the addicts become humanised.***[20]

In this light consider the research by Drake et al (2004) whose review of treatment interventions included analysis of 26 controlled studies of treatment programs for dual diagnosis patients. They comment that the most successful interventions for dual diagnosis clients are those "...with more flexible programs encouraging people who are not yet abstinent to enter gradually without requiring abstinence" (p. 368). They also note that the extensive research on dual diagnosis treatments they have made indicates that people who remain in treatment long term achieve better outcomes, and the reason for this is partly "...that effective programs are flexible enough to manage relapses without dismissals and therefore to prolong retention"(p.369). This is consistent with the experience in Australia where harm minimisation, rather than abstinence provides the framework for drug user treatment. The National Drug Strategy (1997) outlines the following principles of harm minimisation:

- Focus on the harms caused by drug use, rather than drug use per se.
- Maximise the intervention options.
- Choose appropriate goals, giving priority to those that are practicable and realisable.
- Respect the rights of persons with drug-related problems.

The key indicator of success of the harm minimisation approach is net reduction of harm, whether or not there is reduction of use. A harm minimisation framework accepts that the user may not be ready to cease their use and works within that fact. Services adopting this approach identify several stages of behaviour change from pre-contemplation to maintenance and see lapse and relapse as a normal part of the change process. By treating the user with dignity and respect, and focusing on building trust, such programs have been successful in engaging them in treatment programs. (cited in Youth Substance Abuse Service training manual)

(ii) Seeing and addressing what drug use covers up

Programs that would insist on abstinence, which remove clients for breaches, and which in general are disconnected from the underlying reasons for drug use, will fail to see what drug use may be covering up. They will therefore fail to address the substantive issues which revolve around absence or losses of meaning and valued long-term goals, such as close relationships or significant activities.

An American study of two treatment programs for homeless mentally ill drug abusers brings into sharp focus the disconnection between the program philosophy, structures, and expectations, and the actual daily lives of their clients (Weinberg and Kogel 1995). The programs were both heavily influenced by the so-called 12 step approach with its focus on client powerlessness, self-criticism, making reparations, confronting 'excuses' for drug use, and bad ways of thinking. Such programs tend to pathologise what are in fact strategies to enable one to function on the street and take little account of the difficulties of street life. For example tiredness (from sleeping rough) can be seen as lack of commitment to the program. Such programs feature a lack of integration of mental health and substance use treatment with other supports, a lack of follow up, or the capacity to support lasting change. The low success rates—Weinberg and Koegel (1995, p.208) report that only 15% 'graduated' from the residential program, and significantly less from the day program, and these figures do not include any follow-up to check for longer-term success—are indicative of an approach which fails to connect with the genuine problems of clients. Recovery was seen in terms of abstinence, and participants were expected to take personal responsibility for their recovery. This seems like a very top down approach—client involvement within preset parameters—with very few, or no opportunities for negotiations on goals, approaches, etc.

At the centre of this kind of treatment failure is the recognition by clients that their substance misuse masks greater problems of loneliness, depression, social dislocation, unemployability, and homelessness, and that treatment programs which miss these substantive features while focusing on drug use fundamentally misunderstand what is at issue. As Weinberg and Kogel (1995, p.216) point out, the evidence for this was that "…many [clients] eventually confronted the disappointing realisation that much of what they disliked about their lives would remain even if they won the struggle to remain sober." They point out in addition that "…sometimes sobriety and stability just made [their problems] more blatantly apparent and harder to face"(p. 216). Thus clients recognising the problems of their "living situations, their families, friends, and acquaintances, the inability to sustain employment, their poverty, and their future prospects"(p. 216), had the reasonable hope that treatment would include these issues within its purview. And as Weinberg and Kogel (1995, p.217) put it, "Conversely, the recognition that toeing the line would not necessarily ensure their disappearance often threatened commitment to treatment." These results are exactly what would be predicted by the SMH and by our account of the agential values threatened in mental illness. In this connection it is worth considering a pastiche of quotes from interviewed clients.

Charlie says,

> *…first and foremost is I'm extremely lonely…I'm totally unemployable. I'm over the hill, got no references, no appreciable skills, patchy work history at best, former alcoholic and addict, homeless…it's very depressing. I mean [participating in treatment] is not the answer to all my problems. Recovery is not going to make my problems go away. (Weinberg and Kogel, 1995, p. 217)*

Many clients viewed their substance misuse as escape from insurmountable difficulties or boredom. Giving up drugs was therefore, from their point of view, elimination of a synchronic benefit—the relief conferred by the drug—without any compensating improvement in either synchronic or diachronic welfare. As one client put it,

> *…it's hard for me to stay clean, because my life when I'm clean is so horrible. They say it gets better, but for me it never got better. I knew when I relapsed that it wasn't the answer, that I was gonna be even worse off, but I didn't care. I just wanted relief from that misery, even if it was only going to be a temporary fix and was going to make things worse in the end. (Weinberg and Kogel, 1995, p. 218)*

Finally, it is noteworthy that for all of the dangers and long-term deleterious effects of drug taking, for many clients within this homeless group their drug-using lifestyle provided a vestige of social connectedness which they lost during phases of abstinence. Says one,

> *I've got 32 days [of sobriety] and really happy about that, but since I'm not drinking anymore, I can't go to all the places I used to go to drink. I mean I don't want to go to those places, but on the other hand now all I do is sit around and watch TV all day, and it's lonely as hell. I mean it sounds awful, but I turn on the TV even though there's nothing I want to watch because it's kind of company….(Weinberg and Kogel, 1995, p. 220)*

Effective treatment programs must therefore address in a practical way the need for accommodation, community, and meaningful activity. Targeting drug use in isolation is not the answer because it is not usually the primary problem.

(iii) Strengthening self-control

Some philosophers see drug dependence or addiction as a disorder of control, and this suggests that the answer to problematic drug use is to strengthen the agent's capacities for self-control. Some philosophical discussions and psychological analyses of self-control see the will as a kind of muscle. Levy and Bayne (2004), for example, refer to some experiments by Baumeister et al (1998) which suggest the will may suffer depletion. Accordingly, in what the latter call 'ego-depletion',

> *...self-control, apparently, is 'used up', and must be recharged before it is available again. And as with muscle strength, regular exercise of self-control over the longer term can build up its resources. (Levy and Bayne, 2004, p. 461)*

Thus it might be thought one approach would have therapy focus on building a strong will through regular exercises for the ego. The tried and true techniques of self-control constitute such exercises—avoiding situations of temptation, distraction, self-binding, focusing on the goods to be obtained by abstaining, aggregation of motives opposed to satisfying the desire for the drug and so forth. The trouble is that the glimpse we have had at the chaotic and difficult lives of those with co-occurring substance abuse and mental disorder should indicate that a focus on these techniques is not likely to succeed in the first instance, though it might be a useful adjunct to treatment. A central problem is that aspects of one's mental illness disable one's attempts at utilizing these techniques. According to one dual diagnosis patient,

> *[For] 4 years I had been experiencing mild cravings, I would often have dreams about...scoring and taking drugs...Then, when I was suffering with depression (around this time I was actually diagnosed as having manic-depression) the depression severely impaired my self-control, concentration, thinking, rationality.*[21]

As the example of the cocaine users with ADHD suggests, it is most effective to address the underlying causes of drug use in dual diagnosis clients. Sometimes, as in the ADHD cases, this will involve finding appropriate medication for the client's mental illness but medication alone is not always enough. As one of Robinson's respondents says: "They're using what they call the medical model, which is basically medication and that's it...there's more to treating the illness than medication" (2003, p. 29). Our view is that agents need resources in order to exercise self-control and when they have enough of them, when they are strongly attached to worthwhile projects, to other individuals, and to the community, the need for self-control is likely to diminish, because the reasons driving drug use diminish.

Programs that work

(i) Integrated Programs

The constitutive connection between a person and their ground projects that we have argued for above suggests that addressing drug use in people with mental illness requires explicit attention to the disruption and loss of social roles, relationships, and projects upon which our identity and self-esteem are built, suffered by those individuals. All available research points to the importance of an integrated approach to therapy. As

Drake et al (2004, p. 367) remark, "The most consistent finding across recent studies is that effective dual disorders treatments are integrated, which means that they combine mental health and substance misuse interventions at the clinical coalface." The elements of this approach support our view of the importance of building and supporting the capacity for effective agency and assisting the agent to access the central social goods. According to Drake et al (2004) these elements include (ideally) provision of the same clinician to deal with the dual problems in a coordinated fashion; modifications of, and combinations of, treatments for the different disorders; social skills training for developing relationships; education programs for families addressing the interacting aspects of mental illness and substance misuse; and finally, the modification of pharmacological interventions to address both conditions in ways which do not leave the client vulnerable to abusing medications, which may interact with alcohol and other substances. We would suggest that successful programs also must address in an integrated way the institutional exclusion and disadvantage which prevents re-engagement with the community. A person without a home is unlikely to be able to maintain themselves in treatment, let alone progress to the point where they can engage in work, education, and enjoy stable relationships.[22]

(ii) Stage-Wise Treatments

Drake et al (2004) advocate what they call stage-wise treatments. They claim "[e]ffective programs tailor interventions to the person's stage of treatment or recovery" (p. 367). There are important similarities between this approach and the harm-minimisation approach outlined earlier. The stages here include (i) engagement with another to establish a trusting relationship, (ii) motivating the engaged client to position themselves for recovery, (iii) developing skills and supports for managing both illnesses, and (iv) learning strategies to prevent relapse. This approach recognises that the individual presenting for treatment is more than simply a set of symptoms to be managed or controlled, for it recognises the need to focus on the agency of the person, and to support the person in making changes and building competences, rather than attempting to impose change. The approach thus presupposes both an understanding of the impairments to effective agency dual diagnosis clients have sustained while also showing them due respect and acknowledging their central stake in recovery. In particular, the stage-wise approach is consistent with the need to patiently restore the client into a position of gradually taking over the reins of their life.

Conclusion

The perspective of those with co-occurring mental illness and substance use problems regarding their motivations for drug use and their assessment of treatment methods point to a clear need for professionals to focus on building relationships, extending respect to their clients, eschewing detached managerial approaches, and developing an understanding of their client's lives. Such qualitative research is also supported by the statistical analyses which recognise good outcomes for both the integrated and step-wise programs considered above. The focus in successful programs on building trusting therapeutic relationships is no accident. Such a relationship provides a point of stability for the client; they gain what for many of them is a rare experience of respectful engagement and goal sharing and so the relationship itself is a diachronic good upon which they and those treating them can build the project of recovery. When this occurs clients have the best chance of re-accessing the primary moral and social goods their condition deprives them of and also of controlling or eliminating their drug use.

Steve Matthews Ph.D., Senior Lecturer in Philosophy, School of Humanities and Social Sciences, Charles Sturt University, Wagga Wagga, NSW and Senior Research Fellow, Centre for Applied Philosophy and Public Ethics (an ARC funded Special Research Centre), Charles Sturt University, Canberra, and Visiting Senior Research Fellow University of Melbourne and the Australian National University.

Jeanette Kennett Ph.D., Principal Research Fellow, Centre for Applied Philosophy and Public Ethics (an ARC funded Special Research Centre), The Australian National University, and Visiting Principal Research Fellow University of Melbourne.

References

Alvidrez, J., Kaiser, D., & Havassy, B. (2004). Severely mentally ill consumers' perspectives on drug use. *Journal of Psychoactive Drugs, 36*(3), 347-355.

American Beauty. (1999). Dreamworks. Written by Alan Ball. Directed by Sam Mendes.

Baumeister, R. F., Bratslavsky, E., Muraven, M., & Tice, D. M. (1998). Ego-depletion: Is the active self a limited resource? *Journal of Personality and Social Psychology, 74,* 1252-1265.

Bratman M. (2000). Reflection, planning, and temporally extended agency. *The Philosophical Review, 109,* 35-61

Brown, P.J., Stout, R.L., & Mueller T. (1999). Substance use disorder and posttraumatic stress disorder comorbidity: Addiction and psychiatric treatment rates. *Psychology of Addictive Behaviours, 13*(2), 115-122.

Carrigan, M.H., & Randall, C.L. (2003). Self-medication in social phobia: A review of the alcohol literature. *Addictive Behaviours, 28*(2), 269-284.

Deveson, A. (1998). *Tell me I'm here.* Ringwood, Australia: Penguin Books.

Drake, R. E., Mueser, K. T., Brunette, M. F., & McHugo, G. J. (2004). A review of treatments for people with severe mental illnesses and co-occurring substance use disorders. *Psychiatric Rehabilitation Journal, 27*(4), 360-374.

Gandhi, D.H., Bogrov, M.U., Osher, F.C., & Myers, C.P. (2003). A comparison of the patterns of drug use among patients with and without severe mental illness. *The American Journal of Addictions, 12,* 424-431.

Gelkopf, M., Levitt, S., & Bleich, A. (2002). An integration of three approaches to addiction and methadone maintenance treatment: The self-medication hypothesis, the disease model, and social criticism. *The Israel Journal of Psychiatry and Related Sciences, 39,* 140-151.

Goswami, S., Mattoo, S., Basu, D., & Singh, G. (2004). Substance abusing schizophrenics: Do they self medicate? *The American Journal on Addictions, 13*, 39-150.

Harris, K. M., & Edlund, M.J. (2005). Self-medication of mental health problems: New evidence from a national survey. *HSR: Health Services Research, 40*(1), 117-134.

Hides, L., Lubman, I., & Dawe, S. (2004). Models of co-occurring substance misuse and psychosis: Are personality traits the missing link? *Drug and Alcohol Review, 23,* 425-432.

Human Rights Watch Report. (2002). Ill-equipped: US prisons and offenders with mental illness. Retrieved from http://www.hrw.org/reports/2003/usa1003/3.htm#_Toc51489445

Husak, D, N. (2004). The moral relevance of addiction. *Substance Use and Misuse, 39*(3), 399-436.

Kavanagh, D.J., Greenaway. L., Jenner, L., Saunders, J.B., White, A., Sorban, J., & Hamilton, G. (2000). Contrasting views and experiences of health professionals on the management of comorbid substance misuse and mental disorders. *Australian and New Zealand Journal of Psychiatry, 34,* 279-289.

Kennett. J., & Matthews, S. (2003). The unity and disunity of agency. *Philosophy, Psychology, Psychiatry, 10*(4), 305-312.

Kennett. J. (2002). Talking to your kids. *Meanjin, 61*(2), 34-43

Kennett. J. (forthcoming). Mental disorder, moral agency and the self. In Steinbock, B. (ed.), *The oxford handbook of bioethics*. Oxford: Oxford University Press.

Kessler, R., Nelson, C., & McGonagle, K. (1996). The epidemiology of co-occurring addictive and mental disorders: Implications for prevention and service utilization. *American Journal of Orthopsychiatry, 66,* 17–31.

Khantzian, E.J. (n. d.). Addiction: Disease, symptom, or choice. *Counselor: The Magazine for Addiction Professionals*. http://www.counselormagazine.com/display_article.asp?aid=addiction.asp

Korsgaard, C. (1989). Personal identity and the unity of agency. *Philosophy and Public Affairs, 18*(2), 101-132.

Korsgaard, C. (1999). Self-constitution in the ethics of Plato and Kant. *The Journal of Ethics, 3*(1), 1-29.

Kushner, M.G., Abrams, K., Thuras, P., & Hanson, K.L. (2000). Individual differences predictive of drinking to manage anxiety in non-problem drinkers with panic disorder. *Alcoholism: Clinical and Experimental Research, 24*(4), 448-458.

Lammertink, M., Lohrer, F., Kaiser, R., Hambrecht, M., & Pukrop, R. (2001). Differences in substance abuse patters: Multiple drug abuse alone versus schizophrenia with multiple drug abuse. *Acta Psychiatrica Scandinavia, 104,* 361-366.

Levy, N. *Autonomy and addiction*. Unpulished Manuscript.

Levy, N., & Bayne, T. (2004). A will of one's own: Consciousness, control and character. *International Journal of Law and Psychiatry, 27*(5), 459-470.

Link, B. G. (1982). Mental patients status, work, and income: An examination of the effects of a psychiatric label. *American Sociological Review, 47*, 202-15.

Link, B. G. (1987). Understanding labelling effects in the area of mental disorders: An assessment of the effects of expectations of rejection. *American Sociological Review, 52,* 96-112.

Lowe, A.L., & Abou-Saleh, M.T. (2004). The British experience of dual diagnosis in the national health service. *Acta Neuropsychiatrica, 16*, 41-46.

McKenna, G.J. (1982). Methadone and opiate drugs: Psychotropic effect and self-medication. *Annals New York Academy of Sciences, 398*, 44-53.

NHMCC Fact Sheet. Retrieved from http://www.mhcc.org.au/factsheets/factsheet1_Criminal_justice.htm

Pinikahana, J., Happell, B., & Carta, B. (2002). Mental health professionals attitudes to drugs and substance abuse. *Nursing and Health Sciences, 4,* 57-62.

Plume, D. (1995). The self medication hypothesis: ADHD and chronic cocaine abuse. Retrieved on February 21, 2005, from http://www.addcentre.co.uk/selfmed-cocaine.htm.

Robinson, C. (2003, July). Understanding iterative homelessness: The case of people with mental disorders. Report for The Australian Housing and Urban Research Institute. ISBN: 1 920758 52 6.

Salloum, I.M., Moss, H.B., & Daley, D.C. (1991). Substance abuse and schizophrenia: Impediments to optimal care. *American Journal of Drug and Alcohol Abuse. 17*(3), 321-336.

Siegfried, N., Ferguson, J., Cleary, M., Walter, G., & Rey, J.M. (1999). Experience, knowledge and attitudes of mental health staff regarding patients' problematic drug and alcohol use. *Australian and New Zealand Journal of Psychiatry, 33,* 267-273.

Spencer, C., Castle, D., & Michie, P. (2002). Motivations that maintain substance use among individuals with psychotic disorders. *Schizophrenia Bulletin, 28*, 233-247.

Steele, L.D., & Rechberger, E. (2002). Meeting the treatment needs of multiply diagnosed consumers. *Journal of Drug Issues, 32*(3), 812-823.

Swendsen, J.D., Tennen, H., Carney, M.A., Affleck, G., Willard, A., & Hromi, A. (2000). Mood and alcohol consumption: An experience sampling test of the self-medication hypothesis. *Journal of Abnormal Psychology, 109*(2), 198-204.

Todd, J., Green, G., Harrison, M., Ikuesan, B.A., Self, C., Baldacchino, A., & Sherwood, S. (2004). Defining dual diagnosis of mental illness and substance misuse: Some methodological issues. *Journal of Psychiatric and Mental Health Nursing, 11*, 48-54.

Velleman, J. D. (1991). Well-being and time. *Pacific Philosophical Quarterly, 72.* Reprinted in Velleman, (2000). The Possibility of Practical Reason, 56-84. Oxford: Clarendon Press.

Watts, J. and Priebe S. (2002). A phenomenological account of user's experiences of assertive community treatment. *Bioethics Vol 16*(5), 439-454.

Weinberg, D., & Kogel, P. (1995). Impediments to recovery in treatment programs for dually diagnosed homeless adults: An ethnographic analysis. *Contemporary Drug Problems, 22*(2), 193-236.

Wells, L. (2003). Discontinuity in personal narrative: Some perspectives of patients. *Philosophy, Psychiatry & Psychology, 10*(4), 297-303.

Williams, B. (1981). *Moral luck.* Cambridge: Cambridge University Press.

Withers, R. Methadone Treatment: relief from Heroin Addiction. http://www.geocities.com/HotSprings/9740/methadone.html

Wright. E. R., Gronfein, W. P., & Owens, T. J. (2000). Deinstitutionalization, social rejection, and the self-esteem of former mental patients. *Journal of Health and Social Behaviour, 41*, 68-90.

Youth Substance Abuse Service. Orientation to the alcohol and other drugs sector education and training department manual. Melbourne Australia.

Glossary

agential goods: agential goods are those primary moral and social goods available to persons especially in virtue of their capacity for temporally extended agency. An example of such a good would be a long term relationship or a career.

autonomy: autonomy is the capacity we have to govern ourselves. To govern yourself successfully you need to be able to make sense of yourself at any particular time as implementing the projects, and occupying the roles, of the larger temporal unit to which you belong. It is in virtue of this capacity that individuals are able to constitute themselves into persons.

diachronic and synchronic well-being: diachronic well-being is the value attaching to an aspect of someone's life arising from its extension through time. Diachronic well-being is contrasted with synchronic well-being which is value attaching to a momentary period within a life. An example of synchronic well-being would be the pleasure derived from lying in a warm bath. Diachronic well-being is not the summed total of successive events containing synchronic well-being. An example of diachronic well-being would be the maintenance of a loving relationship through a period of turmoil, and then redemption.

dual diagnosis: a person who misuses a substance while simultaneously exhibiting the symptoms of a mental illness is someone for whom a dual diagnosis is appropriate.

effective agency: to be an effective agent one must have the capacity for unified agency. This is the capacity to fulfil roles and accomplish goals over an extended period of time.

ground projects: our ground projects are those (especially long term) activities which make human lives meaningful; they give human lives their particular shape and character. Ground projects typically include such things as learning a skill, playing a sport, studying, pursuing a career, raising a family, maintaining a friendship, or working for a political or moral cause.

unified agency: effective agents must have the capacity to deliberate, choose, and act in accordance with their choices. In order to act successfully agents must eliminate conflict among their disparate motives and adopt a unity of purpose. Because most of our worthwhile and significant relationships, projects, and roles are longitudinal, judgments about how we manage and balance the demands of each must be made with a temporally extended conception of our agency. Whenever we act for the sake of a project extending over time we unify ourselves; we exhibit unified agency.

Notes

1. The psychoactive substances we are concerned with include prescription drugs such as benzodiazepines, currently illicit drugs, such as heroin and marijuana, and legal recreational drugs, primarily alcohol. We include in 'mental disorders' clinically significant anxiety and depression as well as psychotic disorders and dissociative disorders. We use the term 'dual diagnosis' for co-occurring mental disorders and problematic substance use because it is the term applied in the literature to the group we wish to discuss. We do not thereby endorse the 'medicalization' of substance use or its validity as a diagnostic category.
2. We owe this terminology to Michael Bratman (2000).
3. Our discussion of synchronic and diachronic welfare draws on David Velleman's paper "Wellbeing and Time". Velleman argues there, against Michael Slote, that diachronic well-being is not reducible to synchronic wellbeing. "How the value of one's life is affected by a period of failure combined with a period of success …depends on the narrative relations among the successes and failures involved. Were one's travails in the political wilderness ended by ascent to high office? Or were they ended by a lucky ticket in the lottery and a round the world cruise? Our evaluative intuitions about the importance of learning from misfortunes, or of salvaging one's projects thus imply that the value of a life is more strongly irreducible than Slote supposes."
4. The account we offer thus draws partly on Christine Korsgaard's (1989) response to Derek Parfit's reductionist account of personal identity. Korsgaard argued that it is features of extended human agency – including especially human deliberation and practical reason – which provide the building blocks for personal identity.
5. Korsgaard writes (1999, p.27): "For Kant, as for Plato, deliberative action by its very nature imposes unity on the will. It is only when you ask whether your maxim can be a universal law that you exercise the self-conscious causality, the autonomy, that yields an action that can be attributed to you as a whole person. So whatever else you are doing when you choose a deliberative action, you are also unifying yourself into a person. For Kant, as for Plato, action is self-constitution."
6. We would also add that they must be of some worth not just because the agent believes this to be so. There must really be something of value which the agent recognises. After all, the life of a fascist dictator might satisfy the diachronic conditions mentioned above, and such a person might also sincerely believe he has lived a valuable life, when clearly he has not. A full account of the diachronic value of a life would address the issue of what kinds of values should inform how we live.
7. Watts and Priebe say that most of the psychiatric patients in their study of outreach programs had lost significant others 'early in their psychiatric career'. In the words of one patient "I started hearing voices, I started talking to myself, she couldn't take it any more, the relationship broke up…and I ended up on my own" (2002, pp 445-6)

8. By cravings we mean a strong, intrusive, conative state which is relatively (but not wholly) impervious to distraction or defeat by other motives.
9. Neil Levy argues along these lines in 'Autonomy and Addiction' (unpublished manuscript).
10. "Heavy use", even where the person maintains adequate functioning, is obviously a major health issue, and as such can be indirectly morally problematic. But we do not think there is any decent argument to be had that drug use per se is intrinsically morally wrong. In the vast majority of cases moderate drug use by adults - a glass or two a day of red wine, say, or marijuana once a month - is perfectly compatible with a good life. Not all use is misuse and the distinction between licit and illicit drugs is both morally arbitrary and morally obnoxious in many of its effects. It is important to distinguish between those ill-effects of substance use that are directly linked to the pharmacological effects of the drugs eg, states of intoxication, craving and withdrawal, and those that are primarily a function of the circumstances, eg, of prohibition, in which drug use takes place. Many of the ills attributed to heroin addiction, eg, criminal behaviour, poor nutrition, blood borne diseases, unemployment, disruption to relationships, may be traced to criminalisation which means the drug is likely to contain impurities, and will be expensive, time-consuming and sometimes dangerous to procure (Kennett 2002). See Husak (2004) for an analysis and criticism of arguments that drug use is intrinsically morally wrongful.
11. Many readers will think that even in cases where disunified agency has no effects on other persons, there is also a moral disvalue. We remain neutral on this case. Nevertheless, some readers might believe that no moral disvalue would attach to say Robinson Crusoe were he to choose a life of disunity which focussed on synchronic goods only, since no harm would accrue to anyone else and Crusoe ought to be free to live his life as he sees fit. What this would show if it worked is that the unity of agency thesis gets especially moral purchase in situations where disunity results in the net loss of goods which depend on our social relations. However even in the Crusoe case we would argue that a human life containing only synchronic value is impoverished, setting aside the question whether this disvalue is moral disvalue.
12. Salloum et al (1991) accessed at http://www.findarticles.com/p/articles/mi_m0978/is_n3_v17/ai_11249665/pg_2 29/03/05
13. http://www.betterhealthchannel.com.au/bhcv2/bhcarticles.nsf/pages/Dual_diagnosis accessed 4/03/2005
14. Kessler et al. (1996). More recently there have been a number of suggestions that "heavy" marijuana use in adolescence may lead to psychosis and the development of schizophrenia in vulnerable individuals. E.g., report on Four Corners program, Australian Broadcasting Network, 7.03.05. Where the mental illness is clearly secondary to substance abuse this will properly influence the goals of treatment.
15. See for example, Goswami et al. (2004); Carrigan and Randall (2003); Kushner et al. (2000); Swendsen et al. (2000).
16. It is also important to keep in mind that there is great controversy over diagnostic categories. If these categories do not represent real distinctions then the search for patterns of use that fit the categories is a meaningless exercise.
17. http://www.geocities.com/HotSprings/9740/mystory.html.

18. Note we are not here vulnerable to a circularity objection which might claim we are committed to the following: patients should engage in projects, thus extending their agency, which would lead to such values as…projects. To be sure our view is that extended agency is constituted by our projects and roles, and vice versa, but as should be recalled from our earlier discussion, the unity of agency provides at best the necessary conditions under which our projects and relationships may take place. There is always the further question as to the character of those projects and of how well they go.
19. This is not to deny that there may be other initial goals of treatment such as limiting deterioration or maintaining existing functioning. Harm minimisation programs begin by working with the client to identify ways in which they can limit the harms associated with their drug use. Nor is it to deny that clients may value many different things and so may have a variety of particular goals. But the achievement of their various particular goals depends on their effectiveness as agents. Thus their particular goals imply this more fundamental goal of treatment even if it is not articulated.
20. Withers (website) http://www.geocities.com/HotSprings/9740/methadone.html (our emphasis).
21. Withers (website) http://www.geocities.com/HotSprings/9740/methadone.html
22. Kavanagh et al. (2000) report that staff in both mental health and drug services identified rejection from accommodation of their clients and difficulties in accessing work, rehabilitation, and recreation, as posing substantial problems in the treatment of these clients.

2-7 The Prohibition of Sexual Relationships Between Drug Users and Their Counselors: Is It Justified?

Mane Hajdin, J.D., Ph.D.

Abstract

This chapter examines four possible arguments for the prohibition of sexual relationships between counselors of drug users and those counseled by them. The first is that the prohibition counters the special temptations and opportunities for sexual relationships that are created by the phenomenon of transference. The second is that the prohibition contributes to the authority that counselors have to exude if counseling is to accomplish its aim. According to the third reason, the counseling is an extension of law enforcement and is thus subject to the same constraints as law enforcement. The fourth reason is that the prohibition is needed because of the imbalance of power that exists between the counselors and the ones they counsel. The conclusion of the chapter is that each of these four arguments can justify the prohibition in some forms of the counseling of drug users, but only the second one can justify it in all forms of such counseling. That reason, however, appears to be merely a matter of counseling technique, rather than an independent moral constraint on counseling.

Key Words: abuse of power, counseling, drug users, professional ethics, sex, transference

Introduction

The codes of professional responsibility for counselors of drug users typically include an express prohibition of sexual relationships with the drug users. The Ethical Principles of Conduct promulgated by the North Carolina Substance Abuse Professional Certification Board, for example, provide that "the substance abuse professional shall not engage in sexual activity with either a current or former client." The Louisiana State Board of Certification for Substance Abuse Counselors has a Code of Ethics that similarly provides that "a counselor shall not engage in sexual intimacies with any client." Ethical Standards for Counselors by the NAADAC, the National Association for Addiction Professionals, also contain such a prohibition, but express it more emphatically: "The NAADAC member shall not under any circumstances engage in sexual behavior with current or former clients."

As the above examples indicate, the prohibitions may extend to those who were counseled by a particular counselor in the past, but they do not always do so. Sometimes those who were counseled in the past are covered, but only for a specified period after the end of the counseling relation: in Iowa, the Code of Ethics for Alcohol and Drug Counselors prohibits sexual conduct "with a client during a period of time in which a professional relationship exists and for one year after that period of time." The codes typically also prohibit the counseling of drug users with whom the counselor has had a sexual relationship in the past. The prohibition is sometimes specific, as in the rule of the Iowa code that "counselors do not accept as clients anyone with whom they have engaged in sexual conduct," and sometimes implied by some more general rule, as is the Louisiana rule against the counseling of "intimate friends."[1]

The purpose of this chapter is to discuss whether such formal rules against the sexual relationships between counselors and drug users are justified. Throughout the chapter, I shall be using the term "counselor" for the people whose occupation is the subject matter of this volume, regardless of whether they call themselves substance-abuse counselors, drug counselors, substance-abuse professionals, addiction professionals, therapists specializing in drug abuse, or by some other name. Analogously, I will use the term "counseling" for the activity that the counselors engage in, and which could also be called therapy, treatment, intervention, and so forth. I have selected these terms for convenience only: I do not wish to imply that they best capture the nature of this occupation. I will be referring to those who are being counseled by the counselors as "drug users." Although this phrase may not be ideal, it is better than the alternatives: "client" implies more voluntariness and control of the relationship than is sometimes there, "substance abuser" is almost comically overbroad. (Every wrongful act can be characterized as abuse of some substance or other: for example, somebody who commits a murder by means of knife is abusing the substance of the knife. The term "abuse" is also inapposite insofar as it implies that some other use of the drug is its proper, intended use; many of the recreationally used drugs are cultivated or manufactured precisely for recreational use, and have no other use.)

I will now proceed to examine four possible arguments for the formal prohibition of sexual relationships between counselors and the drug users whom they counsel.

- The first is that the prohibition counters the special temptations and opportunities for sexual relationships that are created by the phenomenon of transference, and thus helps to ensure that this phenomenon will be treated as it should.
- The second is that the prohibition contributes to the authority that counselors have to exude if counseling is to accomplish its aim.
- According to the third reason, the counseling is an extension of law enforcement and is thus subject to the same constraints as law enforcement, which includes the prohibition of sexual relationships with those on whom one enforces the laws.
- The fourth reason is that the prohibition is needed because of the imbalance of power that exists between the counselors and the ones they counsel.

As will be seen, each of these four arguments can justify the prohibition in some forms of the counseling of drug users, but only one of them can justify it in all forms of such counseling.

I. Sex and Transference

The idea that the counseling of drug users might constitute a distinct profession, which needs a distinct set of rules of its own, is relatively new and not universally accepted. Most people who are not directly involved with the counseling of drug users probably think of it as simply an application of psychological counseling to a particular subject matter, rather than as a distinct profession. A nonnegligible minority of the practitioners apparently think the same, or at least did so in the early nineties (Banken & McGovern, 1992, p. 46). In determining what rules of professional responsibility are appropriate to a pursuit whose status is thus unsettled, it is natural to look at the rules that govern the larger, better established profession, of which it is arguably a part, and to which it is, in any event, closely related. In this case that is the profession of counseling for psychological problems in general.

Those who practice general psychological counseling are typically prohibited from engaging in sexual relationships with the people they counsel, and that prohibition is relatively uncontroversial. In order to see whether that prohibition should extend to the counselors of drug users, we have to examine the arguments that justify it in the case of general psychological counselors.[2] Some of these arguments appeal to the power imbalance between counselors and those who seek counseling, and these arguments will be examined below, under IV. Another set of arguments for the prohibition, however, has to do with a peculiar phenomenon that was first described and conceptualized about a century ago, within Freud's work that initiated the developments that have led to our having the various forms of psychotherapy that we have today.

According to Freud, at some point in psychoanalysis, a patient comes to experience strong emotions directed at the analyst. This is a regular, predictable feature of psychoanalysis. When the emotions are favorable, as they often are, they may be experienced by the patient as falling in love with the analyst. In fact, to everybody who is not schooled in psychoanalysis, what goes on in such cases may well be indistinguishable from actually falling in love. If the analyst were not educated about this phenomenon, he too could think that the patient is in love with him. Freud, however, insists that what is going on in such cases is not really falling in love but a different phenomenon, which he named *transference*. Analysts must be trained to understand the difference and to not respond to transference as one would respond to real love. Instead, they must use the transference to move the analysis forward, and advance its goal (Freud, 1963, pp. 439-447). When it was observed that analysts often experience pronounced emotions toward their patients, it was analogously concluded that this phenomenon, named countertransference, must also be treated differently from the way in which we treat apparently similar emotions outside therapeutic settings.

Many forms of present-day psychological counseling are, of course, vastly different from Freudian psychoanalysis, but it is still likely that quite a few of them involve interactions of the kind that gives rise to transference. The phenomena of transference and countertransference present psychological counselors with far greater opportunities and temptations for sexual relationships with those they counsel than can be found in most other professional relationships. A definite, unambiguous prohibition of such relationships can be regarded as a device for countering such temptations and reminding counselors that transference must be treated as transference.

Looking at the prohibition of sexual relationships between psychological counselors and the ones they counsel in light of the phenomenon of transference not only explains why the prohibition is there, but also several of its features that might otherwise be puzzling. It explains, for example, why the protection that this prohibition gives to those who are counseled cannot be waived by them: were such waiving possible, the prohibition would not accomplish its purpose, because people in the grip of transference would all too readily waive the protection. It also explains why the prohibition often extends beyond the end of the counseling relationship: were sexual activity permitted immediately upon the end of counseling, the counselors could be tempted to lead the counseling to a premature end, which would again be incompatible with treating transference as transference (cf. Wertheimer, 1996, p. 199). The phenomenon of transference, moreover, provides a ground for the prohibition of counseling people with whom the counselor has a pre-existing emotional relationship: in such counseling it would be impossible to separate transference from the pre-existing emotions, and that would make it impossible to treat transference as transference.

All of this is, however, not a complete justification of the prohibition of sexual relationships between counselors and those they counsel, because the question can still be raised: Why, exactly, must positive transference be treated differently from the love one encounters in other settings? Given that positive transference looks so much like love, why should we believe that it is not genuine love? One could argue, to the contrary, that it is a conceptual truth that, if something is experienced as love, then it is love, and ought to be treated as such.

There are two possible accounts of what makes transference distinct from genuine love, and neither of them is fully convincing. The first is that transference occurs within therapeutic relationships with considerable regularity and predictability, and that this indicates that it is triggered by some aspect of therapy rather than by whatever triggers love. This response is unconvincing for several reasons. It is not obvious that the fact that an emotion is triggered by something different makes it a different emotion. Nor does the predictability of an emotion make it less genuine: most of our emotions are, by and large, predictable. Moreover, it is not obvious that what triggers transference is all that different from what triggers genuine love: uninhibited revelations about one's intimate life and nonjudgmental, compassionate acceptance of these revelations by another person, which are the central features of most forms of psychotherapy, also play a significant role in the development of genuine love. Putting people into nontherapeutic settings in which they make intimate disclosures predictably leads to their feeling close to those who accept the disclosures (Aron et al., 1997).

Being, in spite of his genius, very much a man of his time, Freud was impressed by the fact that transference occurs so regularly that it even appears "under the most unfavourable conditions and where there are positively grotesque incongruities, even in elderly women and in relation to grey-bearded men" (Freud, 1963, p. 442). These "grotesque incongruities" seem to have played a role in his concluding that transference must be something different from apparently similar emotions. In the minds of most people living now, this kind of consideration is unlikely to have much relevance to how transference should be regarded. Thanks largely to the unintended long-term effects of Freud's own work on the culture at large, people have generally ceased to think of the romantic and sexual relationships of elderly people as in any way incongruous.

The second possible reason for thinking that transference is distinct from genuine love is that, as the term "transference" indicates, the emotion is transferred onto the therapist from someone or something else. If one accepts that this is the correct characterization of the phenomenon, then it seems to follow that the emotion is, in some important sense, not really directed at the therapist. Therefore, if the therapist responded to transference as genuine love he would be appropriating something that does not really belong to him. This argument is, however, also invalid. Assuming arguendo that the psychological theory about transference is true, it does not entail that, once transferred, the emotion is not genuinely directed at the therapist. Nor does this account of transference show it to be a significantly different phenomenon from love in other settings. On the contrary, we all come to every new opportunity for love with the full baggage of significant emotions we have already experienced, and whether and how we fall in love is likely to be in various ways colored by these emotions (cf. Wertheimer, 1996, p. 180).

Insisting that transference is different from genuine love therefore fails to generate a convincing argument for the prohibition of sexual relationships between counselors and those they counsel. The regularity with which transference takes place in therapy, however, provides another, more convincing reason for the prohibition. In order to see what that reason is, let us suppose for a moment that the prohibition does not exist, and that counselors feel no inhibitions about responding to the transference by entering into sexual relationships with those they counsel. There are three seemingly possible outcomes of that state of affairs.

One is that the counselors would continue to counsel as many people as they do now, and that, whenever there is the right kind of transference, they would enter into sexual relationships with them. Because of how widespread transference in counseling is, this would probably make counselors the most promiscuous people in the world. In order to accommodate that many sexual relationships in their lives, counselors would either have to keep the relationships very short, or they would have to juggle a large number of relationships running in parallel (or both). In the minds of many people, such large-scale promiscuity is intrinsically immoral, and that is enough to rule this possibility out as unacceptable. But even if one thinks that promiscuity is, generally, not a very bad thing, one has a reason for being opposed to it in this case. The reason is that being in a relationship with another person who has many such relationships running in parallel, or going through the break-up that follows a short-lived sexual relationship, is likely to have a hurtful, destabilizing effect on the person who sought counseling. (We have to remember here that a person would not have sought counseling unless that person was overwhelmed by some difficulties.) Such sexual relationships between counselors and those they counsel would thus be very likely to undo whatever benefit the counseling might otherwise have. This means that counseling would, under this scenario, have no real point: what is usually its point would be cancelled out by widespread promiscuous sexual relationships between counselors and those they counsel.

The second apparent possibility is that counselors would enter into sexual relationships with those they counsel, whenever there is the right kind of transference, but that they would still avoid becoming promiscuous in the way that was described above. That would, however, mean that a counselor could counsel only a very small number of people in a lifetime. That would, in turn, mean that counseling could not be a genuine profession. The body of experience and expertise that is necessary for something to be a profession cannot come into being unless people practice it regularly, repeatedly, and systematically.

Finally, the third apparent possibility is that counselors would continue to counsel as many people as they do now, but that they would avoid becoming promiscuous by having sexual relationships with only a few of the people they counsel. In other words, this possibility would involve counselors picking and choosing their sexual partners from the pool of those who go through the relevant transference. At first sight, this option may seem to be more palatable than the first two. But if, while going through transference, one knew that a consummated sexual relationship was a real possibility, chances are that one would be disappointed and thus hurt by not having been chosen. This disappointment would carry the risk of undoing whatever benefit counseling might otherwise have. This third possibility would thus suffer from the same problem as the first one.

Upon reflection we thus see that each of the three seeming possibilities is incoherent, that it is not a genuine possibility. It thus follows that the practice of counseling is, in general, impossible without some form of prohibition of sexual relationships between counselors and those they counsel. This remains true as long as the phenomenon of transference regularly occurs in counseling.

The argument just made shows not only why such sexual relationships need to be prohibited, but also that it is desirable that the prohibition be well-known to those who are counseled. If the prohibition existed but one did not know about it, one could still wonder whether one's infatuation with one's counselor could lead to a consummated sexual relationship and be disappointed if it does not. Promulgating the prohibition in a set of formal rules helps to ensure that the prohibition is widely known and thus reduces the likelihood of such disappointments.

It should be noted that the argument just made does not depend on any elaborate and potentially controversial account of the nature of the phenomenon of transference; the argument makes only rather uncontroversial assumptions about the setting in which transference occurs. The argument also does not depend on any particularly controversial ethical theory. Those familiar with Kant's ethics are likely to have noticed in the argument an echo of some of Kant's applications of the first formulation of the categorical imperative, but the argument does not depend on Kantianism; it works equally well within the framework of utilitarianism.

Now that the transference-based reason for the prohibition of sexual relationships between the practitioners of general psychological counseling and those who are counseled by them has been clarified, we need to consider whether that reason applies with equal strength to the counseling of drug users. That will depend on answers to a number of questions about the peculiarities of the counseling of drug users.

The first question is whether the phenomenon of transference occurs in the counseling of drug users with the same frequency as in general psychological counseling. Now, most of those who have studied drug use insist that it cannot be fully understood apart from the rest of the user's life. Many of them will take this to imply that an attempt to get the user to discontinue the use can be successful only if it includes efforts at resolution of a wide range of the user's psychological problems that may be related to the drug use. In other words, they will regard the counseling of drug users as something that normally involves general psychological counseling. Under this approach, transference in the counseling of drug users will, of course, be as likely as it is in general psychological counseling. There are, however, other approaches to the counseling of drug users, often inspired by behaviorism, that are more focused on drug use itself, and involve less exploration of the user's psychological background. Within such approaches, transference seems less likely.

The second question is whether the counselor's temptation to respond to positive transference by entering into a sexual relationship is likely to be as strong in the counseling of drug users as in other kinds of psychological counseling. Many of those who seek counseling for drug use do so only when they reach the point at which their lives have been gravely disrupted by drug use, and even then only under the threat of a legal punishment. Finding oneself in such circumstances, in most cases, does not exactly help to make one erotically alluring (at least not to people who are not themselves in a similar position). It is, of course, true that many other forms of counseling also involve people in grave difficulties, but much counseling, at least in developed countries, deals with less disruptive problems. A counselor who is counseling a drug user may therefore be expected to be less tempted to enter into a sexual relationship with the person counseled than, say, a counselor providing assistance with marital problems. This is, of course, only a very rough generalization, and it should not be taken to imply that the counselors of drug users will be free of such temptations.[3]

Finally, there is the question of whether a consummated sexual relationship between a drug user and a counselor is likely to be as harmful to the drug user as an analogous relationship would be in other kinds of psychological counseling. The answer to that question will depend on the kind of substantive psychological theory about drug use that one adopts. The more one thinks of drug use as something that is profoundly related to various other aspects of a person's life, the more concerned one will be about disappointments that the drug users might experience if sexual relationships with counselors were permitted, and about the effect of these disappointments on the success of the counseling. The more one thinks of drug use as a relatively independent phenomenon, the less concerned one will be about such matters.

We thus have to conclude that the extent to which transference provides a reason for the prohibition of sexual relationships between the counselors of drug users and those they counsel depends on one's overall psychological theory about drug use and on the type of counseling that one has in mind. The reason will be particularly strong if drug use is considered to be importantly connected with the rest of the user's life, and if the counseling consequently involves a great deal of general psychological counseling. Such assumptions, however, also weaken the reasons for there being separate codes of ethics for the counselors of drug users, distinct from those for general psychological counselors. There is thus a certain tension (although not an outright contradiction) between relying on transference-based reasons for the prohibition, and insisting that there should be separate codes of ethics for the counselors of drug users.

II. Sex and Counselors' Authority

Instead of relying on transference as the reason for the prohibition of sexual relationships between counselors and drug users, one may argue that this particular kind of counseling can be effective only if the counselor exudes a certain authority, a certain firmness. The counselor's overall demeanor has to make it clear that the goal of counseling, and the important steps toward that goal, are not open to negotiation. Without such firm, authoritative guidance (one may argue) the drug users would all-too-readily succumb to the temptation to continue drug use, and the counseling would not accomplish its purpose. Having sexual relationships with someone is incompatible with exuding such authority and firmness. Shared sexual experiences put people on an equal footing. After one has seen somebody naked, and in the grip of physical passion, it is difficult to take that person's assertions of authority seriously. A sexual relationship between a counselor and the drug users counseled is thus, according to this line of reasoning, incompatible with an important aspect of counseling.

Nor is that all. A realistic possibility of a sexual relationship between two people opens the doors to mutual flirtations, attempts at seduction, general playfulness, and subtle informal negotiations that revolve around that possibility. Such interactions undermine the authority that one party is striving to have over the other, even if the relationship is not consummated. That is why it may be important that the prohibition not only be in place, but that it be embodied in a set of formal rules. Formal codification of the prohibition ensures that it will be known to drug users that a sexual relationship with counselors is not a realistic possibility, and thus discourages an undermining of the counselor's authority by erotically charged give-and-take.

This reason for the prohibition, like the previous one, explains why drug users do not have the option of waiving its protection. If drug users had such a power of waiver, they could, by exercising it, create the same state of affairs as if there were no prohibition. This would open the door to sexually colored exchanges with counselors, which would, even if the relationship is not consummated, undermine the aura of authority that the counselor is trying to create. Moreover, it could be argued that giving drug users the power of such waiver would, on its own, give them a sense of control over the relationship that would subtly weaken the counselor's authority, even in the cases in which the power of waiver is not exercised.

The same considerations can help to explain the prohibition of sexual relationships between counselors and those they have counseled in the recent past. If sexual relationships were permitted immediately upon the termination of the relationship, then the anticipation of their being permitted could give a sexually charged tone to the final stages of the counseling, which would jeopardize the counselor's image of authority, and thus risk undoing whatever had been accomplished in the process thus far. Moreover, the argument that has been made above in discussing the transference-based reasons for the prohibition can be made here as well: if sexual relationships were prohibited during the counseling, but permitted immediately upon its end, that could create a temptation to steer the counseling toward a premature end. It should be noted, however, that neither of these considerations justifies prohibitions of sexual relationships between counselors and those they counseled in the more distant past: the possibility of a sexual relationship several years after the end of counseling is unlikely to significantly affect what goes on within the counseling.

This line of reasoning also explains the prohibition of counseling former sexual partners and intimate friends. Memories of sexual interaction or a close nonsexual friendship with someone make it difficult to take seriously that person's attempts to project an image of authority. If this image of authority is necessary for successful counseling, as this line of reasoning presupposes, then it follows that a counselor cannot successfully counsel those with whom the counselor has a history of intimacy, sexual or nonsexual. It might be objected that, if the only problem with such counseling is that it is unlikely to be successful, that may be a reason for advising against it, but not for prohibiting it by a code of ethics. A counselor's attempt to counsel a former sexual partner that then collapsed because the former partner could not take seriously the counselor's attempts to be authoritative, may, however, make that person less receptive to counseling in general. If so, then attempts at such counseling are not merely a waste of time, but actually harmful. Prevention of such harm is a good reason for promulgating the prohibition in a code of ethics.

This reason for the prohibition can be readily applied to the forms of counseling that are not comfortably covered by the transference-based reasons, including the counseling inspired by hardcore behaviorism. Question may, however, be raised whether this gain in coverage is offset by a loss somewhere else: are there forms of counseling to which this reason cannot be applied?

If there were such counseling, it would have to be counseling in which counselors' exuding authority and firmness plays no role. Given that there are forms of general psychological counseling that do not rely on authority and firmness, one may at first assume that there could be such forms of counseling drug users as well. It is, however, questionable whether the idea of such nonauthoritative counseling is coherent. The counseling of drug users that is the subject matter of this volume is counseling that always has a definite goal. Typically the goal is the cessation of drug use and then the continuation of abstinence from drugs. The counselors measure their success by how many of those they counsel permanently abstain from drugs, and they measure their failure by how many continue using drugs or revert to using them after a brief period of abstinence. Some counseling of drug users may have the less ambitious goal of merely reducing the use and directing the users to less harmful ways of using drugs, but even such "harm-reduction" counseling has a definite goal. No counselor of drug users would take a supportive and nonjudgmental stance if those counseled were to make it clear that they plan to increase their use of drugs and their dependence on them. A counselor who did not steer the users away from drugs would not be engaged in the kind of counseling that is the topic of this volume. This means that it is an essential feature of such counseling that it has specific goals that are not negotiable.

In this respect, the counseling of drug users is unlike many other forms of psychological counseling. The goals of counseling for marital difficulties, for example, are usually much more open-ended. Those who provide such counseling generally do not regard it as their goal that all their clients get divorced, nor do they regard it as their goal that the clients remain married at all costs. All such options are treated as genuine options, worthy of serious exploration. The role of a counselor of drug users, on the other hand, requires that one present the goal of abstinence (or, at least, limiting drug use) to those counseled as something that is beyond genuine doubt. This in turn requires of such counselors at least some authoritativeness and firmness that may not be needed in many other types of psychological counseling. The reason for the prohibition of sexual relationships between counselors and drug users that has been presented in this section thus applies to all counseling of drug users.

It may, however, be debatable whether this reason is, strictly speaking, a moral reason. It is principally based on the considerations of what makes counseling effective, and it could be argued that these are matters of counseling technique rather than independent moral reasons. If this argument is accepted, then it may appear misleading to speak of the prohibition as a rule of ethics. To this it might be responded that, to the extent to which counseling is morally desirable, everything that makes it effective is also morally desirable. The response is, however, problematic, because it implicitly obliterates the useful distinction between ethical rules of a profession and the precepts of professional technique.

III. Counseling as an Extension of Law Enforcement

In the preceding two sections, we have been comparing and contrasting the counseling of drug users with other psychological counseling. It is possible, however, to argue that the *raison d'être* of the counseling of drug users is so vastly different from the *raison d'être* of most other psychological counseling, that we need to take an entirely different approach to our topic.

Here is one possible account of the genesis of the counseling of drug users. For whatever reasons (good or bad), the government has chosen to prohibit recreational drug use. As with any other law, if the prohibition is to be meaningful, there must be some mechanism for its enforcement. The government has thus empowered the police to arrest drug users, judges to sentence them, and jailers to jail them. But then it has been observed that these mechanisms are quite ineffective, in that a substantial number of people keep using drugs in spite of the threat of legal punishment. This observation leads those who support the laws against drugs to wonder whether some different mechanism of enforcing them could be more effective. Somebody then suggests that supplementing the work of police, courts, etc. with the counseling of drug users could, perhaps, be the more effective mechanism sought. Many find that suggestion plausible, and various counseling programs are instituted, funding for them is provided, and counselors are hired to work in them.

This way of looking at the counseling of drug users makes it a part of law enforcement. To be sure, the methods of counselors are more gentle than the methods of police officers and jailers, but their social function is the same: ensuring that the laws are obeyed. Moreover, the gentle methods of the counselors and the harsher methods of traditional law enforcement complement each other. In some cases the complementing is plainly visible, as when a drug user is arrested and sentenced, but then given probation or parole on the condition of undergoing counseling. But even the drug users who enter counseling programs "voluntarily" often do so because they are concerned that continuation of drug use could lead them to be arrested and punished: it can thus be argued that even the counselors who are nominally independent of the law enforcement system can be viewed as extensions of that system. There are good reasons to expect that such a combination of harsher and gentler methods will be more effective in getting people to comply with the law than either of these methods would be on its own: this is, after all, the same kind of combination as in the well-known "good cop, bad cop" technique of getting people to acquiesce in the dictates of the authorities.

If the role of the counselors of drug users is looked at in this light, then the reasons for their being prohibited from engaging in sexual relationships with those they counsel are the same as the reasons for prohibiting police officers, judges, prison guards, and parole officers from engaging in sexual relationships with the criminals they arrest, judge, guard, or supervise. A law enforcer in a sexual (or, more generally, intimate) relationship with a person on whom he is supposed to enforce the law could be tempted to not enforce it on that person. If the temptation were then succumbed to, the law would be undermined in an obvious way. The law would, however, be undermined even were the law enforcer to resist the temptation. The mere existence of such sexual relationships would raise doubts as to how the law is enforced, and such doubts are undesirable in themselves, even if the law does eventually get enforced properly. The doubts would reduce the faith of the public in the legal system; they would detract from the dignity of the law enforcement and thus of the law itself.

If the counseling of drug users is regarded as an extension of law enforcement, then sexual relationships between counselors and those they counsel would similarly undermine the law. The prohibition of the relationships protects the law from being thus weakened. This way of looking at the prohibition is importantly different from those that are discussed in other sections of this chapter, in that, according to it, the prohibition does not in any way aim at serving the interests of the drug users counseled. What the prohibition does aim at, according to this line of reasoning, is the strengthening of the law and maintenance of its dignity, and thus protection of the (putative)[4] interests of the general public.

By treating the prohibition as something that serves the general public and not the drug users themselves, this reason makes it very clear why individual drug users have no control over the way in which the prohibition applies to their respective cases. This reason also explains well why counselors are prohibited from sexual relationships with those they counseled in the recent past, and from counseling those with whom they have had sexual relationships in the past. If sexual relationships were permitted immediately upon the end of the counseling, then the anticipation of their being permitted could create temptations for the counselor in the last stages of counseling, and these temptations would jeopardize the counselor's ability to enforce the law. A counselor who attempted to counsel a former sexual partner would probably find it difficult to approach the task with the decorum that befits law enforcement. These explanations are similar to those given in the preceding section, and that is natural given that both the preceding reason and this one revolve around the need for the counselor's doing his work with an air of authority. This similarity between the two reasons should, however, not prevent one from appreciating the important difference between them: in the reason discussed in this section, the counselor's air of authority is a manifestation of the authority of the law, which the counselor represents to those counseled; in the preceding reason, the counselor's air of authority was merely a tool that was intended to make counseling more effective and more beneficial to those counseled.

Is this third reason for the prohibition of sexual relationships between counselors and those they counsel capable of covering all forms of counseling of drug users? It clearly does cover all counseling that people undergo under explicit legal compulsion, such as counseling that some offenders participate in as a condition of parole. Moreover, as has been observed above, even when the counseling is not thus coerced, its principal purpose often is to ensure compliance with the law; to the extent to which this is true, nominally voluntary counseling can also be regarded as a form of law enforcement and thus as covered by this reason for the prohibition of sexual relationships. The question then arises whether there is counseling of which this is not true, i.e., whether there is counseling that people undergo without any legal pressure, even an indirect one. In other words, are there, among drug users in counseling, some who would have sought counseling even if drug use had been legal? Given that the laws against drugs are so well entrenched, this question is difficult to answer with confidence: in the motivations of people who seek counseling it is difficult to separate those that are law-related from those that are not. Many of the reasons for entering counseling that are not on their face law-related may upon further examination turn out to be so: e.g., a person may enter counseling because drug use causes tensions in his marriage, but the tensions would not be there were the other spouse not concerned about the illegality of the use.

The fact that many people seek counseling for alcoholism even though drinking alcoholic beverages is legal does, however, provide a fairly strong ground for concluding that some of the drug users who now enter counseling would have done the same if drug use had been legal. This means that there does exist some counseling of drug users that is not a form of law enforcement, and to such counseling the reason considered in this section does not apply. How much of the counseling that presently goes on is like that is, however, bound to be a matter of speculation, because of the difficulties in separating law-related motivations for counseling from those that are independent of the law.

IV. Sex and the Power Imbalance between Counselors and Drug Users

Finally, we reach the fourth possible reason for the prohibition. This reason is based on the claim that the relationship of a counselor to a drug user is one in which the counselor has power over the drug user, and that the existence of such imbalance of power precludes the drug user's consent to a sexual relationship from legitimizing the relationship. If one also makes a relatively uncontroversial assumption that it is wrong to enter into a sexual relationship that is not legitimized by the consent of the other party, then it follows that it is wrong for counselors to enter into sexual relationships with the drug users they counsel.

One version of this reason can be expressed by saying that the drug user's consent to the relationship is, because of the power imbalance, merely apparent and not genuine. Alternatively, it may be claimed that the power imbalance renders the drug user's consent to a relationship morally ineffective, even though it may be, in some sense, genuine. The comments that I am about to make about this reason apply to both versions.

In deciding whether to agree that there is a power imbalance between a counselor and the person counseled, and that this power imbalance precludes the user from effectively consenting to a sexual relationship, one should examine carefully what kind of power is referred to here.[5] Let me, therefore, present the multiplicity of the kinds of power that may be implicated in counseling.

It is uncontroversial that the counselor always has a certain kind of power over the person counseled: the counselor determines many aspects of how the counseling proceeds. But this power is limited to that specific subject matter, and it is not obvious why one would expect it to spill over outside its limited domain. A sexual relationship between a grocer and a regular customer would not be suspect just because the grocer has the power to determine how the grocery store operates, and thus the conditions under which the customer buys groceries.

In the cases in which the counseling takes place under direct legal coercion (as when undergoing counseling is a condition of the drug user's parole or probation), the counselor does have much greater power, comparable to that of a parole officer.

In such a case, it could be argued, the drug user may be apprehensive about rejecting the counselor's sexual advances for fear of reprisals. It would then be quite plausible to conclude that the drug user's apparent consent to sex is coerced and thus ineffective. This argument, however, does not prove anything about consent in other types of counseling. It should be noted that this kind of power is present only in the cases of direct legal coercion; it does not extend to the counseling that is a result of only indirect legal pressure. (The fact that a drug user may have been motivated by fear of legal consequences in entering the counseling does not give the counselor any kind of power that could be used for the purposes of reprisal.)

Somebody may argue that the power imbalance in counseling exists because the drug user desperately needs to be counseled, while the counselor has no comparable need to counsel. This, the argument could continue, may make the drug user worried about the possibility that the counselor would discontinue the counseling if the counselor's sexual advances are rejected; this worry may then preclude the drug user's apparent consent to sex from being effective. What makes this line of reasoning problematic is that it is not obvious that its premises are true.

- First, a discontinuation of counseling may have adverse effects on the counselor's reputation and/or income (depending on the setting in which the counseling takes place); thus counselors, in a way, do need the counseling to continue.
- Second and more importantly, even if it is assumed, *arguendo*, that many drug users who enter counseling do so because of a desperate need for it, that does not prove that they desperately need to be counseled by a particular counselor. If a drug user rejects the counselor's sexual advances and that rejection makes it difficult to continue counseling, the drug user may go to somebody else. (The cases in which this option will not be readily available are those in which the counseling takes place under direct legal coercion; these cases have already been discussed in the immediately preceding paragraph.)

The next kind of power imbalance that may be claimed to exist between a counselor and a drug user is the imbalance that is due to their having very different positions in the society. Drug users are often poor, uneducated, without a steady career, and likely to have criminal records. Counselors are, on the other hand, professionals who are well educated, relatively well paid, and generally well respected. The counselors' social status gives them (one may argue) a kind of power that drug users cannot have.

- Now, the first observation to be made about this line of reasoning is that its premises are, at best, true only on the average. Some of the people who seek counseling are movie stars, well-to-do businessmen, and very highly paid professionals, whose overall social status is much higher than that of a typical counselor, and who thus have much more of this kind of power than their counselors.
- Second, the fact that the counselors typically have this kind of power in the society at large does not automatically give them any special power *over* the drug users counseled. (That is, it does not give them any power over the drug users that would be in addition to the kinds of power that have already been discussed in the preceding paragraphs.) In other words, so far as this kind of power is concerned, one's own counselor is on a par with any other similar

professional; the counselor does not have any more of this power over oneself, in virtue of being *one's own* counselor.

- Third, it is not clear why we would believe that this kind of power imbalance between two people entails that sexual relationships between them should be prohibited. People of vastly different social status often do enter into sexual and romantic relationships, including marriages, with each other, and that is generally not prohibited. (In fact, such relationships seem to be widely regarded as specially admirable, as witnessed by the number and popularity of the works of literature that take them as their subject matter.) It is therefore not clear why this kind of power would justify the prohibition of sexual relationships between drug users and their counselors.

We are thus led to the conclusion that this reason for the prohibition is not convincing. If we take it to be about certain kinds of power, it does not support the prohibition at all; if we take it to be about certain other kinds of power it supports it for some counseling settings, but not all. If the reason appears convincing to some people, that is because they do not clearly distinguish the different kinds of power that may be relevant here.

As a supplement to the above arguments, I will, in the remainder of this section, examine whether this reason can account for the features of the prohibition that I have discussed in connection with the other three reasons.

The reason appears to support the inability of drug users to waive the protection that the prohibition gives them. If one thinks that the counselors' power precludes drug users' consent to sex from being effective, then one is likely to think that it would also preclude any waiver of the protection from being effective. Giving drug users such power of waiver would therefore be incompatible with this reason. This is, however, true only of waivers that would take place after the counseling has already started. It does not explain why there would be no power of waiver *ex ante*, i.e., why people would not be able to declare before the counseling starts whether they want the prohibition to apply to them or not. In this respect, the reason we are considering now is different from the preceding three. The preceding three reasons all invoke the purposes of counseling and imply that sexual relationships between the counselors and those counseled are incompatible with these purposes; the incompatibility then rules out all waivers, both those that would be given before the start of counseling and those that would be given while it is in progress. The reason we are considering now does not invoke the purposes of counseling at all, but something that happens while the counseling is in progress; this leaves open the possibility of waivers *ex ante*.

The reason, moreover, does not explain why the prohibition would ever extend beyond the end of the counseling relationship. Once the counseling is over, the counselor loses any power over a particular drug user that he had in virtue of that particular counseling relationship. (The only power that the counselor arguably retains is the general power associated with his social position, but, as we have seen above, that kind of power does not give him any special power over the *particular* people counseled.) After the end of the counseling relationship, there is not much that the counselor can do to retaliate for rejection of sexual advances. The person that he has formerly counseled, therefore, does not have to fear the consequences of such rejection. This means that, if the person consents to sex, there will be no reason to doubt the effectiveness of that consent.

The reason also does not explain why there would be a prohibition of counseling of former sexual partners. If these people have consented to sex before entering into the counseling, and before the counseling was anticipated,[6] then the consent could not have possibly been tainted by any power that the counselor acquires over a person in virtue of counseling that person.

Conclusion

We thus have to conclude that the reason we considered in section II is the most plausible one as a reason for an across-the-board prohibition of sexual relationships between counselors and the drug users they counsel. Each of the other three reasons could arguably support the prohibition in some specific forms of such counseling, but none of the three is a convincing reason for the prohibition in all counseling of drug users.

The reason presented in section II is, however, based on a feature of the counseling of drug users, that many counselors may be reluctant to openly acknowledge, namely its essentially authoritarian character. Moreover, it is a reason that appears to be merely a matter of counseling technique, rather than an independent moral constraint on counseling. This means that the prohibition of the sexual relationship is morally justified only to the extent to which the counseling itself is morally justified. It is an open question what that extent is, but that question is outside the scope of this chapter.

Mane Hajdin, J.D., Ph.D., has taught philosophy at universities in Canada, Papua New Guinea, New Zealand, and the United States. His philosophical research is within the analytic tradition, and covers both theoretical and applied aspects of ethics, philosophy of law, social and political philosophy. He is the author of The Boundaries of Moral Discourse (1994) and The Law of Sexual Harassment: A Critique (2002), co-author (with Linda LeMoncheck) of Sexual Harassment: A Debate (1997), and the editor of The Notion of Equality (2001). He lives in San Francisco.

References

Aron, A., et al. (1997). The experimental generation of interpersonal closeness: A procedure and some preliminary findings. *Personality and Social Psychology Bulletin, 23*, 363-377.

Banken, J.A. and McGovern, T.F. (1992). Alcoholism and drug abuse counseling: state of the art consideration. *Alcoholism Treatment Quarterly, 9*(2), 29-53.

California Rules of Professional Conduct <http://www.calbar.ca.gov/state/calbar/calbar_extend.jsp?cid=10158>.

Freud, S. (1963). *The Standard Edition of the Complete Psychological Works of Sigmund Freud, vol. XVI*, Introductory Lectures on Psycho-Analysis, Part III. Translated and edited by Strachey, J. London: The Hogarth Press.

Gottdiener, W. (2005). *Sexual boundary violations in residential drug-free therapeutic communities*. Unpublished manuscript.

Wertheimer, A. (1996). *Exploitation*. Princeton, New Jersey: Princeton University Press.

Notes

1. In this respect, the rules discussed in this chapter are different from superficially similar restrictions that may apply to some other professions. For example, lawyers in California, are prohibited from "requir[ing] or demand[ing] sexual relations with [their] client[s] incident to...any professional representation," but that rule explicitly exempts "ongoing consensual sexual relationships which predate the initiation of the lawyer-client relationship" (California Rules of Professional Conduct, 3-120).
2. For a more detailed philosophical examination of these arguments, see Wertheimer (1996, pp. 158-202).
3. There is some evidence that sexual relationships between counselors and drug users do, in fact, take place. Interviews with 190 women who spent time in residential "therapeutic communities" aimed at cessation of drug use, revealed that, while in these communities, eight of them had sexual relationships with their primary counselors, and six more had relationships with other counselors or staff members of the community (Gottdiener, 2005). In view of the fact that such relationships are prohibited, these numbers are quite noteworthy. On the other hand, however, it needs to be taken into account that a drug user in a therapeutic community is largely precluded from finding a sexual partner outside it; this fact may be at least a part of the explanation for these relationships. The results, therefore, may not be generalizable to the kinds of counseling in which drug users continue their regular day-to-day lives, with the normal array of opportunities for sexual relationships.
4. Whether the general public really has an interest in the enforcement of the laws against drugs is debatable, but that debate is outside the scope of this chapter.
5. The reason for the prohibition that was discussed in section I of this chapter could also be expressed in terms of a power imbalance between the counselors and drug users. In this section, however, I set that reason aside and explore other kinds of power imbalance that may be claimed to exist between them.
6. The power could arguably affect the person during the period in which the counseling is anticipated but has not yet started, but the prohibitions of counseling former sexual partners are not restricted to those who became sexual partners during that period, which is, in any event, likely to be very brief.

2-8 **Drug User Counseling, Remuneration and Ethics**

Adrian Walsh, Ph.D. and Tony Lynch, Ph.D.

Abstract

In this article we explore the implications that remuneration, in its various forms, might have for drug-user counselors. A long philosophical tradition has it that financial reward and altruism are mutually exclusive. Our view is somewhat different. We argue, contra that tradition, that although financial reward in the guise of either commercial profit or wages is not in and of itself morally pernicious, it does confront counselors with ethical hazards. These are hazards against which those involved in drug-user counseling need to be especially vigilant.

Key Words: distributive justice, commutative justice, ethical hazard, lucrepathic action, lucrephobic action, stipendiary action

1 Introduction

When a person subject to a drug addiction, misuse, or dependency enters counseling, then, all things being equal, something worthwhile, something good, is going on.[1] It is a good thing to want to break such an addiction, and so it is a good thing to help someone do that. But if this much is obvious, it is not so obvious that doing such good on the condition that one is financially rewarded, leaves the moral virtues of the intervention unscathed. What ethical issues, then, does remuneration raise in itself for drug-user counseling?

This is no idle, or gratuitous, matter, for a perusal of the various codes of ethics for drug or substance-user counselors indicates concerns with appropriate fee setting, with the various possibilities for the operation of remunerative motives which may undermine or pervert the proper goals of counseling, and for matters of access to such needed services in the absence of the required financial wherewithal. What is missing from such codes is not a concern with such matters, but a systematically argued and rationally ordered account of the ethical roots of these concerns. We offer such an account here, not merely to clarify the matters at issue, but so that we might be better placed to recognize and deal with such concerns.

2 Is Money Corrupting?

While some economists maintain that money is simply a neutral mechanism for calculation (Robbins, 1937, p. 31; Veblen, 1984, p. 154), there is a long history in the Western philosophical tradition of regarding money as morally corrosive or corrupting. Aristotle (1946, Bk. I, 1256a-b; Meikle, 2000) thought that the pursuit of money for its own sake was unnatural (and hence perverse). In *The Laws*, Plato (1970, pp. 457-58 [918-19]) argued that the pursuit of money as a calling was so corrupting that in his ideal city only foreigners would be allowed to engage in commerce. With this in mind, consider the following three objections to remuneration for counseling drug users. First, it might be argued that money has a pernicious effect upon those who pursue it because it transforms our motivational structures. Once one counsels for money, then any altruistic component to one's motivational set is necessarily evacuated. (Let us call this the Objection from Altruism). Second, it might be argued that taking money for counseling makes it difficult to distinguish morally between the drug dealer and the drug-user counselor (let us call this the Paradox of Remunerative Counseling). The argument runs as follows: If it is wrong to profit from the sale of illegal and often harmful drugs, then surely it is wrong to make money out of the users and victims of the sale of such drugs. Third, it might be argued that any form of fee setting potentially excludes the less wealthy members of society from access to counseling services. If we conceive of such counseling as a need, and if we regard any process that prevents the satisfaction of needs as morally pernicious, then remuneration is morally pernicious. (Let us call this the Objection from Distributive Access). These three objections would have significant consequences for public policy if thought to be valid, since they would seem to imply that counseling services should not be performed for money. Indeed if they were true and we decided to act upon them, then it would appear that drug-user counseling could be provided only by private charity or from the public purse.

Should we view all monetary transactions as involving dealings with filthy lucre, as these objections would seem to imply? Our view—as we develop it below—is that such objections are overstated; money is not necessarily corrupting or morally pernicious as would seem to be implied. Nonetheless we also maintain that the objections contain some considerable elements of truth that are of vital interest to any account of the ethics of drug-user counseling. We argue that although money is not necessarily morally pernicious, it does provide us with a number of "ethical hazards," some of which are imprecisely articulated in the three objections above.

Our aim then is to explicate the nature of these ethical hazards. We do so through an analysis of the motives or incentives involved in commercial activity in general and, before explicating the objections in greater detail, it is to such an analysis we initially proceed.

3 Money Motives, Temptation, and Ethical Hazards

In order to distill the useful elements of the three objections, we require a more nuanced account of morally salient features of the commercial realm, for it is through an analysis of the commercial realm that we will gain insight into the ways in which money and remuneration can have morally considerable effects. In particular, we shall explore the nature and structure of money motives and the modal structure of the moral harm associated with money.

The first piece of conceptual machinery that we wish to introduce involves an analysis of the relationship between the desire for, or the individual aim of, money and other-regarding moral concerns. The analysis is predicated upon the assumption that motives can be (and usually are) mixed. Thus, contrary to some analyses (Titmuss, 1970), it is possible to both be financially motivated and simultaneously to have other-regarding motives.

There are, we suggest, four central ways in which money and the other-regarding motives can be related in action. First, one might be willing to sacrifice all moral concerns with others in order to obtain money. This we term "lucrepathic action," and it refers to forms of action in which seeking money is the sole or dominant consideration in an agent's all-things-considered judgments.

The second form of action here is what we call "accumulative action," and the term refers to cases where one aims to make money but such pursuit must be consistent with certain fundamental other-regarding moral concerns that the agent holds. In this case, while the pursuit of money is a primary aim of action, its pursuit is moderated either by moral goals or by moral side-constraints.[2]

The third action type is what we call "stipendiary action," and in this case the relationship between money and other-regarding morality is the inverse of that which occurs in the case of accumulative action, since here other-regarding morality takes a primary role. In stipendiary action, the profit motive is not so much a goal as a side-constraint upon action and, in the relevant case for our purposes, one of the goals involves some moral other-regarding outcome.

Finally, in addition to these action types that necessarily involve monetary motives, there is what we call lucrephobic action. In lucrephobic action one's goal is other-regarding and there is the view that any financial concern is inherently nonmoral. Thus we have the following taxonomy:

- **Lucrepathic Action**: seeking money is the sole or dominant consideration in an agent's all-things-considered judgments.
- **Accumulative Action**: whilst the money motive is a primary aim of action, its pursuit is moderated either by moral goals that have weight or by moral side-constraints.
- **Stipendiary Action**: the money motive is not a goal, but rather functions as a side-constraint on action directed by other noncommercial goals.[3]
- **Lucrephobic Action**: the money motive is not present at all; instead, in the pursuit of moral goals, the agent repudiates the pursuit of money altogether.

There are further subtleties that might be added here in classifying monetary motives, but for our purposes this fourfold taxonomy is sufficient (Lynch & Walsh, 2003).

It is also worth noticing that in this we have focused solely on the relationship between money seeking in general and morality and not on the different ways in which one might seek money. Typically, money is sought either through wages or commercial profits and, accordingly, we might finesse our taxonomy by distinguishing between wages motives and profit motives (Flew, 1976). There is a case for doing so, but note that it does not affect the general shape of our taxonomy. We can have lucrepathic, accumulative, or stipendiary action in pursuit of either wages or profit. So, in both cases the taxonomy will remain as above. Just as one can singlemindedly (and lucrepathically) pursue profit, a wage worker can perform his job with no aim in mind other than the wages he receives at the end of the week. So even if we redescribe self-employed substance user counselors simply as agents earning a wage for themselves (rather than as commercial profit seekers), the taxonomy still stands. Their actions in pursuit of money in their work can be categorized by the role that the pursuit of money plays in their motivational sets and whether or not moral side-constraints play any part in their decision-making processes.

The second piece of conceptual machinery that we introduce is the notion of an "ethical hazard." The term "ethical hazard" refers to temptations to morally vicious behavior that—given our natural proclivities—certain processes, institutional frameworks, or states of affairs present to us. (The idea is somewhat akin to the Medieval notion of an "occasion of sin"—in which something is not a direct cause of moral vice, but rather is the "occasion" of it.) Ethical hazards are to be distinguished from moral vices, in which the action or state of affairs in question necessarily is to be condemned because its occurrence necessarily involves the pernicious. In the case of the ethically hazardous, in order for vice to arise, the agent in question must yield to the temptations for vicious behavior.

Our suggestion is that the pursuit of money is ethically hazardous rather than being vicious in and of itself. It may well provide the occasions for corruption, but it is not corrupting in and of itself. Still those temptations are very strong. In a passage in the Laws, Plato (1970, Bk XI, 918d-e) suggests that the corrupting power of money is so strong that few resist. He writes:

> *There are not many of us who remain sober when we have the opportunity to grow wealthy, or prefer measure to abundance. The great multitude of men are of a completely contrary temper—what they desire they desire out of all measure—when they have the option of making a reasonable one they prefer to make an exorbitant one.*

Plato, whilst acknowledging the power of money, does not suggest either that it is impossible to "remain sober," or that money necessarily corrupts; rather, it has simply an overwhelming tendency to do so. Plato is driving toward the idea that money is what we term "ethically hazardous," and clearly he thinks the hazards are extremely high.

Note that there will, in all likelihood, be greater hazards for those engaged in counseling for profit than those who do so for wages. In the case of commercial or profit-oriented interventions there is a much closer link between the pursuit of money and one's activities than is evident in the case of those who undertake counseling for wages. As it turns out, most counseling will be undertaken within a public rather than a commercial environment, and so it is to this context that we address the greater proportion of our attention.

What should also be clear is that the category of the ethically hazardous possesses less power to trump other criteria than, say, the morally vicious; that is to say, to be judged ethically hazardous is not to give an action or practice the same argumentative weight as to be judged wrong in and of itself. Accordingly, unless one can show that the hazards of commerce are of a sufficiently high level, it is unlikely that any moral hazards we find in remuneration will provide reasons for repudiating the pursuit of money in counseling. And this is in fact how it will turn out below. What our hazards of remuneration provide are grounds for concern and ethical traps against which one must maintain vigilance, rather than reasons for rejecting money altogether.

We turn now to a closer examination of the objections listed earlier, beginning with the Objection from Altruism.

4 The Objection from Altruism

Drug-user counseling, like many of the caring professions, has a "significant other-regarding" component. It is humanitarian in orientation. However, it might be argued that remuneration undermines this altruistic humanitarian ethos. Certainly there is a long tradition of thinking that altruism and financial rewards are incompatible. For instance, in his seminal work *The Gift Relationship*, Richard Titmuss (1970) famously argues that noncommercial blood donation is to be preferred to commercial collection, since giving to blood banks is one of the few opportunities we have in the modern world for altruistic giving to strangers. Underpinning this is the idea that altruism and remuneration are at odds with one another. Of course, Titmuss's line of argument here is not uncontroversial. At the time of its publication there was an often heated debate about whether or not financial rewards did in fact undermine altruistic giving (Arrow, 1972; Singer, 1973).

In a similar vein, one might argue that the pursuit of money is incompatible with the altruistic aims that are appropriate to ethical interventions in drug use. We have referred to this as the "Objection from Altruism." There are two sides to the objection:

- first, that once money enters the picture we will lose or come to lack the requisite other-regarding goals;
- second, that the advent of money means that those who receive such rewards will have an instrumental mode of regard toward work for which one should be intrinsically motivated.

Both these claims are predicated upon the idea that the mere presence of money evacuates any altruistic content. The first point to make here is simply that it is not clear what status the objection would have if it were true. How important in itself is the quality of the motives from which people do things in our all-things-considered judgments about social policy? Imagine that money did eliminate this other-regarding component. Just because the altruistic dimension is lost, would this matter if the counselor was performing his or her job well? Here, reasons of overall well-being would trump those of concern about transformed motivational structure.

The second point concerns the claim that altruism and remuneration are incompatible. There are in fact reasons for being skeptical about the mutual exclusivity of altruism and remuneration (Walsh, 2001). The mere presence of money does not evacuate an activity of altruistic content. We need think only of those engaged in other caring professions, such as nursing, in which the agents are paid for their services, and yet in which an ethos of other-regarding concern is sustained and, indeed, flourishes. There is no reason why this should not also be true when it comes to drug-user counseling. Part of the problem with the Objection from Altruism is the failure to recognize both the existence and possibility of mixed motives and, furthermore, that altruism and self-interest can often co-exist. We can have both other-regarding and self-interested motives at the same time.

However, the objection is not without content; it is just that it is overstated. While there is no necessity for money to evacuate other-regarding behavior, there are dangers that a focus on money may gradually corrode our attitudes toward work that should be undertaken—in part at least—with a concern for the welfare of others, or may undermine our capacity to pursue actions that ought to be intrinsically motivated. This is not just idle speculation. There has in fact been a great deal of empirical work undertaken to demonstrate that financial rewards can undermine intrinsic motivation (Frey, 1997; Frey & Jegen, 2001; Lepper & Greene, 1978). If we think of altruistic activity as being a form of intrinsically motivated behavior, then it is easy to see how such lessons would also apply to the loss of altruistic motivation.

The pressures on altruism that we have detected in the case of the provider with remunerative motives may be strengthened from a different direction. After all, given that the levels of remuneration for counselors are typically set by accepted professional practice, then some members of the profession may well feel hostility if an individual is willing to provide *pro bono* counseling. This is because such offerings may themselves tend either to suppress or to reduce the "accepted" level of remuneration, or may reduce the income of the supplier of such services by diverting potential clients to the free or cheaper supplier. Or alternatively, the provision of *pro bono* or discounted services may reflect badly and perhaps unfairly on other providers who do not offer the same.

The lesson to take from this is that remunerative goals can, if we are not vigilant, lead us to lose our altruistic motivations for counseling. In setting fees and receiving remuneration, counselors must be careful that they do not fall victim to the dangers of being overly concerned with remuneration and, in so doing, lose contact with the altruistic ethos of their profession.

5 The Paradox of Remunerative Counseling

At this point, one line of criticism that might be raised is that if it is wrong to make money out of selling drugs then it is surely wrong to make money out of the consequences of such selling. If it is wrong for the drug dealer to make money out of others' misery then might we not also think the same about those who make money out of intervention in these cases. We have called this the "Paradox of Remunerative Counseling." (Perhaps it appears a frivolous comparison but we hope that the discussion will shed some light on the ethics of remuneration). This certainly seems a counterintuitive conclusion to draw, because a moral distinction does seem to be had between the substance-user counselor and the drug dealer (or at least the drug dealer as traditionally conceived).[4] Here we might usefully draw a further distinction between dealers who are the original source of the drug (that is, the people who grow or produce the drug) and street dealers who are often substance users themselves. Presumably the street dealer who is also a substance user is less in control of their actions and hence less morally culpable. But, either way, it seems odd to compare drug-user counselors with drug dealers, regardless of whether they are original dealers or street dealers, because drug-user counselors do not seem to be engaged in any morally dubious behavior.

However, consider the following line of reasoning. The counselor, like the dealer, relies on the continued existence of drug addicts or users for his or her continued livelihood. One can be a drug counselor only if there are drug addicts. Once money enters the picture, the counselor, like the drug dealer, has an incentive to maintain the seller/client relationship. There might well then be a perverse incentive for treatment not to be adequately performed or for patients to be deceived about their need for treatment.

Such possibilities are recognized in the various codes of ethics in four ways. First, there is an incentive to prolong treatment, and also, therefore, remuneration, when it should be clear to the provider that further treatment will be ineffective or pointless. In a number of codes, prolonging treatment beyond necessity is explicitly disapproved of, although there is no mention of the commercial incentives for doing so. For example, the National Association for Alcohol and Drug Addiction Counselors (NAADAC) code dictates that NAADAC members shall "terminate a counseling or consulting relationship when it is reasonably clear to the member that the client is not benefiting from the relationship.' (NAADAC 7b) Secondly, there may be an incentive to prescribe extra, and unneeded, products or services. The commercial dangers here are directly addressed by a number of the codes. In the NAADAC code (11d) there is the direction that counselors shall not use their relationship with clients for personal gain or for the profit of an agency or commercial enterprise of any kind. And in the Wisconsin codes there are directives against both the promotion and sale of commercial services and products to one's clients (Wisconsin Certification Board, Counselor Code of Conduct, Section VI. Rules 6.3 and 6.4). Thirdly, there may be a commercial incentive for making unnecessary referrals and this too is addressed in a number of the codes. The Californian Counselors code explicitly rules out money for referrals (CAADAC 11b) as does the Wisconsin Code (Rule 6.6). Finally, there are directives against gratuities. In any case in which a client has a right to services through an institution or agency, counselors should not accept a private fee, gifts, or gratuity for professional work. (NAADAC 11.e; cf. Corey, Corey & Callanan, 2003, pp. 262-63).

Clearly the codes acknowledge the pressures of money on the moral virtue of counselors. But what does this tell us about the moral status of counselors themselves? Although these pressures may be real, the claim that the roles of counselor and dealer are morally equivalent is surely wrong. It has the air of paradox for the very reason that our intuitions tell us that the conclusion must be wrong. How then do we morally distinguish between the drug-user counselor and the prototypical drug dealer? We suggest that this is to be done through an analysis of the ends of activity and that often the difference between the two can be discerned only counterfactually.

Let us begin with the proper ends of intervention in drug use. Intervention here is properly oriented toward the meeting of needs and the realization of a higher level of well-being than is evident prior to the intervention. Drug dealers, however, are (typically) interested only in the pursuit of money, and have a self-interested concern not to lose a valuable source of income, without regard to the consequences of their actions on their clients; in our terminology they will typically be lucrepaths and often exploiting a vulnerability. The fact that the well-being of their customers is often diminished—the complexity of determining comparative levels of well-being notwithstanding—is of little concern to them. To be sure, there might well be some dealers who are concerned with the well-being of the customers and aim to provide clean drugs. They might argue that they continue to deal because they believe that their customers will be less harmed by their provision of relatively clean drugs than would be otherwise the case. But such virtuous dealers are likely to be the exception rather than the rule and, further, their aim will be the realization of the lesser of two evils rather than the realization of well-being.

This distinction in terms of goals or aims can often be discerned only counterfactually. What we mean here is that while treatment is continuing the counselor oriented toward needs is "profiting" from the drug addict's condition just as surely as the drug dealer who has no concern for the well-being of his customers and who often plays a role in keeping them in their "cycle of addiction." However, suppose that the drug-user counselor comes across a "safe treatment" or procedure that will end the addict's condition and accordingly end the need for treatment. In these circumstances, the drug-user counselor oriented toward need will (all other things being equal) take steps toward ending the counseling phase. By contrast, the drug dealer, typically with few qualms for the well-being of his customers, has no interest in ending his commercial relationship with the addict. It is only in these kinds of circumstances that we will be able to distinguish clearly between the goals of the counselor and the dealer.

A second important moral distinction that can be drawn between the counselor and the drug dealer concerns their causal relationship to their clients' condition. Even so-called virtuous drug dealers who claim to be supplying a necessary evil and doing so more safely than other less virtuous dealers play a causal role in generating the very needs that they claim virtuously to meet. This is just to say that counselors, qua counselors, are not causally responsible for the circumstances in which their clients find themselves.

The counselor is to be distinguished from the dealer in terms of her orientation toward the needs of her clients rather than the straightforwardly venal or lucrepathic orientation of many dealers. This need orientation is a point that goes unacknowledged in the formulation of the Paradox of Remunerative Counseling. The failure to recognize the need orientation arises in part because of the way that the remunerative motives are treated as being singular and indivisible. Thus, if two people are both motivated by the desire for remuneration, then we cannot distinguish between their motives because they have the same motive and we therefore cannot draw any moral distinctions between their actions and attitudes in terms of their motivational sets.

However, if we accept the existence of a plurality of remunerative motives along the lines laid out in the previous section, and more importantly accept that certain moral motivations can co-exist with remunerative motives, then the mere fact that two agents both possess a remunerative motive does not render their actions morally indistinguishable. One conclusion that we might draw from this is that it is important to distinguish "profiteering" from "profit taking." Profiteering involves unscrupulously taking advantage of circumstances, especially the material circumstances of others, in order to make a profit. Profit taking, on the other hand, simply involves the making of a profit, and may therefore be moderated by side-constraints in a way that profiteering is not. The mere existence of a desire for remuneration does not entail that the person is oriented only toward money either in the form of wages or profit.

Nonetheless, in saying this we need to be careful. Allowing for the possible co-existence of an orientation toward need with a remunerative motive does not mean that there are no grounds for a concern with remuneration. As was the case in our discussion of altruism, there is a danger that a focus on remuneration could lead one to lose sight of the meeting of needs. It is possible for one's need orientation to be gradually evacuated by the interest in remuneration. Our remunerative motives might well lead us to lose our concern with the needs of others. One might well become a "lucrepath."

Once again, the lesson here is that remuneration provides us with an ethical hazard; in this particular instance it is that we might lose sight of the proper ends of counseling. This will presumably be of more concern in cases in which one is working directly for profit rather than for wages, for in the former case there is a more direct connection between one's provision of services and financial reward.

6 Justice, Fee Setting, and Exclusion: the Question of a Just Price

Ethical issues regarding remuneration and the proper ends of counseling do not end with questions about the proper structure of one's motivational set, for they are much broader than that. It is not only the possibility that one might become what we have termed a lucrepath in pursuing remuneration that is of ethical interest; fee setting also has distributive consequences. This is because money functions not only as a mechanism of reward, but also as part of a larger distributive system. Many money transactions, when combined, make for a market, and market systems are (among other things) systems employed for the allocation of goods and services across whole societies. We should note the positive aspects of this: such market systems have considerable benefits. Markets can provide us with an efficient mechanism for the allocation of goods, linking those with goods to sell and services to provide with those in the community who desire such commodities. The incentives in terms of financial rewards that underpin markets are capable (in the right circumstances) of generating an unparalleled superfluity and variety of goods.

However, it is also true that in the wrong circumstances market systems can give rise to pathological consequences, and nowhere is this truer than in the distributive realm. As a distributive system (at least in its ideal form), the market allocates goods solely on the basis of money. Rank, social status, race, and gender are (ideally) all irrelevant to the allocation of goods in a market; all that matters is that one has the requisite financial resources to buy the goods in question. As Moll Flanders noted in Defoe's eponymous novel, "with money in pocket one is at home anywhere." But equally, if one does not have access to money or access to sufficient financial resources, then one will be excluded from access to whatever goods are for sale. When the goods in question involve fundamental human needs then such exclusion is morally undesirable.

The relevance of this to counseling should be obvious: if the proper ends of counseling are the satisfaction of need, then we can see how fees might well stand in the way of such ends by excluding those without the financial wherewithal. Moreover, given that we are often dealing with addicts who will spend whatever spare money they have on drugs, this increases the likelihood that they will not have that wherewithal (and often their only means of generating income involve criminality). So there are even stronger reasons here for thinking that high fees will exclude those who need the treatment from access to it. Accordingly, one might formulate an objection to fee setting in the counseling context along the following lines. Counseling should be oriented toward the satisfaction of needs. However, fees can prevent some people who need these services from gaining access to counseling. Given that counseling meets a need that is morally significant, then such exclusion from access is also morally significant. This we have called the "Objection from Distributive Access."

To compound the harm here, it may well be the case that those who have successfully completed an abstinence-driven treatment program or a harm-reduction program are not subsequently accepted into what we might take as the conventional community. Often the stereotyping of drug users means that even when they abandon drug-using behavior, they remain stigmatized and hence marginalized. Indeed such people might feel doubly excluded and isolated when they have given up their substance-user social networks at the same time as not being accepted into any non-substance-using social groupings.

What lessons might we draw at this point? A radical conclusion that some might wish to draw, given concerns with distributive access, is that we should reject fees and financial remuneration in counseling altogether. This would involve an absolute repudiation of remuneration. But this is clearly an absurd overreaction. For a start, one could provide remuneration for counselors in a nonmarket context as part of a universal system of health care. Secondly, even within a market system there are means of ensuring that all have access to necessary goods through the provision of safety nets and so on. We might, for instance, provide vouchers or compensation payments for those without sufficient resources. There are a number of such schemes that will typically involve government intervention that can be used to ensure that those who need these services have access them, even in a highly commercial context. Thus, concerns about exclusion from access to counseling services because of an inability to pay any fees that are charged do not provide grounds for rejecting the collection of fees. Remuneration does not necessarily entail exclusion from these services and indeed there are many extant models in place that are aimed at ensuring that such exclusion does not occur. We suggest then that such radical conclusions are wrongheaded.

But whatever the merits of these institutional responses to concerns with distributive access, they lie outside the purview of our discussion. Herein we are interested in the ethical issues for individuals setting fees and so the background questions of what kind of institutional arrangements are best belong to the realm of political philosophy and not applied ethics. The specifically ethical question in which we are interested concerns the problem of how counselors, if they are in a situation in which they need or choose to charge fees, should go about setting such fees, given what we know about the possibility of exclusion via the use of money as a distributive mechanism. How would we determine a just price for counseling services?

Our answer to this question will be of a general nature, focused on the broad considerations that need to be taken into account, rather than attempting to provide any specific mechanism for setting fees. Determining the just price (or the just fee) will involve balancing considerations from two opposing poles. On the one hand there is the concern with the exclusion of potential clients from access to counseling services because of the fees charged. This is something that the counselor must take into account, especially given what we have claimed about the need orientation of counseling. How significant this will be in their calculation will be determined by factors outside of the control of the counselor, such as the relative levels of poverty and so on that exist in the counselor's society. On the other hand, we should not think that issues of justice arise only on the demand side; there are also supply-side considerations. One can talk about just remuneration (either in the form of a just wage or a just profit) as easily as one might talk about just access to goods. Counselors require a level of remuneration that, at the very least, allows a comfortable level of well-being, commensurate with that of other professionals in their society. So the just price for counseling requires that access for clients and fair remuneration for the providers be taken into account. For this reason, counselors cannot be expected to deal with all cases in which clients cannot pay by engaging in pro bono work. Although the performance of such work is admirable, it cannot be required because too much pro bono work would eventually threaten the livelihood of the counselor. One possible work-around would be to engage in barter for services in cases in which clients cannot pay. Barter can often be a useful alternative. However, there are clear and present dangers in pursuing this line of approach, and any counselor who undertook it would need to be extremely careful that exploitative relationships were not being set up.

In summary, then, a third reason that the setting of fees gives rise to ethical issues for counselors is because of the possibility that such fees might exclude some clients from access to their services or prevent them from accessing them over a longer period of time in which longer term treatment is required or in which there might be relapses. Given that counseling provides valuable services that we can, without engaging in hyperbole, readily conceive of as needs, then it follows that a loss of access is of moral concern. In so far as fee setting can lead to exclusion of some from access, then this is a matter of moral concern for counselors. In working through these issues, counselors need to balance the possible distributive effects of fees with what is a just form of remuneration for themselves. Balancing these opposing poles is an important aspect of ensuring that the remunerative aspects of drug-user counseling are handled in an ethically acceptable manner.[5]

There is some recognition of this need in the various codes of ethics in so far as they might counsel providers to "consider the financial status of clients and locality" and ensure that that the fees are fair, reasonable, and commensurate with the services provided. Consideration should be given to the client's ability to pay. However, these concerns are typically expressed not so much as matters of distributive justice, but as matters of commutative justice, or of contractual fairness. In the NAADAC code there is a requirement that members shall inform the client of all financial policies (NAADAC 11a; see also CAADAC 11a). But questions of commutative justice are—as Aristotle (1954, Bk. V) taught us many years ago—distinct from questions of distributive justice. What is noticeable here is a lack of detailed exploration of the obligations of distributive justice of counselors toward their clients.

In so far as there is talk of distributive justice, it involves little by way of positive direction. Counselors are told to "consider the ability" of clients to pay in setting their wages (for example, Michigan 11b), but there is no suggestion that they have an obligation of any kind toward those who are in dire financial straits. Indeed there is no suggestion at any point that there will be times at which counselors have an obligation to perform pro bono work. All of this sits oddly with the fact that at the outset of many of the codes (e.g., NAADAC Principle 1, CAADAC Principle 1) there is an exhortation to avoid discrimination of any kind, including that based on the client's economic condition. In this respect at least the codes seem underdescribed and incomplete.

7 Conclusion: Monetary Hazards and the Ethics of Remuneration

In exploring the ethical issues surrounding remuneration for drug counselors, we started with a series of objections—some of which one might think provide grounds for rejecting money motives altogether. Although in all cases we found these objections too strong, they do point toward ethical hazards of remuneration that should be taken into account. We found three main ethical hazards. First, there is the danger of a possible loss of altruistic motivation; counselors engaged in counseling for remuneration might find the other-regarding component of their work no longer existent. Second, there is the danger of losing sight of the proper ends of counseling, namely, meeting the needs of others. Finally, there is the danger of allowing financial orientations to lead to the exclusion of those who need the treatment and yet are not in a financial position to afford the treatment. All these ethical hazards are to be avoided if fee setting is not to lead to a corruption of the practice of drug-user counseling.

Adrian Walsh, Ph.D. is a Senior Lecturer in Philosophy at the University of New England, in Armidale, Australia. He works mainly in political philosophy and applied ethics and has a particular interest in moral issues surrounding the market, money, and processes of commodification. Unlike the majority of Australians, he lives on the western side of the Great Dividing Range in the small town of Uralla. There, with his wife and five children, he divides his time between philosophizing and looking after their small rural block.

Tony Lynch, Ph.D. is a Senior Lecturer in Politics and Philosophy at the University of New England, and pursues research interests in moral psychology, moral theory, and political and environmental philosophy. With his colleagues he is engaged on a practical attempt to refute Marx's condemnation of the imbecility of rural life. So far things are going well.

References

Aristotle. (1954). *Nicomachean ethics*. (Sir. D. Ross, Trans and Intro.). London: Oxford University Press.

Aristotle. (1946). *Politics*. (Barker, E. Trans. and Intro). Oxford: Clarendon Press.

Arrow, K. (1972). Gifts and exchanges. *Philosophy & Public Affairs, 1*, 1972, 343-362.

California Association of Alcoholism and Drug Abuse Counselors (CAADAC). (2003). *Code of ethics for the certified alcohol and drug counselor*. <http://www.caadac.org/cadcethics.htm>

Child, J.W. (1998, Summer). Profit: the concept and its moral features. *Social Philosophy & Policy, 15*(2), 243-282.

Corey, G., Corey, M.S., & Callanan, P. (2003). *Issues & ethics in the helping professions (6th ed.)*. Pacific Grove, CA.: Brooks/Cole.

Defoe, D. (1722). *Moll Flanders*.

Flew, A. (1976). The profit motive. *Ethics, 86*, pp. 312-322.

Frey, B. (1997). *Not just for the money: an economic theory of personal motivation*. Cheltenham, U.K.: Elgar Publishing.

Frey B., & Jegen, R. (2001). Motivation crowding theory. *Journal of Economic Surveys, 15*, pp. 589-611.

Lepper, M.R., & Greene, D. (Eds.) (1978). *The hidden costs of reward: new perspectives on the psychology of human motivation*. Hillsdale, N.J.: Lawrence Erlbaum.

Lynch, T., & Walsh, A. (2003). The Mandevillean conceit and the profit motive. *Philosophy, 78*, pp.43-62.

Meikle, S. (2000). Aristotle on money. In Smithin, J. (Ed.), *What is money?* London: Routledge.

Michigan Certification Board for Addiction Professionals. (nd). *Code of ethical conduct*. <http://mcbap.com/aoda&arms.htm>

National Association for Alcohol and Drug Addiction Counselors (NAADAC). (1995) *Ethical standards for counselors*.<http://naadac.org/documents/display.php?DocumentID=11>

Plato. (1970). *The Laws* (T.J. Saunders, Trans & Intro.). Harmondsworth, Middlesex: Penguin.

Robbins, L. (1937). *An essay on the nature and significance of economic science*. London: Macmillan and Co.

Singer, P (1973). Altruism and commerce: a defense of Titmuss against Arrow. *Philosophy & Public Affairs, 2*, pp.312-320.

Titmuss, R. (1970). *The gift relationship: from human blood to social policy*. London: George Allen & Unwin.

Veblen, T. (1984). The limitations of marginal utility theory. In Hausmann, D.M. (Ed.), *The philosophy of economics*. Cambridge: Cambridge University Press.

Walsh, A (2001, December). Are market norms and intrinsic valuation mutually exclusive? *Australasian Journal of Philosophy, 79*(4), pp.523-543.

Walsh, A., & Lynch, T. (2002, Fall-Winter). The very idea of justice in pricing. *Business & Professional Ethics Journal, 21*(3 & 4), pp. 3-26.

Wisconsin Certification Board. (1996). *Counselor code of conduct*. <http://wisconsincertificationboard.org/DOCS/CounselorCode.pdf >

Glossary

Accumulative Action: whilst the money motive is a primary aim of action, its pursuit is moderated either by moral goals that have weight or by moral side-constraints.

commutative justice: sometimes called corrective or rectificatory justice, concerns justice in exchange. It includes the justice of exchanges freely undertaken, such as when one is paid for a service as well as compensation for any damage incurred in human interactions.

distributive justice: concerns the right or correct way of allocating benefits and burdens in society.

ethical hazard: a temptation to morally vicious behavior that—given our natural proclivities—certain processes, institutional frameworks, or states of affairs present to us.

Lucrepathic Action: seeking money is the sole or dominant consideration in an agent's all-things-considered judgments.

Lucrephobic Action: the money motive is not present at all; instead, in the pursuit of moral goals, the agent repudiates the pursuit of money altogether.

Stipendiary Action: the money motive is not a goal, but rather functions as a side-constraint on action directed by other noncommercial goals.

Notes

1. By "drug" we simply mean any active chemical substance which affects the structure and/or functioning of any living organism.
2. Note the important difference between morality conceived as a goal and as a side-constraint. In the former, moral outcomes are the specific goal of an action, whilst in the latter, they simply function as side-constraints upon our action. Thus in the

latter case we might pursue the goal of making money but hold that there are certain things we shall not do because of particular side-constraints that we have.

3. Here we focus on actual profit motives where the agent is a commercial agent engaging in standard commercial practices of buying and selling. It would be possible to broaden the analysis to encompass monetary motives more generally, which would include such things as, for instance, being motivated by a monetary wage, but for purposes of simplicity we restrict our attention to profit seeking.
4. The point of talking of the drug dealer "as traditionally conceived" is that there is no reason to believe that all drug dealers are entirely venal…or that suppliers of "social substances" are saints.
5. There is a further question as to whether counselors should engage in political activity to ensure better distribution in cases in which provision is not adequate. Presumably in cases in which there is a clear failure on the part of governments to provide adequate services, then counselors will have obligations to try to improve the situation. However, we would be reluctant to present such duties as being essential elements of their ethical obligations qua counselors.

2-9 Privacy, Confidentiality, and the Treatment of Drug Addicts

Seumas Miller, Ph.D.

Abstract

Underpinning the principle of confidentiality are various considerations, including the right to privacy, trust, and the harmful consequences of disclosure. And the right to privacy itself is underpinned by other moral values, including autonomy. This makes the moral justification for confidentiality a complex one. Our degree of commitment to and the scope of the principle of confidentiality need to be relativized to circumstances. In some cases or categories of drug addicts, some grounds for confidentiality may be lacking, because of diminished autonomy and thus a reduced force or scope of the right to privacy. Nevertheless, it would not automatically follow from this that our commitment to the principle of confidentiality should be weaker.

Key Words: autonomy, confidentiality, craving, drug addiction, medical model, moral model, normative, privacy, well-being

In the first section of this chapter I sketch a view of the moral or ethical dimensions of drug addiction and the treatment thereof; in the second section I offer an account of privacy and confidentiality; and in the third and final section I discuss the nature and limits of privacy and confidentiality in the treatment of drug addicts. Please note that I am using the terms "ethical" and "moral" interchangeably, and principally to refer to properties, relations, actions, and character traits that are intrinsic elements of—and not merely instrumental to—human well-being. Thus compassion, sympathy, autonomy, courage, happiness, fairness, virtue and vice are all ethical or moral terms on this view. As such, they are normative and not merely descriptive. To say that someone is "happy" or "compassionate" or "courageous" or "autonomous" is to describe that person as being in a certain state, having a certain disposition, or possessing a certain property. Moreover, the states, dispositions, or properties in question are desirable; to be happy, autonomous, courageous, or compassionate is—other things being equal—a good thing to be. In short, the terms happy, autonomous, honest, and compassionate are normative as well as descriptive, and the descriptive element is normative in character. So the tradition I am endorsing—the tradition associated with the philosopher Aristotle, among others—rejects the sharp descriptive/normative or fact/value distinction advocated by the philosopher David Hume and his contemporary followers in the social sciences and elsewhere. On my favored conception, many, but not all, descriptive terms are also normative; in particular, many central ethical notions are both descriptive and normative, and the descriptive element—for example, compassion—is normative in character (Foot, 1978).

Ethical Aspects of Drug Addiction and Treatment

The definition of drug addiction is both conceptually problematic and politically controversial; drug addicts are, moreover, a highly variegated group. Some so-called drug addicts appear to use their drug of choice on a recreational basis, and do so without detriment to their well-being; indeed, in some instances their well-being is arguably enhanced. Others are not so fortunate; their addiction first dominates and then destroys their lives. I am not here going to try to offer a definition of drug addiction here, or try to map the rather diverse landscape of drug addicts. Rather, for the purposes of this chapter I will assume that at least the following two propositions are true of at least a significant minority of those referred to as drug addicts.[1]

First, some drug addicts—including some who are addicted to cigarettes, alcohol, heroin, morphine, or cocaine—have cravings for the pleasure afforded by these drugs, and at least partly as a consequence of these cravings are either psychologically unable, or able only with great difficulty, to bring themselves to resist such cravings and thereby cease taking the drugs in question.[2] Note that this is consistent with it being the case that some other drug addicts habitually take their drug of choice—perhaps over many years—and yet are able to resist their craving for this drug and thereby abandon their addiction with relative ease, though not without at least some substantial degree of discomfort.[3] (I take it that an addiction is more than the mere habitual taking of a drug sustained by the pleasure it provides.) Second, I am going to assume that at least in the case of some so-called drug addicts their autonomy is diminished by their addiction. However, I am not going to assume that all drug addicts necessarily suffer a diminution in their autonomy.

The extent to which an addict's autonomy is diminished will depend on the nature, including the strength, of the addiction. Consider a person who is strongly addicted to cigarettes; she finds it almost impossible to give up smoking. This person has a strong addiction, but nevertheless the addiction might make very little difference to her decision making in most of the spheres of her life, for example, her work, friendships, and marriage; her addiction does not dominate her life. So, overall, this person's autonomy is not significantly diminished by her addiction.

Now consider a person who has been smoking marijuana every day for many years. Indeed, he is more often than not "high" on marijuana; marijuana is a dominant element in his life. However, let us assume that though his addiction is life-dominating, it is not very strong; he can, and one day does, give up marijuana smoking with relative ease and without excessive discomfort. Perhaps we think this marijuana addict has wasted years of his life, but surely we would not be justified in claiming that his autonomy is, or was, significantly diminished; rather he freely chose, and continued to freely choose, habitually to smoke marijuana. Finally, consider a heroin addict who is both strongly addicted to heroin—he is unable to resist his cravings for heroin—and whose life is dominated by his addiction; he spends all his time either "high" on heroin or else securing money to pay for his next injection of heroin. This person's autonomy is significantly diminished.

In tying addiction to diminished autonomy in this way, I am in effect assuming that loss of autonomy is a constitutive feature of at least some forms of addiction—namely, those forms of addiction in which the addiction is strong and life-dominating—albeit not necessarily a feature of all forms of addiction.[4] For this reason, loss of autonomy is more closely connected to drug addiction than are various other harms sometimes associated with drug addiction. For instance, someone addicted to smoking may well end up dying of lung cancer. However, damage to a smoker's lungs—and the smoker's consequent death—are not constitutive features of smoking; rather, they are contingently connected, causal effects of smoking. It could have been the case that smoking did not damage the smoker's lungs or cause the smoker's death, for example, if the tissue in human lungs were resistant to the damaging effects of nicotine.

As we have just seen, diminished autonomy is one feature of some drug addiction. Further, I take it that—other things being equal—a significant diminution in one's autonomy is morally undesirable. It is morally undesirable because autonomy is a basic human good. As such, autonomy is both good in itself and as a means to other goods—it is, for example, a means to self-fulfilment.

Drug addiction is, moreover, morally or ethically problematic by virtue of its harmful effects. Some of these harmful effects, such as lung cancer or brain damage, are medical effects. But others are not. Consider a heroin addict whose addiction is life-dominating to the extent that she loses any interest in maintaining deep human relationships (such as friendships), or in pursuing projects that express and extend her talents, and ends up living in a largely solipsistic world that consists of her experiencing by herself an ongoing cycle of drug-induced cravings and "highs." For rational, social animals, such as human beings, this is surely an impoverished existence—and therefore ethically undesirable. Such an addiction, moreover, might in some circumstances have a corrosive effect on her moral character. If she was poor and heroin relatively expensive, theft and deceit might become a way of life and—ultimately—dishonesty a trait of character.[5]

A further set of ethically problematic consequences of some forms of drug addiction pertain to harmful effects on others. Consider in this connection the effects that the above-described drug addict's behavior might have on her parents, her children, her friends, and on those from whom she steals.

I have described various harmful features and effects of some forms of drug addiction. Naturally, many drugs also have beneficial effects—pleasure being one of the main ones—and some drug addicts might be better off addicted than they would be without their addiction. Consider a person who is not able to take morphine without becoming addicted to it but who will suffer ongoing, high level—indeed debilitating—pain if morphine is not taken. Perhaps this person is better off choosing to become a morphine addict.

Having outlined what I hope is a relatively permissive—and therefore in this context a relatively innocuous—account of the ethical or moral dimensions of drug addiction, I now turn to some basic models of the treatment of drug addiction; specifically, the so-called medical and moral models (Morse, 2005).

The medical model, at least in its pure form, treats drug addiction as akin to a disease or other medical condition, and considers that treatment ought therefore to take the form appropriate to a medical condition. As with infection by a disease, drug addiction, in this view, is not a moral condition, and the drug addict's use of drugs is not something for which the addict is morally responsible. (Although, if the medical analogy is to be preserved, the drug addict can be held morally responsible for failing to take drug treatment—assuming it is available.) Accordingly, so the argument runs, the drug addict qua addict is not a fit object of praise or blame, and the appropriate treatment is some form of medical or quasi-medical—especially therapeutic—intervention; for example, participating in a methadone program or drug-user counselling. What is ruled out on this picture is blaming the addict and making negative moral judgments about the addict's addiction.[6]

In relation to blaming the addict, there is a distinction between suspending moral judgments for the purposes of maximizing the chances of successful treatment, and not making moral judgments because there is no rationally appropriate object of moral judgment—as, for example, would be the case if drug addiction is akin to suffering from a disease. Perhaps it is therapeutically desirable for drug user counsellors to suspend moral judgments about their addict clients. However, it is implausible to claim that moral or ethical judgments are not rationally appropriate, given that some addicts have, for example, diminished autonomy as an aspect of their addiction. To judge that someone has diminished autonomy is to make a moral judgment; specifically, a judgment about the moral property of autonomy.[7] Moreover, to try to increase people's self-esteem and get them to take control of their lives, that is, to try to assist them to retrieve their autonomy—a practice involved in many, if not most, drug therapy programs—is a morally informed practice.

The medical model, at least in its pure form, is implausible on a number of counts. For one thing, different forms of drug addiction appear to be sustained by a variety of causal factors, including factors largely unaffected by medical or therapeutic interventions. An alcoholic's addiction might be partly sustained by the drinking culture to which he has belonged all his life, in part by his hard life as an underpaid, late middle-aged laborer, and in part by the fact that his wife of forty years died recently. In short, the cause of his addiction is most likely to include a mix of social and psychological factors, including objectively existing conditions as well as subjectively experienced states. Accordingly, the addict might be largely unaffected by any intervention short of a wholesale rearrangement of his social and personal circumstances.

This is not to deny that drug addiction is in many cases amenable to medical or therapeutic intervention. It is to claim merely that in the light of such social and psychological causal factors the medical model needs to be supplemented.

But there is a second important respect in which the medical model is inadequate. It fails to acknowledge the moral or ethical dimensions of some cases of drug addiction. Consider a young adult whose addiction to heroin is both strong and life-dominating and who, as a consequence, has undergone a process of moral corrosion to the point at which he routinely engages in burglary, assault, and drug dealing—including inducting minors into drug using—to sustain his drug habit. Let us assume that this drug addict could kick his habit, if he chose to, and if he was given appropriate support, including therapeutic and medical treatment. Assume, however, that though he has significantly diminished autonomy, the main barrier to his rehabilitation is his lack of any very strong desire for rehabilitation. He does not find his life as a drug addict-dealer morally repugnant, or even undesirable in terms of his own self-interest. The medical model in its pure form does not accommodate central moral aspects of this kind of addiction—for example, the addict's lack of autonomy and his deficient moral character.

Supporters of the pure form of the medical model might respond to this in one of two ways. First, they might deny that any intervention, medical or otherwise, is called for. If addicts are happy to stay addicted, then so be it; it's their choice not to be treated, as is the case of those suffering from diseases. But this move is a little too swift. For one thing, as is the case with some diseases, if the addiction impairs the decision-making abilities of an addict, then the addict's refusal of treatment is not necessarily a decisive consideration against intervention. Moreover, the response does not address the issue of the harm done to others as a consequence of the drug addict-dealer's addiction.

Second, and alternatively, supporters of the pure form of the medical model might argue that intervention is needed, and in particular a medical or therapeutic intervention that causes the drug addict-dealer to change his behavior toward others; for example, his placement in a methadone program and—in relation to his habit of assaulting people—an anger management program. Unfortunately, such interventions might not be welcomed by the drug addict-dealer; they might need to be coercively imposed. The latter option relies on making use of the criminal justice system to administer, or threaten to administer, punishment in the event that medical or therapeutic treatments ("diversions") are refused. But such reliance on punishment displays an inadequacy in the pure form of the medical model; here again it stands in need of supplementation, this time by recourse to the threat of punishment. Moreover, even if the drug addict-dealer goes along with the treatment programs under duress, the programs might fail. They might fail because the drug addict-dealer is not committed to their success; minimal compliance, as opposed to committed participation, might not be sufficient for rehabilitation. Rather, successful treatment might depend on the addict's understanding and accepting that his addiction is undesirable because it undermines his autonomy and is otherwise harmful to himself and/or others. Such understanding is in part moral understanding, understanding in relation to a moral state of affairs—for example, his diminished autonomy. At any rate, if such moral understanding is required for rehabilitation, then ethics has once again re-entered the picture and displayed the inadequacy of the medical model, at least in its pure form.

The moral model stands in some contrast to the medical model. In the case of our drug addict-dealer, the moral model focuses on his diminished autonomy (as partly constitutive of his addiction) and lack of moral character (as one consequence of his addiction). On one version of the moral model, the drug addict-dealer can reasonably be held morally responsible for his addiction and/or his behavior, and—given the seriousness of the moral harm to himself and others—proponents of this moral model may align themselves with the policy of criminalizing drug use. For, on this view, an addict's continued use of drugs is akin to ordinary criminal behavior; it is harmful behavior for which the addict is morally responsible, and therefore behavior for which he should be held criminally liable.

This version of the moral model denies the obvious fact that many drug addicts have diminished autonomy, and therefore cannot be held fully morally responsible for their continued use of drugs. A modified version of this model would claim that drug addicts are at least morally obliged to seek treatment for their addiction. On this modified view, drug use on the part of addicts operating outside any treatment program ought to be criminalized, but not the drug use of those placed in treatment programs.

This modified version of the moral model does not presuppose that drug addicts are morally responsible for their addiction and continued drug use. Here it is important to make a distinction between blaming people because they are morally responsible for some morally unacceptable action or character trait, and merely offering a negative moral evaluation of their action or character trait. The latter does not presuppose that the person in question was morally responsible for the action or character trait. Yet moral evaluation of actions or traits of character for which people are not morally responsible is a commonplace and perfectly admissible practice. It is quite coherent to claim that a drug addict lacks moral autonomy, or is dishonest or vicious, and therefore has a moral deficiency, while also maintaining that this addict is not morally responsible for being addicted, or for her lack of autonomy, her dishonesty and viciousness, or the behavior consequent upon her addiction. Accordingly, the moral model can, and ought to, uncouple the notion of moral responsibility from the notion of moral deficiency; the former is not a necessary condition for the latter.[8]

Once this move is made, the possibility is opened up of grafting elements of the medical model onto the moral model. If particular drug addicts are not morally responsible for their addiction, or for elements of their character and/or actions consequent upon their addiction, they may stand in need of therapeutic treatment. However, such addicts may be morally obliged to undertake treatment, and may be held morally responsible for failing to do so.[9]

To the extent that this version of the moral model accepts that some addicts suffer from diminished autonomy, and the consequent need for therapeutic and/or medical interventions, it shares common ground with the medical model. However, if the therapeutic treatment is partly directed at a moral deficiency, then this treatment will most likely have a moral dimension, for example, counselling that involves explicit discussion of the moral harms of one's drug addiction to self—including diminished autonomy—and to others. To this extent, the revised moral model does not simply collapse into the medical model.

One might reasonably conclude from this discussion that the medical and moral models are not necessarily mutually exclusive. Perhaps the treatment of drug addicts requires elements of both models—as well as, for that matter, recourse to policies that will ameliorate the social conditions that facilitate addiction, enlightened drug education and judicious use of the criminal justice system to detect and/or deter some categories of drug addict (or at least those who supply them).

Let me now provide an account of privacy and confidentiality.

Privacy and Confidentiality

Privacy has proven a difficult notion to explicate adequately.[10] However, a number of general points can be made (Benn, 1988).

First, as is the case with other key notions that are at issue in this discussion (such as autonomy), the notion of privacy has both a descriptive and a normative dimension. On the one hand, privacy consists of being in some condition of not being interfered with or of having some power to exclude; on the other hand, privacy is held to be a moral right, or at least an important good. Most accounts of privacy acknowledge this much. For example, Warren and Brandeis (1890) gave an early and famous definition in terms of a "right to be let alone." Here the term "right" expresses a normative aspect of privacy.

Second, privacy is a desirable condition or power or a moral right that a person has in relation to other persons—with respect to the acquisition of information by other persons about him/herself or the observation/perceiving of him/herself by other persons. The range of matters regarded as private embraces much of what could be referred to as a person's inner self. A demand—as opposed to a request—by one person to know everything about another person's thoughts, beliefs, emotions, and bodily sensations and states would be regarded as unacceptably intrusive.

Third, privacy is a desirable condition or power or moral right that a person has in relation to other persons with respect to interference in that person's life by those other persons. (It is also taken to include occupancy of "private" space by unwanted physical intrusions.) In particular, a person's intimate personal relations with other people are regarded as private. So, although a lover, friend, or close relation might be entitled to know certain things or to intervene in a particular person's life, others would not be so entitled.

Fourth, certain facts are regarded as private by virtue of the impact that their disclosure would have on a person's various public roles and practices (Benn, 1988). These kinds of facts are apparently regarded as private partly by virtue of their potential, should they be disclosed, to undermine that person's capacity to function in these public roles or to compete fairly in these practices. If others know a person's criminal record, this may undermine that person's job prospects. If business competitors have access to my business plans, they will gain an unfair advantage over me. If a would be employer knows my sexual preferences, he or she may unfairly discriminate against me. If people know that I am an alcoholic, and if alcoholism is widely regarded as contemptible or reprehensible, then my reputation will suffer, and as a consequence my capacity to function in a range of public roles and practices might be significantly diminished.

Fifth, Westin (1967) suggests that privacy is an instrument for achieving individual goals of self realization. Thus, a measure of privacy is necessary simply in order for a person to pursue his or her projects, whatever those projects might be. For one thing, reflection is necessary for planning, and reflection requires privacy. For another, knowledge of someone else's plans can enable those plans to be thwarted. Individual autonomy requires a measure of privacy.

Indeed, the negative impact that infringements of privacy can have on autonomy, both the autonomous pursuit of individual goals as well as (relatedly) autonomous participation in public roles and practices, can lead to the thought that privacy has no moral value independent of autonomy, or at least that privacy has no value independently of autonomy and some other values. I have argued against this claim elsewhere (Miller, n.d.; see also Collingridge, et al., 2001). Here I will simply assume that the moral value of privacy is not exhausted by the moral value attaching to autonomy and/or other goods.

Given the foregoing account of privacy, what can we say of the relation between privacy and confidentiality in the case of human service professionals, including drug user counselors?

There are circumstances under which a professional's knowledge concerning a client's inner self or intimate relations will be in the client's interest. A doctor needs to know about a patient's bodily sensations and states, insofar as this is necessary for successful treatment and insofar as the patient consents to be treated—specifically, insofar as the patient has given informed consent. The same holds for psychologists, social workers, and drug user counselors. This need to know for the benefit of the client gives rise to the principle of confidentiality. For such information, though available to the doctor or drug counselor, should still be unavailable to others, and the doctor or drug counselor who disclosed this information to third parties would breach confidentiality.

There are, however, circumstances under which counselors may justifiably interfere in the lives of their clients in a manner that infringes their privacy and/or confidentiality, notwithstanding that it is not in the clients' interest, or at least notwithstanding that the clients have not given their consent. Such cases include those in which clients are seriously harming, or are likely to seriously harm, some third party. They also include cases in which clients are seriously harming or are likely to seriously harm themselves, but are not able to give their informed consent to treatment. (What constitutes serious harm is a difficult question to which we return below.)

A further point here is that a client's right to privacy may constrain the further disclosure of personal information about that client, notwithstanding the fact that there has already been an infringement of privacy because personal information has already been disclosed by the counselor to some third party who is not entitled to it. In such circumstances, it is required that as far as possible the breach of privacy be contained. Accordingly, the third party is not at liberty to disclose the personal information to additional parties.

The duty to contain infringements of privacy also applies in cases in which counselors or other professionals are not responsible for the infringement of privacy. Consider the problem that occurs in relation to familial genetic diseases where screening or testing has revealed that other members of the family are carriers or recipients of a genetic disorder. Privacy with respect to a genetic disease might not be possible in a family context simply because the testing of one person will necessarily infringe the privacy of another.

I have argued that the right to privacy can underpin the principle of confidentiality observed by many human service professionals. However, there is at least one other justification for this principle. This is an argument from trust. It is claimed that a client's trust of his or her professional practitioner is necessary for effective practice, and that confidentiality is essential for trust. Therefore, the argument runs, confidentiality is a basic and very robust ethical principle for human service practice.

It is important to note that the force of this argument, as distinct from its validity, turns on the moral weight that attaches to effective practice. In what follows I will assume that effective human service work delivers human goods that have very considerable moral weight, or at least that such work does so in a significant number of kinds of case.

The first thing to note about this argument from trust is that it seems to conflate two slightly different, albeit closely related, arguments. The first argument is a quite straightforward one to the effect that if confidentiality is not guaranteed then clients –such as HIV/AIDS sufferers or alcoholics or heroin addicts—will simply refuse treatment, for they fear the consequences of public knowledge of their condition: conviction for a crime, loss of reputation, or loss of employment opportunities.

The second, and related, argument primarily concerns the relationship between trust and effective practice. Arguably, unless the client trusts the professional there will not be effective practice. So far so good. However, one element of this trust is the client's belief that the professional can be trusted not to disclose personal information.

Such information might or might not be embarrassing or harmful to the client—but the point is that the professional can be relied upon not to disclose it. Consider the client of a heart surgeon. As it happens, the client might not be particularly concerned whether it is a matter of public knowledge that he is to have open-heart surgery, nor even whether or not any specific personal medical detail relevant to this operation is a matter of public knowledge (for example, that his history of smoking had contributed to his heart condition). Nevertheless, the trust relationship between professionals and their clients—including this surgeon and this client—rests in part on clients' belief that professionals will respect their right to privacy and that any disclosure of personal information will be under the clients' control. Accordingly, this surgeon's client has a right to expect that the surgeon will not publicly disclose that the client underwent open-heart surgery, unless he explicitly agrees that the surgeon may do so.[11]

Here, the relationship between trust—including the belief that confidentiality will be respected—and effective practice is not quite the straightforward one involved in the first argument: the client may well agree to open-heart surgery, even when he suspects that the surgeon is likely to infringe the confidentiality principle. In the second argument this suspicion is indicative, and in part constitutive, of a degree of distrust, and this distrust might reduce the efficacy of the treatment—for example, if the client experiences a degree of anxiety as a consequence of this distrust of the surgeon, and if this anxiety impacts negatively on the recovery process.

The same degree of suspicion of a breach of confidentiality in a relevantly similar scenario involving a professional offering psychological treatment—as opposed to purely physical treatment—would probably have an even greater negative impact on the treatment process. (Here I am assuming that a relevantly similar case would be one in which public disclosure of the treatment would not in itself be embarrassing or harmful to the client.)

Each version of the trust argument might encounter two kinds of objection. The first objection goes as follows. Let us concede: (1) that sometimes a guarantee of confidentiality is (directly) necessary if consent to treatment is to be given, and (2) that some degree of confidentiality is necessary for trust, and some degree of trust is necessary for effective practice. However, it does not follow from either (1) or (2) (or (1) and (2)) that a very robust principle of confidentiality is necessary for trust and hence for effective practice.

For one thing, it appears there is scant empirical evidence for the claim that confidentiality is directly or indirectly necessary for effective practice. Marcia Neave (1987, p.4), writing about HIV and confidentiality, observes that

> *[u]nfortunately there is little empirical evidence bearing upon this difficult policy question. The extent to which preservation of doctor patient confidence affects willingness of individuals to seek medical help or to provide information about their sexual behavior to their doctors is not really known.…Findings about…the psychotherapists patient/relationship (such as frankness of patients during interviews) have also been inconclusive.*

For another thing, both versions of the trust argument seem to have ignored—and thereby distorted—the motivational relationship between confidentiality and effectiveness, at least from the client's perspective. Perhaps a reasonably high level of both confidentiality and trust is necessary for professional effectiveness. However, perhaps a low level of professional effectiveness can substantially contribute to the desire for a very high level of confidentiality. When the client has a concern that the professional might not be able to solve his or her problem, the client might require airtight guarantees that his unsolved problem will not be disclosed. Consider the high level of confidentiality demanded by HIV patients. On the other hand, if the client knows the problem is going to be solved he or she is less concerned that its existence not be disclosed. If a cure for AIDS was discovered, would not that weaken the demand for confidentiality?

Another reason for demanding a high level of confidentiality between workers and clients could be that it protects professionals from scrutiny of ineffective or immoral practice. Consider the many recent cases in which workers have sexually abused clients during the course of therapy or while the clients were in residential care.

If these lines of reasoning are sound, demands for robust confidentiality are likely to exist in professions in which there is often some doubt as to the effectiveness of their procedures and their practitioners.

The second kind of objection concerns the relative importance of the trust argument. If the trust argument is offered as the sole or primary justification for confidentiality, it ignores—or perhaps fails to accommodate sufficiently—the right to privacy that clients have in relation to information concerning their health, psychological well being, and intimate activities. Such privacy rights—rights that exist prior to the establishment of any relationship between client and human service practitioner—are a large part of the underpinning for the principle of confidentiality. A practitioner ought not to disclose the psychological condition of his or her client because the client has a right to privacy in respect of such information, and the practitioner is privy to the information only on the general (but defeasible) condition that he or she not disclose it to any third party. Respect for the right to privacy is in part constitutive of the more general principle of respect for persons. Having an intrinsic respect for persons consists partly in respecting their right to privacy.

So much for our characterization of confidentiality as it is conceived in the human service professions and the importance attached to the trust argument. I have suggested that the notions of privacy and confidentiality need to be kept separate. I have also argued against placing great weight on the trust argument for client confidentiality. I claim that confidentiality in human service work practice is principally, though not exclusively, based on the more fundamental notion of privacy.

The Nature and Limits of Privacy and Confidentiality in the Treatment of Drug Addicts

At one level, drug addicts are no different from other clients receiving psychological or medical treatment. Drug addicts have a right to privacy from which, along with trust, a right to confidentiality can, as we have seen, be derived. The right to confidentiality can also be grounded in trust. A suspicion or belief that the counselor's commitment to the confidentiality principle is weak or non-existent can contribute to a more generalized lack of trust in the counselor, and thereby reduce the efficacy of the treatment process. Alternatively, or additionally, a drug addict might not even be prepared to undergo treatment unless she or he has a guarantee of the counselor's strict adherence to the confidentiality principle.

Whether or not there are substantial numbers of drug addicts in the latter category is an empirical question. However, one relevant consideration here is that in many societies a social stigma attaches to drug addiction. This makes it plausible to claim that in many societies strict adherence to confidentiality is, if not a requirement, then at least a very weighty consideration for many drug addicts contemplating treatment for their addiction. In this respect, drug addiction appears to be similar to infection with a sexually transmitted disease. Recall, however, that Neave casts doubt on the validity of the empirical claim that HIV/AIDS sufferers—and by analogy drug addicts—generally require strict confidentiality if they are to embark on treatment programs. Moreover, it may be that it is the social stigma that ought to be countered rather than adherence to a strict principle of confidentiality. Indeed, strict adherence to confidentiality arguably tends to make drug addiction less understood in a society than it might otherwise be, and thereby helps to perpetuate the social stigma that attaches to it.

We need to be careful to distinguish between the reasons governing the decisions of the drug addict (subjective reasons) and the moral weight to be attached to the various considerations in play (objective reasons). Let us assume that the drug addict wants treatment, but is likely to refuse treatment if there is no guarantee of confidentiality. Now let us clarify the moral weight that attaches to the principle of confidentiality.

The right to privacy has a certain moral weight, and at least some of this weight also attaches to the principle of confidentiality insofar as the latter is derived from the former. However, because the right to privacy is not an absolute right, neither is the right to confidentiality; or, at least insofar as the right to confidentiality is derived from the right to privacy, the right to confidentiality is not absolute.

Because successful treatment of the drug addict is a morally desirable outcome, a certain moral weight attaches to the principle of confidentiality insofar as compliance with the latter is necessary to realizing this desirable outcome. (Naturally, compliance with the principle of confidentiality might not be necessary for successful treatment, but the assumption here is that in the case of drug addicts it frequently is.)

And further, the moral weight attaching to the principle of confidentiality is the cumulative product of (at least) the weight derived from the addict's right to privacy and the desirability of his or her successful treatment.

On the face of it, there is no problem here. The decision to be made by drug user counselors is clear: comply with the principle of confidentiality. For by doing so addicts' rights to privacy will be respected, they will trust counselors and not, therefore, forgo treatment for fear of breached confidentiality.

However, this is hardly the end of the matter. There are several residual problems. I will consider three of these.

The first problem arises when, as part of the addiction treatment, there is a need for disclosure to persons other than the drug counselor—for example, spouses, close friends, or members of Alcoholics Anonymous. Here, the boundaries of the circle of confidentiality are extended to include non-professionals. Nevertheless, a degree of anonymity can be maintained by, for example, using only first names and restricting discussions to elements of one's addiction. This is the procedure used by Alcoholics Anonymous and similar organizations. Unlike drug user counselors and other professional practitioners, drug addicts do not have their commitment to confidentiality underpinned by professional education, a professional ethos, and the disciplinary procedures of professional associations. On the other hand, drug addicts' commitment to confidentiality is partly based on the mutual benefit indirectly derived therefrom, namely, the beneficial treatment available in confidential sessions with other addicts, and the mutual harm that can be done should that confidentiality be breached.

This still leaves other important categories of persons, such as significant others. Presumably, however, their concern for drug addicts' interests will generally be such that they can be expected to respect addicts' desire for confidentiality.

The second problem I will consider here is that of disclosure in the case of addicts who are harming, or highly likely to harm, others—for example, HIV/AIDS infected drug addicts who engage in prostitution to support their habit, or addicts engaged in drug dealing to support their habit.

Given the non-absolute nature of a drug addict's right to confidentiality, actual or likely serious harm to others may override the principle of confidentiality. This much is clear. In this respect, the situation of a drug addict is no different in principle from that of other clients of professional practitioners. Consider the well-known Tarasoff case (Tarasoff v. Regents of the University of California, 1976). In October 1969, Prosenjit Poddar killed Tatiana Tarasoff. Some two months earlier, Poddar, who was a voluntary outpatient at a hospital attached to the University of California, had confided to a psychologist his intention to kill Tatiana. The psychologist notified the campus police who briefly detained Poddar but later released him because he appeared rational and because he promised to stay away from the girl. At no stage was Tatiana informed either of the threat or of Poddar's detention. Tatiana's parents sued the University because of the failure of the psychologist and campus police to warn her—their failure, in other words, to breach client confidentiality. In their joint judgment the judges said that though there was a need to protect confidences generally, it "must yield to the extent to which disclosure is essential to avert danger to others. The protective privilege ends where the public peril begins."

This is a legal judgment and our concern here is with ethics not law. However, the judgment does raise some difficult ethical questions in relation to breaches of confidentiality designed to prevent harm to others. Specifically, it raises questions about where to draw the line—about how much, and what kind of past, actual, or potential harm to others is necessary to morally justify breaching the principle of confidentiality.

Presumably, the answer to this ethical or moral question will turn partly on the moral weight to be attached to the right to privacy and also to successful treatment in individual cases of drug addicts (or at least individual categories of drug addict). If a young adult is being counseled in relation to his addiction to smoking, and makes known to the counselor his intention to steal cigarettes from a local shop, presumably the counselor is morally entitled to breach confidentiality by, for example, warning the shopkeeper or the police. (Here I am bracketing legal considerations and any moral obligations that they might generate.) After all, in relation to disclosure that one smokes, one's privacy right is weak, and the young adult has many years of opportunity to quit smoking before there is serious damage to his health. Moreover, widespread knowledge of this breach of confidentiality is unlikely to affect the willingness of other smokers to seek counseling in relation to their smoking habit. In short, there is not a great deal at stake in breaching the principle of confidentiality in such cases.[12]

By contrast, disclosure of a past legal offense—such as prostitution, or even intention to commit prostitution—is not a sufficient condition for breaching confidentiality in the case of heroin addicts whose future well-being is substantially dependent on their present participation in treatment programs, and who will not participate if they know confidentiality will be breached at the first sign of any past, present, or future wrongdoing on their part. (Here of course I am assuming that the addict practices safe sex and is not, say, HIV/AIDS infected.) On the other hand, what if the addict/prostitute is HIV/AIDS infected? Surely there is a duty toward those lives that would be put at risk, and this duty would override the addict's right to confidentiality. And what of the case of the drug user-dealer who is careless in relation to the quality of the drugs he deals in—if, for example, there is a risk of death from very pure, high grade heroin or from contaminated heroin?

Another relevant consideration here will be the extent of the breach of confidentiality. In relation to the drug user-dealer, assume that the youth is a minor and therefore the object of certain protections not afforded to adults. If so, the counselor might be obliged to try to contain his breach of confidentiality by, say, communicating the youth's intention only to the juvenile justice officer responsible for the youth's rehabilitation. The officer could be expected to speak in confidence to the youth and discipline him, without—at least in the first instance—alerting the drug using community and therefore, at least potentially, the community at large. So the youth's drug-using and drug-dealing activities would not necessarily become matters of public knowledge to his present and future detriment.

A third relevant consideration in relation to whether or not to breach confidentiality will be the success rate of the sort of treatment being undertaken by the category of drug addicts in question. Suppose that alcoholics are being offered a treatment that consists in, say, exercises in free association in the company of the counselor. Suppose, further, that this treatment is entirely useless; no alcoholic has ever been, or likely ever will be, successfully treated using this method. It is very difficult to see what the basis for strict compliance with the principle of confidentiality would be—other than the alcoholic's right to privacy in the context of the stigma attaching to being an alcoholic.[13] If, instead of alcoholics, this treatment was being offered to smokers, and with equal—that is, no—success, there may well be an obligation to breach confidentiality and disclose the failure of this treatment in order to protect other smokers from wasting their time and money on it.[14]

The third and last issue or problem that I will discuss in relation to confidentiality is one of a more general nature, and concerns the relationship between confidentiality, on the one hand, and the addict's well-being, on the other. We have seen that one important justification for strict adherence to the principle of confidentiality is trust, and especially the unwillingness of some addicts to participate in treatment programs, absent strict adherence to confidentiality. In what follows, I want to ignore this consideration and focus on countervailing reasons, that is, reasons that pull against compliance with the principle of confidentiality.

My focus here is on the other justification for the principle of confidentiality, namely the right to privacy. I will attempt to determine whether or not the right to privacy is suspended, or at least its moral force greatly reduced, in the case of drug addicts who have diminished autonomy. If so, this would have the effect of weakening the commitment to confidentiality in these cases and, specifically, of weakening the commitment to confidentiality in so far as this commitment is based on the right to privacy.

Consider a person whose drug addiction is such that she has significantly diminished autonomy; the addiction is both strong and life-dominating. Why would anyone hold the view that the right to privacy of this drug addict ought to be suspended, or is at best a right with greatly reduced moral force?

One reason is that the addict in question lacks autonomy, or at least that she has suffered a significant diminution in her autonomy. Yet we have seen that the value of autonomy provides one justification for the right to privacy, and therefore is at least one element in the justification of a stringent right to privacy. As indicated above, my own view is that the value of autonomy is not the only justification for the right to privacy; I hold that privacy possesses a degree of moral value independently of autonomy and other moral values. Accordingly—on my view—the addict's right to privacy is substantially intact, notwithstanding her lack of autonomy. However, it might be held that the right to privacy is substantially or even wholly dependent on the value of autonomy. If so, the right to privacy of individuals who lack autonomy, or who have substantially diminished autonomy, is arguably suspended, or at least the force of their right to privacy is greatly reduced.

One way to adjudicate between these different views it to test them against examples. John Kleinig has suggested to me that a person in a coma has a right to privacy, notwithstanding his or her lack of autonomy. This example supports my view against the alternative one.

Naturally, if people have significantly diminished autonomy, they could not be expected to adequately exercise their moral rights, including their right to privacy, in their own interest. Suppose there is a drug addict-prostitute who is aware that she is living only for the next "fix" and who has recently embarked on a treatment program, but whose self-respect and autonomy is so diminished that she is unaware of or largely unconcerned with the issue of privacy, or the harm to her that public knowledge of her situation might cause (for example, in relation to her job prospects should the treatment program she has recently embarked upon succeed). Perhaps her privacy is something the drug counselor needs to try to protect on her behalf.

There is a second reason why someone might hold the view that the right to privacy has greatly reduced force in the case of a drug addict who lacks autonomy. The continued addiction of some drug addicts—for example, some heroin addicts—might be largely dependent on the secrecy surrounding their drug-using and drug-selling activities. Accordingly, insisting on respect for their right to privacy in regard to these activities might serve merely to ensure that the addicts are closed off from the very people—including not only professional drug counselors, but also family and friends—who, had they greater access to the addicts' drug using activities, might be able to assist them. In short, in such cases, respect for privacy is at odds with the addicts' deeper self-interest. However, it is important to note that this consideration does not tell in favor of suspending the general right to privacy, but only in favor of reducing its scope; the right to privacy is overridden only in relation to the addict's drug-using and drug-selling activities.

Conclusion

The principle of confidentiality has various moral grounds, including the right to privacy, the requirement of trust, and the harmful consequences of disclosure. Moreover, the right to privacy is itself partly underpinned by other moral values, including autonomy. As a consequence, the moral justification for the principle of confidentiality is complex.

Further, the degree of commitment to the principle of confidentiality needs to be relativized to circumstances—there is, for example, a relatively weak commitment in the case of the above-described delinquent youth addicted to smoking cigarettes. In addition, the scope of the principle of confidentiality might need to be relativized—for example, it might need to include family members or other addicts, as well as professional counselors, though not the public at large.

Finally, the different moral grounds for confidentiality are not necessarily present in all cases or categories of drug addict—for example, the force, or at least the scope, of the right to privacy might be reduced in the case of drug addicts having substantially diminished autonomy. It would not follow from this that commitment to the principle of confidentiality ought to be weaker: that would depend on the force attaching to the other relevant moral grounds for that principle. For example, the right to privacy (insofar as that right is not based on autonomy) and the harmful consequences of disclosure might dictate strict adherence to the principle of confidentiality.[15]

Seumas Miller, Ph.D. is Professor of Philosophy at Charles Sturt University and the Australian National University (joint position) and Director of the Centre for Applied Philosophy and Public Ethics (an Australian Research Council funded Special Research Centre). He is the author or co-author of a number of books including, Social Action: A Teleological Account (Cambridge University Press, 2001), Corruption and Anti-corruption (with Peter Roberts and Ed Spence) (Prentice Hall, 2005), Ethical Issues in Policing (with John Blackler) (Ashgate, 2005) and Terrorism and Counter-terrorism (Blackwell Publishing, forthcoming).

References

Benn, S. (1988). *A theory of freedom.* Cambridge: Cambridge University Press.

Collingridge, M., Miller, S., and Bowles, W. (2001). Privacy and confidentiality in social work. *Australian Social Work, 54*(2), 3-14.

Foot, P. (1978). *Virtues and Vices.* Berkeley, CA: University of California Press.

Husak, D. N. (2005). The moral relevance of addiction. In this volume.

Miller, S. (n.d.). Privacy, autonomy and identity (unpublished).

Morse, S.J. (2005). Medicine and morals, craving and compulsion. In this volume.

National Institute on Drug Abuse. (2000). Approaches to drug abuse counseling Washington, D.C.: U.S. Department of Health and Human Services, National Institutes of Health) <www.drugabuse.gov/ADAC/ADAC1.html)>.

Neave, M. (1987). AIDS—Confidentiality and the duty to warn. *University of Tasmania Law Review, 9*(1), 1-31.

Tarasoff v. Regents of the University of California, 17 Cal.3d 425; 551 P.2d 334; 131 Cal. Rptr. 14 (1976).

Warren, S.D. and Brandeis, L.D. (1890). The right to privacy. *Harvard Law Review, 4*, 193-220.

Westin, A.F. (1967). *Privacy and freedom.* New York: Atheneum.

Notes

1. A third proposition that is possibly also true is that the drug to which people are addicted is not a substance that their bodies need and which they "crave" because their bodies need it. Thus, humans need to drink water (in some form or other) and become thirsty when their intake of water is too low. But I take it that they need water in the objective sense of need; they do not merely have a thirst for water. (Here thirst is partly a psychological state and partly a bodily one, for example, dry saliva.) By contrast, the alcoholic's 'thirst' for an alcoholic drink is a thirst, but it is not an objective need; indeed, objectively speaking, excessive alcohol damages the body (for example, the liver).
2. The notion of a craving stands in need of a definition, notwithstanding its use in ordinary language. I cannot provide such a definition here. However, I note that the notion of a craving is complex; its complexity consists in part in its being embedded in a complex causal and associational network. I am using it to refer to a subjective felt state lying at the core of such a network, and not seeking to elaborate the complex associations it may typically have nor its standard causal antecedents and effects.
3. The modes of resistance are various, as are the degree to which they are successful. Here, as elsewhere, I have simplified a complex phenomenon.
4. This relationship between drug addiction and diminished autonomy is presupposed in many, if not most, treatment programs, for example, Minnesota Model, CENAPS Model of Relapse Prevention Therapy. See, for example, National Institute on Drug Abuse (2000). It is also presupposed in the programs offered by organizations such as Alcoholics Anonymous and Narcotics Anonymous. However, some writers do not seem to see diminished autonomy as a central feature of drug addiction. See, for example, Husak (2005).
5. I do not mean to imply that such an outcome is typical and irreversible. According to the "natural recovery" literature, the majority of people who use illicit drugs or misuse licit ones eventually stop on their own.
6. Or at least this is ruled out if we assume that addicts, like many—if not most—persons suffering from diseases, do not deliberately take steps to become afflicted (or are otherwise blameless for their affliction).
7. No doubt there is a distinction to be made between moral judgements which are explicitly moral, e.g., "You are a bad person," and ones which are implicitly so. However many of the latter are, nevertheless, moral judgments.
8. More plausibly, persons are to some degree responsible for some of their character traits; this is consistent with their not being able to undertake wholesale re-engineering of their character, and certainly not being able to change character traits at will.
9. This is not necessarily so—for example, the addiction might be such as to causally determine the addict not to seek therapy. In general, addictions do not seem to be fully causally determinative in this respect. Naturally, if a drug addict cannot resist

his addiction by himself, but is able to choose to have treatment, then there is a sense in which he is able to choose—albeit indirectly—to resist his addiction. I am referring to such an addict as, nevertheless, unable to resist his addiction, i.e., unable directly and without assistance from others to resist his addiction.

10. An earlier version of much of the material in this section appeared in Collingridge, Miller, and Bowles (2001).
11. I am assuming the operation is not a matter of public knowledge.
12. Indeed, the youth is not really an addict of the sort principally of interest to us in this chapter. However, the case allows me to conveniently make the point I need to make.
13. The alcoholic might wish to keep things quiet because of feelings of humiliation at being conned; but then again he or she might not.
14. Of course it might not be necessary to breach confidentiality to advertise lack of success; but it might be highly desirable to name names in order to substantiate what would otherwise be a claim that was not able to be verified, e.g., Someone's treatment was a failure.
15. Thanks to John Kleinig, Stan Einstein and Steve Matthews for comments on earlier versions of this chapter.

2-10 Competence in Chemical Dependency Counseling

Theodore M. Godlaski, M.Div.

There is such an enormous gap between our words and our deeds! Everyone talks about freedom, democracy, justice, human rights, and peace; but at the same time, everyone, more or less, consciously or unconsciously, serves those values and ideals only to the extent necessary to defend and serve his own interests, and those of his group or state. Who should break this vicious circle? Responsibility cannot be preached: it can only be borne, and the only possible place to begin is with oneself.

— Vaclav Havel

Abstract

Although clinician competence is universally held to be necessary for ethically correct practice, it is often ill defined. Significant efforts toward a better specification have been made by an expert panel, working under the sponsorship of the Substance Abuse and Mental Health Services Administration of the United States. This group specifies three areas in which adequate capacity is necessary for competence: knowledge, skill, and attitudes. However, virtually all certifying bodies measure knowledge only objectively, leaving skill and attitude to the testimony of clinical supervisors. There is some reason to be concerned about the quality and quantity of supervisory contact on which such judgments are based. Also, there is reason to question whether all knowledge and all skills are of equal ethical value. Further, there are ethical questions about whether a field of substance-user counseling, separate from general counseling, can be justified.

Key Words: codes of ethics, substance use counseling, counselor competence, clinical supervision, evidence-based treatment, ethics, empathy, counseling skills, alcoholism, "drug abuse," substance user treatment, treatment fidelity

Introduction

Although counselor competence is generally held to be necessary for ethically correct practice, there is difficulty in specifying the constituents of competence. This chapter will explore current notions about competence and its components from various codes of ethics and from the work of certifying bodies and expert panels. It will also raise specific questions about whether all those things seen as necessary for competence are of equal ethical importance. Further, it will explore whether current notions of competence are in keeping with the ways in which individuals actually experience substance use disorders.

It is striking that codes of ethics, promulgated primarily by certification boards whose business it is to assure minimum levels of competence in chemical dependency counselors,[1] frequently fail to mention competence altogether. In the Code of Ethics published by The Kentucky Board of Certification of Alcohol and Drug Counselors (2003) the only allusion to competence is:

Section 1. Responsibility to Clients.

(1) An alcohol and drug counselor shall:

(a) Advance and protect the welfare of the client;

(b) Respect the rights of a person seeking assistance; and

(c) Make reasonable efforts to ensure that services are used appropriately. (201 KAR 35:030. p. 7)

It is valuable to note that this code does not go on to define what "used appropriately" means; nor does it contain any discussion of the quality of care that might "advance and protect the welfare of the client."

In the State of Ohio, the Code of Ethics for certified or licensed chemical dependency counselors (Chemical Dependency Professionals Board, nd) states the following,

> *The licensee or certificate holder shall recognize limitations of his or her competency based on professional qualifications, education and experience and shall not offer services or use techniques outside his or her professional competency or scope of practice defined by rules 4758-6-01 through 4758-6-05 of the Administrative Code. (OAR 4758-8-01 p. 27)*

The state of Ohio has a tiered system of certification and licensure – similar to some states and different from others – allowing increasing levels of function and autonomy with increasing levels of academic degree and time in practice. Commendably, the Ohio code requires competency not only of the counselor in practice but also in referral.

> *A licensee or certificate holder shall obtain appropriate consultation or make an appropriate referral when the client's problem is beyond the licensee or certificate holder's area of training, expertise, competency or scope of practice.*
>
> *The licensee or certificate holder shall refer clients to a person or agency that the licensee or certificate holder knows is qualified by training, experience, certification or license to provide such professional services. (OAR 4758-8-01 p. 27)*

Unfortunately, like most codes, the Ohio Code of Ethics does not specify how the counselor is to make such a judgment.

In much the same vein, the Missouri Substance Abuse Counselors Certification Board Code of Ethics states:

> *5. I shall remain aware of my own skills and limitations. I will attempt never to counsel or advise clients on matters outside my area of expertise. I will recognize when it is in the best interest to release or refer the client to another program or professional.*

6. I shall accept responsibility for my continuing education and professional development as part of my commitment to providing quality care for persons who seek my services as a substance abuse counselor and/or supervisor. (Missouri Substance Abuse Counselors Certification Board, nd)

The Connecticut Certification Board, however, addresses competency in a more direct fashion, having a specific heading for it in its Code of Ethics.

PRINCIPLE 3: Competence

Alcoholism and "drug abuse"[2] *counselors shall provide competent professional service to clients. Competent professional service requires thorough knowledge of alcohol and drug abuse, skill in presentation and counseling techniques, thoroughness and preparation reasonably necessary to assure the highest level of quality care to a client, and a willingness to maintain state-of-the-art knowledge through on-going professional education. (Connecticut Certification Board, Inc., nd)*

There might be some concern about how one could operationalize "thorough knowledge of alcohol and drug abuse, skill in presentation and counseling techniques, thoroughness and preparation reasonably necessary to assure the highest level of quality care to a client." And one might also wonder who decides what is "state-of-the-art knowledge".

The North Carolina Substance Abuse Professional Certification Board, Inc. is a bit more explicit. In a section of the North Carolina Administrative Code (Title 21, Chapter 68, Section .0503) there is a heading for "Competence" that states:

.0503 – COMPETENCE.

The substance abuse professional shall recognize that the profession is founded on national standards of competency which promote the best interests of society, of the client and of the profession as a whole. The counselor shall obtain continuing education as a component of professional competency. (North Carolina Substance Abuse Professional Certification Board, Inc., nd)

Unfortunately, it does not reference the "national standards of competency" to which it refers. One might assume that these are the performance domains and core functions published by the International Certification & Reciprocity Consortium/Alcohol and Other Drug Abuse (ICRC). This voluntary organization, established in 1981, sets standards for the certification of chemical dependency counselors and provides training and testing materials that can be used by its member certification boards. The ICRC Mission Statement says:

ICRC's mission is to establish, monitor and advance reciprocal competency standards for credentialing of professionals engaged in prevention and treatment of substance use disorders and related problems. (International Certification & Reciprocity Certification/ Alcohol and Other Drug Abuse, nd)

The standards set by the ICRC and other certifying organizations are not evidence-based. They are set through surveys of individuals already practicing in the field of substance-misuse counseling and employers to identify what levels of education and experience are acceptable for specific levels of function. In this way they may be more likely to reflect the prevailing values of the marketplace than any objective measures of what actually is necessary to constitute competence (Beckett, 2005).

Reviewing the ethical codes of certifying bodies for a definition of "competence" brings to mind a saying of Augustine of Hippo, "I know what time is until you ask me to explain it."[3] But this may be because the purpose of these certifying bodies is to assure minimum levels of competence in chemical dependency counselors. Consequently, they may view their process of certification itself as elucidation of competence. The majority of certifying bodies assure competence by following some version of the guidelines developed by the ICRC.

The ICRC guidelines for assuring competence include a minimum level of education about substance use disorders related to the performance domains of counseling, a minimum amount of clinical supervision in the performance of core functions of counseling, a minimum of work experience, and a written and oral examination. The performance domains identified by the ICRC are assessment, counseling, case management, education, and professional responsibility. The ICRC requires a minimum of 270 clock hours of instruction total in all these areas with a minimum of 6 hours specifically devoted to ethics and professional responsibility. It might be noted that unlike other professions in which academic education leading to a specific degree is required, these hours of education can be done in workshop settings in which no test is administered and no grade is given. The core functions identified by the ICRC for entry-level counselors are screening, intake, orientation, assessment, treatment planning, counseling, case management, crisis intervention, client education, referral, reports and record keeping, and consultation with other professionals. The ICRC requires a minimum of 300 hours of supervised training in these (a minimum of 10 hours in each core function). In addition, the ICRC requires 6,000 hours (3 years) of supervised work experience, the passing of a written examination, an oral case presentation and examination on the core functions, and the signing of a code of ethics.

The standards set by the ICRC and accepted by over 70 certifying bodies internationally evolved out of its experience enriched by the advice of experts and focus groups. The purpose of the standards is to attempt to insure exposure to a sufficient level of information and skill building to constitute essential competence. It could be said that the standards themselves provide an explication of competence in chemical dependency counseling, although not a very concise or rigorous one. It is a fact of human experience that no matter how carefully standards may be developed, they cannot be better than the judgment of the independent certification boards that approve educational programs and workshops to meet the requirements for training hours and decide what forms of supervision are acceptable. Although the ICRC sets standards for supervisors, it is difficult for anyone to assure the quality of clinical supervision especially in a time of decreasing public and private funding. Finally, the tests, both written and oral, developed by the ICRC primarily test knowledge and not actual skill, aptitude, or attitude.

This point about testing being largely about "knowing" as opposed to "knowing how to" is not unique to chemical dependency counseling. Exactly the same issue is being debated concerning medical education (Wass et al., 2001). Indeed, it is not unreasonable to question whether "knowing how to do something" and "being able to actually do it" are not also different things. A well-designed test can verify that someone both "knows" and "knows how to." It is left to the testimony of clinical supervisors that an individual can actually perform the procedure in question with a reasonable degree of facility and can do so in a fairly consistent manner. The ability to function well and consistently would seem to carry the greatest weight of ethical importance and in this area certification of competence relies on the testimony of supervisors.

This is reminiscent of the distinction, in classical philosophy, between action (praxis) as an abstract and the making or crafting (poiesis) of a specific product.[4] Perhaps even more to the point, it is the distinction between scientific knowledge and prudence—with the understanding that the meaning of prudence here contains no hint of timidity, it is the apprehension of the principles that guide the doing of a specific task.[5] Aquinas furthers this discussion by indicating that it is prudence that brings knowledge (speculative knowledge) to fruition in the real word.[6] When certification boards give their stamp of approval to an individual, what they are actually doing is making a promise to society in general and to those who are potential recipients of care at the hands of the one certified in particular, that this individual will act with consistent competence—that he/she not only "knows how" and "knows how to" but will actually skillfully produce the products of counseling case after case. The making of such a promise is a grave matter, especially when it is ultimately based not on direct and observable evidence but on the testimony of others—testimony seldom challenged by examination (Griffin, 2005; Beckett, 2005). It also presupposes that the knowledge of how to produce the products of counseling under varying conditions and in different circumstances is available, at least in some acceptably valid form.

Before any further discussion of performance domains and core functions, it might be worthwhile to reflect on the basis of competence and why it has been generally held to be important for ethical practice. Put generally, we might say that competence has something to do with knowing what needs to be done, along with how and when it needs to be done, together with the skills needed to do it and the aptitudes and attitudes that facilitate doing it well in a consistent fashion. Even those who espouse a principle-based approach to ethics, and most certainly those who take a virtue-based approach, place practitioner competence under the heading of Trustworthiness or Fidelity to Trust (Beauchamp & Childress, 2001; Pellegrino & Thomasma, 1993). This placement has important ethical implications. From the patient's perspective, one part of competence has to do with trusting a system of education and credentialing. This is more accurately a form of reliance rather than of trust (Baier, 1986; Luhmann, 1979) similar to the confidence one might have in an airline pilot or a firefighter. It is not really personal and has nothing in particular to do with character. In the healing professions, however, patients do not just rely on the competence of the practitioner. They trust that he/she will combine the knowledge and skills learned to satisfy the educational and credentialing system with intimate knowledge of the specific patient's life and mind to consistently do what is best and most acceptable. In this way, competence as an ethical factor requires the ability to apply both knowledge and skill with considerable discretionary latitude, but to do so in a consistent fashion that can be grasped by the patient. It is primarily an interpersonal reality. In ethical terms, it is not until the knowledge, skills, and attitudes of the practitioner are combined with the information, values, and goals of a specific patient that competence can be evidenced.

In this way, competence is not simply a matter of technical skill, of the correct performance of procedures. In all forms of counseling and therapy, the ability of counselor and patient to form a therapeutic alliance, of the counselor to engage the patient as a collaborator, is a powerful predictor of positive outcome.

In 1998, The Addiction Technology Transfers Centers Curriculum Committee, under the sponsorship of the Center for Substance Abuse Treatment, and the leadership of David Deitch, published Addiction Counseling Competencies: The Knowledge, Skills, and Attitudes of Professional Practice. In this comprehensive treatment of the elements considered important for competent practice there is the following definition:

> ***Competency:*** *the requisite knowledge, skills, and attitudes to perform tasks and responsibilities essential to addiction counseling. (p.103)*

In this work, the Curriculum Committee took great pains to specify the areas of knowledge, skill, and attitude necessary for competent function in what it termed "Interdisciplinary Foundations" (understanding addiction; treatment knowledge; application to practice; and professional readiness) as well as the "Practice Dimensions of Addiction Counseling" (clinical evaluation; treatment planning; referral, service coordination; counseling; client, family, and community education; documentation; and professional and ethical responsibility). Its purpose was to establish a blueprint for the development of educational and supervisory activity directed toward competent preparation of individuals treating people manifesting substance-use disorders.[7] It succeeded impressively. Additionally, the Northwest Frontier Addiction Technology Transfer Center (2001) developed rubrics to assist supervisors in assessing the level of competence demonstrated by candidates in field placements. The task of the present chapter is not to revisit its work but to examine some of the ethical concerns and challenges related to the "requisite knowledge, skills, and attitudes."

It is a long-standing notion that certain groups of individuals have command of a special body of knowledge as well as a special set of skills—it might also be added certain attitudes or aptitudes that facilitate the graceful and creative application of that knowledge and those skills—in order to perform specific tasks for the benefit of others and of human society at large. These groups have been identified as the professions, not so much because of the knowledge and skills, but because they profess a specific code of ethics that govern their activity and bind them together as a moral community (Pellegrino & Thomasma, 1993). Having demonstrated a requisite level of such knowledge and skill is considered essential before professing the code of ethics and thus entering the profession. Determining what the "requisite level" is and how to measure it has bedeviled committees and boards of licensure/certification for a very long time.

It would seem that the knowledge at issue here is not speculative knowledge —knowledge for its own sake—but rather practical knowledge—knowledge for the sake of doing or accomplishing something. The reason for this is that the knowledge is directed toward the specific end of the activity. Thus the end of all the healing professions—substance user counseling included—is health.[8] The knowledge that is critical for competence is not all knowledge but only knowledge that is useful for establishing health. There may be a good deal of information about substance use, for example, that is of interest to research scientists but has no known direct application to clinical practice. Ignorance of such information does not bear on competence because it does not limit a practitioner's ability to facilitate healing. Also, the knowledge necessary to perform one function may be quite different from the knowledge required to perform another. For example, knowledge about the "natural history of addiction" and the diagnostic criteria of various substance-use disorders are important when doing an assessment but are largely irrelevant when providing individual counseling.

So not all knowledge is of equal importance. The knowledge that is most valuable here would seem to be empirical and descriptive, capable of application to specific cases, rather than general and abstract.[9] Any one who has taught psychopathology can attest to the fact that students who are very fluent in describing and discussing the diagnostic criteria for a specific disorder may be at a loss when given a case presentation of the same disorder and asked to identify which criteria have been met. It is not hard to imagine that the same difficulty might result when going from identifying diagnostic criteria in a written narrative to recognizing them in a face-to-face interview. The point is that the knowledge that can be brought down to the specific case level is the most critical ethically. Knowing that there is a sizable correlation between perpetration of intimate violence and alcohol use in males who are dysphoric and display some characteristics of Borderline Personality Disorder (Holtzworth-Munroe & Stewart, 1994) is likely to be more important than knowing the current street slang for methamphetamine. Likewise, knowing that about one-half of adolescents, nation-wide, referred for outpatient treatment of substance-use disorder, also reported current (within the past 12 months) histories of physical and/or sexual abuse (Adolescent Treatment Models, Cross-site Analysis, 2002) is likely to be more critical to client care than knowing about phenotypic models of addiction.

Knowledge that can be readily applied to a particular situation is not always the knowledge that is assessed by certifying bodies. Take, for example the following sample question from the ICRC written examination.

When an actively-using, alcohol-dependent client presents with depressive symptoms:

A. Cognitive approaches to treating depression should be the focus of treatment.

B. The presence of a primary depressive disorder should be assessed as soon as possible.

C. He/she frequently responds quickly to the use of antidepressant medication.

D. Depressive symptoms in the majority of cases will be significantly diminished after detoxification and abstinence.

E. The client should be referred. (Castle Worldwide, Inc, 2002)

The scoring key indicates that the correct answer is "D." Although there are some differences depending on the population studied, the majority of individuals who display symptoms of Major Depressive Episode while drinking heavily do remit after a few days to a few weeks abstinence; however, 5% of men and 10% of women do not (Kaplan & Saddock, 1995). Given an understanding that the knowledge most critical to competence is that which can be most easily applied clinically to specific cases, would it not be more important to know that a proportion of individuals will not experience remission of depressive symptoms with abstinence, that these will more likely be women than men, and will require further assessment, specialized treatment, and probable referral than simply to know that most will remit?

An interesting question about the scope of knowledge necessary for competence can be raised: is the knowledge necessary for competence general and universal in nature or is it interdependent with the duties that a professional actually performs? This question was raised by Allen Buchanan (1991) in relation to knowledge necessary for medical specialists. When the interdisciplinary foundations and the clinical functions—or whatever name one chooses to call the range of activities that certifying bodies use to set the limits of appropriate knowledge—are examined, it seems clear that every activity that can be performed by a counselor has been identified and included. But in actual fact, it is rare that a counselor, especially one working in an interdisciplinary team setting, would actually be called on to perform all these duties. It certainly could be argued that the general and inclusive scope of this knowledge insures competence in whatever duties a counselor might actually perform. Even though true, it is not ethically relevant in specific cases. Further, general knowledge may not be sufficient to insure competence in those whose function is specialized. If a counselor chooses to work only with adolescent females, general knowledge base measures may not insure that he/she actually knows enough to understand what is in the clients' best interest. The intent here is not to encourage an endless series of super sub-specialty certifications or endorsements, but to point out some concerns with the system as it exists.

The knowledge necessary to provide competent substance misuser counseling changes with how the disorder presents in different groups, at different times, and in different places. A substance misuser counselor practicing in the United States in the early 1960s who knew nothing about the disease caused by Human Immunodeficiency Virus would not be considered incompetent. However, by the mid 1980s the same counselor who did not know enough about the vectors of infection for HIV/AIDS to advise clients when testing was needed or enough about the treatment and progression of the disease to provide at least supportive counseling to those who tested positive would certainly be considered incompetent in at least that area of practice. Given the frequency with which substance-use disorders co-occur with a variety of mental health disorders[10] (Regler et al., 1990; Kendel, 1992; Kessler et al., 1997; Kessler et al., 1996), it would appear that the same could be said even more strongly about knowledge of psychopathology. Given the fact that large epidemiological studies of comorbidity seem to indicate that symptoms of mental health disorder predate substance use in a majority of cases (Kessler et al., 1997; Kessler et al., 1996), that the substance use disorder is secondary—at least temporally—to the mental health disorder, serious questions are raised about whether knowledge and skills specific to substance misuser treatment alone is ever truly adequate for competent practice. Part of the difficulty arises out of the historical origins of substance user counseling as an independent field rather than as a sub-specialty of general mental health practice. Substance Use Disorders are not, as diagnostic entities or syndromal descriptions, anything special among mental health problems. They are no more distinctive than, say Schizophrenia, Bipolar Affective Disorder, or Cyclothymic Disorder. Yet none of these has its own field to treat it. Certainly, there are psychiatrists, psychologists, and social workers that specialize in the treatment of specific disorders but they have a generalist grounding. Substance user counseling arose as a separate field because the traditional practitioners in mental health had little or no interest in treating patients who manifested problems with the use and misuse of alcohol and other drugs (Deitch & Carleton, 1997). However, as understanding of the inter-related nature of mental health disorders, including Substance Use Disorders, has progressed, it is time to question whether what began as a noble attempt to address a specific type of human suffering has not outlived its usefulness. In fact there are movements to provide a tiered certification/licensure with the highest tier requiring a graduate degree in one of the mental health areas. NAADAC, the Association for Addiction Professionals has had such a tiered credential for at least 10 years. It provides three levels of certification, each requiring greater academic credentials together with specialized training and experience. The establishment of this multilevel credentialing scheme was not implemented without controversy that continues even today (Beckett, 2005). It is interesting to note that some, if not most, of the opposition to such efforts has come from provider organizations because they are concerned about the effect on their ability to recruit and pay more qualified practitioners. For example, in Kentucky, the law providing for State certification of chemical dependency counselors, passed in 1996 (KRS 309.080—309.089), required that by 2004 a Master's degree in behavioral science or allied disciplines would be necessary for individuals to be certified. In 2003, the association of community mental health centers lobbied the Kentucky State Legislature to suspend that provision of the law specifically for the reasons already mentioned. They were successful. It seems strange that as knowledge of the complex and interrelated nature of substance use and other behavioral and developmental problems increases, there is no concomitant demand for a broader level of demonstrated knowledge on the part of substance-use counseling professionals.

This suggests a question that is really beyond the scope of this chapter but deserves reflection and debate: is the continued existence of a separate profession of substance-use counseling primarily a matter of beneficence or of self-interest? In other words, does substance-use counseling as a distinct field of activity separate from general counseling serve the good of clients or serve its own good primarily? As has already been mentioned, a large proportion of individuals with Substance-Use Disorders also have other serious mental health problems (Sacks et al., 1997; Compton et al., 2000). If clinicians are competent to address only substance misuse, this necessitates the involvement of at least one, if not more, additional clinicians as well as the smooth coordination of their interaction with that individual and with each other (Center for Substance Abuse Treatment, 2005). In the abstract, this may seem reasonable. However, practically it requires an individual to form relationships with multiple treatment providers, often not working in the same organization,[11] increases the need for the arrangement of additional transportation, childcare, costs, and may require significant additional time away from work.[12] Such a state of affairs might be justified if the knowledge and technical skills required of clinicians were of such a high order that no single individual could be expected to master more than one set of them. For example, this is often the case with specific forms of surgery: ophthalmologists do not perform orthopedic procedures nor do neurosurgeons do cardiac procedures. However, all counseling approaches used in the formal treatment of substance misuse are either derived from or very similar to those used in the treatment of other behavioral and emotional disorders as are the skills necessary (Miller & Rollnick, 2002; Miller, & Brown, 1997). Given the fact that a large proportion of individuals seeking treatment, whether voluntarily or under coercion, for substance-use problems have other serious mental health problems; that beyond the specific medical technology for detoxification and adjunctive treatment of substance-use problems, there is virtually nothing that distinguishes substance-use counseling from the counseling done for other behavioral and emotional problems; and that a separate profession of substance-use counseling creates the need, in individuals having substance use and comorbid psychiatric problems, for simultaneous treatment by multiple clinicians; can it be said that substance-use counseling is in the best interest of most clients? Certainly, having someone who has special knowledge about one's problem and perhaps even a greater degree of likelihood to empathize with one's experience is an asset. [If I am right in thinking that many such counselors are ex-addicts, possibly with limited educational background, but great empathy, and possibly sought after because of that, might there not be a case for creating a special class of addiction counselors?] However, it does not seem that these are sufficient to justify a separate profession. Individuals who wish to help suffering alcoholics and addicts[13] but have no interest in a lengthy process of academic preparation benefit from having a separate profession of substance-use counseling since this allows them to get their training primarily on the job. It is of benefit to treatment provider organizations, primarily in the public sector, since it allows them to pay less to undegreed but certified chemical dependency counselors than to degreed and licensed Social Workers or Psychologists. It is of benefit to managed care and insurance companies because cheaper manpower cost leads to cheaper treatment (Deitch & Carleton, 1997). It might also be argued that state and federal governments benefit because, although other behavioral healthcare providers tend to have very strong and well-funded lobbies, substance-use counselors do not.[14]

It would be remiss not to mention knowledge about how substance misuse differs from culture to culture as well as in the same culture from one period of time to another. However, this knowledge should not be naïve or arrogant. It is important to keep in mind what Hays (1996) pointed out, that, "despite distinct differences in their meanings, the terms race, ethnicity, and culture continue to be used interchangeably and in ways that reinforce Eurocentric assumptions" (p.333). Believing that because people speak Spanish or Portuguese as a primary language they are one culture (Hispanic) is both naïve and arrogant. Further, culture is not defined by ethnicity. People living in rural Appalachia have quite a different culture from people living in rural Nebraska. Individuals living in small towns, have a different culture from those living in large metropolitan areas. Further, there are issues raised by the degree of enculturation. A recent study by Grant et al. (2004) shows significantly different rates of both substance misuse and mental health problems for both Latino and non-Latino whites depending on whether they were born elsewhere and immigrated to the United States or were born in the United States. The one thing that is consistent across groups is that inclusion into American culture is hazardous to one's health. Perhaps counselors who are aware of their own prejudices and reactions while obtaining detailed information about clients' beliefs, values, fears, goals, and aspirations best address the matter of cultural competence (Ashenberg-Straussner, 2001). Likewise, treatment approaches are called for that are clearly client centered and that honor client autonomy. This is not because autonomy is equally honored in all cultures, but rather because it creates the necessary conditions under which the client may teach the clinician what is appropriate.

In another way of viewing cultural competence, what is to be avoided may be more important than what is to be included. What is to be avoided is a kind of clinical fundamentalism or clinical imperialism: a belief that what is most acceptable or effective in the mainstream or dominant culture should be equally acceptable and effective in cultures outside the mainstream.

Knowledge about various treatment approaches is also considered necessary for competent practice.[15] It would be comforting to say that current training allows clinicians to match clients with the treatment approach that is best suited for them. However, although there is much we have learned, such refined differential therapeutics seems currently beyond our reach (Babor et al., 2003). At most, it allows counselors to present options to their clients about how their treatment might proceed or inform counselors about which treatment approaches might increase resistance and anger for clients who have certain personality traits.

The notion that any competent counselor should be able to learn and implement any sound treatment approach might be unrealistic. A specific therapeutic approach requires a specific kind of individual to deliver it—certain dispositional factors in the counselor need to be in harmony with the tenor of the treatment approach. Few developers of treatment technologies seem to acknowledge this, though there are exceptions (Miller & Rollnick, 1991). Further, there is some evidence that therapists self-select for the kind of treatment approaches they utilize (Elkins, 1999). To require that a counselor who is very uncomfortable with ambivalence, uncertainty, and disagreement be proficient in a counseling approach such as Motivational Interviewing—which focuses on client autonomy—in order to be considered competent may be unrealistic. To address this quirk of human nature, treatment developers have recently turned to the use of treatment manuals as a way of insuring compliance with specific treatment approaches. Although this may make for good science in a clinical trial, it does not necessarily make for good treatment. It should go without saying that following a manual does not constitute competence (Elkin, 1999; Dobson & Shaw, 1988). Finally, there is evidence in the psychotherapeutic literature that rigidly adhering to a manual may actually result in poorer client outcomes (Strupp & Anderson, 1997).

Because this is a discussion of ethics, it might be worth pointing out that the measures used to determine the success of a specific treatment approach seldom if ever use measures that have explicit ethical significance. Instead, the measures used are those of social control: abstinence or decreased use of alcohol and other drugs, increased income or employment and/or education, decreased involvement with the criminal justice system, improvement in housing, and decreased use of medical and psychiatric services. Aristotle set as a goal for all ethical activity the "flourishing life," happiness both for individuals and communities (Book I, Chapter iv, line 2, 1994). To be sure, all of the measures already mentioned may have some bearing on the sum total of happiness for a given individual, but they do not necessarily do so. Researchers investigating the outcome of a treatment protocol do not usually, if ever, ask participants if they are happier as a result of their participation. Granted, there is some scientific justification for this since "happiness" is not a measure that can be made objectively or verified, albeit, as with "time" one is likely to know "it" and can experience "it" when "it" happens. Nevertheless, it would be of interest to see what the results would be.

There has been a commendable linkage between responsible practice and use of evidence-based forms of treatment (National Institute on Drug Abuse, 1999). These are treatment approaches that have been tested in controlled studies and have proven themselves to be as or more effective than other treatment approaches. Although it is laudable that treatment approaches based on measures of efficacy rather than on blind faith should be selected, some caveats are in order. Trials of therapeutic approaches designed to show their effectiveness must be conducted under very strictly controlled conditions (Bellg, 2004). This is necessary to control the intervening variables that might affect the outcome but which have nothing directly to do with the treatment protocol under study. Unfortunately, the very strict level of control that allows researchers to demonstrate the effectiveness of a treatment may make it virtually impossible to transfer that same treatment into an actual clinical setting with any fidelity (Leventhal & Friedman, 2004). What is done under laboratory conditions in which the focus is on fidelity to the treatment protocol and control of all other factors, including variability among clinicians and clients, is quite different from what it is possible to achieve in a working clinic in which the focus is quite different and anyone who walks through the door can be a client. Dwayne Simpson (2002) has done initial work on conceptualizing how treatment technologies are transferred from the research to the clinical setting. The factors are multiple, and involve the institutional structure and culture, clinician characteristics, perception of need and value, and resources available. In testing the conceptual model, the factors expected to influence the degree and fidelity of even a very simple treatment technology are not always the ones that one might expect (Roman & Johnson, 2002). Further, successful transfer of evidence-based treatment technologies is time consuming and expensive. Given the supervisor and staff turn-over rates in most clinical settings, the fact that education and supervision are both expensive and non revenue-producing activities, and that substance-misuser treatment is a poorly compensated enterprise, it is doubtful whether evidence-based treatment practices will be implemented with sufficient fidelity to retain their vigor (McLellan et al., 2003). Despite this dismal assessment, it would seem prudent to keep the emphasis on these evidence-based approaches when training and testing for competence. Whether or not they are better than non-evidence-based approaches to treatment in actual practice is uncertain but even in an infirmed and partly implemented form they may retain elements that are of specific benefit to clients.

To this point, the knowledge discussed is that which the counselor has gained as a result of study outside the therapeutic relationship. But there is also a whole world of knowledge that is gained only in interaction with the client. This is knowledge about the perceptions, judgment, beliefs, attitudes, desires, values, agendas, self-experienced and defined needs and wants, goals, and aspirations of an individual client, as well as the social networks of which he/she is a member (Barabasi, 2003; Wasserman & Faust, 1997). Without this information, the body of knowledge gained through study is clinically useless. This sort of knowledge is intimately bound up with the skills necessary to counsel competently. Earlier, it was noted that competence has something to do with knowing what needs to be done, along with how and when and where it needs to be done. Out of this interactive knowledge of the client's unique experience both of the disorder and of life, the competent counselor knows these four things. Unlike the case with certain medications and surgical procedures, there is not one best practice, or one right way to assist someone with a Substance-Use Disorder to achieve a better state of health and happiness. This assistance embraces not only the conventional definitions of "recovery" but extends also to all the varieties of harm reduction. It is here that competence is actually demonstrated. This is where knowledge, skill, attitude, and aptitude meet.

This intimate and interactive knowledge, gained from working with a large number of individuals over time, coming to understand what is helpful for some and not for others, is as essential as any body of knowledge, whether general and theoretical or empirical and statistical. Despite the current dictum that "the plural of anecdote is not evidence," it is specifically this kind of essentially anecdotal evidence that necessarily informs competent practice. The extended period that substance user counseling, and for that matter any profession, requires as a kind of apprenticeship not only provides an opportunity to practice skill but is also directed to the acquisition of such knowledge. It may be an error that the ICRC allows its member certification board the option of waiving the time required when progressively more advanced degrees are pursued (ICRC, nd).

To obtain such knowledge requires skill. The skills are not simply related to the ability to frame questions in an interview or to use structured assessment instruments in an artful fashion; they are primarily the skills of engaging with and listening to the client. The knowledge that clients convey is narrative, stories about their life and experience. The ability to listen well and resonate with the narrative is what is called for (Sky, 2002; Charon, 1993). This may be especially important if the findings of John Strauss in his qualitative work with individuals having schizophrenia apply also to those with other chronic emotional and behavioral problems (Strauss, 2000; 1997): that the way in which individuals cope and recover is idiosyncratic and nonlinear. The challenge remains to be able to transform "therapeutic engagement" and "therapeutic alliance" from concepts into vital and central dimensions of an ongoing relationship.

The Curriculum Committee of the Addiction Technology Transfer Center has enumerated, in some detail, the knowledge, skills, and attitudes necessary for all the functions it identifies with substance use counseling (The Addiction Technology Transfers Centers Curriculum Committee, 1998). The purpose here is not to revisit this very long list of skills specific to various functions but to focus on a small subset that seems especially salient. Under the heading "Screening," subheading "1. Establish rapport, including management of crisis situation and determination of need for additional professional assistance," the following skills are listed:

a. Demonstrating effective verbal and nonverbal communication.

b. Accurately identifying client's frame of reference.

c. Reflecting client's feelings and message.

d. Recognizing and defusing volatile or dangerous situations.

e. Demonstrating empathy, respect, and genuineness. (p.27)

All but d. have been called "facilitative interpersonal skills" (Simmons et al., 1995; Spruce & Snyders, 1982) or "nonspecific skills" (Strupp, 1995): those skills that do not relate to any specific therapeutic approach but are the foundation of the relationship between the counselor and the counseled. Also, in the same document, under the heading "Individual Counseling," subheading "1. Establish a helping relationship with the client characterized by warmth, respect, genuineness, concreteness, and empathy," there is the following list of skills:

a. Active listening, including paraphrasing, reflecting, and summarizing.
b. Conveying warmth, respect, and genuineness in a culturally appropriate manner.
c. Demonstrating empathic understanding.
d. Using power and authority appropriately in support of treatment goals. (p.63)

Although research in this area of substance misuse is scant, the presence of these interpersonal skills, forming the basis for a therapeutic alliance, grounded in empathy, seem to be particularly significant in predicting positive outcomes in substance user treatment (Luborsky et al., 1985; Miller et al., 1980; Valle, 1981; Ritter et al., 2002). The psychotherapy literature is much richer in this area, and these skills are considered the basis of all therapeutic interaction (Strupp, 1996; Greenberg & Elliot, 1997; Watson, 2001; Lambert & Bergin, 1994; Bohart & Greenberg, 1997). It is not that these skills are in themselves sufficient, but they are foundational, in the same way that the ability to make articulate sounds is foundational to oral communication. The knowledge of any number of languages will not suffice to remedy this deficit. So it seems reasonable that before any other skills are determined to be present as a matter of counselor competence, these skills and abilities should be determined to be present.

A reasonable question arises about how, specifically, these foundational skills may be acquired. It would seem that one must have, at least to some minimal degree, the personality apparatus necessary to recognize that the experiences of others are as real and substantial as one's own (Hill & O'Brien, 1999). This may have something to do with what in a Five Factor Model of personality it called "Agreeableness," since abnormally low levels of this factor tend to mark personality disorders in which a lack of empathy is a hallmark (Costa & Widiger, 1994). Then, one must have sufficiently reflected on personal experience to recognize that suffering and troubles are part of all human experience. In order to accomplish this, one must have also sufficiently transcended essential narcissism so as to have an interest in experiences beyond one's own (Mathiasen & Alpert, 1993) Literature may express this better than behavioral science. Herodotus, in this History of the World has Croesus, conquered King of Lydia, give the following advice to Cyrus, King of Persia:

> *Alas! My own sufferings have been my lessons and have taught me to be keen sighted of dangers. If you think yourself an immortal, leading an army of immortals, my counsel will be wasted on you. But if you know yourself to be a man and the leader of men, then take what I say to heart, that there is a wheel on which the affairs of men revolve, and its movement forbids that the same man should always be fortunate. (I, par. 221)*

In Albert Camus' The Plague (1991), we find:

> *"Who taught you all this, Doctor?"*
> *The reply came promptly:*
> *"Suffering." (pp.128-129)*

Further, one must have recognized that the sufferings and joys of others are not alien or essentially different from one's own. As Edith Stein indicates, all these things together allow for the recognition that the experience of suffering or joy is no longer "mine" or "yours," or "his" or "hers" but "ours"—that "I" and "you" and "they" have become "we" (Stein, 1970). This is not to say that one experiences the joy or suffering of another but that one is capable of an intimate understanding of it through one's own similar experiences. This is not a purely affective process—that would be sympathy—but is also, and perhaps even primarily, a cognitive process. If this is true, then it is not difficult to understand why it is basic to engagement and therapeutic alliance.

Finally, one must learn to express this capacity in an effective and understandable fashion. There has been some work done on empathy training for counselors which all points to the fact that this is a long and difficult task, much more so than teaching a narrow, focused therapeutic technique (Nerdrum, 1997; Nerdrum & Ronnestad, 2002).

> *Training of therapist empathy should reflect that initiating trainee change beyond a style of explaining, questioning, arguing, and giving advice, toward a decentered, empathic helping style, is a complex and demanding task for both trainees and trainers. Such changes challenge automatized communication patterns, trainee self-esteem, and trainee sense of therapeutic mastery. (Nerdrum & Ronnestad, 2002, p 626)*

All evidence points to the fact that training therapists to interact more empathically with clients is not something that can be accomplished in a workshop, even a two-day workshop. Given the centrality of the ability to experience and effectively express empathy in the counseling relationship, certifying bodies might consider how it could be better measured, at least as a basic trait.

Theodore M. Godlaski, M.Div.., (USA), is Assistant Clinical Professor of Psychiatry School of Medicine, former member of the staff of the Center on Drug and Alcohol Research at the University of Kentucky and currently a member of the faculty of the School of Social Work. Prior to coming to the University, he developed and directed treatment programs in both the public and private sector. He also consulted both nationally and internationally on program design and operation. He is currently involved in three research projects. Two are directed toward examining the outcome of substance user treatment and one focuses on the affect, for Native Alaskans, of inclusion of traditional Tlingit healing practices in an inpatient treatment program. He is a current member and former Chairperson of the National Ethics Committee for NAADAC. He has a long standing interest in clinical research with rural populations and has been a MESIDU faculty member both in Israel, Italy and in Spain. He is a member of the Editorial Board of Substance Use and Misuse.

References

Adolescent Treatment Models, Cross-site Analysis. (2002). Summary Report from June 27-28 Meeting. Rockville, MD: Northrop Grumman Information Technology Health Solutions and Service Division.

Allyn & Bacon Professional (Producer). (2001). Motivational Interviewing for Addictions with Miller, W.R.: Brief Therapy Series. [Video Tape] (Available from Allyn & Bacon 75 Arlington Street, Suite 300, Boston, MA 02116).

Aristotle. (1994). *Nicomachean Ethics*. Cambridge, Massachusetts: Harvard University Press.

Ashenberg-Straussner, A. (2001). Ethnocultural issues in substance abuse treatment: An overview. In Ashenberg-Straussner, S. (ed.) *Ethnocultural Factors in Substance Abuse Treatment*. New York: Guilford Press, pp. 3-28.

Babor, T.F. & DelBoca, F.K. (eds.). (2003). *Treatment matching in alcoholism*. New York: Cambridge University Press.

Baier, A. (1986). Trust and anti-trust. *Ethics 96*(2): 231-260.

Barabasi, A.L. (2003). Linked. New York: Plume-Penguin Books.

Beauchamp, T.L., & Childress, J.F. (2001). *Principles of biomedical ethics (5th Edition)*. New York: Oxford University Press.

Beckett, S. (2005). Director of Education and Certification, NAADAC. Personal communication.

Bellg, A.J., Resnick, B., Minicucci, D.S., Ogedegbe, G., Ernst, D., Borrelli, B., Hecht, J., Ory, M., Orwig, D., & Czajkowski, S. (2004). Enhancing treatment fidelity in health behavior change studies: Best practices and recommendations from the NIH Behavior Change Consortium. *Health Psychology 23*(5): 443–451.

Bohart, A.C., & Greenberg, L.S. (1997). Empathy: Where are we and where do we go from here? In Bohart, A.C. & Greenberg, L.S. (Eds.), *Empathy reconsidered. New directions in psychotherapy* (pp. 419-449). Washington, DC: American Psychological Association.

Buchanan, A. (1991). The physician's knowledge and the patient's best interest. In Pellegrino, E.D., Veatch, R.M., & Langan, J.P. (eds.). *Ethics, trust, and the professions: Philosophical and cultural aspects*. Washiington, DC: Georgetown University Press, pp. 93-112.

Camu, A. (1991). *The plague*. New York: Vantage, Reissue Edition.

Castle Worldwide, Inc. (2002). Candidate guide: International certification examination for alcohol and other drug abuse counselors. Washington, DC: IC&RC/AODA, Inc.

Center for Substance Abuse Treatment. (2005). Substance Abuse Treatment for Persons With Co-Occurring Disorders. Treatment Improvement Protocol (TIP) Series 42. DHHS Publication No. (SMA) 05-3992. Rockville, MD: Substance Abuse and Mental Health Services Administration.

Charon, R. (1993). The narrative road to empathy. In Spiro, H., Mccrea Curnen, M.G., Peschel, E., & St. James, D. (eds). *Empathy and the Practice of Medicine* (pp. 147-159). New York: Yale University Press.

Chemical Dependency Professionals Board (nd) Ohio Administrative Code. Retrieved from http://ocdp.ohio.gov/pdfs/rules.pdf on December 20, 2004.

Clark, J., Leukefeld, C., Godlaski, T., Brown, C., Garrity, J., & Hays, L. (2002). Developing, implementing, and evaluating a treatment protocol for rural substance abusers. *The Journal of Rural Health, 18*(3), 396-406.

Compton, W.M., Cottler, L.B., Ben Abdallah, A., Phelps, D.L., Spitznagel, E.L., & Horton, J.C. (2000). Substance dependence and other psychiatric disorders among drug dependent subjects: Race and gender correlates. *American Journal of Addictions 9*(2):113–125.

Connecticut Certification Board, Inc (nd). *Alcoholism and substance abuse counselors' code of ethics*. Retrieved from http://Competence\Connecticut Certification Board, Inc.htm, 12/26/2004.

Costa, P.T., & Widiger, T.A. (1994). *Personality disorders and the five factor model of personality*. Washington, DC: Amarican Psychological Association.

Deich, D.A., & Carleton, S.A. (1997). Education and training of clinical personnel. In Lowenson, J.A., Ruiz, P., Millman, R.B., & Langrod, J.P (eds.) *Substance abuse: A comprehensive textbook*; pp. 801-811, Baltimore, MD: Williams & Willkins.

Dobson, K.S. & Shaw, B.F. (1988). The use of treatment manuals in cognitive therapy: Experiences and issues. *Journal of Consulting and Clinical Psychology, 56*: 673-680.

Elkin, I. (1999). A major dilemma in psychotherapy outcome research: Disentangling therapists from therapies. *Clinical Psychology: Science and Practice; 6*(1): 10-32.

Frances, A., First, M.B., & Pincus, H.A. (1995). *DSM-IV Guidebook*. Washington, DC: American Psychiatric Press, Inc.

Grant, B.F., Stinson, F.S., Hasin, D.S., Dawson, D.A., Chou, S.P., & Anderson, K. (2004). Immigration and lifetime prevalence of DSM-IV psychiatric disorders among Mexican Americans and non-Hispanic whites in the United States: Results from the National Epidemiologic Survey on alcohol related conditions. *Archives of General Psychiatry, 61*:1226-1233.

Greenberg, L.S.,& Elliott, R. (1997). Varieties of empathic responding. In Bohart, A.C. & Greenberg, L.S. (Eds.), *Empathy reconsidered. New directions in psychotherapy* (pp. 167-186). Washington, DC: American Psychological Association.

Griffin, S. (2005). Deputy Executive Director, International Certification Reciprocity Consortium, personal communication.

Hays, P.A. (1996). Addressing the complexity of culture and gender in counseling. *Journal of Counseling and Development, 74*(4): 332-338.

Hill, C. E.,& O'Brien, K. M. (1999). Helping skills. Facilitating exploration, insight and action. Washington, DC: American Psychological Association.

Holtzworth-Munroe, A, & Stuart, G.L. (1994).Typologies of male batterers: Three subtypes and the differences among them. *Psychological Bullitin, 116*, 476-497.

ICRC (ND) Standards for certified AODA counselors. Retrieved from http://www.icrcaoda.org/standards_counselor.cfm , 1/3/05.

Kaplan, H.L. & Saddock, B.J. (eds.). (1995). *Comprehensive textbook of psychiatry, sixth edition*. Baltimore, MD: Williams and Wilkins.

Kandel, D.B. (1992). Epidemiological trends and implications for the understanding of addiction. In O'Brian, P. & Jaffe, J. (Eds.). *Addiction Studies*. Research Publication, New York: Vol 70, p23.

Kessler, R.C., Crum, R.M., Warner, L.A., Nelson, C.B., Schulenberg, J., & Anthony, J.C. (1997). Lifetime co-occurrence of DSM-III-R alcohol abuse and dependence with other psychiatric disorders in the National Comorbidity Survey. *Arch Gen Psychiatry, 54*(4):313-21.

Kessler, R.C., Nelson, C.B., McGonagle, K.A., Edlund, M.J., Frank, R.G., & Leaf, P.J. (1996). The epidemiology of co-occurring addictive and mental disorders: Implications for prevention and service utilization. *American Journal of Orthopsychiatry. 66*:17-31.

Lambert, M. J.,& Bergin, A. E. (1994). The effectiveness of psychotherapy. In Bergin, A.E. & Garfield, S.L. (Eds.), *Handbook of psychotherapy and behavior change* (pp. 143-189). New York: John Wiley.

Leukefeld, C., Clark, J., Godlaski, T., Brown, C., & Hays, L. *Structured Behavioral Outpatient Rural Therapy: A Manual for Substance Abuse Treatment*. University of Kentucky Press, Lexington, KY, 2000

Leventhal, H., & Friedman, M.A. (2004). Does establishing fidelity of treatment help in understanding treatment efficacy?: Comment on Bellg et al. (2004). *Health Psychology, 23*(5): 452–456.

Luborsky, L., McLellan, A.T., Woody, G., O'Brien, C.P., & Auerbach, A. (1985). Therapist success and its determinants. *Archives of General Psychiatry 42*: 602 - 611.

Luhmann, N. (1979). *Trust and power*. Ann Arbor, MI: Books on Demand.

Miller, W.R. & Rollnick, S. (1991). *Motivational Interviewing*. New York: Guilford Press.

Mathiasen, H., & Alpert, J.S. (1993). Lessons in empathy: Literature, art, and medicine. In Spiro, H.M., McCrea Curnen, M.G., Peschel, E. & St. James, D. (Eds.) *Empathy and the practice of medicine*. (pp. 135-146). New York: Yale University Press

McLellan, A.T., Carise, D., Kleber, H.D. (2003). Can the national addiction treatment infrastructure support the public's demand for quality care? *Journal of Substance Abuse Treatment 25*: 117–121.

Miller, W.R., & Brown, S.A. (1997). Why psychologists should treat alcohol and drug problems. *American Psychologist 52*(12): 1269-1279.

Miller, W.R., Rolnick, S. (2002). *Motivational interviewing: Preparing people to change – 2nd edition*. New York: The Guilford Press.

Miller WR, Taylor CA, & West JC. (1980). Focused versus broadspectrum behaviour therapy for problem drinkers. *Journal of Consulting Clinical Psychology 48*: 590-601.

National Institute on Drug Abuse.(1999). *Principles of drug addiction treatment: A research based guide*. Rockville, MD: NIH Publication No. 99-4180.

Nerdrum, P. (1997). Maintenance of effect of training in communication skills. Acontrolled follow-up study of level of communicated empathy. *British Journal of Social Work, 27*, 705-722.

Nerdrum, P., & Ronnestad, M.H. (2002). The trainee's perspective: A qualitative study of learning empathic communications in Norway. *The Counseling Psycholigist, 30*(4): 609-629

Northwest Frontier Addiction Technology Transfer Center. (2001). *Guidelines for supervised field experiences in addiction treatment*. Salem, Oregon: Northwest Frontier Addiction Technology Transfer Center.

Pellegrino, E.D., & Thomasma, D.C. (1993). *The virtues in medical practice*. New York: Oxford University Press.

Regler, D.A., et al. (1990). Comorbidity of mental disorders with alcohol and other drug abuse – Results from the Epidemiologic Catchment Area study. *JAMA, 264*, 2511-2518.

Ritter, A., Bowdan, S., Murray, T., Ross, P., Greeley, J., & Pead, J. (2002). The influence of the therapeutic relationship in treatment for alcohol dependency. *Drug and Alcohol Review; 21*, 261-268.

Roman, P.M., & Johnson, A.J. (2002). Adoption and implementation of new technologies in substance abuse treatment. *Journal of Substance Abuse Treatment 22*: 211 –218.

Sacks, S., Sacks, J., De Leon, G., Bernhardt, A.I., and Staines, G.L. (1997). Modified therapeutic community for mentally ill chemical "abusers": Background; influences; program description; preliminary findings. *Substance Use and Misuse 32*(9):1217–1259.

Simmons, J., Roberge, L., Kendrick, S.B., & Richards, B. (1995). The interpersonal relationship in clinical practice: The Barrett-Lennard Relationship Inventory as an assessment instrument. *Evaluation and the Health Professions, 18*(1): 103-112.

Simpson, D.D. (2002). A conceptual framework for transferring research to practice. *Journal of Substance Abuse Treatment 22*: 171– 182.

Sky, D.A. (2002). *Simple storylistenting*. Indianapolis, IN: August Graphics.

Spruce, M.F., & Snyders, F.J. (1982). An assessment of a microcounseling model for nurse training in facilitative interpersonal skills. *South African Journal of Psychology 12*(3): 81-87.

Stein, E. (1970). *On the problem of empathy*. Translated by W. Stein. The Hague: Martinus Nijhoff.

Strupp, H.H. (1995). The psychotherapist's skills revisited. *Clinical Psychology: Science and Practice, 2*(1): 70-74.

Strupp, H.H. (1996). Some salient lessons from research and practice. *Psychotherapy: Theory, Research, Practice, and Training; 33*(1): 135-138.

Strauss, J. (1997). Process of healing and the nature of schizophrenia. In Boker, W. & Hogrefe, H.D. (Eds.). *Toward a Comprehensive Therapy for Schizophrenia* (pp. 252-261); Ashland, OH: Hogrefe & Huber Publishers.

Strauss, J. (2000). The interactive development model revisited. *Acta Psychiatrica Scandinavica; 102* (Supplement 407): 19-25.

Strupp, H.H., & Anderson, T. (1997). On the limitations of therapy manuals. *Clinical Psychology: Science and Practice, 4*(1), 76-82.

The Kentucky Board of Certification of Alcohol and Drug Counselors. (2003). Laws and regulations relating to certification as an alcohol and drug counselor. Frankfort, KY. Retrieved from http://www.state.ky.us/agencies/finance/occupations/alcoholdrug/index.htm on 12/21/2004

The Missouri Substance Abuse Counselors Certification Board (nd) Code of ethics. Retrieved from http://Competence\Missouri Substance Abuse Counselor's Certification Board.htm. 12/26/2004.

North Carolina Substance Abuse Professional Certification Board, Inc (nd). Ethicval principles of conduct. Retrieved from http://Competence\North Carolina Substance Abuse Professional Certification Board.htm. 12/26/2004

International Certification & Reciprocity Certification/ Alcohol and Other Drug Abuse (nd). Mission Statement. Retrieved from http://www.icrcaoda.org/icrcmission.cfm, 12/26/2004.

The Addiction Technology Transfers Centers Curriculum Committee. (1998). Addiction counseling competencies: The knowledge, skills, and attitudes of professional practice. Rockville, MD: UD Department of Health and Human Services, DHHS Publication No. (SMA)98-3171.

Thompson, A. (1990). *Guide to the ethical practice of psychotherapy*. New York: John Wiley & Sons.

Valle, S. (1981). Interpersonal functioning of alcoholism counselors and treatment outcome. *Journal of Studies in Alcohol; 42*: 783-790.

Wass, V., Van der Vleuten, C., Shatzer, J., & Jones, R. (2001). Assessment of clinical competence. *Lancet, 357*: 945-953.

Wasserman, S., & Faust, K. (1997). *Social network analysis: Methods and applications*. New York: Cambridge University Press.

Watson, J.C. (2001). Re-visioning empathy: Theory, research and practice. In Cain, D. & Seeman, J. (Eds.), *The handbook of research and practice in experiential psychotherapy*.Washington, DC: APA Books.

Glossary

addiction counseling: professional and ethical application of basic tasks and responsibilities which include clinical evaluation; treatment planning; referral; service coordination; client, family, and community education; client, family, and group counseling; and documentation.

competence: the requisite knowledge, skills, and attitudes to perform tasks and responsibilities essential to addiction counseling.

counseling: a process involving a therapeutic relationship between a client who is asking for help and a counselor or therapist trained to provide that help.

cultural diversity: an appreciation and recognition of the vast array of different cultural groups based on varying behaviors, attitudes, values, languages, celebrations, rituals, and histories; diversity as it relates to culture includes actions taken by individuals, organizations, and communities to reflect inclusion and representation of diverse groups.

culture: the vast structure of behaviors, ideas, attitudes, values, habits, beliefs, customs, language, rituals, ceremonies, histories, and practices distinctive to a particular group of people.

disorder: an affliction that affects the functions of the mind and/or body, disturbing physical and/or mental health.

multi-disciplinary: a planned and coordinated program of care involving two or more health professions for the purpose of improving health care as a result of their joint contributions.

professionalism: a demonstration of knowledge, skills, and attitudes consistently applied when working with substance users, in addition to maintaining the code of ethics most commonly held by addictions professionals.

recovery: achieving and sustaining a state of health in which the individual no longer engages in problematic behavior and is able to establish and accomplish goals.

Supervision/Clinical Supervision: the administrative, clinical, and evaluative process of monitoring, assessing, and enhancing counselor performance.

Notes

1. This relatively new classification includes a range of professionals representing various disciplines and including ex-addicts, recovered alcoholics, volunteers, etc.

engaged in the treatment of different types of substance users. This taxonomy was created approximately during the same period, in the West as what some consider as the medicalization and pathologizing of substance users – *Substance Use Disorders*. (DSM-III, DSM-III-R). It did not exist, for example, during the eras prior to this, the *Gray Manual of Psychiatric Disorders*. The reader is asked to consider what the implications of this are, or could be, when concepts such as "addiction," "dependency," "chemical dependency counselor" are mystified and empowered, whether or not they are or can be misleading and what are the ethical implications, if any. (William L. Benzon and David G. Hays (1990) The Evolution of Cognition. *Journal of Social and Biological Structures 13*(4): 297-320,)

2. The volume's style utilizes the category substance abuse as a diagnostic category. Substances are used or misused; living organisms are and can be abused . Editor's note.. Similarly, the counselors are treating the "user, who is a person and not the posited pathology of "drug abuse".
3. Augustine, *Confessions*, Book 11, Chapter 14, paragraph 17. A more specific translation is "What, then, is time? If no one asks me, I know what it is. If I wish to explain it to him who asks me, I do not know."
4. See, for example, Aristotle, *Nicomachean Ethics* VI, viii, 2.
5. "Nor is prudence a knowledge of general principles only; it must also take into account particular facts, since it is concerned with action, and action deals with particular things. This is why men who are ignorant of general principles are sometimes more successful in action than others who know them." Aristotle, *Nicomachean Ethics* VI, vii, 7.
6. "Prudence is "right reason applied to action," as stated above. Hence that which is the chief act of reason in regard to action must needs be the chief act of prudence. Now there are three such acts. The first is "to take counsel," which belongs to discovery, for counsel is an act of inquiry, as stated above. The second act is "to judge of what one has discovered," and this is an act of the speculative reason. But the practical reason, which is directed to action, goes further, and its third act is "to command," which act consists in applying to action the things counseled and judged. And since this act approaches nearer to the end of the practical reason, it follows that it is the chief act of the practical reason, and consequently of prudence." Aquinas, *Summa Theologica*, 2/2, 4, 47, 8.
7. The reader is reminded that treatment, however defined, can be usefully categorized as being tradition-bound, professional driven, social control driven, mutual-aid driven (i.e. AA, NA) and self help driven ("natural recovery literature", see H.K.Klingemann and L.C. Sobell (eds.) 2001, Natural Recovery Research Across Substance Use, *Substance Use and Misuse 36*:11). There can be and is a range of ethical issues associated with each of these "models".
8. The reader might consider that both *health* and *sickness* are constructs that attempt to embrace a range of human experience; defined in a variety of ways or models each with its own unique etiologies, concepts, "demands," processes, levels/phases, necessary conditions for "existing," etc. that are all bounded to a large degree by specific time, place, culture, etc.
9. The issue of "general" vs. "specific" continues to be an open, unresolved one which has been explored, for example in the psychiatric literature dealing with Type A

and Type B treaters ; specialists vs. generalists. The demands and implications of such taxonomy can and does raise ethical issues.

10. It should be noted that the notion of "dual diagnosis" or comorbid conditions is, at least in part, an artifact of Nosology. A good deal of the problem comes from the notion that psychiatric disorders are clearly distinct entities rather than understanding that "Most, if not all, mental disorders are better conceived as no more than (but no less than) valuable heuristic constructs"(Frances, A., First, M.B., & Pincus, H.A. (1995) *DSM-IV Guidebook.* Washington, DC: American Psychiatric Press, Inc., p.14.) Additionally, there are those who seem to have difficulty with the concept altogether. William Miller, in a videotaped interview said, *"I don't know about dual diagnosis. If you are addicted to heroin, it seems to me you have all kinds of problems."* [Allyn & Bacon Professional (Producer). (2001). Motivational Interviewing for Addictions with William R. Miller: Brief Therapy Series. [Video Tape] (Available from Allyn & Bacon 75 Arlington Street, Suite 300, Boston, MA 02116)]
11. Aside from the issue of putting the individual in the position of forming therapeutic alliances with multiple providers, it may also require the establishing of multiple medical records, each having its own long list of demographic and assessment questions.
12. Problems with transportation, childcare, and interference with revenue producing activities have all been identified as significant barriers to treatment, especially among individuals in rural communities. See Clark, J, Leukefeld, C., Godlaski, T., Brown, C., Garrity, J., & Hays, L. (2002). Developing, implementing, and evaluating a treatment protocol for rural substance abusers. *The Journal of Rural Health,* 18 (3), 396-406. and Leukefeld, C., Clark, J., Godlaski, T., Brown, C., & Hays, L. (2000) *Structured Behavioral Outpatient Rural Therapy: A Manual for Substance Abuse Treatment.* Lexington, KY: University Press of Kentucky.
13. It is interesting to note this distinction between those who misuse alcohol versus those who misuse other substances. Although diagnostically, the DSM-IV uses a unitary set of criteria for substance dependence and substance abuse irrespective of specific substance and the findings of basic research pointing to a single neural mechanism underlying substance dependence, the distinction is as alive today as it ever was. This distinction is seen in the mutual help groups with the separate existence of Alcoholics Anonymous and Narcotics Anonymous. It is also seen in the US government Institutes of Health with the establishment and maintenance of quite distinct and separate agencies: NIAAA (National Institute on Alcoholism and Alcohol Abuse) and NIDA (National Institute on Drug Abuse).
14. This is no slight to organizations like NAADAC or the National Council on Alcoholism. It is only to note that the AMA, APA, and NASW have far larger, wealthier, and more vocal memberships.
15. It should be noted that this knowledge includes not only the principles and techniques specific to various treatment approaches, it should also include the shortcomings and limitations of those approaches. Most specifically, it should recognize which treatment approaches are most open to "mystification" and, therefore likely to be dependency producing (Thompson, 1990).

2-11 From the Ivory Tower to the Trenches: Teaching Professional Ethics to Substance Abuse[1] Counselors

Daniel Yalisove, Ph.D.

Abstract

This chapter outlines an approach to teaching professional ethics to counselors who treat substance use disorders. It introduces three innovative ideas that have not previously been given consideration in teaching professional ethics: (1) Counselors have confused ethical with other-than-ethical considerations in ethical decision making. It is important to clarify this distinction for students in professional ethics education. (2) There is a special synergy between humanistic counseling and professional ethics. (3) Explicit attention is given to the process of morally educating some clients by helping them to become aware of ethical problems.

Key Words: beneficence, confidentiality, dual relationship, informed consent, justice, moral reasoning, moral sensitivity, non-maleficence, professional ethics, relapse, substance abuse treatment, substance use disorder

Introduction

There are many challenges in successfully translating the highly abstract principles of theoretical ethics into useful guidelines for the everyday reality of the substance abuse counselor (called counselor or student counselor for the rest of the chapter). I will discuss these challenges and my efforts to overcome them.

First, I present a brief description of this type of counseling and the challenges counselors face. Then I discuss the ethical issues with which counselors are confronted, many of which are more fully detailed in other chapters of this volume. Finally, I outline the professional ethics course I teach at John Jay College of Criminal Justice. In this chapter, I introduce three ideas that I believe are important in teaching professional ethics:

(1) I identify a confusion that counselors have between ethical and other-than-ethical considerations in decision making. I believe it is important to clarify this distinction for students for professional ethics education.

(2) I develop the view that there is a special synergy between humanistic counseling and professional ethics. I believe that humanistic counseling concepts are consistent with many ethical principles. I also believe the therapeutic relationship itself can be instrumental in solving some ethical dilemmas where they arise in the treatment situation.

(3) I make explicit the process whereby some clients can be morally educated by helping them to become aware of and to solve ethical problems.

Counseling for those suffering from substance use disorders is a relatively new mental health specialty, created in the 1970s and 1980s (Yalisove, in press) when large numbers of substance abuse treatment programs were developed in the United States (Yalisove, 1998). From this period to the present, the substance abuse treatment system has operated separately from the mental health treatment system. The American substance abuse treatment system includes alcoholism clinics, methadone maintenance clinics (MMTP), inpatient therapeutic communities (TC), inpatient detoxification units, and other substance-abuse treatment settings. Substance abuse counselors are the primary treatment personnel in American substance abuse treatment programs. Unlike other mental health professions, the education and training requirements for counselors vary greatly from state to state (Yalisove, in press). It is noteworthy that this profession has the most modest educational requirements of any human service profession in the U.S. with many states requiring for certification only a high school diploma and a set number of hours of education for alcohol and substance abuse. Further, a large percentage of counselors employed in the field are not certified and thus do not have even this modest level of education. For example, in a recent survey of Northeast U.S. counselors, Knudsen and Gabriel (2003) found that less than half of the counselors had substance abuse certification. Thus, in any given agency, there may be counselors who have state substance abuse credentials and others who do not; typically there are both. Another unusual feature of this profession is that about half of all counselors are in remission from substance use disorder themselves (Yalisove, in press). A large percentage of this group are members of Alcoholics Anonymous (AA) or Narcotics Anonymous (NA), which refer to individuals who have arrested their use of drugs and alcohol as "recovering" (Yalisove, in press).

Although U.S. states differ in the amount of ethics education required for counselor certification, 29 require only 6 hours (St. Germaine, 1997). Similarly, the National Association of Alcoholism and Drug Abuse Counselors (NAADAC), which administers some of the states' credentialing requirements, requires only 6 hours of ethics (Godlaski, 2006). Considering the range of ethical issues that counselors face and which I discuss in this chapter, it should become clear that 6 hours of professional ethics education is insufficient to cover the many important ethical considerations confronting this profession.

Who teaches professional ethics to future counselors? I believe I am rather typical of the group. I have little formal background in ethics except for a wonderful undergraduate 2-semester course on ethics, taken, alas, over 30 years ago. My primary expertise comes from my experience as a professional in the substance abuse treatment field. I believe my background is typical of those providing ethics education for substance abuse counselors since the instruction occurs within specific programs dedicated to counselor education. It is a fair question to ask whether instructors such as I, clinicians or ex-clinicians in the substance abuse field, are the best instructors for professional ethics education. Our understanding of ethics comes largely from our experiences as professionals working in substance abuse treatment as providers, supervisors, and directors of programs. Collaboration with ethicists would be a useful undertaking in reviewing these curricula. I anticipate gaining some valuable insight from the other contributors to this volume.

A challenging profession

Substance abuse counselors are entrusted with being the primary caregivers of clients who manifest substance use disorders. These clients often require enormous patience, empathy, limit setting, crisis management, additional services beyond counseling (such as welfare, health and mental health services), and often have criminal justice involvement. Counselors may have to consult with several other professionals who are involved with a mutual client's treatment. Caseloads are high, and extensive written documentation is required (McLellan, Carise, and Kleber, 2003). Staff turnover is high in substance abuse clinics. The organizational and administrative infrastructure of many programs is inadequate and unstable (McLellan, Carise, and Kleber, 2003). Counseling substance abusers is, by all accounts, a stressful, demanding, and relatively low-paying profession. When ethical problems surface, they can be seen as an additional burden to counselors (Dove, 1995). Thus, I believe, an instructor teaching ethics to counselors is presented with a challenging task—to raise ethical understanding without making this understanding too idealistic to confront the current realities of treatment programs. Hence the title of the chapter: "From the Ivory Tower to the Trenches."

Special challenges for the educator

Counseling is a profession that people often enter without anticipating that ethical responsibility is an important element of their training. Student counselors do not generally sit in the first ethics class eagerly awaiting moral instruction. As someone who has undergone the ethical training for substance abuse counselors, I can say that the content and the instruction were not inspired. Most of my fellow participants were not eager learners. On the other hand, a complicating but potentially helpful factor is that many student counselors are members of AA and NA. Since the teachings of AA and NA are rich in moral instruction, these student counselors have often given thought to moral considerations. Another positive aspect of many student counselors is their idealism and genuine wish to help others (Elman and Dowd, 1997).

There is very little literature on professional ethics in counseling for substance use and even less on the teaching of ethics. The first substance use counseling text on ethics was written by Bissell and Royce in 1987. Although they cover many of the important ethical concerns, their text is heavily influenced by AA philosophy and concepts, reflecting the fact that AA treatment philosophy dominated U.S. alcoholism treatment at that time (Yalisove, 1998). The first relatively comprehensive contemporary article on the topic of counselor ethics education was written by Dove (1995). In that article, he sets out some of the basic issues and suggests learning objectives: to increase counselors' moral sensitivity, improve counselors' ethical reasoning, and help counselors tolerate the ambiguity of ethical decision making. St. Germaine (1997) suggests that teaching counselors professional ethics would be aided by the use of role playing, case studies, and ethical dilemmas.

Since there is such a small literature on counseling ethics specific to substance abuse, I have based my teaching on mental health professional ethics literature and added the special issues relevant for substance use. Following St. Germaine's suggestion, I have used case studies extensively to illustrate ethical issues and dilemmas. The use of case studies has a number of advantages. They are the mainstay of teaching clinical skills and student counselors are therefore familiar with the format. Case studies can concretize a problem such that it is dramatically represented and elicits strong student interest. Case studies elicit problem solving skills that student counselors are developing in all aspects of their counselor training. As we discuss case studies, I am often able to demonstrate how ethical considerations inform good clinical technique. This provides additional motivation for student counselors to learn ethics since they are eager to improve their clinical skills.

Elements in the curriculum

Ethical considerations for mental health professionals.

Because counselors are members of the mental health profession, it is important to review the ethical considerations relevant to all such professionals. Welfel (2002), whose excellent text I have used for several years, has nicely summarized the important ethical content areas for mental health professionals.

First, all professionals must be knowledgeable about and understand their respective ethical canons. This includes an understanding of the rationale for the professional code and the underlying principles and values implicit in that code. This way the spirit of ethics as well as the letter of the canon can be taught.

Second, there is an ethical obligation to be competent to practice. This includes having sufficient knowledge and skill in the area of practice and diligence in performing substance abuse counseling tasks. An important consideration for substance abuse counselors is that they learn to distinguish among personal convictions, professional knowledge, and research knowledge, and that they remain open to new treatment methods (Yalisove, 2004). The term "scope of practice" refers to the types of interventions counselors should be competent to perform as well as delineating areas beyond their purview. The latter is an important consideration for substance abuse counselors since many clients have additional mental health problems that require interventions beyond substance abuse counselors' expertise (Godlaski, 2006). Also bearing on competence for substance abuse counselors is an understanding of counselor impairment. In addition, for those professionals who become supervisors, competence as counselors does not insure competence as supervisors. Thus, supervisors have an obligation to be competent as supervisors. These topics will be considered more fully in a later section (Godlaski, 2005).

Third, counselors must understand the legal and ethical aspects of confidentiality, the protection of client information. This includes an understanding of any laws that offer special confidentiality protection to clients in substance abuse clinics (Legal Action Center, 1995). It is important to clarify the distinction between a law and an ethical principle because, if too much emphasis is placed on legal matters, students may be left with the impression that if an action is not illegal, it is the correct thing to do (Dove, 1995), and they may thus fail to give sufficient weight to ethical considerations (Miller, 2006).

Fourth, counselors must understand the principle of informed consent and be able to provide the proper therapeutic atmosphere for clients to give informed consent. Clients are entitled to knowledge about their illness, the treatments available, and the treatment proposed by the counselor. This should include a discussion of the types of intervention available, such as outpatient treatment, inpatient treatment, and medication treatment as well as the treatment philosophy of programs. In the U.S. substance abuse treatment system, AA-oriented programs, cognitive behavioral programs, TC programs, MMTP, and medically oriented detoxification programs are the most widely available.

Clients must then have the opportunity to freely choose to accept or decline the treatment. Two considerations are of special relevance for substance abuse clients: their possible impairment at the beginning of treatment and court-ordered or otherwise mandated treatment. The former may make the client unable to provide informed consent (see, further, Clarke & Levy, 2006). The latter may not allow the client to feel he has the choice to refuse treatment.

Fifth, counselors must understand how dual relationships can potentially compromise their therapeutic relationships with clients and be able to avoid such relationships when the professional relationship might be damaged or otherwise harm the client. The counselor/client relationship is not an equal one. The counselor has knowledge about the client while the client has little knowledge about the counselor. The counselor may have power over the client's release from prison and/or return to work, and in some cases may have to make a recommendation regarding whether legal charges against the client ought to be dismissed. To safeguard clients from possible abuse of this power and knowledge, counselors must refrain from additional relationships with the client that could be exploitative or damage the client in other ways. The most discussed potentially harmful dual relationship is when a counselor has a sexual relationship with a current client (Welfel, 2002). In substance abuse treatment, other dual relationships are often difficult to avoid: counselors and clients may attend the same self-help meetings and a former client can become a counselor where his former counselor is currently on staff (see, further, Hajdin, 2006; Cohen, 2006).

In like manner, supervisors must be sensitive to the power they have over subordinates and make sure that any unavoidable dual relationships are not exploitative or otherwise harmful to subordinates.

A related issue concerns the distinction between friendships and professional relationships. There is a traditional understanding that professional relationships are more formal and careful than friendships, which are obviously more relaxed and casual (Reisman, 1986). Thus, touching clients is frowned upon in therapeutic relationships (Welfel, 2002). However, in substance abuse treatment, recovering counselors who attend AA/NA are informal and friendly to their fellow members at their meetings. They often import this spirit into the agencies in which they work, which could come into conflict with the more formal professional atmosphere of some programs. Another potential problem is that clients who see their counselors at AA meetings can feel confused if counselors act one way at self-help meetings and another way at the clinic in their professional role.

Sixth, counselors must be sensitive to diversity. This concern was originally framed as an issue of justice: there is an ethical obligation to treat all clients without prejudice; all are entitled to the same standard of care and concern. Counselors must be aware of the diversity of clients they may treat—this includes cultural, religious, ethnic, gender, and life-style choices. Professionals must be sensitive to these issues, be able to assess their effectiveness to treat clients with different backgrounds, and seek consultation when they lack knowledge.

Seventh, counselors must respond to ethical lapses of themselves, their colleagues, and their agencies' administration. The counselor who becomes aware of his or her own lapse has a responsibility to make appropriate reparation where possible, examine the reason for the lapse, and take appropriate steps to insure that similar problems do not arise again. Ethical concerns about colleagues need to be addressed. The issue of reporting ethical violations committed by an agency administration creates dilemmas similar to those confronting whistle-blowers in any organization.

In addition to these content areas, Kitchener (1986) suggests there are four overall goals in the ethics education of professionals: sensitizing them to ethical issues, improving their abilities to reason about ethical issues, developing their moral responsibility, and helping them tolerate the ambiguity of ethical decision making.

Special ethical considerations in substance abuse treatment.

In addition to the issues that are germane to all mental health professionals, there are a number of special ethical concerns that need to be discussed for counselors who treat substance abuse disorders. They are as follows:

Counselor impairment

Counselor impairment was first noted as a special ethical problem for counselors by Kinney (1983). Recovering counselors, who comprise about half of all counselors, are subject to relapse. When relapsed, counselors often become impaired and are not able to provide diligent, helpful, competent interventions and are also less able to serve as role models. Kinney found that 33% of the counselor class at Dartmouth College had relapsed within 6 years of graduation. In St. Germaine's (1997) survey of ethics complaints, counselor impairment due to alcohol or drugs ranked second in frequency, comprising 12.37% of the complaints. Jensen and Peterson's (1992) survey of Minnesota certified counselors found that 40% of the counselors had to confront a situation with an impaired counselor. Impairment due to "burnout" is also an important consideration for substance abuse counselors. "Burnout" refers to counselors who become overwhelmed by the tasks of counseling and lose their effectiveness as a result (Welfel, 2002). The burdens placed on counselors mentioned earlier in this chapter no doubt contribute to this vulnerability.

Counselor-client contact

Counselor-client contact outside of the treatment situation is much more frequent in the substance use treatment field than in other mental health professions. A St. Germaine survey (1996) found that 47.5% of the surveyed counselors reported some outside encounters with clients and 16.8% of counselors reported such contacts as occurring frequently. The reason for this is that counselors in recovery often recover with the help of AA/NA and remain active in their respective self-help groups. Most substance use treatment programs encourage clients to attend AA/NA, and thus it is natural to expect clients and counselors to attend some of the same meetings. The meetings have a social aspect, which can create challenges for the client/counselor relationship. Of course, the most obvious challenge is a romantic and/or sexual involvement with a current client. But other less dramatic boundary issues are in play as well.

Treatment program ideology

A feature of our current substance use treatment system is that a large number of treatment programs adhere to a treatment philosophy which must be uniformly applied by all counseling staff to all clients. Most alcoholism treatment programs are abstinence-based and 12-step-oriented. Drug user treatment programs that run on a Therapeutic Community (TC) model have a confrontational format that is closely adhered to. Counselors who feel that a particular client may need another approach may be subject to strong pressure to adhere to the agency's treatment philosophy, if that philosophy discourages counselors from deviating from the treatment protocol. For example, a counselor may believe that a temporary goal of harm reduction would be the best goal for a client, even though agency policy often forbids it.

Knowledge about misconduct of counselors in the substance abuse field

Little is known about the extent of ethical misconduct by counselors. In the only survey I could find, St. Germaine (1997) surveyed state credentialing boards for instances of ethical violations. Of 40 responding boards, for the period 1991-1992, a total of 327 ethical complaints were filed, with disciplinary action taken in 172 cases. The most frequent ethical complaint filed against counselors was sexual contact with a current client (16.40%). Are counselors any more or less ethical than other mental health professionals? It is difficult to compare the results of this survey with the reporting of other mental health professions' ethical violations because of differences in collecting and analyzing the information in reports of ethical violations from other professions.

Teaching ethics to student counselors

Becoming aware of all of the challenges for counselors on the job, my biggest one has been to find a way of not overwhelming the counselor students by making ethical considerations either an ivory tower exercise or a daunting burden. Substantively, I have relied on the mental health professional ethics literature since there is so little available on counseling ethics, adding topics germane to substance abuse.

Table 2.11.1: Topics covered in the course on ethics for counselors who treat substance use disorders.

First third of the course: Introduction and Basic Concepts
Personal values of students
The Ethical Canon for Credentialed Alcoholism and Substance Abuse Counselors in New York State.
The ethical principles that are the foundation of professional ethics.
Ethical virtues associated with professional ethics.
Moral sensitivity, awareness of moral issues.
Moral reasoning, a systematic way to think about moral problems.
Model for ethical decision making and action, a systematic method for thinking about, resolving, and making ethical decisions and actions.
The term paper assignment can be fully explained at this point.

Second section: Ethical and legal considerations in substance abuse counseling: The core content is discussed in this section of the course, organized by the following areas: Competence Legal issues Informed consent Dual relationships Diversity Ethical misconduct Agency treatment ideology Protecting the public
Last section of the course: Case studies developed by the students provide a means to put the ethical knowledge and model for decision making to use. Students present their role plays and summarize their analysis of the ethical dilemma they have portrayed. Additionally, the following topics are discussed: Helping clients become aware of ethical problems and helping solve some of them Ethical decision making and other-than-ethical motivations. Additional resources for resolving ethical problems.

First section of course: Introduction and basic concepts

I introduce the topic of ethics by asking students to examine their own personal values. I ask them to list their important principles and goals for themselves. After they develop their lists, I ask them to consider how each of these values could interfere with being fair and/or objective with a client. If, for example, the counselor values thrift greatly, can he restrain his feelings when a client runs through a large inheritance? Students develop an insight into their own special values and become aware of how these values can affect their objectivity in relating to clients. They can also develop a perspective on these values. Fairness is a good thing but can be taken too far. I develop the idea that the best way to think about values is one of balance. An exaggerated emphasis on one value may cause more harm than good whereas balancing values such as honesty and empathy often allows us to make the best decisions.

The counselor ethical canon mandated by New York State is reviewed at this point. After discussing each element of the code, I explain the rationale for a professional code of ethics. The counselor canon, like any code of professional ethics, has shortcomings that include inherent contradictions, ambiguities, and gaps (Kitchener, 1984). I illustrate these shortcomings by giving examples of ethical dilemmas that are not resolved by reviewing the canon. In the remainder of the course, as the several ethical topics are discussed, we review the ethical canon for relevant provisions.

In this section of the course, I focus on the ethical principles that counselors should follow and the virtues that are important for good counselors to have. The principles are respect for autonomy, beneficence, nonmaleficence, fidelity to promises made, and justice (Kitchener, 1984). Having introduced ethical principles, the ethical principles underlying the professional code can be discussed at this point. Important virtues for counselors are integrity, prudence, trustworthiness, compassion, and respectfulness (Welfel, 2002). Possessing these virtues helps counselors initiate and complete ethical action to resolve ethical problems. I add an additional virtue that I feel is vital to being a successful counselor: patience. I lead a discussion with students to illustrate how each of these principles and virtues is important for the counselor to use and embody. I also point out where other principles, such as truth and candor, need to be considered. I point out how adherence to these principles and virtues promotes trust in the therapeutic relationship and thus enhances the chances of a successful treatment outcome. In the discussion of ethical principles, it becomes apparent that ethical principles sometimes conflict with each other in specific situations. This dynamic becomes a central aspect of the remainder of the course.

Here I point out that the ethical principles and values discussed above are consonant with humanistic counseling theory. In humanistic psychology, the therapeutic relationship is based on respect for the client's autonomy (Kottler & Hazler, 1991). The importance of counselor trustworthiness, honesty, and candor are stressed in humanistic theory. Humanistic psychology maintains that these traits encourage clients to disclose inner fears and concerns and trust counselors to help them. A counselor who embraces these principles will be inclined to be ethically responsive since so many humanistic counseling principles are ethical principles as well.

Three more elements are introduced in this first section of the course: moral sensitivity, moral reasoning, and a model for ethical decision making and action. Moral sensitivity refers to awareness of potential moral considerations (Rest, 1983, Welfel, 2002). Individuals who tune out moral considerations in their lives are considered low in moral sensitivity. Those who are highly attuned to them are considered high in moral sensitivity. Similarly, good counselors need to have ethical sensitivity if they are to behave ethically. A second step in ethical behavior is to have in place a moral reasoning process to think through the ethical implications of a situation (Rest, 1983). The third step is to go through a process that results in ethical behavior. Welfel (2002) has proposed an excellent 10-step model for ethical decision making and action, which I review in the class.

At the end of this section, then, the student has learned about the ethical canon, the rationale for the canon, the basic principles of professional ethics, and the virtues that are especially important in counseling. The students are prepared to consider ethical considerations in the several topics to be discussed in the next part of the course.

Middle section of course: Ethical and legal considerations in substance abuse counseling.

The core content is discussed in this section, organized by the following areas:

Competence

The first topic is competence. A special consideration for counselors is their scope of practice. Because of their specialized and limited education, it has been emphasized that they are competent to counsel clients only about their addictive illness. Mental health issues, marital problems, health issues, and other underlying problems are generally considered beyond their scope to counsel, despite the fact that most substance abuse clients have some of these additional problems. In interviews with practicing counselors, I have been impressed with their awareness of the scope of their expertise and determination not to go beyond it. On the other hand, counselors may not allow exploration of many important issues their clients face such as childhood sexual abuse, depression, or marital problems because they do not even have minimal training in these areas. In discussing this topic with student counselors, I point out that counselors can go too far in avoiding these areas when they are important issues for the client. On the other hand, counselors must be able to step back and acknowledge when they do not have the expertise to provide help. I believe that we need to develop better guidelines for counselors to deal with these issues and provide the necessary training to allow counselors to provide basic help and make referrals when necessary. My model for this is the primary care physician who listens to the patient's complaint, makes a preliminary determination, and, if necessary, refers the patient to the appropriate specialist. Thus, if childhood sexual abuse is an issue for a client, the counselor should be able to determine whether this was a trauma for the client, whether symptoms have resulted, and whether a referral is therefore appropriate. As it stands now, the most obvious path for substance abuse counselors is to take the position that they should talk only about the addiction. This is unfortunate since I believe a modest amount of training would allow counselors to screen clients for other related conditions, offer reassurance and education, and make appropriate referrals when needed.

Under the heading of competence, counselor impairment and "burn out" is appropriately addressed. Student counselors have no difficulty in seeing that counselors who relapse on alcohol or drugs and become impaired should not provide counseling services because they are not able to provide good care to clients and are not good role models (Bissell & Royce, 1987). Not surprisingly, however, some counselors who become impaired because of drug abuse are unwilling to acknowledge this fact and place colleagues and administration in a difficult situation. If a counselor is removed from clinical work, his clients become curious, the caseload must be reassigned, and the privacy of the counselor must also be protected. Thus, the class discussion centers around how best to deal with a colleague who has relapsed and become impaired.

In the case of "burn out," I emphasize the need for counselors to take proper care of themselves. I point out that in a study conducted by Elman & Dowd (1997) occupational stress and psychological strain are correlated strongly with "burn out." Excessive job demands, lack of proper performance recognition, unclear performance expectations, role conflicts, emotional distress, and frequent physical symptoms are also correlated with "burn out" (Elman & Dowd, 1997). It is essential for student counselors to understand the proper role of the counselor in the client's treatment. Counselors are not responsible for the successful outcome of all their clients' problems but are responsible for providing good professional help; there is an appropriate sense of counselor responsibility, but not one of control; the counselor should maintain an interest in the client but not become over-involved. Idealism, which draws many students to the field, must be tempered with realistic goals and expectations. I also discuss the usefulness of one's own therapy at times to relieve some of the emotional strain of counseling.

Counselors who become supervisors must be competent as supervisors, which includes providing informed consent to their subordinates, and being fair evaluators of the counselors under their authority. Supervisors must balance responsibility for client welfare with fair treatment of subordinate counselors.

Legal issues

The special laws protecting confidentiality are discussed here. U.S. Federal and state laws have provisions that apply specifically to clients in substance abuse treatment. Although knowledge of the details of the law is important, it is also important for the student counselor to appreciate the underlying principles of trustworthiness and loyalty that are at the foundation of confidentiality. Dilemmas occur when the client's confidentiality may have to be broken because of other ethical concerns such as potential harm to others, as, for example in the Tarasoff (1974)[2] decision and in cases in which the client appears to be neglecting or abusing a child (New York Society for the Prevention of Cruelty to Children, 1990). The duty to warn is less clear in other situations—for example, when a client has a transmittable illness and is not taking precautions to insure that his behavior is not spreading the illness. An important segment of this section of the course is a review of those laws that require professionals to break confidentiality.

It is at this point that I explain what an ethical dilemma is: one in which a situation appeals to two competing ethical principles. In the above cases, for example, the principle of confidentiality (trustworthiness and loyalty) comes into conflict with the principle that we should prevent harm to others. I use Welfel's (2002) 10-step model to analyze and resolve specific ethical dilemmas involving confidentiality. In all of the remaining content areas of the course I present relevant ethical dilemmas and analyze them in a similar manner. I then discuss the term paper assignment which requires that students create an ethical dilemma, analyze that dilemma using Welfel's model, present a role play in class that illustrates the dilemma, find and summarize the relevant research on the dilemma, and finally devise and administer a survey to 10 heath-care providers about the dilemma.

Informed consent

In many clinics, informed consent is reduced to obtaining the client's signature in several places, indicating that the client has been informed about the procedures and consents to the treatment. Obviously, this defeats the spirit of the principle of informed consent. Ideally, clients should understand the nature of their illness, the nature of the treatment proposed, the potential hazards of the treatment, the alternatives, and feel free to discuss them with the counselor. Clinic policies should be explained at this time, including billing and fees and provisions of confidentiality as previously discussed (Welfel, 2002). Informed consent is based on a conception of the client's autonomy: the presumption that he or she can make an informed choice. In cases in which the client is currently intoxicated or suffering from withdrawal and thus impaired by drugs/alcohol, or is currently impaired by severe mental illness, the counselor may have to act paternalistically to propose or even insist on what may be necessary treatment such as hospitalization for detoxification. As the client regains his or her cognitive capacities, informed consent should be obtained. I believe that taking the time to insure informed consent improves the therapeutic relationship and in addition increases patient cooperation with the treatment (see, further, Clarke & Levy, 2006).

Since drug user treatment is often mandated by the criminal justice system, it is important to discuss how clients can realistically "consent" to the treatment. Although it is true that the client does have a choice—accept treatment or the negative sanction—this choice is a more limited one than that which voluntary clients face when choosing treatment. All the more important then that clients be fully informed of the nature of the treatment, their rights, the reporting requirements to the legal authority, the consequences of failing to follow the treatment regimen, and of the need to supply positive urine screens. On the other hand student counselors need to know that mandated clients, on average, do as well as non-mandated clients in treatment retention and outcome (Yalisove, 2004). Proper informed consent may be crucial to forming a good relationship with these clients and play a large role in determining the outcome of the treatment.

A related topic here is negotiating a treatment plan—a document that sets out the goals and objectives of the treatment. Traditional programs have paternalistically dictated treatment goals and plans for the patient's treatment. More recently, in accord with respect for the patient's autonomy, the idea of negotiating goals and plans with clients has been advocated (O'Neill, 1998).

Dual relationships

Student counselors have little difficulty in understanding the potential harm of romantic or sexual involvement with clients. We also discuss potential but less obvious harm in other types of dual relationships. What I stress in this discussion is that, when advising the client, additional relationships can create potential threats to objectivity in ways that interfere with promoting the client's welfare (Welfel, 2002).

For example, if a counselor enters into a business relationship with a client, can the counselor remain objective if the client considers ending this business relationship? Although, as mentioned earlier, there is a greater chance for dual relationships in counseling substance users, my students do not report many difficulties in this area nor do they anticipate any. I believe that counselors in recovery and AA actually develop good sensitivity in this area because they see examples of exploitation of newly sober members of AA, informally called the "Thirteenth Step."[3] They see how harmful it is, and can easily extrapolate that to their role of counselor. There are other social interactions that can affect relationships within AA. For example, many new members of AA choose a sponsor. Typically, a sponsor is a member of AA who has at least a year of sobriety and has used the principles of AA to improve his or her life. Sponsors teach newcomers about AA, offer support, and explain how they dealt with certain issues that may be troubling newcomers. Good sponsors are sensitive to many social issues that come up, such as "sponsees" competing for the sponsor's attention. Thus, when recovering counselors meet clients at AA meetings, they are generally relatively adroit in their interactions. One survey of alcoholism counselors found that they had stricter views about protecting the unique counseling relationship than other mental health professions (St. Germaine, 1996).

I point out that dual relationships between supervisors and subordinates have the same potential ethical problems. I make a point to inform female student counselors that they have an ethical right to refuse any romantic or sexual advances of supervisors or, for that matter, any staff. I also discuss how to handle sexual harassment at this point.

The last topic for this section of the course is a discussion of the difference between a friendship and a professional relationship. In AA, warmth and acceptance is often expressed in physical gestures such as hugs and kisses. On the other hand, in professional counseling, there is a tradition of greater formality, especially in regard to touching (Welfel, 2002). An important reason for this is that some clients are not comfortable being touched. Although warmth and friendliness are important aspects of the counseling relationship, I emphasize that nothing should be done that could be misinterpreted as an improper advance.

Diversity

Here I encourage a discussion about the importance of justice—namely, that all clients deserve to be treated fairly and with respect. It is important to be aware of our own beliefs and prejudices and to try to overcome them, and make sure that they do not interfere with treatment. I devote time to discussing with students the types of clients for whom provision of counseling would be difficult. Although education on diversity is part of the required CASAC (Credentialed Alcoholism and Substance Abuse Counselor) education, I am aware of very little of value in helping counselors adapt to the incredible diversity of treatment populations.

Ethical misconduct

It is here that human nature shows itself most clearly. Almost all of my students can identify the ethical misconduct of others. Can't we all? They rarely see it in their own behavior. Yet this is the place to begin. What do we do if we discover that we have harmed a client? A process is outlined and discussed. This provides a perspective from which to begin the discussion of discovering and dealing with the ethical missteps of colleagues.

The degree of potential harm to the client or others and the immediacy of need to intervene must be assessed. If it is a relatively minor infraction, bringing it to the person's attention may be sufficient. If more serious, a carefully planned discussion with the person is warranted, in which the counselor is expected to acknowledge the issue and agree to remedy it. If the potential for causing harm is great, as in sexual involvement with a client, reporting to the supervisor and state agency may be necessary. If the ethical misconduct is endemic in the agency or promoted by the administration, whistle-blowing may be necessary. I make a point of discussing the wide variations among treatment agencies regarding ethical conduct and recommend that this be an important consideration in choosing where to work. In discussions about colleague misconduct, student counselors often base their decisions on other-than-ethical considerations: that is, keeping out of trouble, keeping their jobs, and loyalty to colleagues. I return to this aspect of decision making in a later section.

Agency treatment ideology

As mentioned earlier, many, if not most, substance user treatment programs adhere to a fairly rigid treatment ideology. Counselors are directed to follow these principles closely. For most American programs, abstinence is viewed as the only acceptable goal. Specific techniques are dictated regardless of the special characteristics of the client. Counselors are faced with a dilemma should they feel that a specific client requires a goal or intervention that is not approved by the agency for which they work. My advice to student counselors is to be aware of treatment ideology and the practices of agencies and to be sure that they are compatible with their own views before deciding to work for a specific agency.

Protecting the public

In the topics discussed so far, the focus has been on protecting the client. But this must be balanced against ethical considerations that protect the public. The *Tarasoff* decision (1974) and the obligation to report suspected child abuse and neglect (New York Society for the Prevention of Cruelty to Children, 1990) have already been mentioned in this regard. It is less clear what a counselor should do when a client is exploiting or abusing another person. Little has been written on this topic. In the examples she uses, Welfel (2002) implies that moral education of the client can be an important aspect of handling these situations. Ironically, psychotherapy and social science have largely supplanted moral education. In the 19th and early 20th centuries, alcoholism and substance use were considered moral afflictions and remedy was offered by various morally-based movements such as the Temperance Movement (Lender and Martin, 1987). In today's world, moral education is based on the idea of developing moral awareness rather than indoctrination into any particular moral view (Welfel, 2002). I believe a key element in these interventions is for the counselor to be moral rather than moralistic and judgmental. In the section below, I outline some considerations regarding the moral education of clients.

Final section of course: Case studies developed by the students

The case studies out the ethical knowledge and model for decision making to use. Students role-play their ethical dilemmas. This provides a forum for discussing all of the relevant ethical considerations. Additionally, the following topics are discussed:

Helping clients to become aware of ethical problems and helping to solve some of them

In selected situations, counselors can help some clients to become aware of ethical problems and to solve them. Clients are sometimes morally insensitive, failing to see the negative effects of their actions on others. In other instances, clients are sensitive to moral issues, but are unable to resolve them. In both cases, there is an interaction between clinical and ethical issues. Before proceeding, it is important to assess the nature of the therapeutic relationship, the capacities and motivations of the client, and to estimate the impact that the counselor can have on the client. In some cases, the dilemma can be resolved collaboratively with the client. To resolve the ethical dilemma with a client requires that the client be given an opportunity to solve the problem with the counselor. If it is determined that the client lacks the resources or motivation to address the issue, counselors must decide what their ethical course of action as professionals should be. Welfel (2002, p. 97) creates a hypothetical case that illustrates how moral education might be fostered. Raymond, an HIV-infected college student, has met a young woman and, after seeing her a few times, is hoping to have a sexual relationship with her. He seeks counseling because he is confused and worried about what to do. Welfel nicely captures the anxieties of the counselor and the potential for helping the client, and the elements of the ethical dilemma. The dilemma is clear (simplified for my purposes here): should loyalty and adherence to confidentiality and protecting the therapeutic relationship with Raymond take precedence? Or should the potential harm to the potential sexual partner take precedence? Welfel (2002) indicates that there is no imminent harm to the woman since they are not meeting for a week and Raymond indicates his intention to practice safe sex should it proceed that far. Welfel (2002) continues the ethical analysis, but I want to discuss the situation's potential for moral education. Raymond appears to have moral sensitivity—after all, a large part of the reason he came for counseling was his moral dilemma. He has a difficult life issue to deal with: his HIV status and his desire for an intimate relationship. The counselor has an opportunity to assess Raymond's capacity to develop an ethical plan and to follow it through, at the same time helping Raymond to resolve his life issues. This makes sense, especially from a humanistic counseling approach. If Raymond is serious about the relationship, then the importance of disclosure to an intimate partner can be discussed. What would be the consequences of living with someone without telling her about his HIV status? What would be the consequences of telling her after withholding the information? What about the anxiety of finding out whether your potential partner is able to accept this news and still be interested in the relationship? What if she turns out not to be so? In this manner, the situation can be explored for the benefit of the client and the potential partner. Granted, this is a best-case scenario. On the other hand, the opposite pole response of jumping in with insistence that Raymond's potential sexual partner be notified of his status without exploring it with him runs a serious risk of disturbing the therapeutic relationship to such a degree that the client will flee treatment. Perhaps the most important thing I have learned from my own experience of enduring several crises as a counselor without the benefit of any useful ethical instruction, is that an emotional reaction, though understandable, is often unhelpful. The impulse that we must do something is not always justified. A few moments of reflection or discussion with a colleague can start a process of critical reasoning. An emotional response, though well-intended, could cause a great deal of harm. A key element for this process is a judgment about how quickly any action must be taken. As in the above example if the potential harm is not imminent, there is time for a counselor to use a problem-solving model. If imminent harm is likely, however, the counselor may not have the luxury of this process. The process of ethical reasoning and a model for ethical decision making helps to "inoculate" one against emotional and impulsive actions.

Ethical decision making and other than ethical motivations

Kitchener (1986) notes that there are competing nonmoral values and motives that also influence ethical decision making. Rest (1983) considers this an important factor in moral behavior but indicates that little research has been conducted in this area (Rest, 1994). Having taught a course on professional ethics for counselors for many years, I have observed that my students often do not see a clear distinction between ethical motives and other-than-ethical considerations. It is my impression that counselors often make decisions that are based not so much on ethical considerations or reasoning but rather on other factors. Counselors may believe that taking an ethical stand may be time-consuming and stressful, may create discomfort with clients, may jeopardize relationships with colleagues with whom cooperation is required, may antagonize supervisors, and may trigger retaliation from other staff, including the possibility of loss of employment. Such factors may override counselors' ethical motivation. I do not mean to single out counselors in this regard; I believe that people generally function in much the same way. Still, I believe that the failure to consider these other motivations in ethical decision-making situations is a major shortcoming in current ethical instruction for counselors and other mental health professionals. The obvious danger is that the student counselors may learn the ethical canon and the principles of ethics and then ignore them in their practice.

In my discussion of this topic, I clarify the motivations counselors commonly use to make decisions that have ethical implications. For example, if a counselor decides not to confront a supervisor for fear of losing his or her job, the counselor's decision is not based on ethical considerations, but practical ones. I encourage the students to discuss the pros and cons of making such decisions. Although I make sure that the arguments for acting ethically are articulated, I make no special plea to students to act accordingly. Another way to show the distinction between ethical and non-ethical motivations is to analyze the survey responses to the ethical dilemmas student counselors have administered to mental health professionals. A great deal more needs to be done in this area.

Resources for understanding ethics

There is a variety of resources available to student counselors to illuminate ethical concerns, including writings about relevant laws and regulations, articles about the ethical code, ethics scholarship, and clinical case studies. Often, research that has been conducted illuminates ethical issues: there is, for example, a research literature that has documented the harm caused by sexual exploitation (Welfel, 2002), how often misconduct charges are upheld, and clients' reactions to various informed consent procedures (O'Neill, 1998). I believe that it is important for students to learn how to find and make use of these resources. I encourage them to do so in two ways: first, one component of their term paper is to review relevant research bearing on the dilemma they have chosen; secondly, when an interesting question arises, I encourage an interested student to research the question and report on it to the class.

Summary and Recommendations

In this chapter, I have outlined the important areas that a course on professional ethics for counselors should cover and discuss methods that I have used over the past decade to teach a course on ethics for counselors. What began for me as a required course for the Addiction Studies Curriculum has become a vibrant course for both students and the instructor.

As important background for the reader, I briefly discuss the relatively new mental health profession of counselors who treat substance use disorders. Noteworthy is the modest educational requirements for state certification and the fact that many practicing counselors do not have certification. Twenty-nine U.S. states require only 6 hours of ethics education. Unique to this branch of the mental health profession, about 50% of these counselors are themselves in remission from substance use disorders. Despite the modest educational requirements for certification, counselors are responsible for the care of demanding and often multi-problem clients.

My first objective in teaching the course on professional ethics is to make ethics relevant but not overburdening to student counselors. Many student counselors are idealistic. I encourage idealism, but point out the constraints of the current treatment system.

I outline the content areas covered in the course relevant for all mental health counselors. These include:

1. The ethical canon.
2. The responsibility to be competent.
3. The duty to respect confidentiality.
4. The duty to insure informed consent.
5. The responsibility to avoid dual relationships where they could harm the client.
6. The duty to respond to ethical lapses.
7. The obligation to respect diversity in clients.

I have outlined special ethical concerns for counselors who treat substance abuse:

1. The heightened risk of counselor impairment and "burn out".
2. The increased frequency of extra-therapy counselor-client contact in self-help groups.
3. Special challenges of providing appropriate interventions to clients when they deviate from treatment program ideology.

Key elements of the curriculum:

To build student counselor motivation for learning professional ethics, I trace the close relationship between humanistic counseling principles and professional ethics. I teach the ethical principles relevant for counseling and their inevitable conflict. I develop ethical sensitivity, teach moral reasoning, and a model for ethical decision making and action. Knowledge of the model and developing skill in its application inoculates student counselors against impulsive emotional action. I promote student use of resources, especially relevant research findings. I make extensive use of case studies, such as Raymond's case. These are invaluable for depicting ethical dilemmas and promote student interest. I am impressed by the resource material that is now becoming available to research the ethical problems that surface in substance abuse counseling. With a careful analysis of a situation, the use of relevant resource material, a good path can be chosen by the counselor to solve ethical problems. The term paper promotes the development of all of these areas: the student chooses a specific ethical dilemma; creates a role play illustrating it; reviews relevant literature, especially research findings; creates and administers a survey about the dilemma that investigates mental health professionals' understanding of the dilemma; and, after reviewing all of this information, the student uses moral reasoning to resolve the dilemma.

The paper introduces three innovations in professional ethics education:

(1) There is a special synergy between humanistic counseling and ethics. Although implicit in Welfel (2002), (2) I make the process of morally educating clients explicit by helping clients to become aware of ethical problems and to solve them. (3) Although Rest (1983) and Kitchener (1986) point out that nonmoral motivations can influence ethical decisions, to date there has been no significant discussion about how to incorporate a consideration of this issue in a professional ethics course. I believe this is an

essential component and have made the preliminary step of clarifying this distinction for students.

Many of the elements I have proposed can be applied to any mental health professional ethics course. Others are of special importance to counselors who treat substance abuse:

- In the area of competence, I believe it is important to discuss the appropriate scope of practice, counselor impairment, and "burn out".
- In the area of informed consent, it is important to discuss the ethical way to proceed when the client is impaired or coerced.
- Student substance abuse counselors should know that quite often treatment agencies adhere to a strict treatment ideology.

Recommendations:

The minimal educational requirements for this profession are problematic. Nevertheless, I believe that there should be additional training requirements to include some skill in basic understanding and treatment of mental disorders, screening for mental illness, and instruction on the proper way to refer when necessary. Based on the many complex ethical issues that counselors face as documented in this chapter, I believe there should be an increased training requirement for professional ethics education as well.

Daniel Yalisove, Ph. D., is Coordinator of the Addiction Studies Program and Associate Professor of Psychology at John Jay College of Criminal Justice. He has written one book, Introduction to Alcohol Research: Implications for Research, Practice, and Policy and edited another, The Essential Papers on Addiction. He is a board member of the International Coalition of Addiction Studies Educators and an advocate for addiction studies in higher education. Before entering academic life, he was the director of the Stuyvesant Polyclinic Alcoholism Program for 12 years.

References

Alcoholics Anonymous World Services. (1976). *Alcoholics Anonymous*. New York: Alcoholics Anonymous World Services.

Bissel, L. & Royce, J.E. (1987). *Ethics for addiction professionals*. Hazelden Foundation.

Clarke, S. & Levy, N. (2006). On the competence of substance users to consent to treatment programs. In Einstein, S. & Kleinig, J. (Eds.), *Ethical Challenges for Intervening in Drug use: Policy, Research and Treatment Issues*. Huntsville, TX: OICJ Press.

Cohen, E. (2006). Conceptualizing the Professional relationship in Drug User and Alcohol Misuser counseling. In Einstein, S. & Kleinig, J. (Eds.), *Ethical Challenges for Intervening in Drug use: Policy, Research and Treatment Issues*. Huntsville, TX: OICJ Press.

Dove, W.R. (1995). Ethics training for the alcohol/drug abuse professional. *Alcoholism Treatment Quarterly, 12*, 19-30.

Godlaski, T.M. (2006). Competence in chemical dependency counseling. In Einstein, S. & Kleinig, J. (Eds.), *Ethical Challenges for Intervening in Drug use: Policy, Research and Treatment Issues*. Huntsville, TX: OICJ Press.

Hajdin, M. (2006). The prohibition of Sexual Relationships between Drug Users and Their Counselors: Is it Justified? In Einstein, S. & Kleinig, J. (Eds.), *Ethical Challenges for Intervening in Drug use: Policy, Research and Treatment Issues*. Huntsville, TX: OICJ Press.

Jensen, M.A. and Peterson, T.L. (1992). Ethical dilemmas and ethics preparation of addiction counselors. *Rehabilitation Education, 6*, 139-150.

Kinney, J. (1983). Relapse among alcoholics who are alcoholism counselors. *Journal of Studies on Alcohol, 44*, 744-748.

Kitchener, K.S. (1984). Intuition, critical evaluation and ethical principles: The foundation for ethical decisions in counseling psychology. *The Counseling Psychologist, 12*, 43-55.

Kitchener, K.S. (1986). Teaching applied ethics in counselor education: An integration of psychological processes and philosophical analysis. *Journal of Counseling and Development, 64*, 306-310.

Knudsen, J.R. and Gabriel, R.M. (2003). Advancing the current state of addiction treatment. Salem, Ore. Northwest Frontier Addiction Technology Transfer Center.

Legal Action Center. (1995). *Confidentiality: A guide to the federal law and regulations*. NY: Legal Action Center.

Kottler, J.A. & Hazler, R.J. (1991). The therapist as a model of humane values and humanistic behavior. In Schneider, K.J., Bugental, J.F., and Pierson, J.F. (Eds.) *The handbook of humanistic psychology*. (pp. 355-369). Thousand Oaks: Sage.

Lender, M.E. & Martin, J.K. (1987). *Drinking in America: A history*. NY: The Free Press.

Maslach, C. & Jackson, S.E. (1986). *Maslach burnout inventory: Manual (2nd edition)*. Palo Alto, CA: Consulting Psychologists Press.

Miller, S. (2005). Privacy, Confidentiality, and the Treatment of Drug Addicts. In Einstein, S. & Kleinig, J. (Eds.), *Ethical Challenges for Intervening in Drug use: Policy, Research and Treatment Issues*. Huntsville, TX: OICJ Press.

New York Society for the Prevention of Cruelty to Children. (1990). *Professionals' handbook identifying and reporting child abuse and neglect*. NY: New York Society for the Prevention of Cruelty to Children.

O'Neill, P. (1998). *Negotiating consent in psychotherapy*. NY: NYU Press.

Reisman, J.M. (1986). Psychotherapy as a professional relationship. *Professional Psychology: Research and Practice, 17*, 565-569.

Rest, J.R. (1983). Morality. In Flavell, J.H. and Markman, E. (Eds.) Cognitive Development. In Mussen, P.H. (General Editor) *Manual of Child Psychology*. (Vol. III, pp. 550-629). NY: Wiley.

Rest, J.R. (1994). Background: Theory and research. In Rest, J.R. & Narvaez, N. (Eds.) *Moral development in the professions: Psychology and applied ethics*. Mahwah, NJ: Lawrence Erlbaum.

St. Germaine, J. (1997). Ethical practices of certified addiction counselors: A national survey of state certification boards. *Alcoholism Treatment Quarterly, 15*, 63-72.

St. Germaine, J. (1996). Dual relationships and certified alcohol and drug counselors: A national study of ethical beliefs and behaviors. *Alcoholism Treatment Quarterly, 14*, 29-44.

Tarasoff v. Regents of the University of California, 529 P.2d 553 (Cal. 1974); 551 P. 2d 334, 331 (Cal. 1976).

Toriello, P.J. and Benshoff, J.J. (2003). Substance abuse counselors and ethical dilemmas: The influence of recovery and education level. *Journal of Addictions & Offender Counseling, 23*, pp. 83-98.

Welfel, E.R. (2002). *Ethics in Counseling and Psychotherapy, 2nd ed.*, Pacific Grove, CA: Brooks/Cole.

Yalisove, D.L. (In press). Considerations in the development of a research-to-practice curriculum for alcoholism and substance abuse counselors. *Journal of Teaching in the Addictions*.

Yalisove, D.L. (1998). The Origins and evolution of the disease concept of treatment. *Journal of Studies on Alcohol, 59*, 469-476.

Yalisove, D.L. (2004). *Introduction to alcohol research: Implications for research, practice, and policy*. Boston: Allyn & Bacon.

Glossary

beneficence: the professional ethical principle to do good. When providing professional interventions, counselors have the obligation to provide real help.

"burnout": an emotionally-depleted condition that can afflict mental health workers. It consists of emotional exhaustion, loss of a sense of accomplishment in one's work, and a depersonalization of those served (Maslach & Jackson, 1986).

counselors who treat substance use disorders: commonly called substance abuse counselors in the U.S. Educational and training requirements are variably determined by the states to a much greater degree than for other professions. The requirements are modest in comparison to other mental health professions.

fidelity: the professional ethical principle to be faithful to promises made. Counselors have an obligation to be reliably helpful to their clients and to follow through on commitments made on the client's behalf.

harm reduction: one possible therapeutic goal for substance-using clients. The goal is to help the client modify his or her current drug use patterns so that use is less harmful. For example, needle exchange programs provide clean syringes and needles to drug users who inject drugs in exchange for the dirty ones. In this manner, the spread of infections such as HIV and Hepatitis C can be decreased. Harm reduction goals have not yet been embraced by the American "substance abuse" treatment system.

humanistic counseling: an approach to counseling based on humanistic values in the personality theories of Abraham Maslow and Carl Rogers. Rogers' client-centered counseling is the most common type of humanistic counseling.

impaired counselor: a counselor who is unable to perform his or her duties as a counselor reliably. The impairment can be caused by a variety of factors. In the substance abuse field, it often is caused by relapse to substance abuse in counselors previously in remission.

informed consent: the counselor's obligation to provide to the client a full disclosure about the proposed treatment he or she is to receive and related matters. It is also the counselor's obligation to insure that the client understands the proposed treatment and consents to it.

non-maleficence: the professional ethical principle to do no harm. The counselor is obligated to be sure what he or she is doing is not harming the client or others.

recovering alcoholic/addict: a term used in AA. AA members who are abstaining from alcohol and working the 12-steps of AA are referred to as recovering. Because they view recovery as an ongoing process rather than a status, they use the term recovering rather than recovered. From AA's perspective, this terminology keeps members aware of the possibility of relapse.

respect for autonomy: a professional ethical principle as well as a philosophical principle of humanistic counseling. It means that the client should be afforded the greatest degree of freedom merited in the choices he or she makes. The principle does not mean the client should be afforded boundless freedom. The counselor must temper this principle with the client's cognitive capacities and other ethical considerations.

Thirteenth Step: informal AA terminology. AA members use the 12 Steps as a means to develop a spiritual life and achieve sobriety (Alcoholics Anonymous, 1976). Informally, many AA members have in a somewhat wry manner suggested a 13th Step. It is a mistaken step of becoming romantically and/or sexually involved with a new member of AA, who is viewed as vulnerable to exploitation.

Notes

1. The often used term "substance abuse" is a relatively new term in the field. It is used as a diagnostic category among its various uses. Substances are used or misused; living organisms are and can be *abused*. Editor's note.
2. In this case, the family of a murdered student sued her killer's psychologist for failing in his reposibility to protect their daughter from imminent danger. The patient had confided to the psychologist that he intended to kill her. The California Supreme Court affirmed this professional responsibility and the court decision led to an understanding that, in the U.S., mental health professionals have a duty to warn and protect third parties from imminent danger of which they are aware (Welfel, 2002).
3. AA members use the 12 Steps as a means to develop a spiritual life and achieve sobriety (Alcoholics Anonymous, 1976). Informally, many AA members have, in a somewhat wry manner, suggested a 13th Step. It is a mistaken step of becoming romantically and/or sexually involved with a new member of AA, who is viewed as vulnerable to exploitation.

2-12 Ethical Issues Surrounding Access to Drug User Counseling/Treatment

Barbara C. Wallace, Ph.D.

Abstract

Ethical issues surrounding access to drug user counseling and treatment are quite varied. The range includes the potential for discrimination with regard to access to treatment given a client's race, religion, gender, or condition¬ such as age, pregnancy, geographical location and distance from treatment, poverty, or lack of insurance. Other ethical issues include: the client's disability status, including physical and psychiatric disabilities, for example; how to manage issues of relapse, as verified by ongoing positive urine toxicology reports; the risk of violent acting out by clients in treatment and when to bar access to treatment; and, the use of coercion and mandates to treatment, whether by the criminal justice system, welfare agencies, or child protection agencies¬ as all force clients to gain access to treatment. Recommendations for how to conceptualize and respond to the full range of contemporary ethical issues regarding access to drug user counseling and treatment are offered in this chapter.

Key Words: drug user treatment; drug user counseling; access to treatment; discrimination; advocacy

Introduction

Ethical issues surrounding access to drug user counseling and treatment are quite varied. A model that has been recommended for examining drug abuse health service utilization (Leukefeld, Logan, Martin Purvis & Farabee, 1998) serves as a guide for conceptualizing ethical issues surrounding access to drug user treatment/counseling. Providing a conceptual framework for this chapter, the model builds upon prior work (Andersen & Newman, 1973) and considers three major components:

1) societal determinants, such as the available technology for treatment and prevailing norms for responding to illness (e.g., stigmatization, discrimination);
2) characteristics of the health care system, such as the organization of available resources; and
3) individual determinants, such as client characteristics before illness, attitudes, past experiences, predisposition to use services, income, insurance coverage, having a regular source of care, ability to secure services, perceived barriers to accessing care (e.g., stigmatization), perceived self-efficacy in securing services, and the perception of illness/severity of illness (Andersen & Newman, 1973; Leukefeld, Logan, Martin, Purvis & Farabee, 1998).

Thus, this chapter will present an approach to ethical issues surrounding access to drug user treatment/counseling from a framework that considers societal determinants (social and interpersonal processes between practitioners and drug users), characteristics of the health care system (what is available in the environment as the existing service delivery system infrastructure), and individual determinants (characteristics of the drug user). In addition, this chapter will offer four principles to guide ethical access to drug user treatment/counseling:

- **Principle 1.** Ensure Access to Drug User Treatment/Counseling by Avoiding Stigmatization, Disdain, and Discrimination.
- **Principle 2.** Ensure Access to Drug User Treatment/Counseling by Advocating for Adequate Service Delivery Infrastructure.
- **Principle 3.** Ensure Access for Special Populations to Integrated Models and Multi-Problem Clients' Receipt of Multiple Services.
- **Principle 4.** Ensure Access to Drug User Treatment/Counseling With Increased Compliance Through the Use of Contingency Contracting.

Throughout the discussion, the importance of practitioners engaging in advocacy work is underscored, emphasizing the importance of social action for social justice on behalf of clients, given clients' complex, multiple, and inter-related drug user treatment/counseling needs.

Principle 1. Ensure Access to Drug User Treatment/Counseling by Avoiding Stigmatization, Disdain, and Discrimination

Regardless of what exists as the service delivery infrastructure within a specific geographic region to which clients may gain access, if the practitioner engaged in the screening, assessment, referral, and/or treatment process engages in processes of stigmatization, disdain, and discrimination, then clients may not gain ethical access to drug user treatment/counseling. A consideration of societal determinants, such as the norms for responding to illness, suggest the potential for stigmatization and discrimination to prevent access to drug user treatment/counseling. These issues are addressed within Principle 1: Ensure Access to Drug User Treatment/Counseling by Avoiding Stigmatization, Disdain, and Discrimination.

Well-documented is the risk that clients in the field of drug user treatment/counseling will face stigma (Lamont et al, 2003; Satel, 2002). One compelling analysis of stigma emphasizes how those with the "stigmatized characteristics (the 'marks') as members of a social out-group" can be monitored, controlled, and denied advantages of the dominant in-group (Tucker, 1999, p.32). This may include denial of access to drug user treatment/counseling, as well as health care services (Tucker, 1999, p. 7)—suggesting how discrimination follows from stigma.

The potential for discrimination with regard to access to treatment may occur given a client's race, religion, gender, or condition—such as age, pregnancy, geographical location and distance from treatment, poverty, or lack of insurance. Discrimination based on a client's race or gender can be understood, given how those socialized with regard to the pertinent "marks" in a particular society may become agents for monitoring, social control, and denial of equal access to opportunities reserved as advantages for the dominant group—such as those of a particular race or men. Practitioners may be effectively socialized, in this manner, and engage in discrimination, barring access to drug user treatment/counseling. These socialization processes may occur on the level of family, community, the media, during education and professional training, as well as during employment experiences.

To the extent that substance abuse treatment has been integrated into general health care services, it may become even more important to ensure access to services without any processes of stigmatization or discrimination operating. For example, drug users have a legitimate fear of disclosing drug problems, as it may result in discrimination/denial of services, negatively impacting human service utilization rates, or seeking out health services (Ashery et al, 1995).

Ideally, access to drug user treatment/counseling should never be influenced by the socially conditioned cognitions, affects, or behaviors of those practitioners engaged in the process of screening, assessment, treatment, or any aspect of service delivery. A practitioner's socially conditioned responses can be categorized as maladaptive cognitive, affective, and behavioral responses to a client (Wallace, 2005). Cognitively, practitioners are in danger of engaging in processes of stigmatization, as a maladaptive cognitive response to a client. Affectively, practitioners are in danger of experiencing disdain, as a maladaptive affective response to a client. Behaviorally, practitioners are in danger of engaging in discrimination, as a maladaptive behavioral response to a client; examples include ending sessions early, failing to provide clients with appropriate interventions, or failing to inform clients of an available treatment option—as one would normally do with members of an advantaged race or men, for example. These responses may be seen as maladaptive to the extent that they result in stigmatization, disdain, and discrimination. Alternatively, the training of practitioners can ensure that they avoid such maladaptive cognitive, affective, and behavioral responses to clients. The result of adequate training for practitioners may be the adaptive cognitive response of engaging in optimistic thinking and focusing on a client's possession of strengths. Also, an adaptive affective response would include empathy, respect, and acceptance. And, an adaptive behavioral response to a client would include fidelity in service delivery with adherence to all ethical standards and principles that ensure a client's timely access to the very best treatment available (Wallace, 2005).

Overcoming some maladaptive cognitive, affective, and behavioral responses to client diversity requires the receipt of training in multicultural sensitivity and competence (Sue, 2003; Sue et al., 1998; Wallace, 2002)—especially, in light of the urgent need to avoid further perpetrating racial/ethnic disparities in health in places such as the United States (National Institute on Drug Abuse, 2003) and around the globe (Evans, Whitehead, Diderichsen, Bhuiya & Wirth, 2001). Such a focus is also consistent with paying attention to a client's strengths and building upon them, as well as with a positive psychological approach (van Wormer & Davis, 2003; Aspinwall & Staudinger, 2003; Lopez & Snyder, 2003; Seligman, 2002) in vogue as a refreshing alternative to viewing clients with stigma and disdain.

Stigmatization, disdain, and discrimination can also be embodied in the policies, procedures, and actions of policymakers, governments, and agencies providing funding for drug user treatment/counseling and overall health care. This may be the case, in particular, within places such as the United States, where a current conservative, moralistic, and intolerant historical era prevails—one aptly described as particularly harsh, while emphasizing criminal sanctions, intensive supervision, and zero-tolerance policies with regard to the use of drugs (Tucker, 1999).

The special characteristics/multiple-problems of clients can lead to yet further stigmatization, disdain and discrimination, above and beyond that due to being a drug user and/or criminal offenders of a particular race or gender. Possibilities include practitioners engaging in discrimination in response to a client's possession of mental disabilities (e.g., schizophrenia, bipolar disorder, borderline personality disorder, etc.) and physical disabilities (e.g., paralysis, HIV/AIDS, etc.) (Wallace, 2005; Linton, 1998).

Hence, Principle 1 seeks to ensure clients' access to drug user treatment/counseling by emphasizing how practitioners engaged in the screening, assessment, referral, and/or treatment referral process must be trained to ensure that they do not engage in processes of stigmatization, disdain, and discrimination. The requisite ethical standard embodied in Principle 1 suggests the need for adequate training that fosters practitioners' attainment of adaptive cognitive, affective, and behavioral responses to drug users—ensuring client access to drug user treatment/counseling without experiences of discrimination.

Principle 2. Ensure Access to Drug User Treatment/Counseling by Advocating for Adequate Service Delivery Infrastructure

There are several dimensions to ensuring access to drug user treatment/counseling via advocacy or the taking of social action for social justice (Wallace, 2000) on the part of practitioners in the field. There is also a role for professionals in other agencies, policy makers, government administrators, and members of society at large in advocating for adequate service delivery infrastructure. These issues are addressed via Principle 2: Ensure Access to Drug User Treatment/Counseling by Advocating for Adequate Service Delivery Infrastructure.

Advocacy to Ensure Access to Adequate Treatment Slots

One dimension involves ensuring access to adequate treatment slots within the service delivery infrastructure by advocating for their creation. This follows from a fundamental principle advanced in the United States that drug user treatment needs to be readily available (NIDA, 1999). Readily available drug user treatment/counseling prevents potential treatment applicants from being lost or falling through the cracks when treatment is not immediately available or is not readily accessible in their environment (NIDA, 1999).

This means ensuring that clients have access to adequate drug user treatment slots across a variety of drug user treatment/counseling modalities within reasonable geographic distance from where they are located. Funding for treatment must also increase so that adequate drug user treatment slots are made available, and the time it takes to enter treatment (waiting lists) is reduced to a reasonable level. These goals include having a range of interventions available within a continuum of care that creates a sufficient number of varied treatment slots across diverse treatment modalities, such as those commonly found within the United States:

- mobile crisis units that engage in outreach and emergency screening, assessment, and referral
- crisis centers that engage in triage, including screening, assessment, and emergency referral to and placement within the next level of care—as clients are matched to appropriate evidence-based interventions in light of assessment findings.

The full range of drug user treatment/counseling options that constitute the next level of care to which drug users are matched include the following:

- intensive outpatient programs, day treatment programs, outpatient medically supervised chemical dependence treatment programs, outpatient methadone maintenance treatment programs, outpatient detoxification services, and (within the larger health care delivery system and related insurance plans) there are also drug user, mental health, and psychiatric services provided by practitioners within outpatient clinic and private practice settings;
- inpatient detoxification across days or weeks, and longer-term inpatient rehabilitation (28 days to 45 days);
- short-stay residential therapeutic community programs (several months), longer-stay residential therapeutic community programs (1-2 years), and specialized integrated residential therapeutic community programs for mentally ill chemical abusers (MICA) that provide both drug and mental health services (in MICA residences);
- specialized integrated models that are either outpatient, inpatient, or residential and provide services for numerous "special populations," such as pregnant women/women with very young children, adolescents, the homeless, criminal offenders, the disabled—and those who, in addition to being a member of one of these special populations, are also dually diagnosed/MICA;
- specialized integrated models for criminal offenders that are either outpatient, inpatient, or residential, and may be located in either the jail, prison or community setting, while including drug courts.

Other sources provide a more detailed description of these drug user treatment/counseling modalities (NIDA, 1999; Belenko & Logan, 2003; Marlowe, 2003; Wallace, 2005, 2002, 1996, 1992, 1991; Higgins & Silverman, 1999; Marlatt & VandenBos, 1997). The creation of adequate drug user treatment/counseling slots within each modality might resolve a contemporary puzzle: Data suggests that all those who "need" drug user treatment/counseling in the United States are not accessing treatment. Figures available in 2002 showed that only 8% of the 18.6 million Americans who met criteria for alcohol treatment and only 18% of the 7.7 million Americans who met criteria for drug user treatment actually received it in the prior year (Office of Applied Studies, 2003).

One possible reason for these patterns of drug user health service utilization may include patterns of funding within the United States that favor drug supply reduction (domestic law enforcement, source-country control of coca production, interdiction at United States borders) over demand reduction strategies such as drug user treatment (Tucker, 1999). Funding needs to increase for drug user treatment, going beyond the 15, 124 substance abuse treatment facilities in the United States in 2003, while also growing beyond the 67% of these receiving government funding (SAMHSA, 2004). One goal articulated by the National Institute on Drug Abuse in the United States is for treatment to be immediately available and readily accessible (NIDA, 1999). Practitioner advocacy can assist in ensuring drug users have access to sufficient treatment slots.

Advocacy to Ensure Access to Evidence-Based Treatments

Within contemporary times, ensuring access to drug user treatment/counseling translates into ensuring access to evidence-based interventions. Practitioners must learn to function within the new age of evidence-based practice (Sammons, 2001) and become familiar with what constitutes evidence-based approaches. A menu of evidence-based interventions or effective treatment alternatives for drug users is now available in the United States (NIDA, 1999). In explaining why practitioners must gain knowledge of evidence-based alternatives, Miller, Wilbourne, and Hettema (2003) offer the analogy of facing a life-threatening physical illness; would one want their doctor to select the treatment most likely to give the best chance for recovery, or accept a doctor saying, "I really don't pay much attention to that scientific stuff" (p. 13)? Thus, practitioners must know which treatments have a body of empirical support for their use, advocate for drug user access to these evidence-based treatments, and learn how to deploy these evidence-based alternatives. Practitioners may also have a responsibility to adapt these interventions as needed, given client characteristics, heterogeneity, diverse needs, multiple problems (e.g., high risk sexual behavior, violence, mental disorders, and preferences as consumers—matching clients to appropriately tailored and integrated models in light of these factors (Wallace, 2005).

Practitioners must advocate for the creation of an adequate service delivery infrastructure within the environment that includes evidence-based approaches. This is important, given that there is currently a gap between the evidence of "what works" in addiction treatment and the actual work of practitioners in delivering treatment (Sorensen, Rawson, Guydish, & Zweben, 2003). Practitioners need access to the very best proven technology in the field of addiction treatment, including programs available in the environmental context that are funded so that they contain and/or support evidence-based program components. For example, most programs lack the funding to support many evidence-based treatment components (e.g., the community reinforcement approach with vouchers). Access to the menu of evidence-based options may also be limited by other factors, such as the lack of access to treatment offered by well-funded research centers, the cost of adapting evidence-based interventions to heterogeneous clients in the real world, geographical factors wherein certain regions lack access, or practitioners lacking training in how to deliver the evidence-based intervention (e.g., training in motivational interviewing). Ensuring access to evidence-based drug user treatments may also mean practitioners overcoming any personal bias and receiving new training and/or supervision, as needed. Practitioner bias rooted in their prior training within a particular school of thought (e.g., psychoanalytic/psychodynamic, cognitive, or behavioral) can result in effectively barring clients from accessing contemporary evidence-based drug user treatment/counseling.

Evidence-based drug user treatment/counseling options available in certain parts of the United States include relapse prevention, supportive-expressive psychotherapy; individualized drug counseling; motivational enhancement therapy; the community reinforcement approach (CRA) plus vouchers; day treatment with abstinence contingencies and vouchers, and the Matrix Model (NIDA, 1999). Yet others (Wallace, 2005) have recommended a menu of seven evidence-based options and seven state-of-the-art practices that provide a theoretical rationale to guide the work of practitioners, including a role for harm reduction and abstinence models (See Appendix A). A rather extensive discussion of the rationale for the inclusion of each option on the menu has been provided. Thus, the reader is referred elsewhere for more information (Wallace, 2005).

Other evidence-based interventions include pharmacological treatments that target physical aspects of substance use and dependence (e.g., "craving," tolerance, and comorbid disorders). This may mean practitioners overcoming any philosophical and ideological resistance that it may be wrong to treat drug dependence with drugs (Carroll, 2001). There is, for example, compelling evidence that combined pharmacological-behavior approaches may, in many cases, constitute the "optimal" treatment strategy for substance use disorders (Carroll, 2001). Pharmacotherapy can play a vital role in many instances (Carroll, 2001), as indicated below:

- detoxification in cases where there may be substantial withdrawal symptoms (e.g., alcohol, opioids, sedative-hypnotics);
- where there is a need for stabilization and maintenance (e.g., methadone, nicotine replacement therapies);
- where there is a value in blocking the effects of an opioid (if taken into the body) with a long acting opioid antagonist (e.g., naltrexone); and
- where there are coexisting mental disorders such as affective/mood and anxiety disorders that might respond well to psychiatric medication (e.g., antidepressant medication).

Thus, these, too, are menu options to which clients deserve to have access. This suggests vital work on the part of practitioners in ensuring their availability.

Coordinated Advocacy For Adequate Service Delivery Infrastructure

Advocates must work to ensure that an adequate service delivery system infrastructure exists. This advocacy occurs within the context of a treatment scene in the United States that is best characterized as a "climate in which costs are increasing, funding and resources are limited, and problems are increasing in intensity and severity" (Leukefeld, Logan, Martin, Purvis, & Farabee, 1998, p. 1126). Advocacy in this context may be quite challenging. However, the ethical response of advocacy is needed, nonetheless, and should include coordination with other professionals across agencies (Lamont et al, 2002).

Practitioners and other professionals have failed to engage in sufficient levels of coordinated advocacy. Thus, far too little pressure has been put on government funding agencies to overcome barriers to the creation of an adequate service delivery infrastructure so that quality care is readily available and consistently delivered to this population (Lamont et al, 2002). Those working in the fields of drug user treatment/counseling, mental health, as well as policy researchers, government administrators, and societal members can all work much more effectively through coordinated advocacy (Lamont, et al., 2002). Increased pressure on government funding agencies through coordinated advocacy for creation of an adequate service delivery infrastructure may follow from recognition of how the availability of specialized services may reduce criminal justice expenditures, costs associated with long-term hospital based psychiatric care, and create a safer environment (Lamont et al, 2002).

Thus, a fundamental issue involves the gap between what has already been funded and is available as the service delivery infrastructure and technology in the environmental context versus that which is evidence-based and justifiably needed for inclusion.

This gap underscores practitioners' ethical responsibility to press through advocacy for the availability of an adequate service delivery infrastructure and technology. This goal also necessitates identifying the clear responsibility on the part of policy makers, policy researchers (who must provide pertinent and relevant data upon which decisions can be based), and government administrators (who must make budgetary decisions). Moreover, ethical and wise decision-making is necessary on the part of societal members who can either call for more funding for evidence-based and specialized services within an adequate service delivery infrastructure; or, merely join their voices with those of politicians who engage in "tough on crime" rhetoric—emphasizing incarceration without adequately funding diversion programs that provide treatment services. In sum, practitioners, policy makers, policy researchers, government administrators, and societal members should all engage in coordinated advocacy for the creation and maintenance of an adequate service delivery system infrastructure, even as all will benefit from a safer society. Principle 2 is important in guiding practitioners to engage in such advocacy.

Principle 3. Ensure Access for Special Populations to Integrated Models and Multi-Problem Clients' Receipt of Multiple Services

An adequate service delivery system includes a variety of integrated models that meet the needs of diverse clients, including those who are members of special populations, or those with multiple problems needing multiple services. Resultant ethical issues include how the client's disability status, including physical and psychiatric disabilities, for example, may serve to bar a client's access to drug user treatment/counseling. Yet the range of client characteristics and problems is quite varied. For example, as diverse multi-problem clients, the contemporary special population of criminal offenders seeking access to drug user treatment/counseling in the United States includes those who are under the supervision of the criminal justice system—whether while incarcerated in jail or prison, on parole or probation, participating in a drug court or other program operating in conjunction with the criminal justice system, or mandated to community-based drug user treatment/counseling (van Wormer & Davis, 2003; Farabee & Leukefeld, 2001; Margolis & Zweben, 1998). The criminal justice system is responsible for "40 to 50% of referrals to community-based treatment programs" (Farabee & Leukefeld, 2001). By the year 2003, the courts, probation, parole, or the corrections system accounted for "40-60% of all those entering addiction treatment programs" in the United States (McLellan, 2003, p. 187). Others point out that that these percentages are even higher in minority communities of color (Howard, 2003; Wallace, 2005).

The multiple problems among drug users in places such as the United States include those outlined by Wallace (2005) and shown below:

- felony convictions that can bar them from voting, employment opportunities, access to public housing, and even welfare benefits, in some states;
- traumatic stress from prison isolation experiences;
- separation from family during incarceration, the dissolution of marriages/partnerships due to incarceration;
- the especially traumatic separation from children via loss of child custody, foster care placements, adoption, and termination of parental rights;

- family instability and lack of social support as a consequence of multiple family generations of addiction and/or incarceration;
- traumatic childhood histories or sexual and physical abuse, and adolescent and adult domestic violence;
- multiple severe mental disorders (e.g., substance use disorders, post-traumatic stress disorder and other anxiety disorders, depression and bipolar disorders, borderline and other personal disorders, etc.);
- multiple "addictions" and varied use patterns involving more than one substance;
- multiple problem behaviors, including engagement in more than one problem behavior (e.g., high risk sexual behavior, violence, drug use, etc.);
- combinations of multiple mental disorders, multiple addictions, and multiple problem behaviors, including varied patterns of both victimization and the perpetuation of violence, as well as being homeless and possessing varied health problems (Wallace, 2005).

Another way to categorize contemporary clients is to consider how the population includes those who are members of special populations, such as those including women, pregnant women, adolescents, the homeless, drug offenders, those with physical disabilities, and/or those presenting mental disabilities or comorbid/co-occurring disorders. As a result, there is a rationale for Principle 3. Ensure Access for Special Populations to Integrated Models and Multi-Problem Clients' Receipt of Multiple Services.

Special Populations and Special Considerations In Ensuring Ethical Access to Treatment

A nexus of potential problems involving mental, behavioral, and physical health issues has been described (Wallace, 2005). The common health problems of those presenting drug abuse and drug dependence requires a consideration of access to three sets of services—drug user, physical health, and mental health treatment systems (Leukefeld, et al, 1998). And, comorbidity, for example, requires a consideration of what it takes to access two sets of services, such as the drug user and mental health treatment systems (Leukefeld, et al, 1998; Ouimette & Brown, 2003). Other combinations of client characteristics, including their being multi-problem clients necessitates receipt of interventions to address their behavioral health (e.g., engagement in high risk sex, needle sharing, etc.), physical health, and mental health (Wallace, 2005). The homeless are another special population who not only need access to safe housing, but frequently also need access to drug user, physical health, and mental health treatment (Schumacher, et al, 1999). Many clients also require income support (Lamont, et al., 2002) and need referrals for welfare.

Given such considerations, it is no surprise that integrated models have emerged as the new contemporary standard. Even as the contemporary emphasis on ensuring clients' accessing evidence-based treatment is now the norm (Sammons, 2001), the heterogeneity of contemporary drug user clients in the real world who possess multiple problems (as well as strengths) necessitates that evidence-based interventions be thoughtfully integrated and adapted as treatment is "tailored" for individual clients (Wallace, 2005). The result is integrated models.

Ensuring Access to Integrated Models of Care for Those with Comorbid Disorders

The co-occurrence of mental health disorders, such as posttraumatic stress disorder (PTSD) and substance use disorders (SUDS), requires ensuring ethical access to what has also been described as an integrated model of treatment, combining the simultaneous delivery of drug user and mental health interventions delivered by the same clinician at the same time (versus a sequential model wherein SUDS are treated first, followed by the treatment of PTSD) (Najavits, 2003). Integrated models have been consistently recommended as the treatment of choice for dual disorders, despite the ongoing common practice to tell clients "they need to become abstinent from substances before working on PTSD," which does not work for many patients (Najavits, 2003, p. 152).

Ensuring Access to Integrated Models of Care for Those with Physical Health Problems

Other integrated models address clients' substance use disorders and health problems, including physical disabilities. For example, the presence of physical disability also characterizes many clients entering addiction treatment, as in the case of histories of violence within the drug trade and related gun injuries, including ongoing pain conditions and even paralysis. Pertinent here may be a consideration of the full spectrum of disabilities clients may present, whether mental or physical in origin (Linton, 1998). In addition, contemporary disability studies is different from psychology which "primarily trains practitioners to intervene on the personal level rather than intervene to alter the environment" with the resulting policy addressing "person-fixing" versus "context changing" (Linton, 1998, p. 6). Contemporary disability studies focuses on external variables and related patterns of discrimination that perpetuate a divided and unequal society (Linton, 1998, pp. 6-7).

For example, to accommodate the needs of those with physical disabilities advocacy needs to address environmental changes. The purpose of advocacy is to ensure that clients have access to physical plants that are accessible by those labeled disabled and who may be wheelchair bound, for example.

There is also a need for integrated models that address both substance use disorders and physical health problems. The list of health conditions to be considered includes the following: conditions such as HIV/AIDS, hepatitis B and C virus (HBV and HCV, respectively), and sexually transmitted diseases; tuberculosis; reproductive health problems, smoking-related disease such as asthma, coronary heart disease, and cancer; chronic diseases such as diabetes and hypertension; obesity; problems associated with aging; and other specific disabilities (visual, learning, speaking, hearing, etc…) (Wallace, 2005). Advocacy acknowledges all such issues.

Ensuring Access to Integrated Models of Care for Those Under Criminal Justice Supervision

Integrated models are also the evidence-based norm for the special population of clients who present both substance abuse/dependence disorders and are under criminal justice supervision. The recommended integrated models involve the combination of community-based addiction treatment and ongoing criminal justice supervision, while also conveniently accommodating the preferences within the public health perspective and public safety viewpoint (Marlowe, 2003). Although practitioners typically embrace a public health perspective that focuses upon the delivery of treatment with minimal criminal justice system involvement, public safety proponents typically embrace the notion of criminal offenders being under constant criminal justice system supervision, while the recommended integrated model accommodates both views (Marlowe, 2003). Numerous examples of the integrated approach that are evidence-based include drug-courts and work-release therapeutic communities that provide treatment in the community, the opportunity to avoid incarceration or a criminal record, and close supervision to ensure compliance, while responding to non-compliance with certain and immediate consequences (Marlowe, 2003; Wexler, 2003; Belenko & Logan, 2003).

Co-morbidity and Criminal Justice System Involvement

Another special population includes those who present mental illness, substance use/misuse, and criminal justice system involvement as offenders, suggesting the challenge of client identification, the need for systematic psychiatric screening and psychological assessment, and the matching of clients to appropriate individualized services based on screening/assessment findings (Broner, Borum, Whitmire, & Gawley, 2002; Broner, Borum & Gawley, 2002). This multi-problem population has been found to need diversion from the criminal justice setting for receipt of multiple services and integrated treatment models for co-occurring disorders, given numerous factors, such as the following: a record of poor response to community mental health interventions; severe functional impairments in employment, interpersonal relationships, and physical health; high rates of homelessness; increased risk of violence; more frequent hospitalizations than those with mental illness alone; low rates of treatment compliance; more severe symptomatology; and, higher rates of relapse than those with a single disorder (Broner, Borum, & Gawley, 2002).

Diversion: Ensuring Ethical Access to Drug and Mental Health Treatment

Ideally, diversion provides drug offenders with an alternative to adjudication and incarceration, given their mental illness (Lamont, et al., 2002). Diversion can occur at multiple points in the criminal justice system, beginning with police officers who encounter a person in need of mental health and drug users treatment/counseling, suggesting a collaboration between the police and mental health departments in a city such as New York, including access to pertinent 24-hour hotlines and mobile crises teams. A second point for diversion occurs early in the judicial process, such as the time of arraignment, providing the opportunity to avoid a trial and incarceration. For example, New York City introduced in the year 2000 Arraignment Court Mental Health Diversion Services, given the large number of those being arraigned with psychiatric disorders and histories of homelessness; this model requires coordination between the police, the court, the judge, and programs providing treatment alternatives to incarceration that the prosecutor and judge can consider, as well as linking clients to all needed drug user treatment/counseling, mental health treatment, and housing services; thus, residential placements are frequently needed (Lamont et al., 2002). A third point for diversion occurs after arraignment, involving plans to link jailed clients to needed services (community based services and case management) within discharge plans presented to the judge and prosecutor as an alternative to incarceration (Lamont et al., 2002).

Jail-based mental health services include psychiatric screening and assessments with referral to mental health services, medication management (ensuring clients take psychiatric medication), counseling, drug user treatment/counseling, specialized housing, crisis management, and suicide prevention (Lamont et al, 2002); but a jail stay may last only days or weeks, suggesting the critical role of discharge planning, including the making of appointments for clients. But, because of clients' multiple problems, they may also need assistance with income support and require appropriate referrals. The level of assistance needed could even require someone accompanying clients to community service providers for appointments and helping with the completion of paperwork for income assistance, as well as ongoing case management (Lamont et al., 2002). For those with no means of paying for prescribed psychiatric medication, New York state also has a program where participating pharmacies are asked to fill psychiatric medication prescriptions with special insurance when the client is not enrolled in Medicaid—all in an effort to successfully link clients to essential services (Lamont et al., 2002).

Coordination among agencies with diverse staff working together is essential, while case managers are especially vital in linking clients to all needed community-based programs and service providers, including ongoing tracking of clients to ensure they remain in treatment programs to which they have been referred (Lamont et al., 2002). Despite the progress made in linking clients to services in places such as New York City, other needs remain: the need for immediate placement beds for those released directly from court, transitional beds for those being released from jail or being moved from immediate placement beds, and permanent housing for the chronic mentally ill; an improved system for training police so they take more clients to psychiatric hospitals instead of arresting them, including changing police procedures so they are not punished for electing the route of hospitalization and experience long waits during the hospital admission process, ideally simply filling out a form to leave with psychiatric staff (Lamont et al., 2002). Clients deserve ethical access to this full range of diversion services.

Co-morbidity and Criminal Justice System Involvement Among Women

The overlapping issues of co-morbidity and criminal justice system involvement become even more complicated when this special population of offenders with co-occurring disorders is female. Women typically present the following multiple, complex, interrelated problems: a history of early and repeated trauma, including multiple chronic experiences of sexual and physical abuse; leaving home early; a history of having been very young mothers, having their first child between the ages of 12 and 16; being single parents; histories of violent and unstable relationships; high rates of post-traumatic stress disorder; poor education, poor employment histories, poverty, and homelessness; and, health problems, including a rate of HIV infection that may be twice as high as that of male offenders (DeCou & Van Wright, 2002).

Compared to incarcerated males, incarcerated women and adolescent females have strikingly high rates of psychiatric disorders—with post-traumatic stress disorder (PTSD) and substance use disorders (SUD) being the most prevalent; as many as 64–80% of incarcerated women met criteria for a psychiatric disorder at some point in their lifetime; and, the most commonly used drug was cocaine/crack, followed by marijuana, heroin/opiates, stimulants, depressants, and hallucinogens, while women tended to report "heavier" drug use than men in the month before their offense (Battle et al., 2003). The most universal experience among incarcerated women is a history of traumatic events. Thus, there are links among women's experiences of victimization, substance use, and criminal behavior—including the use of prostitution and other criminal behavior to maintain access to drugs. However, there are few data on the presence of SUD-PTSD comorbidity among incarcerated women, while rates of both PTSD and SUD among female inmates are significantly elevated—being twice as high as rates found for females in the community. There are no empirically validated treatments for incarcerated women presenting both PTSD and SUD, even as promising models have emerged. Meanwhile, the legal response to drug-related behavior has become increasingly punitive, resulting in flooding the criminal justice system with less serious female offenders. There has been a call for gender-specific treatment that addresses the long-term impact of childhood victimization/past trauma. Practitioners have a key role to play in providing comprehensive assessment and treatment of women with PTSD and SUD (Battle, et al., 2003). Ensuring access to drug user treatment/counseling integrated models that have adequate interventions to address both the SUD and PTSD is another responsibility of practitioners, suggesting another critical area for advocacy.

For the special population of women with such problems, it is crucial to assist them in avoiding the revolving door of their return to the criminal justice system; thus, women require coordination of services, as the criminal justice system and mental health systems work in tandem. Improvements in New York City in creating a network of linked programs that target the special population of those with mental health and drug user-related problems who come in contact with the criminal justice system have been described at length (Lamont et al., 2002). Discharge planning and case management in the community are essential elements, ensuring access to all needed services and treatment, including housing, psychiatric treatment upon release from incarceration, and peer support—linking clients to vital services (Lamont, et al., 2002).

Co-morbidity and Criminal Justice System Involvement Among Adolescents

There is a body of research indicating that, among adolescents, roughly two-thirds to nine-tenths are mandated to drug user treatment/counseling. Moreover, involvement with the criminal justice system is the "norm" (Dennis, 2002; Jainchill, 2002).

Work with adolescents who are involved with the criminal justice system includes addressing the youth's developmental needs, socializing them to reject criminal behavior, assisting them in completing their high school education, and preparing them for future goals involving education and employment. Essential elements of working with adolescents involved in the criminal justice system include ensuring adolescents' future economic and social stability, necessitating preparing them to stay drug free (as this and most criminal justice system supported programs endorse the goal of abstinence), pursue a non-violent lifestyle, develop healthy interpersonal relationships, and be role models for others in the community with regard to avoiding what they have been through (Navon, 2002). However, the task becomes even more complicated with adolescents who also present co-morbidity—whether attention deficit disorder, conduct disorder, or other psychiatric disorders along with substance use disorders.

Even though there is little evidence on the exact prevalence of post-traumatic stress disorder (PTSD) and substance use disorders (SUD), there is tremendous evidence that adolescents are at risk for developing these disorders, especially given histories of trauma and substance use (Giaconia, et al., 2003). Practitioners need to anticipate and assess adolescents for traumas, PTSD, and SUD, as these may be associated with greater impairment in psychological, physical, and social functioning; for example, there are high rates among these adolescents of externalizing behavior problems, internalizing behavior problems (anxiety, withdrawn behavior), aggressive behavior, school expulsions/suspensions/absences, criminal arrests in the past year, serious suicidal behavior, poor self-reported health status, and somatic complaints (e.g., headaches) (Giaconia et al., 2003). This underscores how practitioners must ensure that multi-problem adolescents have access to multiple services. Thus, there is a valid rationale for Principle 3, which draws practitioners' attention to the vital work of ensuring clients who are members of special populations and have multiple problems have access to appropriate integrated models and multiple services.

Principle 4: Ensure Access to Drug User Treatment/Counseling With Increased Compliance Through the Use of Contingency Contracting

Other ethical issues include practitioner management of instances of relapse, as verified by ongoing positive urine toxicology reports. Additional ethical issues involve the risk of violent acting out by clients in treatment and when to bar access to treatment. Other ethical issues involve the use of coercion and mandates to treatment, whether by the criminal justice system, welfare agencies, or child protection agencies—as all force clients to gain access to treatment. Pertinent to all of these situations is the use of contingency contracting. Contingency contracting involves the establishment of a Contingency Contract in an initial phase.

During this first phase of contingency contracting, it has been suggested (Wallace, 2005) that two guiding principles be followed by practitioners:

1) establish contingency contracts with clients, at the onset of the relationship, ideally when contact is first made with the client, responding to individual client needs and characteristics; and
2) explain to the client how contingencies function in response to behavior a client performs that is under the client's own personal control, and obtain client oral consent to the contract.

During the second phase, called The Contingency Management Phase, practitioners are urged (Wallace, 2005) to adhere to two additional guiding principles:

3) during the contingency management phase, when a client produces an outcome that the client controls through his or her own personal behavior, consequences follow through the application of sanctions or rewards that are certain, swift and appropriate; and
4) the sanctions and rewards applied over time increase or are graduated, increasing in value (rewards) or response cost (sanctions), as an appropriate response to a client's on-going pattern of producing outcomes that the client controls through his or her own personal behavior.

Hence, all of the ethical issues discussed in the opening of this section are addressed by Principle 4: Ensure Access to Drug User Treatment/Counseling With Increased Compliance Through the Use of Contingency Contracting.

It has also been pointed out how, despite gaining access to treatment, clients need assistance in remaining compliant, avoiding negative consequences such as the following: graduated sanctions, including discharge, and being violated by parole and re-incarcerated; losing child custody or having parental rights terminated; and/or, losing welfare benefits and having no income (Wallace, 2005). Thus, beyond ensuring access to treatment, a next immediate step for practitioners at time of intake is to provide clients with vital assistance with compliance. Clients need assistance fully understanding and, thereby, abiding by the terms and conditions of the following:

- mandates given out by parole, probation, a judge, drug court, or related program;
- contingencies spelled out by a child protection, welfare, or other agency coercing them into treatment; and
- for all voluntary, coerced, and mandated clients, there is a need to understand their new treatment programs' rules, regulations, and contingency contracts into which all clients enter upon program admission, so as to avoid graduated sanctions, including discharge.

This work means that practitioners must assist clients in fully comprehending the kind of graduated sanctions which they may potentially face, depending upon their behavior—such as when urine test results are positive for drug use. Clients need to understand the kind of graduated sanctions they face for relapse, chronic relapse, and repeated positive toxicology results, as well as for violence or threats of violence (Wallace, 2005).

Making Treatment Access Contingent On Client Execution of an Oral Contingency Contract

There are also cases where ethical action on the part of practitioners includes actually making access to drug user treatment/counseling contingent on a client's execution of an oral contingency contract. Such oral contingency contracting has been recommended for use immediately upon completion of a psychiatric screening and psychological assessment, ideally, at the first client contact, before formal program admission—especially where there is a risk of violent acting out behavior, homicidality, or suicidality, as well as the need for ongoing psychiatric treatment and medication so clients are stable and free from psychiatric symptoms that might contribute to the risk of relapse to either drug use and/or violence. Such cases suggest that it is an ethical action on the part of a practitioner to ensure the safety of other staff and program participants, as well as that of the client in question. Indeed, the reward of admission should be made contingent upon clients engaging in an oral contingency contract that addresses such risk factors. Such action is considered ethical, in light of those newly identified risks (based on psychiatric screening/psychological assessment findings) that exist in association with program admission, and the extent to which the oral contingency contract is seen as effectively addressing and reducing that risk. Five such oral contingency contracts have been described in detail (Wallace, 2005), including what practitioners actually say to clients, as presented below:

- Contract # 1. Admission contingent on documenting current psychiatric care. In order for you to be accepted into this program for admission, bring a letter from your psychiatrist indicating your diagnoses and the medication that you are taking. In addition, you will have to continue psychiatric treatment and take prescribed medication; if you stop these behaviors, staff will review your case and make a decision regarding what seems best for you at that time, including transfer to another program. Are you able to make this oral contract? Please repeat what you have to do (Wallace, 2005).

- Contract # 2. Admission contingent on obtaining psychiatric care. In order for you to be accepted into this program: 1) start seeing a psychiatrist; 2) start taking any medication prescribed for you; 3) bring a letter from your psychiatrist indicating the medications you are taking and your diagnoses. In addition, you will have to continue psychiatric treatment and take prescribed medication; if you stop these behaviors, staff will review your case and make a decision regarding what seems best for you at that time, including transfer to another program. Are you able to make this oral contract? Please repeat what you have to do (Wallace, 2005).
- Contract # 3. Admission contingent on obtaining psychiatric care and achieving stability. In order for you to be accepted into this program: 1) start seeing a psychiatrist; 2) take any medication prescribed for you; 3) wait until you are stable on medication before you return to the program; and 4) bring a letter to the program from your psychiatrist indicating the medications you are taking, your diagnoses, and stating that you are stable on that medication. This process may take several weeks, delaying admission to our program. Once you are admitted into the program, you will have to continue psychiatric treatment and take prescribed medication; if you stop these behaviors, staff will review your case and make a decision regarding what seems best for you at that time, including transfer to another program. Are you able to make this oral contract? Please repeat what you have to do. I can write it all down for you (Wallace, 2005).
- Contract # 4. Admission contingent on making a contract for suicidality. If you start feeling suicidal, you must inform staff—telling your counselor, the psychologist, or any available staff member. Staff will make a decision with regard to the next steps that are best for you, talking to you, and including you in this process. If you become suicidal in the evening or over the weekend, go to the emergency room. Inform our program staff about any emergency psychiatric treatment you receive as soon as you can. Are you able to make this oral contract? Please repeat what you have to do (Wallace, 2005).
- Contract # 5. Admission contingent on making a contract for homicidality/violence. Walk away before you become verbally or physically aggressive. You have permission to walk out of groups, the cafeteria, or the building. Once you walk away, do not return to the program until you feel calm again—whether this takes 10 minutes or three days. Once you return to the program, you must inform staff about the incident. A decision will be made with regard to the next steps that are best for you, including transfer to another program. Are you able to make this oral contract? Please repeat what you have to do (Wallace, 2005).

As these oral contingency contracts suggest, there is great value in Principle 4: Ensure Access to Drug User Treatment/Counseling With Increased Compliance Through the Use of Contingency Contracting. This represents a creative and novel dimension to the overall approach suggested in this chapter to ethical issues surrounding access to drug user treatment/counseling. However, future research needs to study the effectiveness of such oral contingency contracts.

Conclusion

The discussion of ethical issues surrounding access to drug user treatment/counseling presented in this chapter used a conceptual framework based on a model that considers societal determinants, specific characteristics of the health care system, and individual client characteristics. Within this framework, four novel principles were introduced to guide practitioners in the vital work of ensuring ethical access to drug user treatment/counseling in contemporary times in places such as the United States. Future research is needed to determine the utility of the four principles—both in the United States and other parts of the world, while focusing on pertinent outcome variables. Special emphasis was also placed on the role of practitioners as advocates throughout the discussion.

The discussion provided in this chapter is not necessarily comprehensive, and no claim is being made that every pertinent ethical dilemma or ethical issue surrounding access to drug user treatment/counseling has been addressed. For example, an issue not addressed in this chapter involves the ethics of clients with no self-reported history of drug use and no documented drug use (via urine toxicology reports) being mandated, nonetheless, to participation in outpatient drug user treatment/counseling. Is this an unethical practice? Are the rights of non-drug users mandated to drug user treatment/counseling being violated? Is the right to access a treatment slot being denied to veritable drug users when a non-drug user is mandated to that treatment slot? Does this create an ethical dilemma? To what extent do such practices reflect the stigmatization of all offenders by assuming they are all drug users? Do such practices also reflect discrimination, as mandated clients are also effectively being denied the ability to use all of their available time during the day to access employment and/or vocational training? Instead of engaging in work or job training, such clients typically have to wait until mandated drug user treatment/counseling is completed across as many as three, six, or nine months of treatment, before they can seek employment and/or vocational training as preparation for employment. Are drug user treatment/counseling practitioners being forced to collude (along with criminal justice system personnel) in an unethical practice that is also discriminatory? To what extent do such contemporary practices within the criminal justice system call for some form of coordinated social action for social justice on the part of practitioners, other professionals across multiple agencies, angry/frustrated parolees, and their families/communities?

Admittedly, a solution is needed for those newly released from incarceration who lack a drug use history. However, an argument can be made that a mandate to outpatient drug user treatment is not the best option for these clients—on what may be a very limited list of available options with limited slots. Meanwhile, given the disproportionate arrest and incarceration of those who are African American and Hispanic for drug crimes within the United States, the majority of these recently released from incarceration and entering drug user treatment/counseling are also African American or Hispanic (NIDA, 2003; Mauer & Chesney-Lind, 2002; Glaze, 2002; Haney & Zimbardo, 1998). Such clients are, therefore, also vulnerable to discrimination and oppression because of these characteristics, suggesting a factor that may also be contributing to their mistreatment via mandates to drug user treatment/counseling in the absence of a pertinent drug history. While a potential form of mistreatment, mandated placement in drug user treatment/counseling may be the best approximation of what clients need, but not the perfect fit. Furthermore, if there are, indeed, limited treatment slots for which contemporary clients must compete, consider the following questions:

- What is the impact on the service delivery system and those presenting genuine urgent instances of current drug dependence with a need to access one of these limited drug user treatment/counseling slots?
- What is the best ethical response to such dilemmas?
- Do such dilemmas even exist, and can we document them?
- And, if such dilemmas do exist, in which specific geographical locations do they occur?
- Finally, how are they being resolved?

In conclusion, this is just one example of an area in which there are unresolved ethical issues, reflecting the extent to which the discourse on ethical issues surrounding access to drug user treatment/counseling is, by necessity, an ongoing dialogue requiring yet more future recommendations. Meanwhile, the recommendations offered in this chapter provide an important foundation and starting point for the ongoing discourse on the ethical issues surrounding access to drug user treatment/counseling.

Barbara C. Wallace, Ph.D., is a New York state licensed Psychologist and tenured Associate Professor of Health Education in the Department of Health and Behavior Studies at Teachers College, Columbia University. Dr. Wallace has been honored with the status of Fellow in Division 50 on Addictive Behaviors within the American Psychological Association. Her books include the following: Crack Cocaine: A Practical Treatment Approach for the Chemically Dependent (1991, Brunner/Mazel, Inc.), The Chemically Dependent: Phases of Treatment and Recovery (Editor, 1992, Brunner/Mazel, Inc.), Adult Children of Dysfunctional Families: Prevention, Intervention and Treatment for Community Mental Health Promotion (1996, Praeger), Understanding and Dealing with Violence: A Multicultural Approach (with Co-Editor Robert T. Carter, Ph.D., 2003, Sage), and Making Mandated Addiction Treatment Work (2005, Jason Aronson/Rowman & Littlefield). In addition, she has published numerous journal articles and chapters in edited books. Dr. Wallace serves as a consulting psychologist to drug user treatment/counseling programs in New York City. She also travels widely as a keynote speaker, conference presenter, and workshop leader, covering a range of topics—chemical dependence, relapse prevention for a range of addictive and problem behaviors, HIV/AIDS, violence prevention, trauma resolution for sexual abuse, physical abuse and domestic violence, community empowerment, as well as multiculturalism/diversity. She is also Founder and Director of the Research Group on Disparities in Health within the Department of Health and Behavior Studies at Teachers College, Columbia University, supporting the work of graduate students, post-doctoral fellows, and colleagues.

References

Andersen, R, & Newman, J.F. (1973). Societal and individual determinants of medical care utilization in the United States. *Milbank Memorial Fund Quarterly, 51*, 95-124.

Ashery, R.S., Carlson, R.G., Falck, R.S., & Siegal, H.A. (1995). Injection drug users, crack-cocaine users, and human service utilization: An Exploratory study. *Social Work, 40*, 75-82.

Aspinwall, L.G., & Staudinger, U.M. (Eds.). (2003). *A Psychology of Human Strengths: Fundamental Questions and Future Directions for a Positive Psychology.* American Psychological Association: Washington, D.C.

Battle, C.L., Zlotnick, C., Najavits, L.M., Gutierrez, M., Winsor, C. (2003). "Post-traumatic Stress Disorder and Substance Use Disorder Among Incarcerated Women," In Ouimette, P. & Brown, P.J. (Eds). *Trauma and Substance Abuse: Causes, Consequences, and Treatment of Comorbid Disorders.* American Psychological Association: Washington, D.C. pp.209-225

Belenko, S., & Logan, T.K. (2003). "Delivering More Effective Treatment to Adolescents: Improving the Juvenile Drug Court Model," *Journal of Substance Abuse Treatment, 25*, 189-211.

Broner, N., Borum, R., & Gawley, K. (2002). "Criminal Justice Diversion of Individuals with Co-Occurring Mental Illness and Substance Use Disorders: An Overview," In. Landsberg, G., Rock, M., Berg, L.K. W., & Smiley, A. (Eds). (2002). *Serving Mentally Ill Offenders: Challenges and Opportunities for Mental Health Professionals,* (pp. 83-106). New York: Springer Publishing Co.

Broner, N., Borum, R., Whitmire, L., & Gawley, K. (2002). "A Review of Screening Instruments for Co-occurring Mental Illness and Substance Use in Criminal Justice Programs," In. Landsberg, G., Rock, M., Berg, L.K. W., & Smiley, A. (Eds). (2002). *Serving Mentally Ill Offenders: Challenges and Opportunities for Mental Health Professionals*, (pp. 289-337). New York: Springer Publishing Co.

Carroll, K.M. (2001). "Combined Treatments for Substance Dependence," In Sammons, M.T. & Schmidt, N.B. (Eds). *Combined Treatments for Mental Disorders: A Guide to Psychological and Pharmacological Intervention.* American Psychological Association: Washington, D.C. pp. 215-237.

DeCou, K., Van Wright, S. (2002). A gender-specific intervention model for incarcerated women: Women's V.O.I.C.E.S. (Validation opportunity inspiration communication empowerment safety). In. Landsberg, G., Rock, M., Berg, L.K. W., & Smiley, A. (Eds). (2002). *Serving Mentally Ill Offenders: Challenges and Opportunities for Mental Health Professionals*, (pp. 172-190). New York: Springer Publishing Co.

Dennis, M.L. (2002). "Long-Term Outcome After the Cannabis Youth Treatment (CYT) Experiment," A Paper presented within a Symposium entitled "Persistent Effects of Adolescent Substance Abuse Treatment," held at the 110th Annual Convention of the American Psychological Association, August 23, 2002, Chicago, McCormick Place, Lakeside Center.

Evans, T., Whitehead, M., Diderichsen, F., Bhuiya, A., & Wirth,M. (Eds.). (2001). *Challenging Inequities in Health: From Ethics to Action.* New York, NY: Oxford University Press.

Farabee, D. & Leukefeld, C.G. (2001). "Recovery and the Criminal Justice System," In F. M. Tims, C.G. Leukefeld, & J.J. Platt (Eds.). (2001). *Relapse and Recovery in Addictions*, New Haven: Yale University Press, (pp. 40-59).

Giaconia, R.M., Reinherz, H.Z., Paradis, A.D., & Stashwick, C.K. (2003). Comorbidity of substance use disorders and posttraumatic stress disorder in adolescents. In. P. Ouimette & P.J. Brown (Eds). *Trauma and Substance Abuse: Causes, Consequences, and Treatment of Comorbid Disorders*, (pp.227-242). American Psychological Association: Washington, D.C.

Glaze, L.E. (2002). "Probation and Parole in the United States, 2002," Bureau of Statistics Bulletin, U.S. Department of Justice, August 2002, NCJ 195669.

Haney, C. & Zimbardo, P. (1998). "The Past and Future of U.S. Prison Policy: Twenty Five Years After the Stanford Prison Experiment, *American Psychologist, Vol. 53*, No 7, 709-727.

Hester, R.K. & Miller, W.R. (Eds.). (2003). *Handbook of Alcoholism Treatment Approaches: Effective Alternatives, Third Edition*, Boston, MA.: Allyn and Bacon.

Higgins, S.T. & Silverman, K. (1999). *Motivating Behavior Change Among Illicit-Drug Abusers: Research on Contingency Management Interventions*, Washington, D.C: American Psychological Association.

Jainchill, N. (2002). "Discussant." A paper presented within a Symposium entitled "Persistent Effects of Adolescent Substance Abuse Treatment," held at the 110th Annual Convention of the American Psychological Association, August 23, 2002, Chicago, McCormick Place, Lakeside Center.

Lamont, S.S., Cohen, N.L., & Broner, N. (2002). New York city' system of criminal justice mental health services, In. Landsberg, G., Rock, M., Berg, L.K. W., & Smiley, A. (Eds). (2002). *Serving Mentally Ill Offenders: Challenges and Opportunities for Mental Health Professionals*, (pp. 144-156) New York: Springer Publishing Co.

Leukefeld, C.G., Logan, T.K., Martin, S.S., Purvis, R.T., & Farabee, D. (1998). A health services use framework for drug-abusing offenders, *American Behavioral Scientist, Vol. 41*, No, 8, 1123-1135

Linton, S. (1998). *Claiming disability: Knowledge and identity*. New York, NY: New York University Press.

Lopez, S.J., & Snyder, C.R. (Eds.). (2003). *Positive Psychological Assessment: A Handbook of Models and Measures*, American Psychological Association: Washington, D.C.

Marlatt, G.A & VandenBos, G.R. (Eds.). (1997). Addictive Behaviors: Readings in Etiology, Prevention, and Treatment," Washington, DC: American Psychological Association. (pp. xi-xxv).

Marlowe, D. B. (2003). "Integrating Substance Abuse Treatment and Criminal Justice Supervision," *Science & Practice Perspectives, Vol 2*, No. 1, 4-14.

Mauer, M, & Chesney-Lind, M (Eds.). (2002). *Invisible Punishment: The Collateral Consequences of Mass Imprisonment*, New York: The New Press.

McLellan, A.T. (2003). "Crime and Punishment and Treatment: Latest Findings in the Treatment of Drug-Related Offenders," *Journal of Substance Abuse Treatment, Vol 25*, 187-188

Miller, W.R., Wilbourne, P.L., Hettema, J.E. (2003). "What Works? A Summary of Alcohol Treatment Outcome Research," In. Hester, R.K. & Miller, W.R. (Eds.) (2003).

Handbook of Alcoholism Treatment Approaches: Effective Alternatives, Third Edition, Boston, MA: Allyn & Bacon. pp. 13-63.

Najavits, L.M. (2003). "Seeking Safety: A New Psychotherapy for Posttraumatic Stress Disorder and Substance Use Disorder," In. Ouimette, P. & Brown, P.J. (Eds). *Trauma and Substance Abuse: Causes, Consequences, and Treatment of Comorbid Disorders*, (pp. 147-169). American Psychological Association: Washington, D.C.

National Institute on Drug Abuse. (2003). Drug Use Among Racial/Ethnic Minorities, U.S. Department of Health and Human Services, NIH Publication No. 03-3888, National Institute on Drug Abuse: Bethesda, MD.

National Institute on Drug Abuse. (1999). Principles of Drug Addiction Treatment: A Research-Based Guide, U.S. Department of Health and Human Services, NIH Publication No. 99-4180, National Institute on Drug Abuse: Bethesda, MD.

Navon, B. (2002). Friends of island academic providing youth with positive opportunities after jail, In. Landsberg, G., Rock, M., Berg, L.K. W., & Smiley, A. (Eds). (2002). *Serving Mentally Ill Offenders: Challenges and Opportunities for Mental Health Professionals*, (pp. 120-127). New York: Springer Publishing Co.

Office of Applied Studies. (2003). Results from the 2002 National Survey on Drug use and Health: National findings (DHHS Publication No. SMA 03-3836, NHSHA Series H-22). Rockville, MD: Substance Abuse and Mental Health Services Administration.

Ouimette, P. & Brown, P.J. (Eds.). (2003). *Trauma and Substance Abuse: Causes, Consequences, and Treatment of Comorbid Disorders*, American Psychological Association: Washington, D.C.

SAMHSA. (2004). National survey of substance abuse treatment services 2002: Profile of all states and jurisdictions. Retrieved from http://www.oas.samhsa.gov/dasis.html#Reports.

Sammons, M.T. (2001). "Combined Treatments for Mental Disorders: Clinical Dilemmas," In Sammons, M.T. & Schmidt, N.B., *Combined Treatments for Mental Disorders: A Guide to Psychological and Pharmacological Interventions*, American Psychological Association: Washington, D.C. pp. 11-32.

Schumacher, J.E., Milby, J.B., McNamara, C.L., Wallace, D., Michael, M., Popkin, S., & Usdan, S. (1999). Effective treatment of homeless substance abusers: The role of contingency management. In Higgins, S.T. & Silverman, K. (Eds). *Motivating Behavior Change Among Illicit-Drug Abusers: Research on Contingency Management Interventions*, pp. 77-94. Washington, D.C.: American Psychological Association.

Satel, S. (2002). "Is Drug Addiction a Brain Disease?" In Musto, D.F. (Ed.) *One Hundred Years of Heroin*, Westport, Conn: Auburn House, pp. 55-63.

Seligman, M.E.P. (2002). *Authentic Happiness: Using the New Positive Psychology to Realize Your Potential for Lasting Fulfillment*, Free Press: New York.

Sorenson, J.L., Rawson, R., Guydish, J., & Zweben, J.E. (Eds.). (2003). *Drug Abuse Treatment Through Collaboration: Practice and Research Partnerships That Work*, American Psychological Association: Washington, D.C.

Sue, D. W. (2003). *Overcoming Our Racism: The Journey to Liberation*, New York: John Wiley & Sons.

Sue, D.W., Carter, R.T., Casas, J.M., Fouad, N.A., Ivey, A.E., Jensen, M., LaFromboise, T., Manese, J.E., Ponterotto, J.G., Vazquez-Nutall, E. (1998). *Multicultural*

Counseling Competencies: Individual and Organizational Development, Thousand Oaks, CA: Sage Publications.

Tucker, J.A. (1999). "Changing Addictive Behavior: Historical and Contemporary Perspectives," In Tucker, J.A., Donovan, D.M., & Marlatt, G.A. (Eds.) (1999). *Changing Addictive Behavior: Bridging Clinical and Public Health Strategies*, New York: Guilford Press. pp. (3-44).

van Wormer, K. & Davis, D.R. (2003). *Addiction Treatment: A Strengths Perspective*, Brooks/Cole: Pacific Grove, CA.

Wallace, B.C. (In press, anticipated October, 2005). *Making mandated addiction treatment work*, Lanhan, MD: Jason Aronson/A division of Rowman & Littlefield Publishers.

Wallace, B.C. (2002). The Healing Power of Groups and the Residential Therapeutic Community: The case of Ms. E—A study in success and mutual transformation. In A. Tatarsky. (Ed.). *Harm Reduction Psychotherapy: A New Treatment for Drug and Alcohol Problems*. Jason Aaronson Inc.; NJ.

Wallace, B.C. (2000). A Call for change in multicultural training at graduate schools of education: Educating to end oppression and for social justice." *Teachers College Record. Vol 102*, No 6, 1086-1111.

Wallace, B. C. (1996). *Adult children of dysfunctional families: Prevention, intervention, and treatment for community mental health promotion*. Praeger: Westport, Connecticut.

Wallace, B.C. (Ed.) (1992). *The Chemically Dependent: Phases of Treatment and Recovery*, New York: Brunner/Mazel.

Wallace, B.C. (1991). *Crack Cocaine: A Practical Treatment Approach for the Chemically Dependent*, New York: Brunner/Mazel.

Wexler, H.K. (2003). "The Promise of Prison-Based Treatment for Dually Diagnosed Inmates," *Journal of Substance Abuse Treatment, Vol 25*, 3: 223-231

Appendix A

(Taken from Wallace, B.C. (2005, in press) *Making Mandated Addiction Treatment Work*. New York: Jason Aronson (imprint of Rowman & Littlefield Publishers)

Menu of Effective Alternatives Available in the Social Context

Category I: 7 Evidence-Based Addiction Treatments

1. Special Focus on Building A Strong Therapeutic Alliance/Social Support Network (TASS)
2. Motivational Interviewing/Motivational Enhancement Therapy (MET)/Brief Interventions
3. Cognitive-Behavioral Therapy (CBT)/Relapse Prevention (RP)/Social Skills Training (SST)
4. Twelve-Step Facilitation (TSF)/Guidance Using Alcoholics and/or Narcotics Anonymous
5. Individual Drug Counseling (IDC) and/or Supportive-Expressive Psychotherapy (SEP)
6. Community Reinforcement Approach (CRA)/Vouchers: Contingency Management (CM)
7. The MATRIX Model—Or, a Day Treatment Approach or "IEC" Outpatient Model That Is "I" or Intensive (4-5 days per week), "E" or Extensive (6-12 months), and "C" or Comprehensive (TASS, CBT/RP, IDC, Group Drug Counseling (GDC), drug testing, etc.).

Category II: 7 Recommended State-of-the-Art Practices

1. Integration of Motivational Interviewing and Stages of Change
2. Integration of Stages of Change and Phases of Treatment and Recovery
3. Integration of Harm Reduction, Moderation Approaches, and Abstinence Models
4. Integration of Psychoanalytic and Cognitive-Behavioral Theory and Technique
5. Acquisition of Affective, Behavioral, and Cognitive Coping Skills—Learning New "A,B,Cs"
6. Integration of Motivational Interviewing, Stages of Change, and Identity Development Theory for a Diverse Identity Involving Race, Sexual Orientation, and/or Disability
7. Incorporating Contemporary Trends in Psychology: Multiculturalism, Positive Psychology, The Strengths-Based Approach, and Optimistic Thinking/Learned Optimism

2-13 Ethical Issues Surrounding Access to Treatment for Substance Misuse

Shelly A. Wiechelt, Ph.D.

Abstract

The many varieties of substance user treatment programs in the United States have provided a plethora of research evidence showing treatment effectiveness. Regardless of increasing knowledge and overall treatment availability, a tremendous gap exists between the number of people identified as needing treatment and those who actually receive treatment. This chapter discusses some of the factors and conditions that contribute to treatment access problems for substance users in the United States. These access issues are explored in light of the existing ethical codes of addiction treatment professionals.

Key Words: addiction, addiction treatment, ethics, access, barriers to treatment

Introduction

Since the inception of the National Institute on Drug Abuse (NIDA) and the National Institute on Alcohol Abuse and Alcoholism (NIAAA) in the 1970's, research on substance use and substance use-related problems has been burgeoning in the United States (US). Existing research provides evidence for effective treatments, and many types of treatment programs are available in the US. Regardless of increasing knowledge and overall treatment availability, a tremendous gap exists between the number of people identified as needing treatment and those who actually receive treatment. In 2003, it was estimated that 22.2 million people aged 12 or older (9.3 % of the total population) needed treatment for an alcohol or illicit drug use problem. Only an estimated 1.9 million of these people (8.5% of the people who needed treatment) received treatment at a substance user treatment facility. The number of people who needed, but did not receive treatment in 2003 was 20.3 million. Approximately one million of them felt that they needed treatment for a drug or alcohol use problem, and 273,000 (26%) of these people sought, but were unable to obtain treatment. The most often reported reasons that they needed, but did not receive treatment were: not ready to stop using (41%), cost or insurance barriers (33%), stigma (20%), and did not feel the need for treatment at that time or could handle the problem on their own (17%) (the total percentage exceeds 100%, as it was possible to select more than one reason.) (Substance Abuse and Mental Health Services Administration, 2004b).

Clearly, treatment access is an issue for individuals with substance use-related problems in the US. Several factors that may be barriers to treatment have been identified. These factors can usefully be categorized as exogenous and endogenous whose dimensions may range from the micro to the macro, from simple to complex, and can entail various levels and phases. They include: individual characteristic variables such as, gender, race, ethnicity, culture, sexual orientation, religion, age, and socioeconomic status; and structural variables such as, organizational structure of the treatment delivery system, geographic location, federal and state funding priorities, payer system, and philosophy of treatment (Council, 2004; Schmidt & Weisner, 1999). These same barriers also seem to impede the ability of some individuals to complete treatment once they start. Such barriers to treatment may place addiction treatment professionals in ethical binds or in frank violation of their ethical codes. The focus of this chapter is to discuss the issue of treatment access and the ethical conundrum that addiction treatment professionals[1] face in light of the current condition of treatment access.

Ethics for the Addiction Treatment Professional

Ethics are standards of conduct and guiding principles that members of a given professional group are expected to follow. Ethics are underpinned by the values of the group. The principles of beneficence (to work to benefit others), non-maleficence (to do no harm), fidelity (to be trustworthy), integrity (to be honest), and justice (to be fair and promote equal access for all) are integral to the values and ethical codes of helping professionals (Beauchamp & Childress, 1994). An individual who violates the ethical standards of his/her profession may be censured by the accrediting professional body.

Addiction treatment professionals include counselors, physicians, social workers, psychologists, and nurses. Paraprofessionals, such as individuals who have obtained an associates degree in a related field, may be credentialed as addiction counselors if they meet the eligibility requirements of their state accrediting body or the National Association for Addiction Professionals (NAADAC). Nonprofessionals, such as "recovering persons", may also be credentialed based on training and experience in some states. There are variations in the level of credential that an individual is eligible for, depending on a combination of training and experience (See www.icrcaoda.org and www.naadac.org. Also, counselor certification is discussed in detail in the chapter by Ted Godlaski in this volume.). Regardless of the level of their credential, individuals are expected to adhere to the code of ethics as outlined by the credentialing body (NAADAC and/or state board). Additionally, individuals who are professionals as listed above are required to adhere to the ethical codes of their respective profession. The complete ethical code of each of these professions can be found on the internet:

National Association for Addiction Professionals	www.naadac.org
National Association of Social Workers	www.socialworkers.org
American Medical Association	www.ama-assn.org
American Psychiatric Association	www.apa.org
American Nursing Association	www.nursingworld.org
American Counseling Association	www.counseling.org
Commission on Rehabilitation Counselors Certification	www.crccertification.com

The ethical codes of state boards of addiction counselor certification can be accessed on the internet, but their various web addresses are too numerous to list here. The interested reader can utilize www.icrcaoda.org for links to many state boards.

Ethics relevant to access

The ethical codes for addiction counselors and the professions of social work, counseling, psychology, medicine, and nursing have standards, principles, policies, or guides that indicate that members of the professions should not engage in discrimination, should endeavor to advocate for social justice so that all individuals have access to care, and should not abandon clients for their inability to pay or for any other reason. If individuals are unable to pay for a service or if service does not appear to be benefiting the individual, it is the responsibility of the professional to arrange for continued care with an appropriate provider. The specific standards for each profession are too numerous to list here, but can be found at the internet addresses listed above. Given that the emphasis of this chapter is on addiction treatment, excerpts from the NAADAC code of ethics that are pertinent to access are presented here (See appendix 1 in this volume for the complete NAADAC code of ethics.):

Principle 1: Non-Discrimination

> The NAADAC member shall not discriminate against clients or professionals based on race, religion, age, gender, disability, national ancestry, sexual orientation, or economic condition.

Principle 2: Responsibility

> The NAADAC member shall espouse objectivity and integrity, and maintain the highest standards in the services the member offers.
>
> a. The NAADAC member shall maintain respect for institutional policies and management functions of the agencies and institutions within which the services are being performed, but will take initiative toward improving such policies when it will better serve the interest of the client.

Principle 7: Client Welfare

> The NAADAC member shall promote the protection of the public health, safety, and welfare and use the best interests of the client as a primary guide in determining the conduct of all NAADAC members.
>
> c. The NAADAC member shall hold the welfare of the client paramount when making any decisions or recommendations concerning referral, treatment procedures, or termination from treatment.

Principle 9: Client Relationships

> It is the responsibility of the NAADAC member to safeguard the integrity of the counseling relationship and to ensure that the client has reasonable access to effective treatment.

Principle 11: Remuneration

> The NAADAC member shall establish financial arrangements in professional practice and in accord with the professional standards that safeguard the best interests of the client first, and then of the counselor, the agency and the profession.

Principle 12: Societal Obligations

> The NAADAC member shall to the best of his/her ability actively engage the legislative process, educational institutions, and the general public to change public policy and legislation to make possible opportunities and choice of service for all human beings of any ethnic or social background whose lives

are impaired by alcoholism and drug misuse. (see NAADAC, The Association for Addiction Professionals, 2005)

Keep the ethical codes, standards, and underpinning values in mind as you read the sections on access.

Access

On the surface the notion of access to treatment for substance misuse (i.e., can people who need help get help?) appears to be a relatively simple concept to study and understand. However, when endeavoring to answer that simple question it becomes apparent that access is a rather complex construct and process with several components whose dimensions are less likely to be linear, cause and effect, and more likely to be non-linear, with all of the implications of this distinction (Buscema, 1998). The components of an access "landscape" include, among other considerations, a culture of giving and receiving help, the availability of services, location of services, range of services, the appropriateness of services to a given population, clear points of entry to obtain services, costs of services, funding levels for services, need for services, demand for services, effectiveness of services, and the personal characteristics and help-seeking behaviors of the individuals and their families who need services (Council, 2004; Titmus, 1970). Schmidt and Weisner (1999) suggest that the interaction of individual, organizational, and sociocultural factors influence access. The extent to which the various factors interact to affect access is likely to fluctuate with changes in individuals and systems (e.g., perceptions about substance use and its derived and related problems, who the user is or could be, and funding for treatment).

The field of health services research examines how social factors, financing systems, organizational structures and processes, health technologies, and personal behaviors affect access to health care as well as the social and economic costs, quality, and effectiveness of health care (Lohr & Steinwachs, 2002). Researchers have endeavored to understand the gap between those who need treatment for substance misuse and those who actually receive treatment.

State by state

In recent years, efforts to understand the treatment gap by gathering and examining state-by-state data have been undertaken (McAuliffe & Dunn, 2004; McAuliffe, LaBrie, Woodworth, Zhange, & Dunn, 2003; Wright & Sathe, 2005). McAuliffe and his colleagues (2003) and McAuliffe and Dunn (2004) found that there are regional variations in treatment need and access problems. In their research, Southern and Southwestern states appeared to have the largest treatment gaps in the country. Southern states were found to have low to moderate levels of substance misuse, but were very low in their treatment services availability. Southwestern states were found to have "exceptionally high levels" of substance misuse with only moderate levels of treatment services available (McAuliffe & Dunn, 2004 p. 1009). States with high percentages of at-risk-groups in their population and states with low per capita income are likely to have gaps between treatment need and treatment capacity. The authors note that the Southern states have high levels of African Americans, and the Southwestern states have high levels of Hispanics and Native Americans. Thus, simply making more treatment services available in those regions of the country would likely have a positive effect on treatment access for minorities in the US. People in rural states appear to suffer disparity between needing and receiving treatment for alcohol use-related problems.

Wright and Sathe (2005) report that New Mexico had the highest percentage and California the largest total number of persons age 12 or older needing, but not receiving, treatment for an illicit drug problem. Also, the upper fifth of states with the greatest disparity between those needing and receiving treatment for an illicit drug problem in persons age 12 or older consisted mainly of five Western states and four Northeastern states (see Figure 1). The upper fifth of states with the greatest disparity between those needing but not receiving treatment for alcohol use-related problems consisted mainly of four Western and five Midwestern states (see Figure 2). Arizona, the District of Columbia, New Mexico, and Rhode Island were in the top fifth of states that have the greatest disparity between those people age 12 or older needing, but not receiving, treatment for an alcohol problem and those people age 12 or older needing, but not receiving, treatment for an illicit drug problem. These findings are congruent with the notion that treatment gaps are wider for states with high concentrations of minority populations or lower per capita income. (McAuliffe & Dunn, 2004; McAuliffe et al., 2003). There are also variations in the types of drugs used in various parts of the country and by different age groups that have implications for appropriate treatment programs (Substance Abuse and Mental Health Services Administration, 2004b; Wright & Sathe, 2005).

The variations in the percentages of individuals needing treatment and those actually receiving treatment reflected in the state-by-state analyses indicate that there are biases inherent to the funding structure for addiction treatment in the US and in the availability of appropriate substance user treatment services. Bias against individuals on the basis of their ethnicity, race, age, and economic condition are in direct violation of the ethical principle of non-discrimination. The NAADAC code of ethics, as well as the other professional ethical codes listed above, indicates that members are responsible to seek social justice by promoting equal access to treatment for all individuals.

Figure 2.13.1: Needing But Not Receiving Treatment for Illicit Drug Use in Past Year among Persons Aged 12 or Older, by State: Percentages, Annual Averages Based on 2002 and 2003 NSDUHs

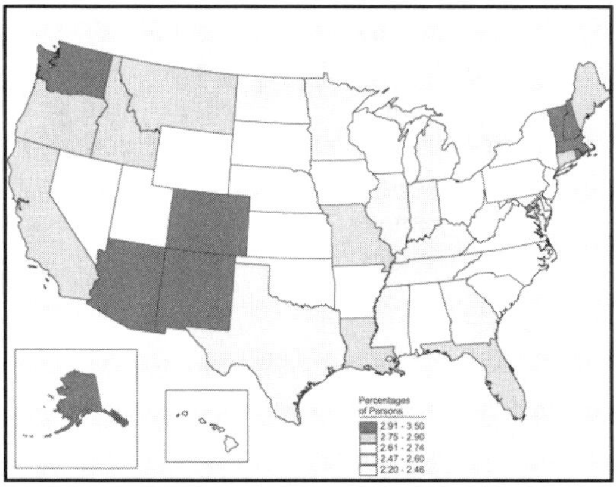

Source: SAMHSA, Office of Applied Studies, National Survey on Drug Use and Health, 2002 and 2003.

Figure 2.13.2: Needing But Not Receiving Treatment for Alcohol Use in Past Year among Persons Aged 12 or Older, by State: Percentages, Annual Averages Based on 2002 and 2003 NSDUHs

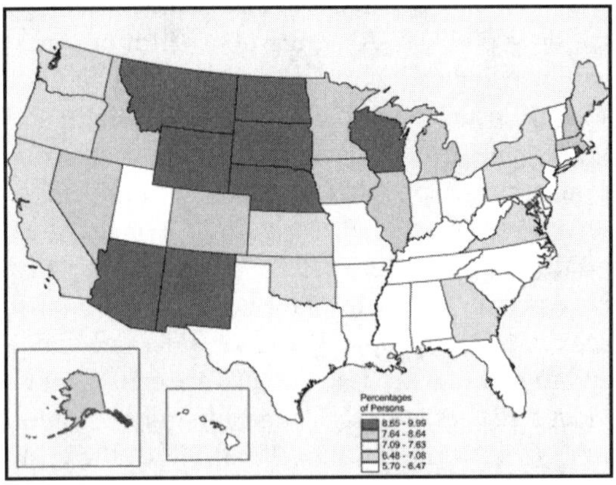

Source: SAMHSA, Office of Applied Studies, National Survey on Drug Use and Health, 2002 and 2003.

Public and private programs

The current treatment delivery system consists of both private sector and public sector treatment programs. The public sector programs are developed and maintained by states. They are funded by state revenues, federal block grants, and Medicaid dollars (Substance Abuse and Mental Health Services Administration, 2004a). The private sector programs are paid for by private insurance, from the individual's pocket, or by private donations. Private entities may sub-contract with state or local governments to provide services. This bifurcation of public and private programs has resulted in a two-tiered treatment system (Council, 2004). Individuals who are either employed or have financial means from other sources are likely to have easier access to substance user treatment in general and utilize private programs. Individuals without financial means, i.e., people who are homeless, mentally ill, elderly, young, female, minorities, indigent, unemployed, or in the criminal justice system, are treated in public programs. Limitations on public funding (i.e., bias toward wealthy states and urban areas in the Substance Abuse Prevention and Treatment Block Grant formula) limit access to treatment for many individuals without financial means (McAuliffe et al., 2003). The bifurcation in the treatment delivery system appears to make access easier for those who have more power in the society to receive treatment. Again, the structure of the treatment delivery and funding systems violates the ethical principle of non-discrimination.

The President's solution

In 2003, President George W. Bush announced a program entitled "Access to Recovery" (ATR) that is intended to increase treatment access for individuals with substance use-related problems who do not have private insurance. The ATR program requires that individuals seeking treatment or support services for their drug or alcohol use-related problems are assessed, provided with a list of treatment options including faith-based and community-based programs, and given vouchers to pay for appropriate treatment services. Individuals choose the programs that they would like to receive services from in order to "recover" from their addiction problem. US states, territories, and tribal groups are eligible to apply for the funds. States must use the funding to supplement current funding and build on existing programs. States may target their efforts to areas of greatest need, areas with a high degree of readiness, or specific populations (see Office of National Drug Control Policy, 2005a, 2005b; Substance Abuse and Mental Health Services Administration, 2004a). Of the 44 states and 22 Native American tribes and US territories that responded to the request for applications, 14 states and 1 tribal group received funds for the 2004 fiscal year (US Department of Health and Human Services, 2004). Outcomes such as abstinence from drugs and alcohol, attainment of employment or enrollment in school, no involvement with the criminal justice system, stable housing, social support, access to care, and retention services are being evaluated. The data on these outcomes are not yet available. In the long run, the ATR initiative may improve access to substance user treatment and provide individuals with an array of services. Given the magnitude of substance use-related problems in the US, however, it seems that much more funding would need to be made available to extend the program across the country and to remediate access problems for individuals seeking treatment in the public sector. Also, the ATR initiative does not address the institutional and individual biases that impede treatment access.

Managed care

Managed care has greatly affected substance user treatment over the past 25 years (Galanter, Keller, Dermatis, & Egelko, 2000). Managed care has its origins in 1929 when physician-owned practices began accepting prepaid contracts from organizations (Kongstvedt, 1989). Managed care began to flourish in the US when exploding increases in health care costs created a vast market for managed care organizations (MCO). The cost of providing health insurance to employees was cutting too far into the profit margins of corporations. The managed care products of insurance corporations and MCOs became increasingly marketable. Employers provided financial incentives for their employees to switch from indemnity plans to managed care plans for their health insurance. Ultimately, consumer choice regarding type of care and provider of care was greatly diminished

Managed care is essentially a structure that is designed to administer health care that is both high quality and cost effective (Sands, 2001). The problem is that these two goals are often competing. The need to provide accessible, comprehensive, continuous, and effective services is tempered by limited resources and the need to contain costs (Wernet, 1999). Individuals who have private insurance are likely to have at least the minimum mandated coverage for substance user treatment, but the oversight of managed care may limit their access to treatment in terms of duration and type of treatment. Managed care has also affected individuals who receive treatment in public programs in that some states have adopted managed care models to contain treatment costs.

Managed care has reduced the number and length of inpatient treatment stays and transferred most care to outpatient programs (Council, 2004). There are various levels of treatment including outpatient individual therapy, group therapy, intensive outpatient programs, partial hospitalization, residential, and inpatient detoxification or rehabilitation programs. MCO's typically use patient placement criteria to determine which level of care they will authorize for initial and continued treatment. Increasingly, the criteria for authorization are based on theoretical and empirical knowledge of the appropriate treatment for an individual. However, the need to contain costs often results in short-term, least-expensive solutions (Galanter et al., 2000). Prior to the mid-1980's, inpatient treatment was the most common form of treatment for substance use. Researchers at that time found that the treatment outcomes were the same in both inpatient and outpatient settings (Miller & Hester, 1986). Given managed care organizations' preference for the less costly outpatient setting and limited resources in general, substance user treatment shifted to outpatient settings. For many individuals, treatment in an outpatient setting is sufficient to meet their treatment needs. For others, particularly those with more severe problems, saving money in the short run ends up costing more in the long run (Council, 2004).

The idea of managed care in and of itself does not necessarily contradict the ethical codes of addiction treatment professionals, but its current emphasis on providing the least expensive rather than the best type of care does contradict them. For example, the NAADAC code's principle of client welfare states that the NAADAC member should use "the best interests of the client as a primary guide…and hold the welfare of the client paramount when making any decisions or recommendations concerning referral, treatment procedures, or termination of treatment" (NAADAC The Association for Addiction Professionals, 2005). This seems to indicate that the best treatment for the client should be the guide to treatment authorization rather than the best treatment for the price. Another ethical concern is that managed care for the employed as well as the "vulnerable populations" in the public system creates a situation in which only the wealthy have a choice regarding the best treatment. Finally, clients should not be abandoned because of an inability to pay, thus the treatment professional is put in the position of providing treatment even if the MCO does not authorize it.

Conclusion

The discussion of access to treatment for substance use-related problems and the associated ethical concerns presented in this chapter are not meant to be and cannot be exhaustive. The factors that contribute to access problems and the ways in which they interact are fluid. That is to say, they change depending on individuals, systems, and conditions. This chapter is intended to raise awareness on the ethical issues that arise when there are access problems in relation to substance user treatment and to stimulate dialogue on ways to resolve access problems in a way that promotes an ethical treatment delivery system to address substance use-related problems. The AMA suggests that the social principle of fair opportunity requires that all people in the society, regardless of their characteristics, have access to "adequate" care (American Medical Association, 1993). An ethical treatment delivery system would likely need to be based on a social value that demands that all people are entitled to the "best" care.

Shelly A. Wiechelt, Ph.D., (USA), Assistant Professor, University of Maryland, Baltimore County, School of Social Work, is a member of the editorial board of Substance Use and Misuse, and a faculty member of the Middle Eastern Summer Institute on Drug Use (MESIDU) in Italy, Spain, and Israel. She conducts research on the interplay of shame, trauma, and substance use among women and Native Americans and endeavors to establish collaborations between researchers and practitioners. She has worked extensively as a clinician in both substance use and mental health treatment settings and teaches continuing education workshops to practitioners. She has multiple publications and presentations on her research and practice interests.

References

American Medical Association. (1993). Ethical issues in health care systems reform: The provision of adequate health care. Retrieved July 11, 2005, from http://www.ama-assn.org/ama1/pub/upload/mm/369ceja_7i93.pdf

Beauchamp, T.L., & Childress, J.F. (1994). *Principles of biomedical ethics*. Oxford: Oxford University Press.

Buscema, M. (1998). Artificial neural networks. *Substance Use & Misuse, 33*(1-3).

Council, C.L., (Ed.). (2004). Health services utilization by individuals with substance abuse and mental disorders, (DHHS Publication No SMA 04-3949, Analytic Series A-25). Rockville: MD: Substance Abuse and Mental Health Services Administration, Office of Applies Studies.

Galanter, M., Keller, D.S., Dermatis, H., & Egelko, S. (2000). The impact of managed care on substance abuse treatment: A report of the American Society of Addiction Medicine. *Journal of Addictive Diseases, 19*(3), 13-34.

Kongstvedt, P.R. (1989). *The managed health care handbook*. Gaithersburg, MD: Aspen Publishers, Inc.

Lohr, K.N., & Steinwachs, D.M. (2002). Health services research: An evolving definition of the field. *Health Services Research, 35*, 375-387.

McAuliffe, W.E., & Dunn, R. (2004). Substance abuse treatment needs and access in the USA: Interstate variations. *Addiction, 99*, 999-1014.

McAuliffe, W.E., LaBrie, R., Woodworth, R., Zhange, C., & Dunn, R.P. (2003). State substance abuse treatment gaps. *The American Journal on Addictions, 12*(2), 101-121.

Miller, W.R., & Hester, R.K. (1986). Inpatient alcoholism treatment: Who benefits? *American Psychologist, 41*, 794-805.

NAADAC, The Association for Addiction Professionals. (2005). Ethical standards for counselors by NAADAC. Retrieved May 19, 2005, from http://naadac.org/documents/print.php?DocumentsID=11

Office of National Drug Control Policy. (2005a). Access to Recovery-Taking action to healing America's substance users. Retrieved July 10, 2005, from http://www.whitehousedrugpolicy.gov/treat/initiative.html

Office of National Drug Control Policy. (2005b). Healing America's drug users: Getting treatment resources where they are needed. Retrieved July 10, 2005, from http://www.whitehousedrugpolicy.gov/publications/policy/ndcs05/healing_amer.html

Sands, R.G. (2001). *Clinical social work practice in behavioral mental health: A postmodern approach to practice with adults*. Boston: Allyn and Bacon.

Schmidt, L.A., & Weisner, C.M. (1999). Public health perspectives on access and need for substance abuse treatment. In Tucker, J.A., Donovan, D.M. & Marlatt, G.A. (Eds.), *Changing addictive behavior: Bridging clinical and public health strategies* (pp. 67-96). New York: The Guilford Press.

Substance Abuse and Mental Health Services Administration. (2004a). Access to recovery: How it will work. Retrieved July 10, 2005, from http://www.samhsa.gov/news/newsreleases/040303bg_howworks.htm

Substance Abuse and Mental Health Services Administration. (2004b). Results from the 2003 national survey on drug use and health: National findings. Rockville, MD: Office of Applied Studies, NSDUH Series H-25, DHHS Publication No. SMA 04-3964. Retrieved July 10, 2005, from http://www.drugabusestatistics.samhsa.gov/NHSDA/2k3NSDUH/2k3Results.htm.

Titmus, R. (1970). *The gift relationship: From human blood to social policy*. London: George Allen and Unwin.

US Department of Health and Human Services. (2004). News Release. Retrieved July 10, 2005, from http://www.dhs.gov/news/press/2004pres/20040803c.html

Wernet, S.P. (1999). Introduction to managed care in human services. In Wernet, S.P. (Ed.), *Managed care in human services*. Chicago: Lyceum.

Wright, D., & Sathe, N. (2005). State estimates of substance use for the 2002-2003 national surveys on drug use and health, (DHHS Publication No.SMA 05-3989, NSDUH Series H-26). Rockville: MD: Substance Abuse and Mental Health Services Administration, Office of Applied Studies.

Glossary

Access to Recovery (ATR): treatment access initiative developed by the Bush administration to provide substance users seeking treatment with assessment, referrals to appropriate programs, and vouchers to pay for the services that the individual chooses (options may include faith-based and community based programs).

barriers to treatment: factors, characteristics, and processes that impede one's ability to seek or obtain treatment such as, personal characteristics, societal bias, and structure of treatment delivery system.

ethics: standards of conduct and guiding principles that members of a given professional group are expected to follow.

effectiveness: treatments that have been shown to improve the condition of individuals in randomized controlled clinical trials.

fair opportunity: moral concept that holds that each member of society should have adequate opportunity to develop without unjust interference; includes having adequate opportunity for good health.

faith-based treatment: treatment that incorporates principles of faith (religion) in the treatment process.

help-seeking: process of initiating a request for services for a problem such as addiction.

health services research: examines how social factors, financing systems, organizational structures and processes, health technologies, and personal behaviors affect access to health care.

managed care: an umbrella term that encompasses a number of structures and processes that are designed to administer health care that is both high quality and cost effective.

recovering persons: individuals who consider themselves to have been addicted to alcohol or other drugs and ceased use via a recovery program, such as Alcoholics Anonymous.

treatment access: a complex construct and process regarding the ability of individuals to seek and obtain treatment services; includes the availability of services, location of services, range of services, the appropriateness of services to a given population, clear points of entry to obtain services, costs of services, funding levels for services, need for services, demand for services, effectiveness of services, and the personal characteristics and help-seeking behaviors of the individuals and their families who need services.

treatment gap: numeric difference between those who need treatment and those who actually receive treatment.

Notes

1. "Addiction" is a loaded "container concept" which can and does mean many different things to many different individuals and systemic stakeholders. It is used in this chapter since this term is the current "politically correct" shibboleth. It is also used in this chapter to designate the treatment of a heterogeneous population of people who use a broad range of licit as well as illicit psychoactive substances in various ways and patterns, on their own as well as with others, with various imputed meanings to the "drug", its use, its anticipated functions, etc. This author is aware that there are voices in the field who posit that "addiction treatment" is a misleading misnomer given the *de facto* reality that at any given time, place, and culture substance users are treated with the same techniques and models as are non-substance users; that there are no unique treatment models for substance user. This is the gist of the chapter by Stan Einstein in this volume.

2-14 Drug Users Can't be Treated, People Can Be! The Creation and Maintenance of Ethical Travesties, or at Least Dilemmas

Stanley Einstein, Ph.D.[1]

And those who were dancing were thought to be insane by those who couldn't hear the music.

— *Nietzsche*

Abstract

Using selected examples, I posit and examine the thesis that contemporary "substance use disorder" (SUD) treatment (both abstinence-oriented and harm-reduction-driven)—which is almost always implemented in sites that are separate from the mainstream of treatment made available to the population-at-large—has the following characteristics: it

- *is in its essence unethical; such beneficence as it displays is overwhelmed by unnecessary "doses" of malfeasance;*
- *is misleadingly characterized since (1) there is no unique "treatment" (models or techniques) for "drug users" that isn't also used for non-drug users, (2) the dimensions of "normed" and "non-normed" treatment sites and their access to other needed treatment support and resource systems can, and does, affect treatment availability, accessibility, quality and patient rights, amongst other considerations, and (3) both "drug users" and non-users constitute heterogeneous populations of PEOPLE and not unique, homogeneous nosologies;*
- *is unlikely to be changed into an ethically-based process because of the positions, agendas, and goals of individual and systemic stakeholders, representing various motivations (power-driven, having been co-opted, going along with established tradition, etc.)*
- *is nourished by "principles of [blind?] faith" which are overlain and undergirded by concepts such as "evidence-based", whose use and misuse have neutralized their scientific veracity and turned them into slogans,*
- *can be, and all-too-often is maintained (inadvertently) by a range of co-opted change agents, who represent a range of disciplines, and include non-professionals "in recovery" or ex-addicts,*
- *operates within an ongoing de facto reality in which new generalizable findings are, more often than not, not introduced and*

not used to treat suitable substance users, supposedly due to "transfer of technology problems."

Key Words: beneficence, compliance, change agents, control agents, cooptation, demonized, dependency, disease, disease models, failure of treatment fit, illegitimate questions, legitimate questions, maleficience, "normed" treatment sites, "principles of faith," stakeholders, "substance use disorder" (SUD), "substance use disorder" treatment, "tame questions," treatment, treatment appropriateness, treatment quality, "wicked" problems

Introduction

People in the substance user treatment field seem to forget that the diagnosis "substance use disorder" (SUD) refers to a relapsing condition that corresponds to many disease models, including non-medical models with unique characteristics and ethical issues. Professionals in SUD ("we") consider persons with SUD ("they", "them", or "those") to relapse due to the effects of their disease or their lack of motivation to get better. There is no agreement on what the professional ("we") needs to know to effectively treat "those" who use drugs, whether legal or illegal. What are the ethical implications of our focusing on the wrong issues for effective treatment planning and implementation? When "they" relapse, are "we" just using public funds to treat "them" to make ourselves feel good about ourselves? Or is it that we don't think "they" are really "sick" so we are just controlling and punishing "them"? "We" are discharging them before they are "cured" or in remission, something "we" wouldn't do to that person with a real "normed" disease, like a diabetic or a schizophrenic. Is there some inappropriate prejudice that leads us to do this, or is there some substantive difference between substance user relapse and the return of elevated blood sugar levels (say)? These questions and issues will be explored in this chapter.

Our socio-political environment largely determines for whom certain actions are permitted and for whom they are forbidden, and what interventions are permitted (see Figure I.1, page xiv), yet this is rarely considered when "we" professionals discuss SUD treatment. Could it be that we just do things because that is what everyone else is doing, even when it doesn't best meet the patient's needs? Maybe we need to find out what patients actually need and then change our ways of treating them instead of just following tradition. Instead of blaming failure on the treatment, we are inclined to blame the patient. Do admissions and re-admissions to treatment produce better results than "natural recovery"? We try to get people with SUD to make major changes in their lives—by asking them to completely re-orient the meaning of their lives as well as their activities—a process that can be very upsetting; yet we are willing to provide help only during normal business hours, even though we know that emotional crises occur at any hour of the day or night. Maybe our interventions are so inadequate and patients' prognosis so poor because we are treating the wrong diagnoses. Or maybe we are just treating a "label" ("alcohol," "drugs" dependence, abuse, addiction, or co-dependence), one, moreover, that is stigmatized, rather than the right diagnosis or a real person. How we treat may be more related to fashions in treatment and the use of a limited number of treatment techniques ("talk therapy", institutionalization). Maybe we need to consider therapies based on other ways of communicating, including art, movement, phototherapy, or music, if we really want to do "treatment matching." The issues of "normed" diseases, treatment and sites of treatment, which are critical to understanding our ongoing treatment of drug users, will be explored in greater depth in the chapter. Do traditional treatment goals really help people to get better, or might they contribute to relapse? If we are really serious about the effectiveness of treatments, why don't we take more account of what happens when people get better by themselves? Moreover, why is there so little concern beyond Magura's (2000) for the effectiveness of quality and appropriateness of treatment staff, techniques, sites, policies, hours of operation, support, and resource systems? In contemporary drug user treatment we marginalize the patient in specialized programs away from mainstream "normed" treatment sites with little regard for differences of degree and type of patients' SUD conditions. But SUD patients aren't so different from us. Consider that, since a range of drug users and misusers have been known since "drugs" have been known by man—which historically is a very long time—and since the drug use disorder is such a relatively new diagnosis (1994, footnote 2), and since we treat drug users with the same techniques and models as we treat non-drug users, a separate (d) kind of treatment being more appropriate has yet to be empirically demonstrated. Even if we don't want to acknowledge it, if we separate 'them' out from 'us' and from other types of patients, maybe they won't be treated as well. If we want real evidence-based treatment that works, we have to evaluate if, by being kept separate, drug users receive less access and fewer treatment opportunities than non-drug users do in traditional, "normed" treatment sites.

WE need to know:

- Who are the traditional foci?
- What is the traditional focus?
- Is abstinence or harm reduction a better treatment model? (The choice is not a simplistic either/or one but exists because the "substance use disorder" treatment field has so structured what is being asked and what is being done.)
- Are the results generally used?

The Traditional Focus: WHO?

How are we going to get the patient to engage in his own treatment and make progress toward getting better? Also, how do we accept [accommodate?] the fact that part of this progress includes relapses?

The Traditional Focus: WHAT?

We have our traditional therapeutic intervention techniques, but what of the patients' adaptational strengths and energy levels and engagement ("compliance") as they get better and relapse or become more fully integrated into society? Failure may be built into the treatment system because of the therapy's and therapist's availability, energy level, and degree of engagement.

SUD Treatment Ideology and Harm Reduction/ Harm Production

Harm reduction (HR) is controversial, and encompasses a wide rage of services, many of which allow a person with SUD to continue using drugs. HR reaches marginalized populations that haven't hitherto been engaged by existing programs and who now don't need to learn about any other available therapeutic interventions that may be of use to them. Are HR therapists no longer change agents, or even agents of control, but have they just been co-opted into perpetuating the status quo? We have to ask hard "legitimate" questions that don't have evident answers (Foerster 1960).

Treatment Assessment Results and the 'Transfer of Technology' Syndrome

Why do we bother to spend public monies to fund research and evaluation of programs that are supposed to be generalizable, when these programs are rarely applied to the real world? The continued funding of research, or "research welfarism", is more related to connections with research funding organizations than with real world applicability of findings. It is being posited that it is not that the research is not applicable to the real world of substance user treatment, but rather that policy makers don't take it into account. The difficulties of moving from scientifically derived data, to analyzed information, to knowledge and wise use of what we know, does not happen often in real world SUD treatment situations.

Is it fair to blame the slowness in moving from the laboratories of science to real life on the problems of 'technology transfer'?

We have generally progressed from treating the disease to treating real people, but only "pathologized", depersonalized, demonized and "homogenized" real SUD PEOPLE!

Among the critical necessary conditions which lead to this situation, is the fact that funders do not consider these issues in research proposals submitted to them, and that researchers, hence, don't include them in their research proposals.

Who are the individual and systemic stakeholders in this SUD treatment assessment process? What are their agendas, and what are their sources of power?

Does this ongoing reality portend ethical dilemmas? And if it does, for whom? For you, for THEM, for US?

All of these issues need to be considered in order to facilitate greater "substance user" treatment beneficence—for THEM—and reduce malfeasance. The ongoing interaction between initiators of treatment, the treatment process, and selected treatment foci (including who is the patient) raises ethical issues in the interactions between models of care, traditional ethical concerns, and substance use(r) disorder treatment process factors.

We need to remember that Drug Users can't be treated; only people can be treated under sufficiently well-known conditions. One of the critical necessary conditions is being able and willing to see the PERSON and not the SUD.

It is important to ask whether these issues of SUD treatment—stemming from the interaction between initiators of treatment, the treatment process, and selected treatment foci—raise ethical issues for the interactions between models of care, traditional ethical concerns and substance use(r) disorder treatment process factors, as well as whether they arise in order to facilitate greater treatment beneficence for THEM and reduce malfeasance?

A Necessary Background

The concept and the process of treatment is value laden. It surely is not value neutral for "social diseases" such as "substance use disorder". "Social disease" is one of numerous models of "disease" categories summarized in Table 1. Given this reality, there is a need to define "treatment" in order to follow this chapter's central theses: we currently treat substance users because we have recently "pathologized" and "diseased" THEM after having initially "moralized" and then "criminalized" THEM. But the manner in which we treat THEM –as an institutionalized system—is ethically flawed.

Were I writing about the treatment of ulcers or neurosis, I would not feel the necessity to include a definition of "treatment". Such diseases–sicknesses–illnesses–ailments have been reasonably well defined, nosologically, over time. Of greater importance is that they have been "normed": they are legitimate sicknesses manifested by legitimate people—like you and me. The status of "drug abuse", "drug misuse" and "drug dependency", in any of their varieties is neither legitimate, nor acceptable. "Recreational use" and "social substances", current categories of licit psychoactive substances such as alcohol, caffeine and tobacco and their usage patterns, are not pathologized. Substance use, recently diagnosed as a "substance use disorder", is part of a social disease nosology which can be problematic in terms of etiology, its process and its prognosis, with or without treatment. Social disease, which can also be read as "deviance", "anti-social", etc, is a label to which the current societal response is to "treat", at the same time that "conventional wisdom" and "common sense" beliefs exist and actively operate among many that, if THEY really wanted to, and really tried, THEY could stop their deviant behavior and life style. We don't seem to believe this about "legitimate", normed diseases.

Table 2.14.1: Models of Disease-Sickness-Illness-Pathology

Type of Model	Definition-Description of Model's Basis
Biochemical	Structural or chemical alterations of a living organism which reduces life expectancy in part or totally (e.g., diabetes, cancer)
Actuarial	Significant deviations from a statistical average in a general population (e.g., obesity, dwarfism, high blood pressure)
Functional	Loss or disturbance of functions in a socially integrated or otherwise well-functioning individual. (e.g., cardiac insufficiency, asthma)
Experiential	Dysphoric experiences which lead to partial or complete incapacitation. (e.g., neurosis, depersonalization)
Social	A-social or anti-social behavior affecting an individual's normal or usual life style. (e.g., phobias, substance use, juvenile delinquency, loss of ambition, social withdrawal)
Consumer	The individual self-defines, for himself and/or for others, the state of his own health/illness, and as a result defines the parameters of his "patient" role(s) (e.g., the person who seeks plastic surgery ["nose-job", "tummy-tuck"] for self-perceived esthetic deficiencies).
Spirit	The state of one's functioning and being is directly related to the quality and types of relationships one has with spirits present in one's environs. An example of this is animism, a belief in the power of spirits and the supernatural world to affect both health and disease; evil spirits can cause illness; illness and disease are likely due to a loss of the whole or part of one's soul.
Political	The direct or indirect result of oppression, repression, exploitation, discrimi-nation and the limiting of opportunities for selected segments of the population. (e.g., Psychiatric hospitalization (treatment?) of dissidents, "sheltered work-shops" for the mentally retarded or the blind)
Metaphor	Illness as a form of expression rather than as a process or course of micro/macro events. A label used by the labeler ("You are sick") or by the labeled ("I am sick").

Note: All these models of disease have been, at one time or another, or are being, currently, applied to what we now term substance use (r) disorder

It is not my intention to beat you, the reader, over the head with an overwhelming numbing set of terms and qualifications in my "treatment" definition, each of which merits clarification and may seem to be no clearer than the term that is being "defined." Yet the definition is necessary because it is the background for why I am positing that SUD treatment, as currently generally practiced in specialized programs away from the mainstream of "normed" treatment of "normed" other diseases, is intrinsically unethical…whatever its positive outcomes for the substance user client-patient, the treatment agent and agency, "significant others", communities, and society-at-large. The issue is not the meaning of "treatment" (which is what dictionaries are concerned with). Nor is this about the kinds of treatment models and/or techniques to which SUDs are subject. Rather, the ethical concerns about SUD treatment derive from the reinforcing of a process of marginalization in specialized treatment programs and the way in which we continue to characterize an SUD, by stigmatizing, homogenizing, dehumanizing, stereotyping, depersonalizing and focusing almost always on "impairment" and not on existing adaptational strengths, skills, abilities, energy levels, etc., of a well-documented heterogeneous population of INDIVIDUAL PEOPLE.

In order to create a line of communication between myself and you, the reader, I offer the following working definition of treatment so that the various "charges" in this brief are as clear as I can make them. You need not accept my definition. Simply consider it as you read my various "charges".

Treatment can be usefully defined and considered to be:

a planned, bounded (in terms of culture-place-time-age-gender-ethnicity-religiosity-SEC [?], etc.), ideologically-driven and/or influenced,

complex,

dynamic,

uni- or multi-dimensional (simple, complex, complicated; linear, non-linear),

phase/level structured,

multi-directional,

goal-driven,

quality,

appropriate and effective change process

which is model-driven (professional, mutual-help [AA, NA], self-help ["natural recovery"], tradition),

"demanding" critical necessary conditions in which

evidence-based "matching" of a range of actual, and potential,

individual and

systemic "constituents" (symptomatized identified patients, targeted prevention recipients, significant others, etc.)

become, and remain, "engaged",

using a range of viable

criteria-based treatment goals and

other objectives,

with suitable techniques

and services

representing a range of assessable

quality,

appropriateness and

effectiveness

for the necessary time (theoretically, empirically and tradition-based),
and number of times,
by individual and multiple "treaters"
of all types,
traditions, and
ideologies,
who represent types and levels of knowledge,
experience,
abilities,
expertise,
values,
mandates,
agendas,
beliefs,
principles of faith, and
energy levels,
who (should) know what they are doing
while being available, and
accessible to new needed knowledge
and experience(s)
in tradition-determined sites, contexts and environments
which foster either "liberating" or
controlled adaptation
effected by facilitating and
interfering policies,
as a function of systemic agendas,
with needed,
available and
accessible formal and
informal,
institutional and
non-institutional support systems
which include, rather than exclude,
the tagged, powerless, and, at times,
disenfranchised
who continue to be "empowered" by myths and
vested interests, and

which can be structured to include
a necessary system to assess and
monitor process (es) and
outcome(s)
in order to make the necessary decisions,
both during and
post- treatment,
regarding all of the treatment components, and
to enable the process and
the processors to learn and
to make needed adjustments.

This definition may have greater meaning, use, and impact if it is read out loud. You, the reader, are referred to a masterful book on graphics as a stimulus for schematizing complex verbiage: Fletcher, Alan (2001), The Art of Looking Sideways, London: Phaidon Press. Indeed looking at SUD treatment "sideways" may be the necessary way to do so.

I originally listed this definition as a long footnote but a graphic artist suggested that a vertical listing is easier for perceiving, paying attention, considering, judging, decision making, accepting, rejecting, changing—for relating to each of these parameters.

Some run-of-the mill dictionary definitions of "treatment" are given below:

Table 2.14.2: Some Dictionary Definitions of "Treatment"

Definition	Source
Care by procedures or applications that are intended to relieve illness or injury	Wordnetdictionary
The application of medical care or attention to a patient.	Concise Oxford Dictionary
Therapeutics; therapy; the medical or surgical care of a patient; the institution of measures or the giving of remedies designed to cure a disease.	Stedman's Medical Dictionary

These definitions do not encompass the complexities of treating a person, or any other living organism, nor do they address the challenges of treatment planning, implementation, and assessment…and surely not of dealing with THEM—the "drug users." One can only imagine the (awful) scenario in which a dictionary may have been used to effect behavioral changes by being used as an interrogation tool to beat someone, to help one to "straighten up and fly right", and, at times, even to learn something.

No doubt I can be criticized for taking what could be considered to be a bit of a misguided shot by perhaps misusing dictionary definitions (and dictionaries). After all, a dictionary is about meanings, not about treatment programs. There is, for example, nothing wrong with the above-noted dictionary definitions—they do what they are intended to do, and they do it just as well for SUDs as for cancer and cystitis. These dictionary definitions are concerned with what it means to treat, not with how to treat. And that's part of the "rub". You are being asked to consider whether the medicalizing-pathologizing of types of substance users, patterns of use, meanings attributed to use and users, or to the use of selected illicit substances and misuse of licit ones, has resulted in ethical –beneficent treatment as has been the general experience with regard to "normed" disease and "normed" treatment. The Soviets, for example, in the recent past, treated people for political deviations; theirs was a political-based disease nosology. One could question whether they understood or misunderstood the meaning of treatment, and/or the nature of political deviations. Need one question if their treatment was ethically-based in the overall beneficence- maleficience balance of things?

Introduction

This chapter begins in about the middle; there is neither a consensus-based beginning nor an end to the ethics of "substance use disorder" treatment. Indeed, the existence of considered, delineated Codes of Ethics by the various organized professional groups whose members are those who treat the range of types of "drug users", is not matched by an extensive, considered theoretical, and empirically-based literature. People in the field—you decide if they are many or few—from policymakers to treatment agents, seem to manifest a memory lapse with regard to ethical implications of "substance use disorder" treatment, given that:

- "substance use disorder" (SUD) has been diagnosed as a chronic disease with relapses and lapses, according to the secular Bible of mental illness: the DSM-IV –REV, (American Psychiatric Association, 1994).
- as previously noted, there are many disease models, not just one.
- each model has its own critical definitions, criteria, goals and agendas, constituencies, indicated and contra-indicated techniques and services, "healers" and change agents, preferred sites for intervention, temporal parameters, and stakeholders. Each has its unique associated ethical issues.
- if the "substance use disorder" is a relapsing process, whatever its etiology, the prognosis that should follow in the linear, "cause and effect," evidence-based, abstinence—aspired-to—world of treating THEM[2], is that THEY will oscillate between "clean"[3] times and "dirty" times,[4] and between "clean urines" and "dirty urines". THEY are expected to "fall". By whom? By almost everyone, including themselves. This appears to be one of the "side effects" of "social diseases" from society's perspective. THEY can, and do, "lapse" and "relapse", notwithstanding the presence, or absence, of THEIR sufficient motivation which is posited as being a critical ingredient for the achievement and maintenance of reified abstinence. Whether or not this prognosis-prediction is an integral dimension of a SUD, or perhaps operates as a self-fulfilling prophecy for the various SUD constituents,[5] it is an important issue which merits exploration. The relationships (actual or potential) between prognosis, as a type of judgment and prediction, and anticipation "demands" (actual or potential) of the various "actors" will not be considered in this chapter. The reader is asked to consider that, whereas in a logical, linear, cause-and-effect world, prediction is fundamentally dif-

ferent from demand (prediction =//= "demand"), in a complex, non-linear, multi-dimensional world, over time, some (or many) substance users have "learned"—through identification, being inducted, reinforcement regimens, etc.—what is expected of them regarding abstinence, lapses, relapses, etc. I have chosen to label this dynamic process of working out ways of adapting to the expectations of others of the SUD as a "demand."

- There does not appear to be a consensus response to the question: WHAT DO I NEED TO KNOW in order to effectively treat PEOPLE who, along with other behaviors,
  — may also use a variety of licit, as well as illicit, psychoactive substances,
  — in a variety of ways and patterns, places, and times,
  — to which various meanings can be, and are, attributed, by the user ("self"), as well as by others,
  — for known, knowable, and unknowable reasons.

Consider the following sample of issues which are connected to one another in terms of their being part of a treatment process that is meant to be effective, keeping in mind the limitations, i.e., the lack of necessary human and non-human resources, which are part of any *de facto* treatment process and reality, but even more so for the treatment of "social diseases" such as SUD. Real "normed" medical diseases, for example, are generally not negatively affected or interfered with by politicalization which continues to be intrinsic to "drug use" and to SUD intervention. The reality that women have often complained that if men suffered from "X", there would be much more research money spent on "it" or examples such as moral-entrepreneur-driven responses to HIV/AIDS and other sexually transmitted diseases (STD) which are related to as if they are not normative do not minimize what is being noted about SUD treatment politicalization. "Normed" diseases and "normed" sites of treatment are an outcome of a complex non-linear process entailing perception, judgment, decision making, choices, overt behaviors, etc. in which social rules and regulations determine the diseases' social status (a run-of-the-mill reality or a "threat" with pejorative dimensions) and the valences (+, +/- -; positive, mixed and negative) attributed to what is being "normed"—its acceptability or rejection by society at large. "Drug use" and particular users continue to be perceived and related to as being "non-normed" by society-at-large.

- Do current SUD screening foci supply what is needed for effective treatment planning and implementation?
- And, if they don't, are there ethical issues that need to be considered?
- What makes it possible for US to react to THEM—by providing treatment mostly using public funds —in a punitive fashion, rather than in a rehabilitative-bound manner or in other accepting ways, when there are limits to public fund resources and all of the public needs to be served by such resources? For some readers the distinguishing between public and private funds to operate beneficent or maleficent interventions, including treatment, may not seem relevant. My own view is that when resources are limited for everyone –the ongoing *de facto* realities of public funding—every one is

equally effected. The use of private funding sources does not seem to be constrained by this concern.

- Consider that "lapse" and "relapse" are often-used concepts which continue to be negatively "loaded" and which are often used against the drug user in treatment. Also consider that learning after only one or two trials-attempts-experiences, in humans, is quite rare in relation to complex, dynamic, multi-dimensional, phase-/level-structured, non-linear processes/phenomena that are also bounded[6] (by culture, time, place, etc.). These factors will be noted and repeated numerous times in this chapter because they are rarely related to in the "drug use(r)" intervention literature.

Each of these parameters-processes-phenomena separately, and in interactive combinations, are heavily weighted, "loaded", and, perhaps, even overloaded, with many actual, as well as potential, meanings! Repetition, which leads to considering them and to utilizable learning, may be necessary.

Figure 2.14.1: Overload

Given that the process of learning, integrating that which is learned, and using what was learned effectively, has been well documented, common sense—which is not too common—suggests that it takes sufficient time[7] to learn, or to relearn, an action, a behavior, a life style, an attitude…if "success" is to be at all feasible…however "success may be interpreted. Ask any coach as s/he prepares a new team for a new season of challenges which involve unlearning, learning, pacing, trying, not doing "it right", etc. The Buddhist saying: "*Fall down seven times, get up eight times is the road to perfection*" beautifully describes a learning process. This "reinterpretation" in meaning of "lapse" and "relapse" doesn't change the "learning" aspects. If there is any merit to the possibility that lapse and/or relapse equal(s) learning [(re)lapse = learning] under certain conditions, then it becomes incumbent upon us to begin to explore what processes facilitate learning from these phenomena, and what are the conditions which can, and do, make this possible, as well as those which interfere with, and/or prevent, such needed learning. And in this exploration we must be careful not to create or remain with "too-early closure", where relapse is equated with badness (relapse = bad)!

A caveat is necessary at this point. One could easily invest time and energy into "lapsing", into considering whether or not the pathological Substance Use(r) Diseases:

- are somehow construed as different from other diseases, without their necessarily being different;
- should necessarily be related to as learning deficiencies of some kind that can be "overcome" by learning paradigms;
- are construed as:
  - — psychological/psychiatric "impairments" which need to be "repaired", if at all possible, and/or
  - — "toxic environmental" outcomes to be reconstructed (through urban planning interventions [?!]).

Figure 2.14.2: "Drug Treatment" and "Alcohol Treatment"

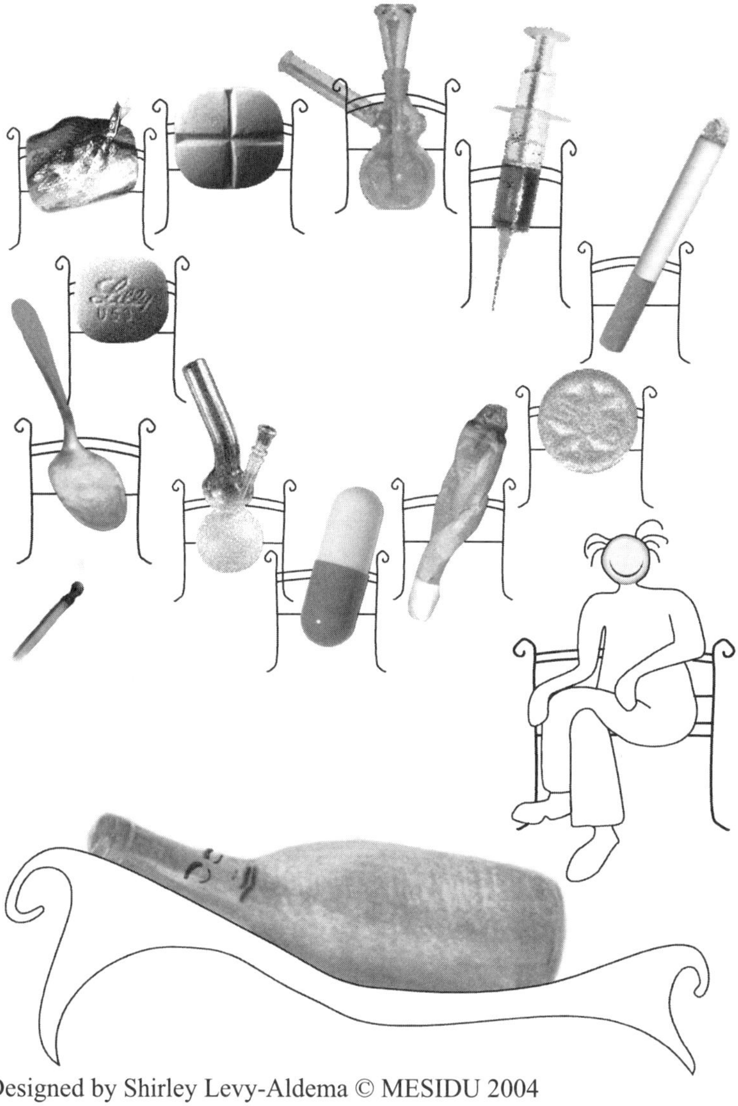

Note: Designed by Shirley Levy-Aldema © MESIDU 2004

The ethical issue being explored does not relate to etiology. It relates to the implications of where "drug users" are being treated, to the availability of necessary, appropriate, quality treatment, and to treatment accessibility, including treatment slots and access[8] to treatment (and to less-than-beneficent treatment policies), in the "normed" havens for health.

Do THEY, after all, or don't THEY, make it possible for US (not to generalize, stereotype and "homogenize", just some of us) to feel a sense of beneficence,[9] of having made the correct SUD diagnosis in the first place. Holding our diagnostic pathologizing abilities, powers and cleverness in abeyance, the issue is not that the substance users' misfortunes are the occasion for our feelings of beneficence, but rather the built-in beneficence which can, and indeed all-too-often does, come about from actually treating the substance user.[10] If THEY were but able to successfully overcome OUR treatment-access barriers. Our initial SUD diagnosis—even if it is followed by THEIR chronic relapsing—can serve to confirm OUR diagnostic ability. THEY lapsed/relapsed as predicted; WE are good diagnosticians. THEY, once again, on the other hand, abstained and/or reduced selected "harms", risk-taking behaviors, etc. And WE are good therapists. WE come out of SUD treatment smelling like a rose—or any other flower that you, the reader, choose. As for THEM…

Consider:

- More often than not, a methadone[11] maintained (MMT) drug user, who is not often considered to be or related to as being a real "normed" patient[12]—whose urine is "dirty"—will have his methadone dose decreased, may even be totally detoxified from methadone, and, in a worst-of-ethical-scenarios world, s/he may be discharged from the program.[13]
- Do we act in the same way with a diabetic (a real genuinely sick human being) patient whose blood sugar level is "dirty"?
- Do we respond in the same manner—administrative discharge from treatment, which is not that rare in MMT—to a schizophrenic patient who has moved from a state of remission to one of active hallucinations? To make things even worse s/he may be speaking to a God. Who is not my God! Oh my God!!

You, the reader, can surely add your own examples of a chronic disease and consider what is generally done when the non-compliant patient (a real "normed" patient manifesting a real disease) raises and manifests his or her non-compliant complaints.

- Do we take back the heart, or parts of it, from those who have been privileged to be given an organ implant (which has not been somatically rejected), and who have relapsed to smoking; perhaps even to overeating—bordering on an "eating disorder" in a "Super Size Me" world (Spurlock 2005)?
- The micro → macro context-environment—which determines: FOR WHOM IS IT PERMITTED, FOR WHOM IS IT FORBIDDEN? as well as WHAT TO DO (treatment?) or not to do? with whom? how? where? when? and for how long?—would appear to rarely be considered in the SUD treatment literature.

Figure 2.14.3: Worlds for Adaptation-Coping-Acting-Reacting

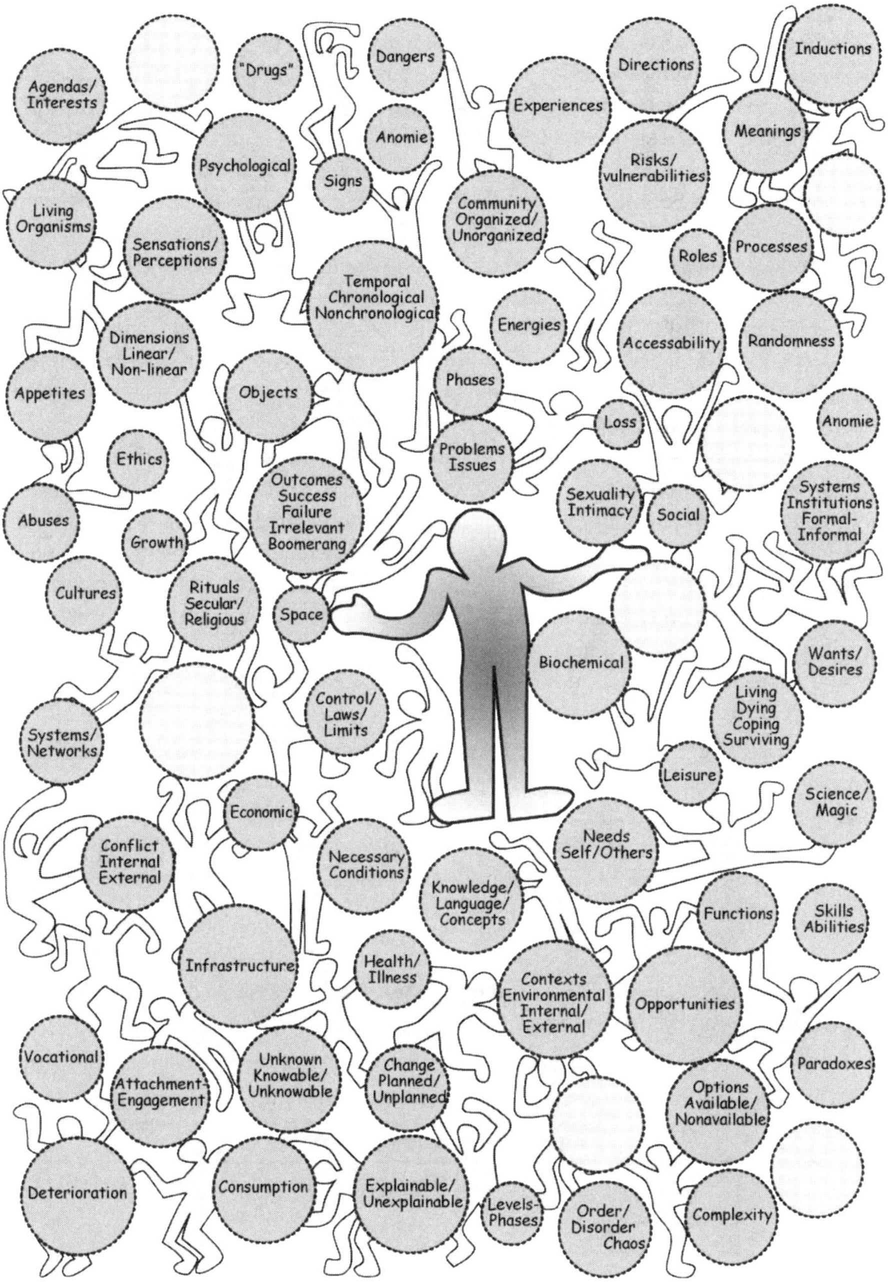

Note: Designed by Shirley Levy-Aldema © MESIDU 2004

Figure 2.14.3 schematically presents this author's views about the dynamic, very crowded, interacting, multi-dimensional contexts within which treatment can and does, or doesn't, operate. Rarely, if ever, do SUD treatment articles and/or books, conferences, etc., note this ever-present background, foreground, center-stage actual/potential FORCE as a critical constituent in, and for, SUD treatment—whatever its processes and outcomes. Consider the following example, rooted in the past. From 1919 to 1923, 43 clinics treated drug addicts (not a pejorative term but rather a description of pre-SUD-addicted Americans)[14] in various parts of the USA by supplying morphine (pre-MMT).[15] The last one, in Louisville, was closed because it was the last one! Based on such professional, scientific-driven organization policies one should never have opened the first one since none existed before!

Sixty years later, Riverside Hospital, the only facility in the USA at that time treating civilly committed drug user minors—situated in a former TB hospital on North Brothers Island, off the shores of the Bronx (borough, New York City), and in front of Rikers Island (a prison)[16]-- was closed after 10 years, for no empirically-based decisions, during a media strike which made protests ineffective. Was this an ethical issue? You, the reader, can decide.

The process of treatment, however defined, can, and does, include various basic phases as well as components. Figure 2.14.8 (in the Appendix) notes them, from the author's perspective, although you, the reader, may not agree with this schematic representation. Figures 2.14.8 to 2.14.10 are designed as schematic tools to help you to explore the actual/potential interactions and relationships between treatment process phases, goal selection criteria, actual/potential treatment foci,[17] initiators of treatment, and selected ethical issues. They are placed in the Appendix to this chapter as a resource for you to manipulate, and "play" with, in order to explore and to create options for ethically-driven substance user treatments.

Because to begin treatment one needs the **?**[18] to treat. The **?** could be micro in its dimensions or macro. Whatever its dimensions, be it actually observable or not observable, thinkable or unthinkable, knowable, unknown or even unknowable, engageable or not engageable, diagnosable or not diagnosable, it needs to exist for the planned, potential change process. SO… treatment could use some sort of an outreach component or program.

Table 2.14.3: An "Average" Treatment Model: Basic Stages and Components and Basic Necessary Components

Table 2.14.3a: An "Average" Treatment Model: Basic Stages and Components

A Planned Treatment Process						
Early case finding/ Outreach"	Initial Stages/ Pre-Engagement	Ongoing/ Engagement	Changes	Planned Cessation	Cessation	"After Care"

Table 2.14.3b: An "Average" Treatment Model: Basic Necessary Components

Stake-holders	Budget Focus	Policies Focus	Micro ↔ Macro Focus	"Treaters"	Diag-nostic System	Goals	Tech-niques	Site	Time	Services

Follow-up and/or monitoring may be an integral part of the planned treatment process.

Necessary resources/support systems (institutional-non-institutional, formal-informal) components for the treatment focus ("the patient") and systems and opportunities for the training of the "healer" (traditional models, professional models, mutual-help models, and "self-healer") are also needed.

There are, of course, individual treaters who choose to treat the pathologized SUD and who, in the process of developing, for example, a "therapeutic alliance", can, and do, over time, relate to the actual PERSON. But the actual, as well as potential, negative impact on drug users, as well as on a range of systems and ethical values of those who have chosen not to do so, is great. Consider, for example, administrators of many of the delivery of care and human services institutions who distance "drug users" from their doors, as well as many of the population-at-large who often have demonized THEM. That such (re)actions may be defense mechanisms doesn't change their dehumanizing outcomes.

- Do most, or many, substance user treatment programs practice such institutionalized "distancing"? I would like to believe that WE/they don't! Unfortunately I have witnessed this "distancing" practice in many parts of the world and in many models of "drug user" treatment. My own "principle of faith" is that a primary factor for this unfortunate reality is the continued misuse of the concept of motivation; a concept whose dimensions are less than clear and whose dimensions for measurement can be, and are, paradoxical, if not actually problematic. WE expect THEM to make the initial efforts to seek treatment in order to clearly demonstrate that it makes sense—indeed that it is justified—to offer them treatment.[19] If, and when, THEY actually do make an overt effort to seek treatment, THEY demonstrate motivation to US—albeit, whether such interpreted motivation is of the necessary quality, stability, temporality, potency, meaning, etc., are issues which merit investigation and concern.[20] If THEY don't make the overt effort they are not motivated.[21] This is a simplistic either/or world whose consequences can be far-reaching and life- and death-determining for the drug user, and ethically challenging for US. If the thesis which is being raised in this chapter—"the malfeasance of treating drug users in "non-normed" treatment sites—has any meaning then it is possible that a program which has an "outreach" component would be making it difficult, if not impossible, to assess the "drug user's" motivation to change as well as to enter treatment.[22]
- Do the various systems, at whatever levels of government authority (local, regional, national and now international in a globalizing European community), generally fund such components? No, they don't! That such efforts and programs for populations such as "drug users" are rarely funded is a reality. Why this continues is an issue meriting investigation; perhaps doctoral students

seeking a topic, human rights advocates seeking a cause, or a new documentary film-maker seeking to create a follow-up to the 2004 film "Super Size Me"[23] with the title "Institutionalizing Harm Production"...

Returning and moving on...if THEY wanted to change...really wanted to..., THEY would make the necessary effort (singular and not plural) and therein demonstrate THEIR motivation to do something (about their non-iatrogenic, self-induced condition). That THEY don't do so is indicative of... That THEY may, at times, indeed often DO (viz., the "natural recovery" literature),[24] in no way mitigates the "chronicity" of the posited "substance use disorder". Architecturally this may result in (revolving) doors for motivated SUDs, unmotivated SUDs, as well as for indecisive SUDs. It is possible that the "natural recovery" literature could be invoked in order to show that what those "suffering" from SUDs really lack is motivation. The self-treaters would exemplify highly motivated people. Various treatment regimens could therefore be characterized as circumventing this lack of or a state of impaired motivation of the SUD client or operating to prop up his or her motivation. Additional topics for MA and Ph. D. dissertations.

For some readers my referring to, perhaps even appealing to, the "natural recovery" literature may appear to border on being something of a mantra. After all don't many, if not most of us, recover[25] "naturally" from common colds? Is that a reason to not go to the doctor for something that may relieve its symptoms?

At issue is not whether the "natural recovery" path—it is not a movement—to a substance user's behavioral and lifestyle changes is better, more efficient, more cost effective, with lesser social costs, and resulting in quicker and/or longer-lasting results, etc., than tradition-based, professional-driven or mutual-help based treatment. These are topics which need to be explored and researched. The key issue is not competitiveness. Rather, the issue is: may a different (or the same) person, with SUD, at different times, points and transitions in the course of their life, their lifestyle, their functioning and adaptation, benefit, or not, from one of these 4 treatment "models"...at any given time or at a particular time. And treatment that is self-sought and self-initiated or which is, for example, jurisprudence-driven, needs to be sensitive, and able and willing to meet, at the very least, basic ethical dimensions. And this position not only refers to the treatment processes but to its agents as well.

Is there an ethical issue which merits consideration about not facilitating the opportunity, accessibility and availability for planned pro-social change[26] to come about? The traditional goals of traditional programs treating drug users—abstinence, employment and/or studying, and no (or diminished) criminality—are, at least in theory, measurable indices of the ("mother" of) meta-goal of pro-social, conventional functioning and adaptation: "normative" behavior as an outcome of "habilitation" for those people with SUDs who never had "the past" to return to for rehabilitation, and rehabilitation for those whose past could still be a basis for a better here-and-now as well as a healthier future. All of this is a very complex, multi-dimensional, dynamic reality.

Consider: Very few special SUD programs offer vocational guidance services, assessment, training, and/or contacts for employment. Recent changes in "disability regulations" for "drug users" in the USA also make it more difficult for drug users as they seek employment and try to change. (See the Benoit and Magura in Part 1, Chapter 8):

The *de facto* reality, generally, for needed "civilian intervention" is one of limited resources –human, conceptual, cognitive, temporal, sites, budgetary, etc.—when these limitations occur in peace-time and are not a side-effect of "national security", conflict, or war conditions. Health, social welfare, education—the areas of daily living—are not as prioritized as are the "merchants of death", or the "saviors of national security". This is the constant reality for substance user treatment as an effective, useable diagnostic/screening process which is critical for effective treatment planning and implementation, and its monitoring and (ongoing) assessment. In simplistic, if not over-simplistic terms, a viable diagnosis (WHAT DO I HAVE TO KNOW IN ORDER TO…) should make it possible for US to understand etiology, process and prognosis. When the diagnosis "delivers the goods" and, if needed and necessary treatment and other contextual and systemic resources are accessible and available, treatment planning and implementation is possible. Prognosis, in a non-linear sense, is not yet predictable.[27] The contemporary field of SUD treatment continues to operate as if there is no difference between a diagnosis and a label.[28] Both are taxonomies but their dimensions, uses, meanings and implications are considerably different. All diagnoses are labels but not all labels are diagnostic. For example, using the concept of "etiology" in the broadest way that you choose to, try to analyze a series of selected labels. What would, or could, each of these labels "tell" you? Probably not much.

In reality—whatever 'reality' can mean—the public, visible, "tagged," depersonalized, stigmatized, (persona non grata), demonized drug user who comes to the specialized "alcohol," "drug," or "dual diagnosis"[29] treatment program, has already been diagnosed before s/he was even met by a staff member and screened. In a variety of ways, we know that s/he, (the singular THEM) suffers from and/or manifests *dependence, abuse* and, in the past, an *addiction*, and that if s/he is not now nor ever was an active "user," possibly suffers from *co-dependence*.[30]

Most, if not all, SUD programs[31] are created with a limited range of treatment techniques which are likely to be culture- and *zeitgeist*-bound. This includes, more often than not in the West, a limited range of verbally-based techniques (individual and group therapies). The use of couple therapy, for example, is relatively rare. Family therapy is, most often in these specialized programs, little more than a term, a lecture, a book. Expressive therapies (art, movement, phototherapy, etc.) are to be found in SUD programs even less often than couple therapy. If the primary purpose of treating a "drug user" is the resolution of an array of resolvable human problems, various techniques will be needed in order to most effectively get the job done. Each treatment model and technique has theoretical-driven as well as evidence-based criteria to be used for its selection or when it is contra-indicated. For example, the power of "group problem solving" is not part of individual therapies. Limiting the types of available and accessible techniques can limit achieving the selected treatment goals. When this takes place due to institutionalized constraints rather than as the *de facto* reality of limited resources for every one, malfeasance may be raising its ugly head again.

Once again, if the screening-intake process doesn't make it possible for the treatment planner to realistically plan—even given that the SUD diagnosis is and will be an active 'given' –, then "treatment matching" remains no more than a Code word to be used at conferences. In this process WE offer THEM what we have, and not necessarily what THEY may (or even actually do) need treatment-wise. In this traditional distorted, institutionalized, "non-therapeutic alliance"-prone, SUD treatment process in a "non-normed" treatment site, WE help THEM to become a (role induction) pathologized-driven less-than-"real patient."[32, 33]

What are the ethical implications of continuing to publicly fund separate and unequal treatment programs for persons manifesting a SUD whom WE have sentenced to a life of chronic lapses and relapses[34] even though it is known that many of THEM change their life styles and behaviors into being pro-social fellow citizens in spite of US? And if all of this isn't 'bad enuf'[35] consider the implications of how many of the staff treating THEM are aware of, have read, and have learned something for their work from the "natural recovery" literature?[36]

In addition, in this pilgrimage of non-parity in the process of planned SUD treatment praxis (to be read out loud for some type of an effect), the tradition-driven, preselected goals have yet to be empirically demonstrated—and not as "principles of faith" or by being stakeholder agenda-driven—as being achievable as well as maintainable by the use of the limited number of techniques which continue to be used. It is almost ironic, if not ethically questionable, that OUR historico-political "War on Drugs" coexists with so few tools for THEIR change in its armamentarium![37] Are we going to TREAT or are we going to treat? This is not a graphic gimmick but rather my attempt at visualizing an important concept. The tools of war and the staffs for battle are so much greater in their types, numbers, potency, availability, accessibility and uses [but not necessarily effectiveness] than are the techniques used for SUD treatment.[38] Does this relate only to drug use(r) intervention? Of course not! This chapter is, however, not about needed interventions to combat poverty, conflicts, illiteracy, inadequate levels and quality of health, mass migration, or various "side effects" of globalization. It is about the unnecessary, built-in violating of a selected part of a population of substance users—wherever—who are visibly tagged, stereotyped… (by now you can fill in the rest of the sentence) in terms of accessible, appropriate, quality treatment (given *de facto* resource realities) in "normed" treatment sites.

An odd reality has continued to exist with regard to substance use(r) treatment—its planning, implementation and assessment. The dimensions of quality and appropriateness are rarely, if ever, reported in peer-reviewed journals or presented at local → international meetings, conferences, symposia, from the level of 'poster sessions' to the Plenary presentation. Does this necessarily signify that these two processes, phenomena and values, etc., are indeed absent from SUD treatment? It is difficult to know. Nevertheless, it is useful to consider that the volume edited by Dr. Stephen Magura (2000)[39] at the turn of this millennium is one of the few publications exploring this topic in the SUD treatment literature…at least in English. Does this, can this, raise ethical issues? Some hackles perhaps?

Perhaps! If the quality and appropriateness of treatment is unknown;

- re-treatment staff,
- re-treatment techniques,
- re-treatment sites,
- re-treatment policies,
- re-temporal parameters of the process/program,

- re-the formal-informal, institutional-non-institutional support/resource systems that are needed to facilitate planned change, and

IF such a reality continues for decades—and is likely to continue—could any of this be less than ethical?

Moving from the treatment process to the schema presented in Figure 2.14.2, I will now focus on the major issue which undergirds the thesis: SUD treatment—treating the visible, 'tagged' THEM, as has been done for many decades—is, in its very essence, unethical.

WE treat a 'homogenized', stereotyped, stigmatized, marginalized, depersonalized THEM in specialized programs away from the "NORMED", mainstream of treating a range of acute ↔ chronic, infectious ↔ non-infectious, good prognostic ↔ lethal prognostic ailments-conditions-diseases-pathologies-symptoms-preventable states. And we do this with the available, empirical-based knowledge that we have

- using the same techniques and models that are available and accessible for both healthy, and less than healthy,[40] "users", and non-users,
- employing the same disciplines—professionals as well as volunteers.[41]

SO...why do we continue to "treat" THEM separately, particularly given the Brown vs. Board of Education, 1954, Landmark Supreme Court Decision that ended educational racial segregation of students in racially separate schools in the US because separate = UNEQUAL?

One can and should ask: "*Is every separation intrinsically a manifestation of inequality?*" Not necessarily! Separation, even isolation, which are necessary for effective, needed treatment would, and should, be warranted and made possible given the necessary available and accessible resources. Treating contagious disease in isolation units is one such example in regards to the infectious patient, other patients, the staff, visitors, etc. Substance use is neither infectious nor contagious, in a medical model sense, -you, she, he, I, we, don't "catch" IT- notwithstanding the use and misuse of such loaded metaphors as "drug epidemics". And if and whether or not the direct as well as indirect consequences of substance use will "catch up" with each and every user is complex and unpredictable.

It is being posited that, after many years of treating a heterogeneous population of "drug users", it is incumbbent upon the "field", as well as on the relevant policymakers, to demonstrate, in a generalizable, evidence-based manner, the beneficence of such an institutionalized, separation-driven treatment for the drug user, non-users, staffs, communities-at-large, and all other relevant individual and systemic constituents. It is not incumbent upon those who challenge such a discriminatory practice to "prove" (with or without reasonable doubt) the inherent malfeasance of this ongoing, traditional, SUD treatment system. Why? Because to:

- "stereotype",
- to "demonize",
- to "depersonalize" and
- "homogenize";
- to offer specialized treatment which is non-existent,
- which all-too-often is lesser in parity,

- quality and appropriateness
- than what is made available and
- accessible
- in mainstream,
- "normed" treatment sites,
- to,
- with, and
- for non-substance users,
- is inherently wrong!
- It is an ethical "no-no"!

Is this accusation unfair? It's as unfair as the ongoing lack of parity in treatment opportunities, accessibility and availability for the large range of disadvantaged, disempowered, marginalized substance users, when compared to OUR treatment in OUR "normed" institutions.

There are issues that need to be separated in order to better explore and understand their dimensions and implications. For example, when one compares psychotherapeutic treatment, generally, with the treatment of "physical" ailments, there often is a great disparity. Is this justified? Of course not, from an ethical perspective. Being aware of, and acknowledging, this *de facto* reality doesn't make it "right", nor does it imply agreement with such a state of affairs. Would SUD treatment be significantly enhanced by bringing it under the umbrella of traditional psychotherapeutic treatment? Perhaps it would. Perhaps it wouldn't. A reality is that this remains an ongoing issue among a range of stakeholders and treatment traditions.

The central issue is not to whom should SUD treatment belong. From an ethical perspective, among others, which you the reader can choose to consider, a key question and issue is: what frame of reference will make it possible for meeting the "meetable" intervention needs of a substance user given his/her strengths and limitations, at given points in time, within a *de facto* institutional-support system reality, within a given society-at-large? A (a "mother" of questions) meta-question. The underlying assumption being posited in this chapter is that, being a substance user, however defined, is not, by definition, a pathological state-condition necessitating treatment.[42]

Another reality is that the mental health field, by and large, chose to remove itself from treating THEM. Substance users who sought treatment for a myriad of reasons didn't separate themselves or file for "divorce" from loving, caring, available, accessible mental health workers representing a range of disciplines.

It is a truism that in order to learn about what we are doing from ITS processes and outcomes, and in order to make "evidence-based" changes, there is the need to evaluate. This relatively long brief is not the appropriate forum for exploring institutionalized, mostly publicly-funded, substance use(r) research. Ongoing, real-time-based, updated tomes would be appropriate. What shall be focused on are five limited dimensions:

- Who are the traditional foci?
- What is the traditional focus?
- In the choice between abstinence-driven SUD treatment models and harm-reduction-based models are the latter 'more ethical' than the former?

- What is the actual/potential nexus between the dimensions of substance use (linear-non-linear) and the treatment of the "drug users" as an ethical issue?
- Are the drug user treatment research results generally used?[43]

The Traditional Focus: WHO?

Just as in traditional SUD treatment, the identified patient (IP) is an active, or about to "fall", "substance user"/drug user and not a range of "significant others" who can, and do, affect his or her seeking and entering treatment, becoming therapeutically engaged, making initial and ongoing pro-social changes, participating in planned treatment cessation, so too, in SUD treatment assessment, it is the same—therapeutically engaged or not engaged IP—who is, by and large, the data source, and not a range, of, equally important treatment constituents.[44] Acknowledging that s/he is programmed to lapse/relapse (genetically-determined, reinforcement-wise, personality-pathology-driven, environmentally-based, etc.), is there nothing to learn from or about:

- the SUD therapist,
- the specialized SUD treatment program (sites and their environmental dimensions,[45] policies, etc.),
- the social networks[46] of users and non-users in which the "drug user" is actively involved in various roles and activities and/or with which he or she identifies, the communities in which each of these individuals and systems (mal-)adapt, (mal-)function, and operate.

It is for you, the reader, to consider whether the issue of the actual, as well as viable and potential, foci for SUD treatment assessment are indeed relevant, or perhaps irrelevant, to the treatment processes and outcomes…to these "drug" interventions. Why? If for no other reason than the reality is that YOU, ME, US [I, WE] are footing the bill for the treatment, and for the consequences of innapropriate treatment and other interventions, as well as for the lack of treatment.

The Traditional Focus: WHAT?

Traditionally WE focus on processes, behaviors, etc., that are associated with the traditional limited goals associated with the drug user IP—abstinence, employment and/or formal studies and (diminished → no) criminality indices.

We have the choice, if we choose to, of:

- focusing on areas of daily (pro-social) functioning and adaptation,
- assessing their levels and qualities and then,
- creating a treatment plan,
- which sets goals (long-, as well as short-term ones),
- with the drug user (as a partner for change), or
- for the drug user (as a compliant patient-client),
- in each area,
- with the help of empirically-based criteria,
- and if the *de facto* reality permits,

- "matched" with
- appropriate techniques,
- time,
- policies,
- etc.
- which are monitored
- in order to permit making changes when needed.

Figure 2.14.4: An AA meeting room in a prison-wing-chairs surrounding the gas chamber.

Our training, professional induction, cultural *zeitgeist*, and stakeholder agendas all-too-often interfere with our even considering the "user's" adaptational strengths, skills, abilities and energy levels as s/he somehow "makes it" as a "user"…for shorter and longer periods of time; even for a life-time—which could also be shorter or longer in terms of the pharmacological consequences of drug use, the effects of what the "non-quality-control" drugs are mixed with, style of life effects and side-effects, as well as other considerations. If we were stimulated by this challenge and were to accept it, we could, for example, ponder the "problem"[47] of viable options for "conventionalizing" burglary skills. If the drug user burglar is really skilled, could s/he not be "rehabilitated" into working as a pro-social locksmith? Absurd! Perhaps? Is this any more absurd, and perhaps any more ethically questionable, than continuing to treat anticipated and predicted SUD treatment "failures", when failure may be built into the treatment system because of both what is done, as well as not done?

Consider, for example, the difference between "dropping out" of SUD treatment and a "failure of treatment fit".[48] The former is obviously the fault of the drug user-patient-client; with the program deciding the number of "no-shows" necessary to be listed and responded to as a "dropped out". A "failure of treatment fit" has to do, in various ways, with the program and those "forces" that are responsible for the program and its policies, etc.

At times we also focus on parameters of the treatment process—"dropping out," "therapeutic *engagement*", "*compliance*", etc. For how long does the PDSU (Pathologized, Disordered, Substance User) remain in treatment, become "engaged" as well as being a compliant patient? These are important questions and issues. So important that one should not take for granted what the answers might be concerning the therapist … whatever his or her experience, ideology, expertise, knowledge, etc. In very simplistic terms:

- Does the SUD therapist/change agent comply with the therapeutic "demands" of a planned treatment program, and even with what has been changed during the process, in the best way that s/he is capable of doing, within the context of the *de facto* program-community reality?;
- To what extent is the SUD therapist "therapeutically engaged" and how is this gauged?
- And what are the parameters of a SUD treatment program "dropping out",[49] how often does this occur, and who really cares?

Whether or not these issues are indeed the current 'norm' in SUD treatment has rarely been adequately assessed, whereas the "user's" engagement and compliance continue to be treatment issues deserving of publicly funded research.

SUD Treatment Ideology and Harm Reduction/ Harm Production

Harm reduction (HR) is the latest SUD treatment model in the West. It is many things to its proponents as well as to its detractors. And there are individual and systemic stakeholders on both sides of the DIVIDE. And a DIVIDE it is indeed!

HR is, among other considerations:

- an ideology and
- a delivery of service system.

HR supplies:

- a range of human needs,
- syringes,
- needles,
- condoms,
- containers,
- information,
- hot showers,
- a brief "time out"
- a respite from the day-to-day hustle and hassle,

- a cup of coffee,
- a meal,
- a smile, and
- an interaction with the program staff professionals
- or volunteers,
- an opportunity to continue being an active drug user but using drugs in a less harmful and/or healthier way;
- an opportunity to give of oneself in a new role as a trained "public health agent" (PHA)[50]
- an opportunity for volunteers and communities to show and to express their concern for an "other" "in need",
- an opportunity for individual and systemic stakeholders to play power games in a new arena.

This is a creative variation of a secondary exchange program (SEP).

Having noted what I have noted about HR, a caveat is also necessary. A potential ethical problem exists which may not have been adequately considered. Harm reduction programs generally, and needle exchange programs more specifically, hopefully reached marginalized individuals and subpopulations who—for a variety of reasons, conditions, forces, having been, or are, participating in being marginalized—have all-too-often not been engaged by existing systems of delivery of services and their communities. This would seem to be considered a success for a program. Read on.

Under conditions in which harm reduction-driven programs, including needle exchange programs (NEPs)/secondary needle exchange programs (SNEPs) deliver their needed services to "users" who continue not to get to know what the system at-large has to offer and which they may need:

- do not learn how to use what is available, and
- do not use "IT"

WE inadvertently may be co-opted into switching roles from change agents promoting client/ patient/person autonomy to functioning as social control agents maintaining the status quo. If this is not to be a fictional scenario for a D-grade film, book, play, etc., this ethically-loaded issue merits consideration. The SUD treatment literature has yet to take up the cooptation challenge.[51]

Consider that:

When WE make it possible for THEM not to use available traditional, "normed" services which could facilitate increased levels of health, functioning, adaptation and autonomy,

WE make it possible for this sub-group of THEMs to live less autonomously. And if, and when, this posited process exists,

WE may, and often do, become co-opted agents of non-change, and, at times, even of regressive changes.

The cyberneticist Heinz Von Foerster posited that there are two types of questions: illegitimate questions and legitimate questions.[52] An illegitimate question is one for which the answer is known. *Legitimate questions* are those for which the answer is not known, may not be knowable, but which, if considered, may stimulate needed efforts.

Such new efforts could include the creation of new concepts, tools, paradigms, etc. The *legitimate questions* which have concerned me for years are:

- whether or not making traditional, "normed" treatment sites available and accessible for treatable substance users would result in more effective, ethically-driven treatment processes and outcomes, and
- what effects would such a change have upon the treatment staff, "significant others, the program, other needed institutional support and resource systems, as well as communities-at-large?

The history of substance use and (re)actions for and against can be divided into the following broad reaction categories by individuals as well as systems:

- "normative" use of more and more psychoactive naturally-grown as well as produced substances,
- morality-driven actions and reactions[53] with its moral entrepreneurs,
- criminalization of selected substances, uses, equipment for use, and users,
- pathologizing" of selected users and uses, and
- most recently, a harm reduction response.

And, over time, more and more people have used, and are using, a broad range of illicit "drugs" along with licit ones such as alcohol, caffeine, nicotine, and "junk foods". Is it possible that the questions which have been asked, to date, have not resulted in the needed intervention planning, implementation and assessment? It is reasonable to conclude that much of the SUD treatment literature appears to be based on—influenced and driven by—illegitimate questions.

Would it be useful to create a Forum which is designed to explore Legitimate Questions for Legitimate Substance Use Intervention?

Who would fund exploring such critically needed legitimate questions in our real world?

The Dimensions of Substance Use and its Treatment as Sources of Ethical Issues

The need to move from the abstract-theoretical to the applied—the actual living "landscapes" of substance use, users and the range of treatment interventions—presents yet an additional ethical challenge, if not a moral morass. SUD treatment planning and implementation has, to date, been structured as, and considered to be, a linear, 'cause and effect' phenomenon by those mandated to do it and those responsible for its policy and budgetary underpinnings. Posited impairments of various types and levels of seriousness (genetic, personality, learning, environmental, etc.),[54] under conditions of "at-risk", "vulnerability", a lack of adequate-sufficient-suitable "protective factors" → substance use; along, all-too-often, with other "risky" behaviors. TREATMENT, currently, is the linear, "magic bullet" response, notwithstanding all of the anticipated prognostic limitations associated with a "substance use disorder".

This scenario overlooks the ongoing reality—noted earlier, pages back—that with the advent, decades ago, of artificial science and its theoretical underpinnings (chaos, complexity, uncertainty and the more recent network theories), it is now posited that much of human behavior is non-linear, complex, dynamic, multi-dimensional, level/phase structured, law-driven and bounded (by culture, time, place, age, gender, ethnicity, etc.). Substance use, of any type and however it is defined and categorized, would be such a behavior/process. From such a perspective, how could its dimensions be linear and/or uni-dimensional?

Notwithstanding this non-linear, empirical-based reality, "drug use" and "drug user" treatment research continue to be designed as linear paradigms for data collection, and the collected data continue to be analyzed using linear tools. In very simplistic terms there are two important issues to consider and which are derived from this:

(1) Using linear models/tools to study non-linear processes/phenomena can, and does, result in misleading conclusions. If and when this is allowed to occur it can and does result in creating, selecting and using inappropriate treatment intervention techniques and models;

(2) In a non-linear model, the concepts prediction and control (having an effect on) have different meanings and dimensions than they do in the more traditional linear 'cause and effect' paradigms.[55] What is the meaning of all of this ethics-wise? The terms linear and non-linear can easily be just a semantic issue; a result of attached letters. This linear-non-linear distinction is not a semantic issue for SUD treatment.

Does the following photograph, for example, taken in a "conflict zone" (a nice euphemism when one considers the never ending "War(s) on Drugs"), graphically "catch" a linear or a non-linear process?

Figure 2.14.5: Linear or non-linear reality?

- What is "cause" and what is "effect"?
- Who are the "actors" (the visible ones?) as well as those not present, but who are surely vital "others"?
- What is the outcome (single → plural → even more than "some" plural; immediate –long term) and for whom?
- Can there be another outcome?

- If there could be, under what necessary critical endogenous as well as exogenous conditions?
- How would YOU choose to "Photo- Shop" this visual virtual reality?
- WHO CARES?

When SUD treatment is considered to be—and is related to as being—a linear process [pre-screened THEM; pre-"goaled" (as in objective and not jail) plans; limited treatment time and techniques used and limiting policies; potentially co-opted control agents as change agent therapists], the realities of its inherent complexities, multi-dimensionality, phase-level structuring, dynamics and boundedness can be, and all-too-often are, minimized, or even not considered at all, in the treatment planning, implementation and ongoing as well as final assessment.

The consequent ethical issue can be/is the creation and/or maintenance of harm(s) rather than beneficence for the:

- substance user-sometimes adjudicated offender-patient,
- his/her "significant" others,
- therapist and,
- his/her program,
- communities-at-large, and a
- wasting of limited human and other resources.

Whether treating "drug users", of whatever types, in separated, "non-normed", specialized substance user disorders programs exacerbates linear-based rather than non-linear-based treatment paradigms, is a topic meriting investigation. Hopefully some readers of this chapter will be challenged and stimulated to do so. The newer transdisciplinary paradigms may even be the preferred choice for such treatment research.[56]

In summary, the dimensions of substance use as a process and its current treatment (linear and non-linear paradigms) is being raised as being yet another potential ethical issue which merits exploration by:

- the "insiders", in the SUD treatment field,
- the policy making stakeholders, and
- the "outsiders"-US- for what is happening as WE oscillate and engage, or don't, as "social problem" solvers.

Treatment Assessment Results and the 'Transfer of Technology' Syndrome

It is an ongoing phenomenon that substance use(r) treatment researchers and other intervention-treatment-change agents and agencies continue to be publicly funded, can, and do, document important generalizable findings, and report them through a range of public and professional media and forums. And, all too often, these generalizable findings, or pilot study outcomes from which researchable hypotheses can be developed, are *not used* as the broader intervention field continues with its institutionalized traditions[57] while being aware of the findings or 'protecting itself' from them. With sufficient reporting, the right "connections" and a viable research design, the researchers, and others, can be, and generally are, re-funded. This can, and does, limit the burden of the Welfare system[58] for researchers, if not for the object of their research—the stereotyped, manipulative "drug user." This process of moving from scientifically-derived data, to analyzed information, on to knowledge and then perhaps even to the wise use of what we now know can, and does, not come about, all too often, in the stakeholder-driven arena of SUD treatment. The fact that this gap is found in many fields, not just that of drug user treatment, does not minimize the contribution which such a reality makes to minimizing the potential beneficence of quality-driven, "new" known treatment models and techniques being made available and accessible, hopefully using empirically-based criteria in the indicated/contra-indicated selection process.

After all, real researchers are not ethically obligated to be concerned about, or to consider, whether their publicly-funded research and its outcomes of generalizable findings will be applied or if they may have a role in moving potential treatment beneficence from the laboratory to real life 'out there'! Again, is this peculiar to SUD research? Of course not! Think of educational research, for example. Why does this process happen again and again? This chapter is not designed to analyze *who* the stakeholders are, what are their sources of power, and what has led to the creation and maintenance of a relatively new system of a plethora of substance use intervention-initiated empires (NIDA, NIAAA, etc.), from local to regional, to national and international levels. And all of this is continuing, as more and more drugs are being used and more and more data and information are available and accessible.

It is possible that the use of a traditional mechanism, such as a Commission of Inquiry, mandated and adequately "resourced" in terms of budgets, staff, time, etc., would help the funding public to learn what is going on and why.

SO, are we treating the "user", his/her "disease" (SUD), both, or even needed "significant others"—individuals as well as communities?

Are we creating harm as we hasten to heal?

Can we "treat" THE DISEASE and not the PERSON? Of course we can. And of course we do… as we continue to "pathologize", depersonalize and "homogenize" real PEOPLE!

Can we "Greek-chorus-like" chant the 'evidence-based' ballad, but not use what we know which is useable, and repeat and repeat and repeat this process? Of course we can. And, of course, we do!

Research welfarism continues to be institutionalized and 'normative'. The above questions can obviously be the ingredients of simply more rhetoric rather than being a stimulus and an opportunity for needed explanations, clarifications and understandings.

SO…

- What makes it possible for all of the aforementioned to continue to happen?
- What are the critical necessary conditions that make it possible for funding agencies such as NIDA, NIAAA, the European Community and large and important foundations not to include legitimate questions and potential and critical foci for assessment as basic criteria in research proposals submitted to them?
- Do SUD treatment researchers consider, as the research is being designed, that generalizable findings are likely, if not more than likely, not to be used?
- Who are the individual and systemic stakeholders in this SUD treatment assessment "research happening," what are their agendas, and what are their sources of power?

Does this ongoing reality portend ethical dilemmas? And if it does, for whom...for you, for THEM, for US?

Conclusion

I could obviously go on...point by point using Figure 2.14.7a and 2.14.7b as well as introducing Figures 2.14.8 and 2.14.9. Figure 2.14.7a is designed as a visual conceptualizing tool to explore the sources of potential/actual ethical issues that have been, and currently are, associated with SUD treatment in the interaction between initiators of treatment, the treatment process and selected treatment foci. The assumption is being made (theory-based, empirically-based, stakeholder agenda-driven, "principle of faith"-based, etc.) that each type of initiator (or preventor) of treatment—each with its own traditions, mandates, agendas, goals, policies, etc.—will result in a unique range of "processes" and "outcomes." That such a sound assumption is generally not the SUD treatment reality can, and does, raise various ethical issues. Triangulating a selected point in each "leg" of Figure 2.14.7a permits one to begin to consider actual, as well as potential, ethical issues and problems which can, and do, arise in the interactions between models of care, traditional ethical concerns, and substance use(r) disorder treatment process factors.

But it really isn't necessary to continue this brief's analysis.

By this point in this long brief, it is possible that I have either lost you, irritated you, bored you, confused you, engaged you or whatever. I would hope that my style is not experienced as being patronizing. If apologies are called for, on my part, then I apologize for whatever harm I may be responsible. Of the various issues that could result, change-wise, from what has been described, is/will agreeing or disagreeing with what has been raised, in order to facilitate greater treatment beneficence for THEM and reduce malfeasance, likely to come about? It is as unlikely to do so as, for example, for Picasso's famous painting Guernica ever to have stopped a bullet from being fired. Or a bomb from being dropped. Or an innocent from being tortured. Only speaking to ourselves, among ourselves—the ongoing *de facto* substance user treatment/intervention reality—is not likely to result in raising the quality, incidence and/or prevalence of ethically-driven treatment, is it?

Indeed I am left concluding[59] with what I began: Drug Users Can't be Treated—People Can Be! Under sufficiently well-known internal and external conditions. One of the critical necessary conditions is being able and willing to see the PERSON and not the "substance use disorder" (SUD).

I am positing that if drug users—who represent a documented heterogeneous population of people who both differ from as well as are similar to US in many ways—were related to as such rather than as pathologized SUDs :

- Our *raison d'être* for treating THEM would be different from what it currently is. The use of illicit substances and misuse of licit ones would be less likely to be responded to, almost automatically, by "treatment"—be it an appropriate, quality-based, autonomy-driven model, or an inappropriate "control"-driven model.
- The information which we gather in "our need to know" would focus on documenting a broad range of actual, as well as potential, strengths of the targeted and/or self-identified PERSON and his/her networks and systems, and not

focus, primarily, as we continue to do, on pathologies and impairments—on the indices of what is wrong.

- The individual substance user, as a PERSON, would be inducted into a change-driven, participatory, partnership, 'pilgrimage' and not trained as, and reinforced into becoming, a compliant, identified and identifiable "patient" (IP) within a traditional medical-model hiearchial system in which, ironically, many physicians choose not to treat the "drug user". This is an ongoing system which continues to anticipate failure, for and by THEM, and not for the "therapist", the program, the community, the policy, the policymakers and other individual and systemic constituents of SUD treatment.

And all of this usually takes place away from US.

Even though the point that I am making, perhaps endlessly, is noted in such generalities that it invites the response of it being little more than rhetorical flourishes, do consider it. You don't have to agree with it. Just as Godlaski has reminded us in Chapter 10 in this volume that the plural of anecdote is not evidence, so too, the mantra-like repetition of homogenized, depersonalized, demonized, dehumanized, and pathologized does not make this so.[60]

So…consider and "interact" with Table 2.14.7a, which is designed to explore people's views, attitudes, opinions, believed in "facts", etc.—including yours—about the relationship(s) between:

- types of and levels of treatment outcomes, prognosis,
- types of "diseases", including, obviously "substance use disorder", and their posited imputed responsibility, and
- attached stigma.

Table 2.14.4a: Types of Disease by Treatment Prognosis, Imputed Responsibility and Stigma

Prognosis	Responsible		Not Responsible	
curable	No stigma	Stigma	No stigma	Stigma
improvable but not curable				
incurable and unimprovable				

As noted earlier, and summarized in Table 2.14.1, there are many disease models, not just one. Each has its own critical definitions, criteria, goals and agendas, constituencies, indicated and contra-indicated techniques and services, "healers" and change agents, preferred sites for intervention, temporal parameters, and stake holders.

Create your own list of "diseases" and place your choices in their "correct" places, from your perspective.

Table 2.14.4b: Types of Disease by Treatment Prognosis, Imputed Responsibility and Stigma

Prognosis	Responsible		Not Responsible	
	No stigma	Stigma	No stigma	Stigma
curable	parking violation	obesity	tuberculosis	leprosy
improvable but not curable	tax violation	burglary	Crippling condition	Manic depression
incurable and unimprovable	Professional mercenary	drug misuse	dwarfism	schizophrenia

Where would you place the non-smoking, non-alcoholic drinker, non-caffeinated, vegetarian, type A personality, 14- hour a day, hi-tech employed, heterosexual, safe-sex practicing, personally trained gym-goer, who is physically healthy, spiritually fulfilled and a long-weekend "retreat" participant?

As you review, and, it is to be hoped, "interact" with, Table 2.14.7b, please consider that, in all likelihood, if the past is any type of predictor of the future, additional "disease models" will be created as circumstances and society "demand" them, or find a need for them. After all, SUD is a relatively new disease!

Returning to Table 2.14.7a, where would you place:

- a "generalized" drug user,
- a specific type,
- a type of alcohol user as well as
- an alcohol "misuser" from the various existing types, and/or
- a chain smoker, MacDonald's' "Super Size Me", "Pepsi generation" coffee guzzler, who has never used "drugs"?

Consider permitting yourself an 'abstentious' or 'non-abstentious' "time-out" in which to explore this exercise and then determine if the posited homogenizing, depersonalizing, demonizing, dehumanizing, and pathologizing processes are simply this author's inflammatory, but unhelpful, rhetoric and overgeneralization, or a reality that makes it possible for the continued unethical treatment of THEM.

And as you do, look at, consider, and respond to the rabbit-duck figure, and its potential relevance to what has been raised and posited in this chapter.

WHAT DO YOU SEE?

Figure 2.14.6: The rabbit duck figure

Source: Jastrow, J. (1899 Readers interested in ambiguous [or reversible, or bi-stable] figures, or illusions are referred to: http://ist-socrates.berkeley.edu/~kihlstrm/Jastrow-Duck.htm)

DO YOU SEE WHAT I SEE?

CAN WE LOOK TOGETHER?

Unresolved Issues?

At first blush there seems to be a tension (or perhaps a paradox) between the positions presented in this chapter. On the one hand you, the reader, are being asked to consider that the ongoing stigmatizing, stereotyping, homogenizing and dehumanizing of a group of heterogeneous PEOPLE who *also use* illicit drugs as well as misuse licit ones results in malfeasance for THEM as well as for many other individuals and systems. It is posited that "treating" them like everyone else (i.e. not in separate "non-normed" facilities, accepting their "lapses" and "relapses" as an integral part of change, growth and development, etc.) would hopefully help to "normalize" SUDs; a beneficent process and end result. On the other hand, the very classification of "drug use" as a "substance use disorder"—a pathologized, chronic impairment with a possibility for intermittent episodes of abstentious "recovery" requires, and, perhaps, even "demands" treatment- is being challenged. That which we call "drug use", in its ordinary day-to-day sense, and SUD, in its medicalized version, is not a "normed" disease but rather an unacceptable "social disease".

- SUD's hosts -THEM- (and from the perspective of some people its "carriers") are to be—and are indeed—marginalized and disempowered. All of THEM? No! As a generalization which you, the reader, can challenge, just those who do not have the status, power and connections to protect[61] themselves from the processes and consequences of public (stereotype) and stigmatizing. As well as those for whom the likelihood of achieving health and treatment parity will remain an open question in a world preferring too early closure for demanding issues, questions and problems.
- THEY are often regarded as being sources and causes of "bad".

What is the problem? If they are sick aren't THEY entitled to be treated?

And if THEY are not sick, then they are not. But by definition, label and diagnosis THEY are sick. Most people would contend that normal, healthy people, etc., etc., etc., do not do what THEY do. Don't live the way that THEY live. Normal healthy people learn from experience…unlike THEM. Not quite! Look around. Do you see what is there to be perceived? Look again.

This chapter is not challenging the definition(s) of disease or of health. Rather, what is being challenged is whether the ongoing consequences of disease models are unchangeable for the "tagged", the "taggers" as well as the micro-macro landscape in which beneficent as well as malfeasant treatment (processes, availability and accessibility) should not have an equal opportunity to co-exist. The historical reality that social diseases are not a post-modern creation or a "happening" and are likely to continue under conditions of institutionalized power imbalances does not mitigate that "diseasing" drug users "socially" is and remains an ethical "no-no".

What this chapter is asking you, the reader, to consider is that the "drug user"—whoever s/he was, is and may become as a human being— should have the opportunity for making needed (pro-social[62] ?) changes in his/her life given the *de facto* cultural-place-historical time realities in spite of a "substance use disorder" pseudo-diagnostic,[63] destructive social label.

If s/he is treated for a myriad of drug-use-related "normed" diseases—as well as for other diseases which are unrelated to drug use --, such treatment should be carried out where the rest of us 'good folk' are treated daily and hopefully at necessary levels of quality and appropriateness given the existing *de facto* relevant resource realities. Some reader may ask: Isn't this what generally happens? Doesn't a person suffering from a drug overdose or cirrhosis of the liver get treated in the same facilities as the rest of us? The reality is that known, "tagged" drug users may not be treated for medical and/or psychiatric diseases, social welfare conditions or for vocational (re)habilitation needs because their diagnosis serves as a barrier rather than being a red light signaling for needed attention. I have referred drug user patients to psychiatric services, who were suicidal, and who were "diagnosed" as "testing boundaries", were not treated and who committed suicide. How often does this happen? Does it really matter? Does such a question signify a condition of "ethical innumeracy"? The reporting in an article or a book, at a conference and through a poster session "that 47.3%" can be a useful way of distancing ourselves from our responsibilities towards and with a fellow human being –albeit their patient-client role and status-, a couple or a family whom WE are treating or not treating. In the landscape of drug user treatment, ethically-driven numbers are usefully limited to 100% or 0 %! Such a treatment culture should be of beneficence to everyone: to the treated, the treaters, their institutions, communities and to society-at-large. "Treatment" used as a control mechanism for "non-normed", "social diseases" are not beneficent to the treated, the treaters, their institutions, their communities and to society-at-large, even if the end result may be positive for some treatment constituents. Why? Because the actual and/or potential harm that was caused was, in all likelihood, not the only available option for achieving the same sought-after end-result had we and the "drug user" not remained trapped by our SUD *weltanschaung*.

We need to *not consider* that those whose behaviors, lifestyles, beliefs, and values we reject (for whatever our reasons), feel threatened by, feel helpless to respond and react to necessarily have a "disease".

There are those who might argue that "diseasing" THEM may entitle THEM to needed assistance which THEY could otherwise not receive. For example there was a time that people with "chronic fatigue syndrome", "post traumatic stress syndrome" or "carpel tunnel syndrome" could not receive access to medical benefits because what they had was not yet seen as being a disease. This type of illegitimate question (à la von Foerster) and point of view can serve to way lay us. This chapter explores:

- whether or not health and treatment parity—dimensions of beneficence- should be available and accessible to people whatever the model of their "disease" and whether such a disease is or can be "normed" or not, given the treatment resource *de facto* reality,
- whether the choices which WE have made until now for treating THEM are the best ones that WE can make given the various documented outcomes,
- whether other choices which are more beneficent-driven are feasible, and
- with what critical necessary endogenous and exogenous conditions?

Why? Because "diseasing" THEM does not, will not, and cannot lower the threat and/or sense of behavioral impotence which we experience. Because dehumanizing other PEOPLE also humanizes the dehumanizer[64] in the process. Why? Because in the process of diluting beneficence (when the dimensions of the help that is given can and does harm the "treated" SUD)—"dehumanizing" is an ethical "no-no". You-me-some-one can, and does, add some malfeasance—hopefully inadvertently—to a process of illusory protection against the stereotyped and feared "other"!

Does this chapter advocate that drug use—however this overloaded concept is defined—should be:

- de-diseased, and/or
- accepted as healthy behavior or functioning adaptation?

No! And in addition, in all likelihood

- the relevant individual and systemic stakeholders will continue to bring about whatever their agendas call for, and
- many, if not most, of the public-at-large—US—will continue to do that which we have generally done in and with our lives re the use and misuse of naturally grown, industrially manufactured and individually designed psychoactive substances.

The "fact" that for many stakeholders "drug use" is not a disease but rather is related to as a crime for which THEY are responsible and should be punished is an ongoing reality. This chapter is not the relevant forum for a needed analysis of this.

What is being raised for consideration as a viable effort—and not as a slick slo-gan—is that PEOPLE who also use and/or misuse "drugs", who also may need and/or want help of various types, which is, and/or can be, available and accessible, have the opportunity to become part of, and even engaged in, a helping process, without being inducted into a client-patient, disease-driven process and role—be it hierarchical-driven or "partner-based".

Stanley (Shlomo) Einstein, Ph.D., (IL) Professor, Institute of Criminology, Hebrew University, has also taught in the USA. He is a clinical and social psychologist, clinical supervisor, researcher, lecturer, journalist, radio interviewer, training films consultant, addictions consultant to industry (ATT, GM), conference organizer (3 regional, 15 national, 15 international); author/editor of 31 books (of which 27 books have been published so far), and many articles in professional journals. He has created and served as chief editor of The International Journal of the Addictions/Substance Use & Misuse; Drug Forum; Altered States of Consciousness; Violence, Aggression & Terrorism and Social Pharmacology. He is a member of the editorial boards of various professional journals and the creator of the monograph series, The Use and Misuse of Drugs, and creator and co-editor of THE UNCERTAINTY SERIES, creator-director of The Middle Eastern Summer Institute on Drug Use (Jerusalem, Israel), co-creator and co-director of The Mediterranean Institute (Rome, Italy), and creator of The Middle Eastern- Mediterranean Summer Institute on Drug Use. He is a recipient of the NIDA Pacesetter Award and the Mayor of Jerusalem Outstanding Volunteer Award, 2001. Areas of interest include: the parameters and processes of failure; creating and disseminating knowledge.

The author within the Berlin Holocaust Memorial June 1, 2005

Dedication

This chapter is dedicated to Eileen G., my teenage Black partner in a therapeutic alliance, who died of a heroin O.D., thus teaching a young-in-age-and-experience, naïve, White psychotherapist that traditional goals selected by stakeholders are all-too-often not met or supported by a reality of discrimination—humiliating, pain-inducing, unavailable, inaccesible, but necessary-for-change support systems, whose "demands" can, and do, make initial and ongoing drug use a viable option for surviving—if not for living—and an O.D. a "time-out" option for the marginalized.

Acknowledgments

I learned a great deal from the helpful and critical comments made by Profs. John Kleinig, Manuella Adrian, Ted Godlaski and by Uri Hurvitz. I am indebted to them for their "being there".

References

American Psychiatric Association. (1994). *Diagnostic and statistical manual of mental disorders (DSM-IV)*, 4th Ed. Washington, DC: American Psychiatric Association.

Barabási, A.L. (2003). *Linked.* New York City: Plume-Penguin Books.

Benzon, W.L. and Hays, D.G. (1990). The evolution of cognition. *Journal of Social and Biological Structures 13*(4): 297-320.

Bernstein, L., Laurents, A. and Sondheim, S. (1961). West Side Story. Sony/Capital.

Bock, J. and Harnick, S. (1964). Fiddler on the Roof. New York: RCA.

Buscema, M. (1998). Artificial neural networks. *Substance Use & Misuse, 33,* 1-3.

Allen, R.E. (Ed.). (1991). Concise Oxford Dictionary of Current English (8th edition) [first edited by H. W. Fowler and F. G. Fowler]. Oxford: Clarendon Press.

Courtright, D. T. (2001). *Forces of habit.* Cambridge, MA: Harvard University Press.

Einstein, S. and Jones, F. (1965). Group therapy with adolescent addicts: Use of a heterogeneous group approach. In Harmes, E. (Ed.), *Drug addiction in youth.* New York: Pergamon Press.

Fletcher, A. (2001). *The art of looking sideways.* London: Phaidon Press

Goffman, E. (1952). On cooling the mark out: Some aspects of adaptation to failure. *Psychiatry 15,* 451-63. Reprinted in: A.M. Rose, (Ed.), *Human behavior and social processes: An interactional approach.* Boston: Houghton Mifflin, pp. 482-50.

Gove, Walter R. (1980). *The labeling of deviance: Evaluating a perspective.* London: Sage Publications

Heschel, A.J. (1959). The patient as a person. In Heschel, A.J. *The insecurity of freedom: Essays on Human Existence.* New York: Schocken Books, pp 24-39.

Hill, J., & Cheadle, R. (1996). *The Bible tells me so: Uses and abuses of holy scripture.* New York: Anchor Books/Doubleday.

Holub, M. (1990). *The dimension of the present moment and other essays.* London: Faber and Faber.

Jastrow, J. (1899). The mind's eye. *Popular Science Monthly, 54*, 299-312.

Kahneman, D., Slovic, P., and Tverskey, A. (1982). *Judgment under uncertainty: Heuristics and biases.* Cambridge Univ.

Klingemann, H.K., and Sobell, L.C. (eds.). (2001). Natural recovery research across substance use. *Substance Use and Misuse, 36,* 11.

Lettieri, D.J., Sayers, M., and Wallenstein, P.H. (1980). *Theories on drug abuse.* NIDA Research Monograph No. 30, Rockville, Md. NIDA.

Lifton, R.J. (1986). *The nazi doctors.* New York: Basic Books.

MacCoun, R.J., and Reuter, P. (2001). *Drug war heresies: Learning from other vices, times and places*. London: Cambridge University Press.

Magura, S. (Ed.). (2000). Special issue on program quality in substance dependency treatment. *Substance Use and Misuse, 34,*12-14.

McAllister, W.B. (2000). *Drug diplomacy in the Twentieth Century: An international history.* London: Routledge.

McCoy, A.W. (2003). *The politics of heroin: CIA complicity in the global drug trade.* Chicago: Lawrence Hill Books.

Meyer, K. and Parssinen, T. (1998). *Webs of smoke.* Maryland: Rowman and Littlefield.

Pollan, M. (2002). *The botany of desire*. New York: Random House.

Porter, R. and Teich, M. (Eds.). (1995). *Drugs and narcotics in history.* Cambridge: Cambridge University Press.

Pulford, J., Adams, P., and Sheridan, J. (In press). Unilateral treatment exit: A failure of retention or a failure of treatment fit? *Substance Use and Misuse, 41.*

Rittel, H., and Noble, D. (1989). Issue-based information systems for design, Working Paper 492. The Institute of Urban and Regional Development, University of California, Berkeley, California.

Shorkey, C.T. (2004). *Spontaneous recovery and chemical dependence: Indexed bibliography of articles published in professional chemical dependency journals.* University of Texas at Austin. <http://128.83.80.200/tattc/spontaneousrecovery.html>.

Spurlock, M. (2005). Super size me. Hart Sharp Video.

Stedman's medical dictionary (Illustrated), 23rd ed. (1976). Baltimore: Williams and Wilkins Co.

Sussman, S., .Stacy A.W., and Anderson Johnson, S. (Eds.). (2004). Transdisciplinary drug misuse prevention research. *Substance Use and Misuse, 39*, 10-12.

Szasz, T. (1985). *Ceremonial chemistry: The ritual persecution of drugs, addicts and pushers.* Holmes Beach, FL: Learning Publications, Inc.

Terry C.E., and Pellens M. (1928). *The opium problem.* New York: Bureau of Social Hygiene.

Tuan, Yi-Fu. (1974). *Topophilia: A study of environmental perception, attitudes and values.* Englewood Cliffs, New Jersey: Prentice Hall.

Von Foerster, H., Mora, P. M., and Amiot, L. W. (1960). Doomsday; Friday, 13 November, A.D. 2026. *Science, 132*, 1291-1295.

Vuchinich, R.E., and Heather, N. (Eds.). (2003). *Choice, behavioral economics and addiction.* New York: Pergamon.

Wallace, B.C. (2005). Ethical issues surrounding access to drug user counseling/ treatment. In: Kleinig, J. and Einstein, S. (Eds.) *Ethical challenges for intervening in drug use: Treatment issues* Vol. 2. Huntsville, TX : Office of International Criminal Justice (OICJ), Sam Houston State University, Criminal Justice Center.

Younge, S.L., Oetting, E.R., Banning, J.H., and Younge, K.A. (1990-1991). Psychological messages from the physical environment: The drug and alcohol treatment center environment. *The International Journal of the Addictions, 25*(7A & 8A), 905-955.

Glossary

demand: the dynamic process of working out ways of adapting to the expectations of others developed by substance users. Substance users have "learned"—through identification, being inducted, reinforcement regimens, etc.—what is expected of them regarding abstinence, lapses, relapses, etc.

meta-goal: an unofficial, latent or unarticulated goal

normed: pertaining to treatments that do not solely treat "substance use disorder" (SUD) and to those patients who are treated in facilities and programs that are not devoted solely to SUD.

Notes

1. This paper was translated from the lengthier English version which follows it to a "Reader's Digest"-like English version which is more reader-friendly by Manuella Adrian, friend and colleague. Many thanks, Manuella.
2. THEM and THEY continue to represent a "homogenizing" and a stereotyping of a heterogeneous population who, by and large, are marginalized, depersonalized and disempowered, as the "drugs" which THEY use, continue to be mystified and empowered, and we continue to be frightened – when we care enough – by manipulating stakeholders. And a profit is made by many! And if not by many, then by some.

3. You, the reader, are asked to consider what relationship, if any, exists between the concepts underlying the expressions "cleanliness is next to Godliness", " clean up your mess", "clean up after yourself", "getting clean", "staying clean", "dirty needles", etc., and the "risk" of becoming and remaining "clean" in a substance-using environment in which "use" is value-laden. In a globalized world of toxic environments and increasing violation of life and liberty and corruption without borders, shame or guilt (?), "clean" = "good" = "healthy" = "normative" are equated under delineated conditions, although not under all conditions. For example, effective primary prevention can result in not permitting a living organism, including the human organism, the necessary opportunity and experience to strengthen its immunity systems and capacities and thereby make it quite vulnerable to being "infected". The cognitions and semantics of a given time, place, and culture can, and do, affect the dimensions of actual, delayed, or non-interventions (Benzon and Hays, 1990). These many points are derivable from what, on the surface, appears to be the value-neutral word clean.
4. If THEY were sufficiently motivated and diagnostically OK (unimpaired) to begin with, they wouldn't be drug users in the first place! Right? And in the 2nd place, this is, notwithstanding the implications of the research by Prof. Daniel Kahneman (recipient of the Nobel Prize in 2002) over 40 years, which demonstrates evidence-based, that human judgment, at its core, is based upon irrationality (Kahneman., et al., 1982). Or the more recent thesis by the "rational addiction" behavioral economists that individuals will not, voluntarily, take actions which they expect will make them worse off (Vuchinich and Heather, 2003). This challenges the moral, criminal, and medical models, which are based upon a posited existing "impairment". Whether these latter two views have merit or not, the "DSM-IV REVniks" continue their efforts, seemingly without taking these challenging positions into consideration. It may be unfair to expect that a diagnostic manual that structures and explicates pathology should, in some manner, remind the reader about healthy parameters of perception, judgment, choices, decision-making, etc. This chapter's thesis does however ask you to consider that whatever the basis of substance use – the relevant perceptions, judgments, choices…which range from being appropriate to being inappropriate, from faulty to reasonable, from intuitive to being well thought out and "weighed" – it does not follow that (1) "drug user treatment" is necessarily indicated, or (2) that it is any more than one of the options to be considered if planned intervention is needed. Readers are referred to Thomas Szasz, (1985) *Ceremonial Chemistry: The ritual persecution of drugs, addicts and pushers for a provocative point of view*. For example, interventions structured to assess and to affect perception, judgment, choices, decisions, etc., without the various values and weights which are socially attributed to "treatment" would /could be more appropriate and useful for some "drug users". For whom? Such is the challenge of "matching". More about this later. Simply consider, that in addition to "normed" relapse training there could be "perception training" (view Figure 6), judgment training (under regular conditions or under conditions of adversity), "decision-making training", "choice "training" (how do YOU choose your doctor, dentist, lawyer, garage mechanic, a friend, your soul mate, etc.?)... Such types of interventions could affect the curriculum for professional training, needed policies, as well

as the criteria used to assess intervention success, failure, irrelevance, as well as "boomerang effects". It is also obvious that terms such as "irrational" and "rational" are loaded terms (see figure 2.14.1). For the behavioral economist, "rational" simply means that an individual expects, on the basis of the information available to him, that he will be better off as a result of doing something. If he is mistaken, and has taken an action that makes him worse off, behavioral economics simply asks that he learn from the experience, and not repeat the same action over and over again in the belief that eventually it will make him feel good. Any individual who acts in accordance with this basic premise is classified as being rational. This term is not used as a diagnostic assessment of a person's mental health status. Responding in a way that is not logical in terms of somebody's "facts" – not rationally but intuitively, or even reflexively – is not equivalent to empirically-based evidence of pathology that needs to be automatically treated. Nor is Kahneman's work about human judgment a prelude for mass psychiatric hospitalization. Consider the following scene: with smoking prohibited at one's employment site, workers go outside for a smoking break even during winter weather conditions, into the cold, perhaps even into the snow or rain. Is this rational or irrational behavior by the non-psychiatrically labeled? At this point, you, the reader, may be thinking doesn't this go too far? Why should you trust this author's judgment and/or analysis any more than Kahneman's or the "rational addictionists"? You shouldn't! This chapter invites YOU to investigate as much as you can, given your limitations in time, energy, interest, etc., what are the issues, the facts, the non-facts, the myths regarding drug use – a "social disease" turned into psychiatric disorders such SUD – who the stakeholders are, and then to make your own assessments and decisions about the ethics of contemporary drug user treatment.

5. SUD constituents represent various individual and systemic vested interests (the drug user, his or her "significant others", therapists, the health care system, the social welfare system, other formal and informal resources and support systems and communities, who may or do have something to gain or lose by a particular view of SUD as well as a change in or maintaining the SUD treatment status quo.
6. It is being posited that culture, place and (period) time do more than influence. They define and bind the what, who, when, where, how, with whom, for how long and how often as meta field forces. The history of substance use and reactions to it exemplify this [see: Pollan, Michael 2002, *The Botany of Desire*, Random House, NY; D. T. Courtright, 2001 *Forces of Habit* Harvard University Press, Cambridge MA); Porter, R. and Teich, M., (1995) eds., *Drugs and Narcotics in History*, Cambridge: Cambridge University Press; MacCoun, R.J. and Reuter, P., *Drug War Heresies: Learning from Other Vices, Times and Places*. (2001) London, Cambridge University Press; McAllister, William B., *Drug Diplomacy in the Twentieth Century: An International History*, Routledge: London 2000; McCoy, Alfred, W., *The Politics of Heroin: CIA Complicity in the Global Drug Trade*, Lawrence Hill Books: Chicago, IL, 2003; Meyer, K. and Parssinen, T., *Webs of Smoke*, Rowman and Littlefield, Maryland, 1998.
7. Sufficient time, in addition to "historical time", which was previously alluded to with culture and place, is not a static, predictable "given" when one needs to unlearn, learn, and relearn. Drug users, for example, don't enter treatment tabula rasa, without preconceived notions. THEY, just as the rest of us, have experienced

a range of successful and unsuccessful treatments (medical, dental, and psychological) both prior to their SUD treatment experience as well as in various "drug" and "alcohol treatments." And these have been partially, or more totally, successful, failures, irrelevant to the drug users' daily adaptation and functioning, or have even created harm for them. It may be politically incorrect to raise treatment "harm production" in an era of increasing "harm reduction" efforts. All of this has taken time; enough time, generally under conditions of never enough time. The two terms, "drug treatment" and "alcohol treatment", which are so common in the literature, raise yet another area for ethical concerns: WHO is being treated? The forbidden substance? The use of a selected drug? A disease? A person? A 'less-than person'? The illustration shown below, Figure 2.14.2, created by my friend the Israeli graphic artist Shirly Levy-Almeda, graphically illustrates a less-than-beneficent treatment reality stemming from sloppy, misinforming conceptualizing.

8. The reader is referred to Prof. Wallace's chapter: Ethical Issues Surrounding Access to Drug User Counseling/Treatment. It masterfully reviews drug user treatment access.
9. In a science-driven world it would be useful to study if the endorphin component of the "drug experience" or "high" has another type of endorphin-like basis for beneficence, for malfeasance or even for "evil."
10. Manuella Adrian, reviewing this chapter, shared the following anecdote with me and which some reader may want to use as one struggles with ethical issues: The Marquis de Sade once explained to a peasant girl whom he was whipping that the reason he got enjoyment out of hurting others is for the same reason she got enjoyment out of helping others. She felt good as a result of doing good (in keeping with morality and religious precepts in France at that time) whereas he felt good as a result of doing evil! Although de Sade's reasoning is hardly convincing this "tale" is included to remind US to consider whose perspectives does one need to be sensitive too.
11. The pharmacological actions of methadone operate with other opiates. Many, if not most, "drug users", at least in the West, are poly-drug users. MMT does not affect, pharmacologically, the theory-based, morally-driven goals of abstinence-non-drug use. Ergo, why should one expect "clean" urines? Unless one's judgment was impaired...which might put one "at risk" for...Secondly, since MMT is not a "drug free" SUD treatment model, this can, and does, raise problems for some professionals in the field who are abstinence-committed, for some policy makers and groups such as Narcotics Anonymous, as well as for numerous others. In Israel an ironic reversal has occurred. The country's only two needle exchange programs, in Jerusalem and in Ashdod, are part of the Ministry of Health's MMT infrastructure. Some MMT patients-clients continue to voice concern about why syringes and needles are being given to active drug users; they object that the program is supporting drug use! Would these issues not be raised if "normed" sites for treating people were also available and accessible for SUDs? We may never know.
12. Heschel, A. J. (1959) The patient as a person, in The Insecurity of Freedom: Essays on Human Existence, Schocken Books, New York pp 24-39. The reader is referred to this very illuminating and challenging essay.
13. "Dirty is not good". IT is a "no, no". Think back to your childhood.

14. "substance use disorder" is a new diagnosis created by a committee of medical experts and published in the DSM-IV in 1994 by the American Psychiatric Association. The APA's previous psychiatric diagnostic manual was used to diagnose the heterogeneous group of substance users as manifesting a full range of psychiatric diagnoses. Now that we have SUD, we also have "dual diagnosis". Is the treated drug user any better off? Have the "ethics" of drug user treatment changed with the advent of SUD diagnoses? What is your considered opinion after reading the many chapters in this volume?
15. Terry C.E. and Pellens M. (1928) *The Opium Problem*. New York: Bureau of Social Hygiene
16. The spatial symbolism – a hospital on North Brothers Island, off the shores of the Bronx borough of New York City, in front of the Rikers Island prison – is amazing. The mainland, with the "good folk" – you and me –; the hospital for teen-age "junkies" who need to be separated from "us"; and, the next stop in the "junky's life-cycle, the prison…: before reaching the cemetery for those with drug overdoses and/or other fatal consequences of drug use.
17. Given the definition of "treatment" on pages 568-570, one has the choice, if not the obligation, of considering a range of micro to macro foci of relevant treatment parameters and individuals (i.e., "significant others," care-givers, employers, etc.) beyond that of the traditional, visible and "tagged" substance user patient-client.
18. The ? is a question mark which looks like a figure or any essential term which you choose to include. Given that the visible, tagged, depersonalized, homogenized (VTDH) – you, the reader, can add "S" for stereotyped) – THEM, has become a symbol for so much that is not good, this taxonomy is so "loaded" that it may be useful to represent THEM as a symbol – which almost looks like a PERSON
19. During the current era of case management delivery of care and treatment, it is as if the person is initially guilty (i.e., getting sick) and has to prove his/her innocence in order to receive needed help. I ponder whether labeling this new model of care "helping people" would have resulted in more cost effective, humane, ethical based treatment?
20. Drug user treatment programs have been known to ask the SUD treatment seeker to return numerous times over a number of days and at different times in order to assess the "addict's" motivation. And do they get reimbursed for their transportation costs and lost wages? An ethical issue?
21. One needs to remember that "motivation", in humans, is not a directly observable phenomenon but rather is an interpreted AFTER-behavior which, in the case of SUD treatment, is then used to predict what will happen in the future in terms of processes as complex, non-linear, dynamic, multi-dimensional and phase-driven as a drug user becoming therapeutically engaged, not-dropping out of treatment, minimizing or ceasing his or her "drug use", getting a job, holding on to a job, going to school, minimizing risk-taking, minimizing aggression, etc. In laboratory rats the indices for measuring motivation have to do with the ability to experience a range of electric shocks on "hot" grids. If the shock indices were used in special populations of non-drug users such as "ordinary" masochists and people living their lives as "victims" we could be challenged by people who were highly motivated, maladapting, and malfunctioning.

22. It is interesting to consider that a range of treatment programs, with public health ideologies among them, practice “early case findings” routinely. This is different from “reaching out”, but with similar goals regarding the targeted population as well as society-at-large and the communities within which THEY live. Apparently “real diseases” merit the opportunity for early intervention.
23. “Filmmaker Morgan Spurlock unravels the American obesity epidemic by interviewing experts nationwide and by subjecting himself to a ‘McDonald’s only’ diet for 30 days straight”. A blurb from the DVD (2004, Kathbur Pictures, Inc.).
24. Klingemann, H.K. and Sobell, L.C. (eds.) (2001). Natural recovery research across substance use, *Substance Use and Misuse, 36*(11); Shorkey, C.T. (2004). *Spontaneous Recovery and Chemical Dependence;* Indexed bibliography of articles Published in Professional Chemical Dependency Journals, University of Texas at Austin <http://128.83.80.200/tattc/spontaneousrecovery.html>. This literature summarizes the cessation of substance use *without* any treatment by or through professional-based, mutual-help (i.e., AA, NA, OA, etc.)-based and/or tradition-based models. The “user” stops on his own.
25. “Recovery” – a label, a state, a status, a path, an outcome, and identification (by oneself as well as by others) – is another overloaded, value-laden term in the substance user treatment field which promises much, raises many images and anecdotes but which needs a great deal of clarification. IT can be a source for ethical concerns given that there are many who are “in recovery” – i.e., “ex addicts” and “former alcoholics” – who are treating SUDs. What they do, to whom, where and how, etc. can result in their being as “vulnerable” to ethical issues as are any other people treating others. “Recoverer’s” views about “recovery” might, however, affect treatment processes and outcomes differently from the views of other “change agents” who are not “in recovery”. This is yet another topic that needs to be empirically investigated.
26. Having entered the “non-field” of drug use, drug users, and lots of etc. in 1960, by chance, I am, at times, moved to demonstrate that I can indeed “walk the walk, and talk the talk”, and write/right the shibboleths. A paradox, if not an irony, is that I created the first drug user treatment center in Jerusalem Israel – The Jerusalem Center for Drug Use Intervention – in 1976, with the agenda of closing it, by demonstrating, empirically, that the range of available non-drug user treatment programs and services could treat THEM just as well. I failed to achieve my goal. The Center continues, and, in so doing, “permits” other programs in the Holy City, in the Holy Land, to have minimal contact with drug users and with their families. It would appear that being in a doubly holy place does not really guarantee ethical behavior. And the journal which I created and edit – Substance Use and Misuse (SUM) –”treats” drugs, their use and misuse, their users, gambling, eating disorders and the various planned interventions, as distinctive arenas of investigation. SUM is now in its 40th year. You, the reader, will have to decide how to assess this possible inconsistency between what I posit in this chapter and what I do professionally.
27. Prediction and control have different meanings in the linear, “cause and effect” world and in the non-linear worlds of chaos, uncertainty, and complexity theories. (See Buscema, M. (1998)-. Artificial Neural Networks, Substance Use & Misuse, 33(1-3). The latter is OUR REAL WORLD. And so? We have yet to consider, as a

"norm", the implications of these theories and of non-linearity for SUD treatment and treatment research. Not using such materials, which could be of benefit for substance users and those treating them, raises ethical issues.

28. Gove, Walter R. (1980) *The labeling of deviance: Evaluating a perspective*, London: Sage Publications presents a useful review of labeling with regard to deviance.
29. It would appear that many of the treatment agents working in the SUD treatment field are ardent environmentalists: in order to save paper as well as trees the terms "use," 'user', "misuser" and the favorite one, "abuser," are rarely inserted. The literature has matched this process with the terms "drug treatment" and "alcohol treatment" which raises interesting images of various types of drugs and alcohol being treated. See Figure 2.14.2 (page 575) again.
30. Do we, who treat THEM, whatever our discipline, status, responsibilities, expertise, etc., manifest some type of "co-dependence", if, or as, our income, participation in conferences, serving as invited experts and consultants, locally, nationally and internationally, is somehow related to THEM? Are WE perhaps, even dependent upon THEM?
31. The SUD treatment program literature continues to promote and maintain a myth, which inadvertently may be misleading, in the manner in which it reports about treatment effectiveness. It posits 6 basic types of treatment models: (1) detoxification/drying out, (2) out-patient, (3) in-patient short-term or (4) long-term residential, (5) drug-free, and (6) "substitute drugs". Their dimensions differ in terms of site (in-patient/out-patient), temporal ranges (short- vs. long-term) and medication culture . With the advent of "Harm Reduction" they can and do also differ in ideology. Their range of techniques is limited. Their essential differences are minimal. These 6 "models" continue to be compared – at times – for process effectiveness ("dropping out" and "treatment retention") and outcome effectiveness (abstinence, employment and/or study and a decrease in or no criminal behavior). But most of these 6 models use the same therapy techniques – whatever these may be at a given point in time, place and culture. Using a taxonomy that is generic for any type of treatment, including SUD Rx – professional-based, tradition-based, mutual-help-based (AA, NA, OA, GA, etc.), and self-help-driven ("natural recovery") models – raises an interesting "fact." Notwithstanding the predictable sentencing of "chronicity," the professional peer-reviewed literature reports that many of THEM stop their drug use with no help from US. There are also lots of THEM who continue their "drug" use notwithstanding our help. And some of THEM are the very same people at different points, times and/or transitions in their lives. How is this possible if our conceptual framework for understanding and treating SUDs is correct?
32. There seems to be a non-complicated historical memory disability manifestation in the SUD field. The processes of historical, cultural and *zeitgeist* reactions to selected drugs (opiates, alcohol, etc.) selected users (the tagged, visible, depersonalized, demonized, "homogenized" THEM) and selected reasons for substance use ("chronic use" vs. OUR recreational use) has moved from 'normative' use to moralizing, to criminalizing, to pathologizing; from moral entrepreneurs to criminal justice intervention (which remains the fastest, expanding 'growth industry' in contemporary USA), to "addictionologists", "narcologists", "alcohologists", and a range of other "addiction" experts and specialists. Should there be this level

of specialization? The writer Robert A. Heinlein has suggested that: *"A human being should be able to change a diaper, plan an invasion, butcher a hog, conn a ship, design a building, write a sonnet, balance accounts, build a wall, set a bone, comfort the dying, take orders, give orders, cooperate, act alone, solve equations, analyze a new problem, pitch manure, program a computer, cook a tasty meal, fight efficiently, die gallantly. Specialization is for insects."* (*Time Enough for Love*, G.P. Putnam's, 1973)

33. Isaac Newton, father of modern science-driven research, noted in his Principia that simplicity should be preferred for explanations. It is obvious that my style of explanation in this chapter has not integrated this principle. That is why the first 5 pages of this chapter are a translation from the English. Returning to "experts", it has been said about this same alchemist, apple-driven theoretician, that when his cat gave birth to a kitten, not wanting to be disturbed by a kitten's need to take care of its basic "needs", Newton simply had another hole in the door added to enable the kitten to exit. SO…is it possible that WE treat THEM because WE have the power, position and opportunity to "pathologize" THEM, and that God and prisons – God-given laws and man-made ones – are not what one offers the "disordered" in a world based on, and driven by, complexity, uncertainty, and chaos theories as well as realities? One could rightfully criticize this chapter's style as being little more than an exercise in rhetoric, and, perhaps, even worse than that, being unfair to an undelineated WE. WE includes those individuals and systems that have helped to create and to maintain SUD as a diagnosis, as a label, as a specialized treatment process and program, which has many built-in discrimination-driven, stereotyping, ethical limitations.
34. Do THEY not have any responsibility for their lives? Are THEY innocent victims while WE are the victimizers? (1) Yes THEY do – for some of it! (2) No THEY are not! This chapter and book is about the ethics of OUR interventions and not about the ethics – or lack thereof – of THEIR lives.
35. Given that the mystified and empowered process of "peer-reviewed" affects the worth of a publishable article, is it unethical to raise the following issue? If/when a publisher's editorial staff are there to correct grammatical and spelling errors and to create clarity in lieu of confusion and professional obfuscation ("galley proof beneficence"), WHO is responsible for preventing and/or minimizing conceptual as well as process maleficience? The editors? The publishers? Or the peers who are doing the reviewing? Or, perhaps, an institutionalized and organized field which permits all of this to begin and to continue? Having refereed journals does not, in and of itself, "guarantee." Nor does the more recent "sacramental-like" Impact Factor score for assessing a journal's status, merit, influence and worth. Sharon Begley (June 5, 2006), Science journals artfully try to boost their rankings. *Wall Street Journal*.
36. "Natural recovery" is the term used to describe a self-help process by a broad range of individuals who, having begun to use various illicit "drugs" and misuse licit, "recreational" or medicinal ones, ceased such use without tradition-based, formal-professionally-driven or mutual-helped based treatment such as AA, NA, OA, etc. The reader is refferd to: Klingemann, H.K. and Sobell, L.C. (eds.) (2001). Natural recovery research across substance use, *Substance Use and Misuse,*

36(11); Shorkey, C.T. (2004). *Spontaneous Recovery and Chemical Dependence;* Indexed bibliography of articles Published in Professional Chemical Dependency Journals, University of Texas at Austin <http://128.83.80.200/tattc/spontaneous-recovery.html>.

37. When one considers that abstinence (behavior, a life-style, or what), employment and/or studying and diminished criminality are more likely to be akin to Protestant ethical values (or come from some other organized value system) than being therapeutic-technique treatment achievable goals, it may follow that yesterday's moral entrepreneurs have changed garb and "gear" to become contemporary social control agents. If this is possibly true – which would merit a transdisciplinary longitudinal cross-cultural study – then the language of contemporary SUD treatment may be Pickwickian-driven or perhaps Alice in Wonderland-based. Communication also has ethical dimensions. Consideer the newish "spin" concept.
38. Reading about a lack in "treatment slots" and "bed slots" is not rare in the professional or even in the mass media. When was the last time you heard or read about missing "bomb slots", "gun slots" "ammunition slots"?
39. Magura, S. (ed.) Special Issue on Program Quality In Substance Dependency Treatment, (2000), SUM, 34:12-14). Personal communication with Dr. Magura, 7/6/05: *"The volume consists of: reviews and critiques of the literature on various topics related to program quality; some original research, some original descriptions of program quality assurance models, and some formal meta-analysis. The purpose was to bring together the research on the subject, as well as to add to it. We didn't miss much. 'Program quality' may often go by other names in the literature. For example, the purpose of evaluating patient outcomes is to determine whether the program delivers what it promises - if patient outcomes are good, one can infer that a quality treatment is being delivered. But research has been weak on identifying the 'active ingredients' of effective treatments, so that treatment may be inefficient – a lot may be done, only some of which is useful. I suppose this is an ethical issue - but the volume addresses it only implicitly – I didn't call it an ethical issue in those terms."*
40. Just as there are various models of sickness (see Table 2.14.1), each with its own criteria, so too there are models of health. Health is a state of complete physical, mental and social well-being and not merely the absence of disease. (World Health Organization: Introduction to Constitution). Do you, the reader, know any healthy substance users, including smokers, alcohol drinkers, caffeine drinkers, etc.? There are both direct and indirect, long-term and short-term, permanent and temporary pharmacological effects from the use of *all* active chemical substances as well as from a range of behaviors and life styles which can and do differ in their 'risk quotient'. What does this have to do with the differential placement of treatment, when needed, in mainstream, "normed", treatment facilities or in programs distanced from the mainstream?
41. It is interesting to note that, whereas a "survivor" of cancer (in remission) who is considered to be successfully treated after remaining alive for five years, and is not labeled as an "ex-cancer", may be active in some role in "support groups", the "ex-addict" and the "recovered-alcoholic" – whose lapse-relapse remains anticipated (and all too often identified with by THEM)—have become institutionalized

paraprofessionals due to their posited existential expertise. The possibility that WE may not want THEM to live, work, study, etc., where WE are, is surely not an issue in this process. Right? The reality that THEIR relative, or not so relative, marginalization and homogenization continues and does not appear to be on any one's agenda in the substance use(r) intervention field, remains as an ethical blemish in a world which values "winners," faults and stains "losers," and stigmatizes "failures." Rumor has it that the 11th Commandment, in the first broken edition, was *Do not get caught.*

42. Readers interested in exploring this viewpoint are referred to historical perspectives covered in: Terry, C.E. and Pellens, M. (1928). *The Opium Problem.* New York: Bureau of Social Hygiene; Courtright, D.T. (2001). *Forces of Habit.* Harvard University Press, Cambridge MA; Porter, R. and Teich, M., (eds.) (1995). *Drugs and Narcotics in History.* Cambridge: Cambridge University Press; Pollan, M. (2002). *The Botany of Desire.* Random House, NY.
43. There is a long list of potential choices to focus on in order to explore and learn about the (un)ethical parameters of SUD treatment. For example, consider that whereas their 6 traditional treatment models are compared and studied, the techniques used – their dimensions and "demands" – generally aren't. These ongoing used techniques appear to be a stakeholder "given," which, it would seem, do not have to be scientifically assessed. The use of other available techniques may be rarely considered. And why, indeed, should they be? They aren't empirically-based! The use of circus skills and techniques may, for example, be a potentially important appropriate medium to offer the SUD treatment "circus." Given that THEY are so often dehumanized, circus skills, in general terms, offer the technique participant an opportunity to be in touch with his soma and psyche, to learn about them, to care about both of them and their sum – him/her self – to learn to work with others, and to trust "the other" and to depend upon them ('basic trust') to create a healthy self and body image, to create needed self-confidence, to keep to a rigorous, but flexible, schedule, and, among other outcomes, to potentially give pleasure to others. And in such a potential SUD circus technique-facilitated treatment, perhaps to achieve, in some manner, the Buddhist aspiration: *"fall down 7 times, get up 8 times, that is the path to perfection."* In a world in which the therapy "tool box" is limited to some metaphorical hammers then many, if not most, of THEM can be, and are, related to as "nails" to be…
44. The issue of data ownership, a complex and sensitive issues, is rarely considered in SUD treatment assessment and is even less likely, if ever, to be reported in the literature. A related ethical issue which merits noting are the implications of collecting data from individuals who then are not very likely to benefit directly from their participation. What's in it for THEM? The fact that an SUD treatment assessment research project has been reviewed and OK-ed by an Institutional Review Board (IRB) describes the well-known process of covering one's _ _ _; this process does not, *ipso facto*, give IT the Good House Keeping Seal of approval for ethical research, nor the kosher/hallal signification of ritual purity. It is possible that some, perhaps even many, researchers may be somewhat resentful of IRBs. One needs to remember that the latter have been foisted upon researchers because

of the liberties which some researchers have taken with patients. If this is so, then the IRB process may not be primarily a device for covering one's _ _ _.]

45. The environmental dimensions and "demands" of programs which can, will, and do (1) promote engagement in treatment; compliance with goals and effective use of techniques, (2) minimize and/or prevent the patient and the staff from not becoming therapeutically engaged as well as not maintaining stereotypic and stereotyped "drug user roles," etc., have rarely been considered in SUD treatment. Such dimensions include (amongst others): a relationship dimension, a personal development dimension, maintenance and change dimensions, emotional catalyzer dimensions, information catalyzer/processing dimensions, environmental perceptions, attitudes and values dimensions, problem-solving/adaptational dimensions, dimension definer-boundary definer, Tuan, Yi-Fu, (1974). *Topophilia A Study of Environmental Perception, Attitudes and Values*. Englewood Cliffs, New Jersey: Prentice Hall; Younge, S.L., Oetting, E.R., Banning, J.H., and Younge, K.A. (1990-1991). Psychological messages from the physical environment: The drug and alcohol treatment center environment. *The International Journal of the Addictions, 25*(7A & 8A), 905-955). Does the photograph (Figure 2.14.5, page 586) of the room given to prisoners in a US prison for an AA meeting in which chairs surround the gas chamber merit concern as an ethical issue or is this simply to be related to as yet another *de facto* reality? Or perhaps another "cheap shot" designed to provoke? Another example from another part of the world. For a two year period during the early 1980's a pharmacist, guarded by Border Police, two hours a day, when his pharmacy was closed for the noon break, not far from Tel Aviv, sold methadone and barbiturates to approximately 1,000 drug addicts at the large official garbage dump. This "Rx program" was a private venture but was indeed known to various government ministries whose budgetary and other needs were met by it. Cab drivers profited since there was no public transportation going to the garbage dump—which has since been turned into an ecological site to be visited. The police knew where this large group of "narkomanim" (Hebrew, plural for "junkies") were. The Ministry of Tourism had less worries about tourists being "bothered" by THEM. The Ministry of Health did not have to supply more staff lines for treatment centers (there were only three in the entire country at that time). What is the point of all of this? A gifted writer could note: *"streets are not just for walking."* A concerned clinician could note: *"rooms are not just for talking."* And you, the reader, could choose to check whether the environments for treating SUDs in your community facilitate, interfere with, or are irrelevant to ethical treatment for the IP, the "significant others", the treatment staff, etc.

46. Barabási, A.L. (2003). *Linked.* Plume-Penguin Books.

47. Horst Rittel has suggested that problems can, and should, be usefully categorized into two types: "tame problems" and "wicked problems". The former are solved in a traditional known and tried "water fall paradigm"; gather data, analyze data, formulate solution, implement solution. The latter "wicked problems" can be responded to only individually, each time anew, with no ultimate, repeatable solution. This distinction, regarding a taxonomy of problems, has yet to be considered in terms of its utility, "demands", and implications for substance use(r) treatment and other programs and processes (Rittel, Horst, and Douglas Noble

(1989) "Issue-Based Information Systems for Design," Working Paper 492, The Institute of Urban and Regional Development, University of California, Berkeley, California, email: iurd@uclink.berkeley.edu). Is SUD treatment "the solution" to "the drug problem"?

48. Pulford, J. et al (in press) Unilateral treatment exit: A failure of retention or a failure of treatment fit? *Substance Use and Misuse 41*:2006
49. Consider the paradox of a "user" client- patient leading a pro-social, conventional life, integrating and identifying with Protestant ethic-driven treatment goals and soberly having to contend with the new reality of not being able to continue his or her needed, engaged-in treatment for "their" myriad of human problems in the specialized program (once an addict always an ...) because the program's hours are the same as conventional work/study hours, despite the 24 hours a day accessibility and availability of hospitals, etc., for legitimate, "normed", "sick" people. When the drug user did not come to his/her treatment sessions for a specific number of times s/he was coded, and related to, as a "drop-out". When the SUD treatment program is designed and operated in such a way as not to be able to meet the on-going treatment needs of a successful pro-social ex-addict/recovering alcoholic, and other "normed", non-specialist SUD programs are not accessible by tradition and/or policy, is this a form of institutional "dropping-out? Or, perhaps, the SUD treatment program may not have really been there to begin with in order to meet the complex needs of a PERSON who also uses drugs?
50. Readers interested in this model can contact Dr. Dickson-Gomez at: Institute for Community Research, 2 Hartford Square, Suite 100, Hartford, CT 06106 USA julia.dickson@icrweb.org.
51. Goffman, Erving (1952) 'On cooling the mark out: some aspects of adaptation to failure', Psychiatry 15: 451-63 (reprinted in: A.M. Rose, ed. Human Behavior and Social Processes: An Interactional Approach. Boston: Houghton Mifflin, 1962: 482-505) presents an intriguing "look" at this issue.
52. Heinz Von Foerster, Patricia M. Mora, and Lawrence W. Amiot, "Doomsday; Friday, 13 November, A.D, 2026," Science, 132, 1960. pp. 1291-1295.
53. The reader is referred to the following stimulating and challenging book: Hill, Jim & Cheadle, Rand, (1996) The Bible Tells Me So: Uses and Abuses of Holy Scripture, New York: Anchor Books/Doubleday
54. Lettieri, D.J. Et Al, (Eds.) 1980, Theories on Drug Abuse. NIDA Research Monograph No. 30, Rockville, Md. NIDA
55. Buscema, M. (1998), Artificial Neural Networks, Substance Use & Misuse, 33(1-3); Barabási, Albert-Lászlo. Linked (2003) Plume-Penguin Books)
56. Sussman, S., Stacy A.W. and Anderson Johnson, S. (Eds.) (2004) Transdisciplinary Drug Misuse Prevention Research Substance Use and Misuse.39:10-12
57. "Tradition" is not only important as a song in the Broadway show "Fiddler on the Roof" (Bock, J. and Harnick, S, (1964) New York: RCA). Consider the following: *De facto* standards occur in many different industries. For example, many *de facto* standards cooperated to dictate why the NASA space shuttle engines are a certain size. The engines are crafted to be able to ride on trains from one side of the country to another. The width of train tracks is the same throughout the United States, and tunnels have certain minimum heights and widths. The engines have to fit through

those tunnels while riding on a train car. Nobody got together to decide how wide the tracks would be. Instead, the first trains were created based on widths common in Europe. The distance between train tracks in Europe happens to be about the same width as the wooden rails that supported horse-drawn wagons in mines. Again, no group got together to decide how far apart to place the wagon wheels or rails. The distance between wagon wheels is the same width as that of the chariots the Romans used all over the Roman Empire, which at one time stretched into England. The width of those chariots was determined by the wheelbase used for chariots that had two horses, side by side. No group collaborated to decide how wide a horse's backside should be. We laid thousands of miles of track all over the United States (and other places on Earth), and the width of the track was based on a *de facto* standard—which ultimately dictated the size of NASA space shuttle engines—the width of a horse's backside! What "tracks" is contemporary SUD treatment on? Are we "on course"? Are we getting "there"— wherever that is? Who are the WE and who should be the WE? Who is tracking SUD treatment – particularly its ethical dimensions? Is the treatment "load" being carried equitably?

58. This process may be usefully considered to be a form of *research welfarism*, which, in theory, could challenge the efficacy of the American Wisconsin plan for overcoming unemployment psychopathy. The majority of American Wisconsin plan participants were reported to be unemployed a year after being "helped" by this program; the majority of "drug use(r)" researchers continue to be employed for many years after entering the field.
59. Consistency and stability are not necessarily virtues. Consider: A Mississippi state senator addressed the legislature thus: *"You have asked me how I feel about whiskey. All right, here is just how I stand on this question: If, when you say whiskey, you mean the devil's brew, the poison scourge, the bloody monster that defiles innocence, yea, literally takes the bread from the mouths of little children; if you mean the evil drink that topples the Christian man and woman from the pinnacles of righteous, gracious living into the bottomless pit of degradation and despair, shame and helplessness and hopelessness, then certainly I am against it with all my power. But, if when you say whiskey, you mean the oil of conversation...the drink that enables a man to magnify his joy and his happiness and to forget, if only for a little while, life's great tragedies and heartbreaks and sorrows; if you mean that drink, the sale of which pours into our treasuries untold millions of dollars which are used to provide tender care for our little crippled children, our blind, our deaf, our dumb, our pitiful aged and infirm, to build highways, hospitals, and schools, then certainly I am in favor of it."* [delivered by Sen. Noah S. "Soggy" Sweat Jr. on April 4, 1952, at a banquet]. Returning to the non-beginning of this chapter's thesis, the above quotation is part of the environment in which an SUD is "treated" and in which a selected substance user may not be related to, engaged by, served by, or treated by mainstream, "normed", public, institutions representing a range of human services and needs. AN ETHICAL TRAVESTY or at the very least an ethical dilemma. You decide.
60. *"Perhaps all the dragons in our lives are merely princesses, waiting for us once to act with beauty and courage. Perhaps fear, in its deepest essence, is something so strangely wanting and needing of our love."* (Rilke, R.M. *"Letters to a Young*

Poet," no. 8, August 12, 1904). How likely is it that THEY will be able to be rid of their frightening dragon- garb and demeanor and WE of our fears, if the traditional SUD treatment continues? I was challenged to deal with this more than 40 years ago at Riverside Hospital when I created a heterogeneous therapy group which mixed hospitalized drug user with non-drug using college students for weekly 90 minute sessions as part of a more traditional, "homogenized" drug user, group therapy research project. Interested readers are referred to Einstein, S. and Jones, F. (1965). Group therapy with adolescent addicts; Use of a heterogeneous group approach in Ernest Harmes (ed) *Drug Addiction in Youth*. Pergamon Press: New York Within a relatively short period of time these 10 young adults, aged 17-26, created "bridges" of communality for communication around issues of personal revelation, peers, the therapist, attitudes to therapy, sexuality, family relationships, search for help, vocational-educational, and last of all – drugs. All of the other groups in this group therapy project spent a great deal of time talking about "drugs," "shooting up," "O.D.s" (over dose), "mainlining," "the works," and "hustling." One of the points being made is that another *de facto* reality can be created, limited as it may be because of traditions and stakeholders, in which basic ethical-bound treatment opportunities are possible…even for and with THEM.

61. The literature on posited substance use "risk" and "protective" factors and processes has absented itself from considering what protective mechanisms an active substance user may or does need in order to seek and become engaged in a change process.
62. A philosopher, a logician and others could obviously and legitimately ask" needed by whom"? Since I don't have THE ANSWER to such a legitimate question I can "cop a plea" by stating my "principle of faith": By those who have the necessary autonomy and/or can achieve it in order to make their own definitions as they distinguish between "needs" and "wants", are able to take adequate responsibility for their perceptions, judgments, choices, decisions and outcomes and all that follows from this.
63. It is necessary to consider that a useful diagnosis should permit one to know a disease's etiology, process and prognosis. "substance use disorder" does not do this task well, which has implications for any type of planned treatment.
64. Referring to this book, (Lifton, R. J., 1986, The Nazi Doctors NYC, Basic Books) which describes such a process very clearly, in no way implies that intervention agents in the field of "drug use" interventions—whatever their ideological commitments, roles and styles of work –, in any way carry out what these in-name-only physicians did. The issue is not whether the infamous Dr. Mengele was a "real physician" or not. A critical issue is what are the necessary conditions and processes which a SUD treater, working in a specialized methadone treatment program (MMT), for example, uses and "needs" in order to detoxify a non-compliant poly drug user from his/her daily methadone because of the drug user's ongoing use of cocaine, barbiturates, amphetamines as documented through random urine testing? Or what endogenous and exogenous conditions enables a professional to "screen out" a methadone-maintained treatment (MMT) patient, employed as a full time staff member in a needle exchange program, from participating in a course training "ex-addicts" to work with addicts in a variety of treatment programs because his MMT "prevents" him from being "drug free"…which is a condition of being accepted into the course.

Appendix A

Figures 2.14.8a and 2.14.8b are designed to help you, the reader, to organize, keep in mind and to explore potential, as well as actual, relationships and interactions between selected basic parameters for any type of treatment process: its planning, implementation, as well as needed assessment.

This **Y** tool, as with any tool, has built-in limitations as well as advantages. One of its major advantages is also a limitation; it only permits the tool's user to "work with" a selected number of the many factors which are part of treatment (a limitation) while permitting one–you-me—to "juggle" with a quantity which WE should be able to reasonably handle without being 'threatened' by the sense of vulnerability-inducing "helplessness" due to the enormity of the multiplicity of ongoing treatment "demands". And, all-too-often, in "defense", WE may chose, in some way, to "give up" on THEM.

Encircling the **Y** (Figure 2.14.7b) and referring back to Figure 2.14.3 (which schematized the "landscape" of substance user interventions, including treatment) also can remind US—a pronoun which is generally missing in traditional SUD treatment—that what is being done treatment-wise with "substance use disorders" as well as with PEOPLE, occurs in interacting contexts and environments which continue to do whatever THEY do, whether or not WE pay attention, acknowledge, deny, distort, etc. Treatment, however one defines the process and the outcomes, is context-driven and bound.

WE can choose to "allow" Figure 2.14.7a's three "legs" to remind US to be aware of the dynamic, interacting, complex multi-dimensionality of a treatment process in terms of:

- Goal heterogeneity and specificity for each treatment phase or level. Treatment is not a homogeneous, static, linear, "cause and effect" "happening".
- The range of types of necessary criteria which are needed and which need to be used for goal selection, and of our resposibility to be aware of their underpinnings (theory-based, empirically-based, stakeholder agenda-driven, "principle of faith-based", *de facto* reality-based, arbitrary, etc.). Each criterion has its own dimensions, "demands" and necessary conditions for it to operate well, to operate not so well, to operate somewhat "sickly", not to operate at all, and perhaps even to operate in a "boomerang" or regressive manner.
- The goal selection process (i.e. hiearchial-driven, partnership-based, etc.).
- The range of potential as well as actual treatment foci, from a micro to a macro level...including, as well as excluding, necessary people, parameters, etc.

As you, the reader, view this **Y** schema you may, or may not, agree with what I have included: my world view/"principle of faith" about treatment. Obviously you don't have to. But do be willing to "play along" with "planned change" (treatment) being:

- process-based and driven,
- in which viable goals,
- which are appropriate,
- available and
- accessible
- for each phase

- can be selected,
- in a benificent and
- not in a malfeasent manner,
- using criteria which help and
- which don't hinder,
- for,
- with,
- against
- a particular treatment focus.

Knowing what is indicated as well as what is contra-indicated, viable as well as illusory, should either be basic knowledge of licenced "change agents" or should be learnable by them/US.

SO...let's begin to "play" the **Y** game keeping in mind that WE—the SUD treatment "constituency"—are not "gaming" with lives.

Select the phase of treatment for your planned intervention, from an outreach-early case finding phase to a post-treatment outcome phase—which may or may not be operating as an "after-care" level—, or to no further treatment following post-treatment follow-up. Then select your primary/initial focus of treatment. Connecting the selected points on each treatment planning "leg" will create a triangle which can, and does, differ from being a "perfectly" shaped △. The resulting imperfect schema matches imperfect realities in our less than perfect context and the worlds in which SUD treatment is initiated, or not, continues, or doesn't continue, changes for all sorts of known, unknown and unknowable reasons, and ceases or is "ceased". What we are exploring are the sources of potential/actual ethical issues that have been, and currently are, associated with SUD treatment in the interaction between treatment process, goal selection criteria, and selected treatment foci. In ethically-based treatment, empirically-based goal criteria would "drive" the goal selection whether the process was tradition-based, hierarchial-professional treatment-based or partnership-mutual help-based, or other stakeholder-based. Keep in mind that since SUD treatment goals, by and large, are traditionally pre-determined—even before the "drug" user 'seeker-needer' of treatment meets the deliverer of care-services-treatment—, with minimal attention given to existing exogenous and endogenous factors and conditions, this process is questionable, ethically.

And now, with YOUR created framework for treatment planning, begin to ask the kinds of necessary questions whose actual/potential answers (total or partial; "legitimate" or "illegitimate" ones, à la Von Foerster, etc.) will permit YOU to move towards, and within, the targeted, ethically-driven, treatment goal-driven direction.

For example:

- What is an appropriate selection criterion to use for a goal or objective before treatment has actually begun which may (or is likely to) be part of the lifestyle of an individual, a couple, or a family, who have been "targeted" for treatment—early-case finding or outreach—and/or who is considering seeking treatment?

- For whom or what does the selection criteria have to be appropriate: the targeted focus of treatment, the therapist, the program, the policy maker or any other potential stakeholders, and/or the context-environment-culture within which the intervention-treatment plans are being made?

Figure 2.14.7a: Exploring Relationships Between GOAL SELECTION CRITERIA, Substance Use(r) Intervention FOCI and TYPES of TREATMENT PHASE GOALS

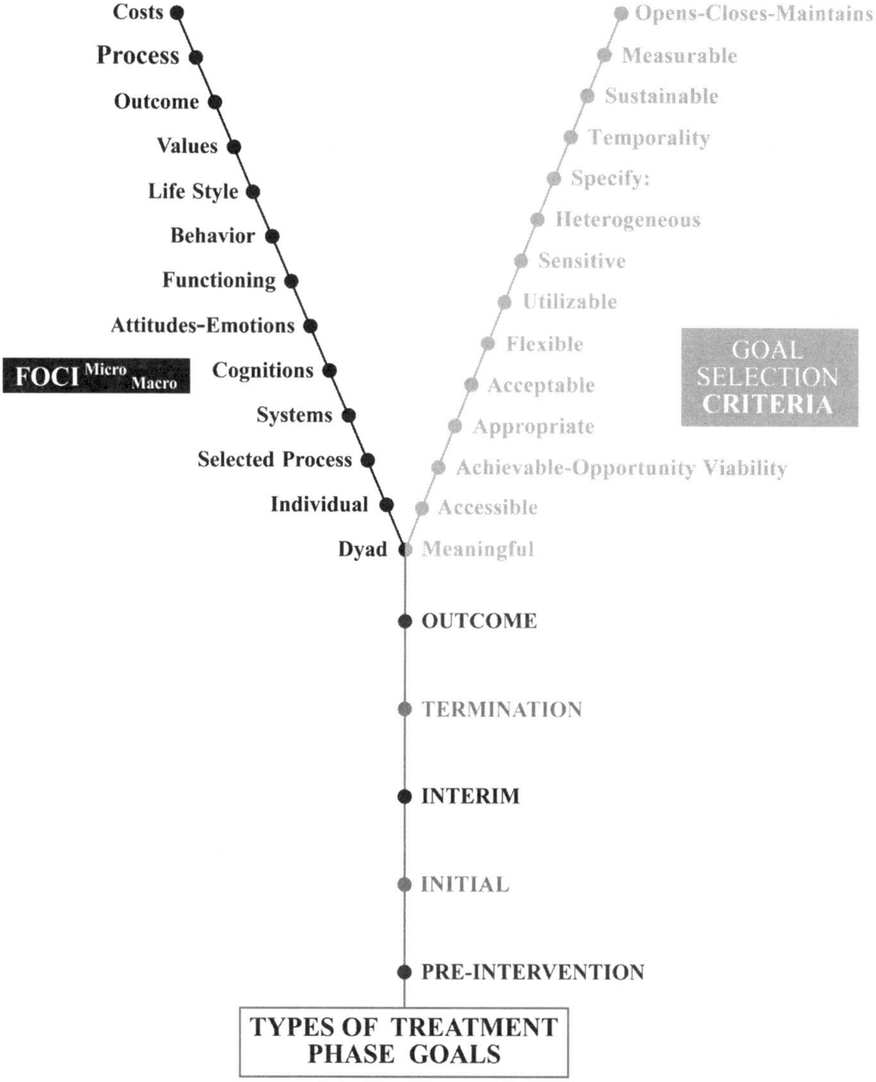

It remains all-too easy to overlook and/or to "forget" that a "treatment landscape" can be/is relatively "crowded"—see Figure 2.14.3—with the needs, agendas and values of many whom WE need to consider, if for no other reason than the *de facto* one that

THEY can help as well as hinder, promote as well as prevent. For example, making medicinally-pure heroin—which has been available and used as a legal pain killer—may be appropriate for a particular user of illicit heroin at a particular phase in his or her life, generally, as well as a phase in their drug using "career". It is unlikely that this will be appropriate for a politician running for office in a particular culture (if it became known to a free electorate). And although all of God's human creatures were made in the image of God, as George Orwell once reminded those who didn't know…some creatures are more equal than others… With all that this implies. Daily.

- What are the posited (theory-based, as well as empirically-based) critical, necessary conditions, for an effective interaction between the three selected "leg"-parameters to begin, continue, change, cease, or not begin at all?
- WHO are the necessary "actors" in this interacting process and outcomes of individuals as well as systems? What are their sources and types of power, their relative status and position in the "hen-pecking" order of being able (or not being able) to have an impact, as well as what is their "survivability" quotient?

Figure 2.14.7a is not an inflexible tool in the sense that if you only have a hammer then you may be prone/"vulnerable"/"at risk" to "nail" everything and everyone. This tool is as flexible as you choose to make it in the manner in which you use it, within the limits of any type of "material fatigue" as well as "human error".

As you manipulate this **Y**—so as not to manipulate an SUD patient-client—using the knowledge which you have, the experience which you have learned from and interpreted (correctly or not), your beliefs, values and "principles of faith", which currently are likely to be an integral part of your multiplicity of roles in your life-style, permit yourself to *go beyond* the human defensive arrogance of being "right" and "flawless", and simply "play" with the given materials—adding your own as you need and want to. Moses erred. He didn't get into the Holy Land. Did he fail?

The goal of this "game"—which is also to be played with the series of additional conceptual schemas-Figures, which have been included in this Appendix—is to move closer to ethically-based-driven treatment for people who "use"…, within our *de facto* contexts, doing the best that WE can with ourselves as well as in partnerships with others. It is possible that the WE -THEY can be changed into an US.

Is this a viable option? "Playing" the tool may result in one or more innovative answers or needed stimuli, which may lead to needed and useable answers.

Just as Figure 2.14.7a serves to organize our focus for planning, implementing and assessing ethically-based treatment of "drug users" in terms of goal selection options for different treatment phases, using measurable, available and accessible criteria whose underpinnings are knowable, for selected micro ↔ macro levels of the planned treatment focus,

- Figure 2.14.7a and 2.14.7b can serve as a checklist for including helpful as well as hindering stakeholders and parameters which we need to remember for a viable treatment plan and to consider their actual as well as potential (inter) relationships,
- Figure 2.14.8 can be used to explore the actual, or potential, nexus-connectedness-inter-relating between selected treatment factors (or phases of treatment if you change this schema), models of care, and selected ethical issues in which

a missing "encirclement" of the **Y** is an everpresent, impacting context-environment, and

- Figure 2.14.9 can be used to explore current, as well as potential, relationships between selected treatment factors (or, if you choose, treatment phases), types of initiators of treatment, and selected ethical issues (or, if you choose, micro ↔ macro treatment foci).

Ethically-created, -based, and -maintained treatment can be, and remains as, no more than a "container concept", a topic for books (such as this one), articles, conferences, Commissions of Inquiry, a focus for research as well as being a vibrant process. WE need to be more and better aware of the necessary critical endogenous and exogenous conditions for this to occur as well as what are likely to be endless relevant and irrelevant answers and responses to: WHAT DO I NEED TO KNOW IN ORDER TO…

Figure 2.14.7b: Exploring Relationships Between GOAL SELECTION CRITERIA, Substance Use(r) Intervention FOCI and TYPES of TREATMENT PHASE GOALS

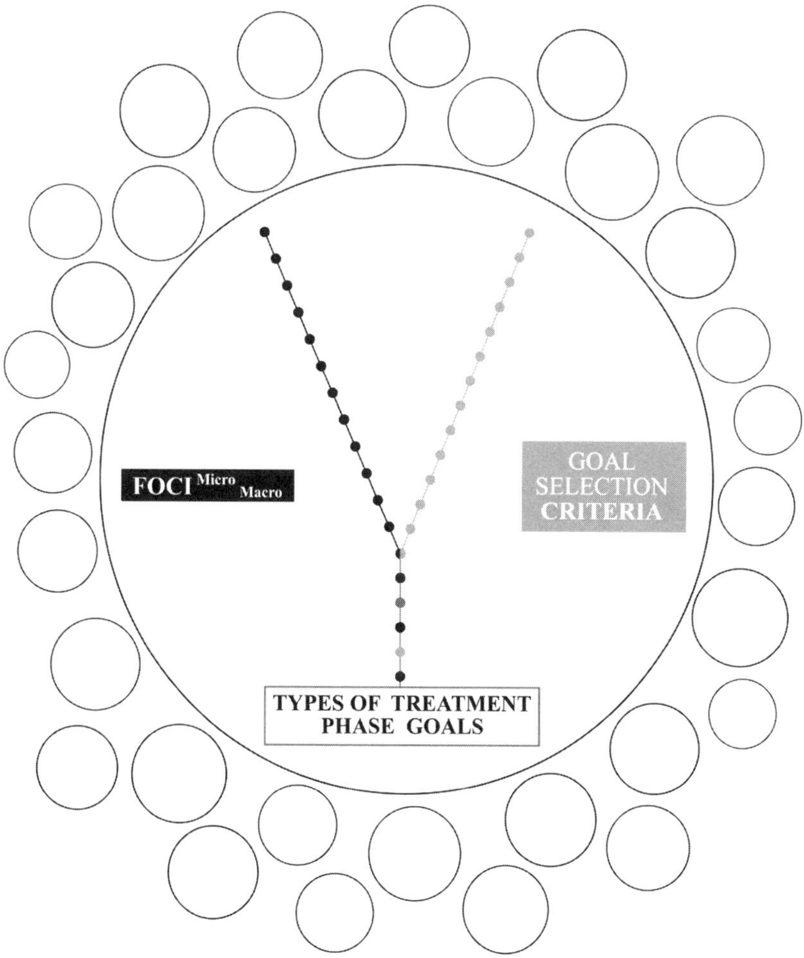

Figure 2.14.8: Exploring Relationships Between MODELS OF CARE, ETHICAL ISSUES and Substance Use(r) Intervention/TREATMENT FACTORS

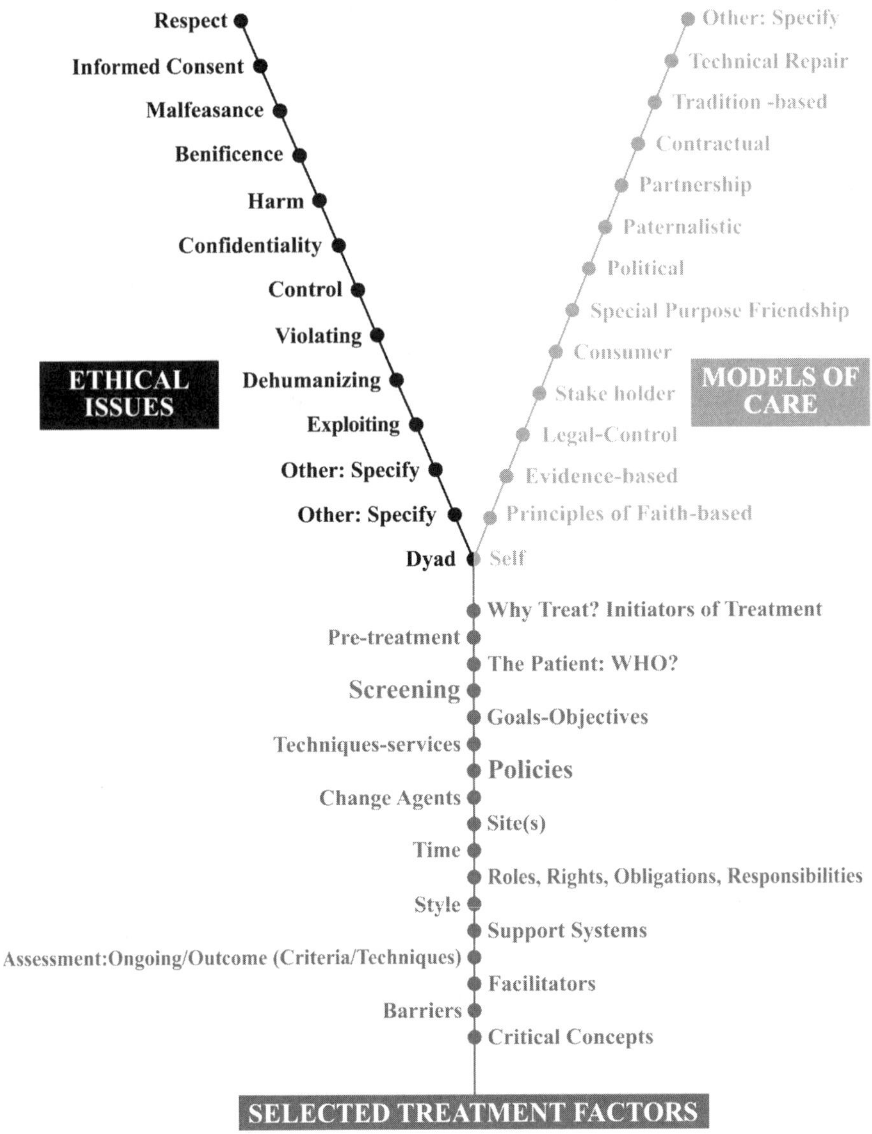

Figure 2.14.9: Exploring Relationships Between INITIATORS OF TREATMENT, Substance Use(r) Intervention FOCI and SELECTED TREATMENT FACTORS

Appendix 1 - Codes of Ethics for Substance User Counselors

Ethical standards for Counselors by NAADAC

NAADAC, The Association for Addiction Professionals is comprised of alcoholism and drug abuse counselors who, as responsible health care professionals, believe in the dignity and worth of human beings. In the practice of their profession they assert that the ethical principles of autonomy, beneficence and justice must guide their professional conduct. As professionals dedicated to the treatment of alcohol and drug-dependent clients and their families, they believe that they can effectively treat its individual and familial manifestations. NAADAC members dedicate themselves to promote the best interests of their society, of their clients, of their profession and of their colleagues.

Specific Principles

Principle 1: Non-Discrimination

The NAADAC member shall not discriminate against clients or professionals based on race, religion, age, gender, disability, national ancestry, sexual orientation or economic condition.

a. The NAADAC member shall avoid bringing personal or professional issues into the counseling relationship. Through an awareness of the impact of stereotyping and discrimination, the member guards the individual rights and personal dignity of clients.

b. The NAADAC member shall be knowledgeable about disabling conditions, demonstrate empathy and personal emotional comfort in interactions with clients with disabilities, and make available physical, sensory and cognitive accommodations that allow clients with disabilities to receive services.

Principle 2: Responsibility

The NAADAC member shall espouse objectivity and integrity, and maintain the highest standards in the services the member offers.

a. The NAADAC member shall maintain respect for institutional policies and management functions of the agencies and institutions within which the services are being performed, but will take initiative toward improving such policies when it will better serve the interest of the client.

b. The NAADAC member, as educator, has a primary obligation to help others acquire knowledge and skills in dealing with the disease of alcoholism and drug abuse.

c. The NAADAC member who supervises others accepts the obligation to facilitate further professional development of these individuals by providing accurate and current information, timely evaluations and constructive consultation.

d. The NAADAC member who is aware of unethical conduct or of unprofessional modes of practice shall report such inappropriate behavior to the appropriate authority.

Principle 3: Competence

The NAADAC member shall recognize that the profession is founded on national standards of competency which promote the best interests of society, of the client, of the member and of the profession as a whole. The NAADAC member shall recognize the need for ongoing education as a component of professional competency.

a. The NAADAC member shall recognize boundaries and limitations of the member's competencies and not offer services or use techniques outside of these professional competencies.

b. The NAADAC member shall recognize the effect of impairment on professional performance and shall be willing to seek appropriate treatment for oneself or for a colleague. The member shall support peer assistance programs in this respect.

Principle 4: Legal and Moral Standards

The NAADAC member shall uphold the legal and accepted moral codes which pertain to professional conduct.

a. The NAADAC member shall be fully cognizant of all federal laws and laws of the member's respective state governing the practice of alcoholism and drug abuse counseling.

b. The NAADAC member shall not claim either directly or by implication, professional qualifications/affiliations that the member does not possess.

c. The NAADAC member shall ensure that products or services associated with or provided by the member by means of teaching, demonstration, publications or other types of media meet the ethical standards of this code.

Principle 5: Public Statements

The NAADAC member shall honestly respect the limits of present knowledge in public statements concerning alcoholism and drug abuse.

a. The NAADAC member, in making statements to clients, other professionals, and the general public shall state as fact only those matters which have been empirically validated as fact. All other opinions, speculations, and conjecture concerning the nature of alcoholism and drug abuse, its natural history, its treatment or any other matters which touch on the subject of alcoholism and drug abuse shall be represented as less than scientifically validated.

b. The NAADAC member shall acknowledge and accurately report the substantiation and support for statements made concerning the nature of alcoholism and drug abuse, its natural history, and its treatment. Such acknowledgment should extend to the source of the information and reliability of the method by which it was derived.

Principle 6: Publication Credit

The NAADAC member shall assign credit to all who have contributed to the published material and for the work upon which the publication is based.

a. The NAADAC member shall recognize joint authorship and major contributions of a professional nature made by one or more persons to a common project. The author who has made the principal contribution to a publication must be identified as first author.

b. The NAADAC member shall acknowledge in footnotes or in an introductory statement minor contributions of a professional nature, extensive clerical or similar assistance and other minor contributions.

c. The NAADAC member shall in no way violate the copyright of anyone by reproducing material in any form whatsoever, except in those ways which are allowed under the copyright laws. This involves direct violation of copyright as well as the passive assent to the violation of copyright by others.

Principle 7: Client Welfare

The NAADAC member shall promote the protection of the public health, safety and welfare and the best interest of the client as a primary guide in determining the conduct of all NAADAC members.

a. The NAADAC member shall disclose the member's code of ethics, professional loyalties and responsibilities to all clients.

b. The NAADAC member shall terminate a counseling or consulting relationship when it is reasonably clear to the member that the client is not benefiting from the relationship.

c. The NAADAC member shall hold the welfare of the client paramount when making any decisions or recommendations concerning referral, treatment procedures or termination of treatment.

d. The NAADAC member shall not use or encourage a client's participation in any demonstration, research or other non-treatment activities when such participation would have potential harmful consequences for the client or when the client is not fully informed. (See Principle 9)

e. The NAADAC member shall take care to provide services in an environment which will ensure the privacy and safety of the client at all times and ensure the appropriateness of service delivery.

Principle 8: Confidentiality

The NAADAC member working in the best interest of the client shall embrace, as a primary obligation, the duty of protecting client's rights under confidentiality and shall not disclose confidential information acquired in teaching, practice or investigation without appropriately executed consent.

a. The NAADAC member shall provide the client his/her rights regarding confidentiality, in writing, as part of informing the client in any areas likely to affect the client's confidentiality. This includes the recording of the clinical interview, the use of material for insurance purposes, the use of material for training or observation by another party.

b. The NAADAC member shall make appropriate provisions for the maintenance of confidentiality and the ultimate disposition of confidential records. The member shall ensure that data obtained, including any form of electronic communication, are secured by the available security methodology. Data shall be limited to information that is necessary and appropriate to the services being provided and be accessible only to appropriate personnel.

c. The NAADAC member shall adhere to all federal and state laws regarding confidentiality and the member's responsibility to report clinical information in specific circumstances to the appropriate authorities.

d. The NAADAC member shall discuss the information obtained in clinical, consulting, or observational relationships only in the appropriate settings for professional purposes that are in the client's best interest. Written and oral reports must present only data germane and pursuant to the purpose of evaluation, diagnosis, progress, and compliance. Every effort shall be made to avoid undue invasion of privacy.

e. The NAADAC member shall use clinical and other material in teaching and/or writing only when there is no identifying information used about the parties involved.

Principle 9: Client Relationships

It is the responsibility of the NAADAC member to safeguard the integrity of the counseling relationship and to ensure that the client has reasonable access to effective treatment. The NAADAC member shall provide the client and/or guardian with accurate and complete information regarding the extent of the potential professional relationship.

a. The NAADAC member shall inform the client and obtain the client's agreement in areas likely to affect the client's participation including the recording of an interview, the use of interview material for training purposes, and/or observation of an interview by another person.

b. The NAADAC member shall not engage in professional relationships or commitments that conflict with family members, friends, close associates, or others whose welfare might be jeopardized by such a dual relationship.

c. The NAADAC member shall not exploit relationships with current or former clients for personal gain, including social or business relationships.

d. The NAADAC member shall not under any circumstances engage in sexual behavior with current or former clients.

e. The NAADAC member shall not accept as clients anyone with whom they have engaged in sexual behavior.

Principle 10: Interprofessional Relationships

The NAADAC member shall treat colleagues with respect, courtesy, fairness, and good faith and shall afford the same to other professionals.

a. The NAADAC member shall refrain from offering professional services to a client in counseling with another professional except with the knowledge of the other professional or after the termination of the client's relationship with the other professional.
b. The NAADAC member shall cooperate with duly constituted professional ethics committees and promptly supply necessary information unless constrained by the demands of confidentiality.
c. The NAADAC member shall not in any way exploit relationships with supervisees, employees, students, research participants or volunteers.

Principle 11: Remuneration

The NAADAC member shall establish financial arrangements in professional practice and in accord with the professional standards that safeguard the best interests of the client first, and then of the counselor, the agency, and the profession.

a. The NAADAC member shall inform the client of all financial policies. In circumstances where an agency dictates explicit provisions with its staff for private consultations, clients shall be made fully aware of these policies.
b. The NAADAC member shall consider the ability of a client to meet the financial cost in establishing rates for professional services.
c. The NAADAC member shall not engage in fee splitting. The member shall not send or receive any commission or rebate or any other form of remuneration for referral of clients for professional services.
d. The NAADAC member ,in the practice of counseling ,shall not at any time use one's relationship with clients for personal gain or for the profit of an agency or any commercial enterprise of any kind.
e. The NAADAC member shall not accept a private fee for professional work with a person who is entitled to such services through an institution or agency unless the client is informed of such services and still requests private services.

Principle 12: Societal Obligations

The NAADAC member shall to the best of his/her ability actively engage the legislative processes, educational institutions, and the general public to change public policy and legislation to make possible opportunities and choice of service for all human beings of any ethnic or social background whose lives are impaired by alcoholism and drug abuse.

Revised: May 20, 1995

NAADAC grants permission for other professionals, associations and certifying bodies to use this code of ethics. NAADAC shall be referenced in writing as the source when using any or all parts of this code. Any changes from NAADAC's original code must be noted.

Reprinted with permission <http://naadac.org/documents/display.php?DocumentID=11>

The NAADAC Standards have been adopted by many state boards, including some of those whose URLS are listed below:

Principles for the Provision of Mental Health and Substance Abuse Treatment Services: A Bill of Rights. American Counseling Association, et al. <http://www.apa.org/pubinfo/rights/rights.html>

Code of Ethics and Standards of Practice. American Counseling Association <http://www.counseling.org/Content/NavigationMenu/RESOURCES/ETHICS/ACA_Code_of_Ethics.htm>

Alcoholism and Substance Abuse Counselors' Code of Ethics. Connecticut Certification Board, Inc. <http://www.ccb-inc.org/ethics.htm>

Code of Ethics for Alcohol and Drug Counselors. The Iowa Board of Substance Abuse Certification <http://www.ibsac.org/counsethics.pdf>

Code of Ethics. Louisiana State Board for Certified Substance Abuse Counselors <http://www.lsbcsac.org/bcsac_app_code.pdf >

Code of Ethics. New Mexico Regulation and Licensing Department Counseling and Therapy Practice Board <http://www.nmcpr.state.nm.us/nmac/parts/title16/16.027.0018.htm>

Ethical Principles of Conduct. The North Carolina Substance Abuse Professional Certification Board, Inc. <http://www.ncsapcb.org/sacode-98.html>

Code of Ethics. Missouri Substance Abuse Counselors' Certification Board, Inc. http://www.msaccb.com/code.htm >

Counselor Code of Conduct. Wisconsin Certification Board. <http://wisconsincertificationboard.org/DOCS/CounselorCode.pdf>

Code of Ethics for the Certified Alcohol and Drug Counselor. California Association of Alcoholism and Drug Abuse Counselors (CAADAC). <http://www.caadac.org/cadcethics.htm>

Code of Ethics. Kentucky Board of Certification of Alcohol and Drug Counselors <http://finance.ky.gov/NR/rdonlyres/756666F2-0965-4B11-A598-5BD2E5D1FBFF/0/lawandregulations.pdf> p. 7.

Code of Ethical Conduct. Michigan Certification Board for Addiction Professionals. <http://mcbap.com/aoda&arms.htm>

Ethics Guidelines of the ICECC. Institute of 12 Step Counselors<http://www.12steprecoveryprogram.com/ethics.html>

Guiding Principles. Florida Alcohol and Drug Abuse Association (FADAA)<http://www.fadaa.org/about/index.htm>

Appendix 2 - The Most Critical Unresolved Ethical Issue Associated with Drug Use Intervention

Some Unresolved Issues with Ethics and Research Data: Data Quality, Missing Data And Failed Experiments.

"Good models are hard to build on the basis of bad data."

— University of California,
Berkeley statistician Freedman (1985: 345)

The point of research is to get a better understanding of the world and how it works. Our understanding should be: more complete, more accurate, more precise and, essentially, more "real" than earlier explanations. 'Better' explanations are also more 'useful' in the case of applied research, and 'elegance' (efficient ways to discover the truth) is preferred.

All results are dependent on data and data quality. However, problems of data quality are not always sufficiently recognized. Our most elaborate models and most sophisticated statistical testing will ultimately prove to be meaningless if we don't take into account --and correct -- problems of data quality, such as inaccurate, incomplete or contradictory responses by a respondent: e.g., the 49-year old who reports their age as 38 to appear younger or as 50 because it's easier to remember round numbers, the person who reports regular drug use over the past month, but no drug use over the past year when, perforce, use over the past month also necessarily means use over the past year, etc.

These sorts of data quality problems are more ubiquitous than we would like to acknowledge, and because they are rarely addressed in the literature, effective methods of data quality checks (e.g., comparing reasonableness of responses from several potentially related questions) and data cleanup techniques (e.g., imputations, proxies using indirect indicators from multiple measures of comparable information) are not well known to many researchers working outside of large statistical bureaus but who are faced with these sorts of problems in their own data. (Some of these issues have been addressed in Adrian 1985:1-8.)

Consider the following situation in the case of the problem of missing data:

Data is collected on 3 variables (Age, Gender, and Education) from a sample of 100 students (student 1 , student 2… student 100). Let us assume that information on variable Age is missing for students 1 to 10, information on variable Gender is missing for students 11 to 20, and information on variable Education is missing for students 21 to 30. This means that 30% of the sample has missing data. There are several options to deal with this:

1. Eliminate those cases with missing data from the analysis. Results would be meaningful for those with complete data, but may lack in external validity if

those 30 students with missing data in our example are somehow different from those 70 with complete data (this is called selectivity bias). Although some consider this the best alternative if subsequent analyses use regression (Haitovsky 1968), we lose the non-missing information on the other two variables for these students.

2. Impute missing data. For example, Age may be missing but proxied by Education, as persons in grade 1 are likely to be aged 6, based on the average age of those who were in grade 1 among the 80 students in the sample who reported both Age and Education. Missing data may also be imputed from the sample average for all of those who do report information for the missing Age variable. A variety of more complex imputation methods are also in use.

Imputation is preferred if the missing data is non-random, although some methods of imputation are better than others depending on the type of missing data. Interestingly enough, imputation may have scant effect on the quality of the results, depending on how much data is missing and the type of analyses done subsequently (see Snedecor & Cochran 1980:274-279, Haitovsky 1968, and Little 1992, for a fuller discussion).

More open and free discussions of problems of data quality and methods that have been used to deal with them, at conferences and/or in published articles, may prove useful in providing solutions to data quality problems encountered by researchers.

Another problem is with the way that we determine if a particular theory or hypothesis is correct. We can never prove a theory or hypothesis, we can only disprove it. If one hundred research projects test a hypothesis or theory and 99 of them cannot invalidate the hypothesis or theory and one does find results that indicate the hypothesis or theory does not hold and is false, then that 100th research project's results are sufficient to invalidate the hypothesis or theory. All scientific glory and honor goes to the 100th researcher! That 100th researcher's results may set the stage for a new better theory. For example, some measurements made by astronomers in about 1900 found inconsistencies with some aspects of Newtonian physics theory, but not incompatible with Einstein's theory. Hence the development of a new branch of physics.

However...

If the hypothesis or theory invalidated by the researcher is the researcher's own hypothesis or theory, little honor accrues to that researcher. There is an impression that journals won't publish negative findings – and researchers may feel embarrassed to be associated with a failed experiment. Results of failed experiments that would disprove a particular hypothesis or theory are essentially unpublicized, and scant research resources can be wasted if other researchers unknowingly repeat the same methods to investigate the same question. A forum or regular brief reports of failed experiments may prove a useful contribution to the field, so that researchers need not re-invent the square wheel.

References

Adrian, M. (1985) Introduction. In: Adrian, M. (Comp.) (1985) *Statistics on Alcohol and Drug Use in Canada and Other Countries-Volume II: Statistics on Drug Use, Data Available by September 1984*. Toronto (Canada): Alcoholism and Drug Addiction Research Foundation, pp. 1-8

Freedman, D.A. (1985) Statistics and the scientific method. In: William, M., Mason, W.M., & Fienberg, S.E. (eds.) (1985) *Cohort Analysis In Social Research: Beyond The Identification Problem*. New York: Springer-Verlag, pp. 342-366.

Haitovsky, Y. (1968) Missing data in regression. *Journal of The Royal Statistical Society, 30*(1):67-82

Little, R.J.A. (1992) Regression with missing 'X's: a review. *Journal of The American Statistical Association, 87*(420):1227-1237.

Snedecor, G.W. & Cochran, W.G. (1980) *Statistical methods. 7th ed.* Ames, Iowa: Iowa State University Press.

Manuella Adrian, M.Sc.Hyg.

***

> *"During many years I have been engaged in a battle for a radical dis-criminalisation of all drugs as the only way out..."*

This quotation, from a brief letter that sociologist Ivan Illich sent to an Italian alcohologist about twenty years ago, describes his passionate position in front of the needs and the rights of people using and abusing drugs and other substances. Illich's engagement is still relevant today. In fact, in spite of the wide diffusion of Twelve–Step Fellowships, that stand on the philosophy that addiction is an existential illness rather than an immoral comportment, behaviours of both drug addicts and alcoholics are still stigmatised in present society—if not identified as crimes. Social deviancy, once characterizing mental illness, is nowadays an attribution of addiction; it defines a special group of people with a sort of lower ethical status, and it elicits practices of both "guarding" and "punishing" among care providers and professionals. The interpretation of addiction as social deviancy stays behind the campaigns against drugs or alcohol and the control-oriented approaches promoted by both treatment clinics and criminal justice programs; it also is at the basis of unresolved ethical issues associated with the treatment of substance users and misusers.

In each culture at any time the prevailing values indirectly point out those underlying behaviours that are not part of the fashionable norms. As a low tide reveals hidden logs and stones on a beach, present times disclose those unfashionable conducts of the individuals who are no more able to play the role of the winner, or of the ones incapable to maintain the expected levels of self-control. Such defeated and defective persons represent the limitations of the contemporary ideal of autonomy and self-sufficiency; they end up highlighting the dramatic condition of being dependent on a substance or on another human being.

Addiction is thought as an immoral or criminal behaviour, and the addicted patient is considered responsible for the physical interpersonal and economic problems due to the use and misuse of alcohol and of other drugs. If they are causing their own problems and harm, we assume, they cannot expect to be treated as normal people. As an example, a drug addict cannot expect to be enrolled in an expensive Hepatitis C treatment program as any other citizen affected by the same disease:(s)he is supposed to be unable to persevere in the lengthy medical therapy needed for a successful outcome.

For the same reason an alcoholic patient affected with hepatic cirrhosis cannot easily be admitted to a liver transplant list—even if recent studies question the common sense statement that there is a better chance of success if a liver transplant is done for a non-alcoholic than for an alcoholic patient.

Criminalizing addictions allows authoritarian behaviours to occur in the professional-client relationship within the context of the out- and in-patient clinic and of therapeutic community programs. Authority-based approaches have been expelled from modern teaching methods at all school-related curricula. However the authoritarian principle, for ages at the base of the doctor-patient interactions, found special shelter in addiction treatment programs. In these programs a high admission threshold, a negative prescription—i.e. prohibiting the use of a substance—the control of both behaviour and biological fluids, and blackmailing and rewarding, are common milestones. In the last analysis, the individual is considered as a means rather than an end; s(he) is a means to reach her/his good, according to the perspective of others. Such an approach raises the issue of addicted persons that are treated as second class citizens, being considered less responsible than a "normal" individual.

Dis-criminalising does not mean not proscribing the misuse of alcohol and other drugs by professionals and by society; it rather means to appreciate and promote that underlying search for meaning that is common among addicts. According to an alcoholic metaphor quoted within Alcoholics Anonymous Fellowship, the addict's quest should then move from "spirit" to "Spirit".

Nowadays, there are at least two critical unresolved ethical issues in the formal treatment of substance users and misusers. First of all, there is inequality in the access threshold to treatment programs between addict and non-addict patients. This is best shown when the treatment is expensive or prestigious, as medical or surgical interventions. Second, there is an abuse of the authority principle by professionals who interact with addicted clients. This is demonstrated by the compulsoriness of many treatment programs and by the control approach of most professionals relating with illicit drug and alcohol misusers. The fact that such problematic behaviours are occurring in the context of clinical and therapeutic practice may be explained by the dependent attitude of the clients, who may find it difficult to express consistent objections to their therapists.

Are such ethical issues, and their related conflictual practices, going to last in the next future? We do not know, but we can hope that in the next decade such challenges to our society find a new way out, so that an equality approach towards the deviant others is achieved by listening to the people who need help.

We can help such a change occur.

Allaman Allamani, M.D. (Florence, Italy)

***

Issues in Cross-Cultural Assessment

Prevention practitioners and researchers alike are concerned about the need to use appropriate and scientifically-based outcome measurements. Among other things, measures can vary with regard to their popularity, availability, scoring, completion time, reading level, developmental appropriateness, reliability, stability, sensitivity to change, generalizability, ease of administration, and cultural appropriateness. Because the demographics of the United States are changing so rapidly, we believe that the serious gaps in appropriate instrumentation for different ethnocultural groups is one of the most important issues in the prevention field to date.

Since the 1960s social scientists and clinicians have underscored the importance of taking cultural variation into account in the prevention of and intervention in health problems and in the treatment of clients from differing cultural groups. The concrete results from recognizing cultural variation as a significant factor in health prevention and treatment, however, have been elusive and limited. Over the past four decades a plethora of scholars from different disciplines have produced a substantial literature addressing issues of acculturation, assimilation, cross-cultural variation, ethnicity, nationalism, and racial variation (Alba, 1990; Banks, 1996; Bee, 1974; Bennett, 1975; Berry et al., 1986; Eller, 1999; Eriksen, 1993; Fenton, 1999; Greeley, 1974; Jenkins, 1997; Westermeyer & Janca, 1997.) This disciplinary richness, though, has resulted in many unsynthesized perspectives, theories, and empirical studies. An effective cross-cultural (or multicultural) assessment, intervention, and treatment approach is thorny because some very difficult questions have not been sufficiently tackled. One particularly critical question is the way in which assessments are made—in other words, the methods of collecting the information and the way in which these data are analyzed and interpreted. This is related to disciplinary distinctions. Psychology and its many sub disciplines and related disciplines (e.g., clinical psychology, social psychology, developmental psychology, school psychology, counseling psychology, etc.) and psychiatry have taken the lead in the applicable assessment instruments and/or identification of best measures. Ostensibly, these instruments could then be used in a more "appropriate" manner with the cultural group/s in mind.

In this approach, a major assumption is made that culturally sensitive health assessments can be completed through developing standardized instruments that accommodate critical cultural differences in the way in which they have been worded and the instructions given to the person who will administer the instrument. This assumption is grounded in the traditional quantitative approach of many of the social sciences. Perhaps this is one reason why there is relatively little communication in the literature between, for example, anthropology and social psychology, with respect to the impact of ethnic variation on clinical assessment. While many anthropologists do use quantitative methods, sociocultural anthropology is grounded most firmly within an ethnographic or qualitative tradition. This tradition argues against the total reliance upon questionnaire-type instruments for assessing such complex entities such as mental health problems in different cultural groups. Instead, ethnographers emphasize the centrality of the person who asks the questions as the "instrument" of data collection (Agar 1980). Thus, it is the experienced researcher or clinician—whatever discipline they happen to come from—and not a piece of paper with questions on it to be completed or to be asked by a research assistant that serves as the assessment instrument.

Obviously, this is a very big difference in research approaches. One reason relatively little communication has taken place between social science disciplines with respect to effective cross-cultural assessments is that there are no easy answers to this question. Various attempts have been made to resolve some of these dilemmas, however. In the assessment of alcohol and drug-related problems, for example, two projects are notable. Helzer and Canino (1992) and their colleagues addressed the application of assessment instruments such as the DIS (Diagnostic Interview Schedule) in cultural groups in North America, Europe, and Asia. In 1990 the World Health Organization, NIAAA, NIDA, and NIMH (the latter three then part of ADAMHA) initiated a study entitled the Cross-Cultural Applicability Research (CAR) Study. The main objective of the study was to examine the applicability of the alcohol and drug sections of two assessment instruments (The Composite International Diagnostic Interview (CIDI) and the Schedules for Clinical Assessment in Neuropsychiatry (SCAN)) cross-culturally. Nine countries from four continents (Asia, Europe, Africa, and North America) were asked to participate; these particular societies were selected on the basis of linguistic and cultural variation (Bennett et al. 1993; Room et al. 1996). This work is a testament to the desire to move the agenda in the direction of cross-fertilization of ideas between disciplines that have a "different take" on how to address this problem.

Many solid arguments can be made in favor of using standardized instruments that have been field-tested in different cultural groups. First, unless we have such data, it is very difficult to make epidemiological comparisons across ethnic groups within particular countries, let alone across nations. While the comparisons may be very suspect no matter how carefully the instruments are developed and field-tested and revised, there is clear value in being able to assess health problems in different cultures. Early identification of particular problems as they are increasing in incidence can offer the opportunity for effective prevention and intervention programs, such as carried out by the World Health Organization. Furthermore, evaluating the effectiveness of different prevention and intervention approaches can be informed by longitudinal data collected through standardized instruments.

In addition to the epidemiological benefits of having well-designed instruments that are appropriate for the cultural groups for which they are administered, there is the very practical problem of the expense in collecting and analyzing the information. The collection of qualitative/ethnographic data is typically, though not exclusively, done by trained ethnographers, often holding the Ph.D. and/or the M.A. degrees and possessing a considerable amount of experience conducting ethnography. The expense of having such professionals collect the information from research/clinical clients usually is prohibitive, especially beyond the pilot stage of a project. Although the training involved in administrating structured instruments such as the Diagnostic Interview Schedule (DIS) is extensive and requires considerable training and practice, the extent and depth of training involved is less than that involved in learning how to skillfully conduct ethnographic interviews.

Another practical consideration in attempting to accommodate cultural diversity in making valid assessments is the difficulty in addressing the myriad of cultural groups in particular societies. This is especially the case in the United States. Typically the most populace cultural (or ethnic) groups are targeted for culturally appropriate instrument development, taking into account linguistic and cultural features. Although considerable progress has been made through focusing work in this manner, gaps will always remain in terms of people who belong to particular cultural groups not being specifically accommodated. While it is extremely helpful to have identified assessment instruments that, for example, apply well to Latino groups or to Native American groups, some groups will not receive such attention.

In summary, we face a dilemma that cannot be resolved by only good intentions and careful construction and revision of standardized instruments in which cultural variation is taken into account. The thorny issues remain regarding who conducts the assessment, how much cross-cultural assessment expertise they have, and the extent of flexibility permitted to reframe and rephrase questions such that they result in culturally valid answers.

Some Modest Recommendations

To help advance our ability to make more culturally appropriate clinical assessments, we offer some recommendations. A multi-pronged approach to resolve the dilemma is suggested. First, the most culturally appropriate possible instruments must be developed for all cultural groups and for specific cultural groups. Typically, standardized instruments that are reviewed for cultural applicability are revised with the intention of being able to use them with all cultural groups. It appears that the bulk of attention to cross-cultural assessment has been given to revising standardized structured instruments into the most culturally appropriate shape possible. This is a necessary, but insufficient, step in carrying out valid cross-cultural assessments. Second, instruments that specifically are designed for assessments in particular cultural groups in which the numbers are sufficiently great to warrant this attention should be identified, developed, or modified. This is an area where qualitatively oriented social scientists and clinicians have much to bring to the enterprise.

Realistically, what can we do?

(1) Increase awareness of how critical an issue culturally appropriate assessments are. This is already occurring, as seen in the notable increase in publications on this topic and in web site materials, especially in psychology, counseling, and medical anthropology.

(2) Improve existing standardized instruments to make them less culturally inappropriate than they are currently for all cultural groups in which they are used. This is an area where careful attention to the translation and back-translation process can be extremely important.

(3) Identify and/or develop instruments that are geared especially well toward particular cultural groups.

(4) Draw upon qualitative/ethnographic research approaches in the development and administration of semi-structured assessment formats that permit flexibility in the way in which questions are framed and rephrased.

(5) At the same time, serious attention needs to be given to the valid administration of assessments by professionals who are familiar with the culture and the language and who are skilled in conducting assessments.

(6) Substantially increase the cross-disciplinary fertilization in the application of concepts, empirical data, and methods to improve cross-cultural assessments of health status.

Linda A. Bennett, Ph.D. (Memphis, TN)
Jeannette L. Johnson, Ph.D. (Baltimore, MD)
A. Aukahi Austin, Ph.D. (Mānoa, Hawai'i)

Linda A. Bennett, Ph.D., is a Professor of Anthropology and Associate Dean of the College of Arts and Sciences at The University of Memphis. She completed her PhD in Anthropology at American University in 1976. Past president of the Society for Applied Anthropology, the National Association for the Practice of Anthropology, and the Washington Association of Professional Anthropologists, and co-founder of the Alcohol & Drug Study Group of the Society for Medical Anthropology, Dr. Bennett is currently a member of the Executive Board of the American Anthropological Association. In collaboration with other leaders in applied anthropology programs in 2000, Dr. Bennett founded the Consortium of Practicing and Applied Anthropology Programs (COPAA). She is co-editor of The American Experience with Alcohol (1985), co-author of The Alcoholic Family (1987), editor of A Russian-English Language Guide for Adopting Families, and author of Personal Choice in Ethic Identity Maintenance: Serbs, Croats, and Slovenes in Washington, D.C. (1978). Dr. Bennett has conducted fieldwork in medical anthropology in the former Yugoslavia, especially Croatia, and in the United States. She has also performed ethnic identity research in Washington, D.C. and Pittsburgh. Recently she has worked on a collaborative study of neighborhood rituals and routines in neighborhoods of Memphis, Tennessee. At The University of Memphis, she received the Meritorious Faculty Award in the College of Arts and Sciences (1999) and the Board of Visitors' Eminent Faculty Award (2003) and gave the Commencement Address at the University of Memphis, August 2003.

Jeannette L. Johnson, Ph.D., Dr. Johnson is a cross-cultural psychologist who has extensive experience in community-based prevention research, with an emphasis on understanding the role of risk and protective factors in high risk youth and examining models of vulnerability. She is currently a Senior Research Analyst at Friends Research Institute in Baltimore, MD. In the past she was a Distinguished Professor at SUNY-Buffalo and the Director of the Research Center on Children and Youth. Dr. Johnson is of Native American heritage (Huron) and has extensive experience with Native American communities. She has conducted community-based substance use and HIV/AIDS prevention research as well as treatment research with chronic substance users. She is a contributing editor for several journals - Substance Use and Misuse; the author and co-author of many professional publications. and a faculty member of the Middle Eastern Summer Institute on Drug Use (MESIDU) in Israel, Italy and Spain.

A. Aukahi Austin received her Ph.D. in clinical psychology from the Clinical Studies Program, University of Hawai'i at Mānoa in 2004. She completed her pre-doctoral internship training at Tripler Army Medical Center, and is currently finishing a post-doctoral fellowship at the University of Hawai'i at Mānoa that encompasses transportation of evidenced-based practices for the treatment of child and adolescent anxiety, depression, and disruptive behavior problems into community settings in Hawai'i. Dr. Austin conducts research on substance use and violence among Native Hawaiians, and is engaged in ongoing research on the prevalence and treatment of mental health disorders among Native Hawaiians in rural medically underserved areas.

References

Agar, M.H. (1980). *The professional stranger*. New York: Academic Press.

Alba, R.D. (1990). *Ethnic identity: The transformation of white America*. New Haven, CT: Yale University Press.

Banks, M. (1996). *Ethnicity: Anthropological constructions*. London: Routledge.

Bee, R.L. (1974). *Patterns and processes: An introduction to anthropological strategies for the study of sociocultural change*. New York: The Free Press.

Bennett, J.W. (Ed.) (1975). *The new ethnicity: perspectives from ethnology.* Saint Paul, MN: West Publishing Co.

Bennett, L.A., Janca, A., Grant, B.F., and Sartorius, N. (1993). Boundaries between normal and pathological drinking: A cross-cultural comparison. *Alcohol Health and Research World, 17*, 190-195.

Berry, J., Trimble, J., and Olmedo, E. (1986). Assessment of acculturation. In Lonner, W. and Berry, J. (Eds.), *Field methods in cross-cultural research.* Newbury Park, CA: Sage.

Eller, J.D. (1999). *From culture to ethnicity to conflict: An anthropological perspective on international ethnic conflict.* Ann Arbor: University of Michigan Press.

Eriksen, T.H. (1993). *Ethnicity & nationalism: Anthropological perspectives.* London: Pluto Press.

Fenton, S. (1999). *Ethnicity: Racism, class and culture*. Lanham, MD: Rowman and Littlefield Publishers, Inc.

Greeley, A.M. (1974). *Ethnicity in the United States: A preliminary reconnaissance*. New York: John Wiley and Sons.

Helzer, J.E., and Canino, G. J. (Eds.). (1992). *Alcoholism in North America, Europe, and Asia.* New York and Oxford: Oxford University Press.

Jenkins, R. (1997). *Rethinking ethnicity: Arguments and explorations*. Thousand Oaks, CA: Sage Publications.

Room, R., Janca, A., Bennett, L.A., Schmidt, L., and Sartorius, N. (1996). WHO Cross-cultural applicability research on diagnosis and assessment of substance use disorders: An overview of methods and selected results. *Addiction, 91*(2), 199-220.

Westermeyer, J. and Janca, A. (1997). Language, culture and psychopathology: Conceptual and methodological essues. *Transcultural Psychiatry, 34*(3), 291-311.

***

Ideology vs. Science in Providing Disability Benefits to the Chronically Addicted

The Social Security Administration's (SSA) experience with addiction as a disability can be seen as a triumph of viability over validity (Conrad and Schneider 1992). That is, a popular image of substance misusers as social parasites persuaded Congress in 1996 to terminate their eligibility for cash benefits from the Drug Addicts and Alcoholics (DA&A) program under Supplemental Security Income (SSI). The widely accepted image of SSI recipients exploiting taxpayer support to buy alcohol and drugs was viable in a political climate that demonized impoverished substance users. But the image was not valid—there was no corroborating evidence for this claim, beyond anecdotes from program administrators and officials (Swartz, Baumohl and Lurigio 2004). This is not to say that SSI payments were never spent on alcohol or drugs, but it seems clear that such behavior was not widespread enough to warrant eliminating the entire program. (At the least, more thorough and systematic investigation should have been conducted.) Indeed, the program's termination culminated years of regulatory changes that had become increasingly based on political ideology rather than the science of addiction.

Little was known about the actual behavior of chronically addicted SSI recipients when the DA&A program ended, and only limited research has been done on how individuals have been affected by the loss of disability benefits. One exception was a longitudinal study conducted by the federal Center for Substance Abuse Treatment (CSAT) in collaboration with a group of independent researchers that interviewed more than 1,700 former recipients in nine cities over for the first two years after they lost benefits. Fewer than half of the study's participants requalified for SSI benefits under another disability category. About nine percent subsequently initiated drug user treatment, and 40 percent reported some illegal drug use at the end of the two years. However, illegal drug use was not higher among those who requalified for disability benefits, casting renewed doubt on the political claim that such benefits encouraged drug use. Overall, in terms of psychological, physical and economic functioning, the investigators found that most former beneficiaries were no worse off than they had been under the DA&A program, although most also reported having to rely on friends, relatives, and other forms of assistance in order to meet even that low standard (Swartz et al. 2004).

Although more research is needed, these findings could be used to support an argument that terminating SSI's DA&A program has done no overall harm, even though that has meant leaving disabled individuals on their own to eke out a marginal existence. From an ethical perspective, however, lack of injury does not justify the double standard applied by the SSA to individuals disabled by substance misuse, first by singling them out in the 1990s for treatment mandates and punitive sanctions that were not applied to other beneficiaries, and later by declaring them ineligible for assistance at all. In crafting such policies, SSA regulators ignored what was known or could have been determined to be the involuntary character of chronic drug addiction. Not only were the facts well established by research, but a federal court had ruled in 1975 that SSA must consider involuntary consumption ("loss of control") when evaluating alcoholism as a disability (Griffis v. Weinberger 1975).

Similarly, SSA regulators ignored the episodic nature of addiction, again despite accumulated evidence that relapse is common among substance users, disabled or not, even among those participating in treatment (see, for example, McClellan, Lewis, O'Brien and Kleber 2000); it is a well-documented characteristic of the condition. The World Health Organization (2004) specifically defines substance dependence as a condition that is chronic and relapsing. Instead of recognizing this, Congress and the SSA imposed a coercive treatment policy without funding to facilitate it, and then expressed outrage when it became clear that relatively few SSI recipients were complying with the treatment mandate.

What would a science-based policy toward addiction and disability look like? To begin with, regulations and benefit schemes would recognize that addiction is an illness that is involuntary, chronic, and relapsing, and that it can prevent individuals from maintaining or perhaps even securing legal employment—in other words, that it is a disabling condition (Erickson and Callaghan 2005). Although there should be incentives for participating in substance user treatment programs, individuals would not lose benefits if and when they failed to do so. Instead, an enlightened disability program would provide uninterrupted benefits, to prevent recipients from turning to criminal activity and other socially and personally detrimental behaviors. It would also provide support services (or referrals to them) in order to help recipients cope with whatever factors contributed to relapse and help them do what is necessary to resume treatment. Finally, a science-based policy would ensure that disabled substance users have access to innovative, evidence-based vocational rehabilitation programs so that the recovery process would bring recipients as close as possible to economic self-sufficiency (Magura and Staines, 2004). The SSA is in the process of reconsidering the central role of work in its definition of disability, to possibly shift the emphasis to what applicants can do, rather than what they cannot do. In explaining the move toward reform, the Social Security Advisory Board (2003) cites the need to resolve contradictions with the Americans with Disabilities Act, to recognize how the nature of work has changed with the economy and to open new possibilities for rehabilitation. If the Social Security Administration would also recognize the accumulated science showing addiction to be a chronic relapsing involuntary illness, disabled substance users would benefit from these anticipated reforms as well.

Ellen Benoit, Ph.D. and Stephen Magura, Ph.D., C.S.W.

References

Conrad, P. and Schneider, J.W. (1992). *Deviance and medicalization: From badness to sickness.* Philadelphia: Temple University Press.

Erickson, P. and Callaghan, R.C. (2005). The likely impacts of the removal of the addiction disability benefit in Ontario. In press, the *Canadian Journal of Community Mental Health.*

Griffis v. Weinberger. (1975). 509 F.2d 837 (9th Cir.)

Magura, S. and Staines, G.L.. (2004). Special issue on contemporary vocational rehabilitation for substance users. *Substance Use and Misuse* 13/14.

McClellan, A., Lewis, D., O'Brien, C. and Kleber, H. (2000). Drug dependence, a chronic medical illness: Implications for treatment, insurance and outcomes evaluation. *Journal of the American Medical Association 284*, 1689-1695.

Social Security Advisory Board. (2003). *The Social Security definition of disability: Is it consistent with a national goal of supporting maximum self sufficiency?* Washington, D.C.: Social Security Advisory Board.

Swartz, J.A., Baumohl, J. and Lurigio, A.J. (2004). Termination of supplemental security income benefits for drug addiction and alcoholism: Results of a longitudinal study of the effects on former beneficiaries. *Social Service Review 78*(1), 96-124.

World Health Organization. (2004). *Neuroscience of psychoactive substance use and dependence.* Geneva: Department of Mental Health and Substance Abuse.

***

Critical Unresolved Ethical Issues in Substance User Treatment

A serious, still often unresolved ethical issue in the provision of substance user treatment, particularly in smaller, local treatment facilities, is about counselor-client boundaries. Issues may arise because of a long-held belief by many in the addictions treatment field that those who have experienced addiction are the most qualified and effective in providing quality, empathetic treatment to those addicted to substances. This is a curious phenomenon not generally seen in the provision of other medical and mental health related services. For example, as a society and as professionals involved in the study and delivery of health care services, we do not generally operate under the belief that it takes someone who has experienced schizophrenia to be able to provide effective, compassionate treatment for the schizophrenic because they have a unique understanding of what the victim of this condition experiences. We would suggest that the practice of treatment delivery by persons in recovery is likely born out of the prejudice with which our society has generally regarded those addicted to substances and the linking in the minds of the general public of addiction with anti-social behaviors such as lack of personal responsibility and criminal activities that are inconsistent with the values of the majority society. Indeed, understanding the pain and consequences of this prejudice is an important element for helping a person in recovery regain their position in their families, work places and society at large, but just as shared experience with addiction can be an asset for the counselor in relating to their client, it can also complicate the counselor-client relationship for some individuals, raising ethical issues of maintaining boundaries.

We acknowledge and applaud the many recovering persons who are scrupulous in the ethical provision of substance user treatment and are not suggesting that recovering persons should not be in the counselor role, but rather raising the point that recovery status of the counselor can, in some circumstances with some individuals, raise ethical issues. Although AA and NA guidelines address this issue, of particular concern in small communities—whether defined by rurality, ethnicity, sexual preference or a host of other factors which define communities—is the likelihood that if the counselor him or herself is involved in an ongoing support group, it may be very difficult to find alternatives to encountering their client attending the same group once the recovery process has begun. Their relationship within the group may often be in conflict with the counselor-client relationship that is required by law and ethical practices. Further, although empathy is necessary for good counseling, when the experience of the counselor and client are too closely aligned, over-identification may cloud judgment, leading the counselor or caregiver to engage in non-standard or even illegal actions in an effort to alleviate what they perceive as unnecessary suffering of their client. An example of this might be to give prescribed medications in larger doses or more frequently than is prescribed by the treatment plan to reduce withdrawal symptoms, an empathetic and nurturing action, but an illegal one. Education of counselors virtually always heavily emphasizes these issues and we would suggest such behaviors are certainly not the norm, but, nevertheless, do occur.

Our challenge is to recognize the potential for boundary issues and systematically educate counselors and directors of treatment facilities to be continually be alert for potential ethical conflicts and be prepared with alternatives.

Ruth W. Edwards, Ph.D. and Kendall Alexander, M.S.W.

Ruth W. Edwards, Ph.D., (USA) is a senior research scientist and director of the Tri-Ethnic Center for Prevention Research at Colorado State University. Her research interests include community interventions particularly in rural and ethnic communities, causes and correlates of substance use, violence and victimization among women and adolescents and principles and methodology for conducting successful community based participatory research. She is a member of the editorial board of Substance Use and Misuse and has served as a faculty member of the Middle Eastern Summer Institute on Drug Use (MESIDU) in Israel and Italy.

Kendall Alexander, M.S.W., (USA), is Executive Director of the Island Grove Regional Treatment Center that serves all of northeastern Colorado, US. He has almost two decades of experience in the mental health and substance use treatment fields. Mr. Alexander is particularly interested in increasing quality of care to rural and diverse populations in this era of decreased funding.

***

A critical unresolved substance use(r) intervention ethical- related, multi-dimensional issue manifests itself, daily, by:

- not considering our responsibility, if not indeed our obligation, as privileged facilitators and agents of change for pro-social opportunities, to be a voice for those who are not heard, to be a story teller for those whose tales were not told, in order create a bridge between US and THEM,
- not having learned to adequately listen to as well as hear the "losers";
- our reluctance to consider that many people working in the field of "substance use disorders" have actively or passively become co-opted into functioning as social control agents—for political and other stake holders—over dehumanized, "homogenized" but in reality heterogeneous populations of INDIVIDUAL PERSONS;
- increasing focusing on human and other resources and investing these into *forms* (i.e. techniques and models) while losing sight of the necessary and viable fundamental *meanings* (the reduction of harms- however defined- to self, to others and to a range of systems, and the production of growth and the development and maintenance of a stable BEING) for substance users as a selected THEM who are kept at a distance from OUR mainstream living.

Stanley Einstein, Ph.D.

***

An Opinion about Ethical Problems in Substance Misuse

I can only address those problems with which I am familiar, and those are the problems in the United States. However, similar factors may create ethical problems elsewhere.

At the core of the most serious ethical problems in substance user counseling in the United States are the cultural/social/political attitudes toward substance misuse and, consequently, toward those who are perceived to misuse substances. Progressively, over the past 20 years, there has been a movement away from social attitudes that understood substance misuse and its concomitant problems as issues of public health and toward not merely a moral but a criminal definition. The effect of mandatory sentences even for nonviolent drug offenders, and the expenditure of vast sums on interdiction and law enforcement as opposed to intervention and recovery are fairly well known. The social cost in almost every way has been staggering while the effect on substance use and misuse has been negligible. It is a testament to the durability of even bad ideas that despite multiple, large-scale, and well-designed studies indicating that this approach not only does not work but is counterproductive, the Government and the people of the United States persist on this course.

Two outcomes of this attitudinal shift that may not be as obvious deserve mention. The first is that the substance misuse treatment system has been largely co-opted as part of the criminal justice system. Through the early 1980's only a small proportion of individuals seeking assistance for substance misuse did so as a result of involvement with the criminal justice system—less than 10%. Today, in publicly funded clinics, upward of 85% of individuals seeking assistance do so under some court mandate. The effect of this on the relationship between those seeking assistance and those offering it has been drastic. In 2000, I did a series of interviews with rural substance user counselors about a variety of subjects. The one thing that stood out most clearly and universally was their struggle and frustration at attempting to establish relationships of trust and honesty with the majority of clients who were court referred and their pain at knowing that whatever they did would be minimally effective without such a relationship. Further, in many cases it is counselors who are also under court mandate to produce monthly progress reports on their clients' progress for the courts. All of this removes them from the traditional role of healer and makes them a kind of more psychologically sophisticated probation officer. You might ask. "Since the court is not paying for treatment, why don't they just refuse?" The simple answer is that their client will be sent back to prison and they don't see this as in their client's best interest.

The second outcome is that insurance companies and managed care entities have felt increasingly less and less obliged to cover the cost of treatment for substance use disorders. After all, they don't pay for treatment of burglary or homicide. As a result, even individuals who are reasonably well-insured for other behavioral conditions may find it impossible to receive anything more than the most cursory and ineffective assistance for substance misuse. Unfortunately, they do not concomitantly lower their premiums as a result.

Theodore M. Godlaski, M. Div.

***

The Most Critical Unresolved Ethical Issue Associated with Contemporary Substance User Treatment (Harm Reduction Psychotherapy)

The single most important ethical issue surrounding Harm Reduction Psychotherapy (HRP) is making the distinction between helping clients reduce the potential of harming themselves via psychoactive substance use and minimizing the harm that psychoactive substances can cause. As a clinician, the HRP therapist's goal is to help his or her clients reduce the potential for self-harm. In order to do this the clinician must take an active role in their clients' treatment, and remain interested in how they treatment themselves. It has been observed that poor self-care dominates the lives of people who are diagnosed with substance use disorder (SUD). Therapists must help their clients take better care of themselves. From a psychoanalytic perspective, the therapist helps strengthen the client's ego functioning that has been diminished by the SUD.

It is paramount that the therapist practicing HRP help clients take better care of themselves. In order to do this, the therapist must take the client's substance use and its concomitant potential for danger seriously. However, it is also easy to forget how dangerous psychoactive substance use can be. A HRP therapist's personal beliefs could create a countertransference problem in which the therapist could minimize the potential dangers of psychoactive substance use and believe that his or her patient's substance abuse is not so bad. However, such an attitude, partially conscious, and partially unconscious, is not what is meant by HRP. Effective HRP must be practiced actively to engage the client in better self-care. This can happen in many ways, including analysis of defense mechanisms, teaching coping and self-care skills, forming social and familial networks, self-help treatment programs, among others.

To prevent these kinds of countertransference problems, the HRP therapist must discuss his or her cases with supervisors, colleagues, and at some point, be in his or her own treatment. Otherwise, the clinician can fail to intervene when the client is behaving dangerously to themselves and, in such a situation, HRP would be harm inducing rather than harm reducing.

William H. Gottdiener, Ph.D.

***

From my perspective as a philosopher of criminal law, the most critical unresolved ethical issue about substance use intervention concerns criminalization: What conditions must be satisfied by a substance before the state is justified in using criminal sanctions against persons who possess and use that substance for recreational purposes? Once we know what criteria a given substance needs to satisfy, we can begin to apply these conditions to existing substances like tobacco, alcohol, cocaine and heroin. In the absence of criteria to distinguish those substances eligible for prohibition from those that are not, our existing policy is suspiciously unprincipled and ad hoc. No legal philosopher should be complacent about this state of affairs.

Douglas N. Husak, J.D., Ph.D.

***

The single most important issue lying at the core of the debate on drugs is the question of the degree to which we should criminalise drug-taking behaviour. There are very good pragmatic reasons for legalising and regulating the supply of currently illicit drugs, and these emerge once we recognise how drugs are simply another commodity subject to the laws of supply and demand. The illegal nature of a drug, along with its attractiveness, provides the essential high price-fixing mechanism needed for big-time drug dealers to thrive. Remove that, and you remove them. Licensing and regulation of production, and control and restriction of supply, such as exists in the pharmaceutical industry, would be far more effective at reducing the supply of currently illicit drugs than is prohibition. As things stand it's easier for a teenager to buy marijuana than alcohol, and easier (at least in big cities) to get hold of heroin than benzodiazepines.

We know that people have always used recreational drugs regardless of the lawfulness of that pursuit; we have good reason to believe they will always do so as long as we occupy a society whose people are not controlled by totalitarian techniques. A free and open society may frown on the taking of substances it regards as harmful or bad in some way; it may legislate against the taking of such substances; but it must accept such behaviour as a statistical certainty. Citizens within liberal democratic societies will take these substances to some degree regardless of what its drug laws proscribe. It follows that a zero tolerance approach to taking drugs is doomed to failure. Given these assumptions, how should drug policy sensibly be conceived?

First we should ask whether the badness of taking any particular drug tracks the current legal status of that drug. Further we should question whether the practice of consuming drugs is in itself the kind of behaviour that is so bad it should be outlawed, for if we cherish a society with real liberties, then we cherish a society where we allow adults to behave in ways we may well disapprove of.

People drink tea and coffee as part of a social ritual and as a stimulant. People drink alcohol to unwind after work, and as a social lubricant. People smoke cigarettes again as part of a social ritual, and for its pleasurable hit, but often also because of its addictive properties. People take amphetamines for a range of reasons, social, work, and because of its addictive qualities. The same can be said for some other recreational drugs, such as cocaine and ecstasy. All of these drugs—both legal and illegal—can cause harm to their users in varying degrees, and in different ways. Of all of these drugs, tobacco is probably the most dangerous, causing, for example, around 16% of all deaths in the US in an average year. If a drug as seriously harmful and addictive as tobacco were to be trialled for legal usage in 2005, those attempting to have it licensed would not make it past the front door of any bureaucratic agency anywhere in the world that wasn't either fundamentally irrational or corrupt.

The point is, then, that there are historical reasons why some drugs are legal and some are not, such that the inference from illegality to immorality is unfounded. The oft-made argument that we should not add to the damage wrought by alcohol and tobacco by legalising or decriminalising recreational use of other drugs is weak. First it ignores the considerable damage caused by criminalisation. Second, it is not a conceptual truth that recreational drug use is damaging. That depends on both the properties of the particular drug and the way it is used. Alcohol in moderate quantities is now thought to be beneficial, in excess it can be a disaster, and the same may be true of some currently illicit drugs. Recreational drugs are taken for their pleasurable effects and for social enhancement. The motivation to design a drug with these desirable properties that lacked all harmful side effects, would be, *prima facie* a rational motivation. If someone wanted to ban such a drug it could only be because they disapproved of this way of gaining pleasure and so forth. But disapproval of an activity is not a sufficient ground for criminalising it. And nor is the fact that it carries some risk.

Drug taking, whether licit or illicit, has risks. But so do many other perfectly licit activities. Sky diving once a week is vastly more dangerous than smoking cannabis (say) once a month. Should we criminalise that? Injuries cause suffering. Should we stop people playing contact sports where the risk of injury is high? Should we prohibit the introduction of new sports or pursuits which carry any risk of injury? The answer is that we don't and we shouldn't. What we do is to try to minimise the risks attached to these voluntary activities through regulating them. We have rules in sport and referees to control the play. People still get injured of course, sometimes seriously, but it is hard to see what good would be served by imposing a legal punishment on participants on top of the injury they have sustained.

Thus we should get a grip on the real problem: the taking of drugs is bad (and more likely to result in a range of harms) when it becomes an end in itself, as exemplified in those who are in the grip of a habit or addiction. For most people, the use of alcohol, tobacco, analgesics, some prescription drugs, and a range of illicit drugs is not problematic. The key test is in the relation between the drug and the person: who is in charge? Is the person using the drug, or is the drug using the person? Those who plan their lives around the taking and securing of their drug(s) of choice have tipped over into problematic use. Is it helpful to criminalise their behaviour at this point? We think it is not.

Substance use may well be morally criticisable when it generates harm to self and others, but not all moral wrongs are appropriately dealt with by the criminal law. That one's family is distressed by the effects of one's drug taking is an important moral consideration against taking drugs, but upsetting one's family is not against the law. A person who steals or deals to support a heroin habit has reached a point where it may be thought that it is legitimate for the law to step in. But notice that a vicious circularity is present here: this person has turned to crime in large part because criminalisation of heroin use has made procuring it risky and expensive. Alcoholics and nicotine addicts are not typically forced into crime to maintain their habits. And criminality is not intrinsically associated with opiate use since it is well known that offending behaviour diminishes among those addicts taking opiates in the form of methadone maintenance therapy. Much of the moral badness associated with heroin use emerges because it is criminally proscribed, not the other way around.

Moreover, the social circumstances which lie behind the taking of both licit and illicit drugs are, as we've indicated in our paper, complex, and the reasons why people engage in such behaviour are similarly complex. Complex problems aren't solved by simplistic solutions, and the imposition of criminal sanctions, especially on the poor, the mentally ill, and those on the margins, only exacerbate an already difficult situation. Criminalising drug use is both immoral and unworkable.

Jeannette Kennett, Ph.D. and Stephen Matthews, Ph.D.

***

Drug Use, Misuse, and Addiction as Free Choice? Autonomy and Drug-Taking Behaviors

While many ethical issues and dilemmas associated with drug use and addiction have been addressed, debated, and some even resolved, there still is a critical ethical issue that remains unresolved. In fact, it never will be resolved, but hopefully a balance between extremes someday can be attained. Autonomy is a primary ethical principle that refers to an individual's liberty of thought, choice, and action. A drug user's autonomy is at the crux of many ethical, as well as interpersonal and socio-political, issues and dilemmas in drug use prevention and treatment.

For young people, any type of drug use is viewed as problematic, as is the use of illicit drugs by adults. Drug education and prevention programs, whether focused on abstinence or harm reduction as the goal, have failed to achieve those goals for most individuals, especially those engaged more "heavily" in drug use. Drug use typically is viewed as a cause of personal and social maladjustments. But perhaps it is the other way around, and drug use, especially "problem drug use", is a symptom of maladjustment (Shedler and Block, 1990). Regardless, current sentiment is that everyone should be tested regularly for the "possibility" of drug use. Yet, most drug testing programs are greatly flawed, ineffective, and identify only a small proportion of actual users.

If an individual is deemed by others to be engaging in a pattern of drug use considered problematic by those others, or uses certain drugs even intermittently, then it is time to intervene. Intervention seemingly has become a common occurrence in our lives. Two recovering drug users in Minnesota "have formed a successful business helping other people stage interventions to get friends and relatives help for alcohol and other drug abuse" (Anon., 2005a). Six offices nationwide design interventions for clients, including businesses and families, at a cost of $2,700 to $5,500 per "event." Intervening into another person's problem behavior has become an obsession for many people, as evidenced by two reality-based television shows on "Intervention" (Arts & Entertainment and Fox) that depict this "event" for interested viewers, as well as another reality show on the PAX network called, "Cold Turkey," which intrusively records users as they try to quit without treatment, but for cash awards (Anon., 2005b). Research on the value and effectiveness of these interventions is inconclusive, and in many instances, interventions have led to extremely negative outcomes, including disrupted or destroyed interpersonal relationships with no change in the targeted problem drug use. For instance, on the "Intervention" reality show, "if the intervention doesn't succeed, viewers will still be witness to a portrait of the unrelenting power of addiction" (Anon., 2005b).

If an individual uses drugs on a regular basis, or certain drugs which are defined as being illegal, then they are addicted. But is addiction a myth (Davies, 1997), or if it is "real," then what is wrong with being addicted (Keane, 2000)? Individuals addicted to drugs must be treated. But how often is the choice to seek and engage in treatment made voluntarily or coerced? Research also has shown that treatment success is limited and an elusive goal for many users. On the other hand, a growing body of "natural recovery" research (Shorkey 2004) suggests that many people addicted to drugs stop using on their own without the help of a treatment program, or move back and forth over time between problem drug use, use, and non-use, and in these cases, the decision to do so and the actual behavior is the choice of that individual.

In all of these examples, instigated or commanded by people other than the drug user, where is the individual drug user's autonomy? Is it that their autonomy is not relevant, or quite simply, does it not exist? Is drug use a disease, moral weakness, illegal activity, psychological disorder, or genetic flaw, and who determines which of these? Or is drug use a behavior in which a person chooses to engage?

Most current efforts at drug prevention and treatment are not effective, probably due to the erroneous focus on symptoms rather than on the psychological syndromes, socio-political contexts, or individual beliefs and reasons underlying the user's decision to engage in any pattern of drug use. Perhaps addiction is not something that happens to people; it is something that people do (Davies, 1997). A more extreme view is that "drugs don't cause addiction. Addiction doesn't mean you can't control your behavior. Drugs are inanimate objects. They have no will or power of their own" (Schaler, 2000). In essence, addiction is an expression of a person's values, and thus, addiction is a choice. The retort, of course, is that a drug's pharmacological activity obscures or destroys the ability to think or choose; the user no longer has freedom of will.

There is a need for "humanity and comprehensibility in a process too often seen as arising from the magical power of drugs to change the very bases of human behavior, regardless of the goals and purposes of the user" (Davies, 1997). The autonomy of drug users has been superseded by the good of society, the will of non-users, the arrogance of the "others" who know what's good for everyone. This imbalance gets us nowhere in drug prevention and treatment efforts (Montagne, 2002). It is time to redress this imbalance.

Michael Montagne, Ph.D.

Michael Montagne, B.Sc. (pharmacy), M.A. (sociology), Ph.D. (social pharmacy), is Professor of Social Pharmacy and Associate Dean of Graduate Studies at the Massachusetts College of Pharmacy & Health Sciences and Adjunct Professor of International Health at Boston University's School of Public Health. He has taught and performed research for 25 years on the social, cultural, and historical aspects of drug effects, drug use and drug discovery.

He has co-authored books on drug development (Searching for Magic Bullets: Orphan Drugs, Consumer Activism, and Pharmaceutical Development, 1994 and Clinical Research in Pharmaceutical Development, 1996), pharmacoepidemiology (Pharmacoepidemiology: Principles & practice, 2001) and has studied drug use and drug advertising from a sociological perspective ("Drug Advertising and Promotion," Journal of Drug Issues, Spring, 1992). He teaches courses on "Drugs and Society," "Drug Education," and "Pharmacoepidemiology." His current research focuses on social pharmacology, media representations of drug use in America, anti-depressant drug effects and use, and literacy issues in medication use. He is a member of the editorial board of Substance Use and Misuse

References

Anon. (2005a, June 29). Minn. pair turn recovery into successful business. *Join Together Online*. (http://www.jointogether.org/y/0,2521,577604,00.html. Accessed 7/28/05).

Anon. (2005b, March 16). Reality TV shows focus on addiction. *Join Together Online.* (http://www.jointogether.org/y/0,2521,576436,00.html. Accessed 7/28/05).

Davies, J.B. (1997). *The Myth of Addiction.* Second Edition. Philadelphia PA: Harwood Academic,

Keane, H. (2002). *What's Wrong with Addiction?* New York: New York University Press.

Montagne, M. (2002). Appreciating the user's perspective: listening to the "Methadonians." *Substance Use & Misuse, 37,* 563-67.

Schaler, J.A. (2000). Addiction is a Choice. Chicago, IL: Open Court.

Shedler, J., and Block, J. (1990). Adolescent drug use and psychological health: A longitudinal study. *American Psychologist;45,* 612-30.

Shorkey, C.T. (2004). Spontaneous Recovery and Chemical Dependence: Indexed bibliography of articles. In *Professional Chemical Dependency Journals.* University of Texas at Austin <http://128.83.80.200/tattc/spontaneousrecovery.html>.

***

Ethical Issues in Drug Dependence Treatment in Resource Poor Settings

The existence of guidelines and state and national level legislation in many developed countries ensures that a discussion of ethical and legal issues in substance user treatment remains on the table. Key areas of ethical and legal consideration in substance use treatment are: confidentiality, informed consent, the duty to care, respecting client self-determination and credentializing mechanisms for service providers. Unfortunately, ethical aspects of substance user treatment receive very little attention in resource poor countries. A review of the literature related to ethics in drug dependence treatment in developing countries does not reveal a mature discussion on the issue. Notably, there are no comparative studies on how different geographically, culturally and legally dissimilar locations interpret and deal with ethical issues. Neither is it clear as to what extent ethical issues vary in response to differing treatment approaches, for example key ethical considerations in a methadone maintenance programme as compared to a therapeutic community model (or in a voluntary versus mandatory treatment programme). In order to understand why this is the case, it is useful to provide a brief sketch of substance user treatment in developing countries. I paint this picture from an Asian perspective.

Historically, substance user treatment in most Asian countries is related to legislation mandating treatment—frequently related to national governments being signatories to the supply-reduction focussed United Nations (UN) Conventions on Psychotropic Substances. In 1961 the UN adopted the Single Convention on Narcotic Drugs. The Convention had 51 Articles and was ratified by 73 states. The Preamble stated that the Parties to the Convention are "*concerned* with the health and welfare of mankind," and "*recognis[e]* that addiction to narcotic drugs constitutes a serious evil for the individual and is fraught with social and economic danger to mankind" and are "*conscious* of their duty to prevent and combat the evil of drug addiction."

(Note: emphasis in the original)

The Single Convention on Narcotic Drugs of 1961 was amended in 1972. The amending Protocol called for the provision of adequate resources to "provide assistance in the fight against illicit traffic" and declared that "one of the most effective methods of treatment for addiction is treatment in a hospital institution having a drug free atmosphere." Thus the themes of the Amendment Protocol focused around the control of drug supply and abstinence based treatment. In 1988 the UN adopted the Convention against Illicit Traffic in Narcotic Drugs and Psychotropic Substances. This Convention broadly followed the principles laid out in the Conventions of 1961 and 1971, but went on to strongly connect criminal activity with drug use. In the preamble it stated that the Parties to the Convention are:

"Aware that illicit traffic generates large financial profits and wealth enabling transnational criminal organisations to penetrate, contaminate and corrupt the structures of government,...and society at all its levels."

In addition to this, the Convention recognised clearly for the first time that there was a need to "eliminate the root causes of the problem of narcotic drugs and psychotropic substances including the illicit demand for such drugs and substances."

However, nowhere in the Convention was a strategy spelt out to deal with how a reduction in the demand for illicit drugs might be effected. Of the thirty-three articles in the Convention, not a single one deals with issues of treatment, rehabilitation and socioeconomic reintegration.

The ethics of "abstinence only"

In country after country, these Conventions led to the enactment of national legislation which criminalised opium and mandated drug dependence treatment for the possession of small amounts of drugs as an alternative to a jail term. As a result, most drug dependence treatment was (and is) abstinence based. The criminalisation of drug use has also led to a strong and dogmatic focus on abstinence being achieved not through pharmacological and psychosocial interventions but through detention and hard physical labour. This model of so-called drug treatment has been witnessed in South and South East Asia, particularly in China, Malaysia, Myanmar and Vietnam.

More recently, these countries have had to review their approach to substance use in the light of massive HIV epidemics among drug user populations. China for example intends to provide large scale methadone treatment to IDUs and Malaysia has admitted that the provision of sterile injecting equipment is a key strategy in preventing HIV epidemics. However, the overwhelming focus remains on abstinence. In the light of the HIV/AIDS epidemic, is it ethical for governments to require complete abstinence from its citizens, despite the enormous relapse rates that abstinence based programmes display? I would argue that it is unethical in the extreme to not allow individuals opportunities to reduce harms to themselves and to others related to drug use. It is also unethical to refuse substitution therapy to HIV positive IDUs who need to comply with lifesaving anti-retroviral therapy. Current legislation in the majority of Asian countries prevents the provision of risk reduction services to those who need them most.

A duty to care—How ethical is "cold turkey?"

Drug dependence treatment in developing countries in many settings (including Therapeutic Community (TC), faith-based organisations and prisons), involves the detoxification of clients "cold turkey." Medication to alleviate withdrawal symptoms such as Catapres (Clonidine) or other pharmacological interventions are treated with great suspicion. Most services provided in such settings do not conform to any standards or substance user treatment guidelines in terms of duration of treatment, client assessment and treatment planning, detoxification procedures, rehabilitation and follow up. Another enduring feature of substance user treatment in many developing countries is the provision of drug user treatment "beds" inside psychiatric units or mental health units. While the levels of psychiatric co-morbidity in drug dependent populations are significant, should drug users be treated in the same fashion as a mentally ill individual? In Bangladesh, for instance, the use of high doses of anti-psychotic medication to keep clients docile during detoxification is widespread and often requires a detoxification from these drugs themselves. Several ethical issues arise in this type of substance user treatment provision.

- First, is it ethical to give the name of "treatment" to what is in effect detention by largely untrained staff, frequently without medication and counselling?
- Do treatment providers have the right to force clients to undergo painful withdrawal and argue that it is part of required behaviour change? Or worse still, prescribe inappropriate medication to unsuspecting clients?

Confidentiality and informed consent

Given the lack of "buy in" into human rights-related principles in many governments in this region, client confidentiality and informed consent is rarely practiced. In a recent survey of 7 drug user treatment providers in India and Bangladesh (by me), not a single one required written informed consent prior to in-patient treatment. While clients are required to sign indemnity forms with provisions to absolve providers of all responsibility in case of death or injury, very little is done to protect client's rights in such settings. Data protection is non-existent. The impact of poor confidentiality on client stigmatisation is immense. Governments have been greatly remiss in not enacting and enforcing legislation that protects client rights and confidentiality.

Equity and access to treatment

The public sector in developing countries has failed miserably to provide accessible and equitable treatment to drug users despite mandating treatment. Countless surveys indicate that the most marginalised and poor are over-represented among drug users. The concept of "rights–based" treatment approaches is a relatively new one in such settings. A large majority of clients needing treatment are unable to afford it, forcing them to seek out sub-standard and humiliating options in their desperation to be rid of drugs. In Manipur (northeast India), poor and hapless parents are known to beg police officials to arrest their sons and daughters so that they can be sent to jail, where they are detoxified by detention. Another issue pertaining to access is gender related. In all of South Asia I am aware of no more than 2 non-governmental agencies that provide affordable abstinence based drug dependence treatment to women.

Treatment by quacks

Drug user treatment is provided by anyone who wishes to do so—including "recovering addicts," members of faith-based organisations, or, quite simply, quacks. No accreditation is required in many countries to provide drug user treatment services. No minimum standards or clinical guidelines exist in many countries. Physical punishment, didactic learning and detention are key features of this type of treatment. Even so, the numbers of treatment slots do not even begin to address the high demand for treatment. The paucity of resources for optimal treatment provision and the lack of basic health insurance options in poor countries often results in clients only achieving detoxification (medically assisted or "cold turkey"), but they believe that they are being treated. It is unjustifiable both from a moral and ethical point of view to force individuals into "drug treatment" without providing a minimum standard of services. Further, service providers and governments have an ethical obligation to inform clients adequately of service options in a context where rehabilitation services either do not exist or cannot be afforded.

In conclusion, the principles of consent, beneficence and justice are rarely incorporated in substance user treatment in developing countries. In fact, the entire discussion on ethical issues remains very poorly developed at this stage.

Mukta Sharma, M.S.C.

Mukta Sharma, M.S.C., (India), completed her Ph.D. in 2006 at the London School of Economics. In 2003 she was elected as the Vice President of the International Harm Reduction Association. Mukta trained as a demographer and is currently based as a Senior Technical Officer, Drug Use-related Interventions, Family Health International in Dhaka, Bangladesh. For the last eight years Mukta has worked in the field of drug use, HIV/AIDS prevention and care in developing and post conflict countries. She is a member of the Editorial Board of Substance Use and Misuse and the International Journal of Drug Policy, and has published numerous articles and made presentations at many international conferences and seminars. Key areas of work include policy analysis, integration of STI treatment in substance use programmes in resource poor countries, evaluation of needle syringe programs, promotion/design of high coverage and quality interventions.

***

Listen to the Voices of the Modern Day Enslaved in the United States Prison Economy: Do You Hear An Ethical Dilemma?

As mentioned in my chapter, given the disproportionate arrest and incarceration of those who are African American and Hispanic for drug crimes within the United States, the majority of these recently released from incarceration and entering drug user treatment/counseling are also African American or Hispanic. Such clients may have been arrested as a consequence of a form of racial profiling wherein the police and undercover narcotics officers have systematically targeted for investigation and arrest those who are African American and Hispanic, and living in particular poor urban neighborhoods in places such as New York City. Some of these individuals may have been drug dealers, but never used drugs. Others may have stopped using drugs once incarcerated; despite having been abstinent for as many as three years and/or having received prison-based drug user treatment, these individuals typically face a mandate to drug user treatment as a condition of their parole. As a result, there is a dilemma involving whether it is ethical for those who have not used drugs in many years to be mandated to and thereby occupy drug user treatment/counseling slots that might be desperately needed by those who are currently actively using drugs.

But, there is also a much larger contemporary ethical dilemma in the United States. The ethical dilemma of which I speak is reminiscent of the American plantation system that held sway in the United States across prior centuries. In the American plantation system there were many who benefited from slavery—some directly and others indirectly. Racism drove the selection of those enslaved and forced to endure unpaid labor and the loss of their freedom for the benefit of others in the United States. The contemporary ethical dilemma in the United States shares certain key features with the prior American plantation system: racism drives the selection of those forced to endure their loss of freedom while incarcerated, and there are many who benefit from the United States prison economy—some directly and others indirectly.

I have listened to the voices of the modern day enslaved in the United States prison economy. Their voices support the assertion that the contemporary United States prison economy is akin to the American plantation system of former centuries. Consider the following cycle my former clients have helped me to appreciate, effectively describing the whole of their experience as the modern day enslaved in the United States prison economy:

1) being arrested for drug sale or drug possession, as well as being caught up in drug sweeps in targeted neighborhoods in New York City, including being charged with loitering in a known drug selling area for merely walking through or living in and around what the police considered an active drug selling area while being totally innocent of any drug involvement;
2) being poor, lacking funds for legal bail and/or representation, receiving inferior/inadequate free legal services, and being pressured to accept a plea bargain where one admits to being guilty of the drug charges, even when not guilty;
3) going to prison for one to several years and sustaining the upstate New York rural economy within communities that have lost other forms of employment, as these communities have become dependent on the prison industrial complex to sustain their communities' economic livelihood;
4) experiencing prison incarceration, including being moved across several prisons, while observing within each prison setting how the majority of inmates are from seven poor urban largely African American and Hispanic neighborhoods in New York City;
5) eventually returning to one of these seven New York City neighborhoods and experiencing considerable difficulty reintegrating back into the lives of partners/spouses, children, and their community;
6) having varied problems such as great difficulty finding work because of a felony status, and being barred from access to public housing because of that same felony status; and,
7) being forbidden to work (as is a practice of many parole officers across many of the early months of being on parole) and being mandated to community-based

addiction treatment as a condition of one's parole, including an arrangement wherein urine toxicology reports may be accessed by parole, and the possibility of being violated by parole and experiencing re-incarceration exists. In listening to the voices of my former clients, the modern day enslaved in the United States prison economy, do you hear an ethical dilemma?

I would like to offer a frank analysis of this 7-step cycle that suggests that there is, indeed, a complex ethical dilemma. This analysis suggests how societal-wide systemic racism built upon the practice of racial profiling has created a modern day United States prison economy that is akin to the former plantation era slavery economy; moreover, this economy benefits many in this society. The direct beneficiaries are the communities in places such as upstate New York that experience a new revitalized economy with employment dependent upon the presence of a prison in their community. But, there are also indirect beneficiaries. Just as with the American plantation system that held sway in the United States across prior centuries wherein mostly Southern masters of slaves seemed to have their hands "tainted" by slavery as direct beneficiaries, the reality was that many others were also indirect beneficiaries of slavery—including banks that accepted slaves as collateral for loans, insurance companies, and the United States economy as a whole. In contemporary times, consider the "others" who indirectly benefit from the painful experiences of the modern day enslaved in the United States prison economy:

1) New York City based police officers and undercover narcotics squads whose employment and income is driven by and dependent upon the arrest of a certain "number" of suspects per month; and,
2) New York City-based drug user treatment/counseling programs whose staff members' employment and income is driven by and dependent upon mandated clients to ensure full caseloads and competition for treatment slots by those who are mandated and not mandated. Thus, New York City-based police officers and drug user treatment/counseling staff members are facing the ethical dilemma of colluding in a racist system of oppression by indirectly benefiting from the contemporary United States prison economy; they are like those working in the banks and insurance companies whose employment was intimately tied up with the enslaved cargo of the American plantation economy.

So, on a very simple level, there is the dilemma involving whether or not it is ethical for a mandated client sent by parole to enter a drug user treatment slot post-incarceration, especially if such slots are limited in number. But, on a much more complex level there is the dilemma of drug user treatment/counseling programs colluding in and benefiting from the new United States prison economy which is based on racism—including the racial profiling of drug user suspects. Having shared with you the voices of the modern day enslaved in the United States prison economy, I leave you with a thought provoking question: Do you hear an ethical dilemma?

Finally, what is a modern day abolitionist to do?

Barbara C. Wallace, Ph.D.

***

Keeping Heart

Addiction to alcohol and other drugs is a serious problem in the United States. In the past addiction was largely viewed as a moral problem. People were seen as "being bad" and "needing to get good". The emergence of Alcoholics Anonymous (AA) in 1935 coupled with the development of the disease model of alcoholism led to a more compassionate view of people who had addiction problems.

Senator Harold Hughes masterfully and passionately brought addiction problems into the public debate in the 1970's. His efforts led to legislation that provided structures and funding to promote treatment, education, and research on alcohol and drug addiction. Consequently, there was a proliferation of addiction treatment programs throughout the US in the 1970's and 1980's. These programs were largely inpatient programs that were based on the twelve steps of AA and the disease model of addiction. The addiction counselors who staffed these programs were often people who were themselves recovering from alcohol or drug addiction. The treatment milieu provided an environment and a process that encouraged people to get honest about who and what they were and make changes where necessary. The process was painstaking, but brought many people new found freedom. There were some problems with these inpatient programs; they used a "one-size-fits-all" approach, were costly, and often used non-professionals as treatment staff.

The body of research on addiction also grew in the in the 1970's and 1980's and continues to grow today. Researchers have developed empirically based knowledge on the etiology and treatment of addiction problems. It has become apparent that addiction is a complex and multiply determined problem that has physiological, psychological, and social causes and consequences. It has also become apparent that addicted individuals have differing treatment needs and that, for many, outpatient treatment is as effective as inpatient treatment.

Treatment programs today are largely outpatient and staffed by professionals. There is a great deal of emphasis on training and motivating addiction treatment professionals to use the evidence-based interventions. The shift away from one-size-fits-all treatment and use of research and evidence based interventions will benefit addicted individuals in the long run. The concern is that in the process of shifting our paradigm we may leave our hearts behind.

The treatment programs of the past emphasized honesty, compassion, responsibility, courage, and love. The addiction treatment field today is under pressure to emphasize technique, thought, and cost containment. Certainly, identifying the most effective treatments for individuals in various conditions and circumstances and getting clinicians to use those treatments with their clients is necessary and important. In my view, it is also necessary and important to appreciate and retain honesty, compassion, responsibility, courage, and love in addiction treatment. The greatest ethical challenge that I see for the addiction treatment field today is keeping its heart while developing its head.

Shelly A. Wiechelt, Ph.D.

***

Let me briefly comment on what I think is today's greatest challenge for substance use educators. I came into the field of substance use treatment as a therapist when the ideology of Alcoholics Anonymous had replaced the ideology of the Temperance Movement. There was no body of research on alcohol or substance use. My treatment methods largely had to conform to or be in opposition to AA beliefs. Substance use education was substantially based on AA convictions. Switch to the present: the substance use knowledge base has exploded. There has been a proliferation of journals dedicated to issues of substance use. My capacity to absorb, synthesize, and teach important knowledge about substance use is under siege. I believe my greatest challenge, and for substance use educators in general, is to responsibly present the most relevant substance use knowledge to students, teach them the skills to evaluate new findings, and to instill in them the importance of following important new findings once they graduate. There are several potential dangers: 1) Educators may adhere to personal convictions and ignore current findings. 2) Educators may resort to over-simplified presentations of new findings and fail to instill appreciation of the objectivity and scope of important research findings. 3) Educators may intimidate students about evaluating knowledge and leave the impression that only the experts can determine the validity and application of research findings. 4) Educators may convey that it is too burdensome for clinicians or policymakers to keep up with current findings.

What can be done to help the substance use educators? Besides the obvious answers—reading the *Journal of the Teaching of Addictions* and joining the professional organization of substance use educators, the International Coalition for Addiction Studies Education, INCASE (INCASE.org)—I believe books like this one are invaluable. I enjoyed collaborating on this project with the editors, John and Stan, and reading the drafts of chapters relevant to mine. I look forward to reading the finished chapters of my colleagues. I felt I was speaking to a community of interested people. One of the best features of the book is the international and wide differences in professional background of the authors. A number of issues are examined from a number of different perspectives. I have certainly learned a lot by participating. Interdisciplinary collaboration on specific topics I believe would help us educators begin to synthesize the many (competing) perspectives in viewing substance use. In addition to the separate chapters in this book, I would like to see in books like this a final chapter where there is a discussion among the contributors of all of the issues raised in the book. Such a discussion could be arranged via internet.

Interdisciplinary conferences could be convened and focus on specific timely topics. I believe we could take a topic such as harm reduction or coerced treatment and convene a group of experts from all the relevant disciplines and create a synthesis which integrates these points of view into a coherent direction with policy implications. I think it's worth a try.

Daniel Yalisove, Ph.D.

Appendix 3 - Foreign Language Abstracts

Schwierige Entscheidungen in der Forschung und in der Ethik: Die Fehlerhafte Anwendendung von Drogenverbrauchsstatistiken

Manuella Adrian, M. Sc Hyg.

Wissenschaftliche Forschung hat uns mit einem der leistungsfähigsten Mittel, das Los der Menschheit zu verbessern versehen. Jedoch kann ihre Macht die Quelle einer Menge moralischer und ethischer Fragen für Forscher sein, die sie benutzen. Die übliche Aufmerksamkeit in die Ethik der Forschung ist z.Z. auf die Verwendung von Menschen als Probesubjekten gerichtet, und wird dahin orientiert, die Wahrscheinlichkeit au vermindern, den Teilnehmern Schaden zuzufügen. Gute Forschungsrichtlinien sind im letzten halben Jahrhundert entwickelt worden. Auch erkennt man heute das ethische Dilemma, das aus der Forschungen zu militärischen Zwecken auftaucht. Weniger bekannt sind ethischen Fragen, die aus der wissenschaftlichen Methode selber entstehen, d.h. von der Deutung von erforschten Daten. Solche Fragen werden in der vorliegenden Arbeit beschrieben werden. Wir überprüfen einige der grundlegenden Lehren der wissenschaftlichen Methode, die im Bereich des Substanzgebrauches und -mißbrauches angewendet werden. Wir beginnen mit den methodischen Grundprinzipien, die von Isaac Newton für die Forschung von Kausalitätsbeziehungen entwickelt worden waren, und dann nehmen wir die neueren Begriffsrahmen in Blick, die dazu verwendet werden, um Stellen zu identifizieren, wo Interventionen gerechtfertigt werden können, in der wir handeln dürfen, um die gewollten Resultate zu erreichen, selbst wenn strenge lineare Kausalität nicht angewendet werden kann. Wir benutzen Beispiele nicht nur vom Bereich des Substanzgebrauches, sondern auch von einem allgemeineren wissenschaftlichen Rahmen, worin solche Beispiele nützlich sein können. Wir betrachten dann die ethischen und moralischen Probleme, die aus dem Wesen des nachgeforschten Themas resultieren können, wie aus seiner Organisation und Finanzierung, sowie aus dem Gebrauch von nicht angebrachten Methoden und Techniken -- einschließlich der Fragen, die aus der Benutzung von Menschen als Probekaninchen entstehen – die zu Fehlschlüsse führen könnten, die für die Patienten, für die Wissenschaftler, und für die Gesellschaft als Ganzes schädlich sein könnten.

Aufgetauchte ethische Themen durch Selbsthilfsgruppen in bezug auf Drogenbenutzertherapie: Die Position der Zwoelf-schritt Organizationen

Allaman Allamani, M.D.

Die wirklichen Unterschiede in der Art in der Selbsthilfgruppen im gegensatz zur Professionellen Behandlung und Institutionen, sich abgeben und arbeiten mit Missbraucher von alkoholischen Getraenke und anderen Drogen, verursachen etische Implikationen. Insbesondere ist die Ethik der Zwoelf-schritt Organizationen ist *Universalistisch, und basiert auf Spiritualitaet Anderstsein und Solidaritaet*. Obwohl man ihren Erfolg in der Abstinenz Erzeugung wissenschftlich studieren kann, sind sie am Besten als "*Heilende*

Gemeinschaften" beschrieben (Seppala, 2001). Auf der anderen Seite, wenn professionelle Drogenbenutzerprogramme sich beteiligen, scheint die Etik Utilitarisch zu sein; sie wird orientiert in Richtung entweder des Einzelnen oder der Sozialengruppe. Sogar wenn diese zwei diverse Richtungen mitwirken, entstehen Spannung und Konflikt, die cooperation zwischen Selbsthilfsprogramme und der Krankenkassensysteme ist heutzutage Weltweit verwischt.

Behinderte und Drogennutzer Behandlungen/Rehabilitation: Ethische Bedenken

Ellen Benoit, Ph.D und Stephen Magura, Ph.D.

In den USA bevor 1996 Personnen, die Drogen oder Alkohol kronisch suechtig waren, konnten als Behinderte anerkannt werden, und somit Soziallohn von der Social Security Administration (SSA) erhalten, in so fern sie i ein Behandlungsprogramm mitmachten. Die gesetzgebung von Maerz 1996, verlangte von der SSA Suechtige zu eliminieren von den anerkannten Behinderten Listen und somit jeden der Sozialhilfe bekam von ihren Listen zu loeschen. Diese Aenderung bringt hervor wichtige ethische Fragen, die wir ansprechen aus der Perspektive der Rechtsverteilung. Wir untersuchen die Unterscheidungspolitik zwischen "erkannte" und unerkannte" Hilfsbeduer ftigen Personnen und analysieren wie die aertzlische zwispaeltige Natur der Sucht hervor bringt gegeneinander prallende Argumente in der Anerkennsungdebate. Zum beispiel ist es ein voluntarischer Akt Behinderte zu werden wegen Missbrauch von Substanzen? Zum Abschluss, wir anylisieren die Konsequenzen der reklassifikation der SSA bezogen auf die politischen Interesanten: Nutzniesser, Behandlungsgeber, und das Publikum.

Ueber die Kompetenz des Substanznutzer und ihre Faehigkeit einen Behandlungsprogramm zu Akzeptieren

Steve Clarke, Ph.D und Neil Levi, Ph.D.

Viele denken das ein normaler Drogennutzer nicht Kompetent ist um eine Behandlungsentscheidung zu treffen. In diesem Artikel moechten wir Basiskriteria fuer Sozialarbeitern aufbauen um die Kompetenz fuer eine informierte Behandlungseinwilligung zu ermessen. Wir behaupten das der normale Drogennutzer, sogar die als Suechtig betrachtet werden, faehig ssind diese Bediengungen einzuhalten. Obwohl Suechitgkeit die Autonomie einschrenkt, beschrenkt sie einen nicht in so ein das die Faehigkeit verlieren zu einer informierten Einwilligung. Benehmensstudien von Suechtigen zeigen das sie im allgemeinen gunuegend Macht ueber ihrem Benehmen und Entscheidungsfaehigkeit behalten um als Kompetent zu gelten um ihre Einwilligung zu geben.

Konzeptualisierung der professionellen Beziehung bei der Beratung von Drogenbenutzer und Alkoholmissbraucher

Elliot D. Cohen, Ph.D.

Etische Codexe, Gesetze und Case Law bringen grundliegende ethische Verpflichtungen oder Forderungen von professionellen, die Drogenbenutzer und Alkoholmissbraucher beraten. Vorausgesetzt das die Therapeuten wirkend beraten moechten, muessen sie erwartungsvoller, auf den Patienten konzertrierte Kriteria mit aufnehmen in ihre Beratungspraktiken. Wir beginen mit der Analyse der fundementalen Werte die fuer eine effektive Therapie eingeschlossen werden muessen; durch die Integration verschiedener professioneller zusammenhaengender Modelle im Gesundsheitswesen, dieser Kapitel baut ein moeglisches eklektiches Model von der Beziehung zwischen Patient und Therapeut.

Etische Bedenken die durch Unbestrafbarkeitspolitik der Drogenbenutzer auftauchen

Stephen Coleman, Ph.D.

Ueber den laezten Jahrzenten ist in verschiedenen Laender eine starke Stroehmung erschienen die die Implementation von Programme und Politik den Benutzer von Drogen nicht den Strafrechtsystem zu uebergeben, um den Drogenabhaengigen zu schuetzen. Dieser kapitel ziehl auf spezifische ethische Probleme dass diese Politik erzeugt. Bestimmte Programme werden betrachtet: Methadon Behandlung, Schpritzen waechsel Programm, Hygienische und sichere Orte die Drogen nehmen zu koennen, Verscheiben von Heroin und dekriminalizieren von Cannabis.

Drogenbenutzer können nicht behandelt werden; Leute Aber Doch!

Stan Einstein, Ph.D.

Die Thesen werden erst gesetzt und dann mit ausgesuchten Beispielen überprüft, daß die aktuelle Behandlung von "Substanzgebrauch-Störung" (die "SUD") – sei es nach Enthaltsamkeit oder sei es nach der Verminderung von Schaden orientiert (doch fast immer in den Behandlungsstellen eingeführt, die von den Hauptströmungen der Behandlungstechniken ganz abgekommen sind) – die für die Bevölkerung im ganzen zugänglich gemacht wird:

1. Ist im wesentlichen unmoralisch, denn das Maß ihrer Wohltätigkeit ist weniger als das Maß ihrer bösen Wirkungen;
2. Ist eine irreführende falsche Bezeichnung, denn (1) es gibt keine einzigartige "Behandlung" (Modelle oder Techniken) für "Drogenbenutzer," die nicht auch für Nichtdrogenbenutzer verwendet wird und (2) "Drogenbenutzer" und "Nichtdrogenbenutzer" gehören einer heterogenen Bevölkerung von *Personen* und nicht einer einzigartigen homogenen Typologie;

3. Ist der Unwahrscheinlichkeit ausgesetzt, daß die SUD wegen der Situation, des Vorhabens, und der Ziele von machthabenden einzelnen und institutionellen Anteilnehmer und wegen systemimmanenter Faktoren, in einen in der Sittlichkeit gegründeten Prozeß verwandelt werden könnte;
4. Ist durch ein "Glaubenssystem" unterstützt, das durch Schlagworte wie "Beweis-begründet" ernährt wird;
5. Kann und wird nur zu häufig durch eine Reihe von kooptierten Veränderungsagenten (versehentlich) unterstützt, die eine Reihe von Disziplinen vertreten, sowie auch von sich von Drogenverbrauch erholten Menschen, oder von ehemaligen Drogenverbraucher aus dem Laienstand;
6. Existiert innerhalb einer fortwährenden tatsächlichen Wirklichkeit, worin neue verwendbare Entdeckungen wegen eines sogenannten "Problems der Technologieübertragung" meistens nicht zur Behandlung von dazu geeigneten Drogenbenutzern eingeführt werden.

Kompetenz in der Beratung wegen Rauschgiftsmißbrauch

Theodore M. Godlaski, M.Div.

Obgleich Klinikerkompetenz allgemein hin eine Bedingung einer ethisch korrekten Praxis angesehen wird, ist sie häufig schlecht definiert. Bedeutende Versuche nach einer besseren Spezifikation des Kompetenzbegriffes wurden durch eine von der U.S. Substance Abuse and Mental Health Services Administration gesponserte Expertengruppe unternommen. Diese Gruppe spezifiziert drei Bereiche, in denen eine ausreichende Kapazität als die Bedingung der Kompetenz notwendig ist: Wissen, Fähigkeit und Haltung. Praktisch alle Instanzen messen jedoch objektiv nur das Wissen, wobei Fähigkeit und Haltung zur Beurteilung der Oberhaupte der Kliniken überlassen werden. Es gibt also Grund dazu, Sorgen über die Qualität und die Quantität des Überwachungskontaktes zu haben, worauf sich solche Urteile basieren. Auch hat man Grund zu fragen, ob alles Wissen und alle Fähigkeiten ethisch vom gleichen Wert sind. Weiter gibt es noch ethische Fragen, ob es ein Substanzberatungsfach, getrennt vom allgemeinen Beratungsfach, noch gerechtfertigt werden kann.

Reflexionen auf ethischen Fragen in der Forschung mit Ureinwohner

Theodore M. Godlaski, M. Div., Jeannette Johnson, Ph.D. und Rodney Haring, LMSW.

Dieses Kapitel setzt sich mit den auffallenden ethischen Fragen aus, die aus der Forschung mit Aboriginesstamme oder einheimischen Völkern entstehen.. Die Primärquelle des ethischen Nachdenkens ist die kulturelle Angemessenheit der Forschung: ihre Zwecke, ihre Gestaltung, ihre Methoden, ihr Protokoll und die Veröffentlichung und Dissemination ihrer Ergebnisse. Obgleich die kulturelle Angemessenheit ein nicht gut definierter Begriff ist, mangende Sorge der Forscher um die Denkweise, die Sozialstruktur, die Kommunikationsmethoden und die Weltansicht der Ureinwohner manifestiert sich in den Schaden, die ein schlecht überlegtes Forschungsvorhaben zur Folge hat. Die Autoren beziehen sich auf neue Arbeit in diesem Bereich in ihre Bemühungen, Forschern für kulturell einfühlsame Forschungsrichtlinien zur Verfügung zu stellen.

Interessen Konflikte in der Bewertung und Beschraenkung von Programme fuer Vorkehrung von Drogenbenutzung

Dennis M. Gorman, Ph.D.

Dieser Kapitel untersucht die Implikationen der letzten Etwicklungen in der Bewertung und Marketing von Drogen Vorkehrungsproramme; insbesondere die Bedrohung die durch die Interessen Konflikte entsehen fuer die vershciedenen Programme. Erstens untersuchen wir was mit dem Interessen Konflikt gemient wird, danach werden die verschieden Konflikte in der Aertzliche und politischen Literatur, der letzten Jahre, besprochen werden. Dies wird befolgt von eine detaillierte Diskussion ueber der indivuduellen und Instutionellen Interessen Konflikte die in der Drogenvorkehrungs-forschung existieren.

Ist Harm Reduction (Gefahr mindernde) Psychotherapie Ethisch?

William H. Gottdiener, Ph.D.

“Harm Reduction Pchychotherapie” (HRP) ist eine Art von Outpatient (Aussenpatient) Psychotherapie fuer Individuelle die mit “Substance Use Disorder” (SUD) diagnostiziert wurden und die noch Psychoaktive Substanzen benutzen. HRP ist ein Weg potenzielle Schaden einzuschreanken die der Gebrauch Schaeden von psychoactive Substanzen begleiten. Nuechternheit ist eine Moglichjkeit Schaeden einzuschrenken, verglichen zu der traditionellen SUD Versorgung die die Nuechternheit als einzig moeglicher Ziehl sieht.. HRP wird benutzt da totale Nuechternheit nicht immer erreichbar ist. Dieser Kapitel untersucht ob HRP fuer SUD Patienten, eine ethische Behanglung ist. Von der Foucoultschen Perspektive her, ist die persoenliche Freiheit ein Grundsatz fuer eine SUD Behandlung, und eine Psychoanalitische Perspektive der Nuechternheit ist nur erreichbar durch ein Patient der diesen Ziehl erreichen moechte, und erst dann wen der Patient die noetige endogene und exogene Anpassungsfaehigkeit hat um sein Lebenstil aendern zu koennen. Der Autor behauptet das HRP die einzig ethische Psychoterapie ist fuer Aussenpatienten die an SUD leiden.

Das Verbot von sexuellen Verhältnissen zwischen Drogenbenutzern und ihren Ratsmitgliedern: Wird es gerechtfertigt?

Mähne Hajdin, J.D., Ph.D.

Dieses Kapitel überprüft vier mögliche Argumente für das Verbot von sexuellen Verhältnissen zwischen den wegen Drogenmißbrauch Beratenen und ihren Ratgebern. Das erste Argument besteht im Satz, daß das Verbot den besonderen Versuchungen und den Gelegenheiten für sexuelle Verhältnisse begegne, die durch das Phänomen von Übertragung verursacht werden. Das zweite besteht darin, daß das Verbot zur Autorität beiträge, die der Berater haben muß, wenn das Beraten sein Ziel erreichen sollte. Nach dem dritten Argument sei die Beratung eine Ausdehnung der Staatsmacht [auf den Berater], der folglich unter denselben Zwang lege wie alle Vertreter der Staatsmacht. Der vierte Grund bezieht sich auf die Überlegung, daß das Verbot wegen der Ungleichheit der Machtverhältnisse erforderlich sei, die zwischen den Ratgebern und den Beratenen besteht. Die vorliegende Untersuchung kommt zum Schluß, daß alle von diesen vier Argumenten das Verbot in einigen Kontexten der Beratung von Rauschgiftsüchtigen rechtfertigen kann, aber nur das zweite kann es in allen seinen Kontexten. Die Grundlage hier scheint aber in der Technik zu liegen, die ein erfolgreiches Beratungsverhältnis ermöglicht, und sie stellt eine unabhängige moralische Begrenzung des Verhaltens der Teilnehmer nicht dar.

Medizin und Moral, Drang und Zwang :Die sittliche Relevanz der Rauschgiftsucht

Douglas N. Husak, J.D., Ph.D.

Ich setze mich hier mit der verbreiteten Ansicht auseinander, daß die Rauschgiftsucht sittlich relevant ist. Ich untersuche einige Darlegungen dieser Ansicht, *wie* vom Standpunkt der Sittlichkeit aus die Rauschgiftsucht als bedeutsam angesehen werden könnte. Obwohl ich Theorien der Tugend kurz behandle, liegt das Schwergewicht der Diskussion auf drei möglichen Darlegungen der Ansicht, daß die Rauschgiftsucht moralischen Tadel verdienen könnte. Erstens, man gebe dem Rauschgiftsüchtigen die Schuld allen wegen der Benützung des Rauschgiftes. Zweitens, der Zustand der Sucht selber könne die Schuld tragen. Drittens die Schuld könnte an den möglichen Risiken liegen, die in Mensch in aller Wahrscheinlichkeit eingeht, wenn er einmal Rauschgiftsüchtiger wird. Ich ziehe den Schluß, daß jede der Darlegungen eine gewisse Plausibilität hat, doch ist keine problemfrei. Wahrscheinlich *hat* die Rauschgiftsucht sittliche Relevanz, trotzdem ist der Grad ihrer Wichtigkeit nicht so groß, wie einige behaupten. Die sittliche Relevanz der Rauschgiftsucht nicht zu der Stufe zu ersteigen, Strafmaßnahmen gegen Rauschgiftsüchtigen zu gerechtfertigen.

Ethik der Forschung nach Rauschgiftsverhütung bei Kindern

Jeannette L. Johnson, Ph.D. und Nancy R. Van De Mark, M.S.W.

Die ethischen Entscheidungen, die in der Forschung über die Verhütung von Drogenmißbrauch auftauchen, können schwierig und auch einfach zu verstehen sein. Verhütungsforschung ist schwierig, weil sie Kinder als Gegenstand nimmt, und die Fragen, die den Schutz des Kindes und ihre Rechte betreffen, lebenswichtig sind. Wenn es um Kinder geht, müssen diese Rechte mit einer Klarheit über den Zwecken der Forschung, einem Respekt für das Kind, und einer Zärtlichkeit in seiner Behandlung zusammengehen. Die Ethik in diesem Bereich ist auch einfach, weil die notwendigen Kenntnisse zum Verstehen der wirkungsvollsten verhütenden Interventionen nur während der Kindheit gefunden werden können. Man kann die Mittel zur Vorbeugung von sozialen, physischen und psychologischen Krankheiten nur dann verstehen, wenn man erst Forschung mit Kindern unternimmt. Es ist dieser Verbindung von Schwierigkeiten und Einfachheit, die alle ethischen Fragen in der Verhütungsforschung heikel macht.

Rauschgiftsucht und die Verantwortlichkeit für die Fürsorge von Rauschgiftsüchtigen

Tziporah Kasachkoff, Ph.D.

Die offene Fürsorge für Menschen, die Gesundheitspflege bedürftig sind, wird von den meisten Bürgern gerne angenommen, soweit die Staatskasse es erlaubt. Muß aber diese Verpflichtung irgendwie dadurch bedingt werden, daß die Krankheiten, von denen eine Person leidet, aus seiner freien Handlung, deren eventuellen Auswirkungen auf seine Gesundheit ihr in voraus wohlbekannt waren, entsprungen sind? Genau gesagt, ist die Verpflichtung der Gesellschaft, Rauschgiftsüchtigen die Krankenpflege anzubieten, irgendwie durch die Tatsache abgeschwächt, daß sie sich freiwillig nach verbotenen Drogen süchtig gemacht haben? Einige behaupten es, doch andere Menschen finden diese These moralisch unbegründet. Diese Arbeit untersucht die Frage, wer recht in dieser Sache haben möchte und warum.

Der Moralische Ziehl der Behandlung in Faellen einer dualen Diagnosis

Jeannette Kennett, Ph.D. und Stephen Matthews, Ph.D.

Drogen Verbrauch und Missbrauch erscheinen oefters unter Menschen die Psychiche Gesundheitsprobleme haben und die Verbindung dieser zwei Zustaende ist komplex.

In diesem Kapitel behaupten wird dass die Behandlung von Drogenbenutzer in Faellen von dualer Diagnose muss dabei anfangen die Verlusste die, die Patienten mit Psychichen Krankheiten erlitten haben zu erortern. Wir beschreiben eine fundamentale Bedingung der effektiven Institution, eine geeinte Institution, die gespalten ist in Faellen von Psychichkranken und zeigen wie wichtig es ist Zugang zu versichern zu zentral sozialen und moralischem Hab und Gut ist so wie das kontinuirliche Arbeiten, und befriedigende Beziehungen zu haben bedeutet. Wir behaupten das Drogen Verbrauch entwertet wird ersteinmal in so fern das es auch den Zugang unterbindet zu diesem institutionalen Hab und Gut und den Bertreuer die Moeglichkeit giebt sich scharf auf das synchrone Wohlergehen einstellen zu koennen und das diachrone auszuschalten. Die Ziehle und Metoden der Behandlung von dual diagnostizierte Patienten reflektiert sich ersteinamal bei der Beschraenkung der nicht geeinten Institutionen.

Ethische Fragen über Interventionen bei Drogenmißbrauch

John Kleinig, Ph.D.

Diese Arbeit bietet einen Überblick über die aus staatlichen und medizinischen Interventionen bei Rauschgiftsnehmern hervorgehenden ethischen Fragen. Mit Bezug auf die staatlichen Einmischungen, wir gehen von der liberalen Annahme aus, daß die zwangläufige Einschränkung der freien Handlungen eines Menschen nur mit Bezug auf die möglichen Schaden, welche die Handlungen anrichten könnte, gerechtfertigt werden kann, doch diese Annahme wird durch etwaige sozialen Erfordernisse begrenzt. In bezug auf die Interventionen der Medizin, stehen die für die Versorger der ärztlichen Behandlung und ihre Klienten bestimmten Vorschriften im Brennpunkt der Forschung. Sie untersucht die ethische Untermauerung ihrer Hauptvorkehrungen: die informierte Einwilligung, die Privatsphäre, die Nichtdiskriminierung, die Maßstäbe des Berufsethos, und die Verantwortlichkeit der Versorger.

Ethisches Denken in bezug auf das Schpritzen waechsel Programm

John Kleinig, Ph.D.

Forausgesehen – nur der Diskussion halber - wir die jaetzige legale Politik akzeptieren in bezug auf Heroin, welche ethische Fragen stellen sich fuer das Programm der Schpritzen waechsel? Schwaechen sie die Drogen Gesetze; senden sie eine falsche Meldung oder vertuschen sie die richtige Meldung; tun sie nich genug um die Drogen Gefahr zu eliminieren; verhindern sie Alternativen und oder beseht das Programm nur aus der Ausichtslosigkeit? Da es an geprueften Alternativen mangelt, sehe ich im Programm der Schpritzen Waechsel ein moralisch akzeptabler Weg, obwohl die weiter kriminalisierung von Drogen voran geht.

Geheimhaltung , Vertraulichkeit und die Behandlung von Drogen Abhaenginge

Seumas Miller, Ph.D.

Das Grundprinzip der Geheimhaltung , bring hervor eine Maenge von Betrachtungen, u.A. das recht auf Gehiemhaltung, Vertrauen und die schadenvolle Konsequezen der Veroeffentlichung. Das Recht zur Geheimhaltung untermauert durch andere moralischen Werte auch die Autonomie. Das heisst die moralische Begruendung zur Vertraulichkeit ist komplex. Der Grad unserer Verplichtung muss relativiert werden den Umstaende etspraechend. In bestimmten Faellen und Kategorien der Drogenabhaenginge, hat die Vertraulichkeit ihre Maengel, verursacht durch die beschrenkte Autonomie und deshalb ein reduziertes Recht zur Vertraulichkeit. Nicht desto Trotz sollte man unsere Verplichtung zu Geheimhaltung nicht dadurch schwaechen.

Medizin und Moral, Drang und Zwang

Stephen J. Morse, J.D., Ph.D.

Zwei Muster dominieren das Denken über die Rauschgiftsucht: Das eine gründet sich auf die Medizin, welche die Rauschgiftsucht als eine Krankheit behandelt, und die Handlugsweisen der Süchtigen als Zeichen und Symptomen der Krankheit ansieht. Das andere bezieht sich auf die Sittlichkeit, und sieht die Rauschgiftsucht und die Handlugsweisen der Süchtigen als Zeichen eines moralischen Versagens an. Die vorliegende Arbeit beschreibt beide Muster und ihre Implikationen, betont aber das moralische. Der Sinn von Zwang oder Druck, die von solchen psychologischen Zuständen wie die Sucht verursacht sein sollen, wird untersucht, um zu bestimmen, ob Rauschgiftsüchtige moralisch und gesetzmäßig für ihre Handlungen z.B. die Suche nach und die Benützung vom Rauschgift für verantwortlich gemacht werden können. Die These wird aufgestellt, daß nicht der Zwang, sondern eine geschwächte Rationalität die Tatsache am Besten erklärt, warum die Rauschgiftsüchtigen für ihre Handlungen entschuldigt werden könnten, doch es wird auch behauptet, daß die meisten Rauschgiftsüchtigen größtenteils für ihre Rauschgift-relevanten Handlangen verantwortlich sind. Trotzdem, die beiden Muster haben wünschenswerte Eigenschaften, und die Sozialpolitik soll sich nicht ausschließlich auf das eine oder auf das andere begrenzen. Die Implikationen für das sich auf beide Muster verlassende Strafrecht werden untersucht.

Ethische Probleme in derForschung der Behadlung von Drogennutzer

Kenneth D. Pimple, Ph.D.

Drogennutzer Forschung sollte gefuehrt werden wie alle anderen Wissenschaftlichen Forschungen, z.B. Ehrlichkeit, Aufrichtigkeit, Kredit respektieren, ohne den Patient zu belestigen, ethische Prinzipien so zitiert wie in dem Belmont Report, nicht boessartig und gerecht. Ein zusaetzlicher Prinzip das nicht im Belmont Report erwaehnt wurde aber weite Zustimmung bekommt ist das Ermoeglichen einer Therapie. Wissenschaftler sind moralisch (und manchmal gesetzlich) dieser Prinzipien gebunden. Die Gemeinschaft fuer die Behandlung von Drogennutzer im ganzen ist dazu verplichtet ihr bestes zu tun um die Forschungs Agenda so wie die Sozialpolitik anhand der oben genannte Prinzipien auszuueben.

Drogennutzer Behandlung – Faire Politik oder Beweissbasierende Politik?

Maurice Rickard, Ph.D.

Es ist etwas daran. das man Entscheidungen bezueglich welcher Behandlungen gegeben werden sollten, die Angelegenheit der oeffentlichen Politik und sozialer Wahl sind. Es ist sinnvoll die Therapeutischen {und ethische} Beweiss basierende Intervention zugaenglich zu machen. Es ist auch berechtigt das die Politik und der soziale Prozess ueber die Behandlungspraktiken fair und gerecht ablaufen soll. Fairness sollte immer present sein bei Entscheidungen, in solch einer Art das der Medizinische Urteil nicht beintreachtigt wird. Das Problem kann enstehen wen der Ziehl der Behandlung von der Weltanschaung des Therapeuten abhaengt, in anderen Worten die Behandlung soll richtig authorisiert sein. Dennoch ist das Problem das die Entscheidung welche die Therapeutiche richtige Behandlung ist in der Hand des Therapeuten und seiner Anschaung bleiben muss.. Die Gefahr besteht darin das man letzt endlich einen kotroversiellen Konzept des fairen Prozesses benutzt statt einer der durch die mehrheit als akzeptabel anerkannt wird..Dieser Kapitel untersucht manche philosophische Themen in bezug auf faire Behandlungspolitiken und gute Behandlungspolitik, inklusive wer die Rolle des Entscheiden tragen soll.

Ethische Fragen betreffend den Zugangs des Drogenkonsumenten zur Beratung / Behandlung

Barbara C. Wallace, Ph.D.

Die ethischen Fragen betreffend den Zuganges des Drogenkonsumenten zur Beratung und Behandlung sind sehr verschiedenartig.. Die Variationsbreite schliesst ein die Faehigkeit zur Diskriminierung im Hinblick auf die Zulassung zur Behandlung aufgrund von Rasse, Religion, Geschlecht, Alter, Schwangerschaft, geographischer Lage oder Entfernung vom Ort der Behandlung, Armut oder Fehlen einer Versicherung des Klienten. Andere ethische Fragen erfassen die Behinderung eines Klienten, physische und psychische Behinderung zum Beispiel. Andere ethische Fragen beinhalten, wie man mit einem Rueckfall und mit permanenten positiven toxischen Urin Testergebnissen zurechtkommt.. Die Faelle, welche die groesste Herausforderung darstellen, sind solche, wo das Leben des Suechtigen durch einen chronischen Rueckfall gepraegt ist. Zusaetzliche ethische Fragen betreffen das Risiko des gewalttaetigen Verhalten von Klienten waehrend der Behandlung und wann man ihnen den Zugang zur Behandlungen verbieten sollte. Andere ethische Fragen beziehen sich auf den Behandlungszwang entweder durch das Strafvollzugssystem, die Wohlfahrtsbehoerde oder die Kinderschutzeinrichtung, da sie alle den Klienten zwingen sich einer Behandlung zu unterziehen. In diesem Kapital werden Empfehlungen angeboten, wie man die gesamte Reichweite an aktuellen ethische Fragen hinsichtlich des Zuganges des Drogenkonsumenten zur Beratung und Behandlung begrifflich erfasst und darauf reagiert.

Drogennutzer Betreung, Honorar und Ethic

Adrian Walsh, Ph.D und Tony Lynch, Ph.D.

In diesem Artikel explorieren wir die Implikationen dass das Honorar in all seiner verschiedenheiten auf die Betreuern von Drogennutzer ausueben kann. Nach einer lange gehaltenen Tradition besteht die Idee das finanzielle Belohnung und Altruismus nicht kompatibel sind. Umsere Weltanschauung ist etwa anderst. Wir behaupten in gegen der Tradition dass obwohl finanzielle Belohnung nicht automatisch negativ ist konfrontiert sie den Therapeuten mit etischen Gefahren. Die die sich mit Drogennutzer abgeben muessen ins besonder aufpassen.

Rauschgiftsucht und Behinderung: Sittliche und sozialpolitische Fragen

David Wasserman, J.D.

Die vorliegende Arbeit behandelt die begrifflichen, sittlichen, und sozialpolitischen Fragen, die der gesetzmäßigen Klassifizierung der Rauschgiftsucht als Behinderung entspringt, und die Behandlung der gegenwärtig drogenfreien Rauschgiftsüchtigen als Behinderten. Sie bezieht sich auf die Fragen (1) welche sittlichen Urteile, wenn es überhaupt solche gibt, die Klassifikation der Rauschgiftsucht als Behinderung zugrunde liegen; (2) ob es sinnvoll ist, die Lasten der Rauschgiftsucht unter chemischen, biologischen, sozialen, politischen, und anderen Ursachen zu teilen; (3) wie Rücksicht auf die ausgleichende Gerechtigkeit zu Maßnahmen zur Verminderung der Last der Rauschgiftsucht führen könnte, oder auch solche Maßnahmen verbieten; (4) ob es gerechtfertigt ist, den gegenwärtigen Rauschgiftsüchtigen rechtmäßigen Schutz zu verweigern, der dem gegenwärtigen Verbraucher von nicht verbotenen Drogen angeboten wird.

Ethische Fragen betreffend den Behandlungszugang Fuer Drogensuechtige

Shelly A. Wiechelt, Ph.D.

Die Vielfalt an Programmen fuer die Behandlung von Drogensuechtigen, welche in den USA angeboten werden, liefert eine Unmenge an forschungsgestuetzten Beweisen fuer die Wirksamkeit der Behandlung.

Unabhenging vom zunehmenden Wissen und der Verfuegbarkeit an Behandlung gibt es eine enorme kluft

zwischen der Anzahl von Personen, welche eine Behandlung benoetigen und denjenigen welche tatsaechlich eine Behandlung erhalten. Dieses Kapitel diskutiert einige der Faktoren und Bedingungen, die zum Problem des Zuganges von Drogensuechtigen zur Behandlung in den USA beitragen Die Zugangsprobleme werden untersucht im Lichte des bestehenden ethischen Verhaltenskodex fuer Fachleute fuer die Behandlung von Drogensuechtigen.

Die Beziehung zwischen dem Klienten und dem Berater und die Rolle der beruflichen Ethik

Kylie Williams, M.A. and Dean Cocking, PhD.

Dieses Kapitels praesentiert eine pluralistische Konzeption hinsichtlich der Rolle, welche die Ethik in der professionellen Beratung spielt. Die Rolle - Verpflichtungen Sensivitaeten und die Reichweite an menschlichen Problemen, welche sich auf die Beratung beziehen, ist sehr weit im Umfang und konflikttraechtig Ein besonderes Problem fuer die Beziehung zwischen dem Klienten und dem Beraterstellt der Charakter und die Situation der unfreiwilligen Behandlung von Drogensuechtigen dar Nach Auffassung vieler Autoren beeintraechtigen diese Probleme die Ethik und die Richtlinien, welche fuer die Beratung wesentlich sind. Wir stimmen zu , das viele Schluesselwerte bei den unfreiwilligen Behandlungen kompromitiert werden Wir argumentieren jedoch, dass der Konflikt in eine pluralistischen Konzeption hineinpasst, ohne dass er eine Gewohnheit der Beratung losgeloest von seinen grundlegenden Zielsetzungen reflektiert.

Vom Elfenbein Turm zu den Graben: Das beibringen von Ethic an Drogennutzer Betreuer

Daniel Yalisove, Ph.D.

Dieser Kapitel beschreibt ein Weg wie man Drogennutzer Betreuer professionelle Ethic beibringt. Es stellt vor drei innovative Ideen: (1) Betreuer haben durcheinander gebracht ethische mit nicht etischen Ruecksichten in primaer ethischen Entscheidungen. Es ist wichtig diesen Unterschied zu erklaeren fuer Studenten in Ihrer Ausbildung. (2) Es besteht eine sonder synergie zwichen humanistischer Betrueung und Professioneller Ethic. (3) Es ist wichtig die Aufmerksamkeit des Patienten zu erwecken in bezug auf die moralich ethischen Probleme einer Behandlung.

Il y a des décisions difficiles dans l'éthique de la recherche qui se sert de données et de méthodes statistiques dans le domaine de la toxicomanie et des toxicomanes.

Manuella Adrian, M.S. Hyg.

La recherche scientifique nous a fourni un des moyens les plus puissants pour améliorer le sort de l'espèce humaine. C'est aussi une source de problèmes éthiques et moraux pour ceux qui font de la recherche scientifique. De nos jours, nous portons une grande attention aux problèmes éthiques de la recherche sur les être humains, cherchant a minimiser les possibilités de faire du mal a quelqu'un: depuis Nuremberg, des règlements stricts ont été établis depuis un demi-siècle à ce but. Nous sommes aussi conscient des problèmes liés à la recherche à but militariste. Moins bien connus sont les problèmes qui surgissent de la méthode scientifique elle-même et de l'interprétation des données. Nous passons en revue les principes de la méthode scientifique tels qu'énoncés par Isaac Newton pour établir une relation de cause à effet, ainsi qu'ils s'appliquent au domaine de la recherche en général et de la recherche sur la toxicomanie et les toxicomanes en particulier. Nous considérons aussi les nouveaux concepts servant à identifier les « points critiques » où l'on peut intervenir, même s'ils ne sont pas « la cause » au sens strict du terme. De plus, nous considérons les problèmes qui découlent de la nature du sujet étudié, de l'organisation et du financement de la recherche, ainsi que de l'usage de méthodes et de techniques de recherche qui ne sont pas adéquates au sujet et qui mènent à des conclusions erronées qui peuvent être nocives aux patients, aux scientifiques et à la société.

Problèmes d'éthique dans les traitements d'entraide aux toxicomanes: la place des organisations àa douze étapes.

Allaman Allamani, M.D.

Les différences intrinsèques entre la façon dont les groupes d'entraide mutuelle et les agents et organismes professionnels de traitement formel se comportent avec ceux qui font un mauvais emploi des boissons alcooliques et d'autres drogues ont des répercussions éthiques. En particulier, l'éthique des groupes à douze étapes (« twelve step ») est universaliste vue qu'elle est basée sur l'idée de spiritualisme, d'autrui, et de solidarité. Même si l'on peut étudier leur efficacité à produire un état d'abstinence vis-à-vis de l'alcool, la meilleure façon de les décrire est en tant que « communautés vouées à la guérison » (Seppala 2001). Cependant, pour les professionnels qui s'occupent des programmes de traitement de ceux qui utilisent des substances toxicomanes, la base éthique semble être l'utilitarisme, axé sur les intérêts soit de la personne individuelle soit du groupe social. Même si lors des interaction de ces deux perspectives différentes il surgit une certaine tension ou un degré de conflit, il existe, actuellement et mondialement, une coopération croissante entre les associations d'entraide mutuelle et du système de soins de santé.

Incapacité et le Traitement des Toxicomanes: Considérations Éthiques

Ellen Benoit, Ph. D. and Stephen Magura, Ph.D.

Avant 1996, aux Etats-Unis, les personnes qui étaient chroniquement dépendantes des drogues ou de l'alcool pouvaient être certifiées comme incapacités, leur donnant le droit à l'appui de revenu de l'Administration de sécurité sociale (SSA), s'ils participaient au traitement. En mars 1996, la législation a exigé que la SSA élimine la toxicomanie de sa liste d'incapacités qualifiées et enlève de ses listes toutes les personnes qui avaient reçu des avantages sociaux en tant qu'incapacités. Ce changement suscite des questions éthiques significatives que nous adressons de la perspective de justice distributive. Nous examinons la distinction de la politique entre les nécessiteux "méritant" et "non-méritant," et nous analysons comment l'ambiguïté de la nature médicale de la toxicomanie encourage les réclamations rivales basées sur la relativité du mérite dans le débat concernant l'éligibilité. Par exemple, le fait de devenir incapacité a cause de la toxicomanie constitue-t-il une forme de comportement volontaire? Finalement, nous considérons les conséquences du reclassement de SSA pour les constituants politiques, y compris les bénéficiaires, les fournisseurs de traitement et le public.

Sur la compétence des utilisateurs de stupéfiants à consentir au traitement medical

Steve Clarke, PhD et Neil Levy, Ph.D.

Beaucoup de penseurs soutiennent que les utilisateurs de stupéfiants réguliers sont incompétents pour consentir au traitement médical. En cet article, nous établons des critères minimaux pour que les agents qualifiénnent comme comptent en tant que compétent au consentement informé, et soutenons que les utilisateurs de drogue réguliers—y compris ceux qui sont considérés toxicomanes—satisfont typiquement ces conditions. Bien que la dépendance altère l'autonomie, il ne l'altère pas à un degré incompatible avec le consentement informé. Les études du comportement des toxicomanes prouvent qu'ils gardent la maîtrise suffisante de leur comportement et de leur prise de décision pour qualifier comme compétente pour consentir.

Conceptualisation de la relation professionnelle entre le soignant et les drogués et alcoliques

E. D. Cohen, Ph.D.

Les codes éthiques, les lois et les jurisprudences fondent les exigences et obligations éthiques que doivent appliquer les professionnels qui accompagnent les alcooliques et les drogués. Cependant, si ces thérapeutes veulent accompagner ces gens effectivement, ils doivent aussi intégrer plus de considérations et de critères, centrant leur pratique sur l'individu. Ce chapitre pose les bases d'un modèle ouvert qui peut s'appliquer à la relation existant entre le patient et le thérapeute. En fait les valeurs fondamentales qui englobent la réalité thérapeutique intègrent différents modèles professionnels relatifs au soin.

Les problèmes d'éthique suscités par les politiques non punitives des personnes qui utilisent des drogues.

Stephen Coleman, Ph.D.

Depuis les quelques dernières décennies, il y a eu une tendance dans bien des pays à mettre sur pied des programmes et des politiques qui prennent une approche non punitive vis-à-vis l'usage et le mésusage des drogues, et qui généralement ont pour but de minimiser le mal causé à ceux qui utilisent des drogues. Ce chapitre tente de montrer et de mettre en valeur les problèmes d'éthique suscités par ces politiques non punitives concernant les drogues. Les politiques que nous examinons comprennent les traitements de maintient à la méthadone, les programmes d'échanges de seringues, l'instauration de locaux où l'on peut injecter en sécurité (« safe injecting »), les prescriptions pour de l'héroïne et la décriminalisation du cannabis.

On n'offre pas des traitements aux toxicomanes : on offre des traitements à la personne.

Stan Einstein, Ph.D.

La thèse est posée en principe, et examinée en utilisant des exemples choisis, que les traitements, que nous offrons actuellement pour les « troubles d'usage de substances » (TUS) – qu'ils soient axe sur l'abstinence ou conduit par l'idée de réduire les maux qui s'ensuivent (« harm reduction ») – et qui sont presque toujours offerts dans des sites à part de ceux où l'on traite la plupart des gens, ont les caractéristiques suivantes:

- Ces « traitements » sont essentiellement non éthiques : leur manque de bienfaisance est plus qu'égalé par leur degré de malfaisance ;
- Le mot « traitement » est un terme mal approprié et propre seulement à nous induire en erreur ; (1) d'abord il n'existe pas de « traitements » (qu'ils soient basés sur des modèles ou des techniques) qui sont uniquement le propre des soit - disant « usagers de drogues » et que l'on n'utilisent pas aussi avec ceux qui n'utilisent pas de drogues, et ensuite, (2) tant les "utilisateurs de drogue" que ceux qui ne les utilisent pas représentent des populations hétérogènes composées de PERSONNES et non seulement des nosologies homogènes ;
- Ces « traitements » sont peu susceptibles d'être changés en un processus à base éthique en raison des positions et des buts (cachés ou formels) des intervenants (individus ou systèmes) mus par le désir d'augmenter leur pouvoir;
- Ces « traitements » sont nourris par des "principes de foi" qui sont imbriqués dans des slogans tels que « basé sur l'évidence »
- Ces « traitements », bien trop souvent, continuent d'exister (comme par hasard, presque) parce que ceux qui eussent été des agents de changements ont été

cooptés, et représentent une gamme de disciplines ainsi que des non professionnels « en état de réadaptation » ou d'anciens toxicomanes

- Dans un monde où, en fait, les nouveaux résultats les plus applicables et les plus appropriés, le plus souvent, ne sont ni présentés ni employés pour offrir des traitements convenables à ceux qui utilisent des substances toxicomanes avec, comme mot d'excuse, les problèmes du « transfert de la technologie ».

La compétence dans les services de conseils pour la dépendance chimique

Theodore M. Godlaski, M.Div.

Bien que la compétence du clinicien soit universellement reconnue comme étant nécessaire pour fournir des services éthiques, elle est souvent mal définie. Il y a eu des efforts importants pour arriver à une meilleure définition, parrainés par l'Administration des services contre l'abus des substances et pour la santé mentale (« Substance Abuse and Mental Health Services Administration ») des Etats-Unis. Ce groupe a identifié trois domaines de compétence nécessaires : les connaissances, l'habilite dans la pratique et l'attitude. Cependant, pratiquement tous les organismes officiels qui émettent des certificats ne mesurent objectivement que les connaissances, laissant les superviseurs cliniques à témoigner de l'habilité dans la pratique et des attitudes. Cependant, nous devrions nous poser des questions tant sur la qualité que sur le nombre de contacts entre cliniciens étudiants et superviseurs qui sont à la base des ces évaluations. De plus, nous devons considérer si toutes les connaissances et tous les aspects de l'habilité dans la pratique ont la même importance. Enfin, il faudrait savoir si un champ d'action pour les services de conseils aux toxicomanes tenu à part de ceux offerts à la population générale peut se justifier éthiquement.

Réflexions sur les questions morales dans la recherche avec les peuples indigènes

Theodore M. Godlaski, M.Div., Jeannette Johnson, Ph.D. et Rodney Haring, LMSW

Ce chapitre est une réflexion sur les questions morales saillantes qui surgissent dans le travail de recherches avec les indigènes ou la source primaire de souci moral est la convenance culturelle du but de recherches, de la conception, des méthodes, du protocole, et du plan de publication/dissemination. Bien que la convenance culturelle ne soit pas une construction bien définie, le manque de souci pour des manières indigènes de la pensée, de la structure sociale, de la communication, et de la vue du monde peut être évident dans le mal fait en raison de maurais conçus de recherches. Les auteurs basent leurs récents travaux dans ce secteur pour fournir des directives pour la recherche culturellement sensible.

Conflit d'intérêts dans l'évaluation et la diffusion des programmes de prévention de l'usage des drogues

Dennis M. Gorman, Ph.D.

Ce chapitre examine les conséquences de certains développements récents dans l'évaluation et le marketing des programmes de prévention de l'usage des drogues sur la probité de la recherche et, surtout, sur l'effet de conflits d'intérêts qui pourraient entraver cette probité. Nous commençons par une description de ce que nous entendons par un conflit d'intérêts ; suit une revue des principaux genres de conflits d'intérêts qui ont été causes de discussions dans les revues médicales ou dans les ouvrages concernant les politiques d'ordre public dans ces dernières années. Enfin, suit une discussion plus détaillée des différents conflits d'intérêts, tant d'ordre individuel qu'institutionnel, dans le domaine de la recherche sur la prévention de l'usage de drogues

La Psychothérapie De Réduction Du Mal Est-elle Morale ?

William H. Gottdiener, Ph.D.

La Psychothérapie De Réduction Du Mal (PRM) représente une sorte de psychothérapie ambulatoire destinée aux personnes qui sont diagnostiquées comme ayant des « troubles liés à l'usage des substances » (TUS) et qui continuent d'utiliser des substances psychotropes. Le but des traitement de type PRM est de réduire la souffrance potentielle qui pourrait accompagner l'utilisation des substances psychotropes. L'abstinence ne représente qu'une des manières de diminuer le mal par rapport aux traitements de TUS traditionnels ou l'abstinence reste le seul but acceptable. On utilise la thérapie PRM justement parce que l'état d'abstinence est un but impossible a atteindre ou a maintenir par toutes les personnes atteintes de TUS ou dans toutes les étapes du traitement. Ce chapitre examine si le traitement de PRM est un traitement éthique a fournir a tous ceux qui ont reçu le diagnostique de TUS. Selon la pensée de Foucault, la liberté individuelle est essentielle dans ces cas. La perspective pyscho-analytique stipule qu'un état de sobriété ne peut être atteint que par un client qui est prêt a se fixer sur ce but et qui possède les caractéristiques nécessaires - tant endogènes qu'exogène – pour mettre en marche et maintenir un tel changement dans leur mode de vie. Ces deux idées mènent l'auteur a penser que la seule forme éthique de psychothérapie ambulatoire a fournis a une personne atteint de TUS est la PRM.

Est-ce justifié d'interdire les rapports sexuels entre les drogués et leurs soignants?

Mane Hajdin, J.D., Ph.D.

Ce chapitre examine quatre arguments possibles en faveur de l'interdiction de rapports sexuels entre soignants et drogués. Premièrement, l'interdiction concerne les tentations sexuelles créées par les phénomènes de transfert. Deuxièmement, il faut que les soignants fassent preuve d'autorité dans l'accomplissement de leur tâche. Troisièmement, il faut reconnaître que le traitement représente une manifestation de la loi et donc reste soumis à ses contraintes. La quatrième raison est que l'interdiction s'impose pour équilibrer le rapport qui existe entre les soignants et les soignés. En conclusion, ce chapitre établit que chacun de ces quatre arguments peut justiifier l'interdiction dans quelques cas mais seul le second peut s'imposer dans tous les cas. Cependant, cette raison apparaît plutôt sous l'aspect technique que sous l'aspect moral.

Role de la moralité dans l'attachment

Douglas N. Husak, Ph.D.

J' essaye de comprendre et estimer la croyance repandue que I' addiction a un rapport avec l'moralite. 1'examine plusiers relations qui demonstrent que l'addiction pourrait etre significative d'un point de vue moral. Bien que je parle brievement des theories de la vertu, je me concentre sur les trois moyens possibles de prouver que l'addiction pourrait ressortir de la responsabilite morale. Premierement la responsabilite pourrait etre conferer a la personne qui est adonnee a la drogue. Deuxiemement le blame pourrait etre conferer pour la condition d'etre adonne a la drogue. Troisiemement, la responsabilite pourrait en outre etre imposee pour les risques que les drogues pouraient encourir. 1'en conclus que chacun de ces cas est plausible, mais aucun d'eux n'est sans probleme. L'addiction a probablement un rapport avec la moralite, bien que son degre d'importance ne soit pas aussi serieux que les commentateurs ne le pensent. Le rapport de l'addiction avec la moralite ne semble pas justifier une prise de sanctions contre les drogues.

Le rôle de l'éthique dans la recherche sur la prévention chez les enfants.

Jeannette L. Johnson, Ph.D. et Nancy R. VanDeMark, Ph.D.

Comprendre les décisions éthiques dans la recherche sur la prévention de l'usage des drogues est à la fois compliqué et simple. La recherche sur la prévention est compliquée parce qu'il s'agit d'enfants et que les problèmes concernant la protection de l'enfance et les droits de l'enfant sont très importants. Les droits de l'enfant doivent être considérés clairement, respectueusement et avec douceur. L'éthique de la recherche de prévention est simple parce que le secret des interventions préventives efficaces ne se trouvent que dans l'enfance. Nous n'avons aucune alternative si nous voulons comprendre comment prévenir la maladie, les désordres, ou les erreurs dans le fonctionnement sans d'abord faire des recherches avec les enfants. C'est le lien entre les complications et la simplicité qui rend difficile les problèmes d'éthique dans la recherche sur la prévention.

La dépendence aux drogues et la responabilité pour les soins de santé des personnes dépendantese aux drogues

Tziporah Kasachkoff, Ph.D.

Prendre soin de ceux qui ont besoin des service de Santé Publique, est quelque chose, que nous, en tant que société, sommes engagé d'assumer jusque dans la mesure où nous avons les moyens financiers publiques de les payer. Est-ce que cet engagement est de quelques manière que ce soit justifié, si la maladie d'une personne est le résultat pour cette dernière poursuivant volontairement une conduite dont elle sait et apprecie à l'avance les risques à conséquence délétère encourus pour sa santé? Est-ce que la société a precisément une obligation de subvenir à la Santé Publique pour ceux qui se sont créés une dependence aux drogues illégales, obligation atténuèe par le fait de leur dépendance? Certains peuvent débattre le point qu'il en est ainsi alors que d'autres considèrent cette prise de position comme moralement intenable. Cette dissertation explore la question de qui a raison et pourquoi.

Le but moral de traitement en cas de diagnostique double

Jeannette Kennett, Ph.D. et Stephen Matthews, Ph.D.

L'usage et l'abus des substances se produisent à un taux très élevé parmi les personnes avec des problèmes de santé mentale, et les liens entre ces deux conditions sont complexes. Dans cet article nous soutenons que le traitement de l'usage de substances chez les clients ayant un tel diagnostic double doit commencer d'une compréhension des pertes que subissent ceux qui éprouvent une maladie mentale. Nous esquissons la condition fondamentale de l'agence efficace : c'est-à-dire l'agence unifiée. C'est celle-ci qui est dérangée dans la maladie mentale, et nous tenons à montrer comme elle est nécessaire pour maintenir l'accès aux bons sociaux et moraux centraux, par exemple l'emploi continu. Puis nous avançons que l'usage de drogues aura une valeur négative principalement en ce qu'il empêche l'accès à cet ensemble de bons agentifs, et en ce qu'il fasse que l'agent se préoccupe du bien-être synchronique à l'exclusion du bien-être diachronique. Ainsi faut-il que les buts et les méthodes de traitement pour les patients à diagnostic double doivent répondre à cet abattement primaire de l'agence unifiée.

L'aspect moral d'intervention dans l'utilisation des substances

John Kleinig, Ph.D.

Cet essai offre une vue panoramique de certaines questions morales soulevèes par les interventions gouvermentales et medicales concernant l'usage de la drogue. En ce qui concerne les premières interventions, il faut commencer par l'hypothèse liberale que des contraintes sur une libre action peuvent être justifiées si l'on songe aux effets nocifs qu'elles ont sur les autres; cependant cette hypothèse liberale doit être qualifiée en notant les exigences sociales d'une action libre. En ce qui concerne les interventions médicales cet essai fait le point sur les codes developpés pour ceaux qui fournissant le traitement medical, ainsi que leurs clients; et il explore également les foundations morales de plusieurs de leurs principales croyances: consentement conscient, vie privée, confidentialité, discrimination injustifiée, professionalisme, et responsabilité de ses actes.

Considérations éthiques à propos des programmes seringue et aiguille.

John Kleinig, Ph.D.

Si nous acceptons notre politique actuelle concernant la consommation d'héroïne, quelles sont les questions éthiques qui découlent des programmes concernant les aiguilles et les seringues? Est-ce que ces programmes affaiblissent la législation anti-drogue, diffusent un message trompeur ou brouillent-ils le vrai message? Sont-ils peu efficaces, empêchent-ils l'adoption d'autres solutions ou sont-ils un facteur de désespoir? Je suggère qu'en l'absence de solutions alternatives, ces programmes représentent une solution moralement acceptable et même dans certains cas une option souhaitable en dépit du maintien de la criminalisation de la consommation de drogues dures. Toutefois, ces programmes doivent être conduits et gérés de manière à ne pas accentuer la contestation sociale.

La vie privée, la confidentialité et le traitement des toxicomanes

Seumas Miller, PhD

A la base du principe de confidentialité il y a plusieurs principes importants dont le droit à la vie privée, la fiabilité et les conséquences néfastes de divulguer certaines informations. De plus, le droit à la vie privée est basé sur certaines valeurs morales dont l'autonomie. Justifier le besoin de confidentialité sur une base morale est donc compliqué. Les circonstances attenantes ont un impact sur notre degré d'engagement à et de la portée du principe du besoin de confidentialité. Dans certains cas ou pour certaines catégories de toxicomanes, il peut ne pas y avoir de raisons pour maintenir la confidentialité étant donne la diminution de l'autonomie, ce qui peut mener à diminuer l'ampleur ou la nécessite du droit à la vie privée. Néanmoins, cela n'implique pas une diminution automatique de notre engagement au principe de la confidentialité.

Explora las implicaciones de la justicia criminal empleando ambos modelos para guiar la política pública.

Stephen J. Morse, J.D., Ph.D.

La discussion sur la dépendance à la drogue est dominée par deux modèles théoriques: le médical, qui traite de la dépendance à la drogue comme une maladie avec des comportements liés aux symptômes; et l'autre modèle qui traite de la dépendance avec des comportements liés comme des indications d'une manque de moralité. Cet essai décrit ces deux modèles theorique avec leurs implications, se concentrant sur le modèle moral de la dépendance. Ce compte-rendu examine la signification del la coutrainte et de la compulsion créées par certaines dispositions psychologiques comme, par example, les envies irrisistible pour établir si c'est justifiable à rendre moralement et legalement responsables les dépendants à la drogue pour leur comportement. Ce compte-rendu préconise qu'une diminution des facultés intellectuelles expliquent mieux que si une compulsion poussait les drogués à excusir leur comportement. Cepandant on peut conclure que la majorité des drogués pouvent être tenus comme responsables de la plupart de leurs comportements vis-à-vis de la dépendance à la drogue. Néanmoins, puisque ces deux théories ont des caractéristiques souhaitables, il faut en conclure qu'une politique publique ne devrait pas être fondée entièrement sur une théorie ou l'autre. Cette essai explore les implications que ces deux modèles ont pour la criminologie et la politique.

Considérations éthiques dans la recherche sur le traitement des consommateurs de drogue

Kenneth D. Pimple, Ph.D.

La recherche sur le traitement des consommateurs de drogue devrait être guidée par les principes éthiques de base qui caractérisent tous les aspects de la recherche scientifique, y compris l'honnêteté et la franchise; la reconnaissance adéquate de la propriété intellectuelle de chaque auteur; une ligne de conduite qui respecte les distances et qui ne ressemble pas à de l'harcèlement; enfin les principes éthiques spécifiques à la recherche utilisant des sujets humains énoncés dans le rapport Belmont tels que le respect des personnes, la bienfaisance (et la non-malfaisance) et la justice. Un autre principe qui n'est pas explicitement mentionné dans le rapport Belmont mais qui devient largement approuvé est le droit à l'inclusion, ou à l'accès aux traitements. Les chercheurs ont l'obligation morale (et dans certains cas légale) de respecter ces principes, et l'ensemble des chercheurs spécialisés dans le traitement des consommateurs de drogue a une obligation de faire de son mieux pour établir un programme de recherche et une politique sociale qui tiennent compte de ces principes.

Traitement des Addictions - Pratique pragmatique ou scientifique ?

Maurice Rickard, Ph.D.

On peut constater que les décisions concernant le choix du traitement des drogués devrait relever de la politique publique et d'un choix de société. Il est logique de souhaiter que la politique rende accessible les interventions thérapeutiques scientifiques (donc éthiques). Il semble également fondé d'espérer que cette politique et ces choix sociaux conernant les pratiques thérapeutiques soient équitables et justes. En d'autres termes, que les décisions soient correctement appliquées. L'une des façons de respecter ces deux attentes légitimes est de concevoir une politique juste en matière de choix du traitement approprié des addictions, de telle façon que ce soit la bonne thérapie qui prime. Le problème est que la détermination d'une thérapie correcte et efficace dépend de l'objectif que chacun se fixe en matière de traitement des addictions. Le danger est d'aboutir à des controverses sur la nature équitable du traitement proposé, au lieu de s'intéresser à celui qui est valable pour tous. Ce chapitre explore quelques interrogations philosophiques concernant une politique positive se penchant sur la question de qui doit prendre et appliquer la décision.

Les problèmes d'éthique concernant l'accès aux services de conseils et de traitements pour ceux qui utilisent des drogues.

Barbara C. Wallace, Ph.D.

Les problèmes d'éthique concernant l'accès aux services de conseils et aux traitements de ceux qui utilisent des drogues varient. La gamme inclut les possibilités de discrimination en ce qui concerne l'accès au traitement étant donne certaines caractéristiques des clients, dont la race, la religion, le genre, ou certaines conditions attenantes telles que l'âge, la grossesse, la position géographique et la distance à parcourir pour se rendre aux services de traitements, la pauvreté, ou le manque d'assurances pour recevoir des soins de santé. D'autres problèmes d'éthique concernent l'état d'incapacité du client, y compris des incapacités physiques ou psychiatriques, par exemple. Comment contrôler le nombre de cas de rechutes, des résultats d'examens toxicologiques d'urine qui continuent à être positifs et, surtout, les cas les plus complexes qui sont caractérisés par une carrière de rechute chronique, tous sont des exemples de problèmes d'ordre éthique. Les risques d'actes violents (« acting out ») par les clients en traitement (ce qui peut mener à la décision de leur barrer l'accès aux traitements) ont aussi leurs aspects éthiques. Enfin, contraindre les utilisateurs de drogues à se faire traiter et leur présenter un mandat de traitement de la part du système légal, des agences d'assistance sociale ou de protection de l'enfant, ont aussi leur aspects de problèmes d'ordre éthique, étant donne que ces actes ont tous pour but de forcer les clients à faire accès aux services de traitement. Ce chapitre suggère comment conceptualiser et répondre à la gamme de problèmes d'ordre éthique liés à l'accès aux services de conseils et de traitements pour ceux qui utilisent des drogues.

Les implications ethiques de la remuneration de l'assistance aux drogues

Adrian Walsh, Ph.D. et Tony Lynch, Ph.D.

Nous aborderons dans cet article les implication de la remuneration, sous toutes ses formes, des conseillers pour personnes a proie a des problemes lies a la drogue. Selon une tradition philosophique de longue date, les recompenses financieres et l'altruisme sont mutuellement exclusifs. Nous ne partageons pas ce point de vue. Au contraire, nous somme de l'avis que bien que la recompense sous forme de benefice ou de salaire n'est pas nocive en elle meme, mais elle confronte cependant les conseillers a des problemes d'ethique. Il y a des dangers dont les personnes impliquees dans l'assistance aux drogues se doivent d'etre vigilantes quant a ces risques.

La dependence aux drogues et la responsabilité pour soins de santé des personnes dependants aux drogues

David Wasserman, J.D.

Ce compte-rendue examine les questions de conception, d'éthique et de politique soulevèes par la classification légale de la dépendance à la drogue comme une diminution de l'integrité de la personne ainsi que la situation de certains dépendants qui n'ont pas recours aux drogues mais considérés comme des invalides. Ce compte-rendu ce concentre sur les questions suivantes: (1) quel est le jugement moral s'il y en a un, qui est à la base de la classification de l'addiction comme un amoindrissement? (2) est-il raisonable de répartir les fardeaux monétaires de l'addiction à la drogue, ayant à choisir entre le causes chimiques, biologiques, sociales, politiques et autres? (3) quelles sont les considerations qui peuvent nous forcer or nous contraindre à prendre les mesures qui facilitent l'appropriation des fardeaux monétaires de l'addiction a la drogue afin de distribuer la justice? (4) est-il justifiable de refuser aux usagers actuels des substances illégales les protections légales qui sont cependant disponibles aux usagers actuels des substances légales?

Les problèmes éthiques concernant l'accès au traitement pour l'abus de drogues

Shelly A. Wiechelt, Ph.D.

La grande variété de programmes de traitements pour les personnes qui utilisent des substances psycho actives aux Etats-Unis nous ont montré que les traitements sont efficaces. Malgré que nos connaissances augmentent de plus en plus et qu'il y a de plus en plus de traitements disponibles en général, il y a un gouffre entre le nombre de personnes identifiées comme ayant besoin de ces traitements et de ceux qui les reçoivent réellement. Ce chapitre présente certains des facteurs et des conditions qui contribuent aux problèmes de l'accès aux traitements pour les personnes qui utilisent des substance aux Etats-Unis. Ces problèmes d'accès sont explorés à la lumière des codes éthiques professionnels sur les traitements de la toxicomanie.

Relations Intervenant-Patient et Ethique professionnelle

Kylie Williams, M.A. et Dean Cocking, Ph.D.

Dans ce chapitre, nous mettons en valeur une conception pluraliste de l'éthique adaptée au rôle d'accompagnement professionnel. Les contraintes inhérantes à la tâche, les sensibilités et le domaine des problèmes humains relevant d'un accompagnement sont multiples et susceptibles d'engendrer des conflits. La nature et le cadre des programmes du traitement de l'usage involontaire des drogues présentent des problèmes spécifiques concernant les relations conseiller-patient. En effet, pour de nombreux analystes, ces problèmes compromettent inévitablement la morale et les objectifs fondamentaux de l'intervention. Nous reconnaissons le fait que certaines valeurs fondamentales sont souvent compromises de manière involontaire. En revanche, nous insistons sur le fait que la plupart des conflits peuvent servir notre conception pluraliste plutôt que de nuire à une pratique de l'accompagnement totalement dissociée de ses véritables objectifs.

De la tour d'ivoire de la théorie aux fossés de la pratique : Comment enseigner l'éthique professionnelle à ceux qui fournissent des services de conseils a ceux qui utilisent des drogues

Par: Daniel Yalisove, Ph.D.

Ce chapitre décrit une approche à l'enseignement de l'éthique aux professionnels qui offrent des services de conseils à ceux qui ont des problèmes liés à l'utilisation de substances psychotropes. Trois nouvelles idées qui n'ont pas reçu à date la considération qu'elles méritent dans l'enseignement de l'éthique professionnelle sont présentées : (1) En voulant prendre des décisions d'ordre éthique les conseillers ont confondu des considérations d'ordre éthiques avec celles qui n'avaient rien à voir avec l'éthique. Ces différences doivent être misent au clair pour les étudiants lors de l'enseignement de l'éthique professionnelle. (2) Il existe une synergie toute particulière entre les services de conseils humanistes et l'éthique professionnelle. (3) Il faut donner une attention toute particulière au processus de l'enseignement de l'éthique pour certains clients en les aidant à se rendre compte des problèmes d'ordre éthique.

Le difficili Decisioni che coinvolgono Ricerca ed Etica: Statistiche degli Abusatori di Droghe

Manuella Adrian, M. Sc. Hyg.

La ricerca scientifica ci ha fornito uno dei mezzi più potenti per migliorare la sorte dell'umanità. Tuttavia, proprio questo potere può esser la fonte di una miriade di dilemmi morali ed etici per coloro che ne fanno uso. La maggior parte dell' attenzione dedicata all'etica della ricerca è attualmente diretta alla ricerca su soggetti umani ed è orientata a ridurre la probabilità dei danni arrecati ai partecipanti, attraverso linee guida ragionevolmente ben sviluppate e che sono emerse negli scorsi cinquant'anni. Sono anche riconosciuti quei dilemmi etici che originano dagli scopi della ricerca, specialmente quella militare. Meno note sono quell'insieme di problematiche etiche che nascono dal metodo scientifico stesso, dai metodi di ricerca e dall'interpretazione dei dati che sono poi descritti in queste pagine. Si passano qui in rassegna alcuni presupposti del metodo scientifico impiegato nelle indagini sull'uso e abuso della sostanze, a partire dai principi di base enunciati da Isaac Newton per stabilire la causalità ed esplorando poi alcune delle più nuove cornici concettuali utili a determinare i punti di intervento dove si possa agire per ottenere i risultati desiderati, anche quando la causalità lineare non è applicabile con rigore, servendosi di esempi provenienti non soltanto dall'ambito dell' uso di sostanze, ma anche da una cornice scientifica più generale, quando tali illustrazioni possono essere utili. Vengono poi considerati i problemi etici e morali derivanti dalla natura degli argomenti oggetto di ricerca, dalla loro organizzazione e dal loro finanziamento, così come dall'uso di metodi e tecniche inadeguati -- compresi alcuni aspetti che devono essere considerati quando si tratta di soggetti umani --, che possono portare a conclusioni errate e potenzialmente nocive a pazienti, scienziati e alla società in generale.

Aspetti etici inerenti l'Approccio del Mutuo Aiuto nel Trattamento di chi fa Uso di Sostanze: il Ruolo delle Organizzazioni dei Dodici Passi

Allaman Allamani, M.D.

I gruppi di mutuo-aiuto, e i trattamenti formali che sono in relazione e lavorano con persone che abusano di bevande alcoliche e di altre sostanze, appartengono a dimensioni etiche che sono diverse secondo la intrinseca differenza di ciascuno dei due settori. In particolare, l'etica dei Dodici Passi è universalistica dato che si basa sui principi di spiritualità, alterità e solidarietà; se pure la loro efficacia nell'indurre astinenza può essere studiata scientificamente, essi sono da considerare come "comunità di guarigione" (Seppiala 2001). D'altro lato l'etica del contesto dei professionisti coinvolti nel trattamento appare utilitaristica, cioè orientata agli interessi dell'individuo o del gruppo. Anche se, quando interagiscono, le due differenti prospettive hanno talvolta creato tensioni o conflitti, la loro co-operazione è oggi diffusa in tutto il mondo.

Disabilità e Trattamento/Riabilitazione di chi fa Uso di Sostanze: Considerazioni etiche

Ellen Benoit, Ph. D. e Stephen Magura, Ph.D.

Prima del 1996 negli Stati Uniti coloro che erano cronicamente dipendenti da droghe o da alcol potevano ricevere un certificato di disabilità, che concedeva loro un sostegno economico da parte della Amministrazione della Sicurezza Sociale (ASS) per tutto il periodo della loro adesione al trattamento. La legislazione del marzo 1996 ha richiesto che l'ASS cancellasse le dipendenze dalle disabilità riconosciute e rimovesse dalle sue liste chiunque avesse ricevuto benefici in quanto faceva uso di sostanze. Questo mutamento solleva significative questioni etiche, che affrontiamo dalla prospettiva della giustizia distributiva. Esaminiamo le politiche che distinguono le persone bisognose in meritevoli e immeritevoli, analizzando come nel dibattito sulla idoneità delle richieste la natura medicalmente ambigua della dipendenza promuova richieste che "cadono nel nulla". Per esempio, il divenir disabile per abuso di sostanze costituisce una forma di comportamento volontaristico? Per concludere, consideriamo le conseguenze che i cambiamenti operati dall'ASS hanno per i referenti delle politiche sanitarie, e cioè gli utenti, i fornitori di trattamento ed il pubblico.

Se chi usa le Sostanze è in grado di dare il Consenso a un Programma di Trattamento

Steve Clarke, Ph.D. e Neil Levy, Ph.D.

Secondo molte opinioni, chi fa uso regolare di droghe non è in grado di acconsentire a un trattamento medico. In questo articolo precisiamo i criteri di minima che valgono perché gli operatori considerino una persona in grado di dare un consenso informato, e sosteniamo che chi fa uso regolare di droghe- incluso chi è considerato dipendente dalla droghe –tipicamente soddisfa tali condizioni. Sebbene la dipendenza riduca l'autonomia, non la riduce fino al punto di rendere una persona inabile a fornire un consenso informato. Gli studi sul comportamento delle persone dipendenti indicano che di solito esse mantengono un sufficiente controllo dei loro comportamenti e una capacità di decidere tali da potersi qualificare come persone in grado di dare un consenso.

Una Concettualizzazione del Rapporto professionale nel Counselling per i Consumatori di Droghe e per gli Abusatori di Alcol

Elliot D. Cohen, Ph.D.

Codici etici, statuti e casi legali danno origine a doveri etici di base o requisisti che spetta ai professionisti che fanno counselling di attuare nei confronti dei consumatori di droghe e degli abusatori di alcol. Tuttavia, onde tali terapisti agiscano efficacemente, debbono anche incorporare nella loro pratica più criteri motivazionali e centrati sulla persona. A partire da un'analisi dei valori fondamentali che sottostanno a un'efficace terapia, e integrando parecchi modelli professionali relazionali dell'assistenza sanitaria, questo capitolo sviluppa un modello praticabile ed eclettico del rapporto terapista - cliente.

Questioni etiche sollevare delle Politiche non punitive nei confronti dei Consumatori di Droghe

Stephen Coleman, Ph.D.

Negli ultimi decenni in molti paesi c'è stata una forte spinta all'attuazione di programmi e di politiche aventi un atteggiamento non punitivo verso i consumatori e gli abusatori di droghe, di solito con lo scopo di minimizzare i danni ad essi causati. Lo scopo di questo capitolo è di precisare e discutere le specifiche questioni etiche sollevate da alcune di queste politiche non punitive, che includono trattamento metadonico di manutenzione, programmi di scambio di aghi, allestimento di spazi opportuni per effettuare le iniezioni, prescrizione di eroina, e decriminalizzazione della canapa.

I Consumatori di Droghe non sono da trattare, ma la Gente sì! –

Stan Einstein, Ph. D.

Viene presupposta ed esaminata, usando esempi selezionati, la tesi che l'attuale trattamento dei "disordini da uso di sostanze" - sia orientato all'astinenza sia indirizzato alla riduzione del danno che è quasi sempre effettuato fuori dai luoghi ove avviene il flusso principale del trattamento – che viene messo a disposizione della popolazione generale:

- è sostanzialmente non etico; la scarsità dei suoi benefici è sopravanzata da una non necessaria "dose" di prevaricazioni;
- è una definizione fuorviante: 1) non c'è un "trattamento" (modelli o tecniche) unico per i "consumatori di droghe" che non sia anche usato per i non consumatori di droghe; 2) tanto i "consumatori di droghe" quanto i non consumatori rappresentano popolazioni eterogenee di GENTE e non nosologie uniche ed omogenee;
- non ha probabilità di essere cambiato in un processo basato sull'etica a causa delle posizioni, degli impegni e dei fini dei referenti individuali e di sistema orientati al potere;
- è nutrito da "princìpi di fede" sovrastati e sottesi da slogan quali "basato sull'evidenza" e
- può essere ed è troppo spesso (involontariamente) mantenuto da una gamma di agenti di cambiamento co-optati e che rappresentano uno spettro di discipline, come pure dai non-professionisti "in recupero" o ex-dipendenti,
- all'interno di una realtà *de facto* in cui nuovi risultati generalizzabili sono, più spesso che no, non introdotti e non usati per curare con adeguatezza i consumatori di sostanze sotto la rubrica di problemi di trasferimento di tecnologia.

Competenza nel Counselling per le Dipendenze Chimiche

Theodore M. Godlaski, M.Div.

Anche se per una pratica eticamente corretta la competenza clinica sia ovunque ritenuta necessaria, essa è spesso mal definita. Un gruppo di esperti, sotto il patrocinio dell'Amministrazione dei Servizi di Salute Mentale e di Abuso di Sostanze degli Stati Uniti, ha compiuto sforzi significativi per una sua miglior definizione, specificando che ci sono tre aree ove per aver competenza è necessaria un'adeguata capacità: conoscenze, abilità ed atteggiamenti. Tuttavia, quasi tutte la istituzioni certificanti si limitano a misure obiettive del sapere, affidando abilità ed atteggiamenti alla dichiarazione di supervisori clinici. C'è qualche motivo di preoccupazione circa la qualità e la quantità del contatto fornito dai supervisori, su cui tali giudizi sono basati. Inoltre, c'è motivo di dubitare che tutta la conoscenza e tutte le abilità siano, eticamente, di pari valore. Infine ci sono domande etiche sulla legittimità della separazione tra l'area del counselling per consumatori di sostanze il counselling in generale.

Riflessioni sugli Aspetti etici nella Ricerca con le Popolazioni Aborigene

Theodore M. Godlaski, M.Div., Jeannette Johnson, Ph.D. and Rodney Haring, MSW

Questo capitolo è una riflessione sugli aspetti etici salienti che nascono durante il lavoro di ricerca con le popolazioni aborigene o nativi. La fonte primaria di preoccupazione etica è l'appropriatezza culturale degli scopi della ricerca, e del suo disegno, metodi, protocollo e programma di pubblicazione e disseminazione. Sebbene l'appropriatezza culturale non sia un costrutto ben definito, la mancanza di attenzione per i modi di pensare dei nativi e per la loro struttura sociale, comunicazione e visione del mondo può essere evidente nel danno fatto come conseguenza di sforzi di ricerca mal concepiti. Gli autori si basano su un recente lavoro compiuto in quest'area per fornire linee-guida per le ricerche sensibili agli aspetti culturali.

I Conflitti di Interesse nella Valutazione e nella Diffusione dei Programmi

Dennis M. Gorman, Ph.D.

Questo capitolo esamina le implicazioni che i recenti sviluppi nella valutazione e nel marketing dei programmi di prevenzione delle droghe hanno per l'integrità della ricerca e in particolare per la minaccia costituita dai conflitti d'interesse. Inizia con una descrizione di cosa significhi conflitto d'interesse e con una rassegna dei principali tipi di conflitti discussi negli ultimi anni nella letteratura medica e in quella delle politiche pubbliche. Segue una discussione più dettagliata sui conflitti d'interesse individuale e istituzionale che esistono nella ricerca relativa alla prevenzione delle droghe.

È etica una Psicoterapia di Riduzione del Danno?

William H. Gottdiener, Ph.D.

La psicoterapia di riduzione di danno (PRD) è una psicoterapia per clienti ambulatoriali con diagnosi di disordine da uso di sostanze (DUS) e che continuano ad usare sostanze psicoattive. L'obiettivo di trattamento della PRD è ridurre il danno potenziale che può accompagnar l'uso delle sostanze psicoattive, e la sobrietà è solo una via per ridurre il danno, rispetto ai tradizionali trattamenti del DUS in cui la sobrieta è l'unico obiettivo accettabile. La PRD è usata dato che la sobrietà non è realizzabile e/o mantenibile in tutti quelli che hanno un DUS o per ogni fase del loro trattamento. Il capitolo discute se la PRD sia un trattamento etico da disporre per chi ha una diagnosi di DUS. L'autore, assumendo in linea con Foucald che la libertà personale è essenziale al trattamento del DUS, e in linea con una prospettiva psicanalitica che la sobrietà può esser realizzata soltanto da clienti pronti per aspirare a quell'obiettivo e forniti di ciò che è necessario – dal punto di vista endogeno ed esogeno – per iniziare e mantenere un tal aggiustamento nello stile di vita, sostiene che la PRD è l'unica forma etica di psicoterapia ambulatoriale da fornire agli individui con DUS.

Proibizione dei rapporti sessuali fra Consumatori di Droga ed i loro Counsellor: è giustificata?

Mane Hajdin, J.D., Ph.D.

Questo capitolo esamina quattro possibili ragioni per la proibizione dei rapporti sessuali fra i counsellor per chi fa uso di droghe e i loro stessi utenti. La prima è che la proibizione contrasta le speciali tentazioni e occasioni di rapporti sessuali generate dal fenomeno del transfert. La seconda è che la proibizione contribuisce all'autorità che i consulenti devono emanare se l'intervento deve raggiungere il suo scopo. Secondo la terza ragione, il counselling è un'estensione di un'applicazione di legge, ed è pertanto soggetta agli stessi vincoli dell'applicazione di una legge. La quarta ragione è che la proibizione è necessaria a causa dello squilibrio di potere che esiste fra i counsellor e i loro utenti. La conclusione del capitolo è che ciascuna di queste quattro ragioni può giustificare la proibizione in alcuni aspetti del counselling per i consumatori di droghe, ma soltanto la seconda può giustificarlo in tutti i suoi aspetti. Tuttavia tale ragione appare essere puramente materia di tecnica di counselling piuttosto che un vincolo morale indipendente dal counselling stesso.

La rilevanza morale della Dipendenza

Douglas N. Husak, J.D., Ph.D.

Il mio è un tentativo di capire e valutare la diffusa credenza che la dipendenza abbia a che fare con la moralità. Esamino parecchie ragioni che spiegano come la dipendenza possa essere significativa dal punto di vista morale. Pur discutendo brevemente delle teorie sulla virtù, ci si sofferma su tre possibili percorsi per cui la dipendenza potrebbe essere importante per la colpa morale. In primo luogo la colpa può essere posta per il fatto di usare sostanze dipendentogene. In secondo luogo, per la condizione di essere dipendenti. In terzo luogo, per gli ulteriori rischi che le persone è probabile che si assumano una volta che sono diventate dipendenti. Concludo che ciascuno di queste ragioni ha una certa plausibilità, ma nessuna è del tutto senza problemi. La dipendenza è probabilmente rilevante in quanto alla moralità, seppur il suo grado di importanza non è grande come alcuni commentatori sembrano ritenere. L'importanza morale della dipendenza non appare raggiungere qualsiasi livello che possa giustificare una risposta punitiva verso i tossicodipendenti.

Tossicodipendenza Etica nella Ricerca sulla Prevenzione con i Bambini

Jeannette L. Johnson, Ph.D. e Nancy R. VanDeMark, Ph.D.

Capire le decisioni etiche implicate nella ricerca sulla prevenzione dell' uso di droghe può essere tanto complicato quanto semplice. La ricerca sulla prevenzione è complicata perché riguarda i bambini, e gli aspetti che hanno a che fare con la loro protezione ed i loro diritti sono estremamente significativi. Con i bambini, tali diritti devono essere seguiti con chiarezza di intenzioni, rispetto e sensibilità. L'etica della ricerca sulla prevenzione è semplice perché la risposta per capire gli interventi preventivi efficaci può essere trovata soltanto durante l'infanzia. Non ci sono alternative a capire come prevenire la malattia, il disordine, o la disfunzione senza prima condurre una ricerca coi bambini. È la congiunzione di complicazione e di semplicità che rende spinosi gli aspetti etici della ricerca sulla prevenzione.

Tossicodipendenza e responsabilità nell'assistenza ai tossicomani

Tziporah Kasachkoff, Ph.D.

Prendersi cura di coloro che hanno bisogno di assistenza sanitaria è qualcosa a cui, come società, ci sentiamo impegnati nella misura in cui i fondi pubblici lo permettono. Questo impegno è in ogni caso qualificato dal fatto che le malattie mediche di una persona dipendono dalla eventualità che essa si sia volontariamente imbarcata in attività delle cui conseguenze, deleterie per salute, era ben informata in anticipo? Specificamente, l'obbligo che ha una società di fornire servizi di assistenza sanitaria a chi si è fatto tossicodipendente è attenuato dalla circostanza della dipendenza? Alcuni sostengono di sì, altri considerano questa posizione insostenibile moralmente.. Questo saggio esplora il punto di chi ha qui ragione e perché.

Lo Scopo morale del Trattamento nei Casi di Doppia Diagnosi

Jeannette Kennett, Ph.D. e Stephen Matthews, Ph.D.

Uso e "abuso" di sostanze sono assai frequenti tra persone con problemi di salute mentale, ed il rapporto fra le due condizioni è complesso. In questo capitolo sosteniamo che il trattamento del consumo di sostanze nei clienti con doppia diagnosi deve cominciare da una comprensione delle perdite sofferte da chi ha una malattia mentale. Delineiamo lo stato fondamentale di un' efficace capacità di agire, o capacità di agire unica, che s'interrompe nella malattia mentale e che si dimostra necessaria per assicurare l'accesso a beni centrali dal punto di vista sociale e morale, quali un'occupazione continuativa e rapporti soddisfacenti. Sosteniamo che l'uso della droghe è un non valore soprattutto finchè impedisce al soggetto anche l'accesso all' insieme dei beni, focalizzandolo sul benessere sincronico a spese del benessere diacronico. Gli scopi ed i metodi di trattamento per i pazienti con doppia diagnosi devono perciò riflettere così il deficit primario nella capacità di agire.

Pensando eticamente ai Programmi di Scambio di Aghi

John Kleinig, Ph.D.

Accettando -- nell'interesse della discussione -- le nostre attuali politiche legali che riguardano l'eroina, quali questioni etiche vengono sollevate per i programmi di scambio di aghi? Forse indeboliscono le leggi sulla droghe? trasmettono il messaggio errato od oscurano quello giusto? non fanno abbastanza per eliminare il danno prodotto dalle droghe? distolgono dalle alternative? e/o costituiscono una risoluzione disperata? Suggerisco che in assenza di consolidate e migliori alternative, tali programmi costituiscono un'opzione moralmente accettabile e perfino desiderabile, malgrado la continua criminalizzazione del consumo di droghe.

Aspetti Etici nell'i ntervento sull' uso di Droghe

John Kleinig, Ph.D.

Questo saggio offre una descrizione di alcune delle questioni etiche sollevate dagli interventi governativi e sanitari nel campo dell'uso della droghe. Riguardo i primi, comincia con il presupposto liberale che i vincoli alla libera azione devono essere giustificati in riferimento al suo deleterio effetto sugli altri, ma successivamente qualifica quel presupposto notando i requisiti sociali della libera azione. Riguardo gli interventi medici, mette a fuoco sui codici che sono stati sviluppati per i fornitori di trattamento ed i loro clienti, ed esplora i sostegni etici di varie delle loro clausole centrali - consenso, segretezza, riservatezza, non-discriminazione, professionalità e responsabilità, consenso informato.

Privatezza, Riservatezza e Trattamento dei Tossicomani

Seumas Miller, Ph.D.

A sostegno del principio di riservatezza stanno varie considerazioni, compreso il diritto alla privatezza, la fiducia e le conseguenze nocive che può avere la divulgazione. E lo stesso diritto alla privatezza è in sé sostenuto da altri valori morali, compresa l'autonomia. Ciò rende complessa la giustificazione morale alla riservatezza. Il nostro grado di coinvolgimento e lo scopo del principio di riservatezza hanno bisognodi essere relativizzati secondo le circostanze. In alcuni casi o categorie di tossicomani, possono difettare le basi per una riservatezza, a causa di una ridotta autonomia, con una conseguente riduzione nella forza o scopo del diritto alla privatezza. Nondimeno, non ne seguirebbe automaticamente che il nostro impegno al principio di riservatezza sarebbe più debole.

Medicina e morali, craving e compulsione

Stephen J. Morse, J.D., Ph.D.

Il campo delle dipendenze è stato dominato da due modelli: il modello medico, che tratta la dipendenza come una malattia ed i comportamenti relativi come segni e sintomi, ed il modello morale, che vede la dipendenza ed i comportamenti relativi come indicazioni di un fallimento morale. Questo articolo descrive entrambi i modelli e le loro implicazioni, con particolare enfasi sul modello morale. Il significato della compulsione o coercizione causata da condizioni psicologiche interne, come il craving, viene esplorato per determinare se i dipendenti possono ragionevolmente essere giudicati moralmente e legalmente responsabili del loro comportamento, quale si riflette nella ricerca e l'uso delle sostanze. Si argomenta che la diminuita razionalità spiega, meglio della compulsione, il perché i dipendenti siano da scusare per il loro comportamento, ma si conclude che la maggior parte dei dipendenti possono essere giudicati responsabili per la maggior parte dei comportamenti legati alla dipendenza.. Ciò nonostante, entrambi i modelli hanno caratteristiche desiderabili e una solida strategia di intervento pubblico non dovrebbe essere basata su uno solo di essi. Vengono esplorate le implicazioni che ha per la giustizia criminale l' impiego di ambedue i modelli.

Aspetti etici nel Trattamento dei Consumatori di Droghe

Kenneth D. Pimple, Ph.D.

La ricerca nel trattamento di chi fa uso di droghe dovrebbe essere guidata dalle considerazioni etiche di fondo che prevalgono in ogni ricerca scientifica, che includono l'onestà e la sincerità; l'accreditamento del vero autore; l'astenersi da condotte intime o moleste verso i soggetti della ricerca; e dai principii etici propri della ricerca su soggetti umani enumerati nel rapporto Belmont quali il rispetto per le persone, l'operare cose buone (e non cose cattive) e la giustizia. Un principio ulteriore non esplicitamente menzionato nel rapporto Belmont, ma che viene ora largamente accettato, è l'inclusione, o accesso ai trattamenti. I ricercatori sono moralmente (ed in alcuni casi legalmente) legati ad aderire a questi principii e la comunità dei ricercatori circa il trattamento per i consumatori di droghe ha nell'insieme l'obbligo di fare il meglio per conformare a questi principi la pianificazione della ricerca e le politiche sociali.

Trattamento dei Consumatori di Sostanze - una Politica corretta o una Politica Basata sull'Evidenza?

Maurice Rickard, Ph.D.

Ci sono ragioni che mostrano che le decisioni su quali tipi di trattamento debbano essere messi in pratica per chi fa uso di sostanze, siano materia di politiche pubbliche e di scelte sociali. Appare sensato volere che i percorsi della politica rendano disponibili interventi terapeuticamente (e moralmente) basati sull'evidenza. Appare poi ragionevole attendersi che i processi delle scelte sociali e politiche circa le pratiche di trattamento siano giusti e corretti, o, in altre parole, che le decisioni siano autorizzate appropriatamente. Un modo per rispettare queste plausibili attese è di concettualizzare la correttezza nella presa delle decisioni circa le politiche di trattamento di chi fa uso di droghe, in modo tale che essa sia concettualmente condizionata dal fatto che le decisioni prese risultino giuste dal punto di vista terapeutico. Il problema qui è che ciò che è terapeuticamente corretto o efficace dipende dal proprio punto di vista su che cosa è lo scopo che ha il trattamento di chi fa uso di droghe. Il rischio è di finire con una concezione controversa dei processi corretti, piuttosto che con una concezione massimamente accettabile da tutti. Il capitolo esamina alcuni aspetti filosofici circa la politica del trattamento corretto e quella del buon trattamento, incluso chi dovrebbe avere un ruolo nel prendere decisioni su tali politiche.

Questioni etiche relative all'Accesso al Trattamento/Counselling dei Consumatori di Droga

Barbara C. Wallace, Ph.D.

Le questioni etiche relative all'accesso al counselling e trattamento dei consumatori di droga sono assai varie e includono una potenziale discriminazione sull'accesso al trattamento secondo la razza, la religione, il genere, o la condizione del cliente -- quali età, gravidanza, posizione geografica e distanza dal trattamento, povertà, o mancanza di assicurazione. Altre questioni etiche riguardano lo stato di inabilità del cliente, comprese ad esempio le inabilità fisiche e psichiatriche, ovvero il modo di controllare i problemi della ricaduta, i referti tossicologici positivi sulle urine e i casi più impegnativi che coinvolgono le carriere dei dipendenti caratterizzate da ricadute croniche. Ulteriori questioni etiche coinvolgono il rischio di acting out violenti di clienti in trattamento e quando viene escluso l'accesso al trattamento. Altre questioni etiche coinvolgono l'uso di coercizione e dell'obbligo al trattamento, attuati sia dal sistema giudiziario, sia dalle agenzie di assistenza sociale, sia dalle agenzie di protezione dei minori, in quanto tutte forzano i loro clienti ad accedere al trattamento. In questo capitolo vengono offerte raccomandazioni per come concettualizzare e rispondere a tutto l'insieme delle questioni etiche contemporanee per quanto riguarda l'accesso al counselling e al trattamento dei consumatori di droga.

Counseling per i Consumatori di Droghe, Remunerazione ed Etica

Adrian Walsh, Ph.D. e Tony Lynch, Ph.D.

Questo capitolo esplora le implicazioni che può avere la remunerazione, nelle sue varie forme, per i counsellor dei consumatori di droghe. Una lunga tradizione filosofica sostiene che ricompensa economica e altruismo si escludono l'un l'altro. Il nostro punto di vista è un po' differente e contro tale tradizione argomentiamo che anche se la ricompensa economica sotto forma o di profitto commerciale o di stipendio non è per sé o da sé moralmente perniciosa, essa pone il counsellor di fronte a dei rischi etici. Nei confonti di tali rischi devono essere particolarmente vigili coloro che sono implicati nel counselling di chi fa uso di droghe.

Dipendenza e Disabilità: Aspetti morali e di Politica Sanitaria

David Wasserman, J.D.

Questo articolo discute gli aspetti concettuali, etici e di politica sanitaria sollevati dalla classificazione legale della tossicodipendenza in quanto menomazione, e di alcuni che non fanno alcun uso di droghe come le persone con disabilità. Si sofferma su alcuni punti (1) quali sono, se mai, i giudizi morali alla base della classificazione della dipendenza come menomazione; (2) se ha significato suddividere il peso della dipendenza tra cause chimiche, biologiche, sociali, politiche ed altre; (3) come le considerazioni di giustizia distributiva possano spingere a misure per alleggerire il peso della tossicodipendenza; e (4) se è giustificabile negare agli attuali consumatori di sostanze illegali le protezioni legali disponibili per gli attuali consumatori di sostanze legali.

Aspetti etici inerenti l' accesso al Trattamento per "abuso" di sostanze

Shelly A. Wiechelt, Ph.D.

Negli Stati Uniti la gran varietà di programmi di trattamento per chi fa uso di sostanze ha prodotto un'abbondante evidenza scientifica che mostra l'efficacia dei trattamenti. Indipendentemente dalle crescenti conoscenze e dalla complessiva disponibilità di trattamento, esiste una tremenda divaricazione fra il numero di persone identificate come bisognose di trattamento e quello di coloro che effetivamente lo ricevono. Questo capitolo discute alcuni tra i fattori e le circostanze che negli Stati Uniti contribuiscono ai problemi di accesso al trattamento per i consumatori di sostanze. Gli aspetti inerenti gli accessi sono esplorati alla luce dei codici etici per i professionisti, relativi al trattamento delle dipendenze.

Interazione tra Counselor e Cliente, e Moralità Professionale di Ruolo

Kylie Williams, M.A. e Dean Cocking, Ph.D.

Questo capitolo presenta una concezione pluralista della moralità di ruolo appropriata al counselling professionale. Gli obblighi di ruolo, le sensibilità e l'area dei problemi umani che sono relativi al counselling hanno una portata particolarmente ampia e sono carichi di conflitti potenziali; la natura e i contesti dei programmi non volontari di trattamento per i consumatori di droghe presentano problemi speciali per le interazioni tra counsellor e cliente. In effetti per molti autori, tali problemi fatalmente compromettono i beni morali e gli scopi basilari che fondano il counselling. Mentre concordiamo che alcuni valori chiave siano spesso compromessi nei contesti non volontari, sosteniamo però che il conflitto di ruolo sia qui meglio capito nel quadro della nostra concezione pluralistica, piuttosto che riflettendo una pratica di counselling complessivamente dissociata dagli appropriati scopi che la costituiscono.

Dalla Torre d' Avorio alle Trincee: Insegnamento dell' Etica professionale ai Counsellor per Abuso di Sostanze

Daniel Yalisove, Ph.D.

Questo capitolo descrive un approccio per insegnare l'etica professionale ai counsellor che trattano i disordini da uso di sostanze, e introduce tre idee innovarici precedentemente non prese in considerazione nell'insegnamento dell'etica professionale: 1) i counsellor hanno confuso considerazioni etiche con altre di natura non etica quando hanno dovuto prendere decisioni di tipo etico. È importante che nella formazione all' etica professionale gli allievi abbiano chiara questa distinzione. 2) C'è uno speciale sinergismo fra il counselling umanistico e l'etica professionale. 3) Si dà esplicita attenzione al processo di educazione morale di alcuni clienti, che avviene quando si aiutano a diventare consapevoli dei problemi etici.

Decisões Difíceis Envolvendo Pesquisa e Ética: Utilizando Mal as Estatísticas sobre o Uso e o Usuário de Drogas

Manuella Adrian, M. Sc. Hyg.

A pesquisa científica tem nos oferecido um dos mais poderosos meios para melhorar o destino da humanidade. Entretanto, este poder pode ser a fonte de uma série de dilemas morais e éticos para aqueles que o utilizam. A maior parte da atenção sobre a ética na pesquisa é atualmente dirigida à pesquisa envolvendo sujeitos humanos e é orientada para reduzir a probabilidade de danos para os participantes, com diretrizes razoavelmente bem desenvolvidas tendo emergido nos últimos cinqüenta anos. São também reconhecidos os dilemas éticos que decorrem das finalidades da pesquisa particularmente com relação à pesquisa militar. Não tão bem conhecidas são áreas de preocupação ética emergindo do próprio método científico, desde métodos de pesquisa e interpretação de dados, que são também descritos neste paper. Nós revemos alguns dos princípios básicos do método científico utilizado na condução de investigações em pesquisa na área de uso e abuso de substância, começando com os princípios básicos enunciados por Isaac Newton para estabelecer causalidade e explorando alguns dos novos quadros conceituais usados para determinar pontos de intervenção onde nós podemos agir a fim de obter os resultados que nós queremos, mesmo quando a causalidade linear estrita não pode ser aplicada, utilizando exemplos não apenas da área do uso de substância, mas também de quadro científico mais geral quando estas ilustrações possam ser úteis. Nós vamos então considerar os problemas éticos e morais que podem resultar da natureza da matéria sendo investigada, sua organização e patrocínio, tanto quanto do uso de métodos e técnicas não apropriadas – incluindo algumas das questões que devem ser consideradas com o uso de sujeitos humanos – que podem resultar em conclusões errôneas e que podem ser danosas para os pacientes e para a sociedade como um todo.

Questões Éticas Levantadas por Abordagens de Auxílio Mútuo para o Tratamento do Usuário de Substância: O Lugar das Organizações de Doze Passos

Allaman Allamani, M.D.

As diferenças intrínsecas entre as maneiras pelas quais grupos de ajuda mútua e agentes e agências de tratamento formal e profissional se relacionam e trabalham com usuários que abusam de bebidas alcoólicas e outras drogas têm implicações éticas. Mais especificamente, a ética dos Grupos de Doze Passos é universalista, baseada em espiritualidade, reconhecimento do outro e solidariedade. Mesmo que sua eficácia em produzir abstinência possa ser cientificamente estudada, eles são mais bem descritos como comunidades terapêuticas (Seppala 2001). Por outro lado, quando profissionais estão envolvidos em programas de tratamento do usuário de substância, a ética parece ser utilitária; é orientada para os interesses do indivíduo ou do grupo social. Mesmo se, quando interagem, as duas perspectivas diferentes possam ter produzido tensão ou conflito, cooperação entre comunidades de ajuda mútua e o sistema de saúde é atualmente difundida e global.

Incapacidade e Tratamento/Reabilitação do Usuário de Substância: Considerações Éticas

Ellen Benoit, Ph.D. e Stephan Magura, Ph.D.

Antes de 1996, indivíduos nos Estados Unidos que eram cronicamente dependentes de drogas ou álcool podiam receber certificação como sendo incapacitados, tornando-os elegíveis para receber apoio financeiro da Administração da Previdência Social (APS), pelo tempo em que eles estivessem participando de tratamento. Legislação de março de 1996 exigiu que a APS eliminasse a dependência da lista de incapacidades com direito a apoio financeiro e removesse das suas listas todas as pessoas que vinham recebendo benefícios como usuários de substância incapacitados. Esta mudança levanta questões éticas significantes, que nós tratamos da perspectiva da justiça distributiva. Nós examinamos nesta política pública a distinção entre pessoas necessitadas "merecedoras" e "não-merecedoras" e analisamos como a natureza médica ambígua da dependência fomenta a competição entre reivindicações de "justo merecimento" no debate sobre elegibilidade. Por exemplo, tornar-se incapacitado como resultado do abuso de substância constitui uma forma de comportamento voluntário? Finalmente, nós consideramos as conseqüências da reclassificação pela APS para os interessados nesta política publica, incluindo beneficiários, provedores de tratamento e o público.

Sobre a Competência de Usuários de Substância para Consentir com Programas de Tratamento

Steve Clarke, Ph.D. e Neil Levy, Ph.D.

Muitos pensadores julgam que usuários regulares de drogas são incompetentes para dar consentimento para tratamento médico. Neste artigo, nós estabelecemos critérios mínimos para agentes serem considerados como competentes para dar consentimento informado, e argumentamos que usuários regulares de drogas – aqueles que são considerados dependentes de uma droga – tipicamente preenchem estas condições. Apesar de que dependência diminuiu a autonomia, ela não a diminui a um grau incompatível com oferecimento de um consentimento informado. Estudos dos comportamentos dos dependentes mostram que eles geralmente retêm suficiente controle sobre seus comportamentos e seu processo decisório para qualificar como competentes para dar consentimento.

Conceitualizando a Relação Professional no Aconselhamento do Usuário de Droga e de Quem Abusa do Álcool

Elliot D. Cohen, Ph.D.

Códigos de ética, estatutos e legislação pousem obrigações ou requerimentos éticos básicos que cabem a profissionais que aconselham usuários de drogas e quem abusa do álcool. Entretanto, se estes terapeutas têm que aconselhar efetivamente, eles têm que incorporar critérios mais ambiciosos, centrados na pessoa, nas suas práticas de aconselhamento. Começando com uma análise dos valores fundamentais que sustentam efetiva terapia, integrando diversos modelos profissionais de relacionamento na área da saúde, este capítulo desenvolve um modelo eclético, viável da relação terapeuta-cliente.

Questões Éticas Levantadas por Políticas Não Punitivas do Usuário de Droga

Stephen Coleman, Ph.D.

Nas ultimas décadas, tem havido uma forte pressão em muitos países para a implementação de programas e políticas que adotam uma atitude não-punitiva em relação ao uso e abuso de drogas, geralmente com o objetivo de minimizar o dano causado aos usuários de substâncias. O objetivo deste capítulo é apontar e discutir questões éticas particulares que algumas destas políticas não-punitivas levantam. Políticas particulares examinadas incluem tratamento de manutenção com metadona, programas de troca de agulhas, disponibilização de estabelecimentos para injeções seguras, prescrição de heroína e descriminalização da maconha.

Os Usuários de Drogas não Podem ser Tratados — As Pessoas Podem! A Criação e a Manutenção de Travestis Éticos — ou, ao Menos Dilemas

Stan Einstein, Ph.D.

Formula-se e examina-se a tese, utilizando exemplos selecionados, de que o tratamento contemporâneo dos "transtornos por uso de substâncias" – seja ele orientado para a abstinência ou direcionado à redução de danos que é quase sempre implementado em lugares que são separados dos principais lugares de tratamento – disponível para a população em geral:

- é, em sua essência, antiético; sua escassez em benefícios é mais do que superada por suas "doses" desnecessárias de malefícios;
- é uma designação enganadora; (1) não há tratamento único (modelos ou técnicas) para "usuários de drogas" que não sejam também utilizados para não-usuários de drogas e (2) "usuários de drogas" e não usuários de drogas representam populações heterogêneas de PESSOAS e não classificações de doenças únicas e homogêneas;
- é improvável que seja alterado no sentido de um processo de base ética em decorrência das posições, agendas e metas dos indivíduos e instâncias sistêmicas que detêm o poder;
- se alimenta de "princípios da fé", que são acobertados e sustentados sobre lugares-comuns, tais como "baseado em evidências"; e
- pode ser e com demasiada freqüência são mantidos (inadvertidamente) por agentes da mudança cooptados representando uma gama de disciplinas assim como não-profissionais "em recuperação" e ex-dependentes;

- dentro de uma contínua realidade de fato em que novos achados generalizáveis são com mais freqüência não introduzidos e usados para tratar usuários de substância aptos sob a rubrica de problemas de transferência de tecnologia.

Competência no Aconselhamento em Dependência Química.

Theodore M. Godlaski, M.Div.

Apesar de que competência clínica é quase universalmente tida como necessária para uma prática correta, é quase sempre mal-definida. Esforços significativos na direção de uma melhor especificação têm sido feito por um painel de especialistas, trabalhando sob o patrocínio da Administração de Serviços de Saúde Mental e Abuso de Substância dos Estados Unidos. Este grupo especifica três áreas em que adequada capacidade é necessária para competência: conhecimento, técnica e atitudes. Entretanto, virtualmente todos os órgãos de certificação medem objetivamente apenas conhecimento, deixando técnica e atitude para o testemunho de supervisores clínicos. Há alguma razão para ter preocupação com a qualidade e quantidade de supervisão sobre a qual estes julgamentos são baseados. Também, há razão para questionar se todo conhecimento e todas as técnicas têm, eticamente, valor igual. Além disso, há questões éticas se o campo de aconselhamento do usuário de substância, separadamente do aconselhamento geral pode ser justificado.

Reflexões sobre Questões Éticas na Pesquisa com Povos Indígenas

Theodore M. Godlaski, M. Div., Jeannette Johnson, Ph.D. e Rodney Haring, LMSW.

Este capítulo é uma reflexão sobre as questões éticas salientes que emergem no trabalho de pesquisa com povos indígenas ou nativos. A primeira fonte de preocupação ética é a propriedade cultural do propósito, desenho, métodos, protocolo e planos de disseminação/publicação da pesquisa. Apesar de que propriedade cultural não é um conceito bem definido, a falta de preocupação com as maneiras de pensar, estrutura social, comunicação e visão de mundo dos Nativos pode ser evidente em danos resultantes de empreendimentos de pesquisa mal concebidos. Os autores trabalham sobre trabalhos recentes nesta área para oferecer diretrizes para pesquisas culturalmente sensíveis.

Conflitos de Interesse na Avaliação e Disseminação de Programas de Prevenção do Uso de Drogas

Dennis M. Gorman, Ph.D.

Este capítulo examina as implicações de desenvolvimentos recentes na avaliação e marketing de programas de prevenção do uso de drogas para a integridade da pesquisa, e especificamente para as ameaças a esta integridade que derivam de conflitos de interesse. O capítulo começa com uma descrição do que se entende pelo termo conflito de interesse e revê os muitos tipos de conflito que têm sido discutidos na literatura médica e política nos anos recentes. Segue uma discussão mais detalhada dos conflitos de interesse individuais e institucionais que existem na pesquisa de prevenção às drogas.

A Psicoterapia de Redução de Danos é Ética?

William H. Gottdiener, Ph.D.

A Psicoterapia de Redução de Danos (PRD) é uma forma de psicoterapia para pacientes não internados que são diagnosticados com portadores de transtorno por uso de substância (TUS) e que continuam a usar substâncias psico-ativas. O objetivo do tratamento de PRD é reduzir o potencial de dano que pode acompanhar o uso de substâncias psicoativas. Sobriedade é apenas um dos meios de reduzir dano, comparado com o tradicional tratamento para TUS em que sobriedade é o único objetivo aceitável. PRD é utilizado porque sobriedade não pode ser atingida e/ou mantida em todos os indivíduos que manifestam TUS ou para todas as fases no tratamento da pessoa. O capítulo discute se PRD é um tratamento ético ou não para ser oferecido a pacientes que são diagnosticados com TUS. Adotando uma perspectiva Foucaldiana que a liberdade pessoal é indispensável para o tratamento do TUS, e uma perspectiva psicanalítica que a sobriedade pode ser atingida apenas por um cliente que está pronto para mirar este objetivo e tem o que quer que seja necessário –endogenamente ou exogenamente– para iniciar e manter a adaptação para este estilo de vida, o autor argumenta que PRD é a única forma ética de psicoterapia para pacientes não internados a ser oferecida a indivíduos com SUD.

A Proibição de Relações Sexuais entre Usuários de Droga e seus Conselheiros: É justificável?

Mane Hajdin, J.D., Ph.D.

Este capítulo examina quarto possíveis argumentos para a proibição de relações sexuais entre conselheiros de usuários de droga e aqueles aconselhados por eles. O primeiro é que a proibição contrabalança tentações e oportunidades especiais para relações sexuais que são criadas pelo fenômeno da transferência. A segunda é que a proibição contribui para a autoridade que os conselheiros têm que externar para que o aconselhamento atinja seus objetivos. De acordo com a terceira razão, o aconselhamento é uma extensão da aplicação da lei e é assim sujeito aos mesmos constrangimentos da aplicação da lei. A quarta razão é que a proibição é necessária por causa do desequilíbrio de poder que existe entre conselheiros e aqueles a quem eles aconselham. A conclusão do capítulo é que cada um destes argumentos pode justificar a proibição em algumas formas de aconselhamento de usuários de drogas, mas apenas o segundo pode justificá-la em todas as formas deste aconselhamento. A razão, entretanto, parece ser meramente uma matéria de técnica de aconselhamento, ao invés de um constrangimento moral independente no aconselhamento.

A Relevância Moral da Dependência

Douglas N. Husak, J.D., Ph.D.

Eu tento entender e avaliar a crença amplamente disseminada de que a dependência é relevante para a moralidade. Eu examino diversas explicações de como a dependência pode ser significativa de um ponto de vista moral. Apesar de que eu discuto brevemente teorias sobre a virtude, eu foco em três maneiras pelas quais dependência pode ser relevante para censura moral. Primeiro, censura poderia ser imposta pelo ato de usar drogas que causam dependência. Segundo, censura poderia sem imposta pela condição de ser dependente. Terceiro, censura poderia ser imposta por riscos adicionais que as pessoas provavelmente incorrerão uma vez que se tornarem dependentes. Eu concluo que cada uma destas explicações tem alguma plausibilidade, mas nenhuma é inteiramente não problemática. Dependência provavelmente é relevante para moralidade, apesar de que o seu grau de importância não é tão grande quanto alguns comentaristas parecem acreditar. A relevância moral da dependência não parece alcançar a qualquer nível que justificaria uma resposta punitiva aos usuários de drogas dependentes.

Ética em Pesquisa de Prevenção com Crianças

Jeannette L. Johnson, Ph.D. e Nancy R. VanDeMark, Ph.D.

Compreender as decisões éticas envolvidas em pesquisa sobre a prevenção do uso de drogas pode ser complicado e simples. Pesquisa sobre prevenção é complicada porque ocorre com crianças e as questões relativas à proteção da criança e seus direitos têm uma significância vital. Com crianças, estes direitos devem receber atenção com clareza de propósito, respeito e suavidade. Ética em pesquisa sobre prevenção é simples porque a resposta pata compreender intervenções preventivas efetivas podem ser encontradas apenas durante a infância. Não há alternativas para compreender como prevenir doença, transtorno, ou disfunção sem primeiro conduzir pesquisa com crianças. È a conjunção de complexidade e simplicidade que tornam espinhosas as questões em pesquisa de prevenção.

Dependência de Drogas e Responsabilidade pelo Cuidado com a Saúde de Dependentes de Drogas

Tziporah Kasachkoff, Ph.D.

Cuidar daqueles que têm necessidade de cuidados com a saúde é alguma coisa com a qual nós, como sociedade, nos sentimos comprometidos na medida em que recursos públicos possibilitem isso. É este comprometimento de alguma forma qualificado pelo fato de que as enfermidades médicas da pessoa são resultados do fato de aquela pessoa ter voluntariamente embarcado em atividades cujas conseqüências deletérias para saúde eram conhecidas e avaliadas por aquela pessoa de antemão: Especificamente, a obrigação da sociedade de oferecer serviços de cuidados médicos para aqueles que se tornaram dependentes de drogas ilícitas atenuado pelo fato desta dependência? Alguns argumentam que sim, enquanto outros consideram esta posição moralmente insustentável. Este ensaio explora a questão de quem está certo neste debate e por que.

O Objetivo Moral no Tratamento de Casos de Duplo Diagnóstico

Jeannette Kennett, Ph.D. e Stephen Matthews, Ph.D.

Uso e abuso de substância ocorrem numa taxa muito alta entre pessoas com problemas de saúde mental e a relação entre as duas condições é complexa. Neste capítulo, nós argumentamos que uso de substância em clientes com dois diagnósticos deve começar pela compreensão das perdas sofridas por aqueles com doenças mentais. Nós delineamos a condição fundamental para agência efetiva, unificada agência, que é rompida na doença mental e mostramos como esta é necessária para assegurar acesso a bens sociais e morais centrais tais quais continuidade no emprego e relações satisfatórias. Nós argumentamos que o uso de droga será desvalorizado primeiramente na medida em que impede acesso a este conjunto de bens agenciais e focaliza o agente em bem-estar sincrônico excluindo o bem estar diacrônico. Os objetivos e métodos de tratamento para pacientes com duplo diagnóstico devem assim refletir o prejuízo primário à agência unificada.

Questões Éticas na Intervenção sobre Uso de Substância

John Kleinig, Ph.D.

Este ensaio oferece uma visão das questões éticas levantadas por intervenções médicas e governamentais sobre o uso de droga. Com respeito ao primeiro, começa com o pressuposto liberal que constrangimentos sobre ações livres têm que ser justificados pela referência aos seus impactos deletérios sobre outros, mas então qualifica este pressuposto notando os requisitos sociais para uma ação livre. Com respeito a intervenções médicas, focaliza nos códigos que têm sido desenvolvidos para os fornecedores de tratamento e seus clientes, e explora a sustentação ética de várias das duas disposições centrais – consentimento informado, privacidade, confidencial idade, não-discriminação, profissionalismo e responsabilização.

Pensando Eticamente Sobre Programas de Troca de Agulhas

John Kleinig, Ph.D.

Aceitando – por questão de argumento – nossas políticas legislativas referente à heroína, que questões éticas são levantadas quanto aos programas de troca de agulhas? Eles enfraquecem leis sobre droga; enviam mensagem errada ou obscurecem a mensagem correta; fazem pouco para eliminar o dano das drogas; depreciam as alternativas; e/ou constituem um conselho que provém de desespero? Eu sugiro que, na ausência de alternativas melhores, programas de troca de agulhas (PTA) constituem uma opção moralmente aceitável e até desejável apesar da continuidade da criminalização do uso de drogas. Mesmo assim. Eles devem ser administrados de modo a não reforçar os preconceitos sociais dominantes.

Privacidade, Confidencialidade e o Tratamento de Dependentes de Droga

Seumas Miller, Ph.D.

Sustentando o princípio da confidencialidade há várias considerações, incluindo o direito à privacidade, confiança, e as conseqüências danosas da divulgação. E o próprio direito à privacidade é sustentado por outros valores morais, incluindo autonomia. Isto torna complexa a justificativa moral para confidencialidade. Nosso grau de comprometimento e a abrangência do princípio da confidencialidade precisa ser relativizado em função das circunstâncias. Em alguns casos ou categorias de dependentes de droga, algumas bases gerais para confidencialidade podem estar faltando, devido à autonomia diminuída, e, portanto, à redução da força ou abrangência do direito à privacidade. Entretanto, não decorre automaticamente disto que nosso comprometimento com o princípio da confidencialidade deve ser enfraquecido.

Medicina e Moral, Avidez e Compulsão

Stephen J. Morse, J.D., Ph.D.

Pensar sobre dependências tem sido dominado por dois modelos: o modelo médico, que trata dependência como uma doença e comportamentos relacionados como sinais e sintomas, e o modelo moral, que vê dependência e comportamentos relacionados como indicações de fracasso moral. Este paper descreve os dois modelos e suas implicações, com ênfase especial no modelo moral. O significado de compulsão e coerção causada por estados psicológicos internos, tal como avidez, é explorado para determinar se dependentes podem ser razoavelmente considerados moralmente e legalmente responsáveis por seus comportamentos, tais como procurar e usar substâncias. Argumenta-se que racionalidade diminuída explica melhor que compulsão porque dependentes podem ser desculpados por seu comportamento, mas conclui-se que a maioria dos dependentes podem ser responsabilizados pela maioria dos comportamentos relacionados à dependência. Entretanto, os dois modelos têm características desejáveis, e políticas públicas dignas de confiança não devem ser baseadas em apenas um deles. As implicações da utilização para a justice criminal do emprego dos dois modelos para guiar políticas são exploradas.

Questões Éticas na Pesquisa do Tratamento do Usuário de Droga

Kenneth D. Pimple, Ph.D.

A pesquisa do tratamento do usuário de droga deve a) ser guiada por considerações éticas básicas que prevalecem em todas as formas de pesquisa científica, incluindo honestidade e candor; designar o crédito de autoria apropriado; e abster-se de comportamento íntimo ou inoportuno em relação aos sujeitos de pesquisa; e b) princípios éticos específicos à pesquisa usando sujeitos humanos enumerados no Relatório Belmont como respeito pelas pessoas, beneficiência (e não maleficiência), e justiça. Um princípio adicional não explicitamente mencionado no Relatório Belmont, mas ganhando ampla aceitação é inclusão, ou acesso a tratamentos. Pesquisadores são moralmente (e em alguns casos legalmente) obrigados a aderir a estes princípios, e a comunidade de pesquisa do tratamento do usuário de droga como um todo tem uma obrigação de dar o melhor de si para moldar a agenda de pesquisa e a política social de acordo com estes princípios.

Tratamento do Usuário de Substância – Política Justa ou Política Baseada em Evidência?

Maurice Rickard, Ph.D.

Há um caso a ser feito de que decisões sobre que tipos de tratamento do usuário de substância devem ser praticados são matérias de políticas públicas e escolhas sociais. Faz sentido querer que o processo político disponibilize intervenções baseadas em evidência (e éticas). Também parece razoável esperar que processos sociais e políticos sobre práticas de tratamento sejam razoáveis e justos. Que as decisões sejam apropriadamente autorizadas, em outras palavras. Uma maneira de respeitar estas duas expectativas plausíveis é conceitualizar razoabilidade no processo decisório sobre a política de tratamento do usuário de droga de maneira que este seja conceitualmente condicionado a que as decisões produzidas sejam as corretas terapeuticamente. O problema com isso é que o que é terapeuticamente correto ou efetivo depende da visão de cada um sobre qual é o propósito do tratamento do usuário de droga. O perigo é acabar com uma concepção controversa de processos razoáveis, ao invés de uma que é conceitualmente aceita por todos. Este capítulo explora algumas das questões filosóficas relacionadas a políticas razoáveis de tratamento e políticas de bom tratamento, incluindo a quem deve ser dado um papel no processo de decisão política.

Questões Éticas em Torno do Acesso a Aconselhamento/Tratamento para Uso de Droga

Barbara C. Wallace, Ph.D.

Questões éticas em torno do acesso ao aconselhamento e tratamento do uso de drogas são bem variadas. O espectro inclui o potencial para discriminação com relação ao acesso ao tratamento devido à raça, gênero ou condição do cliente – tais como idade, gravidez, localidade geográfica e distância do tratamento, pobreza, ou falta de seguro. Outras questões éticas incluem a condição de incapacidade do cliente, incluindo incapacidades físicas e psicológicas, por exemplo. Outras questões éticas incluem como gerenciar questões de reincidência, relatórios toxicológicos de urina positivos, e os casos mais desafiantes envolvendo dependentes de carreira caracterizados por reincidência crônica. Questões éticas adicionais envolvem o risco de comportamentos violentos por parte dos clientes em tratamento e quando barrar acesso a tratamento. Outras questões éticas envolvem o uso de coerção e mandados para tratamento, tanto pelo sistema de justice criminal, por agencias do serviço social ou proteção à criança – como todos os clientes forçados a ganhar acesso a tratamento. Recomendações para como conceitualizar e responder a todo espectro de questões éticas sobre o acesso ao aconselhamento e tratamento relacionado à droga são oferecidos neste capítulo.

Aconselhamento do Usuário de Droga, Remuneração e Ética

Adrian Walsh, Ph.D. e Tony Lynch, Ph.D.

Neste artigo nós exploramos as implicações que remuneração, nas suas várias formas, podem ter para conselheiros do usuário de droga. Uma longa tradição filosófica afirma que gratificação financeira e altruísmo são mutuamente excludentes. Nossa visão é de alguma maneira diferente. Nós argumentamos, contra esta tradição, que apesar de que gratificação financeira na forma de lucro comerciai ou salário não é em si mesmo moralmente perniciosa, ela confronta conselheiros com riscos éticos. Estes são riscos contra os quais aqueles envolvidos no aconselhamento do usuário de droga precisam estar especialmente vigilantes.

Dependência e Incapacidade: Questões Políticas e Morais

David Wasserman, J.D.

Este capítulo discute questões conceituais, éticas e políticas levantadas pela classificação legal da dependência de droga como uma deficiência, e de alguns dependentes não-usuários de droga como pessoas com incapacidade. Focaliza questões de (1) que julgamentos morais, se algum, sustenta a classificação de dependência como uma deficiência; (2) se faz sentido repartir os fardos da dependência da droga entre causas químicas, biológicas, sociais, políticas e outras; (3) como considerações de justiça distributiva podem compelir ou constranger medidas para diminuir os fardos da dependência de drogas; e (4) se é justificável negar aos atuais usuários de substâncias ilegais proteções legais disponíveis para os atuais usuários de substâncias legais.

Questões Éticas em Torno do Acesso ao Tratamento por "Abuso" de Substância

Shelly A. Wiechelt, Ph.D.

As muitas variedades de programas de tratamento para usuário de substância nos Estados Unidos têm oferecido uma grande quantidade de evidência de pesquisa mostrando a efetividade do tratamento. Independentemente do crescente conhecimento e toda disponibilidade de tratamento, uma tremenda distância existe entre o numero de pessoas identificadas como necessitando tratamento e aqueles que de fato recebem tratamento. Este capítulo discute alguns dos fatores e condições que contribuem para problemas de acesso ao tratamento para usuários de substância nos Estados Unidos. Estas questões de acesso são exploradas à luz dos códigos de ética sobre tratamento da dependência existentes para profissionais.

Relações Conselheiro-Cliente e a Moralidade do Papel Profissional

Kylie Williams, M.A. e Dean Cocking, Ph.D.

Este capítulo apresenta uma concepção pluralista do papel da moralidade apropriada para o aconselhamento profissional. O papel das obrigações, sensibilidades e território de problemas humanos relevantes para o aconselhamento são especialmente amplos em abrangência e cheios de conflitos potenciais. A natureza e locais de programas de tratamento do usuário de droga involuntário apresentam problemas especiais para a relação conselheiro-cliente. Na verdade, para muitos escritores, estes problemas fatalmente comprometem os bens morais e as metas orientadoras fundamentais para o aconselhamento. Nós concordamos que alguns valores chaves são frequentemente comprometidos em locais involuntários. Nós argumentamos, entretanto, que muito do conflito de papéis aqui é mais bem compreendido e acomodado dentro da nossa concepção pluralista, ao invés de refletir uma prática de aconselhamento dissociada totalmente de suas metas constitutivas apropriadas.

Da Torre de Marfim às Trincheiras: Ensinando Ética Professional para Conselheiros no Uso de Substância

Daniel Yalisove, Ph.D.

Este capitulo delineia uma abordagem para ensinar ética profissional a conselheiros que tratam transtornos por uso de substância. O capítulo introduz três idéias inovativas que não receberam previamente consideração no ensino da ética profissional: (1) Conselheiros têm confundido considerações éticas e não éticas no processo decisório. (2) Há uma especial sinergia entre aconselhamento humanitário e ética profissional. (3) Atenção explícita é dada ao processo de educar moralmente alguns clientes ajudando-os a se tornar conscientes de problemas éticos.

Hay decisiones éticas difíciles en investigaciones científicas sobre la toxico dependencia que utilizan dados y métodos estadísticos.

Manuella Adrian, M.S. Hyg.

Las investigaciones científicas nos han dado uno de los métodos mas fuertes para ameliorar el bien estar de la humanidad. Pero, es también causa de problemas éticos y morales para los que hacen estas investigaciones. Hoy día, después de Nuremberg, las investigaciones que utilizan seres humanos tienen reglas muy estrictas para minimizar la posibilidad de hacer danos a las personas. También son conocidos los problemas éticos de las investigaciones militares. Menos conocidos son los problemas relacionados al uso del método científico y de la interpretación de dados estadísticos. Hablamos de los principios de Isaac Newton que sirven para establecer una relación de causa y de efecto en investigaciones científicas en general y en investigaciones a propósito de la toxico dependencia. También, consideramos los nuevos métodos para identificar los "puntos críticos" que pueden servir para identificar donde podemos hacer intervenciones para mejorar los problemas sociales aunque no conocemos exactamente la causa. Hablamos de los problemas éticos relacionados a la organización y el financiamiento de las investigaciones científicas, y, además, al uso de métodos y técnicas de investigaciones que no son apropiados a lo que se investiga y que producen resultados y conclusiones que son falsos y que hacen daño a los pacientes, a los científicos y a la sociedad..

Los asuntos éticas levantaron por métodos de la ayuda mutua para el tratamiento del usuario de sustancias: El lugar de las organizaciones de los Doce Pasos

Allaman Allamani, M.D.

Las diferencias intrínsecas entre las maneras de las cuales grupos de la ayuda mutua y los agentes y las agencias profesionales formales del tratamiento se relaciona con y trabaja con los mal usuarios de bebidas alcohólicas y otras drogas tienen implicaciones éticas. Más particularmente, el ética de los grupos de los Doce Pasos es universalistico, basado como está en la espiritualidad, la alteridad, y solidaridad. Incluso si su eficacia en producir abstinencia puede ser estudiada científicamente, se describen lo mejor posible como "comunidades de curación"(Seppala 2001). Por otra parte, donde los profesionales están involucrados en programas del tratamiento de usuarios de sustancias, el ética aparece ser utilitario; se orienta hacia los intereses del individuo o del grupo social. Incluso si cuando el obrar recíprocamente de las dos perspectivas diversas pudo haber producido la tensión o el conflicto, la cooperación entre los compañerismos de la ayuda mutua y el sistema del cuidado médico se difunde actualmente y por todo el mundo.

Incapacidad y Tratamiento de los Drogadictos: Consideraciones Éticas

Ellen Benoit, Ph.D.and Stephen Magura, Ph.D.

Antes de 1996, los individuos en los Estados Unidos que eran crónicamente adictos a drogas o alcohol podrían recibir certificación como incapacitados lo cual les permitia recibir ingresos del Seguro Social (SSA), pero solo si eran ingresados en algun programa de tratamiento. Nueva legislación en Marzo 1996 requiere que el SSA elimine la adicción a sustancias controladas como categoria de incapacitación, tambien suspendiendo toda clase de beneficios a todo ello que lo distinguia como deshabilitado por su previo uso. Este cambio crea varias preguntas éticas significativas, las cuales analizamos de la perspectiva de la Justicia Distributiva. Examinamos la distinción entre personas "merecedoras" y "no merecedoras" creadas por estas politicas y analizamos cómo el estatus médicamente ambiguo de la adicción fomenta reclamos competitivos acerca del debate reclamando "Justicia Merecida" sobre la elegibilidad. ¿Por ejemplo, constituye el ser incapacitado como resultado de la adicción una forma de conducta voluntaria? Finalmente, consideramos las consecuencias de esta reclasificación del SSA para todas personas interesadas, incluyendo beneficiarios, proveedores de tratamiento y el público.

De la Competencia de los Adictos de Substancias de Dar Consentimiento a Programas de Tratamiento

Steve Clarke, Ph.D. and Neil Levy, Ph.D.

Muchos pensadores sostienen que los drogadictos no están capacitados para dar su consentimiento al tratamiento médico. En este artículo damos criterio mínimo para agentes dando consentimiento informado, y argüimos que los usuarios de drogas—hasta los que son considerados adictos—satisfacen estas condiciones. Aunque la adicción sí disminuye la autonomía, no lo hace en un grado incompatible con la provisión de consentimiento informado. Estudios sobre el comportamiento de los adictos muestran que ellos retienen autocontrol suficiente y facultad de decidir para calificarlos como capacitados para dar su consentimiento.

La Conceptualización de La Relación Profesional En El Counseling de Usuarios de Drogas Y Abusivos De Alcohol

Elliot D. Cohen, Ph.D.

Códigos de ética, estatutos, y caso-ley da deberes éticos básicos o requisitos que corresponden a los que da consejos a los usuarios de drogas y abusivos de alcohol. Sin embargo, si estos terapeutas van a aconsejar con éxito, tienen que incorporar criterios más deseados y centrados en la persona en su práctica de counseling. Empezando con un análisis de valores fundamentales que apoyan la terapia eficaz, integrando algunos modelos profesionales relacionados con el cuidado de salud, este capítulo edifica un modelo viable y ecléctico de la relación entre cliente y terapeuta.

Temas Éticas Relacionadas a Políticas No Punitivos del Uso de Drogas

Stephen Coleman, Ph.D.

A lo largo de recientes décadas ha habido un gran esfuerzo en muchos países para la implementación de programas y políticas que adopten una actitud no punitiva ante el uso y abuso de drogas, generalmente con la finalidad de minimizar los daños causados por los usuarios de substancias. La finalidad de este capítulo es señalar y discutir los asuntos éticos que algunas de estas políticas no punitivas sugieren. Políticas individuales que examinamos incluyen tratamiento de mantenimiento de metadona, programas de cambio de jeringas, provisión de lugares seguros para inyección, recetar heroína, legalización de cannabis.

Los usuarios de droga no pueden ser tratados; ¡La Gente Puede Ser! –

Stan Einstein, Ph.D.

Se postula y se examina la tesis, usando ejemplos seleccionados, que el tratamiento contemporáneo del "desorden del uso de las sustancias" (DUS) - sea orientado hacia la abstinencia o conducido por la reducción de daños que se pone en ejecución casi siempre en los sitios que están a parte de la corriente principal del tratamiento -- puesto a disposición de la población en general:

- está en su esencia poco ética; su brevedad en beneficencia es más que emparejado por sus "dosis" innecesarias del hecho delictivo;
- es un nombre equivocado engañoso; (1) no existe ningún "tratamiento" único (los modelos ni las técnicas) para los "usuarios de drogas" que también no se utiliza para los que no son usuarios de drogas y (2) ambos los "usuarios de drogas" y los no usuarios representan las poblaciones heterogéneas de la GENTE y no representan nosologias únicos, homogéneas;
- es poco probable ser cambiado en un proceso basado en el ética debido a las posiciones, las agendas y las metas de tenedores de apuestas individuales y del sistema que son conducidos por el poder,
- es alimentado por los "principios de la fe" que son cubiertos y apoyadados por lemas como "basados en la evidencia", y
- puede ser y es mantenido demasiado a menudo (inadvertidamente) por una gama de agentes del cambio cooptados que representan una variedad de disciplinas tan bien como los no profesionales "en la recuperación" o ex-adictos,
- dentro de una realidad *de facto* en la cual los nuevos resultados generalizables a menudo no se introducen y no se utilizan para tratar a usuarios de sustancias apropriados debajo de la rúbrica de los problemas de la transferencia de la tecnología.

Capacidad en la consejería de la dependencia química

Theodore M. Godlaski, M.Div.

Aunque la capacidad clínica se reconoce universalmente como necesaria para la práctica ético correcta, es a menudo mal definida. Los esfuerzos significativos hacia una especificación mejor han sido hechos por un equipo de expertos, trabajando bajo patrocinio de la administración del abuso de sustancias y de la salud mental (SAMHSA), de los Estados Unidos. Este grupo especifica tres áreas en las cuales la capacidad adecuada sea necesaria para la aptitud: conocimiento, habilidad, y actitudes. Sin embargo, virtualmente todo los cuerpos de certificación solamente miden objetivamente el conocimiento, dejando la habilidad y la actitud al testimonio de supervisores clínicos. Hay una cierta razón de tener preocupación por la calidad y la cantidad de contacto de supervisión en la cual se basan tales juicios. También, hay razón de preguntar si todo el conocimiento y todas las habilidades están, ético, de valor igual. Además, existen las cuestiones éticas que preguntan si un campo de consejería para los usuarios de sustancias, a parte de la consejería general, puede ser justificado.

Reflexiones en ediciones éticas en la investigación con las gentes aborígenes

Theodore M. Godlaski, M.Div., Jeannette Johnson, Ph.D. et Rodney Haring, LMSW

Este capítulo es una reflexión en las ediciones éticas salientes que se presentan en trabajo de investigación con los indígenas aborígenes o. La fuente primaria de la preocupación ética es la conveniencia cultural del propósito de la investigación, del diseño, de los métodos, del protocolo, y del plan de publication/dissemination. Aunque la conveniencia cultural no es una construcción bien definida, la carencia de la preocupación por maneras nativas del pensamiento, de la estructura social, de la comunicación, y de la opinión del mundo puede ser evidente en el daño hecho como resultado de esfuerzos concebidos enfermos de la investigación. Los autores dibujan en trabajo reciente en esta área para proporcionar las pautas para la investigación cultural sensible.

Los conflictos del interés en la evaluación y la diseminación de los programas de prevención del uso de las drogas

Dennis M. Gorman, Ph.D.

Este capítulo examina las implicaciones de progresos recientes en la evaluación y la mercadotecnia de los programas de prevención de las drogas para la integridad de la investigación, y específicamente para las amenazas a esto que nacen de conflictos del interés. Comienza con una descripción de qué es significada por el término conflicto del interés y un repaso de los tipos principales de conflictos que se han discutido en las literaturas médicas y política pública en años recientes. Esto es seguida por una discusión más detallada de los conflictos del interés individuales e institucionales que existen en la investigación de la prevención de drogas.

¿Es Ética la Psicoterapia de Reducción de Daño?

William H. Gottdiener, Ph.D.

La Psicoterapia de Reducción de Daño (PRD) es un tipo de psicoterapia para pacientes externos diagnosticados por un desorden de uso de substancias y continúan usando substancias sicoactivas. La finalidad del tratamiento de PRD es la reducción del daño potencial que puede acompañar al uso de substancias sicoactivas. La sobriedad es solamente una de las maneras para reducir el daño, en comparición con tratamientos tradicionales DUS donde la sobriedad es la única finalidad aceptable. Se usa PRD porque la sobriedad no es siempre alcanzable y/o sostenible en todos los individuos diagnosticados con DUS o en todas las fases de su tratamiento. Saliendo de una perspectiva Foucauldiana en que la libertad personal es esencial para el tratamiento de DUS, y una perspectiva psicoanalítica en que la sobriedad es solamente alcanzable por individuos que están listos para esta finalidad y tienen lo necesario—interior y exteriormente—para imitar y mantener su adaptación a este estilo de vida, el autor sostiene que PRD es la única forma ética de psicoterapia para pacientes externos con un DUS.

La Prohibición de Relaciones Sexuales Entre Usuarios de Drogas Y Sus Consejeros: ¿Es Justificada?

Mane Hajdin, J.D., Ph.D.

Este capítulo examina cuatro argumentos posibles a favor de la prohibición de relaciones sexuales entre los consejeros de usuarios de drogas y los aconsejados por ellos. El primero es que la prohibición contrarresta las tentaciones especiales y las oportunidades para relaciones sexuales creadas por el fenómeno de la transferencia. El segundo es que la prohibición contribuye a la autoridad que los consejeros tengan que exudar si el counseling va a tener éxito. Según la tercera razón, counseling es una extensión del mantenimiento de la ley y así está sujeta a las mismas limitaciones que el mantenimiento de la ley. La cuarta razón es que hace falta la prohibición a causa del desequilibrio de poder que existe entre los consejeros y los que aconsejan. La conclusión del capitulo es que cada uno de los cuatro argumentos pueden justificar la prohibición en algunas formas del counseling a usuarios de drogas, pero solamente el segundo puede justificar tal counseling en todas las formas. Esa razón, sin embargo, parece meramente un asunto de técnica del counseling, en vez de una limitación moral independiente del counseling.

La Relevancia Moral de la Adiccion

Douglas N. Husak, Ph.D.

Intento comprender y evaluar la opinion general de que la adiccion tiene relevancia en la moralidad. Examino varias explicaciones de como puede ser la adiccion importante desde el punto de vista moral. Aunque trato brevemente teorias sobre la virtud, destaco de tres maneras posibles que la adiccion puede tener relevancia en la culpa moral. Primero, la culpa puede ser originada por la utilizacion de drogas que crean adiccion. Segundo, la culpabilidad puede ser consecuencia de la condicion de ser adicto. Tercero, la culpa puede ser causa de los riesgos adicionales que las personas probablemente correnin una vez sean adictas. Mi conclusion es que cada una de estas posiciones tiene alguna probabilidad, pero que ninguna de ellas evitani problemas. Probablemente la adiccion tiene algo que ver con la moralidad, pero su importancia no es tanta como algunos comentaristas opinan. La relevancia moral de la adiccion parece no alcancar a un nivel que justificaria respuesta punitiva a los que usan drogas adictivas.

El ética en la investigación de prevención con los niños

Jeannette L. Johnson, Ph.D. y Nancy R. VanDeMark, Ph.D.

Entender las decisiones éticas implicadas en la investigación sobre la prevención del uso de las drogas puede ser complicada y simple. La investigación de la prevención es complicada porque ocurre con los niños y los asuntos que rodean la protección del niño y sus derechos son de primerísima importancia. Con los niños, estos derechos se deben atender con la claridad del propósito, con respecto, y con dulzura. El ética en la investigación de la prevención es simple porque la respuesta a entender intervenciones preventivos eficaces se puede encontrar solamente durante la niñez. No hay alternativas a entender cómo prevenir enfermedad, desorden, o la disfunción sin primero conducir investigaciónes con los niños. Es la conjunción de ambas las complicaciones y la simplicidad que hace espinosas las cuestiones éticas en la investigación de la prevención.

La Adicción a Drogas y Responsabilidad Para El Cuidado de Salud de Los Drogadictos

Tziporah Kasachkoff, Ph.D.

Cuidar a los que necesitan ayuda de salud es algo a lo que estamos, como sociedad, comprometidos, en cuanto lo permitan fondos públicos. ¿Está este compromiso limitado de alguna manera por el hecho de que las enfermedades que sufre una persona son los resultados de actividades voluntarias cuyos efectos perjudicales para la salud eran anteriormente conocidos y entendidos por esa persona? Específicamente, ¿es obligación de la socieded proveer cuidado de salud a los que se han hecho adictos a drogas ilegales atenuado de alguna manera por el hecho de esta adicción? Algunos proponen que lo es, pero otros consideran que esta postura no tiene justifación moral. Este ensayo explora el asunto de quien tiene razón y por qué.

Jeannette Kennett, Ph.D. y Stephen Matthews, Ph.D.

El uso y abuso de alcohol y otras drogas se da en un alto grado entre personas con problemas de salud mental, y la relación entre ambas afecciones es compleja. En este ensayo, defendemos que el tratamiento del uso de alcohol y otras drogas en clientes con doble diagnóstico debe empezar por entender las deficiencias que sufren aquellas personas con enfermedades mentales. Describimos primero una condición fundamental para la agencia efectiva, a saber, agencia unificada, la cual se perturba en casos de enfermedad mental, y mostramos como es necesaria para asegurar el acceso a bienes morales y sociales centrales, tales como el empleo continuado. Después, argumentamos que el consumo de alcohol y otras drogas tiene un valor negativo primordialmente en la medida en que impide también el acceso a esta serie de bienes agenciales y concentra al agente en su bienestar sincrónico, excluyendo su bienestar diacrónico. Los objetivos y métodos del tratamiento para clientes con doble diagnóstico deberían pues reflejar el daño fundamental a su agencia unificada.

Pensando Éticamente Sobre Programas de Cambio de Jeringas

John Kleinig, Ph.D.

Dado—por causa de argumento—nuestras políticas actuales sobre el uso de heroína ¿qué preguntas surgen sobre los programas de cambio de jeringas? ¿Es que hacen mas ineficaces las leyes sobre drogas; manden un mensaje erróneo u oscurezcan el mensaje correcto; no son suficientes para eliminar el daño de las drogas; quitan mérito a alternativas; y/o constituyen un consejo a la desesperación? Sugiero que, dada la ausencia de mejores alternativas, los programas para el cambio de jeringas constituyen una opción moralmente aceptable y hasta deseable a pesar de la criminalidad continuada del uso de drogas.

Temas Éticos de Intervención Con El Uso de Substancias

John Kleinig, Ph.D.

Este ensayo ofrece una perspectiva general de alguna de las preguntas que surgen acerca de intervenciones gubernamentales y médicas por el uso de drogas. En cuanto a la primera, empieza con la premisa liberal de que restricciones en la acción libre se justifican con las consecuencias perjudiciales para los otros, pero modifica esta premisa refiriéndose a los requistos sociales de la acción libre. Con respecto a las intervenciones médicas, enfoca en los códigos que se han desarollado por los suministradores de tratamiento y sus clientes, y explora alguno de sus puntos centrales--el consentimiento informado, privacidad, confidencialidad, ausencia de discriminación, profesionalismo, y responsabilidad.

Privacidad, Confidencialidad, y el Tratamiento de Drogadictos

Seumas Miller, Ph.D.

Apuntalando el principio de confidencialidad hay varias consideraciones, incluyendo el derecho a la intimidad, confianza, y las perjudiciales consecuencias de divulgación. Y el derecho a la intimidad en sí está apuntalado por otros valores morales, incluyendo autonomía. Por eso resulta complicado justificar la confidencialidad. Nuestro grado de obligación al ámbito del principio tiene que ser relativo a las circunstancias. En algunos casos o clases de drogadictos, pueden faltar algunas de las razones de confidencialidad, dada la autonomía disminuida y por eso al ámbito reducido para el derecho a la intimidad. Sin embargo, no es automático que nuestra obligación al principio de confidencialidad sea más débil.

La Medicina y la Moral, Coacción y Compulsión

Stephen J. Morse, J.D., Ph.D.

La opinión sobre las adicciones ha seguido dos modelos: el modelo médico, que trata la adicción como una enfermedad y su comportamiento relacionado como señales y síntomas; y el modelo moral, que trata la adicción y su comportamiento relacionado como indicación de fracaso moral. Este ensayo describe ambos modelos y sus implicaciones, con especial énfasis en el modelo moral. Se explora el significado de la compulsión o coacción causado por estados psicológicos internos, como ansia, para determinar si los adictos pueden ser justa, legal y moralmente vistos como responsables de su comportamiento, por ejemplo buscando y utilizando substancias. El autór sostiene que la racionalidad disminuida explica mejor que la coacción por qué los adictos pueden ser disculpados por su comportamiento, pero concluye que el adicto puede ser considerado como responsable de la mayoría de su comportamiento relacionado a la adicción. Sin embargo, ambos modelos tienen características atractivas y una política pública buena no debe estar basada ni en el uno ni el otro.

Consideraciones éticas en la investigación del tratamiento del usuario de la Droga

Kenneth D. .Pimple, Ph.D.

La investigación del tratamiento del usuario de droga se debe dirigir por las consideraciones éticas básicas que prevalecen en todas las formas de investigación científica, incluyendo honradez y sinceridad; asignar crédito apropiado al escritor; y refrenándose de comportamiento íntimo o que acosa hacia los sujetos de la investigación; y principios éticos específicos a la investigación usando los temas humanos enumerados en el informe de Belmont, tal como respecto para las personas, la beneficencia (y la non-maleficencia), y la justicia. Un principio adicional que el informe de Belmont no menciona explícitamente, pero que va ganando la aceptación amplia, es la inclusión, o el acceso a los tratamientos. Los investigadores son obligados moralmente (y en algunos casos legalmente) a adherir a estos principios, y en su totalidad la comunidad de investigadores del tratamiento del usuario de droga tiene una obligación a esforzarse en formar la agenda de la investigación y la política social según estos principios.

El Tratamiento del Abuso de Substancias—¿Política Justa o Política Basado en Evidencia?

Maurice Rickard, Ph.D.

Se puede probar la tesis que las decisiones sobre los tipos de tratamiento para el abuso de substancias son asuntos de política pública y elección social. Tiene sentido desear un proceso de política que hace accesible las intervenciones terapéuticas (y éticamente) basado en la evidencia. También parece razonable esperar que la política y elección social sobre métodos de tratamiento sea justa e imparcial. En otras palabras, que las decisiones estén autorizadas de una manera adecuada. Una manera de respetar ambas de esas expectativas plausibles es conceptualizar lo imparcial en hacer decisiones sobre la política del tratamiento de drogas de una manera en que es conceptualmente condicionado a que las decisiones otorgadas sean terapéuticamente correctas. El problema resulta que lo que es terapéuticamente correcto depende del punto de vista sobre la finalidad del tratamiento. El peligro es terminar con una concepción controvertida de lo que son procesos justos en vez de que una sea aceptable máximamente a todos. Este capítulo explora algunas de las cuestiones filosóficas sobre lo que es una política justa y buena, incluso quien debe tener parte en la política de hacer decisiones.

Temas Éticos Sobre El Acceso al Tratamiento de Uso de Drogas

Barbara C. Wallace, Ph.D.

Los temas éticos que tienen que ver con el acceso al counseling y tratamiento son muy variados. Esa gama incluye el potencial por discriminación al acceso a tratamiento basado en la raza, religión, género sexual o condición del paciente—por ejemplo edad, embarazo, lugar geográfico, distancia de tratamiento, pobreza, o falta de seguro. Otros asuntos éticos incluyen el estatus de minusvalía del cliente, incluyendo minusvalías físicas y psiquiátricas, por ejemplo. Otros asuntos éticos incluyen como manejar asuntos de recaídas, actuales pruebas positivas de toxicología de orina, y los casos mas desafiantes que tienen que ver con carreras de adición caracterizados por recaídas crónicas. Otros asuntos éticos adicionales tienen que ver con el riesgo de comportarse mal violentamente en el tratamiento y cuando negar el acceso al tratamiento. Otros asuntos éticos tienen que ver con el uso de coacción y órdenes para tratamiento, si por el sistema de justicia criminal, agencias de bienestar, agencias de protección a niños—como todos exigen a sus clientes que accedan al tratamiento. Recomendaciones de cómo conceptualizar y responder a una gama completo de cuestiones contemporáneas que tienen que ver con el acceso a counseling y su tratamiento están ofrecidas en este capítulo.

El Consejo de Usuarios de Drogas, Remuneración, y la Ética.

Adrian Walsh, Ph.D. y Tony Lynch, Ph.D.

En este artículo, exploramos las implicaciones que la remuneración, en sus variadas formas, puede tener para los consejeros de usuarios de drogas. Una larga tradición filosófica sostiene que la ganancia financiera y el altruismo son mutuamente incompatibles. Nuestro punto de vista es algo diferente. Argüimos, contra esta tradición, que aunque la ganancia en la apariencia de beneficio financiero o de sueldo no es en sí mismo moralmente pernicioso, sí presenta a los consejeros de drogas con peligros éticos. Contra esos peligros quienes están involucrados en aconsejar a los usuarios de drogas han de estar especialmente vigilantes.

La Adicción y Minusvalía: Temas Morales y de Política Pública

David Wasserman, J.D.

Este ensayo trata de los temas conceptuales, éticos, y de política pública que surgen cuando se considera legalmente la adicción a drogas como invalidez, y de algunos adictos que no usan drogas como gente con minusvalía. Destaca estas cuestiones: (1) en que juicios morales, si hay alguno, se basa la clasificación de la adicción como minusvalía; (2) si tiene sentido repartir las cargas de la adicción entre causas químicas, biológicas, sociales, políticos, y otras; (3) como consideraciones de la justicia distributiva pueden forzar o contener medidas para disminuir las cargas de la adicción; y (4) si es justificable negar a las personas que usan substancias ilegales las protecciones legales que tienen los que usan substancias legales.

Los problemas éticos que rodeaban el acceso al tratamiento para los que usan y abusan substancias

Shelly A. Wiechelt, Ph.D.

Hay muchos variedades de programas de tratamiento de la toxicomanía en los Estados Unidos que nos muestran la eficacia del tratamiento. Aun que hay un aumento en nuestros conocimientos y en la disponibilidad total de tratamientos en general, hay mucho mas personas quienes necesitan tratamiento que hay personas que reciben tratamiento en realidad. Este capítulo discute algunos de los factores y las condiciones que contribuyen a los problemas del acceso al tratamiento para las personas que usan substancias en los Estados Unidos. Estos problemas del acceso se exploran en la luz de los códigos éticos profesionales a propósito del tratamiento de la adicción.

La Relación Entre Consejeros y Sus Clientes La Moralidad Del Papel Profesional

Kylie Williams, M.S.W. y Dean Cocking, Ph.D.

En este capítulo, presentamos una concepción pluralista del la moralidad del papel en counseling profesional. El lugar de obligaciones del papel, sensibilidades, y territorio de problemas humanos que tienen que ver con counseling son especialmente anchos en su ámbito y lleno de conflictos potenciales. La naturaleza y lugares del tratamiento involuntario para usuarios de drogas presentan problemas especiales para las relaciones entre consejeros y clientes. En efecto, para muchos escritores, esos problemas comprometen fatalmente los bienes morales y finalidades dirigentes que son fundamentales para counseling. Estamos de acuerdo en que algunos valores claves están algunas veces comprometidos en ambientes involuntarios. Argüimos, sin embargo, que una gran parte del conflicto de papeles aquí puede ser acomodado dentro de nuestra concepción pluralista, en vez de reflejar una práctica de counseling disociado de sus finalidades constitutivas apropiadas.

De La Torre de Hierba a las Trincheras: Enseñando la Ética Profesional a los Consejeros de abusadores de Drogas.

Daniel Yalisove, Ph.D.

Este capítulo bosqueja un método de la enseñanza de la ética profesional para consejeros que traten de trastornos del abuso de substancias. Presenta tres ideas innovadoras que antes no han recibido atención en la enseñanza de la ética profesional: (1) Los consejeros han confundido consideraciones éticas y no éticas en el asunto de tomar decisiones. Es importante clarificar la diferencia para estudiantes de la ética profesional. (2) Hay una sinergia especial entre el consejo humanístico y ética profesional. (3) Damos hincapié especial al proceso de la formación ética de algunos clientes, ayudándoles a estar conscientes de problemas éticos.

القرارات الصعبة المتعلقة بالبحث واخلاقيات المهنة:

مانويلا ادريان / ماجستير

لقد زودنا البحث العلمى بواحدة من اقوىالطرق لتطوير الانسان ، على كل حال ان القوة هي مصدر لجملة من المشاكل الاخلاقية وتلك المتعلقة باخلاقيات المهنة عند اولئك الذين يستخدمونها . ان غالبية الاهتمام باخلاقيات البحث هي موجهة حاليا الى الجانب الانساني في البحث لتقليل احتمالات تعريض المشاركين في البحث للاذى، مع بعض الاسس المتطورة شيئا ما والتى ظهرت خلال نصف القرن الماضي . وكذلك الاعتراف بالاشكاليات الاخلاقية للمهنة والتي تنتج عن اهداف البحث وخاصة البحوث المتشددة . ان مشاكل اخلاقيات المهنة والناتجة عن البحث العامي نفسه ومن خلال اساليب البحث وترجمة المعلومات والتي تتطرق لوصفها هذه الورقة.

بمراجعة بعض المبادئْ الاساسية للاسلوب العلمي المستخدم في اجراء تحقيقات البحث فيما يتعلق باستخدام وسوء استخدام المخدرات بدءا من المبادىء التي يوضحها)
اسحق نيوتن) لتحقيق المصادفة واستطلاع بعض اطر العمل
الذي يستخدم لتقرير نقاط التدخل حيث يمكنمنا من العمل حيث يمكننا من العمل للحصول على النتائج التى نريدها عندما لا يمكن تطبيق عنصر المصادفة ، مستخدمين امثلة ليس فقط في موضوع استخدام المخدرات ، ولكن كذلك في مواضيع البحث العلمي ، عندما يكون تسليط الاضواء امرا نافعا حينه سنعتبر المشاكل المهنية المتعلقة باخلاق المهنة التي قد تنتج عن طبيعة الموضوع المراد بحثه والتحقيق فيه ، من ناحية التنظيم، و التمويل ،وايضا اتستخدام اساليب غير سليمة وكذلك التقنيات لتشمل بعض المشاكل التي يجب اخذها في الاعتبار مع استخدام الانسان كموضوع للدراسة، والتي قد ينتج عنها استنتاجات خاطئة قد تكون ضارة للمرضى من وجهة نظر العلماء والمجتمع ككل.

(مشاكل اخلاقيات المهنة التي تنتج طريقة المساعدة المشتركة(الثنائية " لمعالجة مستخدمي المخدرات "منظمات ال 12 خطوه

علامان الاماني \ ماجستير

ان اختلاف طرق المساعدة المشتركة بين مجموعات المعالجة الثنائية وتلك المعالجة الرسمية المهنية ومؤسساتها التي تعمل مع مستخدي الكحول والمخدرات لها تأثيرات اخلاقية ، وخصوصا ان اخلاق المهنة المعروفة عالميا تعتمد على الروحانيات، قبول الآخر والتضامن ويصبح من الممكن اجراء دراسة علمية على انها تعتمد قيمة وجودية عالية الجودة للانسان تجعله يمتنع نهائيا ، وافضل وصف لها هو "مجتمعات المعالجة والاستشفاء " سابالا 2001 . وفي المقابل حيث يكون الاخصائيون المهنيون في برامج معالجة متعاطي المخدرات ،حبث تكون اخلاق المهنة ذات فائدة وهي تتبع اهتمامات الشخص او المجموعة المجتمعية . حتى وانه عندما يتفاعل هذين الطرفين المتطورين قد لا يكون خاليا من التوتر او

المشاكل فان التعاون الثنائي بين الزمالة المهنية ونظام الرعاية الصحية وهذا منتشر الآن على مستوى العالم.

الاعاقة واعادة تأهيل متعاطي المخدرات : اعتبارات أخلاقية

د . اتين بينويت و د . ستيفان ماجيورا

قبل العام 1996 وفي الولايات المتحدة الأمريكية اعتبر ان مدمني الكحول والمخدرات هم معاقين وبالتالي يستحقون دعما اعاشيا من ادارة الضمان الاجتماعي طتاما واظبوا على حضور جلسات المعالجة من الادمان . وفي شهر أذار(مارس) عام 1996 طالب المشرع الأمريكي ادارة الضمان الاجتماعي على شطب المدمنين من لائحة اصحاب الاعاقات التى تؤهلهم للحصول على الدعم الاعاشي.
وهذا التغيير يثير تساؤلات اخلاقية جمة مثل توزيع العدالة وتتفحص سياسة التفريق أو التمييز بين المستحق للخدمة وبين التقصير في تقديم خدمات الدعم الاعاشي للشخص المحتاج ونحلل كيف أن الادمان الذى هو ذا طبيعة غامضة طبيا وعلى سبيل المثال هل يصبح المتعاطي معاقا نتيجة لتعاطيه المخدرات أو الكحول وهل يفسر ذلك على يصبح نموذج سلوكي طوعي.

قدرة المتعاطي على قبول برامج المعالجة

د. ستيف كلارك و د. نيل ليفي

الكثير من المفكرين يعتقدون ان الشخص الذي يتعاطى الكحول أو المخدرات بشكل منتظم غير قادر على قبول المعالجة الطبية وفي هذه المقالة وضعنا تصنيفا كحد أدنى حيث تضع المدمنين ، حيث ان الادمان يجعل الشخص غير قادر ان يكون ذو استقلال ذاتي ولكن ليس الى درجة عدم التأهل للبرامج العلاجية ، ويحتفظ المدمن عادة بدرجة كافية من السيطرة على سلوكه كي يقبل للاستفادة من البرامج العلاجية.

العلاقة المهنية في العلاج بين المدمن والمعالج

د . اليوت د كوهين

وضعت قوانين اخلاقيات المهنة حيث توجب واجبات اخلاقية ومتطلبات على المختصين المهنيين الذين يعالجون الادمان ان ينضووا تحتها حتى يستطيعون القيام بالعلاج بشكل فعال وأن يوظفوا الطموح الانسان الذي يتمحور حول نفسه في أساليب العلاج . بدءا بتحليل القيم

الأساسية التي تغذي المعالجة الفعالة حيث يتم دمج عدة أساليب علاجية فيما يتعلق بالرعاية الصحية ، وهذا البحث يبنى نموذجا للعلاقة بين المدمن والمعالج.

اشكاليات اخلاقيات المهنة التي تثيرها سياسة عدم معاقبة المتعاطي

د. ستيفن كولمان

خلال العقود القليلة الماضيةوفي كثير من البلدان كان هناك دفعا باتجاه اتخاذ واقرار سياسات غير عقابية لمتعاطي الكحول و/أو المخدرات وبشكل عام فان الهدف هو تقليل الاذى للمتعاطي . وهدف هذا الجزء هو مناقشة وتسليط الضوء على المشاكل المهنية التي تثيرها هذه السياسات غير العقابية . وقد اشتمل فحص هذه السياسات على صيانة واعادة تأهيل العلاج ، وكذلك الاساليب المثلى في حقن الهيروين بهدف علاج المتعاطي وكذلك عدم تجريم متعاطي مادة القنب (حشيش أو ماريجوانا. (

! لا يمكن معالجة المتعاطي : يمكن معالجة البشر

د. ستان (شلومو) آينشتاين

الدراسة واضحة وقد تم فحصها ، مع أمثلة مختارة ، أن العلاج العصري لمتعاطي الكحول و / أو المخدرات ، وحيث أن الاقلاع التام عن التعاطي لتقليل الأضرار والذي يطبق في الكثير من أماكن العلاج المنفصلة والمقدمة
(SUD) "substance use disorder". للجمهور في كل مكان
_هو في الاساسغير أخلاقي بسبب تقصيره في تقديم المنفعة وبهذا يكون مشابها للممارسة الخاطئة والغير ضرورية ان التسمية هي خاطئة (1) لا يوجد أسلوب مميز للعلاج (2) المتعاطي وغير المتعاطي في المجتمع المختلف الاصول والاشخاص وليس متميزا.
_لا يمكن تغيير هذا النظام لاختلاف مواقع وأهداف أولئك الساعين الى القوة في هذا النظام
_أنه يترعرع تحت (مبادىء الايمان) والتي تعتبر بالية وقديمة.
_أنه غالبا يتم العناية به وهو يتأثر بالمتغيرات من عدم المهنية أو أن القائمين عليه هم مقلعون عن التعاطي أو هم مدمنين سابقين.
_في ظل الحقيقة القائمة حيث مايتم اكتشافه من معطيات لا يستخدم في المعالجة الملائمة في ظل التغيرات التكنولوجية ومشاكلها.

" القدرة على معالجة الاعتماد الكيماويات "

ثيودور م . جودالسكي / ماجستير

على الرغم من القدرة العلاجية العيادية التي تعتمد عالميا كأسلوب علاجي أخلاقي صحيح في أغلب الاحيان غير محددة أو واضحة ، فقد بذل طاقم متخصص جهدا في سبيل تحسين المواصفات ، فان العمل تحت رعاية دائرة مكافحة المخدرات في دائرة الخدمات الانسانية الصحية والنفسية في الولايات المتحدة اللأمريكية ، وهذه المجموعة تحددثلاثة اتجاهات حيث تكون ضرورة القدرة الكافية اللازمة في تحديد

القدرة على العلاج ، المعرفة ، المهارة ، والاسلوب . على اية حال فان جميع الجهات تقريبا والمناط بها النظر في أساليب العلاج تقيس المعرفة بشكل موضوعي ،

فانها تترك المهارة والاسلوب لتقدير وتقييم المشرفين على مراكز العلاج .وهناك بعض المنطق في الحذر في نوعية وجودة ومدى هذا الا شراف في التقييم والحكم على الاشياء . وكذلك يوجد مبرر للتحقق من ما اذا كانت المعرفة والمهارة هما ذات قيمة متساوية ، بالاضافة الى أن الاسئلة الاخلاقية منها جدوى الفصل بين العلاج العاموالعلاج المتخصص لمتعاطي المخدرات.

انعكاسات لمشاكل أخلاق المهنة في بالشعوب القائمة منذ بدء الخليقة

ثيودور م . جودالسكي
د. جانيت جونسون
رودني هارينج

في هذا الفصل عرض لانعكاس مشاكل أخلاقيات المهنة الظاهرة والملموسة بشكل واضح ، والتي تظهر في أعمال البحث بخصوص المجموعات البشرية للمحليين . ان المصدر الرئيس للقلق هو القيمة الثقافية لأهداف البحث، التصميم ، الأساليب ، والاجراءات ، وتعميم نشر الخطة.

رغم أن القبول الثقافي هو غير واضح البناء والتشكل ، وان عدم معرفة طرق التفكير المحلية ، وكذلك البنية الاجتماعية ، وطرق التواصل ، ونظرة العالم توضح الضرر الذي تم كنتيجة لعدم فهم محاولة البحث الطموح . يقوم المؤلفون بالحديث والبناء في الأعمال الاخيرة في هذا المجال لتأمين حدود واضحة للأبحاث ذات الحساسية الثقافية.

اشكاليات مهمة في تقييم ونشر برامج معالجة الادمان

د . دينيس م . جورمان

يفحص هذا الفصل النتائج التطويرية الأخيرة في تقييم وتسويق برامج معالجة الادمان من ناحية صحة البحث ، وخصوصا فيما يتهدده والتي قد تنجم عن تداخل المصالح . فهو يبدأ في وصف ما يقصده ويقول(تناقض أوتداخل المصالح)وكذلك مراجعة الاشكال الرئيسية من تناقض المصالح ، والتي تم بحثها في نشرات السياسة العامة في السنوات الأخيرة . ويتبع ذلك نقاش مفصل في تناقض المصالح بالنسبة للفرد والمؤسسات فيما يتعلق بأبحاث مكافحة المخدرات.

هل تقليل الضرر في المعالجة النفسية أمر أخلاقي

د. وليام ه. جوتدنير

ان تقليل الاضرار النفسية هو نوع من معالجة الاشخاص الذين تم تشخيص حالتهم باستخدام أو تعاطي المخدرات والذين يستمرون في تناول العقاقير التي تؤثر على صحتهم النفسية . ان هدف العلاج هو تقليل الضرر ، بالمقارنة مع طرق العلاج التقليدية التي تعتبر أن الاقلاع هو الهدف الوحيد المقبول . ان علاج تقليل الضرر تستخدم لعدم التمكن من تحقيق الاقلاع لأن استمرار استخدام المخدرات من قبل المدمن أو المدمنين لكل مرحلة من مراحل المدمن ويجب ملاحظة أن الحرية الشخصية للشخص مهمة جدا حسب اساليب العلاج التقليدية وكذلك الأسلوب التحليلي في العلاج ، والذي يقول ان الاقلاع يتم بواسطة المدمن الناضج ليحدد هدفه في الاقلاع ويتوفر لديه كل مايلزم لذلك ليبدأ نمط حياة جديدة ، ويناقش المؤلف ان هذه الطريقة هي الطريقة الاخلاقية الوحيدة التي تفيد المدمن.

منع العلاقات الجنسية بين المدمن والمعالج : هل هو مبرر ؟

د. مين حاج دين

يفحص هذا الفصل 4 احتمالات للجدال في منع اقامة علاقات جنسية بين المدمن والمعالج ، حيث أن المنع يقاوم الاغراءات الخاصة ، والفرصة المتاحة لعلاقة جنسية والتي تحدث بسبب ظاهرة الانتقال . أما الثاني فهو أن المنع يساهم في جعل المعالجين اذا كان للعلاج أن ينجح ويحقق هدفه . أما الثالث فهو ان العلاج هو امتدادلمهمة تنفيذ القوانين والسبب الرابع فهو أن منع العلاقات الجنسية هذه ضرورة بسبب عدم تكافؤ القوة بين المدمن والمعالج .ان خلاصة هذا الفصل هي أن كل من هذه الاسباب الاربعة يمكن أن تبرر هذا المنع في بعض علاجات المدمنين ،

ولكن السبب الثاني هو الوحيد الذي يبرر تلك العلاقة ، وهو سبب يبدو أنه مجرد تقنية علاجية بدلا من كونه مانعا أخلاقيا في العلاج.

ألأهمية الاخلاقية للأدمان

د . دوجلاس ن . هوساك

أحاول أن أفهم وأقيم الاعتقاد السائد بأن الا دمان له علاقة بالاخلاق وأفحص عدة حالات وكيف أن الادمان قد يكون مهما من ناحية أخلاقية وعلى الرغم أني أناقش باختصار نظريات المثل العليا ، أركز على ثلاثة طرق محتملة حيث يكون الادمان عرضة للوم الاخلاقي . اللوم الأول يمكن أن يفرض على الممارسة أى تعاطي عقاقير تسبب الادمان.
اللوم الثاني يمكن أن يفرض على حاله كونه مدمنا .اللوم الثالث هو بسبب المخاطر الذي المتعاطي نفسه فيها عندما يصبح مدمنا .وهنا استنتج من التأمل في كل واحد من هذه الاستنتاجات أن أيا منها لا يمكن أن يكون خالي من المشاكل . من الممكن أن للادمان علاقة بالاخلاقيات ولكن درجة أهميته لاتصل الى درجة الأهمية التي يعتقدها المعلقون . ولكن العلاقة بين الادمان والاخلاق لايمكن أن ترقى الى الاعتقاد بعدالة فرض رد فعل عقابي للمدمن.

أخلاق المهنة في أبحاث المكافحة مع الأطفال

د . جانيت ل جونسون
نانسي ر فانديمارك - ماجستير

ان فهم القرارات الاخلاقية التي تتعلق بالأبحاث المتعلقة بمكافحة الادمان ممكن أن تكون معقدة وسهلة في نفس الوقت، ان ابحاث المكافحة معقدة بسبب أنها تكون متعلقة بالاطفال وكذلك المسائل المحيطة بحماية الطفل وحقوقه هي مهمة جدا ،
ويجب الانتباه الى هذه الحقوق بحيث تكون واضحة الهدف ، الاحترام والتعامل الحنون . ان أخلاقيات أبحاث المكافحة بسيطة لأن الجواب لفهم التدخل في المكافحة الفعالة توجد فقط في سنوات الطفولة . ولا يوجد بدائل
لتفهم كيف يمكن مقاومة والحيلولة دون حدوث مرض أو اعاقة بدون أن تقوم أولا باجراء الابحاث على الاطفال . ان تلازم التعقيد والبساطة هو ما يجعل المشاكل المتعلقة بالاخلاق في برامج المكافحة أمرا شائعا.

ادمان المخدرات ومسؤولية العناية الصحية للمدمن

د ز تسيبورا كازاخوف

ان الاهتمام والرعاية الصحية لأولئك الذين يحتاجونها هو أمر يشعرنا كمجتمع أننا ملزمين بتوفيره طالما أن الأموال الحكومية تجعل ذلك ممكنا . وهل هذا الالتزام أيا كان ان ذلك الشخص ذو المشاكل الصحية هي نتيجة أنه دخل الى هذه الممارسات التي لها نتائج مؤذية وأنه كان يعرفها قبل أن يتورط وخصوصا هل التزام المجتمع في تأمين خدمات الرعاية الصحية لهؤلاء الذين أدمنوا على المخدرات الممنوعة والبعض يجادل في ذلك حيث أن البعض يعتبر هذا الموقف يمكن الدفاع عنه بنجاح .
هذه الدراسة تجيب على أن كان هؤلاء على حق ولماذا ؟.

الهدف الاخلاقي من المعالجة في حالات التشخيص المزدوج

د . جانيت كينيث
د. ستيف ماثيو

ان استخدام العقاقير أو سوء استخدامها يحدث على مستويات كبيرة بين الناس الذين لديهم مشاكل عقلية والعلاقة بين الاثنين معقدة وفي هذا الفصل نناقش حالات استعمال المخدرات في حالات التشخيص المزدوج للعملاء ويجب البدء في تفهم أن هؤلاء يعانون من أضرار نتيجة المرض العقلي . ونوضح هنا الحالة الأساسية للوكالة الفعالة ، الوكالة الموحدة ، التي تتداخل مع المرض العقلي وتوضح كيف أنها تلزم من أجل تأمين الانخراط في الجيد من الأعمال والاخلاق مثل استمرارالاستخدام والعلاقات المرضية ، ونحن نناقش أن استخدام المخدرات سيكون غير ذا قيمة بشكل رئيسي كي يمنع من الولوج الى هذه المجموعة من الأعمال الجيدة وتركز النظر في أساليب معالجة مرضى حالات التشخيص المزدوج وهذه الأساليب العلاجية يجب أن تعكس الأضرار لهذه الجمعيات والوكالات العلاجية.

مشاكل أخلاقية في مكافحة المخدرات

د . جون كلينج

يعرض هذا البحث صورة عامة لبعض التساؤلات الاخلاقية التي تثار من التدخل الحكومي في الحد ومكافحة المخدرات ونظرا الى ما قد سبق فانها تبدأ الاسترسال في الاعتقاد الذي يضع قيودا على العمل الحر تبررالضرر الذي يلحق بالآخرين ، ولكن هذا الاعتقاد يعتمد على ملآحظة المتطلبات الاجتماعية للعمل الحر . أما فيما يتعلق بالتدخل الطبي ، تسلط الأضواء على الشيفرات التي طورت لتخدم المعالجين ومؤسساتهم وكذلك زبائنهم

، وتستطلع الالزام الأخلاقي من الكثير من هذه القوانين المركزية ، الموافقة المبنية على المعرفة ، السرية ، الخصوصية ، وعدم التمييز والمهنية وكذلك المساءلة.

التفكير الأخلاقي بما يتعلق ببرنامج نيدل التبادلي

د . جون كلينج

اذا قبلنا على سبيل الجدل سياساتنا القانونية الحالية بما يتعلق بالهيروين فما هي الأسئلة المثارة عن برنامج نيدل التبادلي ؟ وهل تضعف قوانين المخدرات ،
ويرسل رسالة خاطئة أو تمنع الرسالة الصحيحة ، أو لا تفعل ما يكفي اتقليل مضار المخدرات ، تبتعد عن البدائل ، و أو توجب الاستشارة عن اليأس ؟ اقترح أنه في ظل عدم وجود بدائل تشرع خيارا مقبول أخلاقيا ومحبب رغم استمرارية تجريم استخدام المخدرات.

الخصوصية والسرية وعلاج مدمن المخدرات

د . سيوماس ميللر

لتثبيت مبدأ السرية اعتبارات متعددة ، بما فيها الحق في الخصوصية ، الثقة ،
ة\والآثار الضارة المترتبة على عدم الوفاء بمبدأ السرية أو البوح بالسر وكذلك فان الحق في السرية بحد ذاته ، مقيد بقيم أخلاقية ، بما فيها الاستقلالية الذاتية ، وهذا مايجعل التبرير الأخلاقي للسرية تبرير معقد . ان درجة التزامنا بمبدأ السرية يحتاج الى أن يتم ايجاد رابط بينه وبين الظروف وفي بعض الحالات أو التصنيفات لمدمني المخدرات توفر بعض الأرضية أو الأسس للسرية ولكنها ليست الوحيدة بسبب تلاشي الاستقلالية الذاتية وتقلل من أهمية الخصوصية ، وعلى أي حال ، لا يمكن لنا بشكل أوتوماتيكي أن يضعف مدى التزامنا بمبدأ السرية.

الدواء والاخلاقيات ، اشتهاء المخدر والاستسلام له

د . ستيفين جي . مورس

يوجد أسلوبين للنظر الى الادمان ، النمط الطبي الذي يعالج الادمان كمرض ،
والسلوكيات المرافقة كأعراض للمرض . والموديل أو النمط الأخلاقي ، الذي ينظر للأدمان والسلوكيات المرافقة على أنها فشل أو سقوط أخلاقي . تصف هذه الورقة كلا النمطين وتأثيراتهما ، مع تركيز خاص على النمط الأخلاقي . ان معنى الاستسلام بالاكراه الذي يحصل نتيجة أوضاع نفسية داخلية مثل (النهم والاشتهاء° للمخدر) أو الرغبة في التعاطي يتم استطلاعه لتقرير اذا كان المدمن يجب أن يساءل بشكل عادل ويكون مسؤولا أخلاقيا

وقانونيا عن سلوكه ، مثل البحث عن المخدرات واستخدامها ، بينمانجادل بأن العقلانية المتلاشية تفسر بشكل أفضل من الاستسلام بالاكراه للمخدرات ، لماذا يجب اعفاء المدمن من المساءلة عن سلوكهم . ولكن تخلص الورقة الى أن معظم المدمنين يمكن مساءلتهم عن أي سلوك له علاقة بالادمان . ولكن النمطين لهما صفات محببة وان السياسة العامة يجب أن لا تتخذ من أي منهما أساسا . ان تأثيرات النظام الجنائي في توظيف النمطين كدليل لهذه السياسة يجري استطلاعه

مشكلات اخلاقية في أبحاث معالجة المدمنين

د . كينيث د . بيمبل

تكون أبحاث معالجة متعاطي المخدرات خاضعة لاعتبارات أخلاقية أساسية تكون ظاهرة في كافة الأبحاث العلمية بما فيها ، الصدق والامانة وكذلك الصراحة ، واستخدام ناشر مناسب ، والامتناع عن أي علاقات حميمة أو مضايقات للشخص موضوع البحث ،
وكذلك المبادىء الاخلاقية التي تتعلق بالأبحاث التي تستخدم الانسان كموضوع للبحث ، وهي واردة في تقرير بلمونت مثل احترام الأشخاص ، وأن يكون نافعا ،
مفيدا وعادلا . وهناك مبدأ اضافي لم يردذكره في تقرير بلمونت وليس الابتذال الوارد في تقرير بلمونت ولكن يكتسب قبولا واسعا ، أو الوصول للعلاج. وأنه يجب على الباحثين أن يطيعوا هذه المبادىء أخلاقيا وقانونيا ، وعلى الجمعية أو الهيئات التي تقوم بعلا >متعاطي المخدرات أن تفعل ما تستطيع لتشكيل البحث والأجندة والسياسة الاجتماعية طبقا لهذه المبادىء.

معالجة متعاطي المخدرات : أهي سياسة عادلة أم سياسة تقوم على الحقائق

د. موريس ريكارد

ان القضية هنا ، ان القرارات بخصوص أي نوع من برامج مكافحة تعاطي المخدرات يجب تبنيه وهي مسألة سياسة عامة وخيار اجتماعي . ومن المنطق أن تعتمد هذه السياسة على الأدلة والمبادىء الأخلاقية في العلاج .ويبدو من المعقول ان نتوقع ان السياسة والخيار الاجتماعي عن ممارسات المعالجة أن تكون عادلة ، وأن القرارات يجب أن تقر بشكل مناسب . ان الطريقة التي يتم فيها احترام هذين المبدأين هو جعل اتخاذ القرار بخصوص سياسة معالجة
متعاطي المخدرات مبدئيا وعادلا بحيث يكون هذا القرار صائبا . ولكن المشكلة ان ما يمكن أن يكون قرارا صائبا وفعالا ويعتمد على الغرض من برنامج المعالجة هذا . ولكن الخطورة هي أن ينتهي الى جدال ومعضلة حول عدالة.
هذا البرنامج بدلا من أن يكون مقبولا من الجميع . في هذا الفصل نستطلع بعض المشاكل الفلسفية فيما يتعلق بسياسة المعالجة العادلة والجيدة بما فيها تقرير من هو الذي يمنح دورافي سياسة صنع القرار.

مشاكل أخلاقية تحيط بعملية الدخول الى برامج المعالجة

د . باربارا سي . والاس

وهعي (تتنوع المشاكل الاخلاقية فيما يتعلق بدخول برامج المعالجة (الحصول على العلاج موقع السكن تتراوح بين الجنس البشري ، الدين ، الجنس ، الحالة مثل العمر ، الحمل ، المتعاطي الجغرافي ، وبعده عن مراكز العلاج ، الفقر ، عدم وجود تأمين صحي لدى يعاني منها . وهناك قضايا أخلاّقية أخرى، تشمل مدى الاعاقة النفسية أو الصحية التي لتعاطي المتعاطي نفسه وكذلك من المشاكل كيف يتم التعامل مع المتعاطي الذي يعود المزمن المخدرات وكذلك تقارير فحص البول وأخطر هذه المشاكل هو التعامل مع المتعاطي للعلاج أثناء في العودة الى المخدرات . وكذلك مخاطر الضعف من جانب المتعاطي الخاضع زمنية في العلاج العلاج أو عند رفض تقديم العلاج له . وكذلك مشاكل اجبار ووضع برامج الاجتماعي تفرض بشكل سلطوي ، سواء عن طريق القانون الجنائي ، مؤسسات الدعم الى العلاج ، أو مؤسسات حماية الأطفال والتي تكون مجتمعة عاملا ضاغطا على الدخول الاخلاقية الحديثة . في هذا الفصل هناك توصيات حول كيفية الرد والتعامل مع هذه المشاكل

علاج متعاطي المخدرات ، المكفأة وأخلاق المهنة

د. أدريان والش
د. توني لينش

يستطلع هذا الفصل تأثيرات مكافأة القائم على العلاج في صيغها المختلفة وتمشيا مع التقاليد الفلسفية أن مكافأة المعالج هي أمر ثنائي خاص ، ولكن لنا رأي مختلف بعض الشيء . نجادل بأنه على عكس التقاليد وعلى الرغم من أن المكافأة قد تختبيء وراء الكسب التجاري أو كراتب أو أجر وانه في حد ذاتها ليست شيئا محرما ولكنها تبرز أمام المعالج كخطر أخلاقي وهذه اللأخطار توجب على المعالج أن يكون متيقظا لها.

الادمان والاعاقة : مشاكل السياسة واللأخلاق

ديفيد واسيرمان

يعالج هذا الفصل مباية وأخلاقية ومشاكل سياسة المعالجة التي يثيرها التصنيف القانوني للادمان على أنه اعاقة . وكذلك حالات المعاقين ليسي كنتيجة لتعاطي المخدرات ، انها تسلط الضوء على 4 أسئلة : (1) ماهو الحكم الاخلاقي في التصنيف الذي يعتبر الادمان اعاقة (2) اذا عقلانيا توزيع حمل الادمان على أسباب كيماوية ، حيوية ، اجتماعية

وسياسية أو اي أسباب أخرى (3) كيف يمكن لاعتبارات توزيع العدالة أن تعيق الاجراءات التي يفترض أن تقللمن مضار الادمان (4) اذا ما كان من الممكن تبرير عدم اعطاء متعاطي المخدرات الحالي مخدرات ممنوعة وكذلك الحماية القانونية الممنوحة حاليا لمتعاطي المخدرات القانونية.

المشاكل الأخلاقية المحيطة في الدخول الى برامج معالجة الاستخدام السيء للمخدرات

د . شيلي أ ويشيلت
7

ان تنوع برامج معالجة تعاطي المخدرات في الولايات المتحدة لهي دليل مدى فاعلية العلاج . وبغض النظر عن ازدياد المعرفة وتوفر العلاج بشكل عام هناك فجوة كبيرة جدا بين من يحتاجون للعلاج والذين يتلقون العلاج فعلا.

يبحث هذا الفصل بعض العوامل والظروفالتي تساهم في مشاكل عدم استيعاب متعاطي المخدرات في الولايات المتحدة . و نستطلع هذه المشاكل في ضوء قوانين السلوك المهني بخصوص المعالجين المهنيين.

علاقة المستشار بالمتعاطي ودور أخلاق المهنة

كايل وليامز / ماجستير
د . دين كوكنج

يعرض هذا الفصل لعمومية مبدأ دور أخلاق المهنة المناسب للاستشارة وكذلك الالتزام ، الحساسيات واماكن مشاكل الانسان التي لها علاقة بالاستشارة (العلاج (خصوصا في شمولية الصورة تنذر باشكاليات محتملة . ان الطبيعة الاجبارية لبرامج العلاج توجد مشاكل جمة في العلاقة بين المعالج ومتلقي العلاج .في الحقيقة فانه لكثير من المؤلفين وهذه المشاكل تصيب في مقتل أخلاقيات المهنة التي هي أساسية جدا لتقديم العلاج أو المشورة . ونوافق أن بعض القيم الرئيسية يتم التنازل عنها في حالة الاجبار على العلاج . ونجادل على أية حال أن الكثير من المشكلةيفهم بان يتم استيعابه من خلال عمومية المبدأ وليس انعكاس ممارسة العلاج في معزل عن الاهداف الاساسية.

من الأبراج العاجية الى المخبأ الارضي : تعليم أخلاق المهنة لمستشاري العلاج

د . دانييل ياليسوف

يوضح هذا الفصل كيف يتم تعليم الاخلاق المهنية للمعالجين في مجال مكافحة الادمان وهو يظهر 3 أفكار مبتكرة لم يكن قد تم منحها الاعتبار اللازم في تدريس الاخلاق المهنية . (1) خلط المعالجون الاعتبارات المهنية أو غير المهنية في اتخاذقرارات أخلاقية ، وانه من المهم توضيح هذا التميز في تعليم الاخلاق المهنية (2) . يوجد حميمية خاصة بين بين العلاج الانساني وأخلاق المهنة (3) انتباه شديد يعطى لعملية تعليم الاخلاقية المهنية لجميع الزبائن بأن يتم مساعدتهم ليصبحوا مدركين للمشاكل في المهنية الأخلاقية.

החלטות קשות המערבות מחקר ואתיקה: שימוש לרעה בסטטיסטיקה של שימוש/משתמשים בסמים

Manuella Adrian, M. Sc. Hyg.

המחקר המדעי יספק לנו את אחד האמצעים החזקים ביותר לשפר את מצב האנושות. עם זאת, כוחו עצמו עלול לשמש אכסניה לדילמות מוסריות ואתיות לאלו המשתמשים בו. רוב תשומת הלב לאתיקה של מחקר מתמקדת עכשיו בסובייקט האנושי ומכוונת להפחתת אפשרות הנזק למשתתפים, עם קווים מנחים מפותחים באופן סביר, אשר התפתחו בחצי-המאה האחרונה. מזוהות גם הדילמות האתיות אשר עולות ממידעי המחקר במיוחד בכל הקשור למחקר מיליטריסטי. פחות ידועים הם תחומים של דאגות אתיות העולות מהמתודות המדעיות עצמן, ממתודות המחקר ומפרשנות המידע אשר גם הן מתוארות במאמר זה. אנחנו בוחנים כמה מהעיקרים הבסיסיים של המתודה המדעית בהם נעשה שימוש מחקרי בתחום של שימוש ושימוש לרעה בסמים, תוך שאנו מתחילים עם העקרונות היסודיים שהובעו על-ידי אייזק ניוטון בבואו לבסס סיבתיות ובבחינה של מספר מבנים תפיסתיים חדשים יותר המשמשים להחלטה על נקודות התערבות בהן אנו עשויים לפעול על-מנת להשיג את התוצאות הרצויות גם כאשר אי-אפשר ליישם סיבתיות לינארית קשוחה, תוך היעזרות בדוגמאות לא רק מתחום השימוש בסמים אלא גם ממסגרת מדעית כללית יותר כאשר תיאורים כאלה עשויים להיות לעזר. לאחר מכן נבחן את הבעיות האתיות והמוסריות אשר עשויות לעלות מטבעו של נושא החקירה, הארגון שלו ומימון, כמו-גם השימוש במתודות וטכניקות לא ראויות – כולל כמה מן הנושאים שצריכים להילקח בחשבון בשימוש באנשים – אשר עשויות להוביל למסקנות שגויות שעשויות להזיק לפציינטים, למדענים ולחברה בכלל.

סוגיות אתיות שעולות מגישות של עזרה-עצמית בטיפול במשתמש בסמים: מקומם של ארגוני שנים-עשר הצעדים

Allaman Allamani, M.D.

להבדלים המהותיים ביחס אל ובעבודה עם משתמשים לרעה במשקאות אלכוהוליים וסמים אחרים של קבוצות עזרה הדדית ושל גורמי וסוכנויות טיפול רשמיות מקצועיות יש השלכות אתיות. בפרט, האתיקה של קבוצות שנים-עשר הצעדים היא אוניברסלית, מבוססות כמו שהן על רוחניות, אחרו·ת וסולידריות. גם אם יעילותן בגרימת הינזרות יכולה להיות מוכחת מדעית, הן מתוארות באופן הטוב ביותר כ"קהילות של ריפוי" ("communities of healing"(Seppala 2001)). מאידך, במקום שבו מעורבים אנשי מקצוע בתוכניות טיפול למשתמשים בסמים, האתיקה נראית כתועלתנית; היא מכוונת כלפי האינטרסים או של היחיד או של הקבוצה החברתית. גם אם כאשר קיימת ביניהן אינטראקציה שתי דרכים שונות אלו יצרו מתח או קונפליקט, הרי ששיתוף פעולה בקרב אגודות לעזרה עצמית ומערכת הדאגה לבריאות הוא כיום מתפשט והופך לנחלתו של כל העולם.

נכות וטיפול/שיקום של משתמש בסמים: שיקולים אתיים

Ellen Benoit, Ph.D. and Stephen Magura, Ph.D.

לפני 1996, אנשים בארה"ב שהיו מכורים כרוניים לסמים או אלכוהול יכולים היו לקבל תעודה כנכים, אשר זיכתה אותם בהבטחת הכנסה מהביטוח הלאומי - Social Security Administration (SSA), כל עוד לקחו חלק בטיפול. חקיקה במרץ 1996 הביאה את ה-SSA לבטל התמכרות כנכות שמאפשרת זכאות ולמחוק מרשימותיה את כל מי שהיה מקבל תמיכה כמשתמש בסמים נכה. שינוי זה מעלה שאלות אתיות משמעותיות, אליהן אנו מתייחסים מנקודת המבט של צדק חלוקתי. אנו בוחנים את ההבחנה במדיניות בין

אנשים נזקים "שמגיע להם" לאלה "שלא-מגיע להם" איך הטבע המערופל מבחינה רפואית של התמכרות גורר טענות מתחרות של "קיבל מה שבישל לעצמו" בדיון סביב זכאות. לדוגמה, האם היעשותו של מישהו נכה כתוצאה משימוש בסמים מהווה צורה של התנהגות מתוך רצון חופשי? לבסוף, אנו שוקלים את תוצאות המיון מחדש של ה-SSA לבעלי העניין המדיניים, כולל מקבלי הקצבאות, נותני הטיפול והציבור הרחב.

על היכולת של משתמשים בסמים לנתינת הסכמתם לתכניות טיפול

Steve Clarke, Ph.D. and Neil Levy, Ph.D.

הוגי דעות רבים מחזיקים בדעה שמשתמשים רגילים בסמים אינם בעלי יכולת לתת הסכמתם לטיפול רפואי. במאמר זה אנו פורשים קריטריוני מינימום לסוכני-טיפול שיחשבו כמסוגלים למסור הסכמה בידיעה (informed consent), וטוענים שמשתמשים רגילים בסמים – גם אלה שמייחסים להם התמכרות לסם – בדרך-כלל עומדים בקריטריונים האלה. למרות שהתמכרות פוגעת באוטונומיה, היא אינה פוגעת ברמה שלא מאפשרת נתינת הסכמה בידיעה. מחקרים של התנהגות של מכורים מראים שבאופן כללי הם שומרים על שליטה מספקת על התנהגויותיהם ולקיחת ההחלטות שלהם ברמה שעושה אותם כשירים לנתינת הסכמה.

המשגת היחסים המקצועיים בטיפול למשתמש בסמים ולמשתמש לרעה באלכוהול

Elliot D. Cohen, Ph.D.

קודים אתיים, חוקים והלכה הפסוקה (case law) נושאים דרישות או חובות בסיסיות שחלות על אנשי מקצוע המייעצים למשתמשים בסמים ולמשתמשים לרעה באלכוהול. בכל אופן, אם מטפלים אלה מייעצים באופן אפקטיבי, הרי שהם חייבים לכלול בדרכי הטיפול שלהם גם קריטריונים ממוקדי-אדם ושאיפות. בפתיחה עם בחינה של הערכים היסודיים שמעגנים טיפול אפקטיבי; תוך שילוב של מספר מודלים מקצועיים שקשורים בשמירת-בריאות, פרק זה בונה מודל אקלקטי אפשרי של יחסי מטפל-מטופל.

סוגיות אתיות המועלות על ידי מדיניות לא-ענישתית של המשתמש בסמים

Stephen Coleman, Ph.D.

במהלך העשורים האחרונים קיימת דחיפה חזקה במדינות רבות ליישום תוכניות ומדיניות שלוקחות גישה שאינה ענישתית לשימוש והשימוש לרעה בסמים, באופן כללי עם המטרה של הפחתת הנזק הנגרם למשתמשים בסמים. מטרת פרק זה היא להצביע על, ולדון בסוגיות האתיות הספציפיות שדרכי מדיניות סמים שאינן ענישתיות עשויות להעלות. דרכי מדיניות ספציפיות שנבחנות כוללות טיפול אחזקתי במתדון, תכניות להחלפת מזרקים, הספקה של מקומות הזרקה בטוחים, הרואין במרשם ודקרימינליזציה של חשיש.

אי-אפשר לטפל במשתמשים בסמים; באנשים אפשר!

Stan Einstein, Ph.D.

הנחת היסוד המוצגת ונבחנת, תוך שימוש בדוגמאות נבחרות, שטיפול ל"הפרעת שימוש בסמים" (הש"ס) – יהיה זה ממוקד בהינזרות או מונע על-ידי הפחתת נזקים שכמעט תמיד מתרחש באתרים נפרדים מהטיפול "הנורמטיבי" המקובל (מיינסטרים) – אשר מוצע לאוכלוסיה ככלל:

- מישעמ לש תורתוימה "תונמ"ל מיאתממ רתוי מידסח תולימגב ולש רסוחה ;יתא-אל ודוסיב אוה וב שיש מיער;
- (תוקינכט וא מילדומ) דחוימ "לופיט" מייק אל (1) ;משב מלוה אלו העטמ שומיש אוה מג (2) מגו ,מימסב מישמתשמ מניאש ימ מע מג שומישב וניאש "מימסב מישמתשמ"ל אלו מישנא לש תוינגורטה תויסולכוא מיגציימ מישמתשמ מניאש ימ מגו "מימסב מישמתשמ" תולחמ גוויסל תוינגומוהו תודחוימ תורות;
- ןיינע-ילעב לש תורטמהו תודנ'גאה ,תודמעה ללגב תיתא-ססובמ ךילהתל הנתשי אוהש הארנ אל חכ ידי-לע מיענומה מייתכרעמו מייטרפ;
- "החכוה-ססובמ" ומכ תואמסיס לע מיססובמו מיחנומש "הנומא לש תונורקע" ידי-לע ןזומ אוה מגו
- יוניש ינכוס לש ןווגמ ידי לע (הנווכב אלש) קזחותמ ידימ תוברוק מיתעל אוה ןכאו תויהל לוכי מייעוצקמ מניאש מישנא מג ומכ תונילפיצסיד לש חווט מיגציימה (co-opted) מיחפוסמ "המלחהב" ("in recovery") וא מירוכמ-מייקנ;
- אלמ רתוי תוברוק מיתעל הללכהל מינתינה מיאצממ הב רשא וטקפ-הד תכשמתמ תואיצמ ךותב לש הקירבורה תחת ,מימאתמ מימסב מישמתשמב לופיטל שומיש מהב השענ אלו מיגצומ אל "היגולונכט תויעב תרבעה" ("transfer of technology problems")

?קדצומ הז מאה :מהלש מילפטמל מימסב מישמתשמ ןיב ןימ יסחי מויק לע רוסיא תלוכי (Competence) תימיכ תורכמתהל לופיטב

Theodore M. Godlaski, M.Div.

איה תוברוק מיתעל ,תיתא הניחבמ הנוכנ הדובעל השורדכ תילסרבינוא הרוצב תספתנ תינילק תלוכיש תורמל מידבועש ,עוצקמ ישנא לש לנאפ ידי-לע רתוי בוט רואיתל ןויצל מייואר מיצמאמ ושענ .ןוכנ אל תרדגומ ב"הראב שפנה תואירבו מימסב הערל שומישה יתוריש להנמ תוסחב (Substance Abuse and Mental Health Services Administration). מימלוה מידיקפת מהבש מימוחת השולש תראתמ וז הצובק מידדומ מירשאמה מיפוגה לכ טעמכ השעמל ,ןפוא לכב .תושיגו ,תונמוימ ,עדי :תלוכי תחכוהל מישרדנ הביס הנשי .מיינילק מיחנומ לש תודעה ידיב השיגו תונמוימ מיריאשמ מהש דוח ,עדי קר יביטקייבוא ןפואב הנשי ,ךסונב .הלאכש מיטופיש מיססובמ וילעש הייחנה רשק לש תוכיאלו תומכל רשאב הגאדל יהשלכ רשאב תולאש ןנשי מגו .הווש ךרע ילעב יתא ןפואב מה תונמוימ לכו עדי לכ מאה הלאשה תא תולעהל הביס קדצומ תויהל לוכי ,ללכב לופיטמ דרפנ ןפואב ,מימסב שמתשמל לופיט לש מוחת מאה היגוסל.

מיני'גירובא מע רקחמב תויתא תויגוס לע תובשחמ

Theodore M. Godlaski, M.Div., Jeannette Johnson, Ph.D. and Rodney Haring, LMSW

"מידילי" מע וא מיני'גירובא מע רקחמה תדובעב תולועש תובושחה תויגוסה לע הבשחמ אוה הז קרפ תרטמ לש יתוברתה מאותה אוה תיתא הגאדל ינושארה רוקמה .מייוסמ מוקמ לש (native peoples) רדגומ גשומ אל אוה יתוברת מאותש תורמל .הצפה/מוסרפ תינכתו ,לוקוטורפ ,תודותמ ,ובוציע ,רקחמה מקפסמ ,הבשחמ לש "תודילי" מיכרדל רושקה לכב תקפסמ יתלב תוסחייתה (Native ways of thinking), רקחמ תונויסינמ האצותכ קזנל מורגל היושע מלועה לע טבמ תדוקנלו תרושקתל ,יתרבחה הנבמל קפסל ידכ הז מוחתב הנורחאל התשענש הדובעל מיסחייתמ מיבתוכה .הקיפסמ הבשחמ מהל השדקוה אלש תיתוברת שיגר רקחמל מיחנמ מיוק

םימסב שומיש תעינמל תוינכת לש הצפהבו הכרעהב םיסרטניא ידוגינ

Dennis M. Gorman, Ph.D.

שומיש תעינמל תוינכת לש קווישבו הכרעהב הנורחאל ועריאש תויוחתפתה לש תוכלשהה תא ןחוב הז קרפ
אוה .םיסרטניא ידוגינמ ול תוברואה תונכסל רשאב יפיצפס ןפואבו ,רקחמה תוירסומל רשאב ,םימסב
ונודינש םיירקיעה םידוגינה יגוס לש הריקסבו םיסרטניא דוגינ חנומב הנווכה המ לש רואיתב ליחתמ
לש רתוי טרופמ ןויד הוולמ הז תא .תונורחאה םינשב תירוביצה תוינידמה לש וזבו תיאופרה תורפסב
.םימסב שומישה תעינמ רקחמב םימייקש םיידסומהו םייטרפה םיסרטניאה ידוגינ

?תיתא םיקזנ תתחפה לש היפרתוכיספ מאה

William H. Gottdiener, Ph.D.

םישנאל (outpatient) ץוח-ילוח לש היפרתוכיספ לש הרוצ הניה (נ"הפ) םיקזנ תתחפה לש היפרתוכיספ
.םייביטקאוכיספ םירמוחב שמתשהל םיכישממשו (ס"שה) םימסב שומיש לש הערפה ילעבכ םינחבואמה
.םייביטקאוכיספ םירמוחב שומיש תוולל לולעש העיגפה לאיצנטופ תא תיחפהל איה נ"הפ לש לופיטה תרטמ
איה תוחכיפ םהבש ס"שה-ב םייתרוסמ םילופיט םע האוושהב ,םיקזנ תיחפהל תחא ךרד קר איה תוחכיפ
םישנאה לכב תוחכיפ רמשל וא/ו גישהל רשפא-יאש םושמ שומיש השענ נ"הפ-ב .הדיחיה תלבוקמה הרטמה
אל וא יתא מאה הלאשב קסוע קרפה .םיוסמ םדאב לופיטה לש בלש לכל וא ,ס"שה לש םינמיס םיארמש
תישיא תוריחש תינאיוקופ טבמ תדוקנ טקונ אוהש ךות .ס"שה-מ םילבוסה םישנאל לופיטכ נ"הפ קפסל
טניילק ידי-לע קר תגשומ תויהל היושע תוחכיפש תיטילנאוכיספ טבמ תדוקנו ,ס"שה-ב לופיטל תינויח איה
ליחתהל – םיינוציח תורוקממו םיימינפ תורוקממ – ךירצש המ לכ תא ול שישו וז הרטמל ןווכל ןכומש
הדיחיה ץוח-ילוחב היפרתוכיספה תרוצ איה נ"הפ-ש ןעוט בתוכה ,הזכש םייח חרואל תולגתסה רמשלו
ס"שה ילעב םישנאל קפסל רשפאש תיתא איהש

?קדצומ הז מאה :םהלש םילפטמל םימסב םישמתשמ ןיב ןימ יסחי םויק לע רוסיא

Mane Hajdin, J.D., Ph.D.

הלאו םימסב םישמתשמל םילפטמ ןיב ןימ יסחי םויק לע רוסיאל םיירשפא םינועיט העברא ןחוב הז קרפ
םירצוימה ןימ יסחיל תויורשפאהו םידחוימה םייותיפה דגנכ דמוע רוסיאהש אוה ןושארה .םדי-לע םילפוטמש
מא םילפטמל שיש הטירוטואל םרות רוסיאהש אוה ינשה .(transference) הרבעהה תעפות ידי-לע
תחת אצמנ ןכלו קוחה תפיכא לש הבחרה אוה לופיטש רמוא ישילשה ןועיטה .ותרטמ תגשהל לעופ לופיטה
םייקש הכב ןוזיאה רסוח ללגב שורד רוסיאהש אוה יעיברה ןועיטה .קוחה תפיכא לש םיצוליאה םתוא
תא קידצהל יושע םינועיטה תעבראמ דחא לכש איה קרפה תנקסמ .םהב םילפטמ םהש הלאו םילפטמ ןיב
לכב ותוא קידצהל יושע ינשה ןועיטה קרש לבא ,םימסב םישמתשמל לופיט לש םינפוא רפסמב רוסיאה
וניאו ,לופיט תוקינכט לש ןיינע לכה-ךסב אוה הזה ןועיטהש ןפוא לכב הארנ .הזכש לופיט לש םינפואה
.לופיטב יאמצע ירסומ ץוליא

תורכמתה לש תירסומה (Relevance) הקיזהו תועמשמה

Douglas N. Husak, Ph.D.

םיקדבנ .רסומל הקיז תלעבו הרושק תורכמתההש הצופנה הנומאה תא ךירעהלו ןיבהל הסנמ רמאמה
,רוציקב תונודינ יכ םא .תירסומ טבמ תדוקנמ תיתועמשמ תויהל הלוכי תורכמתה דציכ :תוקמנה המכ
הלוכי תורכמתה ןהיפל תויורשפא שולש לע איה תודקמתהה ,(Virtue) ירסומ םייח חרוא לש תוירואית
.םירכמתמ םימסב שומישב לש תוגהנתהה לע המשא ליטהל רשפא ,תישאר .תירסומ המשאל הקיז תלעב תויהל
המשא ליטהל רשפא ,תישילש .(addicted) רוכמ תויהל לש בצמה םצע לע המשא ליטהל רשפא ,תינש
תוריבסה שי (accounts) תוקמנההמ תחא לכל ,םוכיסב .םיחקול ,םירוכמל וכפהש הלאש םינוכיסה לע
יכ םא ,רסומל תיטנבלרו הקיז תלעב איהש אמתסמ תורכמתה .תיתייעב םג איה ןהמ תחא לכ לבא ,תמיוסמ
הלוע הניא תורכמתה לש תירסומה תויטנבלרה .םינשרפ המכ םינימאמש יפכ ההובג הכ הניא הקיזה תמר
.םירכמתמ םימסב םישמתשמל תיתשנוע הבוגת הקידצמש איהשלכ המרל

םידלי לצא יתעינמ רקחמב הקיתא

Jeannette L. Johnson, Ph.D. and Nancy R. VanDeMark, Ph.D.

םגו תכבוסמ םג תויהל הלוכי םימסב שומיש לש העינמה לע רקחמב תוברועמה תויתא תוטלחה לש הנבה
דליה לע הנגהל תועגונה תויגוסהש ללגבו םידלי םע םייקתמ אוהש ללגב ךבוסמ אוה יתעינמ רקחמ .הטושפ
דובכ ,הרטמה תוריהבב ךות הלאה תויוכזל גואדל ךירצ ,םידלי םע .דחוימ ןפואב תויתועמשמ ןה ויתויוכז לעו
תויביטקפא תויתעינמ תויוברעתה ןיבהל תרשפאמה הבושתהש ינפמ טושפ אוה יתעינמ רקחמ .תונידעו
רסוח וא ,תוערפה ,תולחמ עונמל ךיא ןיבהל ידכ תוביטנרטלא תומייק אל .תודליה ליגב רק תולגתהל הלוכי
םרוג רשא תוטשפה לש םגו םיכוביסה לש םג ףוריצה והז .םידלי םע םירקחמ ךורעל לכ םדוק ילב דוקפת
.תוינרקוד תויהל יתעינמ רקחמב תויתאה תויגוסל

םימסל םירוכמ לש םתואירבל תויוריחאו םימסל תורכמתה

Tziporah Kasachoff, Ph.D.

םיבאשמש הדימב ,םיביוחמ םישיגרמ הרבחכ ונא רשא ,והשמ אוה יאופר לופיטל םיקוקזה הלאל לופיטו הגאד
איה םדאה לש יאופרה ובצמש הדבועה ידי לע תלבגומ איה תאז תוביוחמ םאה .תאז םירשפאמ םיירוביצ
?םרשאש םהילע עדיי רשאו ותואירבל תוינסרה תואצות תולעב תויוגהנתהל הנפ ונוצרמ ומצע אוהש האצות
?םתורכמתה לש האצותכ ולחו ורכמתהש הלאל תואירב יתוריש קפסל הרבחה לש התבוח וז םאה ,תיפיצפס
.תירסומ הניחבמ תלבוקמ הניא וז הדמעש םינעוט םירחא דועב ,הרבחה תבוח וז ןיידעש םינעוטש שי

.עודמו הז אשונב קדוצ ימ :היעבב קסוע רמאמה
הלופכ הנחבא לש םירקמב לופיטה לש תירסומה הרטמה (Dual Diagnosis)

Jeannette Kennett, Ph.D. and Stephen Matthews, Ph.D.

םיסחיהו שפנה תואירבב תויעב םע םישנא ברקב דאמ הובג רועישב שחרתמ םימסב הערל שומישו שומיש
הנחבא םהלש םילפוטמב םימסב שומישב לופיטש םינעוט ונחנא הז קרפב .םיבכרומ הם םיבצמה ינש ןיב
יתוהמה בצמה תא םיטטרשמ ונחנא .שפנ תולחמ םהלש הלא םילבוס םהמש םיכסחהמ ליחתהל בייח הלופכ
לש תולוכי תיביטקפא (effective agency), תדחואמ תלוכי (unified agency), רשא תעגפנ תלחמב

מיסחיו הקסעה תויכשמה ומכ מיירסומו מייתרבח מיבאשמל השיג חיטבהל ידכ תשרדנ וז דךיא מיארמו שפנ
לש הז דךרעמל השיג ענומ אוה םגו תויה רקיעב דךרע-רסח היהי מימסב שומישש מינעוט ונא .מיקפסמ
תואירבמ תומלעתה דות תינורכניס תואירבב ןכוסה תא דקממו (agential goods) תלוכי לש מיבאשמ
ינושארה מגפה תא ףקשל ןכל דירצ הלופכ הנחבא ילעב מילפוטמב לופיטל תודותמהו תורטמה .תינורכאיד
תדחואמה תלוכיה לש.

מירכממ מירמוחב שומישב תוברעתהב תויתא תויגוס

John Kleinig, Ph.D.

תויאופרהו תויתכלממה תויוברעתהה ןמ תולעומה תויתאה תולאשה ןמ המכב יללכ ןויד גיצמ רמאמה
מישימשב .מימסב שומישב .לשממה תוברעתהל רשאב .תישפוה הלועפ לש תולבגמש תילרבילה הנהבה ליחתמ ןוידה
תלבגומ וז החנה דךא .מירחא לע מימסב שומיש לש תוילילשה תואצותל תוסחייתה דותמ הקידצהל רשפא
דוקימה ,תויאופרה תויוברועמל רשאב .תישפוה הלועפל תיתרבח תוציחנו דךרוצ לש הדבועה דותמ הנתומו
לש תויתאה דוסיה תוחנה מינודינ דךא ,מהיתוחוקללו לופיט יקינעמל וחתופש מייתא מידוק לע אוה ןוידב
תויעוצקמ ,היילפה רדעה ,תוידוס ,תויטרפ(informed consent) תרהצומ המכסה :לופיטה תונורקעמ המכ
תוירחאו (accountability).

מיטחמ תפלחהל תוינכת לע תיתא הביגש

John Kleinig, Ph.D.

תויתא תולאש וליא ,ןיאורהל תעגונה תיקוחה תוינידמה לש יחכונה בצמה תא – ןוידה דךרוצל – הלבק דותמ
תא תולפרעמ וא העטומ רסמ תוחלוש ;מימס יקוח תושילחמ ןה םאה ?מיטחמ תפלחהל תוינכתל רשאב תולוע
תוננוכמ ואו/ ;תוביטנרטלאמ תוחיסמ ;מימסה לש קזנה תא מילעהל תנמ-לע קיפסמ תושוע אל ;ןוכנה רסמה
הביטנרטלא תווהמ מיטחמ תפלחהל תוינכת ,תוססובמ תוביטנרטלא רדעיהבש ןעוט ינא ?שואיי לש לופיט
.מימסב שומישה לש תכשמתמה היצזיליניימירקה תורמל היוצר תורשפא ףאו ירסומ ןפואב תלבוקמ

מימסב מישמתשמב לופיטו תוידוס ,תויטרפ

Seumas Miller, Ph.D.

הפישח לש תוינסרההה תואצותהו ,ןומא ,תויטרפל תוכזה ללוכ ,מילוקיש רפסמ םנשי תוידוסה ןורקע סיסבב.
ירסומה קודיצה תא דךפוה הז .הימונוטוא ללוכ ,מירחא רסומ יכרע ידי-לע תססובמה המצע תויטרפל תוכזהו
תוביסנלמ מייסחי תויהל מיכירצ תוידוסל ונלש תוביוחמה תגרדו תוידוסה ןורקע ףקיה .בכרומל תוידוסל
,תוידוסל תומיוסמ תוליע תורסח תויהל תויושע ,מימסל מירוכמ לש תומיוסמ תוירוגטק וא מימיוסמ מירקמב
עבונ ןיא ,ןכ יפ לע ףא .תויטרפל תוכזה לש מינטקומ ףקיה וא חוכ דךכמ האצותכו תתחפומ הימונוטואה ללגב
.שלחיהל דירצ תוידוסה ןורקעל ונלש תוביוחמה יטמוטוא ןפואב דךכמ

האופר ,רסומו ההימכ (Craving) היפכו (Compulsion)

Stephen Morse, J.D., Ph.D.

תויוגהנתהה תאו הלחמ תורכמתהב האורה יאופרה לדומה :מילדומ ינש ידי לע טלשנ תויורכמתה לע ןוידה
הב תורושקה תויוגהנתההו תורכמתהב האורה ירסומה לדומהו ;הלש מימוטפמיסו מינמיסכ הב תורושקה

כמציין כשלון מוסרי. המאמר מתאר את שני המודלים הללו ותוצאותיהם, אך מתוך הדגשה על המודל המוסרי. המשמעות של כפייתיות או הכרחה (Coercion) הנוצר בשילוב עם מצבים פסיכולוגיים פנימיים, כמו כמיה, נידונה במאמר כדי לקבוע אם בצדק ניתן ליחס למכורים אחריות מוסרית וחוקית להתנהגותם, כמו החופש לשימוש בסמים. המאמר טוען שהתהליך של רציונליות מופחתת מסבירה טוב יותר, מאשר המושג "כפייתיות" מדוע אפשר לסלוח למכורים על התנהגותם. מן האמור עולה המסקנה, שרוב המכורים אחראים להתנהגותם הקשורה להתמכרות. מאידך, מדיניות ציבורית הגיונית אינה צריכה להתבסס רק על אחד משני המודלים המסקנות לגבי מדיניות במערכת אכיפת החוק והמשפט הנובעות מהפעלת שני המודלים נבחנות בסיכום.

סוגיות אתיות במחקר על הטיפול במשתמש בסמים

Kenneth D. Pimple, Ph.D.

המחקר על הטיפול במשתמש בסמים צריך להיות מונחה על-ידי השיקולים האתיים הבסיסיים שקיימים בכל דרכי המחקר המדעי, כולל יושרה והגינות; רישום זכויות יוצרים ונתינת קרדיט נכונים; והימנעות מהתנהגות אינטימית או מטרידה כלפי הפרטים הנחקרים; וגם (ב) עקרונות אתיים ספציפיים למחקר תוך שימוש באנשים כמצוין בדו"ח בלמונט (Belmont Report) ככבוד לאנשים, גמילות-חסד (ולא-גרימת-נזק), וצדק. עקרון נוסף שלא מצוין במפורש בדו"ח בלמונט אך רוחש הסכמה רחבה הוא כלילת או גישה לטיפולים. חוקרים חייבים באופן מוסרי (ולפעמים גם חוקי) לדבוק בעקרונות אלו, וקהיליית המחקר של הטיפול במשתמש בסמים בכלל היא בעלת מחויבות לעשות ככל יכולתה לעצב את האג'נדה המחקרית שלה כך שתתאים לעקרונות אלה.

טיפול במשתמש בסמים – מדיניות הוגנת או מדיניות מבוססת-הוכחה (Evidence-based Policy)?

Maurice Rickard, Ph.D.

יש מקום לטענה שהחלטות הנוגעות לסוגי הטיפול למשתמש בסמים שבהם יש לעשות שימוש זה עניין למדיניות ציבורית ובחירה חברתית. נראה הגיוני לרצות שתהליך המדיניות יספק את ההתערבויות המבוססות-הוכחה מבחינה תרפויטית (ואתית). כמו-כן נראה הגיוני לצפות שתהליכים של מדיניות ותהליכים חברתיים של בחירה באשר לדרכי טיפול יהיו הוגנים וצודקים. במלים אחרות, שההחלטות יאושרו באופן הולם. דרך אחת לכבד שתי ציפיות מתקבלות על הדעת אלה היא להשיג הוגנות בקבלת החלטות בקשר למדיניות טיפול במשתמש בסמים כך שבאופן מושגי היא מותנית בכך שההחלטות היוצאות ממנה הן הנכונות באופן תרפויטי. הבעיה עם זה היא מה שהוא נכון או אפקטיבי מבחינה תרפויטית תלוי בראיה של אותו אדם באשר למה היא מטרת הטיפול במשתמש בסמים. הסכנה היא להישאר עם תפיסה קונטרוברסיאלית של מהם תהליכים הוגנים, ולא תפיסה שהיא המקובלת על כולם באופן מקסימלי. פרק זה בוחן כמה מן הסוגיות הפילוסופיות הנוגעות למדיניות טיפול הוגנת ומדיניות טיפול טובה, כולל למי צריך להינתן תפקיד בקבלת החלטות הקשורה במדיניות.

טיפול, פיצוי ואתיקה בקשר למשתמש בסמים

Adrian Walsh, Ph.D. and Tony Lynch, Ph.D.

במאמר זה אנחנו בוחנים את ההשלכות שעשויות להיות לפיצוי, על צורותיו השונות, על מטפלים למשתמשים בסמים. מסורת פילוסופית ארוכת שנים מחזיקה בעמדה שפיצוי כספי ואלטרואיזם לא יכולים להיתפס

לש הרוצב יפסכ יוציפש תורמלש ,וז תרוסמל דוגינב ,םינעוט ונחנא .הנוש תצק ונתדמע .תחא הפיפכב ולא .םייתא םינוכיס ינפב םילפטמ דימעמ אוהש ירה ,ומצעשכל תירסומ קיזמ וניא תרוכשמ וא ירחסמ חוור .םהיבגל םיריהז דחוימבו תויהל םיכירצ םימסב םישמתשמל לופיטב ברועמש ימש םינוכיס םה

םימסב שומישל לופיט/לופיטל תושיגנה ביבס תויגוס

Barbara C. Wallace, Ph.D.

הילפהל לאיצנטופה תא ללוכ חווטה .תונווגמ יד םימסב שומישל לופיטו לופיטל תושיגנה ביבס תויגוס ,ןוירה ,ליג אמגודל – ובצמ וא ולש רדגמה ,ותד ,לפוטמה לש ואצומ ןתניהב לופיטל תושיגנל םסחייתהב בצמ תא אמגודל תוללוכ תורחא תויתא תויגוס .חוטיבב רסוח וא ינוע ,לופיטהמ קחרמו יפרגואיג םוקמ בצמ םע תודדומתהה תוללוכ תופסונ תויתא תויגוס .תוירטאיכיספו תויזיפ תויוכנ ללוכ ,לפוטמה לש תוכנה לש רתויב םירגתאמה םירקמהו ,ןתש לש היגולוסקוט לש םיכשמתמ םייבויח םיחוויד ,שומישל הרזח לש לש ןוכיסב תורושק תופסונ תויתא תויגוס .שומישל תינורכ הרזח ידי לע תונייפואמה תורכמתה תוריירק הייפכב שומישב תורושק תופסונ תויתא תויגוס .לופיטל השיג עונמל יתמו םילפוטמ לש המילא תוגהנתה תויה – םידלי לע הנגהה תוכרעמ וא ,החוורה תויושר ,קוחה תפיכא תכרעמ ידי לע םא ,לופיטל םיטדנמו אלמה חווטל הנעמ תניתנלו הגשמהל תוירשפא םיכרדל תוצלמה .לופיטל עיגהל םילפוטמ תובייחמ ןלוכו .הז קרפב תונודינ לופיטו לופיטל השיגב תורושקה תויוושכע תויתא תויגוס לש

תוינידמ לש תוירסומ תויגוס ,תוכנו תורכמתה

David Wasserman, Ph.D.

םגפכ םימסל תורכמתה לש םייקוח םינוימ דותמ תולועה תוינידמ לשו תויתא ,תויגשומ תויגוסב ןד רמאמה .םיכנכ םירוכמה המכ לשו (impairment) הלחמכ ,ירסומ

לש ןוימל סיסב םיווהמ ,ללכב םא ,םימייק םיירסומ םיטופיש הזיא (1) :תואבה תולאשב דקמתמ רמאמה תוימיכ תוביס ןיב םימסל תורכמתהל םירבסהה תא קלחל םעט שי םאה (2) ;הלחמכו םגפכ תויורכמתה ןיב ,תויגולויב ,תויתרבח ,תויטילופ ,תוביס וא תורחא תוביס ;(3) ציכד םילוקיש לש קדצ יתקולח (distribu-tive justice)עשוי ליבגהל תא םיצמאמה לודדתהל םע השקה לש םיישק לש תורכמתהה ;(4) םאה קדצומ לשלול .םייקוח םירמוחב םישמתשמל םויכ תמייקה ,תיקוח הנגה םייקוח יתלב םירמוחב םישמתשממ

םימסב הערל שומישב לופיטל השיגה ביבס תויתא תויגוס

Shelly A. Wiechelt, Ph.D.

לש תויביטקפא תוארמה תובר תוירקחמ תוחכוה וקפיס ב''הראב םימסב שמתשמל לופיטה תוינכת ןווגמ םיקוקזכ םיהדזמה םישנאה רפסמ ןיב לודג רעפ םייק ,לופיט תונימזלו רבטצמה עדיל רשק ילב .לופיט תושיגנב תויעבל םימרותש םיאנתו םיביכרמ רפסמב ןד הז קרפ .ותוא םילבקמ השעמלש הלאו לופיטל לצא םימייקה םייתאה םידוקה רואל םינחבנ ולא תושיגנ יאשונ .ב''הראב םימסב םישמתשמל לופיטה .תויורכמתהב לופיטב עוצקמה ישנא

יעוצקמ דיקפת לש תוירסומו לפוטמ-לפטמ יסחי

Kylie Williams, M.A. and Dean Cocking, Ph.D.

תויושיגר ,דיקפתה תובוח .יעוצקמ לופיטל תירסומ םלוהה דיקפת לש תיטסילרולפ הסיפת גיצמ הז קרפ
םיטקילפנוקב םיכורכו םפקיהב דחוימב םיבחר םה לופיטל תויטנוולרה תוישונא תויעב לש םימוחתו
יסחיל תודחוימ תויעב םיגיצמ ,םימסב שמתשמל תויופכ לופיט תוינכת לש תרגסמהו עבטה .םיילאיצנטופ
םייסיסבה םיחנמה םידעיהו ןיבוטה תא ינפוס ןפואב תוסרוה הלא תויעב םיבר םיבתוכל ,ןכא .לפוטמ-לפטמ
,םינעוט ונחנא .יופכ לופיט תרגסמב חתפמ יכרע רפסמ לע הרשפ תישענש םימיכסמ ונחנא .לופיטל ךד לכ
,ונלש יטסילרולפה גשומה ךותב רשפאתמכ ןאכ הלועה דיקפתה טקילפנוקמ הברה ןיבהל ןתינש ,ןפוא לכב
.םיידוסיהו םימלוההה הידעימ תקתונמ איה ללככש לופיט ךרד ןקשמכ אלו

םימסב םישמתשמל םילפטמל תיעוצקמ הקיתא תארוה :תוח·ושל ןשה לדגממ

Daniel Yalisove, Ph.D.

.םימסב שומישב תורושקה תוערפהב םילפטמש םילפטמל תיעוצקמ הקיתא תארוהל השיג ראתמ הז קרפ
:תיעוצקמ הקיתא תארוה לש רשקהב ןכ-ינפל תעדה םהילע הנתינ אלש םיינשדח תונויער השולש גיצמ אוה
הנחבה ריהבהל בושח .תויתא תוטלחה תלבקב םייתא-םניאש-הלאכ םע םייתא םילוקיש ולבלב םילפטמ (1)
הקיתאו יטסינמוה לופיט ןיב תדחוימ (הלועפ ףותיש) היגרניס הנשי (2) .יעוצקמ יתא ךוניחב םיטנדוטסל וז
םירזוע ךכ ידי-לע םיטנייילק רפסמ לש ירסומה ךוניחה ךילהתל תנתינ הרורב בל תמושת (3) .תיעוצקמ
.תויתא תויעבל םיעדומ ךפיהל םהל

涉及研究和道德的艰难决定：滥用药物(及滥用药物人士)的统计

Manuella Adrian, M. Sc. Hyg.

科学研究为我们提供了其中一种最能改善大部分人类的方法。但是它的威力却能成为使用它的人在操守和道德上面对的困境的来源。现在在研究道德的问题上，大多数的注意力都放在以人类作为研究对象的研究，并透过过去五十年间制定出来的且发展得相当健全的指引，朝着减少参与者所可能受到的伤害这个方向发展。另外一样被指出的是源于研究目标道德困境，尤其是在关于军国主义研究方面。本文同时会描述较为少被注意到的、由科研方法本身、研究方法和数据分析引起的道德问题。我们会以 Isaac Newton 主张的基本原则作开始去重新探讨关于在进行药物使用和滥用的研究调查中所采用的科学方法的基本宗旨以确立因果关系，并在适合的情况下引用在一般科学架构中的例子来探讨一些较新的概念架构，使我们能即使在单纯直接因果关系不能适用的情况下仍能用来决定我们可以介入的情况以得到我们希望得到的结果。我们跟着会考虑可能由被调查主体的性质、组织和财政来源，以及使用不适当方法和技巧 — 包括使用人体作为研究对象时需要考虑的一些问题 — 对病人、科学家，以及社会整体可能导致伤害的错误结论所引起的操守和道德问题。

互助模式的物质使用者治疗引起的道德问题：十二步骤组织的定位

Allaman Allamani, M.D.

互助组织与正规的专业治疗媒介和有关滥用酒精饮品和其它药物的人士的媒介及与这些人士一起工作的媒介之间的内在分别具有道德上的意义。特别是所有十二步骤组织的道德是一致的，是以灵性、它性和团结作为基础的。即使他们产生节制的效力也能被科学化地研究，对他们最佳的形容是“治疗社区”(Seppala, 2001)。另外，当有专业人士参与物质使用者治疗计划时，道德好像是功利的；它是朝着个人或社会团体的利益这个方向发展的。即使当两种不同的角度的互助有可能产生紧张状况或冲突，现时互助团体与保健制度的合作是分散和遍及全球的。

残障与物质使用者治疗/更新：道德的考虑

Ellen Benoit, Ph.D. 和 *Stephen Magura Ph.D.*

1996 年之前，在美国长期依赖药物和酒精的人士可被发出证书证明他们是有残障，让他们在参加治疗期间有资格领取社会保障管理部门发放的收入支助。1996 年 3 月制订的法律要求社会保障管理部门取消成瘾者被视为符合残障人士的资格，并将所有一直以残障物质使用者身份领取福利的人士的名字从其名册中删除。这个改变引起了重大的道德问题，而我们则会对此从分配正义的角度去讨论。我们会探讨在政策上被视为是“值得”和“不值得”的有需要人士的分别，并分析上瘾这个在医学上含糊的性质在关于资格的辩论中如何促进竞争性的公平报应主张。例如由滥用物质引起的残障是否构成一种意志倾向的行为?最后，我们会研究社会保障管理部门这样重新界定对政策受众，包括受益者、治疗提供者和公众的后果。

论药物使用者表示同意接受治疗计划的资格

Steve Clarke Ph.D. 和 *Neil Levy Ph.D.*

很多思想家都认为经常使用药物的人士并没有资格表示是否同意接受医治。在本文中，我们会列出被认为是具有资格表示知情同意的媒介的最低条件，并指出经常使用药物的人士 — 即使是那些被视为是已经对一种药物成瘾的人 — 一般都符合这些条件。虽然成瘾会削弱自主能力，但是其影响力并不足以达至影响作出知情同意的程度。有关成瘾人士行为的研究显示出他们一般会对其行为和决定能力保持足够的控制力以符合有能力作出同意的资格。

把对药物使用者和酒精滥用者的辅导工作中的专业关系概念化

Elliot D. Cohen, Ph.D.

道德规范、法律条文和案例所产生的基本道德责任和要求使辅导药物使用者和酒精滥用者的专业人士裹足不前。但是如果这些治疗师要更有效地提供辅导，他们便必须在其辅导工作中加入更多具期望的和以人为中心的原素。本文首先分析加强有效治疗的基本价值并结合数个关于医疗保健的专业模式 ,建立一个可行和折衷模式的治疗师与客户关系。

毒品使用者非惩罚性政策的道德问题

Stephen Coleman, Ph.D.

在过去数十年间有很多国家一直本着减少对毒品使用者构成的伤害为目的，大力推动对毒品使用和滥用实行非惩罚性的计划和政策。本文旨在指出和讨论一些非惩罚性毒品政策在道德上引起的特定问题。文中所探讨的特定政策包括美沙酮维持使用治疗计划、针具交换项目、提供安全注射设施、海洛因处方和大麻非刑事化。

药物使用者不能被治疗；人们能够!–

Stan Einstein, Ph.D.

本文透过一些经挑选过的例子来探讨现行为大多数人所能得到的(无论是以节制为目标还是以减少伤害作为推动力这些差不多经常在主流治疗场所以外的地方实施的)药物使用障碍治疗，并证实：

- 它的本质是不道德的；它的贡献远比其所制造的不必要不正当行为的“份量”为少；
- 它是一个误导的名称；(1)它根本没有给予“药物使用者”同样没有适用于非药物使用者的独特的“治疗”(模式和技巧)，而且(2) “药物使用者”和非药物使用者都代表着人类中的异质种群而非独特的同质疾病分类；

- 基于权力驱使的个人和系统受众的地位、工作和目标不同，它不太可能转变为一个以道德为基础的过程；
- 它是靠“以证据为基础”等代号覆盖的“诚信原则”维持的；
- 它可能受到且太过经常地受到代表着不同领域和专业人士中的康复中人士或前成瘾者的指定变革倡导者所(非故意地)支持；
- 由于技术转移的问题，在持续的真正现实中，新的可泛化的调查结果经常不会被引入和用于治疗适合的药物使用者。

依赖化学的辅导中的资格问题

Theodore M. Godlaski, M.Div.

虽然人们一致地认为治疗师的资格是在道德上正确的实务工作所必须的，但它却常被不清晰地界定。一个由美国药物滥用与精神卫生服务局资助的专家组一直在制定一个更好的规格的工作上付出重大的努力。这个小组具体指出三个要求足够能力作为付合资格所必须的条件的领域：知识、技术和态度。但是差不多所有的认证机构只会客观地衡量知识，而技术和态度则留给临床监督去证明。关注对作为作出该决定的依据的监督接触的质和量是有一定的理由的。再者，我们亦有理由去问是否所有的知识和技术在道德上都具同等价值。还有的道德问题是关于将药物使用者辅导这一范畴独立于一般辅导工作的做法是否合理。

研究土著的道德问题的反省

Theodore M. Godlaski, M.Div.、*Jeannette Johnson, Ph.D.* 和 *Rodney Harding, LMSW*

本文对在研究土著或本土人士的工作中引起的突出道德问题作出反省。道德考虑源于研究的目的、设计、方法、协议和出版/发表计划在文化方面的适当性。虽然文化方面的适当性并非一个定义明确的概念，但是不考虑本土人士的想法、社会结构、联系和世界观，会在计划不周的研究所产生的伤害中反映出来。作者根据这个领域的新近研究定出在进行文化方面的敏感性研究工作的指引。

评价和宣传防止使用毒品计划中的利益冲突

Dennis M. Gorman, Ph.D.

本文探讨评价和推广毒品预防计划的新近发展对研究诚信的意义，尤其是由利益冲突对这方面造成的威胁。本文首先对利益冲突一词作出解释，并探讨近年来医学和公共政策文献中一直讨论的各种主要冲突。跟着本文会对在毒品预防研究中存在的个人和制度性的利益冲突作详细讨论。

减少伤害精神治疗是否道德？

William H. Gottdiener, Ph.D.

减少伤害精神治疗(HRP)是对被诊断为物质使用障碍(SUD)和持续使用对心理或精神有显着影响的物质的人士的一种门诊精神治疗。HRP 治疗的目标是减少可能伴随使用对心理或精神有显着影响的物质而出现的潜在伤害。节制只是一种减少伤害的方法，但是相对而言在传统 SUD 治疗中节制是唯一一种可接受的目标。使用 HRP 是由于节制的情况未能达到及/或未能在所有被证实患有物质使用障碍的人士中或在有关人士的治疗的每个阶段中维持。本文讨论 HRP 是否对被诊断为 SUD 的人士的一种道德治疗。作者从 Foucaldian 这个强调个人自由对被诊断为 SUD 的人士的必要性的角度和认为只有想达到节制这个目标并具备所有开始和维持这种生活模式改变的必要(内在和外在)条件的人才能达至节制这个精神分析角度，主张 HRP 是对 SUD 人士的唯一一种有道德的门诊精神治疗。

禁止药物使用者与其辅导员发生性关系：是否合理？

Mane Hajdin, Ph.D.

本文对关于禁止药物使用者辅导员与接受其辅导的人士发生性关系的四个有可能的论点作出研究。第一个是有关的禁制防止由转移现象在性关系方面制造出的特别引诱和机会。第二个是有关的禁制是如果希望辅导能完成其有关的辅导目标，辅导员便必须流露。根据第三个原因，辅导是执法的延续并因此与执法受到同样的限制。第四个原因是由于在辅导员与接受其辅导的人士之间存在权力不平衡的情况，因此有关禁制是有必要的。本文的总结是这四个论点中除了第二个论点可以证明对所有药物使用者的辅导实施有关禁制是合理的之外，其余的每一个论点都只能证明对某些药物使用者的辅导的禁制是合理的。但是这个原因似乎只是一个辅导技巧的问题而非在辅导中的一个独立的道德限制。

毒癮與道德的相關性

Douglas N. Husak, J.D. Ph.D.

本文作者嘗試了解及評估毒癮與道德是相關這一普遍看法。本文檢驗幾項論述，這些論述提出道德觀點對毒癮的看法。雖然作者會簡要地討論有關德行的理論，但作□會集中分析三項有關毒癮與道德責備的相關可能性。第一，責備可能會被加諸於使用成癮藥物的行為。第二，責備可能會被加在已成癮的狀況。第三，對於那些一旦成為上癮者的人，他們可能會作出進一步的風險行為，而責備可能會被加於進一步的風險行為。作者認為，各項論述均有一些合理之處，可是無一論述是完全沒有問題的。縱然毒癮有違道德的嚴重性未至於像一些評論者所相信的那麼嚴重，但毒癮與道德問題確是有關的。無論如何，毒癮與道德的相關性並未達致任何嚴重程度可用來合理化對毒癮者採取懲罰性的處理手法。

对儿童进行预防性研究中的道德问题

Jeannette L. Johnson, Ph.D. 和 *Nancy R. VanDeMark, Ph.D.*

要理解在预防使用毒品的研究中所涉及的道德可以同时是一项既复杂又简单的工作。预防性的研究是复杂的，因为它是对儿童进行的，而围绕保护儿童及他们的权利的问题至关重要。由于有儿童涉及，因此我们必须明确地、尊重地和细心地顾及这些权利。预防性研究的道德是简单的，因为有关理解有效的预防性干预的答案只能在孩童时代找到。除了首先对儿童进行研究之外，我们并没有其它的方法去理解如何预防疾病、失调或官能障碍。复杂和简单这两者正是使预防性研究中的道德问题充满障碍的原因。

在双重诊断个案中的治疗道德目标

Jeannette Kennett, Ph.D. 和 *Steve Matthews, Ph.D.*

药物使用和滥用的情况在有精神问题的人士中出现的比率非常高，而这两个条件之间的关系是复杂的。我们会在本文中主张对双重诊断的病人的药物使用治疗必须由理解那些患有精神病的人所承受的损失开始。我们列出被精神病中断的有效媒介和统一媒介的基本状况，并显示出它在保障达到持续就业和满足关系等这些中央社会和道德产物方面的重要性。我们认为药物使用主要会因其同时阻止获得这一系列的媒介产物而被轻视，我们更会将媒介的焦点放在同时的福祉以排除不同时的福祉。治疗双重诊断病人的目标和方法应该能够反映出对统一媒介造成的主要损害。

毒癮與為毒癮者提供醫療保健之責任

Tziporah Kasachkoff, Ph.D.

在公共福利經費充足的可能情況下，作為社會的一份子，我們都有責任為有需要的社會成員提供醫療保健。不過，這承諾對於某些個人的病態是否不適用呢？這些病態源於個人自願地引發一些行為，以及個人已預知及願意□擔這些行為對自身健康所帶來有害的後果。具體來說，社會對毒癮者提供醫療保健服務之責任會否因他們的毒癮而被削減？有些學者支持此立論，但有些學者卻認為此論點在道德立場上是不能成立的。本文會探索於這議題上誰的立論是正確，以及提出立論正確的原因。

物質使用干預服務的道德問題

John Kleinig, Ph.D.

本文對物質使用的政府及醫療干預所引起的一些道德問題提供一個概覽。政府干預建基於自由論的假設，物質使用是自由的行為，對物質使用的約束是基於對他人帶來損害性的影響。不過此假設卻有爭議之處，就是自由行動是社會的必需品。關於醫療干預，本文集中討論醫療干預對服務提供者及其服務對象所建立的一套規程，以及探討數項主要服務的道德基礎，包括獲諮詢的同意、私隱、保密性、非歧視、專業化及問責的問題。

从道德方面思考针具交换计划

John Kleinig, Ph.D.

接受我们现行有关海洛因的法律政策为针具交换计划带来甚么道德问题呢？它们会否削弱关于毒品管制的法律的效力；传播错误信息或混淆正确的信息，在消除毒品祸害方面还未作出足够的贡献；削弱其它选择；和／或构成绝望的辅导呢？作者主张在缺乏其它较好的既定选择的情况下，即使毒品使用仍属刑事化，针具交换计划亦构成了一个道德上可被接受且令人满意的选择。

私隐、保密与吸毒者的治疗

Seuman Miller, Ph.D.

保密原则的基础是各种因素，包括私隐权、信任和披露的损害后果。而私隐权本身的基础亦是其它的道德价值，包括自主权。保密的道德理据因此而变得复杂。我们对保密原则的遵守程度及该原则的范围需要视乎有关情况而定。在对一些案件或一些类型的吸毒者保密时，某些保密原因可能会由于自主权的减弱而有所缺失，因而削弱了私隐权的力量和范围。不过，这并不自动地表示我们对保密原则私遵守应该因此而减弱。

藥物與道德，典癮與強迫

Stephen J. Morse, J.D., Ph.D.

直以來有兩個理論模型支配□對毒癮的看法，這兩個理論模型分別是醫療模型及道德模型。醫療模型視毒癮為一種疾病，以及視與毒癮相關的行為為徵兆和病徵。道德模型視毒癮及相關行為為道德敗壞的指標。本文會描述這兩個理論模型及它們的啟示，尤其會□重道德模型的討論。本文亦會探討由內在心理狀態而導致失去自控或強迫的意思，目的在明確地指出要毒癮者在道德上和法律上對他們的行為(例如尋找和使用藥物)負上責任是否公平？本文認為，理智漸弱的看法會提出較好的解釋說明為何毒癮者可能會為自己的行為辯解，但無論如何大部份毒癮者都應為大部份與成癮相關的行為負責。該兩個理論模型都有其可取之特點，故此要提出可靠的公共政策，不能單靠一個模型。最後本文會探討運用該兩個理論模型作為建立政策的指引對刑事司法之啟示。

药物使用者治疗研究中的道德问题

Kenneth D. Pimple, Ph.D.

药物使用者治疗研究应该依从盛行于所有科研的基本道德考虑，包括(a)正直和坦诚、正确地承认原作者的贡献和禁止威吓或骚扰研究对象；及(b)贝尔蒙特报告中列出规范有关以人体实验作为研究对象的特定伦理道德原则，即尊重人格、行善(及避免伤害)和正义。另外一个贝尔蒙特报告中没有明确提及但却广泛地被接受的原则是纳入或获得治疗。研究员在道德上(在一些个案中同时在法律上)必须遵守这些原则，而作为一个整体而言，药物使用者治疗研究这个领域有责任去尽力依据这些原则去设计研究计划和社会政策。

药物使用者治疗 – 公平政策还是以证据作为基础的政策?

Maurice Rickard, Ph.D.

决定应该使用甚么类型的药物使用者治疗是一个公共政策和社会选择问题的主张是有充分理据支持的。希望制定政策的过程容许以治疗上(和在道德上)的证据为基础的干预是合理的。期望政策和社会在作出有关治疗实务工作的决定的过程是公平和公正的也似是合理的。换言之，有关的决定应是经正当授权而作出的。一个尊重这两个似是正确的期望的方法是将在决定有关药物使用者治疗政策中的公平概念在概念上限制为所作出的决定应在治疗上是正确的。这个做法的问题是，甚么是治疗上的正确或有效视乎个人对药物使用者治疗的目的的看法而有所不同。其存在的危险是最终会引致对公平程序这个概念的争议，而非达至一个大部分人都能接受的概念。本文探讨关于公平治疗政策和优良治疗政策的一些哲学性问题，包括谁有权参与政策的制定。

围绕获得药物使用辅导/治疗的道德问题

Barbara C. Wallace, Ph.D.

围绕获得药物使用辅导和治疗的道德问题的种类颇多，包括基于客户的种族、宗教、性别或条件(例如年龄、怀孕、地理位置和与接受治疗的地方的距离、贫穷或没有购买保险)在其获得治疗方面的潜在歧视。其它道德问题包括客户的残障状况，例如包括肉体上和精神上的残障。其它道德问题包括如何处理旧病复发、尿液毒性测试持续出现阳性反应的报告和涉及长期旧病复发的上瘾经历这最具挑战性的个案。另外的道德问题涉及客户在治疗时实施暴力行为的危险和何时禁止他们接受治疗。其它的道德问题涉及由刑事司法机构、福利机构或保护儿童机构下令使用威迫和强制的治疗 — 因为他们都会强迫客户接受治疗。本文会对如何将所有现行关于获得药物辅导和治疗的道德问题概念化和作出响应提供建议。

药物使用者辅导、回报及道德

Adrian Walsh, Ph.D. 和 *Tony Lynch, Ph.D.*

本文探讨各种形式的回报对药物使用者辅导员所可能带来的意义。在悠久的哲学传统上，金钱上的回报与利他主义是相互排斥的，但是我们的意见却有点不同。与那个传统相反，我们认为虽然商业利益或工资形式的金钱上的回报本身在道德上并无害处，但是这些回报却使辅导员面对道德上的危机。参与辅导药物使用者的人士需要对这些害处提高警觉。

毒癮與傷殘：道德及政策問題

David Wasserman, J.D.

本文討論法律界定毒癮為身體缺陷及界定現非毒癮者為傷殘人士所引起的概念、道德及政策問題。本文集中討論四項問題：(1) 將毒癮分類為傷殘行為是基於什麼道德評審準則？(2) 將毒癮所帶來的負擔分類為化學、生理、社會、政治和其他成因是否合理？(3) 分配正義理念所持的考慮因素如何促使或限制措施之提供以減輕毒癮帶來的負擔？(4) 拒絕現有使用違禁藥物者獲得法律的保障是否合理？

围绕获得滥用药物治疗的道德问题

Shelley A. Wiechelt, Ph.D.

美国那些种类繁多的药物使用者治疗计划已经提供了太多显示治疗成效的研究证据。虽然知识和获得治疗的整体机会都在不断提升，但是在被确认为需要接受治疗的人数与实际接受治疗的人数之间仍存在一个巨大的差距。本文讨论为美国药物使用者带来有关接受治疗的问题的一些原因和情况。我们会从现行对治疗成瘾的专业人士的道德规范的角度去探讨这些有关接受治疗的问题。

辅导员与其客户之间的关系和专业角色的道德

Kylie Williams, M.A. 和 Dean Cocking, Ph.D.

本文描述一个适合专业辅导工作的角色道德的多元化概念。关于辅导的角色义务，敏感性和涉及人的问题的范围特别广泛而且充满潜在的冲突。非自愿性的药物使用者治疗计划的性质和设置为辅导员与其客户之间的关系带来一些特别问题。其实对很多作家而言，这些问题严重地影响辅导的基本道德福祉和指引目标。我们同意一些主要的价值常会在非自愿的设置中被削弱。但是我们认为最好的做法是将大部份的这些角色冲突视为已融入我们的多元化概念中，而非反映一个完全与其适当的建构性目标没有关联的辅导实务工作。

从象牙塔到战壕：教授药物使用者辅导员专业道德

Daniel Yalisove, Ph.D.

本文概述一个教授治疗药物使用障碍的辅导员专业道德的方式。文中介绍三种以前在教授专业道德时从未被考虑过的创新意念：(1)辅导员在作出道德决定时一直把道德和道德以外的考虑混淆。在专业道德教育中对学生解释清楚这个分别是很重要的。(2)人性化的辅导与专业道德之间有着一种特别的协同作用。(3)对有道德地教授一些客户以帮助其注意道德问题的这个过程加以明确注意。

Трудные решения в отношении научных исследований и этики: злоупотребление наркологической статистикой

Мануэлла Адриан, M. Sc. Hyg.

Наука стала одним из самых мощных средств улучшения судеб человечества. Однако, сама ее мощь может стать источником множества моральных и этических дилемм для тех, кто пользуется ей. Большая часть вопросов этики научных исследований в настоящее время связана с использованием человека в качестве объекта научного исследования, и внимание обращается на то, чтобы снизить возможность вреда для участников исследования. За последние полвека в этом направлении были разработаны достаточно хорошие рекомендации. Общепризнанными являются также этические дилеммы, связанные с целями научных исследований, особенно в отношении исследований для военных целей. Менее известны вопросы этики, связанные с самим научным методом, исследовательскими методиками и интерпретацией данных, которые также описываются в данной статье. Мы рассматриваем некоторые из основ научного метода, используемого в исследованиях в области употребления и злоупотребления психоактивными веществами, начиная с основных принципов установления причинно-следственной связи, изложенных Исааком Ньютоном, и приводим обзор некоторых из более новых концептуальных основ, которые используются при определении моментов вмешательства, когда мы можем предпринять действия, чтобы получить желаемые результаты, даже если строгая линейная причинная связь не может быть применена, при этом мы используем примеры не только из области злоупотребления веществами, но также из области науки в целом, если такие иллюстрации могут оказаться полезными. Далее мы анализируем этические и моральные проблемы, которые могут быть обусловлены самим предметом исследования, его организацией и финансированием, а также применением несоответствующих методов и приемов (включая некоторые из вопросов, которые необходимо исследовать с привлечением человека как испытуемого), что может привести к ошибочным заключениям и к вреду пациентам, ученым и обществу в целом.

Лечение наркопотребителей – справедливая политика или политика на основе доказательств?

Морис Рикард, Ph.D.

Необходимо определиться в том, что решения о том, какие виды лечения наркозависимых следует практиковать, являются вопросами общественной политики и социального выбора. Представляется разумным желать, чтобы политика сделала доступными те вмешательства, которые терапевтически (и этически) основываются на доказательствах. Также разумно ожидать, чтобы политика и социальный выбор в отношении методов лечения были справедливыми и обоснованными. Другими словами, решения должным быть соответственно оформлены. Одним из способов удовлетворения этих ожиданий является реализация принципа справедливости в принятии политических решений в отношении лечения наркозависимых с концептуальной опорой на терапевтически правильные решения. Проблема здесь заключается в том, что решение о том, что является терапевтически правильным или эффективным, зависит от конкретных представлений о целях лечения наркозависимых. Опасность же заключается в том, что можно придти к противоречивой концепции справедливых технологий, а не к максимально приемлемой для всех. В главе исследуются некоторые из философских проблем справедливой лечебной политики и хорошей лечебной политики, включая вопрос о том, кто должен участвовать в принятии политических решений.

Является ли психотерапия снижения вреда этичной?

Уильям Х. Готтдинер, Ph.D.

Психотерапия снижения вреда (ПСР) является формой амбулаторной психотерапии для лиц, у которых диагностируется расстройство наркопотребления, и которые продолжают употреблять психоактивные вещества. Цель лечения ПСР состоит в том, чтобы уменьшить потенциальный вред, который может сопровождать потребление психоактивных веществ. Трезвость – это всего лишь один из способов уменьшить вред по сравнению с традиционными видами наркологического лечения, в которых полный отказ является единственной приемлемой целью. ПСР используется потому, что трезвость не является достижимой целью и/или устойчивым состоянием у всех лиц с расстройством наркопотребления или на каждой из стадий процесса выздоровления человека. В главе обсуждается, действительно ли ПСР является этичным лечением для тех, кому поставлен диагноз расстройства наркозависимости. С учетом точки зрения Фуко о том, что личная свобода имеет существенное значение в лечении от наркозависимости, и с психоаналитической точки зрения о том, что трезвость может быть достигнута только тем клиентом, который готов стремиться к этой цели и имеет все необходимое – эндогенно и экзогенно - чтобы инициировать и устойчиво поддерживать такое изменение образа жизни, автор утверждает, что ПСР – это единственная этичная форма амбулаторной психотерапии для больных с расстройством наркозависимости.

Размышления об этике программ обмена шприцев

Джон Клейниг, Ph.D.

Если принять - ради сути спора - нашу текущую правовую политику в отношении героина, какие этические вопросы поднимаются в отношении программ обмена шприцев (ПОШ)? Ослабляют ли они законы о наркотиках; формируют неверное мнение или затеняют правильное мнение; не делают достаточно для устранения вреда от наркотиков, отвлекают от альтернатив и/или представляют собой меру отчаяния? Я считаю, что при отсутствии более хороших альтернатив, ПОШ представляют собой нравственно приемлемый и даже желательный вариант, несмотря на продолжающуюся криминализацию наркотиков.

Этические вопросы, поднимаемые некарательной политикой в отношении наркопотребителей

Стивен Коулман, Ph.D.

В последние несколько десятилетий во многих странах возник импульс к реализации программ и политики, которые основываются на некарательном отношении к употреблению и злоупотреблению наркотиками с общей целью снижения вреда от наркотиков. Цель данной главы состоит в том, чтобы выделить и обсудить конкретные этические проблемы, которые поднимают некоторые из этих некарательных подходов. В частности исследуются программы метадоновой заместительной терапии, программы обмена шприцев, предоставление помещений для безопасного инъецирования, медицинское назначение героина и декриминализация каннабиса.

Конфликт интересов в оценке и распространении программ профилактики наркопотребления

Д.М. Горман, Ph.D.

В главе анализируется значение недавних событий в оценке и маркетинге программ профилактики наркомании в связи с вопросами исследовательской честности, в частности, в связи с угрозой, которую представляет для такой честности конфликт интересов. Она начинается с описания того, что подразумевается под термином «конфликт интересов», и дает обзор главных типов конфликтов, которые обсуждались в медицинской и общественной литературе в последние годы. Затем следует более детальное обсуждение индивидуальных и институциональных конфликтов интересов, которые существуют в исследованиях по профилактике наркоманий.

Инвалидность и лечение/реабилитация наркопотребителей: этические соображения

Эллен Бенуа, Ph.D. и Стивен Магура Ph.D.

До 1996 г. в США лица с хронической зависимостью от наркотиков и алкоголя могли получить свидетельство об инвалидности, которое давало им право на денежное пособие от Администрации социального обеспечения (АСС), если они участвовали в лечении. В марте 1996 г законодатели потребовали, чтобы АСС исключила аддикцию из списка инвалидностей, а также исключила из своих списков всех, кто получал пособие по инвалидности в результате зависимости. Это изменение поднимает значимые этические вопросы, к которым мы обращаемся с точки зрения справедливого распределения благ. Мы исследуем политическое различие между “заслуживающими” и “незаслуживающими” нуждающимися людьми и анализируем, как двоякое с медицинской точки зрения состояние аддикции подпитывает конкурирующие требования “справедливой заслуги” в спорах о праве на получение пособий. Например, составляет ли инвалидность в результате злоупотребления веществами форму волюнтаристского поведения? Наконец, мы рассматриваем последствия реклассификации списка АСС для заинтересованных ведомств, включая бенефициаров, поставщиков лечебных услуг и общественность.

О компетентности согласия наркопотребителей на программы лечения

Стив Кларк Ph.D. и Нил Леви Ph.D.

Многие полагают, что те, кто регулярно употребляет наркотики, не могут дать компетентного согласия на лечение. В данной статье мы излагаем минимальные критерии компетентности на предоставление информированного согласия и считаем, что постоянные наркопотребители, даже те, кто считается зависимым от наркотиков, отвечают этим условиям. Хотя аддикция вредит независимости, она не наносит вред в степени, которая не совместима с предоставлением информированного согласия. Исследования поведения наркозависимых показывают, что они в целом сохраняют достаточный контроль над своим поведением и способность к принятию решений, чтобы их можно было квалифицировать как способных на компетентное согласие.

Отношения «консультант–клиент» и моральность профессиональных ролей

Кайли Уильямс, M.A. и Дин Кокинг, Ph.D.

В данной главе представлена плюралистская концепция ролевой моральности, соответствующей профессиональному консультированию. Ролевые обязательства, тактичность и область человеческих проблем, на которые распространяется консультирование, особенно широки по масштабу и чреваты потенциальными конфликтами. Характер и условия принудительных программ лечения создают особые проблемы для отношений «консультант-клиент». Для многих авторов эти проблемы фатально компрометируют моральные добродетели и основные цели, которые являются фундаментальными в области психологического консультирования. Мы согласны, что некоторые ключевые ценности часто компрометируются в условиях принуждения. Мы считаем, однако, что ролевой конфликт можно лучше понять в контексте нашей плюралистской концепции, не рассматривая практику консультирования как полностью оторванную от ее соответствующих фундаментальных целей.

Концептуализация профессиональных отношений в психологическим консультировании тех, кто злоупотребляет наркотиками и алкоголем

Эллиот Д. Коуэн, Ph.D.

Кодексы этики, уставы и прецедентное право накладывают определенные этические обязательства на специалистов, которые осуществляют психологические консультирование тех, кто злоупотребляет алкоголем и наркотиками. Однако, если они хотят консультировать эффективно, они должны включить в свою практику консультирования более целеустремленные, обращенные на человека критерии. Глава начинается с анализа фундаментальных ценностей, которые лежат в основе эффективной терапии; объединяющей несколько профессиональных моделей отношений в здравоохранении и затем выстраивает жизнеспособную, эклектичную модель отношений врач-клиент.

Этические вопросы, возникающие в связи с подходами к лечению наркопотребителей на основе взаимопомощи: место двенадцати-шаговых организаций

Алламан Алламани, M.D.

Внутренние различия во взаимодействии и работе групп взаимопомощи и официальных специалистов и ведомств с теми, кто злоупотребляет алкогольными напитками и наркотиками, имеют этические аспекты. В частности, этика двенадцати-шаговых групп является универсалистской, базируясь на духовности, учете «другого» и солидарности. И даже если их эффективность в обеспечении абстиненции может изучаться с научной точки зрения, они лучше поддаются описанию как “целительские общины” (Seppala 2001). С другой стороны, когда в программах лечения наркопотребителей участвуют специалисты, этика становится утилитарной и ориентированной на интересы либо индивида, либо социальной группы. Хотя при взаимодействии между этими двумя различными перспективами могут возникать напряженные отношения и конфликты, сотрудничество между группами самопомощи и системой здравоохранения в целом широко распространенно по всему миру.

Этические вопросы, связанные с доступом к лечению по поводу злоупотребления наркотиками

Шелли А. Уичелт, Ph.D.

Разнообразие программ наркологического лечения в США породило массу научных исследований, демонстрирующих их эффективность. Вне зависимости от растущих знаний и общей доступности лечения существует огромный разрыв между числом людей, которые оценены как нуждающиеся в лечении, и числом тех, кто на самом деле получает лечение. В главе обсуждаются некоторые факторы и условия, препятствующие доступу наркопотребителей к лечению в США. Эти вопросы доступа исследуются в свете существующих этических кодексов лечения зависимостей, которыми пользуются специалисты.

Моральная цель лечения в случаях двойного диагноза

Джанетт Кеннетт, Ph.D. и Стив Мэттьюз, Ph.D.

Употребление и злоупотребление психоактивными веществами имеет широкое распространение среди лиц с проблемами психического здоровья, и отношения между этими двумя состояниями сложны. В данной главе мы выдвигаем мнение, что лечение от наркозависимости при двойном диагнозе должно начинаться с понимания потерь, которые понесли лица с психической болезнью. Мы описываем фундаментальное состояние эффективного субъекта, единого субъекта, состояние которого нарушено психической болезнью, и показываем, почему необходимо обеспечить доступ к центральным социальным и моральным благам типа постоянной работы и удовлетворяющих социальных отношений. Мы утверждаем, что наркопотребление не является чем-нибудь ценным прежде всего потому, что оно мешает обладать этим набором благ и сосредотачивает внимание субъекта на синхронном благосостоянии, что приводит к исключению диахронического благосостояния. Цели и методы лечения пациентов с двойным диагнозом должны, таким образом, отразить первичное ухудшение состояния единого субъекта.

Запрет на сексуальные связи между наркопотребителями и их консультантами: оправдан ли он?

Мане Хайдин, Ph.D.

В данной главе исследуются четыре возможных аргумента в пользу запрета сексуальных связей между психологами-консультантами в области химической зависимости и теми, кого они консультируют. Первый состоит в том, что запрет противодействует особым искушениям и возможностям, которые создаются явлением психологического переноса. Второй состоит в том, что запрет усиливает авторитет, который должен излучать консультант, если он хочет, чтобы консультирование достигло цели. Согласно третьей причине, консультирование является продолжением правоохранительной практики, и как таковое оно подпадает под те же ограничения, которые накладываются на охрану правопорядка. Четвертая причина заключается в том, что запрет необходим с учетом дисбаланса власти, который присутствует между консультантом и консультируемым. В заключение утверждается, что каждый из этих четырех аргументов может стать основанием для запрета в некоторых формах консультирования наркопотребителей, но только второй может стать оправданием для всех форм такого консультирования. Эта причина, однако, представляет собой лишь вопрос техники консультирования, а не отдельное моральное ограничение в консультировании.

Психологическое консультирование наркопотребителей, вознаграждение и этика

Адриан Уолш, Ph.D. и Тони Линч, Ph.D.

В данной статье мы исследуем вопрос о том, что может дать вознаграждение в его различных формах тем, кто консультирует наркопотребителей. Длительная философская традиция состоит в том, что финансовая награда и альтруизм взаимно исключают друг друга. Наш взгляд несколько отличается. В противовес традиции мы считаем, что, хотя финансовая награда в виде коммерческой прибыли или заработной платы не является нравственно пагубной сама по себе, она ставит этические трудности для консультантов. Те, кто участвует в психологическом консультировании наркопотребителей, должны быть особенно бдительными по отношению к таким трудностям.

Право на личную жизнь, конфиденциальность и лечение наркозависимых

Сеймас Миллер, Ph.D.

В основе принципа конфиденциальности лежат различные соображения, включая право на личную жизнь, доверие, а также вредные последствия раскрытия информации. А само право на личную жизнь подкреплено другими моральными ценностями, включая автономию. Это делает моральное оправдание конфиденциальности сложным вопросом. Необходимо соотнести нашу степень приверженности принципу конфиденциальности и объем принципа конфиденциальности с обстоятельствами. В некоторых случаях и для некоторых категорий наркопотребителей основания для соблюдения конфиденциальности могут отсутствовать из-за ограничения автономии и, таким образом, снижения силы или объема прав на личную жизнь. Однако, из этого не следует автоматически, что наша приверженность принципу конфиденциальности должна ослабнуть.

Компетентность в области психологического консуль тирования лиц с химической зависимостью

Теодор М. Годласки M.Div.

Хотя клиническая компетентность универсально признается в качестве необходимого элемента этически правильной практики, часто она определяется неудовлетворительно. Существенные усилия были предприняты для выработки более хорошего определения группой экспертов, работающих при поддержке Администрации наркологических и психиатрических служб в США. Эта группа выделила три компонента, в рамках которых требуется адекватный уровень компетентности: знания, навыки и отношения. Однако, фактически все сертифицирующие органы объективно измеряют только знания, оставляя решения о навыках и отношении на усмотрение клинических руководителей. Вызывает обоснованную озабоченность качество и количество супервизионных контактов, на которых такие суждения базируются. Возникает и законный вопрос, все ли знания и навыки этически равноценны. Более того, возникает также этический вопрос, оправдано ли существование психологического консультирования для наркопотребителей в качестве отдельного, независимого от общего психологического консультирования направления.

Из башен в траншеи: обучение профессиональной этике консультантов наркопотребителей

Даниел Ялисов, Ph.D.

В данной главе описывается подход к обучению профессиональной этике консультантов, которые лечат расстройства наркозависимости. Вводятся три инновационных идеи, которые ранее на рассматривались в обучении профессиональной этике: (1) консультанты путали этические вопросы с неэтическими при принятии этических решений. Важно разъяснить слушателям эти различия при обучении профессиональной этике. (2) имеется особый синергизм между гуманистическим психологическим консультированием и профессиональной этикой. (3) Внимание уделяется процессу морального просвещения некоторых клиентов через осознание ими этических проблем.

Этические проблемы, связанные с доступом к психологическому консультированию/наркологическому лечению

Барбара С. Уоллес, Ph.D.

Этические проблемы, связанные с доступом к психологическому консультированию и лечению по поводу употребления наркотиков весьма разнообразны. К ним относятся вопросы доступности лечения, связанные с возможностью дискриминации по расовому признаку, религии, полу или статусу, например, возрасту, беременности, географическому местоположению и расстоянию до места лечения, бедности или отсутствию страховки. К другим этическим проблемам относятся инвалидность, как физическая, так и психическая. Другие этические проблемы включают в себя вопросы действий в случае рецидивов, постоянных положительных результатов текущего контроля мочи и наиболее сложные случаи зависимости, характеризующиеся хроническими рецидивами. К дополнительным этическим вопросам относятся риск буйного поведения клиентов в ходе лечения, а также определение того, когда следует отказать в лечении. Еще один ряд этических проблем связан с использованием принуждения и ордеров на лечение со стороны системы правосудия, органов социальной защиты или органов по защите детства, так как все они используют принуждение в обеспечении доступа к лечению. Даются рекомендации по концептуализации и поиску ответов на целый ряд современных этических проблем доступа к психологическому консультированию и лечению в связи с употреблением наркотиков.

Наркопотребителей вылечить нельзя; а людей можно!

Стэн Эйнштейн, Ph.D.

На основе избранных примеров выдвигается и исследуется тезис о том, что современное лечение “расстройства наркопотребления” (будь то ориентированное на полный отказ или включающее концепцию снижения вреда, которая почти всегда реализуется отдельно от официальной медицины), предоставляемое населению в целом:

- является по сути неэтичным; и недостатку милосердия в нем более чем полно соответствуют ненужные "дозы" зла;
- является вводящей в заблуждение ошибкой названия; (1) не существует единственного "лечения" (моделей или методик) для "наркопотребителей", которые не использовалось бы также и для лечения тех, кто не употребляет наркотики и (2) как "наркопотребители", так и те, кто не употребляет их, представляют гетерогенные популяции ЛЮДЕЙ, а не отдельные, гомогенные нозологии;
- вряд будет заменено основанной на этике технологией с учетом позиций, актуальных вопросов и целей ориентированных на власть заинтересованных лиц и ведомств,
- подпитывается "принципами веры", которые украшены и подперты словесами, такими как "доказательный" и
- может поддерживаться и слишком часто поддерживается (неумышленно) целым рядом кооптированных агентов изменения, представляющих ряд дисциплин, а также неспециалистами из числа "выздоравливающих" или бывших наркопотребителей,
- в рамках текущей реальности de facto, в которой новые, поддающиеся генерализации данные чаще всего не внедряются и не используются для лечения соответствующих наркопотребителей под лозунгом проблем передачи технологий.

Этические аспекты в исследованиях вопросов лечения наркопотребителей

Кеннет Д. Пимпл, Ph.D.

Исследования в области лечения наркопотребителей должны руководствоваться основными этическими соображениями, которые преобладают во всех научных исследованиях, включая честность и искренность; признание надлежащего авторства и отказ от близких или раздражающих отношений с объектами исследования; и (b) этическими принципами, специфическими для исследований с участием человека в качестве объекта исследования, перечисленными в Докладе Белмонта, такие как уважение к человеку, благодеяние (и непричинение вреда) и справедливость. Дополнительным принципом, который явно не упомянут в Докладе Белмонта, но получил широкое признание, является включение или доступ к услугам лечения. Исследователи морально (и в некоторых случаях юридически) обязаны придерживаться этих принципов, а исследовательское сообщество, работающее в области лечения наркопотребителей, обязано приложить все усилия, чтобы сформировать тематику исследований и социальную политику согласно этим принципам.

Этика в профилактической работе среди детей

Джанетт Л. Джонсон, Ph.D. и Нэнси Р. ВанДеМарк, Ph.D.

Понимание этических решений при проведении исследований в области профилактики наркомании может представлять собой одновременно сложный и простой вопрос. Профилактика сложна, так как она проводится среди детей, и вопросы защиты ребенка и его прав представляют собой большую значимость. В случае детей эти права должны соблюдаться при ясности цели, уважении и мягкости. Этика в профилактических исследованиях является простым вопросом, так как ответ на вопрос о понимании эффективных мер профилактики можно найти лишь в детстве. Не существует альтернатив пониманию того, как предотвратить болезнь, расстройство, дисфункцию, не проведя исследование с участием детей. Именно сочетание сложности и простоты придает тернистость этическим вопросам в исследованиях в области профилактики.

Размышления об этических вопросах в исследованиях аборигенов

Теодор М. Годласки M.Div., Джанетт Джонсон, Ph.D. и Родни Харинг, LMSW

Данная глава представляет собой размышления о важных этических вопросах, которые возникают в связи с исследованиями, проводимыми среди аборигенов или коренного населения. Основной причиной этической озабоченности здесь является культурная приемлемость целей исследования, структура, методы, протоколы и планы публикаций/распространения. Хотя культурное соответствие не является достаточно хорошо определенным понятием, игнорирование менталитета коренного населения, социальных структур, способов общения и взглядов на мир может причинить вред в результате плохо спланированного научного исследования. Авторы опираются на недавние работы в этой области, чтобы представить рекомендации по проведению научных исследований, учитывающих особенности местной культуры.

Index

A

B

C

D

H

I

J

K

L

M

N

O

P

R

U

V

W

Y

Z